Turkey

Verity Campbell,
Jean-Bernard Carillet, Dan Elridge, Frances Linzee Gordon,
Virginia Maxwell, Tom Parkinson

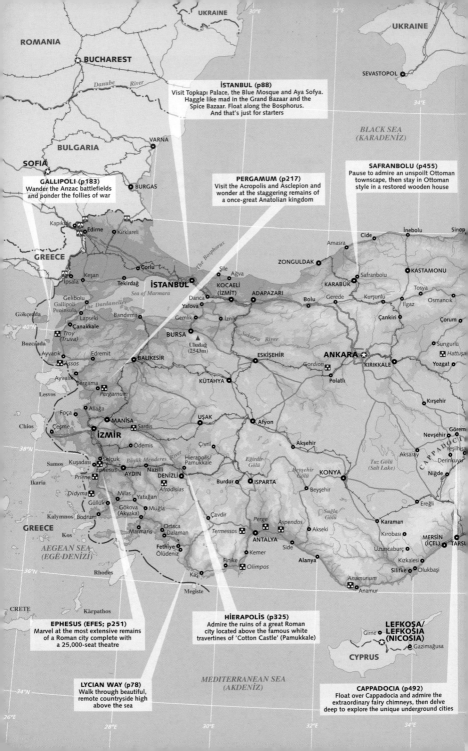

İSTANBUL (p88)
Visit Topkapı Palace, the Blue Mosque and Aya Sofya. Haggle like mad in the Grand Bazaar and the Spice Bazaar. Float along the Bosphorus. And that's just for starters

GALLIPOLI (p183)
Wander the Anzac battlefields and ponder the follies of war

PERGAMUM (p217)
Visit the Acropolis and Asclepion and wonder at the staggering remains of a once-great Anatolian kingdom

SAFRANBOLU (p455)
Pause to admire an unspoilt Ottoman townscape, then stay in Ottoman style in a restored wooden house

EPHESUS (EFES; p251)
Marvel at the most extensive remains of a Roman city complete with a 25,000-seat theatre

HİERAPOLİS (p325)
Admire the ruins of a great Roman city located above the famous white travertines of 'Cotton Castle' (Pamukkale)

LYCIAN WAY (p78)
Walk through beautiful, remote countryside high above the sea

CAPPADOCIA (p492)
Float over Cappadocia and admire the extraordinary fairy chimneys, then delve deep to explore the unique underground cities

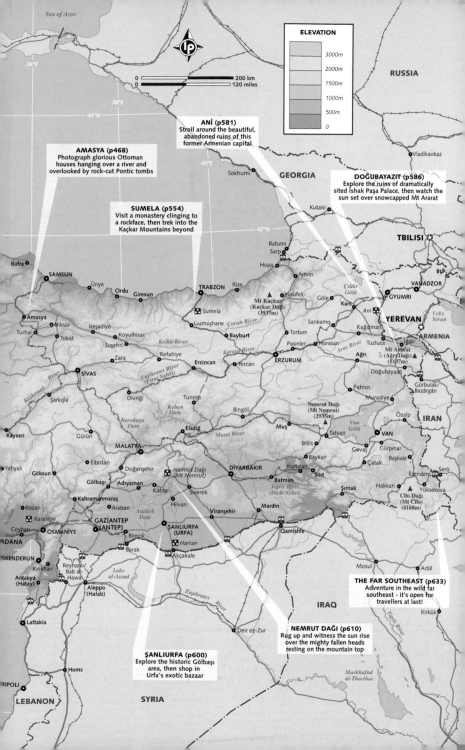

ELEVATION

	3000m
	2000m
	1500m
	1000m
	500m
	0

AMASYA (p468)
Photograph glorious Ottoman
houses hanging over a river and
overlooked by rock-cut Pontic tombs

ANİ (p581)
Stroll around the beautiful,
abandoned ruins of this
former Armenian capital

DOĞUBAYAZIT (p586)
Explore the ruins of dramatically
sited İshak Paşa Palace, then watch the
sun set over snowcapped Mt Ararat

SUMELA (p554)
Visit a monastery clinging to
a rockface, then trek into the
Kaçkar Mountains beyond

THE FAR SOUTHEAST (p633)
Adventure in the wild far
southeast - it's open for
travellers at last!

NEMRUT DAĞI (p610)
Rug up and witness the sun rise
over the mighty fallen heads
resting on the mountain top

ŞANLIURFA (p600)
Explore the historic Gölbaşı
area, then shop in
Urfa's exotic bazaar

Destination Turkey

Turkey might be the world's most contested country. Its landscape is dotted with battlegrounds, ruined castles and the palaces of great empires. This is the land where Alexander the Great slashed the Gordion Knot, where Achilles battled the Trojans in Homer's *Iliad*, and where the Ottoman Empire fought battles that would shape the world. History buffs can immerse themselves in marvels and mementos stretching back to the dawn of civilisation.

Then again, if you want to simply unwind, spend an afternoon being pampered at a *hamam*, or let the warm waters of the Mediterranean lap at your toes. Adventure lovers can head east, to uncover a wild, exotic, Turkey. Bon vivants need look no further than İstanbul, where the markets and bars are among the most stylish and atmospheric, and the mod Ottoman cuisine rates as the tastiest, in the world.

The country's tumultuous history has left a deep legacy. People who've never had to suffer for an idea or fight for a patch of land can be overwhelmed by the passion of ordinary Turks for their country. But for ordinary Turks that passion finds its outlet, not in martial ardour, but in simple pleasures: family, food, music, football, and friendship. Turks have an inspiring ability to keep things in perspective, to get on with everyday life and to have a bloody good time in the process. Sharing their joy in the simple things is a highlight for every visitor.

Treat Turkey as that most quintessential of Turkish dishes, the meze, a table piled high with scrumptious treats. Throw away the menu, order a plate of everything and feast till you can't go on. *Afiyet olsun!*

OPPOSITE: JOHN ELK III

JEFF GREENBERG

Ancient Sites & Ruins

A Roman-built walkway at the Great Theatre is the perfect invitation for the visitor to go and explore, Miletus (p266)

JOHN ELK III

IZZET KERIBAR

Giant stone heads rest in front of the Antiochus I funerary mound, Nemrut Dağı National Park (p610)

The ruins of the tetrapylon make a fine picnic stop, Afrodisias (p329)

SUSAN ST

ADINA TOVY AMSEL

The ancient Library of Celsus graces the best-preserved classical city in the eastern Mediterranean, Ephesus (p251)

JOHN ELK III

Lycian rock-hewn tombs dot the hillside around ancient Myra (p378), near Kale

The Temple of Trajan strikes a dramatic profile at the Acropolis of Pergamum (p220), Bergama

DIANA MAYFIELD

Diverse Landscapes

Springtime adds a sprinkle of colour to a vista of fairy chimneys, Göreme Open-Air Museum (p499)

Barren mountains and verdant valleys are a feature of the the Kaçkar Mountains region (p558), northeastern Anatolia

The resort at Belcekız lies nestled between the mountainous and beach, Ölüdeniz (p359)

A snow-covered field separates brooding Erciyes Dağı (Mt Erciyes) from a surreal rocky landscape, Cappadocia (p492)

Mosques & Palaces

Soft evening lights illuminate the Blue Mosque (p106) in Sultanahmet, İstanbul

The harem (p112) at Topkapı Palace is an absolute must-see, İstanbul

A prayer hall at a mosque awaits the coming of the faithful, Konya (p481)

The Rüstem Paşa Camii (p117) provides a perfect location for some devout contemplation, İstanbul

The 17th-century İshak Paşa Palace (p586), evokes stories from *A Thousand and One Nights*, Doğubeyazıt

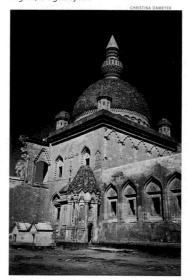

Old mosques lie in varous states of disrepair, Van (p637)

Bazaars

The art of calligraphy is kept alive in the Grand Bazaar (Kapalı Çarşı; p115), İstanbul

PHIL WEYMOUTH

Baharat (spices) and *çay* (tea) make shopping in the Spice Bazaar (p118) a thrill for all the senses, İstanbul

DIANA MAYFIELD

JOHN E

Shops and their offerings spill out into a mall of the Grand Bazaar (p115), İstanbul

Contents

Regional Map Contents

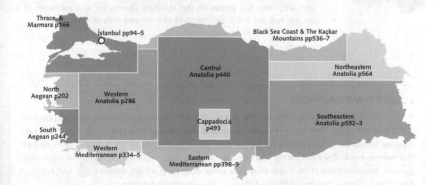

Thrace & Marmara p166
İstanbul pp94–5
Black Sea Coast & The Kaçkar Mountains pp536–7
Northeastern Anatolia p564
North Aegean p202
Western Anatolia p286
Central Anatolia p440
Southeastern Anatolia p592–3
South Aegean p244
Cappadocia p493
Western Mediterranean p334–5
Eastern Mediterranean pp398–9

The Authors

VERITY CAMPBELL Introductory chapters, İstanbul, Directory, Transport

Straight after high school Verity visited Turkey and ended up staying for 18 months, learning the language, teaching English and hitchhiking throughout the country. She crisscrossed Australia and Turkey for the next 15 years until she finally persuaded both husband and toddler they'd enjoy a year in İstanbul. Verity has worked for six years as an author for Lonely Planet in various countries, but no prizes for guessing where her heart lies. As well as coordinating and authoring on this book, Verity has authored the *İstanbul Encounter* guide, several chapters in *Turkey 8*, and the Turkey chapter for *Mediterranean Europe* and *Europe on a shoestring*.

Coordinating Author's Favourite Trip

The southeast is my all-time favourite region of Turkey. Diyarbakır (p621), the Kurdish heartland, is a magical city steeped in ancient history, with its recent turbulent history etched on every face. A visit here is transforming. I then head southeast to Mardin (p626) to explore its dusty laneways, frenzied bazaars, and superb architecture. From Mardin I pay homage to the ancient Tigris and ill-fated Hasankeyf (p632). I then scoot through the seemingly all-male towns of Batman and Bitlis to Van (p637). To me this city is the barometer of Turkey's modernisation. When I first visited in the early 1990s I was virtually the only woman on the street. The optimistic chit-chat of both sexes in the streets, cafés and bars today fuels this liberal metropolis.

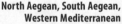

FRANCES LINZEE GORDON North Aegean, South Aegean, Western Mediterranean

Frances' fervour for travel was first sparked by a school scholarship when she was aged 17. More recently, she completed an MA in African & Asian (Middle Eastern) Studies in London, of which Ottoman history formed a major part. Keen to test out her studies, she champed at the bit to travel around Turkey. The combination of history and hedonism, sophistication and simplicity, but above all the absolute charm, wit and welcome of the people saw her soon smitten, and she dreams only of returning.

LONELY PLANET AUTHORS

Why is our travel information the best in the world? It's simple: our authors are independent, dedicated travellers. They don't research using just the internet or phone, and they don't take freebies in exchange for positive coverage. They travel widely, to all the popular spots and off the beaten track. They personally visit thousands of hotels, restaurants, cafés, bars, galleries, palaces, museums and more – and they take pride in getting all the details right, and telling it how it is. For more, see the authors section on www.lonelyplanet.com.

JEAN-BERNARD CARILLET   Northeastern Anatolia, Southeastern Anatolia

Jean-Bernard's love for Turkey was first sparked by a train ride from Paris that ended in İstanbul during his teenage years. Since this initiation, the lure of Turkey has never been tamed. For this edition, he was all too happy to travel the breadth and length of the most remote corners of eastern Anatolia, full of (good) surprises. As an incorrigible Frenchman and foodie, he also ate more *fıstıklı* baklava (pistachio baklava) and kebaps than he cares to remember. A full-time writer and photographer based in Paris, he has contributed to numerous Lonely Planet titles, including the previous edition of *Turkey*.

TOM PARKINSON   Thrace & Marmara, Western Anatolia, Central Anatolia, Black Sea & Kaçkar Mountains

Tom's first experience of Turkish culture was living on a street full of kebap shops in Berlin, Germany, and it was only a matter of time before he graduated to the real thing. Having covered the standard western circuit for Mediterranean Europe, he returned to seek out the varied delights of Turkey, from wrestlers in Thrace and cave dwellings in central Anatolia to mountain rakı (aniseed brandy) in the Kaçkars, with quick incursions into Georgia and Bulgaria for good measure. Thanks to diligent research, Tom remains an unrivalled authority on the relative merits of döners worldwide.

DAN ELDRIDGE   Antalya region, Eastern Mediterranean

Dan first visited Turkey in 2001, when he ferried across the Aegean Sea from Greece in search of odd jobs. After briefly working as a tour guide on a *gulet* (traditional yacht) that sailed between Marmaris and Fethiye, Dan relocated to İstanbul, where he taught English and worked as an editor for a monthly backpackers' magazine. For this edition, Dan explored Antalya and the length of Turkey's eastern Mediterranean, a region blessed with gorgeous ruined cities and sprawling beaches. A native of California, Dan works as a full-time freelance journalist. He lives in Philadelphia.

VIRGINIA MAXWELL   Cappadocia

After working for many years as a publishing manager at Lonely Planet's Melbourne headquarters, Virginia decided that she'd be happier writing guidebooks rather than commissioning them. Since making this decision she's authored Lonely Planet's *İstanbul* city guide and covered Egypt, Spain, Lebanon, Syria and the United Arab Emirates for other titles. She has made multiple trips to Turkey with partner Peter and young son Max, and nominates İstanbul and Cappadocia as her favourite parts of the country.

CONTRIBUTING AUTHORS

Kate Clow Kate has lived in Turkey since 1989, working first in İstanbul and Ankara. After moving to Antalya, she researched Turkey's first long-distance walking route – the Lycian Way – and, with the help of Garanti Bank, opened the route in 1999. Since then she has implemented a second route – the St Paul Trail. Kate also leads trekking groups, flower and birding groups and cultural tours in the Turkish Lake District, Pontic Alps and Van regions. Kate, with her partner, Terry Richardson, has worked as a photographer and contributor to various magazines and books on Turkey, as well as international trekking guides. Kate wrote the Trekking chapter.

Will Gourlay A serial visitor to Turkey, Will first arrived in İstanbul over 15 years ago intending to sit on a Turkish beach. However, he couldn't resist the lure of Anatolia and ended up climbing Nemrut Dağı and traipsing from the Black Sea to the Syrian border. Will subsequently taught in İzmir for a year, learning of the delights of İskender kebap and the perils of rakı. When not obsessing on all things Turkish/Turkic/Ottoman-related he works as a commissioning editor in Lonely Planet's London office. Will wrote the History chapter and contributed some sidebars to the Culture chapter.

Dr Caroline Evans The Health chapter is adapted from text prepared by Dr Caroline Evans.

Getting Started

Travelling in Turkey is a breeze thanks to the laid-back charm of the locals, bus transport that's second to none, and the sheer volume of accommodation options, from friendly cheap-as-chips backpackers to immaculately groomed boutique guesthouses. Only during the height of peak season or on public holidays would you be wise to book ahead; at most times you can just turn up and find your first accommodation choice awaiting.

WHEN TO GO

Spring (April to May) and autumn (September to October) are the best times to visit, since the climate will be perfect for sightseeing in İstanbul and on the Aegean and Mediterranean coasts, and it will be cool in central Anatolia, but not unpleasantly so. Visiting before mid-June or after August may also help you avoid mosquitoes. If your primary drive is for beach-bumming, mid-May to September is perfect for the Aegean and Mediterranean coasts, if a little steamy out of the water. The Black Sea coast is best visited between April and September – there will still be rain but not so much of it. Head to eastern Turkey from late June to September, but not before May or after mid-October unless you're prepared for snow, road closures and bone-chilling temperatures.

See Climate Charts (p653) for more information.

With the exception of İstanbul, Turkey doesn't really have a winter tourism season (see p20 for more details). Most accommodation along the Aegean, Mediterranean and Black Sea and in some parts of Cappadocia is closed from mid-October until late April. These dates are not set in stone and depend on how the season is going. High season is from July to mid-September, and prices are at their peak.

Anticipate crowds along all coastal areas from mid-June until early September. You will need to plan ahead when travelling during the four- or five-day Kurban Bayramı, as banks shut and ATMs may run out of cash (for more details see p660). Also, try not to visit the Gallipoli Peninsula around Anzac Day (25 April) unless it's particularly important for you to be there at that time.

COSTS & MONEY

Turkey is no longer Europe's bargain-basement destination, but it still offers good value for money. Costs are lowest in eastern Anatolia, and Cappadocia,

---

DON'T LEAVE HOME WITHOUT...

- 'Cover-up' clothing for mosque visits. Women might want to bring a scarf, although if you don't you've got a good excuse to go shopping.

- Slip-on shoes or sandals. Highly recommended as they are cool to wear and easy to remove before entering mosques or Turkish homes.

- Books in English. Those available in Turkey are hard to find and can be pricey. Second-hand book exchanges plug the gaps, but you'll need to have something to swap.

- Tampons. They can be hard to find as most Turkish women use pads.

- Universal sink plug.

- An appetite for kebaps.

- First-aid kit including sunscreen, which can be expensive in Turkey.

- Checking your government's travel warnings (see p655).

Selçuk, Pamukkale and Olympos still offer bargain prices. Prices are highest in İstanbul, İzmir, Ankara and the touristy coastal cities and towns. In these places you can get by on €30 to €40 per person per day, provided you use public transport, stay in pensions, share bathrooms and eat out at a basic eatery once a day (add extra for entry to sights). Away from İstanbul, and the Aegean and Mediterranean coasts, budget travellers can travel on as little as €25 to €35 per day. Throughout the country for €35 to €55 per day you can upgrade to midrange hotels with private bathrooms and eat most meals in restaurants. On more than €55 per day you can enjoy Turkey's boutique hotels, take occasional flights, and wine and dine out every day.

We quote all costs in this guidebook in euros. Although inflation has dropped from the stratospheric levels of the 1990s to around 9%, if we quoted Turkish new lira, prices would probably be out of date before the book even emerged from the printers.

TRAVEL LITERATURE

Since time immemorial travellers have written about their rambles across Turkey. Herodotus (5th century BC), Xenophon (5th century BC) and Strabo (1st century BC) have all left us accounts of Anatolia in antiquity. The famous march to Persia by the Greek army, immortalised in Xenophon's *Anabasis*, has been retraced some 2400 years later by Shane Brennan in his fabulous tale, *In the Tracks of the Ten Thousand: A Journey on Foot Through Turkey, Syria and Iraq*. Mary Wortley Montagu's *Turkish Embassy Letters* details the author's travels to Istanbul with her husband, the British ambassador to Turkey, in 1716. It's a surprisingly nonjudgemental account of life at the heart of the Ottoman Empire.

Edmondo De Amicis' *Constantinople*, first published in 1877, has been recently translated into English. While its main focus is İstanbul, this classic beautifully details the exoticism of the city and the cosmopolitan nature of 19th-century Turkey. *Alexander's Path*, by the indomitable Freya Stark, will appeal to those who wish they too could have visited the classical sites of the coast in the early 20th century.

HOW MUCH?

Loaf of bread €0.20

Glass of *çay* €0.20

100km by bus €3-3.50

Short dolmuş trip €0.65

Turkish Daily News €1

TOURING TURKEY IN WINTER

Unlike other Mediterranean hot spots, Turkey doesn't have a winter tourism season. However, for some travellers, winter is the best time to visit İstanbul: expect snow and chilly temperatures, but you get to enjoy the sights without the tourist press, and the touts are too busy savouring the low season to bother you in earnest.

All restaurants and hotels remain open in İstanbul year-round. You also won't have problems finding somewhere to stay in Ankara, İzmir or other big nontouristy cities where the hotels cater primarily to business travellers.

Even during a mild winter most hotels and restaurants along the Aegean and Mediterranean, and many in Cappadocia, close from mid-October to late April. Forget about choice – you may have to stay in the one place in town that's open.

Deep snow is a standard feature of the eastern Turkish winter with mountain passes regularly closed and buses delayed. Even some airports may close because they lack radar equipment. The central and western Anatolian winter is more fickle. One year you can be picnicking in the Ihlara Gorge in January, the following year subzero temperatures, deep snow and lethal ice make it impossible to venture further than the nearest shop.

If you're lucky enough to find a hotel open in winter, you'd be well advised to verify whether the heating is turned on before checking in. If the hot water comes from solar panels, beware – like pipes, the panels freeze up in winter.

TOP FIVE

Festivals

Turks really know how to have a good time, so it should come as no surprise to hear a festival or event is on nearly every other day. These are our top five; see p658 for others.

- Camel wrestling (p246) Bloodless bull-wrestling.
- Nevruz (p658) Kurds, Alevis and everyone else celebrate the ancient Middle Eastern spring knees-up on 21 March with joviality.
- Aspendos Opera & Ballet Festival (p395) Unbeatable Roman-era venue.
- Kafkasör Kültür ve Sanat Festivalı (p575) More bloodless bull-wrestling.
- Kırkpınar Oil Wrestling Competition (p171) Yet more battling, but this time it's greasy buck-wrestling!

Must-Reads

Given Turkey's long history and vibrant culture it's hardly surprising that it has provided copious source material for authors old and new, local and foreign. For more information about Turkish authors and the literary tradition in Turkey, see p55.

- *Birds Without Wings*, by Louis de Bernières. If you only read one book about Turkey, make this it. Superbly written and researched historical fiction.
- *Memed, My Hawk*, by Yaşar Kemal. If this were a movie, it would rival the tear-jerking *Gone with the Wind*.
- *Snow*, by Orhan Pamuk. Pamuk's fictional insight unearths Turkey's contemporary challenges.
- *Atatürk*, by Andrew Mango. Get to know one of the 20th century's most intriguing political figures, virtually unknown outside his homeland.
- *Portrait of a Turkish Family*, by Irfan Orga. This page-turner is so intimate you'll feel like an honorary family member.

R&R

Ooo la la. You've come to the right place with your empty to-do list. In one word: *hamams*. These are our favourite, plus a couple of other options to indulge in some much-needed R&R.

- Çemberlitaş Hamamı, İstanbul (p133) Touristy sure, but sublime architecture and a head-to-toe service make a visit to this ancient institution a must.
- Cağaloğlu Hamamı, İstanbul (p133) Arm-wrestling with Çemberlitaş Hamamı for the title of most beautiful *hamam*. Heck, try both!
- Kurşunlu Banyo, Termal (p287) Soak your toes in steamy, mineral waters, then cool them off in the open-air pool – bliss!
- Kabak (p363) The word's starting to get out about this off-the-beaten-path beach community. Get there fast.
- Sultaniye Hot Springs and Mud Baths (p351) They'd pay a packet for this in Manhattan, a nose-to-tail mineral mud-pack.

In *From the Holy Mountain*, William Dalrymple retraces the journey of 6th-century monk John Moschos who wandered the reaches of eastern Byzantium from Mt Athos, Greece, through İstanbul, Anatolia and the Middle East to Egypt. This is a gripping meditation on the declining Christian communities, and amusing 'ta boot'. İstanbul-based poet John Ash provides a must-read for anyone interested in the Byzantine monuments scattered around İstanbul, Cappadocia and the rest of Turkey in *A Byzantine Journey*.

Balthasar's Odyssey, by Amin Maalouf, is a gripping tale of a Levantine merchant who travels through 17th-century Constantinople in search of the 'hundredth name' of God.

The lives of the disappearing Yörük, once one of Anatolia's largest nomadic tribes, have long captured the imagination of writers. Irfan Orga's superbly evocative *The Caravan Moves On: Three Weeks Among Turkish Nomads,* first published in 1958, details the author's journey and insights into the lives and lore of the nomads in the 1950s. An excellent follow-up read is *Bolkar: Travels with a Donkey in the Taurus Mountains,* by Dux Schneider, a bitter-sweet insight into the lives of the Yörük and Tatars today.

The 8.55 to Baghdad: From London to Iraq on the Trail of Agatha Christie, by Andrew Eames, retraces the crime queen's travels on the *Orient Express* with a chapter dedicated to the author's Turkey adventures.

INTERNET RESOURCES

ExpatinTurkey.com (www.expatinturkey.com) Expats' travel advice including jobs, working visas and eating, drinking and sleeping recommendations. The occasional cattiness makes for great reading.

Lonely Planet (www.lonelyplanet.com) Check out the Thorn Tree bulletin board to find out the latest travellers' tips for travelling the country, especially out east.

My Merhaba (www.mymerhaba.com) Aimed at expats with lots of general information of use to visitors too (such as what's on in İstanbul and restaurant reviews).

Skylife magazine (www.thy.com/en-US/skylife) Click through to the archive of the excellent Turkish Airlines in-flight magazine, *Skylife,* with articles on all sorts of aspects of life in Turkey.

Tourism Turkey (www.tourismturkey.org) Government website with grab-bag of articles and information.

Turkey Travel Planner (www.turkeytravelplanner.com) An ever-growing site with up-to-the-minute information on all aspects of travel in Turkey.

Turkish Daily News (www.turkishdailynews.com.tr) All the latest local news.

Itineraries
CLASSIC ROUTES

FROM THE GOLDEN HORN TO THE SACRED WAY
One Week /
İstanbul to Ephesus

Hold tight for a whiz through the triumphs, glories and tragedies of empires. Begin in İstanbul, once the glittering heart of the Byzantine and Ottoman Empires. Start with the **Topkapı Palace** (p109), one-time home of Ottoman sultans, obelisk-hop the ancient **Hippodrome** (p106), and steam away any aches with a massage at **Çemberlitaş Hamamı** (p133). Late evening, do as the locals do and head to İstiklal Caddesi, heart of modern Turkey, and a helluva place for people-watching. The buzzing *meyhanes* (taverns) behind **Çiçek Pasajı** (p146) are a must. If you needed an excuse to dip into a glass or three of rakı (aniseed-flavoured grape brandy), you'll find plenty of peer pressure here. On day two start with the **Blue Mosque** (p106), then the magnificent **Aya Sofya** (p104). Afterwards head underground at the atmospheric **Basilica Cistern** (p108) and take a charged credit card and plenty of stamina to the labyrinthine **Grand Bazaar** (p115). Weather permitting, on day three you could take a cruise along the **Bosphorus** (p128), and peer over to the Black Sea after you've hiked off your delish fish lunch at **Anadolu Kavağı** (p131).

Come day four rise early and head down to Çanakkale, so you can be touring the **Gallipoli battlefields** (p183) by early afternoon. The devastation witnessed here during WWI needs no introduction. Next morning head to famous **Troy** (p203), worth a visit even without Brad Pitt. You'll need another early start to bus down to Selçuk, the base for visiting the ruins of **Ephesus** (p251), the best preserved classical city in the eastern Mediterranean.

Tick off İstanbul's A-list sights, the Gallipoli battle-fields, and the ruins of Troy and Ephesus in one action-packed week, a journey of 1450km.

COAST & CAPPADOCIA
Three Weeks / İstanbul to Cappadocia

For the first week, follow the first itinerary; see p23. Then, from your base at Selçuk, day-trip to the travertines and ruins of Hierapolis at **Pamukkale** (p324). The brilliant white terraces can be dizzying in the midday sun, but a dip in Hierapolis Termal's swimming pool will restore your cool.

Heading back to the coast, ignore the overblown resorts of Bodrum and Marmaris and head straight for **Fethiye** (p353) and beautiful **Ölüdeniz** (p359). This is the spot to take to the air on a paraglide or lay way low on a beach towel. You're now within kicking distance of the famous **Lycian Way** (p78); hike for a day through superb countryside to overnight in heavenly **Faralya** (p362), and further inroads into the Lycian Way will definitely head up your 'next time' list. Back on the coast, pit stop at laid-back **Kaş** (p371), its pretty harbourside square alive nightly with the hum of friendly folk enjoying the breeze, views, boutique browsing and a beer or two. You may want a few days more unwinding at the famous beach tree house complexes at **Olympos** (p379) close by.

Antalya's old **Kaleiçi quarter** (p384) is well worth a wander against the backdrop of that jaw-dropping mountain range. Then it's time to fold your bikini into a matchbox and head inland. Catch an overnight bus north to claim your cave in **Göreme** (p499). This low-key travellers' hang-out is the best place to base yourself in **Cappadocia** (p492), a surreal moonscape with phallic tuff cones, no less. For most the cones don't overshadow the more orthodox sights including the superb rock-cut frescoed churches of **Göreme Open-Air Museum** (p499) and the spooky underground cities at **Derinkuyu** (p528) and **Kaymaklı** (p528).

This is one trip you won't forget in a hurry. Pack your towel, pumps, pedometer – you're seeing the sights of Old İstanbul, the highlights of the Aegean and the Mediterranean coasts and finishing off in kooky Cappadocia – a whopping 3100km of travel.

ROADS LESS TRAVELLED

EASTERN DELIGHTS
Three to Four Weeks / Trabzon to Nemrut Dağı

Buzzing **Trabzon** (p548) has a handful of sights worth a quick look-see, though most people head straight to nearby **Sumela monastery** (p554), peering down on a forested valley from its precarious-looking rockface. The route from here to Kars is spectacular. First travel from **Trabzon to Erzurum** (p555) and then continue via **Yusufeli** (p571). The route is best done by car or taxi as you'd miss the breathtaking views and ruined churches of medieval Georgia whizzing past in a bus. The onward drive between Yusufeli, Artvin and Kars is one of Turkey's most scenic (see p576), with roadways passing over dramatic mountain ranges, through gorges frothing with white water and past crumbling castles. **Kars** (p577) is beguiling, but its star attraction is **Ani** (p581), close by, once a thriving Armenian capital, but now a field strewn with magnificent ruins overlooked by the border guards of modern Armenia.

Head south to the raffish frontier town of **Doğubayazıt** (p586) and the outstanding **İshak Paşa Palace** (p586).

Further south is **Van** (p637), its proud drawcards the nearby spectacular **Hoşap Castle** (p643) and the 10th-century **Akdamar church** (p636), the sole inhabitant of a teeny island in Lake Van. The church's superbly preserved carvings just pip the wow factor on this church's magnificent setting.

Heading west, don't miss **Hasankeyf** (p632), with its soaring rock-cut castle by the ancient Tigris River, and **Mardin** (p626), a gorgeous, honey-coloured town overlooking the roasting plains of Mesopotamia. From Mardin head north to **Diyarbakır** (p621), the exotic heartland of Kurdish culture, its ancient sights ringed by even older city walls. Finally, see what all the fuss is about at **Nemrut Dağı** (p610), the gigantic stone heads the only image of eastern Turkey that does make it into brochures.

Escape the crowds and hightail it to the Turkey rarely seen in glossy tourist brochures, the other Turkey: the wild, magnificent east. After it casts its spell you'll find western Turkey downright tame. Some 2740km, and never a dull moment.

THE CARAVAN TRAIL
Two Weeks / Kuşadası to Dıyarbakır

Caravanserais (see p57), dotting the routes of ancient trade routes, were once the ancient equivalent of the roadhouse. Today they're renovated as historical sights and hotels, or are sadly crumbling away. All evoke the nights of snorting animals tethered in the courtyard, with the rooms above abuzz with the snores of travellers and merchants.

Spending a night at overblown Kuşadası is worth it for **Club Caravanserai** (p261), the pleasant rooms playing second fiddle to the 'Turkish Nights' show in the courtyard. Plant your tongue in your cheek and enjoy. Head east to famous Pamukkale, but instead of the travertines admire the beautiful carved gateway of the **Ak Han** (p329) and the nearby Kaklık Cave, the underground 'Pamukkale' that tourists rarely see. Head north to **Otel Dülgeroğlu** (p311) in Uşak, now a mighty fine hotel. Continue north to Bursa's **Koza Han** (p296); visit in June or September to join the heaving throng engaging in the age-old haggle of the silk trade.

From Bursa, head east to the **Cinci Han** (p457), as good excuse as any to visit the World Heritage–listed Ottoman town of Safranbolu. From here head south to Cappadocia, a region with more caravanserais than fleas on a camel. Highlights include **Ağzıkara Hanı** (p534), the superb **Sultanhanı** (p491), Turkey's largest caravanserai, and **Sultan Han** (p499), runner up to that title. **Sarıhan** (p515) and **Saruhan** (p527) both offer something slightly different. The first doubles as a set for whirling dervish *sema* and the latter is home to a fine eatery. From Cappadocia head east to pit stop at **Battalgazi** (p619) near Malatya. End your caravan journey in style at the atmospheric **Otel Büyük Kervansaray** (p625) in beguiling Diyarbakır, Kurdish heartland and a soulful city steeped in history.

No camels and very little grunt is required on this 1800km adventure into Turkey's lesser-known but magnificent hinterland. From tourist-trashed Kuşadası to sublimely exotic Diyarbakır, saddle up and hit the hans.

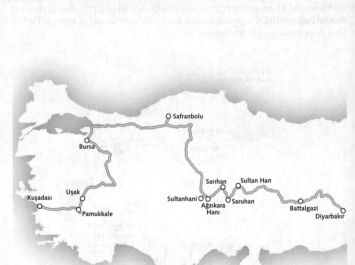

TAILORED TRIPS

NINE WONDERS OF TURKEY   Three Weeks to Tick Off Turkey's A-List

Unesco has applied World Heritage status to nine of Turkey's sights.

Start by soaking up the treasures of **Old İstanbul** (p104), then head to **Troy** (p203) with city layered upon city for the last 5000 years. **Pamukkale** (p324) boasts the famous dazzling white travertines and the ruins of Hierapolis, a city once known for the curative powers of its warm calcium-rich waters.

On the southern coast, **Xanthos** (p366) was once the glittering Lycian capital city, with **Letoön** (p365), close by, its religious sanctuary. Inland, hidden in the fairytale landscape of Cappadocia, **Göreme Open-Air Museum** (p499) is a cluster of rock-hewn Byzantine churches and monasteries. The going gets more rugged when you head to **Nemrut Dağı** (p610) and the proud 'thrones of the gods', which have been standing sentinel for over two millennia. From there head northward to the mosque-*medrese* complex of **Divriği** (p481), the least-visited of Turkey's World Heritage sites yet one of the most rewarding for its out-of-the-way location and the jaw-dropping ornamentation.

The ancient Hittites' magnificent capital was **Hattuşa** (p464) – the gorgeous rural location itself is as enthralling as the remains of the sprawling city. Head back towards İstanbul via the pristine Ottoman townscape of **Safranbolu** (p455), where you can soak up the atmosphere overnight in a meticulously maintained Ottomansion.

TURKEY FOR TASTEBUDS   Time Enough to Ease a Belt Hole or Three

Turks are deservedly proud of their scrumptious cuisine, and different parts of the country are known – and loved – for their specialities.

People may avoid you for days after, but **Tokat kebap** (see p476) – a lamb-basted eggplant kebap boasting a full fist of garlic – is worth every bite. Greasy, but worth it is *İskender* kebap – best sampled in eateries in **Bursa** (p299). The squid caught off the north Aegean coast is the finest in the nation; get it cooked fresh at **Sığacık** (p241) and you'll be boasting for years. If you overindulge, hope that the *mesir macunu* (power gum; p235) sold in nearby Manisa can cure you. Time your visit for the spring equinox to see the townsfolk concocting this tooth-binding elixir.

There ain't nought more experienced at making **lokum (Turkish delight)** than the folk at Ali Muhaddin Hacı Bekir (p153) in İstanbul, ancestors of the shop's namesake who invented the stuff. **Afyon** (p311) is famous for its immense crop of poppies and the rich clotted *kaymak* cream, reputedly so good because the cows graze on the poppies. Gaziantep boasts a trifecta: **fıstık (pistachios), baklava and künefe**. Blending the first two together for an addictive finger-licking treat is İmam Çağdaş **(p597)**. **Kahramanmaraş** (p591) is the *dondurma* (ice cream) capital of Turkey. Served in fist-sized blocks, it's best tackled with a knife and fork.

WE DARE YOU
As Long As You've Got

Travel in Turkey can be 100% pure adventure or soft and gooey like a piece of Turkish delight. You could leave your bathers on the coast and explore the regions and outdoor activities of Turkey unknown even to most Turks; maybe even criss-cross borders to pass a day or two with Turkey's exotic neighbours. We're not encouraging you to do silly things; do your own research and make sure you check out the latest situation (see p655) before you launch out on any adventure.

For those keen to explore places well off the beaten trail, western Anatolia's Phrygian Valley (p304) offers spectacular scenery and Phrygian ruins. And now that the troubles in the southeast are seemingly on the mend, former no-go zones in the east are opening up to visitors (see p644). The **upper valley of the Euphrates**, between Elazığ and Erzincan (p620), is still uncharted territory; as is the stupendous scenery of the wild far southeast surrounding isolated **Bahçesaray (p643)**, **Hakkari (p644)**, and **Şırnak (p633)**. Get there before the tourists do.

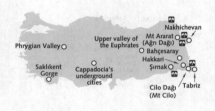

The claustrophobic but compelling underground cities (p528) of Cappadocia were once a haven from invading armies. Today you're lucky enough to be able to play at being a troglodyte. Hire a guide, take a good torch and delve deep into **Özlüce** (p528), **Güzelyurt** (p532) and **Özkonak** (p515), underground cities well off the tourist trail.

Most tourists just ice their toes in the **Saklıkent Gorge** (p364), but there's a full 18km to be explored by white-water rafting, canyoning and hiking. Mountaineers might want to tackle Mt Ararat (p589), which has captivated the imaginations of travellers for centuries, and check out developments at **Cilo Dağı** (Cilo Mountains; p644). Word is out that trekking trips will be starting here any day. See p77 for other trekking possibilities and p648 for other outdoor opportunities.

One of the authors of this book confesses to being a border-crossing junkie. For others out there Turkey has several gnarly border crossings: Georgia–Turkey, Azerbaijan–Turkey, Iran–Turkey and Iraq–Turkey. Spend a night in **Georgia** (p585) with a full-bodied red *wink*. Peep into **Azerbaijan's** (p586) isolated back pocket, Nakhichevan and spend a day in this intriguing oil- and gas-rich nation. Follow the classic hippy overland trail by dropping out in Iran. Enter from Doğubayazıt (p588), or maybe from the more intrepid Esendere–Seró border crossing (p645) and spend a day or two in magical Tabriz. You can even follow Tony Wheeler's footsteps into **northern Iraq** (p631) to see for yourself what's happening in this Kurdish heartland.

Snapshot

True to the topsy-turvy nature of Turkish politics, Turkey's ardour for Europe has cooled somewhat in the last couple of years. Locals are less than impressed with the West over recent policies in the Middle East and are also grumbling that meeting the stringent EU conditions for accession compromises Turkey's autonomy. Given its youthful population base (compared with the EU's ageing population) and key geostrategic location, they argue that Europe needs Turkey more than Turkey needs Europe. 'Let them come to us.' Nevertheless the government pushes doggedly ahead with legislative overhauls and official accession talks, which started at last in October 2005.

The Cyprus issue continues to be a stumbling block. Turkey's refusal to 'abandon' Turkish Cypriots continues to drive a wedge between it and EU member states Greek and Cyprus, whose support it will need if Turkey's bid is to succeed. And the negative press received when Turkey's best-known author Orhan Pamuk was tried for 'insulting Turkishness' (p51) has put the spotlight on the government's declared commitment to freedom of expression. With no guarantee of acceptance into the EU anyway, it seems that Turkey may remain teetering at the edge of Europe for some time.

EU or not, exciting developments are taking place in the country. The government is overhauling the rail network, greatly improving the country's transport infrastructure. İstanbul's mighty cross-Bosphorus tunnel project will relieve road congestion in a city that is in danger of grinding to a halt (p159).

In other respects, too, the government of Prime Minister Erdoğan has much to be proud of. It has trodden a remarkably skilful path through Turkey's minefield of vested interests. The country's economic nemesis, runaway inflation, has been held in check (p46). And despite a few hiccups, including the currency fall of early 2006, employment growth is robust. Relations with traditional rival Greece have been improving, so that a collision of Turkish and Greek military aircraft in May 2006 caused barely a diplomatic ripple. Life for the Kurds of southeast Anatolia is improving at last. EU-pushed government concessions have fostered a growing optimism, and the security forces have largely eased their stranglehold over the Kurdish provinces. While sporadic bombings by a breakaway group of Kurdish rebels act as reminders that the Kurds' problems are far from resolved, most people are confident that Turkey will not fall to the depths it reached during Abdullah Öcalan's reign of terror (p48). There are even signs of a thaw in relations with Armenia.

Erdoğan's greatest test, however, is likely to come as he confronts Turkey's secular institutions, including the all-powerful military clique. All eyes will be turned to the up-and-coming presidential elections, as the role of the president is seen as the arch-defender of secularism in Turkey. If openly religious Erdoğan becomes president this will be a first for the republic. Everyone has an opinion on a president whose wife wears a headscarf (see p52).

FAST FACTS

Population: 70.4 million

Surface area: 779,452 sq km

Highest mountain: Mt Ararat 5137m

Longest river: Kızılırmak 1355km

'Biggest flag flown at greatest height'. Held by Turks

İstanbul's ranking among world's most expensive cities: 18th

Average annual salary: €3500

Life expectancy: men 68, women 73

Percentage of population supporting Turkey's application to join EU: 73% 2004, 43% 2006

History

Fate has put Turkey at the junction of two continents. As a land bridge, a meeting point and a battleground, it has seen peoples moving in both directions between Europe and Asia throughout recorded history. That human traffic has left monuments and debris, dynasties and lasting cultural legacies, all of which have contributed to the character of modern Turkey. Turkish history is such a hugely rich patchwork of overlapping eras and empires that it boasts figures, events and phenomena familiar even to the layperson.

EARLY CULTURES, CITIES & CLASHES

Archaeological finds indicate that the earliest Anatolian hunter-gatherers lived in caves during the Palaeolithic era. By around the 7th millennium BC some folk had abandoned their nomadic existence and formed settlements. Çatalhöyük (p489), which arose around 6500 BC, may well be the first ever city. It was certainly a centre of innovation – here locals developed crop irrigation and were the first to domesticate pigs and sheep, as well as create distinctive pottery and what is thought to have been the first-ever landscape picture. Relics from this settlement can be seen at Ankara's Museum of Anatolian Civilisations (p443).

The Chalcolithic age saw the rise of Hacılar, near current-day Burdur in Central Anatolia, as well as communities in the southeast, which absorbed Mesopotamian influences, including the use of metal tools. Across Anatolia more and larger communities sprung up and interacted – not always happily: settlements tended to be fortified.

By 3000 BC advances in metallurgy allowed power to be concentrated in certain hands, leading to the creation of various Anatolian kingdoms. One such kingdom was at Alacahöyük (p467). Alacahöyük was in the heart of Anatolia, yet even this place showed Caucasian influence, evidence of trade far beyond the Anatolian plateau.

Trade, too, was increasing on the southern and western coasts, with Troy trading with the Aegean islands and mainland Greece. Around 2000 BC the Hatti people created a capital at Kanesh (Kültepe, near Kayseri), ruling over an extensive web of trading communities. Here for the first time Anatolian history emerges from the realm of archaeological conjecture and becomes 'real': clay tablets left at Kanesh provide written records of dates, events and names.

No singular, significant Anatolian civilisation had yet emerged, but the tone was set for the millennia to come: cultural interaction, trade and war were to become the recurring themes of Anatolian history.

AGES OF BRONZE: THE HITTITES

The Hatti were only a temporary presence. As they declined, a new people, the Hittites, assumed their territory. From Alacahöyük, the Hittites shifted their capital to Hattuşa (near present-day Boğazkale; p464) some time around 1800 BC.

The Hittites' legacy consisted of their great capital, as well as their state archives (cuneiform clay tablets) and distinctive artistic styles. By 1450 BC

Anatolia is so named for the Greek word anatolē meaning 'rising of the sun'. The Turkish 'anadolu' translates, very roughly, as 'motherlode'.

Archaeologist Ian Hodder's *Catalhoyuk: The Leopard's Tale* is an account of the excavation of the site, which vividly portrays life as it was during the city's heyday.

Until the rediscovery of the ruins at Boğazkale in the 19th century, the Hittites were known only through an obscure reference in the Old Testament.

---

c 7500 BC	c 1180 BC
Founding of settlement at Çatalhöyük	Fall of Homer's Troy

the kingdom, having endured internal ructions, was reborn as an empire. In creating the first great Anatolian empire, the Hittites were necessarily warlike, but also displayed other imperial trappings – they ruled over myriad vassal states and princelings while also being noted for their sense of ethics and an occasional penchant for diplomacy. This didn't prevent them from overrunning Ramses II of Egypt in 1298 BC, but did allow them to patch things up with the crestfallen Ramses by dividing up Syria with him and marrying him to a Hittite princess.

The Hittite empire was harassed in its later stages by subject principalities, including Troy (p203) on the Aegean coast. The final straw was the invasion of the iron-smelting Greeks, generally known as the 'sea peoples'. The Hittites found themselves landlocked – hence disadvantaged during an era of burgeoning sea trade – and lacking in the use of the latest technology: iron.

Meanwhile a new dynasty at Troy was establishing itself as a regional power. The Trojans in turn were harried by the Greeks, which inevitably lead to the Trojan War (1250 BC). This allowed the Hittites some breathing space. However, later arrivals, from both east and west, sped the demise of the Hittites. Some pockets of Hittite culture persisted in the Taurus Mountains, but the great empire was dead. Later city states created a Neo-Hittite culture, which attracted Greek merchants of the Iron Age and became the conduit through which Mesopotamian religion and art forms were transmitted to the Greeks.

CLASSICAL EMPIRES: GREECE & PERSIA

Post-Hittite Anatolia consisted of a patchwork of peoples, both indigenous Anatolians and recent interlopers. In the east the Urartians, descendants of earlier Anatolian Hurrians, forged a kingdom near Lake Van (Van Gölü). By the 8th century BC the Phrygians arrived in western Anatolia from Thrace. Under King Gordius, he of the Gordian knot, the Phrygians created a capital at Gordion (Yassıhöyük, p454), their power peaking later under King Midas. In 725 BC Gordion was put to the sword by horse-borne Cimmerians, a fate that even King Midas' golden touch couldn't avert, and the Phrygians were no more.

On the southwest coast the Lycians established a confederation of independent city states extending from modern-day Fethiye (p353) to Antalya (p382). Inland the similarly named Lydians dominated Western Anatolia from their capital at Sardis (p235) and are credited with creating the first-ever coinage.

Meanwhile, Greek colonies were steadily spreading along the Mediterranean coast, and Greek cultural influence was spreading through Anatolia. Most of the peoples of the Anatolian patchwork were clearly influenced by the Greeks: Phrygia's King Midas had a Greek wife; the Lycians borrowed the legend of the Chimera and cult of Leto (centred on Letoön, p365); and Lydian art acted as a conduit between Greek and Persian art forms. It seems that at times admiration was mutual: the Lycians were the only Anatolian people whom the Greeks didn't deride as 'barbarians', and the Greeks were so impressed by the wealth of the Lydian king Croesus that they coined the expression 'as rich as Croesus'.

These increasing manifestations of Hellenic influence didn't go unnoticed. Cyrus, the emperor of Persia, would not countenance such temerity in his

Homer, the Greek author of *The Iliad*, which told the story of the Trojan War, is believed to have been born in Smyrna (present-day İzmir), before 700 BC.

The most enduring reminder of the Phrygians is the Phrygian cap, a conical cloth cap with the top jauntily pulled forward. It was recorded on Greek vase paintings and tomb carvings, and was adopted as a symbol of liberty during the French Revolution and in various anticolonial revolutions in Latin America.

For further discussion of the highs and lows of life in ancient Lycia and detailed information on the sites of Turkey's Lycian coast, visit www.lycianturkey.com.

c 1100 BC	547 BC
Fall of Hittite Empire. Greek colonists start to land on coast of Asia Minor.	Cyrus of Persia overruns Anatolia and the Greek colonies

backyard. He invaded in 547 BC, initially putting paid to the Lydians, then barrelled on to extend control to the Aegean. Over a period of years under emperors Darius I and Xerxes the Persians checked the expansion of coastal Greek trading colonies. They also subdued the interior, bringing to an end the era of home-grown Anatolian kingdoms.

Ruling Anatolia through compliant local satrapies, the Persians didn't have it all their own way. They had to contend with periodic resistance from feisty Anatolians, such as the revolt of the Ionian city of Miletus (p268) in 494 BC. Allegedly fomented from Athens, the revolt was abruptly put down and the locals massacred. The Persians used the connivance of Athens as a pretext to invade mainland Greece, only to be routed at Marathon (whence the endurance event arose).

ALEXANDER & AFTER

Persian control of Anatolia continued until 334 BC when a new force stormed across Anatolia. Alexander and his Macedonian adventurers crossed the Dardanelles at Çanakkale, initially intent on relieving Anatolia of the Persian yoke. Sweeping down the coast they rolled the Persians at Granicus, near Troy, then pushed down to Sardis, which willingly surrendered. After later successfully besieging Halicarnassus (modern-day Bodrum; p272) Alexander ricocheted ever-eastwards disposing of another Persian force on the Cilician plain.

In the former Phrygian capital of Gordion, Alexander encountered the Gordian knot. Tradition stated that whoever untied the knot would come to rule Asia. Frustrated in his attempts to untie it, Alexander dispatched it with a blow of his sword. Asia lay before him; he and his men thundered all the way across Persia to the Indus until all the known world was his dominion.

Alexander was seemingly more disposed to conquest than to nation-building, and when he died in Babylon in 323 BC he left no successor. The enormous empire he had created was to be short-lived – perhaps he should have been more patient with that knot – and was divided between his generals in a flurry of civil wars. ,

However, if Alexander's intention had been to cleanse Anatolia of Persian influence and bring it within the Hellenic sphere, he had been monumentally successful. In the wake of Alexander's armies, a steady process of Hellenisation occurred, a culmination of the process begun centuries earlier that had so provoked Cyrus, the Persian king. A formidable network of municipal communities – the lifeblood of which, as ever in the Hellenic tradition, was trade – spread across Anatolia. The most notable of these was Pergamum (now Bergama; p217). The Pergamene kings were great warriors and governors and enthusiastic patrons of the arts. Greatest of the Pergamene kings was Eumenes (r 197–159BC) who ruled an empire extending from the Dardanelles to the Taurus Mountains and was responsible for much of what can still be seen of Pergamum's acropolis. As notable as the building of Hellenic temples and aqueducts was the gradual spread of the Greek language, which came to extinguish the native Anatolian languages over a period of centuries.

All the while the cauldron of Anatolian cultures continued to bubble, throwing up various typically short-lived flavour-of-the-month kingdoms.

According to legend, both of Alexander's parents foresaw his birth. His mother dreamed that a lightning strike had struck her womb, while his father dreamed that his wife's womb had been sealed by a lion. In great consternation they consulted a seer, who told them their child would have the character of a lion.

In 333 BC Persian Emperor Darius, facing defeat by Alexander, abandoned his wife, children and mother on the battlefield. His mother was so disgusted she disowned him and adopted Alexander as her son.

334-323 BC	261-133 BC
Alexander the Great conquers most of Anatolia. On his death his empire splinters into smaller independent states.	Glory days of kingdom of Pergamum. On his death, Attalus III leaves his state to Rome.

In 279 BC the Celts romped in from southeastern Europe, establishing a kingdom of Galatia centred on Ancyra (Ankara). To the northeast a certain Mithridates had earlier established the kingdom of Pontus, centred on Amasya, and the Armenians, long established in the Lake Van region, and thought by some to be descendants of the earlier Urartians, re-established themselves having been granted autonomy under Alexander.

Meanwhile, across the Aegean Sea, the increasingly powerful Romans were casting covetous eyes on the rich resources and trade networks of Anatolia.

ROMAN RULE & THE RISE OF CHRISTIANITY

Ironically, Pergamum, the greatest of the post-Alexandrian cities, became the mechanism by which the Romans came to control Anatolia. The Roman legions had defeated the armies of a Seleucid king at Magnesia (Manisa) in 190 BC, but Pergamum became the beachhead from which the Roman embrace of Anatolia began in earnest when King Attalus III died in 133 BC, bequeathing the city to Rome. In 129 BC Ephesus (p251) was nominated capital of the Roman province of Asia and within 60 years the Romans had overcome spirited resistance from Mithridates of Pontus and extended their reach to Armenia, on the Persian border.

To get the background on the search for, discovery of and ensuing controversy of Mary's final resting place, read Donald Carroll's *Mary's House*.

The reign of Emperor Augustus was a period of relative peace and prosperity for Anatolia. It was in this milieu that the fledgling religion of Christianity was able to spread, albeit clandestinely and subject to intermittently rigorous persecution. Tradition has it that St John retired to Ephesus to write the fourth Gospel, bringing Mary with him. John was buried on top of a hill in what is now Selçuk; the great Basilica of St John (p246) marks the site. And Mary is said to be buried at Meryemana (p255) nearby. The indefatigable St Paul capitalised on the Roman road system, his sprightly step taking him across Anatolia from AD 45 to AD 58 spreading the word.

Julius Caesar made his famous 'Veni, vidi, vici' ('I came, I saw, I conquered') speech at Zile, near Tokat.

As Christianity quietly spread, the Roman Empire grew cumbersome. In the late 3rd century Diocletian tried to steady the empire by splitting it into eastern and western administrative units, simultaneously attempting to wipe out Christianity. Both endeavours failed. Diocletian's reforms resulted in a civil war out of which Constantine emerged victorious. An earlier convert to Christianity, Constantine was said to have been guided by angels in choosing to build a 'New Rome' on the ancient Greek town of Byzantium. The city came to be known as Constantinople (now İstanbul; p88). On his death bed, seven years later in 337, Constantine was baptised and by the end of the century Christianity had become the official religion of the empire.

ROME ASUNDER, BYZANTIUM ARISES

Even with a new capital at Constantinople, the Roman Empire proved no less unwieldy. Once the steadying hand of Theodosius (r 379–95) was gone the impact of the reforms that Diocletian had instituted earlier became apparent: the empire split. The western – Roman – half of the empire eventually succumbed to decadence, sloth and sundry 'barbarians'; the eastern half – Byzantium – prospered, gradually adopting the Greek language and allowing Christianity to become its defining feature.

John Julius Norwich's concise *A Short History of Byzantium* – a distillation of three volumes on the Byzantines – does a fantastic job of cramming 1123 eventful years of history into less than 500 pages.

By the time of Justinian (527–65), Byzantium had taken up the mantle of imperialism that had once been Rome's. History books note Justinian as

AD 330	527-65
Constantine makes New Rome (later Constantinople) the capital of the Eastern Roman Empire (Byzantium)	Reign of Justinian. Byzantines extend control within Mediterranean

*Sailing from Byzantium:
How a Lost Empire Shaped
the World*, by Colin Wells,
brilliantly illustrates the
profound effect the
Byzantines had on all
of the cultures they
came into contact with:
Turkish, Slavic, Western
European and Arabic.

responsible for the Aya Sofya (p104) and codifying Roman law, but he also pushed the boundaries of the empire to envelope southern Spain, North Africa and Italy. It was at this stage that Byzantium came to be an entity distinct from Rome, although sentimental attachment to the idea of Rome remained: the Greek-speaking Byzantines still referred to themselves as 'Romans', and in subsequent centuries the Turks would refer to them as 'Rum'. However, Justinian's exuberance and ambition overstretched the empire. Plague and the untimely encroachment of Avars and Slavic tribes north of the Danube curtailed any further expansion.

Later a drawn-out struggle with their age-old rivals the Persians further weakened the Byzantines, leaving the eastern provinces of Anatolia easy prey for the Arab armies exploding out of Arabia. The Arabs took Ankara in 654 and by 669 had besieged Constantinople. Here were a new people, bringing a new language, civilisation and, most crucially, new religion: Islam.

In 1054 the line along
which the empire had
split in 395 became the
separating line between
Catholicism and Orthodox
Christianity, a fault line
that persists to this day.

On the western front, Goths and Lombards impinged as well, ensuring that by the 8th century Byzantium was pushed back into the Balkans and Anatolia. The empire remained hunkered down until the emergence of the Macedonian emperors. Basil assumed the throne in 867 and the empire's fortunes started heading on the up once more, as Basil chalked up victories against Muslim Egypt, the Slavic Bulgars and Russia. Basil II (976–1025) earned the moniker the 'Bulgar Slayer' after putting out the eyes of 14,000 Bulgarian prisoners of war. When Basil died the empire lacked anyone of his leadership skills – or ferocity, perhaps – and the era of Byzantine expansion was comprehensively over.

THE BYZANTINES & ARABS… & THE RENAISSANCE

Fully 680 years before Constantinople fell to the Ottomans, a Muslim army laid siege to the Byzantine capital. Newly converted, the armies of Islam marched out of Arabia, swept through southeast Anatolia by 654 and by 669 arrived at Constantinople's city walls. The early Arab incursions into Byzantine territory so worried Emperor Constantine III that he withdrew to Sicily in 660. When he then requested that his wife and son come and join him, the citizens of Constantinople refused, believing that if they left the city would lose its imperial status. His son, Constantine IV, succeeded him in 668 and endured five Arabic assaults on Constantinople in 10 years.

The meeting of the Byzantines and Arabs wasn't all acrimonious, however: there was considerable cultural cross-pollination. The Islamic ban on portraying human beings in pictures was adopted by Emperor Leo in 726, thus ushering in the Iconoclastic period that was to last almost a century. More happily, domes were an innovation unknown to Arabs until they saw Byzantine churches. Thereafter the dome entered the repertoire of Muslim architects, and with the passing of time the fabulous voluptuous skylines of Islamic cities – İstanbul not least among them – were born. And in meeting the Byzantines the Arabs also encountered the scientific and philosophical works of the classical Greeks. The Arabic translations of these works eventually made their way to Western Europe, via Muslim Spain, thus providing the spark for the Renaissance.

To Ottoman believers, a relic of the Arab sieges of Constantinople became the fourth most holy site in Islam: the place where the Prophet Mohammed's friend and standard bearer, Ayub Ansari, was buried. The site of his grave was lost during the continuing reign of the Byzantines, but once Mehmet's soldiers took the city in 1453 it was 'miraculously' rediscovered (see p124). Thereafter it became a pilgrimage site for Ottoman sultans on ascending the throne.

663	1071
Muslim Arab armies invade Anatolia, bringing the message of Islam	The Seljuks defeat the Byzantines at the Battle of Manzikert. Start of Seljuk domination of central Anatolia.

THE FIRST TURKIC EMPIRE: THE SELJUKS

During the centuries of Byzantine waxing and waning, a nomadic people, the Turks, had been moving ever westward out of Central Asia. En route the Turks encountered the Arabs and in so doing converted to Islam. Vigorous and martial by nature, the Turks assumed control of parts of the moribund Abbasid empire, and built an empire of their own centred on Persia. Tuğrul, of the Turkish Seljuk clan, took the title of sultan in Baghdad, and from there the Seljuks began raiding Byzantine territory. In 1071 Tuğrul's son Alp Arslan faced down the might of the Byzantine army at Manzikert (modern Malazgırt, north of Lake Van). Although vastly outnumbered, the nimble Turkish cavalry won the day, laying all of Anatolia open to wandering Turcoman bands and beginning the drawn-out, final demise of the Byzantine Empire.

Not everything went the Seljuks' way. The 12th and 13th centuries saw incursions by Crusaders, who established short-lived statelets at Antioch (Antakya; p433) and Edessa (modern Şanlıurfa; p600). In a sideshow to the ongoing Seljuk saga, an unruly army of Crusaders, in 1204, sacked Constantinople, the capital of the Christian Byzantines, ostensibly the allies of the Crusaders. Meanwhile the Seljuks were riven by internal power struggles of their own and their vast empire fragmented.

The Seljuk legacy lived on in Anatolia in the Sultanate of Rum, centred on the capital at Konya (p481). Although ethnically Turkish, the Seljuks were purveyors of Persian culture, art and literature. It was the Seljuks who introduced knotted woollen rugs to Anatolia, and they endowed the countryside with remarkable architecture – still visible at Erzurum (p564), Divriği (p481), Amasya (p468) and Sivas (p477). These Seljuk creations were the first truly Islamic art forms in Anatolia, and they were to become the prototypes on which Ottoman art forms would later be modelled. Celaleddin Rumi (p483), the Sufi mystic who founded the Mevlevi, or Whirling Dervish, order, was an exemplar of the cultural and artistic heights reached in Konya.

In the meantime, the Mongol descendants of Genghis Khan rumbled through Anatolia. They took Erzurum in 1242, then defeated a Seljuk army at Köse Dağ in 1243. At the Mongol onslaught, Anatolia fractured into a mosaic of Turkish *beyliks* (principalities) and Mongol fiefdoms; the shell-shocked Byzantines did not regain Constantinople until 1261. But by 1300 a single Turkish *bey*, Osman, established the Ottoman dynasty that would end the Byzantine line once and for all.

An overview of the various Turkic communities from southeastern Turkey to the deserts of China's Xinjiang region, from 600 BC to the modern day, *The Turks in World History*, by Carter Vaughn Findley, is informed and insightful.

European observers referred to Anatolia as 'Turchia' as early as the 12th century. The Turks themselves didn't do this until the 1920s.

THE FLEDGLING OTTOMAN STATE

The Ottoman Turks were in fact new to Islam, flitting with impunity around the borderlands between Byzantine and formerly Seljuk territory, but once galvanised they moved with the zeal of the new convert. In an era marked by destruction and dissolution they provided an ideal that attracted legions of followers and they quickly established an administrative and military model that allowed them to expand with alacrity. From the outset they embraced all the cultures of Anatolia – as many Anatolian civilisations before them had done – and their culture became an amalgam of Greek and Turkish, Muslim and Christian elements, particularly in the janissary corps, which were drawn from the Christian populations of their territories.

Vigorous, ambitious and seemingly invincible, they forged westward, establishing a first capital at Bursa (p292), then crossing into Europe and

1204	1243
The Fourth Crusade seizes and ransacks Constantinople	Mongols defeat Seljuks at Köse Dağ, effectively ending the Seljuk empire

taking Adrianople (Edirne; p166) in 1362. By 1371 they had reached the Adriatic, and in 1389 they met and vanquished the Serbs at Kosovo Polje, effectively taking control of the Balkans.

In the Balkans the Ottomans encountered a resolute Christian community, yet they absorbed them neatly into the state in the creation of the *millet* system, by which minority communities were officially recognised and allowed to govern their own affairs. That said, neither Christian insolence nor military bravado were countenanced within Ottoman territory, and Sultan Beyazıt resoundingly trounced the armies of the last Crusade at Nicopolis in Bulgaria in 1396. Beyazıt perhaps took military victories for granted from then on. Several years later it was he who was insolent, when he taunted – to his detriment – the Tatar warlord Tamerlane at Ankara. Beyazıt was captured, his army defeated and the burgeoning Ottoman Empire abruptly halted as Tamerlane lurched through Anatolia and out again.

> Murat (r 1421–51) was the most contemplative of the early Ottoman sultans – he abdicated twice to retire to his palace, but both times had to reclaim the throne in order to see off insurgencies in the Balkans.

THE OTTOMANS ASCENDANT: CONSTANTINOPLE & BEYOND

It took a decade for the dust to settle after Tamerlane departed, dragging a no-doubt chastened Beyazıt with him. Beyazıt's sons wrestled for control until finally a new sultan worthy of his predecessors emerged. With Mehmet I at the helm the Ottomans regrouped and got back to the job at hand: expansion. With a momentum born of reprieve they scooped up the remaining parts of Anatolia, rolled through Greece, made a first attempt at Constantinople and beat the Serbs, this time with Albanian sidekicks, for a second time in 1448.

> Bubbling with enthusiasm and *bons môts*, Jason Goodwin's *Lords of the Horizons* is an energetic tilt through Ottoman history.

The Ottomans had fully regained their momentum by the time Mehmet II became sultan in 1451. Constantinople, the last redoubt of the beleaguered Byzantines, stuck out like a sore thumb in the expanse of Ottoman territory. Mehmet, as an untested sultan, had no choice but to claim it. He built a fortress just along the Bosphorus, imposed a naval blockade on the city and amassed his enormous army. The Byzantines appealed forlornly and in vain to Europe for help. After seven weeks of siege the city fell on 29 May 1453. Christendom shuddered at the seemingly unstoppable Ottomans and fawning diplomats likened Mehmet to Alexander the Great and declared him to have assumed the mantle of the great Roman and Byzantine emperors.

> Mehmet's siege of Constantinople coincided with a lunar eclipse (22 May 1453). The defending Byzantines interpreted this as an extremely bad omen, presaging the fall of the city and the impending defeat of all Christendom. Things didn't get quite that bad, but the city did fall within a week.

Thereafter the Ottoman war machine rolled on, alternating campaigns each summer between eastern and western borders of the empire. By this point Ottoman society was fully geared for war. The janissary system, by which subject Christian youths were converted and trained for the military, meant that the Ottomans had the only standing army in Europe. They were agile, highly organised and motivated. Successive sultans expanded the realm, Selim the Grim capturing the Hejaz in 1517, and with it Mecca and Medina, thus claiming for the Ottomans status as the guardians of Islam's holiest places. It wasn't all militarism and mindless expansion, however: Sultan Beyazit II demonstrated the essentially multicultural nature of the empire when he invited the Jews expelled from Iberia by the Spanish Inquisition to İstanbul in 1492.

The Ottoman golden age came during the reign of Sultan Süleyman (1520–66). A remarkable figure, Süleyman was noted as much for codifying Ottoman law (he is known in Turkish as Süleyman Kanunı – law bringer) as for his military prowess. Under Süleyman, the Ottomans enjoyed victories

THE SULTANATE OF WOMEN

The Ottoman Empire may have been the mightiest Islamic empire, but for a time women commanded great influence in the machinations of the empire. More than ever before or after, from the reign of Süleyman the Magnificent until the mid-17th century, some women of the Ottoman court assumed and wielded considerable political clout.

This period, sometimes referred to as the sultanate of women, began with Lady Hürrem, known to the West as Roxelana. A concubine in the harem of Süleyman, Roxelana is believed to have been of Russian or Ukrainian origin. She quickly became Süleyman's favourite consort, and when his mother died, Roxelana became the most powerful woman in the harem. She then proceeded to shore up her own position, persuading Süleyman to marry her – something that no concubine had done before.

A master of the art of palace intrigue, she manoeuvred the sultan into doing away with Mustafa, his son from an earlier coupling, and İbrahim, his grand vizier. This left the way open for Roxelana's son, Selim, to succeed Süleyman as sultan.

Such conniving had a lasting legacy on the fortunes of the empire. Selim proved to be an inept and inebriated leader, and some historians claim that the precedent of behind-the-scenes manipulation, set by Roxelana, contributed to the increasing incompetence and eventual downfall of the Ottoman aristocracy.

over the Hungarians and absorbed the Mediterranean coast of Algeria and Tunisia; Süleyman's legal code was a visionary amalgam of secular and Islamic law, and his patronage of the arts saw the Ottomans reach their cultural zenith.

Süleyman was also notable as the first Ottoman sultan to marry. Whereas previously sultans had enjoyed the multifarious comforts of concubines, Süleyman fell in love and married Roxelana (see the boxed text, above). More remarkably still, he remained faithful to her. Sadly, monogamy did not make for domestic bliss: palace intrigues brought about the death of his first two sons. A wearied Süleyman died campaigning on the Danube in 1566, and his body was spirited back to İstanbul.

THE OTTOMAN JUGGERNAUT FALTERS

Putting a finger on exactly when or why the Ottoman rot set in is tricky, not to say contentious, but some historians pinpoint the death of Süleyman as a critical juncture. Süleyman's failure to take Malta (1565) was a harbinger of what was to come, and the earlier unsuccessful naval tilts in the Indian Ocean aimed at circumventing Portuguese influence in East Africa were evidence of growing European military might.

Indulging in hindsight it is easy to say that the remarkable ancestral line of Ottoman sovereigns – from Osman to Süleyman, inspirational leaders and mighty generals all – could not go on indefinitely. The Ottoman family tree was bound to throw up some duds eventually. And so it did.

Plainly the sultans immediately following Süleyman were not up to the task. Süleyman's son by Roxelana, Selim, known disparagingly as 'the Sot', lasted only briefly as sultan, overseeing the naval catastrophe at Lepanto, which spelled the definitive end of Ottoman supremacy in the Mediterranean. The intrigues and powerbroking that occurred during the 'sultanate of women' (above) contributed to the general befuddlement of later sultans,

Miguel Cervantes was wounded fighting against the Ottomans at the battle of Lepanto. It is said that his experiences served as inspiration for some scenes in *Don Quixote*.

1453	1520-66
Mehmet the Conqueror defeats the last Byzantine emperor and captures Constantinople. Ottoman supremacy in Turkey.	The reign of Süleyman the Magnificent, the high point of the Ottoman Empire

but male vested interests, putting personal advancement ahead of the best interests of the empire, also played a role in this. Assassinations, mutinies and fratricide were the order of the day, and little good came of it.

Further, Süleyman was the last sultan to lead his army into the field. Those who came after him were generally coddled and sequestered in the fineries of the palace, having minimal experience of everyday life and little inclination to administer or expand the empire.

These factors, coupled with the inertia that was inevitable after 250 years of virtually unfettered expansion, meant that the Ottoman military might, once famously referred to by Martin Luther as irresistible, was on the wain. There were occasional military victories, largely choreographed by capable viziers, but these were relatively few and far between.

THE SICK MAN OF EUROPE

The siege of Vienna in 1683 was effectively the Ottomans' last tilt at expanding further into Europe. It failed, as had an earlier attempt in 1529. Thereafter it was a downward spiral, the more bumpy for occasional minor rushes of victory. At the treaty of Karlovitz in 1699 the Ottomans sued for peace for the first time, and were forced to give up the Peloponnese, Transylvania and Hungary. The empire was still vast and powerful, but it had lost its momentum and was rapidly falling behind the West on many levels: social, military and scientific. Napoleon's swashbuckling campaign through Egypt in 1799 was an indication that an emboldened Europe was now willing to take the battle right up to the Ottomans, and was the first example of industrialised Europe meddling in the affairs of the Middle East.

It wasn't just Napoleon who was breathing down the neck of the empire. The Hapsburgs in Central Europe and the Russians were increasingly assertive, while Western Europe had grown rich after several centuries of colonising and exploiting the 'New World' – something the Ottomans had missed out on. In some regards, the Ottomans themselves had to endure a quasi-colonisation by European powers, which dumped their cheaply produced industrial goods in the empire while also building and running much infrastructure: innovations such as electricity, postal services and railways. Indeed, the Ottomans remained moribund, inward looking and generally unaware of the advances that were happening in Europe. An earlier clear indication of this was the fact that the Ottoman clergy did not allow the use of the printing press until the 18th century – a century and a half after it had been introduced into Europe.

Wild Europe: The Balkans in the Gaze of Western Travellers, by Bozidar Jezernik, is a fascinating record of travellers' observations of the Balkans under Ottoman rule.

But it was another idea imported from the West that was to greatly speed the dissolution of the empire: nationalism. For centuries manifold ethnic groups had coexisted harmoniously in the Ottoman Empire, but the creation of nation-states in Western Europe sparked a desire in the empire's subject peoples to throw off the Ottoman 'yoke' and determine their own destinies. So it was that pieces of the Ottoman jigsaw wriggled free: Greece attained its freedom in 1830. In 1878 Romania, Montenegro, Serbia and Bosnia went their own ways, while at the same time Russia was encroaching on Kars (p577) and boldly proclaiming itself protector of all of the empire's Orthodox subjects.

As the empire shrank there were various attempts at reform, but it was all too little, too late. In 1829 Mahmut II had abolished the janissaries, and in so doing had slaughtered them, but he did succeed in modernising the

1699	1876
The Treaty of Karlovitz – the Ottomans lose the Peloponnese, Transylvania and Hungary	Abdül Hamit II takes the throne. The National Assembly meets for the first time.

armed forces. In 1876 Abdülhamid had allowed the creation of an Ottoman constitution and the first ever Ottoman parliament. But he used the events of 1878 as an excuse for doing away with the constitution. His reign henceforth grew increasingly authoritarian.

But it wasn't just subject peoples who were determined to modernise: educated Turks, too, looked for ways to improve their lot. In Macedonia the Committee for Union and Progress (CUP) was created. Reform minded and Western looking, the CUP, who came to be known as the 'Young Turks', forced Abdülhamid in 1908 to abdicate and reinstate the constitution. Any rejoicing proved short-lived. The First Balkans War saw Bulgaria and Macedonia removed from the Ottoman map, with Bulgarian, Greek and Serbian troops advancing rapidly on İstanbul.

The Ottoman regime, once feared and respected, was now condescendingly known as the 'sick man of Europe'. European diplomats and politicians bombastically pondered the 'eastern question', ie how to dismember the empire and cherry-pick its choicest parts.

WWI & ITS AFTERMATH

The military crisis saw a triumvirate of ambitious, nationalistic and brutish CUP paşas – Enver, Talat and Cemal – stage a coup and take de facto control of the ever-shrinking empire. They managed to push back the unlikely alliance of Balkan armies and save İstanbul and Edirne, but there the good they did ended. Their next move was to choose the wrong side in the looming world war. Enver Paşa had been educated in Germany, and because of that the Ottomans had to fend off the Western powers on multiple fronts during WWI: Greece in Thrace, Russia in northeast Anatolia, Britain in Arabia (where Lawrence rose to the fore and led the Arabs to victory) and a multinational force at Gallipoli. It was during this time of confusion and turmoil that the Armenian scenario unfolded (see p40).

It was only at Gallipoli (p183) that the Ottomans held their own. This was due partially to the ineptitude of the British high command but also to the brilliance of Turkish commander Mustafa Kemal. Inspiring and iron-willed, he inspired his men to hold their lines, while also inflicting shocking casualties on the invading British and Anzac forces. Unbeknown to anyone at the time, two enduring legends of nationhood were born on the blood-spattered sands of Gallipoli: Australians see that brutal nine-month campaign as the birth of their sense of nationhood, while the Turks regard the defence of their homeland as the birth of their national consciousness.

The end of WWI saw the Turks largely in disarray. The French occupied southeast Anatolia; the Italians controlled the western Mediterranean; the Greeks occupied İzmir; and Armenians, with Russian support, controlled parts of northeast Anatolia. The Treaty of Sèvres in 1920 ensured the dismembering of the empire, with only a sliver of dun steppe to be left to the Turks. European haughtiness did not figure on a Turkish backlash. But backlash there was. A slowly building Turkish nationalist movement was created, motivated by the humiliation of the Treaty of Sèvres. At the head of this movement was Mustafa Kemal, the victorious leader at Gallipoli. He secured the support of the Bektaşi dervishes, began organising Turkish resistance and established a national assembly in Ankara, in the heart of Anatolia, far from opposing armies and meddling diplomats.

A Peace to End All Peace: Creating the Modern Middle East, 1914–1922, by David Fromkin, is an intriguing account of how the map of the modern Middle East was drawn arbitrarily by European colonial governments in the wake of the demise of the Ottoman Empire.

1908	**1914-15**
Revolution of the Young Turks	Turkey enters WWI on the German side; the Gallipoli campaign begins

In the meantime, a Greek expeditionary force pushed out from İzmir. The Greeks, who, since attaining independence in 1830, had dreamed of recreating the Byzantine Empire, controlling both sides of the Aegean, saw this opportunity to realise their *megali idea* (great idea). Capitalising on Turkish disorder, the Greeks took Bursa and Edirne and pushed towards Ankara. This was just the provocation that Mustafa Kemal needed to galvanise Turkish support. After an initial skirmish at İnönü, the Greeks pressed on for Ankara seeking to crush the Turks. But stubborn Turkish resistance stalled them at the battle of Sakarya. The two armies faced off again at Dumlupınar. Here the Turks savaged the Greeks, sending them in panicked retreat towards İzmir, where they were expelled from Anatolia amid stricken refugees, pillage and looting.

Mustafa Kemal emerged as the hero of the Turkish people. Macedonian-born himself, he had realised the dream of the 'Young Turks' of years past: to create a modern, Turkish nation state. The treaty of Lausanne in 1923 undid the humiliations of Sèvres and saw foreign powers leave Turkey. The borders of the modern Turkish state were set and the Ottoman Empire was no more, although its legacy lives on in manifold nation states, from Albania to Yemen.

THE FATE OF ANATOLIA'S ARMENIANS?

The final years of the Ottoman Empire saw human misery on an epic scale, but nothing has proved as enduringly melancholy and controversial as the fate of Anatolia's Armenians. The tale begins with eyewitness accounts, in autumn 1915, of Ottoman army units rounding up Armenian populations and marching them towards the Syrian desert. It ends with an Anatolian hinterland virtually devoid of Armenians. What happened in between remains a muddied melange of conjecture, recrimination, obfuscation and outright propaganda.

Armenians maintain that they were subject to the 20th century's first orchestrated 'genocide'. They claim that over a million Armenians were summarily executed or killed on death marches and that Ottoman authorities issued a deportation order with the intention of removing the Armenian presence from Anatolia. They allege that Ottoman archives relating to this event were deliberately destroyed. To this day, Armenians demand an acknowledgement of this 'genocide'.

Turkey, though, refutes that any such 'genocide' occurred. It does admit that thousands of Armenians died but claim the Ottoman order had been to 'relocate' Armenians with no intention to eradicate them. The deaths, according to Turkish officials, were the result of disease and starvation, direct consequences of the tumultuous state of affairs during a time of war. A few even go so far as to say that it was the Turks who were subjected to 'genocide' at the hand of the Armenians.

Almost a century after the events the issue remains contentious. In 2005 President Erdoğan encouraged the creation of a joint Turkish–Armenian commission to investigate the events; Orhan Pamuk, Turkey's most famous novelist and 2006 Nobel Prize Laureate, speaking in Germany, claimed that a million Armenians had been killed and that Turkey should be prepared to discuss it; and academics convened in İstanbul to discuss the issue. All three initiatives failed: Armenia flatly refused Erdoğan's offer, Pamuk was pursued by the courts for impugning the Turkish national identity (see p51) and the conference attracted vehement protests from Turkish nationalists.

It seems that even a dialogue between the Turks and Armenians is not possible...and so the tragedy lives on.

1920	1938
Turkish War of Independence; ends with the Treaty of Lausanne (1923) and the founding of the Turkish Republic	Death of Atatürk

ATATÜRK: REFORM & THE REPUBLIC

Left to manage their own affairs, the Turks consolidated Ankara as their capital and abolished the sultanate. Mustafa Kemal assumed the newly created presidency of the secular republic at the head of the CHP (Republican People's Party). Later he would take on the name Atatürk (literally 'Father Turk'). Thereupon the Turks set to work. Given Turkey's many problems, they had a job ahead of them. But Mustafa Kemal's energy was apparently limitless; his vision was to see Turkey take its place among the modern, developed countries of Europe.

Before WWI Mustafa Kemal had served the army in Sofia, Bulgaria; a legacy of his disagreements with the CUP revolutionaries, whom he had helped seize power in 1908.

At the time, the country was impoverished and devastated after years of war, so a firm hand was needed. The Atatürk era was one of enlightened despotism. Atatürk set up the institutions of democracy while never allowing any opposition sufficient oxygen to impede him. He brooked little dissent and indulged an occasional authoritarian streak, yet his ultimate motivation was the betterment of his people. One aspect of his vision, however, was to have ongoing and sorry consequences for the country: his insistence that the state be solely Turkish. To encourage national unity made sense considering the nationalist separatist movements that had bedevilled the Ottoman Empire, but in doing so he denied a cultural existence to the Kurds, many of whom had fought valiantly during the struggle for independence. Sure enough, within a few short years a Kurdish revolt erupted in southeast Anatolia, the first of several such ructions to recur throughout the 20th century (see p47).

The desire to create unified nation-states on both sides of the Aegean also brought about population exchanges after the armistice between Greece and Turkey, whereby whole communities were uprooted as Greek-speaking peoples of Anatolia were shipped to Greece, while Muslim residents of Greece were transferred to Turkey. These exchanges brought great disruption and the creation of 'ghost villages' that were vacated but never reoccupied, such as Kayaköy (see p361). Again, this was a pragmatic move aimed at forestalling outbreaks of ethnic violence, but it became one of the more melancholy episodes of the early years of the republic and, importantly, hobbled the development of the new state. Turkey found itself without much of its Ottoman-educated classes, many of whom had not been Turkish-speakers, and in their stead Turkey accepted impoverished Muslim peasants from the Balkans.

Bruce Clark's *Twice a Stranger* is an investigation of the Greek-Turkish population exchanges of the 1920s. Analysing background events and interviewing Greeks and Turks who were transported, Clark recreates the trauma of the exchanges and shines new light on the fraught relationship of the two countries.

Mustafa Kemal's zeal for modernisation was unwavering, giving the Turkish state a makeover on micro and macro levels. Everything from headgear to spoken language was scrutinised and where necessary reformed. Throughout the 1920s and '30s Turkey adopted the Gregorian calendar (bringing it in line with the West, rather than the Middle East), reformed its alphabet (adopting the Roman alphabet and abandoning Arabic script) and standardised the Turkish language, outlawed the fez (seen as a reminder of the Ottoman era, hence backward), instituted universal suffrage, and decreed that Turks should take surnames, something that they had previously got by without. By the time of his death in November 1938, Atatürk had, to a greater or lesser degree, lived up to that name, having been the pre-eminent figure in the creation of the nation state and having dragged it into the modern era by a combination of inspiration, ruthlessness and sheer weight of personality.

1960-80	1974
Three military coups attempt to bring order to Turkey	Turkey invades northern Cyprus, creating the Turkish Republic of Northern Cyprus

FATHER OF THE MOTHERLAND

To Westerners unused to venerating figures of authority, the Turks' devotion to Atatürk may seem unusual. In response the Turks simply remark that the Turkish state is a result of his energy and vision; that without him there would be no Turkey. From an era that threw up Stalin, Hitler and Mussolini, Atatürk stands as a beacon of statesmanship and proves that radical reform, deftly handled, can be hugely successful.

The Turks' gratitude to Atatürk manifests itself throughout the country. He appears on stamps, banknotes, statues – often in martial pose astride a horse – in town squares across the country. His name is affixed to landmarks and infrastructure projects too many to mention, from bridges to airports to four-lane highways. And seemingly every house where he spent a night from the southern Aegean to the Black Sea is now a museum.

Turkish schoolchildren are well versed in Atatürk's life and achievements – they learn them by rote and can dutifully recite them. But it may be that the history-book image of Atatürk is more simplistic than the reality. An avowed champion of Turkish culture, he preferred opera to Turkish music. Though calling himself 'Father Turk', he had no offspring and a single short and troubled marriage. A recently published biography (in Turkish only) of his wife, Latife Uşşaki, sheds light on aspects of his life previously glossed over, and has raised the ire of duly reverent Turks.

Atatürk died relatively young (aged 57) in 1938. No doubt years as a military man, reformer and public figure took their toll. His friend and successor as president, İsmet İnönü, ensured that he was to be lauded by his countrymen. The praise continues to this day. Indeed, any perceived insult to Atatürk is considered not only highly offensive but is also illegal. Cynicism about politicians may be well and good at home, but it is a no-no in Turkey as regards Atatürk.

There are two outstanding biographies of the great man. Patrick Kinross' *Ataturk: Rebirth of a Nation* is engagingly written and hoves closely to the official Turkish view, while Andrew Mango's *Atatürk* is a detached, objective and highly detailed look at a remarkable life.

DEMOCRATISATION & THE COUPS

Though reform had proceeded apace in Turkey, the country remained economically and military weak and Atatürk's successor, İsmet İnönü, stepped carefully to avoid involvement in WWII. The war over, Turkey found itself allied to the USA. A bulwark against the Soviets (the Armenian border then marked the edge of the Soviet bloc), Turkey was of great strategic importance and found itself on the receiving end of US aid. The new friendship was cemented when Turkish troops fought in Korea, and Turkey was made a member of NATO soon afterwards.

Meanwhile, the democratic process, previously stifled, gained momentum. In 1950 the Democratic Party swept to power. Ruling for a decade, the Democrats had raised the hackles of the Kemalists from the outset by reinstituting the call to prayer in Arabic (something Atatürk had outlawed), but when, as their tenure proceeded, they failed to live up to their name and became increasingly autocratic, the army stepped in during 1960 and removed them. Army rule lasted only briefly, and resulted in the liberalisation of the constitution, but it set the tone for years to come. The military considered themselves the guardians of Atatürk's vision – pro-Western and secular – and felt obliged and empowered to step in when necessary to ensure the republic maintained the right trajectory.

The 1960s and '70s saw the creation of political parties of all stripes, from left-leaning to fascist–nationalist to pro-Islamic, but a profusion of new par-

1983	1985-99
Turgut Özal wins elections; starts to open Turkey to the wider world	Kurdish uprising in southeast, effectively ended by capture of Kurdistan Workers Party (PKK) leader Abdullah Öcalan

ties did not necessarily make for a more vibrant democracy. The late 1960s were characterised by left-wing activism and political violence that prompted the creation of unlikely coalitions and a move to the right by centrist parties. The army stepped in again in 1971 to restore order, before swiftly handing power back in late 1973. Several months later the military was again in the thick of things when President Bulent Ecevit ordered them into Cyprus to protect the Turkish minority, in response to a Cypriot Greek extremist organisation who had seized power and was espousing union with Greece. The invasion effectively divided the island into two political entities – one of which is only recognised by Turkey – a situation that persists to this day.

Political and economic chaos reigned for the rest of the '70s so the military took it upon themselves to seize power again and re-establish order in 1980. This they did through the creation of the highly feared National Security Council, but allowed elections in 1983. Here, for the first time in decades, was a happy result for Turkey. Turgut Özal, leader of the Motherland Party (ANAP), won a majority and, unhindered by unruly coalition partners, was able to set Turkey back on course. An astute economist, and pro-Islamic, Özal made vital economic and legal reforms that brought Turkey in line with the international community and sowed the seeds of its current vitality.

The late 1980s, however, were notable for two aspects – corruption and Kurdish separatism (see p47) – that were to have an impact long beyond Özal's tenure.

THE 1990S: MODERNISATION & SEPARATISM

The first Gulf War kick-started the 1990s with a bang. Turkey played a prominent role in the allied invasion of Iraq, with Özal supporting sanctions and allowing air strikes from bases in southern Anatolia. In so doing, Turkey, after decades in the wilderness, affirmed its place in the international community, while also becoming a more important US ally. At the end of the Gulf War millions of Iraqi Kurds, fearing reprisals from Saddam, fled north into southeastern Anatolia. The exodus caught the attention of the international media, bringing the Kurdish issue into the international spotlight, and resulted in the establishment of the Kurdish safe haven in northern Iraq. This in turn emboldened the Kurdistan Workers' Party (PKK), who stepped up their campaign, thus provoking more drastic and iron-fisted responses from the Turkish military, such that the southeast was effectively enduring a civil war. The Kurdish conflagration continued escalating, with most of the southeast under martial law, until the capture of Abdullah Öcalan in 1999.

Meanwhile, Turgut Özal died suddenly in 1993 thus creating a power vacuum. Various weak coalition governments followed throughout the 1990s, with a cast of political figures flitting across the political stage. Tansu Çiller served briefly as Turkey's first female prime minister, but her much-vaunted feminine touch and economic expertise did nothing to find a solution to the Kurdish issue or to cure the ailing economy. In fact, her husband's name was aired in various fraud investigations at a time when sinister links between organised crime, big business and politicians were becoming increasingly apparent.

In December 1995, to everyone's surprise, the religious Refah (Welfare) Party managed to form a government led by veteran politician Necmettin Erbakan. Heady with power, Refah politicians made Islamist statements that

Voices from the Front: Turkish Soldiers on the War with the Kurds, by Nadire Mater, offers sometimes harrowing first-hand accounts of the Kurdish insurgency during the 1990s.

1999	2001
Twin earthquakes wreak devastation on northwestern Turkey	Economy collapses and Turkish lira loses half its value

raised the ire of the military. In 1997 the National Security Council declared that Refah had flouted the constitutional ban on religion in politics. Faced with what some dubbed a 'postmodern coup', the government resigned and Refah was disbanded.

TOWARDS EUROPE

Former BBC Turkey correspondent Chris Morris ponders the rhythms and cadences of modern Turkish life in *The New Turkey: The Quiet Revolution on the Edge of Europe*

The capture of PKK leader Abdullah Öcalan in early 1999 may have seemed like a good omen after the torrid '90s. His capture offered an opportunity – as yet largely unrealised – to settle the Kurdish question. Later that year the disastrous earthquakes centred on İzmit put paid to any premillennial false hopes. The government's handling of the crisis was woefully inadequate; however, the global outpouring of aid and sympathy – not least from traditional foes, the Greeks – did much to reassure Turks they were valued members of the world community.

An economic collapse in early 2001 seemed to compound the country's woes (see p46), but despite the government securing IMF loans the long-suffering Turks were understandably jaded with their lot.

Things changed dramatically in late 2002 when the Justice and Development Party (AKP) swept to power in such convincing fashion that most old political parties were confined to oblivion, and with them several political perennials long past their use-by date. The electorate held its collective breath to see if the military would intervene to prevent the manifestly pro-Islamic AKP from assuming government but the generals consented to respect the will of the electorate. The AKP's leader, Recep Tayyıp Erdoğan, was initially banned from sitting in parliament due to an earlier conviction for 'inciting religious violence' (reading out a poem that compared the minarets of a mosque to the swords of Islam), but some deft sidestepping ensued, and he was allowed into parliament and into the prime ministership.

Pundits were concerned as to which direction Erdoğan would take the country. Any initial misgivings were swiftly cast aside. Clearly intent on gaining EU entry for Turkey, Erdoğan proved a deft and inspiring leader, amending the constitution to scrap the death penalty, granting greater cultural rights to the Kurds and cracking down on human rights violations. By the end of 2002 the EU was making approving noises and the economy was largely back on track. Turkey was as self-confident and assertive as it had been in many a long year, steadfastly refusing American demands that the country be used as a base for attacking northern Iraq in 2003, then later the same year enduring the horror of terrorist bombings in İstanbul with resilience and solidarity. By January 2005 the economy was considered robust enough to introduce the new Turkish lira (Yeni Türk Lirası) and do away with six zeroes on each and every banknote.

The icing on the cake came when the flirtatious EU finally started accession talks with Turkey in October 2005 after many years of come-ons had come to nothing. However, there are still a number of obstacles to overcome before Turkey achieves EU accession. For more details, see p29.

2002	2005
Recep Tayyip Erdoğan's Islamic Justice & Development Party (AKP) wins landslide election victory	Yeni Türk Lirası introduced (January); EU accession talks start (October)

The Culture

THE NATIONAL PSYCHE

Just as the person who asks 'How are you?' in the street expects you to reply with 'Fine' rather than give a blow-by-blow account of your health and relationship problems, so the Turk who asks 'How is Turkey?' expects the answer '*Çok güzel!*' (Wonderful!) rather than a detailed critique. Turks may grumble and criticise aspects of the country themselves, but they certainly don't want outsiders to do the same thing.

Turkish chauvinism is the ugly side of the national psyche. When Atatürk salvaged a nation from the wreck of the Ottoman Empire, the price for national unity was an ideology in which minorities and outsiders were regarded with suspicion, even hostility. An official veil was drawn over Turkey's cosmopolitan past, and the saying went about: 'A Turk's only friend is another Turk.' Outsiders are frequently dismayed to find that their fluent English-speaking and apparently intelligent new Turkish friend turns out to harbour all sorts of conspiracy theories about how the world plans to do Turkey in.

Happily, there are signs this situation is giving way to a new openness and pluralism. In the streets, hip-hop artists are giving the global phenomenon a very Turkish twist. In the universities, it is common to meet students of Ottoman language and Byzantine history. Crumbling churches dotted throughout the countryside are being restored. And from Ankara to Van, an increasing number of people feel there is no contradiction in being both Turkish and Kurdish.

Eight hundred years of Ottoman empire-building, followed by a century of fighting for survival, forged a people who respect authority and toughness. But it also endowed them with the ability to laugh in the face of adversity, to enjoy the here-and-now, and to show generosity to strangers and the less well off. It's that unique combination of traits that make the Turks, for all their insularity, some of the most warm-hearted and hospitable people in the world.

LIFESTYLE

Increasingly, two completely different lifestyles coexist in Turkey. In İstanbul, İzmir, Bursa, Ankara and along the west coast, people live their lives much like people in the West. Both men and women march off to jobs in city offices and shops, men and women socialise together, and in their homes people sit down to dinner at tables and use 'modern' (ie pedestal) toilets. But move away from the cities (and in particular out east) and you will find a very different, far more traditional lifestyle still alive and kicking. In these areas, men and women rarely sit (let alone socialise) together, women stay at home to look after the children, everyone sits on the floor to eat and toilets are firmly of the squat variety.

The picture has been complicated by massed emigration from the villages of the east to the big cities of the west, which means that alongside the Westernised neighbourhoods there are also pockets of traditionalism. Women in headscarves may be a rarity along İstanbul's İstiklal Caddesi, but they're the norm in the backstreets of Sultanahmet.

Children receive nine years of compulsory education. Doing well on the controversial three-hour University Entrance Exam (ÖSS) is a must to get into university, but only a quarter of high school graduates find a place at university anyway. A World Bank report on Turkish education says the standard of education across the country is in dire need of an overhaul. One of the major reforms needed is to increase high school graduation from just

Turks claim to be able to detect someone's political affiliations from the shape of their moustache. Civil servants are given instructions on how much hair can adorn their upper lip. University students are forbidden to grow beards.

A survey carried out in east and southeast Turkey discovered that one in 10 women was living in polygamous marriages, even though these became illegal in 1926.

ONE BIG, HAPPY FAMILY *Verity Campbell*

One of the cultural habits Turks have in common with their Arabic neighbours is the use of familial titles to embrace strangers into the extended family. This endearing habit is worth keeping an ear out for as it really does charm you. One of my fondest recent memories was when a friend was having a picnic in a park beside the Haliç (Golden Horn) in İstanbul, and I asked an old woman directions (in Turkish). 'Just south of the Fener *iskelesi* (jetty), my daughter' she said. I was so delighted I could have placed a big kiss on her grizzled face right then, though my reaction was also probably mixed with relief that she'd called me 'daughter' *(kızım)* and not 'sister'.

Listen out for slightly older men being called *abi* (big brother) and slightly older women *abla* (big sister). Considerably older men are *amca* (uncle) or *baba* (father); considerably older woman *teyze* (auntie) or *anne* (mother). You'll hear these titles in use when tensions are riding high in order to help to ease the situation.

35% in eastern provinces to 80% (the rate in the EU) and to implement a pre-schooling program. Despite the need for reform, literacy rates are good. According to the Turkish Statistics Institute some 80% of women and 95% of men are literate.

Although people are generally getting wealthier, with a declining number of people living under the poverty line (currently a quarter of the population), the gap between those at the top and bottom of the income pile is wide and growing wider. The average civil servant earns around €450 per month, while the owners of successful private companies throw away equivalent amounts on fripperies every day.

Tourism has had a huge impact on life in Turkey. While bringing in much-needed cash, it has also fostered rapid and all-pervasive social change. Until the 1970s not even a husband and wife could kiss or hold hands in public. Today, with many tourists wandering around in as few clothes as they can get away with, the taboos are breaking down and young Turks in the cities behave in much the same way as young people anywhere. This can cause confusion for tourists who, assuming anything goes these days, are shocked when a fight breaks out over 'possession' of a woman or someone takes offence on seeing a couple kiss in public. If in doubt, the watchword must always be to err on the side of caution, especially in rural areas.

ECONOMY

Turkey is infamous for a galloping inflation rate that tipped 77.5% in the 1990s, with so many zeros regularly added to the currency that having a tea for 1,000,000 Turkish lira no longer seemed a joke.

An economic collapse in early 2001 compounded the country's woes. Inflation skyrocketed and the value of the Turkish lira plummeted. Kemal Derviş, a newly appointed Minister of the Economy, succeeded in sweet-talking the IMF for loans and made much-needed economic reforms, thus avoiding a potentially disastrous downward spiral.

By January 2005, under the direction of the Justice and Development Party (AKP), the economy was considered robust enough to introduce the new Turkish lira (Yeni Türk Lirası) and finally do away with six zeroes on each and every banknote. For a year or so the yeni lira looked fairly stable, but in early 2006 a global downturn saw an exodus of international money and the currency lost some 18% of its value. Investors were left feeling shaky, sadly reminded of Turkey's vulnerability due to its high debt and current-account deficit. While the AKP had been boasting about bettering their IMF repayments, they were left red-faced. With the aid of the Central Bank the currency is back on track – for now.

POPULATION

Turkey has a population of approximately 70 million, the great majority of whom are Turks. The Turks form the largest minority, and there are also small groups of Laz and Hemşin people along the Black Sea coast, and Yörüks and Tahtacıs along the eastern Mediterranean coast.

Since the 1950s there has been a steady movement of people away from the countryside and into the towns, so that today some 66% of Turks live in cities. This process was speeded up by the years of fighting in the southeast when villagers were either forcibly relocated or decided for themselves that the grass was greener elsewhere (predominantly in Turkey's largest cities of İstanbul, Ankara, Bursa and Adana, but also in eastern towns such as Gaziantep and Malatya). The result is that cities such as İstanbul have turned into sprawling monsters, their historic hearts padded out with ring after ring of largely unplanned new neighbourhoods inhabited by the poor from all around the country.

Various (not exactly academically rigorous) theories state that the Turks are descendants of Japheth, the grandson of Noah. The Ottomans themselves claimed that Osman could trace his genealogy back through 52 generations to Noah.

Turks

That the Turks speak Turkish is a given, but what is not perhaps quite so widely known is that Turkic languages are spoken by a much larger group of people of similar ancestry who can be found all the way from Turkey through Azerbaijan and Iran to Turkmenistan, Kazakhstan, Kirghizstan and even Uighur, China. This is because the Turks are the descendants of assorted Central Asian tribal groupings, including the Seljuks, Huns and the nomadic Oğuz. Although academics believe the Turkic languages may have been spoken as early as 600 BC, the Turks definitively first appeared in medieval Chinese sources as the Tujue (or Turks) in 6th-century Mongolia and Siberia. As they moved westwards they encountered the Arabs and converted to Islam.

The Seljuks became Anatolia's first Turkic empire (see p35). It's believed that as news of Seljuk conquests and expansions spread, other nomadic Turkic people moved into Anatolia.

Kurds

Turkey has a significant Kurdish minority estimated at 14 million. The sparsely populated eastern and southeastern regions are home to perhaps seven million Kurds, while seven million more Kurds live elsewhere in the country, more or less integrated into mainstream Turkish society. Virtually all Turkish Kurds are Muslims. Kurds look physically similar to the Turks, but have a separate language, culture and family traditions.

According to the UN, Turkish is one of the world's most widely used languages, spoken in one form or another by around 150 million people from the old Yugoslavia to northwestern China.

Troubles between Kurds and Turks have been well documented. The Ottoman Empire's inclusivity ensured Kurds and Turks fought together during the struggle for independence, but relations soured after the formation of the Republic. Atatürk's reforms fuelled nationalism that left little room for anything other than Turkishness. It was only a matter of time before the Kurds began their separatist struggle.

Unlike the Christians, Jews and Armenians, the Kurds were not guaranteed rights as a minority group under the terms of the Treaty of Lausanne, which effectively created modern Turkey. Indeed, until relatively recently the Turkish government refused to even recognise the existence of the Kurds, insisting they be called 'Mountain Turks'. Even today the census form doesn't allow anyone to identify themselves as Kurdish, nor can they be identified as Kurdish on their identity cards. This is in spite of the fact that many people in the east, particularly women, speak the Kurmancı dialect of Kurdish as their first language (see the boxed text, p621) and may have only a shaky grasp of formal Turkish.

In 1984 Abdullah Öcalan formed the Kurdistan Workers' Party (PKK), which proved to be the most enduring – and bloodthirsty – Kurdish organisation that Turkey had seen. Many Kurds, while not necessarily supporting the early demands of the PKK for a separate state, wanted to be able to read newspapers in their own language, have their children taught in their own language and watch Kurdish TV.

From the mid-1980s the separatist strife escalated until the southeast was in a permanent state of emergency. After 15 years of fighting during the 1980s and '90s, and the deaths of some 30,000 people, Abdullah Öcalan was caught in Kenya in 1999. The 21st century started on a more promising note for relations between the Turks and Kurds when Öcalan urged his followers to lay down their weapons and a ceasefire was called.

The best hope for speedy change lies in Turkey's eagerness to join the EU, which champions the rights of cultural and ethnic minorities. In 2002 the Turkish government approved broadcasts in Kurdish and the go-ahead was given for Kurdish to be taught in language schools. Emergency rule was lifted in the southeast. The government started compensating villagers displaced in the troubles and a conference entitled 'The Kurdish Question in Turkey: Ways for a Democratic Settlement' was held in İstanbul in 2006. Life for Kurds in the southeast has become considerably easier: the press of harsh military rule and censorship has largely been lifted, and optimism has been fuelled by the outlook of accession with the EU. Many Kurds have been delighted with the development of the quasi-independent Kurdish state over the border in northern Iraq, but prefer to see their future with a country tied to the EU.

However, despite the positive accomplishments, this road will not be easy. Some Kurdish activists maintain reforms are inadequate and want an amnesty for PKK militants. The ceasefire was broken in June 2004 and since then low-level fighting has resumed in the southeast. A group believed to be a front for the PKK, the TAK (Kurdistan Freedom Falcons), claims responsibility for the unrest and the sporadic bombings throughout the country. But few feel that these events spell a return to the terror of the 1980s and '90s.

Laz

The 250,000-odd Laz people mainly inhabit the valleys between Trabzon and Rize. East of Trabzon you can hardly miss the women in their vivid red- and maroon-striped shawls. Laz men are less conspicuous, although they were once among the most feared of Turkish warriors: for years black-clad Laz warriors were Atatürk's personal bodyguards.

Once Christian but now Muslim, the Laz are a Caucasian people who speak a language related to Georgian. Just as speaking Kurdish was forbidden until 1991, so was speaking Lazuri, a language that until recently had not been written down. However, the German Wolfgang Feuerstein and the Kaçkar Working Group drew up a Lazuri alphabet (combining Latin and Georgian characters) and dictionary, and there are small signs of a growing sense of Laz nationalism.

The Laz are renowned for their business acumen and many are involved in shipping and construction.

Turkey has the youngest population in Europe; some 22 million (32% of the population) are under 15.

Hemşin

The Hemşin people mainly come from the far-eastern end of the Black Sea coast, although perhaps no more than 15,000 of them still live there; most have long since migrated to the cities where they earn a tasty living as bread and pastry cooks.

The Hemşin may have arrived in Turkey from parts of what is now Armenia. Like the Laz, they were originally Christian – their relatively recent conversion could explain why they seem to wear their Islam so lightly. You won't see any women in veils or chadors in Ayder, although the local women wear leopard-print scarves (even more eye-catching than those worn by Laz women) twisted into elaborate headdresses.

Other

About 70,000 Armenians still live in Turkey, mainly in İstanbul, around Lake Van and in and around Antakya. The controversy surrounding the Armenians and the Ottomans in the final years of the Ottoman Empire ensures that relations between Turks and Armenians in Turkey and abroad remain predominantly sour (see p40).

Although Turkey once had a large ethnic Greek population, after the population exchanges of the early Republic era (p41) most of the ethnic Greeks still living in Turkey settled in İstanbul. A few Pontic Greeks still live in the remote valleys of the eastern Black Sea.

There are also small communities of Circassians, Assyrians, Tatars, Yörük, Arabs, Roma and Jews, as well as a large – and growing – expat community.

SPORT
Football

Turks are simply mad about football (soccer). Every city has a football stadium that heaves with fans on match days. Pre- and post-match, the streets are aflutter with team flags, and the bars and tea gardens buzz with talk of nothing else.

The Turks' love affair with football began in the mid-19th century, after they were introduced to the game by English tobacco merchants. First matches saw English and Greek teams face off, but soon Turkish students from the Galata high school ran on field as the Galatasaray club. Fenerbahçe, Beşiktaş and Galatasaray are the top three teams, all of which are based in İstanbul, and all of which have fanatical national followings. Choose a team at your peril.

Since the 1990s Turkish teams and players have been enjoying greater success and increasingly higher profiles. In 2003, the national team made it to the semi-finals of the World Cup; Turks even outdid themselves when it came to partying hard.

If you are interested in seeing a game, the best place to see one is in İstanbul (p151).

Oil Wrestling

Turkey's most famous *yağlı güreş* (oil wrestling) matches have been taking place near Edirne since 1361 (see the boxed text, p171). Every June, hundreds of amateur wrestlers from all over Turkey gather there to show off their strength.

The wrestlers are organised into classes, from *teşvik* (encouragement) to *baş güreşler* (head wrestlers), with the winner in each class being designated a *başpehlivan*, or master wrestler. Clad only in leather shorts, they coat themselves with olive oil, utter a traditional chant and start going through a warm-up routine consisting of exaggerated arm-swinging steps and gestures. Then they get down to the nitty-gritty of battling each other to the ground, a business that involves some interesting hand techniques to say the least.

On the last day of the festival, the *başpehlivans* wrestle for the top prize. Finally only two are left to compete for the coveted gold belt.

Diminutive weightlifter Naim Süleymanoğlu won a hat-trick of Olympic gold medals in 1988, 1992 and 1996.

Camel Wrestling

Another purely Turkish spectacle is the camel-wrestling matches held in the South Aegean town of Selçuk, late January. Huge male camels are brought together to grapple with each other, which sounds like a frightfully unfair infringement of animal rights. Actually, it all seems rather harmless, with teams of men on hand with ropes like tug-of-war teams to pull the beasts apart at the first sign of anything seriously threatening. It's an amazingly colourful sport, and the picnicking spectators love it. For more information see the boxed text, p250.

MULTICULTURALISM

Under the Ottomans Turkey was well known for its multiculturalism, with many towns all over the country boasting populations of Greeks, Jews and Armenians as large as their Muslim ones. The Ottoman policy was to allow people to go on with their lives in peace provided they paid the requisite taxes. However, the events of WWI and then of the Turkish War of Independence meant that most Turks came to see non-Turkish nationalism within Turkey as a threat (p41), a heritage they have been slow to shake off.

Modern Turks will assure you that theirs is a very cosmopolitan country, an impression that can just about be sustained if you stick to the main tourist areas. However, when it comes to permanent inhabitants the picture looks very different. Take a stroll down İstanbul's İstiklal Caddesi and you'll see a population almost uniformly Caucasian and Muslim. The shortage of restaurants selling anything other than local and daringly 'European' food speaks volumes for this lack of diversity.

In such circumstances Turkey has barely reached first base when it comes to dealing with the realities of multiculturalism. Foreigners wanting to move to Turkey often have trouble persuading officials to let them keep their own names on their ID cards, let alone being allowed to register themselves as Christians or Jews. If anything, despite the government's rhetoric to the contrary, suspicion of 'alien' religions seems to be growing and polls confirm that support for nationalistic parties is on the rise. Even the St Paul Trail came under scrutiny for fear that those beefy trekkers were really missionaries in disguise, while the killing of a Catholic priest amid the Prophet Mohammed caricatures controversy in 2006 was further proof that tensions are rising. It will be a long time yet before Turkey is ready to have its children celebrate alternative religious festivals in school.

Even in its heyday the Ottoman Empire didn't extend beyond Europe, the Middle East and Africa. The result is that Turkey has not come under the same pressures to take in settlers from ex-colonies and accommodate refugees from far-flung places that have so changed the complexion of most Western countries. But all that is changing. In the last few years the numbers of asylum-seekers reaching Turkey have grown, and Turkey's position on

---

LOVE US OR LEAVE US   *Verity Campbell*

While talking to two modern young Turkish girls about their aspirations, we were inevitably drawn to a discussion about travel. They wanted to study English overseas and were discussing which country they'd like to go to. A young man in the group was asked if he'd like to travel: 'No, I love Turkey. Why would I want to leave?' The ridiculous idea seems to be growing in the community, closely tied to increasing nationalism, that if you leave Turkey you don't love it – you're a traitor. Turkish legislation seems to have fostered this trend. Turks were legally allowed to travel overseas for the first time in 1961, and Turkey has the most expensive passports in the world (some €400 for five years), seemingly designed to penalise those who leave.

FREEDOM TO SPEAK

Although Turkey has been implementing a wide range of reforms for its EU membership bid, the country's new penal code still retains the infamous Article 301, which prohibits people from 'insulting Turkishness'. This Article has been the basis for a series of recent high-profile prosecutions of journalists, writers and artists, exposing Turkey's freedom of expression credentials (or lack thereof) to the world.

The most famous case to hit the headlines was Turkey's internationally acclaimed novelist, Orhan Pamuk, who was tried after he mentioned the killing of Armenians by Ottoman Turks at the beginning of the 20th century (see the boxed text, p40). Charges were dropped early 2006, but Pamuk had become a reluctant political symbol and a target for nationalists, and the damage to Turkey's reputation had been done.

Lesser-known but just as important cases have followed. Journalist and author Perihan Mağden was tried for 'turning people against military service' after she wrote an article in the *Yeni Akteul* titled 'Conscientious objection is a human right'. Her case, heard in the Sultanahmet law courts in mid-2006, was a debacle because ultranationalists were allowed to demonstrate loudly outside the courtroom throughout the hearing. Critics claim the fact that security forces did little to quell the protestors makes them complicit. At the time of writing, Turkey's feted literary queen, Elif Şafak, was also due to stand trial for comments made by the Armenian characters in her *The Bastard of İstanbul*.

Even Prime Minister Erdoğan has taken artists to court – and won – for caricatures representing him as an animal. With this level of hypocrisy, it remains to be seen whether continuing pressure and international exposure from the increasing number of cases will eventually force the government into acting on its declared commitment to freedom of expression.

---

the doorstop of Europe has made it one of the major centres for human trafficking in the world (see p107).

Turkey has a large diaspora, with the largest community (some 2.6 million first- and second-generation Turks) living in Germany. Turks arrived in Germany in the 1960s as 'guest workers' at the invitation of the German government. However, the Kohl government's 1983 *Voluntary Repatriation Encouragement Act*, offering Turks financial incentives to return home, goes a long way to show that relations have never been easy. There are also significant populations in Bulgaria, France, Netherlands, UK, USA, Austria and Australia.

MEDIA

Although from the way the Turks slag their governments off in print it may look as if there's little censorship, certain subjects (the 'Armenian genocide', the 'Kurdish problem', negative portrayal of Atatürk, the army etc) still cause problems. Since editors and journalists know the likely penalties of stepping out of line, self-censorship is the order of the day. Still, some 200 journalists, artists and writers have been tried over the last two decades. In response, a freedom-of-speech movement has gained momentum over the last few years (see the boxed text, above).

Although controls over TV have loosened, the public broadcaster, Turkish Radio and Television (TRT), still receives a certain amount of censorship from the government of the day.

RELIGION

The Turkish population is 98% Muslim, mostly of the Sunni creed, with about 20% Alevis and a small group of Shiites (around Kars and Iğdır). İstanbul, İzmir and the coastal resorts have small Christian populations. There's also a small but rapidly declining community of Assyrian Orthodox Christians in and around Diyarbakır, Mardin and the Tür Abdin plateau. Turkey has had a Jewish community since at least 1492 when Sultan Beyazit II invited Jews expelled by the Spanish Inquisition. Today there are some 24,000 Jews in İstanbul, with smaller numbers in cities such as Ankara, Bursa and İzmir.

Turkey is a predominantly Muslim country with a secular constitution. Some 75% of Turks support the separation of state and religion, but nevertheless tensions between state and religion remain high. The urban-elite secularists, who see themselves as defenders of Turkey's republican foundations, fear the country will become an Islamic state (like its neighbour, Iran) if the fiercely guarded principles of the constitution are chipped away. Others say the doggedly secular laws repress basic human rights, including religious expression and duty. The headscarf has become a symbol of ongoing state versus religion tensions – see the boxed text, below.

Biblical Sites in Turkey, by Everett C Blake & Anna G Edmonds, provides detailed coverage of the country's many Christian and Jewish holy places as well as the Muslim ones.

Islam

Many Turks take a fairly relaxed approach in terms of Muslim religious duties and practices. Fasting during Ramazan (Ramadan in many Islamic countries) is usual and Islam's holy days and festivals are treated with due respect, but for many the holy day, Friday, and Islamic holidays are the only times they'll visit a mosque. You can also tell by the many bars and *meyhanes* throughout the country that Turks like a drink or three, another strict no-no for Muslims in other countries. If you've travelled in other Muslim countries where the five-times-a-day prayers are strictly followed, you'll find the practice of Islam in Turkey quite different.

Like Christians, Muslims believe that Allah (God) created the world and everything in it, pretty much according to the biblical account. They also believe that Adam (Adem), Noah (Nuh), Abraham (İbrahim), Moses

---

ISLAMISTS VS THE STATE: THE HEADSCARF CONTROVERSY

Who would have thought a square of cloth could cause such controversy? But for secular Turks the headscarf (*türban* or *eşarp*) worn by religious women is a symbol of everything they despise, of a backward-looking mentality that has rejected everything Atatürk stood for.

The result of this contempt is that people of otherwise impeccable left-wing credentials will behave towards women with headscarves in a way that would be out of the question in the politically correct West. But they have the law on their side. Women are forbidden to wear headscarves while working in public offices (which means schools as well as government buildings), and the start of every academic year sees huge demonstrations on university campuses since, in theory at least, women may not study for their degree while wearing a headscarf.

All this came to a head in 1998 when the elected MP Merve Kavakçı tried to take the oath of office while wearing a scarf, only to be jeered at and slow hand-clapped by her fellow MPs. And it's still not uncommon for government ministers to be denied invitations to presidential receptions if their wives wear headscarves.

Despite all this, in an almost inexplicable decision, the European courts ruled in 2004 that universities were within their rights to refuse to admit adult women who were wearing scarves. The current government has passionately argued for the lifting of the ban, but so far, to no avail.

So do all headscarves indicate fervent fundamentalist faith? Of course they don't, although they may indicate a generally traditional and more conservative approach to life in which a woman's modesty is of utmost importance. Regardless, it does seem ridiculous that a woman should be denied the right to study because she wears a headscarf. That the wife of the current prime minister wears a headscarf was controversial at election time, yet he was voted into office. For the upcoming presidential elections all eyes are on the candidates, and their wives, as the president is seen as the keeper of secularism in Turkey. If the chosen candidate's wife wears a headscarf it's likely that attitudes will be forced to change in the country.

(Musa) and Jesus (İsa) were prophets, although they don't believe that Jesus was divine or that he was a saviour. Jews and Christians are called 'People of the Book', meaning those with a revealed religion (in the Torah and Bible) that preceded Islam.

Where Islam diverges from Christianity and Judaism is in the belief that Islam is the 'perfection' of these earlier traditions. Although Moses and Jesus were great prophets, Mohammed was the greatest and last: *the* Prophet (Peygamber) to whom Allah communicated his final revelation, trusting him to communicate it to the world.

Accordingly, Muslims do not worship Mohammed, only Allah. In fact, Muslim in Arabic means 'one who has submitted to Allah's will'. The *ezan* called from the minaret five times a day and said at the beginning of Muslim prayers says: 'Allah is great! There is no god but Allah, and Mohammed is his Prophet.' Allah's revelations to Mohammed are contained in the Kur'an-i Kerim, the Quran (Koran in Turkish).

Muslims are expected to observe the following five 'pillars' of Islam:

- Say, understand and believe: 'There is no god but Allah, and Mohammed is his Prophet.'
- Pray five times daily: at dawn, noon, midafternoon, dusk and after dark.
- Give alms to the poor.
- Keep the fast of Ramazan, if capable of doing so.
- Make a pilgrimage to Mecca.

Muslim prayers are set rituals. Before praying, Muslims must wash their hands and arms, feet and ankles, and head and neck in running water. Then they must cover their head, face Mecca and perform a precise series of gestures and genuflections. If they deviate from the pattern, they must begin again.

A Muslim must not touch or eat pork, nor drink wine (interpreted as any alcoholic beverage), and must refrain from fraud, usury, slander and gambling. No sort of image of any being with an immortal soul (ie human or animal) can be revered or worshipped.

Islam has been split into many factions and sects since the time of Mohammed, and Islamic theology has become very elaborate and complex. However, these tenets are the basic ones shared by the entire Muslim community (or *umma*).

WOMEN IN TURKEY

Women in Turkey live in polar opposite worlds. Many women in İstanbul and other big coastal cities live a life not unlike their sisters in the West, free to come and go pretty much as they choose, to go out to work and to dress as they wish. But for the majority of Turkish women, especially those in villages out east, no such freedom exists and their lives continue to be ruled by the need to maintain their modesty and the honour of their family for fear of retribution.

Honour killings are an ongoing headache for the country. Over 2000 women were allegedly murdered for 'honour' in the country during the six years since 2000, and police believe these figures are just the tip of the iceberg. In most honour killings the 'dishonoured' family chooses a male family member to murder the woman accused of dishonouring the family, usually by having a child outside marriage or an extra-marital affair. Traditionally the murderers have received reduced sentences due to pleas of provocation, but the government's recent law amendments have increased penalties. However, social ideals also have to change – especially out

While the Ottoman Empire was a Muslim entity, its rulers weren't a particularly pious lot. No Ottoman sultan performed the Haj except Selim I – when he conquered Mecca.

Turkey's answer to England's King Henry VIII, Sultan İbrahim (r 1640–48) had his entire harem of 280 women tied in sacks and thrown into the Bosphorus when he tired of them.

THE ALEVIS

An estimated 20% of the Turkish population are Alevis – Muslims whose traditions differ markedly from those of the majority Sunnis; they have more in common with Shiites. The origins of these differences lie in the quarrels that broke out in 656 between the followers and relatives of the Prophet Mohammed following his death.

The religious practices of Sunnis and Alevis differ significantly. Many Alevi beliefs correspond with those of Hacı Bektaş Veli, the 13th-century Muslim mystic whose tomb is in Hacıbektaş (see the boxed text, p517) in Cappadocia. While Sunnis gather for prayer in a *cami* (mosque) with men and women separated, the Alevis assemble in a *cemevi* (assembly hall) with men and women together. During an Alevi *cem* (ceremony) a sermon is delivered by a *dede* (grandfather; a moral authority in the community) and then men and women begin a *sema*, the whirling ritual dance.

Antipathy between the Sunnis and the Alevis has continued into modern times, with some Turks denying that Alevis are true Muslims. Alevis want their religion included in textbooks (currently only the Sunni faith is covered), their rights recognised and their *cemevi* recognised as places of worship. In 2006 they took their complaints to the European Courts of Human Rights, a move designed, no doubt, to get the Turkish government to sit up and listen.

One of the nastiest manifestations of this antipathy is known as the Madımak tragedy. After lunchtime prayers, one July Friday in 1993, a mob attacked the Madımak hotel in Sivas, killing 37 people. Most of the dead were Alevis and were in Sivas for a local cultural festival; among them was the Turkish publisher of Salman Rushdie's *Satanic Verses* (allegedly the catalyst for the event). Although some of the culprits were captured, their prison sentences were pretty derisory – authorities claimed that those killed had contributed to their own fate by 'provoking' the crowd.

The Alevis in Turkey: The Emergence of a Secular Islamic Tradition, by David Shankland, based on anthropological studies in central Anatolia, sheds light on the relatively unknown traditions of the Alevis.

For more information about women's issues in Turkey, see KA-MER (www.kamer.org.tr) and Flying Broom (http://en.ucansupurge.org/).

east – before this tradition is stamped out. A recent parliamentary commission into honour killings found some 37% of respondents thought women who commit adultery should be killed. Ongoing 'suicide epidemics' of young women out east, as described in Orhan Pamuk's *Snow*, is an ongoing interrelated issue. Activists think the clampdown on honour killings may be partly responsible for encouraging families to push 'dishonourable' women in the family to dispose of themselves.

So it goes without saying that equality for women is a long way off in Turkey. Despite the country granting key rights such as the right to vote and be elected in the 1930s, long before some Western countries did, women still get a raw deal. Studies show women earn an average 40% less than their male equivalents, that women make up only 4.4% of parliamentary representatives, and that 45% of men think they have a right to beat their wives.

Good news is that around one-third of all lawyers and academics in the country are female, and there's a growing pool of talented women taking executive roles in the marketing, banking and retail sectors. Other good news is that the government has recently overhauled its laws with a view to joining the EU. As of January 2003 Turkish women are technically the equal of their menfolk. The new Turkish Civil Code abolished the clause decreeing that men were the heads of every household and ruled that henceforth women will be entitled to half their household's wealth in the event of a divorce. Rape in marriage and sexual harassment are now recognised as crimes. These tougher laws are a good start, but addressing the culture of patriarchy in Turkey, which views women squarely as commodities, is a long way off.

ARTS

Turkey's artistic traditions are rich and diverse, but we only have room to offer a brief introduction to some of them.

Literature
NOVELS

The notion of writer as social commentator took off in Turkey in the early 20th century, in the fertile grounds of WWI, the Russian revolution, the demise of the Ottoman Empire and the blossoming Turkish Republic era. Yaşar Kemal is the internationally best known author of the time, his *Memed, My Hawk* a gut-wrenching, thrilling saga and utterly unputdownable insight into the desperate lives of villagers battling land-grabbling feudal lords. Kurdish Yaşar Kemal has been nominated for the Nobel Prize for Literature on several occasions, and jailed a number of times for supposed proseparatist sympathies. Certainly *Memed, My Hawk* is an insight into the socialist era.

For more background reading on Turkish arts see the US-based Turkish Culture Foundation's website: www.turkish culture.org.

Following in the footsteps of this *agent provocateur* is Turkey's other internationally acclaimed author and 2006 Nobel Prize Laureate, Orhan Pamuk. While the foundation of Yaşar Kemal's work was in the early decades of the Republic, contemporary Turkey has given Pamuk much food for thought. He shot to international headlines in 2005 for mentioning the dreaded Armenian tragedy (see the boxed text, p51). Although he is increasingly widely read, his works seem impenetrable to many. The most accessible, and simply his best read to date, is the award-winning *Snow*, set in the remote eastern town of Kars. It explores a society grappling with female 'suicide epidemics'. *İstanbul, Memoirs and the City* is also well worth reading for those interested in the author and his complex relationship with his beguiling city.

Elif Şafak is being touted as the next Orhan Pamuk. Her novel, *The Flea Palace*, certainly has mental chewing-gum prose akin to Pamuk, so it's probably not the best choice for a beach read. However, this story of an elegant İstanbul apartment building fallen on hard times is a living painting of contemporary Turkish society and beautifully evokes İstanbul. Buket Uzuner is also worth seeking out. Her novels have been blockbusters in Turkey and have been well translated, though you probably won't find them in your local bookshop yet. *Mediterranean Waltz* is an unrequited love story set with the backdrop of civil war. Better yet is her *Long White Cloud, Gallipoli*, describing the fallout after a New Zealand woman claims a soldier revered as a war hero in Turkey is actually her great-grandfather. And in true Buket Uzuner style, the protagonist falls into a tangled love affair.

Irfan Orga's autobiographical *Portrait of a Turkish Family*, set during the late Ottoman/early Republican era, describes the collapse of his well-to-do İstanbullu family and its struggled rebuilding (beautifully mirroring the times). It offers an insider's peep into the culture of the *hamam*, the life of leisure in the Bosporus *yalı* (summer houses) and much more. This one will have you up until 3am.

Louis de Bernières, of *Captain Corelli's Mandolin* fame, wrote *Birds Without Wings*, another blockbusting page-turner inspired by Kayaköy (p361) near Fethiye. It exposes the human side of the intermingling of religions and culture in the Ottoman era, war and the population exchange. A must-read.

Some of the recent novels by expatriates living in Turkey or Turkophiles are worth seeking out, too. *Tales of an Expat Harem* is a compilation of stories dealing with life in Turkey for expatriate women. It's an excellent holiday read, if a little unanimously positive about its host country. Barbara Nadel writes gripping whodunits, usually set in İstanbul around the chain-smoking, stubbled hero, Inspector Çetin İkmen. *Belshazzar's Daughter*, her first, is still one of the best, but the award-winning *Dance with Death* is an easy and enjoyable holiday read, too.

See p20 for more reading recommendations.

POETRY

Turkey's two most famous poets lived roughly seven centuries apart from each other: the mystic poet Yunus Emre lived in the 13th century and Nazım Hikmet in the 20th century.

Nazım Hikmet is not only Turkey's greatest poet but also one of the world's best. Although his work was firmly embedded in Turkey and strongly patriotic, he was also a Communist exiled for his beliefs. His poems written while incarcerated are some of his best. He died and is buried in Russia, and sadly his works are still not allowed to be taught in Turkish schools. Probably the best introduction to his work is *Poems of Nazım Hıkmet*.

Carpets

The oldest-known carpet woven in the Turkish double-knotted Gördes style dates from between the 4th and 1st centuries BC, but it is thought that hand-woven carpet techniques were introduced to Anatolia by the Seljuks in the 12th century. Thus it's not surprising that Konya, the Seljuk capital, was mentioned by Marco Polo as a centre of carpet production in the 13th century.

Traditionally, village women wove carpets for their own family's use, or for their dowry. The general pattern and colour schemes were influenced by local traditions and the availability of certain types of wool and dyes. Patterns were memorised, and women usually worked with no more than 45cm of the carpet visible. Each artist imbued her work with her own personality, choosing a motif or a colour based on her own artistic preferences, and even events and emotions in her daily life. Knowing they would be judged on their efforts, the women took great care over their handiwork, hand-spinning and dyeing the wool.

Jon Thompson's beautifully illustrated and very readable *Carpets: From the Tents, Cottages and Workshops of Asia* is an excellent introduction that may well tempt you into parting with your money.

In the 19th century, the European rage for Turkish carpets spurred the development of carpet companies. The companies, run by men, would deal with the customers, take orders, purchase and dye the wool according to the customers' preferences, and contract local women to produce the finished product. The designs might be left to the women, but were more often provided by the company based on their customers' tastes. Although well made, these carpets lost some of the spirit and originality of the older work.

These days, many carpets are made to the dictates of the market. Weavers in eastern Turkey might make carpets in popular styles native to western Turkey, or long-settled villagers might duplicate the wilder, hairier and more naive *yörük* (nomad) carpets. Many carpets still incorporate traditional patterns and symbols, such as the commonly used 'eye' and 'tree' patterns. At a glance two carpets might look identical, but closer examination will reveal the subtle differences that give each Turkish carpet its individuality and charm.

Village women still weave carpets but usually work to fixed contracts for specific shops. Generally they work to a pattern and are paid for their final effort rather than for each hour of work. A carpet made to a fixed contract may still be of great value to its purchaser. However, the selling price should be lower than for a one-off piece.

Other carpets are the product of a division of labour, with different individuals responsible for dyeing and weaving. What such pieces lose in individuality and rarity is often more than made up for in quality control. Most silk Hereke carpets are mass-produced but to standards that make them some of the most sought-after of all Turkish carpets.

Fearing the loss of the old carpet-making methods, the Ministry of Culture has sponsored several projects to revive traditional weaving and dyeing methods in western Turkey. One such scheme is the Natural Dye Research and Development Project (Doğal Boya Arıştırma ve Geliştirme Projesi; Dobag); see p212 for more details. Some shops keep stocks of these 'project carpets', which are usually of high quality.

For advice about buying carpets, see p663.

THE ORIGINAL ROADHOUSE

The Seljuks built a string of caravanserais (caravan palaces) along the route of the 13th-century Silk Road through Anatolia. These camel caravan staging posts were built roughly a day's travel (about 15km to 30km) apart to provide food and lodging and to facilitate trade. Expenses for construction and maintenance of the caravanserais were borne by the sultan, and paid for by the taxes levied on the rich trade in goods.

The Ottomans were not keen builders of caravanserais like the Seljuks. Instead they built thousands of *hans*, urban equivalents of caravanserais, where goods could be loaded and unloaded near the point of sale. Ottoman *hans* were simpler in design than the caravanserais – just two-storey buildings, usually square, surrounding an open court with a fountain or raised *mescit* at its centre. On the upper level, behind an arcaded gallery, were offices and rooms for lodging and dining.

The most beautiful *hans* are the early Ottoman ones in Bursa – the Koza Han and Emir Han – but in fact every Anatolian town has at least a few *hans* in its market district. İstanbul's vast Grand Bazaar is surrounded by *hans* that are still used by traders and artisans.

For the sake of ease, this book does not really differentiate between caravanserais and *hans*. See p26 for a *han*/caravanserais-hopping guide to the country.

Architecture

The history of architecture in Turkey encompasses everything from Hittite stonework and grand Graeco-Roman temples to the most modern tower-blocks in İstanbul, but perhaps the most distinctively Turkish styles were those developed by the Seljuks and Ottomans.

SELJUK ARCHITECTURE

The Seljuks endowed Turkey with a legacy of magnificent mosques and *medreses* (seminaries), distinguished by their elaborate entrances; you can see the best of them in Konya (p481) and Sivas (p477). They also built a string of caravanserais along the route of the 13th-century Silk Road through Anatolia (see above).

OTTOMAN ARCHITECTURE

The Ottomans also left many magnificent mosques and *medreses*, as well as many more fine wood-and-stone houses.

Before Ottoman times, the most common form of mosque was a large square or rectangular space sheltered by a series of small domes resting on pillars, as in Edirne's Eski Cami (p169). But when the Ottomans took Bursa and İznik in the early 14th century they were exposed to Byzantine architecture, particularly ecclesiastical architecture. Ottoman architects absorbed these influences and blended them with the styles of Sassanian Persia to develop a completely new style: the T-shape plan. The Üçşerefeli Cami in Edirne (p167) became the model for other mosques not only because it was one of the first forays into this T-plan, but also because it was the first Ottoman mosque to have a wide dome and a forecourt with an ablutions fountain.

Each imperial mosque had a *külliye*, or collection of charitable institutions, clustered around it. These might include a hospital, asylum for the insane, orphanage, *imaret* (soup kitchen), hospice for travellers, *medrese*, library, baths and a cemetery in which the mosque's imperial patron, his or her family and other notables could be buried. Over time, many of these buildings were demolished or altered, but İstanbul's Süleymaniye mosque complex (p116) still has much of its *külliye* intact.

The design, perfected by Ottoman's most revered architect Mimar Sinan (see the boxed text, p117) during the reign of Süleyman the Magnificent,

For magnificent mosques and minarets seen from an angle you may not be able to manage yourself, Yann Arthur-Bertrand's gorgeous *Turkey from the Air* provides a bird's-eye view of Turkey's stunning scenery.

The Turkish bathing tradition is in fact Roman. When the Turks ventured into Anatolia they encountered the bath houses of the Byzantines, who in turn had inherited the bathing tradition from the Romans. The Turks so took to the steamy ablutions that they became part of the Turkish way of life.

proved so durable that it is still being used, with variations, for modern mosques all over Turkey.

For information about Ottoman houses, see the boxed text (p457).

TURKISH BAROQUE

From the mid-18th century, rococo and baroque influences hit Turkey, resulting in a pastiche of hammed-up curves, frills, scrolls, murals and fruity excesses, sometimes described as 'Turkish baroque'. The period's best – or some say worst – archetype is the extravagant Dolmabahçe Palace (p121). Although building mosques was passé, the Ottomans still adored kiosks where they could enjoy the outdoors; the Küçüksu Kasrı (p129) in İstanbul is a good example.

NEOCLASSICISM

In the 19th and early 20th centuries, foreign or foreign-trained architects began to unfold a neoclassical blend: European architecture mixed in with Turkish baroque and some concessions to classic Ottoman style. Many lavish embassies were built in Pera (Beyoğlu) as vehicles for the colonial powers to cajole the Sublime Porte into trade and territorial concessions. The in-vogue Swiss Fossati brothers were responsible for the Netherlands and Russian consulates-general along İstiklal Caddesi in İstanbul.

Lovers of Art Nouveau architecture will be able to feast their eyes on several beautiful examples of the style in Eminönü and along İstiklal Caddesi. It was introduced to İstanbul by the Italian architect Raimondo D'Aronco.

Also in the capital, Vedat Tek, a Turkish architect who had studied in Paris, built the central post office (p103), a melange of Ottoman elements such as arches and tilework, and European symmetry. Sirkeci train station (p157), by the German architect Jachmund, is another example of this eclectic neoclassicism.

MODERN ARCHITECTURE

There's little worth mentioning as far as modern architecture goes. The most interesting movement in the last few decades is that Turks have begun to reclaim their architectural heritage, especially those parts of it that can be turned into dollars via the tourism industry. These days, restorations and new buildings being built in Sultanahmet and other parts of İstanbul – and even Göreme, in Cappadocia – are most likely to be in classic Ottoman style.

Music
POP, ROCK, ELECTRONIC, HIP HOP & RAP

Turkey's home-grown pop industry is one of its big success stories. The seal was put on worldwide recognition of Turkish pop in 2003 when Sertab

---

ALL THE EMPTY HOUSES

You won't have been in Turkey five minutes before you notice the extraordinary number of half-built apartment blocks, houses and multistorey car parks littering the landscape. The reason behind this ugliness is usually housing cooperatives, whereby a group of people get together to pay for an apartment in a new development. Since they cannot pay all the money upfront (bank loans are prohibitively expensive), they can take several years to be finished – so at least some of the houses will one day be completed.

Unfortunately a lot can happen between the first breaking of the earth and the completion of the complex. The members of the cooperative may run out of money or the builder may go bankrupt. Worse still, builders have been known to disappear with the money, leaving the work to stand incomplete in perpetuity.

But even that cannot completely account for the sheer quantity of half-built blocks. Of course, some of them are entirely speculative projects, begun in the hope of tax breaks or some such reason, and abandoned just as soon as it suits the builder to pull out.

STOLEN TREASURES

'Every flower is beautiful in its own garden. Every antique is beautiful in its own country.' So reads the sign in the lobby of the Ephesus Museum. They surely have a point. And yet everywhere you go in Turkey you will come across archaeological sites that have been stripped of their finest artefacts, even of their most important structures, by Western countries that now display them proudly in their own museums.

The Sphinx column from Xanthos, the altar from Pergamum, the statue from Hadrian's Library at Ephesus, Schliemann's treasure from Troy: these are just some of the more prominent monuments that you must look for in museums in Britain, Germany, Italy and Russia rather than in Turkey.

Most Western countries justify retention of such treasures by arguing that they acquired them 'legitimately'. Or they claim that we all gain by being able to see a wide range of artefacts in museums worldwide. Finally, they claim that they are better equipped to care for the artefacts than the Turks. And while these arguments had started to wear thin, and several important collections had been returned to Turkey, recent scandals of theft from archaeological museums in the country have ensured that Western governments will keep holding on to their Turkish treasures for a while yet.

In 1993 the 2500-year-old Karun Treasure was repatriated to the Uşak museum (p311) after New York's Metropolitan Museum of Art lost a costly legal battle with the Turkish government. Some 13 years later, in the midst of a scandal about a number of thefts in Turkish museums, news broke that the famed golden winged seahorse brooch, one of the most valuable pieces in the collection, had been replicated and stolen. Investigations fingered the museum's director and nine others with embezzlement and artefact smuggling. The government promptly ordered investigations into 32 other museums, and the minister admitted he wouldn't be surprised if there were thefts from every one of them. With the museums chronically understaffed, underfunded and mismanaged – and the Karun scandal attracting international headlines – it will be a long time before Turkey's archaeological museums have any chance of winning back any more of their treasures.

Erener won the Eurovision Song Contest with her hit song 'Every Way that I Can'.

Sezen Aksu is widely regarded as the queen of Turkish pop music, but it is Tarkan, the pretty-boy pop star, who has achieved most international recognition. His '94 album, *A-acayıpsin*, sold over two million copies in Turkey and almost a million in Europe, catapulting him to Turkey's biggest-selling pop sensation. After several more albums, and tours all over Europe, he recently released the long-awaited *Come Closer*, sung entirely in English. It flopped, leaving fans distraught, but Tarkan's hip-swivelling bisexual brand will take a few more hits before it runs out of steam.

Burhan Öçal (www.burhanocal.com) is one of the country's finest percussionists. His latest work, *New Dream*, is a funky take on classical Turkish music, but we daren't box him by this production: his wide-ranging experimentation with all types of Turkish and foreign music genres has earned him due respect. His recent work with the 'Trakya All-Stars' is well worth looking up.

Turkish rock has long aped the West, but it's finally offering something distinctly Turkish. Look out for Duman, Replikas, 110 (electronica) and most definitely Yakup, a blend of East-meets-West oriental rock. Try to catch them live if you're passing through İstanbul.

On a more electronic jazzy theme is Orient Expressions, mixing Alevi and folk with jazzed-up Turkish melodies. Also well worth looking up is Baba Zula, a fusion of traditional Turkish instruments, reggae, electronic, pop and belly-dancing music – and it works! They've started the international touring circuit, so keep an eye out.

Turkey has a thriving rap slash hip-hop scene alive in the streets of İstanbul. Ceza (www.cezafan.com) is the king – he's literally mobbed by fans. Try to catch him live if you're in the city for a once-in-a-lifetime treat you won't forget. On a side note, all albums in Turkey need pre-release approval by the government, which means swearing is a no-no for Turkish rappers – unless they go underground or swear in English, that is. This ends up being a bonus for travellers, as it means most artists perform in English.

ARABESK

The equally popular style of music known as *arabesk* (that, as its name implies, puts an Arabic spin on home-grown Turkish traditions) started in the 1980s. Playing to *arabesk's* traditional audience is the hugely successful Kurdish singer İbrahim Tatlıses, a burly, moustachioed, former construction worker from Şanlıurfa who pops up on TV as often as he does on radio. Orhan Gencebay is, however, the king of *arabesk,* a prolific artist and also an actor. Start with his *Akma Gözlerimden.*

The Turkish government's Virtual Music Museum (www.kultur.gov.tr) is a newly inaugurated work-in-progress, and currently only in Turkish, but it looks like it'll be well worth checking out.

CLASSICAL & RELIGIOUS

Traditional Ottoman classical and religious (particularly Mevlevi) music may sound ponderous and lugubrious to the uninitiated. These musical forms use a system of *makams,* an exotic-sounding series of tones similar in function to Western scales. In addition to the familiar Western whole- and half-tone intervals, Turkish music often uses quarter-tones, unfamiliar to foreign ears and perceived as 'flat' until the ear becomes accustomed to them.

After the banning of the Mevlevi at the beginning of the Republic, it wasn't until the early '90s that a group called Mevlana Kültür ve Sanat Vakfı Sanatcıları was set up to promote the Sufi musical tradition. Mercan Dede (www.mercandede.com) has taken this music to another level altogether, fusing it with electronic, techno, classic beats.

FOLK, TÜRKÜ, FASIL & GYPSY

Turkish folk music is more immediately appealing to Western ears. Instruments and lyrics reflect the life of the musicians and village so they will be slightly different from village to village. Kurdish big names worth looking out for include Ferhat Tunç, who has produced an album annually since 1987, and Aynur Doğan (www.aynurdogan.net). Aynur, as she is simply known, has started touring internationally and is set for stardom. Both produce enjoyable Kurdish folk.

The documentary *Crossing The Bridge: The Story of Music in İstanbul,* by Fatih Akın, follows the trail of musos, giving you a superb peep into the vibrant and extraordinarily diverse contemporary music scene in İstanbul.

Türkü, a sort of halfway house between folk and pop, directly reflects experiences common to Turks. It became very popular in the 1990s.

Fasıl has been likened to a nightclub or lightweight version of Ottoman classical. This is the music you hear at *meyhanes* (taverns), usually played by gypsies. The music is played with clarinet, *kanun* (zither), *darbuka* (a drum shaped like an hourglass) and often an *ud* (a six-stringed Arabic lute), *keman* (violin) and a *cumbus* (similar to a banjo). It's usually hard to distinguish between fasıl and gypsy music.

Until the 1960s and '70s it was still possible to hear Turkish *aşıklar* (troubadours) in action. Although radio, TV, video and CDs have effectively killed off their art, the songs of the great troubadours – Yunus Emre (13th century), Pir Sultan Abdal (16th century) and Aşık Veysel (1894–1973) – remain popular.

If you're lucky you may spot wandering minstrels playing the *zurna* (pipe) and *davul* (drum). They perform at wedding and circumcision parties, and also congregate in bus stations on call-up day to see off the latest band of conscripts in style.

A BEGINNERS' GUIDE TO TURKISH MUSIC

These are our top picks to start your collection growing:

- *Turkish Groove* (compilation) A must-have two-disc introduction to Turkish music with everyone from Sezen Aksu to Burhan Öçal and from pop and Sufi to drum'n'bass
- *Su* by Mercan Dede (Sufi–electronic–techno fusion) Mercan Dede is a growing name in hip circles in İstanbul and abroad. *Su*, his latest offering, is arguably also his best to date.
- *Keçe Kurdan* by Aynur (Kurdish Folk) Aynur's impassioned *Kurdish Girl* album, sung entirely in Kurdish, was her excellent debut on the international scene. One to watch.
- *Rapstar Ceza* by Ceza (rap) You won't understand a word (unless you speak Turkish), but you don't need to. The energy and passion is palpable.
- *Duble Oryantal* by Baba Zulu (fusion) Baba Zulu's latest, 'Belly Double', was mixed by the British dub master Mad Professor.
- *Divan* by Oriental Expressions (fusion) Along the same vein as Baba Zula, yet a little more folksy.
- *Gipsy Rum* by Burhan Öçal and İstanbul Oriental Ensemble (gypsy) This 1998 production is an excellent, thigh-slapping introduction to Turkey's gypsy music, played by instrumental masters.
- *Buluşma* by Başar Dikici and Bülent Altınbaş (Ottoman classic) Mostly traditional, but with a modern twist, this recent big-seller should appeal to those not quite ready to face the classic Ottoman.
- *Yitik Sesen Peşinde* by Bezmârâ (Ottoman classical) An oldie, but a goodie. But you'll probably have to wait until you get to Turkey to pick this one up.

Cinema

The first screening of a foreign film in Turkey took place at the Yıldız Palace in İstanbul in 1896. In 1914 Turkey showed its first home-made documentary and by the end of WWI several Turkish feature films had appeared. The War of Independence inspired actor Muhsin Ertuğrul to establish a film company to make patriotic films. Comedies and documentaries followed, and within a decade Turkish films were winning international competitions. During the 1960s and '70s films with a political edge were being made alongside innumerable lightweight Bollywood-style movies usually lumped together and labelled *Yeşilçam* movies. A string of cinemas opened along İstanbul's İstiklal Caddesi, only to close again in the 1980s (or turn into porn-movie houses) as TV siphoned off their audiences. The 1990s were an exciting decade for the national cinema, with films being critically acclaimed both in Turkey and abroad.

Several Turkish directors have won worldwide recognition, most notably the late Yılmaz Güney. Joint winner of the best film award at Cannes in 1982, *Yol* explored the dilemmas of a group of men on weekend-release from prison, a tale that manages to be gripping and tragic at the same time, and which Turks were forbidden to watch until 2000. His last film, *Duvar (The Wall)*, made before his untimely death at only 46, was a wrist-slashing prison drama.

Following in Güney's footsteps, many Turkish directors continue to make political films. *Güneşe Yolculuk (Journey to the Sun)*, by Yeşim Ustaoğlu, is about a Turk who migrates to İstanbul and is so dark-skinned he's mistaken for a Kurd and treated appallingly. Nuri Bilge Ceylan's excellent *Uzak (Distant)* is also a bleak meditation on the lives of migrants in Turkey – it won the Jury Prize at Cannes. His latest work, *İklimler (Climates)*, which he also

For hard-to-find Turkish music you can't go past US-based online Turkish shopping emporium, Tulumba.com (www .tulumba.com), shipping right to your door – plus you can hear music samples.

stars in, looks at relationships between men and women in Turkey (plenty of scope there!), though some find it a little self-indulgent.

It's not all politics, though. Ferzan Özpetek received international acclaim for *Hamam (Turkish Bath)*, which skilfully explores cultural nuances after a Turk living in Italy reluctantly travels to İstanbul after he inherits a *hamam*. It's also noteworthy for addressing the hitherto hidden issue of homosexuality in Turkish society. His *Harem Suare (Evening Performance in the Harem)* was set in the Ottoman harem, while his most recent offering, *Karşı Pencere (The Window Opposite)*, ponders issues of homosexuality and marriage.

A relatively new name to watch, Fatih Akin, produced the widely acclaimed *Duvara Karsi (Head On)*, a gripping and often violent spotlight on the Turkish immigrant's life in Germany (Fatih is himself a Turkish–German). His documentary, *Crossing the Bridge: The Story of Music in İstanbul*, is also well worth seeking out.

Osman Hamdi (1842–1910), whose orientalist paintings are very much in vogue, was also the man responsible for establishing the İstanbul Archaeological Museum (p114).

Visual Arts

Until 1923 and the founding of the Turkish Republic, all mainstream artistic expression conformed to the laws of Islam, which forbid representation of any being with an immortal soul (ie animal or human). Sculpture and painting as known in the West did not exist, with the notable exception of Turkish miniature painting, which was for the upper classes only.

By the late 19th century, educated Ottomans were influenced by European-style painting. Atatürk encouraged this artistic expression, and the government opened official painting and sculpture academies, encouraging this 'modern' secular art in place of the religious art of the past.

By the 1930s many Turkish artists were studying abroad, with some becoming expatriates. Fikret Mualla is one of Turkey's most famous contemporary artists; he lived most of his life in Paris. Once again, the best place to see what modern artists are up to is İstanbul. İstanbul Modern (p120) is the country's best modern art gallery, but the small private art galleries along İstiklal Caddesi are well worth checking out as well.

Dance

İznik: The Artistry of Ottoman Ceramics, by Walter Denny, is a coffee-table book (and similarly priced), guaranteed to have regular pick-ups. It gives a superbly photographed run-down on this renowned Islamic art form.

Although it is dying out in the towns, folk dance is still a vibrant tradition in Turkish villages, as you will realise if you attend a traditional wedding.

Folk dance can be divided into several broad categories, including the *bar* from the Erzurum/Bayburt area, the *horon* from the Black Sea and the *zeybek* from the west. Although originally a dance of central, south and southeastern Anatolia, the *halay*, led by a dancer waving a handkerchief (or paper tissue), can be seen all over the country, especially at weddings and in *meyhanes* (taverns) in İstanbul when everyone has downed one rakı (aniseed-flavoured grape brandy) too many. But it may well be the *horon* that you most remember, since it involves the men getting down and indulging in all manner of dramatic kicking, Cossack-style. For a quick taste of these and other dances, pop along to the folk dance shows in İstanbul (see p151); they may be touristy but they're also fun.

The *sema* (dervish ceremony) of the whirling dervishes is not unique to Turkey, but it's here that you are most likely to see it performed; see the boxed texts, p119 and p119.

Belly dancing may not have originated in Turkey, but Turks have mastered the art. Although belly dancers are frequently seen at weddings and, incredibly, at many end-of-year company parties, your best chance of seeing a decent belly dancer is at one of the folk shows in İstanbul (p151). If you're interested in teaching your belly to dance see (p654).

Environment

THE LAND

Turkey has one foot in Europe and another in Asia, its two parts separated by the famous Dardanelles, the placid Sea of Marmara and the hectic Bosphorus. Eastern Thrace (European Turkey) makes up a mere 3% of Turkey's 779,452 sq km land area. The remaining 97% is Anatolia (Asian Turkey).

Boasting 8300km of coastline, snow-capped mountains, rolling steppes, vast lakes and broad rivers, Turkey is stupendously geographically diverse. The Aegean coast is lined with coves and beaches, with the Aegean islands (most of them belonging to Greece) dotted never more than a few kilometres offshore. Inland, western Anatolia has two vast lake districts and the soaring Uludağ (Great Mountain), at 2543m one of Turkey's highest mountains and increasingly popular with ski buffs.

The Mediterranean coast is backed by the jagged Taurus Mountains. East of Antalya, however, it opens up into a fertile plain as far as Alanya, before the mountains close in again. Central Anatolia consists of a vast high plateau of rolling steppe broken by mountain ranges, and Cappadocia, a region of fantastical landscapes created by the action of wind and water on tuff thrown for miles around by volcanic eruptions in prehistory.

Like the Mediterranean, the Black Sea is often hemmed in by mountains, and at the eastern end they drop right down into the sea. At 3937m, Mt Kaçkar (Kaçkar Dağı) is the highest point of the popular Kaçkar trekking and mountaineering area at the far eastern end of the Black Sea. There, *yaylas* (high plateau pastures) come ringed with peaks and glaciers.

Mountainous and somewhat forbidding, northeastern Anatolia is also wildly beautiful, especially around Yusufeli, and around Doğubayazıt, where snow-capped Mt Ararat (Ağrı Dağı; 5137m) dominates the landscape for miles around. Southeastern Anatolia offers windswept rolling steppe, jagged outcrops of rock, and Lake Van (Van Gölü), an extraordinary alkaline lake.

The bad news? Turkey lies on at least three active earthquake fault lines: the North Anatolian, the East Anatolian and the Aegean. Most of Turkey lies south of the North Anatolian fault line, which runs roughly parallel with the Black Sea coast. As the Arabian and African plates to the south push northward, the Anatolian plate is shoved into the Eurasian plate and squeezed west towards Greece. Thirteen major quakes in Turkey have been recorded since 1939; the latest in August 1999 hit İzmit (Kocaeli) and Adapazarı (Sakarya) in northwestern Anatolia killing more than 18,000. Some scientists predict that much of İstanbul would be devastated by any earthquake over 7 magnitude, due to unlicensed, jerry-built construction. Locals remain half-panicked, half fatalistic – but no-one doubts it's coming.

WILDLIFE
Animals

In theory, you could see bears, deer, jackals, caracal, wild boars and wolves in Turkey. In practice you're unlikely to see any wild animals at all unless you're trekking.

Instead you can look out for Kangal dogs, which are named after a dreary small town near Sivas. Kangals were originally bred to protect sheep flocks from wolves and bears on mountain pastures. People wandering off the beaten track, especially in eastern Turkey, are often alarmed at the sight of these huge, yellow-coated, black-headed animals, especially as they often wear

---

Turkey is one of only seven countries in the world that is wholly self-sufficient in agriculture.

Bogazici University and the Kandilli Observatory and Earthquake Research Institute run a website mapping the country's seismic activity (www .koeri.boun.edu.tr/sismo /map/en/index). Don't let it spook you!

For more information on Turkey's wildlife, contact Doğal Hayatı Koruma Derneği (Foundation for the Protection of Nature; ☎ 0212-513 2173; www.dhkd.org, in Turkish) or WWF-Turkey (☎ 0212-528 2030; www.wwf.org.tr).

TAKE ONLY PHOTOS, LEAVE ONLY FOOTPRINTS

Tourism is not the only thing that has had a damaging impact on the Turkish environment, but it is certainly one of them. So what can you do to help?

■ Never drop litter anywhere (although, to be fair, tourists are not the worst offenders when it comes to abandoned rubbish).

■ Don't buy coral or seashells, no matter how lovely they look in a necklace.

■ It goes without saying that you should try to do without plastic bags, even though some bags in Turkey are made from recycled material.

■ Complain to the captain if you think your excursion boat is discharging sewage into the sea or if it's dropping its anchor in an environmentally sensitive area. Even better, complain to **Greenpeace Mediterranean** (☎ 0212-248 2661; www.greenpeace.org/mediterranean).

■ Consider staying in pensions and hotels that have been designed with some thought for their surroundings.

■ Refrain from purchasing water in plastic bottles wherever possible. Water in glass bottles is served in many Turkish restaurants, and you can buy water filtration systems from home before your departure. The very least you can do is to buy the 5L plastic water bottles, which you can keep in your hotel room and use to fill up a re-usable smaller bottle to carry with you during the day.

Walking and Birdwatching in Southwest Turkey, by Paul Hope, is an introduction to some of Turkey's best bird-watching spots.

ferocious spiked collars to protect them against the wolves. Their mongrel descendants live on the streets in Turkey's towns, villages and cities.

Some 400 species of bird are found in Turkey, with about 250 of these passing through on migration from Africa to Europe. It's particularly easy to see eagles, storks, (beige) hoopoes, (blue) rollers and (green) bee-eaters. Enthusiastic bird-watchers should head east to Birecik (p599), one of the last known nesting places in the world of the eastern bald ibis *(Geronticus eremita)*. Also well off the beaten trail is Çıldır Gölü (Çıldır Lake; p585), north of Kars in northeastern Anatolia. It's an important breeding ground for various species of birds. More readily accessible is the Göksu Delta (p420), near Silifke, where some 332 species have been recorded – including the rare purple gallinule – and Pamucak (see p256), home to flamingos from February to March.

ENDANGERED SPECIES

Van cats are said to be able to swim the waters of Lake Van – not that their owners would let these valuable pets out of their sight to do so.

Rare loggerhead turtles still nest on various beaches in Turkey, including İztuzu Beach at Dalyan, the Göksu Delta and Patara Beach (see the boxed text, p352). A few Mediterranean monk seals are just about hanging on in Turkey around Foça (p224), but you would be very lucky to see them.

The beautiful, pure-white Van cat, with one blue and one green eye, has also become endangered in its native Turkey.

PLANTS

Turkey's locaion at the junction between Asia and Europe and its varied geology have made it one of the most biodiverse temperate-zone countries in the world, blessed with an exceptionally rich flora of over 9000 species, a third of them endemic. Some sources report that a new species of flora in Turkey is discovered every five days.

Turkey is the last remaining source of frankincense trees *(Liquidambar orientalis)*, which grow in stands along the southwest coast of the Mediterranean, especially around Köyceğiz (p346). The Egyptians used the trees' resin during the embalming process. Today, it is exported for use in perfume and incense. Also on this coast is the endemic Datça palm (*Phoenix theophrastii*), found on the Datça Peninsula and near Kumluca. Like frankincense, these are also the last remaining populations of these trees in the world.

NATIONAL PARKS & RESERVES

In the last few years, thanks to EU aspirations, Turkey has stepped up its environmental protection practices. It's now a signatory to various international conventions including Ramsar and Cites (International Trade of Endangered Species). The growing number of protected areas includes 33 *milli parkı* (national parks), 16 nature parks and 35 nature reserves. It also includes 58 curiously named 'nature monuments', which are mostly protected trees, some as old as 1500 years. (For more information see www.turizm.gov.tr.) In the parks and reserves the environment is supposedly protected and hunting controlled. Sometimes the regulations are carefully enforced, but at other times a blind eye is turned to such problems as litter-dropping picnickers.

Tourism to national parks is not well developed in Turkey, and they are rarely set up with facilities for visitors. It is not even the norm for footpaths to be clearly marked, and camping spots are rarely available. Most of the well-frequented national parks are as popular for their historic monuments as they are for the surrounding natural environment.

The following national parks are among the most popular with foreign visitors to Turkey:

Gallipoli Historic National Park (p183) Historic battlefield sites on a gloriously unspoilt peninsula surrounded by coves.

Göreme National Park (p499) An extraordinary landscape of gorges and cones ('fairy chimneys') spread over a wide area.

Kaçkar Dağları National Park (Kaçkar Mountain National Park; p558) Stunning high mountain ranges popular with trekkers.

Köprülü Kanyon National Park (p396) Dramatic canyon with spectacular scenery and facilities for white-water rafting.

Nemrut Dağı National Park (Mt Nemrut National Park; p610) Huge historic heads surmounting a man-made mound with wonderful views.

Saklıkent National Park (p364) Famous for its 18km-long gorge.

ENVIRONMENTAL ISSUES

Turkey faces the unenviable challenge of balancing environmental management with rapid economic growth and urbanisation, and to date it's done a pretty sloppy job. Hopeless enforcement of environmental laws, lack of finances and poor education have placed the environment so far down

The Byerley Turk: The True Story of the First Thoroughbred, by Jeremy James, is a fictionalised biography of the Ottoman horse, whose ancestors are the world's finest racing horses today.

The Most Beautiful Wild Flowers of Turkey, by Erdoğan Tekin, is the best field guide on the market with some 700 photos and detailed charts on each flower. It's pricey though.

TOWARDS THE EU

Turkey's intended accession to the EU is thankfully forcing it to lift its environmental standards. The country has started to overhaul environmental practices and laws, and even given indications that it might ratify international conventions such as the Kyoto Protocol (don't hold your breath).

The government aims to harmonise all environmental legislation with the EU by 2010. Initial cost estimates put this ambitious project at some €70.5 billion; €150 million has already been received from the World Bank to kickstart 'green' energy developments in 2004.

Although the Environment and Forestry Minister, Osman Pepe, must be having sleepless nights trying to work out where to start with this most challenging quest for accession, most analysts say improving food safety is a major priority. Currently Turkey isn't authorised to export animal products and most nuts to the EU. The other major priorities are wastewater disposal and water treatment facilities.

The Isparta area is one of the world's leading producers of attar of roses, a valuable oil extracted from rose petals and used in perfumes and cosmetics. See p315 to find out how you can see the harvest in late spring.

the list of priorities that it would pack up and leave if it could. But things are looking up, and it's largely due to the country's desire to join the EU – see boxed text, p65.

One of the biggest environmental challenges facing Turkey is the threat from maritime traffic along the Bosphorus. The 1936 Montreux Convention decreed that, although Turkey has sovereignty over the Bosphorus strait, it must permit the free passage of shipping through it. At that time, perhaps a few hundred ships a year passed along the strait, but this has risen to over 45,000 vessels annually (around 10% are tankers), with some estimates suggesting traffic will grow by a further 40% in the near future.

Many of these ships are tankers or are carrying other dangerous loads. There have already been serious accidents, such as the 1979 *Independenta* collision with another vessel, which killed 43 people and spilt and burnt some 95,000 tonnes of oil (2½ times the amount spilt by the famous *Exxon Valdez*). A new oil pipeline running between Azerbaijan and the Turkish eastern Mediterranean port of Ceyhan has been built to relieve some of the burden. Other pipelines are on the drawing board, but in the meantime toxic substances and most oil continues to be carried along the Bosphorus.

Building development is taking a terrible toll on the environment, especially along the Aegean and Mediterranean coasts. Once pleasant fishing villages, Kuşadası and Marmaris have been near swamped by tacky urban spread and are in danger of losing all appeal. Local environmentalists battling development around Bodrum say the number of secluded valleys the famed Blue Voyage (p356) cruises visit has decreased from 45 to 11 in the last few years. Worse still, much of the development is only used for several months of the year, placing unrealistic strains on the infrastructure.

See Sıfır Yok Oluş (www .sifiryokolus.org) for information on Turkey's 266 Key Biodiversity Areas outlined by Turkey's wing of the international coalition, Alliance for Zero Extinction.

Short of water and electricity, Turkey is one of the world's main builders of dams. Wherever you go you see signs to a new *baraj* (dam) construction, and it doesn't take long to hear about the problems they are causing. Furthermore, recent studies have shown Turkey's soil erosion problems are shortening the dams' life spans considerably anyway. The gigantic Southeast Anatolia Project, known as GAP, is one of Turkey's major construction efforts. Harnessing the headwaters of the Tigris and Euphrates Rivers, it's creating a potential political time bomb with the countries downstream that also depend on this water. For more information, see the boxed text, p608.

NUCLEAR TURKEY

One of the biggest environmental challenges facing Turkey's environmentalists is the current government's plan to build three nuclear power plants by 2015. These plants propose to provide 5% to 10% of Turkey's projected energy needs for the next two decades. The first nuclear reactor is planned for Sinop, on the Black Sea coast. One of its most vocal opponents is **Sinop is Ours** (www.sinopbizim.org), a community-run initiative.

Turkey's government says the country's rising dependence on energy from other countries is the main catalyst for its push for nuclear energy. Turkey currently imports some 75% of its oil and natural gas, and when it was hit, like Ukraine was in 2005, by gas cuts by Russia, internal energy security went firmly on the agenda. Experts also claim that Iran's nuclear program, and its alleged push to develop nuclear weapons, makes it an untenable potential threat on Turkey's doorstep, pushing Turkey to have some nuclear capacity. Environmentalists say reports have shown that Turkey's existing energy infrastructure is outdated, poorly maintained and should be improved, and policies should be enforced to better harvest the current energy demands before looking to implement nuclear energy. They also state that the country's seismic vulnerabilities make any nuclear reactors an unacceptable risk.

Disposal and treatment of industrial waste is a major headache for the government; reports suggest up to 75% of industrial waste is discharged without any treatment whatsoever and only 12% of the population is connected to sewage treatment facilities. Turkey is adopting the EU's 'polluters pay' policy by increasing fines and improving legislation and policing. In early 2006 fines for dumping toxic waste increased from a maximum of €4500 to €1.5 million. However, locals feel this is akin to shutting the gate after the horse has bolted, as these legislative changes were announced only after barrels of toxic waste were discovered in empty lots throughout İstanbul. One of the worst hit suburbs was Dilovası, with deaths from cancer in the area nearly three times the world average and a report saying Dilovası should be evacuated and labelled a medical disaster area (neither happened).

To end on a happy note, Turkey is doing well when it comes to beach cleanliness, with 192 of its beaches qualifying for European Blue Flag awards in 2006; go to www.blueflag.org for the complete list.

A surprising 26.7% of Turkey is covered in forest, 28% is pasture and 2% is wetlands.

Food & Drink

Think Turkish food and you may conjure up a vertically roasting döner kebap, spitting-revolving-spitting-revolving while meat is deftly sliced off and stuffed into a hunk of pide (Turkish-style bread), soaked in a garlicky yogurt, and topped with salad sprinkled with *sumak* (ground purple-red berries). Salivating already? You haven't tasted anything yet. Food from the Turkish homeland is so much tastier and so much more diverse than its most famous exports.

It's down to the crunchy-fresh ingredients, the regional specialities, and the tender loving care taken to plan the flavours of every meal. But most importantly, food in Turkey is not merely fuel but a celebration of community. Meals unfurl with great ceremony – they are joyful, boisterous and always communal. Turks eat because they're celebrating a circumcision, crunching on a handful of green plums heralding the start of spring, or savouring a shared leisurely breakfast with the family before the day begins. Turks drink for community too: endless cups of tea to foster new or old friendships; nights spent drinking rakı (grape spirit infused with aniseed) while debating the merits of Gaziantep's *fıstıks* (pistachios) over Giresun's hazelnuts.

The basics of Turkish cooking may have evolved on the steppes of Central Asia, but as the Ottoman Empire grew it swallowed up the ingredients of Greece, Persia, Arabia and the Balkans, creating a deliciously diverse cuisine you can enjoy every meal. *Afiyet olsun!* (Good appetite!)

STAPLES & SPECIALITIES

Turkey is one of the few countries that can feed itself from its own produce and have leftovers. This is not hard to believe as there's food being grown, sold and eaten wherever you look. Famous favourites are the ubiquitous döner kebap, but regional specialities abound – check out Turkey for Tastebuds, p27.

Turkish *kahvaltı* (breakfast) consists of fresh-from-the-oven white *ekmek* (bread), jam or honey, black olives, slices of cucumber and juicy tomatoes, a hard-boiled egg, a block of white cheese, and innumerable dainty glasses of sweetened black *çay* (tea). Locals eat like this daily, with sometimes a second helping late morning if they've had an early start. Expect this feast at every hotel.

There's not always a lot to choose between what's on offer for lunch and dinner, but both meals frequently start with *çorba* (soup). The most common soups are *ezo gelin* (red lentil and rice) and *domates* (tomato), but you may also meet *balık çorbası* (fish soup), *sebze çorbası* (vegetable soup) and *yayla çorbası* (yogurt soup with mint). Workers who don't have time for a leisurely breakfast at home will often pop into a cheap restaurant for a *mercimek çorbası* (lentil soup) on the way to work.

A night fuelled by rakı and Turkish mezes in a *meyhane* (tavern) often ends up being a visitor's most cherished memory of Turkey. Locals usually savour a procession of mezes throughout the night. The waiter brings out a tray of cold mezes for you to point and choose – select your hot mezes from the menu.

In most restaurants, mezes are usually followed by meat. Beef is the most commonly used meat, though lamb and mutton follow closely behind. Meat is prepared in three main ways: as *köfte* (meat balls); *yahni* (stewed or casseroled meat); and, most commonly, as kebaps. You'll find *şiş* kebaps (marinated

The Complete Book of Turkish Cooking, by Ayla Esen Algar, is widely regarded as the best Turkish cookery book (in English) available.

The Turkish diet has meant that Turks now appear near the top of the world obesity stakes.

Deceptively simple, yet absolutely delicious when done to perfection, the humble *simit*, an O-shaped bread ring sprinkled with sesame seeds, is the number-1 snack for Turks. The magic ingredient in something seemingly so simple – flour, water and salt – is *pekmez*, a grape syrup.

TURKEY'S TOP TASTE SENSATIONS

Obviously we're sticking our necks out here, but out of Turkey's myriad culinary offerings we feel these are the must-tries:

- *Yaprak sarma* (stuffed grape leaves) – Fresh grape leaves from the markets stuffed with spiced rice and rolled into tasty fingers.

- *Kalamar* (calamari) – Fleshy calamari from the northern Aegean is so tender you'll be boasting for years.

- *İmam bayıldı* (the imam fainted) – And so did we when we first tasted it. Aubergines stuffed with a garlicky, oniony mixture.

- Tokat kebap – The greasy Tokat might knock 10 years off your life but it tastes so good you won't care (see p476).

- *Fırın sütlaç* (baked rice pudding) – What Granny did best Turks have elevated to a fine art.

- *Tavuk göğsü kazandibi* (burnt chicken-breast pudding) – This chewy chicken dessert is somewhat kooky but surprisingly tasty.

- Baklava – The dental bills are worth it (see p597).

---

cubes of meat on skewers) everywhere. The different meals are distinguished by the spices, accompanying vegetables and occasionally the sauce (usually tomato, but sometimes yogurt-based). Meat dishes are often named after their places of origin. Guess where Tokat kebap comes from?

Turks love vegetables, eating them fresh in summer and pickling them for winter. *Patlıcan* (eggplant/aubergine) is the darling, cooked in every conceivable manner – Turkish cookbooks list up to 200 recipes for it! Turks also love *dolma* (stuffed vegetables): they stuff rice, currants, all-spice, cinnamon and pine nuts into peppers, tomatoes, cabbage and grape leaves (the tastiest). With the addition of lamb mince, *dolma* is served piping hot. Dishes based on cabbage or cheese are staples of the Black Sea region's unique cuisine (see p556).

If you consider mains to be merely an obligation before the most important course, dessert, you'll be delighted to hear that sweets are an indispensable part of the Turkish meal and culture. Turkish sweets are a mix of super-sweet pastries, syrupy cakes, *helva* (a sweet made from sesame seeds), and milk-based, dried-fruit and pulse puddings. Consider yourself warned.

DRINKS

In the coastal touristy towns, virtually every restaurant serves alcohol, as do more expensive restaurants in the big cities. In smaller towns, there's usually at least one restaurant where alcohol is served, although in religiously conservative cities such as Konya you may have to hunt hard to find it. Although Turks have a fairly relaxed attitude towards alcohol, public drunkenness is a definite no-no.

Turkey's beloved tipple is rakı, a grape spirit infused with aniseed, similar to Greek ouzo; do as the locals do and cut it at least by half with water if you want to surface the next day. Beer is becoming a serious contender to rakı's fame, with national consumption doubling since 2000. The main local brew, Efes, is a popular choice on a summer's afternoon.

Turkey has a small but blossoming viniculture, carrying on the Ottoman–Greek wine-making tradition. Head to Ürgüp (p519) in Cappadocia or the idyllic Aegean island of Bozcaada (p206) to taste-test. Elsewhere *şarap* (wine) is fairly average for the price, but you can't go wrong if you stick with the main wine producers, Doluca and Kavaklıdere. For whites try Kavaklıdere's Kavak

Grumbly tummy? Ask for an ihlamur çay (linden tea). Turks always have it on hand for upset stomachs.

THE BELOVED COFFEE BEAN *Will Gourlay*

The Ottomans, inadvertently, gifted coffee to Europe. When Mehmet IV besieged Vienna in 1683 he was so confident of victory he brought coffee beans in preparation for his victory feast. When the Turkish armies eventually retreated they left behind the coffee, which was discovered by the Viennese who then introduced the coffeehouse to Europe.

---

or Çankaya, or Doluca Nevsah and, for reds, Kavaklıdere Ancyra. Angora is a passable cheapie that becomes more drinkable as the night wears on.

Somewhat surprisingly, *Türk kahvesi* (Turkish coffee) is much less popular than tea. It's ordered according to sweetness since the sugar is mixed in during the brewing. The national hot drink is *çay* (tea), served in dainty tulip-shaped glasses – expect to share many a glass with locals on your travels. No-one puts milk in their tea, but everyone adds sugar. The wholly chemical *elma çay* (apple tea) is caffeine-free and only for tourists – locals wouldn't be seen dead drinking the stuff.

Sahlep, a hot milky drink, takes off the winter chill. It's made from wild orchid bulbs and is reputedly an aphrodisiac. *Ayran*, popular year-round, is a mix of yogurt, water and salt, and a must-have with every meal. You might also want to try *şalgam* (see p427) – the first gulp is a revolting salty shock, but persevere and you may find this turnip-carrot concoction becomes an essential accompaniment to rakı binges.

CELEBRATIONS

Every special occasion in Turkey has concomitant foods, and mostly these are sweets. Some say Turks' adoration of sweets may be attributed to the Koranic verse 'To enjoy sweets is a sign of faith'; a local proverb says 'sweets

---

CHEESE, GLORIOUS CHEESE

Be the envy of every mouse with a taste-test tour of Turkey's cheeses. Do as the locals do and try cheeses before you buy. Serve them at room temperature and buy from reputable-looking market stores (brucellosis can be a problem with unpasturised cheeses so it pays to be a little careful). One of the best places to buy cheese is in the Spice Bazaar in İstanbul (p118).

There are three main storage methods for cheese: *teneke*, cheese squares in metal drums; *tulum*, pressed cheese in bags or, less commonly these days, in hairy goat skins; and cheese pressed into wheels. *Keçi* (goat's) cheese is popular in the west of the country and *koyun* (ewe's) cheese out east (the animals are suited to the climatic conditions of each region). *İnek* (cow's) cheese is becoming increasingly popular too. You'll find a combination of these depending on the season, but early spring cheeses are at their milky-rich best.

The most common Turkish cheeses are *beyaz peynir*, a salty white feta you'll find on every breakfast table, and *kaşar peynir*, a yellowy cheese like a Cheddar. *The Treasury of Turkish Cheeses*, written by a true cheeseaholic, Suzanne Swan, is the best resource in English for like-minded cheese devotees.

Our favourites of the many other cheeses worth seeking out are listed below.

■ *Van otlu peynir* – chewy ewe's cheese laced with freshly picked mountain herbs.

■ *Erzincan peynir* – for novelty value try this dry, crumbly ewe's cheese cured in a *tulum* (goatskin bag). Some say it tastes like a goat's backside!

■ *Niğde peynir* – hard to find but well worth the search, this is one of Turkey's finest. Can be found as a blue cheese, too.

■ *Muhlama* – a large dish overflowing with molten cheese, best sampled in the tiny villages of the Kaçkar Mountains – see p556.

are equated with a kind heart and a sugary tongue'. Despite sweets being such a focus during celebrations and festivities you can enjoy many puddings year-round in a *muhallebici* (milk pudding shop) and all restaurants.

Baklava is a sticky, ultra-sweet, syrupy pastry baked in trays and cut into bite-sized rectangles. It was traditionally reserved for festive occasions such as Şeker Bayramı (Sweets Holiday; p660), the three-day holiday at the end of Ramazan (p659). Baklava is also popular for engagements and weddings, proving sugary stamina for the rollicking hours of party-making ahead and the couple's wedding night (wink, wink). The best two *baklavacıs* in the country are Karaköy Güllüoğlu in İstanbul (p145) and İmam Çağdaş in Gaziantep (**p597**).

Other sweets such as *helva* and *lokum* (Turkish delight) are commonly part of more reflective occasions such as deaths and *kandil* days (the five holy evenings in the Muslim calendar). A bereaved family will make *irmik helvası* (semolina *helva*) for visiting friends and relatives, and *helva* is shared with guests at circumcision feasts.

Aşure (Noah's Ark pudding) is a sacred pudding traditionally made with 40 different dried fruits, nuts and pulses, supposedly first baked from the leftovers on Noah's Ark when food provisions ran low. These days *aşure* is traditionally made after the tenth day of Muharram (the first month of the Islamic calendar), and distributed to neighbours and friends.

Savoury dishes are integral to celebrations in Turkey too, albeit not nearly as many. *Kavurma* is a simple lamb dish cooked with the sacrificial lamb or mutton of the Kurban Bayramı (Feast of Sacrifice; see p660). The meat is cubed, fried with onions and baked slowly in its juices. During Ramazan a special round flat pide is baked in the afternoon and collected in time for the break of fast feast, *iftar*.

WHERE TO EAT & DRINK

Turkey's eateries open from eightish in the morning until late at night. Often there isn't much difference between a €6 meal in an informal *lokanta* (restaurant) and a €15 meal in a more upmarket *restoran* except in terms of the ambience and service. Only at very hip restaurants in cities such as İstanbul do you need to make a reservation.

Hazır yemek (ready-made food) restaurants serve stews, casseroles and vegetable dishes prepared in advance and kept warm in steam trays. These are best at lunchtime when the food will be at its freshest.

If you're after meat, look instead for a specialist *kebapçı*. The *ocakbaşı* (fireside) versions are the most fun, with patrons sitting around the sides of a grill and watching the *kebapçı* preparing their dinner. Often diners take pot luck with what they're served and there's no menu or price list.

Meyhanes are Turkish taverns where you can expect a succession of mezes to be paraded in front of you, then a choice of meat and fish dishes, all to be

Legend has it that in society Ottoman-era houses chefs made baklava with over 100 pastry-sheet layers per tray. The master of the house would test the thickness with a gold coin: if it fell to the bottom of the tray the chef kept the coin.

In the 17th century 1300 people slaved away in the kitchens of Topkapı Palace, which could cook up a big enough feast for around 15,000 people.

CHARGE YOUR CARD & YOUR GLASS

Some of our favourite eating establishments:

360 (p144) Superb mod-Turk cuisine, uberstylish and the best views in İstanbul.

Beyaz Yunus Lokantası (p361) Prepare your stomach at the delightful sunset bar for some of Turkey's finest fish and seafood mezes.

Cercis Murat Konağı (p629) Old-fashioned fare prepared by an all-woman team in a traditional Syrian Christian home in Mardin.

Kocadon Restaurant (p278) Old-world charm and traditional Ottoman cuisine.

Ottoman House Restaurant (p413) Time your visit for a fresh tuna-carving session and you'll see what all the fuss is about.

washed down with copious quantities of rakı. Don't miss a night carousing at the *meyhanes* clustered in the Beyoğlu area of İstanbul (p146).

Turkish *pastanes* (patisseries) have supplies of *börek* and sweet and salty biscuits (*kuru pasta*, dry pastry), but a *muhallebici* (milk pudding shop) is a better bet for puddings, baklavas and other sweet goodies. Don't confuse *pasta* (pastry) with *makarna* (noodles).

For vegetarians, Turkey has few purpose-designed restaurants, but there's no reason why you won't be able to eat well. We have included vegetarian options throughout the book where possible; see the boxed text, below, for more information.

Vegetarian Turkish Cookery: Over 100 of Turkey's Classic Recipes for the Vegetarian Cook, by Carol & David Robertson, will help those who love Turkish cooking but don't care for its normally meaty emphasis.

Prices

Most places will have a printed menu with fixed prices. The one exception is fish: you ask the waiter to show you what's available and then get the fish weighed to find out the price. See the boxed text, opposite, for some tips on fish.

Restaurant prices usually include taxes but not service, but in some tourist areas a service charge may be added to the bill automatically. It's worth checking the bill and questioning anything unexpected, like hitherto unmentioned *kuver* (cover) charges, which then have *servis* charges added on to them. For advice on tipping, see p662.

Quick Eats

The best cheap snack is pide, the Turkish version of pizza, a canoe-shaped dough topped with cheese *(peynirli)*, egg *(yumurtalı)* or mince *(kıymalı)* – the tastiest. A *karaşık* pide will have a mixture of toppings. Döner kebap – the one you'll see being cooked on an upright revolving skewer – is Turkey's national dish, served everywhere from street corners to upmarket restaurants. You should also try *su böreği*, a melt-in-the-mouth lasagne-like layered pastry laced with white cheese and parsley, and *gözleme*, savoury crepes rolled thin and cooked with cheese, spinach and potato – delish!

VEG-A-WHAT? TRAVAILS OF A VEGETARIAN TRAVELLER IN TURKEY   Miriam Raphael

As someone whose favourite part of the day is deciding what to eat, I was salivating at the thought of several months in Turkey. All that glorious bread! All that wonderful cheese! But on arrival in İstanbul I began to think, 'All that meat...'. I recalled my friends warning me that as a vegetarian I would die in Turkey. After a week I had to agree; if something didn't change I was going to die. Not of starvation but of a surfeit of welsh rarebit!

But if you are up for a challenge, being a vegetarian in Turkey can be done.

Firstly, learn the words *'Etli mi?'* (Does it have meat?) and *'Sebze yemekleri var mı?'* (Are there any vegetable dishes?). And get used to walking into the kitchen to check things out for yourself (because Turkish 'vegetarians' sometimes eat no animal but chicken. Then get acquainted with all the vegetarian salads and mezes on offer. A couple of these and some piping hot bread is often more than enough for lunch.

Cheap *lokantas* (restaurants) are great for vegetarians. Not only can you see what you are ordering, but also they offer lots of hearty dishes – stuffed aubergines, plates of green beans, okra and peppers – with an obligatory pile of rice on the side. Better restaurants often have vegetable *güveç* (stew in a clay pot) on the menu. Covered in cheese and baked in the oven, it's nothing short of scrumptious. *Menemen*, a stir-fried omelette with tomatoes and hot peppers, is also popular. Unfortunately, most soups, even *ezo gelin* (lentil and rice), are made with meat stock.

Every town has a *börekci* that serves flaky pastry stuffed with white cheese and parsley. And don't miss *gözleme*, a Turkish pancake filled with spinach, cheese or potato.

If all else fails, there's always dessert!

FISH FORM ON THE COAST

With four seas surrounding the country – the Aegean, the Mediterranean, the Sea of Marmara and the Black Sea – Turkey's hardly short of sources of fresh fish. Visitors to the coasts should take advantage: fresh fish cooked *à la Turquie* – sometimes to old Ottoman recipes – is one of the highlights of visiting this region.

Winter is considered the best season for fish, and each month is known for a different species. At this time many species migrate from the Black Sea in search of warmer waters and also reach maturity.

In Turkish cuisine, certain herbs as well as vegetables are thought to complement particular types of fish. Mackerel is often stuffed with onions, bonito is cooked with celery root, and sea bass or sea bream is poached with tomatoes and green peppers. Bay leaves are popped into almost all fish dishes.

A certain etiquette is usually observed when visiting a fish restaurant. After being seated, it's customary to go and inspect the day's catch displayed either on a counter or – in the smaller restaurants – in the kitchen. After seeing what's on offer and taking your pick, you can discuss the way you want the fish prepared. It's then weighed and you're given a price.

Next stop is the mezes cabinet where you choose your first course. In between these and sips of rakı at your table on the seafront, your fish is freshly prepared.

Frances Linzee Gordon, with thanks to Mustafa Yılmaz, head chef, Foça

---

EATING WITH KIDS

Turkish children rarely eat out so children in restaurants are a welcome novelty – babies especially are made a fuss of. Waiting staff will usually be happy to heat food or drinks and generally help out, but it's rare to find high chairs. You won't find kids' menus either, but this shouldn't be a problem as most Turkish food is child-friendly, and less challenging meals are widely available such as *kuru fasulye* (beans), similar to baked beans, and *domates çorbası* (tomato soup). Ask for *acısız* (no spices) meals if you need to.

Great snacks for kids include the delicious *simit* (O-shaped bread ring sprinkled with sesame seeds), sold by street vendors, and *peynirli tost* (toasted cheese) available in snack booths everywhere. Pide is always a hit too.

Ensure that eggs and meat are well cooked.

HABITS & CUSTOMS

In rural Turkey locals usually eat two meals a day, the first at around 11am and the second in the early evening. In the cities three meals a day is the norm. In urban areas people sit down to meals in the same way as people in the West. However, in villages it is still usual to sit on the floor around a *tepsi* (low round table) with a cloth spread over one's knees to catch the crumbs.

Lonely Planet's *World Food Turkey* gives the low-down on all aspects of Turkish cookery, eating etiquette and regional specialities.

TRAVEL YOUR TASTEBUDS

Like most countries, Turkey has its favoured dishes that only a local could love. Top of the yuck stakes for most visitors must come *kokoreç*, seasoned lamb intestines wrapped around a skewer and grilled over charcoal.

İşkembe (tripe) soup reputedly wards off a hangover, so do as the locals do and head to an *işkembeci* (tripe soup restaurant) in the wee hours – maybe not? You might need to seek out *koç yumurtası* (ram's 'eggs') instead. Served spicy with oregano, they reputedly increase sexual stamina.

You may also want to learn the term for *kelle paça* (sheep's foot) soup, so you don't accidentally order it in a restaurant.

Joan Peterson's *Eat Smart in Turkey: How to Decipher the Menu, Know the Market Foods & Embark on a Tasting Adventure* combines cookbook, language and tasting tips, and regional knowledge.

These days people mostly eat from individual plates, although sometimes there will be communal dishes. Most Turks eat with spoons and forks (rarely with knives).

COOKERY COURSES

Turkey has a handful of operators offering foreign-language cookery courses, but the market is growing, so by the time you read this there could be more. Most courses are based in İstanbul, such as İstanbul Food Workshop and the Sarnıç Hotel. See p653 for details of these and other courses.

EAT YOUR WORDS

Want to know a *köfte* from a kebap? Get behind the cuisine scene by getting to know the language. For pronunciation guidelines, see p692.

Useful Phrases

EATING OUT

I'd like (a/the) ..., please.

... *istiyorum lütfen.* ... ees-*tee*-yo-room *lewt*-fen

menu

Menüyü me-new-*yew*

menu in English

İngilizce menü een-gee-*leez*-je me-*new*

I'd like the local speciality

Bu yöreye özgü bir yemek istiyorum. boo yer-re-*ye* erz-*gew* beer ye-*mek* ees-*tee*-yo-room

Enjoy your meal/Bon apetit!

Afiyet olsun! a-fee-yet ol-soon

This is ...

Bu ... boo ...

(too) cold

(çok) soğuk (chok) so-*ook*

(too) spicy

(çok) acı (chok) a-*juh*

superb

enfes en-*fes*

The bill please.

Hesap lütfen. he-*sap lewt*-fen

DO'S AND DON'TS FOR VISITORS TO A TRADITIONAL TURKISH HOME

Do:

■ Take a small gift, such as a box of baklava or *lokum*

■ Eat only the food nearest to you from a communal dish

■ Eat everything on your plate, but don't overeat. Note the Turkish proverb: 'Eat a little be an angel; eat much and perish'!

■ Say '*Afiyet olsun*' (May it be good for your health). After the meal say '*Elinize sağlık*' (Health to your hands) to compliment your hostess on her cooking (it will always be a hostess who cooks!)

Don't:

■ Eat anything directly from a bowl with your left hand

■ Sit down beside someone of the opposite sex unless your host(ess) suggests it

VEGETARIAN & SPECIAL MEALS
Do you have any dishes without meat?

Etsiz yemek var mı?   et·seez ye·mek·var muh

I'm allergic to ...
... alerjim var.   ... a·ler·zheem var

dairy produce

Süt ürünlerine   sewt ew·rewn·le·ree·ne

eggs

Yumurtaya   yoo·moor·ta·ya

nuts

Çerezlere   che·rez·le·re

DRINKS
(cup/glass of) tea ...

... (bir fincan/bardak) çay   ... (beer feen·jan/bar·dak) chai

(cup of) coffee ...

... (bir fincan) kahve   ... (beer feen·jan) kah·ve

with milk

Sütlü   sewt·lew

with a little sugar

Az şekerli   az she·ker·lee

without sugar

Şekersiz   she·ker·seez

Cheers!

Şerefe!   she·re·fe

Food Glossary
STAPLES

bal	bal	honey
çiğer	jee·er	liver
çorba	chor·ba	soup
ekmek	ek·mek	bread
hamsi	ham·see	anchovy
kalamares	ka·la·ma·res	calamari
midye	meed·ye	mussels
peynir	pay·neer	cheese
piliç/tavuk	pee·leech/ta·vook	chicken
pirinç/pilav	pee·reench/pee·lav	rice
yoğurt	yo·oort	yogurt
yumurta	yoo·moor·ta	egg

CONDIMENTS

kara biber	ka·ra bee·ber	black pepper
şeker	she·ker	sugar
tuz	tooz	salt

COOKING TERMS

ızgara	uhz·ga·ra	grilled
tava	ta·va	fried

MEZES

cacık	ja·juhk	yogurt with grated cucumber and mint
fava salatası	fa·va sa·la·ta·suh	mashed broad bean salad
patlıcan salatası	pat·luh·jan sa·la·ta·suh	aubergine (eggplant) salad

| *yaprak dolması* | yap·*rak* dol·ma·*suh* | stuffed vine leaves |
| *çoban salatası* | cho·*ban* sa·la·ta·*suh* | tomato, onion, cucumber and green pepper salad |

MAIN COURSES

börek	boo·*rek*	flaky pastry parcels
Bursa (İskender)	*kebap* boor·sa ees·ken·*der* ke·*bab*	döner kebap on pide with yogurt, melted butter and tomato sauce
döner kebap	*der*·ner ke·*bab*	meat packed onto a vertical skewer, then roasted and sliced off
gözleme	gerz·le·*me*	savoury crepe laced with spinach, cheese or potato
güveç	gew·*vech*	meat-and-vegetable stew in a clay pot
imam bayıldı	ee·*mam*·ba·yuhl·duh	literally, 'the imam fainted'; aubergine stuffed with ground lamb, tomatoes, onions and garlic
karışık ızgara	ka·ruh·*shuhk* uhz·*ga*·ra	mixed grill (lamb)
köfte	kerf·*te*	meatballs
mantı	man·*tuh*	ravioli (Turkish style)
şiş kebap	sheesh ke·*bab*	cubes of meat grilled on a skewer

FRUIT (MEYVE) & VEGETABLES (SEBZE)

biber	bee·*ber*	capsicum/bell pepper
domates	do·ma·*tes*	tomato
elma	el·*ma*	apple
havuç	ha·*vooch*	carrot
ıspanak	uhs·pa·*nak*	spinach
karpuz	kar·*pooz*	watermelon
kavun	ka·*voon*	cantaloupe melon
kayısı	ka·yuh·*suh*	apricot
kuru fasulye	koo·*roo* fa·*sool*·ye	white beans
muz	mooz	banana
patates	pa·ta·*tes*	potato
portakal	por·ta·*kal*	orange
salatalık	sa·la·ta·*luhk*	cucumber
şeftali	shef·ta·*lee*	peach
soğan	so·*an*	onion
taze fasulye	ta·ze fa·*sool*·ye	green beans
üzüm	ew·*zewm*	grape
zeytin	zay·*teen*	olive

DESSERT (TATLI)

aşure	a·shoo·*re*	'Noah's Ark' pudding made from 40 different fruits, nuts and pulses
baklava	bak·la·*va*	layered filo pastry with honey and nuts
dondurma	don·door·*ma*	ice cream
lokum	lo·*koom*	Turkish delight

DRINKS

çay	chai	tea
bira	bee·*ra*	beer
buz	booz	ice
maden suyu	ma·*den* soo·*yoo*	mineral water
meyve suyu	may·ve soo·*yoo*	fruit juice
rakı	ra·*ku*	grape spirit infused with aniseed
şarap	sha·rap	wine
su	soo	water
süt	sewt	milk

Trekking in Turkey

Turkey's huge, bare central plateau, punctuated by isolated volcanic cones and shimmering, shallow lakes, is hemmed by many mountain ranges. The Taurus ranges, in the central south, are limestone – raising white, weathered ridges above ancient cedar or juniper forests. On the coastal sides of these ranges, below pine-clad foothills, are steep-sided coves, busy harbours and resort towns. On the north are the Pontic Alps with, to the east, the Kaçkars – a sharp, granite range, largely unforested, which separates the misty tea-growing Black Sea slopes from the knife-edge gorges of the Çoruh, and the plateau. To the east, the plateau rises towards Asia, divided by the great Euphrates and Tigris Rivers, and closely hemmed by jumbles of ranges rising towards the volcanoes of Suphan and Mt Ararat (Ağrı Dağı). The west of the country slopes down in soft, dry valleys to the Mediterranean.

The best trekking areas are south and north of the plateau. Although the east has much to offer, maps are a problem and, except for Mt Ararat, guides and organised treks scarce.

Ingrained in the unforgiving landscape of Anatolia are the scars of old roads – some dating from Hittite times – linking towns, mines and markets of the interior with coastal harbours. They wind over passes over the ranges and, of course, some are now modern highways. Subsidiary tracks, trodden twice a year by the migrating flocks of sheep and goats, link summer and winter pastures. The whole forms an elusive but timeless net stretching over the country.

The Walks

The five treks highlighted in this chapter weave the old roads into the fabric of modern Turkey, seamlessly allowing the hiker to traverse from old to new, country to town, mountain to plain. On the way, they pass canyons, mountain pastures brimming with flowers, tiny stone villages and ruins of ancient cities. They also offer much more – during these treks, you can walk in the steps of a saint, raft a white-water river, swim in canyons, lakes and your own private coves and stay with shepherds in their black wool tents.

RESPONSIBLE HIKING

Before embarking on a hiking trip, consider the following points to ensure a safe and enjoyable experience:

■ No permits are required for walking or camping, but obey forestry 'no fire' or 'no entry' signs.

■ Acclimatise to the temperature; learn the symptoms of heatstroke and dehydration (see p689).

■ Know your next water point and carry more than sufficient water to reach it.

■ Be aware that weather conditions and terrain vary considerably with altitude and region. In winter – carry full waterproof equipment and a GPS, if you have one, for finding routes in the snow.

■ Shepherds or villagers may offer food and/or accommodation. Treat them respectfully and pay for what you use. If you become hurt or lost, they are your lifeline.

■ Bury your toilet waste away from water sources and don't litter.

■ Take your insurance details and the phone numbers of your consulate and Turkey's rescue organisation – **AKUT** (☎ 0212-217 0410). It's a good idea to buy a local SIM card for your mobile phone (though there's pretty well no reception on the Kaçkars).

Trekking tourism in Turkey should also be seen as an excellent way of providing income for isolated, marginal mountain villages.

The selected treks average three days and are suitable for a reasonably fit person. Three days is long enough for a taste of trekking but short enough to fit into a hectic holiday programme. Most of these treks can be accomplished with little experience and only basic equipment – a daypack, water bottles and comfortable boots. Two require camping equipment. Four of them follow parts of Turkey's newly waymarked long-distance trails. They are spread from the south to the northeast, and you will find a trail for every season.

See p87 for finding everything from hiking maps and books, camping equipment and guides to trekking companies.

Completing the chapter are cross-references to other walks mentioned in other parts of this book (see p87).

ALINCA TO OVACIK – LYCIAN WAY

Alınca, a tiny village spectacularly perched high above seven headlands, is on the west of the Tekke or Lycian peninsula, which extends between Fethiye and Antalya. From Alınca, mule paths run along the wild Lycian coast to Ovacık, between Fethiye and Ölüdeniz. Most of the walk is through clifftop pines, high above the deep indigo sea, though it does descend to pretty beaches. There is pension or village-house accommodation each night. Fit/fast trekkers could take two days, missing the night at Kabak.

The *Sunday Times* chose the Lycian Way as one of the world's 10 best walks, and *Country Walking* magazine chose it as 15th in the world's 50 greatest walks.

Getting to the Start

The Fethiye–Kaş bus passes through Eşen; get off here and find a taxi to take you to Alınca, about 20km away down a side road, past Boğaziçi. Dolmuşes from Fethiye only go as far as Kabak.

In the upper part of Alınca is a Lycian Way signpost marked to Kabak; follow the marked path up to a level area with picnic tables in front of a house belonging to the headman, Bayram.

Accommodation in Alınca is either in **Bayram's house** (☎ 0252-679 1169; cabin per person half board €13.50) – recommended, or in Selcuk's pension, further up the hill.

Day 1

The Lycian Way footpath continues past Bayram's house, running level with pines on the right, to a pass with views towards the jigsaw of dark islands beyond the pale gold crescent of Ölüdeniz (10 min). Follow the old mule path downhill, up to a second low pass (cumulative time 50 min) and then to an area of terraces planted with olives (1¾ hr). From rocks on your left is a spectacular view of a small golden strip of sand, bordered in turquoise, which merges into the velvety indigo of the sea. There is a well 30m off the path to the right and a tiny shepherd's hut hidden in the rocks.

The path descends right into a narrow, forested valley, first straight, then down newly repaired stone hairpins, to a junction known as Delikkaya (Rock with a Hole) below a cliff face (2 hr). Turn left on narrower path down more hairpins, then left again to a level clearing (2¼-2½ hr). From here the path is wider, and leads towards the beach (2¾-3 hr). Turn right onto a short, steep descent to the valley floor where you turn left along a stream bed to the beach of Kabak (see p363; 3¼-3½ hr).

Behind the beach are three places to stay including Turan's Camping and the Olive Garden.

Day 2

From the north end of the beach, climb a narrow path, which immediately widens, then turn left and up again onto hairpins leading up to farmland. Keep right on a path that leads to the village road and Mama's Restaurant (see p363; 1 hr). Opposite Mama's is a spring. Next to it, turn upwards onto a footpath that runs level to a junction; keep left and continue climbing through woodland to a dirt road (1¾ hr). Turn right, and at a junction turn left and walk around terraces with spectacular views, then downhill to a spring and trough (2½-2¾ hr). About 200m further on, turn right onto a footpath, which follows the edge of woodland to a pass (2¾-3 hr). Descend hairpins through woods to meet the dirt road, and turn right to reach Faralya (see p362; 3½-3¾ hr).

There are three pensions in Faralya; we recommend George House (p362).

Day 3

By a spring on the village road, turn upwards to the Old Mill, now a luxurious hotel. The old cobbled mule path passes in front of the millhouse – you may be able to see the restored mill at work. Follow the stream up the valley, looking back from

> **WALK FACTS**
>
> **Duration** 2-3 days
> **Difficulty** easy
> **Waymarking** yes
> **Best time** February–May, October–November
> **Special equipment**: swimming gear; picnic food

time to time to catch the views down into Butterfly Valley (see p362) below.

At the head of the valley turn left into the village of Kirme, and right to the village spring and sitting platform (2 hr). On the road, turn left to a junction by the old school, and continue right up the hill (2¼ hr). At the pass, take a footpath that drops left into woodland and follow the old road around the head of a deep valley. Rejoin the road and continue past a spring and between loose boulders and stones. Here, in the 1950s, an earthquake demolished part of the mountain and buried several village houses. Turn left to circle the village on footpaths, soon rejoining the road (3-3¼ hr). Turn left and continue upwards towards

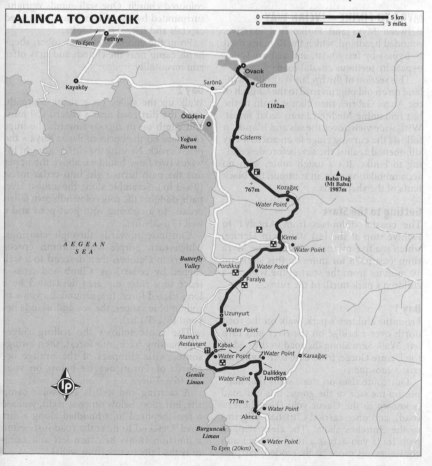

ALINCA TO OVACIK

0 — 5 km
0 — 3 miles

To Eşen — Fethiye
Kayaköy
Sarönü
Ovacik
Cisterns
1102m
Ölüdeniz
Yoğun Burun
Cisterns
767m
Kozağaç
Water Point
Baba Dağ (Mt Baba) 1987m
AEGEAN SEA
Butterfly Valley
Kirme
Water Point
Pordikia
Water Point
Faralya
Uzunyurt
Water Point
Mama's Restaurant
Kabak
Water Point
Karaağaç
Gemile Liman
Water Point
Dalikkya Junction
777m
Water Point
Alinca
Burguncuk Liman
Water Point
To Eşen (20km)

the cliff-tops, following a detour to the cliff edge on the left. Rejoin the road near a new house; just past here are superb views down to the pale crescent of Ölüdeniz (3¼-3½ hr). The cobbled mule path descends a few hairpins, circles a gully and passes two cisterns (4½-4¾ hr). The path, cobbles now gone, continues to another viewpoint, then turns inland, descending gradually through shady pines towards the buildings at the head of the valley. It bears left to a cistern and dirt road (5¾-6 hr). A few minutes later, you reach tarmac and turn left, down to the main Ovacık–Ölüdeniz road (6-6½ hr).

Take a right to reach Ovacık, or take the bus going left down the hill to Ölüdeniz (p359).

MYRA TO FINIKE – LYCIAN WAY

Between Myra and Finike is a massive, rounded headland, which the Romans used to bypass by ferry boat, and visitors today bypass by tortuous coastal road.

This section of the Lycian Way climbs inland on an old pilgrim road to the Church of the Angel Gabriel, then climbs again to the last remaining Mediterranean cedar forest. With wide views over the sea and islands, it follows the curving ridge to an ancient city silhouetted against the sky, before descending to Finike. It's a tough route, with no accommodation save, in summer, the black tents of the shepherds.

Getting to the Start

The coastal dolmuşes from Antalya to Fethiye stop at the bus station in Demre, which is a five-minute walk from the Myra ruins (see p378 for more on this site) and 10 minutes from the start of the walk, at a children's park north of the ruins.

Day 1

From the children's park, walk on the road north over a bridge on the river and turn left. Walk 3km along the road in the bed of the Demre Gorge; from here turn right just past a mosque.

Our route rises on stone walls that hairpin up the side of the gorge; this old road is known as the Gavur yolu (Unbelievers' road), and once carried Christian pilgrims to the churches above. The clear stepped path leads you across a road (1½ hr) and continues up more badly eroded hairpins

on the lower valley wall. Scramble up to meet the road, turn right to tumbledown Belören village (cumulative time 4-4¼ hr), with the remains to two vast churches, once lavishly decorated with carving.

At the fork in the road by a cistern, bear right towards a valley; turn right on a clear path that winds up to a level field; on the road beyond, pass through a cutting to the next valley, Zeytin, bisected by a tiny limestone gorge. Turn left on a dirt road, then go downhill on a path and cross the gorge to regain the dirt road (4¾-5 hr). Over a pass, turn right down a footpath to the ruins of the Church of the Angel Gabriel. The oncefrescoed walls of the church are remembered in the local name: Alakilise – many coloured church. One wall stands upright, surrounded by a jumble of beautiful carved capitals and friezes (5½-5¾ hr).

From the end of May to October, shepherds camp near the church and may offer you hospitality.

Day 2

Walk up the valley on a rising footpath; cross the dirt road near a cistern (20 min) and climb up in zigzags towards the huge rock face on the horizon: Papaz Kaya – the priest's rock. Nearing the cliff, bear right towards two huge boulders; above the upper one the path turns right into cedar forest (2¾-3 hr). Scramble along the almost level path, dodging the roots of windblown fallen cedars, to a clearing with goat pens and a well (3½-3¾ hr).

Continue upwards through clearings, which turn purple with autumn crocus flowers in October, then descend to a well topped by cedar logs. Climb and cross a fence to a ridge-top area devastated by a long-passed forest fire; around are views of rolling blue ranges, the sea and islands beyond (5¼-5½ hr).

The route follows the rolling ridgetop, passing back into forest, then swings south, with glimpses of the orange orchards of Turunçova far below on your left (6½-7 hr).

A clearing and well is a possible camp site, but soon, below on your right, you see a few shepherd huts huddled along a dirt road. Descend to meet the road just before a junction (8-8½ hr), turn left and camp near the huts (water from wells).

Day 3

Keep right at the junction, then turn right onto a footpath that runs along a steep hillside, which overlooks the lagoon at Beymelek, far below. At the end of the ridge, turn left and contour around two valleys, climb another ridge, descend to a well and then meet a newly bulldozed forest road (1½ hr). Continue south and, just before a fenced field, turn right, glimpsing the sea from a low pass. Turn south again down a valley, then up to a ridge crowned with the ruins of Belos (2½-2¾ hr).

All around are remains of huge sarcophagi, some still capped with lids. Rooms are carved out of the rock, ancient walls are topped by later Roman remains and, at the end of the ridge, lie huge cisterns.

After exploring, follow the ridge-top path inland, turning right to contour around a valley, past a fenced graveyard and some shepherds' huts to a new dirt road. Turn right and then left, and follow the road downhill to a pass marked by a length of Roman column (4-4¼ hr).

Keep straight on past the column and, 200m on, turn right down a footpath, which descends into a river bed, running down water-worn steps under arched trees. Turn left on a mule track (5-5¼ hr) that contours around the ridge, with views of Gök Liman beach ahead. At a dirt road, turn left, bear right at a junction and descend past a few houses on the ridge down dirt roads and a narrow track to Finike town, emerging just above the harbour (6½-7 hr).

AKBAŞ TO ÇALTEPE – ST PAUL TRAIL

High above the Köprü River is a migration route (for goats mostly), which follows the Köprülu Kanyon, crossing a Roman bridge, then climbing to Dedegöl mountain, far to

WALK FACTS

Duration 3 days
Difficulty medium
Waymarking yes
Best time April–June, September–November
Special equipment camping gear; string and bucket for wells, food

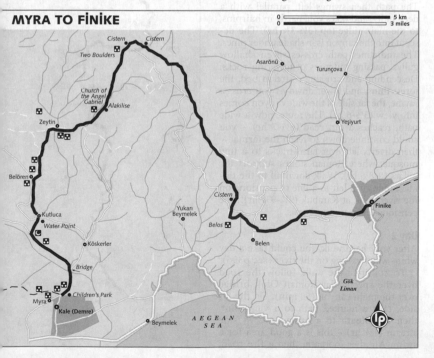

MYRA TO FİNİKE

0 — 5 km
0 — 3 miles

Cistern · Two Boulders · Cistern · Asarönü · Turunçova · Church of the Angel Gabriel · Alakilise · Zeytin · Yeşiyurt · Belören · Kutluca · Water Point · Köskerler · Yukarı Beymelek · Cistern · Belos · Belen · Finike · Bridge · Gök Liman · Myra · Children's Park · Kale (Demre) · Beymelek · AEGEAN SEA

the north. We leave it to scale the terrifyingly sheer canyon side to the ruins of Selge, then descend on Roman roads to rejoin the river at Çaltepe. There are plenty of opportunities to swim, and on day two you could take a rafting trip. Overnight stops are at village accommodation options.

Getting to the Start

Take the daily morning Altınkaya dolmuş or a taxi from Antalya or Serik otogar to Akbaş village. There are also dolmuşes from Serik to Çaltepe that pass by Akbaş. Stay the night at the village shop, from where you can get food.

Day 1

From the village shop at Akbaş, walk on tarmac through the next tiny village, Saraycık, to the end of the track (30 min). Here, follow a stony footpath used by flocks migrating to summer pastures, across a stream through maquis and strawberry trees, up a steep path to a ridge topped by pine forest (cumulative time 1½ hrs). A further climb along the side ridge passes two springs and a shepherd hut. The path then swings left, parallel with a deep gully, and takes you, partly in hairpins, to the main ridge top (3½-3¾ hr). The descent into the canyon is in shade under pines. The indistinct path crosses seven shallow gullys, passing outcrops of towering rocks. Descending and crossing a stream bed, the forest thins, and lower down as you cross a ravine, the far side of the wide canyon comes into view (5½-6 hr). The route, now a wide path, reaches a dirt road (6½-7 hr) – you could continue down to reach the tarmac – then diverts left over farm tracks to a tiny mosque, where Roman stones support the pillars (8-8½ hr). Walk downhill to the tarmac, then turn left to a line of pensions on the river bank at Karabuk (9¼-9¾ hr). The pensions serve evening meals.

Day 2

After your hard walk, you could take a day white-water rafting on the river (see p396).

To continue the walk, follow the road over the spectacular Roman Oluk bridge over the main canyon (50 min). On the far side, take a marked path to a viewpoint, then a footpath to a bridge over a side stream (1¼ hr) – this is a good area for a swim. Another footpath, then a fire road,

leads to the canyon rim. Turn right, down to water level, and continue on the bank to Tevfik's isolated old house (2 hr); you could have a meal (or even stay) here.

Pass the house on a footpath leading to an open field and turn left onto a tractor track. This area was a courtyard of a monastery complex; there are church remains on a

WALK FACTS

Duration 3 days
Difficulty medium
Waymarking yes
Best time: April–June, September–November
Special equipment: swimming gear

AKBAS TO ÇALTEPE   0 — 2km   0 — 1mile

To Kesme; Kasımlar; Adada; Eğirdir
Çaltepe (452m)
Ballıbucak
Kestanelik
Delisarnıç
Oluk
Düzağaç
Selge (918m)
Altınkaya
Tevfit's House
Oluk Bridge
Büğrün Bridge
Köyüler
Karabük
Beşkonak (168m)
Kadir (1698m)
Saraycık
Akbaş
Gökçepınar
Karataş
Gökçeler
To Serilt; Antalya
Bucak

hillock. The track rises past a shepherds' hut on the left, crosses another stream and turns left to cross Yer Köprüsü, a natural bridge (2¾-3 hr). Here the river is wide and shallow, but below the bridge the water emerges to fall, bubbling and churning, into a pool.

Continue to a footpath, which climbs right, approaching the canyon wall; turn up on a steep diagonal, climbing over steps and ledges and, near the summit, pass through a barrier keeping goats out (4-4¼ hr). Looking back, the river lies in bright blue bends below you, amid a patchwork of deep green forests and lighter fields.

The path emerges in a forested area on the canyon rim. Continue through forest on undulating footpath into a narrow valley. A gap between rocks leads to an area of 'fairy chimneys', strange standing rocks eroded into pinnacles. Pass a natural arch among the chimneys and cross a valley to a tractor track (5-5¼ hr).

Turn left, then left again onto a path that bypasses the houses ahead; where this rejoins the road, turn left to the village of Selge (Zerk; 6-6½ hr). The track enters the village on the opposite side from the Roman remains, which are spread on the hill ahead. Walk on the dirt road to the village centre to find the village shop-café.

There is village-house accommodation next to the theatre, further down the road. The villagers are poor, and many will approach you to buy headscarves or jewellery.

Day 3

Leave Selge, passing left of the theatre and continuing on the road to a footpath on the right (25 min), which descends to a beautiful old paved road. At the top of the hill, rejoin the road, turn right past a graveyard and turn right onto a path that rises up a valley (1 hr).

At cross tracks, turn right onto the old road, then right again, rising to a pass. From here a maze of paths leads through delightful green valleys over two passes to a tractor track (2¾-3 hr); turn right for the village of Delisarnıç, where houses are tucked between huge conglomerate boulders.

Walk straight through the village; at the far end is an informal *çay bahçesi* (teahouse) for walkers. As the road bends left, turn right onto a path that follows a stream bed downwards between rocks. When you see telegraph posts (3¾-4 hr), follow them to find the road through the village of Kestanelik. Turn left onto the road, then right under a huge many-branched chestnut tree (4-4¼ hr), following a rising path over a tree-clad ridge. Continue down through woodland, cross a fence (5½-6 hr), then join a stream bed running down for a few hundred metres. Climb left out of the stream bed, then turn right onto a path running diagonally down a huge juniper-clad limestone hill. The path diverts to a well (6¾-7¼ hr) and continues on beautiful cobbled path down the hill flank to the village of Çaltepe, set at the edge of level fields adjoining the river (7¾-8¼ hr).

Erdinç's pretty family pension welcomes you, and there is now another pension in town. In the early morning the daily minibus will take you down the valley to Serik, east of Antalya.

ADADA TO YUKARI GÖKDERE – ST PAUL TRAIL

Adada, a historical site with a superb section of Roman road, is near the start of a route that runs via a small canyon and lovely juniper and oak forest to Yukarı Gökdere, a large village with buses to Eğirdir (p317).

To Reach the Start

Take the Sütçüler–Eğirdir bus to a spring west of the road 2km south of the village of Sağrak.

Day 1

Cross the road and follow a tractor road down into a valley; on the far side of the stream walk uphill, then left and right to the start of the Roman road, which curves up the left slope of the valley ahead (40 min). The Roman road is made up of huge limestone slabs supported on the outer edge by a stone wall. It continues for about 2km before reaching the centre of the site of Adada (1¾ hr). You can walk in the actual footsteps of St Paul on this stretch of well-preserved Roman road leading to Adada.

After exploring the agora and market buildings to your left, cross the road, leave the theatre on your left and continue to the top of the pass on the north of the site. Just over the pass, turn right and follow a path diagonally down to the main road (2¼ hr).

(If you have spent ages exploring, you could take the bus or a lift from here to

Sütçüler – see p321; stay the night there and return to the same spot next day.)

Cross the road and continue down on tracks to the riverside below. Turn right and follow the river until it emerges from a small canyon (3½-3¾ hr). Here your walk becomes a scramble – it's possible (but difficult) to scramble the whole length of the canyon without getting wet, but in summer it's much more fun to paddle and swim in the pools. The canyon ends at a bridge (7-7¼ hr) – turn up the left bank to a spring, then turn right, pass a graveyard, and walk high above the river into the village of Sipahiler (8¼-8¾ hr).

Walk down to the main road, shop and *çay bahçesi*; accommodation for walkers is in a room attached to the mosque.

Day 2

Walk back up the steep road in the centre of the village, bear left onto a path and head for the pass among trees on the skyline to the west (35 min). Cross the next valley, aiming

WALK FACTS

Duration 2-3 days
Difficulty easy
Waymarking yes
Best time April–June, September–November
Special equipment old shoes; swimming gear

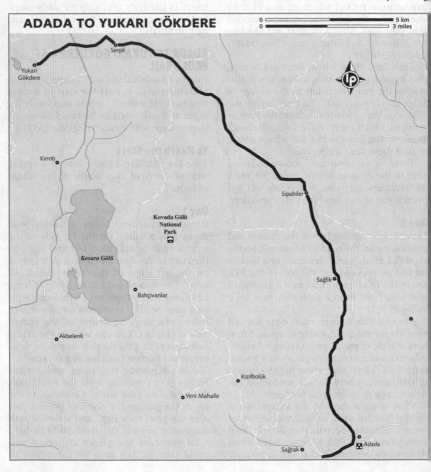

ADADA TO YUKARI GÖKDERE

0 —— 5 km
0 —— 3 miles

Serpil

Yukarı Gökdere

Kırıntı

Kovada Gölü National Park

Kovara Gölü

Sipahiler

Bahçivanlar

Sağlik

Akbelenli

Kızılbölük

Yeni Mahalle

Sağrak

Adada

at a spring on the far side and continue on the path, veering slightly right and climbing the next hill (1½ hr). Descend into a shallow valley, turn left and walk to a tractor track; turn right, continue past a huge well to a pine plantation (2¼ hr). Walk through the pines to a valley, through a wire fence, through more pines to a huge open plain (2¾ hr). Walk down the left side of the plain, cross a low pass, and turn right, passing through forest down to another plain. Cross the plain diagonally right, then over another pass to a tractor track. Turn right for a third plain (3¾-4 hr). Follow the track to a line of telegraph posts, turn left along them and over a final pass (4½-4¾ hr). Follow the paved path down towards the village of Serpil below. Turn left at the path end, and follow tracks around the hillside and down onto the apple orchards below. Cross the orchards to a bridge over the canal and the main road beyond (5¼-5¾ hr). Just opposite are the petrol pumps at Yukarı Gökdere, from where you can get a bus to Eğirdir (p317).

YUKARI KAVRON TO YAYLALAR – TRANS-KAÇKAR TREK

Most trekking in the Kaçkars is above the treeline; routes are well used and quite easy to find. The mountains are notorious for storms and afternoon mists, particularly on the northern slopes; if you experience zero visibility, you should bivouac until the weather clears. Water is never a problem; as long as there are no cattle above you, stream water is safe to drink.

Yukarı Kavron is a summer village on the north slopes of the Kaçkar Mountains (Kaçkar Dağları); from here steep paths lead over the range to Naletleme pass. Often the passes are not open until the third week in July; check at Yukarı Kavron that the Naletleme pass has been used and the snow trodden down. After the pass, you could head straight downriver for Yaylalar, the trailhead on the southern side, but a diversion takes you to the spectacular base camp for Mt Kaçkar. The summit climb isn't covered in this description, as early in the season you need crampons and an ice axe to attempt the climb safely.

To Reach the Start

Take a dolmuş from Pazar or Çamlıhemşin to Ayder and then another to Yukarı Kavron

(there are several per day in season, including one at 9am), where there is accommodation, a café and limited supplies. Accommodation in Ayder is better (see p561).

Day 1

Leave the village heading east, on a footpath that first zigzags, then runs on the right bank of the side-stream bouncing down the steep Çaymakcur valley. The path can be muddy and slippery in the frequent mists. The route crosses the stream, rises left over a lip (2½ hr) and levels as it approaches a small lake, Büyük Deniz (*deniz* literally translates as 'sea'); veer right off the path to the level camp site by the lake (3 hr) set in a grassy basin scooped out of flaking rock and fed by glaciers. Not visible, but a 10-minute walk uphill to the south, is tiny Metenek Gölü (Metenek Lake), swimmable and with a camp site, should the first be full. Take time to explore this area of lush pastures and miniature rhododendrons below the snow-clad peaks.

Day 2

Continue north with Büyük Deniz on the left, and follow the path to the pass east of the lake (20 min). Follow the steep hairpins downhill to the stream that leads to turquoise Kara Deniz lake; cross the stream on a difficult path over boulders and turn upwards (south) to the ridge beyond the stream (1¾ hr). The pass is now ahead, above a rock outcrop. Climb left on a well-used path, which winds in zigzags upwards over scree. Over the outcrop, the gradient eases, although the path remains stony until it reaches the cairn on shady Naletleme pass (3203m), topped much of the year by snow (4-4¼ hr). The view from the top is of wide, green valleys with rounded ranges beyond, and Mt Kaçkar, often capped by cloud, on the right. The descent is first on steep zigzags, then over a snow pocket and scree, then on the left bank of a stream, down a steep, wide valley. As the path veers left to Yaylalar, descend and cross the Düpeduzu stream to a large flat camp site with a spring at 2750m, in the beautiful valley of the same name (6-6½ hr).

Day 3

Head up the valley, first onto a low shelf then southwest into a wide valley penetrating the ridge of Pişovit. The path is a goat track, which gets steeper as you progress, leading in hairpins diagonally over the ridge at about 3100m (2¼ hr). Once over the top, a view opens out over the Hevek valley, with the tiny stone houses of Nastel (or Hastal) Yaylası far below. The narrow path turns right and contours above the spurs of

WALK FACTS

Duration 4 days
Difficulty medium
Waymarking no
Best time mid-July–September
Special equipment wet weather and camping gear, food, compass

the ridge. In places it's indistinct, but you should keep as high as possible, until the base camp of Dilberduzu comes into sight, south-southwest and far below (3¾-4 hr).

In front is a high-point on the ridge. The path starts to descend left down a spur, first with the side-ridge on the right, then on the left. As it descends, the path runs over patches of scree, then through vegetation so lush that in places it is shoulder high.

Cross the Büyük Çay stream (5-5¼ hr) and climb the final 1km to the camp site at the base of the rocks of Şeytan Kaya (Devil's Rocks; 5½-6 hr). The camp site is large enough for 100 or more tents, and is the most popular one in the Kaçkars, as it's the base for climbs to Mt Kaçkar (3937m).

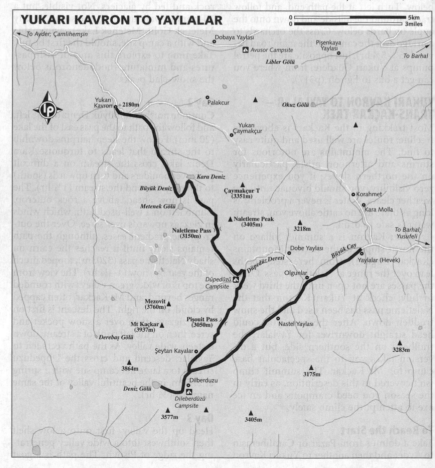

YUKARI KAVRON TO YAYLALAR

TREKKING RESOURCES

Books & Maps
Aladağlar, by Ömer B Tüzel, Homer Kitabevi (publisher, in Turkish)
Kaçkar Dağları, by Tunç Fındık, Homer Kitabevi (in Turkish)
Lycian Way, by Kate Clow, Upcountry
St Paul Trail, by Kate Clow & Terry Richardson, Upcountry
The Mountains of Turkey, by Karl Smith, Cicerone
Walking and Birdwatching in Southwest Turkey, by Paul Hope, Land of Lights

Trekking Companies
Dragoman Turkey (www.dragoman-turkey.com) Trekking holidays mainly in Lycia but also St Paul Trail and Kaçkars.
Middle Earth Travel (www.mountainsofturkey.com, www.middleearthtravel.com) Trekking holidays in Lycia, St Paul Trail, Mt Ararat, Ala Dağlar and Kaçkars. Special itineraries for private groups.
TML travel (www.tmltravel.com) Adventure-holiday base on the St Paul Trail, where they specialise.
Tempo Tur (www.tempotour.com.tr) Tours/adventure holidays, especially Kaçkars and Lycia.
Terra-Anatolia (www.terra-anatolia.com) Self-guided treks in Lycia, also Kaçkars and Cappadocia.
Türkü Turizm (www.turkutour.com) Accommodation and holidays in the north side of the Kaçkars.

Equipment
The following two firms take phone or web orders and deliver promptly.
Adrenalin (www.adrenalin.com.tr, in Turkish) Camping-equipment store that offers mail orders.
Offshop/Adventure Republic (www.offshop.net, in Turkish) Two camping-equipment stores, also offering mail orders.

Trekking Guides & Mules
Middle Earth Travel, Terra-Anatolia and Dragoman can suggest itineraries and provide guides for private groups. In the Kaçkars, mules and their drivers (who double as guides), are organized by Çamyuva Pension in Yaylayar or in Olgunlar (see p574). Mule treks start from Barhal, Yaylalar or Yukarı Kavron.)

Day 4
In the morning, Şeytan Kayalar turn gold as the morning sun strikes them, and alpine choughs shriek from the sheer cliffs. The final day is a short trek down the valley to Yaylalar village. You could first explore the route west to Deniz Gölü (1 hr), where, even in July, icebergs often float on the lake. Retrace your steps and follow the path on the south bank of the stream first towards the *yayla* (here, some buildings in a highland pasture) of Nastel, then Olgunlar (4½-4¾ hr), a permanent village that has two or three inhabitants year-around. In summer it has pensions, a café and occasional minibuses to Yaylalar.

Half an hour's walk beyond is Yaylalar (5-5½ hr), which has a good pension (the Çamyuva; see p574) and a dolmuş to Yusuf-eli (p571), with onward connections.

OTHER TREKS
The walks described earlier in this chapter are only a small sample of the walks that can be done along the Lycian Way, St Paul's Trail and the Kaçkar Mountains. See the books, above, for more details on these walks. Some further information on organising treks in the Kaçkar Mountains is provided in this guidebook, see p558 (from Ayder) and p572 (from Yusufeli). Keep in mind that the snow-free season in the Kaçkars is very short.

You can also trek in the rugged Ala Dağlar National Park (p526), near Niğde, famous for the superb Yedigöller (Seven Lakes).

The spectacular valleys of Cappadocia make another excellent area for hiking, with a range of possibilities lasting from just a few hours to eight days or more. See the boxed text, p502, for short walks and tour operators such as Mephisto Voyage (p511) and ones listed in the boxed text, above, for longer hikes.

Upcountry (Turkey) Ltd (www.trekkinginturkey.com) provides trekking information and offers an online service for buying books.

İstanbul

On an afternoon stroll through İstanbul you can marvel at the greatest examples of Byzantine art and architecture in the world, submerge yourself in the mystique of the seraglio or lose yourself in the labyrinthine Grand Bazaar – a bustling marketplace borne of ancient trade routes. The exquisite legacies of the Ottoman Empire, its mosques, *hamams* (bathhouses), palaces and fountains, are on almost every corner. You can join the throng at a *meyhane* (tavern) heaving with rakı-fuelled song and dance, dine alongside Prada-clad locals enjoying fusion cuisine, wind down in a *çay bahçesi* (tea garden) alongside Anatolian gents puffing nargilehs and witness the ablutions of the faithful summoned by the melodious call to prayer.

Peer beneath the surface and you find a city of immense disparity, a sprawling, heaving metropolis battling the fuelling tensions between the ever-widening haves and have-nots and between those with eyes to the West and those with eyes to the East. A city splitting at the seams as it struggles to deal with a constant influx of migrants from Anatolia and beyond. The life lived by those with wealth alongside the Bosphorus, its romantic hubbub the daily rhythm of their life, couldn't be further from most İstanbullus, whose homes are in airless concrete suburbs far from the coast. For them İstanbul's jewels are forgotten for the working week, only to be reunited on Sunday when the family might picnic under trees at the Hippodrome. These energies and tensions make İstanbul all the more vital and beguiling.

The social challenges facing İstanbul, almost a microcosm of the world's tensions, are played out in one of the world's most historically rich and breathtakingly beautiful and vibrant cities. There simply is no other city like it.

HIGHLIGHTS

- Marvel at one of the world's great buildings, **Aya Sofya** (p104), and its stupendous dome
- Kick up your heels at İstanbul's ongoing eat-street party, **Nevizade Sokak** (p146)
- Admire the extraordinary Byzantine mosaics and frescoes at the **Kariye Müzesi** (p125)
- Take a boat trip along the mighty **Bosphorus** (p128)
- Join the crush and lose yourself in the **Grand Bazaar** (p115), an ancient shopping mecca
- Uncover the secrets of the seraglio at the opulent **Topkapı Palace** (p109)
- Wine, dine and shop along buzzing **İstiklal Caddesi** (p120), the heart of the modern city

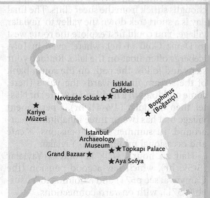

İSTANBUL

If one had but a single glance to give the world, one should gaze on İstanbul

Alphonse de Lamartine

HISTORY

Byzantium

The first historically significant settlement here was founded by a Megarian colonist named Byzas. Before leaving Greece, he asked the Delphic oracle where to set his new colony and received the enigmatic answer: 'Opposite the blind'. When Byzas and his fellow colonists sailed up the Bosphorus in 657 BC, they noticed a small colony on the Asian shore at Chalcedon (modern-day Kadıköy). Looking left, they saw the superb natural harbour of the Golden Horn on the European shore. Thinking, 'Those people in Chalcedon must

---

İSTANBUL IN...

Two Days

Start the day by marvelling at the **Blue Mosque** (p106) and its venerable neighbour, **Aya Sofya** (p104). Next, investigate the watery depths of the **Basilica Cistern** (p108). By this stage you'll be in need of a rest, so make your way up Divan Yolu to the **Grand Bazaar** (p115) and have lunch at **Havuzlu Restaurant** (p142). Shopping is next on the agenda – if you can't find something fabulous to take home you're just not trying hard enough! Mission accomplished, wander north through the bustling mercantile area of Tahtakale to the **Spice Bazaar** (p118) by the water at Eminönü. After taste-testing your way through this historic market, wind up the day by sampling the national dish at **Hamdi Et Lokantası** (p142) – the kebaps here are as impressive as the panoramic views. After dinner return to the Blue Mosque, grab a seat at **Café Meşale** (p147) and sit back to finish the night by enjoying a nargileh (traditional water pipe), listening to live folk music and watching a dervish whirl.

Day two should be devoted to **Topkapı Palace** (p109) and the **İstanbul Archaeological Museum** (p114). Start at the palace and plan on spending at least four hours exploring. Enjoy lunch and the views from the terrace at **Konyalı restaurant** (p141) before making your way down the hill from the First Court to the museum to marvel at its collection. For dinner, you should make your way across the Galata Bridge to cosmopolitan Beyoğlu, promenade down **İstiklal Caddesi** (p120), and enjoy a parade of meze with the locals at party-central, **Nevizade Sokak** (p146).

Four Days

Follow the two-day itinerary, then on your third day hop onto a ferry at Eminönü and explore the **Bosphorus** (p128). At night pamper yourself at a **hamam** (p133) – try Cağaloğlu or Çemberlitaş for maximum Otto-ambiance. Day four should see you heading towards the western districts of Old İstanbul to contemplate the extraordinarily beautiful Byzantine mosaics and frescoes at the **Kariye Müzesi** (p125). In the afternoon, make your way back to Sultanahmet and the impressive **Museum of Turkish and Islamic Arts** (p108), with a stroll along the **Arasta Bazaar** (p106) to the **Great Palace Mosaics Museum** (p106). Wind down the day over a fish dinner with the city's power brokers at **Balıkçı Sabahattin** (p141) or mouth-watering *köfte* (meatballs) at **Tarihi Sultanahmet Köftecisi Selim Usta** (p142) and an after-dinner drink with panoramic views over the twinkling city lights at **Hotel Arcadia** (p138).

One Week

Follow the itineraries above for your first four days. By day five, you could head over to Beyoğlu, spending the morning in **İstanbul Modern** (p120) and/or **Dolmabahçe Palace** (p121). For lunch head to İstiklal Caddesi again and **Leb-i Derya** (p144) or **360** (p144) – both übermodern eateries with knockout views. After, shop till you drop. The delightful **Patisserie Markiz** (p145) offers sugar hits and coffee whenever you run out of stamina. Stay over this side for dinner. On day six the water beckons again and a ferry to the Princes' Islands (p162) is in order. Expect a big but relaxing day wandering around idyllic retreats working off a deliciously indulgent fish lunch. Your last day in the city could start at one of the city's most revered buildings, the magnificent **Süleymaniye Camii** (p116) and end in Asia, with a promenade in Kadıköy with İstanbul's West-focussed youth.

be blind', they settled on the opposite shore, on the site of Lygos, and named their new city Byzantium.

Byzantium submitted willingly to Rome and fought its battles for centuries. But it finally got caught out supporting the wrong side in a civil war. The winner, Sepimus Severus, razed the city walls and took away its privileges in AD 196. When he relented and rebuilt the city, he named it Augusta Antonina.

Constantinople

Another struggle for control of the Roman Empire determined the city's fate for the next 1000 years. Emperor Constantine pursued his rival Licinius to Augusta Antonina, then across the Bosphorus to Chrysopolis (Üsküdar). Defeating his rival in 324, Constantine solidified his control and declared the city the 'New Rome'. He laid out a vast new city to serve as capital of his empire and inaugurated it with much pomp in 330.

Constantine died in 337, just seven years after the dedication of his new capital, but the city continued to grow under the rule of the emperors. Theodosius I ('the Great') had a forum built on the present site of Beyazıt Square, while his son Theodosius II, built the Theodosian walls in 413 when the city was threatened by the maurauding armies of Attila the Hun. Flattened by an earthquake in 447 and hastily rebuilt within two months, the walls he built still surround the old city today.

Theodosius died in 450 and was succeeded by a string of six emperors, the last of whom was Justin, the uncle of the man who was to become one of the famous Byzantine emperors, Justinian (r 527–65). Three years before taking the throne, Justinian had married Theodora, a strong-willed former courtesan. Together they further embellished Constantinople with great buildings, including the famous Aya Sofya (537). Justinian's ambitious building projects and constant wars of reconquest exhausted his treasure and his empire. Following his reign, the Byzantine Empire would never again be as large, powerful or rich.

Much remains of ancient Constantinople, including churches, palaces, cisterns and the Hippodrome. In fact, there's more left than most people realise. Any excavation reveals ancient streets, mosaics, tunnels, water and sewer systems, houses and public buildings buried beneath the modern city centre.

THE CONQUEST

The Ottoman sultan Mehmet II, known as Fatih (the Conqueror), came to power in 1451 and immediately departed his capital in Edirne, to conquer the once-great Byzantine city.

In four short months, Mehmet oversaw the building of Rumeli Hisarı, the great fortress on the European side of the Bosphorus, and the repair of Anadolu Hisarı, built half a century earlier by his great-grandfather Beyazıt I. Together these fortresses controlled the strait's narrowest point.

The Byzantines had closed the mouth of the Golden Horn with a heavy chain to prevent Ottoman boats from sailing in and attacking the city walls on the northern side. Not to be thwarted, Mehmet marshalled his boats at a cove (where the Dolmabahçe Palace now stands) and had them transported overland by night on rollers, up the valley (present site of the Hilton Hotel) and down the other side into the Golden Horn at Kasımpaşa. Catching the Byzantine defenders by surprise, he soon had the Golden Horn under control.

The last great obstacle was the city's mighty walls on the western side. No matter how heavily Mehmet's cannons battered them, the Byzantines rebuilt them by night and, come daybreak, the impetuous young sultan would find himself back where he'd started. Finally, he received a proposal from a Hungarian cannon founder called Urban who had come to help the Byzantine emperor defend Christendom against the infidels. Finding that the Byzantine emperor had no money, Urban instead offered to make Mehmet the most enormous cannon ever seen. Mehmet gladly accepted and the mighty cannon breached the walls, allowing the Ottomans into the city. On 28 May 1453 the final attack began and by the evening of the 29th the Turks were in complete control of the city. The last Byzantine emperor, Constantine XI Dragases, died fighting on the walls.

İstanbul

THE OTTOMAN CENTURIES

Seeing himself as the successor to Constantine, Justinian and the other great emperors, Mehmet the Conqueror at once began to rebuild and repopulate the city. He chose the conspicuous promontory, Seraglio Point, to build his ostentatious palace, Topkapı, and repaired and fortified Theodosius' walls. İstanbul was soon the administrative, commercial and cultural heart of his growing empire.

The building boom Mehmet kicked off was continued by his successors with Süleyman the Magnificent, along with Islam's greatest architect, Sinan, responsible for more construction than any other sultan. The city was endowed with buildings commissioned by the sultan and his family, court and grand viziers including the Süleymaniye Camii (1550), the city's largest mosque. Later sultans also added mosques and in the 19th century numerous palaces were built along the Bosphorus, among them the Dolmabahçe.

As the Ottoman Empire grew to encompass the Middle East and North Africa as well as half of Eastern Europe, İstanbul became a fabulous melting pot of nationalities. On its streets people spoke Turkish, Greek, Armenian, Ladino, Russian, Arabic, Bulgarian, Romanian, Albanian, Italian, French, German, English and Maltese.

However, what was the most civilised city on earth in the time of Süleyman eventually declined along with the Ottoman Empire and by the 19th century İstanbul had lost much of its former glory. Nevertheless it continued to be the 'Paris of the East' and, to reaffirm this, the first great international luxury express train, the famous *Orient Express*, connected İstanbul with the French capital.

TURKISH REPUBLIC & RECENT EVENTS

Mustafa Kemal (Atatürk)'s post-WWI campaign for national salvation and independence was directed from Ankara. In founding the Turkish Republic, Atatürk decided to leave behind the imperial memories of İstanbul and set up his new government in Ankara, a city that could not be threatened by gunboats. Robbed of its status as the capital of a vast empire, İstanbul lost much of its wealth and glitter.

However, since the 1990s İstanbul has undergone a renaissance. Public transport has been upgraded, work on a cross-Bosphorus tunnel is underway and parklands now line the waterways. When İstanbul won the right to become the European Capital of Culture in 2010 other ambitious projects were excitedly placed on the drawing board. There are plans to remodel the Sirkeci shorefront and Saray Burnu, with the latter returned to parklands and the coastal road moved underground.

İstanbul's cultural transformation is just as marked. The seedy dives of Beyoğlu have been replaced by funky cafés, bars and studios, transforming Beyoğlu into a Bohemian hub. İstanbul Modern has opened along the Bosphorus, showcasing Turkey's contemporary art to the world, and galleries seem to open weekly off Beyoğlu's bustling İstiklal Caddesi. The live-music scene in the city has exploded making İstanbul a buzzword for creative, energetic music with a unique East-West twist.

Turkey's bid to join the EU is underpinned by the fact that these days its beloved İstanbul is a cosmopolitan and sophisticated megalopolis, which has reclaimed its status as one of the world's truly great cities.

ORIENTATION

The Bosphorus strait, between the Black and Marmara Seas, divides Europe from Asia. On its western shore, European İstanbul is further divided by the Golden Horn (Haliç) into Old İstanbul in the south and Beyoğlu in the north.

Sultanahmet is the heart of Old İstanbul and it's here that you'll find most of the city's famous sites, including the Blue Mosque, Aya Sofya and Topkapı Palace. The adjoining area, with hotels to suit all budgets, is actually called Cankurtaran although if you say 'Sultanahmet' most people will understand where you mean.

Up the famous Divan Yolu boulevard from Sultanahmet you'll find the Grand Bazaar. To its north is the Süleymaniye Camii, which graces the top of one of the old city's seven hills. Down from the bazaar is the Golden Horn, home to the bustling transport hub of Eminönü.

Over the Galata Bridge from Eminönü is Beyoğlu, on the northern side of the Golden Horn. This is where you'll find the best restaurants, shopping and nightlife in the city, as well as Taksim Sq, the heart of 'modern' İstanbul.

İstanbul's glamour suburbs are Nişantaşı and Teşvikiye, north of Taksim Sq, and its prime real estate is the suburbs lining the Bosphorus, especially those on the European side. However, many locals prefer to live on the Asian side, citing cheaper rents and a better standard of living. Üsküdar and Kadıköy are the two Asian hubs, reachable by a short ferry ride from Eminönü or a drive over the Bosphorus Bridge.

İstanbul's otogar (bus station) is at Esenler, about 10km west of the city centre. The city's main airport, Atatürk International Airport, is in Yeşilköy, 23km west of Sultanahmet; a smaller airport, Sabiha Gökçen International Airport, is 50km southeast. The two main train stations are Haydarpaşa station near Kadıköy on the Asian side and Sirkeci station at Eminönü – though this will change once the Marmaray project comes online (p159). See p159 and p157 for details about getting to and from these transport hubs.

Maps

A free average-quality sheet map of İstanbul, in a number of different languages, is available from tourist-information offices, and it's as good as any sheet map on sale locally. For more detailed guidance, including all minor streets, look for *Sokak Sokak İstanbul* (*İstanbul Street by Street*; €15). You can find it at **Azim Dağıtım** (Map pp96-7; ☎ 0212-638 1313; Klodfarer Caddesi 6, Sultanahmet; ☒ 9am-7pm Mon-Sat) or in **İstanbul Kitapçısı** (see below).

INFORMATION
Bookshops

Bibliophiles will want to head towards the **Old Book Bazaar** (Map pp98-9; Sahaflar Çarşısı, Beyazıt), in a shady little courtyard west of the Grand Bazaar. It dates from Byzantine times. On the Beyoğlu side, you could spend years foraging through the treasure trove of second-hand books (some in English) on the two floors at **Aslıhan Pasajı** (Map pp100-1; Balık Pazar, Galatasaray).

İstanbul's best range and value bookshops are along or just off İstiklal Caddesi in Beyoğlu. Bookshops worth checking out include:

Galeri Kayseri (Map pp96-7; ☎ 0212-512 0456; Divan Yolu 11 & 58, Sultanahmet; ☒ 9am-9pm) Has English-language fiction and glossy books on İstanbul; the other shop over the road – same owner – holds near identical stock.

Homer Kitabevi (Map pp100-1; ☎ 0212-249 5902; Yeni Çarşı Caddesi 28, Galatasaray, Beyoğlu; ☒ 10am-7.30pm Mon-Sat, 12.30-7.30pm Sun) Come here for Homer's unrivalled range of Turkish fiction, plus its enviable collection of nonfiction covering everything from Sufism and Islam to Kurdish and Armenian issues. There's children's books too.

İstanbul Kitapçısı (Map pp100-1; ☎ 0212-292 7692; İstiklal Caddesi 379, Beyoğlu; ☒ 10am-6.45pm Mon-Sat, noon-6.45pm Sun) This government-run bookshop has English-language books on İstanbul, a great selection of

maps and music, and the cheapest prints you'll find in the city (€0.55 to €3.50).

Linda's Book Exchange (Map pp100-1; Şehbender Sokak 18, Tünel, Beyoğlu; ☒ 5-7pm Mon-Fri) Note the limited opening hours of this cosy den of long-term expat, Linda. Unsigned, it's the first door in the building on the left.

Natural Book Exchange (Map pp96-7; ☎ 0212-517 0384; Akbıyık Caddesi 31, Sultanahmet; ☒ 8.30am-8pm) Passable range of second-hand titles with a few gems if you look hard. Swap or buy.

Robinson Crusoe (Map pp100-1; ☎ 0212-293 6968; İstiklal Caddesi 389, Beyoğlu; ☒ 9am-9.30pm Mon-Sat, 10am-9.30pm Sun) Wide range of English-language novels and books about İstanbul – a very close second to Homer Kitabevi.

Emergency

Ambulance ☎ 112
Fire ☎ 110
Police ☎ 155
Tourist police (Map pp96-7; ☎ 527 4503; Yerebatan Caddesi 6, Sultanahmet) Located across the street from the Basilica Cistern.

Internet Access

There are internet cafés all over İstanbul; the following have ADSL connections, English-speaking staff and charge €2 per hour:

Anatolia Internet Cafe (Map pp96-7; İncili Çavuş Sokak 37/2, Sultanahmet; ☒ 9am-9pm) Friendly and mercifully nonsmoking, but not the fastest at times.

Otantik Internet Café (Map pp96-7; Alayköşkü Caddesi 2/B, Sultanahmet; ☒ 9am-midnight) Smoke-free with café attached and printing facilities.

Robin Hood Internet Café (Map pp100-1; Yeni Çarşı Caddesi 24/4, Galatasaray; ☒ 9am-11.30pm) Opposite the Galatasaray Lycée and on the 4th floor up a steep flight of stairs.

You can find wi-fi access at the international terminal at the Atatürk International Airport and at the **Sultan Pub** (Map pp96-7; Divan Yolu Caddesi 2, Sultanahmet; €3.50 per hr; ☒ 9.30am-1am). It's offered free at the café at **World House Hostel** (Map pp100-1; Galipdede Caddesi 117, Galata, Beyoğlu) if you have something to eat or drink there. See the website (www.winet.turktelekom.com.tr) for other locations throughout the city.

Laundry

Clean laundry costs around €2.50 per kilo for washing; add €0.55 per kilo for drying. Good laundrettes are few and far between too.

(Continued on page 103)

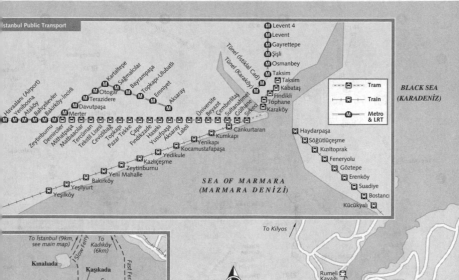

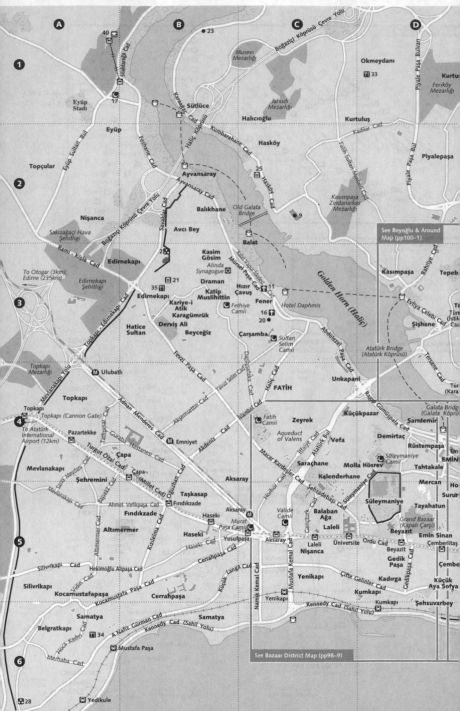

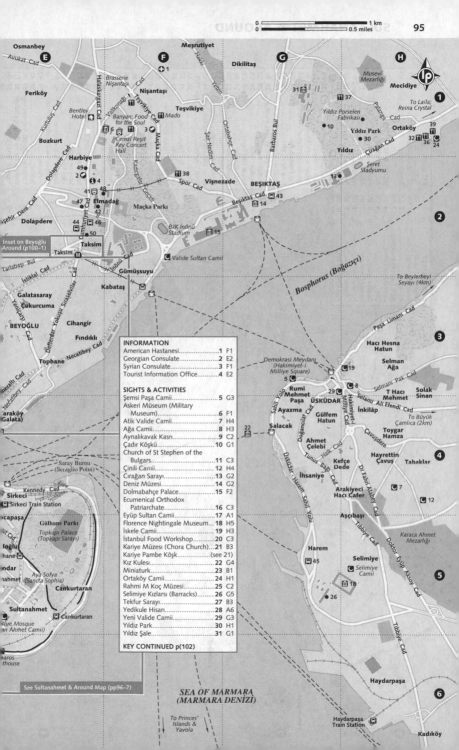

INFORMATION

American Hastanesi	1	F1
Georgian Consulate	2	E2
Syrian Consulate	3	F1
Tourist Information Office	4	E2

SIGHTS & ACTIVITIES

Şemsi Paşa Camii	5	G3
Askeri Müseum (Military Museum)	6	F1
Atik Valide Camii	7	H4
Ağa Camii	8	H3
Aynalıkavak Kasrı	9	C2
Çadır Köşkü	10	G1
Church of St Stephen of the Bulgars	11	C3
Çinili Camii	12	H4
Cırağan Sarayı	13	G2
Deniz Müzesi	14	G2
Dolmabahçe Palace	15	F2
Ecumenical Orthodox Patriarchate	16	C3
Eyüp Sultan Camii	17	A1
Florence Nightingale Museum	18	H5
İskele Camii	19	H3
İstanbul Food Workshop	20	B3
Kariye Müzesi (Chora Church)	21	B3
Kariye Pambe Köşk	(see 21)	
Kız Kulesi	22	G4
Miniaturk	23	B1
Ortaköy Camii	24	H1
Rahmi M Koç Müzesi	25	C2
Selimiye Kızları (Barracks)	26	G5
Tekfur Sarayı	27	B3
Yedikule Hisarı	28	A6
Yeni Valide Camii	29	G3
Yıldız Park	30	H1
Yıldız Şale	31	G1

KEY CONTINUED p(102)

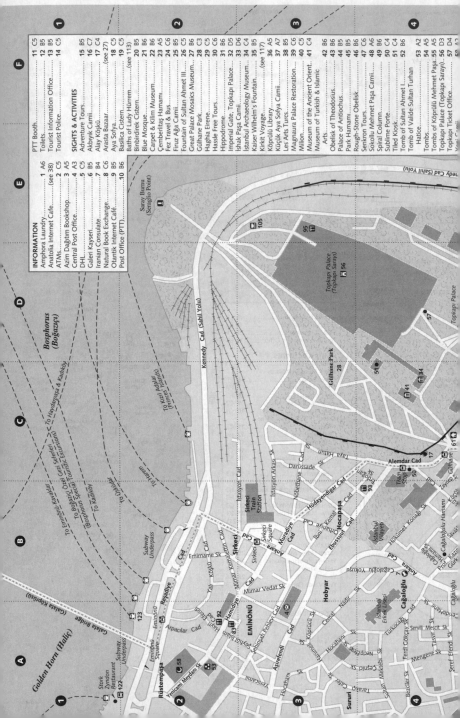

0 |———————| 200 m
0 |———————| 0.1 miles

DRINKING 🍷
Café Meşale............................101 C6
Cheers Bar.............................102 C6
Derviş Aile Çay Bahçesi..........103 C6
Just Bar.............................(see 102)
Legend Hotel.........................104 A6
Set Üstü Çay Bahçesi.............105 E3
Sultan Pub............................106 B5
Yeni Marmara.......................107 B7
Şah Pub & Bar......................108 B5

ENTERTAINMENT 🎭
Şafak Sinemaları.....................109 A5

SHOPPING 🛍
Cağerağa Medresesi................110 C5
Chalcedon.............................111 C5
Cocoon................................112 B7
Coşkun's Bazaar...................(see 61)
Haseki Hamam Carpet & Kilim Sales
   Store...............................113 C6
Istanbul Handicrafts Market..114 C6
İznik Classics & Tiles..............115 C6
İznik Classics & Tiles..............116 C6
Sedir....................................117 C6
Sofa....................................118 A5
Sönmez...............................119 B6
Troy....................................120 C6

TRANSPORT
City Sightseeing Bus..............121 C5
Eminönü Bus Stand (Buses along
   Golden Horn).....................122 A1
Private Ferries for Bosphorus Tours
   and IDO Fast Ferries............123 A2
'T4' Bus to Taksim Square.......124 B5

Orient International Hostel......76 C6
San Konak Oteli......................77 C6
Sarniç Hotel...........................78 B7
Side Hotel & Pension...............79 C6
Stone Hotel & Cafe.................80 A6
Sultan Hostel.........................81 C6
Yeşil Ev................................82 C6

EATING 🍴
Ali Muhiddin Hacı Bekir...........83 A2
Balıkçı Sabahattin...................84 C6
Cennet.................................85 A5
Çiğdem Pastanesi...................86 B5
Doy-Doy...............................87 B7
Dubb...................................88 B5
Erol Taş Kultur Merkez.............89 D6
Giritli...................................90 C7
Greens Supermarket...............91 B4
Hafız Mustafa Şekerlemeleri....92 A2
Hatay..................................93 B4
Karadeniz Aile Pide ve Kebap
   Salonu..............................94 B5
Konyalı.................................95 E3
Oyuncu Sokak Market.............96 C7
Özsüt...................................97 B5
Rami....................................98 C6
Sarniç Restaurant...................99 C4
Tarihi Sultanahmet Köftecisi Selim
   Usta.................................100 B5

SLEEPING 🛏
Ayasofya Pansiyonları.............59 C5
Bahaus Guesthouse................60 C4
Coşkun Pension......................61 C6
Four Seasons Hotel Istanbul.....62 C6
Hotel Ararat..........................63 C6
Hotel Arcadia........................64 A6
Hotel Empress Zoe..................65 C6
Hotel Nomade........................66 B5
Hotel Sultan's Inn...................67 B7
Hotel Turkoman.....................68 B6
İbrahim Paşa Oteli..................69 A6
Istanbul Hostel......................70 C6
Kybele Hotel.........................71 C5
Les Arts Turcs' Rental
   Apartment..........................72 B5
Mavi Guesthouse...................73 C6
Naz Wooden House Inn...........74 C7
Usta...................................75 C7

SEA OF MARMARA
(MARMARA DENİZİ)

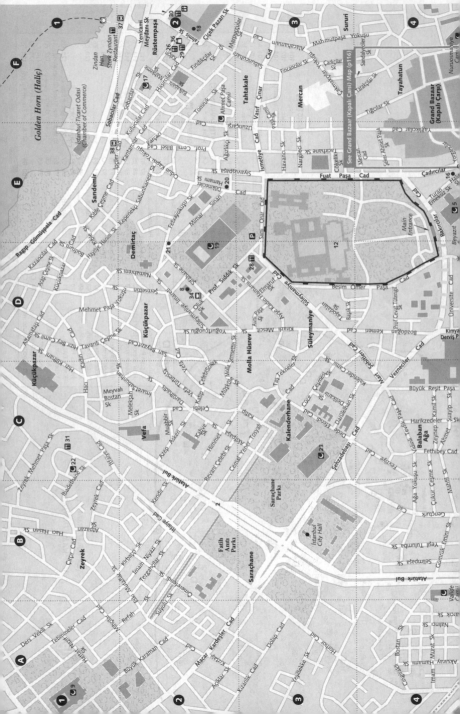

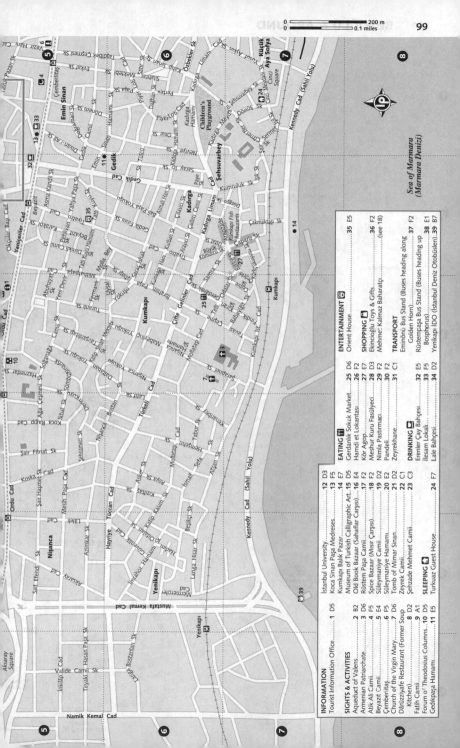

0   200 m
0   0.1 miles

Sea of Marmara
(Marmara Denizi)

INFORMATION
Tourist Information Office...............1 D5

SIGHTS & ACTIVITIES
Aqueduct of Valens..........................2 B2
Armenian Patriarchate.....................3 D6
Atik Ali Camii.....................................4 F5
Beyazıt Camii.....................................5 E4
Çemberlitaş.......................................6 F5
Church of the Virgin Mary................7 D6
Dârüzziyafe Restaurant (Former Soup
    Kitchen)..8 D2
Fatih Camii..9 A1
Forum o' Theodosius Columns.......10 D5
Gedikpaşa Hamamı..........................11 E5
Istanbul University.........................12 D3
Koca Sinan Paşa Medresesi.............13 F5
Kumkapı Balık Pazar........................14 E7
Museum of Turkish Calligraphic Art.15 D5
Old Book Bazaar (Sahaflar Çarşısı)..16 E4
Rüstem Paşa Camii..........................17 F2
Spice Bazaar (Mısır Çarşısı).............18 F2
Süleymaniye Camii..........................19 D2
Süleymaniye Hamamı......................20 E2
Tomb of Mimar Sinan......................21 D2
Zeyrek Camii....................................22 C1
Şehzade Mehmet Camii..................23 C3

SLEEPING
Turkuaz Guest House......................24 F7

EATING
Gerdanlık Sokak Market..................25 D6
Hamdi et Lokantası..........................26 F2
Kör Agop...27 E7
Meshur Kuru Fasulyeci....................28 D3
Nimla Pastırmacı..............................29 D2
Pandeli..30 F2
Zeyrekhane.......................................31 C1

DRINKING
Erenler Çay Bahçesi.........................32 E5
İlesam Lokali.....................................33 F5
Lale Bahçesi......................................34 D2

ENTERTAINMENT
Orient House....................................35 E5

SHOPPING
Ekincioğlu Toys & Gifts...................36 F2
Mehme: Kalmaz Baharatçı.........(see 18)

TRANSPORT
Eminönü Bus Stand (Buses heading along
    Golden Horn)..............................37 F2
Rüstempaşa Bus Stand (Buses heading up
    Bosphorus).................................38 E1
Yenikapı İDO (İstanbul Deniz Otobüsleri).39 B7

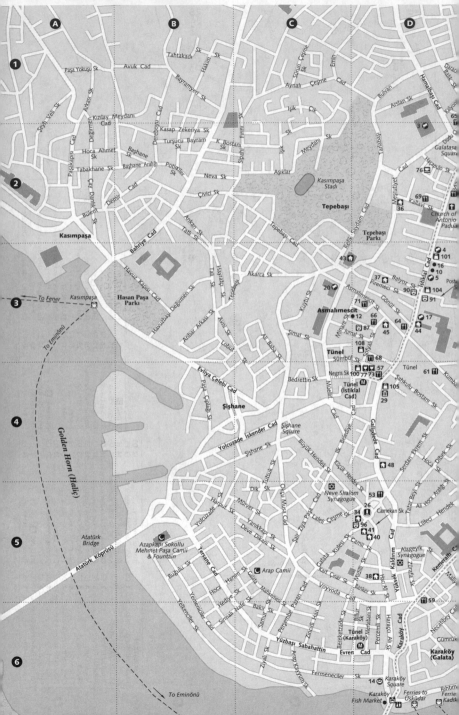

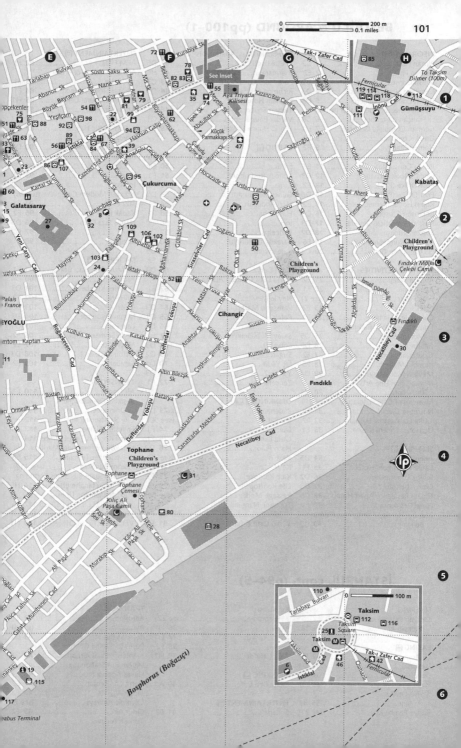

0   200 m
0   0.1 miles

See Inset

Tak-ı Zafer Cad

To Taksim
Dilmer (100m)

E 72 **F** Kurabiye Sk **G** 85 **H**

78

Süslü Saksı Sk

Tarlabaşı Bulvarı

Abanoz Sk Bakkal Sk 82 83 Funicular
Bayram Sk Mis Sk 55 119 114 118
Büyük Nane Sk 35 Aya Triyada 111 7 113
Öğüt Sk 79 74 Kilisesi Kazancı Başı Camii İnönü Cad

54 81 Meşrutiyet Sk Pembe Sk Gümüşsuyu **1**

75 İmam Adnan Sk 99 Necati Bey Sk Sağıroğlu Sk

51 88 92 98 22 62 Abdullah Sk İpek Sk

63 89 94 67 Haşnun Galip Sk Küçük Kabataş
56 107 84 39 Küloğlu Sk Parmakkapı Sk 47

23 86 107 95 Anadolu Geçidi Sk Bilturcu Sk Bol Ahenk

60 Kartal Sk Çukurcuma Hocazade Sk Arslan Yatağı **2**

Galatasaray Turnacıbaşı Sk 97 Somuncu Children's
Playground

9 27 8 32 Liva Soğancı Sk 50 Findıklı Molla
Çelebi Camii

109 102 106 Sıraselviler Cad Children's
103 24 Altıpatlar Sk Playground
Taktak Yokuşu 52 Yeni **3**

Palais Bostanbaşı Cad Çukurcuma Cad **Cihangir** Findıklı
France

BEYOĞLU Külhan Sk Susam Sk 30

Kaptan Sk Defterdar Yokuşu Kumrulu Sk
11 Kasatura Sk Findıklı

Altın Bilezik Sk İlyas Çelebi Sk

Batarya Necatibey Cad **4**

Tophane
Children's
Playground

Tophane 31
Tophane
Çemesi

Kılıç Ali 80
Paşa Camii 28

5

110
Tarlabaşı Bulvarı **Taksim** 0   100 m

112 116
25 **Taksim**
Square
19 Taksim M Tak-ı Zafer Cad
115 46 42
İstiklal Funicular

117 **6**

Bosphorus (Boğaziçi)

eabus Terminal

İSTANBUL cont. (p94–5)

(Continued from page 92)

Amphora Laundry (Map pp96-7; ☎ 0212-638 1555; Pevkhane Sokak 53, Binbirdirek; ✆ 8am-8pm Mon-Sat) Has super-friendly service and a squeaky-clean wash.

Media

The monthly English edition of *Time Out İstanbul* (€2.80) has a large listings section and is the best source for details about upcoming events – you can pick it up at newspaper booths in Sultanahmet.

The glossy *Cornucopia* magazine features many İstanbul-specific articles, including excellent restaurant and exhibition reviews. It is published three times per year (€11). It's impossible to find in Sultanahmet, but you can buy it in the bookshops along İstiklal Caddesi, Beyoğlu.

Medical Services

Although they are expensive, it's probably best to visit one of the private hospitals listed here if you need medical care when in İstanbul. The standard of care at these places is excellent and you will have little trouble finding staff who speak English. All accept credit-card payments and charge around €50 for a consultation.

Alman Hastanesi (Map pp100-1; ☎ 0212-293 2150; Sıraselviler Caddesi 119, Taksim; ✆ 24hr emergency department) A few hundred metres south of Taksim Sq on the left-hand side, this hospital has eye and dental clinics and German administration.

American Hastanesi (Map pp94-5; ☎ 0212-311 2000; Güzelbahçe Sokak 20, Nişantaşı; ✆ 24hr emergency department) About 2km northeast of Taksim Sq, this hospital has US administration and a dental clinic.

Metropolitan Florence Nightingale Hastanesi (Map p93; ☎ 0212-288 3400; Cemil Aslan Guder Sokak 8, Gayrettepe; ✆ 24hr emergency department) This modern facility has a well-respected paediatrics department.

Money

ATMs are everywhere in İstanbul and include those conveniently located in Aya Sofya Meydanı in Sultanahmet (Map pp96–7) and all along İstiklal Caddesi in Beyoğlu.

The 24-hour *döviz bürosu* (exchange bureau) in the arrivals hall at Atatürk International Airport offers rates comparable to those offered by city bureaux. Other exchange bureaux can be found on Divan Yolu in Sultanahmet, near the Grand Bazaar and around Sirkeci Station in Eminönü.

Post

İstanbul's central PTT (post office; Map pp96–7) is a couple of blocks southwest of Sirkeci Train Station. You can make phone calls, buy stamps and send and receive faxes 24 hours a day. All post-restante mail should be sent here (see p663).

There's a convenient PTT booth (Map pp96–7) outside Aya Sofya on Aya Sofya Meydanı in Sultanahmet and PTT branches in the basement of the law courts (Map pp96–7) on İmran Öktem Caddesi in Sultanahmet; off İstiklal Caddesi at Galatasaray Sq (Map pp100-1); near the Galata Bridge in Karaköy (Map pp100–1); and in the southwestern corner of the Grand Bazaar (Map p116).

You can send parcels at the central post office, or parcels less than 2kg at other PTT branches (but not the booth in Sultanahmet). PTTs offer an express post service as well or you could try a carrier such as **DHL** (Map pp96-7; ☎ 0212-512 5452; Yerebatan Caddesi 15, Sultanahmet; ✆ 10am-6pm Mon-Sat).

Telephone

If you are in European İstanbul and wish to call a number in Asian İstanbul, you must dial ☎ 0216 then the number. If you are in Asian İstanbul and wish to call a number in European İstanbul dial ☎ 0212 then the number. Don't use the area codes if you are calling a number on the same shore.

For international calls pick up an IPC phonecard from one of the booths along Divan Yolu in Sultanahmet, or İstiklal Caddesi in Beyoğlu.

Tourist Information

The **Ministry of Culture & Tourism** (www.tourismturkey .org, www.turizm.gov.tr) runs the following tourist information offices:

Atatürk International Airport (✆ 24hr) Booth in international arrivals area.

Beyazıt Sq (Hürriyet Meydanı; Map pp98-9; ☎ 0212-522 4902; ✆ 9am-5pm)

Elmadağ (Map pp94-5; ☎ 0212-233 0592; ✆ 10am-5pm Mon-Sat) In the arcade in front of the İstanbul Hilton Hotel, just off Cumhuriyet Caddesi about a 10-minute walk north of Taksim Sq.

Karaköy International Maritime Passenger Terminal (Map pp100-1; ☎ 0212-249 5776; ✆ 9am-5pm Mon-Sat)

Sirkeci Train Station (Map pp96-7; ☎ 0212-511 5888; ✆ 9am-5pm)

Sultanahmet (Map pp96-7; ☎ 0212-518 8754; ✆ 9am-5pm) At the northeast end of the Hippodrome.

DANGERS & ANNOYANCES

İstanbul is no more nor less safe a city than any large metropolis, but there some dangers worth highlighting. Some İstanbullus drive like rally drivers, and there is no such thing as right of way for pedestrians, despite encouragement from the little green man. As a pedestrian, give way to cars and trucks in all situations, even if you have to jump out of the way. The other main issue is a scam concerning men, bars and women. What could possibly go wrong you ask? See p655 for the low-down.

SIGHTS
Sultanahmet & Around

Many visitors to İstanbul never leave Sultanahmet, which is a shame, though understandable. This is 'Old İstanbul', a Unesco-designated World Heritage site packed with so many wonderful sights you could spend several weeks here and still only scratch the surface.

AYA SOFYA

Called Sancta Sophia in Latin, Haghia Sofia in Greek and the Church of the Divine Wisdom in English, **Aya Sofya** (Map pp96-7; ☎ 0212-522 0989; Aya Sofya Meydanı, Sultanahmet; adult/child under 7 €5.50/free, official guide (45 mins) €20; ☿ 9am-5pm Tue-Sun Nov-May, until 7.30pm Jun-Oct; upper gallery closes 4.30pm, or 6.45pm Jun-Oct) is İstanbul's most famous monument. Arrive early to avoid peak-season crowds.

Emperor Justinian (r 527–65) had the Aya Sofya built as part of his effort to restore the greatness of the Roman Empire. It was completed in 537 and reigned as the greatest church in Christendom until the Conquest in 1453. Mehmet the Conqueror had it converted into a mosque and so it remained until 1935, when Atatürk proclaimed it a museum. Ongoing restoration work (partly Unesco funded) means that the dome is always filled with scaffolding, but not even this can detract from the experience of visiting one of the world's truly great buildings.

On entering his great creation for the first time almost 1500 years ago, Justinian exclaimed, 'Glory to God that I have been judged worthy of such a work. Oh Solomon! I have outdone you!' Entering the building today, it is easy to excuse Justinian's self-congratulatory tone. The interior, with its magnificent domed ceiling soaring heavenward, is so sublimely beautiful that many seeing it for the first time are quite literally stunned into silence.

As you walk into the **inner narthex**, look up to see a brilliant mosaic of Christ as Pantocrator (Ruler of All) above the third and largest door (the Imperial Door). Once through this door the magnificent main dome soars above you. This, the greatest of all domes, is supported by 40 massive ribs, constructed of special hollow bricks made in Rhodes from a unique light, porous clay, resting on huge pillars concealed in the interior walls. (Compare the Blue Mosque's four huge 'elephant's feet' pillars to appreciate the genius of Aya Sofya.)

The curious elevated kiosk screened from public view is the **Sultan's loge**. Ahmet III (r 1703–30) had it built so he could come in, pray and leave again unseen, thus preserving the imperial mystique. The ornate **library**, on the west wall, was built by Sultan Mahmut I in 1739.

In the side aisle to the northeast of the imperial door is the **weeping column**, with a worn copper facing pierced by a hole. Legend has it that the pillar is that of St Gregory the Miracle Worker and that putting one's finger in the hole can lead to ailments being healed if the finger emerges moist.

The large 19th-century **medallions** inscribed with gilt Arabic letters are the work of master calligrapher Mustafa İzzet Efendi, and give the names of God (Allah), Mohammed and the early caliphs Ali and Abu Bakr.

Mosaics

From the floor of Aya Sofya, 9th-century mosaic portraits of St Ignatius the Younger (c 800), St John Chrysostom (c 400) and St Ignatius Theodorus of Antioch are visible high up at the base of the northern tympanum (semicircle) beneath the dome. Next to these three, and seen only from the upstairs east gallery, is a portrait of Alexandros. In the apse is a wonderful mosaic of the Madonna and Child; nearby mosaics depict the archangels Gabriel and Michael, although only fragments of Michael remain.

The upstairs galleries house the most impressive of Aya Sofya's mosaics and mustn't be missed. They can be reached via a switch-back ramp at the northern end of the inner narthex. The magnificent *Deesis Mosaic (The Last Judgement)* in the south gallery dates from the early 14th century. Christ is at the

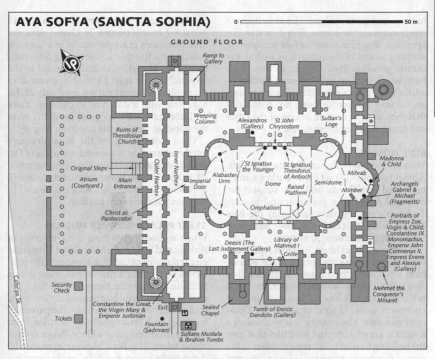

AYA SOFYA (SANCTA SOPHIA)

0   50 m

GROUND FLOOR

Ramp to Gallery

Weeping Column

Alexandros (Gallery)

St John Chrysostom

Sultan's Loge

Ruins of Theodosian Church

Outer Narthex

Inner Narthex

St Ignatius the Younger

St Ignatius Theodorus of Antioch

Madonna & Child

Original Steps

Atrium (Courtyard)

Main Entrance

Imperial Door

Alabaster Urns

Dome

Semidome

Mihrab

Raised Platform

Mimber

Archangels Gabriel & Michael (Fragments)

Christ as Pantocrator

Omphalion

Portraits of Empress Zoe, Virgin & Child, Constantine IX Monomachus, Emperor John Comnenus II, Empress Eirene and Alexius (Gallery)

Deesis (The Last Judgement Gallery)

Library of Mahmut I

Grille

Security Check

Cataeye Sk.

Mehmet the Conqueror's Minaret

Constantine the Great, the Virgin Mary & Emperor Justinian

Exit

Sealed Chapel

Tomb of Enrico Dandolo (Gallery)

Tickets

Fountain (Şadırvan)

Sultans Mustafa & İbrahim Tombs

centre, with the Virgin Mary on the left and John the Baptist on the right.

At the apse end of the southern gallery is the famous mosaic portrait of the Empress Zoe (1028–50), who had three husbands and changed this mosaic portrait with each one. The portrait of the third Mr Zoe, Constantine IX Monomachus, survives because he outlived the empress.

To the right of Zoe and Constantine is another mosaic depicting characters with less saucy histories: in this scene Mary holds the Christ child, centre, with Emperor John (Johannes) Comnenus II (the Good) to the left and Empress Eirene (known for her charitable works) to the right. Their son Alexius, who died soon after this portrait was made, is depicted next to Eirene.

As you leave the museum from the narthex, make sure you turn and look up above the door to see one of the church's finest late 10th-century mosaics. This shows Constantine the Great, on the right, offering Mary, who holds the Christ child, the city of Constantinople; Emperor Justinian, on the left, is offering her Aya Sofya.

BATHS OF LADY HÜRREM

Traditionally, every mosque had a *hamam* included in or around its complex of buildings. Aya Sofya was no exception and this elegant symmetrical building known as the Haseki Hürrem Hamamı or **Baths of Lady Hürrem** (Map pp96–7; ☎ 0212-638 0035; Aya Sofya Meydanı 4, Sultanahmet; admission free; ☺ 9am-5.30pm Tue-Sun, until 6.30pm Jun-Oct), designed by Sinan in 1556–57, was built just across the road from the great mosque by Süleyman in the name of his wife Hürrem Sultan, known to history as Roxelana. The *hamam* was one of 32 designed by Sinan and is widely thought to be his best. It operated until 1910 and now houses a carpet shop run by the Ministry of Culture.

Designed as a 'double *hamam*' with identical baths for men and women, the centre wall dividing the two has now been breached by a small doorway. Both sides have separate entrances and the three traditional rooms: first the square *camekan* for disrobing (the men's side has a pretty marble fountain and stained-glass windows); then the long *soğukluk*, usually a passageway but also sometimes for washing; and finally the octagonal *hararet* for sweating, massage and more washing. The most impressive features are the domes, with their star-like apertures. Also of note are the four semiprivate washing rooms in the *hararet*, as well as the central *göbektaşı* (belly stone) in the men's bath, which is inlaid with coloured marble. In all, the place gives a good idea of how *hamams* are set up – perfect for those not convinced that they want to bare all in one of the city's still-functioning establishments.

BLUE MOSQUE
With his eponymously named mosque, Sultan Ahmet I (r 1603–17) set out to build a monument that would rival and even surpass the nearby Aya Sofya in grandeur and beauty. Today it's more widely known as the **Blue Mosque** (Sultan Ahmet Camii; Map pp96–7; Hippodrome, Sultanahmet; ☾ closed during prayer times).

The mosque's architect, Mehmet Ağa, managed to orchestrate the sort of visual whambam effect with the mosque's exterior that Aya Sofya achieved with its interior. Its curves are voluptuous, it has six minarets and the courtyard is the biggest of all of the Ottoman mosques. The interior is conceived on a similarly grand scale: the blue tiles that give the building its unofficial name number in the tens of thousands, there are 260 windows and the central prayer space is huge.

To appreciate the mosque's design, approach it via the Hippodrome rather than straight from Sultanahmet Park through the crowds. Once inside the courtyard, which is the same size as the mosque's interior, you'll appreciate the building's perfect proportions. The mosque is such a popular attraction that admission is controlled so as to preserve its sacred atmosphere. Only worshippers are admitted through the main door; tourists must use the south door.

Inside, the stained-glass windows and İznik tiles lining the walls immediately attract attention. Although the windows are replacements, they still create the luminous effects of the originals, which came from Venice. You will also see immediately why the Blue Mosque, constructed between 1606 and 1616, more than a millennium after Aya Sofya, is not as daring: four huge 'elephant's feet' pillars hold up the dome, a less elegant but sturdier solution to the problem of support.

From May to October there's a free sound and light show on the north side: check the board for times and languages.

The tile-encrusted **Tomb of Sultan Ahmet I** (Map pp96–7; donation expected; ☾ 9.30am-4.30pm), the Blue Mosque's great patron, is in a separate building on the north side facing Sultanahmet Park. Ahmet, who had ascended to the imperial throne aged 14, died one year after the mosque was constructed, aged only 28. He rests here with a dozen or so children, more evidence that wealth and privilege didn't make the imperial family immune from tragedy.

Up a stone ramp on the Blue Mosque's northeastern side is the underwhelming **Carpet & Kilim Museum** (Halı ve Kilim Müzesi; Map pp96–7; ☎ 0212-518 1330; Blue Mosque, Sultanahmet; admission €2; ☾ 9am-noon & 1-4pm Tue-Sat), which is housed in the mosque's imperial pavilion.

GREAT PALACE MOSAICS MUSEUM
When archaeologists from the University of Ankara and Scotland's St Andrews University dug at the back of the Blue Mosque in the mid-1950s, they found a mosaic pavement dating from early Byzantine times (c AD 500). Covered with wonderful hunting and mythological scenes and emperors' portraits, the pavement was part of a triumphal way that led from the Byzantine emperor's Great Palace (which stood where the Blue Mosque now stands) down to the harbour of Bucoleon to the south. It is now displayed *in situ* in the **Great Palace Mosaics Museum** (Büyüksaray Mozaik Müzesi; Map pp96–7; ☎ 0212-518 1205; Torun Sokak, Sultanahmet; admission €3; ☾ 9am-4.30pm Tue-Sun Nov-May, to 6.30pm Jun-Oct), where there are informative panels documenting the floor's rescue and renovation.

Other 5th-century mosaics were saved when Sultan Ahmet I had an Arasta (row of shops) built on top of them. The **Arasta Bazaar** (Map pp96–7) now houses numerous carpet and ceramic shops that provide rental revenue for the upkeep of the Blue Mosque.

Enter the Great Palace Mosaics Museum from Torun Sokak behind the mosque and the Arasta.

HIPPODROME
The Hippodrome (Atmeydanı; Map pp96–7) was the centre of Byzantium's life for 1200 years and of Ottoman life for another 400-odd years. It was the scene of countless political dramas during the long life of the city. In Byzantine times, the rival chariot teams of 'Greens' and 'Blues' had separate political connections. Support for a team was akin to membership of a political party and a team

victory had important effects on policy. A Byzantine emperor might lose his throne as the result of a post-match riot.

Ottoman sultans also kept an eye on activities in the Hippodrome. If things were going badly in the empire, a surly crowd gathering here could signal the start of a disturbance, then a riot, then a revolution. In 1826 the slaughter of the corrupt janissary corps (the sultan's personal bodyguards) was carried out here by the reformer Sultan Mahmut II. And in 1909, there were riots here that caused the downfall of Abdül Hamit II and the rewriting of the Ottoman constitution.

Although the Hippodrome might be the scene of their downfall, Byzantine emperors and Ottoman sultans outdid one another in beautifying it, adorning it with statues from the far reaches of the empire. Unfortunately, only a handful of these statues remain. Chief among the thieves responsible were the soldiers of the Fourth Crusade, who sacked Constantinople, supposedly a Christian ally city, in 1204.

Near the northern end of the Hippodrome, the little gazebo in beautiful stonework is actually **Kaiser Wilhelm's Fountain**. The German emperor paid a state visit to Abdül Hamit II in 1901, and presented this fountain to the sultan and his people as a token of friendship.

The immaculately preserved pink granite **Obelisk of Theodosius**, the oldest monument in İstanbul, was carved in Egypt during the reign of Thutmose III (r 1549–1503 BC) and erected in the Amon-Re temple at Karnak. The Byzantine emperor, Theodosius, had it brought from Egypt to Constantinople in AD 390. The original obelisk was cut down for transit – the top segment was placed on the ceremonial marble base Theodosius had made. Look at the north side of the base to see a relief depiction of the engineering feat of transporting the obelisk here.

South of the obelisk is a strange column rising out of a hole in the ground. Known as the **Spiral Column**, it was once part of a golden basin supported by three entwined serpents cast to commemorate the victory of the Hellenic confederation over the Persians at Plataea. It stood in front of the temple of Apollo at Delphi from 478 BC until Constantine the Great had it brought to his new capital city around AD 330. Historians suspect the bronze serpents' heads were stolen during the Fourth Crusade.

İSTANBUL'S BOOMING POPULATION

As the main destination for migrants in the country, İstanbul's population has exploded over the last few decades. For those displaced by the war in the southeast and for those from impoverished rural areas looking for better work prospects, İstanbul, and many other big Turkish cities like it – Ankara, Adana, İzmir – offer work opportunities and the hope for a better life.

Turkey's position on the doorstep of the EU has made it one of the largest human trafficking centres in the world. Official estimates put the number of people illegally crossing Turkey's borders at around 100,000 annually – up from just 11,000 a decade ago – though some say the numbers could be as high as 250,000. Those who risk their lives hidden in ships or by crossing the long and rugged mountain border with Turkey's Middle Eastern neighbours, hope to eventually continue their journey by boat to Greece or Italy, or cross by land into Greece. Many get stuck in İstanbul and stay as long as it takes to get asylum visa applications accepted or to earn enough money to fund the next leg of their perilous journey. Most are forced to stay in filthy hotels in Aksaray or slum in overcrowded rooms in Kumkapı or Tarlabaşı (west of Taksim), work illegally (women are often forced into prostitution) and to seek whatever help they can get from religious institutions and the grossly over-patronised social services.

For a city already struggling to cope with the infrastructure and social-support demands of its growing number of migrants, the arrival of increasing numbers of refugees, asylum seekers and illegal migrants has not been met with much enthusiasm. Tensions have increased over the battle for the few jobs and services available.

Meanwhile, the EU continues to apply pressure on Turkey to stem the illegal immigrant tide. Recent clamp downs include the 110 foreigners found in a warehouse in an outer İstanbul suburb. Many worry, with Turkey's already shaky human-rights record, that these and other people with similar plights may be being deported or jailed indefinitely without their cases being heard properly.

İSTANBUL

Little is known about the 4th-century **Rough-Stone Obelisk**, except that in 869 an earthquake toppled the bronze pine cone from its top, and it was clad with sheets of gilded bronze by Constantine VII Porphyrogenitus (r 913–59), commemorated in the inscription in its base. Its bronze plates were ripped off during the Fourth Crusade, but you can still see the bolt holes where they would have been attached.

Note the original ground level of the Hippodrome at the base of the obelisks and column, some 2.5m below ground.

MUSEUM OF TURKISH & ISLAMIC ARTS

This impressive **museum** (Türk ve İslam Eserleri Müzesi; Map pp96-7; ☎ 0212-518 1805; Hippodrome 46, Sultanahmet; admission €3; ⊗ 9am-4.30pm Tue-Sun) is housed in the palace of İbrahim Paşa, built in 1520 on the western side of the Hippodrome.

İbrahim Paşa was Süleyman the Magnificent's close friend and brother-in-law. Captured by Turks as a child in Greece, he had been sold as a slave into the imperial household in İstanbul and worked as a page in Topkapı, where he became friendly with Süleyman, who was the same age. When his friend became sultan, İbrahim was in turn made chief falconer, chief of the royal bedchamber and grand vizier. This palace was bestowed on him by Süleyman the year before he was given the hand of Süleyman's sister, Hadice, in marriage. Alas, the fairy tale was not to last. İbrahim's wealth, power and influence on the monarch became so great that others wishing to influence the sultan became envious, chief among them Süleyman's wife, Roxelana. After a rival accused İbrahim of disloyalty, she convinced her husband that İbrahim was a threat and Süleyman had him strangled in 1536.

Inside, the most interesting exhibits are the floor-to-ceiling Uşak carpets, the beautifully illuminated Qurans and the relief map of the Ottoman Empire (in the room just before the carpets). Don't miss the fascinating ethnographic collection downstairs.

Labels are in Turkish and English. The coffeeshop in the lovely green courtyard of the museum is a welcome refuge from the press of crowds and touts in the area.

BASILICA CISTERN

When those Byzantine emperors built something, they certainly did it properly! This extraordinary **cistern** (Yerebatan Sarnıçı; Map pp96-7; ☎ 0212-522 1259; Yerebatan Caddesi 13, Sultanahmet; admission €5.50; ⊗ 9am-6.30pm Apr-Sep, til 5.30pm Oct-Mar), built by Justinian in AD 532, is a great place to while away half an hour, especially during summer when its cavernous depths stay wonderfully cool.

Like most sites in İstanbul, the cistern has a colourful history. Known in Byzantium as the Basilica Cistern because it laid underneath the Stoa Basilica, one of the great squares on the first hill, it was used to store water for the Great Palace and surrounding buildings. Eventually closed, it seems to have been forgotten by the city authorities some time before the Conquest. Enter scholar Petrus Gyllius, who was researching Byzantine antiquities in 1545 and was told by locals that they could obtain water miraculously by lowering buckets in their basement floors. Some were even catching fish this way. Intrigued, Gyllius explored the neighbourhood and discovered a house through whose basement he accessed the cistern. Even after his discovery, the Ottomans (who referred to the cistern as Yerebatan Sarayı) didn't treat the underground palace with the respect it deserved and it became a dumping ground for all sorts of junk, as well as corpses. It has been restored at least three times.

The cistern is 65m wide and 143m long, and its roof is supported by 336 columns arranged in 12 rows. It once held 80,000 cubic metres of water, pumped and delivered through nearly 20km of aqueducts.

Constructed using columns, capitals and plinths from ruined buildings, the cistern's symmetry and sheer grandeur of conception is quite extraordinary. Don't miss the two columns in the northwestern corner supported by upside-down Medusa heads or the column towards the centre featuring a teardrop design.

Walking on the raised wooden platforms, you'll feel water dripping from the vaulted ceiling and may catch a glimpse of ghostly carp patrolling the water. Lighting is atmospheric and the small café near the exit is certainly an unusual spot to enjoy a cup of çay (tea).

BİNBİRDİREK CISTERN

Binbirdirek (Binbirdirek Sarnıçı, Cistern of 1001 Columns; Map pp96-7; ☎ 0212-518 1001; İmran Öktem Caddesi 4, Binbirdirek; admission incl one drink €5.50; ⊗ 9am-6pm) was built by Constantine in AD 330, and is mainly noteworthy for its custom-built columns, which feature round discs designed to absorb seismic shocks. They've been remarkably successful given only 12 of the original 224 columns have been replaced. During the Ottoman era it was used as a *han* (inn) for silk manufacturers as it could be safely locked up at night, but the false floor that was put in at the time definitely detracts from the space. At the time of writing work was underway to open it as a Byzantine museum, displaying computer-animated re-creations of the city's Byzantine monuments, including the Hippodrome.

KÜÇÜK AYA SOFYA CAMİİ

Justinian and Theodora built this **church** (Little Aya Sofya, SS Sergius & Bacchus Church; Map pp96–7; Küçük Aya Sofya Caddesi; donation requested) sometime between 527 and 536 (just before Justinian built Aya Sofya). It was named after the two patron saints of Christians in the Roman army. Its dome is architecturally noteworthy and its plan – that of an irregular octagon – unusual. Like Aya Sofya, its interior was originally decorated with gold mosaics and featured columns made from fine green and red marble. The mosaics are long gone, but the impressive columns remain. The church was converted into a mosque by the chief white eunuch Hüseyin Ağa around 1500; his tomb is to the north of the building.

At the time of research extensive renovations were near completion. The mosque should be open to visitors by the time you read this.

After visiting Küçük Aya Sofya, go north along Şehit Mehmet Paşa Sokak and back up the hill to see the stunning little **Sokollu Mehmet Paşa Camii**, designed by Sinan in 1571.

TOPKAPI PALACE

Home to Selim the Sot, who drowned in the bath after drinking too much champagne; İbrahim the Mad, who lost his reason after being locked up for four years in the infamous palace *kafes* (cage); and Roxelana, beautiful and malevolent consort of Süleyman the Magnificent, the famous **Topkapı Palace** (Topkapı Sarayı; Map p110 unless otherwise stated; ☎ 0212-512 0480; Soğukçeşme Sokak, Sultanahmet; adult/child under 7 €5.50/free; harem admission adult/child under 7 €5.50/free; ☾ 9am–7pm Wed-Mon Apr-Oct, closes 5pm Nov-May) would have to be the subject of more colourful stories than most of the world's museums put together. No wonder it's been the subject of an award-winning feature film (Jules Dassin's *Topkapı*), an opera (Mozart's *The Abduction from the Seraglio*) and a blockbuster social history (John Freely's wonderful *Inside the Seraglio*).

Mehmet the Conqueror started work on the palace shortly after the Conquest in 1453 and

---

LEAVE YOUR GUIDEBOOK AT THE HOTEL

Scrape away the tourist-friendly veneer of Sultanahmet and the glamorous Bosphorus-side suburbs to see another side of İstanbul. Leave your guidebook behind and explore parts of the city left off most tourists' itineraries. Your adventures will be amply rewarded.

Well worth exploring is the **Kadırga/Kumkapı area** (Map pp98–9). This historic Old İstanbul quarter is begging to be added to İstanbul's World Heritage listing before it crumbles away – and it's only a five-minute walk from Sultanahmet. Explore the streets south of Kadırga Limanı Caddesi to see the hubbub of daily life in teetering Ottoman houses with fluttering washing spanning narrow, cobbled lanes; children kicking balls; fruit sellers pushing carts calling out their wares; *simit* (O-shaped bread rings) sellers balancing towers of fresh *simits* on trays on their heads. The Kumkapı Balık Pazar (fish market) by the shore is one of İstanbul's busiest and best. Most fish winds up at the *meyhane* district, close by, which is fabulous on Friday and Saturday nights (and deathly quiet at other times). You can't go wrong eating at long-timer, **Kör Agop** (Map pp98-9; Ördekli Bakkal Sokak 32). You may want to avoid wandering the side streets after dark, as Kumkapı's *meyhane* district can be pretty seedy – catch a taxi back to your hotel.

If you can, time your visit for the Thursday street market when the locals spill out of their dens. This is one of İstanbul's main migrant suburbs, and at the market you'll see all kinds, from African refugees (see p107) selling rip-off watches, leech sellers peddling their slippery wares, grizzled Anatolian gents in baggy pants, to Russians selling vodka. This area is also home to a large proportion of İstanbul's Armenian population. Pay a visit to the **Armenian Patriarchate** (Map pp98-9; Şarapnel Sokak 2) and the Church of the Virgin Mary, opposite.

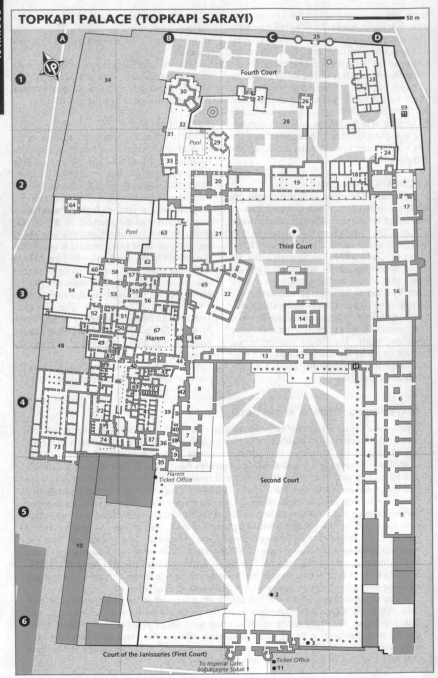

TOPKAPI PALACE (TOPKAPI SARAYI)

0 ——— 50 m

ISTANBUL

Fourth Court

Pool

Third Court

Pool

Harem

Second Court

Harem
Ticket Office

Court of the Janissaries (First Court)

To Imperial Gate;
Soğukçeşme Sokak

Ticket Office

lived here until his death in 1481. Subsequent sultans lived in this rarefied environment until the 19th century, when they moved to ostentatious European-style palaces such as Dolmabahçe, Çırağan and Yıldız that they built on the shores of the Bosphorus. Mahmut II (r 1808–39) was the last sultan to live in Topkapı.

Seeing Topkapı requires at least half a day but preferably more. If you are short on time see the harem, treasury and the rooms around the İftariye Baldachin. Buy your tickets to the palace and the treasury at the main ticket office just outside the gate to the second court. Tickets to the harem are available at the ticket box outside the harem itself. Guides to the palace congregate next to the main ticket office. A one-hour tour will cost you €10 per person (minimum three people or €30). Alternatively, an audio-guide costs €5. These and maps of the palace are available at the booth just inside the turnstile entrance to the second court.

Before you enter the Imperial Gate (Bab-ı Hümayun) of Topkapı, take a look at the ornate structure in the cobbled square near the gate. This is the **Fountain of Sultan Ahmet III** (Map pp96–7), built in 1728 by the sultan who so loved tulips that his reign was dubbed the Tulip Age.

First Court

Topkapı grew and changed with the centuries, but the palace's basic four-courtyard plan remained the same. The Ottomans followed the Byzantine practice of secluding the monarch from the people: the first court was open to all; the second only to people on imperial business; the third only to the imperial family, VIPs and palace staff; while the fourth was the 'family quarters'.

As you pass through the great Imperial Gate behind the Aya Sofya, you enter the First Court, the Court of the Janissaries. On your left is the Byzantine **Haghia Eirene** (Aya İrini Kilisesi, Church of the Divine Peace; Map pp96–7), built in the 4th century, and rebuilt next century by Justinian, so the church you see is as old as Aya Sofya. It's usually only open for concerts during the İstanbul International Music Festival. Also on the left is the gate to the Imperial Mint (Darphane-I

Amire) where there are often temporary exhibitions.

Second Court

The **Middle Gate** (Ortakapı or Bab-üs Selâm) led to the palace's Second Court, which was used for the business of running the empire. Only the sultan and the *valide sultan* (mother of the reigning sultan) were allowed through the Middle Gate on horseback. Everyone else, including the grand vizier, had to dismount. The gate was constructed by Süleyman the Magnificent in 1524.

To the right after you enter are models and a map of the palace. Beyond them, in a nearby building, you'll find a collection of imperial carriages.

The second court has a beautiful, park-like setting. Topkapı is not based on a typical European palace plan – one large building with outlying gardens – but is a series of pavilions, kitchens, barracks, audience chambers, kiosks and sleeping quarters built around a central enclosure.

The great **Palace Kitchens**, on your right, hold a small portion of Topkapı's vast collection of Chinese celadon porcelain. In a building close by are the collections of silverware and glassware. The last of the kitchens, the Helvahane, in which the palace sweets were made, now hosts occasional temporary exhibitions.

On the left (west) side of the second court is the ornate **Imperial Council Chamber**, also called the Divan Salonu. The Imperial Divan (council) met in the Imperial Council Chamber to discuss matters of state while the sultan eavesdropped through a grille high on the wall at the base of the **Tower of Justice** (Adalet Kulesi) in the harem. North of the Imperial Council Chamber is the **Inner Treasury**, which today exhibits arms and armour, including a massive sword that belonged to Mehmet the Conqueror.

The entrance to the palace's most famous sight, the **harem**, is beneath the Tower of Justice.

The Harem

If you decide to tour the harem – and we highly recommend you do – you have no option but to take a guided tour; tickets are available from the ticket office outside the harem's entrance. There are usually lengthy queues and numbers are limited to 60 for each 30-minute tour, so it's a good idea to head this

way as soon as you enter Topkapı or try to arrive in time for the 9.30am tour. Tours depart every 30 minutes from 9.30am to 5pm (4pm in winter) and are in English and Turkish.

Multilingual audio-guides (€4) to the harem are available at the ticket booth outside, though these aren't much use as you're whipping through the tour with barely enough time to listen to the tour guide let alone the audio-guide. A better option may be the combined harem and treasury audio-guides for €5.

As popular belief would have it, the harem was a place where the sultan could engage in debauchery at will (and Murat III did, after all, have 112 children!). In reality, these were the imperial family quarters, and every detail of harem life was governed by tradition, obligation and ceremony. The word 'harem' literally means 'private'.

The women of Topkapı's harem had to be foreigners as Islam forbade enslaving Muslims, Christians or Jews. Girls, too, were bought as slaves (often having been sold by their parents at a good price) or were received as gifts from nobles and potentates.

On entering the harem, the girls would be schooled in Islam and Turkish culture and language, as well as the arts of make-up, dress, comportment, music, reading and writing, embroidery and dancing. They then entered a meritocracy, first as ladies-in-waiting to the sultan's concubines and children, then to the sultan's mother and finally, if they were the best, to the sultan himself.

Ruling the harem was the *valide sultan* (mother of the sultan). She often owned large landed estates in her own name and controlled them through black eunuch servants. Able to give orders directly to the grand vizier, her influence on the sultan, on the selection of his wives and concubines and on matters of state was often profound.

The sultan was allowed by Islamic law to have four legitimate wives, who received the title of *kadın* (wife). He could have as many concubines as he could support – some had up to 300, although they were not all in the harem at the same time. If a sultan's wife bore him a son she was called *haseki sultan; haseki kadın* if it was a daughter. The Ottoman dynasty did not observe primogeniture (the right of the first-born son to the throne), so in principle the throne was available to any imperial son. Each lady of the harem struggled to have her son proclaimed heir to the throne, which would assure her own role as the new *valide sultan*.

Although the harem is built into a hillside and has six levels, the standard tour takes you through or past only a few dozen of the most splendid rooms on one level. Interpretive panels in Turkish and English have been placed throughout the building, although you are hurried through at such a pace that there is little time to read them.

Highlights of the tour include the narrow **Black Eunuchs' Courtyard** (39), the marble and gold **Sultan's Hamam** (50), the **Concubines' & Consorts' Courtyard** (46), the **Valide Sultan's Quarters and Courtyard** (49), the ornate **Privy Chamber of Murat III** (58), the **Library of Ahmet I** (60), the **Dining Room of Ahmet III** (61) and the **Double Kiosks** (62).

Third Court

If you enter the Third Court after visiting the harem you should head for the main gate into the court and enter again to truly appreciate the grandeur of the approach to the heart of the palace. This main gate, known as the **Gate of Felicity** or Gate of the White Eunuchs, was the entrance into the sultan's private domain.

Just inside the Gate of Felicity is the **Audience Chamber**, constructed in the 16th century but refurbished in the 18th century. Important officials and foreign ambassadors were brought to this kiosk to conduct the high business of state. Seated on divans whose cushions were embroidered with over 15,000 seed pearls, the sultan inspected the ambassador's gifts and offerings as they were passed through the small doorway on the left.

Right behind the Audience Chamber is the pretty **Library of Ahmet III**, built in 1719.

To the right of the Audience Chamber (ie on the opposite side of the harem exit) are the rooms of the **Dormitory of the Expeditionary Force**, which now house rich collections of imperial robes, kaftans and uniforms worked in silver and gold thread. Next to the Dormitory of the Expeditionary Force is the **Treasury**. See right for details of its collection.

Opposite the Treasury on the other side of the Third Court is another set of wonders: the holy relics in the Suite of the Felicitous Cloak, nowadays called the **Sacred Safekeeping Rooms**. These rooms, sumptuously decorated with İznik tiles, constitute a holy of holies within the palace. Only the chosen few could enter the Third Court, but entry into the Suite of the Felicitous Cloak was for the chosen of the chosen, and then only on ceremonial occasions.

In the entry room, notice the carved door from the Kaaba in Mecca and, hanging from the ceiling, gilded rain gutters from the same place. To the right a room contains a hair of Prophet Mohammed's beard, his footprint in clay, his sword, tooth and more. An imam is often sitting in a glass booth here and chanting passages from the Quran. The 'felicitous cloak' itself resides in a golden casket in a small adjoining room.

Also in the Third Court are the **Quarters of Pages in Charge of the Sacred Safekeeping Rooms**, where the palace school for pages and janissaries was located. These days the building features exhibits of Turkish miniature paintings, calligraphy and portraits of the sultans.

The Treasury

The Treasury, with its incredible collection of precious objects and simply breathtaking views, is a highlight of a visit to the palace. The building itself was constructed by Mehmet the Conqueror in 1460 and has always been used to store works of art and treasure. In the first room, look for the jewel-encrusted **sword of Süleyman the Magnificent** and the **Throne of Ahmet I**, inlaid with mother-of-pearl and designed by Mehmet Ağa, architect of the Blue Mosque. In the second room, the tiny **Indian figures**, mainly made from seed pearls, are well worth seeking out, as are the bizarre and vaguely sinister relics of the **Arm and Skull of St John the Baptist**, which are encased in jewels.

After passing through the third room and having a gawk at the enormous gold and diamond **candlesticks** you come to a fourth room and the Treasury's most famous exhibit – the **Topkapı Dagger**. The object of the criminal quest in the 1964 movie *Topkapı*, it features three enormous emeralds on the hilt and a watch set into the pommel. Also here is the **Spoonmaker's Diamond** (Kaşıkçı'nın Elması), a teardrop-shaped 86-carat rock surrounded by several dozen smaller stones. First worn by Mehmet IV at his accession to the throne in 1648, it is the world's fifth-largest diamond. It is called the Spoonmaker's Diamond because it was originally found in a rubbish dump in Eğrıkapı and purchased by a street peddler for three spoons.

Fourth Court

Pleasure pavilions occupy the northeastern part of the palace, sometimes called the Tulip Gardens or Fourth Court. A late addition to Topkapı, the **Mecidiye Köşkü** was built by Abdül Mecit (r 1839–61). Beneath it is the Konyalı restaurant (p141); if you plan to eat here, try to arrive before noon or after 2pm to be sure of a table on the terrace.

Up the stairs at the end of the Tulip Garden are two of the most enchanting buildings in the palace, joined by a marble terrace with a beautiful pool. Murat IV (r 1623–40) built the **Revan Kiosk** in 1636 after reclaiming the city of Yerevan (now in Armenia) from Persia. In 1639 he constructed the **Baghdad Kiosk**, one of the last examples of classical palace architecture, to commemorate his victory over that city. Notice the superb İznik tiles, the mother-of-pearl and tortoiseshell inlay, and the woodwork.

Jutting out from the terrace is the golden roof of the **İftariye Baldachin**, the most popular happy-snap spot in the palace grounds. İbrahim the Mad built this small structure in 1640 as a picturesque place to break the daily Ramazan fast.

At the west end of the terrace is the **Circumcision Room** (Sünnet Odası), used for the ritual that admits Muslim boys to manhood. Built by İbrahim in 1641, the outer walls of the chamber are graced by particularly beautiful tile panels.

GÜLHANE PARK

Once the park of the Topkapı Palace, crowds of locals now come to Gülhane Park (Map pp96–7) at weekends to enjoy its shade. Do as the locals do and head to the north end of the park to the **Set Üstü Çay Bahçesi** (see p147), with superb views over the Bosphorus.

To the left of the south exit is a bulbous kiosk built into the park wall. Known as the **Alay Köşkü** (Parade Kiosk), this is where the sultan would sit and watch the periodic parades of troops and trade guilds commemorating great holidays and military victories.

Across the street from the Alay Köşkü (not quite visible from the Gülhane gate) is an outrageously curvaceous rococo gate leading into the precincts of what was once the grand vizierate, or Ottoman prime ministry, known in the West as the **Sublime Porte**. Today the buildings beyond the gate hold various government offices.

İSTANBUL ARCHAEOLOGICAL MUSEUM

It may not pull the number of visitors that flock to nearby Topkapı, but this **museum** (Arkeoloji Müzeleri; Map pp96-7; ☎ 0212-520 7740; Osman Hamdi Bey Yokuşu, Gülhane; admission €3; ☼ 8.30am-5pm Tue-Sun) shouldn't be missed. It can be reached easily by walking down the slope from Topkapı's First Court, or by trudging up the hill from the main gate of Gülhane Park. Allow at least two hours.

The complex is divided into three buildings: the Archaeology Museum (Arkeoloji Müzesi), the Museum of the Ancient Orient (Eski Şark Eserler Müzesi) and the Tiled Kiosk (Çinili Köşk). These museums house the palace collections, formed during the 19th century by archaeologist Osman Hamdi (1842–1910) and added to greatly since the republic was proclaimed. Excellent interpretive panels are in both Turkish and English.

The first building on your left as you enter is the **Museum of the Ancient Orient**. Overlooking the park, it was designed by Alexander Vallaury and built in 1883 to house the Academy of Fine Arts. It displays Anatolian pieces from Hittite empires and pre-Islamic items collected from the Ottoman Empire.

A Roman statue of the god **Bes** greets you as you enter the **Archaeology Museum** on the opposite side of the courtyard. Turn left into Room 1 and walk into the dimly lit rooms beyond, where the museum's major treasures – sarcophagi from the **Royal Necropolis of Sidon** – are displayed. Osman Hamdi unearthed these sarcophagi in Sidon (Side in modern-day Lebanon) in 1887, and in 1891 persuaded the sultan to build the museum to house them.

In Room 2 you will see a sarcophagus that is Egyptian in origin, but which was later reused by **King Tabnit of Sidon**; his mummy lies close by. Also here is a beautifully preserved **Lycian Sarcophagus** made from Paros marble and dating from the end of the 5th century. Next to this is the **Satrap Sarcophagus**.

After admiring these, pass into Room 3 to see the famous marble **Alexander Sarcophagus**, one of the most accomplished of all classical artworks and known as the Alexander Sarcophagus because it depicts the Greek general among his army battling the Persians. (It was actually sculpted for King Abdalonymos of Sidon, not Alexander, though.) Truly exquisite, it is carved out of Pentelic marble and dates from the last quarter of the 4th century

BC. One side shows the Persians (long pants, material headwear) battling with the Greeks. Alexander, on horseback, sports the Nemean Lion's head as a headdress, symbol of Hercules. The other side depicts the violent thrill of a lion hunt. Remarkably, the sculpture has remnants of its original red-and-yellow paintwork.

At the end of this room the **Mourning Women Sarcophagus** also bears traces of its original paintwork. Its depiction of the women is stark and very moving.

Turn back and walk past Bes to Room 4, the first of six **galleries of statues**, which are all worth visiting. Copies of some statues have been painted with gaudy colours as they would have appeared originally.

The annexe behind the main ground-floor gallery has the **Children's Museum**. While children will be bored stiff with the naff dioramas of early Anatolian life, they will no doubt be impressed by the large-scale model of the Trojan horse, which they can climb into. Beside the Children's Museum is the **Neighbouring Cultures of İstanbul** gallery, with a Byzantium collection including a stunning mosaic depicting Orpheus, and an equally impressive small mosaic of St Eudocia. If you have even a passing interest in İstanbul's rich archaeology, don't miss the mezzanine level above showcasing 'İstanbul Through the Ages'. After seeing the displays here you can appreciate how much of the ancient city remains covered.

The last of the complex's museum buildings is the gorgeous **Tiled Kiosk** of Sultan Mehmet the Conqueror. Thought to be the oldest surviving nonreligious Turkish building in İstanbul, it was built in 1472 as an outer pavilion of Topkapı Palace and was used for watching sporting events.

Bazaar District

Crowned by the city's first and most evocative shopping mall – the famous Grand Bazaar (Kapalı Çarşı) – the bazaar district is also home to two of the grandest of all Ottoman buildings, the Süleymaniye and Beyazıt Camiis. For details on exploring a much lesser-known part of this district, see the boxed text, p109.

GRAND BAZAAR

The labyrinthine, chaotic, chintzy **Grand Bazaar** (Kapalı Çarşı, Covered Market; Map pp98-9 for location, Map p116 for detailed map; ⊗ 8.30am-7pm Mon-Sat) is the heart of İstanbul and has been for centuries. No visit to İstanbul would be complete without a stop here.

With over 4000 shops and several kilometres of lanes, as well as mosques, banks, police stations, restaurants and workshops, the bazaar is a covered world. Although there's no doubt that it's a tourist trap *par excellence,* it's also a place where business deals are done between locals and import/export businesses flourish.

Starting from a small masonry *bedesten* (market enclosure) built during the time of Mehmet the Conqueror, the bazaar grew to cover a vast area as neighbouring shopkeepers decided to put up roofs and porches so that commerce could be conducted comfortably in all weather. Finally, a system of locked gates and doors was provided so that the entire minicity could be closed up tight at the end of the business day.

Before you visit, prepare yourself properly. Make sure you're in a good mood and energised, ready to swap friendly banter with the hundreds of shopkeepers who will attempt to lure you into their establishments.

When you get to the bazaar, leave the main streets for tourists, tuck your guidebook in your daypack, and explore the alleys concentrated around the western end. Peep through doorways to find hidden *hans* (caravanserai), take every sidestreet to dig out those teeny boutiques and workshops. Get dizzy on *çay* (tea), compare price after price and try your hand at the art of bargaining. Allow at least three hours here; some travellers spend three days!

On your wanderings you may pass the crooked **Oriental Kiosk**, and, just north from it up Acı Çeşme Sokak, the gorgeous pink **Zincirli Han**.

BEYAZIT SQUARE & İSTANBUL UNIVERSITY

The Sahaflar Çarşısı (Old Book Bazaar) is next to **Beyazıt Camii** (Mosque of Sultan Beyazıt II; Map pp98–9). Beyazıt specified that an exceptional amount of marble, porphyry, verd antique and rare granite be used in this mosque, which he had built between 1501 and 1506.

The large cobbled square here is officially called Hürriyet Meydanı (Freedom Sq), although everyone knows it simply as Beyazıt. Under the Byzantines this was the Forum of Theodosius, the largest of the city's many

GRAND BAZAAR (KAPALI ÇARŞI)

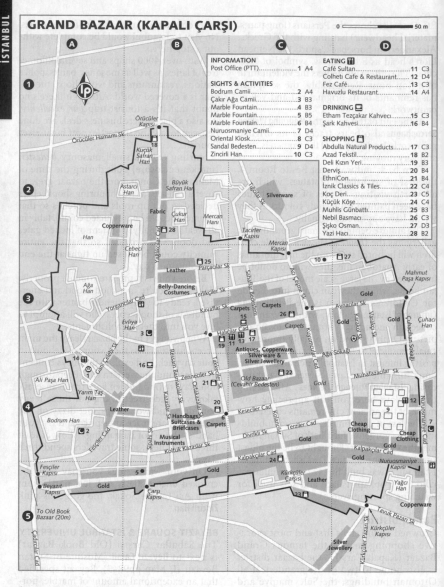

INFORMATION
Post Office (PTT)..................1 A4

SIGHTS & ACTIVITIES
Bodrum Camii........................2 A4
Çakır Ağa Camii.....................3 B3
Marble Fountain....................4 B3
Marble Fountain....................5 B5
Marble Fountain....................6 B4
Nuruosmaniye Camii..............7 D4
Oriental Kiosk......................8 C3
Sandal Bedesten....................9 D4
Zincirli Han.........................10 C3

EATING 🍴
Café Sultan.........................11 C3
Colheti Cafe & Restaurant......12 D4
Fez Café............................13 C3
Havuzlu Restaurant...............14 A4

DRINKING 🍷
Etham Tezçakar Kahvecı..........15 C3
Şark Kahvesi.......................16 B4

SHOPPING 🛍
Abdulla Natural Products........17 C3
Azad Tekstil.......................18 B2
Deli Kızın Yeri.....................19 B3
Derviş...............................20 B4
EthniCon............................21 B4
İznik Classics & Tiles.............22 C4
Koç Deri............................23 C5
Küçük Köşe..........................24 C4
Muhlis Günbattı....................25 B3
Nebil Basmacı......................26 C3
Şişko Osman........................27 D3
Yazi Hacı............................28 B2

---

forums, built by the emperor in AD 393. The square is backed by the impressive portal of İstanbul University.

SÜLEYMANIYE CAMİİ

The **Süleymaniye** (Mosque of Sultan Süleyman the Magnificent; Map pp98-9; Prof Sıddık Sami Onar Caddesi; donation requested) crowns one of the seven hills dominating the Golden Horn and provides a magnificent landmark for the entire city. It was commissioned by the greatest, richest and most powerful of Ottoman sultans, Süleyman the Magnificent (r 1520–66), and was the fourth imperial mosque built in İstanbul.

Although it's not the largest of the Ottoman mosques, the Süleymaniye is certainly the grandest. It was designed by Mimar Sinan, the most famous and talented of all Imperial architects. Although Sinan described the smaller Selimiye Camii in Edirne as his best work, he chose to be buried here in the Süleymaniye complex, probably knowing that this would be the building by which he would be best remembered. His tomb is just outside

---

THE GREAT SİNAN

Sultan Süleyman the Magnificent's reign is known as the golden age of the Ottoman Empire, but it was not only his codification of Ottoman law and military prowess that earned him respect, but also his penchant for embellishing İstanbul with architectural wonders. But Süleyman couldn't have done this without Mimar Sinan (c 1497–1588), Turkey's best-known and greatest architect. Together they perfected the design of the classic Ottoman mosque.

A Sinan mosque has a large forecourt with a central *şadırvan* (ablutions fountain) and domed arcades on three sides. On the fourth side stands the mosque, with a two-storey porch. The main prayer hall is covered by a large central dome rising much higher than the two-storey façade, and surrounded by smaller domes and semidomes.

İstanbul's superb **Süleymaniye Camii** (opposite) is the grandest and most visited work of Sinan's, so if you only have time to visit one of Sinan's masterpieces make this it. The smaller, tile encrusted **Rüstem Paşa Camii** (right) and **Sokollu Mehmet Paşa Camii** (Map pp96–7) are both exquisite, well rewarding anyone who makes the effort to see them.

Sinan did not only design and construct mosques. The **Çemberlitaş Hamamı** (p133) is one of his works, giving you a perfect excuse to blend your architectural studies with a pampering session. He also built the **Baths of Lady Hürrem** (p105) and the **Caferağa Medresesi** (p154).

Sinan's works survive in other towns of the Ottoman heartland, particularly Edirne, the one-time capital of the Empire. Sinan considered that city's **Selimiye Camii** (p167) to be his finest work.

The tomb of Mimar Sinan (Map pp98–9) can be found to the north of the Süleymaniye Camii.

---

the mosque's walled garden in the northern corner.

Inside, the mosque is breathtaking in its size and pleasing in its simplicity. There's little decoration except for some fine İznik tiles in the *mihrab* (niche indicating the direction of Mecca), gorgeous stained-glass windows done by one İbrahim the Drunkard, and four massive columns, one from Baalbek, one from Alexandria and two from Byzantine palaces in İstanbul.

If you are lucky enough to visit when the stairs to the gallery on the northeast side (facing the Golden Horn) are open, make sure you go upstairs to the balcony. The views from this vantage point are spectacular. You can enjoy similar views from the terrace outside.

The *külliye* (mosque complex) of the Süleymaniye, which is outside the walled garden, is particularly elaborate, with the full complement of public services: soup kitchen, hostel, hospital, theological college etc. Today the soup kitchen, with its charming garden courtyard, houses the Darüzziyafe Restaurant. Although a lovely place to enjoy a cup of tea (€0.50), the food was all but inedible on our recent visits. **Lale Bahçesi** (p148), located in a sunken courtyard next to Darüzziyafe, is an atmospheric hang-out for uni students, here for a chat, *çay* and nargileh.

Near the southeast wall of the mosque is its cemetery, home to the **tombs** (☽ 9.30am-4.30pm) of Süleyman and Roxelana. The tile work in both is superb.

RÜSTEM PAŞA CAMİİ

Plonked in the middle of the busy Tahtakale district to the west of the Spice Bazaar, the little-visited **Rüstem Paşa Camii** (Mosque of Rüstem Paşa; Map pp98-9; Hasırcılar Caddesi; donation requested) is an absolute gem. Built in 1560 by Sinan for the son-in-law and grand vizier of Süleyman the Magnificent, it is a showpiece of the best Ottoman architecture and tile work, albeit on a small scale.

At the top of the entry steps there's a terrace and the mosque's colonnaded porch. You'll notice at once the panels of İznik tiles set into the mosque's façade. The interior is covered in similarly gorgeous tiles and features a lovely dome, supported by four tiled pillars.

The preponderance of tiles was Rüstem Paşa's way of signalling his wealth and influence to the world, İznik tiles being particularly expensive and desirable. It may not have assisted his passage into the higher realm, though, because by all accounts he was a loathsome character. His contemporaries dubbed him Kehle-I-Ikbal (the Louse of Fortune) because he was found to be infected with lice before his marriage to Mihrimah, Süleyman's favourite daughter. He is best remembered for plotting with Roxelana to turn Süleyman against his favourite son, Mustafa. They were successful and Mustafa was strangled in 1553 on his father's orders.

The mosque is easy to miss because it's not at street level. Look to the left of the ablutions block on the street and you'll see a stone doorway marked by a silver plaque. A flight of steps next to this leads up to the mosque.

SPICE BAZAAR

Need a herbal love potion or some natural Turkish Viagra? İstanbul's **Spice Bazaar** (Mısır Çarşısı, Egyptian Market; Map pp98-9; 8.30am-6.30pm Mon-Sat) is the place to find them, although we wouldn't vouch for the efficacy of either! The market was constructed in the 1660s as part of the Yeni Cami complex, the rents from the shops going to support the upkeep of the mosque and its charitable activities. It was called the Egyptian Market because it was famous for selling goods shipped in from Cairo.

As well as *baharat* (spices), nuts, honeycomb and olive-oil soaps, the bustling spice bazaar sells truckloads of *incir* (figs), *lokum* (Turkish delight) and fruit pressed into sheets and *pestil* (dried). Although the number of shops selling tourist trinkets increases annually, this is still a great place to stock up on edible souvenirs, share a few jokes with the vendors and marvel at the well-preserved building. Make sure you visit shop number 41, the atmospheric **Mehmet Kalmaz Baharatçı**, which specialises in henna, teats, potions, lotions and the Sultan's very own aphrodisiac. Most of the shops offer vacuum packaging which makes getting souvenirs home easy.

This is also the place to come to try some of Turkey's cheeses. Erzincan's famous *tulum* cheeses are sold here; look for the hairy goat skin (see p70). The bazaar is also home to one of the city's oldest restaurants, Pandeli (p142).

YENİ CAMİ

Only in İstanbul would a 400-year-old mosque be called 'New'. The **Yeni Cami** (New Mosque; Map pp96-7; Yenicami Meydanı Sokak, Eminönü; donation requested) was begun in 1597, commissioned by Valide Sultan Safiye, mother of Sultan Mehmet III (r 1595–1603). Safiye lost her august position when her son the sultan died, and the mosque was completed six sultans later in 1663 by Turhan Hadice, mother of Sultan Mehmet IV (r 1648–87).

In plan, the Yeni Cami is much like the Blue Mosque and the Süleymaniye Camii, with a large forecourt and square sanctuary surmounted by a series of semidomes crowned by a grand dome. The interior is richly decorated with gold, coloured İznik tiles and carved marble, and has an impressive *mihrab*.

In the courtyard near the Spice Bazaar is the **tomb of Valide Sultan Turhan Hadice**. Buried with her are no fewer than six sultans, including her son Mehmet IV.

GALATA BRIDGE

Nothing is quite as evocative as walking across the Galata Bridge (Map pp96–7). At sunset, when the Galata Tower is surrounded by the silhouettes of shrieking seagulls and the mosques atop the seven hills of the city are thrown into relief against a soft red-pink sky, it is spectacularly beautiful. During the day, it carries a constant flow of İstanbullus crossing between Beyoğlu and Eminönü, a long line of hopeful anglers trailing their lines into the waters below and a constantly changing procession of street vendors hawking everything from fresh-baked *simit* to Rolex rip-offs.

Underneath the bridge, fish restaurants and cafés on its lower level serve drinks and food all day. Come here to inhale the evocative scent of apple tobacco wisping out from the nargileh cafés and to watch the passing parade of ferry traffic plying the waters. The eateries below the bridge are much of a muchness, and frankly shameless tourist traps, but the treat of having a meal or a late afternoon beer here and soaking up the views is worth the cultural cringe.

This bridge was built in 1994 to replace an iron structure dating from around 1910, which in turn had replaced three earlier structures. The 1910 bridge was famous for its seedy fish restaurants, tea houses and nargileh joints that occupied the dark recesses beneath its roadway, but it had a major flaw: it floated on pontoons that blocked the natural flow of water and kept the Golden Horn from flushing out pollution. In 1992 the iron bridge was damaged by fire and dragged up the Golden

Horn to RIP; you pass it on the ferry on the way to Eyüp.

Beyoğlu & Around

The suburb of Beyoğlu (*bey*-oh-loo) rises from the shoreline north of the Galata Bridge, and incorporates both Taksim Sq and the grand boulevard, İstiklal Caddesi. By the mid-19th century it was known as Pera, the 'European' quarter of town, home to diplomats and traders, and buzzing with the latest European fashions, European-style patisseries, restaurants, boutiques and embassies all built following the European architectural style of the day. Beyoğlu had telephones, electric light and the one of the first electric tramways in the world, the Tünel.

However all this changed in the decades after the Republic when the embassies moved to the country's new capital, Ankara, the glamorous shops and restaurants closed, the grand buildings crumbled, and Beyoğlu took on a decidedly sleazy air. Fortunately the '90s brought about a rebirth. Beyoğlu is once again the heart of modern İstanbul, ground-zero for galleries, cafés and boutiques, with hip new restaurants opening almost nightly, and more bars then a bar-hopper could hope to prop at in a lifetime. Beyoğlu is a showcase of cosmopolitan Turkey at its best – miss Beyoğlu and you haven't seen İstanbul.

The best way to experience Beyoğlu is to spend an afternoon or day exploring by foot. You can walk across the Galata Bridge from Eminönü and up through Galata, the city's historic Genoese neighbourhood, and along heaving İstiklal Caddesi to Taksim Sq (from where you can catch the T4 bus back to Sultanahmet if you wish). All up it's a walk of two to three hours allowing for breaks along the way.

GALATA TOWER

The **Galata Tower** (Galata Kulesi; Map pp100-1; Galata Meydanı, Karaköy; admission €5.50; ☺ 9am-8pm), originally constructed in 1348, was the highest point in the Genoese fortifications of Galata and has been rebuilt many times. It has survived several earthquakes, as well as the demolition of the rest of the Genoese walls in the mid-19th century. Today it holds a forgettable restaurant/nightclub but a pleasant cafeteria on the 8th floor where you can enjoy a drink (tea €0.80, beer €3). There's also a vertiginous panorama balcony offering spectacular 360-degree views of the city.

MEVLEVİ MONASTERY

The **Museum of Court Literature** (Divan Edebiyatı Müzesi; Map pp100-1; ☎ 0212-245 4141; Galipdede Caddesi 15, Tünel; admission €2; ☺ 9.30am-4.30pm Wed-Mon), in the Mevlevi Monastery, is one of only a

---

SEEING THE DERVISHES WHIRL

The Mevlevi have always welcomed all who wished to witness the *sema* (ceremony), including foreign, non-Muslim visitors. Although banned for a short period in the 1920s by Atatürk, the tradition remained strong and continues today.

There are a growing number of opportunities in İstanbul to see the dervishes whirl, but frankly most of them are little more than tourist shows. The best place to see an authentic *sema*, where a handful of travellers join local followers in this spiritual rite, is in one of the few practicing *tekke* in İstanbul at Fatih, some 4km west of Sultanahmet. It's usually only on Monday nights and it's best to come here with a local escort. You could ask at your hotel, or Les Arts Turcs (see p135) takes travellers from their studio, after giving them a one-hour information session about Sufism and the ceremony (€22).

The second-best option is at the Museum of Court Literature (see above), where *semas* (tickets €14; ☺ 5pm Sat & Sun May-Sep, 3pm 1st & last Sat of month Oct-Apr) last for 90 minutes, starting with a live performance of Sufi music. It's a good idea to buy tickets from the monastery a few days beforehand as the shows are often booked out. Make sure you arrive early and enter the *tekke* (dervish lodge) as soon as the door is opened so that you can get a seat. The best seats are those near the rear windows, on the opposite side to the entrance.

There is also a **performance** (☎ 0212-458 8834; tickets adult/student €17/14; ☺ 7.30pm Wed, Fri & Sun) in the atmospheric exhibition hall on platform 1 at Sirkeci Train Station in Sultanahmet.

Remember that the ceremony is a religious one – by whirling the adherents believe that they are attaining a higher union with God – so don't talk, leave your seat or take flash photographs while the dervishes are spinning. For more information on the whirling dervishes, see p486.

handful of functioning *tekkes* (dervish lodges) remaining in İstanbul. It's a slightly run-down compound and is really only worth visiting if you're here to see the *sema* (ceremony; see p119 for details), and/or you feel like catching respite from the hubbub of Beyoğlu in the pleasant, shady gardens.

As you approach the *tekke*, notice the grave-yard on the left and its stones with graceful Ottoman inscriptions. The shapes atop the stones reflect the headgear of the deceased, each hat denoting a different religious rank. The tomb of Galip Dede, the 17th century Sufi poet who gave his name to the street, lies here.

Inside the *semahane* (ceremonial hall), the central area is for the whirling *sema* (ceremony), while the galleries above were for visitors. Separate areas were set aside for the orchestra and for female visitors (behind the lattices). These days, the upstairs is only for the musicians who play during the ceremony. In the display cases surrounding the central area there are exhibits of Mevlevi calligraphy, writing and musical instruments.

İSTANBUL MODERN

Opened in 2004, **İstanbul Modern** (İstanbul Modern Sanat Müzesi; Map pp100-1; ☎ 0212-334 7300; www.istanbul modern.org; Meclis-i Mebusan Caddesi, Fındıklı; admission €4, free admission Thu; ◷ 10am-6pm Tue & Wed, 10am-8pm Thu, 10am-6pm Fri-Sun) is an excellent introduction to contemporary art in Turkey.

The collection is small but well curated, with everything from the photography of Ara Güler to Eren Eyüboğlu and Fikret Mualla. The 1st floor hosts permanent exhibits, while the ground floor shows largely international touring works, retrospectives and photography. There's a well-stocked shop, a **cinema** that shows arthouse films and a really great-looking café-restaurant with superb views of the Bosphorus. Allow at least an hour.

İSTIKLAL CADDESİ

Stretching from Tünel Sq to Taksim Sq, in the late 19th century **İstiklal Caddesi** (Independence Ave; Map pp100-1) was known as the Grande Rue de Pera, carrying the life of the modern city up and down its lively promenade. It's still the life and soul of the party and a stroll along its length is a must. Come between 4pm and 8pm daily – especially on Friday and Saturday – and you'll see İstiklal at its busiest best.

About half-way along İstiklal Caddesi is the **Galatasaray Lycée** (Map pp100-1), founded in 1868 by Sultan Abdülaziz as a school where students were taught in French, as well as Turkish. Today it's a prestigious public school.

Closeby is the famous **Çiçek Pasajı** (Flower Passage; Map pp100-1). When the *Orient Express* rolled into Old Stamboul and prom-enading down İstiklal Caddesi was all the rage the Cité de Pera building was the most glamorous address in town. Built in 1876 and decorated in Second Empire style, it housed a shopping arcade as well as apartments. As Pera declined, so too did the building, its styl-ish shops giving way to florists and then *mey-hanes* where enthusiastic revellers caroused the night away. In the late 1970s parts of the building collapsed; once rebuilt, the passage was 'beautified' and its raffish charm was lost. These days locals bypass the touts and the mediocre food on offer here and make their way behind the passage to İstanbul's most col-ourful and popular eating precinct, **Nevizade Sokak** (see the boxed text, p146).

Next to the Çiçek Pasajı you'll find Şahne Sokak and Beyoğlu's **Balık Pazar** (Fish Market), with stalls selling fruit, vegetables, pickles and other produce. Leading off the Balık Pazar you'll find the neoclassical **Avrupa Pasajı** (European Passage), a small gallery with marble paving and shops selling tourist wares and some antique goods; and **Aslıhan Pasajı**, a two-storey arcade bursting with second-hand books.

TAKSİM SQUARE

The symbolic heart of modern İstanbul, this busy square (Map pp100-1) is named after the stone *taksim* (reservoir) on its western side, once part of the city's old water-conduit system. The main water line from the Belgrade Forest, north of the city, was laid to this point in 1732 by Sultan Mahmut I (r 1730–54). Branch lines then led from the *taksim* to other parts of the city.

Hardly a triumph of urban design, the square is a bit of a chaotic mess. At its western end, the İstiklal Caddesi tram circumnavigates the **Cumhuriyet Anıtı** (Republic Monument), created by an Italian architect-sculptor team in 1928. It features Atatürk, his assistant and successor İsmet İnönü and other revolutionary leaders.

On the square's north side is the hectic bus terminus (where you can catch the T4 to Sultanahmet); on its east the **Atatürk Cul-**

tural **Centre**, and the west, the Marmara hotel (p140). In the middle is the metro running up to Levent 4, and the funicular tram running down to Kabataş.

ASKERI MÜZESİ (MILITARY MUSEUM)

For a rousing experience, present yourself at this splendid **Military Museum** (Map pp94-5; ☎ 0212-233 2720; Vali Konağı Caddesi, Harbiye; adult/student €3/1.50; ☑ 9am-5pm Wed-Sun), 1km north of Taksim.

The museum is spread over two very large floors. On the ground floor are displays of medieval weapons and armour, military uniforms, and glass cases holding battle standards, both Turkish and captured. Some of the most interesting exhibits are the *sayebanlar* (imperial pavilions). These luxurious cloth shelters, heavily worked with fine silver and gold thread, jewels, precious silks and elegant tracery, were the battle headquarters for sultans during the summer campaign season.

Our favourite exhibit is a length of the chain that the Byzantines stretched across the Golden Horn in the fateful siege of 1453. For military memorabilia, only a plank from the Trojan horse could beat that!

The upper floor has displays on WWI and the War of Independence, including a hall devoted to Atatürk.

The easiest way to get to the museum is to walk up Cumhuriyet Caddesi from Taksim Sq. This will take around 15 minutes. Alternatively, take any bus heading up Cumhuriyet Caddesi from Taksim Sq. Try to visit in the afternoon so that you can enjoy the concert given by the Mehter, the medieval Ottoman Military Band, which occurs between 3pm and 4pm daily.

Beşiktaş & Ortaköy
DOLMABAHÇE PALACE

These days it's fashionable for critics influenced by the form-is-function aesthetic to sneer at buildings such as **Dolmabahçe Palace** (Dolmabahçe Sarayı; Map pp94-5; ☎ 0212-236 9000; Dolmabahçe Caddesi, Beşiktaş; admission selamlık only €8.50, harem-cariyeler only €7, selamlık & harem-cariyeler €12, crystal palace & clock museum €3; ☑ 9am-4pm Tue-Wed & Fri-Sun). Enthusiasts for Ottoman heritage also decry this flourish of the imperial dynasty, finding it shares more in common with the Paris Opera than Topkapı Palace. But whatever the critics may say, judging by the queues the 19th-century imperial residence is a clear crowd favourite.

More is less was certainly *not* the philosophy of Sultan Abdül Mecit, who, deciding that it was time to give lie to talk of Ottoman military and financial decline, decided to move from Topkapı to a lavish new palace on the shores of the Bosphorus. For a site he chose the *dolma bahçe* (filled-in garden) where a predecessor Sultan Ahmet I (r 1607–17) had built an imperial pleasure kiosk surrounded by gardens. In 1843 Abdül Mecit commissioned architects Nikoğos and Garabed Balyan to construct an Ottoman–European palace that would impress everyone who set eyes on it. Construction was completed in 1856. Traditional Ottoman palace architecture was rejected in favour of baroque and neoclassical. Eschewing pavilions, the palace turns in on itself – sadly, given what might have been splendid Bosphorus views. But clearly nothing was to detract from the palace's extravagant interior.

The palace, which is set in well-tended gardens and entered through an ornate gate, is divided into two sections, the over-the-top **selamlık** (ceremonial suites) and the slightly more restrained **harem-cariyeler** (harem and concubines' quarters). You must take a guided tour to see either section (*selamlık* half-hour tour, *harem-cariyeler*, one hour tour). If you only have enough time for one tour, be sure to make it the *selamlık*. Tours are in English and Turkish.

At the end of your tour, make sure you visit the **Crystal Palace**, with its fairy tale–like conservatory featuring etched-glass windows, crystal fountain and myriad chandeliers. There's even a crystal piano and chair. It's next to the aviary on the street side of the palace.

Finally, don't set your watch by any of the palace clocks, all of them stopped at 9.05am, the moment at which Atatürk died in Dolmabahçe on 10 November 1938. When touring the harem you will be shown the quarters he used when he spent time here. Most restrained by Dolmabahçe standards.

The tourist entrance to the palace is near the ornate **clock tower** built by Sultan Abdül Hamit II in 1890–94. There is an outdoor café near here with premium Bosphorus views.

If you want to visit Beylerbeyi Sarayı (see p129) on the Asian shore after the Dolmabahçe, you can take a **guided tour** (☎ 0212-296 5240; tour €30; 9am from the Dolmabahçe summer only, book ahead), which includes a return crossing of the Bosphorus in a replica of an imperial caïque.

DENİZ MÜZESİ

Although this **museum** (Naval Museum; Map pp94-5; ☎ 0212-261 0040; cnr Cezayir & Beşiktaş Caddesi, Beşiktaş; adult/student €2/1; ☒ 9am-12.30pm & 1.30-5pm Wed-Sun) is picturesquely situated on the Bosphorus shore, most landlubbers (including us) find it a tad dull. Compasses, guns, ensigns, model ships, yada yada. Still, those of the naval persuasion will no doubt feel like dropping anchor here for an hour or so.

Those with a particular interest in things military may also be pleased to know that if they come out of the museum and walk straight down to the shore they'll find a line of dolmuşes waiting to run them straight to the Military Museum in Harbiye.

To get here, catch the T4 bus from Sultanahmet to Dolmabahçe and walk the last 10 minutes; or take 40T from Taksim Sq and alight in Beşiktaş.

YILDIZ PARK

A pretty, leafy oasis alive with birds and picnickers, **Yıldız Park** (Yıldız Parkı; Map pp94-5; Çırağan Caddesi; admission free) is the place to come if you need to escape İstanbul's hullabaloo. Once the imperial gardens of nearby Çırağan Palace, it has two grandiose *köşkü* (pavilions), where the sultans could enjoy their surrounds in style, and another Ottoman-European palace, Yıldız Şale.

If you enter from the main entrance, at Çırağan Caddesi, walk 10 minutes up the steep main road to the T intersection at the top. Turn left for the **Çadır Köşkü**. Built between 1865 and 1870, this ornate kiosk is now a low-key café beside a lake.

Turn right at the T intersection to find the entrance to **Yıldız Şale** (Yıldız Chalet Museum; Map pp94-5; ☎ 0212-259 4570; admission €3; ☒ 9.30am-5pm Tue-Wed & Fri-Sun Apr-Oct, to 4pm Nov-May). Sultan Abdül Hamit II (r 1876-1909) didn't allow himself to be upstaged by his predecessors. He built his own fancy chalet here in 1882, expanded it in 1898 for a state visit by Kaiser Wilhelm II of Germany. As you enter, a guide will approach and give you a half-hour tour. Although the chalet isn't as plush as Dolmabahçe, it's a lot less crowded.

Around 500m past the turn-off to Yıldız Şale you'll come to the **Malta Köşkü** (Map pp94-5; ☎ 0212-258 9453; mains €8.50-10; ☒ 9am-10.30pm). Built in 1870, this was where Abdül Hamit imprisoned the deposed Murat V and his family. With its views of the Bosphorus, the terrace café here is a great place for a light lunch.

If you come to the park by taxi, have it take you up the steep slope to Yıldız Şale; you can visit the other kiosks on the walk down. A taxi from Sultanahmet to the top of the hill should cost around €5.

ORTAKÖY CAMII

Ortaköy (Middle Village; Map pp94-5) is a charming waterside suburb with church, synagogue and mosque surrounding a jumble of Ottoman buildings renovated as stylish boutiques, bars and eateries. On balmy nights the restaurants and cafés lining the teeny cobbled square by the water overflow with locals enjoying tea, a fish meal and some of the city's best people-watching.

Right on the water's edge, the decorative **Ortaköy Camii** (Büyük Mecidiye Camii) is the work of Nikoğos Balyan, one of the architects of Dolmabahçe Palace. A strange mix of baroque and neoclassical influences, it was designed and built for Sultan Abdül Mecit III in 1853-55. With the supermodern Bosphorus Bridge looming behind it, the mosque provides the classic photo opportunity for those wanting to illustrate İstanbul's 'old meets new' character. On the Bosphorus Bridge side of the mosque is an excellent (by İstanbul standards) children's playground and a handful of second-hand book stalls (with titles in English, German and French).

Try to time your visit for Sunday, when the bustling street market fills the cobbled lanes. Early risers make it for breakfast, then pick through the market's beaded jewellery, hats, and other crafty trinkets, before heading home around midday to avoid the afternoon traffic crush. See p145 for our favourite eating picks.

To get here catch bus Nos DT1, 40, 40T from Taksim Sq or bus No 25E from Eminönü (get off at the Kabataş Lisesi bus stop). If you're coming from Sultanahmet, you could catch the tram to Kabataş, and then jump on bus No 25E or catch a taxi (€3) the rest of the way to Ortaköy.

Golden Horn

In Byzantine times the Golden Horn provided a perfect natural harbour for the city's commerce, with fresh vegetables, fruit and grains sold in markets along the water's edge. At the height of the Ottoman Empire, the northern shore was used for pleasure and business. **Aynalıkavak Kasrı** (Map pp94–5) was an imperial lodge built as a rural retreat for the Sultans, while the area around Kasımpaşa and Hasköy became the Empire's docklands, arsenal, foundry and admiralty. The shorelines were dotted with villages and gardens, home to thriving Jewish and Greek neighbourhoods.

By the mid-20th century, however, the villages had merged, the forests were lost and the water had silted to become a forgotten, polluted waterway. It wasn't until the old Galata Bridge was replaced with a new one in 1994 that the pollution could be properly addressed, with parklands planted along its length and surrounding neighbourhoods on the road to recovery. The small local ferry that travels up its length is the best way to explore the Golden Horn (see p124). Some travellers find exploring this delightful little-visited pocket of İstanbul is a highlight of their visit.

FENER & BALAT

Once wealthy Greek and Jewish neighbourhoods, since the Republic, Fener and Balat had been left to decay. Recently, Unesco offered a grant to help restore these districts that harbour some of central İstanbul's last remaining traditional residential streets. These two interesting old suburbs are well worth a couple of hours of backstreet exploration.

The **Ecumenical Orthodox Patriarchate** (Map pp94–5; ☎ 0212-531 9670/6; Sadrazam Ali Paşa Caddesi, Fener; ⏰ 9am-5pm) is home to the Ecumenical patriarch. He is the ceremonial head of the Orthodox Church, though most of the churches in Greece, Cyprus, Russia, Romania and other countries have their own patriarchs or archbishops who are independent of İstanbul. Nevertheless, the symbolic importance of the patriarchate, here in the city that saw the great era of Byzantine and Orthodox influence, is considerable. After the conquest of Constantinople, the patriarchate moved from the buildings it used in Aya Sofya and finally found a home here around 1600. The Church of St George, inside the compound, dates from around 1730, and is well worth seeing. Every weekend busloads of pilgrims come for the Sunday morning divine literature.

Right on the waterfront near the Patriarchate stands one of the city's most intriguing architectural curiosities: the Gothic Revival cast-iron **Church of St Stephen of the Bulgars** (Map pp94–5). This was constructed in Vienna, then shipped down the Danube and assembled here in 1898. It's not normally open to visitors, but if you stand at the gates, the caretaker will usually invite you in (well worth the effort). A donation is appreciated.

Les Arts Turcs (p135) and Istamboul Insolite (p135) run informative walking tours of these suburbs.

HASKÖY & SÜTLÜCE

The suburbs of Hasköy and Sütlüce on the northern shore of the Golden Horn are home to two attractions: Rahmi M Koç Müzesi and Miniatürk. If you're coming by the Golden Horn ferry, the closest stop to both sights is Sütlüce.

Miniatürk

To be frank, we're at an absolute loss as to why this **theme park** (Map pp94–5; ☎ 0212-222 2882; İmrahor Caddesi, Sütlüce; admission adult/child or student €4/2; ⏰ 9am-6pm) has been such an enormous hit with locals. Marketed as a miniature park that showcases 'all times and locations of Anatolia at the same place at the same time', it's a cheesy tiny town stocked with models of Turkey's great buildings – everything from the Celsus Library at Ephesus to Atatürk International Airport – set in manicured lawns dotted with fake rocks blasting a distorted recording of the Turkish national anthem. Children are disappointed with the models as they have to look from a distance but the miniature train that traverses the paths and the (none-too-safe) playground equipment is some recompense. Visit with tongue firmly in cheek.

The museum is about a 20-minute walk north of the Sütlüce ferry stop.

Rahmi M Koç Müzesi

This slick **museum** (Rahmi M Koç Industrial Museum; Map pp94–5; ☎ 0212-369 6602; www.rmk-museum.org.tr; Hasköy Caddesi 27; adult/child or student €4/2; ⏰ 10am-5pm Tue-Fri, 10am-7pm Sat & Sun) was founded by the head of the Koç industrial group to exhibit artefacts from İstanbul's industrial past. Its collection is highly eclectic, giving the impression of being a grab-bag of cool stuff collected over the decades or stuff that has been donated to the museum by individuals, organisations or companies at a loss as to what else to do with it. This might sound as if we're damning the place with faint praise, but this is certainly not

İSTANBUL

the case. In fact, this is a corker of a museum that children in particular will love.

The museum is in two superbly restored sections: a historic docklands by the Golden Horn and a one-time Ottoman foundry opposite. Exhibits are largely concerned with forms of transport: a horse-drawn tram; an Amphicar (half car, half boat) that crossed the English Channel in 1962; Sultan Abdül Aziz's ornate railway coach; cars (everything from ugly Turkish Anadol models to fabulous pink Cadillacs); and a 1960 Messerschmitt. Other exhibits look at how appliances work and illustrate mechanical principles – young children in particular will love the levers, buttons and pulleys of these hands-on exhibits.

On weekends the historic Liman II tugboat takes 40-minute tours of the Golden Horn (ticket €5.50) at 1pm, 2.30pm, 4pm and 5.30pm.

Unlike most of the city's museums, wheelchair access is offered throughout the complex and excellent interpretive panels in Turkish and English are provided. A private guide costs €25. There are two excellent restaurants (Halat restaurant, overlooking the Golden Horn, is the perfect spot for lunch), a café and a bar. The submarine exhibit, from which children under eight years of age are barred, requires an extra ticket (€2.50/1.50).

The museum is a 10-minute walk southeast of the Sütlüce ferry stop.

EYÜP

The conservative district of Eyüp is named after Ayub Ansari, a standard-bearer to the Prophet and a revered member of Islam's early leadership. His tomb by the **Eyüp Sultan Camii** (Mosque of the Great Eyüp; Map pp94-5; Camii Kebir Sokak, Eyüp; admission by donation; ☉ tomb 9.30am-4.30pm) makes this complex an extremely sacred place for Muslims, ranking fourth after the big three: Mecca, Medina and Jerusalem. Don't miss the richly decorated tomb, but make sure you observe Islamic proprieties when visiting (note how pilgrims exit by walking backwards so they don't turn their back on Ayub Ansari). You should avoid visiting on Friday or on other Muslim holy days.

The original mosque built by Mehmet the Conqueror, just five years after the Conquest, was where Ottoman princes came to gird the Sword of Osman before their accession to the throne. The mosque you see today was built by Sultan Selim III in 1800. It's a popular place for boys to visit on the day of their circumcision.

A cemetery meanders up the hill behind the mosque. Follow the path cutting up through the cemetery (or catch the cable car, north of the mosque) to the famous **Pierre Loti Café**, where the famous French novelist is said to have come for inspiration. And who could blame him? The views over the Golden Horn are magnificent.

GETTING THERE & AWAY

Ferries run from Üsküdar, via Karaköy and Eminönü, all the way up the Golden Horn to Eyüp. Ferries stop at Kasımpaşa, Fener, Balat, Ayvansaray, Sütlüce and Eyüp. The first ferries leave Eminönü at 7.50am, 8.50am then hourly until 6.50pm and 8.05pm. To find the tiny ferry station at Eminönü, walk down the path between the Eminönü bus stand and the huge Stork Zyndan Restaurant.

Going the other way, the first from Eyüp leaves at 7.30am then hourly until 4.40pm, then 5.35pm, 6.30pm and 7.45pm. On weekends the late services may differ slightly – check the timetable. Consider hopping on and off the ferry, visiting sights along the way.

You can also catch buses along both shores of the Golden Horn. Buses 399B/C/D from Eminönü or bus Nos 55T and 55ET from Taksim Sq run via Fener and Balat to Eyüp. Bus 47 from Eminönü and 54HT from Taksim Sq run via the sights in Hasköy and Sütlüce (the northern shore).

Western Districts

Broadly described as the district between the city walls and Sultanahmet, this old part of İstanbul was once dotted with the churches of Byzantium. While most of the churches have been converted to mosques, and many of the houses are tumble-down or have been razed for ugly apartment blocks, a few hours' exploration in this area will give you a taste of work-a-day İstanbul. There are several sights worth visiting if you have the time, but the Kariye Müzesi is a must for any visit to İstanbul.

AQUEDUCT OF VALENS

It's not certain that the aqueduct (Map pp98-9) was constructed by the Emperor Valens (r 364–78), though we do know it was repaired in 1019, in later times by several sultans, and in the late 1980s. It's thought that the aqueduct carried water over this valley to a cistern at Beyazıt Sq before finally ending up at the Basilica Cistern and the Great Byzantine Palace. After the Conquest it supplied the Eski (Old) and Topkapı Palaces with water.

ZEYREK CAMİİ

Originally part of an important Byzantine sanctuary comprising two churches, a chapel and a monastery is **Zeyrek Camii** (Church of the Pantocrator; Map pp98-9; İbadethane Sokak). The monastery is long gone and the northernmost church is derelict, but the southern church, built by Empress Eirene before her death in AD 1124 (she features in a mosaic at Aya Sofya with Emperor John II Comnenus), still has some features intact, including a magnificent mosaic floor. It and the attached chapel, built by John II, now function as a mosque. Outside prayer times a caretaker is usually available to show visitors around and will gratefully accept a donation in return. Ask him to open the trapdoor in the floor to reveal part of the mosaic floor. The mosque and the crumbling but charming houses in the surrounding streets are Unesco World Heritage listed – it's a great spot for a wander.

The Ottoman building to the east houses the **Zeyrekhane** restaurant (p146).

After you've visited Zeyrek, a very pleasant 15-minute walk can take you along a length of the Aqueduct of Valens northwest to Fatih Camii.

FATIH CAMİİ

This **mosque** (Mosque of the Conqueror; Map pp98-9; Fevzi Paşa Caddesi, Fatih), 750m northwest of the historic Aqueduct of Valens, was the first great imperial mosque to be built in İstanbul. Set in extensive grounds, the mosque complex was enormous and included 15 charitable establishments – religious schools, a hospice for travellers, a caravanserai and more. The mosque was finished in 1470 but was destroyed by an earthquake, rebuilt and then burnt down in 1782. What you see today dates from the reign of Abdül Hamit I (r 1774–89).

Be sure to look at the fine **tomb of the Conqueror** (9.30am-4.30pm Tue-Sun) in the cemetery behind the mosque, though Mehmet is actually buried under the *mimber* in the mosque itself.

On Wednesday both the courtyard and the surrounding streets host a huge mar-

ket selling fresh produce and clothing. This is the best time to visit; at other times you may find the 18th-century mosque relatively unimpressive.

KARIYE MÜZESI

Many visitors to İstanbul are amazed to discover that one of the highlights of their trip, the extraordinary **Kariye Müzesi** (Map pp94-5; ☎ 0212-631 9241; Kariye Camii Sokak, Edirnekapı; admission €5.50; 9am-4.30pm Thu-Tue, until 6.30pm Jun-Oct), is tucked away in the little-visited western districts of the city.

The original name of this building was Chora Church, or the Church of the Holy Saviour Outside the Walls, but what you see today is not the first church-outside-the-walls on this site. Rather, this one was built in the late 11th century, with repairs, restructuring and conversion to a mosque in the succeeding centuries. Virtually all of the interior decoration dates from 1312 and was funded by Theodore Metochites, a poet and man of letters who was auditor of the treasury under Emperor Andronikos II (r 1282–1328). One of the museum's most wonderful mosaics, found above the door to the nave in the inner narthex, depicts Theodore offering the church to Christ.

The mosaics, which depict the lives of Christ and Mary, are simply stunning. Look out for the Deesis, which shows Christ and Mary with two donors: Prince Isaac Komnenos and Melane, daughter of Mikhael Palaiologos VIII. This is under the right dome in the inner narthex. On the dome itself is a wonderful depiction of Jesus and his ancestors *(the Genealogy of Christ)*. On the narthex's left dome is a serenely beautiful mosaic of Mary and the Child Jesus surrounded by her ancestors.

In the nave are three mosaics: of Christ; of Mary and the child Jesus; and of the Dormition (Assumption) of the Blessed Virgin – turn around to see this as it's over the main door you just entered. The 'infant' being held by Jesus is actually Mary's soul.

To the right of the nave is the Pareclesion, a side chapel built to hold the tombs of the church's founder and his relatives, close friends and associates. It is decorated with frescoes that equal the mosaics in quality and depict Old Testament scenes.

The Kariye is one of the city's best museums and deserves an extended visit. On leaving, we highly recommend sampling the delectable Ottoman menu at the Asitane restaurant (p146), which is in the basement of the next-door Kariye Oteli. Alternatively, a *peynirli tost* (toasted cheese sandwich, €3) or Turkish coffee (€2) can be enjoyed at the Kariye Pembe Köşk in the plaza overlooking the museum.

Finally, a plea: despite signs clearly prohibiting the use of flashes in the museum, many visitors wilfully ignore this rule. Please don't do the same – the future of these exquisite and delicate mosaics and frescoes is at stake.

To get here, catch bus Nos 28 or 36KE from Eminönü or bus No 87 from Taksim Sq to Edirnekapı. A taxi from Sultanahmet should cost €4, from Taksim €5.

YEDİKULE & THE CITY WALLS

Yedikule Hisarı (Fortress of the Seven Towers; Map pp94-5; ☎ 0212-585 8933; Kule Meydanı 4, Yedikule; admission €2), looming over the old city's southern approaches, has a history as impressive as its massive structure.

In the late 4th century Theodosius I built a triumphal arch here. When the next Theodosius (r 408–50) built his great land walls, he incorporated the arch into it. Four of the fortress' seven towers were built as part of Theodosius II's walls; the other three, which are inside the walls, were added by Mehmet the Conqueror. Under the Byzantines, the great arch became known as the **Golden Gate** and was used for triumphal state processions into and out of the city. For a time, its gates were indeed plated with gold.

In Ottoman times the fortress was used for defence, and as a repository for the imperial treasury, a prison and a place of execution. After the Republic, Yedikule was neglected, becoming an overgrown green oasis, complete with goat herd. Recent renovations have disappointingly replaced the leafy greenery with acres of gravel. Still, the views from the battlements are the highlight of any visit.

It's possible to spend a day walking on top of or beside the walls all the way from Yedikule to Ayvansaray on the Golden Horn (6.5km), wandering past the late-13th-century **Tekfur Sarayı** (Palace of the Sovereign, Palace of Constantine Porphyrogenetus; Map pp94-5; Hocaçakır Caddesi) on the way. Be warned, though, that the walls are in a bad condition in many spots and go through some less-than-salubrious neighbourhoods. Don't consider doing this walk by yourself.

Yedikule is a long way from most other İstanbul sights and involves a special trip. Situated where the great city walls meet the Sea of Marmara, it's easily accessible by train from Sirkeci or Cankurtaran (the closest stop to Sultanahmet). Hop off the train at Yedikule (15 minutes), turn left as you come out of the station and walk about 500m to the entrance of the fortress.

You can also take bus 80 from Eminönü (these run approximately every 40 minutes) or bus 80T from Taksim (approximately every 25 minutes). The bus stop is across from the small park in front of the castle.

Asian Shore
ÜSKÜDAR

Üsküdar (*oo*-skoo-dar) is the Turkish form of the name Scutari. The first colonists lived in Chalcedon (now Kadıköy), to the south, and Chrysopolis (now Üsküdar) became its first major offshoot; both towns existed about two decades before Byzantium was founded. It soon became clear that the harbour at Chrysopolis was superior to Chalcedon and, as Byzantium blossomed, Chrysopolis outgrew Chalcedon to become the largest suburb on the Asian shore. Unwalled and therefore vulnerable, it became part of the Ottoman Empire at least 100 years before the Conquest.

Today Üsküdar is a bustling suburb with a handful of B-list sights worth seeing if you have a spare half-day. If you feel like a bite to eat, pop into the famous **Kanaat Lokantası** (Map pp94-5; ☎ 0216-553 3791; Selmanı Pak Caddesi 25; mains €6-9), offering some of İstanbul's best traditional meals. It's in the street behind the Ağa Camii.

Kız Kulesi

İstanbul is a maritime city, so it's appropriate that the **Kız Kulesi** (Maiden's Tower; Map pp94-5; ☎ 0216-342 4747; www.kizkulesi.com.tr; ⌚ noon-7pm Tue-Sun), one of its most distinctive landmarks, is on the water. Arriving at Üsküdar by ferry, you'll notice the squat tower on a tiny island to the south, just off the Asian mainland. In ancient times a predecessor of the current 18th-century structure functioned as a tollbooth and defence point; the Bosphorus could be closed off by means of a chain stretching from here to Seraglio Point. Some think its ancient pedigree goes back even further, referring to it as Leander's Tower after the tragic youth who drowned after attempting to swim across a strait to Europe to visit his lover, Hero (a story more usually associated with the Gallipoli peninsula). More recently, the tower featured in the 1999 Bond film *The World is Not Enough*.

The tower is open to the public during the day as a café. At night it functions as a pricey **restaurant** (☎ 0216-342 4747; ⏰ 8.30pm-1am Tue-Sun) serving a set menu (about €50 per person excluding drinks) with folk music or DJs, depending on the night. Small boats run from Salacak to the tower every 15 minutes from noon to 1am Tuesday to Sunday for €3 return. There are boats from Ortaköy at 1pm, 3pm and 5pm (€3.50); guests booking for dinner can catch a boat from Kabataş at 8.30pm, returning at 11.15pm or 12.15am.

Mosques

Judging that Scutari was the closest point in İstanbul to Mecca, many powerful Ottoman figures built mosques here to assist their passage to Paradise. Every year a big caravan sets out from here en route to Mecca and Medina for the Haj, further emphasising its reputation for piety.

As you leave Üsküdar dock, the main square, Demokrasi Meydanı, is right in front of you. Its northeastern corner is dominated by the **İskele Camii** (Map pp94–5), sometimes referred to as the Mihrimah Sultan Camii. This mosque was designed by Sinan for Süleyman the Magnificent's daughter in 1547–48.

South of the square is the **Yeni Valide Camii** (New Sultan's Mother Mosque; Map pp94–5). Featuring a wrought-iron 'birdcage' tomb in its overgrown garden, it was built by Sultan Ahmet III in 1708–10 for his mother Gülnuş Emetullah. East of the square is the **Ağa Camii** (Map pp94–5).

West of the square, overlooking the harbour, is the charming **Şemsi Paşa Camii** (Map pp94–5). Designed by Sinan and built in 1580 for Grand Vizier Şemsi Paşa, its modest size and decoration reflect the fact that its benefactor occupied the position of grand vizier for only a couple of months under Süleyman the Magnificent. Its *medrese* (seminary) has been converted into a library.

The **Atik Valide Camii** (Map pp94–5; Çinili Camii Sokak) is another of Sinan's works. It was built for Valide Sultan Nurbanu, wife of Selim II (the Sot) and mother of Murat III, in 1583. Nurbanu was captured by Turks on the Aegean island of Paros when she was 12 years old, and

went on to be a successful player in the Ottoman court. Murat adored his mother and on her death commissioned Sinan to build this monument to her on Üsküdar's highest hill. It has a pleasant courtyard and impressive interior galleries.

The **Çinili Camii** (Tiled Mosque; Çinili Camii Sokak; Map pp94–5) is the hidden jewel among Üsküdar's mosques. This little building is unprepossessing from the outside, but just wait until you see the interior, which is brilliant with İznik tiles, the bequest of Mahpeyker Kösem (1640), wife of Sultan Ahmet I (r 1603–17) and mother of sultans Murat IV (r 1623–40) and İbrahim (r 1640–48).

To find the Atik Valide Camii and Çinili Camii, walk up Hakimiyet-i Milliye Caddesi until you get to the traffic circle. Continue up Dr Fahri Atabey Caddesi for about 1km until you get to little Sarı Mehmet Sokak, on your left. From here you'll spot the minarets of Atik Valide Camii. To get to Çinili Camii from Atik Valide Camii, walk east along Çinili Camii Sokak for about 300m, after which it turns north and runs uphill. Çinili Camii is about 200m up the hill. All up it's about a 20-minute walk to the Çinili Camii from the main square.

Florence Nightingale Museum

The experience of visiting the Selimiye Kızlarsı (Army Barracks), where this modest **museum** (Map pp94–5; ☎ 0216-553 1009, fax 0216-310 7929; Nci Ordu Komutanliği 1; admission free; ⏰ 9am-5pm Mon-Sat) is housed, is even better than the museum itself. The barracks, built by Mahmut II in 1828 on the site of a barracks originally built by Selim III in 1799 and extended by Abdül Mecit I in 1842 and 1853, is the headquarters of the Turkish First Army, the largest division in the country. It's an extremely handsome building, with 2.5km of corridors, 300 rooms and 300 windows. During the Crimean War (1853–56) the barracks became a military hospital where the famous lady with the lamp and 38 nursing students worked. It was here that Nightingale put in practice the innovative nursing methods that history remembers her for. Although they seem commonsensical from a modern perspective, it is hard to overstate how radical they seemed at the time; it's really amazing to hear that before she arrived here, the mortality rate was 70% of patients but that by the time she left it had dropped to 5% (though others also contributed to this decrease).

The museum is on three levels in the northwest tower of the barracks. Downstairs there is a display charting the history of the First Army and concentrating on the Crimean War. On the two upstairs levels you see Nightingale's personal quarters, including her surgery room with original furnishings (including two lamps) and her living room, with great views across to Old İstanbul.

Unfortunately you need to fax a letter requesting to visit and nominating a time. Include a photocopy of your passport photo page. Do this 48 hours before you wish to visit and make sure you include your İstanbul phone number so that someone can respond to your request.

The museum is about halfway between Üsküdar and Kadıköy, near the fairy tale–like clock towers of the TC Marmara University. To get here, catch a dolmuş from in front of the ferry terminals in Üsküdar to Harem and ask locals to point you towards the Selimiye Kızlarsı Harem Kapısı (the barracks' Harem Gate), a short walk away. A taxi from the ferry shouldn't cost more than €4.

Getting There & Away

If coming to Üsküdar from Sultanahmet, catch the ferry from Eminönü, which runs every 15 to 30 minutes (depending on the time of day) between 6.35am and 11pm.

Ferry services also operate between Beşiktaş (from beside the Deniz Müzesi) and Üsküdar. Ferries start at 6.30am and run every 15 to 30 minutes until 10.30pm. From nearby Kabataş, just south of Dolmabahçe Palace, ferries run to Üsküdar every 30 minutes from 7.15am until 9.15am and from 4.15pm until 8.15pm.

Slower buses and dolmuşes also run to and from Taksim Sq.

KADIKÖY

Although there's nothing to show of its historic beginnings and it has few headline sights, Kadıköy is well worth visiting if you find yourself with a spare afternoon. It has a youthful, modern vibe, which can provide some respite from conservative Old İstanbul over the water. There are shops galore a few steps south of the dock around the old-fashioned **Baylan Pastanesi** (Muvakkithane Caddesi 19) – everyone knows it – and English-language schools on every corner (need a job?). **Café Antre** (Miralay Nazım Sokak 10) roasts the best espresso beans in the city; head to Kadife Sokak for eateries and

bars. If you time your visit for Tuesday, you can scrabble through the goodies on sale in the city's biggest street market, the **Salı Pazarı** (Tuesday Market).

To the north of Kadıköy is the neoclassical **Haydarpaşa Train Station** (Map pp94–5), resembling a German castle. In the early 20th century when Kaiser Wilhelm of Germany was trying to charm the sultan into economic and military cooperation, he presented the station as a small token of his respect. Today it's the subject of a controversial development plan to turn the station and its surrounds into a recreation and trade precinct, boasting seven high-rise towers. Ask a Kadıköy local for their opinion on the project and you'll be in for a long afternoon of çay drinking. Most ferries travelling between Kadıköy and Eminönü or Karaköy make a quick stop here.

Getting There & Away

If you're coming from Sultanahmet, hop on the ferry from Eminönü, which runs every 15 to 20 minutes (depending on the time of day) between 7.30am and 10.35pm.

From the ferry terminal at Karaköy (the Beyoğlu side of the Galata Bridge) services run from 6.10am every 10 to 30 minutes (depending on the time of day) until 11pm.

A ferry service also operates from Beşiktaş (catch it from beside the Deniz Müzesi), starting at 7.15am and running every half-hour until 10.45pm.

Buses and dolmuşes also run to and from Taksim Sq, but they take forever.

Bosphorus

Divan Yolu and İstiklal Caddesi are certainly always awash with people, but neither is the major thoroughfare in İstanbul. That honour goes to the mighty Bosphorus strait, which runs from the Sea of Marmara (Marmara Denizi) all the way to the Black Sea (Karadeniz), 32km to the north.

The strait's name is taken from ancient mythology. *Bous* is cow in ancient Greek, and *poros* is crossing place, so 'Bosphorus' is the place where the cow crossed. The cow was Io, a young girl with whom Zeus, king of the gods, had an affair and got pregnant. When his wife Hera discovered his infidelity, Zeus tried to make up for it by turning his erstwhile lover into a cow. Hera, for good measure, provided a horsefly to sting Io on the rump and drive her across the strait. Proving that there was no true justice on Olympus, Zeus managed to get off scot-free. Io's child, Ceroessa, became the mother of the first founder of the city, Byzas.

In 1973 the Bosphorus Bridge, the fourth-longest suspension bridge in the world, was opened. For the first time there was a physical link across the straits from Europe to Asia. Traffic was so heavy over the new bridge that it paid for itself in less than a decade. Now there is a second bridge, the Fatih Bridge (named after Mehmet the Conqueror, Mehmet Fatih), just north of Rumeli Hisarı and a third is on the drawingboard.

Most visitors to İstanbul explore the Bosphorus suburbs by taking the ferry trip from Eminönü to Anadolu Kavağı.

EMINÖNÜ TO BOSPHORUS BRIDGE

As you start your trip up the Bosphorus, watch out for the small island and tower of **Kız Kulesi** (p126), just off the Asian shore near Üsküdar. Just before the first stop at Beşiktaş, you'll pass the grandiose **Dolmabahçe Palace** (p121). Shortly after Beşiktaş, **Çırağan Sarayı**, (Map pp94–5) once home to Sultan Abdül Aziz and now the luxury Çırağan Palace Hotel Kempinski, looms up on the left. On the Asian shore opposite is a string of *yalı*. The word *yalı* derives from the Greek word for 'coast', and is used to describe the waterside wooden summer residences along the Bosphorus built by the Ottoman aristocracy and foreign ambassadors in the 17th, 18th and 19th centuries. All are now protected by the country's heritage laws.

On the European side, just before the majestic **Bosphorus Bridge** (Map pp94–5), is the pretty **Ortaköy Camii** (p122).

BOSPHORUS BRIDGE TO FATIH BRIDGE

Just after the bridge, on the Asian side, is the grand **Beylerbeyi Sarayı** (Beylerbeyi Palace; Map p93; ☎ 0216-321 9320; Abdullah Ağa Caddesi, Beylerbeyi; admission €4.50; ☉ 9.30am-5pm Tue-Wed & Fri-Sun Apr-Oct, 9.30am-4pm Tue-Wed & Fri-Sun Nov-Mar). Look for its two whimsical marble bathing pavilions on the shore, one of which was for men, the other for the women of the harem. Every sultan needed a little place to get away to, and this 30-room palace was the place for Abdül Aziz (r 1861–76). These days it's musty but still impressive, particularly on a sunny afternoon when golden light floods the rooms. A compulsory guided tour whips you past

room after room filled with Bohemian crystal chandeliers, French (Sèvres) and Ming vases and sumptuous carpets.

Past the suburb of Çengelköy on the Asian side is the imposing **Kuleli Military School** (Map p93), built in 1860 and immortalised in Irfan Orga's wonderful memoir, *Portrait of a Turkish Family*. Look for the two witch hatlike towers.

Almost opposite Kuleli on the European shore is **Arnavutköy**, a suburb boasting a number of well-preserved frilly Ottoman-era wooden houses, including numerous *yalı*. On the hill above it are buildings formerly occupied by the American College for Girls. Its most famous alumna was Halide Edib Adıvar, who wrote about it in her 1926 autobiography *Memoir of Halide Edib*.

Arnavutköy runs straight into the glamorous suburb of **Bebek**, famous for upmarket restaurants and waterside cafés. Its shops surround a small park and a mosque; to the east of these is the ferry dock, to the south the **Egyptian consulate** (Map p93), a gorgeous Art Nouveau minipalace built by the last *khedive* (viceroy during the Ottoman Empire) of Egypt, Abbas Hilmi II, who also later built Hıdiv Kasrı above Kanlıca on the Asian side of the Bosphorus. Above Bebek you'll notice the New England 19th-century-style architecture of the **Boğaziçi Üniversitesi** (Bosphorus University; Map p93).

Between Bebek and Kandilli headland the Bosphorus narrows. Kandilli means 'place of lamps', as lamps were lit here to warn ships of the particularly treacherous currents at the headland. Among the many *yalı* here is the small **Kırmızı Yalı** (The Red Yalı; Map p93), constructed in 1790 and one of the oldest still standing; a little further on is the long, white **Kıbrıslı Mustafa Emin Paşa Yalı** (Map p93). Next to the Kıbrıslı Yalı are the Büyük Göksu Deresi (Great Heavenly Stream) and Küçük Göksu Deresi (Small Heavenly Stream), two brooks that descend from the Asian hills into the Bosphorus. Between them is a flat, fertile delta, grassy and shady, which the Ottoman elite thought just perfect for picnics. Foreign residents, referring to the place as 'the Sweet Waters of Asia', would often join them.

If the weather was good, the sultan joined the party and did so in style. Sultan Abdül Mecit's version of a picnic blanket was the wedding cake–like **Küçüksu Kasrı** (Map p93; ☎ 0216-332 3303; Küçüksu Caddesi; admission €2.50; ☉ 9.30am-5pm

Tue-Wed & Fri-Sun Apr-Oct, 9.30am-4pm Tue-Wed & Fri-Sun Nov-Mar), an ornate lodge built in 1856–57. Earlier sultans had wooden kiosks here, but architect Nikoğos Balyan designed a rococo gem in marble for his monarch.

Just before the **Fatih Bridge** (Map p93) are the majestic structures of Rumeli Hisarı, the Fortress of Europe, and the low towers peeping over trees of the Anadolu Hisarı, the Fortress of Asia.

Mehmet the Conqueror had **Rumeli Hisarı** (Map p93; ☎ 0212-263 5305; Yahya Kemal Caddesi 42; admission €2.50; ☾ 9am-4pm Thu-Tue) built in a mere four months during 1452, in preparation for his planned siege of Byzantine Constantinople. For its location he chose the narrowest point of the Bosphorus, opposite Anadolu Hisarı, which had been built by Sultan Beyazıt I in 1391. By doing so he was able to control all traffic on the strait, so cutting off the city from resupply by sea and brilliantly assisting his invasion strategy.

The mighty fortress's useful military life lasted less than one year. After the conquest of Constantinople, it was used as a glorified Bosphorus tollbooth for a while, then as a barracks, later as a prison, and finally as an open-air theatre hosting concerts every summer.

Within Rumeli Hisarı's walls are parklike grounds, an open-air theatre and the minaret of a ruined mosque. Steep stairs (with no barriers, so beware!) lead up to the ramparts and towers; the views of the Bosphorus from here are magnificent. Just next to the fortress is a clutch of cafés and restaurants. Atmospheric **Sade Kahve** (☎ 0212-358 2324; Yahya Kemal Caddesi 36) is best.

Although it's not open as a museum, visitors are free to wander about **Anadolu Hisarı**'s ruined walls.

Past Anadolu Hisarı (almost directly under the Fatih Bridge) is the recently renovated **Köprülü Amcazade Hüseyin Paşa Yalı** (Map p93) built right on the water in 1698 and the oldest *yalı* on the Bosphorus.

FATIH BRIDGE TO ANADOLU KAVAĞI

Past the bridge, still on the Asian side, is the charming suburb of **Kanlıca**, famous for its rich and delicious yogurt. You can sample it in the **Asırlık Kanlıca Yoğurdu** (İskele Meydanı, Kanlıca; yogurt with honey €1.75, çay €1) on the shady waterfront square. The unprepossessing Gâzi İskender Paşa Camii in the square dates from 1560 and was designed by Sinan.

One of İstanbul's most famous seafood restaurants, **Körfez** (☎ 0216-413 4314; Körfez Caddesi 78, Kanlıca; mains €16-44; ☾ 11am-4pm Tue-Sun, 6pm-midnight daily), is on Kanlıca's outskirts, almost directly under the bridge. Just near Körfez is the late-19th-century **Ethem Pertev Yalı**, with its boathouse and ornate wooden decoration.

High on a promontory above Kanlıca is **Hıdiv Kasrı** (Khedive's Villa; Map p93; ☎ 0216-258 9453; Hıdıv Yolu 32, Kanlıca; admission free, parking €1.50; ☾ 8am-11pm), a grand Art Nouveau villa built by the last *khedive* of Egypt as a summer residence for use during his family's annual visits to İstanbul. Its tower stands high above the foliage.

Restored after decades of neglect, Hıdiv Kasrı now functions as a restaurant and garden café. The villa is a gem and the extensive and lovely garden is superb. It's a few minutes by taxi (€2.50) uphill from Kanlıca or a 20-minute walk. To walk, go north from Kanlıca's main square and mosque and turn right at the first street (Kafadar Sokak), which winds up towards the villa car park. Turn left at Dere Sokak and shortly you'll come to a fork in the road. Take the left fork and walk up past Kanlıca Hekımler Sitesı on the corner. You'll soon see the villa's car park and extensive wooded garden.

On the opposite shore is the wealthy suburb of **Emirgan**. In late April to early May, Emirgan Park, just above the town, is decked out in tulips. North of Emirgan, is the small yacht-lined cove of **İstinye**.

Just north of İstinye, **Yeniköy** is on a point jutting out from the European shore. It was first settled in classical times and later became a favourite summer resort, as indicated by the lavish 19th-century Ottoman *yalı* of the one-time grand vizier, **Sait Halim Paşa**. Look for its two small stone lions on the quay. On the opposite shore is the suburb of **Paşabahçe**, once famous for its glassware factory; and a bit further on is the fishing suburb of **Beykoz**, which has a graceful ablutions fountain dating from 1746 near the village square, as well as several fish restaurants.

Originally called Therapeia for its healthy climate, the little cove of **Tarabya** on the European shore has been a favourite summer watering place for İstanbul's well-to-do for centuries, although contemporary development has sullied some of its charm.

North of the village are some of the old summer embassies of foreign powers. When the heat and fear of disease increased in the warm months, foreign ambassadors and their staff would retire to palatial residences, complete with lush gardens, on this shore. Such residences extended north to the village of **Büyükdere**, notable for its churches, summer embassies and the **Sadberk Hanım Müzesi** (Map p93; ☎ 0212-242 3813; www.sadberkhanimmuzesi.org .tr; Büyükdere Caddesi 27-9, Sarıyer; admission €3; ⓨ 10am-5pm Thu-Tue). Named after the wife of the late Mr Vehbi Koç, founder of Turkey's foremost commercial empire in 1926, the museum, which occupies two restored *yalı*, contains her private collection of Anatolian antiques and Ottoman heirlooms.

Sarıyer, the next suburb up from Büyükdere on the European shore, is noted for its fish restaurants. Turn right as you leave the ferry dock, staying as close to the shore as possible, and you will pass the seabus terminal and several fish restaurants before coming to the Tarihi Balıkçılar Çarşısı, the historic fish market.

The ferry's second-last stop is at **Rumeli Kavağı**, a sleepy place that gets most of its excitement from the arrival and departure of the ferry. There's a small public beach named Altınkum nearby, with a small restaurant serving mezes and beer, but not much else. To the south is the shrine of the Muslim saint Telli Baba, reputed to be able to find suitable husbands for young women who pray there.

Anadolu Kavağı is where the state-run Bosphorus excursion ferry finishes its journey. Surrounded by countryside, it's a pleasant spot in which to wander and have a seafood lunch. Unfortunately restaurant touts can be a bit pushy. It's best to make your choice after inspecting the freshness of the fish; the best restaurants overlook the water by the ferry dock; cheaper ones are in the backstreets. Perched above the village are the ruins of **Anadolu Kavağı Kalesi**, a medieval castle that originally had eight massive towers in its walls. First built by the Byzantines, it was restored and reinforced by the Genoese in 1350, and later by the Ottomans. It will take you 30 to 50 minutes to walk up to the fortress from the town. Alternatively, taxis wait near the fountain in the town square just east of the ferry dock; they charge €5.75 for the return trip with 30 minutes' waiting time. Whichever way you get there, it's worth the effort for the spectacular Black Sea views. Unfortunately, the site is strewn with litter discarded by picnicking groups.

GETTING THERE & AWAY

There are numerous ways to explore the Bosphorus. Most people take the public excursion boat (below), which allows a lovely, relaxing day-trip with a stop for fish lunch up in a pleasant village by the Black Sea (you can walk up to a castle for views over the Bosphorus heads and the Black Sea). You could also take this boat most of the way north up the Bosphorus, then make your way back down the Bosphorus by bus and even local ferry, stopping for sightseeing along the way – see Buses and Public Ferries (p132). This is a great option, too, but it can be marred by the ubiquitous traffic jams along the coastal roads, especially after 3pm. Don't let this put you off, just steel yourself. You can choose between coming back along the European or Asian sides of the Bosphorus, or even a bit of both: both options are gorgeous, but the European side has more frequent public transport and more sights; the Asian side is quieter, with gorgeous village-like suburbs along its length but more hassle to get around.

The third option is the private excursions (p132).

Public Excursion Boats

The most popular way to explore the Bosphorus is by ferry. Most day-trippers take the state-run **Boğaziçi Özel Gezi Seferleri** (Bosphorus Special Touristic Excursions; one way €2, return €4; ⓨ 10.35am year-round & noon & 1.35pm Jun-Oct) ferry up its entire length. These depart from the Boğaz İskelesi dock at Eminönü (Map pp96–7) and stop at Beşiktaş, Kanlıca, Yeniköy, Sarıyer, Rumeli Kavağı and Anadolu Kavağı (the turnaround point). The journey takes 90 minutes each way with a three-hour stop for lunch and exploration of Anadolu Kavağı. Boats leave Anadolu Kavağı for the return journey at 3pm, 4.15pm and 5pm (June to October), arriving back in Eminönü at 4.30pm, 5.30pm and 6.30pm respectively. On summer weekends the last ferry leaves Anadolu Kavağı at 7pm, not 5pm. It is not possible to get on and off the ferry at stops along the way using the same ticket.

The boats fill up early in summer, especially over weekends, so buy your ticket and walk aboard at least 45 minutes prior to departure to get a seat outside or next to a window. During the trip, waiters will offer you fresh orange juice (€1.75), tea and other drinks.

Buses & Public Ferries

You can also take the Boğaziçi Özel Gezi Seferleri ferry from Eminönü up the Bosphorus and travel back by bus along the European or Asian side (or a bit of both if you want to be creative and determined).

There is also a passenger ferry service between Sarıyer and Anadolu Kavağı with 15 ferries a day from 7.15am to 11pm; seven of them stop at Rumeli Kavağı on the way.

If you want to travel back by bus along the European side, consider taking the Boğaziçi ferry as far as Sarıyer, then hopping on a southward bound bus and stopping at Rumeli Hisarı for sightseeing and lunch and perhaps at Ortaköy, Çırağan Sarayı or Dolmabahçe Palace. The ferry arrives at Sarıyer at 11.45am and also at 2.45pm, between June and October. From Sarıyer, bus 25E makes the slow trip back to Eminönü, bus 40 to Taksim Sq and bus 40B to Beşiktaş. Dolmuşes also ply these routes.

If you want to travel back by bus along the Asian side, you'll need more fortitude, but it's still doable. Take the ferry all the way to Anadolu Kavağı, then consider stopping at Hıdiv Kasrı or Körfez Restaurant for lunch, or Küçüksu Kasrı or Beylerbeyi Sarayı on your way back to Üsküdar. Bus No 15A, which leaves from the square in front of the Anadolu Kavağı ferry terminal, will take you along the coast as far as Hıdiv Kasrı or the Körfez Restaurant. From Hıdiv Kasrı or Körfez you can

catch bus No 15 all the way to Üsküdar, from where you can catch a ferry to Eminönü or Beşiktaş, or you could even take a taxi across the Fatih Bridge to Rumeli Hisarı, and continue your journey along the European side.

From Kanlıca it's also possible to catch a passenger ferry back towards town. These stop at Anadolu Hisarı, Kandilli, Bebek and Arnavutköy. Departures from Kanlıca are generally at 8.40am, 10.25am, 1.10pm, 2.40pm, 4.10pm, 5.40pm and 7.20pm. The trip to Arnavutköy takes 30 minutes.

Private Excursion Boats

These excursion boats aren't as good as the public excursion boat trip, as they only take you as far as Rumeli Hisarı (without stopping), although you do travel closer to the shoreline. The whole trip takes about three hours: one hour of travel each way and an hour at Rumeli Hisarı, which is just long enough to have lunch or to see the castle, but certainly not long enough to do both.

Touts are always found selling tickets for these trips around the Eminönü docks for €14 each, but try bargaining. Tours are on smaller boats (60 to 100 people), each with a small sun deck. These boats leave from beside the İstanbul Deniz Otobüsleri dock (Map pp96–7) every 1½ to two hours from 11am, with the last one at 8pm from June to September (4pm at other times). Note that departure times change, as boats tend to leave when they fill up.

BOSPHORUS NIGHT CRUISES

One of the most enjoyable, and certainly most romantic, night-time activities in İstanbul is to take a Bosphorus ferry. It doesn't really matter where – as long as you don't end up on the southern coast of the Sea of Marmara or on the Princes' Islands because you will find it difficult getting back again. Enjoy the view back to the Old City, the twinkling lights, the fishing boats bobbing on the waves and the powerful searchlights of the ferries sweeping the sea lanes.

Perhaps the best ferry to catch for this purpose is the one from Karaköy (just over the Galata Bridge from Eminönü) to **Kadıköy**. Just go to Karaköy, buy two tokens (for the voyages out and back) and walk on board. When you reach Kadıköy you could head into the backstreets and grab a bite to eat (p128). Return ferries leave on the hour and half hour, with the last ferry leaving Kadıköy (or the nearby Haydarpaşa stop) for Karaköy at midnight; make sure you confirm this at the ticket booth when you first arrive. You could also catch the Eminönü–Karaköy ferry, but the last service returns from Kadıköy at 8.40pm.

A shorter ride is the one from Eminönü to **Üsküdar**. When you alight in Üsküdar, you could have a delicious feed at Kanaat Lokantası (p126), or turn right and walk around the coast to the çay bahçesi (tea gardens) near the Şemsi Paşa Camii. After a tea or two, continue on the popular waterside promenade past the famous Kız Kulesı (see p126) – a gorgeous walk on a summer's evening. Return ferries leave every half hour, with the last ferry leaving Üsküdar at 11pm. Again, make sure you confirm this when you first arrive.

HAMAMS

A visit to a *hamam* is a quintessential Turkish experience, and İstanbul's *hamams* are superb. If you're only going to visit one or two while in town, we suggest you choose the 'Big Two' – Cağaloğlu and Çemberlitaş. While these touristy *hamams* are pricey, they're worth it for the gorgeous historic surrounds, their squeaky-clean maintenance and as most clientele will be having their first *hamam* experience, you won't feel out of place. Allow at least an hour. For more information about bath etiquette see the boxed text, p651.

Built over three centuries ago, **Cağaloğlu Hamamı** (Map pp96–7; ☎ 0212-522 2424; Yerebatan Caddesi 34; bath & massage €17, bath only €10; ☼ 7am-10pm men, 8am-8pm women) is one of the city's most beautiful *hamams*. The surroundings are so impressive they've featured in everything from soap ads to an Indiana Jones film. Separate baths each have a large *camekan* (reception area) with private, lockable cubicles where it's possible to have a nap or a tea at the end of your bath. There's also an inviting bar-café. The 'Oriental Luxury Service' costs €30 and includes bath, massage and exfoliation, but you're probably just as well off with the 'Complete' service (€20). A tip is appreciated.

The **Çemberlitaş Hamamı** (Map pp96–7; ☎ 0212-522 7974; Vezir Hanı Caddesi 8, Çemberlitaş; bath & massage €20, bath only €13.50; ☼ 6am-midnight) was designed by Sinan in 1584. Like Cağaloğlu, it's a double *hamam* (separate baths for men and women) and is similarly popular with tourists. The splendid *camekan* is unfortunately for men only. Women must put up with a utilitarian corridor filled with lockers and benches. This makes Cağaloğlu a better bet for women, unless you fancy the full works, including a 30-minute oil massage (€27), or a clay facial (€5). Tips are supposedly included in the price and there's a 20% discount for ISIC holders.

It may be old (c 1475 in fact), run down and a bit grubby, but the masseuses at the local **Gedikpaşa Hamamı** (Map pp98–9; ☎ 0212-517 8956; Hamam Caddesi 65-7, Gedikpaşa; bath & massage €15, bath only €5.50; ☼ 9am-midnight), a short walk from Sultanahmet, know what they're doing.

It's hard to recommend the **Tarihi Galatasaray Hamamı** (Historic Galatasaray Turkish Bath; Map pp100–1; ☎ 0212-244 1412; Turnacıbaşı Sokak 24, Çukurcuma; bath & massage €31, bath only €25; ☼ 6am-10pm men, 8am-8pm women), as it's outrageously overpriced. However, if you're over this side of town, this is one of İstanbul's best *hamams*. It's famous

for having one of the hottest *hararets* in town (that sounds rude but we mean it literally). Note that staff have a reputation for hassling for tips, and the women's section is mostly a 1960s add-on – women would definitely be better off going elsewhere.

WALKING TOUR

Divan Yolu, the main thoroughfare of the old city, was laid out by Roman engineers to connect the city with Roman roads heading west. This tour will have you following in their footsteps.

Start your walk at the **Milion (1)**, at the south side of the park near the Basilica Cistern. This is the marble milestone from which all distances in Byzantium were measured. The tower beside it was once part of the Aqueduct of Valens (p124), delivering water to the Basilica Cistern. Head west along Divan Yolu to the little **Firuz Ağa Camii (2)** built in 1491 during the reign of Beyazıt II (r 1481–1512). Just behind it are the ruins of the 5th-century **Palace of Antiochus (3)**. Continue along Divan Yolu and turn left into İmran Öktem Caddesi to find the 4th-century **Binbirdirek Cistern** (4; p108). Back on Divan Yolu, you'll see an impressive enclosure at the corner of Babıali Caddesi, which is a cemetery housing the **tombs (5)** of the Ottoman high and mighty.

Exit the cemetery and cross the road to find the tiny stone **Köprülü library (6)** built by the Köprülü family in 1661. Stroll a bit further along Divan Yolu and into the Çemberlitaş district where Divan Yolu changes name to Yeniçeriler Caddesi. On the left are some more buildings from the Köprülü *külliyesi*. The **tomb (7)** is that of Köprülü Mehmet Paşa (1575–1661), and the octagonal mosque on the corner was a lecture and study room. Across the street, that strange building with a row of street-front shops is actually an ancient Turkish bathhouse, the **Çemberlitaş Hamamı** (8; left).

The column, under renovation at the time of writing, rising up from the pigeon-packed plaza is, surprisingly, one of İstanbul's most ancient and revered monuments. The **Çemberlitaş (9)**, the Banded Stone or Burnt Column, was erected by Constantine in 330 to celebrate the dedication of Constantinople as capital of the Roman Empire. A bit further on is the **Atik Ali Camii (10)**, built in 1496 by a eunuch and grand vizier of Beyazıt II. Beyond Atik Ali Camii on the right (north) side is the

Koca Sinan Paşa Medresesi (11), resting place of Grand Vizier Koca Sinan Paşa. After you've seen the tomb here, head past the cemetery and to the right, where you'll find the quiet gardens of the **İlesam Lokalı** (**12**; p148), a great place to enjoy a tea-break and nargileh.

Continue along Yeniçeriler Caddesi until you see the **Beyazıt Camii** (**13**; p115). Its *medrese* houses the **Museum of Turkish Calligraphic Art** (**14**; Türk Vakıf Hat Sanatları Müzesi; ☎ 0212-527 5851; Hürriyet Meydanı, Beyazıt; admission €2; ⏰ 9am-4pm Tue-Sat), with a somewhat neglected collection. After exiting the mosque, head towards the right of the grandiose main entrance of İstanbul University. Following the university's walls along Fuat Paşa Caddesi, turn left up Prof Sıddık Sami Onar Caddesi and you will come to one of the most majestic of all Ottoman mosques

---

WALK FACTS

Start Milion, near Basilica Cistern
Finish Süleymaniye Camii
Distance 1.5km
Duration two hours

---

and the last stop on this tour, the **Süleymaniye Camii** (**15**; p116). Reward your efforts with a tea at Lale Bahçesi (p148) or a quick, tasty bite to eat at Meshur Kuru Fasülyeci (p143).

İSTANBUL FOR CHILDREN

Children of all ages will enjoy the sensational **Rahmi M Koç Müzesi** (p123); nearby **Miniatürk** (p123) may amuse them for an hour or two. The spooky **Basilica Cistern** (p108), with its obese fish, is always a hit, as is the ferry trip down the Bosphorus, particularly if it's combined with a visit to the fortress of **Rumeli Hisarı** (p130) – beware of the steep stairs here, which have no barriers. On **Heybeliada** (p162), one of the Princes' Islands, you can hire bikes or circle the island in a *fayton* (horse-drawn carriage). The Mehter band playing at the **Askeri Müzesi** (p121) is always a winner, too.

If you're staying in Sultanahmet, there are two teeny playgrounds near the Cankurtaran train station, and a bigger, busier one in Kadırga park close by. If you're staying in Beyoğlu, the limited options are at least better quality: there's one in Tophane, a better one at Cihangir Park (paid for by locals) and one

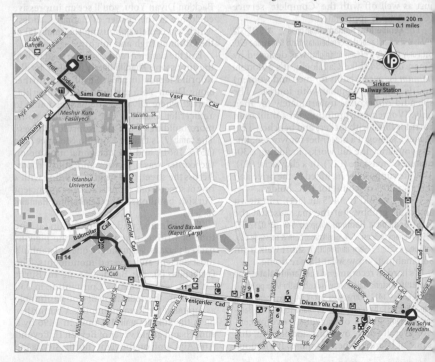

at the Fındıklı station of the tramline, right by the water's edge – very scenic!

If you need to resort to bribery to ensure good behaviour, there's a toyshop area in Eminönü. The biggest and best shop here is **Ekincioğlu Toys & Gifts** (Map pp96-7; ☎ 0212-522 6220; Kalçın Sokak 5; Eminönü; ⌚ 9am-7pm). There's a small shop in Beyoğlu too, **İyigün Oyuncak** (Map pp100-1; ☎ 0212-243 8910; İstiklal Caddesi 415; ⌚ 9am-9pm).

TOURS
City Tours
Adventure Tours (Map pp96-7; ☎ 0212-520 8720; www.adventuretours.com.tr; Şeftali Sokak 12, Sultanahmet) One of the few agents in town offering a full-day beach tour to the Black Sea (€65), which might be just what you need when it's stinking hot in İstanbul.

City Sightseeing bus (☎ 0212-458 1800; one-day ticket adult/student/child 5 & over/child under 5 €18/12/10/free) This is the typical naff hop-on-hop-off bus service. Ticket booths are opposite Aya Sofya and in Taksim Sq or you can purchase tickets on the bus. The full circuit takes 90 minutes or you can get on and off the bus at any of the 63 stops around town, but buses only run a few times a day. Departure times change regularly so double check. Expect traffic congestion on the Beyoğlu section.

Fez Travel (Map pp96-7; ☎ 0212-516 9024; www.feztravel.com; Akbıyık Caddesi 15, Sultanahmet, İstanbul) Backpacker tours around Turkey, including Gallipoli tours. Also operates the Fez Bus; see the boxed text, p680.

Hassle Free Tours (Map pp96-7; ☎ 0212-458-9500; www.hasslefreetour.com; Akbıyık Caddesi 10, Sultanahmet; tours €60) Runs tours to Gallipoli, including an overnight stay at Anzac House in Çanakkale (p193), before visiting the ruins at Troy and either travelling on to Selçuk or back to İstanbul.

İstamboul Insolite (Map pp94-5; ☎ 0212-531 4811; www.istanbulguide.net/insolite; Sadrazam Ali Paşa Caddesi 26, Fener; tours €40-75) This small home-based agency in Fener runs a variety of full- and half-day off-beat tours from the intriguing 'superstitious İstanbul', and a 'caravanserais' tour, to a walk through Fener and Balat. English, German and French are spoken.

İstanbul Food Workshop (Map pp94-5; ☎ 0212-534 4788; www.istanbulfoodworkshop.com; Yıldırım Caddesi 111, Fener) This cookery school also runs walking tours for foodies, divulging the city's best eateries, spice merchants and *pastanes* (patisseries).

Kirkit Voyage (Map pp96-7; ☎ 0212-518 2282; www.kirkit.com; Amiral Tafdil Sokak 12, Sultanahmet; tours €30-75) This small agency specialises in small-group walking tours of the must-see sights as well as 'İstanbul the Unusual Way'. It's one of the only companies to offer an 'Asian İstanbul and its Markets' tour. English and French are spoken. Kirkit also organises overnight Gallipoli and Troy tours.

Les Arts Turcs (Map pp96-7; ☎ 0212-511 2296; www.lesartsturcs.org; İncili Çavuş Sokak 37/3, Sultanahmet; tours & lessons €25-50; ⌚ 9am-11pm) If you've ever wanted to learn *ebru* (paper marbelling), belly dance like a gypsy or become a calligrapher, Les Arts Turcs can make it happen. This isn't a standard tour operator, it's a collective of artists, writers and historians who come and go from a welcoming studio in Sultanahmet. Some of the courses and tours on offer include seeing the whirling dervishes at Fatih Tekke, private Turkish lessons (€22 per hour), and an 'İstanbul Modern Art' tour.

Plan Tours (Map pp96-7; ☎ 0212-234 7777; www.plantours.com; information booth opposite Aya Sofya, Sultanahmet; tours €40-120) Offers a standard range of professionally run half- and full-day tours of the city, the Bosphorus, the Princes' Islands and long day trips to Troy & Gallipoli. There's a 30% discount for children aged from two to seven years.

Senkron Tours (Map pp96-7; ☎ 0212-638 8340; www.senkrontours.com; Arasta Caddesi 51, Sultanahmet; tours €20-45) Aimed squarely at budget travellers, Senkron offers well-priced tours of İstanbul including a combined Golden Horn and the Bosphorus boat trip.

FESTIVALS & EVENTS
During the warmer months İstanbul is buzzing with arts- and music-festivals events, giving the visitor plenty of options when it comes to entertainment. Most of the big-name arts festivals are organised by the **İstanbul Foundation for Culture & Arts** (☎ 0212-334 0700; www.istfest.org). Tickets to most events are available from Biletix (see p150). Headline events include the following:

APRIL & MAY
International İstanbul Film Festival (www.iksv.org)
International İstanbul Theatre Festival (www.iksv.org) Every two years.

JUNE & JULY
Efes Pilsen One Love (www.pozitif-ist.com)
International İstanbul Jazz Festival (www.iksv.org)
International İstanbul Music Festival (www.iksv.org)

SEPTEMBER TO NOVEMBER
Akbank Jazz Festival (www.akbankcaz.com)
Efes Pilsen Blues Festival (www.pozitif-ist.com)
Filmekimi Autumn Film Festival (www.iksv.org)
International İstanbul Biennial (www.iksv.org) Every two years.
Minifest, the Children's Festival (www.iksv.org)
Rock'n Coke (www.rockncoke.com)

SLEEPING

Every accommodation style is available in İstanbul. You can live like a sultan in a world-class luxury hotel, doss in a friendly hostel dorm, or relax in a stylish boutique establishment.

Hotels reviewed here have rooms with private bathroom and include breakfast, usually of the Turkish variety, in the room price. Exceptions are noted in the reviews. All prices given are for high season and include 18% value-added tax (*katma değer vergisi*, KDV). During low season (October to April, but not around Christmas or Easter) you should be able to negotiate a discount of at least 20% on the price. Before you confirm a booking, ask if the hotel will give you a discount for cash payment (usually 10% but can be higher), whether a pick-up from the airport is included (it often is if you stay more than three nights) and whether there are discounts for extended stays. Book ahead from May to September.

For more accommodation reviews by Lonely Planet authors for İstanbul, check out the online booking service at www.lonelyplanet.com.

Sultanahmet & Around

The Sultan Ahmet Camii (the Blue Mosque), gives its name to the quarter surrounding it. This is the heart of Old İstanbul and the city's premier sightseeing area, so the hotels here, and in the adjoining neighbourhoods to the east (Cankurtaran), west (Küçük Aya Sofya) and north (Binbirdirek and Çemberlitaş) are supremely convenient. The area's only drawbacks are the number of carpet touts around, the lack of decent places to eat, and that it's a ghost town at night (no quality nightlife).

BUDGET

Mavi Guesthouse (Map pp96-7; ☎ 0212-517 7287; www .maviguesthouse.com; Kutlugün Sokak 3, Sultanahmet; dm €7-11, s €20, d €24-28; 🖳) Teeny Mavi is a perennial favourite. Don't come for partying, but for night-long backgammon battles in the pint-sized kilim-clad lounge. Rooms are basic but clean enough – get one facing the street – and all share so-so toilets. There's also a communal kitchen. You'll make friends aplenty if you stay on the rooftop bunk beds – almost sleeping on your neighbour is guaranteed to kick-start a conversation! An added bonus is the views: Aya Sofya and a bird's-eye view of the Great Byzantine Palace excavations. You'd pay a packet for this elsewhere!

İstanbul Hostel (Map pp96-7; ☎ 0212-516 9380; www .istanbulhostel.net; Kutlugün Sokak 35, Sultanahmet; dm/d €10/30; ⊠ 🖳) This well-appointed hostel has some of the cheapest and cleanest facilities in town. Six to nine-bed dorms are a little cramped but cheery. There are only two doubles, rooms 6 and 7 – avoid damp-smelling room 7. All rooms share well-kept bathrooms. There's a cellar bar, a leafy courtyard, and a terrace with lovely views – snuggle into a comfy sofa and enjoy. On the minus side, the management gets mixed reviews.

Bahaus Guesthouse (Map pp96-7; ☎ 0212-638 6534; www.travelinistanbul.com; Bayramfırın Sokak 11-13, Cankurtaran; dm €10-12, s €25, d €32-40; ⊠ 🖳) Laid-back, fun and very friendly, the Bahaus is a great choice. Assets include the lovely rooftop terrace; the inviting lounge (inspired wall colour choice fellas!); and the rooftop BBQs for €6, with a pint of beer thrown in (the bar doesn't gather dust at Bahaus). The rooms themselves are fine – not immaculate, but well maintained – but avoid the ones in the bunkerlike basement.

Coşkun Pension (Map pp96-7; ☎ 0212-526 9854; www .coskunpension.com; Soğukçeşme Sokak 40, Sultanahmet; s/d €25/35; ⊠ 🖳) This laid-back, friendly option is a cosy guesthouse gripping Topkapı Palace's walls. Rooms are teensy but homely. This was once the home of the Coşkun family (the other brothers own shops downstairs and we dare you not to hang out with these lads). Beware the treacherous stairs you'll have to scale to reach the rooftop terrace with its ceiling of grape-vine leaves in summer. The pension is a favourite with Japanese travellers.

Stone Hotel & Cafe (Map pp96-7; ☎ 0212-517 6331; www.stonehotel.net; Şehit Mehmet Paşa Yokuşu 34, Binbirdirek; dm/s/d €10/30/40; ⊠) An excellent choice, the Stone Hotel has an eight-bed dorm with proper mattresses and excellent, cheery doubles (rooms 401 and 402 have terrific views). There's a small rooftop terrace overlooking the Sea of Marmara and Sokullu Mehmet Paşa Mosque (er…yes, brace yourself for the early morning call to prayer…). Challenge the locals to a game of *tavla* (backgammon) and a puff-a-thon with a nargileh in the shade-dappled stone-walled courtyard out the back.

Side Hotel & Pension (Map pp96-7; ☎ 0212-517 2282; www.sidehotel.com; Utangaç Sokak 20, Sultanahmet; pension s/d €35/45, hotel s/d €45/60, apt €60-80; ⊠ 🖳) Choose Side for quality rooms, squeaky-clean bathrooms (some with en suite, some shared) and management who know their stuff. The

Turkuaz Guest House (Map pp98-9; ☎ 0212-518 1897; www.hotelturkuaz.com; Cinci Meydanı Sokak 36, Kadırga, Kumkapı; s/d €35/45) Not for the faint-hearted nor for lovers-of-less, this extravagant Ottoman mansion has barely been touched since it was built in the 1850s. The communal spaces are simply mind-blowing: a frenzied pastiche of marble, stained-glass and İznik tiles topped by ornate wooden ceilings heaving with extravagant chandeliers. It's easy to see why the Turkuaz has often been used for film sets. The rooms themselves are over the top as well, but are well kept with good, roomy bathrooms. When you stay in the Sultan's room (€80) you really feel the part. Turkuaz is 15-minutes' walk from Sultanahmet by the Sea of Marmara, in an original, non-touristy neighbourhood of tumbledown houses. Hooray for this delightful dash of eccentricity.

hotel's rooms are top-notch and some have private balconies: rooms 15 and 16 are our fave picks. Next door, the pension's rooms are pleasant, too, but avoid those at the back. The Side has a fabulous terrace (ditto the views), a welcoming hang-out spot with sofas. The fully equipped but dark apartments sleep one to six people.

Orient International Hostel (Map pp96-7; ☎ 0212-518 0789; www.orienthostel.com; Akbıyık Caddesi 13, Cankurtaran; dm €10-11, r €45-65; ☒ 🖳) Always packed, no-frills Orient is backpacker central. The basement bar draws crowds ogling the belly dancer practising her moves into the wee hours. The rooftop restaurant-bar has terrific views and very friendly staff – Happy Hour (5pm to 8pm daily) here is a must. The breakfasts at the Orient get the thumbs up, too (but eat your other meals elsewhere). The simply furnished rooms are generally fine, but housekeeping can be lax at times and the carpets in the dorms (four and eight-bed) are simply appalling. Bathrooms pass the sniff test – just. A good option if you want to be in the heart of the action and you don't mind less than perfect service.

MIDRANGE

Hotel Sultan's Inn (Map pp96-7; ☎ 0212-638 2562; www.sultansinn.com; Mustafa Paşa Sokak 50, Küçük Aya Sofya; s/d €45/60; ☒ ☒ 🖳) Tucked in a pleasant

neighbourhood away from the hullabaloo of Sultanahmet, but still within walking distance to all the sights, the Sultan's Inn is an excellent choice. The biggest drawcard here is the simply stunning 360-degree views from the rooftop terrace. The rooms are a fairly tight squeeze but pleasantly decorated with four-poster beds, wooden furniture and ochre feature walls.

Hotel Ararat (Map pp96-7; ☎ 0212-516 0411; www.ararathotel.com; Torun Sokak 3, Sultanahmet; r €65-75; ☒ 🖳) The Ararat is tiny but its charming host and cosy rooftop terrace-bar in the shadow of the Blue Mosque make it a popular choice. Dark wooden floors, Byzantine-inspired artwork and a clever use of space-enhancing mirrors are the decorative hallmarks. The trick here is to pick the right room – request number 6, 12 or 14 for space and killer views.

Naz Wooden House Inn (Map pp96-7; ☎ 0212-516 7130; www.nazwoodenhouseinn.com; Akbıyık Değirmeni Sokak 7, Cankurtaran; s €70-90, d €70-110; ☒ 🖳) This delightful gem, in a lovely neighbourhood of tumbledown wooden houses, offers traditional hospitality and style, complete with doilies! Our choice is Room 7 overlooking the Sea of Marmara, but you can enjoy the same view from the rooftop terrace. The one downside to Naz is the rail line out back – trains tootle past from 7am to 11pm.

Kybele Hotel (Map pp96-7; ☎ 0212-511 7766; www.kybelehotel.com; Yerebatan Caddesi 35, Sultanahmet; s €60-70, d €80-100; ☒ 🖳) No you haven't walked into a lamp store, but the lobby of the charming Kybele Hotel. Nearly every ceiling in this loopy gem is studded with hanging lamps and public rooms are jam-packed with curios and antique furniture. The rooms themselves are simple, comfortable and roomy with kilims on the floors. There's no roof terrace but a lovely courtyard compensates.

Hotel Nomade (Map pp96-7; ☎ 0212-513 8172; www.hotelnomade.com; Ticarethane Sokak 15, Sultanahmet; s/d €70/85; ☒ 🖳) Cosy and contemporary, Nomade is a well-priced boutique option for lovers of style. The checked-floor terrace up top has tree-top views. Propped at the chunky timber bar up here is obviously the place to be for an afternoon martini. The rooms themselves are a tight squeeze and minimalist, and we must confess, a tad disappointing compared with the cool style of the communal spaces.

Sarı Konak Oteli (Map pp96-7; ☎ 0212-638 6258; www.sarikonak.com; Mimar Mehmet Ağa Caddesi 42-46, Cankurtaran; r €89; ☒ 🖳) With its Ottoman style and not a hair out of place, Sarı Konak Oteli also boasts a lovely stone-walled courtyard, and a terrace with excellent views ringed by white sofa lounges. What better place to watch the sunset? The deluxe rooms are the best value: 203 with its bay window stuffed with a comfy couch is our favourite. The service is both friendly and unflappable.

Hotel Empress Zoe (Map pp96-7; ☎ 0212-518 2504; www.emzoe.com; Adliye Sokak 10, Cankurtaran; s/d budget €50/60; s/d standard €70/95; ☒) Empress Zoe is an excellent choice. Immaculate and supremely tasteful rooms in adjoining buildings share a gorgeous pebbled garden and a wisteria-bedecked terrace offering terrific views. The suites are delightful, especially the 'deluxe garden suite', but the 'special double with terrace' is probably best value for money. If there's a downside to Zoe it's that some of the rooms in the original building are a tight squeeze. Book well ahead.

Hotel Turkoman (Map pp96-7; ☎ 0212-516 2956; www.turkomanhotel.com; Asmalı Çeşme Sokak 2, Sultanahmet; s/d €79/99; ☒ ☒) You'll feel as if you've booked into a private club when you walk into the Turkoman. In a fantastic position up the hill a few steps off the Hippodrome, this renovated 19th-century building features spacious rooms that are simply but tastefully decorated with kilims, reproduction antique furniture and brass beds. Ask for room 4A, which has a balcony and Blue Mosque view. The rooftop terrace has knock-out views of the Princes' Islands. This is the superb setting for the buffet breakfast, but rise early to get the best seats at the front of the terrace.

Hotel Arcadia (Map pp96-7; ☎ 0212-516 9696; www.hotelarcadiaistanbul.com; İmran Öktem Caddesi 1, Sultanahmet; s/d €80/100; ☒ ☐) The piped Michael Bolton music in the foyer was disconcerting, but all was forgiven when we were shown the rooftop café-restaurant with its outstanding views of the Blue Mosque, Aya Sofya, Topkapı Palace and the Sea of Marmara – the best view from any hotel in Sultanahmet. The room décor is chintzy, but appointments are four-star standard. Book rooms 702 to 706 for a view.

TOP END

Ayasofya Pansiyonları & Konuk Evi (Map pp96-7; ☎ 0212-513 3660; www.ayasofyapensions.com; Soğukçeşme Sokak, Sultanahmet; s/d €80/110; ☒ ☐) If you're keen to play out Ottoman fantasies during your stay, choose a room in one of the nine lovingly restored wooden houses lining Topkapı Palace's outer wall (or at Konuk Evi, a stunning mansion hidden away in spectacular private gardens behind the Aya Sofya). These places are both operated by the same company. Rooms have original Ottoman-style furnishings complete with brass beds, simple chandeliers and ruffled curtains. Enjoy the most glamorous breakfast in town, served in a glass conservatory complete with chandeliers.

İbrahim Paşa Oteli (Map pp96-7; ☎ 0212-518 0394; www.ibrahimpasha.com; Terzihane Sokak 5, Sultanahmet; r standard/deluxe €125/175; ☒ ☒ ☐) No doubt İbrahim Paşa would have given the nod to this mod Ottoman renovation borrowing his name. This trés-chic guesthouse successfully combines Ottoman style with contemporary décor. The best standard rooms are 301, 302, 401 and 402. Room 404 is the best deluxe option, with a fabulously plush Ottoman recliner you'll never want to leave. Given the many plusses of this place it's a shame about the rooftop, that the staircase steals the best views, and that the rooms are tipping being overpriced. Tsk Tsk.

Yeşil Ev (Map pp96-7; ☎ 0212-517 6785; www.istanbulyesilev.com; Kabasakal Caddesi 5, Sultanahmet; s/d €125/165; ☒ ☐) Totally rebuilt in the '70s, this late-19th-century Ottoman mansion has been restored to its former glory as a splendid top-end option with a delightful courtyard – you won't want to leave it. Brass beds and chintz furnishings feature, but the bathrooms are a bit cramped.

Four Seasons Hotel İstanbul (Map pp96-7; ☎ 0212-638 8200; www.fourseasons.com; Tevkifhane Sokak 1, Sultanahmet; r €280-500; ☒ ☒ ☐) What used to be the infamous Sultanahmet prison (remember *Midnight Express*?) is now İstanbul's swankiest hotel. The Four Seasons is known for its service (extraordinary), history (deliciously disreputable), location (right in the heart of Old İstanbul) and rooms (wow). Been sentenced to time at the Four Seasons? Get them to throw away the key.

If you prefer a fully furnished apartment you can't go wrong with the **Les Arts Turcs apartment** (Map pp96-7; ☎ 0212-511 2198; www.istanbulrentals.com; İshakpaşa Caddesi 6, Sultanahmet; apt night/week €200/900; ☐): three bedrooms on three floors, fully furnished kitchen, İznik-tiled bathrooms and free ADSL. But the best thing is the rooftop terrace offering ooh-la-la views of the Princes' Islands, Sea of Marmara and on to the Topkapı walls. We'd love to move in ourselves. Bargain for a better rate.

Beyoğlu & Around

Most travellers to İstanbul stay in Sultanahmet, but Beyoğlu is becoming a popular alternative. Stay here to avoid the tout press in Sultanahmet, and because buzzing, bohemian Beyoğlu has the best wining, dining and shopping in the city. Unfortunately there isn't the range or quality of accommodation options here that you'll find in Sultanahmet, but options are opening. Some apartments are included following, or you could check out www.istanbulrentals.com.

Getting to/from the historical sights of Old İstanbul is easy: either walk about half an hour, catch the Taksim Sq–Kabataş funicular and tram a few stops, or take a ride on the comfy T4 bus (see p160).

BUDGET

Saydam Hotel (Map pp100-1; ☎ 0212-251 8116; saydam@istanbulguide.net; Sofyalı Sokak 1, cnr Asmalımescit Sokak, Asmalımescit; s/d €15/25) Located a few steps off İstiklal and a short hip-swaying saunter to some of Beyoğlu's grooviest cafés and galleries, no-one would complain about the location. The same can't be said about the office-like décor, but heck, at this price who's complaining! Rooms are simple, small and reasonably well kept, provided you don't inspect too closely.

Chillout Hostel (Map pp100-1; ☎ 0212-249 4784; www.chillouthc.com; Balyoz Sokak 17, Asmalımescit; dm/s/d €10/15/27; 🖳) If you're in İstanbul to party, you probably already know about Chillout. Offering cheap booze and rooms, Beyoğlu's first hostel is also a great place to hook up with like-minded travellers and locals primed to sample Beyoğlu's wicked nightlife. The squishy dorms are OK at a pinch, especially if you don't plan on spending too much time in them. Ditto the communal bathrooms: they're so small you can shower, go to the loo and preen yourself all at the same time!

World House Hostel (Map pp100-1; ☎ 0212-293 5520; www.worldhouseistanbul.com; Galipdede Caddesi 117, Galata; dm €10-14, s/d €35/40; 🖳) With an unbeatable foothold betwixt the hushed sights of Sultanahmet and the commotion of Beyoğlu, this colourful hostel is the best new kid on the block. Staff are welcoming, rooms generously sized, bathrooms shipshape, and the cosy street-level café serves up cheap, tasty grub and offers free wi-fi. The top dorms, rooms 10 and 11, share a balcony overlooking the Galata Tower, but a planned rooftop terrace will give all superb views of the Bosphorus. The only downside is the minaret right next door – bring earplugs.

Bahar Apartment Hotel (Map pp100-1; ☎ 0212-245 0772; fax 244 1708; İstiklal Caddesi 61; 2-/3-bed apt €45/60) Fancy the idea of sitting in your own apartment with a bottle of wine and viewing the early evening promenade along İstiklal? You can do this at the Bahar. These basic apartments, which can sleep up to four, have enough room to park all your shopping bags, and are reasonably clean, but unfortunately have no kitchen facilities. Location is great if you're planning to party in the surrounding bars, hopeless if you want an early night.

Hotel Residence (Map pp100-1; ☎ 0212-252 7685; www.hotelresidence.com.tr; Sadri Alışık Sokak 19; s/d €40/50; 🏋) If you're here to party, and you want a cheapish, clean hotel to doss in then this no-nonsense place is for you. Note that Sadri Alışık Sokak is one of the busiest streets in the area, lined with cubby-hole bars, and has a vaguely sleazy air – not a great prospect for lone females. Negotiate to get better rates.

MIDRANGE

Büyük Londra Oteli (Map pp100-1; ☎ 0212-245 0670; www.londrahotel.net; Meşrutiyet Caddesi 117, Tepebaşı; s/d €55/70) The highlight of the 1892 Büyük Londra is its wonderfully preserved sitting room, which has barely been touched since its heyday as a dining room for well-heeled passengers fresh off the *Orient Express*. We love the ruffled curtains dangling with tassels, the gilded mouldings, the deep maroon carpets – and the bar. The gilded staircase, complete with mammoth Bohemian crystal chandelier, leads up to the rooms…. And this, folks, is the disappointing news. Rooms are a tad dusty and worn (very *Addams Family*), so ask for one that's been renovated.

Vardar Palace Hotel (Map pp100-1; ☎ 0212-252 2888; www.vardarhotel.com; Sıraselviler Caddesi 54, Taksim; s/d €60/75; 🏋 🖳) Dried flower arrangements and faded carpets may remind you of your grandma's house, but this immaculately clean, small hotel just off Taksim Sq offers excellent value-for-money. Rooms at the rear are darkish but quiet; front rooms are light but face onto a noisy nightclub strip. Service can be so-so: it depends who you approach.

Galata Residence Apart Hotel (Map pp100-1; ☎ 0212-292 4841; www.galataresidence.com; Bankalar Caddesi, Felek Sokak 2, Galata; 1-/2-bed apt per day €65/110, per week €400/650; 🖳) A few steps down from the Galata Tower, this historic building has been refurbished as an apart-hotel with a top-floor Greek restaurant and a bland modern annexe (for the one-bedroom apartments). Apartments are spacious and fully equipped, though you may have to chase up staff for kitchen utensils. Top marks go to the daily servicing and the extremely helpful staff. To find it, ask taxi drivers to drop you in front of the Oyak Bank at the corner of Voyvoda Caddesi and Haraçci Ali Sokak, and walk up the steep stairs.

İstanbul Holiday Apartments (Map pp100-1; ☎ 0212-251 8530; www.istanbulholidayapartments.com; apt per night €70-180 minimum stay three nights, per week €500-1200; ☐ ☒) Bereket Building (Camekar Sokak, Tünel) Glorya Building (Galata Kulesi Sokak, Tünel) Saying that holiday apartments in İstanbul are easy to find is like saying the sultans were celibate, which is why these apartments in two separate blocks near the Galata Tower are such a find. All have undergone a quality renovation and are beautifully kitted out with washer/dryer, fully equipped kitchen (with dishwasher), CD player and every other mod-con you can think of. Book well ahead for the best-value apartments (Glorya garden suite, with a private courtyard; the Penthouse Terrace; and the Duplex View). A great choice for families, but prime yourself for steps. Ask about the newly opened apartments in Cihangir.

Taksim Square Hotel (Map pp100-1; ☎ 0212-292 6440; www.taksimsquarehotel.com.tr; Sıraselviler Caddesi 15, Taksim; s/d €80/100; ☒ ☒) With a fabulous location right by Taksim Sq, this ugly duckling is an excellent pick, so ignore its hideous façade. The modern, comfortable rooms have super views over the square or the Bosphorus. Arrive early for breakfast in the top-floor restaurant to grab a window-side table. Popular with locals.

TOP END

Anemon Galata (Map pp100-1; ☎ 0212-293 2343; www.anemonhotels.com; cnr Galata Meydanı & Büyükhendek Caddesi 11, Galata; s/d €100/120; ☒ ☐) In the shadow of the Galata Tower, Anemon Galata is a magnificent historic building converted into a lovely, intimate hotel. The rooms are individually decorated and impeccably tasteful in elegant Ottoman style. Some rooms have small wrought-iron balconies overlooking Galata Sq; others overlook the Golden Horn. But it's worth staying here for the restaurant alone, which boasts one of the best views in the city. Book well ahead.

Pera Palas Oteli (Map pp100-1; ☎ 0212-251 4560; www.perapalace.com; Meşrutiyet Caddesi 98-100, Tepebaşı; s/d €150/170; ☒) Built in 1894 to house passengers from the *Orient Express*, the grand old Pera has bedded a veritable roll-call of famous politicians, stars and artists. Built in grand European style, it's dripping with mammoth chandeliers, marble columns, acres of ruffled velvet curtains and painted ceiling mouldings – a ride in the wrought-iron 'birdcage' lift is an adventure in itself. The bedrooms are fabulously old-world too – ask for a room at the back on the 2nd or 3rd floor for views of the Golden Horn. Admittedly Pera's glory days have faded and you pay a premium for nostalgia here, but most guests who enjoy the buffet breakfast in the grand dining hall say any time spent in this living museum is money well spent. Check the Internet for specials.

Richmond Hotel (Map pp100-1; ☎ 0212-252 5460; www.richmondhotels.com.tr; İstiklal Caddesi 445, Tünel; s/d €135/165; ☐ ☒) We were in two minds whether to include this place, but the location convinced us. Right on bustling İstiklal Caddesi, there are few better places to base yourself for a pleasure or business visit to Beyoğlu. Standard rooms are comfortable if characterless, but the suites (€230) are knockouts, with modernist décor, great workstations, Jacuzzis and plasma TVs. Book a room at the back of the building for Bosphorus views and to ensure a good night's rest.

Marmara (Map pp100-1; ☎ 0212-251 4696; www.the marmarahotels.com; Taksim Sq; s €240-260, d €275-300; ☒ ☒ ☐ ☒) Perfectly positioned right by Taksim Sq, this very popular hotel is an İstanbul institution. It's slick, plush and has all the five-star mod-cons you'd expect in a very friendly, laid-back, professional package. The splendid views (10th floor and up) and extremely comfortable rooms make it a good choice for tourists and businesspeople alike. There's a highly regarded rooftop restaurant and bar, a pool, a gym and a *hamam*. Breakfast costs an extra €21.

EATING

İstanbul is a food-lover's paradise. Teeming with affordable quick-eats joints, cafés and restaurants, it leaves visitors spoiled for choice when it comes to choosing a venue.

Unfortunately, the area where most visitors to the city stay – Sultanahmet – is disappointing when it comes to food. With the exceptions of top-class Balıkçı Sabahattin, the Tarihi Sultanahmet Köftecisi Selim Usta and a handful of *pidecis* (pide-makers), there are few restaurants worth writing home about. There are other pockets of Old İstanbul worth investigating – Eminönü has the wonderful Hamdi et Lokantası and Sirkeci has the excellent Hatay. On the whole, though, visitors should cross the Galata Bridge and join the locals eating in Beyoğlu. Nothing can beat the enjoyment of spending a night in a *meyhane* on Nevizade Sokak or dining at one of the übercool restaurants overlooking the Bosphorus.

If you are planning to explore Üsküdar or the upper reaches of the Bosphorus, some possibilities for dining are listed from p126 and p130, respectively.

Close to Sultanahmet there are a number of small supermarkets. The best is **Greens** (Map pp96–7; Nuriosmaniye Sokak 1, Cağaloğlu; 7am-8.30pm). Beyoğlu also has many small supermarkets (including Gima) open daily; most are along Sıraselviler Caddesi, running off Taksim Sq.

Sultanahmet & Around
RESTAURANTS

Konuk Evi (Map pp96–7; 0212-517 6785; Soğukçeşme Sokak, Sultanahmet; mains €4-8; closed winter) In the hotel of the same name (p138), a secluded flower-filled garden and fairy tale–like glass conservatory around the corner from Aya Sofya are waiting just for you. Walk down Caferiye Sokak and go through the gate opposite Ayasofya Pansiyonları and you'll find the Konuk Evi, one of the most relaxing places in the city to enjoy an alfresco lunch. Salads, burgers, sandwich and grills are all good value considering the surrounds.

Hatay (Map pp96–7; 0212-522 8513; İbni Kemal Caddesi 9-11, Hocapaşa; mains €5-11) It's a short stroll north of Sultanahmet's hotel district, but after one mouthful here all will be forgiven. Known for its fresh, quality meze – try the meze platter (€8.50) to sample a bit of everything – this is one of the few restaurants around here that caters as much for locals as it does for travellers. Service is fabulous, thanks to the friendly owner hovering in the background to make sure everything is just so. Grab a street-side table in fine weather.

Konyalı (Map pp96–7; 0212-513 9696; Topkapı Palace, Sultanahmet; mains €5-17; lunch) With its fabulous position in the grounds of Topkapı Palace and its charmingly down-at-heel-Riviera feel, Konyalı is a perennial favourite. There are few more pleasant experiences than sitting in its glass pavilion or on the outdoor terrace, both

of which overlook the Bosphorus and Sea of Marmara. You can enjoy a full-service meal, or choose from the buffet (meals €5 to €6).

Balıkçı Sabahattin (Map pp96–7; 0212-458 1824; Seyit Hasan Koyu Sokak 1, Cankurtaran; mains €8-20) The solid stream of chauffeur-driven limousines stopping outside Balıkçı Sabahattın is testament to its enduring popularity with the city's establishment. Indoor eating is in a wooden Ottoman house but most prefer to eat outside under a leafy canopy. The menu offers a limited range of delicious mezes and good-quality fresh fish. It's tucked away in a ramshackle street just near the train line.

Giritli (Map pp96–7; 0212-458 2270; Keresteci Hakkı Sokak, Cankurtaran; mains €8-20) A relatively new but very welcome addition to the local eatery scene, Giritli serves up Cretan dishes in a pretty walled garden or indoors in a creaky renovated Ottoman. You can order from the menu, but the restaurant specialises in its set banquet (€31) offering over 10 types of hot and cold meze, octopus, fish and more. It's a meal you won't forget in a hurry.

Dubb (Map pp96–7; 0212-513 7308; İncili Çavaş Sokak 10, Sultanahmet; mains €10-18) One of İstanbul's few Indian restaurants, Dubb serves a tepid tandoori, but it makes the grade for the simply stunning terrace with a full-view of Aya Sofya – book a table here. Tandooris are the speciality but there are curries and plenty of choices for vegetarians including the vegie banquet (€17). If you like your curries spicy, say so.

Rami (Map pp96–7; 0212-517 6593; Utangaç Sokak 6, Cankurtaran; mains €13-15) This restored Ottoman house has several quaint dining rooms decorated with impressionist-style paintings by Turkish painter Rami Uluer (1913–88), but the favoured spot for dinner is the rooftop terrace, which has a full view of the Blue Mosque – make sure you request a table there when you book. Ottoman specialities such as *kağıt kebap* (lamb and vegetables cooked in a paper pouch) are served; the service can be a little hit and miss.

Sarnıç Restaurant (Map pp96–7; 0212-512 4291; Soğukçeşme Sokak, Sultanahmet; mains €16-18; dinner) Opposite the Konuk Evi, and run by the same people, the Sarnıç is also wonderfully atmospheric being set in a candle-lit Byzantine Cistern. You must reserve in advance.

CAFÉS

Çiğdem Pastanesi (Map pp96–7; 0212-526 8859; Divan Yolu Caddesi 62A, Sultanahmet; börek €1) People have been grazing the goodies here since 1961, and it's still going strong. Come here for a cappuccino that could hold its own on Via Veneto in Rome (€2) and a serve of their crunchy fresh cheese *börek*. Çiğdem's desserts sometimes look better than they taste, so stick to savouries.

Özsüt (Map pp96-7; ☎ 0212-512 7780; Hacı Tahsınbey Sokak 48, Sultanahmet; fırın sütlaç €2.50) Rice pudding devotees, your search is over. Özsüt makes the best *fırın sütlaç* in the city, and its other sweet offerings are worth the dental bills, too. There's a rooftop terrace with excellent views – if you can brave the stairs or squishy lift – and street-side seating. Tea and coffee are available as well.

QUICK EATS

Tarihi Sultanahmet Köftecisi Selim Usta (Map pp96-7; ☎ 0212-520 0566; Divan Yolu 12; mains €2.50-5) Don't get this place confused with the other *köfte* (meatballs) places along this strip purporting to be the *meşhur* (famous) *köfte* restaurant: No 12 is the real McCoy. Hungry locals in-the-know flock here for a serve of the best *köfte* you'll ever grease your palate with, followed by a serve of its equally famous semolina. Do yourself a favour and ease your belt a notch or two.

Karadeniz Aile Pide ve Kebap Salonu (Map pp96-7; ☎ 0212-528 6290; Hacı Tahsınbey Sokak 1, Sultanahmet; mains €2.50-5) This long-timer, off Divan Yolu, serves a tasty *mercimek* (lentil soup), perfect for breakfast, and is also known for its pide (€2.50 to €4). Around the corner is an alley packed with Karadeniz pide joints, all hoping to cash in on the original Karadeniz' success.

Erol Taş Kultur Merkez (Map pp96-7; ☎ 0212-518 1257; Cankurtaran Meydanı 18, Cankurtaran; mains €2.50-5) Erol Taş, one of Turkish cinema's most famous personalities, acted the villain in some 800 films. He ran this café as a hang-out for his contemporaries until his death in 1998. Today it's still the area's most popular hangout, inevitably filled with locals drinking *çay*, playing backgammon and puffing on nargileh. *Patlıcanlı kebap* (eggplant kebap) costs €3 and pides range from €2.50 to €3.

Cennet (Map pp96-7; ☎ 0212-513 5098; Yeniçeriler Caddesi 90, Çemberlitaş; kebaps €4) Only the cheesy nightclubs offering 'live Turkish shows' come near to emulating the kitsch of this 'Anatolian' restaurant. Set in part of the historic Çemberlitaş Hamam, it encourages diners to don Ottoman costumes, recline 'Ottoman-style' and listen to 'Ottoman' musicians (noon to 9.30pm) while noshing on *gözleme* (savoury filled pancakes), the restaurant's speciality. Consider yourself warned.

Doy-Doy (Fill up! Fill up!; Map pp96-7; ☎ 0212-517 1588; Şifa Hamamı Sokak 13; mains €3-8) You'd have to describe the food as stodgy but the fans don't care at this no-fuss traveller-friendly stalwart. Backpackers come for the superb top-floor terrace views and the extensive menu, which has something for everyone, including vegetarians. No alcohol is served.

Bazaar District
RESTAURANTS

Havuzlu Restaurant (Map p116; ☎ 0212-527 3346; Gani Çelebi Sokak 3, Grand Bazaar; mains €6-13; ⏱ 11.30am-5pm Mon-Sat) There are few more pleasant experiences than parking one's shopping bags and enjoying a meal at the Grand Bazaar's best eatery. A lovely space with vaulted ceiling, pale lemon walls and ornate central light-fitting, Havuzlu serves up excellent fare to hungry hordes of tourists and shopkeepers. Ask the waiter to recommend a dish to ensure the best eating experience.

Pandeli (Map pp98-9; ☎ 0212-522 5534; Mısır Çarşısı 1, Eminönü; mezes €3-5, mains €7.50-15; ⏱ lunch Mon-Sat) What a shame that the food and who-cares service at this İstanbul institution don't live up to the beautiful surrounds. Three salons encrusted with stunning turquoise-glazed İznik tiles and furnished with chandeliers and richly upholstered banquettes are perched above the main waterside entrance to the Spice Market;

AUTHOR'S CHOICE

Hamdi Et Lokantası (Hamdi Meat Restaurant; Map pp98-9; ☎ 0212-528 0390; Kalçın Sokak 17, Eminönü; kebaps €4.50-8) A favourite İstanbullu haunt since 1970, Hamdi's phenomenal views, overlooking the bustling Golden Horn and Galata, are matched by some of the city's best kebaps. Ignore the meze menu and choose from the meze platter presented with a flourish by the waiter: the *şuksuka* (roasted eggplant and tomatoes) and *haydari* (yogurt with roasted eggplant and garlic) are resolutely to-die-for. The kebaps are all so good it's impossible to choose, but luckily you don't have to with the excellent mixed kebap (€6). Book ahead and request a spot on the terrace.

FOLLOW YOUR NOSE

Many visitors are pleasantly surprised to discover İstanbul has superb cheeses, olives, pickles, seasonal and dried fruits, sweets, nuts and *pastırma* (dried beef) available everywhere. Exploring the taste sensations in the city's markets and *şarküteri* (delicatessens) is a must.

In Eminönü, the streets around the **Spice Market** (Mısır Çarşısı, Map pp98–9) are pungent with the scent of freshly ground coffee, fresh fish, peaks of fragrant cumin and chilli, rolled *pestil* (sun-dried fruit pulp sheets), and much more. You could put on several kilos smelling the air here. Make sure you wedge your way into a queue at **Nimla Pastırmacı** (below), which has been serving happy customers since the 1920s.

In Beyoğlu, the streets around the **Balık Pazar** (Fish Market; Map pp100–1), next to the Çiçek Pasajı on İstiklal Caddesi, are well worth following your nose to. You'll have fun discovering your own favourites, but we recommend you don't pass by **Petek** (Map pp100-1; Dudu Odaları Sokak 7), a cubby-hole-sized pickle emporium, and the famous rose jam (*gül reçel;* €2.50) at **Üç Yıldız** (Map pp100-1; Dudu Odaları Sokak 15).

For the city's best Turkish delight head to **Ali Muhiddin Hacı Bekir** (p153) – its delight with crunchy coffee beans is particularly tasty. For the best baklava in the city take your sticky fingers to **Karaköy Güllüoğlu** (p145).

For seasonal fruit and vegetables and home-made produce such as pickles, cheese and olives you should take your elbows to joust at the street markets. **Oyuncu Sokak** (Map pp96–7), near the lighthouse in Cankurtaran (near Sultanahmet) has a street market on Wednesday; even better is the Thursday **Gerdanlık Sokak** (Map pp98–9) market west of Kumkapı fish restaurants, which can be found on or near Çapariz Sokak. The markets are busiest during the early evening.

climb the stone stairs to enter. Once inside, we recommend the *patlıcan böreği* (eggplant pielike pastry) and the Pandeli *tatlı* for dessert, but not much else.

CAFÉS

Colhetı Cafe & Restaurant (Map p116; ☎ 0212-512 5094; Sandal Bedesteni 36, Grand Bazaar; 🕑 breakfast & lunch Mon-Sat) This café is inside the bazaar's former auction hall; enjoy lunch here, and the historic atmosphere will flavour your meal. Guests sit in comfortable cane chairs and enjoy döner kebaps (€4.50), sandwiches (€3) and salads (€4 to €5). The best thing about the place is that it's licensed. A beer costs €2.50.

Fez Café (Map p116; ☎ 0212-527 3684; Halıcılar Caddesi 62; 🕑 breakfast & lunch Mon-Sat) Set in a rough-stone den, the popular Fez is a modern Western-style café on one of the bazaar's most atmospheric streets, but you'll pay a premium to sit at the flower-adorned tables (sandwiches cost €4 and salads €4.50 to €6).

Café Sultan (Map p116; ☎ 0212-527 3684; Halıcılar Caddesi; 🕑 breakfast & lunch Mon-Sat) Next door to the Fez, it offers similar fare for slightly cheaper prices.

QUICK EATS

Hafız Mustafa Şekerlemeleri (Map pp96-7; ☎ 0212-526 5627; Hamidiye Caddesi 84-86, Eminönü; sweets €2-3) Since 1864 Hafız has been satisfying happy customers and we know why. This shrine to sugar serves baklava so delicious you'll be thankful you don't live locally or you could make yourself a nuisance here. Hafız is also known for its Meshur Tekirdağ Peynir Helvası, a yellow, goopy cheese *helva* made in only a handful of places around the country, and sold here by the tray load.

Meshur Kuru Fasülyeci (Map pp98-9; ☎ 0212-513 6219; Prof Sıddık Sami Onar Caddesi 11, Süleymaniye; mains €2-3) Join the crowds of hungry locals at this long-time institution in the former *kütüphanesi medrese* of the Süleymaniye mosque. It has been dishing up its spicy signature *fasulye* (broad bean) dish for some 80 years. Best enjoyed with *ayran* (yogurt drink).

Nimla Pastırmacı (Map pp98-9; ☎ 0212-511 6393; Hasırcılar Caddesi 14, Eminönü; mains €3-4; 🕑 7am-7pm Mon-Sat) Delicatessens don't get any better than this. Nimla's mouth-watering selection of cheeses, *pastırma* and meze are known throughout the city. Fight your way to the counter and order a tasty fried *pastırma* roll packed with your choice of point-and-choose ingredients (€3) or a takeaway container of meze. Those-in-the-know eat what they've bought upstairs in the floral cafeteria or find a seat up there for a quick, scrumptious feed.

TOP 5 BARS/RESTAURANTS WITH VIEWS

5 Kat, Cihangir (below) Locals' favourite high haunt.

360, Galatasaray (right) Glam restaurant and open-air bar with, you guessed it, 360-degree views.

Hotel Arcadia, Sultanahmet (see p138) Average hotel, knockout views: leaves all others in shadow.

Legend Hotel, Binbirdirek (p148) Peer out over the Sea of Marmara.

Leb-i Derya, Tünel (right) Not quite up with 360's views, but here you'll keep your hairdo.

Beyoğlu & Around

RESTAURANTS

Karaköyüm (Map pp100-1; ☎ 0212-244 6808; Kemeraltı Caddesi 4, Karaköy; mains €4-8.50) Locals come here when they're homesick and feel like a bit of *anne's* (mama's) hearty home cooking. Regularly featured in the 'best of' lists in İstanbul, the Karaköyüm dishes up perennial favourites such as *limonlu tavuk* (lemon chicken) as well as Ottoman classics. All in pleasant, stylish surrounds with views over the Golden Horn. If mama had a view like this you'd drop in for dinner more often! It's on the 6th floor.

Zencefil (Map pp100-1; ☎ 0212-243 8234; Kurabiye Sokak 8, Beyoğlu; mains €5-9; ⏰ lunch & dinner Tue-Sun) This popular vegetarian café is comfortable and quietly stylish, with a lovely leafy courtyard. Go for the daily and weekly specials to get crunchy-fresh produce (all organic) and guilt-free desserts. A slab of the home-made bread is a definite highlight. There's a great range of herbal teas, too.

5 Kat (Beşinci Kat; Map pp100-1; ☎ 0212-293 3774; 5th fl, Soğancı Sokak 7/5, Cihangir; mains €6-10; ⏰ 10am-2am Mon-Fri & 10.30am-3am Sat & Sun) This long-timer is a local's hang-out on lazy weekend mornings when the mixed crowd leaf through the complimentary liberal *Radikal* newspaper. But even this won't allow an expat's English breakfast (€8) with fried pork sausages go cold. All the international-style meals are excellent – welcoming service and sublime views over the Bosphorus complete the picture. At night it's an excellent bar (p149).

Hacı Abdullah (Map pp100-1; ☎ 0212-293 8561; Sakızağacı Caddesi 17, Beyoğlu; mezes €3.30, mains €6-12) Just thinking about Hacı Abdullah's sensational *imam bayıldı* (eggplant stuffed with ground lamb, tomatoes, onions and garlic) makes our taste buds go into overdrive. This İstanbul institution (established in 1888) is probably

the city's best *lokanta* (Turkish restaurant) and one of the essential gastronomic stops you should make when in town. No alcohol.

Hacı Baba (Map pp100-1; ☎ 0212-244 1886; İstiklal Caddesi 49, Beyoğlu; mezes €3, mains €6-12; ✗) While not as old as nearby rival Hacı Abdullah, the food and surroundings here are just as impressive, though it's firmly on the package-tour itinerary. There's a large nonsmoking section overlooking the main strip and a vine-garlanded terrace for alfresco dining. Best of all, you can order a beer, rakı (aniseed-flavoured grape brandy) or wine with your meal.

Leb-i Derya (Map pp100-1; ☎ 0212-293 4989; Kumbaracı Yokuşu 115/7, Tünel; mains €7-15; ⏰ 11am-2am Mon-Fri, 8.30am-3am Sat & Sun) You can guage the gastro-calibre of an expat or local if they know about stylish Leb-i Derya. Those *not*-in-the-know obviously haven't surrendered to the delights of the *mahmudiye* (€11), an inspired blend of spices over succulent chunks of chicken. There aren't many places in this city to get a darn fine breakfast, but this is one of them. The 'greenpeace' (€7) is a yogurt muesli mix with fresh OJ and *lor*, the melt-in-the-mouth Turkish ricotta. This is one restaurant in İstanbul where you want to avoid the meze (especially the Ottoman starters), and save yourself for mains and dessert. And did we mention the knock-out views? Go.

360 (Map pp100-1; ☎ 0212-251 1042; İstiklal Caddesi 32/309, Galatasaray; mains €8-15; ⏰ 1-3pm & 7.30pm-3am Tue-Sun) This is fine dining at its best. A rooftop with a panorama envied by all in the trade starts 360-degrees ahead of the pack and it just keeps running. From the unflappable staff divining your every desire to superb meals such as melt-in-the-mouth goat-cheese balls with grilled pear, steaks, no-fuss pastas, and Miss Piggy Pizza, there's something for everyone. Ignore the somewhat menacing doorman and head straight to the table of your choice; for drinks only, swagger your way to the terrace. The 360 is on the top floor of the Mısır Apartments; take the stairs to make the most of this gorgeous apartment block. Book ahead on weekends.

CAFÉS

İnci (Map pp100-1; ☎ 0212-243 2412; İstiklal Caddesi 124, Beyoğlu) İstanbullus' naughty secret is to side-step into vintage İnci for a sinful fix of the city's best profiteroles (€2), and then to reappear on İstiklal as if nothing ever happened. Join the sinners – it's standing room only.

kaffeehaus (Map pp100-1; ☎ 0212-245 4028; Tünel Meydanı 4, Tünel) A perennial favourite, welcoming, stylish kaffeehaus is always humming with a local arty set, who monopolise its tables for long breakfasts and a coffee hit (€2.50) whenever the shakes set in. In warmer weather the café's front opens onto Tünel Sq and provides great people-watching opportunities.

Saray Muhallebicisi (Map pp100-1; ☎ 0212-292 3434; İstiklal Caddesi 173, Beyoğlu; sweets €2-4) This *muhallebici* (milk pudding shop) has been dishing up puddings since 1935, and we can't fault them. And it's always packed with locals scratching their heads trying to decide which of the 35-odd varieties of sweets it's to be. If you've wanted to try an *aşure* or *kazandibi*, this is the place to do it.

Patisserie Markiz (Map pp100-1; ☎ 0212-245 8394; İstiklal Caddesi 360-2, Beyoğlu) Everything at Markiz is a work of art: the gloriously restored Art Nouveau interior, the delectable cakes and pastries, and the starched aprons on the suitably glamorous staff. Sipping a Turkish coffee (€3) and devouring a piece of the chocolate gateau (€4) here feels very civilised.

QUICK EATS

Güney Restaurant (Map pp100-1; ☎ 0212-249 0393; Kuledibi Şah Kapısı 6, Tünel; mains €3-7; ✆ Mon-Sat) You won't write home about the food here but Güney is a no-fuss eatery popular with travellers and locals alike. It's a good pick for female travellers, too. Grab a windowside seat in the rustic ground-floor salon or fall into the comfy red couches in the more upmarket salon upstairs.

Konak (Map pp100-1; ☎ 0212-252 0684; İstiklal Caddesi 259, Beyoğlu; mains €3.50-7) Despite the cheesy exterior this long-time no-fuss favourite serves up a parade of surprisingly good kebaps with piping-hot pide in delightfully old-fashioned surrounds. This is also a great place to try Turkey's famous, but hard-to-find, Maraş ice cream. There's another branch near Tünel, but this one is much better.

Musa Usta Ocakbaşı Adana Kebap Salonu (Map pp100-1; ☎ 0212-245 2932; Küçük Parmakkapı Sokak 14, Beyoğlu; mains €5-7) Three floors of old-fashioned atmosphere, plus excellent food, have kept this buzzing place in business for years. An excellent spot to sit alongside the *ocakbaşı* (grill), while you watch your meat grilled to perfection. You can drink beer or rakı here, too.

Beşiktaş & Ortaköy

Vogue (Map pp94-5; ☎ 0212-227 4404; BJK Plaza, A Blok Kat 13, Spor Caddesi, Akaretler, Beşiktaş; mains €15-30) Grace Jones purrs on the sound system, trained Japanese sushi chefs perform wonders with a sliver of tuna and well-trained waiters make sense of a large and thoughtful wine list. The food here is as sensational as the views over the Bosphorus. Ask for a table on the terrace.

While Ortaköy's restaurants specialise in tasty weekend breakfasts, **Zeliş Cafe'de** (Map pp94-5) sets the standard with its great-value open buffet (€5). Ortaköy's other speciality is *kumpir* (baked potato) stuffed with sour cream, olive paste, cheese, chilli, bulgur, and anything else you can squeeze in (€3.50). Buy these by the church. **Çınar** (Plane Tree; Map pp94-5; ☎ 0212-261 5818; İskele Meydanı 42, Ortaköy; meze €3.50-6, mains €5.50-8) is our favourite of the waterside restaurants for a dinner of seafood mezes (yum). Afterwards, slip into **Mado** (Map pp94-5; İskele Meydanı, Ortaköy, cone €2-50-3.50), next door, for a cone of Turkey's famous Maraş *dondurma* (ice cream).

Western Districts

Develi (Map pp94-5; ☎ 0212-529 0833; Gümüşyüzük Sokak 7, Samatya; mains €7-12) This place has been serving up kebaps to hungry locals since 1912, so it really knows what it's doing when it comes to the national dish. Near the city wall at Samatya, its five floors (including a roof terrace) are always full of happy punters enjoying the flavours of southeastern Anatolia. Try the *çiğ köfte* (raw ground lamb, bulgur, onions and spices) and the *fıstıklı kebap* (pistachio kebap) and you'll feel happy too. To get here, catch a taxi along the coastal road (Kennedy Caddesi)

SHRINE TO BAKLAVA

Karaköy Güllüoğlu (Map pp100-1; ☎ 0212-293 0910; Rıhtım Caddesi, Katlı Otopark Altı, Karaköy; ✆ Mon-Sat) We're going to stick our necks out here and say this divine toothkiller makes İstanbul's, and maybe even Turkey's, best baklava. The Güllü family's first shop fittingly opened in Gaziantep, Turkey's baklava capital, before they brought their delectable offerings to ever-grateful İstanbullus. Fill a box with their classics – *fıstıklı* (pistachio) and the rich, custardy *sütlü nuriye* – and win the heart of any prospective mother-in-law.

from Sultanahmet or the train from Sirkeci Train Station (get off at Kocamustafapaşa Station). You'll find the Develi inland from the station in a plaza filled with parked cars.

Asitane (Map pp94-5; ☎ 0212-635 7997; Kariye Oteli, Kariye Camii Sokak 18, Edirnekapı; mains €8-12) It's not often that you'll get to taste Ottoman dishes devised for the 16th-century royal circumcision feast, but that's what's on offer here. The food is magnificent, served in modern, elegant surrounds with a charming outdoor courtyard in summer. Vegetarians are well catered for, too.

Zeyrekhane (Map pp98-9; ☎ 0212-532 2778; İbadethane Arkası Sokak 10; mains €11-15; ☺ Tue-Sun) This place, adjacent to Zeyrek Camii, has an outdoor garden with cushioned couches on which you can recline and soak up the superb view of the Süleymaniye Camii and the Golden Horn. It serves tasty mains (fancy quail kebap served with eggplant?) and snacks.

DRINKING

It may be the biggest city in a predominantly Muslim country, but let us assure you that İstanbul's population likes nothing more than a drink or three. If the rakı-soaked atmosphere in the city's *meyhanes* isn't a clear enough indicator (below), a foray into the thriving bar scene around Beyoğlu will confirm it. You could spend a month bar-hopping in Beyoğlu and still only scratch the surface.

MEYHANE: THE BIGGEST PARTY IN TOWN

If you only have one night out on the town when you visit İstanbul, make sure you spend it a *meyhane* (tavern) in Beyoğlu. Buried in the maze of narrow streets behind the historic Çiçek Pasajı (Flower Passage) on İstiklal Caddesi, **Nevizade Sokak** is one of the most famous eating precincts in the city and it's certainly the most atmospheric. On any night of the week its taverns will be full of chattering locals sampling the dizzying array of mezes and fresh fish on offer, washed down with a never-ending supply of rakı (aniseed-flavoured grape brandy). Vendors wander from table to table selling fresh almonds and at some places small groups of musicians entertain diners with *fasıl* music (Ottoman classical, usually played by gypsies) and wisecracks in return for tips (anything less than €3 per musician would be insulting). The whole experience is enormous fun. On summer Friday and Saturday evenings the street literally heaves with people looking for a table, grabbing a drink at one of the bars along the strip or just wandering past.

Other *meyhanes* are along Sofyalı Sokak, opposite the Tünel, or in Kumkapı, near Sultanahmet (see p109). These are some of the best *meyhanes* in the city:

Boncuk Restaurant (Map pp100-1; ☎ 0212-243 1219; Nevizade Sokak 19, Beyoğlu; meze €3-6, fish €4-11) Armenian specialities differentiate Boncuk from its Nevizade neighbours. Try the excellent, super-fresh *topik* (mezes made with chickpeas, pistachios, onion, flour, currants, cumin and salt).

Despina (Map pp94-5; ☎ 0212-247 3357; Açikyol Sokak 9, Kurtuluş; meze €4.50-7; ☺ noon-midnight) Established in 1946 by the glamorous Madame Despina, whose stylish photograph greets guests at the entrance, Despina is one of the best *meyhanes* in the city. The Armenian–Greek food is good, but plays second fiddle to the live *fasıl* music, which is played by some of the country's most accomplished musicians. Large tables of locals join in the singing and everyone has a great time. Get here by taxi (€8 from Sultanahmet, €5 from Beyoğlu).

Ney'le Mey'le (Map pp100-1; ☎ 0212-249 8103; Nevizade Sokak 12, Beyoğlu; meze €2-6, fish €5-9) Opposite the Boncuk, it's always one of the busiest restaurants in town.

Refik (Map pp100-1; ☎ 0212-243 2834; Sofyalı Sokak 10, Tünel; meze €3-6, fish €7-10; ☺ lunch Mon-Sat, dinner daily) Refik is the original *meyhane* in the Asmalımescit area. It's a convivial cubby-hole famous for both its genial host, Refik Arslan, who will make you feel welcome the minute you set foot through the door, and its speciality, Black Sea fish.

Sofyalı 9 (Map pp100-1; ☎ 0212-245 0362; Sofyalı Sokak 9, Tünel; meze €4-8, grills €5-10; ☺ Mon-Sat) Tables here are hot property on Friday and Saturday nights, and no wonder. This gem of a place serves up some of the best *meyhane* food in the city, and does so in surroundings as welcoming as they are attractive. Regulars swear by the *Arnavut ciğeri* (Albanian fried liver, €5).

Yakup 2 (Map pp100-1; ☎ 0212-249 2925; Asmalımescit Caddesi 35/37, Tünel; meze €4.50-7; ☺ dinner Tue-Sat) This darkly lit den is a long-time favourite for locals who don't want to limit their *meyhane* carousing to the summer months: come here when it's cool as the outdoor area isn't atmospheric, but indoors its shoulder-to-shoulder carousing on Friday and Saturday nights. It offers grills but stick to a parade of meze.

GAY & LESBIAN İSTANBUL

The gay scene in İstanbul has been characterised as homely rather than raunchy; 'all about boys going out in trousers neatly pressed by their mothers who have no idea that they are gay', is how one aficionado summed it up. That said, there is a group in pursuit of the hirsute, the **'bears'** (www.ayilar.net). The lesbian scene is typically harder to pin down: it's here, there, a little bit everywhere. One of the best options for lesbians is to contact Lambda (p659), which regularly hosts events.

There are an increasing number of openly gay bars and nightclubs in the city, mainly around the Taksim Sq end of İstiklal Caddesi. See the Gay & Lesbian section in the monthly *Time Out İstanbul* to find out what's on. For accommodation options, you may want to check out **Gay Friendly Hotels of İstanbul** (www.istanbulgay.com).

Hamams are a gay fave, though as they're unofficially gay, don't expect much slap and tickle. Despite being a little run-down, **Çukurcuma Hamamı** (Map pp100-1; ☎ 0212-243 2401; Çukurcuma Caddesi 57, Çukurcuma; bath & massage €23, bath only €12; ☯ 10am-9pm) is the city's *hamam* most favoured by gays. **Park Hamam** (Map pp96-7; ☎ 0212-513 7204; Dr Emin Paşa Sokak 10, Sultanahmet; bath & massage €20, bath only €11.50; ☯ 7am-midnight), off Divan Yolu, is popular with local and travelling gay men – and a few straights too.

Follow the fluttering rainbow flag to the laid-back **Sugarclub** (Map pp100-1; ☎ 0212-245 0096; Sakasalim Çıkmazı 7, Beyoğlu; mains €5-8; ☯ 11am-midnight). Bag a beanbag and lie back for a damn fine spot of grazing – food that is. Late evening, head to **Bar Bahçe** (Map pp100-1; ☎ 0212-245 1718; www.barbahce.com; Soğancı Sokak 7/1, Cihangir; ☯ 10pm-2am Sun & Tue-Thu, 10pm-4am Fri & Sat), beloved hang-out of a super-looking 20-something set, or the outrageously fun **Cahide on5** (Map pp100-1; ☎ 0212-292 2425; Meşrutiyet Caddesi 193, Beyoğlu; ☯ noon-4am Wed, Fri & Sat; admission €12) with drag shows and cheeky butt pinching aplenty. Cahide takes its naughty self to a close by outdoor venue (Maçka Demokrasi Parkı 13) during the steamy summer months.

Alternatively, you could go check out the alcohol-free, atmosphere-rich *çay bahçesi* (tea gardens) or *kahvehanes* (coffeehouses) dotted around the Old City. These are great places to relax and sample that Turkish institution, the nargileh, accompanied by a cup of *Türk kahvesi* (Turkish coffee) or *çay*. Although there are many spots to sample nargilehs in the Old City, the most popular nargileh spot in İstanbul is beside the Nusretiye Camii (Map pp100-1) just off Necatibey Caddesi in Tophane, below Beyoğlu.

Tea Gardens & Coffeehouses

SULTANAHMET & AROUND

Set Üstü Çay Bahçesi (Map pp96-7; Gülhane Parkı, Sultanahmet; ☯ 10am-11pm) Locals know this place is special, which is why on weekends they parade all the way through Gülhane Park to get there. Order a pot of *çay* (€4.50), a *tost* (toast) and join the congregation in admiring İstanbul's magnificent Bosphorus.

Yeni Marmara (Map pp96-7; ☎ 0212-516 9013; Çayıroğlu Sokak, Küçük Ayasofya; ☯ 8am-midnight) This cavernous tea house is always packed with locals playing backgammon, sipping *çay* (€1) and puffing on nargilehs (€3). The place has

bags of character, featuring rugs, wall hangings and low brass tables. In winter a wood stove keeps the place cosy; in summer patrons sit on the rear terrace and look out over the Sea of Marmara.

Café Meşale (Map pp96-7; ☎ 0212-518 9562; Arasta Bazaar, Utangaç Sokak, Sultanahmet; ☯ 8am-1am) Generations of backpackers have joined locals in claiming one of Meşale's cushioned benches under coloured lights and enjoying a *çay* (€1) and nargileh (€5). In the summer months there's live Turkish music and whirling dervish performances at 8pm nightly. It's in a sunken courtyard behind the Blue Mosque.

Derviş Aile Çay Bahçesi (Dervish Family Tea Garden; Map pp96-7; Mimar Mehmet Ağa Caddesi, Sultanahmet; ☯ 9am-11pm, closed winter) Locations don't come any better than this. Directly opposite the Blue Mosque, the Derviş' paved courtyard beckons patrons with its comfortable cane chairs and shady trees. Efficient service, reasonable prices and peerless people-watching opportunities make it a great place for leisurely *çay*, nargileh and game of backgammon. There are two-hour dervish performances nightly from 8pm mid-May to October.

BAZAAR DISTRICT

Erenler Çay Bahçesi (Map pp98-9; ☎ 0212-528 3785; Yeniçeriler Caddesi 36/28; ⏰ 9am-midnight, later in summer) Packed to the rafters with students from nearby İstanbul University doing their best to live up to their genetic heritage (ie develop a major tobacco addiction), this nargileh place is set in the leafy courtyard of the Çorlulu Ali Paşa Medrese. There are a handful of carpet shops here, which makes it a little touristy, but it's a delightful spot nonetheless.

Etham Tezçakar Kahveci (Map p116; Halıcılar Caddesi, Grand Bazaar; ⏰ 8.30am-7pm Mon-Sat) This teeny tea and coffee stop is smack-bang in the middle of Halıcılar Caddesi. Its traditional brass-tray tables and wooden stools stand in stark contrast to the funky Fez Café opposite.

İlesam Lokalı (Map pp98-9; ☎ 0212-511 2618; Yeniçeriler Caddesi 84; ⏰ 7am-midnight, later in summer) Set in the courtyard of the Koca Sinan Paşa Medrese, this club was formed by the enigmatically named Professional Union of Owners of the Works of Science & Literature. Fortunately, members seem happy for strangers to infiltrate their ranks. It's a great place to enjoy a cheap *çay* (€0.80) and nargileh (€3). After entering through the gate to Koca Sinan Paşa's tomb, go past the cemetery and it's the second tea house to the right.

Lale Bahçesi (Map pp98-9; Sifahane Sokak, Süleymaniye; ⏰ 8am-midnight) In a sunken courtyard that was once part of the Süleymaniye *külliye* (mosque complex), this charming tea garden is always full of students from the nearby theological college and İstanbul University, who come here to sit on cushioned seats under trees and relax while watching the pretty fountain. In winter they huddle inside the warmly lit kilim-clad *külliye*. It's one of the authentic and atmospheric spots in the area to enjoy a *çay* and nargileh.

Şark Kahvesi (Map p116; ☎ 0212-512 1144; Yağlıkçılar Caddesi 134, Grand Bazaar; ⏰ 8.30am-7pm Mon-Sat) The Şark has had a long pedigree as a popular spot for stall-holders to come and enjoy a

---

TOP THREE TEA GARDENS

Set Üstü Çay Bahçesi, Sultanahmet (p147)
Park setting with Bosphorus views.

Haco Pulo, Beyoğlu (right) Maximum atmosphere, a few steps off İstiklal Caddesi.

Erenler Çay Bahçesi, Bazaar District (above)
Historic setting and welcoming staff.

---

tea-break. These days they have to fight for space with tourists, who love the quirky 'flying dervish' murals, old photographs on the walls and cheap *çay* (€0.80).

BEYOĞLU

Haco Pulo (Map pp100-1; ☎ 0212-244 4210; Passage ZD Hazzopulo; İstiklal Caddesi; ⏰ 9am-midnight) There aren't nearly as many traditional tea houses in Beyoğlu as there are in atmospheric Old İstanbul, but this one can hold its own in any tea-house-off with its neighbour. Set in a delightfully picturesque, cobbled and leafy courtyard, on early summer evenings its stool-to-stool 20- to 30-somethings here. Walking from İstiklal Caddesi through the skinny arcade crowded with offbeat shops adds to the experience. A must.

Bars

SULTANAHMET

Put simply, there isn't a lot going on in Sultanahmet, and what is here certainly isn't frequented by locals. Off season, the bars are empty. Beyoğlu is where it's at.

Cheers Bar (Map pp96-7; ☎ 0532-409 6369; Akbıyık Caddesi 20, Cankurtaran; ⏰ 10am-2am) Slap-bang in the middle of backpacker central, this ugly timber-clad bar offers chilled street-side drinking and a late-night knees-up if there are plenty of travellers in town. Just Bar, next door, offers more of the same.

Şah Pub & Bar (Map pp96-7; ☎ 0212-519 5807; İncili Çavaş Sokak 11, Sultanahmet; ⏰ 10am-3am) If you're looking for Sex on the Beach or a Long Slow Screw Against the Wall (the cocktails, of course), you'll be happy here. With indoor and street-side lounging options this place is either jumping or deathly quiet. At least you can stroll past and deduce the verve before committing. When it buzzes, it's mostly backpackers here enjoying a beer (€2) and nargileh (€4.50).

Legend Hotel (Map pp96-7; ☎ 0212-518 3348; Peykhane Caddesi 16, Binbirdirek; ⏰ 3-11pm) As a hotel, Legend doesn't really make it on the radar, but its outdoor rooftop bar is well worth visiting for the simply awe-inspiring views over the Sea of Marmara – and its reasonable prices (beer €2). Don't come here to party, come here to quietly toast another day.

Sultan Pub (Map pp96-7; ☎ 0212-511 5638; Divan Yolu Caddesi 2, Sultanahmet; ⏰ 9.30am-1am) Sultanahmet's version of Ye Olde English Pub, the Sultan has been around for years and continues to attract 30- or 40ish crowds due to the rooftop terrace (super views) and people-watching from the street-side tables. The pub grub is what you would expect from a place like this (ie stodge).

Yeşil Ev (Map pp96-7; ☎ 0212-517 6785; Kabasakal Caddesi 5, Sultanahmet; ⏰ noon-10.30pm) The rear courtyard of this historic hotel (p138) is an oasis for those who want a quiet drink in elegant Ottoman-era surrounds. A beer costs €4, a glass of wine €5 and a *çay* €2.50.

BEYOĞLU

There are hundreds of bars in Beyoğlu with new ones opening up seemingly every night. We've listed the first-rate stayers here with a mix of newbies, but the best thing to do is to go explore yourself. Before you get too adventurous, make sure you assess bars carefully before entering. Most are very welcoming, but there are a few dodgy ones you don't want to stumble into (see p655). The no-windowed, ad-plugged, letterboxed, basement bar is probably going to bring you surprises you'd prefer not to have.

Most bars in Beyoğlu are packed in the side streets up the northern end of İstiklal Caddesi, near Taksim Sq. İmam Adnan Caddesi is lined with street-side drinking holes such as Türkü Cafe and Bar, Life Rooftop, and old-timer Kaktüs. Beyoğlu's hippest watering holes are down the Tünel end; explore around Sofyalı Sokak.

Badehane (Map pp100-1; ☎ 0212-249 0550; General Yazgan Sokak 5, Tünel; ⏰ 9am-2am) This teeny (unsigned) watering hole is a favourite with locals, and no wonder. On a balmy evening the laneway is heaving with chattering, chain-smoking artsy folk, sipping a beer or three. Dress down and come ready to enjoy an attitude-free evening.

5 Kat (Beşinci Kat; Map pp100-1; ☎ 0212-293 3774; 5th fl Soğancı Sokak 7/5, Cihangir; ⏰ 11am-2am) Everyone knows 5 Kat, which is a credit to its longevity, hospitality and consistent quality. One of the city's best bars, it's also an excellent restaurant (see p144). The 'boudoir-chic' décor features deep-red walls, satin ceiling, velvet chairs and candles galore. The Bosphorus views from the picture windows are simply breathtaking, and in warmer weather you can enjoy them from the breezy rooftop terrace.

KeVe (Map pp100-1; ☎ 0212-251 4338; Tünel Geçidi 10, Tünel; ⏰ 8.30am-2.30am) Is this the most atmospheric bar in the city? In a plant-filled Belle

---

TOP 5 NARGILEH JOINTS

Raft of nargileh joints, Tophane (p147) İstanbul's busiest scene.

Lale Bahçesi, Süleymaniye (opposite) Peaceful and pretty.

Yeni Marmara, Küçük Ayasofya (p147) Perfect for a chilly night.

Erenler Çay Bahçesi, Bazaar District (opposite) Amateurs welcome.

Café Meşale, Sultanahmet (p147) Groups welcome.

Epoque arcade opposite the Tünel station, KeVe is invariably full of 30- to 40-somethings enjoying supreme people-watching from its corner side vantage. An excellent spot for a pre- or post-meal beer (€3).

Gizle Bahçe (Map pp100-1; ☎ 0212-249 2192; Nevizade Sokak 27, Beyoğlu; ⏰ 3pm-2am Tue-Sun) Comfy and casual, this homely option is the perfect pick when you want to check out the action on busy Nevizade Sokak, but you don't want to eat. Locals bag a street-side table for a beer or two to imbibe the feel-good vibe before heading off elsewhere. Beers are cheap at €2.

Dulcinea (Map pp100-1; ☎ 0212-245 1071; Meşelik Sokak 20, Taksim; ⏰ 3pm-2am) Beyoğlu bars come and go, but Dulcinea keeps going thanks to its recent refurbishment from a stylish bar into a happening late-night venue. Grab one of the bar stools and strike up a conversation with a regular – you're bound to enjoy yourself.

Klub Karaoke (Map pp100-1; ☎ 0212-293 7639; Zambak Sokak 15, Beyoğlu; admission €12; ⏰ 5pm-2am Mon-Sat) It had to happen. Some bright spark knew Turks would take to Karaoke like ducks to water and recently opened İstanbul's first Karaoke venue. Locals come in large gaggles and book out the huge private rooms but the 'İstanbul Central' room is a free-for-all, so check your pride in at the door and enjoy. A fun night with new friends guaranteed.

ENTERTAINMENT

There's an entertainment option for everyone in İstanbul. With its array of cinemas, almost religious devotion to all forms of music and great love of dance, it's rare to have a week go by when there's not a special event, festival or performance scheduled. In fact, the only thing that you can't do in this town is be bored.

For an overview of what's on in town make sure you pick up a copy of *Time Out İstanbul*

İSTANBUL

(see p103) and check out **Biletix** (☎ 0216-556 9800; www.biletix.com). You can buy tickets for most events either at the venue's box office or through Biletix. Biletix outlets are found in many spots throughout the city, but the most convenient for travellers is the **Ada Bookshop outlet** (Map pp100-1; İstiklal Caddesi 330, Beyoğlu). Alternatively, it's easy to buy your ticket by credit card on Biletix's website and collect the tickets from either Biletix outlets or the venue before the performance.

A night out carousing to *fasıl* music is a must while you're in İstanbul. The best place to do this is at a *meyhane* – see p146.

Nightclubs

İstanbul has a killer nightlife. Sure, some of the DJs still spin bad mid-90s techno and spray-on-jeans are still fashion *de rigueur*, but the locals know how to have a bloody good time and the open-air club scene is second to none. The live-music scene is sensational as well – see p135 for festivals and right for local venues.

When İstanbullus go out clubbing they dress to kill. If you don't do the same, you'll be unlikely to get past the door bitches (usually buffed young hunks) at the mega venues on the Bosphorus.

As is the case with bars and restaurants, most of the clubbing action is in Beyoğlu or along the Bosphorus. Clubs are busiest on Friday, and especially Saturday nights, and the action doesn't really kick off until 1am.

Crystal (☎ 0212-229 7152; www.clubcrystal.org; Muallım Nacı Caddesi 65, Ortaköy; Fri & Sat €17; ☺ 11pm-5.30am Fri & Sat) This is the second home to the city's house aficionados, who come here to zone in to sets by some of the best mixmasters from Turkey and the rest of Europe. Those in the know go to Reina (right) first, then come here to afterparty. Turn up before 2am at your peril. Both indoor and outdoor bars (super views) provide plenty of nooks for you and your new friend.

Indigo (Map pp100-1; ☎ 0212-245 1307; www.livingindigo .com in Turkish; Arkasu Sokak 1-5, Galatasaray; admission varies; ☺ midnight-5am Thu-Sat) A relatively new but very welcome addition to the live-electronic club circuit, Indigo's no-fuss charm has ensured it a permanent fixture in the diaries of all Beyoğlu clubbing darlings. Expect an eclectic music scene – rock, acid-jazz and electro-house – of local and international DJs. Lots of fun.

Reina (☎ 0212-259 5919; www.reina.com.tr; Muallım Nacı Caddesi 44, Ortaköy; admission free Mon-Thu & Sun, €14 Fri & Sat; ☺ 7pm-3am) During the summer months some 4000 cashed-up beautiful people party hard here until the wee hours alongside spectacular views of the Bosphorus in this open-air megaclub-cum-'entertainment complex'-cum-eatery-cum-pickup-joint. The Reina is a good first port of call for those new to the İstanbul scene. Frock up or you won't get in.

Live Music
WESTERN CLASSICAL MUSIC & OPERA

İstanbul has a lively Western classical music scene. The İstanbul Symphonic Orchestra and the Borusan İstanbul Philharmonic Orchestra perform frequently and international ensembles are regulars in İstanbul too – check *Time Out İstanbul* and the website of **Biletix** (www .biletix.com) to see what's on.

The highlight of the year for classical devotees is undeniably the International İstanbul Music Festival (p135) in June. If you can time your visit for the festival don't miss the concerts held in the ancient Haghia Eirene (p111). Mozart's *The Abduction from the Seraglio*, performed in Topkapı Palace, is unfortunately only really an option for German or Turkish speakers.

ROCK, ELECTRONIC, RAP & REGGAE

If you're European you've probably heard about İstanbul's burgeoning live-music scene. For the rest of us here's an introduction: in the last few years İstanbul has witnessed a creative renaissance in the arts arena that's seen new venues opening almost weekly and the sound of garage-band rehearsals almost a fact of life in Beyoğlu's streets. Check out *Crossing The Bridge – The Story of Music in İstanbul*, by Fatih Akin, and the monthly *Time Out İstanbul* to prime yourself.

It almost goes without saying that there's no need to dress up too much.

Babylon (Map pp100-1; ☎ 0212-292 7368; www.baby lon.com.tr; Şehbender Sokak 3, Tünel; admission varies; ☺ 9.30pm-2am Tue-Thu, 10pm-3am Fri & Sat) Babylon is İstanbul's No 1 live venue: any international and local act worth listening to has played in its dark recesses. One night it's the DJ-spun 'Oldies but Goldies', so grab your spangled thong, the other it's Burhan Öçal with his blend of oriental-acid jazz. Every night it's a fun-loving Boho crowd. Buy tickets at the **box office** (☺ 11am-7pm, 7.30pm-start of event) opposite.

Roxy (Map pp100-1; ☎ 0212-249 1283; www.roxy.com.tr; Arslan Yatağı Sokak 7, Taksim; admission varies; 🕑 9pm-3am Wed & Thu, 10pm-4am Fri & Sat) Long-time, beloved haunt of an intoxicated grungy set, Roxy arm wrestles Babylon for the title of the city's best live-music club and usually is just pipped at the finish line. Come to Roxy for sweaty, crowd-surfing nights – forget glam frocks as nights here usually get messy. Expect anything from rap and hip-hop through to jazz fusion and electronic – and '80s on the weekends.

Kapak Rock Bar (Map pp100-1; ☎ 0212-245 4229; Sadri Alışık Sokak 32, Beyoğlu; 🕑 4pm-4am) A newcomer on the scene, on the busiest nights (Friday and Saturday), you'll hear up-and-coming alternative rock bands on stage doing their thing; other nights are more like intimate jam sessions between the rockers on stage and their mates in the crowd – a very friendly scene. You can eat here too.

Balans Music Hall (Map pp100-1; ☎ 0212-251 7020; www.balansmusichall.com, in Turkish; Balo Sokak 22; Beyoğlu; admission €5.50-14; 🕑 9pm-4am Mon-Sat) This three-levelled space, with a great sound system, regularly hosts big and small-name local rock bands. It's a friendly, mixed crowd: join the crush up front to make friends fast.

JAZZ

Jazz Café (Map pp100-1; ☎ 0212-245 0516; www.jazzcaféistanbul.com, in Turkish; Hasnun Galip Sokak 20, Beyoğlu; admission free; 🕑 8pm-4am Tue-Sat) This old favourite is popular with a mix of mainly 30-something expats and locals. Expect laid-back jazz sessions with mostly local musos and occasionally the odd '80s disco thrown in. If you're a jazz purist you might want to look elsewhere. The live music starts at 10pm.

Nardis Jazz Club (Map pp100-1; ☎ 0212-244 6327; www.nardisjazz.com; Kuledibi Sokak 14, Galata; admission €9-13; 🕑 music 10pm-1am Mon-Thu, 11pm-2am Fri & Sat) Just downhill from the Galata Tower, this venue is where the real aficionados go. Run by jazz guitarist Önder Focan, it's small and if you want a decent table you'll need to book. There's a great sound system, as you'd expect, and a restaurant too, but those in-the-know eat elsewhere. It hosts international acts.

Cinemas

İstiklal Caddesi, between Taksim and Galatasaray, is the heart of İstanbul's *sinema* (cinema) district, so you can simply cinema-hop until you find something you like. The only cinema close to Sultanahmet is the Şafak Sinemaları at Çemberlitaş. Foreign films are mostly shown in English with Turkish subtitles, but double-check at the box office in case the film has *Türkçe* (Turkish) dubbing, which sometimes happens with blockbusters and children's films.

When possible, buy your tickets a few hours in advance. Depending on the venue, tickets cost €5 to €7 for adults, €3 or €4 for students – many places offer reduced rates on Wednesday.

City cinemas include:

AFM Fitaş (Map pp100-1; ☎ 0212-251 2020; İstiklal Caddesi 24-26, Beyoğlu)
Alkazar Sinema Merkezi (Map pp100-1; ☎ 0212-293 2466; İstiklal Caddesi 179, Beyoğlu)
Atlas (Map pp100-1; ☎ 0212-252 8576; İstiklal Caddesi 209, Atlas Pasajı, Beyoğlu)
Beyoğlu (Map pp100-1; ☎ 0212-251 3240; İstiklal Caddesi 140, Beyoğlu)
Emek (Map pp100-1; ☎ 0212-293 8439; İstiklal Caddesi, Yeşilçam Sokak 5, Beyoğlu)
İstanbul Modern Cinema (Map pp100-1; ☎ 0212-334 7300; www.istanbulmodern.org; Meclis-i Mebusan Caddesi, off Necatibey Caddesi, Beyoğlu) Excellent selection of arthouse movies.
Rexx (☎ 216-336 0112; Sakızgülü Sokak 20-22, Kadıköy)
Şafak Sinemaları (Map pp96-7; ☎ 0212-516 2660; Divan Yolu 134, Çemberlitaş)
Sinepop (Map pp100-1; ☎ 0212-251 1176; İstiklal Caddesi, Yeşilçam Sokak 22, Beyoğlu)

Folk Dance

There are a number of touristy 'Turkish Shows' around town providing a snapshot of Turkey's folk dances (with belly-dancing), usually accompanied by dinner. Beloved by package-tour operators, they are expensive and the food is usually mediocre at best. Still, if you are keen to see some folk dance while you're in town these places are usually the only ones you'll be able to do it. The two most popular are **Orient House** (Map pp98-9; ☎ 0212-517 6163; www.orienthouseistanbul.com; Tiyatro Caddesi 27, Beyazıt; adult/child €70/35; 🕑 9pm-midnight) and **Sultana's** (Map pp94-5; ☎ 0212-219 3904; www.sultanas-nights.com; Cumhuriyet Caddesi 16, Elmadağ; €75; 🕑 dinner 7.30pm, show 9pm, finish midnight).

Sport

There's only one spectator sport that really matters to Turks: football. Eighteen teams from all over Turkey compete from August to May. Each season three move up from the second division into the first and three get

İSTANBUL

demoted. The top team of the first division plays in the European Cup.

Matches are usually held on weekends, normally on a Saturday night. Almost any Turkish male will be able to tell you which is the best match to see. Tickets are sold at the clubhouses at the *stadyum* (stadium) or at **Biletix** (☎ 0216-556 9800; www.biletix.com) and usually go on sale between Tuesday and Thursday for a weekend game. For open seating you'll pay around €12; for covered seating – which has the best views – anywhere from €17 to €70. If you miss out on the tickets you can get them at the door of the stadium, but they are usually outrageously overpriced.

Some level of violence at games is a fact of life. It's not usually punch-ups or worse, but more likely to be breaking and throwing of seats or fierce fist-waving recriminations to the referee (who may be escorted off by riot police at the end of the game). Sadly, this seems to be seen as all part of the fun of football games and no-one thinks anything of it. It goes without saying that you can count the number of women at matches on one hand. If you're worried about violence, avoid the clashes of arch rivals, Galatasaray and Fenerbahçe. Beşiktaş is another team with a large following.

SHOPPING

If you love shopping you've come to the right place. Despite İstanbul's big-ticket historic sights, many travellers come here and find the highlight of their visit was searching and bantering for treasures in the magnificent **Grand Bazaar** (p115). Come here for jewellery, leather, textiles, ceramics and trinkets. And if you're still standing after a serious session in the Grand Bazaar, İstanbul offers plenty of other opportunities to put your credit rating in jeopardy. **Arasta Bazaar** (p106), behind the Blue Mosque in Sultanahmet, is lined with an excellent range of carpet and ceramic shops – come to this minimum-hassle spot for a leisurely window-shop.

Tahtakale, the area between the Grand Bazaar and Eminönü, is the best place to fossick for good-value haberdashery, manchester, kitchen goods, and especially dried fruits, spices and lotions in the Spice Bazaar – locals say if you can't find it in Tahtakale it doesn't exist. Over in Beyoğlu, **İstiklal Caddesi** (p120) is lined with clothing, shoe, book and music shops; around the Tünel end you'll find old books and prints. A few steps away is **Çukurcuma**, the city's best antique and curios district; on Sunday afternoons there's a flea market here.

Come energised, come with maximum overdraft, come with an empty suitcase.

Art & Antiques

Sofa (Map pp96-7; ☎ 0212-520 2850; Nuruosmaniye Caddesi 85, Cağaloğlu; 9.30am-7pm Mon-Sat) As well as its eclectic range of prints, ceramics, calligraphy and Ottoman and Byzantine curios, Sofa sells contemporary Turkish art and books. The range of jewellery made out of antique Ottoman coins and 24-carat gold is extraordinarily beautiful, but an heirloom piece will start at €400. It's well worth coming in just to browse.

Artrium (Map pp100-1; ☎ 0212-251 4302; Tünel Geçidi 7, Tünel; 9am-7pm Mon-Sat) This Aladdin's cave is crammed with antique ceramics, Ottoman miniatures, maps, prints and jewellery.

Galeri Alfa (Map pp100-1; ☎ 0212-251 1672; Faikpaşa Sokak 47, Çukurcuma; 11am-6pm) What makes this shop special is its range of charming, colourful toy Ottoman soldiers and court figures. It's worth popping in just to see them.

Nebil Basmacı (Map p116; ☎ 0212-520 9504; Halıcılar Caddesi 97, Grand Bazaar; 9am-7pm Mon-Sat) One of myriad shops selling a mix of curios and carpets in the Grand Bazaar, Nebil Basmacı does a nice line in Russian icons, antique İznik tiles (from €40) and quality Anatolian carpets.

Şamdan (Candle; Map pp100-1; ☎ 0212-245 4445; Altıpatlar Sokak 20, Çukurcuma; 11am-5.30pm) Located in the city's best antique and curio district, this small shop stocks quality antique furniture, china and glassware.

Carpets & Textiles

Cocoon (Map pp96-7; ☎ 0212-638 6271; www.cocoontr .com; Küçük Aya Sofya Caddesi 13, Sultanahmet; 8.30am-7.30pm) There are so many rug and textile shops in İstanbul that isolating individual shops is usually incredibly difficult. We had no problem in singling this one out, though. Four floors of felt hats and antique costumes and textiles from Central Asia are artfully displayed next to rugs from Persia, Central Asia, the Caucasus and Anatolia. There's another, smaller shop in the nearby Arasta Bazaar.

EthniCon (Map p116; ☎ 0212-527 6841; Takkeciler Sokak 58-60, Grand Bazaar; www.ethnicon.com; 9am-9pm Mon-Sat) One of the frontrunners in the contemporary kilim trend, EthniCon has a leading

İSTANBUL

TURKISH DELIGHT

You mustn't leave İstanbul without sampling its *lokum* (Turkish delight). The stuff you get here is the best in the world, and you can even buy it from the original shop of **Ali Muhiddin Hacı Bekir** (Map pp96-7; ☎ 0212-522 0666; Hamidiye Caddesi 83; 9am-8pm Mon-Sat), inventor of the gorgeously gooey gloop. There's another store on İstiklal Caddesi in Beyoğlu (Map pp100–1) and one in Kadıköy.

The story goes that Ali Muhiddin came to İstanbul from the Black Sea mountain town of Kastamonu and established himself as a confectioner in the Ottoman capital in the late 18th century. Dissatisfaction with hard candies and traditional sweets led him to invent a new confection that would be easy to swallow, and he called his creation *rahat lokum*, the 'comfortable morsel'. *Lokum*, as it soon came to be called, was an immediate hit with the denizens of the imperial palace and soon the translucent jellied jewels had fans all over the country.

Ali Muhiddin elaborated on his original confection, as did his offspring (the shop, which was established in 1777, is still owned by his descendants); and now, as well as enjoying it *sade* (plain), you can buy *lokum* made with various fillings, including *cevizli* (walnut) and the classic *şam fıstıklı* (pistachio), or flavoured with *portakkallı* (orange), *bademli* (almond), *roze* (rose-water) or even crunchy coffee beans. You can also get a *çeşitli* (assortment).

---

range of patchwork kilims well matched to a modern home. You'll pay around €180 per metre here.

Haseki Hamam Carpet & Kilim Sales Store (Map pp96-7; ☎ 0212-638 0035; Haseki Hürrem Hamamı, Aya Sofya Meydanı 4; 9am-5pm Tue-Sun winter, 9am-6.30pm Tue-Sun summer) Located in the historic Baths of Lady Hürrem, this Ministry of Culture shop sells new carpets replicated from museum pieces. Although prices are fixed and clearly marked, you can get better deals elsewhere. However, this is a good place to come to get an idea of prices before you launch out into the carpet shops.

Muhlis Günbattı (Map p116; ☎ 0212-511 6562; Perdahçılar Sokak 48, Grand Bazaar; 9am-7pm Mon-Sat) One of the most famous stores in the Grand Bazaar, Muhlis Günbattı specialises in *suzani* (needlework) fabrics from Uzbekistan. These spectacularly beautiful bedspreads and wall hangings are made from fine cotton embroidered with silk. They're commonly sold throughout İstanbul now, but the range and quality here is unbeatable. Quality bedspreads start from €300.

Sedir (Map pp96-7; ☎ 0212-458 4702; Mimar Mehmet Ağa Caddesi 39, Sultanahmet; 9am-10pm) There can't be too many rug shops in town with Byzantine mosaics in the basement but this one has just that. After looking through Sedir's excellent and affordable range of kilims, ask the friendly staff if you can have a peek at the mosaics and the sacred spring.

Şişko Osman (Fatty Osman; Map p116; ☎ 0212-528 3548; www.siskoosman.com; Zincirli Han 15, Grand Bazaar; 9am-6pm Mon-Sat) The Osmans have been in the rug business for four generations and their popularity has seen their original shop triple its size. The range and customer service here is certainly hard to beat.

Troy (Map pp96-7; ☎ 0212-458 0892; Arasta Bazaar 39, Sultanahmet; 9am-9pm) One of the many rug shops in the Arasta Bazaar, Troy is noteworthy for its quality stock and the delightful owner, whose shop seems to be filled with customers when all the others are empty. If you're after a hassle-free 'what-to-look-for-when-buying-a-carpet' primer, come here.

Yazi Hacı (Map p116; ☎ 0212-526 7748; Yağlıkçılar Caddesi 16, Grand Bazaar; 10am-7.30pm Mon-Sat) Locals in-the-know come here when they want that special something. This den has wall-to-wall textiles with everything from hand-made scarfs, silk, satin, *suzani* to hand-painted bedspreads. Textile aficionados will think they've died and gone to heaven.

Handicrafts & Ceramics

İstanbul has no end of shops stocking a mixed range of handicrafts and ceramics, but we thought two are worth singling out – both are hassle-free and have the rare find of fixed and clearly marked prices.

Sönmez (Map pp96-7; Atmeydanı Sokak 19, Sultanahmet) Has a seemingly never-ending cavern of goodies.

Coşkun's bazaar (Map pp96-7; Soğukçeşme Sokak 20, Sultanahmet) Is owned by two charismatic brothers in an old house stuck to the side of the Topkapı Walls.

The following places are more specialist:

Chalcedon (Map pp96-7; ☎ 0212-527 6376; Caferiye Sokak 2, Sultanahmet; ☽ 9am-6pm) The azure chalcedony stone, mined in Eskişehir in western Anatolia, reputedly brings calm to its wearer. Used since ancient times in Anatolia, it was named after Chalcedon, modern-day Kadıköy. This small boutique offers the stone crafted into a very appealing range of jewellery. Come here if you want something a little different from what's on offer elsewhere.

Deli Kızın Yeri (Map p116; ☎ 0212-511 1914; Halıcılar Caddesi 42, Grand Bazaar; ☽ 9am-7pm Mon-Sat) Don't let the name – the Crazy Lady's Place – put you off. This is the spot to pick up something for so-and-so's new baby, with a good line of hand-made Turkish teddies and puppets on offer and even a cardboard 'Build Your Own' Aya Sofya. The best thing is that some of these goodies are made by village women on consignment. The Crazy Lady has another shop close by, but this one is better.

İstanbul Handicrafts Market (Map pp96-7; İstanbul Sanatlar Çarşısı; ☎ 0212-517 6782; Kabasakal Caddesi, Sultanahmet; ☽ 9am-6.30pm) Set in the small rooms surrounding the quiet, leafy courtyard of the 18th-century Cedid Mehmed Efendi Medresesi, this handicrafts centre is unusual in that local artisans work here and don't mind visitors watching them. This lovely oasis is a hassle-free place to purchase calligraphy, embroidery, glassware, miniature paintings, ceramics and costumed dolls.

Caferağa Medresesi (Map pp96-7; ☎ 0212-513 3601; Caferiye Sokak, Sultanahmet; ☽ 9am-6.30pm) Near Aya Sofya, it's similar to the handicrafts market, but also runs handicraft and music lessons (in Turkish only).

İznik Classics & Tiles (Map pp96-7; ☎ 0212-517 1705; Arasta Bazaar 67 & 73, Sultanahmet; ☽ 9am-8pm) Arguably the best selection of ceramics in the city, İznik Classics offers everything from superb hand-painted collector's items to very affordable, mass-produced, yet still lovely tiles, platters and vases. With two shops in Arasta Bazaar, another in the Grand Bazaar (Map p116) and a four-floored gallery in Sultanahmet, if you can't find it here you're not looking hard enough.

Homewares & Clothing

Azad Tekstil (Map p116; ☎ 0212-512 4202; Yağlıkçılar Caddesi 16, Grand Bazaar; ☽ 9am-7pm Mon-Sat) If you're after simple but stylish 100% cotton bed spreads, tablecloths or peştemals (hamam wraps, from €3) for arguably the best price and range in the city, this is the place for you. Double-bed spreads go for around €25.

Derviş (Map p116; ☎ 0212-514 4525; www.dervis .com; Keseciler Caddesi 33-35, Grand Bazaar; ☽ 9am-7pm Mon-Sat) Follow the delicious clove scent into Derviş, a stylish gem awash with clothing, shawls, towels and sheets. You'll find raw cotton and silk peştemals, and traditional Turkish dowry vests and engagement dresses. It's all quality stuff but it's aimed at travellers so expect to pay a premium – herbal soaps are €3.50, a peştemal is €15 and the throws start at €200. There's another shop in Halıcılar Cad.

Abdulla Natural Products (Map p116; ☎ 0212-522 9078; Halıcılar Caddesi 53, Grand Bazaar; ☽ 9am-7pm Mon-Sat) On a similar vein to Derviş it's a hanky-sized shop specialising in quality cotton bed linen, silky goat-hair and sheepskin throws, and towels.

eviHAN (Map pp100-1; ☎ 0212-244 0034; Altıpatlar Sokak 8, Çukurcuma; ☽ 10am-7pm Mon-Sat) If you're after a special something you know no-one else will have back home look no further. The owner's range of quality, Ottoman-inspired, but contemporary funky clothing looks simply fantastic with a wristful of her handmade beads.

Leyla Seyhanlı (Map pp100-1; ☎ 0212-293 7410; Altıpatlar Sokak 10, Çukurcuma; ☽ 10am-7pm) If you love old clothes, you'll adore Leyla Seyhanlı's boutique. Filled to the brim with piles of Ottoman embroidery and outfits, it's a rummager's delight. There's no sign, but it's right next door to eviHAN.

Leather

Koç Deri (Map p116; ☎ 0212-527 5553; Kürkçüler Çarşısı 22-46, Grand Bazaar; ☽ 9am-7pm Mon-Sat) If you fancy a leather jacket or coat, Koç is bound to have something that suits. It's one of the bazaar's busiest and longest-running stores.

Küçük Köşe (Little Corner; Map p116; ☎ 0212-513 0335; Kalpakçılar Caddesi 89-91, Grand Bazaar; ☽ 9am-7pm Mon-Sat) If you've always wanted a Kelly or Birkin but can't afford Hermès, this place is for you. Its copies of the work of the big-gun designers are good quality and at around €200 they're a lot more affordable.

Music

Lale Plak (Map pp100-1; ☎ 0212-293 7739; Galipdede Caddesi 1, Tünel; ☽ 9am-7pm Mon-Sat) This long-standing magnet for music aficionados is crammed with

CDs of jazz, Western and Turkish classical, plus Turkish folk and some electronica.

Mephisto (Map pp100-1; ☎ 0212-249 0687; İstiklal Caddesi 197, Beyoğlu; 🕙 9am-midnight) This is the spot to pick up Turkish pop, rap and hip-hop.

Old Books, Maps & Prints

Denizler Kitabevi (Map pp100-1; ☎ 0212-249 8893; İstiklal Caddesi 395; 🕙 9.30am-7.30pm) A charmingly eccentric shop specialising in old maps and books, it also stocks antique prints.

Ottomania (Map pp100-1; ☎ 0212-243 2157; Sofyalı Sokak 30-32, Tünel; 🕙 9am-6pm Mon-Sat) An old map or print can be a great souvenir to bring home from İstanbul and with Ottomania's quality stock you won't have trouble sourcing one. Prices are clearly marked.

GETTING THERE & AWAY

All roads lead to İstanbul. As the country's foremost transport hub, the question is not so much how to get there but how to negotiate the sprawling urban mass when you arrive.

Air

İstanbul's main international airport is the **Atatürk International Airport** (Atatürk Hava Limanı; ☎ 0212-465 3000; www.dhmiata.gov.tr), 23km west of Sultanahmet. The international *(dış hatlar)* and domestic terminals *(iç hatlar)* are side by side. Check the website for flight arrivals and departure times.

There are car hire desks, money-exchange offices, a pharmacy, ATMs and a PTT in the international arrivals area. There's also a **tourist information desk** (🕙 24hr) that supplies a very limited range of maps, advice and brochures. The **left-luggage service** (per suitcase per 24hr €5; 🕙 24hr) is to your left as you exit customs.

For domestic flights it's a good idea to arrive at least an hour before your departure time, especially on weekends and during public holidays, as check-in and security queues can be long.

One of the few annoying things about the airport is that travellers must pay €0.55 to use a baggage trolley. You must pay in Turkish liras, euros or US dollars; fortunately, attendants give change.

İstanbul also has a smaller airport, **Sabiha Gökçen International Airport** (SAW; ☎ 0216-585 5000; www.sgairport.com), some 50km east of Sultanahmet, on the Asian side of the city. It's increasingly popular for cheap flights from Europe, particularly Germany.

INTERNATIONAL AIRLINE OFFICES

Aeroflot (Map pp94-5; ☎ 0212-296 6725; Cumhuriyet Caddesi 26, Taksim)

Air France Taksim (Map pp100-1; ☎ 0212-310 1919; Emirhan Caddesi 145\4, Dikilitaş); Atatürk International Airport (☎ 0212-465 5491)

Azerbaijan Airlines (Map pp94-5; ☎ 0212-296 3530; Cumhuriyet Caddesi 30, Harbiye)

British Airways 4 Levent (☎ 0212-317 6600; Büyükdere Caddesi 209\17, Tekfen Tower); Atatürk International Airport (☎ 0212-465 5682)

Corendon Airlines (☎ 0216-658 7250)

Cyprus Turkish Airlines Mecidiyeköy (☎ 0212-274 6932; Büyükdere Caddesi 56) Atatürk International Airport (☎ 0212-465 3597)

Emirates Airlines Gümüşsuyu (☎ 0212-334 8888; İnönü Caddesi 96); Atatürk International Airport (☎ 0212-465 5814)

Fly Air (☎ 0212-444 4359)

German Wings (☎ 0212-354 6666 call centre only)

Iran Air (Map pp94-5; ☎ 0212-225 0256; Vali Konağı Caddesi 17, Harbiye)

Japan Airlines Elmadağ (Map pp94-5; ☎ 0212-233 0840; Cumhuriyet Caddesi 107/2)

Lufthansa (☎ 0212-315 3434 call centre only)

Olympic Airways Elmadağ (Map pp94-5; ☎ 0212-296 7575; Cumhuriyet Caddesi 171/A); Atatürk International Airport (☎ 0212-465 3388)

Onur Air Elmadağ (Map pp94-5; ☎ 0212-233 3800; Cumhuriyet Caddesi 141/147); Atatürk International Airport (☎ 0212-663 0685)

Pegasus Airlines (☎ 0212-697 7777 call centre only)

Singapore Airlines Harbiye (Map pp94-5; ☎ 0212-232 3706; Halaskargazi Caddesi 113); Atatürk International Airport (☎ 0212-465 3473)

Most of the city's airline offices are along Cumhuriyet Caddesi between Taksim Sq and Harbiye, but Turkish Airlines has offices around the city. Travel agencies can also sell tickets and make reservations for most airlines.

For details of international flights to and from İstanbul, see p671. For information on flights from İstanbul to other Turkish cities, see p679.

Boat
KARAKÖY

Cruise ships arrive at the **Karaköy International Maritime Passenger Terminal** (Map pp100-1; ☎ 0212-249 5776) just near the Galata Bridge.

YENİKAPI

Yenikapı (Map pp98–9) is the dock for the **İDO** (İstanbul Deniz Otobüsleri; www.ido.com.tr) fast ferries across the Sea of Marmara to Yalova (for Bursa) and Bandırma (for İzmir). A new fast ferry line is planned to run between Yenikapı and Mudanya (for Bursa). For more details on services to Yalova see p287, and for Bandırma, see p202.

İDO also operates a commuter ferry between İstanbul (Bostancı) and Mudanya (near Bursa).

KABATAŞ

İDO ferries run services from Kabataş to Yalova (for Bursa).

Bus

BUS STATIONS

The **International İstanbul Bus Station** (Uluslararası İstanbul Otogarı; Map p93; ☎ 0212-658 0505) is the city's main bus station for both intercity and international routes. Called simply the 'otogar', it's in the western district of Esenler, about 10km northwest of Sultanahmet.

The easiest way to get to the otogar is to catch the tram from Sultanahmet to Aksaray and then connect with the Light Rail Transit (LRT) service which stops at the otogar on its way to the airport – all up a half-hour trip. If you're coming from Taksim or Beyoğlu, bus No 830 leaves about every 20 minutes from around 6.30am to 8.40pm from Taksim Sq, taking about an hour to reach the centre of the otogar. Many bus companies run a free *servis* (shuttle bus) between the otogar and Taksim Sq or Sultanahmet. Ask if there's a *servis* when you buy your ticket or when you arrive at the otogar. A taxi from Sultanahmet to the otogar will cost around €12 (20 minutes); from Taksim Sq around €15 (30 minutes).

The otogar is a monster of a place, with over 150 ticket offices all touting for business. Buses leave from here for virtually everywhere in Turkey and for countries including Azerbaijan, Armenia, Bulgaria, Georgia, Greece, Iran, Romania and Syria. For details of international bus services, see p673 to p677.

Excluding holiday periods, you can usually come to the otogar, spend 30 minutes comparing prices and departure times and be on your way within the hour. There's no easy way to find the best fare; you have to go from one office to another asking prices and inspecting the buses parked around the back.

If you plan to leave sooner rather than later, make sure you ask about departure times as well as fares. Touts will be happy to sell you a cheap fare on a bus leaving in four hours' time, but in the meantime several buses from other companies offering similar rates could have seen you on your way.

There is a much smaller bus station on the Asian shore of the Bosphorus at **Harem** (Map pp94-5; ☎ 0216-333 3763), south of Üsküdar and north of Haydarpaşa Train Station. If you're arriving in İstanbul by bus from anywhere in Anatolia (the Asian side of Turkey) it's always quicker to get out at Harem and take the car ferry to Sirkeci (ferry from 7am, then every half-hour until 9.30pm daily). If you stay on the bus until the otogar, you'll add at least an hour to your journey (and then you'll still have to travel into town).

SERVICES FROM İSTANBUL'S OTOGAR

Destination	Fare	Duration	Distance
Alanya	€40	16hr	860km
Ankara	€18-26	5-5½hr	450km
Antakya	€22 (day)	18hr	1115km
	€25 (night)		
Antalya	€36	12½hr	740km
Bodrum	€35-40	12½hr	860km
Bursa	€9	4hr	230km
Çanakkale	€9-14	6hr	340km
Denizli	€20-23	12hr	665km
(for Pamukkale)			
Edirne	€9	2½hr	235km
Fethiye	€40	12hr	820km
Göreme	€18-22	11hr	725km
İzmir	€22-30	8hr	575km
Kaş	€28	12hr	1090km
Konya	€20	10hr	660km
Kuşadası	€37	9hr	555km
Marmaris	€35-40	12½hr	805km
Trabzon	€35	24hr	970km

BUS COMPANIES

The top national lines, offering premium service at marginally higher prices, are:

Kamil Koç Otogar (☎ 444 0567 country-wide; www.kamil koc.com.tr, in Turkish; ticket office No 144-6) Beyoğlu ticket office (Map pp100-1; ☎ 0212-252 7223; İnönü Caddesi 31)

Ulusoy Otogar (☎ 444 1888 country-wide; www.ulusoy .com.tr; ticket office No 128) Beyoğlu ticket office (Map pp100-1; ☎ 0212-244 6375; İnönü Caddesi 59)

Varan Turizm Otogar (☎ 444 8999 country-wide; www .varan.com.tr; ticket office No 16) Beyoğlu ticket office (Map pp100-1; ☎ 0212-251 7474; İnönü Caddesi 29/B)

Car & Motorcycle

The E80 Trans-European Motorway (TEM) from Europe passes about 10km north of Atatürk International Airport, then as Hwy 02 takes the Fatih Bridge across the Bosphorus to Asia, passing some 1.5km north of the Sabiha Gökçen International Airport. This will be your main route for getting to and from İstanbul, but try to avoid rush hours (7am to 10am and 3pm to 7pm Monday to Saturday) as the traffic is nightmarish and the Bosphorus bridges come to a standstill.

Don't plan to use your car in İstanbul; park it for the duration of your stay (p160). If you want to hire a car for your travels, we recommend you hire it from either of the airports on your way *out* of İstanbul. This will mean lugging your baggage by taxi or public transport to the airport, but it won't mean navigating İstanbul's manic roads in an unfamiliar vehicle – you'll be comfortably on your way out of the city before you even get behind the wheel. Alternatively, you could catch public transport to your next destination, and then rent.

Recommended car rental agencies include:

Avis Taksim (☎ 0212-297 9610; www.avis.com.tr; Abdülhak Hamit Caddesi 84) Atatürk International Airport (☎ 0212-465 3455; ☼ 24hrs) Sabiha Gökçen International Airport (☎ 0216-585 5154; ☼ 9am-7pm)

Hertz Taksim (☎ 0212-225 6404; www.hertz.com.tr; Yedikuyular Caddesi 4) Atatürk International Airport (☎ 0212-465 5999; ☼ 24hrs) Sabiha Gökçen International Airport (☎ 0216-349 3040; ☼ 9am-7pm)

National Taksim (☎ 0212-254 7719; www.nationalcar .com; Şehit Muhtar Mahallesi, Aydede Sokak 1/2) Atatürk International Airport (☎ 0212-465 3546; ☼ noon-midnight)

Train

At the time of writing, all trains from Europe were terminating at **Sirkeci Train Station** (Map pp96-7; ☎ 0212-527 0051). Outside the station's main door there's a convenient tram that runs up the hill to Sultanahmet or the other way over the Golden Horn to Kabataş, from where you can travel by funicular rail up to Taksim Sq. Note, that after the Marmaray project is finished (see p159), Sirkeci station will become a museum and trains will terminate at Yenikapı.

Trains from the Asian side of Turkey and from countries east and south terminate at **Haydarpaşa Train Station** (Map pp94-5; ☎ 0216-336 4470), on the Asian shore close to Kadıköy. Ignore anyone who suggests you should take a taxi to or from Haydarpaşa. The ferry between Eminönü and Haydarpaşa/Kadıköy is cheap and speedy; taxis across the Bosphorus always get stuck in traffic. Haydarpaşa has an *emanet* (left-luggage room), a restaurant serving alcoholic beverages, numerous snack shops, bank ATMs and a small PTT. Tickets for trains leaving from Haydarpaşa Train Station can also be purchased from Sirkeci Train Station. Note that as part of the Marmaray project (see p159), Haydarpaşa Train Station will close

MAIN TRAIN SERVICES TO\FROM İSTANBUL

From Sirkeci Train Station

All the following services are express trains. The fares quoted are for a bunk in a sleeper.

Destination	Train	Fare	Frequency	Departs	Arrives	Duration
From İstanbul						
Belgrade	Bosphorus/Balkan	from €58	daily	10pm	8.18pm	22hr
Bucharest	Bosphorus/Balkan	from €48	daily	10pm	5.30pm	19½hr
Budapest	Bosphorus/Balkan	from €81	daily	10pm	10.12am	36hr
Salonika	Dostluk/Filia	from €48	daily	8pm	7.54am	12hr
Sofia	Bosphorus/Balkan	from €26	daily	10pm	11.39am	13½hr
To İstanbul						
From Belgrade	Bosphorus/Balkan	from €58	daily	8.40am	8.25am	22hr
From Bucharest	Bosphorus/Balkan	from €48	daily	2.10pm	8.25am	19½hr
From Budapest	Bosphorus/Balkan	from €81	daily	7.15pm	8.25am	36hr
From Salonika	Dostluk/Filias	from €48	daily	8pm	7.45am	12hr
From Sofia	Bosphorus/Balkan	from €26	daily	6.30pm	8.25am	13½hr

İSTANBUL

MAIN TRAIN SERVICES TO\FROM İSTANBUL *Continued*

From Haydarpaşa Train Station

Other trains not in the table that originate in İstanbul include: *Doğu Ekspresi* (Kars via Ankara, Sivas, Erzurum); *Güney Ekspresi* (Diyarbakır via Ankara, Keyseri, Sivas, Malatya), *İç Andalou Mavi* (Adana via Konya), *Pamukkale Ekspresi* (Denizli via Eğirdir).

There are a number of services between İstanbul and Ankara; only two are shown below.

Destination	Train	Fare	Frequency	Departs	Arrives	Duration
From İstanbul						
Aleppo	*Toros*	€25 (sleeper)	Thu	8.55am	2.34pm	29hr (via Gaziantep, Adana, Konya, Eskişehir)
Ankara (day)	*Baskent*	€12 (pullman chairs only)	daily	10am	4.30pm	6½hr
Ankara (night)		€36/25 (1st-/2nd-class sleeper)	daily	10.30pm	8.04am	9½hr (via Eskişehir)
Kayseri	*Vangölü*	€19/40/34 pullman/1st-/2nd-class sleeper	Mon & Fri	8.05pm	2.48pm	19hr (via Ankara)
Konya	*Meram*	€20/56/45 (pullman/1st-/2nd-class sleeper)	daily	7.20pm	8.21am	13hr (via Afyon)
Tatvan	*Vangölü*	€35/71/60 (pullman/1st-/2nd class sleeper)	Mon & Fri	8.05pm	1.09pm	41hr (via Ankara, Kayseri, Malatya)
Tehran	*Trans-Asya*	€38 (couchette)	Wed	10.55pm	6.45pm	66hr (via Ankara, Kayseri, Van)
To İstanbul						
See above for details of major stops along the way.						
From Aleppo	*Toros*	€25 (sleeper)	Tue	11.05am	5.55pm	29hr
From Ankara (day)	*Baskent*	€12 (pullman only)	daily	10.20am	4.50pm	6½hr
From Ankara (night)		€36/25 (1st-/2nd-class sleeper)	daily	10.30pm	8am	9½hr
From Kayseri	*Vangölü*	€19/40/34 (pullman/1st-/2nd-class sleeper)	Wed & Fri	4.40am	11pm	19hr
From Konya	*Meram*	€20/56/45 (pullman/1st-/2nd-class sleeper)	daily	5.50pm	6.30am	13hr
From Tatvan	*Vangölü*	€35/71/60 (pullman/1st-/2nd-class sleeper)	Tue & Thu	7.20am	11pm	41hr
From Tehran	*Trans-Asya*	€38 (couchette)	Thu	8.15pm	3.45pm	69hr

and trains are proposed to depart from a new station to be built in Üsküdar.

The national rail system has received a much-needed injection of funds and fast-rail projects that are on the drawing board may be running by the time you read this. See p684 for more information.

GETTING AROUND

Moving 16 million people around İstanbul is a challenge but the government has begun to implement ambitious projects aimed to ease the city's horrendous traffic problems. The Marmaray project (see opposite) is planned to bring İstanbul world-class public transport.

THREE CHEERS FOR MARMARAY

Marmaray (www.marmaray.com) is an ambitious public transport project aimed to relieve İstanbul's woeful traffic congestion. Plans show the rail line, which presently follows the coast to Yeşilköy near the airport, going underground at Yedikule, travelling to underground stations at Yenikapı and Sirkeci. From Sirkeci it will travel some 5km under the Bosphorus to another underground station on the Asian side at Üsküdar, before finally coming to ground level some 2km east of Kadıköy.

The project is slated to be completed by 2010, but the deadline is looking increasingly shaky. Old İstanbul is built on layers upon layers of history. No sooner had workmen commenced digging when they found an ancient port and bazaar in Üsküdar, and a 4th-century Byzantine harbour in Yenikapı. Diggers were replaced by brushes, and archaeologists got to work.

Other issues such as the safety of this tunnel being so close to the North Anatolian fault line leave many nervous, though authorities assure state-of-the-art technology will keep commuters safe.

To/From the Airports

ATATÜRK INTERNATIONAL AIRPORT

Getting from the airport to Sultanahmet by public transport is cheap and easy. There are a couple of options, but the most convenient and quickest is to take the LRT service from the airport six stops to Zeytinburnu (€0.60), from where you connect with the tram that takes you directly to Sultanahmet – the whole trip takes about 50 minutes. The airport station is on the lower ground floor beneath the international arrivals hall – follow the 'Hafif Metro – Light Rail System' signs down the escalators and right to the station. Services depart every 10 minutes or so from 6am until 12.40am.

Most hotels and hostels in Sultanahmet book minibus transport from the hotels to the airport for €4 a head. Unfortunately, this option only works going *from* town to the airport and not vice versa. Buses leave at 3.30am, 5.30am, 7.30am, 11am, 1pm, 3pm, 4.30pm and 9pm. Reserve your seat in advance and allow lots of time for the trip as the minibus may spend up to an hour collecting all its

passengers before heading out to the airport (30 to 45 minutes).

If you are staying near Taksim Sq, the **Havaş airport bus** (Map pp94-5; ☎ 444 0487; €5) is the easiest option. This departs from outside the arrivals hall, then goes to Yenikapı (30 minutes) and on to the Havaş ticket office on Cumhuriyet Caddesi just off Taksim Sq (45 to 60 minutes). Buses leave the airport at 5am, 6am and then every 30 minutes until 11pm; going from Taksim Sq to the airport, buses depart daily at 5am, 6am and then every 30 minutes until 1am. Alternatively, you could take the LRT all the way to Aksaray (€0.60), and catch Bus 83MT (€0.60) which runs direct to Taksim Sq.

A taxi between the Atatürk International Airport and Sultanahmet or Taksim Sq costs between €12 and €15, more between midnight and 6am or if there's heavy traffic.

SABIHA GÖKÇEN INTERNATIONAL AIRPORT

Some 50km east of Sultanahmet and Taksim Sq, **Sabiha Gökçen International Airport** (www.sgairport.com) is a lot less convenient to get to than Atatürk International Airport – no matter which mode of transport you take, it's at least an hour-long trip.

There is limited public transportation to/from the airport. You can catch a seabus to Bostancı, and then a connecting privately run bus (☎ 0212-465 7975 for info) to the airport. At least six ferries daily run from Eminönü and Karaköy to Bostancı; see www.ido.com.tr for timetable information. At least 11 buses run from Bostancı to the airport from 4.30am to 6.30pm (with extra services at 9pm and 10.45pm Friday to Monday). Tickets for the bus cost €3.

A much more convenient option is to ring your airline and find out about its transfer arrangements. Many airlines provide a transfer bus, timed to connect with flights, between Sultanahmet or Taksim Sq and the airport from €5 to €11 per person. Alternatively, you could catch the **Havaş airport bus** (☎ 444 0487; €5), with departures timed to connect with Turkish Airlines flights. These buses run from the airport via the Harem bus station (Map pp94-5) to the Kozyatağı Havaş **office** (Atatürk Caddesi 22, Kozyatağı), near Kadıköy ferry dock. Going to the airport, the buses leave the Kozyatağı Havaş office at 4am, running every hour until 10am; then from 1pm buses run hourly until 9pm. The final bus is at 11pm.

Most hotels and hostels in Sultanahmet book minibus transport from the hotels to Sabiha Gökçen for €15 a head, but there's only one departure daily, at 12.30am.

A taxi between Sabiha Gökçen International Airport and Sultanahmet or Taksim Sq costs around €45, more between midnight and 6am or if there's heavy traffic.

Boat

The most enjoyable and efficient way to get around town is by ferry. **İstanbul Deniz Otobüsleri** (☎ 0212-444 4436; www.ido.com.tr) has timetable information or you can pick up a printed timetable at any of the ferry docks. *Jetons* (transport tokens) cost €0.60 and it's possible to use Akbil (opposite) on all routes.

The main ferry docks are at the mouth of the Golden Horn (Eminönü, Sirkeci and Karaköy) and at Kabataş, 2km northeast of the Galata Bridge, just south of Dolmabahçe Palace. Ferries travel many routes around the city, but the routes commonly used by travellers include:

Beşiktaş–Kadıköy (every half-hour from 7.15am-10.45pm)
Eminönü–Anadolu Kavağı (Boğaziçi Özel Gezi; Bosphorus Excursions Ferry; once or twice a day)
Eminönü–Haydarpaşa and Kadıköy (approximately every 20 minutes from 7am-8pm)
Eminönü–Üsküdar (approximately every 20 minutes from 6.35am-11pm)
Kabataş–Üsküdar (around every half-hour from 7am-9.30am & 4.30-8pm)
Karaköy–Kadıköy and Haydarpaşa (approximately every 20 minutes from 6.15am-11pm)
Sirkeci–Harem (daily car ferry from 7am, then every half-hour until 9.30pm)
Sirkeci–Kadıköy–Kınalıada–Burgazada–Heybeliada–Büyükada (Princes' Islands ferry; at least eight ferries a day)
Üsküdar–Karaköy-Eminönü-Kasımpaşa-Fener-Balat-Ayvansaray–Sütlüce–Eyüp (approximately every hour, from 7.30am to 7.45pm)

There are also seabus services, which are more expensive but faster than ferries. One useful route is Bostancı–Karaköy–Eminönü, which has at least six services a day from 7.15am to 5pm).

For more information check with İstanbul Deniz Otobüsleri.

Bus

İstanbul's bus system is extremely efficient. The major bus stations are at Taksim Sq, Beşiktaş, Aksaray, Rüstempaşa-Eminönü, Kadıköy and Üsküdar. Most services run between 6.30am and 11.30pm. Destinations and main stops on city bus routes are shown on a sign on the kerbside of the *otobus* (bus) or on the electronic display at its front.

İETT (www.iett.gov.tr) buses are run by the city and you must have a ticket (€0.65) before boarding. You can buy tickets from the white booths near major stops or from some nearby shops for a small mark-up (look for 'İETT *otobüs bileti satılır'* signs). Think about stocking up a supply to last throughout your stay in the city or buying an Akbil (see opposite). Blue private buses regulated by the city called *Özel Halk Otobüsü* run the same routes; these accept cash (pay the conductor) and Akbil.

The most useful bus for travellers is the T4 bus that runs between Sultanahmet and Taksim Sq. It leaves from Sultanahmet Meydanı, near the Sultanahmet tourist information office, and stops at Karaköy and near Dolmabahçe en route to Taksim – all up usually a half-hour trip. If you're getting on at Sultanahmet Meydanı you can buy tickets from the newspaper booth close by.

Car & Motorcycle

Driving in İstanbul is a nightmare: constant traffic jams, careless drivers, traffic lanes habitually ignored, thin streets choked with parked cars – and you're expected to be able to turn on a postage stamp. Put simply, we recommend you park your car and use İstanbul's cheap and efficient public-transport system instead.

Top-end and a handful of midrange hotels offer undercover parking for guests, and most midrange and budget options have a streetside park or two that is nominally theirs to use. However other parking near your accommodation is easy to find.

There are few undercover long-term car parks in the city. Instead, car parking is dotted all over the city in empty blocks overseen by a caretaker, or roadside, in which case it'll be free or you'll be required to pay an hourly rate to a fee collector. There is no fixed system one street can be free; turn the corner and a fee collector will be waiting. There are also no street signs to tell you where parking lots are. Your best bet is to ring your accommodation and, upon arrival, ask them to point out the nearest and/or cheapest option. Negotiate a rate for the duration of your stay. Expect to pay around €6 for a 24-hour period.

If you baulk at the thought of even driving into the city to park, consider parking at Atatürk International Airport, and catching public transport or a taxi into the city to your accommodation. Parking costs €30 for four days, €45 per week. See the website www .ataturkairport.com for more information. You can could also park at Sabiha Gökçen International Airport.

Dolmuş

İstanbul dolmuşes are minibuses running on defined routes at a set price. As a short-term visitor to the city, you won't have much, if any, cause to use them.

Funicular Railway

The Tünel was built in the late 19th-century to save passengers the steep walk from Karaköy up the hill to İstiklal Caddesi in Beyoğlu. The service still runs today from 7am to 9pm Monday to Friday (from 7.30am on weekends), every five or 10 minutes and the fare is €0.50.

Another funicular railway runs through a tunnel from the Bosphorus shore at Kabataş, where it connects with the tram, up the hill to the metro station at Taksim Sq. Services run around every three minutes for €0.65.

Light Rail Transit (LRT)

An LRT service connects Aksaray with the airport, stopping at 16 stations including the otogar along the way. Services depart every 10 minutes or so from 6am until 12.40am and cost €0.65, no matter how many stops you travel. In line with the Marmaray project (see p159) there are plans to extend this service to Yenikapı.

Metro

İstanbul's underground metro system runs north from Taksim Sq, stopping at Osmanbey, Şişli-Mecidiyeköy, Gayrettepe, Levent and Levent 4. Plans are on the drawing board to extend this north to Ayazağa. Services run every five minutes or so from 6.15am to 12.30am (€0.65).

Taxi

İstanbul is full of yellow taxis. A base rate is levied during the *gündüz* (daytime); the *gece* (night-time) rate, from midnight to 6am, is 50% higher. Meters, with LCD displays, flash *'gündüz'* or *'gece'* when they're started. Oc-

casionally, drivers try to put the *gece* rate on during the day, so watch out.

Taxi rates are very reasonable, from Sultanahmet to Taksim Sq should cost around €5; ignore any taxi driver who insists on a fixed rate as these are invariably much higher than you'd pay using the meter. Double check the money you give the driver too: drivers have been known to insist they were given a 5YTL note for payment, when they were really given 20YTL.

Few of the city's taxis have seatbelts. If you catch a taxi over either of the Bosphorus bridges it is your responsibility to cover the toll. The driver will add this to your fare.

As far as tipping goes, locals usually round up the fare to the nearest 0.5YTL.

Train

İstanbul has two *banliyö treni* (suburban train lines). The first rattles along the Sea of Marmara shore from Sirkeci Train Station, around Seraglio Point to Cankurtaran (Sultanahmet), Kumkapı, Yenikapı and a number of stations before terminating past Atatürk International Airport at Halkala. The second runs from Haydarpaşa Train Station to Gebze via Bostancı. The trains are a bit decrepit,

---

AKBİL

If you're staying in the city for more than a day or so you should consider getting yourself an Akbil, a computerised debit fare tag, which will save you time and money when hopping on and off trams, trains, ferries and buses all around the city. Akbil tags are available at the Akbil Gişesi booths at Sirkeci, Eminönü, Aksaray or Taksim Sq bus stands for a €3 deposit. When you have your tag, you can charge it with any amount from €3 at any Akbil booth or at machines at the Tünel or metro stations. Press the card's metal button into the fare machine on a bus, ferry, Light Rail Transit (LRT), train, tram or funicular and – beep – the fare is automatically deducted from your line of credit. It's perfectly acceptable if one person in a group buys an Akbil and presses it the appropriate number of times when everyone boards together. Akbil fares are 10% lower than cash or ticket fares. You'll get your deposit back when you return the device.

but are reliable (nearly every half-hour) and cheap (€0.65).

Note that after the Marmaray project (p159) is completed, both these train lines will be slightly shortened.

Tram

A tram runs from Kabataş (where the tram connects with a funicular to Taksim Sq), crossing the Golden Horn to Eminönü and Sirkeci, and then on to Sultanahmet, and along Divan Yolu to Çemberlitaş, Beyazıt (for the Grand Bazaar) and Aksaray (to connect to the otogar), then out through the city walls to Zeytinburnu (to connect with the airport). Trams run every five minutes or so from 6am to midnight (€0.65). Works are currently under way to extend the line in both directions. The most useful of these extensions for travellers will be past Kabataş to Beşiktaş, passing Dolmabahçe Palace along the way.

A quaint antique tram rattles its way up and down İstiklal Caddesi in Beyoğlu every day, beginning its journey just outside the Tünel station and travelling to Taksim Sq. Tickets aren't available on board – you must use an Akbil or purchase a ticket (€0.65) from the Tünel station.

AROUND İSTANBUL

If you're staying in İstanbul for a while you may want to consider taking a day trip to the Princes' Islands, a peaceful antidote to the hustle and bustle of the big city.

PRINCES' ISLANDS

☎ 0216

Most İstanbullus refer to the Princes' Islands as 'The Islands' (Adalar). They lie about 20km southeast of the city in the Sea of Marmara and make a great destination for a day's escape.

In Byzantine times, refractory princes, deposed monarchs and others who had outlived their roles were interned on the islands (rather like Abdullah Öcalan, the ex-PKK leader, marooned today on Imrali Island in the Sea of Marmara). A ferry service from İstanbul was started in the mid-19th century and the islands became popular summer resorts with Pera's Greek, Jewish and Armenian business communities. Many of the fine Victorian villas built by these wealthy merchants survive today.

A few minutes after landing you'll realise the Princes' Islands' big surprise: there are no cars! Except for the necessary police, fire and sanitation vehicles, transport is by bicycle, horse-drawn carriage and foot, as in centuries past. After the hustle and bustle of İstanbul, this comes as a very pleasant change.

All of the islands are extremely busy in summer, particularly on weekends, so we recommend avoiding a Sunday visit. If you wish to stay overnight during the summer months it is imperative that you book ahead. Many of the hotels are closed during the winter.

There are nine islands in the Princes' Islands group, only five of them populated. The ferry stops at four of these; the fifth, Sedef, has only recently attracted a resident population. Year-round there are 20,000 permanent residents scattered across the five, but numbers swell to 120,000 during the summer months when İstanbullus – many of whom have holiday homes on the islands – come here to escape the city heat.

The ferry's first stop is **Kınalıada** (a favourite holiday spot for İstanbul's Armenian population), which is sprinkled with low-rise apartments, all sporting red tiled roofs and oriented towards the water. The island has a few pebble beaches, a modernist mosque and an Armenian church to the left of the ferry station. The second stop, **Burgazada**, has always been favoured by İstanbullus of Greek heritage. Sights include a hilltop chapel, mosques, a synagogue, a handful of restaurants and the home of the late writer Sait Faik, now a modest **museum**. While Kınalıada offers little reward for the trouble of getting off the ferry, Burgazada is worth considering if you want to escape all crowds.

In contrast, the charming island of **Heybeliada** (Heybeli for short) has much to offer the visitor. Home to the Turkish Naval Academy (you'll see it to the left of the ferry dock), it has several restaurants and a thriving shopping strip with bakeries and delicatessens selling picnic provisions to day-trippers, who come here on weekends to walk in the pine groves and swim from the tiny (but crowded) beaches. The island's major landmark is the hilltop **Haghia Triada Monastery**. Perched above a picturesque line of poplar trees, the monastery functioned as a Greek Orthodox school of theology where priests were trained until 1974, when it was closed on the government's orders. The Ecumenical Orthodox Patriarchate in Fener has applied for permission to reopen the school.

Heybeliada has a couple of hotels, including the Merit Halkı Palace (right), which is perched at the top of Rafah Şehitleri Caddesi and commands wonderful views over the water. The absolutely delightful walk up to this hotel passes a few antique shops and a host of large wooden villas set in lovingly tended gardens. There are many lanes and streets leading to picnic spots and lookout points off the upper reaches of this street. To do this walk, turn right as you leave the ferry and make your way past the waterfront restaurants and cafés to the plaza with a central newsstand. From here walk up İşgüzar Sokak, veering right until you hit Rafah Şehitleri Caddesi.

If you don't feel like a walk (this one's uphill but not too steep), you can hire a bicycle from one of the shops in the main street (€3 per hour) or a *fayton* (horse-drawn carriage) to take you on a tour of the island. A 25-minute tour (*küçük tur*) costs €10, a one-hour tour (*büyük tur*) €15. Some visitors choose to spend the day by the **pool** (weekdays/weekends €17/25) at the Merit Halki Palace, but most locals swim at the beaches around the island, though it pays to check the cleanliness of the water before you join them.

The largest island in the group, **Büyükada** (the 'Great Island'), shows an impressive face to visitors arriving on the ferry, with gingerbread villas climbing up the slopes of the hill and the bulbous twin cupolas of the Splendid Otel (right) providing an unmistakable landmark.

The **ferry terminal** is a lovely Ottoman-style kiosk. Inside there's a pleasant tile-decorated café with an outdoor terrace, as well as a **tourist information office** (10am-4pm) staffed by volunteers. There are eateries serving fresh fish to the left of the ferry terminal, next to an ATM.

The island's main tourist attraction is the Greek **Monastery of St George**, in the saddle between Büyükada's two highest hills. To get here, walk from the ferry straight ahead to the clock tower in İskele Meydanı (Dock Sq). The shopping district (with cheap eateries) is to the left along Recep Koç Sokak. Bear right onto 23 Nisan Caddesi, from where you can head along Kadıyoran Caddesi up the hill to the monastery. The enjoyable walk, which takes at least 50 minutes, takes you past a

long progression of impressive wooden villas set in gardens. After 30 minutes or so you will reach a reserve called 'Luna Park' by the locals. The monastery is a 20-minute walk up an extremely steep hill from here; some visitors prefer to hire a donkey to take them up the hill and back down again (€6.50). As you ascend you will see hundreds of pieces of cloth tied onto the branches of trees along the path – each represents a prayer, mostly offered by female supplicants who are visiting the monastery to pray for a child.

When you reach the monastery, there's not a lot to see. A small and gaudy church is the only building of note, but there are fabulous panoramic views from the terrace, as well as a small restaurant (see p164). From here it's possible to see all the way to İstanbul, as well as over to the nearby islands of Yassıada and Sivriada.

Bicycles are available for rent in several of the town's shops, and shops on the market street can provide picnic supplies, although food is cheaper on the mainland.

Just off the clock tower square there is a *fayton* stand. Hire one for a long tour of town, the hills and shore (one hour, €15) or a shorter tour of the town only (€10). It costs €6 to be taken to Luna Park. A shop just near the *fayton* stand hires out bicycles for €3 per hour.

Sleeping & Eating
HEYBELIADA
Halki Prenset Pansiyon (351 0039; www.halkiprenset .com in Turkish; Ayyıldız Caddesi 40-42; r Sun-Thu €40, Fri & Sat €50) Its friendly and welcoming, which is just as well since the rooms are uninspiring and frankly overpriced for what they offer. Stay here if you can't get a room somewhere else.

Merit Halki Palace (351 0025; www.merithotels .com; Refah Şehitleri Caddesi 94; s/d Sun-Thu €65/85, s/d Fri & Sat €80/100;) This comfortable hotel is a popular spot for a weekend break for İstanbullus. The pool area is particularly impressive and the restaurant serves meals and drinks (mains €13 to €17, beer €3) on its poolside terrace.

Başak Et Balık Restaurant (351 1289; Ayyıldız Caddesi 26; mezes €3-4.50, fish €4.50-8.50) One of a string of carbon-copy eateries along the shorefront, but it's always popular.

BÜYÜKADA
Splendid Otel (382 6950; www.splendidhotel.net; Nisan Caddesi 23; s/d €50/85;) This atmospheric,

landmark building is indeed splendid. Rooms aren't quite as impressive as the exterior or the common rooms, but are comfortable enough. It's well worth forking out the extra €15 for the front rooms with small balconies and sea views (not available for singles). Prices are the same for weekends and weekdays.

Hotel Princess Büyükada (☎ 382 1628; www.buyu kadaprincess.com; İskele Meydanı 2; r Sun-Thu €70, Fri & Sat €85; ☒ ☒) This recently refurbished hotel is right in the heart of things on the clock tower square. Rooms are large and pleasant enough. Seaview rooms are worth the €10 extra.

Monastery of St George Restaurant (mezes €2-4, grills €3-6, beer €2) Simple but appetising food is served at outdoor tables here.

Alibaba Restaurant (☎ 382 3733; Gülistan Caddesi 20; mezes €3-5, fish €6-12) is a popular, friendly spot and one of the many licensed waterside restaurants next to the ferry terminal.

Getting There & Away

At least nine daily ferries run to the islands between 6.50am and 9pm, departing from Sirkeci's 'Adalar İskelesi' dock (Map pp96–7), about 150m east of the dock for car ferries to Harem. The most useful departure times for day-trippers are 8.30am, 10am and 11.30am – but timetables change, so check beforehand. The trip costs €1.50 to the islands, and the same for each leg between the islands and the return trip. The cheapest and easiest way to pay is to use your Akbil (see p161). Note that the ferries seem dangerously overcrowded on summer weekends; time your trip for weekdays or make sure you board the vessel and grab a seat at least half an hour before departure unless you want to stand the whole way.

The ferry steams away from Sirkeci, out of the Golden Horn and around Seraglio Point (Saray Burnu), offering fine views of Topkapı Palace, Aya Sofya and the Blue Mosque on the right, and Üsküdar and Haydarpaşa to the left. After 20 minutes it makes a quick stop at Kadıköy on the Asian side before making its way to the first island, Kınalıada. It's not uncommon to see dolphins on this leg of the trip (25 minutes). After this, it's another 10 minutes to Burgazada, another 15 minutes again to Heybeliada and another 10 minutes to Büyükada.

Many day-trippers stay on the ferry until Heybeliada, stop there for an hour or so and then hop on another ferry to Büyükada, where they have lunch and spend the rest of the afternoon.

You can also take a fast catamaran from Eminönü or Kabataş to Bostancı on the Asian shore, then another from Bostancı to Heybeliada and Büyükada, but you save little time and the cost is much higher.

Thrace & Marmara

Despite its easy access to İstanbul, Turkey's northwest corner is not a common stop on the tourist circuit. Perhaps it's not surprising: after all, Thrace, the solitary Turkish foothold in Europe, and Marmara, the Asian mainland around the sea of the same name, cover just a small proportion of the country's total area. Also, there are no major cities here whose names might mean anything to an international audience. Why head west from İstanbul when the whole country's waiting to the east?

Well, newsflash. There's plenty to occupy all but the most casual of visitors here, and you don't even have to go through İstanbul to see the sights. As well as offering a quick and easy gateway to Greece, Eastern Europe and the Med, Thrace has piles of classic Ottoman architecture, lashings of strong liquor and the world's oldest sporting event bar the Olympic Games. Marmara, meanwhile, straddles the Dardanelles, is littered with beaches and fishing villages, and preserves the memory of one of WWI's fiercest battles, on the tragically beautiful Gallipoli peninsula.

Above all, this area is the place to come to see real modern Turkish life in all its mixed-up, idiosyncratic glory; to swap Greek recipes for Bulgarian dishes at Seljuk mosques, scramble in the scree on one of the Aegean's few undervisited islands, or ponder life, death, health, wealth, war and peace in the marks they've left on ancient scraps of land. This is where Turkey meets Europe, and until you can appreciate that fusion, you'll never understand the rest of this big, crazy country.

HIGHLIGHTS

- Jostle for the best minaret shot of Edirne's famous **Selimiye Camii** (p167)
- Ogle the slick-shiny oil wrestlers at the June festival in **Kırkpınar** (p171), near Edirne
- Feel the blood- and tear-soaked history of the **Gallipoli battlefields** (p183)
- Tuck into a quaint fish dinner at the dinky harbour in **Gelibolu** (p183)
- Relish the perfect valley-village seclusion of **Tepeköy** (p199), on the stunning island of Gökçeada

★ Edirne
Gelibolu ★
★ Gallipoli Battlefields
Tepeköy ★

EDİRNE

☎ 0284 / pop 120,000

The main conurbation in Turkey's European territory, Edirne is rarely considered by tourists as anything other than a stopover on the road to İstanbul. Luckily the town seems entirely unperturbed by this 'neglect', and remains a bustling centre of modern Turkish life in all its forms, with the added colour of constant through-traffic from Greece and Bulgaria. Visitors who do pause to take an interest will find a surprising amount of impressive architecture – Edirne was briefly the capital of the Ottoman Empire, and many of the key buildings are still in excellent shape.

History

The Roman emperor Hadrian founded Hadrianopolis (later shortened to Adrianople) in the 2nd century AD. During Roman and Byzantine times it was important as a waystation on the Via Egnatia that connected Rome with İstanbul, but by the mid-14th century the growing Ottoman state was looking for new conquests. In 1363 the Ottoman army crossed the Dardanelles, skirted Constantinople and captured Adrianople, which they made their capital.

For almost 100 years, this was the city from which the Ottoman sultan launched his campaigns in Europe and Asia. When at last the time was ripe for the final conquest of the Byzantine Empire, Mehmet the Conqueror (Mehmet Fatih) set out from Edirne for Constantinople along the Via Egnatia.

When the Ottoman Empire disintegrated after WWI, the Allies granted Thrace to the Greeks and declared Constantinople (now İstanbul) an international city. In the summer of 1920, Greek armies occupied Edirne, only to be driven back by Mustafa Kemal's army. The Treaty of Lausanne eventually granted Edirne and eastern Thrace to the Turks.

Orientation

The centre of town is Hürriyet Meydanı (Freedom Sq), at the junction of the two main streets, Saraçlar/Hükümet Caddesi and Talat Paşa Caddesi. Going east along Talat Paşa Caddesi and northeast along Mimar Sinan Caddesi you come to the Selimiye Camii. Down the hill and across Talat Paşa Caddesi is the Eski Cami,

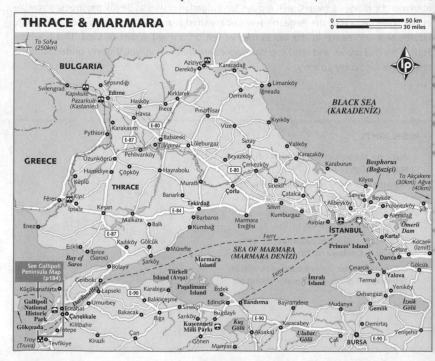

and south of Hürriyet Meydanı is the Ali Paşa Bazaar – Edirne's largest covered bazaar.

The otogar (bus station) is 9km east of the city centre on the access road to the Trans-European Motorway (TEM). Buses to the otogar and dolmuşes to the Bulgarian border at Kapıkule leave from opposite sides of the road in front of the tourist office on Talat Paşa Caddesi.

South of the town centre, two graceful Ottoman bridges lead across the Tunca and Meriç Rivers to a cluster of inviting restaurants. The Kırkpınar stadium, where the annual oil-wrestling contests are held (see p170), is northeast of the town centre.

Information

Araz Döviz (Ali Paşa Bazaar, Talat Paşa Caddesi) Changes cash and travellers cheques.

Aşkin Net (Kaleiçi; per hr €0.55; ☾ from 10am) Internet access.

Post office (PTT; Saraçlar Caddesi)

Tourist office (☎ 213 9208; Talat Paşa Caddesi; ☾ 9am-6pm Mon-Fri) Reasonably helpful, with some English brochures.

Sights

SELİMİYE CAMİİ

It's impossible to miss the **Selimiye Mosque** (1569–75), Edirne's grandest and most central mosque, designed by the great Ottoman architect Mimar Sinan (see p117). Constructed for Sultan Selim II (r 1566–74) and finished just after his death, it is smaller but more elegant than Sinan's tremendous Süleymaniye Camii (1550) in İstanbul, and it's said that Sinan himself considered it his finest work.

To best appreciate the mosque you should enter from the west, as the architect intended, rather than through the terraced park and the *arasta* (row of shops) to the south.

The broad, lofty dome – marginally wider than that of İstanbul's Aya Sofya – is supported unobtrusively by eight pillars, arches and external buttresses, creating a surprisingly spacious interior. As they only bear a portion of the dome's weight, the walls are sound enough to hold dozens of windows, allowing the mosque to be flooded with light, which in turn brings out the colourful calligraphic decorations of the interior.

Beneath the main dome is a prayer-reader's platform, and beneath that a small fountain. All the fittings, from the delicately carved marble *mimber* (pulpit) to the outstanding

İznik tile work around the *mihrab* (niche pointing towards Mecca), are exquisite.

Part of the Selimiye's effect comes from its four very tall (71m), slender minarets, fluted to emphasise their height. Each tower also has three *üçşerefeli* (balconies) – Sinan's respectful nod, perhaps, to his predecessor, the architect of the Üçşerefeli Cami (below).

One of the Selimiye's *medreses* (seminaries) houses the **Turkish & Islamic Arts Museum** (Türk-İslam Eserleri Müzesi; admission €1.10; ☾ 8am-noon & 1-5.30pm Tue-Sun), which has a variety of stone inscriptions and early Ottoman artefacts, plus a display on oil wrestling.

The ruined **Sultan Selim Saray Hamam**, just north of the mosque, is still awaiting restoration (originally scheduled for 2004!), though the houses next to it have been renovated in a 'modern Ottoman' style and look set to open as shops or cafés in the near future.

EDİRNE MUSEUM

This **museum** (☎ 225 1120; admission €1.10; ☾ 8am-noon & 1-5.30pm Tue-Sun) is opposite the Selimiye Camii to the north, with a garden of gravestones in front. The grounds contain all kinds of jars, sculptures, dolmens and *menhirs* (standing stones), as well as replicas of the sort of wattle-and-daub huts that may have been used by Thrace's Stone Age inhabitants.

Inside, the slightly crowded displays include local history, embroidery, textiles and home furnishings. There are several reconstructions of rooms in old houses, including a circumcision room and bridal corner. The archaeological section runs from prehistory through to the classical period of Hadrianopolis, and has also acquired the finds from recent digs around the Macedonian Tower (see p169).

URBAN HISTORY MUSEUM

Housed in the restored Hafızağa Mansion, a particularly fine 19th-century wooden Ottoman villa, this small new **museum** (admission €1.10; ☾ 8.30am-noon & 1-7pm) has poster displays on Edirne's historic buildings, local governors, and some old postcards. As there are currently no English captions it's not an essential stop for visitors, but the house itself is nice and offers great views onto the west side of the Selimiye Mosque (across a car park).

ÜÇŞEREFELİ CAMİ

This mosque, with its four strikingly different minarets all built at different times, dominates

THRACE & MARMARA

THRACE & MARMARA

EDİRNE

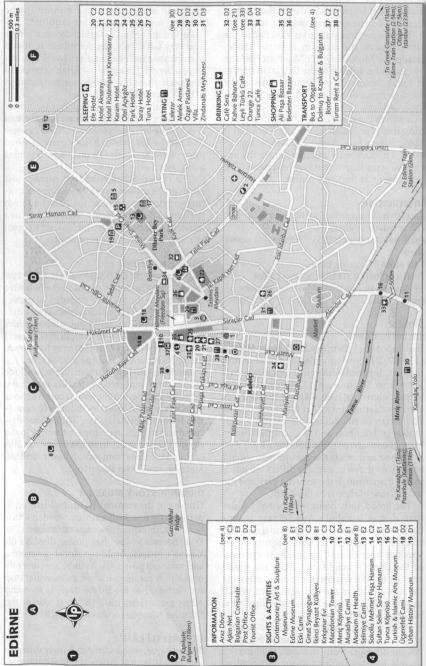

0 ————— 500 m
0 ————— 0.3 miles

To Kapıkule,
Bulgaria (18km)

To Sarayiçi &
Kırkpınar (1km)

To Kapıkule
(18km)

To Karaağaç (1km);
Pazarkule (Kastanies);
Greece (11km)

To Greek Consulate (2.1km);
Edirne Train Station (2.5km);
İstanbul (233km)

To Edirne Train
Station (2km)

Gazi Mihal
Bridge

Tunca River

Meriç River

INFORMATION
Araz Döviz........................(see 4)
Aşkın Net..........................1 C3
Bulgarian Consulate............2 E3
Post Office........................3 C3
Tourist Office....................4 C2

SIGHTS & ACTIVITIES
Contemporary Art & Sculpture
    Museum........................(see 8)
Edirne Museum..................5 E1
Eski Cami.........................6 D2
Great Synagogue................7 C3
İkinci Beyazıt Külliyesi.........8 B1
Kırkpınar Evi.....................9 C3
Macedonian Tower...............10 C2
Meriç Köprüsü....................11 D4
Muradiye Camii..................12 E1
Museum of Health...............(see 8)
Selimiye Camii...................13 E2
Sokollu Mehmet Paşa Hamam..14 C2
Sultan Selim Saray Hamam....15 E1
Tunca Köprüsü...................16 D4
Turkish & Islamic Arts Museum..17 E2
Üçşerefeli Camii.................18 D2
Urban History Museum..........19 D1

SLEEPING
Efe Hotel..........................20 C2
Hotel Aksaray....................21 C2
Hotel Rüstempaşa Kervansaray..22 D2
Karam Hotel......................23 C3
Otel Açıkgöz......................24 C3
Park Hotel........................25 C2
Saray Hotel.......................26 D3
Tuna Hotel........................27 C2

EATING
Lalezar............................(see 30)
Melek Anne.......................28 C2
Özge Pastanesi...................29 D2
Villa................................30 C4
Zindanaltı Meyhanesi...........31 D3

DRINKING
Café Sera.........................32 D2
Kahve Bahane.....................(see 21)
Leyli Türkü Café..................33 D4
Orange 22.........................34 D2
Tunca Café........................34 D2

SHOPPING
Ali Paşa Bazaar...................35 C2
Bedesten Bazaar..................36 D2

TRANSPORT
Bus to Otogar....................(see 4)
Dolmuş to Kapıkule & Bulgarian
    Border.........................37 C2
Turizm Rent a Car................38 C2

Hürriyet Meydanı. The name means 'Mosque with Three Galleries', a reference to the three balconies on the tallest minaret.

It was built between 1440 and 1447 in a design halfway between the Seljuk Turkish–style mosques of Konya and Bursa and the truly Ottoman style, which would be perfected in İstanbul. In the Seljuk style, smaller domes are mounted on square rooms, whereas here the 24m-wide dome is mounted on a hexagonal drum and supported by two walls and two pillars. The courtyard, with its central şadırvan (ablutions fountain), was another innovation that came to be standard in the great Ottoman mosques.

The mosque has been undergoing renovation for years, and unfortunately will be filled with scaffolding for the foreseeable future.

Across the street from the mosque is the atmospheric, unrestored **Sokollu Mehmet Paşa Hamam** (wash & massage €3.50; ☾ 6am-10pm for men, 10am-5pm for women), designed by Mimar Sinan for Grand Vizier Sokollu Mehmet Paşa in the 16th century. Some people may find a visit to the unrestored women's side a little too 'authentic' for comfort.

MACEDONIAN TOWER

Near the mosque and baths stands the restored **Macedonian Tower**, which dates back to Roman times. In the 19th century it served as Edirne's clock tower. Around its base, excavations have uncovered parts of the old city wall, a necropolis and the remains of a Byzantine church. Artefacts and smaller finds can be seen in the Edirne Museum (p167). There are bilingual signs and ladders down among the excavations, but unfortunately the site usually seems to be locked.

ESKİ CAMİ

From Hürriyet Meydanı, walk east along Talat Paşa Caddesi to the **Eski Cami** (Old Mosque; 1414). Behind it is the Rüstem Paşa Hanı, a *han* (caravanserai) built a hundred years later and now the Hotel Rüstempaşa Kervansaray.

The Eski Cami exemplifies one of the two classic mosque styles used by the Ottomans in their earlier capital, Bursa. Like Bursa's great Ulu Cami, the Eski Cami has rows of arches and pillars supporting a series of small domes. Inside, there is a marvellous *mihrab* and huge calligraphic inscriptions on the walls. The columns at the front of the mosque were 'borrowed' from a Roman building.

KALEİÇİ

The Kaleiçi area, framed by Saraçlar Caddesi, Talat Paşa Caddesi and the railway line, was the original medieval town, with its narrow streets laid out on a linear grid plan.

Exploring at will is easy, but you could start by walking south along Maarif Caddesi, which takes you past some fine examples of ornate wooden houses and finishes at the ruins of Edirne's **Great Synagogue**. Other notable specimens grace Cumhuriyet Caddesi, which crosses Maarif Caddesi north of the synagogue.

MURADİYE CAMİİ

A walk of 10 to 15 minutes northeast of the Selimiye along Mimar Sinan Caddesi brings you to the **Muradiye Camii**, built for Sultan Murat II and topped with an unusual cupola. Finished in 1436, it once housed a Mevlevi whirling dervish lodge. The mosque's T-shaped plan, with twin *eyvans* (vaulted halls) and fine İznik tiles, are reminiscent of Ottoman work in Bursa.

The small cemetery harbours the tombstone of Şeyhülislâm Musa Kâzım Efendi, the Ottoman Empire's last chief Islamic judge, who fled the British occupation of İstanbul after WWI and died here in 1920.

İKİNCİ BEYAZIT KÜLLİYESİ

Edirne's last great imperial mosque, the **Beyazıt II complex** was built by the Ottoman architect Hayrettin for Sultan Beyazıt II (r 1481–1512) between 1484 and 1488. Today it stands in splendid isolation to the north of Edirne, which means you get wonderful, uninterrupted views of it as you approach.

In style, the mosque lies midway between the Üçşerefeli and Selimiye designs: its large prayer hall has one large dome, similar to the Selimiye, but it also has a courtyard and fountain, like the earlier Üçşerefeli.

The complex is extensive and includes a *tabhane* (travellers hostel), *medrese,* bakery, *imaret* (soup kitchen), *tımarhane* (asylum) and *darüşşifa* (hospital). The *darüşşifa* has been converted into the award-winning **Museum of Health** (admission €2; ☾ 9am-6pm). Although most of the exhibits are labelled only in Turkish, some of the recreated old rooms are fascinating, particularly the in-patients room illustrating treatment techniques – a surprisingly enlightened selection of quasi–New Age concepts such as music, scent therapy and, yes, basket-weaving.

Another part of the complex houses the **Contemporary Art & Sculpture Museum** (Çağdaş Resim ve Heykel Müzesi; admission €2; 9am-6pm) which, while not wildly exciting, is worth a quick look to see what sort of thing the local talent is turning out.

To get to the complex, walk along Hükümet Caddesi from Hürriyet Meydanı, passing the Üçşerefeli Cami on your right, and turn left immediately after its baths. Walk one block and turn right at the fountain. This street, Horozlu Bayır Caddesi, becomes İmaret Caddesi and takes you across the Tunca River via an Ottoman bridge (1488) to the complex. It's well worth coming out here for the walk alone.

SARAYİÇİ
Translated as 'Inner Palace', **Sarayiçi** is actually a scrub-covered island that was once the private hunting reserve of the Ottoman sultans. Today it's the site of the famous Kırkpınar oil-wrestling matches (see opposite).

Near the ugly modern stadium stands the **Adalet Kasrı** (Justice Hall; 1561), a stone tower with a conical roof that dates from the time of Süleyman the Magnificent. In front of it are two stones: on the Seng-i Hürmet (Stone of Respect) people would place petitions to the sultan, while the Seng-i İbret (Stone of Warning) would display the heads of any high-court officers who had offended the sultan.

Behind the Justice Hall is another small bridge. Cross it and on your right you'll see a memorial and museum dedicated to the Balkan Wars. To the left, the path winds past the scattered and scant ruins of the **Edirne Sarayı** (Edirne Palace). Begun by Sultan Beyazıt II in 1450, this palace once rivalled İstanbul's Topkapı Palace in size and luxury, although you'd be hard-pressed even to visualise the place now.

To get here from Hürriyet Meydanı, walk along Hükümet Caddesi and cross the Tunca River via the Kanuni Bridge. Alternatively, it's a scenic 1km walk along the flood-control embankment from the II Beyazıt Külliyesi (left).

SOUTH OF THE CENTRE
To get away from the busy town centre, simply follow Saraçlar Caddesi south under the railway line and across the **Tunca Köprüsü**, an Ottoman stone humpback bridge that spans the Tunca River. Further south the longer **Meriç Köprüsü** crosses the Meriç River and offers wonderful views from a frescoed Ottoman kiosk in the middle.

The whole area around these bridges is packed with restaurants, tea gardens and bars, all great places to come for a drink or a meal in warm weather. The best ones are those on the southern side of the Meriç Köprüsü, which offer perfect sunset river vistas, great views of the lit-up Selimiye Camii and atmospheric frog background noise on the walk back to town.

From the Meriç Köprüsü, Karaağaç Yolu (also signed as Lozan Caddesi) leads on to the suburb of **Karaağaç**, where there are more old houses, the original station building and a monument to the Treaty of Lausanne.

Sleeping
Edirne's main concentration of hotels is along Maarif Caddesi; note that several places at the northern end have lively (ie noisy) late-closing music bars.

BUDGET
Hotel Aksaray (212 6035; Alipaşa Ortakapı Caddesi; s/d/tr with shared bathroom €12.50/19.50/25.50, s/d/tr/q €18/25/31/38) The cheapest option in town, with basic rooms and bathroom cubicles forcibly rammed into small spaces. The original ceiling fresco in room 103 is an unexpected bonus. Breakfast not included.

Saray Hotel (212-1457; Eski İstanbul Caddesi 28; s/d/tr €14/22.50/28) It may look like a smart business-class option from the outside, but inside the Saray is simply a good modern hotel at reasonable prices. Breakfast is an extra €2.80.

Tuna Hotel (214-3340; Maarif Caddesi 17; s/d/tr/q €19.50/28/36/42;) The layout's slightly strange, especially the elongated triples on the ground floor, but otherwise there's nothing fishy about the Tuna, which does its best to welcome foreign visitors at the quieter southern end of Maarif Caddesi. The neat little courtyard provides a perfect spot for breakfast.

MIDRANGE
Park Hotel (225 4610; www.parkotel.com, in Turkish; Maarif Caddesi 7; s/d/tr €25/44.50/59;) There's nothing spectacular about the Park's rooms, but the facilities go a long way to make it an attractive option, with restaurant, café-bar and barber on site and a big lounge centred around a fireplace. German is spoken and wireless Internet access is offered.

Otel Açıkgöz (☎ 213 1944; www.acikgoz.com, in Turkish; Tufekciler Çarşısı 76; s/d/tr €28/44.50/61; ⊠) The better of two hotels run by the Açıkgöz bathroom company, enjoying a quiet but very central location. The dedicated family room is a particularly good deal.

Efe Hotel (☎ 213 6080; www.efehotel.com; Maarif Caddesi 13; s/d/tr €33.50/44.50/56; ⊠) The Efe is a touch smarter than most of the other choices here, especially in the lobby, and wi-fi Internet is free. The second-floor doubles are by far the nicest, and have fridges as well as the usual TV and phone. The hotel's 'English Pub' opens in summer only.

Karam Hotel (☎ 225 1555; Maarif Caddesi, Garanti Bankası Sokağı 6; s/d/tr €36/47/59; ⊠) Set in a fine restored house, the dubious green colour scheme lets the spacious rooms down slightly, but all in all it's a good place to stay, and prices may be negotiable. There's an appealing courtyard restaurant and a music bar, which stays loud late on Wednesday and at weekends.

Hotel Rüstempaşa Kervansaray (☎ 225 7195; www.kervansarayhotel.net; İki Kapılı Han Caddesi 57; s/d/tr €26/47.50/61, ste €86; ⌨) Facing the park next to the Eski Cami, this *han* was built for Süleyman the Magnificent's grand vizier Rüstempaşa in about 1550. Its inner courtyard offers a romantic setting for breakfast, plus an Internet café and pool hall, but despite the potential of the building the bedrooms are distinctly underwhelming, especially the cheapo singles, and prices don't even include breakfast.

Eating
RESTAURANTS

Edirne's delicacy of choice is *ciğer* (fried liver), sold by small shops all over town, which also usually serve *köfte* (meatballs). There's a wide assortment of eateries along Saraçlar Caddesi. The riverside restaurants south of the centre are more atmospheric, but most only open from June to September and are often booked solid at weekends for wedding and circumcision parties.

Özge Pastanesi (☎ 212 2333; PTT Arkası; dishes from €0.55; ☺ 8am-10pm) Upstairs seating and a good selection of cakes and fast food have kept the Özge's popularity up, where its neighbour the Saray seems to have waned.

Melek Anne (☎ 213 3263; Maarif Caddesi; dishes from €1; ☺ 8am-9pm) A whitewashed old house provides the location for Mama Melek's good home cooking including *mantı* (ravioli) and

---

EDİRNE WRESTLEMANIA

If you like the idea of watching muscular men in leather shorts coat themselves with olive oil and throw each other around for a few days, then Sarayiçi is the place to come towards the end of June, when the **Tarihi Kırkpınar Yağlı Güreş Festivali** (Historic Kırkpınar Oil Wrestling Festival) takes place.

The origins of this oleaginous contest go back almost 650 years to the early days of the Ottoman Empire, making it the world's oldest sporting event after the Olympic Games. Before the conquest of Edirne in 1361, sultan Orhan Gazi sent his brother Süleyman Paşa with 40 chosen men to conquer the Byzantine castle of Domuzlu at Rumeli, a feat they achieved overnight. Besides their soldiering prowess, all 40 were keen wrestlers and regularly challenged each other to bouts; the legend goes that two of them were so evenly matched that they fought for days without any clear result, until both of them finally dropped dead. When the bodies were buried under a nearby fig tree, a spring mysteriously appeared, and the site was given the name Kırkpınar, or 40 Springs, in honour of the 40 warriors who first wrestled there.

Today the original Kırkpınar actually falls within Bulgarian borders, but the Turks seem happy enough with their modern equivalent and the annual matches are the highlight of the Edirne calendar. Fighters compete in 11 categories over the seven-day festival, with dozens of matches taking place simultaneously in the large Sarayiçi stadium. Bouts can last up to 30 minutes, after which they enter 'sudden death' one-fall-wins extra time. When all the fights are decided, prizes are awarded for gentlemanly conduct and best entry technique, as well as the coveted and hotly contested head wrestler title.

During the festival the streets are crowded, the hotels are jam-packed and you may have to wrestle yourself just to get a parking space, but it's unquestionably a spectacle worth seeing, and the atmosphere can be fantastic. For more information visit the **Kırkpınar Evi** (www.kirkpinar .com) on Maarif Caddesi or surf to www.turkishwrestling.com.

grills. Plenty of local women and couples also come for breakfast.

Zindanaltı Meyhanesi (☎ 212 2149; Zindanaltı Caddesi 127; dishes from €1.70; ☺ 11am-midnight) Behind the fake stone cladding, this is three storeys of authentic and friendly *meyhane* (Turkish pub) experience, offering plenty of appetising mezes and meat to accompany the well-iced Efes and piped Turkish pop.

Villa (☎ 225 4077; Karaağaç Yolu; mains €3.50-8.50; ☺ 11am-11pm) One of the best riverside options, boasting a breezy open terrace past the southern end of the Meriç Köprüsü. The bilingual menu covers stews, grills and mezes, plus fish (price varies) and the intriguing 'chicken diversity'. Euros are accepted here if you're strapped for Turkish cash.

Lalezar (☎ 213 0600; Karaağaç Yolu; mains €3.50-8.50; ☺ 11am-11pm) Lalezar is right next to Villa and follows much the same formula, slightly more spread out with a larger play area for kids.

Drinking & Entertainment

Café Sera (Talat Paşa Caddesi) This big, open-air café in front of the Selimiye Camii is a great place to sit out by the fountains and watch the people coming and going, with the added benefit of being above street level.

Tunca Café (☎ 212 4816; Hurriyet Meydanı) This inviting, wood-filled tea garden is set around a duck pond facing the Kadın Kakları Parkı (Women's Rights Park).

Kahve Bahane (Alipaşa Otakapı Caddesi) It's a modern-style coffeehouse in a restored wooden building, complete with internal courtyard and full menu of fancy coffees.

Orange 22 (☎ 213 0066; Karaağaç Yolu) The Orange is a bit of an unusual bar-club option amid the pub and restaurant strip south of town, opting for a slick modern metallic style with vintage car pics and lots of spirits at the front terrace.

Leyli Türkü Café (☎ 214 0039; Karaağaç Yolu) Right next door, this student favourite opts for a much more traditional café-pub vibe, attracting daytime coffee-sippers as well as live music crowds.

Shopping

The most atmospheric places to shop are Edirne's restored Ottoman covered bazaars. The **Ali Paşa Bazaar**, off Saraçlar Caddesi, was designed by Mimar Sinan in 1569, while the **Bedesten Bazaar**, across the road from the Eski Cami, dates from 1414. Traditional local sou-

venirs include fruit-shaped soaps and miniature brooms decorated with mirrors and beads.

Getting There & Around
BUS & DOLMUŞ

The otogar is 9km east of the city centre on the access road to the TEM. There are frequent buses for İstanbul (€6.70 to €8.35, 2½ hours) and at least five daily buses to Çanakkale (€11.10, 3½ hours). City bus 5 (€0.28) and frequent minibuses (€0.55) run to the otogar from in front of the tourist office.

If you're heading for the Bulgarian border crossing at Kapıkule, catch a dolmuş (€1.40, 25 minutes) from opposite the tourist office.

Pazarkule, the nearest Greek border post, is 13km south of Edirne, but there are no longer direct dolmuşes to take you there. You could catch a dolmuş to Karaağaç and then take a taxi, but it's easier just to pick up a taxi all the way from the centre (€5.50 to €8.50, 15 minutes).

For more information on all Bulgarian and Greek border crossings in this area, see p673.

CAR

The main highway connecting Europe and Edirne travels along the river valleys past Nis and Sofia, in between the mountain ranges of the Stara and Rhodopes to Plovdiv, and then along the Meriç River into Edirne, following the route of the ancient Via Egnatia from Rome to Constantinople.

From Edirne, the old highway (D100) continues east across the rolling, steppe-like terrain of eastern Thrace, still following the Via Egnatia. However, the E80 Avrupa Otoyol/ TEM offers a far quicker and safer route to İstanbul, and is used by the majority of bus companies. If you're driving yourself, the toll of about €5 is a small price to pay.

You can hire a car from **Turizm Rent A Car** (☎ 214 8478; www.turizmrentacar.com; Talat Paşa Caddesi). Prices start at around €35 per day for a small sedan.

TRAIN

Edirne train station is 4km southeast of the Eski Cami. Bus 2 comes right here but any dolmuş or city bus along Talat Paşa Caddesi can drop you on the road 200m away. A taxi will cost around €5.55.

(Continued on page 181)

174

Overleaf:
Paper-windmill seller waits for a customer,
İstanbul (p88)

IZZET KERIBAR

Cherry-juice vendors outside the Aya
Sofya (Sancta Sophia; p104), İstanbul

DIANA MAYFIELD

PHIL WEYMOUTH
The İstanbul Archaeology Museum (p114) displays
exhibits from all over the country, İstanbul

The ornate Gate of Felicity (p113), entry point to the Third Court of Topkapı Palace, İstanbul

PHIL WEYM

IZZET KERIBAR

Beyoğlu's fashionable İstiklal Caddesi (p120), İstanbul

CORINNE HUMPHREY

A carpet maker works with patience and skill, Grand Bazaar (p115), İstanbul

Çay (tea; p70) for sale at a street market beside the Bosphorus, İstanbul

GREG ELMS

Familiar worldwide, the ritual of preparing a döner kebap is performed in Karaköy, İstanbul (p88)

Vendor stretches out *dondurma* (Turkish ice cream), Taksim, İstanbul (p88)

Fruit preserves tempt prospective buyers, İstanbul (p88)

Boys enjoying hot corn on the cob beside the
waterfront in Eminönü, İstanbul (p88)

Those with a sweet tooth can indulge in
delicious baklava (p71), İstanbul

After finishing a tray of *mantı* (Turkish ravioli), a woman makes *gözleme* (savoury pancakes) in Taksim,
İstanbul (p88)

Turkish men play backgammon outside a
café, İstanbul (p88)

GREG ELMS

CHRIS MELLOR

A shoeshiner and his compact and ornate kit rests
beside the road, İstanbul (p88)

Western Anatolian dancers perform at the historic Hippodrome (p106), İstanbul

SUSAN

Village women carry water from a well, Lake Van area (p634)

IZZET KERIBAR

Overleaf:
Interior of the dome of the İnce Minare Medresesi (p485), now a museum, Konya

JOHN ELK III

Men gather for a chat on the pavement, İzmir (p226)

HANAN ISACHAR

In Cappadocia, *soğlanı* dolls are popular with tourists and locals alike, Nevşehir (p515)

WES WALKER

(Continued from page 172)

The *Edirne Ekspresi* connects Edirne and İstanbul (€5.85), leaving Edirne at 7.30am and returning from Sirkeci station at 3.50pm. It makes 31 stops and takes 5½ hours. The *Bosfor Ekspresi* to Sofia and Bucharest passes through Edirne at 2.35am.

UZUNKÖPRÜ
☎ 0284 / pop 36,000

About 36km south of Havsa along the E87/ D550, the farming town of Uzunköprü (Long Bridge) sits on the banks of the Ergene River. Amazingly, the long Ottoman bridge (1427–43; 1270m) after which the town is named is still standing, with all its 173 arches intact. It remains the town's main access road from the north, an impressive feat after nearly 600 years of continuous use.

Apart from the bridge there's little to see here, unless you pass through on Thursday for the weekly **market**.

GETTING THERE & AWAY
Uzunköprü is the border-crossing on the railway line connecting İstanbul with Greece; the *Dostluk-Filia Ekspresi* passes through at midnight, heading back to Sirkeci at 3.50am. The *Uzunköprü Ekspresi* offers a more convenient trip to İstanbul at 4.40pm (€6, 5½ hours). The station is 4km north of town – get a bus to Edirne to drop you off or take a taxi for €2.50.

Most days you can easily pick up a bus to Edirne (€2, one hour) from near the bridge.

TEKİRDAĞ
☎ 0282 / pop 118,000

You'd think a town famous for rakı (aniseed-flavoured brandy) and *köfte* would have no end of loyal fans, but as most travellers are passing through on their way to or from Greece, Tekirdağ is often no more than a pit stop. It doesn't have the historical or architectural clout of Edirne, but if you do pause for more than lunch you'll find there's plenty to like about this modest coastal centre.

Sights
The **waterfront** *(sahil)* is the focal point for leisure time in Tekirdağ, with a long promenade running right the way round the bay, punctuated by cafés, restaurants, parks and playgrounds. There's a small tourist information booth, which may or may not be staffed.

The **Rakoczy Museum** (☎ 263 8577; Barbaros Caddesi 32; admission €1.10; ◷ 9am-5pm Tue-Sun) is the unusual legacy of Prince Francis II Rakoczy (1676–1735), a Hungarian folk hero who led his rebel countrymen in their struggle against Hapsburg repression during the Hungarian War of Independence (1703–11). Forced into exile in 1711, he eventually turned up in Turkey and was given asylum by Sultan Ahmet III. In 1906 Rakoczy's remains were returned to Hungary, along with the interior fittings from his house. Between 1981 and 1982, however, these were painstakingly reproduced and displayed to the public in a surprisingly informative museum; what you see now was once the dining hall of his home. It's worth seeing just to admire the lovely watercolours of old Tekirdağ by Aladar Edivi Illes (1870–1958). To get here, walk west along the waterfront until you see the large wooden Namık Kemal Kütüphane (library) above you to the right. Cut up and past it along Rakoczy Caddesi and you'll find the museum on the left.

Continue along Barbaros Caddesi/Rakoczy Caddesi until you come to the **Museum of Archaeology & Ethnography** (☎ 261 2082; Vali Konağı Caddesi 21; admission €1.10; ◷ 9am-5pm Tue-Sun), housed in a fine late-Ottoman building. Here you can see the finds from several local *tumuli* (barrows) and from a site at Perinthos (Marmara Ereğli). The most striking exhibits are the marble tables and chairs set with bronze bowls from the Naip *tumulus*, and a wonderful pottery brazier in the form of a mother goddess from the Taptepe *tumulus* (both 5th century BC).

Further east, past the brown stone **Orta Camii** (1855), you'll find the cute wooden **Namık Kemal Evi** (Namık Kemal Caddesi 7; ◷ 8am-5pm Mon-Sat), a small ethnographical museum built to commemorate Tekirdağ's most famous son, who was born nearby. Kemal (1840–88) was a poet and advocate of national freedom, and had a strong influence on Atatürk, who called him 'the father of my ideas'. The house is beautifully restored, and holds occasional craft markets in the garden.

To get back to the waterfront, cross over to Mimar Sinan Caddesi and head downhill, past the small, square **Rüstem Paşa Külliyesi** (1553), built by the great Mimar Sinan for Rüstem Paşa, one of Süleyman the Magnificent's grand viziers. At the bottom of the hill there's a **statue** commemorating another famous Tekirdağan, the great oil wrestler Hüseyin Pehlivan.

Sleeping & Eating

Yat Hotel (☎ 261 1054; İskele Caddesi; r €7.50-23) Not remotely yachtlike, this unfancy hotel offers a bewildering range of randomly shaped rooms with dated décor; upper floors are brighter and have balconies. Rates depend on your chosen combination of sea or town view, private, shared or shower-only bathroom, and so on. Breakfast costs €2.

Rodosto Hotel (☎ 263 3701; www.rodostohotel.com; İskele Caddesi 34; s/d/tr €33.50/44.50/67; 🖭) If you value comfort over price, the Rodosto is a good bet, banking on a touch of class to win over guests. Two rooms come with Jacuzzis, or at the other end of the scale you can opt for a boxy 'economy' single (€22.25). The conservatory restaurant above the lobby is an added plus.

Buses to Greece often pause for lunch in Tekirdağ, pulling up at the row of *köftecis* (*köfte* restaurants) just inland from the harbour. Meals are much of a muchness at these places, but the **Liman Lokantası** (☎ 261-4984; Yali Caddesi 40; mains €2.80-5.60; 🕙 8am-10pm) has been reliable for years, and also has a posher harbour outlet opposite.

Getting There & Away

Buses for İstanbul (€6.70, two hours), Edirne (€6.70, two hours) and Çanakkale (€11.10, four hours) drop off and pick up on the waterfront. Some Edirne buses stop at offices along Muratlı Caddesi, on the other side of the town centre about 1.5km north of the promenade.

GELİBOLU

☎ 0286 / pop 23,130

This pretty little harbour town must get plenty of its visitors by mistake – Gelibolu is not the same as Gallipoli, it's simply the largest town on the peninsula with the same name, some 60km from the famous battlefield sites. Luckily, if you do fall prey to such confusion you'll find that Gelibolu is a nice stop in its own right, particularly if you stay over for dinner.

Everything you will need – hotels, restaurants, a PTT, banks – is clustered around Gelibolu harbour, which is also where the ferry to Lapseki docks.

Sights

The **Piri Reis Museum** (donation requested; 🕙 8.30am-noon & 1-5pm Tue-Sun) is housed in a stone tower overlooking the harbour walls, the sole remainder of the Byzantine town of Kallipolis, which gave the present town and peninsula their name. The tower is named after the Turkish cartographer Piri Reis, whose statue stands on the coast near the otogar, looking out to sea. The fruit of his life's work, dating back to 1513, was the first known map to show the Americas in their entirety. Inside there's a large, shallow well and an upstairs chamber displaying copies of pages from Reis' famous map, together with a hotchpotch of historical exhibits and remnants from the Gallipoli battles.

The road north past the Hotel Yılmaz veers uphill, behind several military buildings. After 800m you pass the pretty shrine of **Ahmed-i Bican Efendi** on the left. Cross the road behind it and you'll find a mosque and the tomb of **Mehmed-i Bican Efendi**, author of a commentary on the Quran called the *Muhammadiye*.

Return to the south road and eventually you will come to a small **türbe** (tomb) on the right. Take Fener Yolu beside it on to the headland and you'll see steps on the left leading down to the **Bayraklı Baba Türbesi**, a uniquely Turkish memorial. Karaca Bey was an Ottoman standard bearer who, in 1410, ate the flag in his keeping piece by piece rather than let it be captured by the enemy. When his comrades found him they asked where the flag was but refused to believe him; Karaca duly split open his stomach to prove the point and immediately became a local legend, renamed Bayraklı Baba (Flag Father). His pretty tomb is decked out with hundreds of Turkish flags – the attendant will sell you one to add to the collection.

At the edge of the headland, not far from the lighthouse tea garden, is the small but fascinating **Azebler Namazgah**, built in 1407. An unusual outdoor mosque complete with white marble *mihrab* and *mimber*, it is vaguely Mughal in appearance.

Return to the main road and continue downhill until you see, on the left, a **French Cemetery** from the Crimean War (1854–56), which also houses an ossuary containing the bones of Senegalese soldiers who died in the Gallipoli campaign. The road continues down to **Hamzakoy**, the resort part of town, which has a thin strip of sandy beach.

Sleeping

Hotel Oya (☎ 566 0392; Miralay Şefik Aker Caddesi; s €14, d €22.50-25) A good central choice with a mild nautical theme. All rooms have digital TV and some have small bathtubs. Breakfast is served in the bright lobby restaurant.

Hotel Yılmaz (☎ 566 1256; Liman Meyki 8; r per person €14) The Yılmaz is convenient and very friendly, if not the smartest or quietest place in town, and rates may be negotiable. Skip the daily cassette-guided Gallipoli tours though – you'll get a much better deal in Çanakkale.

Otel Hamzakoy (☎ 566 8080; www.hamzakoy.8m .com; s/d €28/39) This pink-tinged block overlooking the bay is Gelibolu's sole resort hotel, and can be very quiet out of season. Rooms are light and spacious with modern furnishings, TVs, fridges and balconies. There is a licensed restaurant on site and two beach bar-restaurants.

Eating

The best reason to linger in Gelibolu is to have dinner in one of the harbourside restaurants, where you can tuck into fresh *sardalya* (sardines) while gazing out over bobbing fishing boats and being serenaded by wandering musicians. Your best bet is to stroll past them all and see which seems to be the happening place that evening. Most dishes cost from €2 to €5.50, although if you opt for fish your bill could rise to around €10 with alcohol.

İlhan Restaurant (☎ 566 1124; Balikhane Sokak 2; mains €2.80-6.70; ⏱ 11am-10pm) This is easily the smartest of the harbour eateries, and also the largest, with a prime location giving it the benefit of sea as well as harbour views (when the Lapseki ferry's not in the way). The menu's also that bit more adventurous – in case you fancy chancing some cold scorpion fish.

Kumsal Restaurant (☎ 566 3626; Hamzakoy; mains from €2.80; ⏱ 11am-10pm) A good alternative to the Otel Hamzakoy restaurants, Kumsal has indoor and outdoor tables right on the beach, offering a range of meat and fish dishes. The menu has no prices so check before ordering fish.

Getting There & Away

The otogar is 500m southwest of the harbour on Kore Kahramanları Caddesi, the main Eceabat road, served by buses to İstanbul (€10, 4½ hours) and Edirne (€8.35, 2¾ hours). You can pick up minibuses to Eceabat (€1.70, 50 minutes) and Çanakkale (€1.70, one hour, via Lapseki) from here or beside the harbour.

The Gelibolu-Lapseki car ferry (€0.85, bicycles and scooters €2, cars €4.75, 30 minutes) runs every hour on the hour in either direction between 9am and midnight, with five departures each way between 1am and 8.15am.

To get to the Gallipoli battlefields, go to Eceabat then look for a dolmuş to Kabatepe. To get to Çanakkale, take the Gelibolu-Lapseki ferry then a bus or dolmuş, or take the minibus to Eceabat and then the ferry to Çanakkale.

GALLIPOLI (GELİBOLU) PENINSULA

The slender peninsula that forms the northwestern side of the Dardanelles, across the water from Çanakkale, is called Gallipoli (Gelibolu in Turkish). For a millennium it has been the key to İstanbul: any navy that could break through the straits had a good chance of capturing the capital of the Eastern European world. Many fleets have tried to force the straits, but most, including the mighty Allied fleet mustered in WWI, have failed.

Today the Gallipoli battlefields are peaceful places covered in scrubby brush and pine forests. However, the battles fought here nearly a century ago are still alive in many memories, both Turkish and foreign. The Turkish officer responsible for the defence of Gallipoli was none other than Mustafa Kemal, later to become Atatürk, and his success is commemmorated in Turkey on 18 March. The big draw for visitors, though, is Anzac Day on 25 April, when a dawn service commemorates the anniversary of the Allied landings, attracting thousands of travellers from Down Under and beyond (see p191).

Most of the peninsula is national park, and even if you're not well up on the history, it's still worth visiting for the rugged natural beauty of the site.

On the hillside by Kilitbahir, clearly visible from Çanakkale, gigantic letters spell out the first few words of a poem by Necmettin Halil Onan commemorating the struggle for Gallipoli in 1915:

Dur yolcu! Bilmeden gelip bastığın
bu toprak bir devrin battığı yerdir.
Eğil de kulak ver, bu sessiz yığın
bir vatan kalbinin attığı yerdir.

Traveller, halt! The soil you heedlessly tread
once witnessed the end of an era.
Listen! In this quiet mound
there once beat the heart of a nation.

The nearest base for visiting the battlefields is Eceabat on the western shore of the Dardanelles, although Çanakkale, on the eastern shore, has a much wider range of accommodation. Gelibolu, 45km northeast of Eceabat, is a less popular option.

For a detailed guide to all the Gallipoli sites, pick up the excellent bilingual *Gallipoli Bat-*

tlefield Guide (*Çanakkale Muharebe Alanları Gezi Rehberi;* Gürsel Göncü & Şahin Doğan, 2006), which includes satellite-accurate maps. You can find it in bookshops in Çanakkale.

Many people visit Gallipoli on a guided tour (see p190).

History

Just 1.4km wide at its narrowest point, the Strait of Çanakkale (variously known as Çanakkale Boğazı, Hellespont or the Dardanelles) has always offered the best opportunity for travellers – and armies – to cross between Europe and Asia Minor.

King Xerxes I of Persia crossed the strait here on a bridge of boats in 481 BC, as did Alexander the Great 150 years later. In Byzantine times it was the first line of defence for Constantinople, but by 1402 the strait was under the control of the Ottoman sultan Beyazıt I, allowing his armies to conquer the Balkans. Mehmet the Conqueror fortified the strait as part of his grand plan to conquer Constantinople (1453), building eight separate fortresses. As the Ottoman Empire declined during the 19th century, England and France competed with Russia for influence over these strategic sea passages.

Hoping to capture the Ottoman capital and access to Eastern Europe during WWI, Winston Churchill, then British First Lord of the Admiralty, organised a naval assault on the straits. In March 1915 a strong Franco-British fleet tried to force them, but failed. Then, on 25 April, British, Australian, New Zealand and Indian troops landed on Gallipoli, and French troops near Çanakkale. Both Turkish and Allied troops fought desperately and fearlessly, and devastated one another. After nine months of ferocious combat but little progress, the Allied forces withdrew.

The Turkish success at Gallipoli was partly due to bad luck and leadership on the Allied side, and partly due to reinforcements to the Turkish side brought in by General Liman von Sanders. But a crucial element in the defeat was that the Allied troops landed in a sector where they faced then Lieutenant-Colonel Mustafa Kemal (later Atatürk).

A relatively minor officer, Mustafa Kemal had General von Sanders' confidence. He managed to guess the Allied battle plan correctly when his commanders did not, and stalled the invasion in spite of bitter fighting that wiped out his regiment (see p188).

GALLIPOLI (GELİBOLU) PENINSULA

0 —————— 10 km
0 —————— 6 miles
Approximate Scale

INFORMATION
Kabatepe Information Centre & Museum	**1** A4
Kilia Bay Information Centre	**2** B4

SIGHTS & ACTIVITIES
7th Field Ambulance Cemetery	**3** A3
Çanakkale Şehitleri Anıtrı (Çanakkale Martyrs Memorial)	**4** A5
Cape Helles British Memorial	**5** A5
French War Memorial & Cemetery	**6** A5
Gallery of the Gallipoli Campaign	(see 14) A5
Hill 60 New Zealand Memorial	**7** B3
Lalababa Hill	**8** A3
Lancashire Landing Cemetery	**9** A5
Nuri Yamut Monument	**10** A5
Picnic Area	**11** A5
Pink Farm Cemetery	**12** A5
Redoubt Cemetery	**13** A5
Salim Mutlu War Museum	**14** A5
Sargı Yeri Cemetery	**15** A5
Skew Bridge Cemetery	**16** A5
Twelve Tree Copse Cemetery	**17** A5
'V' Beach Cemetery	**18** A5
Yahya Çavuş Şehitliği	**19** A5
Şahindere (Falcon Stream) Cemetery	**20** A5

Kireç Tepe
Azmak   Beşyol
Suvla   Hill 10   Yolağzı
Bay   *Salt Lake*   Green   Küçükanafarta
8   *(Tuz Gölü)*   Hill   Kumköy
'B' Beach   Büyükanafarta
3   Kocaçimentepe   Yalova
Hill Q
See Battlefields Map (p186)   To Gelibolu (20km); İstanbul (200km)
Ferry to Gökçeada   Anzac Cove (Anzac Koyu)   Bigalı (Boğhalı)
Kabatepe   2   E-87
Eceabat   To Bandırma (125km); Bursa (300km)
Kum Limanı   **Gallipoli National Historic Park**   Kilitbahir   Çanakkale
AEGEAN SEA (EGE DENİZİ)   Behramlı   Havuzlar
10   20
15   Alçıtepe (Krythia)
17   14   Kepez
13   Dardanos
16   6   11
12   E-87
9   Abide
5   *Morto* 4
19   *Bay*
Cape 18   Seddülbahir   Güzelyalı
Helles   *Dardanelles (Çanakkale Boğazı)*
Kumkale   İntepe   To Troy (10km); Ayvacık (50km); İzmir (325km)

Throughout the campaign, though suffering from malaria, he commanded in full view of his troops and of the enemy, and miraculously escaped death several times. At one point a piece of shrapnel hit him in the chest, but was stopped by his pocket watch. His brilliant performance made him a folk hero and paved the way for his promotion to *paşa* (general).

The Gallipoli campaign lasted until January 1916, and resulted in a total of more than half a million casualties. The British Empire suffered over 200,000 casualties, with the loss of some 36,000 lives. French casualties of 47,000 made up over half the entire French contingent. Half the 500,000 Ottoman troops became casualties, with more than 55,000 dead. Despite the carnage, the battles here are often considered the last true instance of a 'gentleman's war', with both sides displaying respect towards their enemy. Many of the smaller memorials illustrate tales of unusual bravery and fair play.

Orientation & Information

The Gallipoli Peninsula is a fairly large area to tour, especially without your own transport; it's over 35km as the crow flies from the northernmost battlefield to the southern tip of the peninsula.

There are currently 34 war cemeteries on Gallipoli. The principal battles took place on its western shore, near Anzac Cove and Arıburnu, and in the hills just to the east. Anzac Cove is about 12km from Eceabat and 19km from Kilitbahir. If time is tight or you're touring by public transport, head for Anzac Cove and Arıburnu first, which is also what the tours do.

Shops and stalls in every town here sell maps and guides to the battlefields. You can also find plenty of practical and background information on the internet at www.gallipoli-association.com and http://user.online.be/~snelders.

Battlefield Sites

Gallipoli National Historic Park (Gelibolu Tarihi Milli Parkı) covers much of the peninsula and all of the significant battle sites. Park headquarters is 2km southwest of Eceabat at the Kabatepe Information Centre & Museum (Kabatepe Tanıtma Merkezi Müzesi), where there's also a picnic ground.

The national park has several different sign systems: the normal Turkish highway signs,

the national park administration signs and the wooden ones posted by the Commonwealth War Graves Commission. This can lead to confusion because the foreign troops and the Turks used different names for the battlefields, and the park signs don't necessarily agree with the ones erected by the highway department. We've used both English and Turkish names in the text and on the Anzac Battlefields map.

On weekends from April to mid-June and again in September you'll find the battlefield sites overrun with school groups.

NORTHERN PENINSULA

About 3km north of Eceabat a road marked for Kabatepe and Kemalyeri heads west into the park. We describe the sites in the order most walkers and motorists are likely to visit them, although the tours often change the sequence to suit their narrative.

KILIA BAY INFORMATION CENTRE

Opened in 2005, this **centre** (Kilya Koyu Ana Tanıtım Merkezi; Map p184; admission free; 🕙 9am-noon & 1-5pm) is intended as the main information point for visitors to the battlefields. The complex includes the information centre, several exhibition areas, a cinema, library and café. It's about 2km outside Eceabat, 100m off the İstanbul highway.

KABATEPE INFORMATION CENTRE & MUSEUM

This older **centre** (Kabatepe Tanıtma Merkezi Müzesi; Map p184; admission €0.75; 🕙 8am-noon & 1-5pm), roughly 1km east of the village of Kabatepe, holds a small museum with old uniforms, rusty weapons and other battlefield finds, including the skull of a luckless Turkish soldier with a bullet lodged in the forehead. Perhaps the most touching exhibit is a letter from a young officer who had left law school in Constantinople to volunteer in the Gallipoli campaign. He wrote to his mother in poetic terms about the beauty of the landscape and of his love for life. Two days later he died in battle.

The road uphill to Lone Pine (Kanlısırt) and Chunuk Bair begins 750m west of the information centre. Anzac Cove is about 3.5km from the centre.

KABATEPE (GABA TEPE) VILLAGE

The small harbour here (Map p184) was probably the object of the Allied landing on 25

April 1915. In the dark of early morning it's possible that uncharted currents swept the Allies' landing craft northwards to the steep cliffs of Arıburnu – a bit of bad luck that may have sealed the campaign's fate from the start. Today there's little in Kabatepe except for a camping ground and the dock for ferries that go to the island of Gökçeada (see p198).

ANZAC COVE (ANZAK KÖYÜ) & BEACHES

Heading northwest from the information centre, it's 3km to the **Beach (Hell Spit) Cemetery** (Map p186). After another 90m a road cuts inland to the Shrapnel Valley and Plugge's Plateau Cemeteries.

Follow the coastal road for another 400m and you'll come to Anzac Cove, beneath and just south of the Arıburnu cliffs, where the ill-fated Allied landing was made on 25 April 1915. Ordered to advance inland, the Allied forces met with fierce resistance from the Ottoman forces under the leadership of Mustafa Kemal, who had foreseen where they would land and disobeyed an order to send his troops further south to Cape Helles. After this failed endeavour, the Anzacs concentrated on consolidating and expanding the beachhead while awaiting reinforcements.

In August the same year a major offensive was staged in an attempt to advance beyond the beach up to the ridges of Chunuk Bair and Sarı Bair. It resulted in the bloodiest battles of the campaign, but little progress was made.

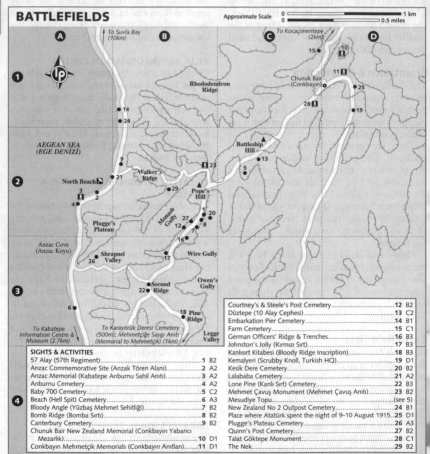

BATTLEFIELDS

Approximate Scale

To Suvla Bay (10km)
To Kocaçimentepe (2km)
Rhododendron Ridge
Chunuk Bair (Conkbayırı)
AEGEAN SEA (EGE DENİZİ)
Walker's Ridge
North Beach
Plugge's Plateau
Pope's Hill
Monash Gully
Anzac Cove (Anzac Koyu)
Shrapnel Valley
Wire Gully
Battleship Hill
Second Ridge
Owen's Gully
Pine Ridge
Legge Valley
To Kabatepe Information Centre & Museum (2.7km)
To Karayörük Deresi Cemetery (500m); Mehmetçiğe Saygı Anıtı (Memorial to Mehmetçik) (1km)

THRACE & MARMARA

PRESERVING GALLIPOLI

Most of the Gallipoli peninsula is a protected national park, but its popularity with visitors makes effective site conservation challenging, and many people feel that the local government and park administration don't always handle the situation effectively. In recent years the flow of traffic has become particularly heavy, particularly around the most-visited monuments, and supposed 'improvements' such as car parks and road-widening have caused considerable damage to certain areas, most shockingly at Anzac Cove.

Of course seeing the entire peninsula on foot or by bike isn't feasible for all visitors, but if possible you should at least try (or encourage your tour driver) to leave your vehicle in Alçıtepe, Seddülbahir or Kabatepe when exploring the areas around these towns, rather than insisting on motoring right up to each and every site.

The other major problem is the proliferation of rubbish all over the peninsula, dumped by careless visitors and locals. As well as the inevitable food wrappers and plastic bottles, all kinds of domestic refuse and even large items such as old furniture crop up even at some of the most important memorial sites. What can you do? Easy: just don't drop your own litter, and feel free to pick up other people's!

Anzac Cove is marked by a Turkish monument, another 300m along, which repeats Atatürk's famous words of 1934:

'To us there is no difference between the Johnnies and the Mehmets…You, the mothers, who sent your sons from faraway countries, wipe away your tears; your sons are now lying in our bosom… after losing their lives in this land they have become our sons as well.'

A memorial reserve, the beach is off-limits to swimmers and picnickers. Sadly erosion and roadworks have damaged the cove considerably, and the beach is now little more than a narrow strip of sand. In 2005 witnesses reported seeing human remains uncovered and construction debris dumped on the beach, prompting outrage among preservation campaigners and war-grave officials. For more on conservation issues, see the boxed text, above.

A few hundred metres beyond Anzac Cove is **Arıburnu Cemetery** (Map p186) and, 750m further along, **Canterbury Cemetery**. Between them is the **Anzac Commemorative Site**, where the dawn services are held on Anzac Day. Less than 1km further along the seaside road are the cemeteries at **No 2 Outpost**, set back inland from the road, and **New Zealand No 2 Outpost**, next to the road. The **Embarkation Pier Cemetery** is 200m beyond the New Zealand No 2 Outpost.

LONE PINE

Retrace your steps to the Kabatepe Information Centre & Museum and follow the signs just under 3km up the hill for Lone Pine (Kanlısırt; Map p186), perhaps the most poignant and moving of all the Anzac cemeteries. It's another 3km uphill to the New Zealand Memorial at Chunuk Bair.

This area saw the most bitter fighting of the campaign. Ironically, a disastrous forest fire of 1994 stripped away the pines, which had been planted after the war, returning the area to what it must have looked like in 1915. Today reforestation is once again underway.

The first monument, **Mehmetçiğe Saygı Anıtı**, on the right-hand side of the road about 1km from the junction, is dedicated to 'Mehmetçik' (Little Mehmet), the Turkish 'Johnnie' or 'GI Joe'. Another 1200m brings you to the **Karayörük Deresi Cemetery** and the **Kanlısırt Yazıtı**, which describes the battle of Lone Pine from the Turkish viewpoint.

At Lone Pine itself, 400m uphill, Australian forces captured the Turkish positions on the evening of 6 August. In the few days of the August assault, 4000 men died here. The trees that shaded the cemetery were swept away by the fire in 1994, leaving only one: a lone pine planted years ago from the seed of the original tree that stood here during the battle. The tombstones carry touching epitaphs: 'Only son', 'He died for his country', 'If I could hold your hand once more just to say well done', and include the grave of the youngest soldier to die here, a boy of just 14.

JOHNSTON'S JOLLY TO QUINN'S POST

Progressing up the hill from Lone Pine, you quickly come to understand the ferocity of the battles. At some points the trenches were only a few metres apart. The order to attack meant certain death to all who followed it, and virtually all – on both sides – did as they were ordered.

At Johnston's Jolly (Map p186), 200m beyond Lone Pine, at Courtney's & Steele's Post, another 300m along, and especially at Quinn's Post (Bomba Sırt, Yüzbaşı Mehmet Şehitliği), another 400m uphill, the trenches were separated only by the width of the modern road. Some of the crumbling trenches have been refaced with wooden struts to give an idea of what they would have looked like in 1915.

On the eastern side at Johnston's Jolly is the Turkish monument to the soldiers of the 125th Regiment who died here on Red Ridge (Kırmızı Sırt/125 Alay Cephesi). At Quinn's Post is the memorial to Sergeant Mehmet, who fought with rocks and his fists after he ran out of ammunition, and the Captain Mehmet Cemetery.

57 ALAY (57TH REGIMENT) CEMETERY

Just over 1km uphill from Lone Pine is another monument to Mehmetçik on the western side of the road and, on the eastern side, the cemetery and monument for officers and soldiers of the Ottoman 57th Regiment, led by Mustafa Kemal, and which he sacrificed to halt the first Anzac assaults (see right). The cemetery (Map p186) has a surprising amount of religious symbolism (including an outdoor mosque reminiscent of the Namazgah at Gelibolu) for a Turkish army site, as historically the republican army has been steadfastly secular. The statue of an old man showing his grand-daughter the battle sites portrays Hüseyin Kaçmaz, who fought in the Balkan Wars, the Gallipoli campaign and at the fateful Battle of Dumlupınar during the War of Independence. He died in 1994, aged 110, the last of the Turkish survivors of Gallipoli.

Down some steps from here, the new **Kesik Dere Cemetery** holds the remains of a further 1115 Turkish soldiers from the 57th and other regiments.

MEHMET ÇAVUŞ MONUMENT & THE NEK

About 100m uphill past the 57th Regiment Cemetery, a road goes west to the monument for Mehmet Çavuş (another Sergeant Mehmet; Map p186) and The Nek. It was at The Nek on 7 August 1915 that the 8th (Victorian)

and 10th (Western Australian) regiments of the third Light Horse Brigade vaulted out of their trenches into withering fire and certain death, an episode immortalised in the Peter Weir film *Gallipoli.*

BABY 700 CEMETERY & MESUDİYE TOPU

About 300m uphill from the road to The Nek is the Baby 700 Cemetery (Map p186) and the Ottoman cannon called the Mesudiye Topu. Baby 700 was the limit of the initial attack, and the graves here are mostly dated 25 April.

DÜZTEPE (10 ALAY CEPHESI)

Another 1.5km uphill brings you to a monument (Map p186) marking the spot where the Ottoman 10th Regiment held the line. The views of the strait and the surrounding countryside are superb.

TALAT GÖKTEPE MONUMENT

About 1km further along from Düztepe is the monument (Map p186) to a more recent casualty of Gallipoli: Talat Göktepe, Chief Director of the Çanakkale Forestry District, who died fighting the forest fire of 1994.

CHUNUK BAIR (CONKBAYIRI)

At the top of the hill, 600m past the Talat Göktepe Monument, is a T intersection. A right turn takes you east to the spot where, having stayed awake for four days and nights, Mustafa Kemal spent the night of 9–10 August directing part of the counterattack to the August offensive, and also to **Kemalyeri** (Scrubby Knoll), his command post.

A left turn leads after 100m to **Chunuk Bair** (Map p186), the first objective of the Allied landing in April 1915, and now the site of the New Zealand Memorial.

As the Anzac troops made their way up the scrub-covered slopes on 25 April, Mustafa Kemal, the divisional commander, brought up the 57th Infantry Regiment and gave them his famous order: 'I am not ordering you to attack, I am ordering you to die. In the time it takes us to die, other troops and commanders will arrive to take our places'. The 57th was wiped out but held the line and inflicted equally heavy casualties on the Anzacs below.

Chunuk Bair was also at the heart of the struggle for the peninsula from 6 to 9 August 1915, when 28,000 men died on this ridge. The peaceful pine grove of today makes it difficult to imagine the blasted wasteland of almost a century ago, when bullets, bombs and shrapnel mowed down men as the fighting went on day and night despite huge numbers of casualties. The Anzac attack on 6 to 7 August, which included the New Zealand Mounted Rifle Brigade and a Maori contingent, was deadly, but the attack on the following day was of a ferocity which, according to Mustafa Kemal, 'could scarcely be described'.

On the western side of the road is the **New Zealand Memorial** and some reconstructed **Turkish trenches**. There's a giant statue of Mustafa Kemal and signs to indicate the spots where he stood to give the order for the crucial attack at 4.30am on 8 August 1915; where he watched the battle's progress; and where shrapnel would have hit his heart, had it not been stopped by his pocket watch. Practically, it's unlikely that these were the actual locations, but the power of his legend is such that it doesn't really matter.

To the east a side road leads to the Turkish **Conkbayırı Mehmetçik Memorial** (Map p186), five giant tablets with Turkish inscriptions describing the battle.

Beyond Chunuk Bair the road leads to Kocaçimentepe, less than 2km along.

SOUTHERN PENINSULA

Far fewer people visit the sites of the southern peninsula (Map p184), which makes it a good place to come to escape the traffic and tour groups. It's easiest to get round these sites with your own transport. A taxi driver from Eceabat will charge you around €40 (negotiable) to whisk you around them for two hours.

From near the Kabatepe Information Centre & Museum a road heads south past the side road to **Kum Limanı**, where there's a good swimming beach.

From Kabatepe it's about 12km to the village of **Alçıtepe**, formerly known as Krythia or Kirte. Close to the village's main intersection is the privately run **Salim Mutlu War Museum** (admission free; ⏰ 8am-noon & 1-5pm), which houses relics from the northern and southern battlefields. Nearby, the **Gallery of the Gallipoli Campaign** (admission free; ⏰ 8am-noon & 1-5pm) takes a more illustrative approach to events. In the village, signs point southwest to the **Twelve Tree Copse** and **Pink Farm Cemeteries**, and north to the Turkish **Sargı Yeri Cemetery** and **Nuri Yamut Monument**. The new **Şahindere (Falcon Stream) Cemetery**, opened in 2005, is about 3km north.

Heading south, the road passes the **Redoubt Cemetery**. About 5.5km south of Alçıtepe, south of the **Skew Bridge Cemetery**, the road divides, the right fork heading for the village of Seddülbahir and several Allied memorials. **Seddülbahir** (Sedd el Bahr), around 2km from the intersection, is a sleepy farming village with a few pensions, a PTT, a ruined Ottoman/Byzantine fortress and a small harbour. The old castle, formerly an army base, is currently under restoration.

Follow the signs for Yahya Çavuş Şehitliği to reach the **Cape Helles British Memorial**, 1km beyond Seddülbahir village square. Today there are fine views of the straits, with ships cruising placidly up and down, but in 1915 half a million men were killed, wounded or lost in the dispute over which ships should go through.

The initial Allied attack was two-pronged, with the southern landing at the tip of the peninsula on 'V' Beach. Yahya Çavuş (Sergeant Yahya) was the Turkish officer who led the first resistance to the Allied landing on 25 April 1915, causing heavy casualties. The cemetery named after him, **Yahya Çavuş Şehitliği**, is between the Helles Memorial and 'V' Beach.

Lancashire Landing Cemetery is off to the north; another sign points south to **'V' Beach**, 550m downhill.

Retrace your steps from the Helles Memorial back to the road division and then head east following signs for Abide or Çanakkale Şehitleri Anıtı (Çanakkale Martyrs' Memorial) at Morto Bay. Along the way you will pass the **French War Memorial & Cemetery**. French troops, including a regiment of Africans, attacked Kumkale on the Asian shore in March 1915 with complete success, then re-embarked and landed in support of their British comrades-in-arms at Cape Helles, where they were virtually wiped out. The French cemetery is rarely visited but quite moving, with rows of metal crosses and five white concrete ossuaries each containing the bones of 3000 soldiers.

At the foot of the hill is a pine-shaded picnic area. The **Çanakkale Şehitleri Anıtı** (Çanakkale Martyrs Memorial) or Abide monument is a gigantic four-legged stone table almost 42m high that commemorates all the Turkish soldiers who fought and died at Gallipoli. It's surrounded by landscaped grounds, including a rose garden planted to commemorate the 80th anniversary of the conflict in 1995, and stands above another **war museum** (closed at the time of research). Translated, the poem on the altarlike stone beneath the monument's legs reads:

> Soldiers who have fallen on this land defending this land!
> Would that your ancestors might descend from the skies to kiss your pure brows.
> Who could dig the grave that was not too small for you?
> All of history itself is too small a place for you.

Tours

Tours can be a good idea, as this way you get the benefit of a guide who can explain the battles as you go along. The typical four- to six-hour tour includes transport by car or minibus, driver and guide, picnic lunch and a swim from a beach on the western shore. Most of the regular Gallipoli guides come in for lots of praise from readers, but ask around to be on the safe side.

Several agencies in Çanakkale and Eceabat organise tours and competition is at times aggressive.

Hassle Free Tours (☎ 0286-213 5969; www.hassle freetour.com; €27) Operates tours out of Anzac House in Çanakkale (p193) and a secondary office in Eceabat (☎ 0286-814 2431). Hassle Free also runs tours out of İstanbul to Gallipoli for €60, inclusive of a stay of one night at Anzac House before visiting the ruins at Troy and either travelling on to Selçuk or back to İstanbul. However, visiting the battlefields straight after a five-hour bus ride from İstanbul is not much fun – it might be better to take the tour from Çanakkale.

TJs Tours (☎ 0286-814 3121; www.anzacgallipolitours .com; €23) Based at the Eceabat Hotel (opposite), TJs comes highly recommended. İlhami Gezici, also known as TJ, marries historical knowledge with genuine enthusiasm. A private two-person tour can cover the less visited sites at Cape Helles and around Suvla Bay for around €100. TJ also has a copy of the Commonwealth War Graves Commission's register to help visitors find a particular grave.

Trooper Tours (☎ 217 3343; www.troopertours.com; €23) Run by Fez Travel, the people behind the Fez Bus, this latest addition to the competition operates from the Yellow Rose Pension in Çanakkale (p195), benefiting from the captive market of travellers on other Fez packages. Having 'poached' popular veteran guide Ali Efe from Hassle Free, standards should be high too.

Troy-Anzac Tours (☎ 0286-217 5849; www.troyanzac .com; Saat Kulesi Meydanı 6, Çanakkale; €23) Facing the clock tower, this place has been in business the longest but doesn't seem to be as popular as the others, perhaps because it is not associated with a hostel.

Diving to examine the wrecks off the western coast of the peninsula is an increasingly popular pastime. TJs Tours charges €60 for two dives or €15 for snorkelling off Anzac Cove, including all equipment.

Sleeping

There are some excellent accommodation options inside the park itself, including a number of well-equipped camp sites. The majority are around Seddülbahir and can be tricky to get to without your own transport, so they're most popular with cyclists and caravaners. Apart from overnight tour groups, most other travellers stay in Çanakkale or Eceabat.

Mocamp Seddülbahir (☎ 862 0056; camping €5.60, tr €17) One of the more convenient options, right next to the beach in Seddülbahir. As well as the camping area, there are a few rooms above the site café.

Pansiyon Helles Panorama (☎ 862 0035; s/d with shared bathroom €14/28) In Seddülbahir, this welcoming guesthouse has the incongruous air of an English B&B. The eponymous panorama is of the Abide monument, which might not be the most elaborate sculpture in the world but is certainly dramatic on its clifftop perch.

Hotel Kum (☎ 814 1455; www.hotelkum.com; s/d €35/52; ☐) At Kum Limanı, south of Kabatepe, the Hotel Kum is virtually a resort complex, right on a sandy beach with facilities including restaurant, bar, disco and dive centre. The plain white décor is nothing special, and the whole idea of a 72-room hotel amid the war memorials is perhaps a little unseemly, but the setting is beautiful and standards are high. Camping costs €4, caravan parking €10.

Abide Motel (☎ 862 0010; s/d full board €28/56) Another reasonably priced establishment in a great location at Morto Bay, northwest of Seddülbahir near the Abide monument and the French Cemetery. The food is highly rated.

Getting There & Around

With your own transport you can easily tour the battlefields in a day. Touring by public transport is also possible, but dolmuşes serve only a few sites and villages. In summer, you might be able to hitch around the peninsula,

---

WARNING: ANZAC DAY CROWDS

In recent years the Anzac Day memorial service has become one of the most popular events in Turkey for foreign visitors. In 2005 more than 20,000 people came to mark the 90th anniversary of the Gallipoli landings, overwhelming the peninsula's modest infrastructure. In Çanakkale, hotels are usually booked out months in advance.

As well as the traffic, which reaches all-day jam proportions, many people report being ripped off on package deals. In particular, some tour operators claim to drive from İstanbul in time for the dawn service, when in fact even people coming from Çanakkale can't always make it in time. Book as early as possible with a reliable agency, and be wary of last-minute deals, especially in İstanbul.

The individual Australian and New Zealand ceremonies at Lone Pine and Chunuk Bair attract smaller crowds than the dawn service at Anzac Cove, and there are plans for a video link so visitors can view all three from one place, but even so, the sheer weight of numbers makes getting around a nightmare.

It's easier to appreciate Gallipoli's poignant beauty at almost any other time, and many visitors find their emotional experience completely different if they take the time to explore at leisure away from the crowds. Maybe the answer is to come for the dawn service and then come back for a quieter, calmer look on another day.

---

but in other seasons there may not be enough traffic. The most important group of monuments and cemeteries, from Lone Pine uphill to Chunuk Bair, can be toured on foot, an excellent idea in fine weather.

Ferries run from Çanakkale on the eastern side of the Dardanelles to Eceabat and Kilitbahir on the peninsula; see p197 for information. See p200 for information on ferries to Kabatepe.

Taxi drivers in Eceabat will happily run you around the main sites for around €40 but they take only two to 2½ hours and few of them speak English well enough to provide a decent commentary.

ECEABAT (MAYDOS)

☎ 0286 / pop 4500

Across the Dardanelles from Çanakkale, Eceabat is a small, easy-going waterfront town with good access to the main Gallipoli sites, offering a convenient base for battlefield visits if you don't fancy the bustle of Çanakkale. Ferries dock by the main square, Cumhuriyet Meydanı, which has restaurants, hotels, ATMs, bus company offices, and dolmuş and taxi stands.

Like most of the peninsula, Eceabat is swamped with groups of students over weekends from April through to mid-June and again in late September.

Sleeping

TJs Hostel (☎ 814 3121; www.anzacgallipolitours.com; Cumhuriyet Caddesi 5; dm €8.50-11; ✗ 💻) In a multistorey building 100m from the main square,

TJs is Eceabat's original backpacker hostel. Since TJs Tours opened the nearby Eceabat Hotel, the ageing hostel has been used mainly as a back-up option for busy periods.

Otel Boss (☎ 814 1464; Cumhuriyet Meydanı 14; s/d/tr €8.50/17/23; ❄) A small, narrow budget hotel right on the main square, with a café downstairs. Opt for a corner room to get a bit more space.

Hotel Boss II (☎ 814 2311; dm €6, s/d/tr €8.50/17/23) Finally, a sequel that's better than the original. The bigger Boss has a choice of accommodation options, including some pleasant wooden bungalows, though the location's less convenient, a 10-minute walk west from the town centre. The on-site restaurant and bar save the hike back into town for refreshment.

Eceabat Hotel (☎ 814 2458; www.anzacgallipolitours.com; Cumhuriyet Meydanı 20; dm €8.35, hostel s/d/tr €18/24/35, hotel s/d/tr €28/39/50; ✗ ❄ 💻) Making the most of its commanding central position, the Eceabat has rooms to suit every budget, from the basic hostel bunk rooms and dorms to the smarter air-con hotel rooms, which boast balconies, parquet floors, TV and phone. The roof bar, Ottoman-styled lobby, tour office and regular barbecues round off the range of traveller services.

Aqua Hotel (☎ 814 2864; www.heyboss.com; İstiklal Caddesi; s/d/tr/q €22.50/39/56/67; ❄) The third part of the Boss trilogy, this low castlelike building (actually a former tomato-canning factory) on the waterfront has a touch of style in its neat rooms and terraced restaurant, though the carpets are a bit worn. The Vegemite bar-club seems a bit out of sync with the largely nonbackpacker clientele.

Free camping is possible on a grubby stretch of sand at the Boomerang Bar (below), but the facilities are pretty rough.

Eating & Drinking

Hanımeli (☎ 814 2345; İskele Caddesi; mains €1.10-4.50; ☯ 8am-10pm) Favoured by smaller tour groups at lunchtime, this little brown café serves up breakfast, *mantı* and traditional dishes, and also sells local produce such as olive oil. It's opposite the waterfront west of the centre.

Gül Aile Kebab Salonu (☎ 814 3040; Hanım Meydanı; mains €2-5.50; ☯ 8am-10pm) A typical family-friendly kebap and pide canteen in the middle of the row of shops and cafeterias leading west from the main square.

Maydos Restaurant & Bar (☎ 814 1454; İstiklal Caddesi; mains €2.50-5.50; ☯ 11am-10pm) Out on the waterfront past the Aqua Hotel, the Maydos is popular with tour groups, sporting a fine, vined terrace and a grill-heavy menu.

Boomerang Bar (☎ 814 2144; ☯ from 5pm) Apart from the hotel bars, this place at the northern end of town is your only option for a not-so-quiet drink if you can't be bothered with the ferry hop to Çanakkale. It's aimed mainly at thirsty young Antipodeans, and stays open as long as there are customers still standing.

Getting There & Away

Long-distance buses pass through Eceabat on the way from Çanakkale to İstanbul (€12.50, five hours).

The Çanakkale–Eceabat ferries (€0.85, bicycles €2, cars €5.50, 25 minutes) run on the hour every hour from 7am to midnight (every 30 minutes in summer), with four services in each direction between 1am and 6am.

Hourly buses or minibuses run to Gelibolu (€1.70, one hour). In summer there are several dolmuşes daily to the ferry dock at Kabatepe (€1.10, 15 minutes) on the western shore of the peninsula. These can drop you at the Kabatepe Information Centre & Museum, or at the base of the road up to Lone Pine and Chunuk Bair.

Dolmuşes also run down the coast to Kilitbahir (€0.55, 10 minutes).

KİLİTBAHİR

A small ferry from Çanakkale sails to Kilitbahir, the 'Lock on the Sea': a tiny fishing harbour completely dominated by a massive **castle** (admission €1.10; ☯ 8.30am-noon & 1.30-6.30pm Wed-Sun) built by Mehmet the Conqueror in 1452 and given a grand seven-storey interior tower a century later by Süleyman the Magnificent. It's well worth a quick look around – and a climb onto the walls if your nerves will stand it. Afterwards, check out the collection of defensive **bunkers** behind it.

There are a few small pensions, tea houses and restaurants here, as well as a row of souvenir stalls for the tour groups, but most people barely pause in Kilitbahir. From the ferry, dolmuşes and taxis run to Eceabat and Gelibolu, and to the Turkish war memorial at Abide, although you may have to wait for them to fill up.

ÇANAKKALE

☎ 0286 / pop 75,900

This sprawling harbour town is the busiest in the Gallipoli region, and is easily the most frequented stopover for groups and individuals visiting the battlefields and memorial sites (for local tour companies, see p190). It's also a good place to hang around in its own right, with a rare concentration of nightlife in its centre, and a sweeping waterfront drag that heaves with activity throughout the summer months.

Çanakkale is the most popular base for visiting the ruins at Troy (see p203), as well as Gallipoli, and has become a very popular destination for weekending Turks. To have your pick of the hotels you're better off coming midweek.

Orientation

Çanakkale is centred on its harbour, with a PTT booth, ATM machines and public phones right by the docks, and hotels, restaurants, banks and bus offices all within a few hundred metres. The otogar is 1km inland, with a Gima supermarket right beside it. From the otogar, turn left, walk to the first set of traffic lights, and follow the 'Feribot' signs, which will bring you to the town centre and docks.

The dolmuş station for getting to Troy and Güzelyalı is also 1km inland, beneath the bridge over the Sarı (Yellow) River.

Information

Maxi Internet (Fetvane Sokak 51; per hr €0.55; ☯ 10-1am) The best of the many Internet cafés around the centre.

Tourist office (☎ 217 1187; ☯ 8am-noon & 1-7pm Mon-Fri) By the harbour; little information but may have a photocopied map.

Sights

MILITARY MUSEUM

The pretty park in the military zone at the southern end of the quay now houses the **Military Museum** (Askeri Müze; admission €1.70; ✆ 9am-noon & 1.30-5pm Tue-Wed & Fri-Sun) and all sorts of military paraphernalia.

A sea-facing late-Ottoman building contains informative exhibits on the Gallipoli battles and some artfully displayed war relics, including fused bullets that hit each other in mid-air – apparently the chances of this happening are something like 160 million to one, which gives a chilling idea of just how much munition was flying around.

Nearby is a replica of the **minelayer** *Nusrat,* which played a heroic role in the sea campaign. The day before the Allied fleet tried to force the straits, Allied minesweepers proclaimed the water cleared. At night the *Nusrat* went out and picked up and relaid loose mines. Three Allied ships struck the *Nusrat's* mines and were sunk or crippled.

Mehmet the Conqueror built the impressive **Çimenlik Kalesi** fortress in 1452. The cannons surrounding the stone walls are leftovers from assorted battles; many were made in French, English and German foundries. Inside are more reminders of Atatürk and some fine paintings of the battles of Gallipoli.

ARCHAEOLOGY MUSEUM

Just over 2km south of the ferry pier on the road to Troy is Çanakkale's **Archaeology Museum** (Arkeoloji Müzesi; admission €1.10; ✆ 9am-5pm Tue-Sun).

The best exhibits here are those from Troy and Assos, although the finds from graves in Dardanos, an ancient town near Çanakkale, are also of interest. Unfortunately the displays look lost in this cavernous, mostly empty building, and could do with some beefing up.

Dolmuşes heading towards İntepe or Güzelyalı from Atatürk Caddesi run past the museum (€0.30).

OTHER ATTRACTIONS

The landmark five-storey Ottoman **clock tower** *(saat kulesi)* near the harbour was built in 1897. Vitalis, an Italian consul and Çanakkale merchant, left 100,000 gold francs to be used for the purpose when he died in France.

At the **Yalı Hamam** (Çarşı Caddesi; ✆ 6am-11.30pm for men, 8am-5pm for women), the full works cost about €8.50.

In Cumhuriyet Bulvarı, the broad main street, stands a **monument** of old WWI cannons. The inscription reads: 'Turkish soldiers used these cannons on 18 March 1915 to ensure the impassability of the Çanakkale Strait'. Nearby is an outsize copy of a Çanakkale pot – a rather kitschy 19th-century style that is slowly gaining popularity. Look for more modestly sized examples in shops around town.

East of the harbour, the waterfront promenade widens out and you're greeted by an impressive, full-sized **Trojan Horse**, as seen in the movie *Troy* (2004), with a model of the ancient city and some information displays beneath it.

Festivals & Events

Every March and April Çanakkale commemorates the great WWI battles of Gallipoli. **Turkish Victory Day** (Çanakkale Deniz Zaferi), when Ottoman cannons and mines succeeded in keeping the Allied fleet from passing through the Dardanelles, is celebrated on 18 March.

Most Australians and New Zealanders choose to visit on **Anzac Day**, 25 April, the anniversary of the Allied landings on the peninsula in 1915. A dawn service near Anzac Cove begins a day of commemorative events. This is when Çanakkale is at its most unbearably overcrowded – see the boxed text, p191. Unless the date has particular personal significance, you would be well advised to pick another date.

Sleeping

Çanakkale has hotels to suit all pockets, except on Anzac Day, when rip-offs and complaints are rife. If you do intend to be in town around 25 April, check prices carefully in advance.

BUDGET

Anzac House (✆ 213 5969; www.anzachouse.com; Cumhuriyet Bulvarı; dm €5, s/d/tr with shared bathroom €8.50/14/17; 🖳) Not to be confused with the smarter Anzac Hotel, Anzac House is the first place most backpackers head for – it's big, cheap and is the base for Hassle Free tours. Unfortunately many of the rooms are little more than cupboards.

Pansiyon Sera Palas (✆ 217 4240; Cimenlik Kalesi Karşısı; s/d €13/26) Skip east from the naval museum to grab one of the four unexpectedly spacious family-run rooms here. The owner is a professional English-speaking tour guide. The showers aren't great, but it's worth the money.

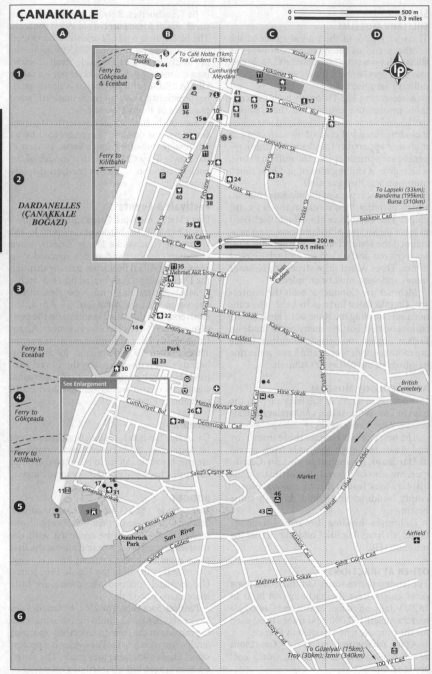

Hotel Efes (☎ 217 3256; Aralık Sokak 5; s/d €14/20) Behind the clock tower, the Efes is an excellent choice with cheery, rather feminine décor. The larger couples/family rooms are nicer than the dodgily plumbed standard singles, with TVs and even orthopaedic mattresses. The breakfasts are great, and there's a sunny little back garden with a fountain.

Yellow Rose Pension (☎ 217 3343; www.yellowrose.4mg.com; Yeni Sokak 5; dm €5.50, s/d/tr €14/22.50/25; 🖳) Increasingly popular with travellers, this bright, attractive guesthouse has a quiet location and lots of extras, from laundry and kitchen to book exchange and video library. It's also the local agent for Fez Travel and Trooper Tours.

Hotel İlion (☎ 212 4411; www.hotelilion.com; İnönü Caddesi 151; s/d/tr €23/34/48; 🍴) A slim tower block facing towards the peninsula, offering modest two-star standards in simple rooms above a marble lobby.

MIDRANGE

Maydos Hotel (☎ 213 5970; Yali Caddesi 12; www.maydos.com.tr; s €22.50-34, d €45-68; 🍴 🖳) The latest venture from the people behind Hassle Free Tours, this brand-new hotel looks a world away from the cramped budget lodgings at the Anzac House, especially in the superswish minimalist lobby with its stylish seats and plasma-screen TV. At these prices it's quite a bargain.

Anzac Hotel (☎ 217 7777; www.anzachotel.com; Saat Kulesi Meydanı 8; s/d €25/35; 🅿 🍴) It's been a while since its last major renovation but the Anzac's two-star improvements still hold good, and you could hardly get a better central location. There's a wheelchair ramp in the lobby.

Hotel Temizay (☎ 212 8760; Cumhuriyet Meydanı 15; s/d/tr €25/39/50; 🍴) It looks posh from the outside, but inside this one-star establishment is nothing more or less than a reasonable, good-value hotel with tiny but shiny bathrooms and some street-facing balconies.

Otel Anafartalar (☎ 217 4454; www.hotelanafartalar .com; İskele Meydanı; s/d €25/40; 🍴) A big pink block in a prime location near the ferry docks, the Anafartalar has fine views of the straits if you can bag a front room. It also has a popular waterfront restaurant.

Hotel Artur (☎ 213 2000; www.hotelartur.com; Cumhuriyet Meydanı 28; s/d/tr €25/40/50; 🍴 🖳) This upper-end hotel has a nicely designed lobby with wireless Internet access and a bar. The spacious modern rooms have sofas as well as the usual amenities, and there's a restaurant downstairs.

Hotel Helen (☎ 212 1818; www.helenhotel.com; Cumhuriyet Meydanı 57; s/d €25/50/65; 🍴 🖳) Just next to Anzac House, the Helen aims for a sophisticated classical air in the marble lobby, and while the rooms may never launch a thousand ships, they have everything you need for a break on your own personal odyssey.

Çanak Hotel (☎ 214 1582; www.canakhotel.com; Dibek Sokak 1; s/d €28/45; 🍴) This is another good tourist-class option tucked just off Cumhuriyet Meydanı, with facilities including roof bar and games room and a skylit atrium connecting the floors. The smart but low-key rooms tick all the right boxes.

TOP END

Büyük Truva Oteli (☎ 217 1024; www.truvahotel.com; Mehmet Akif Ersoy Caddesi 2; s/d/tr €44/54/65, ste €81; 🍴) A discreet side entrance takes you into this

THRACE & MARMARA

AUTHOR'S CHOICE

Hotel Kervansaray (☎ 217 8192; www.hotel kervansaray.org; Fetvane Sokak 13; s/d/tr €25/45/62; 🔀 🖳) Now that it's finally open, Çanakkale's first real boutique hotel is as lovely as you could hope for, laying on plenty of Ottoman touches in keeping with the restored paşa's house it occupies, even in the TV lounge. The rooms have a dash of character without being overdone, and the inviting courtyard and garden really sell the whole package.

---

elegantly old-fashioned three-star block on the waterfront road. The rooms range from comfy and modern to vaguely period, with some good sea views, and the big front terrace restaurant holds occasional special events.

Hotel Akol (☎ 217 9456; www.hotelakol.com.tr; Kordonboyu; s/d/tr €45/67/89, ste €111; 🔀 🖳 🗷) Also on the main bay road, this balcony-studded grey concrete tower is much easier on the eyes from the inside, where you can catch the straits views and admire the slightly overblown classical-themed lobby. It's mainly used by tour groups, so has plenty of high-capacity facilities to feed and entertain.

Eating

For a quick snack or cheap eat, there are small stalls and shops all over town, and street vendors set up along the waterfront in the evening selling corn on the cob, mussels and other simple items. Several shops on Yali Caddesi sell *peynirli helva,* a local variety of helva faintly flavoured with cheese. The whole waterfront is lined with licensed restaurants, whose terraces pack out every evening as long as the weather permits.

Köy Evi (Yalı Caddesi 13; dishes €0.85-1.70; 🕘 8am-9pm) Proper home cooking rules in this tiny shop, where you can watch headscarved local women making *mantı, börek* (filled pastry) and other dishes before serving them to hungry customers.

Özsüt (☎ 213 3773; Kayserili Ahmet Paşa Caddesi 2/A; cakes from €1.10; 🕘 11am-11.30pm) The austere black-and-white décor of this patisserie chain belies the sheer indulgence of the sweet treats sold within. You'll pay more to eat in, but it's worth it for the extra presentation.

Yemek (☎ 217 0154; Cumhuriyet Meydanı 32; mains €2-8.50; 🕘 24hr) Across the road from Anzac

House, Yemek is a straightforward all-hours outlet for kebap, pide and cafeteria meals, with inside and outside seating for all seasons.

Rıhtım Restaurant (☎ 217 1770; Eski Balıkhane Sokak; mains €2.80-7; 🕘 11am-11.30pm) An old favourite in the waterfront restaurant strip south of the harbour, Rıhtım, also known as Çekiç, after its owner, has a varied menu of Turkish and Western dishes along with the usual fish and meat.

Café Notte (☎ 214 9111; Kayserili Ahmet Paşa Caddesi 40/1; mains €4-8; 🕘 11am-11.30pm) At the heart of the trendier northern waterfront strip, the 'Night Cafe' achieves a relaxed but smart bar-bistro feel, with a cosmopolitan menu and some competent cocktails (€3 to €5).

Hünnaphan (☎ 214 2535; Mehmetçik Bulvarı 21; mains €4.50-8.50; 🕘 11am-11.30pm) You don't always have to follow the crowds to get a good meal: set in a purple restored house away from the busy waterfront, this charming restaurant has fantastic ceilings, a beautiful patio garden and two semiprivate balconies for couples to enjoy park views, Turkish or Western dishes and an extensive wine list (bottles €10 to €140). The same firm runs a small hotel in Adatepe, south of Çanakkale.

Drinking & Entertainment

As well as all the waterfront restaurants, Çanakkale has some pleasant tea gardens, most notably those occupying the strategic sunset spots at the southern and northern ends of the quay.

The town also has an unusually busy bar scene, catering for local youth and student crowds, and marauding young Aussies and Kiwis in season. Many venues have regular live music, and most of the liveliest places are clustered around Fetvane Sokak. Lone men may be refused entry, though this won't always apply to tourists. Average opening hours are 9pm to 1am or 2am; any admission charges usually include one drink.

Han Bar (Fetvane Sokak 26; admission €2.80) Upstairs in the old Yalı Han, this is a very popular music venue where the bands may play anything from Turkish rock to the *Ghostbusters* theme tune. The outside gallery also overlooks the equally popular courtyard tea garden.

Hedon (Yali Caddesi) This big bar-venue attempts a spot of lounge sophistication up front, until you get to the barn-like dancefloor. Admission depends on the night, usually around €4 when there's a band on. The clientele also varies – on one memorable night the bar had to close early because the entire crowd was underage!

TNT Bar/Hayal Kahvesi (☎ 217 0470; Saat Kulesi Meydanı 6) Facing the clock tower, this dual-identity bar and coffeehouse isn't always overfilled in the evenings, but does offer live music and cold beer.

Depo (☎ 212 6813; Fetvane Sokak 19; admission €2.80) The biggest and rowdiest of the Fetvane venues, with a warehouse vibe and a fantastic open courtyard full of funky beanbag chairs, Depo favours upfront Western dance tunes.

Getting There & Away
BUS & DOLMUŞ

Çanakkale's otogar is 1km east of the ferry docks but you probably won't need to use it as most buses pick up and drop off at the bus company offices near the harbour. If you do need to go there, walk straight inland from the harbour to Atatürk Caddesi and turn left. The otogar is 100m along on the right.

You can buy bus tickets at the otogar or at the bus-company offices. There are regular services to Ankara (€19.50, 10 hours), Ayvalık (€8.50, 3½ hours), Bandırma (€6.10, 2½ hours), Bursa (€11.10, 4½ hours), Edirne (€11.10, 4½ hours), İstanbul (€14, 5½ hours) and İzmir (€14, 5½ hours).

Dolmuşes to Troy (€1.40, 35 minutes) and Güzelyalı (€0.85, 20 minutes) leave from a separate dolmuş station under the bridge over the Sarı River.

To get to Gelibolu (€2.50, one to two hours), take a bus or minibus from the otogar to Lapseki then the ferry across the Dardanelles; alternatively, take the ferry to Eceabat or Kilitbahir and then a minibus. For Lapseki (€1.70, 30 minutes), grab any bus bound for Gönen, Bandırma or Bursa, but make sure you will be allowed to get off at Lapseki.

If you're heading for Çanakkale from İstanbul, the quickest way is to hop on a ferry from Yenikapı then take a bus from Bandırma, rather than trekking out to İstanbul's otogar for the direct buses.

Many travellers opt to come here on tours from İstanbul. Packages usually include transport and guided tours of the battlefields and Troy; you can then either return to İstanbul or arrange to be dropped in İzmir or Selçuk. The typical cost is around €60, including one night's accommodation; see p135.

BOAT

Two car ferries cross the Dardanelles from Çanakkale to the Gallipoli Peninsula. One goes to Kilitbahir, the other to Eceabat. Timetables are posted outside the ferry ticket office by the harbour.

See p192 for information about Çanakkale–Eceabat ferries.

The smaller Çanakkale–Kilitbahir ferry (€0.55, cars €2.80, 15 to 20 minutes) can carry only a few cars.

From Monday to Friday a single daily ferry runs from Çanakkale to Gökçeada (€1.70, cars €10, 2½ hours), leaving at 5pm and returning at 8am. Check times in advance.

AROUND ÇANAKKALE
Güzelyalı

Güzelyalı is a tiny resort strung out along a thin strip of sandy beach, southwest of Çanakkale off the road to Troy, and can be a handy standby in high season, when Çanakkale's at its most crowded. The views across the Dardanelles are wonderful because no development is allowed on the site of the Gallipoli National Park.

The focal point of the beach for daytrippers is the **Günü Birlik Alan** picnic area, towards the far end of the road, which has changing-cubicles, showers, toilets, picnic tables, beach umbrellas and a small café. The village of Güzelyalı itself also has a few facilities and a pretty **harbour**.

SLEEPING & EATING

Sohbet Camping (☎ 0544 466 5897; tents €5) Sohbet is about 1.5km along the track heading south from Güzelyalı. Unfortunately, when you get there you find that the small bay is hemmed in by buildings and loud Turkish pop music is rife.

Tusan Otel (☎ 232 8746; www.tusanhotel.com; s/d €50/75; 🛇 🖭) The four-star Tusan is a collection of low green blocks in a wonderful hillside location amid pine trees and a landscaped garden, just past the Günü Birlik Alan. The rooms have fairly modern décor, TV, minibar and balcony; there's an 'English pub' on site, and the sea is just down the steps at the back.

Ida Kale Resort Hotel (☎ 232 8332; www.kaleresort.com; s/d €70/100; 🛇 🖭) Back up the main road, the mock-castle design here is a little laughable, but the massive tiled rooms should snap you out of it, especially the individually decorated bathrooms and combined pool and sea views. Some rooms offer disabled access. Discount rates may be available at quiet times.

Koşebaşı (☎ 232 8314; dishes from €2.80) A pleasingly rustic tea garden and café opposite Güzelyalı's small mosque.

GETTING THERE & AWAY
Dolmuşes head for Güzelyalı from Çanakkale at least once an hour (€0.85, 20 minutes).

GÖKÇEADA
☎ 0286 / pop 8900

At the entrance to the Dardanelles, rugged, sparsely populated Gökçeada (also known as Windy Isle) is Turkey's largest island, and one of only two inhabited Aegean islands belonging to Turkey. Its landmass measures roughly 13km from north to south and 30km from east to west, with some surprisingly dramatic scenery packed into that small area.

Originally called İmvros, Gökçeada was once a predominantly Greek island. During WWI it was an important base for the Gallipoli campaign, as Allied commander General Ian Hamilton stationed himself at the village of Aydıncık (formerly Kefalos) on the island's southeast coast. Along with its smaller neighbour Bozcaada (p206), Gökçeada was retained by Turkey but exempted from the population exchange after 1923. However, in the 1950s the Cyprus issue prompted the government to put pressure on local Greeks to leave, and today only a few remain.

Gökçeada's inhabitants mostly earn a living through fishing, farming the narrow belt of fertile land around Gökçeada town, and from tourism. Apart from some semideserted Greek villages, olive groves and pine forests, the island boasts fine beaches and craggy hills. For now it is a rare example of an Aegean island that hasn't been overtaken by mass tourism.

Foreign visitor numbers are clearly picking up, judging by the flurry of new accommodation options, but for the moment most visitors are still well-off İstanbullus or former Greek islanders and their descendants. Public transport is limited to taxis and a couple of bus routes, so if you don't mind a little expense, this is a great place to escape.

Information
Most facilities, including ATMs, taxis, Internet cafés and a small cinema, are found in Gökçeada town, where 85% of the island's population lives. The island's only petrol station is 2km from the town centre, on the Kuzulimanı road.

There's a **tourist office** (☎ 887 4642; www .gokceada.com; Barbaros Caddesi 56) by the Kaleköy harbour, though it wasn't operating at the time of research.

Sights
Gökçeada town itself is useful but not particularly inspiring, although crumbling remains of the old village hide on the hill behind the main square.

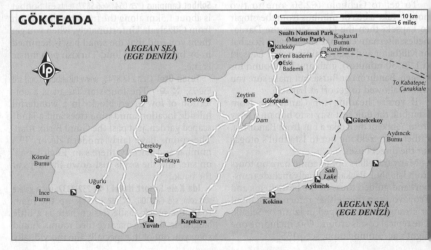

THRACE & MARMARA

DAIRY TALES

As you approach Kuzulimanı by sea, look out for a spectacular geological feature just south of the harbour, strangely resembling a large stack of cheese. This is Kaşkaval Burnu, also known by locals as Peynir Kayalıklari, or Cheese Rocks.

Naturally there is a legend to go with this quirk of geography, and it's a strange one even by Turkish standards. The story goes that a greedy old lady lived on the coast here with her large herds of sheep and goats, whose milk she used to make vast quantities of cheese. Rather than give any to her poorer neighbours, though, she piled all the cheeses on top of each other, in the hope that this would allow her to reach heaven. Seeing such selfishness, God grew angry and sent a mighty blizzard, which froze both the old woman and her tower of dairy. The frozen cheese, of course, became the rocks you see today.

Presumably the lesson in all this is learn to share, and don't mess with the Big Cheese, or you might experience the wrath of Gouda... After all, who wants to end up as a Roquefort-mation?

Most people head straight for **Kaleköy**, which has a so-so small beach, a hillside old quarter and the remains of an Ottoman-era castle, but its harbour setting has been blotted by a large new resort hotel, and a yacht marina is also due for construction. The coastline between Kuzulimanı and Kaleköy is a **marine national park** (Sualtı Milli Parkı).

There are smaller beach resorts at **Kapıkaya, Kokina** and **Yuvalı** along the south side of the island, although you'll need your own transport to reach them.

Heading west you'll skirt the Greek villages of **Zeytinli** (3km west of Gökçeada), **Tepeköy** (10km west) and **Dereköy** (15km west), all of them built on hillsides overlooking the island's central valley to avoid pirate raids. Nowadays many of the houses are deserted and falling into disrepair, and the churches are usually locked. However, Tepeköy and Zeytinli are both discovering the benefits of small-scale tourism thanks to a couple of inspired accommodation options, and either village is worth a visit in itself. Tepeköy in particular is absolutely gorgeous, surrounded by the green and grey of the island's scree-covered hills, with views over villages, valleys and lakes to the sea, plus a dash of Greek heritage in its main square and vine-shaded taverna.

The road west runs out at tiny **Uğurlu**, with nothing much to recommend it apart from another small beach.

Festivals & Events

During the **Yumurta Panayırı** (Egg Festival) in the first week of July many former Greek inhabitants, including the current Orthodox Patriarch of İstanbul, return to the island.

Sleeping & Eating

The old-fashioned *ev pansiyonu* (home pension), which has virtually died out elsewhere, is still alive and kicking on Gökçeada, and it's not unusual for locals to approach and offer you a spare room in their house, usually for around €8.50 a head including breakfast. Yeni Bademli in particular seems to be popular for this kind of deal, with virtually every house sporting a *pansiyon* sign!

Note that single rooms are in short supply, especially during the July and August peak season.

GÖKÇEADA

Otel Taşkın (☎ 887 2880; Zeytinli Caddesi 9; s/d/tr €14/23/31) The better of Gökçeada's two central hotels, this new establishment has a blue mosaiced exterior and spacious, good-value rooms with TV, balcony and lots of light. The triples could happily sleep four. Add €2.80 per person during high season (15 July to 31 August).

Places to eat include the **Meydan Restaurant** (☎ 887 2393; mains €1.70-8.50), a terraced place decked with international flags off the main square, and **Taylan Aile Lokantası** (☎ 887 2451; Atatürk Caddesi; mains €1.70-6), next to the Pegasus Otel; both have extensive menus of the usual Turkish staples. For snack food, ice cream or desserts the nearby **Meydanı Café** (Atatürk Caddesi) is big and airy, with a jukebox playing to the young crowd.

KALEKÖY

Yakamoz Pansiyon (☎ 887 2057; s/d/tr €17/28/34) Perched on the hill overlooking the harbour in Yukarı Kaleköy (Upper Kaleköy), this multiterraced pension has a pleasant terrace restaurant.

Gökçe Motel (☎ 887 2726; s/d €14/28) At the foot of the hill, just before the harbour, this quirky site is less a motel than a collection of neat little huts around a garden, with solar power, bright linen and a small kitchen.

Kale Motel (☎ 887 4404; www.kalemotel.com; Barbaros Caddesi 34; r €11-70; ✷) Arguably the best of the half-dozen hotel-restaurants that line Kaleköy harbour, though there's no need to rule the others out. Plus points here include a range of rooms, cool marble corridors and broad shared balconies. Prices drop considerably out of season.

Gökçeada Resort Hotel (☎ 887 4040; www.gokcead aresorthotel.com; Barbaros Caddesi 16; s/d/tr half board €50/67/89; ✷ 🖳 🐀) Not the most sensitively designed island resort ever, but if you set store by facilities then there's nowhere else this side of the mainland that can offer gym, sauna, hairdresser, games room, basketball court and roof bar.

ZEYTİNLİ

Zeydali Hotel (☎ 887 3233; www.zeydalihotel.com; s/d €42/70, Jul & Aug €49/84; ✷) A cobbled street winds up through Zeytinli to this delightfully stylish hotel inside a restored stone building and with its own restaurant on the ground floor. Rooms are imaginatively decorated in a style that mixes old and new. The hotel closes in winter, when only around 80 people remain in the village.

TEPEKÖY

Barba Yorgo Pension (☎ 887 4247; www.barbayorgo .com; s/d €17/34; ☺ mid-Apr–mid-Sep) Rather than a formal pension, this is actually a group of lovely restored houses overlooking the valley, with wood floors, sparrows in the rafters and a glowering mountain right out back just begging for a morning scramble. Advance reservation can be advisable, especially during August, as it's a long way back if you arrive to find it full.

The same owners also run the village taverna, a very friendly monopoly. Dishes cost around €1.70 to €14, including plenty of mezes and fresh fish; be sure to try the easy-drinking local wines.

Getting There & Away

There are two boat services to Gökçeada: one from Kabatepe on the northern side of the Dardanelles, the other from Çanakkale on the southern side. The summer timetable is fairly reliable, but high winds in winter can prevent boats sailing for up to 10 days at a time.

From Monday to Friday a ferry runs from Çanakkale to Gökçeada (€1.70, cars €10, 2½ hours), leaving at 5pm and returning at 8am.

More frequent daily ferries (€1.40, cars €8.50, 1¾hr) leave from Kabatepe to Gökçeada at 11am and 6pm, returning to Kabatepe at 7am and 4pm. Tickets are also valid for the Eceabat–Çanakkale ferry, so you don't have to pay again to cross the straits.

Getting Around

Ferries dock at Kuzulimanı, where dolmuşes should be waiting to drive you 6km to Gökçeada town (€0.85, 15 minutes), or straight through to Kaleköy, 5km further north (€1.70, 30 minutes). A bus service runs between Kaleköy, Gökçeada and Kuzulimanı roughly every two hours, though it doesn't always stick to the timetable.

Otherwise, the island is tricky to get around without your own transport. Taxis in Gökçeada charge around €2.80 to Kaleköy or Zeytinli, €5.50 to Tepeköy and €12 all the way to Uğurlu.

North Aegean

Once the scene of some of the bloodiest and most epic battles in human history – and with the ruins and remains to prove it – the North Aegean is a very different place today.

As the road takes a turn through scented mountain pines, you may have to stop to let a Turkish tortoise cross the road or a shepherd marshal his woolly charges. Farmers with thick moustaches sit by the roadside selling jars of mountain honey, and in the meadows women in heavy skirts and patterned headscarves gather wild herbs for the evening's stockpot.

Around another corner, a sheltered cove or beautiful beach beckons from the cliffs far below. The Aegean, ever darkening with the day, provides a dramatic backdrop to the beautiful old stone houses of the mountain villages. Out at sea, a couple of *gülets* (wooden yachts) slowly head eastwards, shimmering and hazy in the heavy heat of the afternoon.

Combining some spectacular ancient sites such as Bergama's Pergamum with the lovely low-key coastal resorts of Foça, Yeni Foça or Sığacık, the region also boasts some postcard-perfect villages, including Alaçatı, and pretty landscapes such as those found on the Biga Peninsula.

Then there's laid-back Bozcaada, the ultimate island getaway with good beaches, luscious local wines and charming cobbled streets, and lively İzmir with its buzzing bazaar, cafés and bars, and a fascinating old quarter a world away from the new. Many travellers also find the people of the north friendlier than their more visited southern neighbours. Certainly you'll soon get to sample the legendary Turkish hospitality. For one region, the North Aegean offers a complete package.

HIGHLIGHTS

- Roam the ruins of ancient **Pergamum** (p217), among the Mediterranean's most magical

- Explore the cobbled alleyways of **Alaçatı** (p239) and lap up luxury in its boutique hotels

- Idle away hours, or sip the village vino on beautiful, laid-back **Bozcaada** (p206)

- Hunt out **İzmir**'s (p226) heart in its beguiling, bustling bazaar, or captivating old quarter

- Wander the pretty fishing town of **Foça** (p224) and feast on fish at the seafront

- Admire the amazing **Temple of Athena** (p210) at Behramkale and its stunning sea setting

Bozcaada ★

★ Behramkale & Assos

★ Pergamum (Bergama)

★ Foça

★ İzmir

★ Alaçatı

BANDIRMA

☎ 0266 / pop 109,670

The port town of Bandırma is one of Turkey's many 20th-century *betonvilles* (concrete cities). However, it's an important transit point as the junction between İzmir trains and the Bandırma–İstanbul ferry line, so you may well need to pass through it.

The otogar (bus station) is 1.8km southeast of the centre, out on the main highway and served by *servis* (shuttle minibuses) from the centre.

Getting There & Away

At least two daily **İstanbul Deniz Otobüsleri fast ferries** (İDO; ☎ 444 4436; www.ido.com.tr; per car €52.50

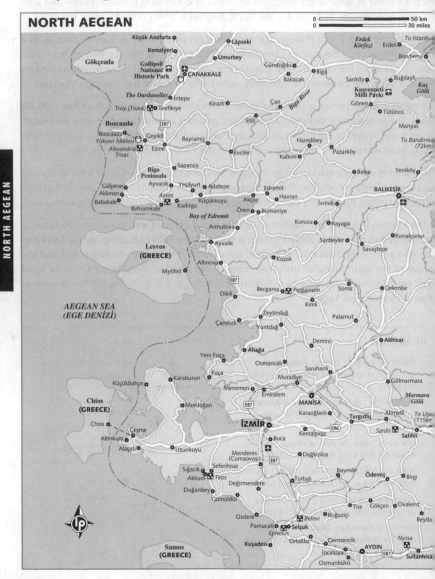

NORTH AEGEAN

er pedestrian or passenger €12) connect Bandırma
vith İstanbul's Yenikapı docks (two hours).
t's a comfortable service, with assigned seats,
rolley-dollies selling fresh orange juice and
heesecake, a business-class lounge and a lift
or disabled passengers.

In theory, the ferry connects with the
norning train from İzmir. However, in real-
y it does so only from mid-July until August.
'he rest of the year you'll have to cool your
eels in Bandırma for a couple of hours.

The *Marmara Ekspresi* train to İzmir's
asmane station (€8.35, 6½ hours, 342km)
eparts from Bandırma *Gar* (the main sta-
ion) at 4.02pm daily and arrives in İzmir at
0.39pm.

Bandırma is midway on the bus run be-
ween Bursa (€5.55, two hours, 115km) and
Çanakkale (€6.65, 2¾ hours, 195km).

ROY (TRUVA) & TEVFİKİYE
☎ 0286

'he ruins of ancient Troy may not be as
reathtaking as those of Ephesus (Efes; p251)
r Afrodisias (p329) but, for anyone who has
ver read Homer's *Iliad* or who has heard the
ales of the Trojan Wars, they have a romance
ew places on earth can hope to match. It's
ardly surprising that Troy is one of Turkey's
Vorld Heritage sites.

Today the approach to Troy is across what
vas once the Troad, an area of low, rolling
rain fields dotted with villages. But until
German-born Californian amateur archae-
logist Heinrich Schliemann (1822–90) came
long it had always been assumed that the
reat poetry of Homer was based on legend,
ather than history. But Schliemann got per-
nission from the Ottoman government to dig
t a site that resembled Homer's description
f Troy and where evidence of buried ruins
ad been uncovered. His excavations, made
t his own expense, uncovered four ancient
owns, but he more or less destroyed three
thers in the process.

At the site, Schliemann is sniffily dismissed
s a 'treasure-hunter' who learnt on the job,
nd certainly his primary interest lay in un-
overing the treasure of King Priam. On the
ast day of excavations he quite literally hit
old. However, what he at first thought dated
ack to Homeric Troy he eventually had to
ccept belonged to a queen or princess liv-
ng in Troy II. Schliemann's treasure disap-
eared during WWII and was only recently

rediscovered in Russia. It's now in Moscow's
Pushkin Museum, the subject of an ongoing
ownership dispute.

Recently, Troy has become a popular destination for weekending school parties. Do
yourself a favour and visit midweek.

History

Troy is an especially tricky site to understand
because excavations have revealed nine ancient cities, built one on top of another and
dating back to 3000 BC. The first people lived
here during the Early Bronze Age. The cities
called Troy I to Troy V (3000–1700 BC) had
a similar culture, but Troy VI (1700–1250
BC) took on a different character, with a new
population of Indo-European stock related
to the Mycenaeans. The town doubled in
size and carried on a prosperous trade with
Mycenae. As defender of the Dardanelles,
it also held the key to the prosperous trade
with the Greek colonies on the Black Sea.
Archaeologists argue over whether Troy VI
or Troy VII was the city of King Priam who
engaged in the Trojan War. Most believe it
was Troy VI, arguing that the earthquake that
brought down the walls in 1250 BC hastened
the Achaean victory.

Troy VII lasted from 1250 to 1000 BC.
The Achaeans may have burned the city in
1240 BC. An invading Balkan people moved
in around 1190 BC, and Troy sank into a
torpor for four centuries. It was revived as
a Greek city (Troy VIII, 700–85 BC), then
as a Roman one (Novum Ilion; Troy IX, 85
BC–AD 500). Before eventually settling on
Byzantium, Constantine the Great toyed with
the idea of building the capital of the eastern
Roman Empire here. As a Byzantine town,
Troy didn't amount to much.

The misguided Fourth Crusaders sometimes claimed that their behaviour in Turkey
was justified as vengeance for Troy, and when
Mehmet the Conqueror visited the site in
1462 he, in turn, claimed to be laying those
ghosts to rest. After that, the town simply
disappeared from the records.

Ruins of Troy

The ticket booth for the ruins of **Troy** (☎ 283
0536; admission per person/car €5.55/2.25; ☒ 8.30am-7pm
May-15 Sep, to 5pm 16 Sep-end Apr) is 500m before
the site.

Two guides are available for tours (€40
to €50 per group depending on the size, 1½

hours); enquire at the ticket booth or restaurants. You can also email in advance Mustafa Askin, author of one of the guidebooks (troyguide@hotmail.com). Illustrated guidebooks (€5 to €34) and maps (€2.75) are sold at the souvenir shops.

The first thing you see as you approach the ruins is a huge replica of the wooden Trojan horse, built by the Ministry of Tourism and Culture, and now a tourism attraction for children in its own right!

Excavations House, to the right of the path, was used by earlier archaeological teams. Today, it holds models and superimposed pictures to give an idea of what Troy looked like at different points in its history, as well as information on the importance of the Troy myth in Western history. Opposite is the sma **Pithos Garden**, with a collection of outsize stor age jars and drainage pipes.

Although the site is still fairly confusing the circular path around the ruins has sign boards to help you understand what you'r seeing.

As you approach the ruins, take the ston steps up on the right. These bring you ou on top of what was the **outer wall of Troy VIII/I** from where you can gaze on the fortification of the **east wall gate** and **tower of Troy VI**.

Descend the stairs and start followin the path round the walls to the right. Even tually, more steps lead up to a knoll from where you can look at some original an some reconstructed red-brick **walls of Troy II/II**

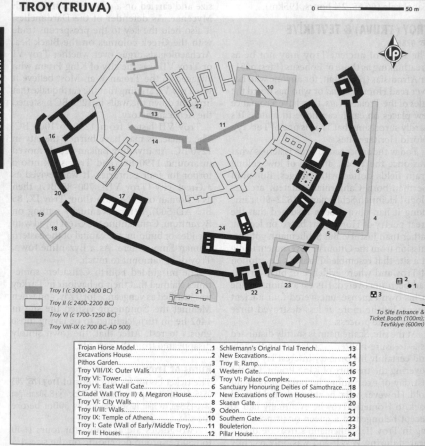

TROY (TRUVA)

0 — 50 m

Legend:
- Troy I (c 3000-2400 BC)
- Troy II (c 2400-2200 BC)
- Troy VI (c 1700-1250 BC)
- Troy VIII-IX (c 700 BC-AD 500)

To Site Entrance &
Ticket Booth (100m);
Tevfikiye (600m)

Trojan Horse Model.................................1	Schliemann's Original Trial Trench..............13	
Excavations House....................................2	New Excavations......................................14	
Pithos Garden...3	Troy II: Ramp..15	
Troy VIII/IX: Outer Walls...........................4	Western Gate...16	
Troy VI: Tower..5	Troy VI: Palace Complex............................17	
Troy VI: East Wall Gate..............................6	Sanctuary Honouring Deities of Samothrace...18	
Citadel Wall (Troy II) & Megaron House.......7	New Excavations of Town Houses...............19	
Troy VI: City Walls....................................8	Skaean Gate..20	
Troy II/III: Walls.......................................9	Odeon...21	
Troy IX: Temple of Athena.......................10	Southern Gate..22	
Troy I: Gate (Wall of Early/Middle Troy).....11	Bouleterion...23	
Troy II: Houses..12	Pillar House...24	

THE TROJAN WAR

Everyone knows the tale of the Trojan War – most probably from the silver screen with Brad in the starring role. A rapid retell goes something like this: claiming that Aphrodite has awarded him this prize, Paris, a Trojan prince, steals Helen, a woman world-famous for her beauty. But she's already married to Menelaus, the king of Sparta, who's not amused. Miffed Menelaus appeals to the Achaeans for help and so begins the epic, decade-long battle.

Hector kills Patroclus. Achilles kills Hector. Paris kills Achilles. Bored with the bloodshed and fed up with the siege's lack of success, the Achaeans finally formulate a cunning plan. Building a huge wooden horse, they stuff it with soldiers and wheel it to the walls of Troy. Brought in by the trusting Trojans, the Achaean soldiers inside the horse emerge in the night and torch the Trojan town. Troy falls at last to the Greeks.

That Homer's story is more fairytale than fact is well known. Indeed some historians hold that it was in fact the earthquake of 1250 BC that brought down Troy's tremendous walls. But desirous of demonstrating their great gratitude to Poseidon, the Achaeans did apparently build an incredible construction. A monumental wooden statue of a horse…

---

mmediately above them was the site of a Graeco-Roman **Temple of Athena**, of which only races of the altar remain.

Continue following the path, past traces of the **wall of Early/Middle Troy (Troy 1 Gate)**. Opposite are remains of the **houses of Troy II**, inhabited by a literal 'upper class' while the poor huddled on the plains.

The path then sweeps past **Schliemann's original trial trench**, carved straight through all the layers of the city. Wooden steps lead down past ongoing excavations to a great stone **ramp** that is believed to have led into Troy II.

Just round the corner is a stretch of wall from what is believed to have been the two-storey-high Troy VI **Palace Complex** and then, to the right, traces of an ancient **sanctuary** to unknown deities. Later, a new sanctuary was built on the same site, apparently honouring the deities of Samothrace. Nearby are remains of the **Skaean Gate** in front of which Achilles and Hector fought the duel that is the focal point of the film *Troy*. Eventually, the path passes in front of the Roman **Odeon**, where concerts were held, and the **Bouleterion** (Council Chamber). Finally you pass the stone slabs of the road that lead into Troy VI before arriving back where you started.

Sleeping & Eating

Most visitors stay in Çanakkale (p192) and visit Troy in passing, leaving their gear at the ticket office or at one of the restaurants opposite the gate. However, the atmosphere of the nearby farming village of Tevfikiye, 500m north of the gates, makes a pleasant change from the hassle of Çanakkale, especially if you want to spend longer at Troy.

Varol Pansiyon (☎ 283 0828; s/d €14/28) Right in the heart of the village, this pension is clean, lovingly cared-for and homely. Rooms are of a decent size, and guests can also use the kitchen.

Hotel Hisarlık (☎ 283 0026; thetroyguide@hotmail.com; s/d €21/31) Opposite the gate to the ruins, this hotel has comfortable rooms with the names of characters from Greek myths. The restaurant (open 8am to 11pm), though popular with tour buses, serves good Turkish home cooking. Try the hearty *güveç* (beef stew) or the delicious *imam bayıldı* (stuffed eggplant).

Getting There & Away

From Çanakkale, dolmuşes leave from a dolmuş station under the bridge over the Sarı River. Dolmuşes to Troy (€1.65, 35 minutes, 30km) leave every hour on the half hour from 9.30am to 5.30pm.

From Troy to Çanakkale, dolmuşes leave every hour on the hour from 7am to 5pm in high season and from 7am to 3pm in low season. If you miss the last bus, try the Hotel Hisarlık minibus (€1.65), which ferries the shopkeepers back to their homes in Çanakkale. It leaves at 7pm to 8pm in high season, 5pm in low season.

The travel agencies offering tours to the Gallipoli battlefields also offer tours to Troy if enough people sign up (around €25 per person). This is worth considering if you want a guided tour of both sites at an affordable rate. For details of the various tour companies, see p190.

NORTH AEGEAN

BOZCAADA

☎ 0286 / pop 2700

Beautiful little Bozcaada. The second of Turkey's two inhabited Aegean islands, it's the sort of place where you arrive planning to spend a night and wind up wishing you could stay forever. A trip here also makes a good break from the usual tourist trail.

Windswept Bozcaada (formerly Tenedos) has always been known to Anatolian oenophiles for its wines (Ataol, Talay and Yunatçilar), and vineyards still blanket its sunny slopes. As in Bodrum (p272), a huge medieval fortress towers over the harbour. In its wake huddles one of Turkey's least-spoilt small towns, a warren of picturesque vine-draped old houses and cobbled streets.

The island is small (about 5km to 6km across) and easy to explore. Lovely unspoilt sandy beaches line the coast road to the south.

Be warned that outside the school-holiday period (mid-June to mid-September) you may find cafés and the like closed, except at weekends and on Wednesdays, when a market fills the main square.

Information

A tourism office (as well as some information panels) are planned for the island in the near future. Until then, you can pick up a rough map (€0.85) from some of the hotels, pensions and cafés.

There's a Ziraat Bankası ATM in Bozcaada town, right beside the PTT. The **Captain Internet Café** (☎ 697 8567; Trüya Sokak; per hr €1.10; 9am-midnight) is a new place.

Sights

Bozcaada is a place for hanging out, rather than doing anything specific. The one official tourist attraction is the impressive **fortress** (☎ 0543-551 8211; admission €0.55; 10am-1pm & 2-7pm May-Nov), in Bozcaada town, which dates back to Byzantine times. Most of what you see survives from the reconstructions of the Venetian and Genoese castle by assorted sultans. Inside the double walls you will find traces of a mosque, several ammo dumps, a barracks and an infirmary.

The **church**, in the old Greek neighbourhood directly behind the castle, is sadly rarely open.

Though not officially open for tours, some **wineries** allow visits. **Talay** (☎ 697 8080; www.talay.com.tr; Lale Sokak 5; 8.30am-6pm), founded in 1948, is one. It lies one block west of th *belediye* along Lale Sokak. You can visit th bottling unit and fermentation tanks and als taste and buy wines (€3.40 to €11) at the littl shop opposite.

The best **beaches** – Ayana, Ayazma an Habbele – straggle along the south coast although Tuzburnu and Sulubahçe, to th east, is also passable. Ayazma boasts severa cafés and a small, abandoned **Greek monaster** uphill.

Sleeping

BUDGET

In summer – particularly at weekends – you'r advised to reserve a room well in advance.

Kale Pansiyon (☎ 697 8617; www.kalepansiyon.ne per person high/low season €22/17) Uphill behind th Ege Otel, the Kale has simple but fastidiousl clean rooms and an open-buffet breakfast (o a terrace with lovely views) that gets top mark from travellers. Pakize, the owner, is keen t please and makes delicious jam.

Güler Pansiyon (☎ 697 8454; Tuzburnu Yolu Üze per person €23) Though simple, the 120-year-ol farmhouse has an authentic island feel an a beautiful setting amid vineyards. There's quiet beach 100m away with tables, sunloungers and a shower. It lies about 2.5km fron town on the Tuzburnu road.

Apart Akarsu Otel (☎ 697 0435; www.akarsuapa pansiyon.com.tr; Gürsel Sokak 36; per person incl breakfa €25; ❄) With four spotless, quiet and spacious one-bedroom apartments, this plac also boasts a fabulous rooftop terrace wit views over the fortress and sea. Reserve a least two weeks in advance.

Gümüs Otel (☎ 697 8252; gumusotel@ttnet.tr; Ya Caddesi 28; s/d high season €25/50, low season €20/40; ❄ If the others are full, try this place. It has clear quite spacious rooms.

Rengigül (☎ 697 8171; rengigul2@superonline.con Atatürk Caddesi 31; s/d with shared bathroom €28/56) Positively infested with trinkets and old antique this characterful 130-year-old Greek hous has five traditionally decorated rooms an a lovely, peaceful, walled garden where yo can eat breakfast.

MIDRANGE

Otel Ege Bozcaada (☎ 697 8189; www.egehotel.con Bozjaada Kale Arkası; s/d €39/78; 10 Apr-15 Nov; ❄) A old 19th-century primary school, this cavernous hotel has 35 attractively furnished rooms each with the name of a poet engraved on th

BOZCAADA

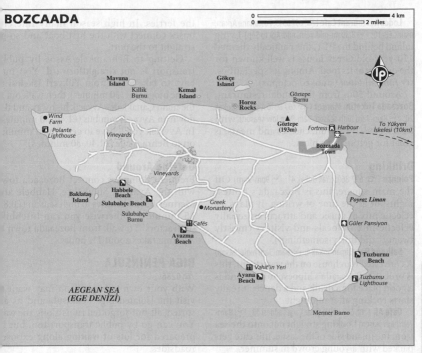

0 / 4 km
0 / 2 miles

Mavuna Island
Killik Burnu
Kemal Island
Gökçe Island
Göztepe Burnu
Horoz Rocks
Göztepe (193m)
Fortress
Harbour
To Yükyeri İskelesi (10km)
Wind Farm
Polante Lighthouse
Vineyards
Bozcaada Town
Vineyards
Baklataş Island
Habbele Beach
Sulubahçe Beach
Sulubahçe Burnu
Greek Monastery
Cafés
Poyraz Liman
Güler Pansiyon
Ayazma Beach
Tuzburnu Beach
Vahit'in Yeri
Ayana Beach
Tuzburnu Lighthouse
AEGEAN SEA (EGE DENİZİ)
Mermer Burno

oor. Six rooms have balconies with gorgeous iews over the fort.

Otel Kaikias (☎ 697 0250; www.kaikias.com in Turkh; per person €42; 🛎) Though the building's ew, it's artfully decorated to appear old and legant, complete with antique Greek furni- ıre, paintings and photos. Rooms boast four- oster beds (draped with bronze-coloured oile!) and marble bathrooms. Four rooms ave fort views.

ating

ahit'in Yeri (☎ 697 0130; Plaj Sokak; snacks €1.90-5.50; 🕒 8am-midnight mid-May to Oct) Overlooking the each at Ayazma 7km from town, this is a ood quick-eats option, or you can just drop y for a sundowner and soak up the view.

Café at Lisa's (☎ 697 0182; Liman; 🕒 8am-9pm) \t the southern end of the harbour 200m rom the disembarkation point, this charming afé is run by Lisa, an Australian, who also uns the local rag (so is very au fait with all ne island goings-on!). It's a great place for reakfast (€1.95 to €4.75) – Lisa's omelettes are egendary – cake (€1.95 to €3), soup (€2.50) r salad (€4 to €5).

Koreli (☎ 697 8098; Yali Caddesi 12; 🕒 9am-midnight) Near the Yakamoz, this charming little place is another excellent choice. It roars with regulars who come for the köfte (€2.80) or fresh sea- food such as kalamar tava (fried squid; €5.55) or stewed fish (€8 for 0.5kg).

Yakamoz Restaurant (☎ 697 0398; Yalı Caddesi 10; fish mains €4.45-6.65; 🕒 9am-1am) At the southern end of the seafront, this new and atmospheric place is packed with locals who come for deli- cious fish dishes at decent prices.

Sandal Restaurant (☎ 668-1025, Alsancak Sokak 31; 🕒 6.30am-10pm) Decorated like a Mediterra- nean café, complete with checked tablecloths and a whole boat strung up on the wall, this place does good fish dishes. The kalamar tava (€4.50) are finger-lickin' good.

Güverte (☎ 668-9582; İstiklal Caddesi Sokak 7; 🕒 8am-10pm) The bistro-style Güverte offers similar food and prices to the Sandal, which is diagonally opposite.

Ada Cafe (☎ 697 8795; Çınar Çeşme Sokak 4; meals €5-8; köfte €3.45, beer €1.95; 🕒 8am to noon May-Sep) Popular locally, the café also serves breakfast and good snacks. The red poppy cordial (€8 for a bottle) is a speciality.

Lodos Restaurant Café (☎ 697 0545; Postahane Arkası; mains €8-10; ☼ 8.30am-midnight, mid-Apr to Sep) Lying inland behind the PTT, this nautically themed 110-year-old Greek house is well known for the quality of its food. Among its specialities, try *füme ahtapot* (smoked octopus).

Around 50m from the Sandal restaurant, **Bozcaada Tüketim Market** (☎ 697 8046 Alsancak Sokak 20; ☼ 8am-1am high season, 9am-9pm low season) with fresh bread, fresh fruit, cheeses and meats, is great for getting up a picnic.

Drinking

Polente (☎ 697 8605; Yali Sokak 41; ☼ 9pm-2am) Off the main square, this is Bozcaada's hottest nightspot at the time of writing. It plays an eclectic mix of music and attracts an equally eclectic mix of locals and visitors (mostly twenty- and thirty-somethings).

Salhane Bar (Liman Sokak 4; ☼ 9am-3am high season) A converted warehouse on the waterfront, this is probably Bozcaada's hippest hotspot and is a good place for a drink and a dance; it really starts rocking after midnight

Café Ali (☎ 697 8001; Çınar Çarşı Caddesi 12; ☼ 8am-2am high season) Looking straight out onto the sea from the inland side of the castle, this café gets packed with a young crowd in summer.

Getting There & Away

Ferries depart from Yükyeri İskelesi (Yükyeri harbour) 4km west of Geyikli, south of Troy. Dolmuşes from Çanakkale otogar run to Geyikli (55km) about every 45 minutes during the day (€2.50, one hour); tell them to drop you off at the harbour. Coming back from Bozcaada, minibuses from the harbour go to Çanakkale, Geyikli and Ezine.

In low season, boats leave Yükyeri İskelesi daily at 10am, 2pm and 7pm. In high season, there's an extra daily service at 9pm, and on Friday to Sunday at midnight. From Bozcaada to Yükyeri İskelesi, boat leave at 7.30am, noon and 6pm in low season. In high season, there's an extra daily service at 8pm, and on Friday to Saturday at 11pm. Note, however, that the 6pm service becomes a 4.30pm service in August. Return tickets per person/car cost €1.65/12.20 and the journey takes 35 minutes.

For confirmation of ferry departures and times, phone **Geyikli ticket office** (☎ 0286-632 0263) or **Bozcaada ticket office** (☎ 0286-697 8185).

If you're coming to Yükyeri İskelesi with public transport from the south, go first to Ezine where dolmuşes usually connect with

the ferries. In high season many interci buses connect with the first boat and so g straight to the port.

Getting to Behramkale/Assos by publi transport is not straightforward. You ma have to take a bus from Yükyeri İskelesi t Ezine otogar (€1, 30 minutes), then walk out t the main Çanakkale–Ayvacık highway and fla down an Ayvacık minibus (€1.40, 30 minutes In Ayvacık you'll have to get a third minibu on to Behramkale (€1.40, 30 minutes).

Getting Around

Frequent dolmuşes connect Bozcaada tow with the Ayazma, Sulubahçe, Habbele an Mermer Burno beaches in high season (€0.8 15 minutes). Otherwise you can hitchhik on tractors. To walk from Bozcaada town t Ayazma takes about 1½ hours.

BIGA PENINSULA
☎ 0286

With your own transport you may want t visit the isolated Biga Peninsula and its a sorted, all-but-forgotten ruins along the wa You can go by public transport too, but b prepared for lots of waiting along expose roadsides.

Alexandria Troas

Ten kilometres south of Geyikli, take a peek a **Alexandria Troas** (admission €2.50), ruins scattere around the village of Dalyan.

After the collapse of Alexander the Great empire, Antigonus, one of his generals, too control of this land, founding the city of Ar tigoneia in 310 BC. Later, he was defeated i battle by Lysimachus, another of Alexander generals, who took the city and renamed it i honour of his late commander. After a perio of Roman occupation, an earthquake eventu ally destroyed much of the city.

Archaeologists have identified bits of th theatre, palace, temple, agora (marketplace baths, necropolis, harbour and city walls, bu for most visitors Alexandria Troas is an a mospheric place that conjures up a feeling o great antiquity slowly fading away.

Infrequent dolmuşes run between Ezin and Dalyan, or you can get here by bus fro Çanakkale otogar.

Gülpınar

Gülpınar is a one-street farming town sout of Geyikli with few services beyond a petr station. However, it was once the ancient city of **Khrysa**, famous for its 2nd-century BC Ionic temple to Apollo and its mice. An oracle had told Cretan colonists to settle where 'the sons of the earth' attacked them. Awaking to find mice chewing their equipment, they decided to settle here and built a temple to Smintheion (Lord of the Mice). The cult statue of the god, now lost, once had marble mice carved at its feet.

The remains of the **Apollon Smintheion** (admission €2.80 including museum; ⊙ 8am-5pm) lie 300m down a side road off the main road (look for the sign 100m after the post office if coming from Babakale). The wonderful reliefs with illustrated scenes from the *Iliad* found amid the ruins are kept in the site's **museum** (⊙ Jul-end Aug).

Buses to Gülpınar run from Çanakkale and Ezine. From Gülpınar there are buses to Babakale (€0.60, 15 minutes) and onwards to Behramkale (€1.50, one hour).

Babakale (Lekton)

From Gülpınar a road heads 9km west for Babakale, passing through a line of coastal development. Babakale itself is a small village clustered at the base of a vast Ottoman **fortress** (recently restored) overlooking an attractive small harbour.

The fort was built to combat pirates and is important as the last Ottoman castle built in present-day Turkey. There's not much else to look at, but it's a pleasant place to unwind for a day or two.

The **Uran Hotel** (☎ 747 0218; s/d €14/28; ⌘) on the seafront has simple but sea-breeze-fresh rooms of a reasonable size. Three have direct harbour views. There's also a large terrace overlooking the fortress ramparts and harbour and a good and very reasonably priced **fish restaurant** (☎ 747 0218; ⊙ 7.30am-midnight). Try the speciality, *kalamar* (€4).

Buses from Gülpınar (€0.60, 15 minutes) to Behramkale (€1.50, one hour) stop at Babakale.

BEHRAMKALE & ASSOS
☎ 0286
Behramkale is a pretty little village that straggles up a hill towards the ruins of a famous temple to Athena. Assos is the name given to a cluster of half a dozen old stone houses-turned-hotels overlooking a picture-perfect harbour reached by a zigzag road down from behind Behramkale (see boxed text, p210).

From the beginning of April to the end of August, avoid the weekends and public holidays if you can, when İstanbullus and İzmirlis pour in by the coachload to visit both the temple and the Hüdavendigar Camii mosque.

Villagers set up quaint stalls all the way up the hill to the temple, touting herbs, woollen socks and locally made kilims (woven rugs). Look out for women in vividly coloured dresses and headscarves, the descendants of nomads who were forced to settle in nearby villages by previous governments.

History
The Mysian city of Assos was founded in the 8th century BC by colonists from Lesvos, who later built its great temple to Athena in 530 BC. The city enjoyed its greatest prosperity under the rule of Hermeias, a one-time student of Plato who also ruled the Troad and Lesvos. Hermeias encouraged philosophers to live in Assos. Aristotle himself lived here from 348 to 345 BC and ended up marrying Hermeias' niece, Pythia. Assos' glory days came to an end with the advent of the Persians, who crucified Hermeias.

Alexander the Great drove the Persians out, but Assos' importance was challenged by the ascendancy of Alexandria Troas to the north. From 241 to 133 BC the city was ruled by the kings of Pergamum.

St Paul visited Assos briefly during his third missionary journey, walking here from Alexandria Troas to meet St Luke before taking a boat to Lesvos.

In late-Byzantine times the city dwindled to a village. Turkish settlers arrived and called the village Behramkale. However, only the coming of tourism revived its fortunes.

Orientation & Information
Approaching the village from Ayvacık, look out for the 14th-century Hüdavendigar bridge, to the left of the road. At the crossroads, the road left leads to the scruffy beach at Kadırga (4km), the road right to Babakale and Gülpınar. Go straight ahead until you reach a fork in the road, then left (uphill) along the rough road for the old village, or straight on (downhill) to the harbour.

The village road winds up through a small square, with a tea house and a bust of Atatürk, to the peak of the hill, which offers a spectacular view towards the Greek island of Lesvos (Mytilini or Midilli in Turkish).

NORTH AEGEAN

Note that there's no bank or ATM, no post office, no petrol station, no tourist office and no pharmacy in Behramkale or Assos.

Sights & Activities

Right on top of the hill in Behramkale village is the 6th-century Ionic **Temple of Athena** (admission €2.75; ☯ 8am-dusk), with its particular Doric features. The short tapered columns with plain capitals are hardly elegant, and the concrete reconstruction hurts more than helps, but the site and the view out to Lesvos are spectacular and well worth the admission fee.

Beside the entrance to the ruins, the 14th-century **Hüdavendigar Camii** is a simply constructed Ottoman mosque – a dome on squinches set on top of a square room – built before the Turks had conquered Constantinople and assimilated the lessons of Sancta Sophia. The lintel above the entrance bears Greek inscriptions incorporating parts filched from a 6th-century church. It's one of just two remaining Ottoman mosques in Turkey (the other is in Bursa).

Ringing the hill are stretches of the **city walls** of medieval Assos, among the most impressive mnedieval fortifications in Turkey. Scramble down the hillside to find the **necropolis**. Assos' sarcophagi (flesh-eaters) were famous. According to Pliny the Elder, the stone was caustic and 'ate' the flesh off the deceased in 40 days. There are also remains of a late-2nd-century BC **theatre** and **basilica**. An exit gate emerges on the road that winds down to the harbour.

VILLAGE OF MULTIPLE NAMES

If asking directions or chatting to locals, be aware of the village's various names. Assos is actually the old Greek name, Behramkale the Turkish one. The town's official name is in fact Behram Köyü. The villagers sometimes refer to *Köyü* ('village') for the upper town and *İskele* ('port') for the harbour area of the lower town, which is also Assos. They also talk of *Yukarıya* ('upstairs') and *Aşağıda* ('downstairs') and *Eski* ('old' – on the hill), and *Yeni* ('new' – where the modern buildings are). Got it?

With thanks to Diana Elmacioğlu, of Behramkale or Assos or whatever for clarifying the situation!

Sleeping

Where you sleep depends on whether you prefer the picturesque and lively Assos harbour, or the more peaceful and atmospheric Behramkale village.

In high season, virtually all the hotels around the harbour insist on *yarım pansiyon* (half-board), though you can try negotiating, as the food is rarely anything to write home about.

ASSOS

Çakır Pansiyon (☎ 721 7048; s/d incl breakfast €14/28, half-board €20/39; camp site per person €4; ✸) Around 100m along the seafront from Hotel Assos Deluxe, the pansiyon has very simple but clean rooms in MDF-made bungalows. It also has a small camping site (with a shower) and rents out three two-person tents (€10). Set right on the beach, you can hear the water lapping on the shore. It also has a delightful lantern-lit restaurant of the same name.

Hotel Nazlıhan (☎ 721 7385; www.assosedengroup .com; s/d with half-board from €31/44) Traditional-meets-modern in this comfortable hotel, which is spread across two restored stone houses with rooms around central courtyards. It's part of a hotel group and is well managed, but gets busy with tour groups.

Yıldız Saray Hotel (☎ 721 7025; www.yildizsaray-hotel .com; s/d incl breakfast €20/39; with half-board €28/56; ✸) Though rooms are on the small side, they're traditionally furnished, attractive and good value. All eight have direct sea views overlooking the harbour, and three have access to a small terrace. The brasserie-style restaurant has a good reputation and boasts its own nesting swallow in spring.

Hotel Assos Kervansaray (☎ 721 7093; www.assos kervansaray.com; s/d with half-board high season €61/84, low-season €39/67; ✸ ▣ ▣) Rooms, set around a covered neoclassical-style courtyard, are comfortable albeit a little dated; 22 have sea views. The big attraction here is the lovely outdoor pool set amid the stone houses, and a stretch of beach it calls its own.

Hotel Assos Deluxe (☎ 721 7017, www.assosgroup .com; s/d/ste with half-board from €47/94/156; ✸) Set back from the seafront, the boutiquey Assos is a slightly quieter option, and its rooms are very attractively decorated in an Orientalist style, all with four-poster beds. Four also have Jacuzzis and six have sea views.

Biber Evi (☎ 721 7410, www.biberevi.com; s with half-board €110-139, d €139-167; ✸) Newly restored, this old stone house boasts a peaceful courtyard, a small terrace with lovely views and a gourmet restaurant. Rooms are Ottoman-rustic in style complete with *gusulhane* – washing facilities hidden in a cupboard! – and under-floor heating. Bed and breakfast is €28 less per person than the half-board prices quoted. From mid-June to mid-August bookings need to be for a minimum of two nights.

BEHRAMKALE

Dolunay Pansiyon (☎ 721 7172; s/d €14/28) Right in the centre of the village, the Dolunay is a homely affair with six spotless, simple rooms set around a pleasant courtyard. There's also a pretty terrace with sea views where you can have a scenic breakfast.

Timur Pansiyon (☎ /fax 721 7449; timurpansiyon@yahoo.com; s/d €17/33; ☼ Apr–mid-Sep) Remote, rustic and rather ramshackle, the 200-year-old Timur's not unlike a shepherd's croft. Its best asset is its fabulous setting above the village right beside the temple, with gorgeous seaviews towards Lesbos (Lesvos in Turkish). Its characterful rooms may prove a bit basic for some, but a drink (beer €2.75) on the blissfully peaceful vine-shaded terrace is well worthwhile.

Old Bridge House (☎ 721 7426; www.assos.de/obh; dm €10, d high season €50-70, low season €30-50, bungalow per person €15; camp sites €5; ☼ Mar-Nov; ☒ ▯) Near the Ottoman bridge at the entrance to town, the Old Bridge House is a long-time travellers' favourite. The helpful and hospitable owner, Diana, is a mine of information about the area and is happy to offer travel tips. It has a cosy salon, a garden (where BBQs happen and fires are lit), a library, free internet access, free use of two mountain bikes, free excursions and even a telescope for star- or moon-gazing! Call ahead during low season.

Eris Pansiyon (☎ 721 7080; www.assos.de/eris; Behramkale Köyü 6; s €45, d €56-67; ☼ Apr-Nov) Set in a stone house with pretty gardens at the far end of the village, the Eris has fairly ordinary (at the price) but pleasant and peaceful rooms. Afternoon tea is served on a terrace with spectacular views over the hills, and it claims the best breakfast in town. It also has a library and book exchange, and Clinton, the retired American owner, needs only the smallest excuse to tell you all about the history of the area. There's a minimum stay of two nights and a deposit is usually required.

Assos Konuk Evi (☎ 721 7081; s/d/t €60/100/150) In a lovely, rather aristocratic-looking old stone house hidden away behind heavy wooden doors, the Konuk Evi offers traditionally and attractively decorated rooms in either the main building or the cosy self-catering cottages. The garden and some rooms have good views towards the mosque and temple. The charming owners show you typical Turkish hospitality.

Eating & Drinking
ASSOS

Uzunev (☎ 721 7007; meze €2; mains €5-6; ☼ 10am-midnight) Considered the best fish restaurant in town, Uzunev has pleasant tables on the terrace and seafront. Try the succulent speciality 'Sea Bass à l'Aristotle' (steamed in a special stock) or the delicious seafood meze (€5.55 to €6.65). In high season after 10pm, it metamorphoses into a disco-bar.

Çakır Pansiyon (☎ 721 7048; meze €1.65, fish €6-9; ☼ 7am-midnight) Also serves fresh fish in its charming, lantern-lit, beach-hut style restaurant right above the water.

BEHRAMKALE

Assos Kale Restaurant (☎ 721 7430; ☼ 8am-1am Apr-Oct) Centrally located in Behramkale and with a pleasant shaded terrace, the Kale is a great place for a quick eat, offering good home cooking at unbeatable prices. Try the delicious *mantı* (Turkish ravioli, €1.95) or homemade creamy *ayran* (yogurt).

Assos Restaurant (☎ 721 7050; köfte & kebabs €3.90-4.45; Main Square; ☼ 7am-midnight) Widely recommended and much-loved, the diminutive but endearing Assos provides excellent home cooking at pleasing prices. It offers no less than 25 dishes including veggie options. Take a table on the tiny terrace overlooking the main square.

Öğretmenin Yeri (Assos Köyüm Restaurant; ☎ 721 7145; Main Square; ☼ 7.30am-midnight Jul-Sep) Offering enticing home cooking at pleasing prices, the Yeri competes with the Assos next door.

Biber Evi Restaurant (☎ 721 7410; Biber Evi hotel; meze €4-7, mains average €11; ☼ 7.30am-10pm) Taking third prize recently for 'Best Meze in Turkey', this new restaurant serves superb Turkish cuisine made from ingredients fresh from its kitchen gardens. It even smokes its own fish. The charming owner, Lütei (an ex-actor and theatre director), also boasts a famous collection of malt whiskies.

For a coffee or Coke on the main square, the **Assos Alle Çay Bahçesi** (☎ 721 7221; soft drinks

€0.85; 7am-midnight) has a pleasant shaded terrace offering attractive views. It serves *gözleme* (savoury crepes, €1.40) good enough to gobble, and drinks.

Shopping

Behramkale is a good place to find some traditional craftwork. Though made for the tourism market, the quality is high and prices are quite reasonable. One supplier with a good reputation for carpets is **Öz Antik Hanlıcilik** (618 7480; kilims €20-350; 9am-dusk) on the main street just off the main square. Ask for Yusuf.

For decent-quality silver jewellery made with local minerals, head for **Pyramit** (721 7207; jewellery €11-33; 9am-5pm). The talented Levent, a geologist, makes 80% of the pieces.

Getting Around

In summer, there's a regular shuttle service throughout the day between Behramkale and Assos (€0.55), which also connects with buses from Assos to Ayvacık. When there's demand, an extra dolmuş is put into service that leaves when it's full. The latter can also act as a contract taxi (€2.75 from the port to Behramkale). In winter, workers shuttle to and forth and you can normally jump on one of their buses.

Getting There & Away

Regular buses run from Çanakkale (€3.50, 1½ hours) to Ayvacık, where you can pick up a dolmuş (which leaves when full) to Assos (€1.50, 20 minutes).

Alternatively, you can get to Behramkale from Gülpınar (€1.50, one hour) or Küçükkuyu (€2, one hour).

Off season, dolmuşes run much less frequently and you can have trouble getting away from Behramkale. If you do visit then try to get to Ayvacık as early in the day as you can to catch a dolmuş to Behramkale. If you miss the last one, Ayvacık has a couple of hotels, or a taxi will cost around €25 to €30.

At the time of writing, boat services to Lesvos had been suspended by the Turkish army. Services may resume in the future; in the meantime, you can get to Lesvos from Ayvalık.

AYVACIK

0286 / pop 6950

Heading to or from Behramkale you may have to transit Ayvacık, which has a big **Friday market** where women from the surrounding villages sell fruit, vegetables and baskets.

Look out for those in long satiny overcoats or brightly coloured headscarves; they are the descendants of Turkmen nomads who settled in this area.

In the centre of Ayvacık near the bus station, there's an excellent **carpet cooperative** (9am-5.30pm) run by the municipality. Quality is controlled and the prices are excellent. All revenue (minus 10%, which goes to the cooperative) goes to the women weavers.

Two kilometres out of Ayvacık on the Çanakkale road you can also visit the **Doğal Boya Arıştırma ve Geliştirme Projesi** (Dobag, Natural Dye Research & Development Project; 712 1274, fax 712 1705; 9am-6pm), which was set up in 1981 to encourage villagers to return to weaving carpets from naturally dyed wool. At about €245 per sq metre, the rugs in the upstairs exhibition hall are certainly not cheap (about five times the prices in the Ayvacık carpet cooperative) and the great majority are exported, but it's quite an interesting place to visit. Unfortunately, the women weavers are paid little, their working conditions aren't great and they are tied to the project. Nevertheless, the project has achieved some good things for the women and community. For more information on traditional weaving, check out www.returntotradition.com.

Getting There & Away

Regular buses run to/from Çanakkale (€3.50; 1½ hours). There are also regular buses to Ayvacık from Ezine, Behramkale and Küçükkuyu.

BAY OF EDREMİT

0286

From Behramkale a new four-lane highway heads east along the shores of the Bay of Edremit. There are several camping grounds out here and several hotels right on the lengthy beach at **Kadırga**, 4km east of Behramkale (firmly package-holiday territory).

The road continues east to rejoin the main coastal highway at **Küçükkuyu** where you could pause to inspect the **Adatepe Zeytinyağı Museum** (admission free; 9am-5pm). Housed in an old olive-oil factory, it explains the process of making olive oil.

From Küçükkuyu, head 4km northeast up into the hills to visit the pretty village of **Adatepe**, a cluster of old stone houses, many of them restored as second homes for wealthy İstanbullus. Here the blissfully tranquil **Hünnap Han** (752 6581; hunnaphan@mynet.com; half-board per person €39.50) is a wonderfully restored house with a lovely garden and stone courtyard.

Alternatively, you could travel 4km northwest into the hills to **Yeşilyurt**, which has not been quite so sensitively restored but where the **Öngen Country Hotel** (☎ 752 2434; www.ongen country.com; s/d with half-board €64/104) offers rooms with attractive modern décor and spectacular views over the wooded hillside.

In high season, four or five buses a day run back and forth between Behramkale and Küçükkuyu, passing through Kadırga. To get to Adatepe and Yeşilyurt from Küçükkuyu you'll need to take a taxi (around €6 return to either).

The road continues east along the Bay of Edremit, passing a depressing sprawl of holiday villages, hotels and second-home developments aimed at the domestic tourist market. Around 2km inland is the **Etnografya Galerisi** (☎ 266-387 3340; admission €0.55; ⏱ 9am-5pm) in Tahtakuşlar village, which has a small collection of local clothing and artefacts, many of them Turkmen.

At Edremit, the road turns south towards Ayvalık. **Edremit** is little more than an important local transport hub. Coming from Ayvacık to Ayvalık, or from Bandırma via Balıkesir, you may well have to change in Edremit. South of Edremit there's a fine, 5km-long beach with sulphur springs at **Akçay**, while the beach at **Ören** stretches for 9km, making either of them possible places to break your journey.

AYVALIK
☎ 0266 / pop 35,830

Ayvalık (meaning Quince Orchard) is a seaside resort, fishing town, olive oil- and soap-making centre, and a terminus for boats to and from the Greek island of Lesvos. The coast is cloaked in pine trees and olive groves, and the offshore waters sprinkled with islands. But there has also been some unfortunate high-rise development, especially around Sarımsaklı.

Ayvalık is also proud of the fact that it was here that the first shot of the Turkish War of Independence was fired. Until after WWI the town was inhabited by Ottoman Greeks, but during the exchange of populations between Greece and Turkey in 1923 (see p41 and the boxed text, p214), Ayvalık's Turkish-speaking Greeks went to Greece, and Greek-speaking Turks came here from Lesvos, the Balkans and Crete. A few locals still speak Greek, and most of the local mosques are converted Orthodox churches: the Saatlı Camii was once the church of Agios Yannis (St John); Çınarlı Camii used to be the Agios Yorgos (St George) church.

Olive-oil production is still big business around here, and lots of shops sell the end product. The skyline is studded with the tall brick chimneys of abandoned olive-oil factories. One such factory now houses the Tansaş supermarket.

Orientation & Information

Ayvalık is small and manageable, although the otogar is 1.5km north of the town centre and the **tourist office** (☎ 312 2122; Yat Limanı Karşısı) is 1.5km south of the main square, just beyond the yacht marina. In high season, you can get information from a **kiosk** (Yat Limanı; ⏱ Jun-Sep) on the waterfront south of the main square, Cumhuriyet Meydanı. New and decent town maps are available. The post office lies to the north of town just to the west of the main street, Atatürk Caddesi.

C@fein Café Net (☎ 312 3597; Cumhuriyet Meydanı; per hr €0.85; ⏱ 8am-midnight) is a few doors north of the police station.

Alibey Island (Alibey Adası), known to the locals as Cunda, faces the harbour. It's linked to the mainland by a thin causeway, although it's more pleasant getting there by boat.

DIVING OFF AYVALIK

Ayvalık is famed among the diving fraternity for its red coral. Lying at depths between 30m and 42m, it's not for beginners, however. The best dive sites to see it are at Deli Mehmetler, Ezer Bey and Kerbela. Other marine life you might come across includes moray eels, grouper, octopus, encrusting anemones and, occasionally, sea horses. There are various dive companies in Ayvalık who can organise trips to see the coral including **Korfez Diving Center** (☎ 312 4996; www.korfez diving.com; ⏱ Mar-Nov). A day's diving (including two dives, lunch, all equipment hire and insurance) costs €50 per person. For those keen to learn or to improve, the company runs various PADI courses, including the four-day open-water course (€450).

MOVING MEMORIES

My grandmother was a young girl of just 13 when she first heard that there was going to be an exchange. Her home at that time was in a small village near the town of Drama, Thessaloniki.

'After the agreement was signed by the officials, they started sending Greeks to my grandmother's village. For a while they actually had to share their house with the Greek immigrants who were arriving.

'Every week we had to give up another of our rooms. In the end we were all confined to one room. The family was large: me, my four brothers and sisters, my parents, grandparents, aunts and uncles…

'Of my grandmother's last day in the village she said: 'We packed up everything and loaded it onto the carts. I thought we were all going together with our animals and all, but they told me that I couldn't take my dog along. The only thing I could do was to leave him a loaf of bread. I cried all the way.'

'She also told me about her cousin. Like my grandmother, she had to leave her village with her family on carts to board the ship to İzmir. There was chaos at the harbour, and as they were boarding my grandmother's cousin suddenly realised that one of her twins was missing. There was absolutely nothing the mother could do, and the ship left without her missing daughter. Months after they had arrived at İzmir, a relative found the child and brought her to their new home. My grandmother used to cry every time she told us about the joy in the family that day.

'My mother still has a copper pan that my grandmother brought with her from their house in Greece. It's a black, worn-out old pan, but my mother still likes to use it. She says that no other pan is as good as that pan for frying aubergines…

In 1924, a total of two million people had to leave their homes. The majority were Turkish people living mainly in northern Greece and the Aegean islands and Greeks living in Anatolia.

With thanks to Zeynep Ozis who recounted this story about her grandmother, Ayse Yalaz

A road lined with grand mansions leads a few kilometres south of Ayvalık to Çamlık and Orta Çamlık, which have a scattering of pensions and camping areas popular with holidaying Turks. Sarımsaklı Plaj (Garlic Beach), also called Küçükköy, is 6km south of the centre. Packed with hotels and pensions, Sarımsaklı is hard-core, package-holiday country, although the beach gets wilder and more deserted if you stay on the bus to the end of its run.

Driving through the narrow and one-way streets of Ayvalık is stressful and there are few places to park. Car parks (marked on the map) generally cost €3/7.50 per day/night.

Sights & Activities

In summer, boats jostle on the quay to offer daytime or evening **cruises** (incl meal per person/with student card around €8/€5.50; ☺ May-Oct) around some of the bay's islands. Some can be visited or you can stop to swim. The bigger boats have a party atmosphere; for a quieter trip, you'll need to pay more for a smaller boat. Sunday excursions to Assos and back cost a similar bargain price.

Named after a hero of the Turkish War of Independence, **Alibey Island (Cunda)** boasts abandoned Greek churches, seaside restaurants in old stone houses and hundreds of condominiums. The northern part of the island forms the **Patriça Nature Reserve**; you'll see the ruins of the Greek **Ayışığı Manastırı** (Moonlight Monastery) on an offshore island as you head out there.

The place to be at sunset is **Şeytan Sofrası** (Devil's Table), a hilltop 9km south of town that offers panoramic views of the surrounding islands. Dolmuşes travel here only from July to mid-September. Otherwise, you'll have to walk, hitch (unlikely) or take a taxi. A couple of cafés wait to serve drinks and light meals to sunset-watchers.

Sleeping
AYVALIK

Bonjour Pansiyon (☎ 312 8085; Fevzi Çakmak Caddesi, Çeşme Sokak 5; www.bonjourpansiyon.com s/d with shared bathroom €13/26; ☒) Centrally located in a lovely house that once belonged to a French priest who was ambassador to the sultan, it boasts a pleasant courtyard, simple but immaculate rooms and, above all, a terrific welcome from Hatice and Yalcin, the friendly owners. Two rooms have bathrooms. Breakfast is available for €4.50. To find the pension, take the side street off the main road bang opposite the post office and follow the signs.

Yalı Pansiyon (☎ 312 2423; fax 318 3819; PTT Arkası 25; s/d with shared bathroom €14/28; ⊙ mid-May–Oct) Though an Ebenezer-like figure may open the imposing doors of this grand old house, don't be put off. And although the sweeping staircase, *trompe-l'oeil* paintings and chandeliers contrast with rather ordinary rooms, the waterfront garden with its own jetty is a gem. Four rooms have direct sea views and breakfast is available for €3. It's on the seafront, behind the PTT.

Annette's House (☎ 312 5971; annstei@hotmail .com; Neşe Sokak 12; per person incl breakfast €22) Owned by the efficient Annette, a retired German teacher, the hotel lies oasis-like amid a war-ren of streets about 250m east of Atatürk Bulvarı. Rooms are simple, but the garden is the biggest boon. Cool, verdant and peaceful, it's a million metaphorical miles from the city centre. If you can't find it, ask for *köyü pazarinda* (the villagers' market) or the *pazar yeri* (bazaar), which is next door.

ALİBEY ISLAND

Alibey has some decent places to stay, though most are over the restaurants and likely to be noisy. In a lovely location right beside Cunda's Taksiyarhis church, **Zehra Teyze'nin Evi** (☎ 327 2285; www.cundaevi.com; Namik Kemal Mahellasi 7; r high season €61, s/d low season €28/39; ☒) is a pension in a 136-year-old house with attractive, traditionally decorated rooms.

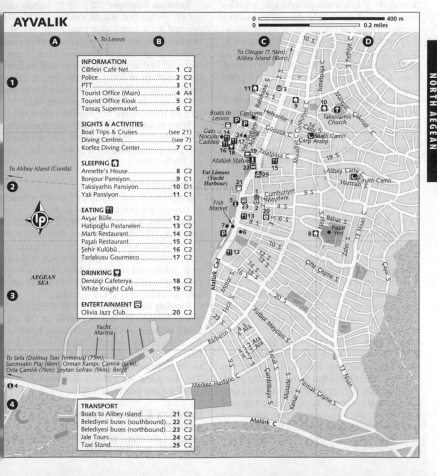

AYVALIK

NORTH AEGEAN

The best camping is on Alibey Island, with the camp sites located inconveniently but quietly outside the village, mostly to the west. The ubiquitously advertised **Ada Camp** (☎ 327 1211; www.adacamping.com; Alibey Adası; per person/car €4/1.50 per tent €1.50-4.50, r in caravan/bungalow €23/34; ☯ Apr-Nov) lies 3km to the west. The air-conditioned bungalows are simple but spotless. Clean, well-run and with its own beach (with pedalos and rowing boats too) and restaurant, this is a great place. Guests can also use the kitchen. Yufuk, the manager, is friendly and accommodating.

Eating

AYVALIK

Restaurants

Paşalı Restaurant (☎ 312 5018; off Fotografçilar Aralığı 18; meals €4; ☯ 5.30am-midnight high season, to 8pm low season) Tucked down side streets, but with a devoted following among those in the know, the new Paşsh does great Turkish home cooking at unbeatable prices. Dishes (including good veggie options for €1.10 to €2.75) change every day, and there's a useful pick-and-point counter.

Şehir Kulübü (☎ 312 1088; Yat Limanı; fish mains €4-10; ☯ 10am-2am) With a gorgeous setting jutting into the sea, this restaurant is the top local pick for fresh fish at feasible prices.

Martı Restaurant (☎ 312 6899; Gazinolar Caddesi 9; mains €5-8; ☯ 7.30am-midnight). A smart new place with an excellent reputation, it specialises in Ayvalık and regional specialities as well as fish.

Cafés & Quick Eats

Hatipoğlu Pastaneleri (☎ 312 2913; Atatürk Caddesi 12; tea/coffee €0.55/1.10; ☯ 6.30am-midnight; ⚇) With a great selection of traditional Turkish puds, pastries and cakes served in the air-conditioned interior or on tables on the seafront, this popular patisserie makes a terrific breakfast or tea stop. Try the Ayvalık speciality, *lok* (sponge oozing honey, €1.40) or baklava (1kg €10).

Avşar Büfe (☎ 312 9821; Atatürk Caddesi 67; tost €0.85-1.10; ☯ 24 hr high season, 8am-2am low season) Famous throughout Turkey is *Ayvalık tost* (Ayvalık 'toast') and this is the place to get it. Traditionally they're filled with *sucuk* (Turkish sausage), cheese, tomato, ketchup and mayonaise, but you can opt just for one or two ingredients if you prefer! Though not exactly *haute cuisine*, they're delicious if you're hungry enough.

Tarlakusu Gourmeco (☎ 312 2141; Gazinolar Caddesi 4/C; ☯ 8am-10pm Mon-Sat, 8am-6pm Sun) Newly opened by a burnt-out İstanbullu couple, this fabulous, mellow, traditional coffeehouse serves a large range of flavoured Turkish coffees and herbal teas (€1.40), as well as food fashioned from local ingredients, ranging from to-die-for *brovna* (chocolate brownies; €2.50) to *otlu piliç* (chicken with veg). It's located underneath the Ayvalık Palas Otel.

White Knight Café (☎ 312 3682; Cumhuriyet Meydanı 3; iced coffee €1.65; ☯ noon-midnight) Has previous-day European newspapers as well as the *Turkish Daily News*.

ALİBEY ISLAND

Taking a boat over to Alibey Island for lunch or dinner is a favourite local pastime.

Bay Nihat (Lale Restaurant; ☎ 327 1063; seafood meze €6.50; ☯ noon-midnight) In a very attractive 150-year-old Greek house, this restaurant is considered Alibey's best for fish and has well-positioned seafront tables. It has a huge range of excellent mezes (its fish mezes have won several pan-Turkey awards).

Papalina Restaurant (☎ 327 1041; Sahil Boyu 7; meze €3, fish mains €11-28) For a table on the seafront without paying a premium, head for the cheerful and popular Papalina on Alibey Island, with its chequered tablecloths and lovely position right next to the fishing boats. Try the *papalina balik*, a fish speciality of Ayvalık (one portion €3.50).

Drinking & Entertainment

AYVALIK

Deniziçi Cafeterya (☎ 312 1537; Gazinocular Caddesi 1; beer €1.95; ☯ 7.30am-12.30am) At the far end of the quay, past the fish restaurants, it has a fabulous position on the corner of the seafront and is great for a sundowner.

Olivia Jazz Club (☎ 327 1750; ⊗ 8pm-3am Jun-Sep) Currently considered Ayvalık's brightest nightly star, it plays live music daily. It lies one block off Atatürk Bulvarı; take the side street bang opposite the fish market then take the first left onto 2 Sokak.

ALİBEY ISLAND

Dinazor Bar (☎ 327 2194; Sahil Boyu 49; beer €3; ⊗ 8pm-4am high season, to 2am low season) Set in a 19th-century olive oil warehouse, this stunning and super-cool bar is Ayvalık's best. In summer, there's live music nightly from 11pm to 2am.

Nargileli Kahwe (☎ 327 1186; Ayvalık Caddesi 16; coffee €1.10, nargileh €7; ⊗ noon to 11pm) If it's mellow you're after, head for this old stone house where you can chill out on cushion- and kilim-covered benches.

Taş Kahve (☎ 327 1166; Sahil Boyu 20; coffee €0.40; ⊗ 7am-midnight) In a 180-year-old building, it's a local institution. Smoky, cavernous and very atmospheric, all the town tittle-tattle takes place here. It's also good for a cheap Turkish breakfast (€3.30).

Getting There & Away

BUS

Coming from Çanakkale (€6, 3¼ hours, 200km) some buses drop you on the main highway to hitch to the centre. Çanakkale/Truva and Metro bus companies should have a *servis* to run you into town. Coming from Edremit (€3, one hour, 56km) you'll be dropped in a smaller terminal, just 200m from the harbour.

When leaving Ayvalık, you can hop on a bus to Edremit and transfer there to services for Çanakkale. Alternatively, book your ticket in advance at one of the bus company offices around the main square and use their *servis* to get you out to the highway again. Buses leave roughly every hour (until around 7pm).

There are frequent buses from İzmir to Ayvalık (€5, three hours, 240km).

It's also possible to make a day trip to Bergama from Ayvalık (€3, 1¾ hours, 45km). Hourly Bergama buses leave from the main terminal and drive slowly south through town so you can pick them up in the main square.

BOAT

From June to September, at least one boat sails daily to Lesvos, Greece (passenger one way/return €40/50, car €60/70, 1½ hours). From October to May, boats sail twice a week (Wednesday and Thursday), returning from Lesvos to Ayvalık on Thursday and Friday. Note that you *must* make a reservation (in person or by telephone) 24 hours before. When you pick up your tickets, bring your passport (details need to be noted).

For information and tickets, contact **Jale Tours** (☎ 312 2740; www.jaletour.com; Gümrük Caddesi 24).

CAR

You can hire a car from **Avis** (☎ 312 2456; Talatpaşa Caddesi).

Getting Around

Ayvalık *belediyesi* (town) buses run right through town from the otogar to the main square, then south to the tourist office and on to Çamlık, Orta Çamlık and Sarımsaklı, for €0.40. They also run to Cunda (€0.40) via the causeway. On summer weekends there is a bus service to Patriça as well.

New in 2006 are the dolmuş taxis (white with red stripe running around them) which behave like little buses, stopping to put down and pick up passengers. They run back and forth along the same route from a spot known as 'Sefa' 100m south of the marina, to Armutçuk, 1km to the north of town; they don't go to Alibey Island. All journeys cost €0.55.

Minibuses (€0.70 to €0.85) depart for the beaches from beside the Tansaş supermarket sign south of the main square. Küçükköy Belediyesi buses also run to the beaches.

Boats to Alibey Island (€0.85, 15 minutes; June to August) leave from behind the tourist kiosk just off the main square.

A taxi from the otogar to the town centre costs €4; to Alibey Island from the town centre costs €6.

BERGAMA (PERGAMUM)

☎ 0232 / pop 58,170

The bustling market town of Bergama is most famous as the home of the Asclepion. Though arguably it has as much as Ephesus to occupy travellers, it's far less visited. This, together with its laid-back and friendly feel and excellent attractions, make it a must for the independent traveller. Many visitors end up falling for Bergama.

There has been a town here since Trojan times, but Pergamum's heyday was during the period between Alexander the Great and the

Roman domination of all Asia Minor when it was one of the Middle East's richest and most powerful small kingdoms.

History

Pergamum owes its prosperity to Lysimachus, one of Alexander the Great's generals, and also its downfall. Lysimachus took control of the Aegean region when Alexander's far-flung empire fell apart after his death in 323 BC. In the battles over the spoils Lysimachus captured a great treasure, which he secured in Pergamum before going off to fight Seleucus for control of Asia Minor. But Lysimachus lost and was killed in 281 BC, whereupon Philetarus, the commander he had posted in Pergamum to protect the treasure, set himself up as governor.

Philetarus was a eunuch, but he was succeeded by his nephew Eumenes I (263–241 BC), and Eumenes was followed by his adopted son Attalus I (241–197 BC). Attalus declared himself king, expanded his power and made an alliance with Rome.

During the reign of his son Eumenes II (197–159 BC), Pergamum achieved its greatest glory. Rich and powerful, Eumenes added the library and the Altar of Zeus to the buildings already crowning the acropolis, and built the 'middle city' on terraces halfway down the hill. He also expanded and beautified the Asclepion. Inevitably, much of what the Pergamese kings built hasn't survived the ravages of the centuries (or the enthusiasm of Western museums), but what has is impressive, dramatically sited and well worth visiting.

Eumenes' brother Attalus II kept up the good work but under his son, Attalus III, the kingdom began to fall apart again. With no heir, Attalus III bequeathed his kingdom to Rome, and the kingdom of Pergamum became the Roman province of Asia in 129 BC.

Orientation & Information

The most handsome part of town flanks the Galinos River to the north: the Muslim neighbourhood is on the west bank, the Ottoman Greek one on the east.

Of Bergama's four main sights, only the museum is located in the town centre. The two main archaeological sites are several kilometres out of town.

Modern Bergama largely consists of one long main street, İzmir Caddesi, along which almost everything you'll need can be found,

including hotels and restaurants, the banks, PTT, museum and otogar (though the otogar may move; see p223). Most of the pensions and hotels allow guests internet access.

The **Tourist Office** (☎ 631 2851; İzmir Caddesi 54), just north of the museum, offers little more than a sketch map.

Sights & Activities

Bergama's attractions open in high season from 8.30am to 6.30pm daily and from 8.30am to 5pm in low season (except the museum, which is closed on Monday). Parking at the acropolis or Asclepion costs €1.65.

ARCHAEOLOGY MUSEUM

Right in the centre of town, the **Archaeology Museum** (☎ 632 9860; Arkeoloji Müzesi; İzmir Caddesi; admission €2.75) boasts a small but substantial collection of artefacts for so small a town. Look out for the sculptures from Pergamum, influenced by the Afrodisias school, which was known for its expressive features and lavish detailing. Look out also for the model of the Altar of Zeus (the original is in Berlin).

Also housed here are finds from the site of Allianoi (see p223). The ethnography section (currently under restoration) will reopen by the end of 2006. It contains textiles, costumes, rugs and manuscripts dating from the Ottoman period.

ASCLEPION

An ancient medical centre, the **Asclepion** (Temple of Asclepios; admission €5.55) was founded by Archias, a local citizen who had been cured at the Asclepion of Epidaurus (Greece). Treatments included massage, mud baths, drinking sacred waters and the use of herbs and ointments. Diagnosis was often by dream analysis.

Pergamum's centre came to the fore under Galen (AD 131–210), who was born here, studied in Alexandria, Greece and Asia Minor, and set up shop as physician to Pergamum's gladiators. Recognised as perhaps the greatest early physician, Galen added considerably to knowledge of the circulatory and nervous systems, and also systematised medical theory. Under his influence, the medical school at Pergamum became renowned. His work was the basis for Western medicine well into the 16th century.

Two roads head up to the Asclepion. One runs from the centre of town. The other is

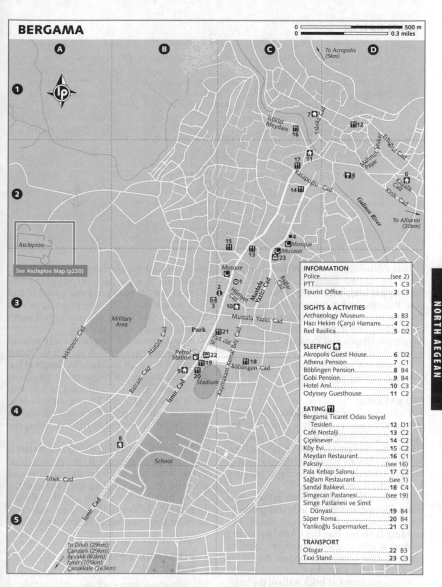

BERGAMA

INFORMATION
Police...(see 2)
PTT...**1** C3
Tourist Office............................**2** C3

SIGHTS & ACTIVITIES
Archaeology Museum................**3** B3
Hacı Hekim (Çarşı) Hamamı.......**4** C2
Red Basilica...............................**5** D2

SLEEPING
Akropolis Guest House...............**6** D2
Athena Pension..........................**7** C1
Böblingen Pension......................**8** B4
Gobi Pension..............................**9** B4
Hotel Anıl...................................**10** C3
Odyssey Guesthouse..................**11** C2

EATING
Bergama Ticaret Odası Sosyal
  Tesisleri.................................**12** D1
Café Nostalji..............................**13** C2
Çiçeksever.................................**14** C2
Köy Evi......................................**15** C2
Meydan Restaurant....................**16** C1
Paksoy....................................(see 16)
Pala Kebap Salonu.....................**17** C2
Sağlam Restaurant...................(see 1)
Sandal Balıkevi..........................**18** C4
Simgecan Pastanesi................(see 19)
Simge Pastanesi ve Simit
  Dünyasi.................................**19** B4
Süper Roma...............................**20** B4
Yanikoğlu Supermarket.............**21** C3

TRANSPORT
Otogar......................................**22** B3
Taxi Stand.................................**23** C3

at the western edge of town, cutting up in front of the Böblingen Pension. Taking the latter road, the ruins are about 2km from the otogar. This road passes through a large Turkish military base; be off it by dusk and don't take photos.

A Roman **bazaar street**, once lined with shops, leads from the car park to the centre where you'll see the base of a column carved with snakes, the symbol of Asclepios (Aesculapius), god of medicine. Just as the snake sheds its skin and gains a 'new life', so the patients at the Asclepion were supposed to 'shed' their illnesses (but not take on new ones). Signs mark a circular **Temple of Asclepios**, a **library** and a **Roman theatre**.

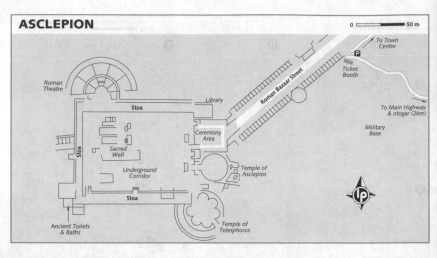

ASCLEPION

0 ▭▭▭ 50 m

To Town Centre

Roman Theatre

Library

Stoa

Roman Bazaar Street

Ticket Booth

To Main Highway & otogar (2km)

Military Base

Ceremony Area

Sacred Well

Stoa

Underground Corridor

Temple of Asclepios

Stoa

Ancient Toilets & Baths

Temple of Telesphorus

Take a drink from the **Sacred Well**, then pass along the vaulted underground corridor to the **Temple of Telesphorus**, another god of medicine. Patients slept in the temple hoping that Telesphorus would send a cure or diagnosis in a dream. The names of Telesphorus' two daughters, Hygeia and Panacea, have passed into medical terminology.

You can buy soft drinks at the Asclepion, although at a hefty premium.

RED BASILICA

The cathedral-sized **Red Basilica** (Kinik Caddesi; admission €2.75) was originally a temple to the Egyptian gods Serapis, Isis and Harpocrates built in the 2nd century AD. In Revelations, St John the Divine wrote that this was one of the seven churches of the Apocalypse, singling it out as the throne of the devil.

Look for a hole in the podium in the centre, which allowed someone to hide and appear to speak through the 10m-high cult statue. The building is so big that the Christians didn't convert it into a church but built a basilica inside it. One tower now houses the neatly converted, small Kurtuluş Camii.

The curious red flat-brick walls of the large, roofless structure are visible from midway down the road to the acropolis. You can easily walk to the Red Basilica, or stop your taxi there on your way to or from the acropolis.

ACROPOLIS

The road up to the **acropolis** (admission €5.55; ⊙ 8.30am-5.30pm) winds 5km from the Red Ba-

silica, around the northern and eastern sides of the hill, to a car park (€1.50) at the top. Next to the car park are some souvenir and refreshment stands. If you're planning to walk to the site, take plenty of water as you won't be able to stock up on the way.

Blue dots mark a suggested route around the main structures, which include the **library** as well as the marble-columned **Temple of Trajan**, built during the reigns of the emperors Trajan and Hadrian and used to worship them as well as Zeus. It's the only Roman structure surviving on the acropolis, and its foundations were used as cisterns during the Middle Ages.

The vertigo-inducing, 10,000-seat **theatre** is impressive and unusual. Its builders decided to take advantage of the spectacular view and conserve precious building space on top of the hill by building the theatre into the hillside. In general, Hellenistic theatres are wider and rounder than this, but at Pergamum the hill-

---

PERGAMUM'S PHENOMENAL PHYSICIAN

Under the guidance of Galen (AD 131–210), chief physician to the gladiators, the Asclepion (Pergamum's ancient medical centre) grew to achieve world renown. So also did Galen. His knowledge of the nervous and circulatory systems remained the basis for Western medicine right up to the 16th century.

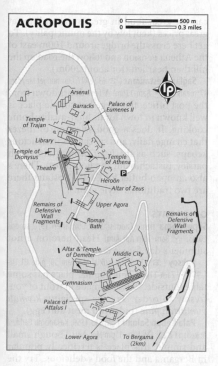

ACROPOLIS

0 — 500 m
0 — 0.3 miles

Arsenal
Barracks
Palace of Eumenes II
Temple of Trajan
Library
Temple of Dionysus
Temple of Athena
Theatre
Heroön
Altar of Zeus
Remains of Defensive Wall Fragments
Upper Agora
Roman Bath
Remains of Defensive Wall Fragments
Altar & Temple of Demeter
Middle City
Gymnasium
Palace of Attalus I
Lower Agora
To Bergama (2km)

side location made rounding impossible and so it was increased in height instead.

Below the stage is the ruined **Temple of Dionysus**. The **Altar of Zeus**, south of the theatre and shaded by evergreen trees, has an idyllic setting. Originally, it was covered with magnificent friezes depicting the battle between the Olympian gods and their subterranean foes, but the sultan allowed 19th-century German excavators to remove most of this famous building to Berlin, leaving only the base behind.

Piles of rubble on top of the acropolis are marked as the **Palaces of Attalus I** and **Eumenes II**, and there's an **Upper Agora**, as well as fragments of the once-magnificent defensive **walls**.

To see everything, walk down the hill behind the Altar of Zeus, passing the **Roman bath**, the **Middle City** and the **Altar & Temple of Demeter**, the **gymnasium** (with bath, auditorium and cult hall) and **Lower Agora**. Take care as the path down is steep and not always clearly marked.

While you're on the acropolis, look across the valley to the Asclepion in the west. You'll also see the ruins of two **theatres** (one small

and one large), an **aqueduct** and a **stadium** in the valley below.

HAMAM

Situated near the Kulaksız Cami, **Hacı Hekim (Çarşı) Hamamı** (🕑 8am-11pm; men only) charges €10 for the full works.

Sleeping

In Bergama, there are really two options: to sample Turkish hospitality in one of the excellent family-run pensions, or opt for one of the lovely, characterful hotels converted from old houses.

Odyssey Guesthouse (☎ 653 9189; www.odyssey guesthouse.com; Abacıhan Sokak 13; dm high/low season €5.50/4.50, s/d without bathroom high season €8/16.50, low season €5.50/11) In a converted 180-year-old Greek house in the heart of the old town, this tranquil guesthouse has seven rather sparse but clean and atmospheric rooms. Run by the bookish Ersin, it also has a good selection of books, as well as a pleasant tea salon and small terrace with views,

Gobi Pension (☎ 633 2518; www.gobipension.com; İzmir Caddesi 18; s with/without bathroom €14/11, d €20/22; 🖵) On the main road around 150m south of the otogar, the family-run Gobi is set in a modern block but is spotless, well maintained and very welcoming. Mustafa, the helpful son, speaks English and often plays guide. Rooms are traditionally decorated, and all have wireless internet connection; five have air con and four have balconies over the little garden at the back.

Böblingen Pension (☎ 633 2153; dincer-altin@hotmail .com; Asklepion Caddesi 2; s/d €14/28; 🍴 P 🖵) Run by

---

LIBRARY WARS

Under Eumenes II, Pergamum's library became world renowned. Said to have held more than 200,000 volumes, the library soon came to challenge the world's greatest, Alexandria's library in Egypt. Afraid that Eumenes' library would attract famous scholars away from Alexandria, the Egyptians decided to cut off Pergamum's supply of papyrus from the Nile. Eumenes simply set his scientists to work, and they soon came up with *pergamen* (Latin for parchment), a writing surface made from animal hides, which quickly did away with the need for pressed papyrus reeds.

the friendly Altın family, this pension is also spotless and well looked after. Set on the hill (just off Asklepion Caddesi) above the main road, it's also quieter than most and has a comfy sitting room. To find it, watch for the sign to the Asclepion off the main road.

Athena Pension (☎ 633 3420; www.athenapension.8m. com; İman Çıkmazı; d with shared/private bathroom €17/28, dm €8, airbed on roof terrace €5) Situated just off Fabrika Caddesi near the foot of the acropolis, the Athena has eight characterful rooms around a pretty courtyard. Aydin, the friendly manager, is also pretty characterful. Room 3 has distant views of the acropolis, as does the roof terrace. To find it, head down Fabrika Caddesi and it's on the left.

Hotel Anıl (☎ 631 1830; www.anilhotelbergama.com; Hatuniye Caddesi 4; s/d €34/45; ❈) The Anıl's attraction is its central location (near the BP station). If you're after peace, privacy or anonymity, it's a good choice and rooms are comfortable if rather soulless. The covered roof terrace has great panoramic views.

Akropolis Guest House (☎ 631 2621; www.akropo lisguesthouse.com; Kayalik Caddesi 5; s/d €20/49, f €44; ❈ 🖳) This 150-year-old stone house is the closest Bergama gets to boutique. Eight attractively decorated rooms surround a peaceful pool and garden. There's also a restaurant set in a lovely old barn and a terrace at the top of a small tower with views of the acropolis. It's a gem and is good value too.

Eating
RESTAURANTS

Sandal Balıkevi (☎ 631 6116; Böblingen Caddesi 51; fixed menu €2.25; ❈ 8am-midnight) A new fish restaurant with tables inside and out, it's well run, clean and popular locally. Fish is fresh and prices are reasonable. Try the speciality sardines (400g €3.90 to €5). There's live music on some evenings.

Meydan Restaurant (☎ 633 1793; İstiklal Meydanı 4; mains €2.25-2.75; ❈ 6am-midnight) One of Bergama's oldest restaurants and a local institution, this simple but sparkling place serves good, regional food at fair prices. It also has tables outside. Try the Bergama speciality, *lahmaçun* (wheat cakes with minced meat).

Bergama Ticaret Odası Sosyal Tesisleri (☎ 632 4522; Ulucamii Mahallesi; meze €1.65, mains €3.35 ❈ 10.30am-11pm) Set up and run by Bergama municipality, this new restaurant is located in a beautifully restored 200-year-old Greek house 100m north of the Ulu Camii (mosque) where you

can eat great food in great surroundings at great prices (kept low by the municipality). To get here cross the bridge around 100m east of the Athena Pension and follow the road up the hill then bear left (for about 200m).

Sağlam Restaurant (☎ 632 8897; Cumhuriyet Meydanı 47; meals €5; ❈ 8am-11pm) A few doors down from the post office, this large but simple place is well known in town for its high-quality home cooking. It does a good selection of mezes that change daily, and specialises in delicious kebaps, such as the *beyti sarma* (lamb with parsley, pistachio nut and hot spices). There's also an open buffet for €4.45. Upstairs there are two traditional-style salons.

QUICK EATS

Süper Roma (İzmir Caddesi, Sitat Dükkarleri 19; 2 scoops €0.85; ❈ 8am-1am Apr-Aug) Head here on a hot summer's day for ice cream.

Paksoy (☎ 633 1722; İstiklal Meydanı 39; pide €1.10-1.95; ❈ 7am-11pm) This popular place has some tables outside. Pides are made in front of you, freshly to order. Try the speciality *kıymalı yumurtalı pide* (pide with meat and egg).

Pala Kebap Salonu (☎ 633 1559; Kasapoğlu Caddesi 4; kebap €2.20; ❈ 8am-11pm Mon-Sat) Though small and simple, this place is terrifically popular in Bergama and the food's delicious. Try the spicy Bergama *köfte* (€1.95).

Çiçeksever (☎ 633 3822; Banklar Caddesi 71; ❈ 7.30am-10.30pm) Near and similar to the Pala.

CAFÉS

Köy Evi (Village House; ☎ 632 4816; Galinos Caddesi 12; ❈ 7.30am-9pm) This is a new, fabulous family-run traditional place with cosy seating inside or among the family out in the courtyard. Menus change daily, but regular specialities include *gözleme* (crêpes, €0.85) and *mantı* (Turkish ravioli).

Café Nostalji (☎ 632 7910; Ahmet Kuduğ Çikmazi 3; soft drinks €1.10; coffee €0.85-1.10; ❈ 9am-2am high season, to midnight low season) Lying 20m north of the post office, this gem of a place lies hidden down a side street off Bankalar Caddesi. With walls decorated with musical instruments and old records, it has a great atmosphere particularly at night. There's live Turkish music on Thursdays and Saturdays from 9pm to midnight (to 2am in high season). Alcohol is not served.

For a coffee and a cake in between the sightseeing, the **Simge Pastanesi ve Simit Dünyası** (☎ 631 1034; İzmir Caddesi 19; couple of pastries €1; ice cream €0.55; ❈ 7am-midnight) and, next door, the

Simgecan Pastanesi (☎ 631 1034; Böblingen Caddesi 4; ⊗ 7.30am-1am) are considered the best patisseries in town and are run by two brothers. There's a good selection of pastries, cakes and Turkish puddings. The baklava is delicious.

SELF-CATERING

Bergama has a bustling Monday **market** (⊗ 8am-6pm), which stretches for about 3km from the otogar to the Red Basilica. It's great for fresh fruit and veg. Böblingen Caddesi and the area around the old bus station is good for picnic-hunting. Cheese, olives, fresh bread and dried fruit are all sold. Near here also is **Yanikoğlu Supermarket** (☎ 632 7942; Merkez Çamipark Karş 21, İzmir Caddesi; ⊗ 8am-midnight).

Getting There & Away

Buses run to İzmir (€4.45, two hours, 110km) every 45 minutes, to Ayvalık (€3.35, 1¼ hours, 60km) at least every hour, to Ankara (€21, eight to nine hours, 916km). For İstanbul, there are nightly (and daily too in high season) buses, but it's cheaper and quicker, surprisingly, to go to İzmir first and take an express bus from there. For Bursa, take the Ayvalık bus.

A new otogar is currently under construction at a junction 7km from town. It should be ready by the end of 2007 (though wrangling between the municipality and bus companies are holding things up). A dolmuş service should shuttle regularly between the new otogar and town (€1 to €1.50). A taxi should cost around €8 during the day, €12 at night. Dolmuşes to Dikili, Ayvalık and Çandarli also leave from here at least every half hour.

Getting Around

Bergama's sights are so spread out that it's hard to walk round them all in one day. The Red Basilica is over 2km from the otogar, the Asclepion is 2km away and the acropolis is over 6km away. If you like walking but have limited time, take a taxi to the top of the acropolis (€8 to €9 from the town), then walk down the hill to the Red Basilica, either following the tarmac road or cutting down the slope beneath the theatre. Then stroll through the shopping area into town, have lunch and take another taxi, or hitch or walk to the Asclepion. Bergama's taxis have meters, but it's much better to try and negotiate a rate for a 'City Tour'. From the centre to the acropolis, basilica, Asclepion and museum, it should

cost around €25 to €28 in high season, €20 to €23 in low season. Taxis wait near some of the mosques and around the otogar.

AROUND BERGAMA
Allianoi

In 1999 local farmers made an exciting discovery in the Valley of Kaikos at Allianoi, 20km east of Bergama. Excavation began and the remains of a Roman spa town were discovered. Although not dramatic as those in Bergama itself, they are nonetheless interesting and impressive. The fine statue of Aphrodite on display in Bergama Museum (p218) came from Allianoi.

Unfortunately, at the time of writing the archaeological site is at the centre of controversy. The Valley of Kaikos is the proposed site for the new Yortanlı Dam, which will bring vital water reserves to the region but submerge the archaeological site under 17m of water in the process. There is a campaign to save Allianoi, but ultimately it will depend on the politicians; it's not looking too hopeful. In the meantime, 90% of the site remains unexcavated, and Turkish archaeologists and students continue to come here each summer. For more information on Allianoi, visit www.europanostra.org/save_allianoi.html.

There is no bus service, but you could try taking the infrequent bus from Bergama to Paşakoy (€2, 45 minutes), which can drop you at the turn-off to Paşaka, and then walk the 1km to Allianoi. Returning to Bergama is tricky. You can only try hailing a passing bus. A taxi here from Bergama costs €34 to €39.

ÇANDARLI
☎ 0232

The small and tranquil resort town of Çandarlı (ancient Pitane) stands on a peninsula jutting into the Aegean, 33km south of Bergama. It's dominated by a small but stately 14th-century restored Genoese **castle** (admission free; ⊗ 24 hr Jul-Aug), which has sporadic opening hours outside the high season, and it has a sandier beach than some of its neighbours. It makes a good base for a couple of days off.

Local tourism fills most of the pensions in high summer. From late October to April/May it's pretty much a ghost town.

Most of the shops, internet cafés and the PTT are within spitting distance of the bus stop. The castle, the restaurants and the pensions line the seashore. Market day is Friday.

Sleeping

Most of the hotels and pensions lie west of the castle, facing a thin strip of coarse sand.

Bağış Pansiyon (☎ 673 2459; Barbaros Sokak 19; s/d €10/20) If the others are full, this place, one block inland and two blocks west of the Samyeli, swaps the sea views of the swankier places for a verdant courtyard and lower prices.

Hotel Samyeli (☎ 673 3428; www.otelsamyeli.com; Sahil Caddesi 18; s/d high season €17/33, low season €14/28; ❄) Located in the middle of the bay, it is simple, spotless and smiley rooms painted canary yellow; 20 have little balconies, 14 also with direct sea views. Reserve one in advance (a week in summer).

Hotel Emigran (☎ 673 2500; www.otelsamyeli.com; Talat Emmi Caddesi 1; s/d half-board €22/44; ❄) This new place 150m west of Hotel Samyeli is situated right on the beach. It's tranquil and quiet and all rooms have direct sea views; from some you can hear the waves lapping on the shore. There are future plans to build a pool and sunbathing terrace.

Eating

For fresh fruit, the daily *çarşı* (market), in the shadow of the town mosque, is a good place to replenish.

Ünal Usta'nın (☎ 673 2772; PTT Sokak 1; ❄ 7am-2am) This quick-eats place is three doors from the post office just off the market square and specialises in delicious pide (€1.95 to €2.75).

Köşem (☎ 673 2132; Çarıçı 14; ❄ 5.30am-midnight, 24 hr high season) With little benches and parasols right on the market square, it serves locally loved soups (€1.35) and kebaps (€2.25 to €3.35).

Samyeli Restaurant (☎ 673 3428; Sahil Caddesi 18; small portion fish & seafood €4.45-5.55; ❄ 8am-midnight) Belonging to the hotel of the same name, but with a good reputation for fish, the restaurant has tables right on the seafront. Prices are good value, and the obliging owner can also tailor your meal to your budget! Try the house speciality *karides* (prawns; €8.35).

Drinking & Enterntainment

Pitaneou Cafe-Bar (☎ 673 3916; Sahil Plaj Caddesi 27; beer €2.75; ❄ 11am-midnight, to 3am high season) A trendy hangout with pleasant tables under vines on the seafront, it claims to play 'the best music in Turkey'. Snacks are available.

Musti Bar (☎ 673 3991; Sahil Plaj Caddesi 38/A; beer €2.75 ❄ 11am-3am) On the seafront one block west of the castle, this is currently Çandarlı's one and only dancing 'hot spot'.

Getting There & Away

Frequent buses run between Çandarlı and İzmir (€4.15, 1½ hours) via Dikili (€0.85; 15 minutes). At least six minibuses run daily to and from Bergama (€1.95, 30 minutes).

YENİ FOÇA

☎ 0232 / pop 3470

A delightful small resort set around a harbour, Yeni Foça boasts a strip of coarse beach and an unusually large number of crumbling Ottoman mansions and old Greek stone houses. Long-discovered by second-home hunters, Yeni Foça now has its fair share of marvels alongside monstrosities, enough to make the great Ottoman architect Sinan himself shudder. Nevertheless, it's a pleasant place to laze away a day or two.

The traditionally styled **Otel Naz** (☎ 814 6619; Sahil Caddesi 113; s/d €17/33) is at the far, western end of the bay about 500m from the harbour. It has large, quite attractively decorated rooms, seven with sea views and three with balconies. It's good value, and there's a café-bar out front.

On the far eastern side of the bay, the endearing little **Tansay Restaurant** (☎ 814 8080; Kordon Caddesi 11; meals €8-12; ❄ 9am-10pm) looks like a kind of Turkish bistro. There are a couple of tables on the seafront, and the food and prices are impressive. Try the *karides güvec* (prawn casserole; €8) or *kalamar dolma* (stuffed squid, €9). A more upmarket (and slightly pricier) alternative is **Veli Usta Orfoz Balık Ve Et Restaurant** (☎ 814 9192; Kordon Caddesi 16; meals €8-12; ❄ 8am-midnight) with a pleasant salon and lots of tables right on the harbour front.

Buses leave every half hour to İzmir (€3.35, 1¾ hours) and every two hours to Eski Foça (€1.95). Taxis to Eski Foça cost around €16.

FOÇA

☎ 0232 / pop 14,600

If Çandarlı is a bit too quiet and Kuşadası too noisy, Foça could be just the ticket. Sometimes called Eski Foça (Old Foça) to distinguish it from its newer, smaller neighbour (Yeni Foça) over the hill, Foça hugs twin bays and a small harbour. Graceful old Ottoman–Greek houses line a shoreline crowded with fishing boats and overlooked by a string of restaurants and pensions.

Eski Foça, the ancient Phocaea, was founded before 600 BC and flourished during the 5th century BC. During their golden age, the Phocaeans were great mariners, sending swift vessels powered by 50 oars into the Aegean, Mediterranean and Black Seas. They were also great colonists, founding Samsun on the Black Sea, as well as towns in Italy, Corsica, France and Spain.

More recently, this was an Ottoman–Greek fishing and trading town. It's now a prosperous, middle-class Turkish resort with holiday villas gathering on the outskirts.

Foça is also famous for the rare Mediterranean monk seals that lurk on the offshore islands (currently around Siren Kayalıkları and Hayırsız islands in particular), but as there are thought to be only 400 of them left in the world you shouldn't bank on seeing one; they're also very shy.

Orientation & Information
Foça's circular bay is partially divided by a peninsula cutting in from the southeast, dividing the eastern part of the bay into the Küçük Deniz (Small Sea) to the north and the Büyük Deniz (Big Sea) to the south. The Küçük Deniz, ringed with restaurants, is the more picturesque part, while bigger fishing vessels pull into the Büyük Deniz.

The otogar, on the edge of the Büyük Deniz, is just south of the main square. Walk north through the square, passing the **tourist office** (☎ /fax 812 1222; Cumhuriyet Meydanı), the PTT and several banks. After 350m you'll arrive at the bay and the restaurants and, just behind them, **Kaptan Net** (☎ 812 3411; Fevzi Paşa Mahallesi 210 Sokak 26/A; per hr €0.85; ☒ 9am-1am); continue along the right-hand (eastern) side to find the pensions.

For more information on the Mediterranean monk seals, visit the **Mediterranean Seal Protection Office** (Akdeniz Foku Foça Yerel Komitesi Bürosu; ☎ 812 3062; Atatürk Mahallesi 123) in the same building as Foça library.

Sights & Activities
Little remains of **ancient Phocaea**: a little remains theatre, remains of an aqueduct near the otogar, an anıt mezarı (monumental tomb), 7km east of town on the way to the İzmir highway, and traces of two shrines to the goddess Cybele, one on the hillside on the road to İzmir, the other not far from the Anfitiyatro Café.

Recently, the townsfolk made an exciting new discovery near Foça high school. Known as the Temple of Athena, the site was found to contain, among other things, a beautiful

griffin and horse's head believed to date to the 5th century BC. Excavations continue there every summer.

If you continue past the outdoor sanctuary of Cybele you'll come to a partially rebuilt fortress called **Beşkapılar** (Five Gates), which was built by the Byzantines and repaired by the Genoese and the Ottomans in 1538–39. Another fortress, the **Dışkale** (External Fortress), guards the town's approaches from the end of the peninsula that shapes the southwestern arc of the bay. It's best seen from the water (on a boat trip) as it's inside a military zone.

Foça's **hamam** (bathhouse; ☎ 812 1959; Atatürk Mahallesi 115 Sokak 22; massage €15; ☒ 8am-11pm) has separate men's and women's sections.

BOAT TRIPS
In summer (beginning of May to end of September) boats leave daily between 10.30am to 11.30am from both the Küçük Deniz and Büyük Deniz for day trips around the outlying islands. Trips cost €8 to €11 (but negotiate prices) and include lunch and water.

Sleeping
Foça has plenty of budget sleeping places but few mid- or top-range options. At the time of writing, billed to open soon was the four-star, British-run **Club Phokaia** (☎ 812 8080; 3 Merkinsak); call to check progress and prices.

İyon Pansiyon (☎ 812 1415; www.eskifoca.com; 198 Sokak 8; d high/low season €22/17) Inland from the seafront, it's run by the enterprising tourism graduate, Umut. Small, simple but endearing rooms are set around a garden-courtyard and there's a sunbathing terrace. Six windsurfers can be rented to guests (€30 per day). Guests can also use the kitchen, and future plans include a beer and BBQ garden.

Siren Pansiyon (☎ 812 2660; www.sirenpansiyon.com; 161 Sokak 13; s/d €14/25) Set off the seafront and so quiet, the Siren makes a spotless, pleasant and good-value choice. Guests also have use of the kitchen. Seven rooms have balconies, and there's a roof terrace.

Hotel Villa Dedem (☎ 812 2838; Sahil Caddesi 66; dedemomer@yahoo.com; s/d from €17/28; 20% more in high season ☒) Though not the cheapest in the budget category, its central location and lovely quayside views over the boats are well worth the price. Just eight rooms have balconies with seaviews – be sure to bags one.

Hotel Grand Amphora (☎ 812 3930; İsmetpaşa Mahallesi 206 Sokak; s/d high season €33/44, low season €23/34;

✖ ✖) The only hotel in town with a pool (albeit small), it's good for sun-soaking on the sunloungers. Rooms are small but comfortable. It's located just beyond Foça hospital on the seafront.

Foçantique Boutique Hotel (☎ 812 4313; www .focantiquehotel.com; Sahil Caddesi 154; d high season €98-118, low season €85-98) Lying at the far end of Küçük Deniz, this beautiful old Greek stone house is well worth the walk. Rooms are individually decorated with genuine 19th-century Turkish antiques, and compete for the most-beautiful-bathroom-in-Turkey prize.

Eating

Foça has a decent Tuesday market, which is a good place to stock up for a picnic. There are also various grocery stores.

Ridvan Ustanın Yeri (☎ 812 6867; İş Bankası; stews €1.40-2.25; ☯ 24 hr) One door down from the post office, the perennially popular chain serves good staple cooking at pleasing prices at outdoor tables just off the main square.

Fokai Restaurant (☎ 812 2186; Sahil Caddesi 11; ☯ 10am to midnight) Recommended for fish, it's a little cheaper than Celep. Specialities include fish slow-cooked in yogurt and garlic (€5.50).

Celep (☎ 812 1495; Sahil Caddesi 48; meals €25-35 ☯ 9am-midnight) If you're after atmosphere or romance and fancy some fish, head here: it's considered the best restaurant in town. Tables are right on the seafront, and waiters pluck lobsters direct from the pots!

Drinking

Anfitiyatro Café (☎ 812 3334; Sahil Caddesi 33; köfte/ kebap €2.25, cappuccino €1.10; ☯ 8am-10pm) A good place to break a stroll along the seafront, this peaceful place is about 60m beyond the Atatürk statue on Büyük Deniz.

Kokoloz Café (☎ 812 5255; Atatürk Mahallesi 194 Sokak 14; köfte €1.65, beer from €1.95; ☯ 9.30am-midnight) Owned by two archaeologists and set in an old Greek warehouse, this café is mellow, atmospheric and fun.

Neco Café & Bar (☎ 812 5020; Sahil Cad 10; snacks €1.10, beer €2.25; ☯ 24hr) For refreshments on the seafront without paying for the privilege, head here. It's relaxed, unpretentious, cheap and much-loved locally.

Keyif Café & Bar (☎ 812 2313; Sahil Caddesi 42/A; beer €2.25; ☯ 9am-4am) Slightly trendier and livelier than Neco, it often plays Western music.

Getting There & Away

Frequent buses connect Foça with İzmir (€3.33, 1½ hours, 86km), passing through Menemen (for connections to Manisa). To get to Bergama, go to Menemen, wait on the highway and flag down any bus heading north.

Three to five city buses run daily from Foça to Yeni Foça (€1.95, 30 minutes, 25km); the timetable is in the otogar. These buses also pass the pretty, small coves, beaches and camping grounds north of Foça.

If you're staying in the area for a few days you might want to hire a car from **1Bir Tour** (☎ 812 5050; www.birtour.com; Favzi Paşa Mahallesi 193/1), near the harbour.

İZMİR

☎ 0232 / pop 2.6 million
Although it has a dramatic setting around a bay backed by mountains, most of İzmir is modern, which makes it a hard city in which to fall in love at first sight. Give it a chance and you may find Turkey's third-largest city growing on you.

İzmir owes a huge debt to the late, much-lamented mayor, Ahmet Piriştina, who saved it from potentially disastrous plans to run a motorway along the seafront and gave large parts of the centre back to the locals by overseeing pedestrianisation schemes. Nowadays the sea-facing Kordon is a great place for jogging, cycling, walking the dog and just plain lounging about, while the northern district of Alsancak is being steadily restored, its lovely old houses reminiscent of the Greek island of Chios, metamorphosing into inviting restaurants and bars.

With a day to spare, you can take in the few antiquities and museums, loiter in cafés along the waterfront, and enjoy the sweeping views from Kadifekale castle. The labyrinthine bazaar also remains a colourful area to get lost in.

History

İzmir used to be Smyrna, the most Westernised and cosmopolitan of Ottoman–Turkish cities, where more citizens were Christian and Jewish than Muslim, and where there were thousands of foreign diplomats, traders and sailors.

The first settlement, at Bayraklı near the eastern end of the bay, was begun in the 10th century BC, but there were probably people here as far back as 3000 BC. Things really began to look up for Smyrna after the Ottomans grabbed it in 1415. In 1535 Süleyman the Magnificent signed a commercial treaty with François I of France, permitting foreign merchants to reside in the sultan's dominions. Smyrna rapidly became Turkey's most sophisticated commercial city, and its streets and buildings took on a quasi-European appearance.

After the collapse of the Ottoman Empire at the end of WWI, the Greeks invaded Smyrna. In fierce fighting on the outskirts of Ankara, they were eventually repelled. Unfortunately, during mopping-up operations, a disastrous fire destroyed most of the old city. But the day that Atatürk recaptured Smyrna (9 September 1922) marked the moment of victory in the Turkish War of Independence, and it's now the biggest local holiday. The events of 1922 are commemorated in the rather top-heavy monument gracing the waterfront.

Orientation

İzmir's two main avenues run parallel to the waterfront. The waterfront street is officially Atatürk Caddesi (Birinci Kordon or First Cordon), but locals just call it the Kordon. Just inland is Cumhuriyet Bulvarı, the İkinci Kordon (Second Cordon).

The city's two main squares – Konak Meydanı (Government House Sq) to the south and Cumhuriyet Meydanı – are along these two parallel avenues.

Konak opens onto the bazaar and Anafartalar Caddesi, the bazaar's main street, winds all the way to the train station, Basmane Garı, which is also linked to Konak by the metro. The Basmane–Çankaya area is home to dozens of small and medium-priced hotels, restaurants and bus ticket offices.

İzmir's shopping, restaurant and nightclub district of Alsancak is to the north, while the UFO-like otogar stands in splendid isolation, 6.5km northeast of the centre.

Information

There are branches of the PTT on Cumhuriyet Meydanı and on Fevzipaşa Bulvarı. Banks with ATMs can be found on Fevzi Paşa Bulvarı in Basmane and around Cumhuriyet Meydanı.
Artı Kitabevi (☎ 421 2632; Cumhuriyet Bulvarı 142/B) English-speaking, friendly bookshop with a good selection of English-language books.
Internet Café (1369 Sokak 9; per hr €0.83; ☼ 8am-1am) New, friendly and helpful.

İzmir Döviz (☎ 441 8882; Fevzi Paşa Bulvarı 75, Çankaya; ☼ 7am-7pm Mon-Sat) Moneychanger where no commission is charged.
T@şkın Internet C@fé (Fevzi Paşa Bulvarı 118; per hr €0.85; ☼ 8am-1am) Opposite the hospital (Şifa Hastanesi) up a spiral staircase on the 1st floor, it's smoky and noisy but has quick connections.
Tourist office (☎ 483 5117; fax 483 4270; Akdeniz Mahallesi 1344 Sokak 2) Inside the ornately stuccoed İl Kültür ve Turizm Müdürlüğü building just off Atatürk Caddesi. Has English-, German- and French-speaking staff who are keen to help.
Yuk@rınet (☎ 463 9308; Kıbrıs Şehitleri Caddesi 68, Alsancak; per hr €0.83; ☼ 9am-1am) Internet access, on the 2nd floor.

Dangers & Annoyances

İzmir is a fairly safe town, but travellers should take care around the train station at night. Bag snatchers have been reported in the alleyways. The area's also something of a red-light district, so lone women should take care. In the bazaar, be alert to pickpockets and thieves.

Sights & Activities
THE KORDON

By the Alsancak docks and further south near Konak Meydanı, huge concrete struts stand as a monument to the human folly of a mayor who thought building a motorway right along İzmir's waterfront would be a great idea. He was stopped in the nick of time, and the Kordon is now one of İzmir's main attractions, a great place to come to watch the sun setting over the bay.

During İzmir's 19th-century heyday the Kordon was lined with stately offices and the fine houses of the wealthy. Most of these have long since vanished, although at the Alsancak end of the waterfront the preserved wooden **Atatürk Evi** (admission free; ☼ 8.30am-noon & 1-5pm) gives an idea of what the homes of the wealthy would have looked like.

KONAK MEYDANI

A pedestrianised plaza named after the Ottoman **government mansion** (*hükümet konağı*), **Konak** has been landscaped with a rather unexpected cactus garden. Also here is a late Ottoman **clock tower** (*saat kulesi*) given to the city in 1901 by Sultan Abdül Hamit II. Its ornate Orientalist style may have been meant to atone for 'infidel Smyrna's' European ambience. Beside it the pretty **Konak Camii**, dating from 1748, is covered in Kütahya tiles.

İZMİR

0 ——— 500 m
0 ——— 0.3 miles

INFORMATION
Artı Kitabevi	1 B3
Banks	2 C5
Internet Café	3 C5
İzmir Döviz	4 C5
PTT	5 B4
PTT	6 C5
Sifa Hastanesi (Hospital)	7 C5
T@şkın Internet C@fé	8 C5
Tourist Office	9 B4
Yuk@rınnet	10 C2

SIGHTS & ACTIVITIES
Agora	11 C5
Archaeology Museum	12 A6
Atatürk Evi	13 C2
Clock Tower	(see 17)
Ethnography Museum	(see 12)
Government Mansion	(see 17)
İzmir Kültür Vakfı	14 A6
Kadifekale (Castle)	15 D6
Kızlaragası Han	16 B5
Konak Camii	17 A5
Museum of History & Art	18 C4
Şifalı Lux Hamam	19 C5

SLEEPING
Grand Zeybek Hotel	(see 20)
Güzel İzmir Oteli	20 C5
Hilton İzmir	21 B4
Hotel Alican 2	22 C5
Hotel Baylan	23 C5
Hotel İsmira	24 B4
Imperial Hotel	25 C5
İzmir Palas Oteli	26 B3
Otel Antik Han	27 C5
Otel Hikmet	28 C5
Otel Karaca	29 B4
Otel Kilim	30 B4

EATING
Balık Pişiricisi	31 C3
Café de Bugün	32 B4
Deniz Restaurant	(see 26)
Dört Mevsim et Lokantası	33 C5
Gül Kebap	34 B5
Güney Doğ	35 C5
Kemal'in Yeri Deniz Mahsülleri	36 C2
Kırçiçeği	37 C2
Neşe Köfte	38 B5
Rıza Aksüt	39 B5
Selanik Lokantası	40 B6
Simorg Café	41 B5
Tabaklar	42 B5
Tuğba	43 C5

DRINKING
Dergah Nargile Ve Çay Evi	44 C5
Emin Çay Evi	45 C5
Kalamış	(see 32)
Passport Café & Bar	(see 32)

ENTERTAINMENT
Barcelona	46 B4
Café Baryum	47 C3

SHOPPING
Alp	48 B5
Sipahi Okey	49 B5

TRANSPORT
Bus Companies City Offices	50 B5
Bus to Kadifekale	51 A6
Green Car	52 C4
Konak Bus Terminal	53 A6
Montrö Meydanı Bus Terminal	54 C4
Taxi Stand	55 B4
Turkish Airlines	56 C5

Alsancak
(Yeni)
Limanı

Alsancak

To Manisa (30km);
Sardis (90km)

Alsancak Gan
(Train Station)

Stadium

Mahmut Esat Bozkurt Cad

Alsancak İskelesi
(Alsancak Pier)

Talatpaşa Bul

Dr Mustafa Enver Cad

Kültür
Park

Pasaport
Pier

Cumhuriyet
Meydanı

Nevresbey Bul

Montrö
Meydanı

Vasıf Çınar Bul

BAY OF İZMİR
(KÖRFEZİ)

Akdeniz Cad

Kazım Paşa Bul

To Otogar (6km);
Çanakkale (340km);
Ankara (600km);
İstanbul (610km)

Şair Eşref Bul

Hürriyet Bul

Mürselpaşa Bul

Gazi Bul

Dokuz
Eylül Meydanı

To Adnan Menderes
Airport (16km);
Selçuk (18km);
Bodrum (250km)

Kemal Lettin Cad

Fevzi Paşa Bul

Çankaya

Train Station

Mosque

Police

Gaziler Cad

Mosque

Mosque

Anafartalar Cad

Hatuniye Camii

Basmane

Cannopied
Market

Konak
Pier

Konak
Meydanı

Konak

Dr Muhittin
Adam Cad

Bazaar

Hacı Aliefendi Cad

Turgutreis
Park

To Asansör Restaurant (1km);
Café Moreno & Synagogues (1km);
Üçkuyular Bus Terminal (5km);
Çeşme (85km)

Üçyol — Konak — Çankaya — Basmane — Hilal — Italkapınar — Stadyumu — Sanayi — Bölge — Bornova

NORTH AEGEAN

AGORA

The ancient **Agora** (Marketplace; Agora Caddesi; admission €1; ⏲ 8am-5pm), built for Alexander the Great, was ruined in an earthquake in AD 178, but rebuilt by the Roman emperor Marcus Aurelius. Colonnades of Corinthian columns, vaulted chambers and a reconstructed arch give you a good idea of what a Roman bazaar must have looked like. Later, a Muslim cemetery was built on the site and you can see many of the old tombstones around the perimeter of the Agora. Ask for the free brochure, which gives a good introduction.

To reach the Agora, walk down Anafartalar Caddesi, the bazaar's bustling main street, then skirt the perimeter of the site to find the gate.

BAZAAR

İzmir's **bazaar** (⏲ 9.30am-9pm Mon-Sat high season, to 5pm low season) is a little slice of fast-vanishing Turkey; this is also the place to head for İzmir's heart and soul. It's a great place to get lost for a few hours amid the stalls, sound of caged songbirds, wedding dress shops and spice stalls. Seek out if you can the flower and bead markets, then stop for a reviving shot of Turkish coffee in one of the delightful cafés at its core.

On the Konak side it's fun trying to find the restored **Kızlarağası Han** (⏲ 9.30am-9pm Mon-Sat high season, to 5pm low season), a covered market built in 1744 and rather like a smaller, calmer version of İstanbul's famous Covered Bazaar. When you're ready to be found again, ask the way back to Basmane or Konak.

SYNAGOGUES

Newly restored and open to the public are some of İzmir's beautiful old **synagogues** (guided tour €23-31) located in the same quarter as the Asansör Restaurant. To visit or tour, call the tourist office (p227), which can arrange access.

ARCHAEOLOGY, ETHNOGRAPHY & HISTORY OF ART MUSEUMS

İzmir's Archaeology and Ethnography Museums are a short, unsignposted walk up the hill from Konak along Anafartalar Caddesi and Millikütüphane Caddesi.

The **İzmir Archaeology Museum** (Arkeoloji Müzesi; ☎ 489 0796; Arkeoloji Müzesi Caddesi; admission €2.75; ⏲ 8am-5pm Tue-Sun) contains a fine collection of Greek and Roman artefacts. The displays are a little dry in places, but look out in particular for the beautifully decorated sarcophagi, the head of a gigantic statue of Domitian that once stood at Ephesus, and the impressive frieze depicting the funeral games from the mausoleum at Belevi (250 BC). To get here, exit the metro and at the crossroads head left up the hill towards the red-tiled, grand building half way up the hill.

More interesting is the **İzmir Ethnography Museum** (Etnografya Müzesi; ☎ 489 0796; admission €1.65; ⏲ 8am-5pm Tue-Sun), next door. Originally built in 1831 as the St Roche Hospital, this lovely old four-storey stone building houses colourful displays (including dioramas, photos and information panels) demonstrating local arts, crafts and customs. You'll learn about everything from camel wrestling, pottery and tinplating to felt-making, embroidery and the art of making those curious little blue-and-white 'evil eye' beads (see also the boxed text, p232). Other displays include weaponry, jewellery and beautiful illustrated manuscripts.

A newly opened museum in the Kültür Park is the **Museum of History & Art** (Tarih ve Sanat Müzesi; ☎ 489 7586; admission €2.75; ⏲ 8am-5pm Tue-Sun). Containing three separate departments, Sculpture, Ceramics, and Precious Artefacts, it gives a good overview of the region's artistic heritage. Look out in particular for the 2nd-century AD high relief of Poseidon and Demeter and the large hunting mosaic from Kadifekale. It also has a small but quite well stocked bookshop with publications on Turkish art, cooking and culture.

KADIFEKALE

Alexander the Great refounded Smyrna on Kadifekale (Mt Pagus) in the centre of the modern city, erecting the fortifications that still crown the hill. It's well worth taking a bus up to the 'Velvet Fortress' to see the view, especially just before sunset. During the day you can watch women migrants from Mardin in southeastern Turkey hard at work on horizontal carpet looms, an increasingly rare sight.

Bus 33 from Konak will carry you up the hill and you can easily walk some of the way back down again. However, the surrounding neighbourhood is pretty rough – don't walk back alone after dark.

HAMAM

If bathing facilities at your hotel are rudimentary, you can patronise the **Şifalı Lux Hamam** (bath/massage €5.50/11; ⏱ 7am-11pm for men, 8am-6pm for women) off Anafartalar Caddesi. It's clean, with a lovely domed and marble interior.

Festivals & Events

From mid-June to mid-July the annual **International İzmir Festival** offers performances of music and dance in Çeşme and Ephesus as well as İzmir (in the Kültür Park). Call the **İzmir Kültür Vakfı** (İzmir Culture Foundation; ☎ 463 0300; Mithatpaşa Caddesi 50/4) south of town to find out what's on where.

Sleeping

İzmir's hotels are often holed up with local businessmen attending trade shows; reserve a few days in advance, more in high summer.

There are lots of small, cheap hotels and several mid-priced places close to the train station. Recently the municipality helped fund the restoration of some old Ottoman houses (now converted hotels) immediately southwest of the train station (1296 Sokak) and, though the façades are very pretty, the interiors are unfortunately generally grungy and uninviting.

BUDGET

Otel Hikmet (☎ 484 2672; 945 Sokak 26; s with/without shower €11/8, d €22/16) If you're after 'atmosphere with authenticity', head for the Hikmet. Tucked away in cobbled streets in old İzmir near the Agora, this simple, family-run three-storey house is chock-full of character. Though longing for a lick of paint, the rooms are spotless.

Imperial Hotel (☎ 425 6883; fax 489 4688; 1294 Sokak 54; s/d €14/22; 🖳) Though the grandiose entrance columns, marble floors and purple carpets all live up to the hotel's name, the rooms are much more modest. But they're still of a decent size, spotless and terrific value.

Güzel İzmir Oteli (☎ 483 5069; 1368 Sokak 8; s/d €14/28; 🖳) Quieter than many, this characterful place (with its carpet-clad walls and rose-tinted statuettes) offers small but clean rooms at good value. Rooms vary; ask to see several.

MIDRANGE & TOP END

İzmir's best hotels boast all the usual bells and whistles but aren't great value; check whether a travel agent can't get you a better deal.

Vaunted to open soon (possibly with a new name) is the freshly refurbished, five-star Grand Ephesus Hotel, a Swiss–Turkish venture, which aspires to be İzmir's best.

Hotel Alican 2 (☎ 425 2912; alicanotel@hotmail.com; 1367 Sokak; s/d €19/31; 🖳) Off the main road, conveniently located, newly opened (and so in good nick), and with decent-sized rooms and modern bathrooms (complete with scalloped sink and toilet!), the 13-room hotel offers great value. Breakfast is included.

Hotel Baylan (☎ 483 1426; hotelbaylan@ttnet.net.tr; 1294 Sokak 8, Basmane; s/d €28/45; 🖳) Built by two brothers to fulfil their father's dream, the Baylan prides itself on its reputation as a 'well-managed place with a friendly, family feel'. Off the main street and so quieter than most, it's also got a small but attractive terrace at the back. Ask for a room with a window on the outside. It costs €11 to have an extra bed in the room. To find it, walk up 1294 Sokak (entry opposite the Basmane mosque) and enter through the car park on the left.

Grand Zeybek Hotel (☎ 441 9590; www.grandzeybekhotels.com; Fevzi Paşa Bulvarı 1368 Sokak 5-7, Basmane; s/d €28/50; 🖳) Central, but quieter than many, it's less grand than it purports to be but is a good option if the others are full.

Otel Kilim (☎ 484 5340; www.kilimotel.com.tr in Turkish; Atatürk Caddesi, Çankaya; s/d €47/56; 🖳) Apart from the central, seafront location, recent renovation and good value, the real draw of this hotel is the lovely views from the rooms and restaurants. Only 12 rooms have full sea views, so book one week in advance.

Otel Antik Han (☎ 489 2750; www.nisanyan.com.tr; Anafartalar Caddesi 600; s/d €40/65) Once belonging to Atatürk's father, this is one of İzmir's very few historic hotels. Boutique in style and stylish in décor, it's set around a tranquil courtyard and is a world away from the hustle and bustle of the bazaar outside. The hotel also has six charming little 'flats' (in fact rooms with a mezzanine floor) that cost the same price as rooms.

İzmir Palas Oteli (☎ 465 0030; www.izmirpalas.com.tr; Atatürk Caddesi 2, Çankaya; s €53-64, d €72-83; ✗ 🖳) Established in 1927, the Palas is İzmir's oldest hotel. Modern-oriental in style, it's elegant and well run. Its biggest boon is its location; most rooms have balconies overlooking the bay.

Hotel İsmira (☎ 445 6060; www.hotelismira.com; Gaziosmanpaşa Bulvarı 28; s/d €75/100; Ⓟ 🖳) If you're after the comfort and anonymity of an international, three-star hotel, the İsmira hits the mark. It also boasts good facilities including a sauna, massage service, jazz bar and restaurant with good views.

Otel Karaca (☎ 489 1940; www.otelkaraca.com.tr; 1379 Sokak 55, Sevgi Yolu; s/d €110/138; **P** 🔀) Offering three-star comfort but with a local flavour, the cosy Karaca resembles an Ottoman official's home. Neighbouring a park, it's also quieter than most.

Hilton İzmir (☎ 497 6060; www.hilton.com; Gazios manpaşa Bulvarı 7; s/d €267/295; 🔀 🖳 🔀) Luxuriating in grey marble, the Hilton stands out above all for fabulous views from rooms, restaurants and bars, and good facilities (including health club, pool, tennis and squash courts).

Eating

For fresh fruit, veg or freshly baked bread and delicious savoury pastries (€0.13), head for the canopied market along Anafartalar Caddesi.

RESTAURANTS

The place to be seen on a summer's evening, but also atmospheric, romantic (if you're so inclined) and fun is the sea-facing Kordon. Though you pay for the location – most restaurants have streetside tables with views of the bay – some serve excellent food as well.

In Alsancak, you lose the sunset views but gain on atmosphere. Try in particular 1453 Sokak (Gazi Kadinlar Sokağı).

Kemal'ın Yeri Deniz Mahsülleri (☎ 422 3190; 1453 Sokak 20/A; meals €15-17; 🕑 6am-midnight) Friendly, informal and fun, this restaurant in the Alsancak district prides itself on 'customer satisfaction', and serves good fish dishes at great prices. Try the grilled *kalamar* with the secret – and sumptuous – house 'mayonnaise'.

Balık Pişiricisi (☎ 464 2705; Atatürk Caddesi 212/A; meals €17-23; 🕑 noon-11.30pm) The queues of diners on the street and waiters galloping from table to table tell much about this fish restaurant. Though simple and modern, its reputation for good seafood at reasonable prices is unsurpassed. Try the speciality, *dil şiş* (grilled sole).

Asansör (☎ 261 2626; Dario Moreno Sokağı; meals €20-30; 🕑 8am-midnight) Housed at the top of a 40m lift (built in 1907 by a local philanthropist to help people travel between the Karataş and Halil Rifat Paşa areas of town), the location is İzmir's best. Apart from the stunning panoramic views, it also makes a cool refuge in summer. There's live Turkish music nightly from 8pm to midnight. If you can't afford to eat at the main restaurant, try the smaller Café Moreno opposite (meals €6 to €10, open for the same hours) or come for a beer (from €3). It's about 2km from the town centre.

Deniz Restaurant (☎ 464 4499; Atatürk Caddesi 188/B; meals from €30; 🕑 11am-11pm) Founded by a father and run by his three sons, the family has firmly held onto Deniz's ranking as İzmir's premier fish restaurant. Try the house speciality, *tuzda balık* (fish baked in a block of salt that's dramatically broken at your table) or the sumptuous seafood.

QUICK EATS

Güney Doğ (☎ 446 7662; 1294; Sokak 39; meals €2; 🕑 10am-midnight) Away from the hustle and bustle of the train station on a pretty street under a leafy wall, the charming, elderly owner serves delicious *köfte* and meat and veggie kebaps at heart-breakingly modest prices.

Gül Kebap (☎ 425 0126; Anafartalar Caddesi 415, Kemeraltı; meals €2-3; 🕑 6.30am-5pm Mon-Sat) For a fuel stop in the bazaar, head for this perennially popular place, feeding the good people of İzmir since 1949.

Neşe Köfte (☎ 445 3868; 906 Sokak 28; meal €3; 11am-6pm Mon-Sat) At the other end of the bazaar, this place claims İzmir's 'best-*köfte*-in-town' crown. Try also the *piyas* (white beans and onion in olive oil and lemon juice) – an Aegean speciality. Later, have a coffee at one of the pretty cafés nearby.

Kırçiçeği (☎ 464 3090; Kıbrıs Şehitleri Caddesi 83; kebaps €4-5; 🕑 24hr) Simple, large and bright but spotless and with exemplary service, this is the place in Alsancak to come for good Turkish food at great prices. The pick-and-point menu may help new arrivals or those keen to try out other dishes.

Selanik Lokantasi (☎ 446 5378; 851 Sokak 9; meals €5-6; 🕑 7.30am-5.30pm) Another local favourite is Selanik, which serves hearty, homemade fare.

Tabaklar (☎ 482 2708; 872 Sokak 132, Kemeraltı; meals €5-8; 🕑 11am-7pm Mon-Sat) In the thick of the bazaar, and serving fish at affordable prices, this simple but hugely popular place is one of İzmir's best kept culinary secrets. Try the speciality: *dil şiş* (grilled sole).

Dört Mevsim Et Lokantası (☎ 489 8991; 1369 Sokak 51/A; meals €6-10; 🕑 9.30am-midnight) Famous as far afield as Ankara and İstanbul, this award-winning *lokanta* serves excellent food at reasonable prices. From the open *ocakbaşı* (grill), try the delicious chargrilled-melted cheese, stuffed aubergine kebap or *köfte* with chilli (the house specialities).

THE EVIL ALL-SEEING EYE

However short your trip to Turkey, you can't fail to notice the famous 'evil eye' watching you wherever you go. This age-old superstition is thought to find its roots in pre-Islamic Anatolia. Though ancient, the belief is still remarkably persistent throughout Turkey today, and the beads, pendants and other artefacts emblazoned with the eye are made just as much for the local market as they are for the tourists. No wedding, funeral or baptism, party or any other event goes by without its manifestation in multiple forms.

In a nutshell, certain people are thought to carry within them a malevolent force that transmits to others via the eyes. This destructive – sometimes fatal – force is considered harmful to humans (particularly children) as well as to animals, houses and even individual objects. To combat it, eyes are made to reflect the evil look back to the originator.

Look out for the eyes handmade in many materials ranging from glass, shell and wood to gold, silver and leather, and keeping safe everything from cars to hotel lobbies, restaurant kitchens and *hamams*.

When in Rome… we bought one to dangle from her hired-car mirror! Given the coast's high accident rate, and her safe return (bar one minor incident), it seemed to do its job!

The majority of the evil eye production takes place in the Aegean region, and İzmir is a great place to buy them (see opposite).

NORTH AEGEAN

CAFÉS & PÂTISSERIES

Tuğba (☎ 441-9622; Gazi Osman Paşa Bulgarı 56, Çankaya; 🕑 8.30am-11pm). For dried fruit, Turkish delight and all things nice.

Rıza Aksüt (☎ 484-9864; 863 Sokak 66, Kemeraltı; homemade ice cream €4; pastries €1.40-2; 🕑 8am-8pm Mon-Sat) Open since 1957 and hugely popular locally, the patisserie offers stunning Turkish puds and pastries. Try the swoon-inducing *bal kaymak* (buttermilk drizzled with honey) or *supangle* (chocolate and milk pudding).

Café de Bugün (☎ 425 8118; Atatürk Caddesi 162 1-2; 🕑 8am-11pm) Along the seafront and in complete contrast to the little cafés and patisseries in the bazaar is the posh Café de Bugün, which rather resembles a French Regency salon.

Simorg Café (☎ 445 7449; 895 Sokak 2/A; meals €5; 8am-9.30pm Mon-Sat) With its Orientalist interior (complete with carpets, old maps and portraits of sultans and their harems), this café makes a great place to recline and rest after a run around the bazaar. The 'coffee made in cup' is a speciality of the area as is the *mantı* (Turkish ravioli). There's live Turkish music on Wednesday, Friday, Saturday and Sunday from 7pm to 9.30pm.

Drinking

Emin Çay Evı (☎ 484 0820; Anafartalar Caddesi; coffee €0.25; 🕑 24 hr) A great, old-fashioned teahouse set on a lovely square, this place is in the heart of the bazaar. You can join the locals for a nargileh (water pipe; €2), gossip and people-watch.

Dergah Nargile Ve Çay Evı (☎ 441-0937; Anafartalar Caddesi; 🕑 5am-9pm) Nearby and similar is the Dergah with little tables on the street.

Kalamiş (☎ 425 3901; Atatürk Caddesi 144, Konak; nargileh €3; 🕑 24 hr) For a nargileh over a game of backgammon or *okey* (kind of Turkish dominoes) head for this atmospheric institution. Old men line the yellowed interior, but students (of both sexes) occupy the 1st floor.

Passport Cafè & Bar (☎ 489 9299; Atatürk Caddesi 140; beer €1.65; 🕑 8am-2am) More modern and more central is this new and funky place with tables on the seafront.

Entertainment

The locals start their evening's entertainment with a *passegiata* (stroll) along the Kordon, which is also good for a sundowner on the seafront. For more trendy café-bars, head for the Kordon and Alsancak. Spots particularly popular currently are the row of bars around the Balık Pişiricisi Restaurant and along Sokak 1482 in Alsancak. For dancing, head for Alsancak, the hub of the club scene.

Barcelona (☎ 464 1936; Atatürk Caddesi 220/C; admission free, beer €5.55; 🕑 11pm-4.30am Wed, Fri, Sat Oct-Apr) Split new, this chrome and blue club boasts a large – and usually heaving – dance floor and a good mix of Turkish and European music.

Café Baryum (☎ 463 4902; Atatürk Caddesi 230/A; beer inside/outside €2.25/2.75; 🕑 8am-2am) The lively and popular Baryum plays live music from 9pm to 2am nightly.

Shopping

İzmir's bazaar is a great place for a spot of shopping at sensible prices.

Sipahi Okey (☎ 446 0830; Anafartalar Caddesi 447) For traditional Turkish souvenirs, try this place with lovely *tavla* (backgammon sets from €8), strings of Turkish chillies to cheer up your kitchen or your cuisine, or lovely beaded jewellery.

Alp (☎ 487 0317; 856 Sokak 51, Kemeraltı; ⏱ 8am-6pm Mon-Sat) This amazing shop specialises in the famous evil eye beads (€1 to €5.5; see the boxed text, opposite).

Getting There & Away

AIR

İzmir's airport is expanding rapidly. Recently both British Airways and KLM started flying here directly from Europe.

Turkish Airlines (☎ 484 1220; www.thy.com; Halit Ziya Bulvarı 65, Çankaya) offers nonstop flights to İstanbul (€85, 50 minutes) and Ankara from **Adnan Menderes Airport** (☎ 274 2424), with connections to other destinations.

Onur Air (www.onurair.com.tr), **Atlasjet** (www.atlasjet .com), **Fly Air** (www.flyair.com.tr), the new domestic carrier **Sun Express Airlines** (www.sunexpress.com.tr) and İzmir Airlines (about to be launched at time of writing) also fly to İzmir. See p679 for more details.

A good local ticketing agent for all these airlines is **Green Car** (☎ 446 9131; www.greenautorent .com; Şair Eşref Bulvarı 18/A, Çankaya).

There are also flights between İzmir and Europe on various European airlines (see p672). With the launch of İzmir Airlines, direct flights to Europe will greatly increase, and İzmir is billed to become one of Turkey's biggest hubs.

BUS

İzmir's mammoth otogar lies 6.5km northeast of the city centre. Inside you'll be confronted with a bow-shaped row of bus companies, cheek-by-jowl and all fiercely competing for business. Choose a reputable company (rather than letting them find you – see p679). For travel to coastal towns on Friday or Saturday, buy your ticket a day in advance; in the high season, two days in advance. Tickets can also be bought from the bus company offices in the city centre.

Long-distance buses and their ticket offices are found on the lower level; regional buses (Selçuk, Bergama, Manisa, Sardis etc) and their ticket offices are on the upper level. City buses and dolmuşes leave from a courtyard in front of the lower level.

From İzmir there are frequent local buses to Bergama (€4.45, two hours, 110km), Çeşme (€4.45, 1½ hours, 116km), Foça (€3.35, 1½ hours, 86km), Kuşadası (€4.70, 1¼ hours, 95km), Manisa (€2.20, 50 minutes, 45km), Salihli (for Sardis; €3.35, 1½ hours, 80km) and Selçuk (€2.75, one hour, 80km).

Short-distance buses (eg to the Çeşme Peninsula) leave from a smaller local bus terminal in Üçkuyular, 6.5km southwest of Konak. Recently short-distance buses started picking up and dropping off at the otogar also.

Details of daily long-distance bus services to important destinations are listed in the table, below. There's a **left-luggage office** (emanetçi; depending on size of bag per 24hr €0.85-1.65; ⏱ 24 hr) on the ground floor.

SERVICES FROM İZMİR'S OTOGAR

Destination	Fare	Duration	Distance	Frequency (per day)
Ankara	€14	8hr	550km	every hour
Antalya	€14	7hr	450km	at least hourly
Bodrum	€8	3¼hr	286km	every 30 min in high season
Bursa	€9	5hr	300km	every hour
Çanakkale	€14	6hr	340km	at least hourly
Denizli	€8	3¼hr	250km	every 30 min
İstanbul	from €20-30	9hr	575km	at least every hour
Konya	€17	8hr	575km	every one to two hours
Marmaris	€11	4hr	320km	hourly

TRAIN

Though İzmir has two train stations, **Alsancak Garı** (☎ 464 7795) and **Basmane Garı** (☎ 484 8638 information, 484 5353 reservations), most intercity trains as well as the airport train arrive at the latter.

The *Marmara Ekspresi* train to Bandırma (€8.35, 6½ hours) departs from İzmir Basmane at 8.35am and arrives in Bandırma Gar (main station) at 2.50pm.

The Express trains run to Ankara (sleeper €35.60, 13 to 15 hours) daily at 5.45pm, 6.25pm and 7.30pm via Eskişehir (sleeper €7.20 to €8.90, 11½ to 13½ hours). For İstanbul, change at Eskişehir.

Express trains also depart for Denizli (for Pamukkale, €5, five hours) three times daily at 9am, 3.15pm and 6.30pm; Selçuk (€1.70; 1½ hours) at 9am, noon, 3.15pm, 6.30pm and 9.30pm; Nazilli (for Afrodisias, €2.80, four hours) at 9am, noon, 3.15pm, 6.30pm and 9.30pm; Isparta (€7.20, 10 hours) at 9.30pm; Burdur (€6.10, nine hours) at 9.30pm; and Kütahya (€6.70 to €7.80, eight hours) at 1pm and 7.30pm.

For trains to northern or eastern Turkey, change at Ankara.

Getting Around
TO/FROM THE AIRPORT
The airport is 18km south of the city near Cumaovası on the road to Ephesus and Kuşadası. Frequent Havaş airport buses (€7, 30 minutes) leave from Gaziosmanpaşa Bulvarı, north of the Hilton, and from the airport (where they meet flights).

More or less hourly suburban trains (€1.10, 30 minutes) connect the airport with Basmane Garı (€1.10), but a taxi (€20 to €30, 30 minutes) is likely to be faster and more dependable.

TO/FROM THE BUS STATIONS
If you've arrived at the main otogar on an intercity bus operated by one of the larger bus companies, a free shuttle *servis* is provided to Dokuz Eylül Meydanı in Basmane. If you arrive on a local bus, you can catch a dolmuş (€0.80, 25 mins) that runs every 15 minutes between the otogar and both Konak and Basmane Garı, or you can take buses 54 and 191 (every 20 minutes), bus 64 (every hour) to Basmane (€0.85) or bus 505 to Bornova (€0.85). Tickets can be bought either on board the bus or at the white booth beside the bus stop.

To get to the otogar, the easiest way is to buy a ticket on an intercity bus at Dokuz Eylül Meydanı and then take the bus company's *servis*. However, if you need to take a local bus from the otogar (eg to Salihli), you'll need to take a dolmuş or bus from Basmane or Bornova.

To get to the bus station at Üçkuyular, catch bus 11 (€0.85) from the Konak bus terminal. Soon, you can also take the metro (right).

BOAT
The nicest way to get about İzmir is by **ferry** (🕒 7am-11pm). Frequent timetabled services link the piers at Konak, Pasaport and Al-

sancak. *Jetons* (transport tokens) cost €1.10 each.

BUS
City buses lumber along the major thoroughfares, but the one-way system and lack of numbering on the bus stops makes them hard for outsiders to use. Two major terminal or transfer points are Montrö Meydanı, by the Kültür Park, and Konak, beside the Atatürk Evi. You can buy a ticket (€0.85) from a white kiosk in advance or on board from the driver.

CAR
The large international car-hire franchises and many smaller companies all have desks (open 24 hours) at the airport, and many have a desk in town.

Avis (☎ 274 2174; www.avis.com.tr)
Europcar (☎ /fax 274 2163)
Green Car (☎ 446 9131; www.greenautorent.com; Şair Eşref Bulvarı 18/A, Çankaya) A good local company and the largest in the Aegean region.
Hertz (☎ 274 2193; fax 274 2099)

METRO
İzmir's **metro** (🕒 6.30am-11.30pm; jeton €0.83) is clean and quick, but there is no route map. It runs from Üçyol to Bornova via Konak (though you're most likely to use it to get from Basmane station to Konak or Bornova). When the new extension opens, it will also run between Üçyol and Üçkuyular (the short-distance bus terminal).

TAXI
You can either hail a taxi or pick one up from a taxi stand or from outside one of the big hotels. Fares start at €0.70 and depend on distance; prices are 50% more at night. Make sure the meter is switched on.

AROUND İZMİR
If you are staying in İzmir for a few days, a number of destinations make good day or half-day excursions. Local buses leave from the upper level of İzmir otogar.

Manisa
☎ 0236 / pop 250,080
Backed by craggy mountains, the mainly modern town of Manisa was once the ancient town of Magnesia ad Sipylus. Although early Ottoman sultans left Manisa many fine

mosques, retreating Greek soldiers wreaked terrible destruction during the War of Independence. Today the main reasons to visit are to inspect the mosques and the finds from Sardis in the museum or to take in the Mesir Şenlikleri festival.

SIGHTS & ACTIVITIES

Of Manisa's many old mosques, the **Muradiye Camii** (1585), the last work of the famous architect Sinan, has the most impressive tilework. The adjoining building, originally constructed as a soup kitchen, is now **Manisa Museum** (admission €1.10; ☻ 9am-noon & 1-5pm Tue-Sun), which houses some fine mosaics from Sardis.

More or less facing the Muradiye, the **Sultan Camii** (1522) features some gaudy paintings. The **hamam** (admission €5; ☻ 10am-9pm) next door has separate entrances for men and women. Perched on the hillside above the town centre is the **Ulu Cami** (1366), ravaged by the ages and not as impressive as the view from the teahouse next to it.

FESTIVALS & EVENTS

Should you be able to visit during the four days around the spring equinox, you would be able to catch the **Mesir Şenlikleri**, a festival in celebration of *mesir macunu* (power gum).

According to legend, over 450 years ago a local pharmacist named Müslihiddin Celebi Merkez Efendi concocted a potion to cure Hafza Sultan, mother of Sultan Süleyman the Magnificent, of a mysterious ailment. Delighted with her swift recovery, the queen mother paid for the amazing elixir to be distributed to the local people. In fact, the Ottomans had a long-standing custom of eating spiced sweets at Nevruz, the Persian New Year.

These days townsfolk in period costumes re-enact the mixing of the potion from sugar and 40 spices and other ingredients, then toss it from the dome of the Sultan Camii. Locals credit *mesir* with calming the nerves, stimulating the hormones and immunising against poisonous stings.

GETTING THERE & AROUND

It's easiest to get to Manisa by hourly bus from İzmir (€2.25, 45 minutes, 30km). You can continue direct from Manisa to Salihli (€1.60, 1½ hours) to see the ruins at Sart.

To get to Manisa's historic mosques, take dolmuş 5 from in front of the otogar (€0.25) and hop off at Ulu Parki.

Sardis (Sart)

Sardis was once the capital of the wealthy Lydian kingdom that dominated much of the Aegean before the Persians came along. Its ruins, 90km east of İzmir, make a particularly worthwhile excursion destination.

Sardis was near the Pactolus River, which carried specks of gold that the Lydians collected with fleece sieves. Croesus (560–546 BC) was a king of Lydia, and the Greeks presumably thought him abnormally rich because he could store so much wealth in his seemingly bottomless pockets rather than in the form of vast estates and livestock. Coinage seems to have been invented here, hence the phrase 'rich as Croesus'. Sardis became a great trading centre partly because its coinage facilitated commerce.

The then Persian town was sacked during a revolt in 499 BC. After the Persians, Alexander the Great took the city in 334 BC and embellished it even more. Unfortunately, an earthquake brought down its fine buildings in AD 17, but it was rebuilt by Tiberius and developed into a thriving Roman town. The end for Sardis happened soon after Tamerlane visited in 1401 in his usual belligerent mood.

The ruins of Sardis are scattered around the village of Sart (Sartmustafa) in a valley overshadowed by a strikingly craggy mountain range.

SIGHTS

The most extensive **ruins** (admission €1.10; ☻ 8am-5pm, high season to 7pm) lie at the eastern end of Sart village, immediately north of the road. Information panels dot the site.

You enter the site along a **Roman road**, past a well-preserved **Byzantine latrine** and rows of **Byzantine shops**, many of which once belonged to Jewish merchants and artisans because they backed onto the wall of the great synagogue. Note the elaborate drainage system, with pipes buried in the stone walls. Some of the buildings have been identified from inscriptions and include a restaurant, Jacob's Paint Shop, an office, a hardware shop, and shops belonging to Sabbatios and Jacob, an elder of the synagogue. At the end of the Roman road an inscription on the marble paving stones was done in either AD 17 or 43 to honour Prince Germanicus.

Turn left from the Roman road to enter the **havra** (synagogue), impressive because of its size and beautiful decoration: fine geometric mosaic paving and coloured stone on the walls.

Beside the synagogue is the grassy expanse of what was once the *hamam* and gymnasium. This complex was probably built in the 2nd century AD and abandoned after a Sassanian invasion in AD 616.

Right at the end is a striking two-storey building called the **Marble Court of the Hall of the Imperial Cult**, which, though heavily restored (and somewhat hideous), gives an idea of the former grandeur of the building. Note the finely chiselled Greek inscriptions and the serpentine fluting on the columns. Behind it you'll find an ancient **swimming pool** and rest area. Look out also for the Roman altar with two Roman eagles on either side and lions back-to-back.

Across the road from the enclosed site continuing excavations have uncovered a stretch of the **Lydian city wall** and a **Roman house** with painted walls right on top of an earlier Lydian residence.

TEMPLE OF ARTEMIS

A sign points south down the road beside the teahouses to the **Temple of Artemis** (admission €1.25; ⊗ 8am-5pm), just over 1km away. Today, only a few columns of a once magnificent but never completed building still stand. Nevertheless, the temple's plan is clearly visible and very impressive. Next to it is an **altar** used since ancient times, refurbished by Alexander the Great and later by the Romans. Clinging to the southeastern corner of the temple is a small brick **Byzantine church**.

As you head back to İzmir, look to the north of the highway and you'll see a series of softly rounded **tumuli**, the burial mounds of the Lydian kings.

GETTING THERE & AWAY

Buses for Salihli (€3, 1½ hours, 90km) leave from İzmir otogar at least every 30 minutes. You must then take an onward dolmuş to Sart (€0.35, 15 minutes, 9km) from the back of Salihli otogar.

Buses also run between Salihli and Manisa (€1.60, 1½ hours), making it possible to visit both places in the same day.

ÇEŞME PENINSULA

The Çeşme Peninsula is İzmir's summer playground, which means that it can get very busy with Turkish tourists at weekends and during the school holidays. The main place to visit is Çeşme itself, which is also a transit point for getting to the Greek island of Chios. Alaçatı, with its lovely Greek-village feel, is well worth an excursion; it's also fast becoming a mecca for windsurfers. There are pleasant beaches all around the peninsula.

ÇEŞME
☎ 0232 / pop 21,300

Çeşme, 85km due west of İzmir, has perked up considerably in recent years and now makes a good base for a few days' holiday, especially when travelling to and from the Greek island of Chios, 8km away across the water. Inevitably it's popular with weekending İzmirlis and can get busy during the school holidays, when prices rise accordingly.

Orientation & Information

The **tourist office** (☎ /fax 712 6653; İskele Meydanı 6), ferry and bus ticket offices, banks with ATMs, restaurants and hotels are all within two blocks of Cumhuriyet Meydanı, the main square near the waterfront with the inevitable statue of Atatürk.

Just off the main square is the new **Triatek** (3048 Sokak; per hr €1.65; ⊗ 10am-1am) internet café with fast connections and modern machines.

The otogar is almost 1km south of Cumhuriyet Meydanı, although you can just as easily pick up transport to İzmir, Ilıca or Alaçatı from the western end of İnkilap Caddesi.

Sights

The Genoese **fortress**, whose dramatic walls dominate the town centre, was built in the 16th century and repaired by Sultan Beyazıt, son of Sultan Mehmet the Conqueror (Mehmet Fatih), to defend the coast from attack by pirates. Later the Knights of St John of Jerusalem based on Rhodes also made use of it. The battlements offer excellent views of Çeşme but otherwise the interior is disappointingly empty. The one exception is the north tower, which houses the **Çeşme Museum** (Çeşme Müzesi; admission €1.65; ⊗ 8am-5pm), displaying some archaeological finds from nearby Erythrae.

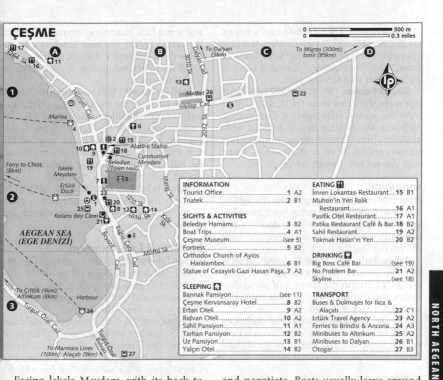

ÇEŞME

INFORMATION
Tourist Office...1 A2
Triatek...2 B1

SIGHTS & ACTIVITIES
Belediye Hamamı.....................................3 B2
Boat Trips...4 A1
Çeşme Museum...............................(see 5)
Fortress...5 B2
Orthodox Church of Ayios
   Haralambos...6 B1
Statue of Cezayirli Gazi Hasan Paşa...7 A2

SLEEPING
Barınak Pansiyon.............................(see 11)
Çeşme Kervansaray Hotel.....................8 B2
Ertan Oteli..9 A2
Rıdvan Oteli...10 A2
Sahil Pansiyon.......................................11 A1
Tarhan Pansiyon...................................12 B2
Uz Pansiyon..13 B1
Yalçın Otel..14 B2

EATING
İmren Lokantası Restaurant....15 B1
Muhsin'in Yeri Balık
   Restaurant...........................16 A1
Pasifik Otel Restaurant............17 A1
Patika Restaurant Café & Bar..18 B2
Sahil Restaurant.....................19 A2
Tokmak Hasan'ın Yeri.............20 B2

DRINKING
Big Boss Café Bar................(see 19)
No Problem Bar......................21 A2
Skyline................................(see 18)

TRANSPORT
Buses & Dolmuşes for Ilıca &
   Alaçatı.................................22 C1
Ertürk Travel Agency...............23 A2
Ferries to Brindisi & Ancona....24 A3
Minibuses to Altınkum.............25 A1
Minibuses to Dalyan...............26 B1
Otogar..................................27 B3

Facing İskele Meydanı, with its back to the fortress, is a **statue of Cezayirli Gazi Hasan Paşa** (1714–90), who was sold into slavery but became a grand vizier. He is shown caressing a lion.

To the north, the imposing but redundant 19th-century **Orthodox Church of Ayios Haralambos** (İnkilap Caddesi) is used for temporary exhibitions of arts and crafts during the summer months.

Past the Çeşme Kervansaray Hotel on Bağlar Çarşı Caddesi is Çeşme's restored 18th-century **Belediye hamamı** (712 5386; Bağlar Çarşı Caddesi; 10am-10pm Jun-Sep; wash & massage €18). With its dome and marble interior, it's an attractive place. Bathing is mixed (though *peştemals* – *hamam* bathtowels – are used). Opening hours are sporadic at other times of the year.

Boat Trips

From June to September, *gülets* offer one-day **boat trips** (€12 to €14 including lunch) to the nearby islands of Wind Bay, Black Island and Donkey Island, where you can swim and snorkel. Browse the waterfront to compare prices

and negotiate. Boats usually leave around 10am and return around 5pm.

Sleeping

BUDGET

Yalçın Otel (712 6981; www.yalcinhotel.freeservers.com; 1002 Sokak 10; s/d €17/22; May-Oct;) Perched on the hillside overlooking the harbour, the hotel has 18 spotless, well-maintained rooms. The biggest drawcards are the two large terraces with sunbeds and fabulous views, and its midrange quality for a budget price. Out of season, you may be able to stay here if you call in advance.

Uz Pansiyon (712 6579; Sokak 3010 11; s/d high season €14/28, low season €11/19;) Close to the bus station and 450m from the centre, this is one of Çeşme's cheapest, but it's spotless and terrific value.

Sahil Pansiyon (712 6934; www.sahilpansiyon.com; 3265 Sokak 3; d high/low season from €28/22;) This is a peaceful place up the stairs beside the Barınak in a rambling house and garden. The immaculate rooms have small balconies, some with sea views (ask for room 9). The family's very accommodating and keen to please.

Tarhan Pansiyon (☎ 712 6599; Kervansaray Yanı; s/d €14/28) Lying 30m off Beyazıt Caddesi, this tiny but rather sweet pension clings to the hillside. Basic, cheap but clean and central, it also has a pretty little roof terrace.

Barınak Pansiyon (☎ 712 6670; 3052 Sokak 58; s/d high season €17/33, low season €14/28; ☒) Uphill from the marina, 600m north of Cumhuriyet Meydanı, this is a family-run pension with glorious vistas of the whole bay from the two terraces shared by six of the rooms – make sure you get one. Rooms are simple.

MIDRANGE

Ertan Oteli (☎ 712 6795; Hurriyet Caddesi 12; d high/low season €50/33; ☒) Though rather institutional in smell and feel, the rooms have decent-sized balconies from where you can see and hear the sea lapping the shore.

Rıdvan Oteli (☎ 712 6336; ridvanotel@ttnet.net.tr; Cumhuriyet Meydanı 11; s/d high season €39/56, low season €22/33; ☒) Slap in the centre and somewhat smart, the real boon is the room balconies with side views of the sea.

The old **Çeşme Kervansaray Hotel** (Bağlar Çarşı Caddesi), formerly the town's top hotel, is currently closed, but may reopen in the distant future under private ownership.

Eating

There's a row of cheap eateries along İkilap Caddesi. For self-caterers, there's a **Migros** (☎ 712 6668; Atatürk Bulvarı 68; ☺ 8am-8pm) supermarket about 1km from the city centre heading northeast on the İzmir road.

Tokmak Hasan'ın Yeri (☎ 712 0519; Çarşı Caddesi 11; mains €1.65-3.35; ☺ 7am-8pm Mon-Sat) Hidden away except to those in the know, this simple place serves terrific home cooking at unbeatable prices. Head straight for the little garden at the back; it's cool and quiet and oasis-like.

İmren Lokantası Restaurant (☎ 712 7620; İnkilap Caddesi 6; meals €6; ☺ noon-9pm) Çeşme's first restaurant and set in a bamboo-roofed atrium with fountain and plants, it's famous locally for its traditional, high-quality Turkish food, which changes daily.

Patika Restaurant Café & Bar (☎ 712 6357; Cumhuriyet Meydanı; meals €5-10; ☺ 3pm-midnight) A well-kept local secret, this is the place for fish at affordable prices. Alcohol is not served. Between 9pm and 1am daily there's live Turkish music and sometimes belly dancing.

Pasifik Otel Restaurant (☎ 712 7465; 3264 Sokak; fish & salad €6; ☺ noon-9pm) If you fancy a walk and some fish, head here, around 1km from the centre on the seafront. It offers a great-value three-course fixed menu (with fish) for €7.25 on tables just metres from the beach; the locals love it.

Sahil Restaurant (☎ 712 8294; Cumhuriyet Meydanı 12; meals €10-12; ☺ 8am-midnight) Right on the waterfront, this Mediterranean-styled place is known for its fish (though its meat dishes are also good). But make sure you ask the fish prices in advance; for some travellers, the bill's been a nasty surprise. *Barbun* (red mullet, €20) is the house speciality.

Muhsin'in Yeri Balık Restaurant (☎ 712 9405; 3264 Sokak 3; meals €14; ☺ 10am-midnight) This new place to the north of town is also recommended for its fish.

Drinking & Entertainment

Big Boss Café Bar (☎ 712 1886; seafront; beer €1.65, coffee €1.40; ☺ 8am-midnight) With tables on the seafront and English newspapers, this new café is a relaxed and (with its competitive prices) cheap way to enjoy the seafront.

Skyline (☎ 712 7567; Cumhuriyet Meydanı; beer €2.75; ☺ 10am-3am, later in high season) Calling itself a 'dance-bar', this tiny place (in the same building as Patika Restaurant Café Bar) was Çeşme's best when we visited. It has a lovely terrace.

No Problem Bar (☎ 712 9411; Çarsı Caddesi 14; beer €1.65; ☺ 7.30am-3am high season only) Unashamedly traveller-trapping, it nevertheless offers beer at competitive prices and bacon butties to boot!

Getting There & Away

BUS

Unfortunately, you have to transit İzmir to get to Çeşme (and from Çeşme to most other places) as there's no longer any onward public transport from Urla to Çeşme.

Buses from Çeşme's otogar run at least every 45 minutes to İzmir's main otogar (€4.45, two hours) and its smaller, western Üçkuyular terminal (€4.15, 1¼ hours, 85km).

There are daily direct buses to İstanbul (€25, nine hours) and to Ankara (€45, seven hours).

Dolmuşes for Ilıca and Alaçati leave from a spot 200m northeast of the town centre; minibuses to Dalyan from near the Hükümet Konağı (Government Building) on Dalyan Caddesi. Minibuses to Altınkum leave from near the tourist office.

FERRY

Many travellers visit Çeşme on their way to or from the nearby Greek island of Chios. Ferries sail between Çesme and Chios (one way €25, day return €40, open day return €50, car €70 to €90, 50 to 60 minutes) at least five times weekly in high season and twice a week in low season (usually Tuesday and Saturday), generally leaving Çesme at 9.30am and returning from Chios at 5pm. You don't need to buy your ticket in advance unless you have a car.

During the summer (and sporadically throughout the rest of the year) ferries also leave at least once a week to one or more of the Italian ports of Ancona (low season from €77 to €102, high season €255 to €306, car high/low season €158/122, 36 to 40 hours), Brindisi or Bari. Prices and journey durations to Brindisi and Bari are similar to Ancona. As times (and destinations) change every year, check the current timetables. Note that the ferries to Italy do not currently stop off in Greece.

Buy tickets direct from the ferry companies along Turgut Özal Bulvarı such as **Marmara Lines** (☎ 712 2223; www.marmaralines.com; Turgut Özal Bulvarı) as travel agents usually charge commission. Tickets to Chios can be bought from **Ertürk Travel Agency** (☎ 712 6768, www.erturk.com.tr; Beyazıt Caddesi 6/7).

AROUND ÇEŞME
Altınkum

Southwest of Çeşme, Altınkum consists of a series of delightful sandy coves easily reachable by regular dolmuşes that leave from behind Çeşme tourist office (€1.10, 15 minutes, 9km).

There's mercifully little development out here, just simple restaurants and camping grounds (open June to end of September). A few places offer rental equipment for water sports, especially windsurfing (boards from €40/140 per day/week). **Tursite** (☎ 722 1221; per tent/caravan €10/15), 8.5km from Çeşme and 500m before Altınkum, is pleasant and clean with a nice beach and camping ground.

Alaçatı
☎ 0232

Southeast of Çeşme, Alaçatı is a lovely village of old stone houses populated by Ottoman Greeks a century ago. The nearest beach is 4km away (see the boxed text, p240).

Alaçatı is now one of Turkey's most unabashedly upmarket holiday spots, catering primarily for well-heeled İstanbullus and İzmiris. Many of the hotels and restaurants have been done up in almost painfully good taste. It's still a lovely place to wander – through the cobbled streets, antique shops, boutiques, cafés and old stone houses decorated with colourful flowerpots and window baskets.

Note that most hotels (and restaurants) open only from mid-May to mid-October and for Christmas and New Year. Some restaurants open at weekends in low season. Reservations in hotels are recommended; they're essential in the high season.

SLEEPING

Hünnap Pansiyon (☎ 716 7686; bistrohannover@hotmail.com; Kemalpaşa Caddesi 67/A; d with/without bathroom high season €83/67, low season €56/42; ❄) Almost the only 'cheap' option in town, it's nevertheless spotless, traditionally decorated, friendly and pleasant.

Değirmen Otel (☎ 716 6714; info@alacatidegirmen.com; Değirmen Sokak 3; d high/low season €111/89) Signposted off Kemalpaşa (at the western end about 50m from the post office) is this new boutique hotel set in three converted windmills. Rustic in feel but beautifully decorated – right down to old telephones and original stone hearths – it's a gorgeous place.

Alaçatı Taş Otel (☎ 716 7772; www.tasotel.com; Kemalpaşa Caddesi 132; s/d high season €95/117, low season from €67/89; ❄ P) At the eastern end of Kemalpaşa, rustic meets refinement in this lovely old Greek mansion furnished like a private house – which it also is. Zeynep, the dynamic owner, attends to every detail and is a mine of information on the town. It's also got a lovely walled garden, pool and peaceful shaded terrace and is open all year.

O Ev Hotel (☎ 716 6150; www.o-ev.com, in Turkish; Kemalpaşa Caddesi; d with half-board high/low season from €158/128; ❄) In a restored olive-oil warehouse, this beautiful boutique hotel now rather resembles a small Moorish palace. There's a small pool set in pretty walled gardens and the gourmet restaurant has an excellent reputation.

EATING

Rasim (☎ 716 8420; Kemalpaşa Caddesi 44; meals with salad €3.35-5; ◷ 8am-11pm) Established in 1962, this simple but cheerful restaurant (the town's

WINDSURFING IN ALAÇATI

Made up of a strip of sand around a small bay, Alaçatı beach (4km from the town of Alaçatı, 70km from İzmir) is fast becoming known among the windsurfing fraternity as one of the best places in and outside Europe for windsurfing.

The bay's natural geography is said to provide good windsurfing conditions. In some areas, the water is just 1m deep, the wind generally blows from the north (allowing for a surfing angle of 19°) and keeps a constant speed: at least 16 to 17 knots (though it can blow up to 27 knots). Waters are also relatively flat.

The main season is from mid-May to the beginning of November. A few hotels and around a dozen windsurfing clubs have sprung up. Note that, in high season, equipment and lessons should be booked at least one week in advance:

The largest windsurfing club in Turkey, the German-run **ASPC** (Alaçatı Surf Paradise Club; ☎ 716 6611; www.alacati.de; Liman Yolu; boards per day €40-60, per week €140-220, harness per day/week €12/40; storage €12/50; ☼ 15 Mar-Oct) is well designed and professionally managed. It offers good courses and high-quality equipment, with over 160 boards and sails for rent (including kites). A 10-hour beginners' course costs €180; a four-hour advanced course €100; kite instruction costs €180 for six hours. There's also a surf shop, a good café serving drinks and meals, and a spot for caravans (€10 to €15). A camping site is due to open in 2008. For a group of five or more, the centre can also open outside the season.

Orsa Club (☎ 0532 336 3355) boasts a beautiful and peaceful setting on the other side of the bay and is attractively designed and ever-expanding. There's also a windsurfing school, which charges similar prices for courses and equipment to the ASPC, and a camping ground (€10 per person per day). It lies 4km from Alaçatı and 2½km off the main road (signposted) to the bay, along a gravel road.

Hotels are on the main road, between 250m and 700m from the ASPC. Most open from mid-March to mid-December, but some open out of season upon reservation. Most can also pick you up from İzmir's airport (€20).

Çark Pansiyon (☎ 716 7309; fax 716 9738; Liman Yolu 3; s/d with shared bathroom €25/50, 3-person apt €100) Run by a friendly Turkish family, the hotel is modest but quiet and peaceful with good views across the bay. There's also a small restaurant.

Shaka Pension & Bar (☎ 716 0506; Liman Yolu 5; www.shaka-alacati.com; s/d high season €60/70, low season €50/60; ✕) This whitewashed Greek-style house is set in attractive gardens and offers guests regular BBQs, parties, live music and movie shows.

Herman Hotel (☎ 716 6295; www.hermanpension.com; Liman Yolu 4; r Jun-Sep €85, s/d May & Oct €60/75; ✕) With its blue and orange décor and stripy curtains, the place is summery, bright and cheerful. Though simple, the 11 rooms are spotless and have pleasant balconies overlooking the bay.

The only restaurant currently on the bay is the nautically themed and family run **Fahri'nin Yeri Liman Restaurant** (☎ 716 7691; Liman Yolu; meal €20, beer €2; ☼ 10am-11pm all year) serving fish only. Set off the main road near the seafront around 100m from the Çark Pansiyon and with tables under a large willow and awnings, it's a pleasant and peaceful place.

Dolmuşes (€0.85, 10 minutes) run every 30 minutes between Alaçatı bus terminus and Alaçatı bay, normally from the beginning of May to the end of September.

first) is still serving hearty Turkish fare at excellent prices. There's also a 'point-and-pick' counter.

Şişarka (☎ 716 8902; Kemalpaşa Caddesi 97; mains from €2.50; ☼ 9am-1am) With tables shaded by fig trees beside a well in a pleasant open courtyard, it serves good, local home cooking at good prices. Try the speciality *güveç Alaçatı* (casserole served in a clay pot). It also has

Turkish/European pizza for €3/5 and is open all year.

Delice (☎ 716 6260; Kemalpaşa Caddesi; meals €5-12) This is an arty little café, boasting a small but attractive garden. Try the delicious home-baked cakes.

Lavanta (☎ 716 6891; Kemalpaşa Caddesi 99; meals €23; ☼ 9am-midnight) If you're tired of Turkish, this Mediterranean bistro-style place serves good

Italian- and French-inspired dishes. There are also tables outside.

Cafe Agrilia (☎ 716 8594; Kemalpaşa Caddesi 75; meals €20-25; ☺ 9am-midnight) Considered Alaçatı's best restaurant, the Agrilia has an impressive setting in a cavernous old tobacco warehouse. Italian-inspired, the speciality is homemade ravioli (€8).

Tuval Butik Restaurant (☎ 716 9808; Kemalpaşa Caddesi 83; meals €25-30) With its lovely wooden beams and whitewashed interior, the Tuval serves good Mediterranean-style food in lovely surroundings.

GETTING THERE & AWAY
Frequent dolmuşes run from Çeşme to Alaçatı (€0.95, 10 minutes, 9km), and from İzmir to Çeşme via Alaçatı (€4.45, one hour, 75km).

SIĞACIK
☎ 0232
More remote and much less spoilt than many coastal towns, Sığacık is a pretty port village, tucked inside crumbling medieval walls. With no beach (which deters the crowds), there's not much to do here except stroll the picturesque waterfront, take a boat trip and watch the fishermen returning with their catch. But, tranquil and peaceful, it's a lovely place to relax.

Sığacık is also famous for its fish, particularly *barbun*, and *kalamar*. If you haven't yet indulged in Turkey's wonderful fresh fish, now might be the time.

Sleeping & Eating
Sığacık's hotels are situated on the waterfront. To find them head towards the harbour then follow the waterfront promenade to the right beside the city walls.

With a great family feel and well-maintained, attractive rooms, **Teos Pansiyon** (☎ 745 7463; 126 Sokak 14; d €28; ☒) is great value. Four rooms have sea views, six are like little suites. You can also buy fresh fish from the market and ask the obliging family to cook it for you.

Around 60m beyond the Teos at the far end of the bay, **Sahil Pansiyon** (☎ 745 7199; fax 745 7741; 127 Sokak 48; d small/large €22/28) has 10 simple but cheerful rooms, five with gorgeous Aegean views.

Dominating the harbour, the **Yeni Bur Restaurant** (☎ 745 7305; Liman Meydanı 17; ☺ 8am-

1am) and **Liman** (☎ 745 7011; Liman Meydanı 19; ☺ 9am-11pm) are slightly soulless and touristy. They're not cheap (€5.5 to €14 for 500g of fish), but the fish is fresh and seafront views are good.

Without the views but serving great Turkish food with French flair is **L'Escale** (☎ 745 7650; Liman Meydanı 15; ☺ 8am-midnight). The restaurant specialises in fish, and the fixed menus (€10/15/20/35) with wine, salad and fruit are excellent value.

For cheaper eats, cut inland behind the Burg Pansiyon to find **Çerkezağa** (☎ 745 7421; Sığacük Çarşı içi 7; kebaps €3.35-3.80; ☺ 8.30am-midnight) next to the teahouse, with tables in a delightful courtyard around an old drinking fountain.

Getting There & Away
To get to Sığacık from İzmir you must first take a bus to Seferihisar from the Üçkuyular otogar (p233; €1.95, 50 minutes); buses leave every 20 minutes. From Seferihisar there are regular dolmuşes and buses to Sığacık (€0.55, 10 minutes, 5km).

Coming from Çeşme you will have to travel via İzmir; no dolmuşes run along the coast road from Çeşme to Urla.

AKKUM & TEOS
☎ 0232
Two kilometres over the hills from Sığacık is the turn-off west to Akkum. A protected cove, it used to attract windsurfers in their thousands in summer but has recently been rather eclipsed by Alaçatı (see opposite). Because of this, it's quieter and cheaper here than in Alaçatı and Akkum has larger waves (for wave-jumpers).

Of its two smooth, sandy beaches, Büyük Akkum has the better facilities, but Küçük Akkum is likely to be quieter.

A few kilometres past Akkum are the scattered **ruins** at Teos, primarily a few picturesque fluted columns re-erected amid grass and olive groves left over from a temple to Dionysus, the Greek god of wine. Teos was once a vast Ionian city, and you can roam the fields in search of other remnants (including a theatre and an odeon). It's a good place to come for a picnic.

To get here, follow the road from Sığacık, turn left off the main road where signposted, then keep left all the way to the bottom of the hill (around 5km from Sığacık).

Sleeping & Eating

A couple of large resorts dominate the bay.

With two pools, a PADI dive centre, wind-surfing school, mountain biking, water sports facilities, fitness centre, beach volleyball, basketball and tennis courts, **Club Resort Atlantis** (☎ 745 7456; www.club-resort-atlantis.de; s/d high season from €68/90, low season from €45/60; ❄) is a great place for an activity holiday! Windsurfer hire (all inclusive) costs €20/50 per hour/day. A beginners' course lasting six hours costs €110.

From Akkum, head up to the main road and turn right to the **Teos Orman İçi Dinlenme Yeri**, a pine-shaded forestry department picnic grove about 1km east of the turn-off. Here you can buy snacks and cold drinks to enjoy beneath shady pine trees overlooking the sea.

Getting There & Away

In summer, frequent dolmuşes and city buses run to Akkum from Seferihisar (€1, 20 minutes) via Sığacık.

Taking a taxi to Teos (3km) shouldn't cost more than €10 to €15 including waiting time (but negotiate).

South Aegean

Turkey's south Aegean can convincingly claim more ancient ruins per square kilometre than any other region in the world. Since time immemorial, conquerors, traders and travellers have beaten a path to the mighty monuments, yet few leave disappointed.

However large and loud the crowd (particularly when the local schools are out), the ruins rarely appear overwhelmed. Huge, majestic and aloof they tower above everything, colonised only by the wild poppies and butterflies in spring, or a stork shaping a shabby nest atop a colossal column.

As the sun begins to sink and the coach parties push off, the ruins are suddenly silent again. Turned crimson by the last rays of the setting sun, they seem as tremendous, timeless and enduring today as they must have done millennia ago. For many travellers, these sites supply the enduring memories of their trip.

Turkey's south Aegean sites are special not just for their sheer age, but also for their state of preservation. History isn't just brought to life here, it's kicking and screaming. As well as Ephesus, the ruined Ionian cities of Priene, Miletus and Didyma are also well worth a wander. Lying quite close to the main coastal road, they're all easily accessible.

In between the ruins and providing a welcome rest from them are some clean sandy beaches such as at Pamucak, some ravishing rural villages such as Şirince or little Herakleia, and some attractive, easy-going towns such as Selçuk providing good hotels at great prices. Perhaps the best antidote of all to the culture-vulturing are the full-on, brash and boisterous coastal resorts of Bodrum and Kuşadası, perfect for some partying or for some cool café culture.

HIGHLIGHTS

- Explore extraordinary **Ephesus** (p251), the best-preserved classical city in the eastern Mediterranean
- Shimmy up to **Şirince** (p256), a heavenly hillside village set amid peach and apple orchards
- Admire the Underwater Archaeology Museum, then dance till dawn in **Bodrum** (p272)
- Wander the wilderness of **Dilek National Park** (p263) and swim in the secluded coves
- Hang out in **Herakleia** (p267) and experience the bucolic bliss of rural Turkey
- Roam the remarkable but less-visited ruins of **Priene** (p265), **Miletus** (p266) and **Didyma** (p266)

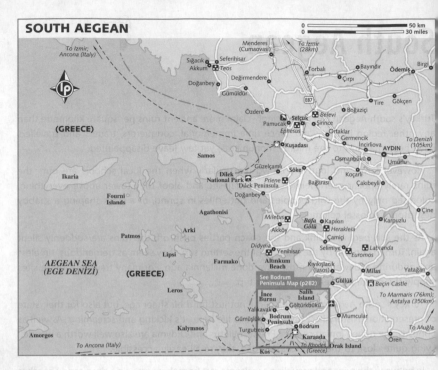

History

The Mycenaean and Hittite civilisations were the earliest recorded along the south Aegean. From 1200 BC, Ionians fleeing Greece established themselves in the area along the coast and founded important cities at Ephesus, Priene and Miletus. South of Ionia was mountainous Caria where the great King Mausolus' tomb, the Mausoleum of Halicarnassus, became one of the Seven Wonders of the Ancient World. Caria was also home to Herodotus, the 'Father of History'. Roman Ephesus prospered with rich trade and commerce, becoming the capital of Asia Minor. The city also attracted a sizeable Christian population. St John settled here with the Virgin Mary, where he is said to have written his gospel. In 1402 the Knights of St John captured the area now called Bodrum where they started building the castle, which today is synonymous with this part of the coast.

SELÇUK

☎ 0232 / pop 25,410

An excellent museum, a fine old basilica and mosque, a stork nest–studded aqueduct, dozens of pleasant, small pensions and the ruins

of Ephesus on its doorstep – Selçuk really does seem to have it all. These days the town more or less lives on the proceeds of tourism, albeit of the smaller-scale, independent-traveller kind.

Orientation

Selçuk otogar (bus station) lies just east of the İzmir–Aydın road (Atatürk Caddesi), with the town centre and some pensions immediately north of it. Three pedestrianised shopping streets – Namık Kemal, Cengiz Topel and Siegburg Caddesi – run east from a round fountain on the main road, north of the otogar, through to the train station.

On the western side of the main road a park spreads out in front of one wing of the famous Ephesus Museum. Many more small pensions can be found in the quiet streets between the museum and Ayasuluk Hill, northwest of the town centre.

Information

There are banks with ATMs and foreign exchange offices along Cengiz Topel and Namık Kemal Caddesis. The internet cafés on Cengiz

SELÇUK

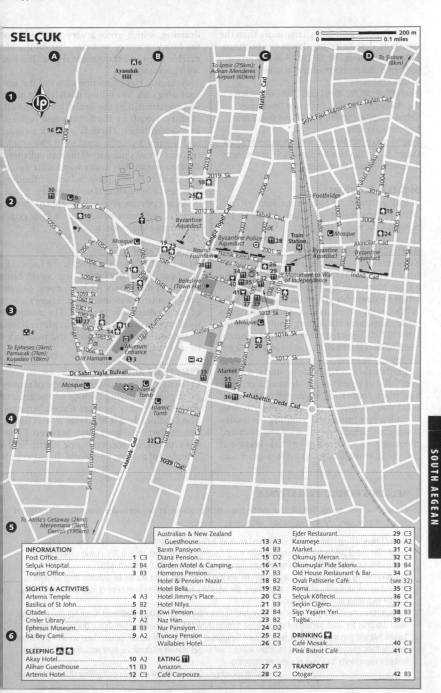

0 — 200 m
0 — 0.1 miles

SOUTH AEGEAN

Topel Caddesi generally charge more than the pensions, despite having slower connections.

Ephesus Assistance (☎ 892 2500) A 24-hour hotline, and services that are recognised by most major travel insurance companies.

Post office (☎ 892 2841; Cengiz Topel Caddesi) Will also change cash, travellers cheques and Eurocheques.

Selçuk Hospital (☎ 892 9814; Dr Sabri Yayla Bulvarı) Near the tourist office.

Tourist office (☎ 892 6945; www.selcuk.gov.tr; Agora Caddesi 35; ☉ 8am-noon & 1-5pm Mon-Fri winter, daily in summer) Opposite the museum.

Sights & Activities

Selçuk's attractions open from 8am to 7pm May to September and 8am to 5pm (or 5.30pm) the rest of the year.

BASILICA OF ST JOHN

St John is said to have come to Ephesus twice: once between AD 37 and AD 48 with the Virgin Mary, and again at the end of his life, when he wrote his gospel on Ayasuluk Hill. A 4th-century tomb was believed to house his remains, so in the 6th century Emperor Justinian (527–65) erected a magnificent church, the **Basilica of St John** (St Jean Caddesi; admission €2.80), on top of the tomb.

Earthquakes and building-material scavengers left it as a heap of rubble until a century ago when restoration began; virtually all of what you see now is restored. Nevertheless, it's still a very impressive building (in its day it was considered a near-marvel and attracted thousands of medieval pilgrims). Look out for the information panel with a plan and

drawing, which gives a very good idea of the building's once-vast size – as do the old marble steps and monumental gate. It's well worth a wander.

Ayasuluk Hill offers fine views of the surrounding sites. The hilltop **citadel** to the north was constructed by the Byzantines in the 6th century, rebuilt by the Seljuks and restored in modern times. There is a Seljuk mosque and a ruined church inside but the citadel remains closed since part of the wall collapsed. Restoration work is under way and it should eventually reopen, though lack of funding appears to be holding it up currently.

As at Ephesus, you may be approached to buy 'ancient' coins, which despite their grimy appearance are modern.

İSA BEY CAMİİ

At the foot of Ayasuluk Hill is the imposing and beautiful **İsa Bey Camii** (St Jean Caddesi), built in 1375 by the Emir of Aydın in a post-Seljuk/pre-Ottoman transitional style. There's a bust of İsa Bey diagonally opposite. The mosque is usually open to visitors except at prayer times. Leave your shoes at the door and remember to cover up properly.

TEMPLE OF ARTEMIS

Ephesus used to earn sizeable sums of money from pilgrims paying homage to the ancient Anatolian fertility goddess Cybele/Artemis. The fabulous **Temple of Artemis** (Artemis Tapınağı; admission free; ☉ 8.30am-5.30pm), between Ephesus and Selçuk, was once one of the Seven Wonders of the Ancient World. In its prime it

---

SELÇUK'S FABULOUS FESTIVALS

For such a tiny town, Selçuk has more than its fair share of fab festivals. The following lists its finest. If you can, try and coincide with one.

Camel Wrestling (Third Sunday in January) From all across Turkey, camel owners marshal their male camels for Selçuk. The eve of the festival is celebrated with much feasting, drinking and dancing. It's a great opportunity to hear traditional Turkish folk music. For more on the wrestling itself, see the boxed text, p250.

Oil Wrestling (First Sunday in May) Famous oil wrestlers from right across the region summon their strength to descend on Selçuk. Known in Turkish as *pehlivan,* the wrestlers rub themselves from head to foot with olive oil then wrestle each other until one gives up.

Selçuk/Efes Festival (First week of September) Showcasing not just Turkish traditional dance but also that from other countries too, each participant stages a spectacular show of their homeland's highlights. During the festival, Turkish folk and pop music concerts are also held throughout the city. In the bazaar, Selçuk's best artisans also set up shop: potters, glass makers, carvers, furniture makers and carpet makers all showcase their sensational skills. It's a fantastic opportunity for a spot of souvenir shopping.

With thanks to Osman Bölük for help compiling this information

was larger than the Parthenon at Athens, with 127 columns, all with figures carved around the base. Unfortunately, little more than one pillar now remains, but it's well worth a visit. It's a lovely tranquil place and the enormous pillar gives you a good idea of the vast size of the temple. You can visit the temple on your way to/from Ephesus.

EPHESUS MUSEUM

This excellent **museum** (☎ 892 6010; Uğur Mumcu Sevgi Yolu Caddesi; admission €2.50) houses a striking collection of artefacts brought to life by some good information panels, photos and dioramas. Don't miss the delightful figure of Cupid riding a dolphin, and the exquisitely carved marble statues of Cybele/Artemis. Look out also for the unsettlingly realistic busts of the Roman emperors, including a huge one of the unpleasant Emperor Domition, and the effigies of Priapus, the phallic god plastered on every postcard from İstanbul to Antakya.

There's also a very interesting exhibition based on the excavations of the gladiators' cemetery discovered in 1993. In the future, a 'Religions and Inscriptions' room should open. Go early in the morning to avoid the schools and tour groups, and ideally after seeing Ephesus.

CRISLER LIBRARY

A new arrival to Selçuk, **Crisler Library** (☎ 892 8317; www.crislerinstitute.com; Prof Anton Kallinger Caddesi 40; admission free; ✆ 10am-7pm) is the result of a bequest from a respected American biblical scholar and archaeologist, B Cobbey Crisler. Proving to be a terrific source of information on the ancient, classical, biblical and Islamic history of the area, it also boasts a full lecture program, a well-stocked bookshop and a coffee shop. Set up in order to 'build cross-cultural bridges through the medium of education and scholarly exchange', it's worth a visit – for neophytes as much as hard-core Ephesus fanatics.

BYZANTINE AQUEDUCT

Running east–west intermittently along Namık Kemal Caddesi and Inönü Caddesi stand the impressive remains of a Byzantine aqueduct, which serve today as a handy nesting place for storks who return to the same spots on it year after year. Eggs are laid in late April or May, and the birds stay right through to September.

Sleeping
BUDGET

Competition between Selçuk's many pensions is intense, and the standard of service and value offered by these places is higher here than perhaps anywhere.

Pension and hotel prices are set by the municipality, so proprietors tend to compete on extras. Most offer the following: free breakfast, home-cooked meals at good prices, free transport to Ephesus and Meryemana (and sometime Şirince), free use of bicycles, good-value excursions and free internet access. If any of these are particularly important to you, check first. Many hotels charge extra (say €1.65 per person per day) for use of air-conditioning or fans in summer and heating in winter.

Garden Motel & Camping (☎ 892 6165; info@galleria selcuki di.com; Kale Altı 5; per adult/child €4/2, per tent/car/ campervan €4/2/5, tent hire for 1/2 people €5/6; 🖳) Located 200m north of the mosque, this green and grassy camping ground is large, well designed and well provided with facilities including kitchen, pool, laundry facilities, a pleasant restaurant and amusements for children.

Atilla's Getaway (☎ 892 3847; www.atillasgetaway .com; dm €10, bungalows with shared bathroom €12.50, r with bathroom €16.50; 🖳 🖳) About 2.5km south of Selçuk is Atilla's, a place so lively and buzzing that it feels like a kind of cool holiday camp for 20- and 30-somethings. Its namesake, Atilla, a proactive Turkish-Australian, is very welcoming and keen to please. Facilities include a pool table, table tennis, a volleyball court, travel office and a fun, poolside bar. Horse riding is planned for the future. Accommodation is simple and clean, and all prices are per person and include half-board. Air-con in the rooms is €4.50 extra per day.

Western Selçuk

Australia & New Zealand Guesthouse (☎ 892 6050; www.anzguesthouse.com; 1064 Sokak 12; dm €8, d with shared bathroom €11, d with bathroom €19-22; 🖳 🖳) The rooms, set around a slightly chaotic courtyard covered with international flags are simple (some on the small side), but clean and bright. The drawcard here is the party-feel in summer and the good facilities, including movie nights and BBQs. The roof terrace, covered to resemble a large nomad's tent, is relaxed and mellow.

Barım Pansiyon (☎ 892 6923; barim_pansiyon@ hotmail.com; 1045 Sokak 34; r per person €11; 🖳) Don't

---

AUTHOR'S CHOICE

Naz Han (☎ 892 8731; nazhanhotel@gmail
.com; 1044 Sokak 2; r €50, Jun €61, Jul & Aug €67;
❂ 🖳) Meaning 'coy', the Naz Han is well
named. Hidden away behind high walls
like a precious jewel, this 100-year-old
Greek house has five simple but comfortable rooms arranged around a small but
enchanting courtyard filled with trinkets,
artefacts and antiques. A small roof terrace grants quite good views over Selçuk's
scenic surrounds. Cemil, a retired İstabullu
textile engineer and a fervent foodie, also
has high hopes for his new kitchen.

---

be put off by the hideous exterior that hides
the characterful 140-year-old stone house
behind. Though simple, rooms are comfortable and filled with the wrought-iron work
of Adnan, the owner. There's also a pleasant
courtyard. Neither try-too-hard-traditional-
Turkish nor overly keen to please, this is a
relaxed, understated and tranquil place.

Homeros Pension (☎ 892 3995; www.homerospen
sion.com; 1050 Sokak 3; r per person €11; ❂) With a firm
family feel, as well as a quirky character, the
Homeros boasts two terraces with good views.
The owner, Derviş, is welcoming and eager to
please. A carpenter, he has cobbled together
from his flea-market finds much of the pretty
furnishings in the comfortable rooms.

Hotel & Pension Nazar (☎ 892 2222; www.nazarhotel
.com; 2019 Sokak 14; s/d €17/22, s/d with air-con €22/31,
f with/without air-con €53/39; ❂ 🖳) The mantra
of owner Osman is 'clean and welcoming',
but Nazar is much more besides: there's a
pool set in a courtyard-garden, a large terrace
with stunning views of the fort, and superb
home-cooking courtesy of Ayse, his mother.
Nothing is too much trouble for the charming family and you'll leave feeling part of it.
Rooms are well equipped, well maintained
and comfortable.

Akay Hotel (☎ 892 7249; www.hotelakay.com; 1054
Sokak 7; s €14-25, d €28-33; ❂ 🖳) Spread over two
buildings, the hotel's main asset is its small
pool set in a peaceful garden full of birdsong.
The large roof terrace also has good views, and
there's a small courtyard.

Also recommended if the above are full:

Tuncay Pension (☎ 892 6260; www.tuncaypension.com;
2019 Sokak 1; r per person from €10; ❂) Friendly and welcoming, with rooms around a cool courtyard with fountain.

Alihan Guesthouse (☎ 892 9496; alihanguest
house@yahoo.com; 1045 Sokak 34; r with shower per
person €11; ❂) Newly renovated by the keen-to-please
Isa, his wife Melissa and Sheila the dog, it's a mishmash of
styles but is friendly, informal and cheap.

Eastern Selçuk

Kiwi Pension (Alison's Place; ☎ 892 4892; www.kiwipen
sion.com; 1038 Sokak 26; dm €4-7, s/d without bathroom
€8/16, with bathroom €11/22, air-con €5 extra; 🖳) Owned
by the energetic Alison, an English woman,
and her Turkish husband, the Kiwi Pension is
well run, friendly and fun. Rooms are simple
but spotless and bright (complete with fresh
daisies in a bedside glass), and a few have balconies. Guests can use the pool table, kitchen
and laundry facilities and have access to a
large and lovely private pool set 1km away in
a mandarin orchard. The pension's located in
a quiet neighbourhood of modern apartments
south of the centre.

Diana Pension (☎ 892 1265; brothers_place@mynet
.com; 3004 Sokak 30; s/d with shared bathroom €7/14, with
bathroom €8/17; ❂ 🖳) If you're counting your
Turkish lira, the Diana is cheap and cheerful
with a pretty courtyard and terrace. It's also
quite close to the train station.

Nur Pansiyon (☎ 892 6595; 3004 Sokak 16; www
.nurpension.com; ❂ 🖳) Near Diana Pension, the
Nur has similar rooms and prices.

Hotel Jimmy's Place (☎ 892 1982; www.artemisguest
house.com; 1016 Sokak 19; deluxe r for 1-3 people €39, s €14-19, d
€17-25; ❂ 🖳) Well travelled themselves, the
friendly, efficient and accommodating Turkish-
Australian couple who run this hotel claim to
know 'what travellers want'. They do: there's a
pool, a terrific Turkey-focused 'Travel Library',
a travel agency, a roof terrace with views and a
lift large enough for wheelchair access. Bron,
the Australian co-owner and a trained nurse,
is 'happy to help those with special needs'.
Rooms are bright, cheerful and comfortable
with orthopaedic mattresses. It lies just a few
minutes from the bus station.

If the above are full, try **Wallabies Hotel**
(☎ 892 3204; www.wallabieshotel.com; Cengız Topel
Caddesi 2; s/d €11/22; ❂ 🖳) where some rooms
have aqueduct views, or **Artemis Hotel** (☎ 892
6191; www.artemisguesthouse.net; 1012 Sokak 2; s/d €8/17;
❂), which is good value and has an enclosed
courtyard and serves a good breakfast.

MIDRANGE

Hotel Bella (☎ 892 3944; www.hotelbella.com; St Jean
Caddesi 7; s/d €20/28; ❂ 🖳) Less than 100m from

the basilica entrance, the hotel is convenient and central. Rooms are decorated with attractive flourishes à l'Ottoman including ceramic work, kilims and carvings. Best of all is the large roof terrace (which also serves as the restaurant): closed-in and cosy in winter, or open, bright and breezy in summer. There's a bird's-eye view – literally – of the storks' nests on the aqueduct and over the basilica. The set menus for €7 are good value and get consistently good reports from travellers.

Hotel Nilya (☎ 892 9081; www.nilya.com; 1051 Sokak 7; s/d €31/47; 🖳) Close to the St John Basilica and a step back from the bustle of town is the calm and collected Nilya. Good-sized rooms are well decorated in a traditional style. Those on the 1st floor share a pretty veranda overlooking the lovely, verdant and lantern-lit walled garden. If you're after some R&R, go no further.

Eating

RESTAURANTS

Selçuk Köftecisi (☎ 892 6696; Şahabettin Dede Caddesi; köfte €2.20; 🕒 8am-9pm winter, 8am-midnight summer) Being recently discovered by tour groups, doesn't detract from the superb home cooking of this family-run place. If you want a table outside, come early or later. The prices are unbeatable too.

Old House Restaurant & Bar (Eski Ev; ☎ 892 9357; 1005 Sokak 1/A; mains €2.75-5.55; 🕒 8am-midnight) With tables set in a little courtyard amid grapefruit and pomegranate trees, and decorated with lanterns, bird cages and wicker chairs, this is a pretty, cool and intimate place that does tasty Turkish dishes. Try the appetising speciality 'Old House Kebap' (€4.45) served sizzling on a platter.

Ejder Restaurant (☎ 892 3296; Cengiz Topel Caddesi 9/E; köfte €3-4.45; 🕒 8.30am-11pm) Receiving warm words from travellers, this simple little place is picturesquely set near a fountain with views of the aqueduct. Run by a welcoming husband-and-wife team, Mehmet does the meat, his wife the veg. All of the food is pretty tasty.

Amazon (☎ 892 3879; Prof Anton Kallinger Caddesi 22; mains €6-8; 🕒 10am-midnight) With its classical music and stools around a bar, the brand-new Amazon looks more wine-bar than restaurant, but the İzmiri chef has a great reputation and serves good international dishes using fresh local ingredients. The set lunch (€5 to €6) is great value. The paintings hung on the walls

are by young local artists and are for sale. Outside there are a few tables with distant views of the Artemis temple.

Okumuş Mercan Restaurant (☎ 892 6196; 1006 Sokak 44; meze €1.65; mains €2.75-4.45; 🕒 7am-11pm) Set in a small courtyard beside a fountain in the shade of a 100-year-old mulberry tree, this place is loved locally for its traditional home fare at good prices.

Turkish puds can be fetched later from the neighbouring **Ovalı Patisserie Café** (☎ 892 4882; 1006 Sokak 43; 🕒 8am-midnight). Another place, still smaller and simpler, but with an equally good reputation for food, is **Seçkin Ciğerci** (☎ 892 3546; Tahsin Başaran Caddesi 4; köfte or kebap €2.75; 🕒 6am-10pm). Going since 1956 and run by four generations of the same family from the cosiest kitchen you've ever seen, it's a great place.

CAFÉS & QUICK EATS

Sişçi Yaşarın Yeri (☎ 892 3487; Atatürk Caddesi; 🕒 9am-10pm winter, 10am-midnight summer) As well as the stall on the street, there's also a delightful shaded area around the back with a few tables. This place is hugely popular with those in-the-know for its delicious köfte and kebaps (all €1.95).

Okumuşlar Pide Salonu (☎ 892 6906; Şahabettin Dede Caddesi 2; pide €1.40-2.25; 🕒 10am-11pm) Next door to the bus station (and one of several branches), this place does fabulous pides (including veggie ones).

If you fancy a cuppa, gözleme (savoury crêpe, €1.40 to €1.95) or even a snooze in between the sightseeing, amid cool and verdant rambling gardens, pop into the **Karameşe** (☎ 892 0466; St Jean Cadessi 18; meals about €5; 🕒 9am-midnight) across the road from the mosque.

Roma (☎ 892 6436; Siegburg Caddesi 21; 1 scoop €0.40; 🕒 8am-midnight Apr-Dec) Having learnt the art of ice cream–making from his father, Feridun, the owner, now produces some heavenly homemade flavours. His particular recommendations are: walnut, black mulberry and mixed chocolate.

Café Carpouza (☎ 892 9264; Argenta Caddesi 8; snacks €0.90-3; 🕒 9am-midnight) Housed in the 133-year-old former railway workers' lodging in the middle of a large green square, this is a cool, tranquil and relaxing place for breakfast (€2.75), a beer (€1.10) or a cup of coffee (€0.55) either on the veranda or inside the atmospheric building. Run by the municipality, prices are kept low; this place offers the best value in town.

SELF-CATERING

Tuğba (☎ 892 1773; 1006 Sokak; ⌚ 9am-midnight) Recently awarded second prize for the 'Best Turkish Delight in Turkey', this well-known chain sells Turkish delight in all colours, flavours and forms, as well as dried nuts, seeds and fruit (great for long bus journeys). They also gift-wrap if you want to cart a year's supply home (€3.85 for 450g). Try the exquisite *duble anterplı* (pistaccio-studded variety).

Every Saturday, Selçuk holds a fantastic **market** (Şahabettin Dede Caddesi; ⌚ 9am-5pm winter, 8am-7pm summer) behind the bus station. With its fresh fruit, veg, cheese and olives, it's a great place to stock up for a picnic.

Drinking

Pink Bistro Café (☎ 892 9801; Siegburg Caddesi 24; beer/spirits €1.65/2.75; ⌚ 10am-2am winter, 10am-4am summer) The oldest drinking establishment in Selçuk, it's called a café, looks like a pub, but functions as a bar-cum-nightclub. Ask Mesut, the bar tender, to demonstrate some magic tricks.

Café Mosaik (☎ 892 6508; 1005 Sokak 6/B; beer/nargileh €1.65/2.75; ⌚ 10pm-1am winter, 9.30pm-3am summer). New on the scene and like a kind of open-ended den, it's carpet-clad and cushioned and decorated *à la Turquie*. It's a fun place for beer or a nargileh with a good mix of European, Turkish and Arabic music.

Getting There & Around

BUS & DOLMUŞ

Selçuk's otogar is across the road from the tourist office. While it's easy enough to get to Selçuk direct from İzmir (€2.10, one hour, 80km), coming from the south or east you generally have to change at Aydın, from where buses leave almost hourly to other destinations (such as Bodrum, Marmaris, Fethiye, Denizli and Antalya). Dolmuşes to Aydın (€2.25, one hour) leave every 40 minutes from Selçuk.

There are direct buses from Selçuk nightly for İstanbul (€20, 11 hours) via Bursa, and in summer at least one bus daily to Pamukkale (€8.35).

CAMEL WRESTLING

Though camel wrestling exists throughout Turkey, it's primarily found along the Western Mediterranean and particularly Aegean coasts. Selçuk holds an annual festival (see the boxed text, p246), which is a great place to witness this ancient sport.

Wrestling camels known as *tülüs* are bred by crossing two distinct breeds. During winter, these camels undergo certain physiological changes that make them inclined to mate with females and fight off any male rival. Harnessing the behaviour that this brings – aggression and energy – the locals bring together the animals to 'wrestle'.

Though the camels fight hard, ancient rules and practices govern the sport. First and foremost, camels must use accepted 'techniques' for wrestling. A board of judges and referees presides over the match and 14 *urganci* (ropers) are close at hand to step in and separate the camels if required. The camel's mouths are also bound tightly with string so that they cannot bite one another. Instead, the camels must use their heads, necks and bodies to overcome their opponents.

One of the requirements of the referees is to match camels equally, not just for the safety of the animals themselves but also in order to provide a much more entertaining wrestle. Camels are matched by their experience, past prizes they may have won, their weight, their wrestling skill and the wrestling styles they use.

For a camel to be declared a winner, he must either force his opponent to flee the ring or force him to fall on to his side. Sometimes the fighting is ferocious, but so high is the confidence of the owner in his camel that he will let him continue wrestling even when the fight looks hopeless. Very often the 'losing' camel does indeed turn out victorious. It is also said that top-grade champions never ever flee the ring.

If you get the chance to watch a wrestle, do so: it's a colourful event. Town criers publicise the event, then the *tülüs* – decked out in all their finery – are proudly paraded through the streets by their owners, accompanied by drummers and musicians. Locally, camel wrestling has a large and devoted following. Fans know their camels' names as they do their favourite footballer or pop star. Camels usually take their names from the places they were born, from Turkish folkloric heroes or even from TV or film stars. When we visited, we met camels called 'David Beckham' and 'Colonel Gaddafi'…

Dolmuşes run to Kuşadası every 20 minutes (€1.65, 30 minutes) and Pamucak (€1.10, 10 minutes). There are no buses or dolmuşes to Söke; either change at Kuşadası or take a train (below).

If you're going to Priene, Mila or Didyma, the easiest way is to go to Söke and get one of the many buses from there.

TAXI

Taxis charge €5.60 per carload to Ephesus. For a day's tour from Selçuk to Meryemana, then Ephesus and back, count on €33.

One good plan is to take a taxi to Meryemana for a short visit, then have it drop you at the southern entrance to Ephesus (€28). You can spend as long as you like at Ephesus, then walk the 3km back to Selçuk or flag a passing minibus.

Taxi rides around town usually cost €2.80 and to İzmir airport €100 (though many pensions can organise it for less). You can usually find taxis around the bus station.

TRAIN

Six trains run daily from **Selçuk train station** (☎ 892 6006) to İzmir (adult/child €1.65/1.10, two hours), the first at 6.25am and the last at 7pm year-round. Trains also leave every evening to Söke (one hour) – the first at 7am, the last at 6pm – and five leave daily to Denizli (four hours): the first at 9.39am, the last at 11.05pm.

EPHESUS (EFES)

The best-preserved classical city in the eastern Mediterranean, **Ephesus** (☎ 892 6010; admission/parking €5.50/1.65; ☒ 8am-5pm Oct-Apr, 8am-7pm May-Sep) is *the* place to get a feel for what life was like in Roman times. For information on the two different entrance gates, see Getting There & Away (p255).

Ancient Ephesus was a great trading city and a centre for the cult of Cybele, the Anatolian fertility goddess. Under the influence of the Ionians, Cybele became Artemis, the virgin goddess of the hunt and the moon, and a fabulous temple was built in her honour. When the Romans took over and made this the province of Asia, Artemis became Diana and Ephesus became the Roman provincial capital.

To avoid the heat of the day, come early in the morning or in the late afternoon, when it's less crowded with tour groups. If you can, avoid public holidays altogether. Note that the

terrace houses cost an extra €8.35 (and take about an hour) to visit. Though they were closed at the time of writing for restoration, they should reopen soon.

If your interest in ruins is slight, half a day may suffice, but real ruins buffs will want to make a day of it. Bring water with you as drinks at the site are expensive.

Try and borrow an illustrated guide from your pension or hotel; it will really enhance the experience. Or you can hire one of the 15 Ephesus guides (two hours for two to 20 people for €39) that hang around the ticket barriers. Between them, they speak six European languages.

There are also new (and quite good) one-hour **audio guides** (adult/student €4.45/2.25) available. Note that only Turkish lira are accepted for the admission fee. An exchange office operates opposite the ticket office if you need to change money.

History
EARLIEST TIMES

According to legend, Androclus, son of King Codrus of Athens, consulted an oracle about where to found a settlement in Ionia. The oracle answered in typically cryptic style: 'Choose the site indicated by the fish and the boar'.

Androclus sat down with some fishermen near the mouth of the Cayster River and Mt Pion (Panayır Dağı), the hill into which Ephesus' Great Theatre was later built. As they grilled some fish for lunch, one of the fish leapt out of the brazier, taking with it a hot coal, which ignited some shavings, which in turn ignited the nearby brush. A wild boar hiding in the brush ran in alarm from the fire and the spot at which the fishermen killed it became the site of Ephesus' Temple of Artemis (see p246).

In ancient times the sea came much further inland, almost as far as present-day Selçuk. The first settlement, of which virtually nothing remains, was built on the hill's northern slope and was a prosperous city by about 600 BC. The nearby sanctuary of Cybele/Artemis had been a place of pilgrimage since at least 800 BC.

CROESUS & THE PERSIANS

Ephesus prospered so much that it aroused the envy of King Croesus of Lydia, who attacked it around 600 BC. The Ephesians, who had neglected to build defensive walls, stretched a rope from the Temple of Artemis to the town, a distance of 1200m, hoping to win the goddess' protection. Croesus responded to this quaint defensive measure by giving some of his famous wealth for the completion of the temple. But he destroyed Ephesus and relocated its citizens inland to the southern side of the temple, where they built a new city.

Neglecting again (or perhaps forbidden) to build walls, the Ephesians were forced to pay tribute to Croesus' Lydia and, later, to the Persians. They then joined the Athenian confederacy, but later fell back under Persian control.

In 356 BC the Temple of Cybele/Artemis was destroyed in a fire set by Herostratus, who claimed to have done it to get his 15 minutes of fame, proving that modern society has no monopoly on a perverted sense of celebrity.

The Ephesians planned a grand new temple, the construction of which was well under way when Alexander the Great arrived in 334 BC. Much impressed, Alexander offered to pay for the cost of construction in return for having the temple dedicated to himself. The Ephesians declined his offer, saying tactfully that it was not fitting for one god to make a dedication to another. When finished, the temple was recognised as one of the Seven Wonders of the World.

LYSIMACHUS & THE ROMANS

After Alexander the Great's death, Ionia came under the control of Lysimachus, one of his generals. As the harbour silted up, it became clear the city would have to move westwards. Unable to convince the Ephesians to budge, Lysimachus blocked the old city's sewers during a downpour, causing major flooding. The Ephesians then moved reluctantly to the western side of Mt Pion, where the Roman city remains.

Little survives of Lysimachus' city, although it finally got a defensive wall almost 10km long, which served it well as it allied itself with the Seleucid kings of Syria, then with the Ptolemies of Egypt, later with King Antiochus, then Eumenes of Pergamum, and finally with the Romans. Long stretches of the wall survive on top of Mt Coressos (Bülbül Dağı), the high ridge of hills on the southern side of Ephesus. A prominent square tower, nicknamed 'St Paul's Prison', also survives on a low hill to the west.

With its brisk sea traffic, rich commerce and right of sanctuary in the Temple of Artemis, Roman Ephesus was the capital of Asia Minor and its population rapidly grew to around 250,000. Successive emperors vied with one another to beautify the city and it drew immigrants from all around the empire. Despite the fame of the cult of Diana, Ephesus soon acquired a sizeable Christian congregation. St John supposedly settled here with the Virgin Mary, and St Paul lived in the city for three years (probably in the AD 60s).

THE END

Unfortunately, despite efforts by Attalus II of Pergamum, who rebuilt the harbour, and Nero's proconsul, who dredged it, the harbour continued to silt up. Emperor Hadrian tried diverting the Cayster, but eventually the sea was forced back to Pamucak. Ephesus began to decline. It was still an important enough place for the Third Ecumenical Council to be held here in AD 431, but by the 6th century AD, when the Emperor Justinian was looking for a site to build a basilica for St John, he chose Ayasuluk Hill in Selçuk.

Sights
GYMNASIUM OF VEDIUS & STADIUM

As you walk along the side road from Dr Sabri Yayla Bulvarı, the first ruin you will pass on your left was once the Gymnasium of Vedius (2nd century AD), with exercise fields, baths, toilets, covered exercise rooms, a swimming pool and a ceremonial hall. A bit further along is the Stadium, dating from the same period. The Byzantines removed most of its finely cut stones to build the castle on Ayasuluk Hill. This 'quarrying' of precut building stone from older, often earthquake-ruined structures was, unfortunately, a constant feature of Ephesian history.

DOUBLE CHURCH

At the car park, which is ringed with çay bahçesis (tea houses), restaurants and souvenir shops, to the right of the road are the ruins of the Church of the Virgin Mary, also called the Double Church. The original building was a museum, a Hall of the Muses – a place for lectures, teaching and debates. Destroyed by fire it was rebuilt as a church in the 4th century. Later it served as the site of the third Ecumenical Council (AD 431) which condemned the Nestorian heresy. Over the centuries several

EPHESUS (EFES)

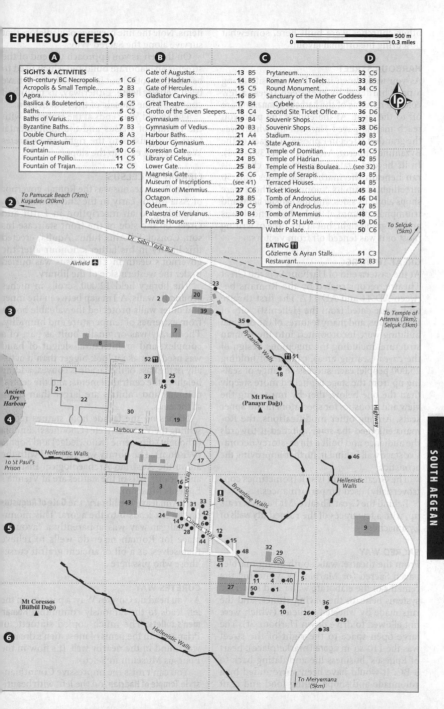

0 ———— 500 m
0 ———— 0.3 miles

To Pamucak Beach (7km);
Kuşadası (20km)

Dr. Sabri Yayla Bul

Airfield ✈

To Selçuk
(5km)

To Temple of
Artemis (3km);
Selçuk (3km)

Byzantine Walls

**Mt Pion
(Panayır Dağı)**
▲

Ancient
Dry
Harbour

Highway

Harbour St

Hellenistic Walls

To St Paul's
Prison

Sacred Way

Byzantine Walls

Hellenistic
Walls

Curetes Way

**Mt Coressos
(Bülbül Dağı)**
▲

Hellenistic Walls

To Meryemana
(5km)

SOUTH AEGEAN

other churches were built here, somewhat obscuring the original layout.

HARBOUR STREET

As you walk down into the main site along a path bordered by evergreen trees, a few colossal remains of the **harbour gymnasium** are off to the right. At the end of the path you reach marble-paved Harbour St, which was the grandest street in Ephesus, a legacy of the Byzantine emperor, Arcadius (r AD 395–408). In its heyday, water and sewerage channels ran beneath the marble flagstones and 50 streetlights lit up its colonnades. There were shops along its sides, and the **harbour baths** and triumphal columns at the harbour end. It was and is a grand sight, but at the time of writing most of it was fenced off from visitors.

GREAT THEATRE

At the eastern end of Harbour St is the Great Theatre, reconstructed by the Romans between AD 41 and AD 117. The first theatre on the site dated from the Hellenistic city of Lysimachus, and many features of the original building were incorporated into the Roman structure, including the ingenious design of the *cavea* (seating area), capable of holding 25,000 people: each successive range of seating up from the stage is pitched more steeply than the one below, thereby improving the view and acoustics for spectators in the upper seats. Among other modifications, the Romans enlarged the stage, pitched it towards the audience and built a three-storey decorative stage wall behind it, further improving the acoustics.

The Great Theatre is still (sometimes controversially) used for performances.

Behind the Great Theatre, Mt Panayır rears up, with a few traces of the ruined **city walls** of Lysimachus.

SACRED WAY

From the theatre, walk south along marble-paved Sacred (or Marble) Way, noting the remains of the elaborate water and sewerage systems beneath the paving stones, and the ruts made by wheeled vehicles (which were not allowed to drive down Harbour St). The large open space to the right of the street was the 110-sq-m **agora** (marketplace), heart of Ephesus' business life and dating back to 3 BC. It would have been surrounded by a colonnade and shops selling food and craft items. Note the fine carvings of gladiators that survive along the Sacred Way.

On the left as you approach the end of the street is an elaborate building, which used to be called a brothel but is now believed to have been a **private house**. Either way, its main hall contains a fine mosaic of the *Four Seasons*.

The Sacred Way ends at the embolos, with the Library of Celsus and the monumental Gate of Augustus to the right, and Curetes Way heading east up the slope.

LIBRARY OF CELSUS

Celsus Polemaeanus was the Roman governor of Asia Minor early in the 2nd century AD. According to an inscription in Latin and Greek on the side of the front staircase his son, Consul Tiberius Julius Aquila, erected this library in his father's honour after the governor's death in 114. Celsus was buried under the western side of the library.

The library held 12,000 scrolls in niches around its walls. A 1m gap between the inner and outer walls protected the valuable books from extremes of temperature and humidity. The library was originally built as part of a complex, and architectural sleight of hand was used to make it look bigger than it actually is: the base of the façade is convex, adding height to the central elements; and the central columns and capitals are larger than those at the ends.

Niches on the façade hold statues representing the Virtues: Arete (Goodness), Ennoia (Thought), Episteme (Knowledge) and Sophia (Wisdom). The library was restored with the aid of the Austrian Archaeological Institute and the originals of the statues are in Vienna's Ephesus Museum.

As you leave the library, the **Gate of Augustus** on the left leads into the agora. This monumental gateway was apparently a favourite place for Roman ne'er-do-wells to relieve themselves, as a bit of ancient graffiti curses 'those who piss here'.

CURETES WAY

As you head up Curetes Way, a passage on the left leads to the famously communal **Roman men's toilets**. The much-copied statuette of Priapus, with the penis of most men's dreams, was found in the nearby **well**. It's now in the Ephesus Museum in Selçuk.

You can't miss the impressive Corinthian-style **Temple of Hadrian**, on the left, with beautiful friezes in the porch and a head of Medusa to keep out evil spirits. It was dedicated to Hadrian, Artemis and the people of Ephesus in AD 118 but greatly reconstructed in the 5th century. Across the street a row of shops from the same period are fronted by an elaborate 5th-century mosaic.

Across from the Temple of Hadrian are the magnificent **Terraced Houses** (Yamaç Evleri; admission €9.50). It's a crying shame that the off-putting admission fee will deter most people from visiting a site that offers the next best chance after Pompeii (Italy) to appreciate the luxury in which the elite of the Roman world lived. In places, the Terraced Houses still stand to two storeys; their walls are covered in frescoes and their floors in elaborate mosaics. To add insult to injury, only the 1st floor of the terraces was open at the time of writing. Some small finds from the houses are on display in the Ephesus Museum in Selçuk (p247).

Further up Curetes Way on the left is the **Fountain of Trajan**. Of the huge statue of the emperor (AD 98–117) that used to tower above the pool, only one foot now remains.

UPPER EPHESUS

Curetes Way ends at the two-storey **Gate of Hercules**, constructed in the 4th century AD, with reliefs of Hercules on both main pillars. To the right a side street leads to a colossal **temple** dedicated to the emperor Domitian (r AD 81–96), part of which serves as a rarely accessible **Museum of Inscriptions**.

Up the hill on the left are the very ruined remains of the **Prytaneum** (a municipal hall) and the **Temple of Hestia Boulaea**, in which a perpetually burning flame was guarded. Finally, you reach the **Odeum**, a small theatre dating from AD 150 and used for musical performances and meetings of the town council. The marble seats at the bottom suggest the magnificence of the original.

To the east of the Odeum are more **baths** and, further east, the **East Gymnasium**. There is a second **site ticket office** across from the slight remains of the **Magnesia Gate**.

Festivals & Events

During the **International İzmir Festival** (see p230) in mid-June to early July many events take place at Ephesus. The world-class acts – opera, ballet and music – are certainly worth getting tickets for. Tickets are sold at the Ephesus Museum (p246) in Selçuk.

Getting There & Away

Many pensions in Selçuk offer free lifts to Ephesus. Note that there are two entry points roughly 3km apart. You may prefer to be dropped off at the upper entrance (the southern gate or *güney kapısı*) so that you can walk back downhill through the ruins and out through the lower main entrance. It's a pleasant 30- to 45-minute walk from the tourist office in Selçuk to the main admission gate.

Frequent Pamucak and Kuşadası minibuses pass the Ephesus turn-off (€0.50, five minutes, 3km), leaving you with a short walk to the main ticket office.

A taxi from Selçuk to the main entrance should cost about €5.55.

AROUND SELÇUK
Meryemana (Mary's House)

Believers say that the Virgin Mary came to Ephesus with St John towards the end of her life (AD 37–45). In the 19th century, nun Catherina Emmerich of Germany had visions of Mary at Ephesus. Using her descriptions, clergy from İzmir discovered the foundations of an old house on the wooded slope of Mt Coressos (Bülbül Dağı), not far from Ephesus. Pope Paul VI authenticated the site on a visit in 1967 and it quickly became a place of pilgrimage. A service to honour Mary's Assumption is held in the chapel every 15 August. Mass is held at 7.15am Monday to Saturday (evening service at 6.30pm), and at 10.30am on Sunday. Note that 'appropriate dress' is required to enter.

The tiny **chapel** (☎ 894 1012; admission per person/car €6/1.65; ⏰ 8am-7pm) is usually mobbed by coach parties. There are information panels in various languages, but if you are interested in why over a million people visit here each year, we recommend *Mary's House* by Donald Carroll, which traces the extraordinary history of the site over 2000 years. You can also write to the **American Society of Ephesus, Inc, George B Ovatiman Foundation** (327 North Elizabeth St, Lima, Ohio, 45801, USA). A small shop also sells brochures (€1.65 to €2.75).

To Muslims, Mary is Meryemana, Mother Mary, who bore İsa Peygamber, the Prophet Jesus. Below the chapel a wall is covered in rags: Turks tie the bits of cloth (or paper or plastic – in fact anything at hand) to a frame and make a wish.

If you want refreshments, head for **Café Turca** (☎ 894 1010; Meryemana Evi; coffee/breakfast €1.10/3.85;

SOUTH AEGEAN

(☽ 7.30am-7pm). Otherwise, the site is a great spot for a picnic – it's cool, verdant and full of birdsong.

The site lies 7km from Ephesus' Lower (northern) Gate and 5.5km from the Upper (southern) Gate. There's no dolmuş service so you'll have to hire a taxi (around €28 return from the otogar) or take a tour.

Grotto of the Seven Sleepers

If you're driving from Meryemana to Ephesus you'll pass the road leading to the Grotto of the Seven Sleepers. According to legend, seven persecuted Christians fled from Ephesus in the 3rd century AD and took refuge in a cave on the northeastern side of Mt Pion. Agents of their persecutor, Emperor Decius, found the cave and sealed it. Two centuries later an earthquake brought down the wall, awakening the sleepers who ambled into town for a meal. Finding all their old friends long dead, they concluded that they had undergone some sort of resurrection. When they died they were buried in the cave and a cult following developed.

The grotto is actually a Byzantine-era **necropolis** (admission free; ☽ 24hr) with scores of tombs cut into the rock. It lies around 200m from the car park (1.5km from Ephesus); follow the well-trodden path up the hill.

It's probably not worth a special trip, although the shady and kilim-covered *ayran* (yogurt drink) and *gözleme* places by the junction make great places for a spot of R&R after Ephesus. The *gözleme* are famous.

Çamlık Steam Locomotive Museum

Trainspotters will delight in this open-air **museum** (☎ 894 8116; Köyü Selçuk; admission €1.65; ☽ 8am-5pm Oct-Apr, 8am-6pm May-Sep), 10km from Selçuk on the Aydin road. The attractively landscaped site has over 30 steam locomotives, some as old as the 1887 C-N2 from the UK, and all of which you are free to climb on. Atatürk had his headquarters here and kept his special white train at this station during Aegean manoeuvres. A new restaurant has opened here but it's open to tour groups only.

Pamucak

☎ 0232

Pamucak beach, a long, wide crescent of soft sand that's reasonably clean, lies about 7km west of Selçuk. The beach is crowded on summer weekends with free campers and Turkish families, but mostly deserted at other times. From February to March, the estuary wetlands (a 15-minute walk from the beach) attract flamingos.

Dereli Motel Restoran (☎ 893 1205; www.dereli -ephesus.net; per tent & per person €10, s/d cabin €28/70; ☽ May-Oct) offers inviting cabins with private bathrooms, some with fridge, and little verandas right on the beach (just 50m from the sea) or overlooking a rose garden. This well-run, German-managed complex also incorporates a restaurant, shop and shady camping area. The beach is kept litter-free, and the restaurant is very reasonably priced. Bring mosquito repellent though!

Minibuses run every half-hour from Selçuk (€1.10, 10 minutes, 7km) in summer and every hour in winter. To/from Kuşadası, go to Selçuk first.

ŞİRİNCE

☎ 0232 / pop 960

Up in the hills 9km east of Selçuk, amid grapevines and peach and apple orchards, sits Şirince, a perfect collection of stone-and-stucco houses with red-tiled roofs. It was probably originally settled when Ephesus was abandoned but what you see today mostly dates from the 19th century. The story goes that a group of freed Greek slaves settled here in the 15th century and called the village Çirkince (Ugliness) to deter others from following them. In 1926 a governor of İzmir decreed that its name be changed to the more honest Şirince (Pleasantness).

A century ago a much larger and more prosperous Şirince was mainly inhabited by Ottoman Greeks and acted as the economic focus for seven monasteries in the hills around. The villagers, who moved here from Salonica and its vicinity during an exchange of populations in 1924, are ardent fruit farmers who also make interesting fruit wines (€3.90 to €5.55), which range from melon to black mulberry. They're delicious served cold as an apéritif.

It is an idyllic place, but in recent years the cruise ships with their 'Authentic Turkish Village' day trips have all but turned it into a parody with high prices and souvenir shops cheek-by-jowl the entire length of the main street. Of course, if you ignore this and stay the night (at a stiff premium of course) you'll be well rewarded with the chance to see the real village after the tour buses have gone.

The minibus from Selçuk drops you at the centre of the village near the restaurants.

Sights & Activities

Although you may want to drop into the ruined **Church of St John the Baptist** and examine its fast-fading frescoes, the real pleasure of a visit to Şirince lies in wandering its pretty backstreets and looking at the lovely old houses.

If you're interested in lace and other textiles, Şirince is also a good, if not exactly cheap, place to shop. Incidentally, if a local woman invites you to inspect her 'antique house', you should assume she'll have lace for sale.

Sleeping

Şirince is a captive market and prices, with a few exceptions can be ludicrously inflated for what you get. Rooms are with bathroom and breakfast is included.

Doğa Pansiyon (☎ 898 3004; r €16.50-33.50) Lying around 200m southwest of the main street up the hill on the periphery of the village, the tiny Doğa has minute but homely and clean rooms and is one of the better 'value' places to stay. There's also quite a pleasant terrace.

Dionysos Pension (☎ 898 3130; www.sirincerehber.com; r €44.50) A tiny but delightful old village house, the Dionysos has four well-maintained and spotless rooms that have retained some of their original features. It's not great value, but the pension has tonnes of character and a dear little garden-terrace outside. Follow the signs from the village centre and look out for the two churches – it lies between.

Kırkınca Pansiyon (☎ 898 3133; www.kirkinca.com; r €50-72, apartments €83-111) Composed of a collection of old houses (offering 15 rooms) and six 'apart houses', the Kırkınca is attractively kitted-out (three of the apartments have four-poster beds) and has lots of character. The biggest boon is the shaded roof terrace of the main building with lovely views overlooking the hills and town. The sitting room contains an ancient Greek amphora with crystallised wine inside.

Nişanyan Evleri (☎ 898 3208; www.nisanyan.com; s/d from €58/89; 🖳) Worth the fairly steep 250m climb to the top of the village is this very attractive, 19th-century, renovated stone house. It's Şirince's smartest place to stay. The five rooms are individually decorated à l'Ottoman, there's a library, several sitting areas, a 'gourmet restaurant' (mains €7 to €13) and a pretty terrace with gorgeous views. Three smaller, restored village houses can also be rented out nearby (€92/139 for one/two people per night). If you don't want to walk here from the village, call for a lift.

Eating

Artemis Şirince Şarapevi Restaurant (☎ 898 3240; pides €1.10-3.35, salad €1.50-2.25, grilled mains €3.85-7; 🕐 8am-midnight) Housed in the old Greek school overlooking the valley, this is a great place for a bite to eat. The interior has old stoves and darkened floorboards; outside there's a lovely, large terrace with great views. It looks expensive but isn't, and the food is good. You can also come here for a drink.

Arşıpel Café (☎ 898 3133; meze €1.65-2.75, mains €5.50-7.25; 🕐 9am-11pm) Part of the Kırkınca Pansiyon is the new Arşıpel Café, which offers an excellent and imaginative menu at reasonable prices. Try the delicious speciality: *kırkınca kebap* (sliced sirloin steak with green pepper, onion and mushroom served with yogurt and garlic and fried aubergine). There are tables outside.

Overlooking the main square where the buses stop with a pleasant shaded terrace and serving both mains and snacks at good prices is **Sultan Han Restaurant** (☎ 898 3179; snacks €1.40-2.25, mains €2.75-5.50; 🕐 8am-11pm).

Getting There & Away

Minibuses (€1.10) leave from Selçuk to Şirince every 15 minutes in summer, and every half-hour in winter.

TİRE, KAPLAN, ÖDEMİŞ & BİRGİ

Pleasant as Selçuk is, no-one could call it undiscovered. However, it's possible to make a straightforward day trip into the Aegean hinterland, which will give you a fascinating insight into less-touristy Turkey. You can do this by dolmuş, but it really works best if you hire a car.

Tire is a modern town with a fascinating old bazaar quarter. Head uphill to find the Tahtakale neighbourhood where it's possible to inspect *hans* (caravanserai) dating back to the 15th century and still in use as shopping centres. Poke around the backstreets and you will be able to watch felt-makers hard at work at a craft that has all but died out elsewhere in Turkey. There are also several interesting 15th-century mosques. Tour groups are brought here for the big Tuesday market, a

---

FILLING FISH

One day, all the fish of the sea came together to plead with God not to be eaten. But God said: 'All creatures must eat and be eaten. What will men eat if they cannot eat fish?' 'All right then,' replied the fish, 'let them eat us but not be filled!' And so it was that men never feel full after eating fish... (And why many Turks today prefer meat!)

Traditional Turkish tale transcribed by Frances Linzee Gordon, with thanks to Mustafa Kemal Gobi

---

great place to stock up on lunch supplies for a relaxing picnic.

About 1km off the Selçuk–Tire road (26km from Selçuk and 15km from Tire) is a restaurant that's well-known in the area. It's a great – and reasonably priced – place to stop for lunch or dinner. **Değirmen** (☎ 529 0066; meals €5; ☺ 8.30am-9pm) is set in expansive gardens full of climbing roses, pools, waterfalls and old trees. Cold meze (€1.65) and grills (€3.35) are the specialities.

Alternatively, take the road to **Kaplan**, a tiny village perched high in the hills, and enjoy a meal and the sensational views from **Kaplan Restaurant** (☎ 512 6652; meals €6; ☺ 8am-10pm).

Ödemiş is less interesting except on Saturday when there's a lively market. But from Ödemiş you can take a dolmuş or drive on to **Birgi**, an undeveloped village that's home to the gorgeous **Çakıroğlu Konağı** (admission €0.75; ☺ 8.30am-noon & 1-5.30pm Tue-Sun), one of the finest historical houses open to the public in Turkey. The three-storey wooden house, completely covered in frescoes, was probably built in 1761 for Şerif Aliağa, a tradesman who owned the local tanning yards and had two wives, from İstanbul and İzmir. To keep them happy he had vistas of their home towns painted on the upstairs walls. Next door, **Konak** (☎ 531 6069; Çakırağa Sokak 6) is a café in a restored house.

Birgi also has a fine **Ulu Cami** (1311) with carved doors and windows and an old stone lion incorporated into the stonework, and the **Birgivi**, a shrine on the outskirts of town that is popular with devout Muslims.

Getting There & Away

There are hourly minibuses to Tire from Selçuk (€1.50) and hourly onward buses from Tire to Ödemiş (€1, 34km). Dolmuşes

leave for Birgi from Ödemiş otogar (€1.50, 20 minutes, 8km).

KUŞADASI

☎ 0256 / pop 47,660

About 22km southwest of Selçuk lies Kuşadası, which suffers from the double indignity of being a cruise-ship port and a major package-holiday resort. English-style pubs and karaoke bars are filled with football strips signed 'Elaine and Gary from Tredegar, South Wales', 'The Essex Police' and 'The Catholic Girls'. Then there are the tattoo parlours and shopping centres. Prices are also higher than other towns (particularly alcohol because of high municipality tax). Rip-offs are all too common, and you'll get plenty of 'Hi, where are you froms' from the carpet touts near the cruise-ship port. For the first time, too, the traditional Turkish hospitality seems a little jaded.

Nevertheless, outside high season it is a laid-back town with some lovely beaches and stunning views. A room at a nice pension with a rooftop terrace also makes a decent base for excursions to the ancient cities of Ephesus, Priene, Miletus and Didyma. Plus, the nightlife is cheesy but full-on. And if you look hard enough, the old Kuşadası is not too far beneath the surface either: there are some lovely bars in the old quarter.

There are also signs that the city fathers have at last cottoned on to the need to clean up their act, with the building of an attractive new waterfront esplanade.

Orientation

Kuşadası's central landmark is the Öküz Mehmet Paşa Kervansarayı, an Ottoman caravanserai that is now a hotel, known as Club Caravanserai. It lies 100m inland from the cruise-ship docks, at the intersection of the waterfront boulevard, Atatürk Bulvarı, and the town's main street, the pedestrianised Barbaros Hayrettin Bulvarı, which cuts inland.

Just beyond the PTT on the northern side of Barbaros Hayrettin Bulvarı, a passage leads to the old Kaleiçi neighbourhood (part of old Kuşadası) of narrow streets packed with restaurants and bars.

Turn right off Barbaros Hayrettin Bulvarı to find raucous Barlar Sokak (Bar St) and the hillside pensions overlooking the harbour.

The most useful dolmuş stand is 1.5km inland on Adnan Menderes Bulvarı. The otogar is right out on the bypass road.

SOUTH AEGEAN

Information

INTERNET ACCESS

B@h@ane Internet Café (Öge Sokak 4/A; per hr €1.40; ⏰ 8.30am-midnight) You can take drinks up here from the downstairs café.

Funny Internet Café (İsmet İnönü Bulvarı 16/A; per hr €1.10; ⏰ 24hr) A couple of doors down from Anker Travel.

MEDICAL

Özel Kuşadası Hastanesi (☎ 613 1616; Anıt Sokak, Turkmen Mahallesi) Kuşadası's excellent private hospital is 3km north of the centre on the Selçuk road, and has English-speaking doctors.

MONEY

There are several banks with ATMs on Barbaros Hayrettin Caddesi.

POST

PTT (☎ 612 3311; Barbaros Hayrettin Paşa Bulvarı 23-25; ⏰ 8.30am-12.30pm & 1.30-5.30pm Mon-Sat winter, 8am-midnight daily summer)

TOURIST INFORMATION

Tourist office (☎ 614 1103; fax 614 6295; İskele Meydanı, Liman Caddesi; ⏰ 8am-noon & 1-5pm Mon-Fri) Near the wharf where the cruise ships dock, about 60m west of the caravanserai.

Sights & Activities

Kuşadası (Bird Island) gets its name from the small Güvercin Adası (Pigeon Island) connected to the mainland by a causeway. Unfortunately, the small stone **fortress** that is its most prominent feature is usually locked,

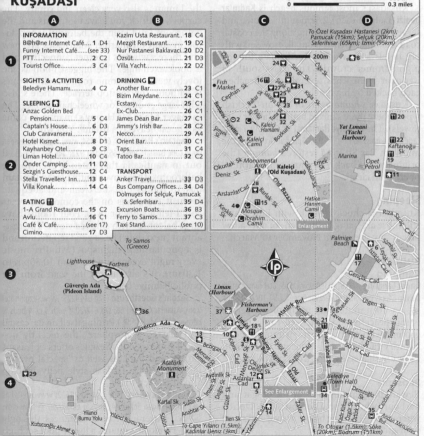

but that doesn't stop it from being a popular stroll for Turkish families. Kids will love the pigeon, duck and rabbit quarters.

The town's most prominent landmark is the **caravanserai** near the harbour. In the early 18th century, Öküz Mehmet Paşa, sometime grand vizier to sultans Ahmet I and Osman II, ordered the building of this caravanserai, together with the Kaleiçi Camii and *hamam* (bathhouse), and the city walls. Today, it's a hotel (opposite) hosting regular 'Turkish Nights'.

You can swim from the rocky shores of Güvercin Adası, but **Cape Yılancı** (Yılancı Burnu), the peninsula less than 1.5km to the south, is more enticing. Alternatively, catch the *şehiriçi* (intracity) dolmuş to the northern beach near the yacht marina or further north to the beach opposite the Tur-Yat Mocamp in Kuştur.

Kuşadası's most famous beach is **Kadınlar Denizi** (Ladies Beach), 2.5km south of town and served by dolmuşes running along the coastal road. Kadınlar Denizi is small, crowded with big hotels and woefully inadequate for the high summer crowds. The coast south of Kadınlar Denizi has several small beaches, each backed by big hotels.

Kuşadası's *hamams* are of the 'un-Turkish type', where there's mixed bathing (albeit with towels). The **Belediye Hamamı** (☎ 614 1219; Yildirim Caddesi 2; admission €14; ☽ 9am-7pm Apr-Oct) is up the hill from Bar St. It's a restored *hamam* (the original dates back 600 years) and is atmospheric and clean.

Sleeping

Kuşadası is chock-a-block with hotels and still more are being built. Even so, only a few places stay open from November to March.

BUDGET
Camping

Önder Camping (☎ 618 1590; www.onderotel.com; Atatürk Bulvarı 84; per person/tent/caravan/car €2.20/1.10/2.20/1.10; ☒) A 10-minute walk north of the centre is this peaceful and quite well-run camping ground with tennis court, swimming pool, laundry facilities and a decent restaurant. Plots are shaded by pine trees and olives.

Pensions

Beware the pension touts at the otogar and harbour (who are paid commission). Decide where you're heading before arrival and stand your ground.

Anzac Golden Bed Pension (☎ 614 8708; www .kusadasihotels.com/goldenbed; off Aslanlar Caddesi, Uğurlu 1 Çıkmazı 4; dm €8-11, s with shared bathroom €11, s/d with bathroom €17-20/22-25; ☒ ☐) Bright, light and spotless, the pension's biggest attraction is its lovely terrace lined with geraniums in flowerpots where you can have breakfast while admiring the views over town. Tucked away in a cul-de-sac (follow the signs from Aslanlar Cadessi), it's peaceful and tranquil and you'll be warmly welcomed by Yusuf and Sandra, the Turkish-Australian owners, and their Shitzu dog, Zia. The pension is on a hill, but the owners happily reimburse taxis (up to YTL5).

Liman Hotel (Mr Happy's; ☎ 614 7770; www.liman hotel.com; Kıbrıs Caddesi, Buyral Sokak 4; s €11-17, d €14-25, f €31; ☒ ☐) With a great location close to the ferries, beaches, town centre and bazaar, the Liman is also very clean and comfy. The carpet's so thick you leave footprints and the bathroom (and even the balcony) is top-to-toe in maroon marble. Mattresses are new and there's wireless internet connection and a book exchange. The biggest boon is the lovely view from some rooms and, if yours is without, the rooftop terrace. There's also a lift large enough for wheelchair access. The manager's (aka Mr Happy's) mantra is 'come as a guest; leave as a friend'. You will.

Captain's House (☎ 614 4754; www.captainshousepan siyon.com; İstiklal Caddesi 66; s/d €11/22; ☒ ☒) Decked out in nauticalia that extends even to the bathrooms, the conveniently placed Captain has 18 rooms that are clean and adequate (even if the stains on the common carpets could tell a story or two). Four rooms have large balconies with side sea views. The restaurant (next door) has a good reputation and is a popular local nightspot (with live music every night except Sunday from 10.30pm to 1.30am). It's also across the road from the public Palmiye beach.

Sezgin's Guesthouse (☎ 614 4225; www.sezginhotel .com; Aslanlar Caddesi 68; s/d €12/20, f with 3 or 4 beds & kitchen €40; ☒ ☐ ☒) Priding itself on its 'casual and relaxed atmosphere', the recently updated and expanded Sezgin's offers a pleasant garden and pool, as well as 'special events' including BBQs Turkish-style, belly dancing and organised tours.

Stella Travelers' Inn (☎ 614 1632; www.stellahos tel.com; Bezirgan Sokak 44; dm/s/d €8/22/28; ☽ Apr-Nov; ☐ ☒) Never judge on appearances: this ugly modern block contains a lovely pool set high on a terrace with simply stunning views. The hotel's a bit 70s-student-common-room, but the 20 rooms are clean, spacious and have direct sea views and balcony. It's good value. To get here, take a taxi (for which you'll be reimbursed on arrival).

MIDRANGE & TOP END

Villa Konak (☎ 612 2170; www.villakonakhotel.com; Yıldırım Caddesi 55; s/d with half board €47/62; 🅿 🖭) Hidden away from the hubbub in the old quarter of town is the Villa Konak, a restored 140-year-old stone house. Rooms, simple but attractively done with the odd Orientalist flourish, are arranged around a large and rambling courtyard-garden complete with pool, ancient well, and citrus and magnolia trees. It's peaceful and cool and there's a bar, restaurant and library.

Club Caravanserai (☎ 614 4115; www.kusadasihotels.com/caravanserail; Atatürk Bulvarı; s/d €47/70; 🕙 1 Mar-15 Nov; 🖭) Constructed by a grand vizier in 1618, this is an attractive caravanserai that boasts a supremely central location and four-star prices at reasonable rates. Unfortunately, the central courtyard is rather ruined by the carpet shops, and the 'Turkish Nights' shows at summer weekends – unless of course you like this kinda thing (€40 with dinner, €30 without).

Hotel Kısmet (☎ 618 1290; www.kismet.com.tr; Atatürk Bulvarı 1; s/d €87/124; 🕙 15 Mar-15 Nov; 🅿 🖭) Who would have thought in Kuşadası? Created by a descendant of the last sultan, the electric gates and avenue give an inkling of what lies beyond: minutely manicured grounds, a gorgeous pool and stylish décor all in neutrals. Be sure to bag a room with a balcony or veranda overlooking the seafront. The only downer is the piped music of cheesy crooners.

If the above are full, try the new **Kayhanbey Otel** (☎ 614 1190; www.ksyhanbey.com; Güvercin Ada Caddesi; s/d €75/100; 🖭 🖨 🖭) with 72 comfortable (albeit anodyne) rooms with balconies with lovely sea views. There's also a *hamam*, and outdoor pool on the roof terrace.

Eating

For cheaper options, it's simple: head inland. The Kaleiçi, the old part of Kuşadası behind the PTT, has some atmospheric dining rooms as well as a few cheap and cheerful joints.

The town's prime dining location is down by the picturesque harbour but competition keeps bills down. Always ask in advance the price of seafood, check wine prices (and ensure you get the bottle, quantity and type you ordered), and always check your bills after a meal.

RESTAURANTS

Avlu (☎ 614 7995; Cephane Sokak 15; stews with free coffee or tea €1.40-1.95; 🕙 8am-midnight) Hidden in the old town amid a maze of streets, this *lokanta* (restaurant) is well worth seeking out. It offers 1st-class home cooking in a clean and cheerful environment at unbeatable prices. A long-standing local fave, in recent times it's been discovered by the more daring cruise-ships tourists too; if you don't want to queue at lunchtime, come earlier or later. There's a great pick-and-point counter for those unsure what to order. It's a good choice for veggies too, as well as for sampling delectable Turkish puds.

1-A Grand Restaurant (☎ 614 8409; Yıldız Sokak 1/A; mains €5-6; 🕙 9am-2am 20 Apr-1 Nov) Set in a square just off Bar St, this lovely place is a whole world away from it. Tables are set in a garden-courtyard under old fig and orange trees and the place is so mellow and laid-back that even the dogs are asleep curled up on the benches. There's a daily happy hour from 10pm to 11pm (all cocktails €3). The food (both European and Turkish) has a good reputation and it claims to do the best steaks in town. There's also free internet access to customers.

Mezgit Restaurant (☎ 618 2808; Atatürk Bulgarı 86; meze €1.65; 500g fish €8-10 🕙 9am-midnight) A new, family-run place, it's already established itself locally as a great place for fresh fish at fair prices – it's half the price of the port. Daily prices are chalked up on the board.

Kazim Usta Restaurant (☎ 614 1226; Liman Caddesi 4; 500g fish €11-20; 🕙 6am-midnight) Opposite the tourist office, this restaurant is now considered the top fish restaurant in town, though it's not cheap. The sumptuous fish soup (€4) is a speciality. If you want a table on the waterfront, reserve at least a day in advance.

CAFÉS & QUICK EATS

Nur Pastanesi Baklavaci (☎ 612 3926; Atatürk Bulvarı, Liman Apt 106; puddings €1.40; 🕙 7am-midnight) Brand new and family-run, this patisserie is a fabulous place for homemade pastries and puds at a quarter of the price of town. There's also good ice cream (€0.30 per scoop). Try the exquisite baklava (four pieces €1.55).

Özsüt (☎ 612 0650; İsmet İnönü Bulvarı 30; 🕙 9.30am-midnight; 🖭) Also new, this well-known İzmiri

SOUTH AEGEAN

chain has the usual delicious selection of traditional Turkish puds served up in smart surrounds, as well as great coffee and ice cream (€0.85 per scoop). Try the wonderful *aşure* (Noah's pudding) or *tavuk göğsü kazandibi* (burnt chicken breast pudding!) for €1.95.

Cimino (☎ 614 6409; Atatürk Bulvarı 56/B; ⊙ 10am-midnight) A place to meet-and-eat locally, this mellow bistro-cum-café serves good cappuccino (€2.75) and mainly Italian-style fare (€2.75 to €14). It's opposite the seafront and plays good jazz music.

Nearby but a little livelier is **Café & Café** (☎ 612 5191; Atatürk Bulvarı 52; beer €2.75; ⊙ 9am-midnight), which is also a great spot for a sundowner, while the **Villa Yacht** (☎ 618 1577; Marina Karşisi, Atatürk Bulvarı 94; beer/nargileh €1.65/2.25; ⊙ 8.30am-3am) is a good, new place if you fancy trying a nargileh.

Drinking & Entertainment

What you'll make of the famous Barlar Sokak (Bar St) probably depends on your penchant for Irish-theme pubs, karaoke bars and cheesy pick-up lines, but it's a good place to meet up with other travellers. For local bars with bags of character and atmosphere, head for old Kuşadası. Everywhere the party never gets going before midnight. From October to March, it shrinks to almost nothing.

Orient Bar (☎ 612 8838; Kışla Sokak 14; beer €2.20; ⊙ 1am-4am 15 Apr-Oct) With white-washed walls covered in trinkets, and wooden tables under vines, rustic meets raucous in the highly popular local hang-out. The music is European and the price of a beer is not prohibitive.

Jimmy's Irish Bar (☎ 612 1318; Barlar Sokak 8; beer €3.35; ⊙ 8pm-4am 5 Apr-Nov) Love it or loathe it (and the burly bouncers with radio earplugs say everything about the clientele), Jimmy's is a popular get-together for travellers. Large screens beam in the compulsory football matches.

In the old town, there's a string of fabulous bars-cum-nightclubs that are well designed, glam and much more Turkish than tourist. Beer costs €4.50 and all are open 10pm to 4am May to September, though a few sporadically open at weekends in winter. The most popular currently are the following.

Another Bar (☎ 614 7552; Tuna Sokak 10) Converted from an old citrus orchard, tables and stools are dotted among the remaining trees and a large, central palm. There's also a large screen and a dance floor.

Ex-Club (☎ 614 7550; Tuna Sokak 13) More club than bar and with a sound system, disco balls and laser lights to prove it, this partly open-air place is crammed with dancers on the floor as well as around the balustrade above.

James Dean Bar (☎ 614 3827; Sakarya Sokak 14) Set in a 200-year-old building, this club is open-air amid orange trees and beautiful bars draped with beautiful people.

Ecstasy (☎ 612 2208; Sakarya Sokak 10) bar is similar. Known to be gay-friendly are **Tattoo Bar** (☎ 612 7693; Tuna Sokak 7) and the British pub-style **Taps** (☎ 612 1371; Tuna Sokak 4).

MEYHANES

Kaleiçi (the old part of Kuşadası) is home to several *meyhanes* (taverns) where meze and rakı (aniseed-flavoured grape brandy) are served up accompanied by live music.

Bizim Meyhane (☎ 614 4152; Kışla Sokak; beer/rakı €2.75/2.20; ⊙ 8.30pm-4am) Low-beamed and draped with musical instruments on the old stone walls, this place looks more barn than bar. Run by a sister and brother who themselves sing and play instruments, it's atmospheric, infectious and fun. Join the locals tossing back the rakı, singing, dancing or scribbling little messages on the wall!

BEACH CLUBS

Recently, a new phenomenon has come to Kuşadası: the beach club. Functioning as a beach club during the day, they transform themselves by night into a restaurant, followed by a lavish nightclub-on-the-sea.

Two such places can be found on the way to Pigeon Island. Considered the hippest (and the first on the scene) is **Necco** (☎ 613 3055; Yilancı Burnu; admission weekday €5.50, weekend with drink incl €11, beer from €4; ⊙ 10am-7pm & 8pm-midnight end May-end Sep). It's very popular with the well heeled and well–dolled up.

To get here, take a dolmuş towards Kadınlar Denizi (Ladies Beach; €0.55). It can drop you at the roundabout from where it's a short walk. On foot, ask the locals for the handy shortcut (about 1km from town).

Getting There & Away

BUS

Kuşadası's otogar is at the southern end of Kahramanlar Caddesi on the bypass highway. Several companies have ticket offices on İsmet İnönü Bulvarı and offer *servis* (shuttle minibuses) to save you the trek out there. Note that dolmuşes leave from the centrally located Adnan Menderes Bulvarı.

In summer, three buses run daily to Bodrum (€7 to €8, 2 to 2½ hours, 151km); in winter, take a dolmuş to Söke (€1.65, at least every 30 minutes all year). For Didyma, Priene and Miletus, change also at Söke. For more information about getting to the 'PMD' ruins, see p264.

For Selçuk, (€1.65, 25 minutes), dolmuşes run every 15 minutes. For Pamucak or Ephesus, take the Selçuk dolmuş (which can drop you off there). For Seherihisar (€2.80; 70 minutes), dolmuşes leave every 45 minutes all year.

BOAT

All Kuşadası travel agents sell tickets to the Greek island of Samos.

From 1st April to 31st October, boats depart daily from Kuşadası to Samos at 8.30am. From 1 May, there's an additional boat at 5pm. Note that ferries do not operate in winter. Tickets cost €32 for a single, €38 for a same-day return and €59 for an open return.

If you stay the night you will be landed with a €9 tax for leaving Greece and another €9 tax for coming back into Turkey. Some pensions discount these tickets, so ask, and flash your student card. You must be at the harbour 45 minutes before sailing time for immigration formalities.

A recommended travel agency is **Anker Travel** (☎ 612 4598; www.ankertravel.net; İnönü Bulvarı 14; ☾ 9am 7pm winter, 9am-9pm summer). It's also a licensed ticketing agent so can sell domestic and international flights.

Getting Around

For Adnan Menderes airport, note that buses can no longer drop you off (since the building of the highway about 10 years ago). You must now take a bus to İzmir otogar (€4.70, 1¼ hours, 80km), take the free shuttle service to the centre, then take a bus (see p234, or a taxi (€67).

Şehiriçi minibuses (€0.85) run every few minutes in summer (every 15 to 20 in winter) from Kuşadası otogar to the town centre, and up and down the coast. Kadınlar Denizi minibuses speed along the coast road south to the beach. You can pick up a minibus heading north along the coast to Kuştur (€1.85) at the junction of İstiklal Sokak and Atatürk Bulvarı.

SÖKE

☎ 0256 / pop 69,370

Söke is a modern town that's enlivened only by Wednesday and Sunday markets. However, it's the main transport hub for this part of the region and you may be forced to come here to change buses as you travel around the coast.

If you get stuck here, the **Hotel Haymanali** (☎ 518 1726; www.hotelhaymanali.com; Sekiler Caddesi 55; s/d €17/28, summer extra €5.50; ⚂), about 70m from the bus station on the main road, is the best of the very few options in town and is comfortable and well run.

You can also base yourself here for visiting the Dilek Peninsula or Priene, Miletus and Didyma, cutting out the transport time from Selçuk or Kuşadası.

Buses run to İzmir (€4.45 to €5.55, usually every 15 minutes), to Denizli (for Pamukkale; €5.55, three times daily), Bodrum (€6.65, every hour) and to Ayden (€2.50, every 20 minutes). For dolmuş services see the table, below. For Selçuk, go to Kuşadası and change.

DOLMUŞ SERVICES FROM SÖKE'S OTOGAR

Destination	Fare	Distance	Frequency (per day)
Bafa	€2.75	30km	every 20 min
Balat (for Miletus)	€2.20	35km	every 30 min
Didyma	€2.50	56km	every 20 min
Güllübahçe (for Priene)	€1.40	17km	every 20 min
Güzelçamlı	€1.95	22km	every 20 min
Kuşadası	€1.65	20km	every 20 min
Milas	€3.35	82km	every 20 min

DİLEK PENINSULA

About 26km south of Kuşadası, the Dilek Peninsula juts westwards into the Aegean, almost touching the Greek island of Samos. West of the village of Güzelçamlı is **Dilek National Park** (Dilek Milli Parkı; admission per person/car €1.65/4.75; ☾ 8am-8pm), a peaceful, mountainous nature reserve with some fine walking and horse-riding areas, and unspoilt coves for swimming.

Just outside the park entrance, look out for a brown sign with 'Zeus Mağarası' written on it, which indicates the location of a cave where you can swim in water that's icy-cool in summer and warm in winter.

National park dolmuşes drop you off at **İçmeler Koyu**, a protected cove with a small but cigarette butt-strewn beach, lounge chairs and umbrellas. About 3km beyond İçmeler Koyu an unpaved road heads 1km downhill on the right to **Aydınlık Beach**, a quieter pebble-and-sand strand about 800m long with surf and backed by pines.

Less than 1km further along is a *jandarma* (police) post. Shortly afterwards a turn on the left is signposted **Kanyon**. If you follow this path all the way it will eventually bring you back to Güzelçamlı, after about six hours' stiff walking through beautiful, peaceful pine forest. Alternatively, you can just take a turn up and down the hill and then return to the main road.

After another 500m you reach the turn-off for **Kavaklı Burun** (also known as Kalamaki Beach and the last dolmuş stop), a sand-and-pebble surf beach. As at Aydınlık, there's a second entrance to the beach at the far end, another 1km along. It's 8.5km back to the park entrance.

Sleeping & Eating

Ecer Pension (☎ 646 2737; necipecer@mynet.com; s/d with or without private bathroom & breakfast €11/22) Though you'd be forgiven for mistaking it for a ramshackle farmhouse, the pension's rooms are simple, tidy and clean. Run by a charming Turkish-German couple, Anneliese and Necdet, you can sip their homemade wine in their rambling garden. It lies 200m east of the bus station on the main road. You can request a wild boar dinner for €6.50.

The owners' son can also arrange horses and guides (€20 to €22 per person for three hours) or take you on a trek (from one hour to eight hours) in the park. The scenery is beautiful and you can hope to see among other things ruined Byzantine monasteries and wildlife including wild horses and boar.

Although camping is not allowed in the national park, there are several sites near the gate at Güzelçamlı.

Outside the park are several, similar fish restaurants perched right on the water; choose the most popular when you visit. The beaches in the park have small cafés selling cold drinks and simple meals, as well as picnicking facilities.

Getting There & Away

Minibuses from Söke travel as far as İçmeler Koyu (€1.65, 35 to 40 minutes); minibuses from Kuşadası continue right down the peninsula to Kavaklı Burun (€1.95). You pay the park entrance fee while on the bus. Minibuses generally run from 7am to midnight in summer and 7am to 6.45pm in winter, but the later dolmuşes fill up quickly, especially at weekends.

You can walk the 2km from Güzelçamlı to İçmeler Koyu in 30 minutes.

PRIENE, MILETUS & DIDYMA
☎ 0256

Ephesus may be the *crème de la crème* of the Aegean archaeological sites, but south of Kuşadası lie the ruins of three other, much-less-frequently visited (but still important) ancient settlements. Priene occupies a dramatic position overlooking the plain of the Büyük Menderes (Meander) River; Miletus preserves a spectacular theatre; and Didyma has a Temple of Apollo vaguely reminiscent of the great temples at Karnak in Egypt.

Beyond Didyma lies **Altınkum Beach**, one of Turkey's finest and busiest beaches, its swathe of 'golden sand' popular with the English package-holiday brigade for whom innumerable British-style cafés dish up the tastes of home. If you end your tour of the ruins at Didyma, you might want to take a quick dip in the sea at the beach before returning to base.

Getting There & Around

If you start early in the morning from Kuşadası or Selçuk, it's just about possible to get to Priene, Miletus, Didyma and Altınkum Beach in the same day using public transport. However, it can be awkward and time-consuming as dolmuş services are patchy and you may have to keep backtracking to Söke. To avoid worries about connections you might prefer to opt for an organised tour from Selçuk or Kuşadası.

If you do want to do it yourself, start out by catching a dolmuş from Kuşadası (€1.65, 20km) to Söke and then another to Güllübahçe (for Priene; €1.40, 17km). When you've finished at Priene, wait for a passing dolmuş heading for Miletus or Söke, hitch the 22km across the flood plain to Miletus or return to Söke and set out again.

Getting from Miletus to Didyma can be tricky. Dolmuşes do run from Miletus to Didyma (€1.65) but if there's no sign of a dolmuş from Miletus to Akköy, you will either have to try hitching or return to Söke and start out all over again. From Akköy, there are dolmuşes every 20 minutes to Didyma (€1.40) and Altınkum.

Lost already? If so it's easy to pick up an organised tour (around €20 per person) from Selçuk otogar, at least in high summer. Minibuses usually leave around 9am, and spend one hour at Priene, 1½ hours at Miletus, 2½ hours at Didyma and 1½ hours at Altınkum Beach, before returning to Selçuk at about 6pm.

In high summer, tours may run daily and you may need to book in advance. At other times, however, they may only operate when enough people have expressed an interest. In winter, note that there are fewer direct dolmuşes and you have to change more frequently from town to town.

Without a doubt, hiring a car is the easiest way to visit these places! There are a multitude of agencies competing for business in the town centre or ask at your hotel. Most international agencies rent out cars for around €50 a day, while a host of smaller travel agencies do it for about half that. Shop around.

Priene (Güllübahçe)

An important city around 300 BC when the League of Ionian Cities held congresses and festivals here, **Priene** (☎ 547 1165; admission €1.10; ◷ 8.30am-6.30pm May-Sep, 8.30am-5.30pm Oct-Apr) was smaller and less important than nearby Miletus. As such, its Hellenistic buildings did not vanish beneath newer Roman ones.

Priene was laid out on a grid plan, an idea that originated in Miletus. Of the buildings that remain, the five standing columns of the **Temple of Athena**, designed by Pythius of Halicarnassus and regarded as the epitome of an Ionian temple, form its most familiar landmark. The **theatre** is one of the best-preserved examples from the Hellenistic period. It had a capacity to seat 6500 people; look out for the finely carved front seats for VIPs. Also worth seeking out are the remains of the **bouleuterion** (council chamber), a **Byzantine church**, the **gymnasium** and the **stadium**.

Although the Priene ruins are interesting there's a strong chance that what will most linger in your mind is their beautiful setting beneath steep Mt Mykale.

Various factories and workshops sell onyx at quite good prices.

SLEEPING & EATING

All of the following are on or just off the main road, Atatürk Caddesi.

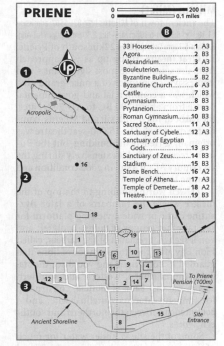

PRIENE

0 ____ 200 m
0 ____ 0.1 miles

33 Houses	1 A3
Agora	2 B3
Alexandrium	3 B3
Bouleuterion	4 B3
Byzantine Buildings	5 B2
Byzantine Church	6 A3
Castle	7 B3
Gymnasium	8 B3
Prytaneion	9 B3
Roman Gymnasium	10 B3
Sacred Stoa	11 A3
Sanctuary of Cybele	12 A3
Sanctuary of Egyptian Gods	13 B3
Sanctuary of Zeus	14 B3
Stadium	15 B3
Stone Bench	16 A2
Temple of Athena	17 A3
Temple of Demeter	18 A2
Theatre	19 B3

Priene Pension (☎ 542 8787; fax 547 1565; camping per person €5.50, s/d winter €14/28, summer €22/28) Currently the only hotel in town, the Priene boasts a beautifully kept garden. Rooms are simple but quite spacious and clean.

Around 30m beyond the Priene, where the dolmuş stops is the **Şelale Restaurant** (☎ 547 1009; ◷ 8am-11pm). Attractively positioned in the shadow of a ruined Byzantine aqueduct, it serves tasty trout (€5.60), which you can net yourself – if you have the stomach – from the restaurant's pool. Next door is the brand-new **Vila Sultan Café Bar Restaurant** (☎ 547 1204; köfte €2.75, kebap €3-4; ◷ 8am-11pm) in a converted kilim factory. The tables are set in a lovely courtyard with a fountain and orange trees and it offers excellent traditional fare. There are plans to rent rooms (probably €20 per person) and family bungalows (€33 to €50) here in the future.

GETTING THERE & AWAY

Dolmuşes run every 15 minutes between Priene (Güllübahçe; €1.40, 17km) and Söke; the last one back to Söke leaves Priene at 7pm.

Miletus (Milet)

The ancient town of **Miletus** (☎ 875 5562; admission €1.10; ☺ 8.30am-6.30pm May-Jun, 8.30am-7.30pm Jul-Aug, 8.30am-5.30pm Oct-Apr) lies 22km south of Priene. Its **Great Theatre,** rising up as you approach from the south, is the most significant – and impressive – reminder of a once-grand city, which was a commercial and governmental centre from about 700 BC to AD 700. Later, the harbour filled with silt and Miletus' commerce dwindled. The 15,000-seat theatre was originally a Hellenistic building, but the Romans reconstructed it extensively during the 1st century AD. It's still in good condition and exciting to explore.

It's well worth climbing to the top of the theatre where the ramparts of a later Byzantine castle provide a viewing platform for several other groups of ruins. Look left and you'll see what remains of the **harbour**, called Lion Bay after the stone statues of lions that guarded it. Look right and you'll see the **stadium**; the northern, western and southern **agoras**; the vast **Baths of Faustina**, constructed for Emperor Marcus Aurelius' wife; and a **bouleuterion** between the northern and southern agoras.

Some of the site is under water for much of the year and although it may make it hard to walk around, it also makes it more picturesque.

South of the main ruins stands the fascinating **İlyas Bey Camii** (1404), dating from a period after the Seljuks but before the Ottomans, when this region was ruled by the Turkish emirs of Menteşe. The doorway and *mihrab* (niche indicating the direction of Mecca) are exquisite, and you'll probably have them to yourself.

Across the road from the Great Theatre, there are a couple of cafés (open 7am to 6pm) serving reasonably priced snacks including delicious *gözleme* (€1.10) and refreshing freshly squeezed orange juice (€0.85). With such fabulous views, it's a great place for a break.

GETTING THERE & AWAY

From Söke take a dolmuş (€1) to Balat and ask to be dropped at the Miletus turn-off, from where it is about a 1km walk. From Miletus there are no dolmuşes anywhere. As there's not much traffic about, it may be quicker to return to Söke (€2.50) and start out again for Didyma. For current information on local

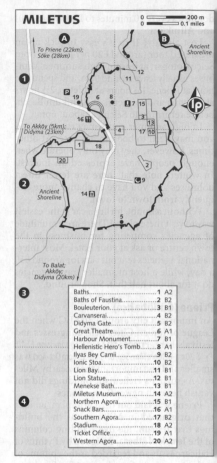

MILETUS

Baths	1 A2
Baths of Faustina	2 B2
Bouleuterion	3 B1
Carvansarai	4 B1
Didyma Gate	5 B2
Great Theatre	6 A1
Harbour Monument	7 B1
Hellenistic Hero's Tomb	8 A1
İlyas Bey Camii	9 B2
Ionic Stoa	10 B2
Lion Bay	11 B1
Lion Statue	12 B1
Menekse Bath	13 B1
Miletus Museum	14 A2
Northern Agora	15 B1
Snack Bars	16 A1
Southern Agora	17 B2
Stadium	18 A2
Ticket Office	19 A1
Western Agora	20 A2

timetables (which change regularly), ask the ticket office at Miletus. If you get stuck, they can sometimes call the Balat dolmuş station and request a pick-up.

Didyma (Didim)

Didyma was the site of a stupendous temple to Apollo, occupied by an oracle as important as the one at Delphi. But ancient Didyma was never a real town; only the priests who specialised in oracular temple management lived here. Modern Didim is a popular stop for tour groups, and carpet shops gush forth touts at the approach of each new bus. No guides are available at the site.

The ruins of the **Temple of Apollo** (☎ 811 0035; admission €1.10; ☺ 8.30am-7.30pm 15 Apr–Sep, 9am-5.30pm

Oct-14 Apr) that you see today belong to a late-4th-century BC temple built to replace the original one (destroyed by the Persians in 494 BC), and a later construction sponsored by Alexander the Great. It was never finished, although its oracle and priests continued hard at work until Christianity became the state religion, thereby bringing pagan practices to an end.

The temple porch held 120 huge columns with richly carved bases reminiscent of Karnak in Egypt. Behind the porch is a great doorway where oracular poems were written and presented to petitioners. Covered ramps on both sides of the porch lead down to the *cella* (inner room), where the oracle sat and prophesied after drinking from the sacred spring. The grounds contain fragments of rich decoration, including a photogenic head of Medusa (she of the snake hairdo). There used to be a road lined with statues that led to a small harbour, but after standing unmoved for 23 centuries the statues were taken to the British Museum in 1858.

Lovely Altınkum Beach (p264) is nearby.

SLEEPING & EATING

Medusa House (☎ 811 0063; www.medusahouse.com; s/d €28/56) Just around the corner from the temple on the Altınkum road is this restored stone village house with five pleasantly decorated rooms set in a very attractive garden (complete with original Greek urns and shaded terraces).

Oracle Pension (☎ 811 0270; s/d €17/28) Next door to Medusa House, the Oracle has simple, rather weary-looking rooms, but this is more than made up for by the stunning views over the temple just next door from the shaded terrace.

Apollon Café & Bar (☎ 811 3555; snacks €1.40-4, mains €5.50-11; ⊙ 8pm-midnight) Across from the temple entrance, the Apollon is located in a traditional stone house and has seating either in the cool interior or on the pleasant terrace overlooking the temple. The menu is extensive and prices reasonable.

Getting There & Away

Dolmuşes run frequently between from Söke and Didim (€3.35, one hour) and Altınkum (€3.35, 1½ hours). There are also frequent dolmuşes from Didim to Akköy (€1.40, 30 minutes) from where you may be able to hitch to Miletus.

HERAKLEIA (LATMOS)
☎ 0252

About 30km south of Söke, the highway skirts the southern shore of the huge Bafa Gölü (Lake Bafa), once a gulf of the Aegean but left behind as a lake as the sea retreated. At the southeastern end of the lake is a village called Çamiçi (Bafa), from which a paved road is signposted 10km north for Kapıkırı (for Herakleia). Watch carefully for the sign, which is easily missed.

At the end of a twisting, rock-dominated road, you'll come to the ruins of Herakleia ad Latmos in and around the village of Kapıkırı, a wonderful spot where rocks and ruins are so closely entwined it's hard to tell where the one ends and the other begins.

Above the village looms dramatic **Beşparmak Dağı** (Five-Fingered Mountain; 1500m), the ancient Mt Latmos that featured in Greek mythology as the place where the hunky shepherd boy Endymion happened to fall asleep. While he was napping, the moon goddess Selene glanced down and fell in love with him. Endymion had asked Zeus to grant him eternal youth and beauty in exchange for staying asleep for eternity. The unfortunate Selene could only gaze down at him night after night, as the moon is forever fated to look down on us mere mortals.

Bafa Gölü is an area where Christian hermits took refuge during the 8th-century Arab invasions (note the many ruined churches and monasteries in the vicinity). The monks reputedly considered Endymion a saint for his powers of self-denial.

Much of the pleasure of visiting Herakleia comes from the chance it offers to observe traditional Turkish life in action. During the day women sit by the road making lace; in the evenings villagers herd their cattle along the main street. Beehives dot the fields, and camomile flowers grow wild by the roadsides in spring and summer. In the morning you'll awaken to the sound of clucking chickens or braying donkeys.

Note that there's only one small shop and no bank or ATM in the village.

Sights & Activities

As you enter the village in summer, you may be asked to pay an admission fee of €2.80 (if the ticket attendant is around). Bear right at the ticket booth, and you'll come to the Agora Pension.

A path behind the Agora car park leads westwards to the large **Temple of Athena**, on a promontory overlooking the lake. Though only three walls remain, the large and beautifully cut building blocks (put together without cement) are impressive. Other signposted paths lead eastwards to the **agora**, the **bouleuterion** and, several hundred metres through stone-walled pastures and across a valley, to the unrestored and oddly sited **theatre**; its most interesting features are the rows of seats and flights of steps cut into the rock. Stretches of **city wall** dating from around 300 BC are also dotted about the village.

Afterwards, you can stroll down the road to the lake, passing: the **Temple of Endymion**, partly built into the rock; the ruins of a **Byzantine castle**; and the city's **necropolis**.

At the lakeside, near the ruins of a **Byzantine church**, there's a small beach of white coarse sand. The island just offshore can sometimes be reached on foot as the lake's water level falls. Around its base can be seen the foundations of several ancient buildings.

The Agora Pension offers boat trips around the lake to see the birds and the ruins and to swim. Half-day tours cost €30 and full-day tours €50. The restaurants by the lake also offer tours.

Sleeping & Eating

Pensions offer half-board, but you can normally request bed and breakfast only if you so wish.

Haus Yasemin Pansion (☎ 543 5598; www.bafa-see .de; s/d €22/45) Greeted by discarded toys and lines of washing, this welcoming place has a firm family feel. The traditionally styled rooms are simple but spotless and there's a nice terrace with views over the village. It's better value than most.

Agora Pension (☎ 543 5445; www.herakleia.com; s/d with shower & half board €45/60, bungalows half-board €39/67; 🍽 🖳) Though rooms are quite attractively decorated with traditional touches, prices are rather too steep. The hotel's setting is its biggest asset, with flower-filled gardens and a peaceful outlook (rural views complete with sheep and cows guaranteed!). There's also a *hamam* and shaded terrace with hammocks. Mithat, the son of the owner, can act as guide to the area and take you hiking (€10, four hours).

Herakleia Selene Restaurant (☎ 543 5579; fish mains €5.55; köfte €2.75; 🕖 7am-midnight) This is a great restaurant (with unbeatable prices), with a lovely position right on the waterfront. A fine spot for either a meal or, as the locals do, a beer at sunset. You can also come here to swim and have lunch. The friendly owner, Güray, rents out boats at reasonable prices (€11 for the whole boat, maximum six people, for two hours). Camping is also possible here (€1.40 per tent including use of bathrooms).

The **Kaya Restaurant & Pansiyon** (☎ 543 5380; meals €5.55; 🕗 8am-midnight) is another good restaurant. To get to both, take the road that forks left down to the water just before the ticket booth if entering the village.

Getting There & Away

Minibuses from Bodrum (€3), Milas (€1.50, 45 minutes) or Söke (€2.30, one hour) will drop you at Bafa. Unfortunately dolmuşes no longer run from Bafa to Herakleia but you can get a taxi (€5.55), or if you've decided where to stay, you can call the pensions for a free pick-up. From Bafa, dolmuşes run to Milas and Söke only.

MİLAS

☎ 0252 / pop 44,260

As Mylasa, Milas was capital of the Kingdom of Caria, except during the period when Mausolus ruled the kingdom from Halicarnassus (present-day Bodrum). Today, it's a fairly sleepy but still sizeable agricultural town, with many homes where carpets are handwoven. Don't be put off by what you see from the otogar – the town is actually quite attractive and makes a pleasant break from the bright lights of the coastal resorts. On Tuesday there's an excellent local market.

Since Milas is actually closer to Bodrum's international airport than Bodrum itself, you could stay the night in Milas if you arrive late in the day during high season when Bodrum is likely to be full.

Orientation

Approaching Milas from Söke, you pass the otogar 1km before reaching the road to Labranda on the left. To the right, İnönü Caddesi is marked for 'Şehir Merkezi' (city centre). It's another 1km to the centre of town at the Milas Belediye Parkı.

Sights & Activities

Coming into town along İnönü Caddesi, watch for signs pointing to the right for the belediye; opposite the belediye turn left for the **Baltalı Kapı** (Gate with an Axe). Cross a small bridge and look left to see the well-preserved Roman gate, which has marble posts and lintel, plus Corinthian capitals. The eponymous double-headed axe is carved into the keystone on the northern side.

Return to the road and continue south, turning right at the traffic roundabout next to the shady Milas Belediye Parkı, in the centre of which is a model of the Gümüşkesen monumental tomb.

Continue straight on for three blocks, turn right, then turn again at Gümüşkesen Caddesi to reach the tomb, 1.4km from the roundabout on a hill west of the centre.

The **Gümüşkesen** ('That Which Cuts Silver' or 'Silver Purse'; admission €2.50) is a Roman tomb dating from the 2nd century AD and thought to have been modelled on the Mausoleum at Halicarnassus. As in the Mausoleum, Corinthian columns support a pyramidal roof, beneath which is a tomb chamber with fine carvings on the ceiling. A hole in the platform floor allowed devotees to pour libations into the tomb to quench the dead souls' thirst. There's no reason to pay to go inside the enclosure as you can see everything perfectly adequately over the wall.

You might also want to see some of Milas' fine mosques, especially the **Ulu Cami** (1378) and **Orhan Bey Camii** (1330), built when Milas was capital of the Turkish principality of Menteşe. The larger, more impressive **Firuz Bey Camii** (1394) was built shortly after Menteşe was incorporated into the new and growing Ottoman Empire.

Milas has kept some of its older houses and there is some very impressive Ottoman and early-20th-century architecture, especially along Atatürk Bulvarı and behind the belediye.

Sleeping & Eating

Yazar Otel (☎ 512 4203; Kadıağa Caddesi 70; s/d €17/25; 🔀) Conveniently located for the Tuesday bazaar (which starts at its steps), this new hotel is small but cheerful, comfortable and clean. Rooms have TV and minibar. It lies right next door to the Halk Bank.

Akdeniz Otel (☎ 512 2217; Kadıağa Caddesi 32; s €5.55, s/d with bathroom & air-con €14/22; 🔀) Around 120m from the Yazar on the same street, Akdeniz is quite clean and good value. Worth considering if the Yazar is full.

Bacanaklar Sofrasi (☎ 512 1134; Menteşe Caddesi 15; köfte €2.75; 🕑 6.30am-11pm) Around 100m from the Yazar Otel (exit and then turn first right), it does excellent home-cooked Turkish fare (including veggie dishes) at pleasing prices.

Dilek Pastaneleri (☎ 512 4140; Kadıağa Caddesi 32; coffee from €1.10, ice cream €0.85; 🕑 7.30am-midnight) On the same street as Yazar Otel, this is a pleasant place for breakfast, snacks or coffee and cake. A portion of pizza costs €1.65.

Getting There & Away

The otogar is on the main Bodrum to Söke road, 1km from the centre, although dolmuşes from Bodrum (€2.80, one hour) drop off in town as well. There are also frequent dolmuş services from Söke (€3.35, 82km).

A small **dolmuş station** (☎ 512 4014; Köy Tabakhane Garaji) in the town centre offers timetabled minibus services to Ören (€1.65) and Iasos (€2).

AROUND MİLAS
Beçin Castle

Just over 1km along the road from Milas to Ören (watch for the brown sign immediately after a corner), a road on the right leads to **Beçin Kalesi** (Beçin Castle; admission €2.75; 🕑 8am-dusk), a Byzantine fortress on a rocky outcrop that was largely remodelled by the Turkish emirs of Menteşe who used Beçin as their capital in the 14th century.

Although the walls are striking, there's not a lot to see inside. Press on for another 500m for other remnants of the 14th-century Menteşe settlement, including the **Kızılhan** (Red Caravanserai), **Orhan Bey Camii** and the **Ahmet Gazi tomb** and **medrese** (seminary).

Labranda

Set into a steep hillside in an area that once supplied the ancient city of Mylasa with its water, the site of ancient Labranda is surrounded by fragrant pine forests peopled by beekeepers. Late in the season (October) you can see their tents pitched in the groves as they go about their business of extracting the honey and rendering the wax from the honeycombs. It's a beautiful place to visit that's well worth seeking out, not least because so few people make it up here.

Labranda (admission €2.50; 🕑 8am-5pm) was a holy place, where worship of a local god was going on by the 6th century BC and perhaps long before. Later it became a sanctuary to Zeus, controlled for a long time by Milas. The great

Temple of Zeus honours the god's warlike aspect (Stratius, or Labrayndus, which means 'Axe-Bearing'). There may have been an oracle here; certainly festivals and Olympic Games were held at the site.

Two men's banqueting halls, the **First Andron** and **Second Andron**, are in surprisingly good condition, as is a fine 4th-century **tomb** and other buildings. Excavated by a Swedish team in the early 20th century, the ruins are interesting enough but it's the site itself, with its spectacular views over the valley, which is most impressive.

Labranda seems to have been abandoned around AD 1000. Today, a caretaker will show you around; he speaks only Turkish, but the site is well labelled.

GETTING THERE & AWAY

The junction for the road to Labranda is just northwest of Milas on the road to Söke. It's 14km to the site. The road passes through the village of Kargıcak, 8km along, but even if you could find a dolmuş going as far as that you'd still have a long walk ahead of you. Hitching is possible but not reliable, particularly later in the day.

A taxi from Milas shouldn't cost more than €16 – the drivers near the Otel Arı seem more willing to negotiate than those near the Ören dolmuş station. Be sure to agree on a price that includes at least an hour's waiting time.

Euromos

The ancient city of Euromos once stood on a site about 12km northwest of Milas and 1km from the village of Selimiye. Today, almost all that remains of it is the picturesque **Temple of Zeus** (admission €2.75; ⊗ 8.30am-5.30pm Oct-Apr, to 7pm May-Sep) with some unfluted columns, which suggest it was never completed.

First settled in the 6th century BC, Euromos originally held a sanctuary to a local deity. With the coming of Greek (then Roman) culture, the local god's place was taken by Zeus. Euromos reached the height of its prosperity between 200 BC and AD 200. Emperor Hadrian, who built so many monuments in Anatolia, is thought to have also built the temple here.

If you're interested in ruins, you can clamber up the slopes to find other bits of the town. Look up behind the ticket booth at the big stone-fortification wall on the hillside. Climb up through the olive groves, go over the wall and continue at the same altitude (the path dips a bit, which is OK, but don't climb higher). After 100m you'll cross another stone wall and find yourself on flat ground that was once the stage of the ancient **theatre**. It's badly ruined, with olive trees poking up from the few remaining rows of seats. The town's **agora** is down by the highway, with only a few toppled column drums to mark it.

Soft drinks are sold at the site in summer.

GETTING THERE & AWAY

To get here, take the Milas to Söke bus or dolmuş and ask to get out at the ruins. Alternatively, take a dolmuş from Milas to Kıyıkışlacık, get out at the road junction for Iasos and walk the short distance north along the highway until you see the Euromos ruins on the right.

Kıyıkışlacık (Iasos)

☎ 0252

About 4km southwest of Euromos (8km northwest of Milas) a road on the right (west) is marked for Kıyıkışlacık ('Little Barracks on the Coast'), which is about 20km further on. Iasos was originally built on a hill at the tip of a peninsula framed by two picture-perfect bays. Today, it's a sleepy Aegean fishing village set amid the tumbled ruins of the ancient city.

The small harbour is crowded with fishing boats. A handful of small pensions and restaurants cater for travellers who want to get away from it all for a few days.

SIGHTS

About 100m before your reach Iasos proper, the road forks. Bear right along the gravel road where the large yellow sign reads: 'Balık Pazarı Açık Hava Müsei', and you should come to the **Balıkpazarı Iasos Müzesi** (Iasos Museum; admission €2.75; ⊗ 8.30am-5.30pm Tue-Sun) and, opposite it, a small cabin (the ticket office). Housed in the old fish market, the museum holds the village's most interesting ruin, a monumental Roman tomb (as well as various other Classical fragments).

If, instead, you bear left, the road continues to the port, then up over the hill and along the coast. The hill above the port is covered with ruins, including a walled **acropolis-fortress** (admission €2.75; ⊗ 8.30am-5.30pm Tue-Sun). Excavations have also revealed the city's bouleuterion and agora, a gymnasium, a basilica, a Roman temple of Artemis Astias (AD 190) and numerous other buildings.

SLEEPING & EATING

Climb the hill behind the restaurants to find the delightful **Cengiz** (☎ 537 7181; cengiz1955@gmail .com; s/d €11/22), the **Zeytin** (☎ 537 7008; s/d €11/22; ☻ Apr–20 Oct) and **Kaya Pension** (☎ 537 7439; www .iasos.de; s/d €14/28; ☒). All have simple, spotless rooms and lovely terraces with gorgeous views. The rooms of the Cengiz and Zeytin have balconies (some with sea views – ask for Nos 1, 2 or 6 at the Cengiz), but the Kaya has a nice pool. At the Zeytin, you can learn how to make mosaics. All places lie on Kıyıkışlacık Köyü, the main road, on the hill above the harbour.

If you haven't yet feasted on Turkish fish, here's your chance. Restaurants offer delicious fresh fish at feasible prices. The **Dilek Restaurant** (☎ 537 7307; meals around €7; ☻ 9am-midnight May-Sep) has a great, open meze buffet (with around 20 different types of meze) for €8, and fish (such as sea bream) for around €5. **Iasos Café Bar** (☎ 537 7073; meals about €7-8; ☻ 10am-midnight) also serves fish as well as snacks (from €1.10).

GETTING THERE & AWAY

In theory, during summer and on Thursdays during the rest of the year (for the Güllük market), municipality boats sail from Güllük to Iasos (€2.75, 15 minutes) and back. In practice, they often don't, so check. You can also hire a fishing boat yourself (€11 one way, 20 minutes) if you want to.

Between Iasos and Milas (€1.65), dolmuşes run every hour in summer (every 1½ hours in winter).

ÖREN
☎ 0252

Though Ören has tried hard to hang on to the tranquil atmosphere once common to villages all along the Turkish coasts, it seems to be slowly going over to the enemy. Look around and you'll see building sites and new buildings everywhere. Nevertheless, outside the high season it can still seem tranquil and quiet.

The actual village – with the PTT, shops and old Ottoman houses with geranium-filled gardens – is about 1.5km inland from the beach, surrounded by the ruins of the ancient city of **Keramos**, which flourished from the 6th century BC until at least the 3rd century AD. Bring funds with you unless you want to have to trek about 4km back along the road to Milas to use the ATM machines outside the gates of the Kemerköy power station.

Hamile Dağı (Pregnant Woman Mountain) soars above the village. With a bit of imagination the jagged western hump becomes the face, the swollen middle hump the belly, and the long ridge closest to town the legs of the woman. Paragliders launch from the 'knees', now sprouting radio towers.

Ören's 1km-long **beach** is especially popular with long-staying Turkish holidaymakers.

Sleeping & Eating

Ören has a handful of pensions and hotels near the waterfront.

Hotel Alnata (☎ 532 2813; www.alnatahotel.com; per person with half/full board winter €19/22, summer €25/35; ☒ ☲) Ören's top hotel, the three-star Alnata is decked out in white marble and Aegean blue and is comfortable and well run. All rooms have balconies, some with direct sea views. There's a nice pool as well as a pebble beach with sunlounges. Various water activities are offered, along with boat trips. Bikes and windsurfers can also be hired.

Hotel Keramos (☎ 532 2250; otelkeramos@ttnet.net .tr; Atatürk Bulvarı; s/d low season €11/22, high season €14/28; ☻ May-Oct; ☒) Where the modern-meets-neoclassical, the curiously designed Keramos has small but sparkling rooms with nice balconies overlooking gardens.

Hotel Kardelen (☎ 532 2678; www.orenkardelen .com; Yalı Mevkii Milas; s/d winter €8/16, summer €16/31; ☒) Across from the minibus stop, the Kardelen has simple and rather stark but spacious rooms. Its biggest bonus is the large rooftop terrace, as well as the good value it offers – it's hard to find cheaper.

In summer, there's a mass of places along the seafront selling pide, kebaps and fish. You're best advised to browse and pick the most popular: places change fast in Ören.

Kerme Restaurant (☎ 532 2065; Atatürk Bulgarı 22; meze €1.65-1.95; ☻ 10.30am-midnight winter, 8.30am-midnight summer) Well established, reliable and open all year, Kerme serves good meze as well as fresh fish at fair prices (€11 to €13 per 500g). Try the flavoursome *barbun* (red mullet), the restaurant's speciality.

Getting There & Away

Minibuses run from Milas to Ören village and beach and back (€1.95, one hour), every hour. To Bodrum (€3.35) and Muğla (€3) three minibuses leave daily.

SOUTH AEGEAN

BODRUM

☎ 0252 / pop 40,870

Bodrum may be just as much of a hyperresort as Kuşadası and Marmaris, but with its sugar-cube houses, draped in bougainvillea, and the palm-lined streets it has been more successful at clinging to its original charm.

Despite the influx of charter deals and lager louts in high summer, a short walk along the waterfront will show Bodrum is gaining a reputation as the Monte Carlo of the Aegean, with a smart new marina, sophisticated restaurants and millions of dollars worth of sailing craft laying over for a night or two. Bodrum's outstanding Museum of Underwater Archaeology is also well worth a stop in itself.

But it's certainly not a place for those whose idea of a dream holiday revolves around peace and quiet. For years the outdoor Halikarnas disco revelled in its fame as the loudest disco in the Med and these days it has competitors too. Come in spring or autumn, however, and Bodrum reverts to a pleasant, relatively low-key resort.

Not surprisingly, tourism is the local economy's lifeblood, although there's a plentiful tangerine crop in winter.

History

Aeons ago Bodrum rose to fame on the back of the Mausoleum, the spectacular tomb of the Carian King Mausolus that Roman historian Pliny the Elder designated one of the Seven Wonders of the World. Sadly, not much remains to be seen today. Most visitors will be more impressed by the Castle of St Peter, standing sentinel over the town's twin bays.

Herodotus (c 485–425 BC), the 'Father of History', was Bodrum's most famous son. Between the two World Wars, writer Cevat Şakir Kabaağaç lived in political exile here and wrote an account of idyllic voyages along the Carian and Lycian coasts, then completely untouched by tourism. The 'Fisherman of Halicarnassus' called his most famous book *Mavi Yolculuk* (Blue Voyage), a name since co-opted for all cruises along these shores. More recently, the late singer Zeki Muran settled in Bodrum, putting it on the map for gay travellers.

Orientation

The road to Bodrum winds through pine forests before cresting a hill to reveal a panorama of the town with its striking Crusader castle.

The otogar is around 400m inland from the sea, on Cevat Şakir Caddesi, the main road into the town centre. Walk down towards the sea, passing the fruit market, and you'll come to a small white mosque called the Adliye Camii (Courthouse Mosque). Turn right, and you'll be heading west on Neyzen Tevfik Caddesi towards the Marina, passing several pensions. If you turn left at the Adliye Camii and cut through the bazaar to walk along Dr Alim Bey Caddesi (which later becomes Cumhuriyet Caddesi to the east), you reach the hotels and pensions facing the western bay.

If you head straight on from the Adliye Camii towards the castle you'll be walking along Kale Caddesi, which is lined with boutiques. At the end of Kale Caddesi, beneath the castle walls, is the main plaza, Kale (İskele) Meydanı. Here you'll find the tourist office, teahouses and the day-excursion boats. Some ferry ticket offices are here. Others are further out along the pier beyond the castle.

Information

There are many ATMs and currency exchanges along Dr Alim Bey Caddesi and Cevat Şakir Caddesi.

Can Laundry (☎ 316 4089; Türkkuyusu Caddesi 99; per 5kg/10kg load €2.50/3.85; ◷ 8.30am-9pm Mon-Sat, 10am-9pm Sun)

Cybernet Internet Café (☎ 316 3167; Üçkuyular Caddesi 7; per hr €1.10; ◷ 24hr)

Minik Laundry (☎ 316 7904; Neyzen Tevfik Caddesi 236; 4kg wash & dry €4.15)

PTT (☎ 316 2760; Cevat Şakir Caddesi; ◷ post office 8.30am-5pm, telephone exchange 8am-midnight)

Tourist Office (☎ 316 1091; Kale Meydanı; ◷ 8am-5pm Mon-Fri, daily in summer)

Sights & Activities

CASTLE OF ST PETER

When Tamerlane invaded Anatolia in 1402, throwing the nascent Ottoman Empire temporarily off balance, the Knights Hospitaller based on Rhodes took the opportunity to capture Bodrum. They built the Castle of St Peter, which defended Bodrum (not always successfully) until the end of WWI. It was later used as an informal storage space for the booty collected during underwater archaeology missions, and then became Bodrum's **Museum of Underwater Archaeology** (☎ 316 2516; admission €5.55; ◷ 9am-noon & 1-7pm Tue-Sun summer; 8am-noon & 1-5pm winter).

BODRUM

0 _____ 400 m
0 _____ 0.2 miles

INFORMATION	
ATMs	(see 4)
Can Laundry	**1** C4
Cybernet Internet Café	**2** C5
Minik Laundry	**3** A5
Money Change Offices	(see 4)
Police Station	(see 5)
PTT	**4** C4
Tourist Office	**5** B5

SIGHTS & ACTIVITIES	
Ancient Theatre	**6** A3
Bardakçı Hamam	**7** D4
Bodrum Hamam	**8** C4
Castle of St Peter	**9** B5
Mausoleum	**10** A4
Museum of Underwater Archaeology	(see 9)
Shipyard	**11** A5
Snorkel & Dive Center	**12** C4
Yachts (for Boat Trips)	**13** B5

SLEEPING	
Antik Tiyatro Hotel	**14** A3

Artemis Pansiyon	**15** D5
Baç Pansiyon	**16** C5
Bahçeli Ağar Aile Pansiyonu	**17** A4
Bodrum Backpackers	**18** C5
Mars Hotel	**19** B3
Merve Park Suites Hotel	**20** D5
Sedan Pansiyon	**21** C4
Sevin Pansiyon	**22** C4
Su Otel	**23** B4

EATING	
06 Lokantası	**24** C5
Atmaca Döner Salonu	**25** C4
Banka Sokak (Traditional Restaurants)	**26** B5
Berk Balık Restaurant	**27** B5
Covered Market	(see 35)
Fruit Market	**28** C4
Kırmızı	**29** B4
Kocadon Restaurant	(see 30)
Kortan Restaurant	(see 37)
Liman Köftecisi	**30** A4
Mado	(see 16)
Marina Yacht Club	**31** A4
Nazık Ana	**32** C4

Özsüt	**33** B4
Sünger Pizza	**34** A4
Tansaş Supermarket	**35** C4
Tarihi Yunuslar Karadeniz Pastanesi	**36** C5
Tranca	**37** C5
Yağhane	(see 30)

DRINKING	
Campanella Bar	**38** C5
Fora	(see 42)
Halikarnas	**39** D5
Kef Bar	**40** C5
Küba Bar	**41** B4
Marine Club Catamaran	**42** C5
Old Café	(see 40)

TRANSPORT	
Avis	**43** B4
Bodrum Ferryboat Association	**44** B5
Otogar	**45** C4
Taxi Stand	**46** C4
Taxi Stand	**47** C4
Taxi Stand	(see 31)

SOUTH AEGEAN

This excellent museum, arguably the most important underwater archaeological museum in the world, is a veritable lesson in how to bring ancient exhibits to life. Items are imaginatively displayed and well lit, and good information panels, maps, models, reconstructions, drawings, murals, dioramas and videos all help to animate them. It's undoubt-edly one of the best museums in Turkey and in the Mediterranean (and could also teach some of the Victorian, cupboard-like museums in the West a thing or two!).

The views from the battalions are spectacular and worth coming for that alone. As the museum is spread throughout the castle, you need two hours to do it justice. Arrows suggest routes around it (red for long; green for short), but guides are not available. In the future, there are plans to open a Mycenaean room, and to install a lift.

As you head up the stone ramp into the castle past a **Crusader coats of arms** carved in marble and mounted on the stone walls, keep an eye out for bits of marble filched from the ancient Mausoleum. The ramp leads to the castle's main court, centred on an ancient mulberry tree. To the left is one of the biggest collections of **amphorae** in the world, dating from the 14th century BC and recovered from the waters of southwest Turkey. The castle'd courtyard café, amid displays of Greek and Roman statuary, provides a shady resting place.

The chapel contains a full-sized reconstruction of the stern half of a 7th-century eastern **Roman ship** discovered off Yassıada. Visitors can walk the decks, stand at the helm, look below decks at the cargo of wine and peek into the galley.

Follow the path to the left of the chape to ascend to the towers. Up the ramp is the **Glass-Shipwreck exhibit** (admission €2.75; ☺ 10-11am & 2-4pm Tue-Fri). As you enter, look for the castle-shaped dovecote on the castle wall. Discovered by a sponge diver in 1973 and excavated by Professor George Bass and a team of marine archaeologists, the 16m-long, 5m-wide ship sank in AD 1025 while carrying 3 tonnes of mainly broken glass between Fatimid Syria and the Black Sea.

Further up in the castle are the **Snake Tower** with an amphora exhibit, and the **German Tower**, decked out in medieval European style.

Descend past the Ottoman toilets to the **Gatineau Tower** and the dungeons beneath Over the inner gate is the inscription 'Inde Deus abest' (Where God does not exist). The

---

A WEEK IN THE LIFE OF BAHADIR BERKAYA

Early one morning, a local man was out spear-gun fishing around Karataş off the western Mediterranean coast. Suddenly, he was shaken to spot what he thought was a dead body lying on the seabed. Frightened, he fled for home as fast as he could to his wife. Managing to summon his strength later, however, he returned to take a closer look. Lying in just 5m of water was a shimmering statue.

As news of the find spread, Bodrum's Museum of Underwater Archaeology finally sent three of their top archaeologists to investigate. There they were astonished to discover that the statue was neither stone nor marble – but bronze. Deciding to keep the find strictly secret, they made camp and during three days and three nights, they slowly freed the statue from the sea bottom. On the fourth day, they raised it. Standing over 2m high and dating back some 2000 years, the statue was a sensational find and soon hit the international headlines.

Returning to Bodrum exhausted but exhilarated, the archaeologists stopped for a coffee in Kaş. There in the harbour they got chatting to an old sponge diver, who told them of the strange, 'biscuit-shaped' objects he had seen underwater. Promising to investigate, they returned a few days later to Kaş where they were shown the spot by the sponge diver some 10km out to sea.

Diving deep, first to 50m, then to 52m, the archaeologists were astonished to discover the remains of an incredible wreck. Collecting from it a biscuit-shaped copper ingot, they dispatched it for dating.

When the results returned, they discovered it dated to earlier than the 14th century BC! That night, the wife of one of the archaeologists had a child. They named her 'Tunc' (bronze) after the Bronze Age site they had discovered.

In the course of the subsequent excavations, a veritable treasure trove was unearthed: a gold chalice, a gold medallion and the gold scarab of Queen Nefertiti, as well as no fewer than 10 tonnes of copper and 1½ tonnes of tin – enough to equip an entire army with bronze weapons. *Uluburun,* as it's now known, was one of the world's largest archaeological discoveries in the last two centuries.

It can be seen today displayed in Bodrum's Museum of Underwater Archaeology (p272).

With thanks to Bahadir Berkaya (Archaeologist, Bodrum Museum of Underwater Archaeology) and one of the three archaeologists involved in the tremendous discoveries of October 1982

dungeon was used as a place of confinement and torture by the Knights from 1513 to 1523. A sign warns that the exhibits of torture implements might not be suitable for children, but most video game–hardened visitors will find the display dummies and the taped groans more laughable than disturbing.

The **English Tower**, built during the reign of King Henry IV of England (whose coat of arms is displayed above the entrance to the uppermost hall), is now fitted out as a medieval refectory. The standards of the Grand Masters of the Knights Hospitaller and their Turkish adversaries hang from the walls. Look for the suits of Turkish chain mail and the graffiti carved into the stone swindow ledges by Crusaders.

See if you can seek out the extraordinary **Bronze Age shipwrecks**, which yielded finds including Canaanite gold jewellery, bronze daggers, ivory and the gold scarab of Queen Nefertiti of Egypt. Look out in particular for the 14th-century BC *Uluburun*, the oldest excavated shipwreck in the world. The *Tektaş Burnu* is the only ancient Greek shipwreck (thought to date around 480 BC to 400 BC) from the Classical Period to be fully excavated in the world. The Treasure Room containing the artefacts occasionally closes if the humidity is high.

Inside the **French Tower** (admission €2.75; 10am-noon & 2-4pm Tue-Fri) are the remains of a great and powerful woman. Though popularly said to belong to Queen Ada (a Carian princess who died sometime between 360 BC and 325 BC aged 29, and whose tomb was discovered by Turkish archaeologists in 1989), there is no concrete evidence for this. Buried with a gold crown, necklace, bracelets, rings and an exquisite wreath of gold myrtle leaves, her identity doesn't lessen the incredible value of the find. Using modern reconstruction techniques, experts at Manchester University have modelled what she might have looked like; a video in Turkish explains their work.

MAUSOLEUM

Following the Persian invasion, Caria was ruled by a satrap (or 'king') named Mausolus (c 376–353 BC), who moved the capital here from Mylasa and called this town Halicarnassus. After the satrap's death, his wife undertook construction of a monumental tomb, as planned by Mausolus himself. The Mausoleum, an enormous white-marble tomb topped by a stepped pyramid, came to be considered one of the Seven Wonders of the Ancient World and stood relatively intact for almost 19 centuries, until it was broken up by the Crusaders in 1522 and the pieces used as building material.

Though most of the **Mausoleum** (Turgutreis Caddesi; admission €2.75; 8am-5pm Tue-Sun) is long gone, the site is still worth visiting. It's a few blocks inland from Neyzen Tevfik Caddesi. Coming from the castle, turn right near the Tepecik Camii on the shore of the western bay onto Hamam Sokak, which leads up to Turgutreis Caddesi. Turn left and follow the signs.

The site has pleasant gardens, with the excavations to the right and a covered arcade to the left. The arcade contains a copy of the famous frieze partly recovered from the castle walls; the original is now in the British Museum in London. The four original fragments on display were discovered more recently. Models, drawings and documents give an idea of why this tomb made Pliny's list of Wonders. Other exhibits include a model of Halicarnassus at the time of King Mausolus, and a model of the Mausoleum and its precincts.

A description written in 1581, supposedly taken from an eyewitness account of 1522, describes how the Knights Hospitaller discovered the buried Mausoleum, uncovered it, admired it and then returned to the castle for the night. During the night, pirates broke in and stole the tomb treasures, which had been safe as long as they had been buried. The next day the knights returned and broke the tomb to pieces for use as building stone. In reality, modern research suggests that tomb robbers had already beaten the knights to the treasure and that earthquakes had shattered it long before they ever set foot in Turkey.

Don't hold your breath in expectation over the actual site. Of the remains, only a few pre-Mausolean stairways and tomb chambers, the Mausolean drainage system, the entry to Mausolus' tomb chamber, a few bits of precinct wall and some large fluted marble column drums survive.

OTHER RUINS

A restored **ancient theatre** (Kıbrıs Şehitler Caddesi; admission €2.75; 8am-5pm Sat-Thu), which could originally seat 13,000 people, is cut into the rock of the hillside behind town on the busy main road to Gümbet. Recently, tombs dating to before the theatre were discovered here.

Just beyond the marina are the recently restored remains of the **Shipyard** (Şafak Sokak; ⊙ 9am-6pm). In 1770 the entire Ottoman fleet was destroyed by the Russians at Çeşme and had to be rebuilt from scratch in boatyards like this. The shipyard was fortified as a defence against pirates, and the restored tower was finished in 1829. The site is mainly used as a children's playground and is memorable for the views from the top, where several old tombstones date from the period when the Latin alphabet was replacing Arabic.

Also newly restored are the remains of the **Myndos Gate** (Myndos Kapısı) at the far western end of Turgutreis Caddesi. This is the only surviving gate in what were originally 7km-long walls probably built by King Mausolus in the 4th century BC. In front of the twin-towered gate are the remains of a moat in which many of Alexander the Great's soldiers drowned in 334 BC.

HAMAMS

Across from the otogar, **Bodrum Hamam** (☎ 313 4129; Cevat Şakir Caddesi, Fabrika Sokak 42; full massage €25; ⊙ 6am-midnight) is convenient and clean with separate sections for men and women. Though the exterior looks unpromising, the **Bardakçı Hamam** (☎ 313 8114; Omurça Dere Sokak 22; bath/massage €8/17; ⊙ 7am-midnight), founded in 1749, has a lovely marble-clad interior and great atmosphere. Bathing is mixed.

BOAT TRIPS

Dozens of yachts are moored along Neyzen Tevfik Caddesi on the western bay and around the ancient harbour for day trips around the bay. Most excursions depart at 10am, return at 5pm to 5.30pm, and cost around €14, including lunch plus afternoon tea and a cake.

Usually, you sail to **Aquarium**, a small cove with beautiful clear water that's good for swimming; then to **Karaada** (Black Island), where hot springs gush out of a cave and swimmers rub the orange mud from the springs onto their skin; followed by **Tavşan Burnu**, a pleasant bay for swimming. The boat then visits the other side of Karaada, before visiting **Meteor** with its 15m-deep pool that's good for diving in, before returning home. Boats sometimes also go to **Ortakent Bay**, a pretty cove backed with beachfront restaurants and hotels.

A nice alternative idea is to take a water taxi (€1.40, five minutes) to **Bardakçı** where there is a pleasant beach, which is generally uncrowded and a good place to relax.

Festivals & Events

For two weeks in August each year, the Castle of St Peter hosts national and international ballet stars at the **International Ballet Festival** (☎ 313 7649), which showcases classical, modern and experimental dance. Check out www.biletix.com for information on tickets. In the first week of October, there is a colourful international **Yacht Festival**.

BODRUM'S BIG BLUE

With its good visibility (up to 20m or 25m on a good day), clean water, and pleasant and steady temperatures, Bodrum is a good place for diving or snorkelling; it's also a very good place to learn.

Marine life sometimes spotted includes octopus, turtle, barracuda, jack fish (usually end of June) and parrot fish. Sadly, coral life doesn't start much before 40m (limiting it to advanced divers only), but the diving clubs are pushing hard for something else: to be granted permission to dive some of the hundreds of incredible wrecks lying just off Bodrum's coast (at depths of 12m to 25m). If permission were ever granted, Bodrum could comfortably claim the best wreck diving in the world. Most likely, permission will eventually be granted to visit one or two wrecks (in an effort sensibly to conserve them); keep your ears to the ground.

The **Snorkel & Dive Center** (☎ 313 6017; www.snorkeldiveshop.com; Cevat Şakir Caddesi 5; ⊙ 10am-6pm winter, 9am-midnight summer) is an excellent source of current information and also sells good-quality snorkelling and diving equipment (mask/snorkel €19/6) in Bodrum, as well as organising dives (full day's diving with two dives, boat, all equipment, insurance, hotel transfers and lunch per person €45). All-day snorkelling trips cost €17 per person. The company also runs PADI, NAUI and CMAS courses. A PADI Open Water course costs €350 per person (including all equipment, tuition and books). It normally takes four days, though three days is possible at a push.

Sleeping

In high summer, especially at weekends, Bodrum fills up quickly, so try to arrive early in the day. If you're planning to stay a week or so and thinking hotel rather than pension, check the package-holiday brochures in case they offer a cheaper deal.

When picking somewhere to stay, bear in mind how close you are to the clubs if you want a good night's sleep – action rarely kicks off before midnight and usually goes on until 4am. Theoretically, double-glazing cuts down on the noise, but unless your room also has air-con you will need to sleep with the windows open in summer. Nowadays, the western bay is as noisy as the eastern bay.

Regrettably, few places bother to stay open for the trickle of winter visitors.

BUDGET

There are various camping grounds on the Bodrum Peninsula's northern shore. Check with the tourist office for information and bookings.

Sevin Pansiyon (☎ 316 7682; sevinpansiyon@hotmail.com; Türkkuyusu Caddesi 5; s €8-14, d €14-17 in winter, s €19-22, d €25-36 in summer; ✖ 🖳) Behind the post office, the Sevin's biggest asset is its central position. It's also a friendly place with good facilities (including laundry services and free internet access). Its 37 rooms vary considerably so check out several (though the smaller ones are cheaper).

Bodrum Backpackers (☎ 313 2762; www.bodrumbackpackers.com; Atatürk Caddesi 31B; dm/s/d €8/11/22, mattress & bedding on terrace with/without breakfast €5.60/3.40; 🖳) Founded by a former backpacker, this clean and well-run place now caters to them. With a pleasant and chilled-out roof terrace (draped with snoozing backpackers when we visited!), it can also organise boat trips, airport pick-up and car hire. Tariq, the manager, is helpful, friendly and efficient. With a British-style pub next door, however, don't come here for a good night's kip.

Sedan Pansiyon (☎ 316 0355; off Türkkuyusu Caddesi 121; s/d with bathroom €11/22, with shared bathroom €8/16) Rooms are arranged around a ramshackle but peaceful courtyard, tucked away off the street. Some rooms are better than others, but it's friendly and good value, and guests can use the kitchen.

Bahçeli Ağar Aile Pansiyonu (☎ 316 1648; 1402 Sokak 4; s/d €17/33) This endearing little pension is located in a passageway off Neyzen Tevik Caddesi, opposite the marina. Run by İbrahim and family, and with a little courtyard filled with chirruping canaries, it has an intimate feel, and guests have use of the kitchen. Rooms are small and simple, but spotless, quiet and peaceful; all have balconies.

Mars Hotel (☎ 316 6559; Araplar Sokak 29; dm €5.50, s/d low season €14/22, high season €22/36, without air-con €8 less; ✖ 🖳) Set back from the road, the Mars is quiet, peaceful and good value. Rooms, though simple and smallish, are clean and bright, and eight look over the pleasant, medium-sized pool. Murat, the owner, is keen to please and there's free bus station transfers.

MIDRANGE

Artemis Pansiyon (☎ 316 1572; www.artemispansiyon.com; Cumhuriyet Caddesi 121; s/d €22/33, plus €5.50 per person in summer; ✖) Rooms though simple boast brand-new bathrooms, and four have direct sea views. The biggest boon is the terrace with panoramic views over the bay.

Baç Pansiyon (☎ 316 2497; bacpansiyon@turk.net; Cumhuriyet Caddesi 14; s €28-33, d €44-50, plus €10 per person in summer) Small but stylish and all in marble, wood and wrought iron, this centrally situated hotel also boasts about the best hotel views in Bodrum. A gem amid the market maelstrom, it sits right above the water and four of its 10 comfortable room have delightful balconies over the water.

Su Otel (☎ 316 6906; www.suhotel.net; Turgutreis Caddesi, 1201 Sokak; s/d €45/72; ✖ 🖳) Down a cul-de-sac, this brightly coloured, modern construction looks a bit like Legoland scaled up. Nonetheless, it's well designed, comfortable and tranquil and has a pleasant pool set in gardens. Rooms – again in primary colours – have balconies, with some overlooking the pool. If you're in Bodrum for more than a week, the Su also has a couple of lovely old cottages (from €105 for up to three people) for rent. One of the cottages holds up to eight people.

Merve Park Suites Hotel (☎ 313 7013; www.mervesuiteshotel.com; Atatürk Caddesi 73; s/d winter €23/39, summer €46/78; 🖳) Despite the rather pretentious name, this small hotel has tasteful rooms around a pretty courtyard decorated with antiquities collected by the İstanbullu owner-antique dealer. It also boats two lovely terraces (one with a pool).

TOP END

Antik Tiyatro Hotel (☎ 316 6053; www.antiquetheatrehotel.com; Kıbrıs Şehitler Caddesi 243; s/d in summer from

€92/120, winter €72/90;) Rooms, arranged around a lovely pool set on the edge of a terraced hillside, have stunning views over the castle and sea. They're simple but stylishly decorated with original art work and antiques. Double-glazing keeps out most of the noise of the busy nearby road.

Eating

In July and August prices are double those of İstanbul. As elsewhere, check prices before ordering fish (see also the boxed text, p73).

Restaurants open and close all the time. Those described here have proved more longstanding and dependable.

WESTERN BAY

Liman Köftecisi (☎ 316 5060; Neyzen Tevfik Caddesi 172; meze €2.20; 8am-midnight) Famous nationally, the trendy Liman has a lovely position on the seafront, yet serves delicious food at very decent prices. *Köfte* (grilled meatballs) are the speciality. Of the six types (€3 to €6.65), try the *Liman köfte* – served with yogurt, tomato sauce and butter. The service is also exemplary.

Kırmızı (☎ 316 4918; Neyzen Tevik Caddesi 44; meze €2.50-5.55, mains €5-12; 11.30am-midnight) Serving Mediterranean food made from the freshest local ingredients, the Kırmızı is a small but characterful place spread over three floors. The walls are used to exhibit the works of local artists, and Duygu, the charming owner, will accord you a warm welcome. The €2.75 three-course fixed lunch is astonishing value.

Sünger Pizza (☎ 316 0854; Neyzen Tevfik Caddesi 218; pizza for one person €3.35-6, salads €2.25-4; 8am-midnight) Named after the owner's grandfather who was a *sünger* (sponge) diver, this place packs out to its rafters with locals who are after the 'best pizza in Bodrum'. Grab a table on the rooftop if you can.

Marina Yacht Club (☎ 316 1228; Neyzen Tevfik Caddesi 5; beer €2.75, mains €7-14; 8am-2am) Despite the rather grand entrance and chichi yachting surrounds, the food and prices are quite reasonable here and there's live music every night from 9pm to 1am. It serves either traditional Turkish food or Italian food in the Café Vela.

Yağhane (☎ 313 4747; Neyzen Tevfik Caddesi 170; mains €9.50-17; 10.30am-midnight) Housed in an old olive mill built in 1894, this is an attractive and atmospheric place, with the walls hung with the works of local artists. The menu, which specialises in old Ottoman and Mediterranean dishes, is select and imaginative. Try the delicious regional speciality *et çökertme* – sliced beef with garlic yogurt, grated potatoes and butter (€11). The wine list is also impressive.

Kocadon Restaurant (☎ 316 3705; Saray Sokak 1; meals €15-25; dinner May-Oct) Set back from Neyzen Tevfik Caddesi in the cobbled courtyard of a very attractive 200-year-old stone house, is this highly civilised and atmospheric place that specialises in old Ottoman cuisine. The excellent three-course set menu (for lunch or dinner, €19), which includes an open buffet of 12 meze and a fish dish, is fab for a splurge. The à la carte menu is select and enticing. This claims to be Bodrum's best; it may well be.

Özsüt (☎ 313 6033; Neyzen Teyfik Caddesi 122; 8am-2am summer, 9.30am-11pm winter) Brand-new on the scene, this ever-popular and award-winning İzmiri chain does the usual delicious traditional Turkish puds and cakes and ice cream (€0.69 per scoop). Try the delectable *Özsüt'un Aynası* (mirror of Özsüt).

CENTRE

At the very southern end of the bazaar, Banka Sokak (locally known as Meyhaneler Sokak – Tavern St) is a lovely narrow alleyway shaded by foliage, and filled with attractive, traditionally decorated restaurants. It's firmly on the tourist trail but is still pleasant if you don't mind forking out an extra lira or two.

Nazik Ana (☎ 313 1891; Eski Hukumet Sokak 7; meat mains €2.25, veg mains €1.40; 9am-10pm, closed Sun in winter) Housed in an attractive 100-year-old stone house with walls decorated with photos of old Bodrum, this simple but atmospheric place is a huge hit locally, particularly with the policemen from next door. With its point-and-pick counter, it's a great place to sample different Turkish dishes. If you don't like something, it's so incredibly cheap it doesn't really matter. It lies off Cevat Şakir Caddesi.

Atmaca Döner Salonu (☎ 313 4150; Cevat Şakir Caddesi 39; beer €1.10; 11am-10pm) Very popular locally for its delicious *döner kebaps* (sandwiches €1.65, plate €3 to €3.65), at dirt-cheap prices, this place also has a secret, shaded garden behind the stall front. It's clean and cool and the food's delicious.

EASTERN BAY

Catering to the package tourists, the area along Dr Alim Bey Caddesi and Cumhuriyet Caddesi is packed with bars, pubs and restaurants. Though the restaurants have pleasant seaside table, they can be very pricey, particularly in summer.

06 Lokantası (☎ 316 6863; Cumhuriyet Caddesi 115; meze €1.65, mains €2.50-4.45; ☯ 9am-3am winter, summer 24 hrs) Though simple, the Lokantası is clean, well run and much-loved locally; its prices are unbeatable. Fresh fish is also served as are good veggie options.

Tranca (☎ 316 6610; Cumhuriyet Caddesi 36; mains €11; ☯ 11am-midnight) Jutting out into the bay, the family-run Tranca probably boasts about the best views of anywhere. Its specialities are *tuzda balik* (fish baked in salt) and *testi kebabı* (casserole served in a clay pot that's broken at your table), both cost €25 to €30 with a minimum of two people. Reserve a seafront table if you can.

Kortan Restaurant (☎ 316 1300; Cumhuriyet Caddesi 32; ☯ 9am-1am Apr-Sep) Worth a visit just to see the interior of this lovely, 350-year-old former tavern, the Kortan also boasts five tables on a pretty terrace (phone to reserve one). The speciality is grilled fish (€11 to €22 for 500g). Try the delectable *barbun* (red mullet).

Berk Balık Restaurant (☎ 313 6878; Cumhuriyet Caddesi 167; meze €2.25, all fish €20 per kilo; ☯ noon-1am) Run by a group of friends, this restaurant specialises in fish and seafood, served on a terrific upstairs terrace that buzzes like a village taverna. It's absolutely packed with locals tossing down octopus in garlic and butter or excellent fresh fish at pleasing prices.

Mado (☎ 313 5655; Cumhuriyet Caddesi 24; pastries & puds €3.35; ☯ 9am-1am) With a gorgeous terrace right on the waterfront, this high-quality chain serves the usual range of tantalising Turkish puds and pastries as well as ice cream (scoop €0.85).

SELF CATERING

The large covered market about 250m north of the bus station is a great place for picnic-hunting, selling very fresh fruit and veg as well as Turkish sweets, dried fruit and nuts at great prices (though you may want to bargain a bit). Around the back of the market there is also a large **Tansaş supermarket** (☎ 313 4932; Garaj Üstü; ☯ 8.30am-10pm).

Tarihi Yunuslar Karadeniz Pastanesi (Cumhuriyet Caddesi 13; ☯ 7.30am-midnight) does great fresh bread (good for a picnic or breakfast *en plein air*).

Drinking & Entertainment

In summer, bars and clubs sprout up everywhere. The roads east of Adliye Camii are dotted with pubs and café-bars that come thicker and faster the further east you go. The beachside cafés have big-screen TVs and happy hours before the clubs open around 10pm. In all these places local beer, rakı and spirits will be much cheaper than imported liquor.

Halıkarnas (The Club; ☎ 316 8000; www.halikarnas .com.tr; Cumhuriyet Caddesi; admission weekday/weekend €17/20; beer & spirits from €5.55; ☯ 10pm-5am 18 May–31 Oct) Since the 1970s, the Halıkarnas has been a clubbers' institution. With top-quality sound and light equipment (including two Class IV lasers you can see in Greece), it's an extraordinary experience, particularly when at capacity (5000 people). Internationally known DJs are billed as well as world-touring shows. On Monday to Wednesday, there's free alcohol from 10pm to 1am. Note that it doesn't get going much before 1am.

Marine Club Catamaran (☎ 313 3600; www.club catamaran; Hilmi Uran Meydanı 14; admission weekday/weekend €17/22, beer €5.55; ☯ 19 May–Sep) This floating nightclub sets sail at 1.30am for 3½ hours of frenzied fun. Its transparent dance floor can pack in no fewer than 1500 clubbers and attendant DJs. Between 3am and 5am, a free shuttle operates every half-hour back to the Eastern Bay. Day trips (€30, 10.30am to 5.30am) are also offered. It lies on Hilmi Uran Meydanı (square) off Dr Alim Bey Caddesi.

Kef Bar (☎ 313 3937; Cumhuriyet Caddesi 134; ☯ 9am-3am or later) A new, multipurpose place with tables right on the beach, you could pass the whole day here if you so fancied. From 9am to 8pm, it behaves as both café and beach club (with its own shower and changing rooms); from 8pm to 11pm, it's a bar (with happy hour); and from 11pm it's a club-cum-bar.

Fora (☎ 316 2244; www.forabar.com; Hilmi Uran Meydanı 10; ☯ 10am-4am May-Oct; ☒) Right above the water, this modern and minimalist place boasts great views over the marina. It's cool and peaceful during the day and fast and fun during the night. There's a happy 'hour' between 9am and 11am daily.

Küba Bar (☎ 313 4450; Neyzen Tevfik Caddesi 62; beer €8.35, meals €25; ☯ 9am-4am summer, 9am-2am winter, Wed-Sat only Dec & Feb) With its chic black and marble counters, this place is popular with İstanbul socialites and fashionistas tempted out from their peninsula summer homes. It's fun but a tad expensive.

Campanella Bar (☎ 316 5302; Cumhuriyet Caddesi; ☯ noon-4am) Though small, this Orientalist-style bar is full of atmosphere and usually has live music playing.

If you fancy a puff on a nargileh, the **Old Café** (☎ 316 1928; Cumhuriyet Caddesi 110; nargileh €5.55, beer €2.75; ☺ 10am-midnight winter, 24hr summer) has comfortable seats in either the Ottoman-style salon or on the beach outside.

The castle and the antique theatre are often used for cultural events such as opera and ballet performances. Check out www.biletix .com to see if anything is on while you're in town.

Getting There & Away

AIR

The **Bodrum international airport** (☎ 523 0101), 60km away, is nearer to Milas than Bodrum. Check the charter-flight brochures for bargains, especially at the start and end of the season, but prepare to be disappointed as there are fewer flights than you might expect. **Turkish Airlines** (THY; ☎ 317 1203; fax 317 1211; Kıbrıs Şehitler Caddesi) is in the Oasis Shopping Centre, about 2km out of town off the Gümbet road. To get here, take a dolmuş (€0.55) from the otogar asking for 'Oasis'.

To get to the airport, you can take the Havaş (airport) **bus** (☎ 523 0040; €7.25) run in conjunction with Turkish Airlines, which leaves two hours before all Turkish Airlines departures from the Turkish Airlines office. It also meets flights and drops passengers at the otogar. If you're not flying with Turkish Airlines, an expensive taxi (€39 to €45 from the centre) is really your only option.

BOAT

Ferries for Datça and the Greek islands of Kos and Rhodes leave from the western bay. For information and tickets contact the **Bodrum Ferryboat Association** (☎ 316 0882; www.bodrumfer ryboat.com; Kale Caddesi Cümrük Alanı 22), on the dock past the western entrance to the castle. Check times as they can change.

For Kos, hydrofoils (€30 one way, €35 same-day return, €60 open return, 20 minutes) and ferries (€25 one way or same-day return, €50 open return, cars €100/200 for one way/return, one hour) leave Bodrum daily May to October at 9.30am (returning at 4.40pm). Only ferries operate from November to April, on Monday, Wednesday and Friday (weather permitting).

For Rhodes, hydrofoils (€50 one way, €60 same-day return, €100 open-day return, 2¼

hours) leave Bodrum daily from June to September at 8.30am on Monday and Saturday and return at 4pm the same day.

For Datça, hydrofoils (single/return €10/13, €26/52 for cars, two hours) leave Bodrum daily either at 9am or 5pm from April to May, and twice a day at 9am and 5pm from June to October. No same-day returns are available. The ferry docks at Körmen on the peninsula's northern coast, and the onward bus journey to Datça (15 minutes) is included in your fare.

You don't need to book in advance unless you have a car (on the ferries only).

SERVICES FROM BODRUM'S OTOGAR

Destination	Fare	Duration	Distance	Frequency (per day)
Ankara	€19	12hr	689km	1 nightly
Antalya	€14	8 hr	496km	2
Denizli	€11	5hr	250km	1
Fethiye	€10	6hr	265km	2
İstanbul	€22	12hr	851km	2 nightly
İzmir	€8	4hr	286km	3
Konya	€17	12hr	626km	6
Kuşadası	€7	2½hr	151km	2
Marmaris	€8	3hr	165km	hourly
Milas	€3	1hr	45km	hourly
Muğla	€6	2hr	149km	hourly
Söke	€6	2hr	130km	2 nightly

BUS

Bodrum has bus services to more or less anywhere you could wish to go. The table (above) lists some useful summer daily services. For Gökova, change at Muğla. For Pamukkale, change at Denizli and go from there (€2.75, 10 minutes, 14km).

CAR

Major car-rental agencies can be found on Neyzen Tevfik Caddesi. **Avis** (☎ 316 2333; www .avis.com; Neyzen Tevfik Caddesi 92/A) rents compact cars without air-conditioning from €30 per day. **Thrifty Car Rental** (☎ 313 1802; www.thrifty .com; Neyzen Tevfik Caddesi 58/A) is another. Officially cars start at €40 per day, but shop around and you should be able to bring it down to €30 to €35 or less, depending on the season and length of hire.

Getting Around

Short hops around town in a dolmuş cost €0.55.

BODRUM PENINSULA
☎ 0252

The Bodrum Peninsula consists of high hills, dramatic rocky outcrops and unexpected marine vistas but, as Bodrum's backyard, it is entirely given over to tourism, with grim patches of Legoland-like housing eroding the hillsides. These range from the seriously scary at Gümbet to the more low-key at pretty little Gümüşlük. There is little to entice the independent traveller except for a sunset swim and fish meal, or a stay at one of the boutique hotels, whose style and luxury are unrivalled along the coast.

Getting Around
Several of the beach villages make for enjoyable day trips from Bodrum. Dolmuşes from Bodrum's otogar ply back and forth to most places on the peninsula and fares rarely rise above €1. In low season, you need to watch out for the departure times of the last minibuses back to Bodrum. Alternatively, you can hire a scooter and ride around the peninsula, although the main road from Bodrum to Turgutreis is basically a highway.

Note that there's no dolmuş from Gümüşlük to Yalıkavak and no dolmuş service from Yalıkavak to Gölköy, so you'll have to keep returning to Bodrum to proceed along the northern coast.

Gümüşlük
About 18km from Bodrum is Gümüşlük, a hamlet on the shore of a fine natural harbour protected by high headlands. New building work is prohibited, ensuring that the actual village retains its quiet charm. However, that hasn't been enough to protect the views. Ranks of half-built villas massing on the hillside opposite illustrate the difficulty of shielding anywhere on the coast from developers.

SIGHTS & ACTIVITIES
Gümüşlük makes the best day trip from Bodrum. Come here to swim or climb the headlands and to take lunch on the shore; or come for an afternoon swim and stay for a sunset dinner.

Little remains of ancient **Mindos** apart from slight ruins on Tavşan Island, the rocky islet to the north, which is reachable on foot or by swimming from in front of the Fenerci Restaurant.

The **beach** to the south is long and generally uncrowded. Though weedy in places, the sea is fine for swimming.

SLEEPING
In the off season (mid-October to mid-May) most of Gümüşlük's pensions are closed. If you want to visit early or late in the season, phone first.

Özak Pansiyon (☎ 394 3388; fax 394 3037; Yalı Mevkii 95; camp site €5.55, r €36; ☾ May–20 Sep) At the quiet southern end of the bay, this place with its conical huts and palm roofs has a real beach-camp feel to it. It's friendly and lively and has a bar and volleyball court. Rooms are around a large courtyard and though simple are white, bright and very clean.

Hera Pansiyon (☎ 394 3065; fax 394 4021; Yalı Mevkii 89; apt for 2/4 people €44/55) Well run by a charming family, the Hera has eight simple but spotless and pleasant apartments set in a garden on the seafront. There's also a reasonably priced restaurant and a shaded lounging area. It lies just over halfway along the bay.

Sysyphos Pansiyon & Restaurant (☎ 394 3016; www.gümüşlük.net; Yalı Mevkii 97; s/d €28/39, s/d bungalows €28/39, 2-bedroom apt €56; ☾ May-Oct) Next door to the Özak and perched almost on the waterfront is this 80-year-old, bougainvillea-clad pension. With a large, rambling garden that's filled with birdsong, this is the right place for some R&R. The 15 rooms boast

SOUTH AEGEAN

PENINSULA PECULIARITIES
As you potter around the peninsula, look out for the interesting architectural anomalies. The odd-looking igloo-shaped buildings are *gümbets* (stone cisterns) once used to store fresh water for times of need. On many hilltops, old windmills still wave, though most are redundant, making way for modern living. More unusual are the *kule evleri* (stone tower houses), similar to those seen on the Mani Peninsula in Greece. In Ortakent, you can find two fine 17th-century examples – on the older stone house, look out for the turned-up corners of the roof. It's an architectural affect that can be traced to Minoan Greece. The 'horns' are said to hark back to the cult of the Minoan bull and were probably put on the houses to ward off the evil eye.

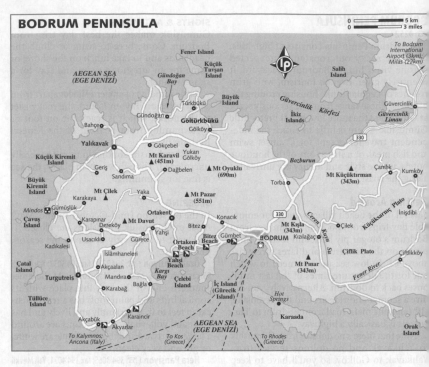

BODRUM PENINSULA

delightful balconies, some directly overlooking the sea.

Taka.com (☎ 394 3045; Yalı Mevkii 19; r winter/summer €17/28) For those on a budget, this is the best option. Though rooms are small and poorly maintained, they have direct sea views.

EATING & DRINKING

Batı Restaurant (☎ 394 3079; meals €6; ◷ 8am-3am May-Oct) An old travellers' favourite, this is a great place for both eating and drinking. A 120-year-old fig tree leans on the restaurant and provides shade for its customer. There's also a fun, cushion-clad chilling area in one corner. The friendly owner is a mine of information about the town and his güveç (casseroles; €6.65 to €8.85) are well worth sampling. There are veggie varieties too (€4.45).

For a mellow drink in the evening under giant, grass-roofed parasols, try the new **Gusta Restaurant Café Bar** (☎ 394 4228; Yalı Mevkii 95; beer €1.65; ◷ 8.30am-2am summer only) or **Club Gümüşlük** (☎ 394 3401; beer €1.65; ◷ 6.30am-2am) at the northern end of the bay, which is a popular haunt for younger locals (and is open all year).

GETTING THERE & AWAY

Dolmuşes run from Gümüşlük to Bodrum (€1.40, 30 to 40 minutes) at least every half-hour and to Turgutreis (€0.85, 15 minutes) every 20 minutes. Vehicles are banned from entering the village, but there is a municipal car park (€2.75 per 12 hours) 300m from the waterfront. The last dolmuş to Bodrum departs at midnight (10pm out of season).

Yalıkavak

In the northwestern corner of the peninsula, 18km from Bodrum, is Yalıkavak. As Datça is to Marmaris, so Yalıkavak is to Bodrum: a smaller, quieter version with the constant threat of similar development looming over it. In the meantime it's remarkably pleasant, with no high-rise buildings to spoil the harbour and several attractive hotels and restaurants.

Yalıkavak's köfte are rightfully famous throughout Turkey; there's no better place to try them.

SLEEPING

Adahan (☎ 385 4759; www.adahanotel.com; Seyhulisla Ömer Lütfü Caddesi 55; s/d €78/100; ◷ May-Oct; ▓ ▓

With its imposing wooden doors that conceal the jewel within, this newly built hotel is designed like an old caravanserai. Spacious and comfortable rooms are arranged around an arcaded courtyard containing a lovely pool. Anatolian antiques furnish some corners and from the kitchen come scintillating smells – the charming owners also run a gourmet restaurant. It lies around 80m from the new yacht harbour on the road to Gümüşlük.

4 Reasons Hotel (☎ 385 3212; www.4reasonshotel .com; Bakan Caddesi 2; d low/high season €110/165, 3-4 person apt €165-200; 🐾 🔁) Set atop a hill 2km from Yalıkavak, the hotel's mantra and 'four reasons' to visit – serenity, design, attitude and quality – are all in evidence here. The almost Zenlike feel starts with the tranquil setting and spacious, neutral rooms (complete with tree branch placed above the bed!) and extends to the yoga classes on Saturdays. There's a lovely pool set in gardens.

Otel Windmill (☎ 385 4805; www.windmillotel.com; s/ d winter €17/28, in summer €28/44, 4-person apt €83; 🐾 🔁) Named after the converted windmill (containing an attractive apartment) in the corner, the hotel's biggest attraction is its pool that appears to 'flow' riverlike around the hotel. Rooms are simple but furnished with nice Orientalist flourishes.

Miray Hotel (☎ 385 4920; www.e-mirayhotel.com; Begonvil Sokak 17; s/d €28/39; 🐾 🔁) If the Windmill is full try this place, with comfortable rooms and a pool.

EATING & DRINKING
All of the following are found at the northern end of the bay.

Cumbalı (☎ 385 4995; İskele Meydanı 126; 400g fish €8; 🕒 8.30am-midnight) A favourite for fish, Cumbalı does delicious dishes at pleasing prices 'to attract locals as well as tourists' as the patron puts it. The seafood meze (€2.75 to €9) are sumptuous, which you can eat right on the seafront.

Kavaklı Köfteci (☎ 385 9349; Çarşı İçi Yalıkavak; meatballs €3.35; 🕒 7.30am-midnight) Around 50m inland from the Café Yalıkavak, this place is famous for its Yalıkavak meatballs served up on simple wooden tables with garlic bread. Smoky-flavoured, slightly spiced and succulent, they're gorgeous! Fight for a table if you have to.

Café Yalıkavak (☎ 385 4095; İskele Meydanı 13; coffee €2, 🕒 7am-1am) Next door to the Cumbarlı, this café sells traditional Turkish pastries and puds

and is fabulous for coffee-and-cake or an ice cream on the seafront.

Değirmenci (☎ 385 2419; Yeldeğırmenı Yani; 🕒 8am-1am) Right beside the old windmill on the seafront, this new place has live music daily from 9pm to midnight.

GETTING THERE & AWAY
Dolmuşes go to Bodrum (€1.40, 25 minutes) every half-hour in summer (but only when full in winter). Surprisingly, although the road is good, there's no dolmuş to Göltürkbükü. You'll have to take a taxi for around €14 to €17 daytime and €22 to €25 at night, or return to Bodrum and catch another dolmuş (€1.40, every 45 minutes) from there.

Göltürkbükü
About 18km north of Bodrum, the twin villages of Gölköy and Türkbükü have decided to merge their names in a cunning plan to fool visitors (www.golturkbuku.com).

GÖLKÖY
Gölköy is set around a narrow beach backed by a sprawl of tourist accommodation. In July and August family pensions open to accommodate most arrivals. Unfortunately, these simply furnished places have the monopoly in summer and if you won't pay €50 for a double, someone else will. Many also have restaurants.

Set right on the waterfront, the newly renovated **Salba Beach Club** (☎ 357 7170; www .salbabeachclub.com; Sahil Sokak 13; s/d €25/50; 🐾) has a sunbathing platform and a nice garden. Rooms are small but quite attractively decorated and have lovely views over the bay. The upper rooms share a balcony.

Made up of a series of modern buildings decorated traditionally, **Sultan Hotel** (☎ 357 7260; fax 357 7261; Sahil Sokak 3; s/d €39/67; 🕒 Apr-Nov; 🐾) is set in a peaceful garden. Rooms are simple but spotless and have little balconies from where you can hear the water lap. There's also a sunbathing platform.

Opposite the Salba Beach Club, **Yör & Mutfak** (☎ 357 7033; Sahil Sokak 14; 🕒 8am-midnight May-Oct) is a good antidote to the expensive hotel restaurant. It does good, home-cooked snacks such as *mantı* (ravioli; €3.35) and *köfte* (€3.85).

TÜRKBÜKÜ
About 1.5km around the point from Gölköy is Türkbükü, a gated wonderland of summer

homes for Turkey's rich and infamous. In July and August the A-listers are flown in by sea plane to their luxurious digs and yachts are packed in tight in the small harbour. There's not much to do apart from people-watch.

SLEEPING & EATING

Much beloved by the fashionable, the rich and the beautiful, **Maki Hotel** (☎ 377 6105; www .makihotel.com.tr; Kelesharimi Mevkii; d from €100; 🅿 🖩) offers comfort *and* style. There's a gorgeous pool set just above the sea, a restaurant with a fine Italian chef and rooms that are hyper-hip (right down to the chrome and orange-painted balconies). Out of season, room rates drop dramatically.

Though built in the 1990s (but designed to look much older), the **Ada Hotel** (☎ 377 5915; www.adahotel.com; Tepecik Caddesi 128; d €238-277; 🅿 Apr-Oct; 🅿 🖩) has already established an enviable reputation. Designed to resemble an old stone house, the hotel boasts a hamam, library, pool and movie theatre. Room adornments

range from real antiques to candles and CD players.

Famous throughout Turkey, the restaurant at **Divan Hotel** (☎ 377 5601; Keleşharım Caddesi 6; meze €4.45-14, fish mains €11-27; 🕑 11.30am-1am) is considered by many as the top table in town. With an İstanbullu chef with a reputation for creativity, the dishes are superb. Try the sole wrapped in shrimp, sautéed Mediterranean herbs and saffron. It even has its own patisserie from where it dreams up its own designs.

Perennially popular **Ship Ahoy** (☎ 377 5070, meze €4-12, fish mains €10-14; 🕑 8am-6am May-Aug), a pretty place on the seafront, serves up superb fish and meze. A famous Turkish singer occupied one table when we visited. From 11pm to 6am it magically metamorphoses into a nightclub.

Another place with a redoubtable reputation is **Mey** (☎ 377 5118; Atatürk Caddesi 61; fish mains €20-22; 🕑 11.30am-2am May-Sep), popular in particular for its lavish fixed menu (which includes three types of fish).

Western Anatolia

Look on the map and it may seem that Western Anatolia falls between at least two stools – it doesn't quite reach the Mediterranean or the Black Sea, stops just short of Ankara, and can only gaze across the Sea of Marmara at İstanbul. Luckily the diversity of the region comes together to create an identity all its own, relatable to Central Anatolia yet distinct from it, and once you've travelled through it and seen the many attractions, you'll start to see the natural progression that connects it to the rest of the country.

The key experiences here lie in the landscape, from the strange vagaries of calcium around Pamukkale to the rich wetlands of the southern lake district. There's no shortage of excuses to get to grips with the great outdoors, but even if you are cruising through on wheels, your senses will keep your brain busy absorbing the colours of poppy fields, the sounds of winds over waterfalls or the sensation of a good mineral bath.

Many of these sites are next to deserted even in season, but don't be fooled into thinking you're a pioneer: people have been treading this ground since ancient times, and whether it's Neolithic settlers near İznik, Phrygian cave carvers around Afyon or Roman pilgrims at Afrodisias, you'll find traces of your predecessors everywhere. If you want to feel connected to the world at large, and Turkey at its best, take a breath, take a chance and take a trip into the hidden heart of the familiar yet alien west.

HIGHLIGHTS

- Blend ancient architecture and modern streetlife in bustling **Bursa** (p292)
- Take a walk through the city walls and catch sunset over **İznik** (p288)
- Sip a brew with a view from a hammock in the fortress at **Kütahya** (p308)
- Investigate the hidden delights and sights of the rock-strewn **Phrygian Valley** (p304)
- Pad or paddle up calcium travertine pools to visit the ruins of **Hierapolis** (p325)
- Relish remote ruins at **Afrodisias** (p329) and at **Sagalassos** (p315)
- Reward yourself with a fish dinner after a day's walking or exploring around **Eğirdir Gölü** (Lake Eğirdir; p317)

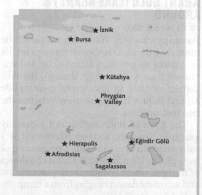

WESTERN ANATOLIA

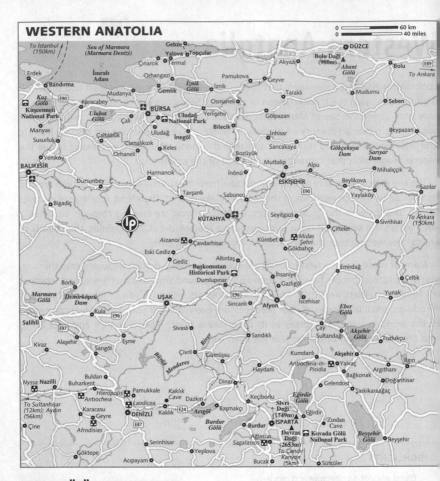

ABANT GÖLÜ (LAKE ABANT) & AROUND

☎ 0374 / pop 6000

For many travellers, Western Anatolia is little more than the area they speed through on the motorway to get from İstanbul to Ankara. Should they wish to stop, though, the lake district nestling in lush, green countryside around Bolu is handily midway between the two metropolises.

The town of Bolu itself is not especially exciting. However, around 30km west is a turn-off south to Abant Gölü, a gorgeous spot for a picnic. It's a 5km walk round the shores of the lake, which is dotted with places to eat and accommodation ranging from a camp site to two five-star hotels.

Even if you don't divert to Abant you should plan to stop on the slopes of **Bolu Dağ** (Mt Bolu), where there are lots of good restaurants offering tasty food and panoramic views. Keen skiers may also want to investigate the resort at **Kartalkaya**, which has good powder from December to March.

MUDURNU

Another 25km southwest of Abant Gölü is the lovely small town of Mudurnu, which used to be famous for its chicken dinners, but is now being feted as an Ottoman revival town. Slowly but surely the old houses are being restored and repurposed to attract visitors. There's a lively old bazaar area and the **Yıldırım Beyazıt hamam** (Büyükcami Caddesi; ☯ 8am-7pm; Mor

Wed, Sat for women) is a real find, charging just €1 if you forego the scrub and massage (not available to women anyway).

Sleeping

Prices at Mudurnu hotels are higher at weekends, when you should also book ahead.

Hacı Abdullahlar Konağı (☎ 421 2284; www.mudurnukonaklari.com, in Turkish; Belediye Yanı 3; s/d €28/39) Just off the main square, this hotel has gorgeous Ottoman-style rooms (some with shared bathroom) in a restored house. There's an inviting upstairs sitting area and a small garden.

Yarışkaşı Konağı (☎ 421 3604; www.yariskasi.com; r €20-30) On the edge of town as you come in from Bolu, this long hotel is in the old style but newly built, with mod cons such as wifi Internet. Rooms are comfortable if quite simple, but there's a large restaurant and some great forest views.

Değirmenyeri Konakları (☎ 421 2677; www.degirmenyeri.com; Kilözü Köyü, Dağ Mevkii; r €39-50) On the Bolu road 8km northeast of Mudurnu, this cluster of mountain cabins is an absolute gem if you want to stay in rustic splendour away from it all.

Getting There & Away

This is an area best explored with a car or motorbike. However, there are regular buses to Bolu from İstanbul and Ankara, and then from Bolu on to Mudurnu (€2, one hour). In summer, there are also several direct buses from Bolu to Abant Gölü.

YALOVA

☎ 0226 / pop 71,000

The town of Yalova is of little interest to travellers except as a terminal for the fast ferries across the Sea of Marmara, the quickest and easiest route between Bursa and İstanbul. Yalova was badly damaged in the earthquake of 1999 and even now has not yet managed to rehouse everyone displaced by the disaster.

Getting There & Away

BOAT

The dock for **İDO fast ferries** (☎ 444 4436; www.ido.com.tr) to İstanbul is just off Yalova's main square; most buses drop you right in front of it. Ferries leave roughly every two hours between 7.30am and 11.30pm for Yenikapı docks (€4.50, car and driver €28, additional passengers €6.70, one hour). A second service runs every 1¼ hours for the port at Pendik

(€2.80, car and driver €22.50, additional passengers €2.25, 45 minutes), south of Bostancı – but if you take this you'll still have a 100km drive or three more pedestrian ferry hops into İstanbul itself.

A cheaper alternative is the older **car ferry** (car and driver €12, 25min), between Topçular, east of Yalova, to Eskihisar, near Gebze. Ferries run every 20 minutes around the clock. However, taking this route leaves even more driving into İstanbul.

BUS

Arriving by ferry from İstanbul you will find the main bus station immediately to the right of the terminal. This is where you pick up one of the frequent dolmuşes (shuttle minibuses) to Termal (€0.55, 30 minutes). Buses to Bursa (€3.35, 1¼ hours) leave every 30 minutes. Dolmuşes to İznik (€2.80, one hour) leave from across the road roughly every hour.

TERMAL

☎ 0226 / pop 2600

About 12km southwest of Yalova, off the road to Çınarcık, Termal consists of a lovely spa resort and a very so-so village with cheap pensions and eateries.

First exploited by the Romans but developed by the Ottomans and then by Atatürk, the baths here take advantage of hot, mineral-rich waters that gush from the earth. They lie in the middle of a beautiful valley, which Atatürk developed as an arboretum, and there are several pleasant walking trails.

Sights & Activities

Termal offers all sorts of bathing possibilities. The main spa complex, the **Kurşunlu Banyo** (☎ 675 7400; ⏱ 7am-10.30pm Mon-Wed & Fri-Sat, 7am-8pm Sun, 7am-noon Thu), features an open-air pool for €5, an enclosed pool and sauna for €4, and small private cubicles for €5 to €7.50. At the **Valide Banyo** (admission €1.50) men and women bathe separately in indoor pools, while at the **Sultan Banyo** (1 person/2 people €6/9) you can rent a private bath by the hour.

Sleeping & Eating

The Çınar and Çamlık **hotels** (☎ 675 7400; s/d from €20/35) in the middle of the spa are run by the same company, Yalova Termal Kaplıca Tesisleri. Rooms at the Çamlık are more expensive but both are quiet and inviting, if slightly old-fashioned and masculine in decoration. Use of the baths is included in the room price. The Çınar has a plane tree–shaded courtyard café while the Çamlık has a proper restaurant.

The smaller hotels in Termal village mostly cater for visitors from the Gulf States.

Getting There & Away

There are frequent buses and dolmuşes (€0.75, 30 minutes) from Yalova. The İDO fast ferry (p287) makes it possible to visit Termal as a day trip from İstanbul.

İZNİK

☎ 0224 / pop 20,000

If all you know about İznik is its reputation for fine tile-making, chances are this isn't what you were expecting. Far from being a commercial hub, today's town has changed surprisingly little since its Ottoman heyday, slumbering peacefully within its historic walls. The town's hilly, rustic surrounds are punctuated by tall, spiky cypress trees and peach orchards, cornfields and vineyards. Development has been largely kept under control here, and the whole place has a relaxed, traditional atmosphere even amid the more modern buildings.

Badly damaged in the War of Independence, İznik has since perked up and offers a welcome retreat for İstanbullus over summer weekends. An increasing number of shops now sell İznik ceramics, but many people still earn their living from either farming or forestry.

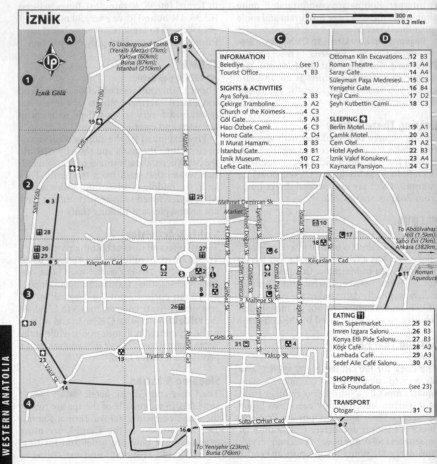

İZNİK

0 — 300 m
0 — 0.2 miles

INFORMATION
Belediye.........................(see 1)
Tourist Office.........................1 B3

SIGHTS & ACTIVITIES
Aya Sofya.........................2 B3
Çekirge Tramboline.........................3 A2
Church of the Koimesis.........................4 C3
Göl Gate.........................5 A3
Hacı Özbek Camii.........................6 C3
Horoz Gate.........................7 D4
II Murat Hamamı.........................8 B3
İstanbul Gate.........................9 B1
İznik Museum.........................10 C2
Lefke Gate.........................11 D3

Ottoman Kiln Excavations.........................12 B3
Roman Theatre.........................13 A4
Saray Gate.........................14 A4
Süleyman Paşa Medresesi.........................15 C3
Yenişehir Gate.........................16 B4
Yeşil Cami.........................17 D2
Şeyh Kutbettin Camii.........................18 C3

SLEEPING
Berlin Motel.........................19 A1
Çamlık Motel.........................20 A3
Cem Otel.........................21 A2
Hotel Aydın.........................22 B3
İznik Vakıf Konukevi.........................23 A4
Kaynarca Pansiyon.........................24 C3

To Underground Tomb (Yeraltı Mezarı) (7km);
Yalova (60km); Bursa (87km); İstanbul (210km)

İznik Gölü

Kılıçaslan Cad

Mehmet Demircan Sk
Market

Kılıçaslan Cad

To Abdülvahap Hill (1.5km); Sahçı Evi (7km); Ankara (382km)

Roman Aqueduct

Lale Sk

Maltepe Sk

Çelebi Sk

Tiyatro Sk

Yakup Sk

EATING
Bim Supermarket.........................25 B2
İmren Izgara Salonu.........................26 B3
Konya Etli Pide Salonu.........................27 B3
Köşk Café.........................28 A2
Lambada Café.........................29 A3
Sedef Aile Café Salonu.........................30 A3

SHOPPING
İznik Foundation.........................(see 23)

TRANSPORT
Otogar.........................31 C3

Sultan Orhan Cad

To Yenişehir (23km); Bursa (76km)

History

İznik may have been founded as early as 1000 BC, but it became a town of any significance only under one of Alexander the Great's generals in 316 BC. A rival general, Lysimachus, captured it in 301 BC and named it rather romantically after his wife, Nikaea. The name stuck, and Nicaea became the capital city of the province of Bithynia, which once spread out along the southern shore of the Sea of Marmara.

Nicaea lost some of its prominence with the founding of Nicomedia (today's Kocaeli/İzmit) in 264 BC, and by 74 BC the entire area had been incorporated into the Roman Empire. It flourished under the Romans, but invasions by the Goths and the Persians brought ruin by AD 300.

With the rise of Constantinople, Nicaea once again acquired importance. In AD 325, the first Ecumenical Council was held here, producing the Nicene Creed, the statement of the basic principles of Christianity. More than four centuries later, the seventh Ecumenical Council was held in Nicaea's Aya Sofya (Hagia Sofia) church.

During the reign of Justinian I (527–65), Nicaea was refurbished with grand new buildings and defences that served the city well when the Arabs invaded. Like Constantinople, Nicaea never fell to its Arab besiegers, but did eventually fall to the Crusaders. From 1204 to 1261, when a Latin king sat on the throne of Byzantium, the true Byzantine emperor, Theodore I (Lascaris), reigned over the empire of Nicaea. When the Crusaders left, the imperial capital returned to Constantinople.

On 2 March 1331, Sultan Orhan conquered İznik, and the city soon possessed the first Ottoman theological school. In 1514 Sultan Selim I captured the Persian city of Tabriz and sent all its artisans west to İznik. They brought with them their skill at making coloured tiles, and soon İznik's kilns were turning out faïence (tin-glazed earthenware) unequalled even today. The great period of İznik tile-making continued almost to 1700, before going into a decline that lasted until 20th-century fashion (and business sense) brought about a revival.

Orientation & Information

Historic İznik is still neatly enclosed within its crumbling city walls and, with the exception of a few hotels and restaurants on the lake-facing side of town, everything that a visitor is likely to want can be found inside the walls. Right in the centre of town, the ruins of the Aya Sofya stand at the intersection of the two main boulevards, Atatürk Caddesi and Kılıçaslan Caddesi. These two roads lead to the four principal gates (kapılar) in the city walls.

The otogar (bus station) is a few blocks southeast of the Aya Sofya.

The **tourist office** (☎ 757 1454; www.iznik.bel.tr; 130 Kılıçaslan Caddesi; ☺ 9am-noon & 1-5pm Mon-Fri) is in the belediye (town hall) building.

Sights & Activities

AYA SOFYA

What was once the **Aya Sofya** (Church of the Divine Wisdom; admission €3.50; ☺ 9am-noon & 1-6pm Tue-Sun) is now a crumbling ruin slumbering in an attractively landscaped rose garden. However, what looks on the outside like one building actually encompasses the ruins of three completely different ones. A mosaic floor and a mural of Jesus with Mary and John the Baptist survive from the original church. Built during the reign of Justinian and destroyed by an earthquake in 1065, it was later rebuilt with the mosaics set into the walls. With the Ottoman conquest, the church became a mosque, but a fire in the 16th century destroyed everything once again. Third time around, reconstruction was carried out under the supervision of the great architect Mimar Sinan, who added İznik tiles to the decoration.

Unfortunately, the church isn't always unlocked during official opening hours.

YEŞİL CAMİ

Built between 1378 and 1387 under Sultan Murat I, the Yeşil Cami (Green Mosque) has Seljuk Turkish proportions influenced more by Iran (the Seljuk homeland) than by İstanbul. The green- and blue-glazed zigzag tiles of the minaret foreshadowed the famous industry that arose here a few decades later.

İZNİK MUSEUM

Opposite the Yeşil Camii is **İznik Museum** (İznik Müzesi; ☎ 757 1027; Müze Sokak; admission €1.10; ☺ 8am-noon & 1-5pm Tue-Sun) housed in the old soup kitchen that Sultan Murat I had built for his mother, Nilüfer Hatun, in 1388. Born a Byzantine princess, Nilüfer had been married to Sultan Orhan to cement a diplomatic alliance.

The grounds of the museum are filled with marble statuary and other archaeological flotsam and jetsam. Inside, the lofty whitewashed halls contain examples of original İznik tiles, with their milky bluish-white and rich 'İznik red'. Among the other displays are 8000-year-old finds from a nearby tumulus at Ilıpınar, believed to show links with Neolithic Balkan culture.

Across the road to the south of the museum is the restored **Şeyh Kutbettin Camii** (1492).

The museum also administers a beautiful, frescoed Byzantine **Underground Tomb** (Yeraltı Mezar) outside town, discovered by accident in the 1960s. Unfortunately staffing and funding problems mean it hasn't been open to the public for years.

CITY WALLS & GATES

It is still possible to make a 5km circuit round most of İznik's walls, which were first erected in Roman times, then rebuilt and strengthened under the Byzantines. Four main gates – İstanbul Kapısı, Yenişehir Kapısı, Lefke Kapısı and Göl Kapısı – still transect the walls. It is possible to make out the remains of another 12 minor gates and 114 towers, some round, some square. In places, the walls still rise to almost their original height of 10m to 13m.

The **Lefke Gate** to the east actually comprises three gateways dating from Byzantine times. The middle one bears a Greek inscription that says it was built by Proconsul Plancius Varus in AD 123. You can climb to the top of the walls here – a good vantage point for inspecting the lie of the land.

The **İstanbul Gate** is similarly imposing, with huge stone carvings of heads facing outwards. However, little remains of the **Göl (Lake) Gate**. To the southwest are the remains of the more minor **Saray (Palace) Gate** – Sultan Orhan (1326–61) had a palace near here in the 14th century. If you head back inside the walls from here you will come to the abandoned ruins of a 15,000-seat **Roman theatre**.

The walls between the **Yenişehir Gate** and the Lefke Gate still stand at a considerable height, and you can follow a footpath for some of the way beside them. However, this is a rather isolated area so it may be wise to explore it in company.

If you cut back inside the walls from the ruins of the minor **Horoz (Rooster) Gate** you will come to the scant ruins of the **Church of the Koimesis** (c AD 800) on the western side

of Kaymakam S Taşkın Sokak. Only some foundations remain, but the church was once famous as the burial place of the Byzantine emperor Theodore I (Lascaris). When the Crusaders took Constantinople in 1204, Lascaris fled to Nicaea and established his court here. It was Lascaris who built Nicaea's outer walls, supported by over 100 towers and protected by a wide moat – no doubt he didn't trust the Crusaders, having already lost one city to them. In a harsh final twist, the church was dynamited after the War of Independence.

OTHER SIGHTS

To the southeast of Aya Sofya, the brick-built **Il Murat Hamamı** (☎ 757 1459; ☽ 6am-midnight, 1-5pm Mon, Thu & Sat for women; wash & massage from €5) was constructed during the reign of Sultan Murat II in the first half of the 15th century.

Across the road from the women's section are the overgrown remains of the 15th- to 17th-century **Ottoman kilns**. The finds are in the İznik Museum.

In the centre of town on Kılıçaslan Caddesi, **Hacı Özbek Camii**, dating from 1332, is one of İznik's oldest mosques.

For something more energetic, **Çekirge Tramboline** (Sahil Yolu; admission €0.85; ☽ 11am-midnight) runs a seasonal trampoline marquee, a surreal counterpoint to İznik's general gravitas. Admission buys you 10 minutes of bouncing.

There is a cluster of minor sights around **Abdülvahap Hill**, outside the Lefke Gate, including the remains of a Roman aqueduct, an open-air Arab *namazgah* mosque, several tombs and a shady cemetery. For a perfect evening stroll, head out an hour or so before sunset to peruse these features and climb the hill itself, where as well as great views you'll find the Berber Rock, a shattered monumental mausoleum carved from a single rock, and the tomb of Abdülvahap Sancaktari, the Turkish-Arab flag bearer who gave his name to the hill after dying during an 8th-century siege.

Sleeping

İznik has a couple of accommodation gems that are perfect for short stays, but they fill up quickly over summer weekends, when advance booking may be a good idea. Bursa has a bigger selection of hotels and restaurants, so you might prefer to stay there and visit İznik as a day trip.

BUDGET

Kaynarca Pansiyon (☎ 757 1753; www.kaynarca
.net; Kılıçaslan Caddesi, Gündem Sokak 1; dm €8.50, s/d/tr
€14/23/34; ▣) Local character Ali Bulmuş's
cheerful, slightly eccentric pension is just
the ticket for budget travellers. It's clean and
central, the TVs show BBC World and there's
a cute little rooftop terrace. Breakfast costs
€2.30. No advance reservations are taken,
but if it's full the staff will help you find an
alternative.

Berlin Motel (☎ 757 3355; www.berlin-motel.com; Göl
Sahil Yolu 36; s/d/tr €17/34/50; ⊠) Don't worry, you
haven't wandered into Germany by accident –
the Turkish owners of this friendly four-storey
block are long-term residents of the Teutonic
capital, hence the name. There are some larger
family rooms (€14 per person), the *Preis-
Leistungsverhältnis* is *ausgezeichnet* (in other
words, it's good value), and of course *man
spricht hier Deutsch.*

Cem Otel (☎ 757 1687; www.cemotel.com; Göl Sahil
Caddesi 34; s/d €23/34; ⊠) Close to the lake and
the city walls, a recent refit has made the Cem
really good value, with TV, phone, minibar
and plenty of space. If you can't land a room
overlooking the lake, hang out for a seat on
the restaurant terrace downstairs.

Hotel Aydın (☎ 757 7650; www.iznikhotelaydin.com;
Kılıçaslan Caddesi 64; s/d/tr €23/34/45) The Aydın is
best known locally for its excellent onsite *pastanesi* (patisserie/bakery), which also dishes
up the hotel breakfasts on the front terrace.
The smallish rooms come with TV, phone,
balcony and chintzy bedspreads.

MIDRANGE

Çamlık Motel (☎ 757 1631; Göl Sahil Yolu; s/d €25/45; ⊠)
Quietly located at the southern end of the road
along the lakeshore, this neat Western-style
motel is a good modern choice with a licensed
restaurant overlooking the lake. It's popular
with tour groups.

İznik Vakıf Konukevi (☎ 757 6025; info@iznik.com;
Vakıf Sokak 13; per person €34) A charming guesthouse set in a delightful rose garden just inland from the lake. The rooms are managed
by the İznik Foundation, which was set up in
1993 to foster the art of İznik tile-making, and
are as cool and stylish as you might expect.
Bizarrely, Foundation staff don't always seem
to know it's there.

Salıcı Evi (☎ 315 4536; www.salicievi.com; Çamoluk;
cabins €56-195) If you have transport, this collection of three character-laden wooden cabins is

the ultimate rural retreat, squirreled away in
the hills 7km southeast of İznik. Cabins sleep
two to six people.

Eating

İznik has an adequate selection of places to eat
but nowhere that really stands out.

İmren Izgara Salonu (☎ 757 3597; Atatürk Caddesi 75; mains from €1.70; ◷ 8am-9pm) A favourite lunchtime spot for locals, who fund a
constant procession of juicy *köfte* and other
grills with dense hunky bread and sweet, hot
green peppers.

Konya Etli Pide Salonu (☎ 757 3156; Kılıçaslan Caddesi; meals €2-3; ◷ 8am-9pm) This is one of several
small eateries opposite the Aya Sofya, serving
among other things good, freshly made pide
(Turkish-style pizza).

In summer the best places to dine (mosquitoes permitting) are the open-air cafés
and restaurants on Sahil Yolu overlooking the
lake. The Köşk Café, Sedef Aile Café Salonu
and Lambada Café are all good for drinks or
simple meals for around €4. In high summer more places open, and the best way to
choose between them is probably to follow
the crowds.

Self-caterers can stock up at the **Bim supermarket** (☎ 411 2216; Atatürk Caddesi; ◷ 8.30am-9.30pm
Mon-Sat, 9am-9pm Sun).

Shopping

Recently, tile-making in İznik has been undergoing a revival, and that the town is proud
of this fact is evident from the posters of tiles
on display in many of the town's restaurants
and hotels. Original İznik tiles are antiquities
and cannot be exported from Turkey, but new
tiles make great, if not particularly cheap,
souvenirs. Good places to start looking are
the small workshops along Salim Demircan
Sokak, and the workshop belonging to the
İznik Foundation (☎ 757 6025; www.iznik.com; Vakıf
Sokak 13).

The **Süleyman Paşa Medresei**, founded by Sultan Orhan shortly after he captured Nicaea,
was the first Ottoman theological seminary,
and it now houses half a dozen ceramic and
craft workshops.

Getting There & Away

There are hourly buses from the otogar to
Bursa (€2.25, 1½ hours) until about 7pm or
8pm, plus frequent buses to Yalova (€2.80,
one hour).

BURSA
☎ 0224 / pop 1.2 million

Sprawling off the slopes of Uludağ (Great Mountain), Bursa may seem at first glance like a purely modern metropolis. In fact, as the first capital of the Ottoman Empire (during the 14th century), the city can be considered the birthplace of modern Turkish culture. Its innumerable ancient buildings, including those of the old spa suburb of Çekirge, a centuries-old tourist draw, are a reminder of Bursa's weighty past.

Today, automobile and textile factories provide the majority of local jobs, and there's affluence in abundance. The local government maintains an admirable record of environmental and progressive initiatives.

Besides its rich history, Bursa is renowned in Turkey for the Bursa, or İskender, kebap – döner kebap on a bed of fresh pide bread, topped with tomato sauce, yogurt and melted butter. Yum... You'll find it all over the country, but here you can really go direct to the source.

History

Bursa dates back to at least 200 BC. According to legend, it was founded by Prusias, the King of Bithynia, but soon came under the sway of Eumenes II of Pergamum and thereafter under Roman rule.

Bursa first grew to importance in the early centuries of Christianity, when the thermal baths at Çekirge (p297) were first developed.

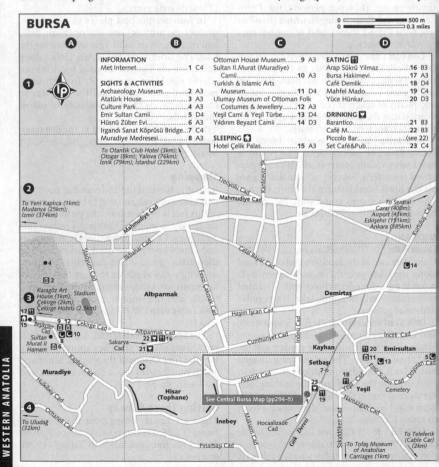

BURSA

0 ————— 500 m
0 ————— 0.3 miles

INFORMATION	
Met Internet	1 C4

SIGHTS & ACTIVITIES	
Archaeology Museum	2 A3
Atatürk House	3 A3
Culture Park	4 A3
Emir Sultan Camii	5 D4
Hüsnü Züber Evi	6 A3
Irgandı Sanat Köprüsü Bridge	7 C4
Muradiye Medresesi	8 A3

Ottoman House Museum	9 A3
Sultan II.Murat (Muradiye) Camii	10 A3
Turkish & Islamic Arts Museum	11 D4
Ulumay Museum of Ottoman Folk Costumes & Jewellery	12 A3
Yeşil Cami & Yeşil Türbe	13 D4
Yıldırım Beyazıt Camii	14 D3

SLEEPING	
Hotel Çelik Palas	15 A3

EATING	
Arap Sükrü Yilmaz	16 B3
Bursa Hakimevi	17 A3
Café Demlik	18 D4
Mahfel Mado	19 C4
Yüce Hünkar	20 D3

DRINKING	
Barantico	21 B3
Café M	22 B3
Piccolo Bar	(see 22)
Set Café&Pub	23 C4

However, it was Justinian I (r AD 527–65) who really put Bursa on the map.

With the decline of the Byzantine Empire, Bursa's location near Constantinople attracted the interest of would-be conquerors, including Arabs and Seljuks. Having seized much of Anatolia by 1075, the Seljuks took Bursa (then Prusa) with ease. But 22 years later the First Crusade arrived, and the city entered a cycle of conquest and reconquest, changing hands periodically for the next 100 years.

After the Turkish migrations into Anatolia during the 11th and 12th centuries, small principalities arose around individual Turkish warlords. One such warlord was Ertuğrul Gazi, who formed a small state near Bursa. In 1317 Bursa was besieged by his son Osman's forces and was starved into submission on 6 April 1326. Under the rule of Osman Gazi, Bursa became the capital of the nascent empire that took Osman's name, Osmanlı (Ottoman).

Osman was succeeded by Orhan Gazi (r 1326–59), who expanded the empire to include everything from what is now Ankara to Adrianople (Edirne), effectively encircling the Byzantine capital at Constantinople. Orhan took the title of sultan, struck the first Ottoman coinage, and, near the end of his reign, was able to dictate to the Byzantine emperors, one of whom, John VI Cantacuzene, became his close ally and father-in-law.

Although the Ottoman capital moved to Edirne in 1402, Bursa remained an important city. Both Osman and Orhan were buried here; their tombs are still important monuments (p296).

With the founding of the Turkish Republic, Bursa started to develop as an industrial centre. In the 1960s and '70s boom times arrived as Fiat (Tofaş) and Renault established factories here. Today it's still a major commercial centre and one of Turkey's wealthiest cities.

Orientation

Bursa's main square is Cumhuriyet Alanı (Republic Sq), usually known as Heykel (Statue) because of its large Atatürk monument. Atatürk Caddesi runs west from Heykel through the commercial centre to the Ulu Cami (Great Mosque). Further west stands the striking blue-glass pyramid of the Zafer Plaza shopping centre, a handy landmark to look for as you approach the city centre.

Heading northwest, Atatürk Caddesi becomes Cemal Nadir Caddesi, then Altıparmak Caddesi and afterwards Çekirge Caddesi, which leads to the spa suburb of Çekirge, about a 10-minute bus ride away. Çekirge is where you'll find many of the spa hotels.

East of Heykel, at Setbaşı, Namazgah Caddesi crosses the Gök Stream (Gök Deresi), which tumbles through a dramatic gorge. Just after the stream, Yeşil Caddesi branches off to the left to the Yeşil Camii and Yeşil Türbe, after which it changes names to become Emir Sultan Caddesi.

From Heykel, Setbaşı and Atatürk Caddesi you can catch dolmuşes and buses to all parts of the city.

Information

There's a post office and numerous banks with ATMs on Atatürk Caddesi (Map pp294–5), and plenty of exchange offices in the Kapalı Çarşı (Covered Market; Map pp294–5).

Discover Internet Centre (Map pp294–5; Taşkapı Caddesi; per hr €0.70; ⏰ 9am-midnight)

FiMa Bookshop (Map pp294–5; Atatürk Caddesi) Sells English-language newspapers.

Met Internet (Map p292; Yılmazsoy İşhanı 6, Hocalizade Caddesi; per hr €1.10; ⏰ 9am-midnight)

Tourist Office (Map pp294–5; ☎ 220-1848; ⏰ 8am-noon & 1-5pm Mon-Fri) Beneath Atatürk Caddesi, in the row of shops at the north entrance to Orhan Gazi Alt Geçidi.

Dangers & Annoyances

Heavy traffic makes it almost impossible to cross Atatürk Caddesi, so you will have to use the *alt geçidi* (pedestrian underpasses). The Atatürk Alt Geçidi (the one nearest to Heykel) has a lift for disabled people; the nearby florist has the key to operate it.

Sights & Activities
EMİR SULTAN CAMİİ
Rebuilt by Selim III in 1805 and restored in the early 1990s, the **Emir Sultan Camii** (Map p292) echoes the romantic decadence of Ottoman rococo style, rich in wood, curves and painted arches on the outside. The interior is surprisingly plain, but the setting, next to a large hillside cemetery surrounded by huge trees and overlooking the city and valley, is as pleasant as the mosque itself.

To reach the mosque, take a dolmuş heading for Emirsultan or any bus with 'Emirsultan' in its name. If you walk between here and the Yeşil Camii and Yeşil Türbe, you'll pass a cemetery, which contains the **grave of Kebapçı İskender**, the kebap maestro himself.

YEŞİL CAMİİ & YEŞİL TÜRBE

A few minutes' walk uphill from Setbaşı, the **Yeşil Camii** (Green Mosque; Map p292), built for Mehmet I between 1419 and 1424, is a supremely beautiful building that represents a turning point in Turkish architectural style. Before this, Turkish mosques echoed the Persian style of the Seljuks, but in the Yeşil Camii a purely Turkish style emerged, and its influence is visible in Ottoman architecture across the country. Note the harmonious façade and the beautiful carved marble work around the central doorway.

As you enter, you pass beneath the sultan's private apartments into a domed central hall with a 15m-high *mihrab* (niche indicating the direction of Mecca). The greenish-blue tiles on the interior walls gave the mosque its name, and there are also fragments of a few original frescoes.

Inside the main entrance a narrow staircase leads up to the sumptuously tiled and deco-

rated *hünkar mahfili* (sultan's private box) above the main door. This was the sultan's living quarters when he chose to stay here, with his harem and household staff in less plush digs on either side.

In the small park surrounding the mosque is the **Yeşil Türbe** (Green Tomb; Map p292; admission free; 8am-noon & 1-5pm), which unlike the mosque is not actually green; the blue exterior tiles were added during restoration work in the 19th century, although the interior tiles are original. Walk round the outside to see the tiled calligraphy above several windows. Inside, the most prominent tomb is that of the Yeşil Camii's founder, Mehmet I (Çelebi), surrounded by those of his children. There's also an impressive tiled *mihrab*.

Down the road from the Yeşil Camii is its *medrese* (seminary), which now houses the **Turkish & Islamic Arts Museum** (Map p292; admission €1.10; 8am-noon & 1-5pm). The collection includes pre-Ottoman İznik ceramics, the original door and *mihrab* curtains from the Yeşil Camii, jewellery, embroidery, calligraphy and dervish artefacts, most with unusually coherent English captions.

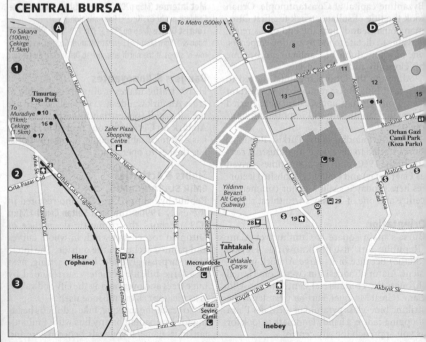

CENTRAL BURSA

To Sakarya (100m); Çekirge (1.5km)

To Metro (500m)

Timurtaş Paşa Park

To Muradiye (1km); Çekirge (1.5km)

Zafer Plaza Shopping Centre

Orhan Gazi Camii Park (Koza Parkı)

Yıldırım Beyazıt Alt Geçidi (Subway)

Tahtakale

Hisar (Tophane)

Mecnundede Camii

Tahtakale Çarşısı

Hacı Sevinç Camii

İnebey

WESTERN ANATOLIA

YILDIRIM BEYAZIT CAMİİ

Gazing across the valley from the Emir Sultan Camii, you'll spot the twin domes of the **Yıldırım Beyazıt Camii** (Mosque of Beyazıt the Thunderbolt, 1391; Map p292), which was built earlier than the Yeşil Camii but forms part of the same architectural evolution.

Next to the mosque is its *medrese*, once a theological seminary, now a public health centre. Here, too, are the tombs of the mosque's founder, the thunderous Sultan Beyazıt I, and his son İsa.

IRGANDI SANAT KÖPRÜSÜ

Crossing the river just north of the Setbaşı road bridge, the **Irgandı Bridge** (Map p292) has been restored in Ottoman style as a charming dual row of tiny yellow shops, selling handicrafts and other items under their tiled roofs. A couple of little cafés make it a nice spot for a browse and a cuppa.

TOFAŞ MUSEUM OF ANATOLIAN CARRIAGES

A short uphill walk south from Setbaşı, along Sakaldöken Caddesi, will bring you to what was once a silk factory and is now a small

museum (Map p292; ☎ 329 3941; Kapıcı Caddesi, Yıldırım; ⏰ 10am-5pm Tue-Sun). It exhibits old carts alongside old cars, and could be somewhere to bring the kids when they get tired of mosques. The museum grounds are laid out as an Ottoman garden – great for picnicking.

BURSA CITY MUSEUM

Bursa has a state-of-the-art **City Museum** (Bursa Kent Müzesi; Map pp294-5; ☎ 220 2486; www.bursakent muzesi.gov.tr; admission €0.85; ⏰ 9.30am-6pm Mon-Fri, 10am-6.30pm Sat & Sun), housed in what was once the old courthouse at Heykel. Ground-floor exhibits whip through the history of the city, with information on the sultans most closely associated with it. Unfortunately, the labelling is in Turkish only, apart from the section headings. Luckily the cultural and ethnographical collections upstairs need little explanation, while down in the basement the reconstructions of old shops are wonderful, with films showing old-fashioned artisans at work. Newspaper clippings also show a couple of local characters to look out for: Deli Ayten, the banjo-playing bag lady, and 'Tarzan Ali', 59-year-old former action hero.

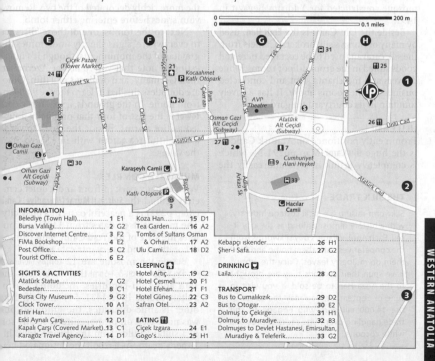

MARKETS

Behind the Ulu Cami, Bursa's sprawling **Kapalı Çarşı** (Covered Market; Map pp294-5) is a great place to while away a few hours, especially if you find İstanbul's Grand Bazaar too touristy. At the centre of the Kapalı Çarşı, the *bedesten* (vaulted, fireproof enclosure for valuable goods) was built in the late 14th century by Yıldırım Beyazıt, although it was reconstructed after an earthquake in 1855. The market is renowned for its high-quality towels and bathrobes, should you have space in your luggage for such bulky items.

As you wander around, look for the **Eski Aynalı Çarşı** (Old Mirrored Market), which was originally the Orhangazi Hamam (1335) – the bathhouse of the Orhan Camii Külliyesi – as indicated by the domed ceiling with its skylights. This is a good place to shop for Karagöz shadow puppets and other traditional items.

The Kapalı Çarşı tumbles out into the surrounding streets, but at some point you will find the gateway into the **Koza Han** (Cocoon Caravanserai), which was built in 1490. Unsurprisingly, the building is full of expensive *ipek* (silk) shops. In the courtyard is a small mosque constructed for Yıldırım Beyazıt in 1491.

Beside the Ulu Cami is the **Emir Han**, used by many of Bursa's silk brokers. Camels from the silk caravans used to be corralled here and goods stored in the ground-floor rooms, while drovers and merchants slept and conducted business in the rooms above. It has a lovely fountain in its courtyard tea garden.

ULU CAMİ

Prominently positioned on Atatürk Caddesi is the huge **Ulu Cami** (Map pp294-5), which is completely Seljuk in style and easily the most imposing of Bursa's mosques. Yıldırım Beyazıt put up the money for the monumental building in 1396. Twenty small domes and a minaret of daunting girth augment the exterior, while inside the size theme continues with immense portals and a forest of square pillars. Notice the fine work of the *mimber* (pulpit) and the preacher's chair, as well as the calligraphy on the walls.

TOMBS OF SULTANS OSMAN & ORHAN

A steep cliff riddled with archaeological workings overlooks Cemal Nadir Caddesi. This section of town, the oldest in Bursa, was once enclosed by stone ramparts and walls, parts of which still survive. From the Ulu Cami, walk west and up Orhan Gazi (Yiğitler) Caddesi a ramplike street that leads to the section known as Hisar (Fortress) or Tophane.

In a little park on the summit are the **Tombs of Sultans Osman and Orhan** (Osman Gazi ve Orhan Gazi Türbeleri; Map pp294-5; admission by donation), founders of the Ottoman Empire. The original structures were destroyed in the earthquake of 1855 and rebuilt in Ottoman baroque style by Sultan Abdül Aziz in 1868. Osman Gazi's tomb is the more richly decorated of the two. Remove your shoes before entering either tomb.

Next to the tombs, one of those 'distance to everywhere' signs slightly undermines the gravitas of the monuments, though it's interesting to note that you're nearer Azerbaijan than Germany, and denizens of Tiffin, Ohio are doubtless thrilled to learn they're 9,600km from home. In the grounds, a six-storey **clock tower** is the last of four that originally doubled as fire alarms. Beside the clock tower is a delightful **tea garden** with fine views over the valley.

MURADİYE COMPLEX

With a shady park in front and a quiet cemetery behind, the **Sultan II Murat (Muradiye) Cami** (Map p292) is a peaceful oasis in a busy city. The mosque itself dates from 1426 and imitates the style of the Yeşil Cami, with painted decorations and a very intricate *mihrab*.

Beside the mosque are 12 **tombs** (admission €2; 8.30am-noon & 1-5pm) that date from the 15th and 16th centuries, including that of Sultan Murat II (r 1421–51) himself. Like other Islamic dynasties, the Ottoman one was not based on primogeniture, so any son of a sultan could claim the throne upon his father's death. As a result the designated heir

---

THE SILK TRADE

Silkworm-raising is a local cottage industry, with a history almost as long as the city itself. Each April, villagers buy silkworms from the cooperatives, take them home and feed them on mulberry leaves. Once the worms have spun their cocoons they are brought to the Koza Han to be sold. If you visit in June or September, you may see some of the 14,000 villagers who engage in the trade haggling over huge sacks of precious white cocoons.

KARAGÖZ & HACİVAT

Bursa is regarded as the birthplace of the Turkish Karagöz shadow puppet theatre, a Central Asian tradition brought to Bursa, from where it spread throughout the Ottoman lands. The puppets – cut from camel hide and treated with oil to make them translucent, then brought to life with coloured paint – are manipulated behind a white cloth onto which their images are cast by back-lighting.

Legend has it that one of the foremen working on Bursa's Ulu Camii was a hunchback called Karagöz. He and his straight man Hacivat indulged in such humorous antics that the other workers abandoned their tasks to watch. This infuriated the sultan, who had the two miscreants put to death. Their comic routines were immortalised, however, in the Karagöz shadow puppet shows. In 2006 the pair was brought to further prominence in Ezel Akay's film comedy *Hacıvat & Karagöz* (released as *Killing the Shadows* in English), starring Haluk Bilginer and Beyazit Öztürk.

In Bursa, Şinasi Çelikkol has worked hard to keep the tradition of Karagöz puppetry alive and was instrumental in the setting up of the **Karagöz Sanat Evi** (Karagöz Art House; Çekirge Caddesi; ☎ 233 8429; admission €5; ☯ shows 11am Wed & Sat, 7.30pm Fri), opposite the Karagöz monument. It houses a small museum of puppetry with some magnificent examples from Uzbekistan. Şinasi Çelikkol's ethnographical collection is also on display here. If you would like to see the collection privately call into his shop – called, inevitably, Karagöz – in the Eski Aynalı Çarşı for an appointment.

(or strongest son) would often have his brothers put to death rather than risk civil war, and many of the occupants of tombs here, including all the *şehzades* (imperial sons), were killed by close relatives.

The custodian will open certain buildings for you, and it's well worth having a look at the beautiful decoration in some of the tombs.

Across the park from the mosque is the **Ottoman House Museum** (Osmanlı Evi Müzesi; admission €1.30; ☯ 10am-noon & 1-5pm Tue-Sun), which should now be open, although it's pot luck whether you find anyone there even during normal opening hours. On the western side of the tombs is the 15th-century **Muradiye Medresesi**, a theological seminary restored in 1951 as a tuberculosis clinic.

Also nearby is the **Ulumay Museum of Ottoman Folk Costumes & Jewellery** (Osmanlı Halk Kıyafetleri ve Takıları Müzesi; İkincimurat Caddesi; admission €2.80; ☯ 9am-7pm), an impressive private collection opened in the restored 1475 Sair Ahmet Paşa *medrese* in 2004. Affable owner-curator Esat Ulumay, a former economist and sword-dancer now considered a leading expert in Ottoman costume, likes to take visitors round the displays personally.

A short walk uphill behind the Sultan Murat II Hamam (follow the signs) brings you to the restored Ottoman **Hüsnü Züber Evi** (Uzunyol Sokak 3; admission €1.30; ☯ 10am-noon & 1-5pm Tue-Sun). Like the Ottoman House it's sporadically staffed, but worth a try anyway.

To get to the complex from Heykel catch a bus or dolmuş to Muradiye. Some buses from Çekirge to Heykel also pass this way.

CULTURE PARK

The **Culture Park** (Kültür Parkı; Map p292) lies north of the Muradiye complex but some way down the hill. The whole park was re-landscaped in 2006, and may take a couple of seasons to recover. As well as tea gardens and playgrounds, the park houses the **Archaeological Museum** (Arkeoloji Müzesi; admission €1.10; ☯ 8am-noon & 1-5pm Tue-Sun), a predominantly classical collection of finds from local sites with little in the way of context or English signage.

Across the road is **Atatürk House** (Atatürk Evi; admission free; ☯ 8.30am-noon & 1.30-5pm Tue-Sun), a swish 1895 chalet in a pretty garden, with restored rooms set up as they would have been during the Father of Turkey's occasional visits (complete with freaky stuffed dog).

You can reach the Culture Park from Heykel by any bus or dolmuş going to Altıparmak, Sigorta or Çekirge.

ÇEKİRGE

An old suburb west of the busy city centre, **Çekirge** is Bursa's spa centre. The warm mineral-rich waters that spring from the slopes of Uludağ have been famous for their curative powers since ancient times, and even today the ailing and infirm come here for several weeks at a time to soak. Most people stay in hotels that have their own mineral baths, although there are several independent *kaplıcalar* (thermal baths) as well.

The **Yeni Kaplıca** (☎ 236 6955; Mudanya Caddesi 10; ⏱ 6am-11pm), on the northwestern side of the Culture Park, was renovated in 1522 by Sultan Süleyman the Magnificent's grand vizier, Rüstem Paşa, on the site of a much older bath built by Justinian. Besides the Yeni (New) bath itself, you'll also find the Kaynarca (Boiling) baths, limited to women; and the Karamustafa baths, with facilities for family bathing. Last admission is at 10pm; the full massage costs €11.10 per half hour.

Perhaps the most attractive bath is the beautifully restored **Eski Kaplıca** (Map p292; ☎ 233 9300; admission €11.10; ⏱ 7am-10.30pm) on Çekirge's eastern outskirts, managed by the next-door Kervansaray Termal Hotel. The bath is done out in creamy marble, and the hot rooms have plunge pools. You'll be charged for everything right down to the soap, so figure on spending up to €30 for the full bath, scrub and massage.

For the lowdown on *hamam* etiquette, see p651.

Çekirge's other main feature is the unusual **I Murat (Hüdavendiğar) Camii**, behind the Ada Palas Oteli. Its basic design is the early-Ottoman inverted 'T' plan, which first appeared in the Nilüfer Hatun *imaretı* (soup kitchen) in İznik (p289). Here, however, the 'T' wings are barrel-vaulted rather than dome-topped. On the ground floor at the front are the rooms of a *zaviye* (dervish hostel). The 2nd-floor gallery on the facade, built as a *medrese*, is not evident from within except for the sultan's loge (box) in the middle at the back of the mosque.

The huge **sarcophagus of Sultan Murat I** (r 1359–89), who died at Kosovo quelling a rebellion by his Albanian, Bosnian, Bulgarian, Hungarian and Serbian subjects, can be viewed in the tomb across the street.

Çekirge's main street is I Murat Caddesi (Birinci Murat Caddesi). To get here, take a bus or dolmuş from Heykel or Atatürk Caddesi to Çekirge or SSK Hastanesi. Bus No 96 goes direct from the otogar to Çekirge.

Festivals & Events

The renowned **Uluslararasi Bursa Festival** (www.bursafestivali.org, in Turkish), Bursa's long-standing citywide music and dance festival, runs for three weeks in June and July.

Every November the **Karagöz Festival** draws Karagöz shadow puppeteers (see p297), Western puppeteers and marionette performers to Bursa for five days of festivities and performances.

Tours

Karagöz Travel Agency (Map p294-5; ☎ 221-8727; www.karagoztravel.com; Kapalıçarşı, Eski Aynalı Çarşı 4) offers an interesting range of local tours, including city tours and trips to Cumalıkızık (p302).

Sleeping

Though a little pricier than elsewhere, Çekirge (3km east of Central Bursa) offers the most attractive sleeping options in Bursa. The majority of hotels here have their own bathing facilities. You may find that your bathroom runs only mineral water, or there may be private or public bathing rooms in the basement. Baths are usually included in the room price, so do take advantage of them.

ÇEKIRGE & SOĞANLI

Yeşil Yayla Termal Otel (☎ 239 6496; Selvi Sokak 6) This original 1950s hotel was being renovated at time of research, but will hopefully remain Çekirge's cheapest choice.

Çekirge Termal Hotel (☎ 233 9335; Hamam Sokak 25 s/d/tr €23/39/50) It won't win any design prizes, but as big orange blocks go, you could probably do worse. The rooms are functional rather than impressive, so make the most of the free baths.

Termal Hotel Gold 2 (☎ 235 6030; www.otelgold.com I Murat Cami Aralığı; s/d/tr €28/50/67; ✖) This restored 1878 house next to the I Murat Camii is a great choice in a quiet location, decked out in full wooden interiors, 'period' furniture and deep red drapery. Baths and parking are included, and the roof terrace is a bonus.

Boyugüzel Termal Otel (☎ 239 9999; www.boyuguzel.com; Uludağ Caddesi; s/d/tr €39/62/75; ✖ 💻) Mostly modern but with a few character touches around the lobby bar; rooms here are smart and well put-together. Rates include a daily mineral bath.

Atlas Termal Hotel (☎ 234 4100; www.atlastotel.com.tr; Hamamlar Caddesi 29; s/d/tr €45/67/84; ✖) Another restored building blending modern and traditional style, with lots of pine fittings and a sunny internal courtyard. Prices include thermal bath.

Hotel Çelik Palas (Map p292; ☎ 233 3800; Çekirge Caddesi 79; s/d €134/150; ✖ 💻 ✖) Overlooking the Culture Park midway between Çekirge and Heykel, this is a huge, partially Art Deco hotel with a gorgeous indoor swimming pool, a *hamam*, two restaurants and rooms with all mod cons. Atatürk had it built right beside his house to accommodate his guests, piping the mineral water all the way from Çekirge. Unfortunately, you'll usually wind up staying in the modern annexe.

Otantik Club Hotel (☎ 211 3280; www.otantikclub hotel.com; Soğanlı; d €78, ste €130; ⊠ ⊇) One of Bursa's best hotels, tucked away in a botanical garden in the suburb of Soğanlı. All the rooms are gorgeous, but the suites, with the sun streaming through their stained-glass windows onto gorgeous Ottoman-style fabrics, are exquisite. Extras include a children's play area, bicycles for loan and a small cinema.

CENTRAL BURSA

Hotel Güneş (Map pp294-5; ☎ 222 1404; otelgunes@yahoo .com; İnebey Caddesi 75; s/d/tr/q with shared bathroom €13/23/25/34) In a restored Ottoman house, the friendly family-run Güneş is Bursa's best budget pension. The small, neat rooms have new laminate floors, the bathrooms have squat toilets and the walls have tourist-board photos of Turkey. There's a pleasant sitting area downstairs with lots of information for travellers.

Hotel Çeşmeli (Map pp294-5; ☎ 224 1511; Gümüşçeken Caddesi 6; s/d €25/38) Named for the ablutions fountain outside, the Çeşmeli is friendly, clean and conveniently located, plus the entire staff is female, making it an excellent choice for women travellers. The buffet breakfast is excellent, and you even get a minibar and hairdryer.

Hotel Artıç (Map pp294-5; ☎ 224 5505; www.artichotel .com; Ulu Camii Karşısı 95; s/d/tr €28/45/62; ⊠) A de-

cent new arrival towards the western end of Atatürk Caddesi. Rooms are light and fairly spacious, though the décor's drab and the singles substandard. The communal areas are best, with Ulu Camii views from the breakfast salon. Posted rates are considerably higher and not really worth it.

Hotel Efehan (Map pp294-5; ☎ 225 2260; www.efehan .com.tr; Gümüşçeken Caddesi 34; s/d €31/48/56) Revelling in a spot of modern style with plenty of marble, the Efehan has all-round appeal and is definitely good value for the central location. At certain times school-age staff may barely register your presence, but the grown-ups are more professional.

Safran Otel (Map pp294-5; ☎ 224 7216; safran_otel@ yahoo.com; Arka Sokak 4, Tophane; s/d €31/56; ⊠) Opposite the Osman and Orhan tombs, the Safran is housed in a characterful restored house in a historic neighbourhood. The Ottoman trappings don't extend to the rooms, but it's an inviting place and has a decent restaurant next door.

Eating

As well as the legendary İskender kebap, Bursa is well known for İnegöl *köftesi*, a rich grilled meatball named after nearby İnegöl. Other culinary specialities include fresh fruit (especially *şeftali* – peaches – in season) and *kestane şekeri* (candied chestnuts).

RESTAURANTS

It's surprisingly hard to find a good İskender in Bursa. Prices start around €3.50 for *bir porsyon* (one serving) or €4.50 if you pig out and order *bir buçuk porsyon* (1½ portions).

Çiçek Izgara (Map pp294-5; ☎ 221 6526; Belediye Caddesi 15; mains €1.70-6; ☯ 11am-9.30pm) One block from Koza Parkı, behind the half-timbered *belediye*, the Çiçek grillhouse is bright and modern (good for lone women), with a 1st-floor salon to catch the flower-market action.

Şehr-i Safa (Map pp294-5; ☎ 222 8080; Atatürk Caddesi 29; meals from €2.80; ☯ 9am-10pm) Get high on fast food: this popular canteen occupies a high-rise terrace up above the trees and houses of Atatürk Caddesi, overlooking Heykel. Meal deals usually include a main, salad and soft drink.

Bursa Hakimevi (Map p292; ☎ 233 4900; Çekirge Caddesi 10; mains €2.50-5; ☯ noon-10pm) It's taken a while, but this restored Ottoman house on the edge of the Culture Park has finally reopened in tastefully low-key restaurant form. The menu's unchallenging but the garden terrace is perfect.

Gogo's (Map pp294-5; ☎ 223 1113; Kirişçi Kız Sokak; mains €2.80-5.50; ⏲ 10.30am-10.30pm) It may sound like a strip club, but Gogo's is actually a characterful backroad restaurant with a lovely terrace full of random baroque Ottoman odds and ends. Occasional art shows and events are held here.

Kebapçı İskender (Map pp294-5; ☎ 221 4615; Ünlü Caddesi 7; mains €4-16.50; ⏲ 10am-10pm) This legendary kebap shop dates back to 1867 and its owners claim to be descendants of İskender Usta himself. However, at €7.50 a portion you're paying a *lot* for a bit of history. There are several branches around town, including on Atatürk Caddesi, in Zafer Plaza and a 'museum restaurant' out in Soğanlı.

Yüce Hünkar (Map p292; ☎ 327 8910; Yeşil Cami Yanı 17-19; meals €9-17; ⏲ 11am-10pm) The Hünkar has a wonderful location overlooking a valley in front of the Yeşil Cami, which just about makes up for the tourist-trap prices.

Formerly part of Bursa's Jewish quarter, **Sakarya Caddesi** (Map p292) acquired new fame from one Arap Şükrü, who opened a restaurant here decades ago. It was so successful that his descendants followed him into the business, and the street now has no less than five family restaurants of the same name, plus the inevitable copycat competitors. The whole upper end of the narrow lane is crammed with tables, so you can wander down and check the buzz before making your choice. Fish is the speciality, starting around €6 per portion, but meat and mezes are also available. **Arap Şükrü Yılmaz** (Map p292; Sakarya Caddesi 4; ⏲ 11am-11pm) is reliably popular.

The street is on the northern side of the Hisar district, just south of Altıparmak Caddesi. It's about 10 minutes' walk from the Ulu Cami, or you can take a Çekirge-bound bus or dolmuş from Heykel to the Çatal Fırın stop, opposite the Sabahettin Paşa Camii.

CAFÉS & QUICK EATS

Café Demlik (Map p292; ☎ 326 4483; Yeşil Caddesi 25; dishes from €1; ⏲ 11am-9pm) This charming old house has been converted into an Ottoman-style eatery where you can sit on floor cushions and get stuck into *gözleme* (savoury pancakes) .

Mahfel Mado (Map p292; ☎ 326 8888; Namazgah Caddesi 2; mains €2.50-4.50; ⏲ 8am-11pm) Now part of the national Mado chain, Bursa's oldest café is open from breakfast to dessert. It also

has live music at its riverside terrace and an art gallery in the basement.

SELF-CATERING

Self-caterers should head straight for **Tahtakale Çarsısı** (Tahtakale Market; Map pp294-5) near Hotel Güneş, for a great choice of fresh fruit vegetables and cheeses.

Drinking & Entertainment

After eating in Sakarya Caddesi, amble down the road to take in one of its smart bars or studenty cafés. The bar clientele is often heavily male, and many places post signs reading 'Damsız Girilmez' (no men without ladies) However, this applies mostly to groups of young Turkish guys.

Barantico (Map p292; ☎ 222 4049; Sakarya Caddes 55; drinks from €1; ⏲ 11am-10pm) Tucked away in a courtyard, this is the place to dabble in all things occult, with tarot readings, séances and the reading of coffee grains the order of the day.

Café M (Map p292; ☎ 220 9428; Altıparmak Caddesi 9/D) Modern, orange and generally rather cool, M attracts a hip, mixed crowd of fashionable young folk.

Piccolo Bar (Map p292; ☎ 223 5658; Sakarya Caddes 16) A cosy pub that has live music most nights and seems to be popular with cigar-puffers.

Set Café&Pub (Map p292; ☎ 225-1162; Köprü Üstü) Across the stream from the Mahfel Mado, this multi-terraced pub has live music, Fosters lager and an entertainingly confusing layout.

Laila (Map pp294-5; Atatürk Caddesi 91) Pitched as a one-stop nightlife shop, Laila has an impressive four floors of self-contained entertainment, including all-day restaurant, café, internet, live music room and disco.

Getting There & Away

Bursa's otogar is 10km north of the centre on the Yalova road. See opposite for information on getting from the otogar to the city centre and Çekirge. Information on some major bus routes and fares is provided in the table, opposite.

The fastest way to get to İstanbul (€5, 2½ to three hours) is to take a bus to Yalova, then the **İDO fast ferry** (☎ 444 4436; www.ido.com.tr) to İstanbul's Yenikapı docks. Get a bus that departs Bursa's bus terminal at least 90 minutes before the scheduled boat departure.

Karayolu ile (by road) buses to İstanbul drag you all around the Bay of İzmit and take four to five hours. Those designated *feribot ile* (by ferry) take you to Topçular, east of Yalova, and then by ferry to Eskihisar, a much quicker and more pleasant way to go.

The table below lists daily services from selected routes from Bursa.

Getting Around

TO & FROM THE OTOGAR

City bus No 38 crawls the 10km between the otogar and the city centre (€0.85, 45 minutes). Returning to the otogar, it leaves from stop 4 on Atatürk Caddesi. Bus No 96 from the otogar goes direct to Çekirge (€0.85, 40 minutes).

A taxi from the otogar to the city centre costs around €8, to Çekirge about €9.

CITY BUS

Bursa's city buses (BOİ; €0.85) have their destinations and stops marked on the front and kerb side. A major set of yellow bus stops is lined up opposite Koza Parkı on Atatürk Caddesi. Catch a bus from stop 1 for Emirsultan and Teleferik (Uludağ cable car); from stop 2 for Muradiye; and from stop 4 for Altıparmak and the Culture Park. You can also pick up buses to the Botanik Parkı (No 15) and Cumalıkızık (No 22) from here.

All city buses now run on a prepay system; you can buy tickets from kiosks or shops near most bus stops (look out for the BursaKart sign). If you're staying for a few days there are various multi-trip options available.

DOLMUŞ

In Bursa, cars and minibuses operate as dolmuşes. The destination is indicated by an illuminated sign on the roof. The minimum fare is €0.70.

Dolmuşes go to Çekirge via the Culture Park, Eski Kaplıca and I Murat Camii from a major dolmuş terminal immediately south of Heykel. Other dolmuşes wait in front of Koza Parkı.

METRO

Bursa has an efficient modern metro system, but as it serves only the outskirts of town rather than the centre, it is seldom used by visitors.

TAXI

A ride from Heykel to Muradiye costs about €2, to Çekirge about €4.

AROUND BURSA

Uludağ

☎ 0224

You may be surprised to discover that Turkey's nascent ski industry flourishes even this far west, with Uludağ (Great Mountain; 2543m), on the outskirts of Bursa, at its heart. A *teleferik* (cable car) runs up to Sarıalan, 7km from the town of Uludağ and the main hotel area, which springs to life during the ski season from December to early April and then slumbers throughout the summer. Even if you don't plan to go skiing or do the three-hour hike to the summit, you might still want to head up to take advantage of the view and the cool, clear air of Uludağ National Park. With pine forests and distant snowy peaks, the scenery is almost reminiscent of Scotland, apart of course from the 30°C summer temperatures here, which would really leave the

SERVICES FROM BURSA'S OTOGAR

Destination	Fare	Duration	Distance	Frequency (per day)
Afyon	€10	5hr	290km	8
Ankara	€11.50	6hr	400km	hourly
Bandırma	€5	2hr	115km	12
Çanakkale	€11.50	5hr	310km	12
Denizli	€11.50	9hr	532km	several
Eskişehir	€5.50	2½hr	155km	hourly
İstanbul	€8.50	3hr	230km	frequent
İzmir	€8.50	5½hr	375km	hourly
İznik	€2.80	1½hr	82km	hourly
Kütahya	€7	3hr	190km	several
Yalova	€3.50	1¼hr	76km	every 30 min

Scots wondering what to wear under their kilts.

At the cable-car terminus at Sarıalan there are a few snack and refreshment stands and a national-park camp site (usually full).

GETTING THERE & AWAY
Cable Car

Take a Bursa city bus from stop 1 or a dolmuş marked 'Teleferik' (€0.60) from behind the city museum to the lower terminus of the cable car, a 15-minute ride from Heykel. The cable cars (€3.50 return, 30 minutes) depart every 40 minutes between 8am and 10pm in summer and between 10am and 5pm in winter, wind and weather permitting. At busy times they'll leave whenever there are 30 people on board.

The cable car stops first at Kadıyayla, then continues upwards to the terminus at Sarıalan (1635m). Stand at the rear of the car for the best views of Bursa as you go up.

Dolmuş

Dolmuşes from central Bursa to Uludağ (€2.80) and Sarıalan (€4) run several times daily in summer and more frequently in winter.

At the 11km marker you must stop and pay an admission fee for the **national park** (€0.30, car & driver €1). The hotel zone is 11km up from the entrance.

The return ride can be difficult in summer, with little public transport about. In winter dolmuşes and taxis are usually eager to get at least some money before they head back down, so you may be able to get back to Bursa for less.

Cumalıkızık
☎ 0224 / pop 700

This gorgeous slice of Turkeyana on the slopes of Uludağ, about 16km east of Bursa, was settled 700 years ago by the Turcoman Kızıks and is chock-full of superbly preserved early Ottoman rural architecture. Wander around to enjoy the peaceful atmosphere, see brightly painted traditional houses amid their crumbling unrestored neighbours, or watch local children chase ducks as water run-off cascades down the narrow cobbled streets.

Sadly TV tourism has put paid to some of the quiet – Cumalıkızık was the location for the popular series *Kınalı Kar (Henna in the Snow)*, and countless fans now drop by to see where the magic happens, with a resultant

flurry of souvenir stalls springing up to try and cash in.

SLEEPING & EATING

There are only two accommodation options in the village, both of which serve food. A couple of small cafés and informal *gözleme* joints provide alternative eating.

Konak Pansiyon (☎ 372 4869; d €28) Take the right fork up into the village to reach this beautifully restored guesthouse, which has just eight rooms, ranging from Ottoman-style floor mattresses to some huge double beds. The restaurant opposite offers standard kebaps, salads, mezes, and *gözleme* for lunch.

Mavi Boncuk (☎ 373 0955; www.cumalikizik-mavi boncuk.com; Saldede Sokak; d/tr €34/50) Heading left instead of right, signs lead you to another old house, less meticulously restored but swamped in appealing gardens. The six rooms are simple but inviting, the food gets great reports, and there are plenty of sitting areas both indoors and out.

GETTING THERE & AWAY

From Bursa take bus No 22 (€0.85, 50 minutes) from stop 3 on Atatürk Caddesi. Buses leave roughly every two hours between 7.30am and 9pm. The last bus back to Bursa usually leaves at 8.30pm. More frequent dolmuşes (€0.70) also run to and from the Sentral Garaj, which is connected to Atatürk Caddesi by other dolmuşes and buses.

ESKİŞEHİR
☎ 0222 / pop 483,000

Ironically, Eskişehir (Old City) is a thoroughly modern town, built over the scant remnants of the Greco-Roman city of Dorylaeum. A small Ottoman district does still survive, but for the most part the city is staunchly new-built, and has a bustling atmosphere enlivened by a large student population.

Like Bursa, the area is rich in mineral springs, and the town centre has several hotels offering thermal water in their bathrooms, as well as innumerable *hamams* utilising the same springs. In 2003 Hamamyolu Caddesi was pedestrianised and landscaped, making the thermal district by far the most appealing place to stay.

Orientation & Information

Most people will want to stay around pedestrianised Hamamyolu Caddesi, which runs

north–south between Yunus Emre and İki
Eylül Caddesis. Odunpazarı, the Ottoman
old-town district, is just beyond the southern
end of the street.

The train station is northwest of the centre, the otogar 3km east of the centre. Trams
and buses run from the otogar to Köprübaşı,
the central district just north of Hamamyolu
Caddesi.

There are banks all over town, and several
internet cafés at the south end of Hamamyolu
Caddesi.

Sights & Activities

Eskişehir is famous for its 'white gold': **meerschaum** (luletaşı), a light, porous white stone,
which is mined in local villages and then
shaped into pipes and other artefacts. To see
some examples, head for the Yunus Emre
Kültür Sarayı, next to the post office, which
contains the **Lületaşı Museum** (İki Eylül Caddesi). This
informal collection includes fine old and new
meerschaum pipes and photos of the mining
process. You may have to wait for someone
to find the key, and having them hover while
you look around hardly encourages you to
linger.

Head south past the imposing yellow **Anadolu Üniversitesi Cumhuriyet Müzesi** (admission free;
8.30am-6pm Mon-Fri, 9am-5pm Sat), a sepia-heavy
collection of Atatürk memorabilia, to find
eski Eskişehir, the old Ottoman quarter. At
its centre, the large **Kurşunlu Camii** (1525) retains most of its külliye (mosque complex),
including an aşevi (cookhouse) bristling with
chimneys and an okuma odası (reading room)
with pillars that incorporate capitals from ancient Dorylaeum. It's surrounded by a pretty,
flower-filled garden and old tombs.

The surrounding streets are lined with
crumbling, colourful old Ottoman houses,
many of which are being restored as part of an
ongoing rejuvenation project. The **Beylerbeyi
Konağı** (Kurşunlu Camii Sokak 28; 10am-noon) is supposedly open to the public, although you'll be
lucky to find it unlocked.

Further west, the **Archaeological Museum**
(Arkeoloji Müzesi; admission €1.10; Hasan Polatkan Bulvarı
36; 8.30am-noon & 1.30-5pm Mon-Fri) contains finds
from Dorylaeum, including several crude mosaic floors and Roman statuettes of Cybele,
Hecate and Mithras.

While in Eskişehir you may want to take
a dip in one of the thermal baths around the
north end of Hamamyolu Caddesi. Most of

them are men-only, but the **Kadinlar Kaplıca**
(admission €3; 5.30am-10pm), near the Has Termal Hotel, is open to women. And it gets the
whole range: from breast-feeding mamas to
arthritic old ladies.

Sleeping

Not many people stay in Eskişehir, but if you
do want to linger, by far the best places to
stay are the hotels with thermal baths in and
around Hamamyolu Caddesi.

Termal Otel Sultan (231 8371; Hamamyolu Caddesi
1; s/d/tr €18/25/31) Everything about the Sultan
looks a bit worn, but the bathrooms are clean
and it's comfortable enough.

Has Hotel Termal (221 4030; www.hasotel.com;
Hamamyolu Caddesi 7; s/d/tr €25/34/39;) Unless
you're a bull, or have some similar aversion
to the colour red, the Has is a decent option,
particularly the marble kuvvet (bathtub) for
those long soaks in thermal water. Use of the
in-house hamam costs €11.

Uysal Otel (221 4353; Asarcıklı Caddesi 7; s/d €28/39)
Just off Hamamyolu Caddesi; the bedrooms
here don't really live up to the flashy atrium,
and the so-called 'minibars' are laughable,
but it still has the edge on the Sultan, at least.
Guests can use the hamam next door.

Eating

Other than the usual kebap and grill places,
Eskişehir is virtually devoid of interesting
restaurants – perhaps student budgets don't
run to such luxuries.

Şomine Et Lokantası (220 8585; Köprübaşı Caddesi
18; mains €1.70-7; 9am-10pm) Smart, shiny and
boasting an open-sided first-floor salon for
warm evenings, this is the pick of the cafeteria
restaurants, with an absolutely massive menu
of Turkish dishes.

Osmanlı Evi (221 5460; Yeşil Efendi Sokak 22; mains
€2-10; 11.30am-9pm) The Ottoman House was
one of the first in Odunpazarı to be restored,
and now functions as a fine café-restaurant.
It's up a side street behind the Kurşunlu
Camii.

Luckily, self-caterers fare much better than
gourmands: there are numerous pastirmacis
(delicatessens) piled high with local cheeses,
sucuk (garlic sausage) and salam (salami), and
even more pastanes (patisseries) for dessert.

Shopping

Eskişehir is the place to come to buy meerschaum pipes, as well as cigarette-holders,

prayer beads and other items made out of *lületaşı*. Some of the hotels sell meerschaum but you would probably be better off looking in local shops.

Eskişehir is also stuffed full of sweet shops. If you want to try something local go for rolls of *med helvası* or chunks of *nuga helvası* (two types of nougat).

Getting There & Away

Like Bursa, all official city transport runs on a prepay system – buy tickets (€0.70) from a booth or kiosk before you travel. Trams, city buses and dolmuşes serve the vast otogar; look for signs saying 'Terminal' or 'Yeni Otogar'. A taxi from Köprübaşı costs around €3.

From the otogar there are regular buses to Afyon (€6.70, three hours), Ankara (€6.70, 3¼ hours), Bursa (€6.70, 2½ hours), İstanbul (€11, six hours), İznik (€7, three hours) and Kütahya (€3.50, 1½ hours).

Eskişehir **train station** (☎ 255 5555) is an important railway terminus, and there are various services from İstanbul (four to six hours) and Ankara (2½ to four hours) throughout the day and night.

AROUND ESKİŞEHİR

Seyitgazi

☎ 0222 / pop 3300

This small town 43km southeast of Eskişehir is dominated by a hill on the top of which stands the vast 13th-century **Battalgazi mosque complex** (admission €1.10). The complex combines Seljuk and Ottoman architecture, and includes pieces of marble presumably taken from the ruins of the Romano-Byzantine town of Nacolea. The mosque commemorates Seyit/Seyyid Battal Gazi, a warrior who fought for the Arabs against the Byzantines and was killed in 740. His tomb sits in a side chamber off the main mosque; it's so long it resembles a drag racer although Battal Gazi himself was of normal height.

Features of the *külliye* include an *aşevi* whose eight chimneys pierce the skyline; a *semahane* (dance hall) where dervishes would have gathered; and a *medrese* containing several grim *çilehanes,* or 'places of suffering' – cells in which the devout lived (and died) like hermits with only their Qurans for company. Numerous calligraphic inscriptions, mostly singing the praises of Battal Gazi, are also visible around the walls, with convenient translations for non-Arabic speakers.

GETTING THERE & AWAY

There are regular Seyitgazi Belediyesi buses from Eskişehir to Seyitgazi (€2, 45 minutes). Some buses from Eskişehir to Afyon also pass through.

PHRYGIAN VALLEY

The rock-hewn monuments in the so-called Phrygian Valley (Frig Vadisi) between Eskişehir and Afyon are some of the most impressive relics to survive from Phrygian times. It's not easy to explore them without a car, although certain parts can be reached by bus and/or taxi (see p306). Hitching would not be a good idea since vehicles are very thin on the ground.

THE PHRYGIANS

Emigrants from Thrace to central Anatolia around 2000 BC, the Phrygians spoke an Indo-European language, used an alphabet similar to Greek and established a kingdom with its capital at Gordion (p454), 106km west of Ankara. The empire flourished under its most famous king, Midas (c 725–675 BC), one of many Phrygian monarchs to have had that name, until it was overrun by the Cimmerians (676–585 BC).

You might not think it, considering they lived in rock dwellings, but the Phrygians were a sophisticated, cultured people who set great store by the arts. Phrygian culture was based on that of the Greeks, but with strong Neo-Hittite and Urartian influences, and they're credited with inventing the frieze, embroidery and numerous musical instruments, including cymbals, double clarinet, flute, lyre, syrinx (Pan pipes) and triangle.

Phrygian civilisation was at its most vigorous around 585 to 550 BC, when the rock-cut monuments at Midas Şehri – the most impressive Phrygian stonework still in existence – were carved. Relics from the period can be seen in museums all over Anatolia, providing fascinating insights into a culture that bridged the gap between 'primitive' and 'advanced' amid the scrub and rocks of central Turkey.

It's well worth coming out here even if you're not much interested in the Phrygians, since this is a beautiful part of Turkey, virtually untouched by tourism. The scenery is as spectacular as anything in Cappadocia and can be even more varied, with inviting picnic places on all sides. To catch the unspoilt countryside at its best, visit in early June, when the opium poppies bloom in white and purple patches amid the green-grey-brown surrounds.

Midas Şehri

What archaeologists call Midas Şehri (Midas City) is actually the village of **Yazılıkaya** (Inscribed Rock), 32km south of Seyitgazi. Don't confuse this Yazılıkaya with the one near the Hittite capital of Hattuşa (p465), to the east of Ankara.

The sights at Yazılıkaya are clustered around a huge rock. Tickets (admission €1.10) are sold at the local library, in front of the steps leading up to the site; if your German's up to it you can also buy or borrow an excellent map-guide (€2.80) detailing 91 separate points of interest.

The so-called **Midas Tomb** is a 17m-high relief covered in geometric patterns, which is carved into the soft tufa and resembles the facade of a temple. At the bottom is a niche where an effigy of Cybele would be displayed during festivals. Inscriptions in the Phrygian alphabet – one bearing Midas' name – ring the tomb.

Opposite the inscribed rock is another huge rock riddled with caves that is believed to have been a **monastery**.

If you walk behind the Midas Tomb the path winds past worn steps leading down to a tunnel, then passes a second **smaller tomb**, high up in the rock, which was probably never finished. The path continues upwards until it emerges on top of the rock, which was an **acropolis**. Here you will find a stepped stone, labelled an **altar**, which may have been used for sacrifices, and traces of walls and roads. Even with a map following the paths can be confusing, but the main features are easy to spot.

As you head back down the steps notice a portion of the **ancient road**, identifiable from the wagon-wheel ruts worn into the rock.

Kümbet

Heading 15km west from Midas Şehri you'll come to the village of Kümbet, which boasts a Seljuk *kümbet* (tomb) with old Byzantine marble carvings reused around its doorway and a storks' nest on the roof. Near the *kümbet* is a rocky outcrop into which are cut several magnificent **rock fireplaces**. Also nearby is the **Arslanlı Mezarı** (Lion Tomb), another rock-cut Phrygian tomb, which has lions carved into its pedimental facade.

Other Sites

The Phrygian Valley separates itself neatly into two sections, the northern area near Kütahya and the southern sector around Afyon, though you could conceivably travel its entire length in a day if you had your own transport.

Most of the sites are along dirt tracks and some can be hard to find, even when they're right beside you. Navigation should slowly be getting better in the southern Afyon section, as local authorities have designated the area a 'Turizm Kuşağı Yolu' (Tourism Zone Route) and embarked on a programme of road improvements along its 170km length.

We've organised the sites here in north–south order for ease of reference and a straightforward drive, but you can tackle the routes any way you like. Remember, these are just a selection of the treasures hidden in them there hills, so the more you explore, the more you'll find!

Heading south from Seyitgazi you will find yourself on a road with brown tourist signs pointing to left and right. One on the right leads 2km along a rough track to the **Doğankale** (Falcon Castle) and **Deveboyukale** (Camel-Height Castle), both of them plugs of rock riddled with caves that were obviously once inhabited.

A little further south another rough track to the right leads 1km to the **Mezar Anıtı** (Monumental Tomb), where a restored tomb resembling a tiny temple is cut into another chunk of rock.

Further south again you'll see yet another temple-like tomb, called the **Küçük Yazılıkaya** (Little Inscribed Stone), cut into the rock at Arezastis.

At the small village of Doğer, which boasts a *han* (caravanserai) dating back to 1434 (usually locked), the two tourist routes come together. From here, dirt tracks run out to beautiful, lily-covered **Emre Gölü** (Lake Emre), a perfect picnic place overlooked by a small stone building once used by dervishes, and a rock formation with a rough staircase called the Kirkmerdiven Kayalıkları (Rocky Place with 40 Stairs). The dirt track then runs on to **Bayramaliler** and Üçlerkayası where you can see dozens of the crazy rock formations called *peribacalar* (fairy chimneys), just like the more famous examples in Cappadocia.

After Bayramaliler you come to the **Göynüş Vadisi** (Göynüş Valley), where there are fine Phrygian rock tombs decorated with lions (Aslantaş) and snakes (Yılantaş). However, the valley is more easily accessible from the main Eskişehir to Afyon road (2km).

Continuing southeast, be sure to stop at **Ayazini** village, where there was once a rock settlement called Metropolis. Here there are more cave-riddled rock formations like those in Cappadocia. In particular, look out for a huge church with its apse and dome cut clear out of the rock face, and a series of rock-cut tombs with carvings of lions, suns and moons.

There are a number of sights around the village of Alanyurt, including some more caves at **Selimiye** and fairy chimneys at **Kurtyurdu**. Finally, another heavy concentration can be found around Karakaya, Seydiler and İscehisar; one must is the bunker-like rock **Seydiler Castle** (Seydiler Kalesi).

Getting There & Around

You really need a car to explore this area properly. The usual starting points are Afyon and Eskişehir, or it's just as easy to head east from Kütahya. Brown signs show the way to many sites, but they're not always as clear as they could be, so be prepared to get lost quite regularly. For the southern sites, it's worth picking up the excellent pictorial brochure and map provided at the Afyon tourist office (p312).

If you don't want to rent a car, you could hire a taxi from any fair-sized town in the region; Seyitgazi and İhsaniye are good bets and conveniently located. Rates start around €25 for a short tour, but are entirely negotiable depending on where you want to go and how long for.

It would be possible to visit Göynüş and Ayazini by hopping off buses between Eskişehir and Afyon, then walking or hitching (with all due caution) the last few kilometres. It is also possible to visit the area around İhsaniye and Doğer by taking a dolmuş or minibus north from Afyon. However, most other sites were inaccessible by public transport at the time of writing.

KÜTAHYA

☎ 0274 / pop 167,000

Like İznik, Kütahya is known for its coloured tiles (*çini*) and pottery. Where İznik claims the artistic high ground, however, Kütahya's factories take pride in the prosaic. Industrial ceramics are big business here, overshadowing the collectible trade. Even on the decorative side there's no kind of snobbery, with tiles cropping up on facades, floors, fountains, car parks and anywhere else they fit.

As a town, too, Kütahya is much nearer Bursa's modern urban energy than İznik's traditional rustic languor, throwing up enough hip cafés and bars to stay street-smart. History lovers are also catered to, with an imposing hilltop fortress and a charming old quarter, lined with crumbling Ottoman-era mansions.

The town's other big hitter is the fine Dumlupınar Fair (Fuarı), Turkey's largest handicrafts fair, held each year in the fairgrounds near the otogar.

History

Kütahya's earliest known inhabitants were Phrygians. In 546 BC it was captured by the Persians, and then saw the usual succession of rulers, from Alexander the Great to the kings of Bithynia and the emperors of Rome and Byzantium, who called the town Cotiaeum.

The first Turks to arrive were the Seljuks in 1182. They were pushed out by the Crusaders, but returned to found the Emirate of Germiyan (1302–1428), with Kütahya as its capital. The emirs cooperated with the Ottomans in nearby Bursa, and when the last emir died his lands were incorporated in the growing Ottoman Empire. When Tamerlane swept in at the beginning of the 15th century he upset everyone's applecart, made Kütahya his headquarters for a while and then went back to where he came from.

After Selim I took Tabriz in 1514, he brought all of its ceramic artisans to Kütahya and İznik and set them to work. Since then the two towns have consistently rivalled one another in the quality of their tilework.

Orientation

A huge vase-shaped fountain in the middle of a roundabout marks Zafer (Belediye) Meydanı, the town's main square, which is overlooked by the *vilayet* (provincial government building) and *belediye* (town hall). The

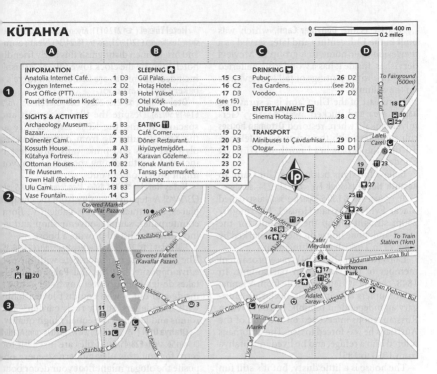

KÜTAHYA

0   400 m
0   0.2 miles

To Fairground (500m)

INFORMATION
Anatolia Internet Café........... 1 D3
Oxygen Internet.................... 2 D2
Post Office (PTT)................... 3 B3
Tourist Information Kiosk....... 4 D3

SIGHTS & ACTIVITIES
Archaeology Museum............ 5 B3
Bazaar................................. 6 B3
Dönenler Cami...................... 7 B3
Kossuth House....................... 8 A3
Kütahya Fortress.................... 9 A3
Ottoman Houses................... 10 A3
Tile Museum......................... 11 A3
Town Hall (Belediye)............. 12 B3
Ulu Cami.............................. 13 B3
Vase Fountain....................... 14 C3

SLEEPING
Gül Palas............................. 15 C3
Hotaş Hotel.......................... 16 C3
Hotel Yüksel......................... 17 D3
Otel Kösk............................. (see 15)
Qtahya Otel.......................... 18 D1

EATING
Café Corner.......................... 19 D2
Döner Restaurant.................. 20 A3
İkiyüzyetmişdört................... 21 D3
Karavan Gözleme.................. 22 D2
Konak Mantı Evi.................... 23 D2
Tansaş Supermarket.............. 24 C2
Yakamoz.............................. 25 D2

DRINKING
Pubuç.................................. 26 D2
Tea Gardens......................... (see 20)
Voodoo............................... 27 D2

ENTERTAINMENT
Sinema Hotaş....................... 28 C2

TRANSPORT
Minibuses to Çavdarhisar....... 29 D1
Otogar................................. 30 D1

To Train Station (1km)

Covered Market (Kavaflar Pazarı)

Germiyan Sk

Mollabey Cad   Kapan Cad

Covered Market (Kavaflar Pazarı)

Adnan Menderes Bul

Zafer Meydanı

Abdurrahman Karaa Bul

Azerbaycan Park

Fatih Sultan Mehmet Bul

Hürriyet Cad

Pazar Pekmez Cad

Cumhuriyet Cad

Asım Gündüz Cad

Yesil Cami

Belediye Sk

Adalet Sarayı   Fuatpaşa Cad

Hükümet Cad Market

Ali Enbati Sk

Gediz Cad

Sultanbağı Cad

Lise Cad

Laleli Cami

---

otogar, Kütahya Çinigar (Tile Station – you'll
see why), is less than 1km northeast of Zafer
Meydanı, along Atatürk Bulvarı. Hotels, res-
aurants, banks with ATMs and tile shops
cluster around the square.

The town's main commercial street is
Cumhuriyet Caddesi, which runs southwest
from the *vilayet*, past the PTT and on to the
Ulu Cami.

nformation

Anatolia Internet Café (Belediye Caddesi 9; per hr
€0.50; ⏰ 9am-midnight)
Oxygen Internet (Atatürk Bulvarı; per hr €0.50;
⏰ 9am-midnight)
Tourist information kiosk (☎ 223 6213; Zafer
Meydanı; ⏰ 9am-1pm & 2-6pm) Little English spoken
but a good map supplied and plenty of brochures.

Sights & Activities

The turreted **Ulu Cami**, at the far end of Cumhuriyet Caddesi, has been restored several
times since it was built in 1410, and features
some minor anachronisms such as modern
doors, windows and a digital clock. Take a
look at the fine marble panels incorporated

into its ablutions fountain and the lovely sun-
burst woodwork above the side door.

The **Archaeology Museum** (Arkeoloji Müzesi; ☎ 224
0785; admission €1.10; ⏰ 9am-12.30pm & 1.30-5pm Tue-Sat)
is next door to the Ulu Cami in the Vacidiye
Medresesi, which was built by Umur bin
Savcı of the Germiyan family in 1314. The
centrepiece of the collection is a magnificent
Roman sarcophagus from Aizanoi's Temple
of Zeus (p309), carved with scenes of battling
Amazons, but there are also finds from the
Phrygian Valley and some interesting Roman
votive stellae.

The **Tile Museum** (Çini Müzesi; ☎ 223 6990; admission
€1.10; ⏰ 9am-12.30pm & 1.30-5pm Tue-Sun) is housed
in the İmaret Camii on the opposite side of
the Ulu Cami, beneath a magnificent dome.
Most of the collection consists of Kütahya
pottery, including some work by the master
craftsman Hacı Hafız Mehmet Emin Efendi,
who worked on İstanbul's Haydarpaşa station. In deference to the town's main rival,
there are also some wonderful İznik tiles and
a lot of beautiful but unlabelled embroidery.
To one side is the 14th-century, blue-tiled
tomb of one Yakup Bey.

WESTERN ANATOLIA

Nearby is the **Dönenler Cami**, which was built in the 14th century and later served as a *mevlevihane* or home to a group of Mevlevi dervishes. Inside it has a wonderful, galleried *semahane* with paintings of tall Mevlevi hats on the columns.

Northeast of the Ulu Cami is a sprawling **bazaar** area and, tucked away nearby, Germiyan Sokak, where restored **Ottoman houses** rub shoulders with their crumbling fellows. To find the bazaar head north up Hürriyet Caddesi.

Follow the signs behind the Ulu Cami to **Kossuth House** (Kossuth Evi; ☎ 223 6214; admission €1.10; ☼ 8am-noon & 1.30-5.30pm Tue-Sun), also called Macar Evi (Hungarian House). It's roughly 250m straight on up the hill; look for the wood-and-stone house on the left, marked by plaques in Turkish and Hungarian.

Lajos Kossuth (1802–94) was a prominent member of the Hungarian parliament. In 1848, chafing at Hapsburg rule from Vienna, he and others rose in revolt, declaring Hungary an independent republic in 1849. When Russian troops intervened on the side of the Austrians he was forced to flee. The Ottomans offered him a refuge, and he lived in Kütahya from 1850 to 1851.

The house is a little dusty, but it's still fun to peer into the various rooms and get an idea of how upper-class Kütahyans lived in the mid-19th century. The 1st-floor veranda, overlooking a rose garden with a statue of Kossuth, offers lovely views of the encircling hills.

Looming above the town, **Kütahya fortress** was built in two stages by the Byzantines, then restored and used by the Seljuks, the Germiyan emirs and the Ottomans. The latest building work seems to have taken place in the 15th century, the most recent restoration in the 1990s. One look at the remains of dozens of round towers makes it clear what a formidable obstacle this would have been to any army. It's a long walk up to the fortress so you might want to take a taxi (around €3). Afterwards you can walk back down along a steep, scree-covered path that eventually deposits you near the Ulu Cami.

Sleeping

Kütahya isn't exactly overrun with accommodation options, but you can generally find a bed without having to resort to the worst cheapies.

Hotel Yüksel (☎ 212 0111; Afyon Caddesi 2; s/d/tr with shared bathroom €12/15/21, s/d/tr €18/24/34) Neat rooms and bright linen distinguish this fairly friendly hotel opposite the clock tower. Breakfast isn't included, but prices are flexible and there's a bakery right next door.

Otel Köşk (☎ 216 2024; Lise Caddesi 1; s/d/tr €14/19.50/28) Despite the tiled reception and spacious rooms, the Köşk isn't as nice as the Yüksel, suffering from dodgy showers, plywood beds and pink walls. Breakfast is included, but the dining room is so dim you might prefer to head out.

Hotaş Hotel (☎ 224 8990; Menderes Caddesi 5; s/c €23/34/45) A step up in quality from the cheaper places: an attractive lobby, cable TV, floral counterpanes, sauna, souvenir shop and an industrial-size lift all provide a boost.

Gül Palas (☎ 216 2325; Zafer Meydanı; s/d/tr €23/36/45) The tiled facade can't compete with the *belediye* opposite, but the Gül Palas definitely takes design honours over any hotel in town, inside and out – who couldn't love a lobby with chandeliers and a rock garden? The rooms and facilities are equally high quality.

Qtahya Otel (☎ 226 2010; www.q-tahya.com; Atatürk Bulvarı 56; s/d/tr €28/45/62) If tiles are just a bit too retro for you, this ultramodern sleepery opposite the otogar might float your décor boat. Western hotel standards reign, and the roof restaurant's an asset.

Eating

Kütahya is a good place to do a deal on a döner, with dozens of shops and restaurants vying for business. A basic kebap can start at €0.40, while a set meal with drink, salad, side order and dessert could be as little as €1.40. There's a good range of other options, especially down Atatürk Bulvarı.

RESTAURANTS

Konak Mantı Evi (☎ 223 9209; Hafız Müezzin Sokak 3/A; dishes €0.50-2; ☼ 8am-8pm) Omelettes, breakfasts, *börek* and of course *mantı* (ravioli) are the mainstays at this little café. It's done up like the outside of an Ottoman street, so you can get that street-seating feel whatever the weather.

Karavan Gözleme (☎ 226 4045; Atatürk Bulvarı 12/A set meals €1.10-4.50; ☼ 9am-10pm) It may serve 15 types of *gözleme*, from *haşhaşlı* (poppy-seed) to chocolate, but the Karavan is more than just a pancake place, offering a full menu of snacks and mains. Pop upstairs to find a small terrace with kitschy fake greenery and an inviting *nargileh* (water pipe) lounge with wireless internet.

Café Corner (☎ 224 0078; Atatürk Bulvarı 53/B; dishes €1.70-5; ☺ 9.30am-9.30pm) One of the quirkiest manifestations of coffeehouse culture outside İstanbul, resplendent in fuchsia tones with a logo suspiciously close to Chanel. Light meals, flavoured coffees, music, TV and wi-fi are the order of the day.

Döner Restaurant (☎ 226 2176; mains €2.50-6; ☺ 11am-9pm) Inside the ruins of the fortress, the Döner used to be a revolving nightclub (no, really), but is now simply the most atmospheric eatery in Kütahya. Run by the Karavan chain, the food's decent and the garden area's superb, dotted with hammocks, chimeneas (ceramic with a bulbous base and chimney that is filled with charcoal for use as a heater) and one perfect spot on a turret. And yes, it does still revolve occasionally.

Yakamoz (☎ 223 0926; Atatürk Bulvarı; mains from €3; ☺ 11am-11pm) This vast café-restaurant, with indoor and outdoor tables, is extremely popular with young Kütahyalıs. Its extensive menu covers everything from pizzas to Turkish puddings.

ikiyüzyetmişdört (☎ 224 0200; Belediye Sokak 3; mains €2.80-6; ☺ 6pm-11pm) About as sophisticated as a kebap restaurant can ever get, the '274' is favoured by men in suits for its indoor charcoal grill, copious mezes, extensive wine list and enclosed outdoor terrace. Try the sausage-studded special kebap.

SELF-CATERING
For fresh fruit, vegetables and picnic supplies, browse the open-air **market** up the hill on Lise Caddesi; it's at its liveliest on Saturday. Alternatively, there's a **Tansaş supermarket** (Adnan Menderes Bulvarı; ☺ 9am-10pm).

Drinking & Entertainment
Atatürk Bulvarı is Kütahya's drinking strip, with a handful of venues crammed together around Yakamoz. On busy nights they may stay open until 1 or 2am.

Voodoo (☎ 226 4146; Atatürk Bulvarı 26) The most publike of the bars, complete with wooden beams, 0.7-litre beers and clear blues leanings.

Pubuç (Atatürk Bulvarı) Proclaiming itself Kütahya's prime spot for 'public drink and dance', this is more of a bar-club, with a big dancefloor.

There are several good **tea gardens** around Zafer Meydanı and Azerbaycan Parkı, but the best views are from the outdoor cafés inside Kütahya fortress.

The three-screen **Sinema Hotaş** (☎ 216 6767; admission €3.50) is opposite the Hotaş Hotel.

Shopping
You can find Kütahya pottery in just about any Turkish souvenir shop, but it's still fun to browse the small stores around Zafer Meydanı. Beside the usual tourist stuff, shops have fine, midrange pieces in a variety of designs, and often a few masterworks for connoisseurs. Out of town towards Eskişehir or Afyon, you'll find vast porcelain warehouses geared to the coach-party trade.

Getting There & Away
Kütahya is a provincial capital with a busy otogar. There are regular services to Afyon (€3.50, 1½ hours), Ankara (€10, five hours), Bursa (€7.50, three hours), Eskişehir (€3.50, 1½ hours), İstanbul (€13.50, six hours) and İzmir (€11, six hours).

Minibuses to Çavdarhisar, for Aizanoi (€2.50, one hour), leave from the local bus stand next to the otogar.

AİZANOİ (ÇAVDARHİSAR)
☎ 0274 / pop 4100
The pretty but fading farming village of Çavdarhisar, about 60km southwest of Kütahya, is home to c, the site of one of Anatolia's best-preserved Roman temples. Long after the Romans had vanished, a group of Çavdar Tartars used the site as a citadel, giving the village its present name: 'Castle of the Çavdars'.

There are virtually no facilities here, but it shouldn't take much more than an hour or two to have a good look at all the ruins.

Temple of Zeus
The great **Temple of Zeus** (admission €1.10; ☺ 8am-5.30pm) dates from the reign of Hadrian (r AD 117–138), and was dedicated to the worship of Zeus (Jupiter) and the Anatolian fertility goddess Cybele.

The temple stands in proud isolation on a raised hill in a bare field, founded on a broad terrace created to serve as its precinct. Like some ancient Hollywood set, the north and west faces of the temple have their double rows of Ionic and Corinthian columns intact,

---

USAK MUSEUM THEFTS

In 2006 Turkey's cultural establishment was shaken when an inspection of the Uşak museum's Lydian Hoard collection revealed that certain priceless items had been removed and replaced with copies. The story made headlines instantly, especially when nine people (including the director of the museum) were arrested in connection with the crime, and despite threats of 28-year sentences, so far no sign of the original pieces has been uncovered. Uşak wasn't the only place to suffer, either: subsequent checks revealed a similar switch incident at the much more high-profile Topkapı Palace in İstanbul.

Ironically, this isn't the first time these objects were 'stolen' – the original 1960s American excavators removed them from tumuli in the valley of the Gediz River and promptly dispatched them back to the States, where they stayed until 1993, when a landmark court ruling that they should be returned to their country of origin. As many commentators have observed, it's ironic that Turkey should put so much effort into retrieving its lost treasures, only to lose them from its own museums.

---

but the south and east rows have fallen into a picturesque jumble. The three columns at the northeastern corner were toppled by the disastrous Gediz earthquake of 1970, but have since been re-erected. The cella (inner room) walls are intact enough to give a good impression of the whole. An enclosure beside the ticket office holds some of the best pieces of sculpture found here, and a small exhibition hut has displays, diagrams and photos of the original 1926 excavations. Sadly, as these first digs were undertaken by German archaeologists, the informative explanatory captions and the accompanying booklet are in German or Turkish only!

If the ticket office is empty, the custodian will catch up with you to sell you a ticket. He'll also take you into the cryptlike sanctuary of Cybele beneath the temple, and may be able to show you around the various ruins nearby, assuming there are no other visitors around.

Other Ruins

When you've finished at the temple, leave the precinct and turn left then right along a path into the fields opposite the temple. You'll quickly come across the remnants of a 2nd-century AD **Roman bath**, then the more substantial ruins of a splendid **theatre** and **stadium**. The stones have crumbled badly and now provide a home for innumerable wheatears and the odd woodpecker. Look out on the right for a stretch of wall with the names of ancient Olympic winners inscribed in medallions.

Çavdarhisar village is dotted with chunks of fallen Roman masonry. Black-on-yellow signs also point to more specific sights such

as a **Roman bridge** over a small stream (go down beside it and you'll see that much of the stonework dates back to Hadrian's reign). Follow the signs into the village and you'll come to the remains of a 2nd-century AD **bath complex**. The shed contains a fine mosaic pavement, mostly covered with geometric patterns but also with a picture of a satyr and maenad. It's kept locked, so you'll need the temple custodian to let you in; he'll also throw some water on the mosaic to bring out the colours, which should probably not be encouraged.

Another sign near the temple points to what it calls a colonnaded street but which is probably the remains of the Roman **forum**, or marketplace, with fine standing columns and a marble pavement. Nearby is an unusual **circular market building** with a little turret reconstructed beside it, which dates back to 301 AD, during the reign of Diocletian. Look closely at the walls and you'll see fixed prices for market goods inscribed in Roman numerals, an attempt to combat inflation. One of these prices apparently reads 'two horses for a strong slave, three slaves for a horse, both equalling 30,000 dinars'. This is one of the earliest known buildings of its type.

There's some English signage around these sites, but they're hopeless translations of the Turkish and, as at the temple, the German captions are far better.

Getting There & Away

Çavdarhisar is on the Kütahya–Gediz road. There are minibuses to Çavdarhisar from Kütahya otogar (€2.50, one hour) or you can take a Gediz or Emet bus, which passes through Çavdarhisar; tell the driver you're going to Aizanoi and they'll drop you right at the site.

UŞAK
☎ 0276 / pop 137,000

Few visitors stop in the provincial town of Uşak, but those who do can seek out a pair of unexpected treats, best appreciated on an overnight stay.

The first is the fine collection of Lydian art, gold and silver treasures on display in the **Archaeology Museum** (Doğan Sokak; admission €1.10; ☯ 8.30am-noon & 1.30-5pm Tue-Sun), just off the main square. The beautiful silver bowls, incense burners, jugs and vases were discovered in tumuli around the Gediz river valley, and date back to the second half of the 6th century BC. Even more evocative are the eerily Egyptian-style wall paintings from the tombs. For added spice, there's still the whiff of recent scandal about the place – see the boxed text, opposite.

At the far end of the town centre, past the 1406 Ulu Camii, discerning sleepers can find Uşak's second selling point, the **Otel Dülgeroğlu** (☎ 227 3773; Cumhuriyet Meydanı 1; s/d €39/56, ste €73; ⌘). Housed in a *han* designed by a 19th-century French architect, it's a superbly conceived and executed project, offering extremely comfortable rooms in a gallery overlooking a courtyard pierced by convincing fake palm trees. Rooms fill up with business travellers midweek but are empty at weekends.

Getting There & Away
Frequent minibuses connect Uşak with Afyon (€4.50, 1½ hours), and there are periodic buses from İzmir (€7.50, 2½ hours). If you get dropped on the highway (Dörtyöl) follow the signs for the *şehir merkezi* (city centre); it's about 1.5km to the Otel Dülgeroğlu. From the otogar, a taxi should cost around €3.

AFYON
☎ 0272 / pop 129,000

Sometimes known by its full name of Afyonkarahisar, modern Afyon is a provincial capital lounging in the shadow of its ancient castle, which occupies a vast rock at the back of town. If you can tear your gaze away from this mighty citadel, Afyon also boasts a fine museum, a magnificent mosque and some original Ottoman housing.

Despite its reputation as a conservative town, Afyon has a young population and is governed by people who like to get in on the ground floor of any trend. It's one of the first towns in Turkey to have recycling bins on every street corner, cycle racks, and posters exhorting its citizens to abandon their cigarettes (not that anyone takes much notice of that one).

Turkey's current president, Ahmet Necdet Sezer, was born in Afyon. His name is now attached to the local research hospital and one campus of Afyon Kocatepe University.

History
As with so many Anatolian towns, Afyon's history started some 3000 years ago. After occupation by the Hittites, Phrygians, Lydians and Persians, it was settled by the Romans then the Byzantines. Following the Seljuk victory at Manzikert in 1071, Afyon was governed by the Seljuk Turks. The important Seljuk vizier Sahip Ata took direct control of

---

OPIATE OF THE PEOPLE

Afyon's proper name, Afyonkarahisar, actually means Black Fortress of Opium, an epithet that not only characterises the castle's appearance but also tips its hat to the area's main cash crop. As unlikely as it may seem, the peaceful countryside around Afyon produces more than a third of the world's legally grown pharmacy-grade opium, and for two weeks in mid-June the fields dance with white and mauve *haşhaşlı çiçekleri* (hash or opium poppies).

The trade is of course strictly regulated, and Afyon is one of only 12 provinces permitted to cultivate the poppies. Most growers are small-scale farmers who use the flowers as a convenient spring crop to bridge the gap between autumn grain harvests. It's not easy work, either: it will take an average labourer 72 hours to pick and process enough poppies to produce 1kg of opium. The end product is then bought by the government and used to manufacture morphine.

Visitors, too, can benefit from the opium trade: Afyon is renowned for its *kaymak* (thick cream), which is said to be so good because the cows from which it comes have been grazing on the magic poppies. So if you find yourself jonesing for another dairy fix, you'll know why…

the town, and it was called Karahisar-i Sahip through Ottoman times (1428–1923).

During the War of Independence, Greek forces occupied the town on their push towards Ankara. During the Battle of Sakarya, in late August 1921, the republican armies under Mustafa Kemal (Atatürk) stopped the invading force within earshot of Ankara in one of history's longest pitched battles. The Greek forces retreated and dug in for the winter near Eskişehir and Afyon.

On 26 August 1922 the Turks began their counteroffensive along an 80km front, advancing rapidly on the Greek army. Within days Atatürk had set up his headquarters in Afyon's *belediye* building and had half the Greek army surrounded at Dumlupınar, 40km to the west. This decisive battle destroyed the Greek army as a fighting force and sent its survivors fleeing towards İzmir. Like Gallipoli, the battlefields are now protected, forming the Başkomutan National Historical Park.

Orientation

The main square, called Hükümet Meydanı and marked by a statue of Atatürk, is northeast of the citadel, at the intersection of Ordu Bulvarı and Milli Egemenlik (Bankalar) Caddesi. About 250m to the southeast another traffic roundabout marks the starting point for Kadınana Caddesi, which runs 2km northeast to the otogar.

Almost everything important lies between the two traffic roundabouts, including the PTT, banks with ATMs, and several hotels and restaurants.

The train station is 2km from the centre, at the northeastern end of Ordu Bulvarı.

Information

AVM Kadinana Internet (Bankalar Caddesi 19; per hr €0.55; ☻ 9.30am-11pm) In Afyon's central department store.

Ferah Internet Café (Bankalar Caddesi; per hr €0.55; ☻ 10am-11pm)

Tourist office (☎ 213 5447; Hükümet Meydanı; ☻ 8am-noon & 1.30-5.30pm Mon-Fri) An unusually useful office with decent city maps and a detailed brochure on the Phrygian Valley; can help arrange day trips to Midas Şehri and other Phrygian sites.

Sights & Activities

CITADEL

Jutting up from otherwise flat surroundings, the craggy rock with the *kale* or *hisar* (citadel)

on top dominates Afyon like a giant with a bullwhip. If you want to get a closer look you'll need to find the lane across the street from the Ulu Cami, where brown signs and green paint point the way. At the end of the lane is the first of some 700 steps to the summit, passing through a series of guard towers – there's no easier way up, and it seems incredible that people managed, voluntarily, to build such a large fortress somewhere so inaccessible.

The Hittite king Mursilis II is thought to have built the first castle by around 1350 BC, and every subsequent conqueror added their own features. However, despite its eventful history, there's little left to see inside, and recent restorations broke clumsily with the original *kara hisar* (black citadel) look by using white stones.

The views from the summit (226m) are spectacular, and it's well worth coming up here at prayer time to listen to the wraparound calls of the muezzins from Afyon's many mosques. Note that the castle isn't lit at night, which is surely missing a trick in PR terms, and can also make it tricky coming down if you leave it too late.

For the best photos of the castle from below, head to the **Kültür ve Semt Evi** (Zaviye Türbe Caddesi), a restored *hamam* with unobstructed views from its raised terrace.

ARCHAEOLOGICAL MUSEUM

Take a dolmuş along Kurtuluş Caddesi, the continuation of Bankalar Caddesi, and eventually you'll arrive at Afyon's **Archaeological Museum** (Arkeoloji Müzesi; admission €1.10; ☻ 8am-noon & 1.30-5pm Tue-Sun), near the intersection with İsmet İnönü Caddesi. Externally, there's not much to distinguish this museum from many other run-of-the-mill local collections. However, for once your money will be well spent since the collection here is both extensive and varied, with the Hittite, Phrygian, Lydian and Roman finds among the most interesting. There are lots of marble statues, a reflection of the fact that the marble quarries at what was then Dokimeon (now İscehisar) were the most important in Anatolia back then, as indeed they still are today. Outside, priceless chunks of marble litter the grounds like discarded gravel.

OTHER SIGHTS

The **İmaret Camii**, Afyon's major mosque, is just south of the traffic roundabout at the southern end of Bankalar Caddesi. Built for Gedik Ahmet Paşa in 1472, its design shows the transition from the Seljuk to the Ottoman style, with the spiral-fluted minaret decorated, Seljuk-style, with blue tiles. The entrance on the eastern side is like an *eyvan* (vaulted recess) and leads to a main sanctuary topped by two domes, front and back, a design also seen in the early Ottoman capitals of Bursa and Edirne. The shady park beside it provides a peaceful refuge from bustling Bankalar Caddesi.

Next door, the **İmaret hamamı** (5am-midnight for men, 8am-8pm for women), housed in a former church, is still well patronised and retains some of the precious old stone basins. Look for the strange 'rusty screwdriver' pillar protruding from the roof.

The **Mevlevihane Camii** was once a dervish meeting place and dates back to Seljuk times (13th century), when Sultan Veled, son of dervish founder Celaleddin Rumi, established Afyon as the empire's second-most important Mevlevi centre after Konya. The present mosque, with twin domes and twin pyramidal roofs above its courtyard, dates from only 1908, when it was built for Sultan Abdül Hamit II.

Afyon's **Ulu Cami** (1273) is one of the most important surviving Seljuk mosques, so it's a shame that it's usually locked outside prayer times. If you do manage to get inside you'll find 40 soaring wooden columns with stalactite capitals and a flat-beamed roof. Note the green tiles on the minaret.

The area around the Ulu Cami has many old **Ottoman wooden houses**. Safranbolu (p455) may be in better repair, but Afyon showcases an interesting variety of styles, and still teems with everyday life. If you're feeling really flush, some of the old residences are even up for sale.

Just along from the tourist office, the **Zafer Müzesi** (Victory Museum; Hükümet Meydanı; admission €0.30; 8am-noon & 1.30-5.30pm) was the first building Atatürk stayed in after liberating Afyon in 1922, and it now has some modest displays of photos, battle plans and military relics from the battlefields.

Sleeping

Sinada Oteli (212 1250; Ambaryolu 25; s/d €11/20) Just off Kadinana Caddesi above an Arçelik electrical store, most things about the Sinada have seen better days, but staff are friendly and the rooms are a decent size (especially the corner ones).

Otel Hocaoğlu (213 8182; Kadinana Caddesi, Ambaryolu 12; s/d/tr €12.50/23/25) Five storeys of surprisingly bright accommodation near the İmaret Camii. The lift's a bit coffin-like but it's all in a marginally better state than the Sinada.

Hotel Soydan (215 2323; Turan Emeksiz Caddesi 2; s/d/tr €20/28/34) Behind the calming green façade, this nominal two-star has little to justify the extra expense besides a dim but comfy bar-salon and a good grocer's next door.

Çakmak Marble Otel (214 3300; www.cakmak marblehotel.com; Süleyman Gonçer Caddesi 2; s/d €33/59, ste €84-92;) One block east of Hükümet Meydanı, the Çakmak, formerly the Grand Ozer, is the only option that even vaguely pulls its weight, offering four-star Western standards throughout the spacious rooms, marble bathrooms and refined public areas. Family rooms come with cute cots, there's a swimming pool and Jacuzzi in the basement, and the *hamam* is wonderfully tricked out in Kütahya tiles and Afyon marble.

Eating & Drinking

İkbal Lokantası (215 1205; Uzunçarşı Caddesi 21; mains €1-3; 9am-10pm) Southwest of Hükümet Meydanı, the İkbal first opened its doors in 1922, and still holds its own against neighbouring competition. There's a good choice of kebaps, stews and desserts, and a separate deli shop opposite.

Emreyunus Art Centre Café (212 1011; mains €1.10-4; 10am-midnight) In the former İmaret *medrese*, the leafy courtyard here must be the most romantic spot in town, though it's mysteriously underfrequented. The menu's fairly limited, concentrating on snacks and a few grills.

AVM Kadinana (214 7900; Bankalar Caddesi 19; mains €2-4; 9.30am-11pm) The top two floors of this department store cater for a multitude of whims, incorporating a restaurant, *pastane*, big-screen TV lounge and rooftop café-nargileh terrace with live music. It's hugely popular, and not just for the great views.

Self-caterers should head straight to the daily **market** beside the otogar for fresh fruit and veg. Otherwise, every other shop around town is draped with necklaces of locally made *sucuk* (sausage) and padded out with pillows of cheese.

Don't forget to pop into one of the local *şekerleme* (sweet shops) for a taste of Afyon's famous *lokum* (Turkish delight). To try something, just point and say *Deneyelim!* (Let's try it!)

WIT VS WISDOM

Nasreddin Hodja (or Hoca) is a semi-legendary figure, central to the Turkish sense of humour, whose quirky epigramatic tales could be compared to Aesop's fables or the antics of Central European character Till Eugenspiegel. He is often depicted riding backwards on a donkey, a reflection of the off-kilter but acerbic world view he represents. Or, as the man himself would put it: 'It's not me that is sitting backwards, but the donkey that is facing the wrong way'...

More than 350 stories are attributed to Hodja, but very little is known about the man himself. The historical imam on whom the myth centres is believed to have been born near Sivrihisar in 1208, then moved to Akşehir in 1237, where he stayed until he died. However, there is little or no biographical evidence to back this up, and the legend has quickly surpassed reality, a situation that a true Hodja would doubtless have relished.

Whether or not the man was real, his idiom has become an entrenched part of Turkish culture, and you'll find plenty of books recounting favourite tales, some of which have quite patently been written by more modern wags. A typical Hodja story will see the turbaned one using his trademark counterintuitive twists of logic to befuddle greedy neighbours, save his own cash or explain away a tricky situation. Beggars, qadis (magistrates), Hodja's own wife (or wives) and even the local sultan are favourite butts of the jokes, as is Hodja himself.

For instance, when asked about the noise from his house the previous night, Hodja says that he had a fight with his wife, who threw his robe down the stairs.

'Really? A robe made that much noise?'

'Well, of course it did,' says Hodja. 'I was wearing it at the time.'

There are pleasant **çay bahçesi** (tea gardens) in Anıt Parkı, overlooking Hükümet Meydanı.

Getting There & Away

Afyon is on the inland routes connecting İstanbul with Antalya and Konya, and İzmir with Ankara and the east. There are regular buses from the otogar to Ankara (€8, four hours), Antalya (€9.50, five hours), Denizli/Pamukkale (€7.50, four hours), Eskişehir (€7, three hours), Isparta (€5.50, three hours), İstanbul (€16, eight hours), İzmir (€9.50, 5½ hours), Konya (€9.50, 3¾ hours) and Kütahya (€4.50, 1½ hours).

The **train station** (☎ 213 7919) is 2km north of the town centre. Three or four express trains a day run to İstanbul Haydarpaşa (€5.50, nine hours), mostly at night; a sleeping compartment costs from €27. There are also daily services to Eskişehir (three hours), via Kütahya (two hours), and Konya (five hours).

To get to the centre from the otogar look for dolmuşes marked 'Çarşı' (€0.60); a taxi would cost about €3. To get to the otogar look for a dolmuş marked 'Garaj' in Gazlıgöl Caddesi, near the tourist information kiosk.

AKŞEHIR

☎ 0332/62,000

Heading southeast from Afyon, the main road passes through **Sultandağı**, which has the remains of an imposing caravanserai right in the town centre, before arriving in Akşehir, a pleasant small town ringed with hills.

Not many places in the world feature an outsize cooking pot as a monument, but then Akşehir was the long-time home of Nasreddin Hodja, Turkey's original funny man (see above). The pot is a reference to one of his best-known tales; ask any local to fill you in. There are lots of other statues of the famous storyteller, on and off his donkey, and devotees can visit his **tomb** (admission €0.25; ☑ 6.30am-8pm) in the local cemetery. The date reads 386, which should be reversed to give his death as 683 (1284) – apparently the eternal joker couldn't resist one final Hodja twist.

Sleeping & Eating

Grand Bal Otel (☎ 811 0270; Anıt Meydanı; s/d €23/34; ☑) If you want to stay over, the Grand Bal is a comfortable modern hotel with colour-coordinated fabrics, decent bathrooms, sauna and Jacuzzi.

Eating options are fairly limited, but if you follow signs down the back streets you'll find the **Akşehir Evi**, a late-19th-century house open to visitors, where you can tuck into home cooking in a pleasant courtyard garden.

Getting There & Away

There are regular minibuses to Akşehir from Afyon otogar (€4.50, two hours).

LAKE DISTRICT

As if having over 7000km of coastline wasn't enough, Turkey also enjoys a swathe of inland waterlife. The Anatolian Lake District consists of three main lakes (*göller*) – Burdur, Eğirdir and Beyşehir – and several smaller ones. The town of Eğirdir, on the lake of the same name, is a popular holiday haven ringed with mountains. Beyşehir is worth a visit for its wonderful 13th-century lakeside mosque and old town.

The ruined cities of Antiocheia-in-Pisidia and Sagalassos provide interest for the historically minded, while outdoor enthusiasts can trek or ski in the nearby mountains, visit Çandır Kanyon in the Yazılı Nature Park or Lake Kovada National Park, and embark in the footsteps of an apostle along the St Paul's Trail.

Compared with the dusty plains further east, this water-rich region is a lush haven of varied greenery, and all its best features are highlighted by the seasons. Spring is a great time to visit the lakes: the apple trees burst into blossom in April, while the annual rose harvest begins in mid-May. By mid-July, however, much of the area fills with holidaying Turkish families, so plan ahead if you prefer flowers to crowds.

ISPARTA

☎ 0246 / pop 149,000

A largely functional town famous for its attar of roses (see boxed text, below), Isparta marks an important junction on the road east to Eğirdir, though there's little to stop for in itself. Turkey's ninth president, Süleyman Demirel, was a local boy, and there's a quirky statue of him in the town centre.

If you end up with some spare time here, look at the **Ulu Cami** (1417) and the **Firdevs Bey Camii** (1561) with its neighbouring **bedesten** (covered market), the latter two buildings attributed to the great Mimar Sinan (see boxed text, p117). Also wander into the huge **Halı Saray** (Carpet Palace; Mimar Sinan Caddesi). Four days a week, between 8am and 10am, you can watch fine Isparta carpets being auctioned to dealers.

Getting There & Away

Although Isparta's otogar is the main transit point for the lakes, the most frequent services to Eğirdir leave from the Çarşı terminal (also called the *köy garaj*) in the town centre, as do dolmuşes for Ağlasun (for Sagalassos). Coming north from Antalya you may find yourself dropped on the outskirts of Isparta and ferried to the otogar on a *servis* (minivan).

To get to Eğirdir (€1.70, 30 minutes) from the otogar, take any Konya-bound bus. Minibuses from the Çarşı terminal run every 30 minutes (€1.40).

There are daily services from Isparta otogar to Afyon (€5.60, three hours), Antalya (€4.50, two hours), Burdur (€2.25, 45 minutes), Denizli (€5.60, three hours), İzmir (€11, six hours) and Konya (€8.50, four hours).

To get to the Çarşı terminal catch a Çarşı city bus (€0.30) from in front of the otogar. Note that the hourly minibus service to Burdur leaves from the otogar.

SAGALASSOS

Dramatically sited on the terraced slopes of Ak Dağ (White Mountain), **Sagalassos** (admission €2.80; ☀ 7.30am-6pm) is a ruined ancient city backed by sheer, ragged rock. Since 1990 a Belgian team of archaeologists has been

---

ROSE TOURS

Every May and June the roses in the fields around Isparta come into flower, and the farmers make haste to pluck the petals at daybreak so that they can be made into attar of roses, a valuable oil used in making perfume. The petals are placed in copper vats, and steam is passed over them. This is then drawn off and condensed, leaving a thin layer of oil floating on the surface of the water that is skimmed off and bottled. A hundred kilos of petals produces just 25g of attar of roses, leaving a vast amount of by-product rosewater, which is sold locally.

If you would like to see the process in action, the Lale Pension (p320) in Eğirdir organises factory tours for around €20 per person, or you may be able to arrange something direct with a manufacturer. **Gülbirlik** (☎ 218 1288; www.gulbirlik.com) is the world's biggest source of rose oil and the main player in Isparta, with four processing plants handling – so they claim – 320 *tonnes* of petals every day! Tours usually take place in May each year, at the height of the rose season.

excavating parts of the city, making it one of the largest archaeological projects in the Mediterranean region, and it's hoped the site may one day rival Ephesus or Pergamum in splendour. The researchers are also reconstructing some of the buildings, taking advantage of the fact that the site was never pillaged for material. Surrounded on three sides by mountains, the spectacular backdrop and views down over the fertile valley are unforgettable, but the rugged geography comes with its own problems, and quite a number of the ruins are inaccessible to visitors.

Sagalassos dates back to at least 1200 BC, when it was founded by a warlike tribe of 'Peoples from the Sea'. Later it became an important Pisidian city, second only to Antiocheia-in-Pisidia near Yalvaç. The Pisidians liked their cities perched high up on easily defensible mountains; Termessos (p392) is another example. The oldest ruins on the site date from Hellenistic times, although most of the surviving structures are Roman. Though the Roman period was the city's most prosperous, plague and earthquakes blighted its later history, and Sagalassos was largely abandoned after a massive quake in the 7th century.

The ticket office at the car park sells an informative map-guide (€2.50). From the entrance the path leads along a path to the **lower agora**, with massive reconstructed Roman **baths**, dating from AD 180, to the left. A flight of steps lead down from the lower agora to a paved street and the **Temple of Antoninus Pius**, built to honour the cult of the Roman emperors. Heading back to the lower agora, you can climb up the slope to the **upper agora**. Facing the agora is a huge **fountain complex**, while on the hillside to the right lies the **bouleuterion** (council meeting-place), with some of its seating intact. The **heroon** (hero's shrine) used to be decorated with carvings of dancing girls. Copies are slowly being reinstated at the site while the originals await rehousing in an annexe to Burdur Museum (right). It may once have housed a statue of Alexander the Great, who captured the city in 333 BC.

Sagalassos's biggest structure is the 9000-seat Roman **theatre**, one of the most complete in Turkey, on a slope below the area known as the Potters' Quarter. Earthquakes have disturbed the rows of seats but otherwise it is largely intact. Nearby is the late-Hellenistic **fountain house** and the Roman **Neron library**

with a fine mosaic floor. Both have been rebuilt, and the fountain house is functioning again using the original water supply, but the shedlike structure protecting the library is usually locked. .

The stark cliffs above Sagalassos are dotted with tombs. Except during the summer months when the archaeologists are at work, you're likely to share the site only with wheatears and corn buntings. It's treeless and exposed, so aim for an early start to avoid the midday sun. There are soft drinks for sale at the ticket office. Walking the entire site via the 'scenic' route could take up to 3½ hours, or you can see the most significant structures near the ticket office in about an hour.

Getting There & Away

To get to Sagalassos take a dolmuş south from Isparta's Çarşı terminal to Ağlasun (€1.10, one hour, hourly from 6am to 5pm). The last dolmuş from Ağlasun to Isparta leaves at 8pm in summer.

From Ağlasun a signposted turn-off points 7km up the mountain. If you're fit, you could walk up, but it's probably easier to pay the dolmuş driver an extra €8.50 to drive you there, wait for an hour and bring you back down again. To get the driver to wait longer you will probably have to agree on a higher fee.

BURDUR

☎ 0248 / pop 63,400

Despite its proximity to saltwater Burdur Gölü (Lake Burdur), Burdur is an unexciting, entirely modern small town you're likely to want to visit only to see the finds from Sagalassos in the museum. Buses from Isparta drop you on the eastern outskirts. Come out of the otogar, turn right and walk along Gazi Caddesi for 15 minutes to the town centre, or catch a city bus from just outside.

To find the **Burdur Museum** (Burdur Müzesi; admission €1.10; ☽ 8am-noon & 1.30-5pm Tue-Sun), turn right opposite the Hacı Mahmut Bey Camii in Gazi Caddesi. If you can cope with the irritating auto-timer lighting, the most impressive exhibits are ceramics and Hellenistic and Roman statues from Kremna and Sagalassos (p315), although there are also Neolithic bits and pieces from the nearby Hacılar and Kuruçay mounds, a 2nd-century bronze torso of an athlete, some fine bronze jugs and several carved 'man and wife' sarcophagi. The terrace **çay bahçesi** in the front is great for a relaxing drink once you've finished with the museum.

Hourly minibuses run to Burdur from Isparta (€2.25, 45 minutes).

DAVRAZ DAĞI (MT DAVRAZ)

The skiing season on the slopes of Mt Davraz (2635m) usually runs from mid-December to March, depending on the snow. Both Nordic and downhill skiing are possible and there's one 1.2km-long chairlift. A day's skiing, with equipment hire and lift pass, costs around €30; summit treks are also possible, or, if adrenaline's more your thing, you could try out 'slope parachute' (paragliding).

Accommodation is available at the main ski centre and the five-star Sirene Davraz Mountain Resort, though, unless you're a hardcore dusk-to-dawn skier it's just as easy to stay in Isparta and Eğirdir.

In season there are regular dolmuşes from Isparta and less frequent ones from Eğirdir (€1, 30 minutes) on weekends. At other times, a taxi up to the resort should cost around €23.

EĞİRDİR

☎ 0246 / pop 17,000

While many of the lake towns here come as a disappointment, you could hardly wish for a setting as perfect as Eğirdir (eh-*yeer*-deer), which lies contentedly near the southern tip of Eğirdir Gölü (Lake Eğirdir), overlooked by Davraz Dağı (Mt Davraz; 2635m). In Lydian times it straddled the Royal Road, the main route between Ephesus and Babylon, and since it was a beautiful and convenient place to stop, Eğirdir quickly prospered.

Today it's still handily placed, on the road from Konya to the Aegean, and tourism has become a major part of the local economy. The main selling points are the sweeping views, fresh fish dinners and boat trips on the silvery-blue waters of Turkey's fourth-largest lake (517 sq km). However, Eğirdir is also increasingly important as a trekking and climbing base for people who want to explore Sivri Dağı (Mt Sivri), walk through the Yazılı Kanyon or trek some part of the St Paul Trail (see p83).

As you approach from Isparta you'll pass a large Turkish mountain commando training base with a slogan emblazoned in

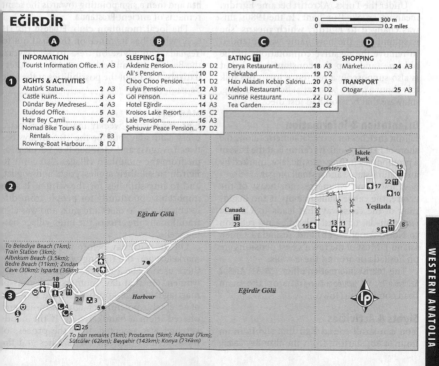

EĞİRDİR

| | 0 — 300 m |
| | 0 — 0.2 miles |

	A		B		C		D
INFORMATION		**SLEEPING** 🏠		**EATING** 🍴		**SHOPPING**	
Tourist Information Office..**1** A3		Akdeniz Pension..............**9** D2		Derya Restaurant..............**18** A3		Market..............**24** A3	
		Ali's Pension..................**10** D2		Felekabad.......................**19** D2			
SIGHTS & ACTIVITIES		Choo Choo Pension........**11** D2		Hacı Alaadin Kebap Salonu...**20** A3		**TRANSPORT**	
Atatürk Statue....................**2** A3		Fulya Pension................**12** A3		Melodi Restaurant............**21** D2		Otogar..............**25** A3	
Castle Ruins.......................**3** A3		Göl Pension...................**13** D2		Sunrise Restaurant...........**22** D2			
Dündar Bey Medresesi........**4** A3		Hotel Eğirdir.................**14** A3		Tea Garden....................**23** C2			
Etudosd Office...................**5** A3		Kroisos Lake Resort........**15** C2					
Hızır Bey Camii..................**6** A3		Lale Pension...................**16** A3					
Nomad Bike Tours &		Şehsuvar Peace Pension..**17** D2					
Rentals.........................**7** B3							
Rowing-Boat Harbour......**8** D2							

İskele Park

Cemetery ●

Eğirdir Gölü

Canada

Yeşilada

Sok 11

Sok 3

Sok 5

To Belediye Beach (1km);
Train Station (3km);
Altınkum Beach (3.5km);
Bedre Beach (11km); Zindan
Cave (30km); Isparta (36km)

Harbour

Eğirdir Gölü

To han remains (1km); Prostanna (5km); Akpınar (7km);
Sütçüler (62km); Beyşehir (143km); Konya (236km)

gigantic letters on the scree slope above: Komandoyuz – Güçlüyüz, Cesuruz, Hazırız ('We're Commandos – We're Strong, We're Brave, We're Ready'). On their days off, these army tough guys are a common sight about town, and over summer weekends their visiting parents often fill the pension rooms.

History

Founded by the Hittites, Eğirdir was taken by the Phrygians (c 1200 BC) and then the Lydians, captured by the Persians and conquered by Alexander the Great. Alexander was followed by the Romans, who called the town Prostanna. Contemporary documents suggest that it was large and prosperous, but no excavations have been done at the site, which lies within a large military enclave.

In Byzantine times, as Akrotiri (Steep Mountain), it was the seat of a bishopric. Later, it became a Seljuk city (c 1080–1280) and then the capital of a small principality ruled by the Hamidoğulları tribe (1280–1381). The Ottomans took control in 1417, but the population of Yeşilada remained mostly Greek Orthodox until the 1920s.

Under the Turks, Akrotiri became Eğridir, meaning 'crooked' or 'bent'. In the 1980s, this was changed to Eğirdir, which means 'she is spinning' – the new name was intended to remove the negative connotations of the old one (and stop the constant jokes), but is also supposedly a reference to an old folk tale about a queen who sat at home spinning, unaware that her son had just died.

Orientation & Information

Eğirdir stretches for several kilometres along the shore of Eğirdir Gölü. Its centre is at the base of a promontory jutting into the lake, marked by an Atatürk statue and a small otogar.

A few hundred metres northeast of the centre, the castle walls rise up at the beginning of the causeway that leads to Canada (jahn-ah-da, or 'Soul Island' – no relation to North America, eh) and Yeşilada ('Green Island'). Most of the town's best pensions are on Yeşilada or around these walls.

The **tourist information office** (☎ 311 4388; 2 Sahilyolu 13; ☼ 8am-6pm Mon-Fri) is on the main road coming into town.

Sights & Activities

You can stroll round Eğirdir's sights in an hour or so, starting from the **Hızır Bey Camii**, built as a Seljuk warehouse in 1237 but turned into a mosque in 1308 by the Hamidoğulları emir Hızır Bey. The mosque is quite simple, with a clerestory (row of windows) above the central hall and new tiles around the mihrab, but note the finely carved wooden doors and the bits of blue tile on the minaret.

Opposite the mosque, the **Dündar Bey Medresesi** was built as a caravanserai by the Seljuk sultan Alaeddin Keykubat in 1218 but converted into a medrese in 1285 for the Hamidoğulları emir, Felekeddin Dündar Bey. In the modern era it's lost its religion entirely and is now a bazaar filled with shops. An unusual walk-through minaret with an arch in its base connects the complex to the mosque.

A few hundred metres out towards Yeşilada stand the massive walls of the ruined **castle**. Its foundations were probably laid during the reign of Croesus, the cash-happy 5th-century BC king of Lydia, but it was restored by the Byzantines, the Hamidoğulları, the Seljuks and the Ottomans.

As you head out of town towards Konya you will pass the crumbling walls of an old **han** and then a sign pointing towards the scant remains of ancient **Prostanna**.

The local mountain club, **Etudosd** (☎ 311 6356), which has its office on the road out to Yeşilada, can advise on treks to Mt Davraz, the Barla massif and other good spots. Alternatively, ask about the possibilities at the Lale Pension (p320).

MARKETS

Eğirdir's normal weekly market takes place every Thursday, but for the 10 Sundays between August and October the Yörük people from the mountain villages also come to Eğirdir to sell their apples, goats and yogurt, and to buy supplies for the winter. It's an important opportunity for people from different villages to meet and mix, and was also traditionally the crux of the inter-village dating scene.

On the Saturday before the last Sunday market, when the trading was nearly done there used to be a market attended only by women. On that day, mothers with sons of marriageable age approached the mothers of acceptable potential daughters-in-law and offered them a handkerchief. If the handkerchief was accepted, then the process of introductions between the families and the prospective bride and groom could begin, and if all went well, the marriage took place in the spring of the following year.

BEACHES

Yeşilada has no real beaches, although there's nothing to stop you swimming off the rocks around the island. To sunbathe you need to head out of the centre. The following local beaches have changing cabins and food stands or restaurants.

The free, sandy **Belediye Beach** is at Yazla, less than 1km from the centre on the Isparta road.

Pebbly **Altınkum Beach** (admission €0.40) is several kilometres further north, near the train station. In high summer, dolmuşes run here every 15 minutes (€0.30) from in front of the otogar.

Even further north, 11km out on the road to Barla, **Bedre Beach** with 1.5km of sand is the best of all. You can walk or cycle here, or a taxi costs about €4.50 each way.

Tours

Most pensions offer **boat trips** with the brother, cousin or son of a pension owner, and if you don't plump for one of them then chances are you'll be offered a trip by anyone who stops you near the waterfront. Some such jaunts are fishing trips, at night or in the early morning. How much you enjoy them may depend more on the weather and the force of the wind than on the boat or owner, but most people seem to have fun. Some trips are free with accommodation, though usually you'll pay up to €17 per person.

Cycle hire is available at many pensions or from **Nomad Bike Tours & Rentals** (☎ 311 6688; www.nomadbiketours.com; Ata Yolu Üzeri), who can suggest itineraries and organise custom tours as well as hiring out mountain bikes at €11 per day.

For information on local rose tours, see p315.

Sleeping

You can choose between staying on Yeşilada, at the end of the promontory, or in the mainland part of town. Handy yellow signs point the way to most of the different pensions.

If you arrive at the start or end of the season, remember that nights can be cold, so look for a pension with central heating. Most places have hot water, although you may need to ask your host to turn it on.

In high season (from mid-June to mid-September), Eğirdir pension owners, especially on Yeşilada, are reluctant to take single travellers. Even if you offer to pay the double rate, they may still turn you down because they won't be able to sell two meals.

YEŞİLADA

Yeşilada has a dozen or so family-run pensions and restaurants, interspersed with second homes for the İstanbul elite who come here for a fortnight every year. It may seem immediately appealing because of its island position, but it's a long walk every time you want to get off it. Most of the pensions are fairly similar and none is in a particularly inspiring building, but the island is small enough to walk around in 15 minutes so you could make a quick circuit before choosing.

Şehsuvar Peace Pension (☎ 311 2433; www.peacepension.com; r €8-20) Aiming at the backpacker end of the market, the name reflects the slightly hippy family ethos here: real budget types can even sleep on the roof terrace for €4. The quiet courtyard is a treat, and there's a bar for louder nights. Breakfast costs around €3.

Akdeniz Pension (☎ 311 2432; s/d €14/20) This pension is run by an elderly couple who don't speak much English. It has four simple but spotless balcony rooms with a light, homey feel to them and a vine-shaded terrace.

Choo Choo Pension (☎ 319 4926; s/d/tr €14/23/28) Eğirdir's newest arrival, the Choo Choo steams its way onto the scene in a vaguely castle-like building. The rooms are typically simple and well formed, but the best feature is the big Halikarnas conservatory restaurant out front.

Ali's Pension (☎ 311 2547; www.alispension.com; s €14-17, d €25) Ali's is a comfortable little pension on the far side of the island with nine attractive, wooden-floored rooms and a pleasant terrace. Run by a genuine fishing family, it's one of the most welcoming places here.

Kroisos Lake Resort (☎ 311 5006; www.kroisoshotel.com; s/d €28/36) This conventional hotel, done out in a few too many dubious shades of green, lacks the personal family atmosphere of the better pensions but makes up for it with the selection of facilities, including ski and bike hire, a lounge with piano and regular live music in the restaurant.

Göl Pension (☎ 311 2370; ahmetdavras@hotmail.com; r €28-39; 🖳) With just six rooms you'll have to get in early to bag the best spots here – the

WESTERN ANATOLIA

two upstairs rooms with private terrace are nicer but pricier than the downstairs shared-bathroom alternatives. It's a family place, and owner Ahmet is invariably popular with guests.

MAINLAND

Lale Pension (☎ 311 2406; www.lalehostel.com; Kale Mahallesi 5 Sokak 2; dm €5.60, r €11-23; 🖳) One of several options up behind the castle, the Lale dominates Eğirdir's backpacker market thanks to its neat, compact rooms, family atmosphere and savvy management by the helpful and knowledgeable İbrahim. There are great lake views from the narrow pine-striped rooftop lounge, where guests meet and mingle like old friends over a nargileh. You can also get plenty of info on local excursions, tours and treks. Bike hire is €7 per day, boat tours start at €14 per person, breakfast is €2.80 and set meals cost €7.

Fulya Pension (☎ 311 2175; dm €8, s/d €13/17; 🖳) The Fulya, operating much like the Lale, has the advantage of a roof terrace offering a 360-degree panorama, perfect for star-gazing and lake-snapping. Rooms are spacious, and the owner is a fisherman who takes guests out on his boat. Breakfast costs €2.80.

Hotel Eğirdir (☎ 311 3961; www.hotelegirdir.com; 2 Sahil Yolu 2; s/d/tr €25/34/46) The main port of call for tour groups, this big three-star block has an impressive lobby and modest but adequate rooms with appealing linen and small balconies overlooking the lake. The large restaurant has three old trees actually growing through the ceiling.

Eating

Virtually every pension and hotel has a restaurant attached, and these often provide the best-value meals, but there are other dining options if you want a bit of variety. Don't miss the chance to eat *istakoz* (crayfish) straight from the lake in season.

Hacı Aladdin Kebap Salonu (☎ 311 4154; Belediye Caddesi 17; mains €1-4; ⏰ 9am-10pm) Tucked in amid the shops in the town centre, this reliable kebap joint also sells that weird Eğirdir speciality, *şekerli pide* (cheese pide sprinkled with sugar).

Derya Restaurant (☎ 311 4047; mains €2-5; ⏰ 9am-10pm) Across the street from the Hotel Eğirdir, the Derya has outdoor tables set by the water and a rather mauve dining room serving a standard range of grills and salads.

Felekabad (☎ 311 5881; Yeşilada; mains €2-6; ⏰ 11am-10pm) A simple family restaurant with a conservatory section and lakefront seating enjoying a faint garden ambience.

Sunrise Restaurant (☎ 311 5852; Yeşilada; mains €4-8; ⏰ 11am-10pm) Next to the Felekabad, the Sunrise is a slightly slicker affair popular with Turkish visitors from the city and, unlike its neighbour, serves alcohol.

Melodi Restaurant (☎ 311 4816; Yeşilada; mains €4-8; ⏰ 11am-10pm) Next to the Akdeniz Pension at the tip of the island, the Melodi is often regarded as the best restaurant in town, with a range of fresh mezes and delicious grilled fish. The lake views are pretty good too.

The popular *çay bahçesi* on Canada makes a fine place to stop for a drink or a snack, and also has a children's playground.

Getting There & Away

BUS

There are daily buses to Ankara (€11, seven hours), Antalya (€5.60, 2½ hours), Denizli (€6, three hours), İstanbul (€17, 11 hours), İzmir (€11, seven hours), Konya (€9.50, four hours), Nevşehir (€14, eight hours), Sütçüler (€4, 1½ hours) and Yalvaç (€2.80, one hour).

If there's no bus leaving straightaway for your destination, hop on a minibus to Isparta (€1.40, 15 minutes) and catch one from there (see p315).

TRAIN

The **train station** (☎ 311 4694) is on the Isparta road 3km from the centre. Daily trains go to Istanbul (€12, 13 hours) and İzmir (€8.50, 10 hours) via Isparta.

AROUND EĞİRDİR
Sivri Dağı (Mt Sivri) & Akpınar

Sivri Dağı ('Sharp Mountain'; 1749m) dominates views southwest of Eğirdir. High up on its steep slopes, the tiny village of Akpınar offers apple orchards and photogenic views over the lake. To get there, head 3km south of Eğirdir along the lakeshore road to the suburb of Yeni Mahalle, where a road starts to wind 4km up the mountain to the village. It's a steep walk, which should take about two hours if you're in reasonable shape. The village has two small tea houses poised to scoop the lake views; one has a battered old tent to shelter in, though you can't actually see anything from it! Both places serve *ayran* (yogurt drink) and freshly made *gözleme*.

Serious hikers can continue to the top of the mountain, but some of the rocks are unstable and there have been fatalities in the past – seek local advice before setting out and take great care. Don't try climbing from the commando base (north) side, as chances are the boys in green won't appreciate it.

Kovada Gölü National Park, Yazılı Nature Park & Çandır Kanyon

Noted for its flora and fauna, **Lake Kovada National Park** (Kovada Gölü Milli Parkı) surrounds a small lake connected to Lake Eğirdir by a channel. It's a pleasant place for a hike and a picnic. The St Paul's Trail passes nearby (see p83 for details). Close by is the **Kasnak Forest**, visited by botanical enthusiasts for its rare orchids.

About 73km south of Eğirdir, the **Yazılı Canyon Nature Park** (Yazılı Kanyon Tabiat Parkı; admission €0.55, car €0.70) protects a forested gorge deep in the mountains separating the Lake District (ancient Pisidia) and the Antalya region (Pamphylia). After paying the admission fee at the car park, you follow a path 1km upstream through the glorious **Çandır Kanyon** to some shady bathing spots; the water is icy cold even in late spring. In July and August the canyon heaves with sunbathing Turkish families; at other times you may well have it to yourself.

The park takes its name from the inscriptions carved in the rocks lining the gorge (*yazılı* means 'written'), which are still clearly visible, though most have been vandalised. Look out for a slightly self-aggrandising poem on the origins and nature of man by the 1st-century poet Epiktitus; whatever his virtues, it's unlikely he lived to be 188, as the dates on the signboard suggest!

The **Yazılı Kanyon Restaurant and Kamping Alanı** (2-person tent €8.50), in the car park at the entrance, offers meals of fresh trout, salad and a drink for €3. When it's not busy, the entrance fee may be waived if you're eating or staying here.

GETTING THERE & AWAY

The easiest way to get to Kovada Gölü and the Çandır Kanyon is to sign up with a tour from one of the pensions. Out-of-season taxi tours, including a three-hour wait, will cost around €28 to the lake or €40 to the lake and the canyon. You could also try hitching on a summer Sunday when locals head out for picnics.

Zından Mağarası (Zından Cave)

Another possible excursion is to Zından Mağarası, 30km southeast of Eğirdir and 1km north of the village of Aksu, across a fine Roman bridge. The 1km-long cave has Byzantine ruins at its mouth, lots of stalactites and stalagmites, and a curious room dubbed the Hamam. There's a pleasant walk along the river if caves aren't your thing.

Pensions organise tours to the cave in summer, or taxis charge about €28 per carload.

Sütçüler
☎ 0246 / pop 3700

The area around Eğirdir is increasingly popular with walkers, particularly now the newly waymarked St Paul Trail (see p83) passes through the area. Easily accessible from Eğirdir, Sütçüler is a fairly unremarkable small town spread out along a winding mountain road. The views, though, should really whet the appetite for a good trek, and the location makes it a good base for a few days' walking.

As well as the walking possibilities, buses from Eğirdir pass within 1km of the romantically deserted ruins of the Roman town of **Adada**, where recognisable remnants include a dramatic Roman road entrance, a 1000-seat agora and the temple of Trajan.

Sütçüler's single pension, **Pension Karacan** (☎ 351-2411; Atatürk Caddesi; gulaykaracan@mynet.com; half board r €11-23; 💻), has spacious rooms, some with shared bathroom, a garden terrace and an indoor restaurant with big windows to take in the green vistas below. Meals are prepared with organic produce, and the owners are thoroughly helpful.

GETTING THERE & AWAY

Seven daily buses run between Isparta and Sütçüler (€3.50, 1½ hours), passing through Eğirdir.

YALVAÇ & ANTIOCHEIA-IN-PISIDIA
☎ 0246 / pop 31,000

You might want to pause in the market town of Yalvaç to visit the extensive ruins of Antiocheia-in-Pisidia, located on a stark mountainside to the northeast.

Antiocheia-in-Pisidia

About 1km from Yalvaç centre lies the site of **Antiocheia-in-Pisidia** (admission €2.80; ☉ 9am-6pm), an ancient city that was abandoned in the

8th century after Arab attacks. Unfortunately, there are no signs on the site.

From the gate, a Roman road leads uphill past the foundations of a triumphal archway, then turns right to the **theatre**. Further uphill, on a flat area surrounded by a semicircular wall of rock, is the city's main **shrine**. This was originally dedicated to the Anatolian mother goddess Cybele, then later to the moon god Men, but in Roman times it featured an imperial cult temple dedicated to Augustus. A path heads left to the **nymphaeum**, once a permanent spring but now dry.

Several arches of the city's **aqueduct** are visible across the fields. Downhill from the nymphaeum are the ruins of the **Roman baths**. Several large chambers have been excavated and much of the original ceiling is intact. On the way back to the entrance you pass the foundations of **St Paul's Basilica**, built on the site of the synagogue. The itinerant tent-maker and apostle's preaching here provoked such a strong reaction that he and St Barnabas were expelled from the city.

After exploring the site you may want to drop into **Yalvaç Museum** (Yalvaç Müzesi; admission €1.10; ☑ 8.30am-5.30pm Tue-Sun) in the town centre, which has a plan of the ruins and a modest collection of finds from the ruins. Its ethnography section has a fine recreation of the Ottoman-era living room of a wealthy household.

Getting There & Away
A few daily buses link Yalvaç with Eğirdir (€2.80, one hour) and Akşehir (€2, 45 minutes).

BEYŞEHİR
☎ 0332 / pop 41,700
The main town on this region's third major lake, fast-growing Beyşehir has preserved its Ottoman heart against the waves of modernity, and is home to one of Anatolia's best medieval mosques. Founded around the 6th century BC, Beyşehir has changed hands innumerable times in the course of history (including 20 times between just 1374 and 1467!), but was most favoured under the 13th-century Seljuks, who considered it a second capital.

In 1296 Şeyheddin Süleyman Bey was responsible for creating the newly restored **Eşrefoğlu Camii**, which, with its 42 soaring wooden pillars, coloured mosaics and beautiful blue-tiled mihrab, is second only in architec-

tural importance to Afyon's Ulu Cami. Originally, it was open to the skies and used only on Friday; nowadays, however, the roof has been covered over. Süleyman Bey is buried beside the mosque. Other key old-town buildings are nearby, including the many-domed **Dokumacılar Hanı** *bedesten* (Cloth Hall; storage chamber), the **Çifte Hamamı** and the **İsmail Ağa Medrese**.

The mosque is right on the lakeshore, reached from the town centre by crossing the impressive arched 1908 railway bridge and following the waterline. You could also take an evening boat tour with **Eşrefoğlu Yat** (☎ 0542 841 8784; tour €1.70), which lets you see the lake-facing side mosque while nibbling some dirt-cheap *köfte* (€0.85).

There are a couple of accommodation options in town if you need to stay over; the **Beyaz Park Motel** (☎ 512 4535; s €11, d €20-25), by the bridge, has a great terrace café-restaurant.

Getting There & Away
There are regular buses to Eğirdir (€5, two hours) and Konya (€3.50, one hour). City buses (€0.30) serve the otogar twice hourly, passing near the mosque.

PAMUKKALE REGION

The region around Pamukkale and Denizli is the natural spa centre of Turkey, encompassing no fewer than 17 different thermal springs at temperatures between 36°C and 100°C. Of these, Pamukkale itself must be the most heavily marketed attraction in the whole of Western Anatolia, with endless tourist posters flashing brighter-than-life images of bathers in clear blue water on the sparkling white travertines that make the town famous.

Sadly the hype worked just a bit too well in the days before conservation was a business concept, and the reality is somewhat different these days as local authorities struggle to undo the damage, or at least prevent any further degradation of a truly unique site. Luckily the extensive ruins of the Roman spa town of Hierapolis still make Pamukkale well worth a visit, whether you paddle (but not bathe) in the ridges or not.

NYSSA (NYSA)
East of the dull modern town of Aydın, you're deep into the fertile farming country of the Büyük Menderes River valley. Cotton

fields sweep away from the road, and during the late October harvest the highways are jammed with tractors hauling trailers laden with the white puffy stuff. Other important crops grown locally include pomegranates, pears, citrus fruits, apples, olives and tobacco.

About 31km east of Aydın stands the town of Sultanhisar. A 3km uphill walk to the north brings you to ancient **Nyssa** (admission €1.10; ☺ daylight hr), set on a hilltop amid olive groves. On arrival you'll find public toilets, a soft-drink stand and a custodian who will show you around the **theatre**. There's also a 115m-long **tunnel** beneath the road and parking area that was once the ancient city's main square. Walk another five minutes up the hill, along the road and through a field, and you'll come to the **bouleuterion**, with some attractive sculpture fragments. But what you'll probably remember most about Nyssa is the site's peaceful beauty, so different from the hubbub at Ephesus.

Getting There & Away

İzmir–Denizli trains stop in town, and many east–west buses run along the highway. Dolmuşes run to Sultanhisar from Nazilli every 15 minutes (€0.55).

NAZİLLİ & AROUND
pop 113,000

If you're driving to Afrodisias you might transit the market town of Nazilli, 14km east of Nysa and Sultanhisar. However, most people visit Afrodisias from Pamukkale.

On the road between the main Nazilli–Denizli highway and Karacasu, look for signs pointing to **Antiocheia**. To get there, turn north at the centre of Başaran village, 18km northwest of Karacasu, and drive 1km to the impressively sited and extensive but completely unexcavated and unrestored ruins of an ancient hilltop city.

Return to the Nazilli–Denizli highway, 6km to the north, by continuing past Antiocheia across the fertile floodplain of the Büyük Menderes River and through the farming village of **Azizabat**, which has some fine stone houses. You regain the highway at a point 5.6km east of the Karacasu turn-off, 21km east of Nazilli. Turn right for Denizli.

Alternatively, continue on to the town of **Karacasu**, which is surrounded by tobacco fields, fig trees and orchards. Karacasu is famous for its potters; to see them at work, ask to be directed to the *çanakçı ocakları* (potter's kiln).

DENİZLİ
☎ 0258 / pop 275,500

The prosperous town of Denizli is famous for its textiles. For most travellers, however, it's just a place to hop off a bus or train and onto a bus or dolmuş heading north to Pamukkale.

Getting There & Away
AIR

Turkish Airlines has daily flights to Denizli, although most travellers arrive by bus or train.

SERVICES FROM DENİZLİ'S OTOGAR

Destination	Fare	Duration	Distance	Frequency (per day)
Afyon	€6.70	4hr	240km	8
Ankara	€11	7hr	480km	frequent
Antalya	€8.50	5hr	300km	several
Bodrum	€11	4hr	290km	several
Bursa	€1418.50	9hr	532km	several
Fethiye	€7.50	5hr	280km	several
Isparta	€5.60	3hr	175km	several
İstanbul	€20	12hr	665km	frequent
İzmir	€6.70	4hr	250km	frequent
Konya	€14	6hr	440km	several
Marmaris	€8.50	3hr	185km	several
Nevşehir	€17	11hr	674km	at least 1 nightly
Selçuk	€8.50	3hr	195km	several, or change at Aydın

BUS

There are frequent buses between İzmir and Denizli via Aydın and Nazilli. The Denizli otogar has an *emanetçi* (left-luggage office) next to the PTT.

You can catch a bus from Denizli to virtually any major city in Turkey. Some daily services are listed in the table on the previous page.

The local bus service to Pamukkale leaves from inside the otogar and runs roughly every 30 minutes, with no waiting about for it to fill up. Touts taking commissions from hotels may try to get you to take the dolmuşes that wait beside the otogar instead of the bus. In summer these fill up quickly, but at other times you'll be waiting around. Buses and dolmuşes to Pamukkale cost exactly the same (€0.85).

TRAIN

The train station is on the main highway, across the road from the otogar and a short distance from the Üçgen roundabout.

On arrival at the train station, walk out of the front door, cross the highway, turn left and walk one block to the otogar to catch a dolmuş or bus to Pamukkale.

The nightly *Pamukkale Ekspresi* (seat €12, couchette €16.50, sleeper €27 to €55, 15½ hours) travels between Denizli and İstanbul via Afyon (€5.30, six hours). It leaves from İstanbul (Haydarpaşa) at 5.35pm and from Denizli at 5pm.

Many people enjoy the relatively short run from Denizli to Selçuk (€3.60, two hours), which passes through attractive countryside and leaves/arrives during sensible daylight hours.

Four trains a day connect Denizli with İzmir (€5, 4½ to 5½ hours), also via Afyon.

PAMUKKALE

☎ 0258 / pop 2500

Calcium's not just good for bones. If the many habitués of the spa town of Pamukkale are to be believed, it works wonders on muscles and sinews too. 'Cotton Castle', 19km north of Denizli, has built a centuries-long reputation on the restorative qualities of its calcium-rich waters. The unique formations of travertine (calcium carbonate) shelves, pools and sta-

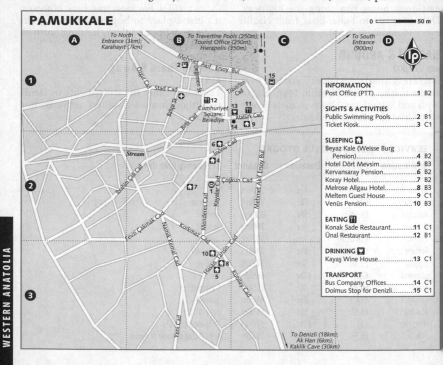

PAMUKKALE

0 ——— 50 m

To North Entrance (3km); Karahayıt (7km)
To Travertine Pools (250m); Tourist Office (250m); Hierapolis (350m)
To South Entrance (900m)
To Denizli (18km); Ak Han (6km); Kaklık Cave (30km)

Mehmet Akif Ersoy Bul
Oğur Cad
Stad Cad
Baliç Sk
Değirmen Sk
Travertin Cad
Cumhuriyet Square; Belediye
Atatürk Cad
Birlik Cad
Stream
İnönü Cad
İbrahim Çallı Cad
Mehmet Akif Ersoy Bul
Coşkun Cad
Kayalar Cad
Menderes Cad
Fevzi Çakmak Cad
Namık Kemal Cad
Korkmaz Cad
Hacı Tahsin Cad
Yeni Cad
Kuşbay Cad

INFORMATION	
Post Office (PTT)......................1 B2	

SIGHTS & ACTIVITIES	
Public Swimming Pools.............2 B1	
Ticket Kiosk...............................3 C1	

SLEEPING	
Beyaz Kale (Weisse Burg	
Pension)...............................4 B2	
Hotel Dört Mevsim....................5 B3	
Kervansaray Pension.................6 B2	
Koray Hotel................................7 B2	
Melrose Allgau Hotel................8 B3	
Meltem Guest House.................9 C1	
Venüs Pension.........................10 B3	

EATING	
Konak Sade Restaurant...........11 C1	
Ünal Restaurant.......................12 B1	

DRINKING	
Kayaş Wine House...................13 C1	

TRANSPORT	
Bus Company Offices..............14 C1	
Dolmus Stop for Denizli..........15 C1	

WESTERN ANATOLIA

lactites, which hug the ridge above town like a white scar, were created by the area's warm mineral water, which cools as it cascades over the cliff edge and deposits its calcium. It's a strange piece of landscape unlike anything else you'll see in Turkey, and it now appears on the Unesco World Heritage list.

Long before Unesco, the Romans recognised the appeal of the site and built a large spa city, Hierapolis, to take advantage of the water's curative powers. The tourist boom of the 1980s and 1990s had a detrimental effect on the site, as a line of hotels above the travertines drained away the waters, leaving the travertines dry, dull and dirtied. In a drastic attempt to preserve the site, all the hotels have been demolished and visitors can no longer bathe in the pools; however, the flow of water is still very slow, and it may be that the real culprits are the many swimming pools in the village below.

Pamukkale village has some charming hotels and pensions, and despite the constant coach parties it's a good place to get a taste of village life, if you steer clear of the main road. Several other attractions are within easy reach, including Afrodisias (p329), one of Turkey's most complete and absorbing archaeological sites, and Laodicea (p328), one of the biblical Seven Churches of Asia.

Orientation & Information

Together Pamukkale and Hierapolis make up a national park, with entrances to north and south. Cars can reach the southern entrance (güney girişi) via Pamukkale village (1km), or the northern entrance (kuzey girişi) via the dismal resort of Karahayıt. It's a short walk from the southern entrance to the centre of the site, but 2.5km from the northern entrance.

Pamukkale **tourist office** (☎ 272-2077; www .pamukkale.gov.tr; ⏰ 8am-noon & 1-5.30pm Mon-Sat) is on the plateau above the travertines, along with a PTT, ATM, police and first-aid post. The nearest banks are in Denizli.

Travertines

Most people come to Pamukkale to see its famous **travertines** (admission €2.80; ⏰ 24hr). Walking around them is enjoyable even now that access is restricted – though you'll never get a photo quite like the ones on the postcards. The route up to the northern entrance is about 3km long but is on tarmac, whereas from the

southern ticket kiosk you have to walk 250m barefoot up to the plateau, along a calcium path through the travertines themselves. Tiny ridges of calcium make this tough on tender feet. Since the site is open 24 hours you can visit for sunrise and sunset. Some pensions also organise trips to view the Hierapolis theatre and the travertines after dark.

You can swim in the Antique Pool in Hierapolis (see below), or there are several pleasant **public swimming pools** with views of the travertines on the main road past Pamukkale village.

Hierapolis

If you're disappointed by the state of the travertines, the ruins of Hierapolis should more than make up for it, since they brilliantly evoke life in the early centuries of the modern era. It was here that the mix of pagan, Roman, Jewish and early Christian elements evolved into a distinctly Anatolian whole. The ruins sprawl over a wide area. To inspect everything carefully could take the best part of a day, although most visitors settle for an hour or two.

Founded around 190 BC by Eumenes II, King of Pergamum, Hierapolis was a cure centre that prospered under the Romans and even more under the Byzantines, when it gained a large Jewish community and an early Christian congregation. Sadly, recurrent earthquakes regularly brought disaster, and after a major one in 1334 the locals called it a day and moved away.

The centre of Hierapolis may originally have been the sacred pool, which is now the swimming pool in the courtyard of the Antique Pool spa. You can still bathe in the **Antique Pool** (adult/child €10/4) amid submerged sections of original fluted marble columns. The water temperature is a languid 36°C. There are lockers for your gear, and the pool is surrounded by a number of café-bar kiosks.

Near the Hierapolis Archaeology Museum stand a ruined **Byzantine church** and the foundations of a **Temple of Apollo**. As at Didyma and Delphi, the temple had an oracle tended by eunuch priests. The source of inspiration was an adjoining spring called the Plutonium, dedicated to Pluto, god of the underworld. As if to confirm its direct line to Hades, the spring gave off toxic vapours, lethal to all but the priests, who would demonstrate its potent

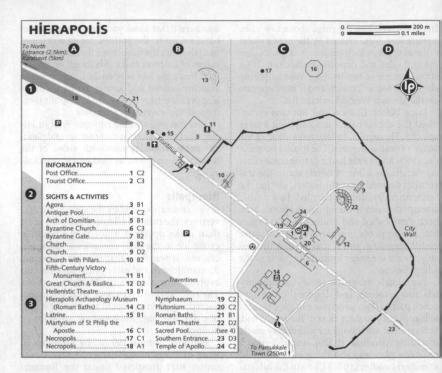

HİERAPOLİS

To North
Entrance (2.5km);
Karahayıt (5km)

0 .... 200 m
0 .... 0.1 miles

To Pamukkale
Town (250m)

Travertines

City
Wall

Frontinus St

powers by tossing small animals and birds in to watch them die.

To find the spring, walk up towards the Roman theatre, enter the first gate in the fence on the right, then follow the path down to the right. To the left, in front of the big, block-like temple, is a small subterranean entrance closed by a rusted grate and marked by a sign reading 'Tehlikelidir Zehirli Gaz' (Dangerous Poisonous Gas). Listen and you will hear the gas bubbling up from the waters below. Note that it is still deadly poisonous, and before the grate was installed there were several fatalities among those with more curiosity than sense.

The spectacular **Roman theatre**, capable of seating more than 12,000 spectators, was built in two stages by the emperors Hadrian and Septimius Severus. Much of the stage survives, along with some of the decorative panels and the front-row 'box' seats for VIPs. It was restored by Italian stonecutters in the 1970s. The new wooden rails are intended to stop people toppling down the tiers.

From the theatre, take one of the rough tracks heading uphill and eventually you'll come to the extraordinary octagonal **Martyrium**

of St Philip the Apostle, built on the site where it's believed that St Philip was martyred. The arches of the eight individual chapels are all marked with crosses. Views from here are wonderful, and few of the regular tours bother to bring visitors up this far.

Hack across the hillside in a westerly direction and eventually you'll come to a completely ruined **Hellenistic theatre** along unmarked goat tracks. Looking down you'll see the 2nd-century **agora**, one of the largest ever discovered. Marble porticoes with Ionic columns surrounded it on three sides, while a basilica closed off the fourth.

Walk down the hill and through the agora, and you'll re-emerge on the main road along the top of the ridge. Turn right towards the northern exit and you'll come to the remains of the marvellous colonnaded **Frontinus Street**, with some of its paving and columns still intact. Once the city's main north-south commercial axis, this street was bounded at both ends by monumental archways. The ruins of the **Arch of Domitian**, with its twin towers, are at the northern end, but just before them don't miss the surprisingly large **latrine** building, with two channels cut into its floor, one to carry away sewage, the other for fresh water.

Beyond the Arch of Domitian you come to the ruins of the **Roman baths**, then to the Appian Way of Hierapolis, an extraordinary **necropolis** (cemetery), extending several kilometres to the north, with many striking, even stupendous, tombs in all shapes and sizes. In particular, look out for a cluster of circular tombs, supposedly topped with phallic symbols in antiquity. In ancient times Hierapolis was a place where the sick came for a miracle cure, but the size of the necropolis suggests the local healers had mixed success.

HIERAPOLIS ARCHAEOLOGY MUSEUM
Housed in what were once the Roman baths, right by the travertines, this excellent **museum** (admission €1.10; ☺ 9am-12.30 & 1.30-7.15pm) has three separate sections, one housing spectacular sarcophagi, another small finds from Hierapolis and nearby Afrodisias, and the third friezes and Roman-era statuary from the Afrodisias school. Those depicting Attis, lover of the goddess Cybele, and a priestess of the Egyptian goddess Isis, are especially fine.

Festivals & Events
If you're here in early June, look out for the annual **Turkish-Greek Friendship Festival** (Türk–Yunan Dostluk Festivali), now in its sixth year. Pamukkale is twinned with Samos in Greece, and a series of talks, concerts and performances are held in both locations over several days, often using the travertines as a venue.

Sleeping
At first glance it seems like almost every building in Pamukkale village is a hotel or pension, and most visitors will stay here, although larger tour groups tend to put up in Karahayıt. Prices vary according to season, reaching their peak in July and August, but heavy competition ensures surprisingly good value for money, with services such as internet access, book exchanges, multilingual TV, in-house catering and swimming pools all commonplace. You'll have no problem finding a room, as pension owners will crowd around your bus and flood you with offers, and anyone with rooms still available after this initial onslaught will intercept you on the street. If you have your heart set on somewhere specific, call in advance and they'll probably collect you from Denizli otogar for free.

CAMPING
There are several **camp sites** (camping per person about €3) set around swimming pools beside the highway as you come into Pamukkale from Denizli. Some pensions also allow camping on their grounds.

PENSIONS & HOTELS
Several welcoming, family-run pensions are clustered at the junction of İnönü and Menderes Caddesis. As you come into town from Denizli there are several more pensions grouped together in a quiet location.

Hotel Dört Mevsim (☎ 272 2009; www.hoteldort mevsim.com; Hasan Tahsin Caddesi 19; s/d €6/12; ✗ ▯ ▣) The 'Four Seasons' bears very little relation to its top-end namesakes, but does provide simple, cheap family-run accommodation and food. Camping is possible at €5.50 for two people, internet access is free and you can hire scooters for €11 per day.

Meltem Guest House (☎ 272 2413; www.meltem guesthouse.com; Kuzey Sokak 9; dm €6; budget s/d/tr €8.50/17/23, deluxe s/d/tr €14/28/34; ✗ ▯ ▣) Aimed firmly at backpackers, the Meltem has a slightly dodgy air when it's not busy, but gives you a choice of reasonably comfortable rooms and plenty of services, including free bike hire and 'bloody cold beer'. Trading up to deluxe gets you air-con, bathtub and basic minibar.

Melrose Allgau Hotel (☎ 272 2767; www.allgau hotel.com; Hasan Tahsin Caddesi; s/d €8.50/17; ✗ ▯ ▣) Unusual name, unusual building. A touch of alpine style informs everything about this yellow-hued German-run pension, and the rooms have a touch of charm in the simple décor and shady gardens.

Venüs Pension (☎ 272 2152; www.venushotel.net; Hasan Tahnsin Caddesi; s/d/tr €8.50/17/25; ✗ ▯ ▣) Our personal favourite right now, this lovely pink house is run by a friendly young Turkish-Australian couple, and it's hard to imagine the eponymous Aphrodite not smiling on a bit of romance beneath the wood ceilings. Home-cooked food and a nice terrace and lounge add to the appeal.

Kervansaray Pension (☎ 272 2209; kervansaray2@ superonline.com.tr; İnönü Caddesi; s/d €10/15; ▯ ▣) Mevlüt Kaya's pension is a honeysuckle-scented place offering cheerful rooms and a friendly, family atmosphere. It's been a favourite for years, and the central-heating system makes it a year-round possibility.

Beyaz Kale (Weisse Burg Pension; ☎ 272 2064; weis seburg@yahoo.com; Menderes Caddesi; s/d €10/20; ▣)

Whether you prefer it in Turkish or German, the 'White Castle' is handy for town without being too close, and has a long record of keeping its guests happy, particularly in the rooftop restaurant. All the rooms have fans.

Koray Hotel (☎ 272 2300; www.hotelkoray.com; Fevzi Çakmak Caddesi 27; s/d €23/34; 🏖 🖳) With the facilities of a hotel but much of the charm of a pension, the Koray Hotel could sell itself just on its inviting courtyard pool, restaurant and bar. The hotel stays open year-round and offers tour services to all the surrounding sites.

Eating & Drinking

Pensions and group travel dominate the market here so much that conventional restaurants have struggled to hold their own. There are a couple worth trying, but it's not a bad idea to take a room with dinner included – chances are that your pension will serve you better food with larger portions at lower prices than the restaurants.

Ünal Restaurant (☎ 272 2451; Belediye Altı; mains €3.50-7.50; 🕙 11am-10pm) By the main square, this smartish licensed restaurant has all the usual standards such as şiş kebap and grills, as well as daily specials.

Kayaş Wine House (☎ 272 2267; Atatürk Caddesi 3; mains €3.50-7.50; 🕙 from noon) As well as a wide-ranging multilingual menu, the Kayaş' terrace offers plenty of scope for a night out, with cocktails (€5.50 to €11), a nargileh corner and satellite TV coverage of big football matches.

Konak Sade Restaurant (☎ 272 2002; mains €3.50-8; 🕙 9am-10pm) Attached to the hotel of the same name; travertine views and garden water features add a little flavour to more of the usual dishes.

Getting There & Away
BUS
In summer, Pamukkale has several direct buses to and from other cities. At other times of year it's best to assume you'll have to change in Denizli.

Pamukkale has no proper otogar. Buses drop you at the Denizli dolmuş stop. Ticket offices are on the main street.

Buses run between Denizli and Pamukkale every 30 minutes or so, more frequently on Saturday and Sunday (€0.85, 30 minutes). The last bus runs at 10pm for most of the year, but check before leaving it late. A few buses

continue to the top of the ridge for minimal extra charge.

In summer dolmuşes run more frequently, but see p324 for a warning on pension touts and delays.

TAXI
A taxi between Denizli and Pamukkale costs about €10, but don't take one until you're *sure* the bus and dolmuş services have stopped for the day, as drivers will probably try to take you to a hotel where they can claim commission.

AROUND PAMUKKALE
Laodicea (Laodikya)
Once a prosperous commercial city at the junction of two major trade routes, Laodicea was famed for its black wool, banking and medicines. It had a large Jewish community and a prominent Christian congregation, and was one of the Seven Churches of Asia mentioned in the New Testament Book of Revelation. Cicero lived here for a few years before being put to death at the behest of Mark Antony.

Although the spread-out **ruins** (admission free 🕙 daylight hr) suggest a city of considerable size, there's not much of interest left for the casual visitor. The outline of the **stadium** is visible, although most of the stones were purloined to construct the railway. One of the two **theatres** is in better shape, with most of the upper tiers of seats remaining – though the bottom ones have collapsed. More striking are the remains of the **agora**, with the ruins of the **basilica church** mentioned in the Bible right beside it. The site is littered with discarded chunks of beautifully carved marble, each one of which would be a major exhibit anywhere not so overflowing in antiquities.

Heading from Pamukkale to Denizli by bus, you'll pass two signs to Laodicea leading off on the right. If you take the first of these it will bring you to a large explanatory sign and then to the agora after about 1km. The second sign leads you to the stadium first – it's quite a walk from there to the agora.

Alternatively, you might want to sign up for a tour from Pamukkale, which will take in other local sites as well.

Kaklık Mağarası (Kaklık Cave) & Ak Han
Inconspicuously hidden away beneath a field, Kaklık Mağarası (admission €1.10) is like a second Pamukkale tucked away underground. Here

calcium-rich water flows from near the surface into a large sinkhole, creating a bright, white pyramid, with warm travertine pools at the bottom, which you walk past on a metal walkway. Guides claim that the deposits became white only after the local earthquake of the mid-1990s. Afterwards, drinks are on sale around a small pool where you can swim (although it doesn't look especially inviting).

En route to or from the cave, pause to inspect the **Ak Han** (White Caravanserai; admission free; ☾ daylight hr), a Seljuk *han* just 1km past the Pamukkale turn-off on the main Denizli–Isparta highway. It's in great shape considering that it dates from around 1251, and has a beautifully carved gateway.

Getting to the cave without your own transport is time-consuming, and it's usually easiest to take a tour from Pamukkale. To visit independently, catch a bus or dolmuş (€1.70) west from Denizli on the Isparta highway until you approach the village of Kaklık, where a huge sign points left (north) to the cave. Unless you can hitch a ride on a farm vehicle, you face a 4km walk along this road to the cave.

Afrodisias

Afrodisias is one of Turkey's finest archaeological sites. Some people even prefer it to Ephesus, if only because it is less overrun with coach parties. While there are certainly finer individual ruins elsewhere, it's the scope of the surviving remains that distinguishes Afrodisias, as so much of it is preserved that

you can get a real sense of the grandeur and extent of the lost classical cities. Come in May or June and you'll find the ruins awash with blazing red poppies.

HISTORY

Excavations have proved that the Afrodisias acropolis is a prehistoric mound built up by successive settlements from around 5000 BC. From the 6th century BC its famous temple was a popular pilgrimage site, but it wasn't until the 2nd or 1st century BC that the village grew into a town that steadily prospered. By the 3rd century AD Afrodisias was the capital of the Roman province of Caria, with a population of 15,000 at its peak. However, under the Byzantines the city changed substantially: the steamy Temple of Aphrodite was transformed into a chaste Christian church, and ancient buildings were pulled down to provide stone for defensive walls (c AD 350).

During the Middle Ages Afrodisias continued as a cathedral town, but it seems to have been abandoned in the 12th century. The village of Gcyre sprang up on the site some time later. In 1956 an earthquake devastated the village, which was rebuilt in its present westerly location, allowing easier excavation of the site. The pleasant plaza in front of the museum was the main square of pre-1956 Geyre.

Although other archaeologists worked on the site before him, Afrodisias will always be associated with the work of Professor Kenan T Erim of New York University, who directed work at the site from 1961 to 1990. His book

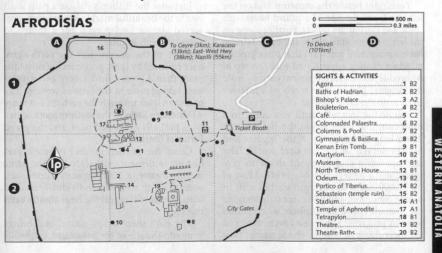

SIGHTS & ACTIVITIES		
Agora	1	B2
Baths of Hadrian	2	B2
Bishop's Palace	3	A2
Bouleterion	4	B2
Café	5	C2
Colonnaded Palaestra	6	B2
Columns & Pool	7	B2
Gymnasium & Basilica	8	B2
Kenan Erim Tomb	9	B1
Martyrion	10	B2
Museum	11	B2
North Temenos House	12	B1
Odeum	13	B2
Portico of Tiberius	14	B2
Sebasteion (temple ruin)	15	B2
Stadium	16	A1
Temple of Aphrodite	17	A1
Tetrapylon	18	B1
Theatre	19	B2
Theatre Baths	20	B2

AFRODİSİAS

To Geyre (3km); Karacasu (13km); East-West Hwy (38km); Nazilli (55km)

To Denizli (101km)

Ticket Booth

City Gates

WESTERN ANATOLIA

MIGHTY APHRODITE

The name Afrodisias quickly evokes the word 'aphrodisiac', which is hardly surprising since both are derived from the Greek name for the goddess of love, Aphrodite. Known as Venus to the Romans, Aphrodite was many things to many people. As Aphrodite Urania she was the goddess of pure, spiritual love, but as Aphrodite Pandemos she was the goddess of sensual love and lust – married to Hephaestus but lover also of Ares, Hermes, Dionysus and Adonis. Her children, Harmonia, Eros, Hermaphroditus, Aeneas (the founder of Troy) and Priapus, the phallic god, reflect aspects from both sides of Aphrodite's dual nature.

Unsurprisingly, these qualities didn't always sit well together, and while Aphrodite could be a champion of true lovers and a defender of humanity, she could also be a mischievous, capricious force in the lives of men. Her presence in classical legend almost always serves to shake up a situation and, often enough, introduce a little chaos. Most notably the entire Trojan war can be attributed to her manipulation of Paris, who was 'persuaded' to declare her the winner in a celestial beauty contest when she promised him the love of the beautiful Helen.

Taken as a whole, the message of the Aphrodite legend is a clear and familiar one: love is a powerful thing, with the potential to change the world or make fools of us all. Small wonder that the Romans here chose to dedicate their city to the goddess they saw pulling those strings.

Afrodisias: City of Venus Aphrodite (1986) tells the story. After his death, Professor Erim was buried at the site that he had done so much to reveal.

RUINS

Most of what you see at **Afrodisias** (admission €4; ⊗ 9am-7.30pm May-Sep, 9am-5pm Oct-Apr) dates back to at least the 2nd century AD. The site is well laid out, with good, clear notices in English and Turkish, and a suggested route marked by yellow-and-black arrows. If you follow the route we give here you will be going against the flow of the regular tour groups, which arrive around 11am most days.

Turn right beside the museum and on the left you'll see the site of a grand **house** with Ionic and Corinthian pillars. Further along on the left is the magnificently elaborate **tetrapylon** (monumental gateway) that once greeted pilgrims as they approached the Temple of Aphrodite, reconstructed almost entirely from the original blocks. The tomb of Professor Erim is on the lawn nearby.

Follow the footpath until you come to a right turn that leads across the fields to the 270m-long **stadium**, one of the biggest and best preserved in the classical world. The stadium has a slightly ovoid shape to give spectators a better view of events. Most of its 30,000 seats are overgrown but still in usable condition, and you can easily imagine the football-crowd atmosphere when games were in progress. Some seats were reserved for individuals or guilds, whose names they

still bear. At some stage, the eastern end of the stadium was converted into an arena for gladiatorial combats.

Return to the main path and continue to the once-famous **Temple of Aphrodite**, completely rebuilt when it was converted into a basilica (c AD 500). Its cella was removed, its columns shifted to form a nave and an apse added at the eastern end, making it hard to imagine how it must have been in the years when orgies in celebration of Aphrodite were held here. Near the temple-church is the **Bishop's Palace**, a grand house that may have accommodated the Roman governor long before any bishops turned up.

Just after the Bishop's Palace, a path leads east to the beautiful marble **bouleuterion**, preserved almost undamaged for a thousand years in a bath of mud.

South of the odeum was the **north agora**, once enclosed by Ionic porticoes but now little more than a grassy field where excavations were taking place at the time of writing. The path then leads through the early 2nd-century AD **Hadrianic Baths** to the **southern agora**, with a long, partially excavated pool, and the grand **Portico of Tiberius**.

Climb the earthen mound (where a prehistoric settlement existed) to find the white marble **theatre**, a 7000-capacity auditorium complete with stage and individually labelled seats. South of it stood the large **theatre baths** complex.

The path then wraps round and brings you onto the site of the **Sebasteion**, originally a temple to the deified Roman emperors. In its heyday this was a spectacular building, preceded by a three-storey-high double colonnade decorated with friezes of Greek myths and the exploits of the emperors; 70 of the original 190 reliefs have been recovered, an excellent ratio for an excavation of this size.

When you've finished looking at the ruins it's worth wandering round the **museum**, admission to which is included in the entry price. During Roman times, Afrodisias was home to a famous school for sculptors – who were attracted by the beds of high-grade marble 2km away at the foot of Babadağ (Mt Baba). The museum collection reflects the excellence of their work, and the birds flying around the rafters add a bit of atmosphere! Noteworthy works include a 2nd-century cult statue of Aphrodite, a series of shield portraits of great philosophers (deliberately vandalised by early Christians), and depictions of the mysterious Caius Julius Zoilos, a former slave of Octavian who not only won his freedom but also gained enough wealth to become one of Afrodisias' major benefactors.

GETTING THERE & AWAY

Afrodisias is 55km from Nazilli and 101km from Denizli. You can get there by public transport, but only by taking one bus from Denizli to Nazilli, then another to Karacasu and then a dolmuş to the site. It's more sensible to arrange a tour or private transport (€15, 1½ hours) from Pamukkale.

WESTERN MEDITERRANEAN

Western Mediterranean

While the development – some would say destruction – of Turkey's Western littoral is well documented, it doesn't take much to discover what drew the developers here in the first place. Just a step inland will take you tumbling back to the Turkey of the pre-'70s. From around a corner trots a dusky donkey chivvied on by its headscarfed owner, off to sell her half-dozen cheeses at the local market.

And even amid the highways, high-rises and discos, the beauty of the place still manages to shimmer through. Marmaris is as shocking for the stunning beauty of its natural harbour as it is for the concrete jungle engulfing its once-charming old town.

Named the 'Turquoise Coast' by early visitors, you can see why when skimming through the surf on board a *gület* – the region's traditional wooden yacht. And most development has its upside, or so some would see it. The region has recently become something of a Mecca for activities and adventure. You can walk the beautiful Lycian Way, paraglide over Ölüdeniz's lovely lagoon, scuba dive at Kaş, or go canyoning at Saklıkent.

Best of all is the region's seamless mix of history and holiday. A stroll at midnight along a beach in Olympos or Patara will suddenly send you back thousands of years as you pass a Lycian tomb or a tremendous Corinthian temple. And between the two extremes lie some quaint coastal towns still clinging to their original charm, such as Kalkan, Kekova, Kaş or the very beautiful Kaleköy. There are signs too that things are a-changing as the region's authorities at last awaken to the importance of sensitive development.

HIGHLIGHTS

- Sea-kayak over the stunning sunken city of **Üçağız** (Kekova; p376)
- Hire a scooter and hit the high roads and hidden coves of the **Hisarönü Peninsula** (p342)
- Marvel at the mythical flames of the **Chimaera** (p379) on a moonless, peopleless night
- Bargain for a boat and take a trip around the islands off **Fethiye** (p354) or **Kaş** (p371)
- Explore the Lycian ruins at **Xanthos** (p366), **Kaunos** (p348) and **Myra** (p378)
- Take flight with a paraglider and soar over the sea at **Ölüdeniz** (p359) and sample a section of the Lycian Way hike
- Potter around the ruins of **Patara** (p366) before plunging into the sea on its beautiful beach

MUĞLA

☎ 0252 / pop 49,000

If only all of Turkey's provincial capitals were like Muğla, a compact, tree-lined city set in a rich agricultural valley that prides itself on having appointed Turkey's first female *vali* (governor).

Drop your bags at the otogar and walk around the historic quarter for a couple of hours – Muğla's old Ottoman neighbourhoods, *çay bahçesi* (tea gardens) and markets are a breath of fresh air after the many concrete resorts.

Orientation & Information

Muğla's centre is Cumhuriyet Meydanı, the traffic roundabout with the statue of Atatürk. Everything you are likely to need is within walking distance: the otogar is 1km downhill (south), and the bazaar and historic quarter 500m uphill (due north) along İsmet İnönü Caddesi.

The **tourist office** (☎ 214 1261; fax 214 1244; Marmaris Bulvarı 24/1) is 100m past the Hotel Petek in İl Turizm Müdürlüğü (Provincial Tourism Directorate), on the main road running east (on the right as you face uphill) from Cumhuriyet Meydanı. It has a useful map of the town centre (free).

Sights & Activities

Go north along İsmet İnönü Caddesi from Cumhuriyet Meydanı to the **Kurşunlu Cami**, which was built in 1494, repaired in 1853 and had a minaret and courtyard added in 1900. Nearby is the **Ulu Cami** (1344), dating from the time of the Menteşe emirs, although repairs made in the 19th-century have rendered its pre-Ottoman design almost unrecognisable.

Continue walking north into the **bazaar**, its narrow lanes jammed with artisans' shops and small local restaurants. Giant plane trees add shade. Proceed up the hill to see Muğla's **Ottoman houses**, many of them in good condition. The winding alleys between whitewashed walls give it a classic Mediterranean ambience. Centuries ago there was a small fortress at the top of the hill, but not a stone remains now.

Muğla's **museum** (☎ 214 4933; Eski Postahane Caddesi; admission €1.10; ☒ 8am-noon & 1-5pm) is close to the *belediye* (town hall) and contains a small but quite interesting collection of Greek and Roman antiquities (with captions and information panels in English) displayed in rooms around a courtyard. There's also a

room containing traditional arts and crafts. The museum faces the beautiful **Konakaltı İskender Alper Kültür Merkezi**, which houses a community centre.

The **Vakıflar Hamam** (☎ 214 2067; Mustafa Muğlalı Caddesi 1; bath/massage €5/14; ☒ 6am-midnight), built in 1344, has mixed bathing, though there's a separate women's area too.

Sleeping & Eating

Otel Tuncer (☎ 214 8251; Saatlı Kule Altı, Kütüphane Sokak 1; d €17) A long block northeast of the Kurşunlu Cami (follow the signs), the hotel has simple but clean and spacious rooms; four have balconies.

Hotel Petek (☎ 214 1897; fax 214 3135; Marmaris Bulvarı 27; s/d €25/45) Though the three-star Petek's a bit characterless, it's comfortable and professionally run.

Muğla Lokantası (☎ 212 3121; İsmet İnönü Cadessi 51; mains €0.85-1.65; ☒ 6.30am-10pm) With a great pick-and-point counter containing a delicious selection of traditional Muğla dishes at rock-bottom prices, this place is permanently packed.

Doyum 98 (☎ 214 2234; Cumhuriyet Caddesi 22; ☒ 9am-11pm) Next door to the tourist office, this new place has become a favourite locally for its delicious pides (€1.40 to €1.95) and *köfte* (grilled meatballs, €2.50). It has a few tables outside.

Muğla Belediyesi Kültür Evi (Muğla Culture House; ☎ 212 8668; İsmet İnönü Caddesi 106; breakfast €1.65, coffee €0.28; ☒ 8am-8.30pm) Recently opened by the municipality after restoration, this 200-year-old house is a lovely place to come for breakfast or coffee. Peaceful and tranquil, it's popular with the locals who read or play backgammon here. Prices are kept low by the municipality.

Sanat Evi (☎ 213 0220; Hekimbaşı Sokak 9; breakfast €2.75, mains €2-3.50, beer €2.20; ☒ 7am-2am) In a 150-year-old Ottoman house, this café is great for a drink or bite to eat. At the back there's a delightful shaded terrace beside a small pool that resonates with birdsong or the strains of classical Turkish music. The chef serves different Muğla dishes daily.

Getting There & Away

Muğla's busy otogar runs services to all major destinations in the region. For points along the Mediterranean coast east of Marmaris, you may have to take a bus to Marmaris first and change there. Buses leave every half-hour (one

WESTERN MEDITERRANEAN

hour in low season) to Marmaris (€2.75, one hour, 55km), to Bodrum (€6.10, 2½ hours) every half-hour (one an hour in low season).

GÖKOVA (AKYAKA)

☎ 0252

About 30km north of Marmaris the road from Muğla comes over the Sakar Geçidi (Sakar Pass; 670m) to reveal breathtaking views of the Gulf of Gökova. It then switchbacks down into a fertile valley.

At the base of the hill, signs point the way to Akyaka, often called Gökova after the beautiful bay nearby. Backed by pine-clad mountains, this village descends to a little grey sand beach beside a river mouth. There are attractive two-storey houses with pantile roofs and intricate wooden balconies.

Every Saturday there is a busy **market** in the centre of town. The local boat cooperative runs tours of beaches along the gulf, which make a nice day trip for around €15.

Yücelen Hotel Sports Club (☎ 243 5434; www .gokovaruzgar.com) offers windsurfers seakayaks, canoes, pedalos, sailing boats and mountain bikes for rent, as well as tuition and courses. Canyoning and paint-balling is also possible.

Sleeping & Eating

Susam Otel (☎ 243 5863; www.mepartours.com; Lütfiye Sakıcı Caddesi; s/d high season €25/31, low season €17/25; ❄) On the same road as the Şirin, the Susam has immaculate and pleasant rooms, as well as a small garden with a pretty pool. It's great value.

Otel Yücelen (☎ 243 5108; www.yucelen.com.tr; s €42-83, d €56-111 depending on room & season; ❄ ⊠) Large, well managed and well designed, the Yücelen is not unlike an upmarket holiday camp. Facilities include two pools, a fitness centre, a *hamam* and table tennis, as well as the excellent and well-managed Yücelen Hotel Sports Club. Avoid the weekends if possible; it's packed with Muğla students.

Şirin Lokanta (Lütfiye Sakıcı Caddesi 45; mains €1.65-2.20; ❄ 8am-2am) Around 25m from the Golden Roof, this place does great home cooking at unbeatable prices. Dishes change daily and it's a good choice for veggies.

Golden Roof Restaurant (☎ 408 9898; Lütfiye Sakıcı Caddesi 43; meze €1.95, mains €4.70-11; ❄ 8am-1am Apr-mid-Nov) About 250m west of Otel Yücelen, this is considered Gökova's best. It's a simple, family-run affair, but mamma's cooking is good and the prices are fair too.

About 750m beyond the village is the **Gökova Orman İci Dinlenme Yeri** (picnic & camp ground; ☎ 243 4398; admission per person/car €0.40/3.80, camp site per tent/car €4.70/5.55; bungalow up to 6 people €83).

Another 500m beyond that is the port hamlet of İskele, with a few basic restaurants serving the tiny beach at the end of the small cove. **Club Çobantur** (☎ 243 4550; www.asuhancobantur .com; Eski İskele Mevkii; s €42-56, d €56-75 depending on room & season; ❄ ⊠), housed in an old seamen's lodging and beautifully set on the seafront amid gardens, a cool mountain stream and a pool, is a tranquil and pretty place. Rooms are smallish but comfortable and 13 have sea views. It's great value.

Getting There & Away

Minibuses run from Gökova to Muğla (€1.10, 30 minutes, 26km) every half-hour, and to Marmaris (€1.40, 30 minutes) twice a day in high season only. Minibuses coming from Marmaris can drop you at the highway junction, from where it's about a 2.5km walk down to the beach or you can wait for a minibus.

MARMARİS

☎ 0252 / pop 35,160

The once-sleepy fishing village of Marmaris sits on the marvellous natural harbour where Lord Nelson organised his fleet for the attack on the French at Abukir in 1798. The setting may still be glorious but the picturesque old part of town around the harbour and castle is now all but lost in the concrete sprawl trailing off to the west.

In the summer the town's population swells to around 200,000, mostly package holidaymakers. The bazaar is full of expensive souvenirs and budget tourists, the streets are full of traffic, and the restaurant scene is based on fish and chips with beer by the gallon. But, to its credit, the town council has woken up and the harbourside promenade now boasts some handsome albeit modern stone buildings. The town also has a disarmingly liberal attitude – there aren't many other places in Turkey where a bikini-clad, tattooed tourist draining a can of beer on the main street at noon doesn't raise an eyebrow.

If it's a last night out, a boat cruise or a ferry to Greece you're after, this is the place.

Marmaris still has Turkey's largest and most modern yacht marina and is consequently the country's busiest yacht-charter port; and the bar district and harbour have a great range of places to drink.

The rugged coastline around Marmaris is an undiscovered gem – only 10km from Marmaris' bright lights, the deeply indented coastline holds bays of azure sea backed by pine-covered mountains. When you need to escape, hire a car or motorcycle and cruise around the rugged Reşadiye and Hisarönü Peninsulas.

Orientation

The otogar is about 3km north of the town centre. From there, dolmuşes run down the wide Ulusal Egemenlik Bulvarı and deposit arrivals at the Tansaş Shopping Centre, which is a useful landmark, as well as at the Siteler dolmuş stop.

At the end of Ulusal Egemenlik Bulvarı, marked by the obligatory Atatürk statue, Yeni Kordon Caddesi veers left along the waterfront for 300m to the İskele Meydanı, the harbourside plaza with the tourist office. The conservation area behind, above and south of the office has some of Marmaris' few remaining old buildings, including its small castle (now a museum).

Inland from İskele Meydanı stretches the çarşı (bazaar) district, much of it a pedestrianised covered bazaar.

Also known as Hacı Mustafa Sokak and – popularly – Bar St, 39 Sokak runs from the bazaar to a canal from where a bridge leads over to the marina.

Uzunyalı, a beach district full of hotels and tourist restaurants, is about 3km west of İskele Meydanı; Siteler, also called Şirinyer, is about 5km southwest of İskele Meydanı; and İçmeler, another beach resort area, is 8km southwest.

About 1km southeast of town is the harbour for ferries to Rhodes; 3.5km southeast of the centre is Günlücek Park, a forest park reserve; and just beyond it is Aktaş, a relatively unspoiled seaside village with several hotels and camping grounds.

Information

There is a cluster of internet cafés in the alley beside the PTT. There are plenty of banks with ATMs and money-exchange offices on Ulusal Egemenlik Bulvarı and Yeni Kordon Caddesi.

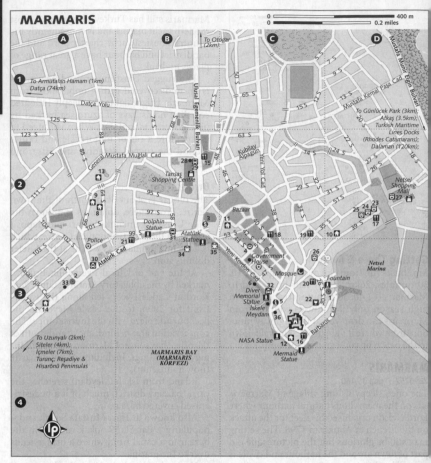

MARMARIS

To Armutalan Hamam (1km);
Datça (74km)

To Otogar
(2km)

To Günlücek Park (3km);
Atkaş (3.5km);
Turkish Maritime
Lines Docks
(Rhodes Catamarans);
Dalaman (120km);

Netsel
Shopping
Mall

Tansaş
Shopping Centre

Bazaar

Dolphin
Statue

Atatürk
Statue

Police

Government
House

Netsel
Marina

Mosque

Fountain

Diver
Memorial
Statue

İskele
Meydanı

NASA Statue

Mermaid
Statue

To Uzunyalı (2km);
Siteler (4km);
İçmeler (7km);
Turunç; Reşadiye &
Hisarönü Peninsulas

MARMARİS BAY
(MARMARIS
KÖRFEZI)

CED Internet C@fé (☎ 413 0193; 28 Sokak 63B; per hr €1.65; ☻ 10am-midnight low season, to 2am high season) A new place. You can buy drinks from the café below.

Internet C@fe (☎ 412 0799; Atatürk Caddesi, Huzur Apt 30; per 30 mins €1.10; ☻ 10am-1am) More expensive than the CED.

Post Office (PTT; 51 Sokak; ☻ 8.30am-midnight) Phones are accessible 24 hours a day.

Tourist Office (☎ 412 1035; İskele Meydanı 2; ☻ 8am-noon, 1-5pm Mon-Fri mid-Sep–May, daily Jun–mid-Sep) Right near the castle.

Sights & Activities
MARMARİS CASTLE
The small **castle** on the hill behind the tourist office was built during the reign of Süleyman the Magnificent. In 1522 the sultan massed 200,000 troops here for the attack and siege of Rhodes, which was defended by the Knights of St John. The fortress is now the **Marmaris Museum** (Marmaris Müzesi; ☎ 412 7420; admission €1.10; ☻ 8am-noon & 1-5pm Tue-Sun). Exhibits are predictably nautical, historical, ethnographic and fairly unexciting, though the building itself, draped in bougainvillea, and the views over the marina and out to sea are lovely.

BEACHES
For such a major holiday resort it's strange that there aren't any good beaches near town. Hotel swimming pools provide the solution.

The beaches at İçmeler and Turunç (p341) can be reached by dolmuşes from outside the Tansaş Shopping Centre, and water taxis from

Yeni Kordon Caddesi southeast of the Atatürk statue. The beach at Günlücek Park is also accessible by dolmuş from outside Tansaş. Dolmuşes to İçmeler cost €0.85, to Turunç €2.75.

HAMAM

The clean and modern **Armutalan Hamam** (☎ 417 5375; 136 Sokak 1; bath & scrub €14, with massage €19.50; ⏱ 8.30am-10pm May-Oct) lies behind the government hospital just off Datça Caddesi about 2km from the town centre. Go after 6pm when the *hamam* is empty of tour groups. There's a frequent free shuttle service from outside the Tansaş Shopping Centre and back, as well as from some hotels and the tourist office.

BOAT TRIPS

Besides the daily boats to Rhodes (p340), yachts, cheek-by-jowl along the waterfront, offer day tours of Marmaris Bay, its beaches and islands. They cost around €175 to €200 per boat (up to four people – around €24 to €28 per person), but you'll need to negotiate. Yachts sail from May (some from April) to October.

Boats usually leave between 9.30am and 10.30am and return at around 5pm to 5.30pm.

Before signing up, check where the excursion goes, its cost and whether lunch is included and, if so, what's on the menu.

Bay excursions usually visit Paradise Island, Aquarium, Phosphoros Cave, Kumlubuku, Amos, Turunç, Green Sea and İçmeler.

Two-day trips (around €385 for the boat) and three-day trips (€555) popularly go to Dalyan and Kaunos. You can also charter longer, more serious boat trips to Datça and Knidos, west of Marmaris.

DIVING

Several centres offer scuba diving excursions and courses from April to October. The **Deep Blue Dive Center** (☎ 412 4438; Yeni Kordon Caddesi) charges €280 for a PADI Open Water course over two to four days. Day excursions cost €35 including two dives, all equipment, a divemaster and lunch.

Sleeping

Interyouth Hostel (☎ 412 3687; interyouth@turk.net; 42 Sokak 45; dm or s without bathroom with/without ISIC card €5.60/7, d without bathroom €14; 🖳) Located inside the covered bazaar (signposted up the

---

SAIL YOUR OWN GÜLET

If you want to charter a boat, Marmaris and Fethiye are good places to ask around the yachting companies. If you can get a party of up to 16 people together, you can hire a *gület* (wooden yacht) complete with skipper and cook. In May, chartering the whole boat is likely to cost around €350 per day, with prices rising to €600 in August.

Experienced sailors can opt for a bareboat charter where you do the crewing (and cooking) yourself. To hire a bareboat sleeping six to 11 passengers for one week in spring costs around €2000. In high summer expect to pay €2700. Extra charges for one-way journeys, employing a skipper, cleaning up at the end of the voyage and so on can bump up the price even more.

The boxed text, p356, describes other *gület* cruises and, for a cautionary tale, see the boxed text, p357.

stairs), this hostel is efficiently run by the helpful Halit who's also a great source of travel information. Rooms, though smallish and rather Spartan, are spotless and well maintained. It also has a laundry service, café, small bookshop and book exchange. From June to September there's a free pasta night on the rooftop. Scooters can be hired (€17 per day), and boat tickets to Rhodes and for *gület* cruises (see the boxed text, p356) are sold here.

Bariş Motel (☎ 413 0652; barismotel@hotmail.com; 66 Sokak 10; s/d €17/22; ☻ high season only) With its clean and quite spacious rooms and its firm family feel, this is a pleasant choice. Rooms have balconies.

Özcan Pension (☎ 412 7761; 66 Sokak 17; s/d high season from €11/17, low season from €5.50/14) Appearing rather elderly, tired and unwelcoming, this pension's nevertheless a clean and good-value place. A few rooms have balconies and there's a pleasant garden terrace.

THE SPONGE DIVERS OF MARMARIS

'Before tourism came, our main source of income in Marmaris was sponge diving. I remember that every year, in early April or May when the seas were calm, most of the men of the village would say goodbye to their families and leave to go diving. We didn't see them again for six months. Working along the reef from Marmaris to Antalya and around Bodrum too, they covered maybe 600km.

'Each diving team basically had three boats, a mother boat where the divers slept and ate, a working boat that pumped air directly to them as they dived, and a rowing boat taking the divers to and from their fishing.

'When they dived, they would walk along the sea bed at depths of 35m or 40m, collecting as many sponges in their baskets as they could. When their dive time was up or they began to go too deep, the captain would pull on the pilot string attached to their lead casket.

'But because they were paid by the kilo, many divers went well beyond their safety limits. Sometimes they went as deep as 50m or 60m or more! If a diver lost consciousness or stopped responding to the pilot string, they'd haul him up to a shallower depth and leave him in the water until he began to respond again.

'Yes, serious accidents did unfortunately happen and divers were injured – or even killed – every year. Maybe the air pipe would get caught in a propeller or the air pump would break down, but usually it was the divers themselves that got themselves into trouble.

'I remember all the women and children at the quayside keeping their eyes on the Straits of Marmaris waiting for their husbands or fathers to return. When a diver didn't come home, all of Marmaris went into mourning. It would be the talk of town for weeks. All of us boys had uncles who had been injured or died. Usually they were paralysed – sometimes from the waist down. I had a neighbour who was crippled.

'But it wasn't just for the money that they took these risks. There was terrible competition not just between the different boat crews but also between the divers themselves. There was huge prestige in the amount of sponges a diver collected – his daily tally was chalked up on a board on the boat. Also how deep he dared to go and how long he dared to dive for. After the dives, many divers would drink. I remember them buying lots of bottles of rakı. My father had a grocery shop in Marmaris where they used to come. But they never paid their bills and in the end my father went bankrupt.

'We all knew that it was a hard job and I guess we thought that they were brave and in a way heroic. They were definitely richer than the rest of us (though I don't think any died rich – though the agents did) and they dressed in a certain way, walked in a certain way, and spent money. Sometimes you'd see them building quite big houses. There were many folk songs about them too – or about their families and the losses they endured.'

The 1970s saw the final demise of Marmaris' divers, but some are still alive and still full of tales of their diving days. You can ask to meet them if you like, though none speak English. Look out also for the diver memorial statue in Marmaris.

With thanks to Erol Uysal, local guide and historian, for agreeing to be interviewed in Marmaris.

Ayçe Otel (☎ 412 3136; fax 412 3705; 64 Sokak 11; s €17-20, d €22-28 depending on season; ❌ �🅡) Central, friendly, family-run and with good facilities, this is a two- or three-star hotel at one-star prices. With comfortable rooms with balconies, a medium-sized pool and a pleasant roof terrace, it's terrific value.

Royal Maris Otel (☎ 412 8383; www.royalmarisotel com; Atatürk Caddesi 34; s €22-50, d €39-83 depending on season; ❌ �🅡) Comfortable and stylish (with a roof terrace that's designed to resemble a ship's deck), this hotel is great value. Facilities include two pools, a private beach, a *hamam* and a fitness centre. All rooms have balconies and 50 have direct sea outlooks. The views from some rooms and from the roof terrace are stunning.

Marina Hotel (☎ 412 0010; www.marmarismarina hotel.com; Barbaros Caddesi 39; s €28, d €40-44; ⏱ Apr-Oct) Don't be put off by the castle-cut-out entrance. The rooms, canary-yellow with frilly curtains and doilies in the bathroom, are homely and comfy. The biggest boon is what the hotel claims is the 'best terrace in Marmaris' with wonderful panoramic views over the marina and castle. There's even a fixed telescope for serial boat-spotters.

Hotel Begonya (☎ 412 4095; fax 412 1518; 39 Sokak 101; d high/low season €34/17; ❌) With seven cosy rooms set around a shaded courtyard, this place is beguilingly peaceful. But set slap-bang in the middle of Bar St, it's for party-goers only, as the owner freely admits! Do as they do and snatch a siesta during the day.

Eating

RESTAURANTS

If you're planing a feast of fish, be sure to ask about prices before ordering, particularly on the waterfront. For something cheap and cheerful, try the bazaar area between the post office and the mosque, the old town area around the castle where there's a host of small Turkish restaurants, and along 39 Sokak (Bar St), where stalls cater to the ravenous late-night revellers.

Meryem Ana (☎ 412 7855; 35 Sokak 62; mains €1.40-2.25 ⏱ 8am-11pm) Though simple and under-stated, this place serves terrific traditional home cooking. A firm family affair, you can see the mother and aunt hard at work in the kitchen stuffing vine leaves. It has an excellent reputation locally and is a good choice for veggies too (a large mixed plate of many dishes costs €4.45).

Liman Restaurant (☎ 412 6336; 40 Sokak 38; ⏱ 8.30am-1am) Though something of an institution and well known for its mezes (€2.50 to €8), this lively restaurant inside the bazaar is not the cheapest of places. But the fish soup (€4) is famous, and the *buğlama* (steamed fish, €19 for 500g) a sumptuous speciality.

Fellini (☎ 413 0826; Barboras Caddesi 61; meals €10; ⏱ 9am-midnight) Perennially popular with both locals and visitors in the know, this attractively set waterfront restaurant does great thin-crust pizzas (€7 to €9) and also has pasta (€5 to €9).

Ney Restaurant (☎ 412 0217; 26 Sokak 24; meze €2.20, mains €5-11) Tucked away off the street up some steps is this tiny but delightful restaurant set in a 250-year-old Greek house. Decorated with seashells and wind chimes, it's run by the charming Birgül, owner and cook, who offers delicious home cooking at pleasing prices. Try the *mantı böreği* (Turkish ravioli).

CAFÉS & QUICK EATS

Café Yavuz Patisserie (☎ 412 6876; Atatürk Caddesi 34/A; ice cream per scoop €0.85, ⏱ 6.30am-9.30pm low season, to 1.30am high season) Also offering an appetising array of Turkish tantalisers, this place is particularly known for its baklava (€1.65 for four pieces), made daily.

Özsüt (☎ 413 4708; Atatürk Caddesi 4; ice cream per scoop €0.70, puddings €1.95-2.20; ⏱ 9am-midnight) With tables set on the seafront, this is the perfect place to tuck into a Turkish pud or two. This ever-popular chain offers the usual freshness and high quality that will have you moaning for more. Try the delightfully named *aşure* (Noah's pudding).

Doyum (☎ 413 4977; Ulusal Egemenlik Bulvarı 17; ⏱ 24 hr) Serving fresh home cooking at fabulous prices, the Doyum is all-too-rare in Marmaris. Perhaps that's why it's packed with appreciative locals. Clean, friendly and always open, it's a good place for an early breakfast (€2.20), and also serves an array of tasty veggie dishes (€1.10 to €2.20)

İdil Mantı Evi (☎ 413 9771; 39 Sokak 140; meze 2.20-2.75, mains €5.50-10; ⏱ 4pm-4am) Conveniently located in Bar St, this is a great place if you get the night-nibbles. With simple wooden tables around a traditional oven, it's a delightful and atmospheric place. Guests leave little messages or their names on the wooden panels of the interior. Veggie dishes (€3.35 to €6.65) are available. The *gözleme* (crêpes, €2.75 to €4.45) make a great snack.

Drinking & Entertainment

Marmaris' nightlife rivals anything on the Turkish coast. The aptly named 'Bar St' (39 Sokak, also known as Hacı Mustafa Sokak) has a string of places that are wildly popular in summer.

Unless stated otherwise, the following bars open from 7pm to 4am daily. Beers cost €3.90, spirits €4.40 and there are foam parties every night as well as dance and laser shows.

Bars 'in' when we visited included the ever-popular **Back Street** (☎ 412 4048; 39 Sokak 93) and a close second, **Areena** (☎ 412 2906; 39 Sokak 54; beer €4.50), with its bar elevated above a large dance floor and high-quality lasers. Ranking number-three in the trendy stakes is **Crazy Daisy** (☎ 412 4048; 39 Sokak 121; ☽ 3pm-4am May–mid-Sep) with its raised terraces (good for dancing on), as well as the cavernous **Greenhouse** (☎ 412 8792; 39 Sokak; beer €3.90).

The **Panorama Bar** (☎ 413 4835; Hacı İmam Sokağı 40; beer €2.75; ☽ 9am-midnight mid-Apr–Oct), off 30 Sokak, is more of a permanent fixture and less of a club. Its terrace, though not large, more than justifies the bar's name – it probably boasts the best views in Marmaris. To find it, follow the signs from left of the museum and castle.

At the eastern end of Bar St, near the Netsel Marina, there is also an **open-air cinema** (tickets €3.85; ☽ Jun-Sep) behind the Keyif Bar. All movies are English-language releases and are screened at sunset. At the time of writing it was closed, but there were plans to reopen it in the future.

Getting There & Away

AIR

The region's principal airport is at Dalaman, 120km east of Marmaris. Turkish Airlines runs an airport bus (known as the Havaş bus; (€3) for their passengers from the Turkish Airlines office in Marmaris, departing about 3½ hours before each Turkish Airlines flight. Otherwise, take one of Marmaris Coop's buses to Dalaman (€3.90) from Marmaris otogar, and take a short but quite expensive taxi ride (€14) from there.

Turkish Airlines (☎ 412 3751; Atatürk Caddesi 26-B) has an office about 400m west of the Atatürk statue on the waterfront. See p351 for info on flights.

BOAT

Catamarans sail daily to Rhodes Town in Greece (one way/same-day return/open re-turn €42/42/73 including port tax, 50 minutes) from 15 April to 1 November, leaving at 9am. They return from Rhodes at 4.30pm. Cars cost €150/180/250 for a one-way/same-day return/open-return ticket.

Greek catamarans also sail during the same period from Rhodes to Marmaris (one way/same-day return/open return €57/57/75) at 8am daily, returning from Marmaris at 4.30pm. Cars cost €150/180/180 for a one-way/same-day return/open return.

Turkish cargo boats (carrying up to 78 passengers) also sail once a week in high season to Rhodes (same prices as the catamarans; two hours; departures usually 12.30pm), and two to three times a week in low season, depending on weather (departures usually 9am). They either return the same day or stay in Rhodes for a period of two or three days.

Note that catamarans do not operate from November to mid-April, and there are no Greek cargo boats.

Tickets can be bought from any travel agency including **Yeşil Marmaris Travel & Yachting** (☎ 412 2290; www.yesilmarmaris.com; Barbados Caddesi 13; ☽ 7am-midnight Mon-Sat high season, 8.30am-6.30pm low season).

Book tickets at least one day in advance (more if you have a car) and bring your passport. You need to be at the ferry dock one hour before departure. Some agencies provide a free pick-up service from hotels in the town centre. Note that when you return from Rhodes (even if you've just been for a day trip) you'll still need to buy a new Turkish visa from the immigration authorities in front of Customs in Rhodes.

BUS

Marmaris' otogar lies 3km north of the centre of town. Dolmuşes run to and from the otogar along Ulusal Egemenlik Bulvarı every few minutes in high season. Bus companies have ticket offices around the Tansaş Shopping Centre.

Buses run to Bodrum (€6.70, 3½ hours, 165km) every one to two hours in high season, every three hours in low season. All year round, buses run to İstanbul (€25, 13 hours, 805km) four times a day, to İzmir (€10.65, 4¼ hours, 320km) every hour, to Fethiye (€5.55, three hours, 170km) every half-hour, and to Antalya (€15, six hours, 590km) twice a day.

For Datça (€3.90, 1¾ hours) dolmuşes run every hour in high season and every 1½ hours n low season. For Köyceğız (€2.80, 40 minutes) take the Fethiye bus. For Dalyan, take the Fethiye bus and change at Ortaca (€3.40, 1½ hours) and take the dolmuş.

Getting Around
Frequent dolmuşes run around the bay, beginning and ending at the Tansaş Shopping Centre on Ulusal Egemenlik Bulvarı. Recently, they have been colour-coded to denote their different routes: the green dolmuşes go to Uzunyalı (€0.55, 3km) and Turban-Siteler (€0.90, 6km), and the orange ones to İçmeler (€1.70, 11km).

AROUND MARMARIS
Once a separate fishing village, İçmeler, 8km west and south around the bay, is now merely a beach suburb of Marmaris. However, it feels a much classier place, not least because it has been better planned and has a relatively clean beach.

Turunç is the next beach resort, but its isolated position has given it some protection from massive overdevelopment. It is popular with British tourists seeking a more relaxed atmosphere than the Marmaris scene. Dolmuşes make the trip over the mountains and down a steep hillside to the cove every 40 minutes (€3.40).

From May to the end of October, water taxis run from various points on the waterfront between the tourist office and the Atatürk statue to İçmeler (€4.15, 30 minutes, every 30 minutes) and Turunç (€5.55, 50 minutes, every hour).

REŞADİYE & HISARÖNÜ PENINSULAS
A narrow, mountainous finger of land stretches west from Marmaris for about 100km into the Aegean Sea between the Greek islands of Kos and Rhodes. Known in ancient times as the Peraea, it is now called the Reşadiye or Datça Peninsula; its southern branch is known as the Hisarönü or Daraçya Peninsula, with the ruins of the ancient city of Loryma at its tip.

The peninsulas have some of Turkey's most beautiful coastline, with deep blue bays, rugged mountains and islands shimmering in the distance, and some excellent, well-priced pensions where you can laze for days.

A road twists its way from Marmaris west to the tip of the Reşadiye Peninsula, perfect for hiring a scooter, although a voyage by boat is

preferable. Aside from the joy of sailing near the peninsula's pine-clad coasts and anchoring in some of its hundreds of secluded coves, visitors come to explore Bozburun (a fishing town 56km from Marmaris), Datça (a resort town about 60km west of Marmaris) and the hamlet and ruins of Knidos (the ancient city of the great sculptor Praxiteles) 35km west of Datça. Here there are ferry connections to Rhodes and the neighbouring Greek island Simi (Symi).

Selimiye
☎ 0252

About 9km south of Orhaniye is an intersection with roads to Bayır and Bozburun. Follow the Bozburun road to reach the village of Selimiye, a traditional boat-builders' village on its own lovely bay facing an islet topped by bits of ancient ruin. Some hotels have been built beside the beach here.

SLEEPING & EATING
Hotel Begovina (☎ 446 4292; fax 446 4181; s/d low season €11/17, high season €14/28) Run by Zeki, a retired shoemaker, this hotel offers good-sized, spotless rooms with direct sea views (some with large balconies). All have fridges and a few have kitchenettes. It lies just metres from the shingle beach and is excellent value.

Hydas Otel (☎ 446 4297; fax 446 4298; Selimiye Köyü; s/d €20/42; ☿ Apr-Oct; ⚡) Despite the rather lurid Mediterranean colours and twee towels arranged like bows, rooms are spotless and comfortable. Those on the upper level share a large zigzag terrace overlooking the café and seafront. It lies around 100m east of the Yakana, and has a medium-sized pool.

Sardunya Bungalows (☎ 446 4003; s €20-26, d €33-45 depending on season; ⚡) Nestled behind the Sardunya Restaurant, these attractive stone bungalows are set around a garden less than 50m from the water. A good choice for travellers with children.

Yakana Beach Hotel (☎ 446 4360; www.yakana.com; Selimiye Köyü; s/d €22/44; ⚡ ⚡) East of the Begovina, the Yakana is a modern, well-designed hotel by the beach. There are 35 rooms around a pleasant pool; some have balconies and sea views.

Beyaz Güvercin Motel (White Pigeon; ☎ 446 4274; www.beyazguvercin.com; Selimiye Köyü; s €34-56, d €45-75 depending on season; ⓟ ⚡) Perched on a hillside at the end of the bay 3km from the town centre, the hotel has a peaceful location amid large and attractive gardens that stretch over 6500 sq m. The chalet-style rooms are simple but some have glimpses of the sea. Windsurfing and sailing are possible and there's a floating restaurant aboard a *taka* (Black Sea boat).

Sardunya Restaurant (☎ 446 4003; meals around €6) It's not quite as pretty as the Aurora but serving even better food. Local organic products are used and it specialises in fish and seafood. Its *kalamar* (squid) stuffed or fried (€6.65) are famous. Try also the delicious *buğulama* (fish casserole, €14).

Aurora Restaurant (☎ 446 4097; Bahçeıçı; meals €17-22; ⏰ 9am-1am Apr-Oct) With a good reputation locally, the Aurora is very prettily set in a 200-year-old stone house with a shaded terrace as well as tables on the seafront. Fish is its speciality; the mezes are mouthwatering too.

Falcon Restaurant & Pansiyon (☎ 446 4105; Selimiye Köyu; ⏰ 9am-midnight) Offering similar fare to the Aurora, this is a new, family-run restaurant about 100m from the town centre and 40m from the sea.

GETTING THERE & AWAY

Dolmuşes run to and from Marmaris (€2.75) every two hours. For Bozburun, you can hop on the Bozburun to Marmaris bus (which passes through Selimiye) if there's space.

Bozburun

☎ 0252

From Selimiye the road twists onwards until, after 12km, you reach Bozburun, a sleepy seaside village and one of the biggest boat-building ports on the Mediterranean. Bozburun is a perfect antidote to the tourist madness of Marmaris. Fishing and farming still employ most villagers, though some work in bars and shops set up to serve the yachties who drop anchor in Sömbeki Körfezi (Sömbeki Bay). There are a few small, well-run pensions and a PTT. Some of the shops exchange currency.

Bozburun is not known for its beaches, but you can dip into the startlingly blue water from the rocks by the primary school southeast of the bust of Atatürk, and charter private vessels to explore the surrounding bays. There are also many interesting walks in the surrounding countryside.

SLEEPING

Yilmaz Pansiyon (☎ 456 2167; www.yilmazpansion.com; İskele Mahallesi 391; s/d €11/22) This convenient and

---

HISARÖNÜ PENINSULA BY SCOOTER

The mountainous, deeply indented Hisarönü Peninsula is the perfect place to escape the madness of Marmaris.

It's a rugged place with remarkably varied landscapes; lush pine forests on a high plateau inland from Turunç give way to steep bare rocky hillsides as you approach Bozburun. You can go via the main road to Bozburun but it's more fun to do a loop, heading down on village roads and coming back on the main road.

Setting off from Marmaris head for İçmeler along Atatürk Caddesi. In İçmeler the main road branches; take the right-hand road, which leads around the back of the town and begins a steep, winding ascent towards Turunç. Take the unpaved road to the right through the pine forest before you get there. The road narrows and gets steeper, slowly winding down to the inland village of **Bayır**. There couldn't be a sharper contrast between the concrete houses of Marmaris and İçmeler and rustic Bayır. The village square is at the foot of an ancient plane tree and has pleasant restaurants with terraces overlooking the valley. After Bayır the landscape becomes much drier, and the land falls steeply away into inaccessible coves. From tiny Söğüt the road is relatively level on the way to **Bozburun**, which has several good cafés for lunch.

From Bozburun a good road leads back along the western side of the peninsula, past the idyllic bays of Selimiye and Hisarönü, before rejoining the main Datça–Marmaris road.

The whole circuit of the peninsula is about 120km, and takes about six hours with rests, swims and photo stops. Many places in Marmaris rent scooters by the day, most for around €14 to €17. The roads are steep and winding, so speed is hardly an asset. Just bear in mind that Turkey has one of the highest road traffic accident rates in the world; it's necessary to wear a helmet, and appropriate clothing is advisable to protect against road rash if you come off.

The only petrol stations on the peninsula are at Bozburun and Turunç, so it's best to fill up in Marmaris before setting out.

friendly little pension is around 100m from the centre and 200m from the dolmuş station. Rooms are simple but cheerful and there's a vine-covered terrace metres from the sea. Six rooms have direct sea views and the hotel boasts a good breakfast.

Pembe Yunus (Pink Dolphin; ☎ 456 2154; www.pembe yunus.net; Kargı Mahallesi 37; s/d €14/22; ⌚ Apr–Oct; ❄ 🖵) Around 700m from the dolmuş station (though you can ask to be dropped here) is this delightful pension run by a mother and her ex-model daughter. Rooms, lavender blue as if sponged with rugs and rustic-style furniture, are clean and homely. Four have stunning sea views. Fatma, the mother, cooks famously. Set-menu dinners cost €14.

Dolphin Pansiyon (☎ 456 2408; Plaj; www.dolphinpen sion.com; Kargı Mahallesi 51; s/d €22/44) A four-year labour of love built stone by Bozburun stone by Yılmaz (son of the indefatigable Fatma from Pembe Yanus), this well-designed place has 10 good-sized and pleasantly decorated rooms with balconies and sensational sea views. There's also a verdant terrace and sundeck above the water. From May to September Yılmaz runs daily boat excursions (€8 per person, minimum two people) around the bay. Swimming, snorkelling and fishing are all available.

Sabrinas Haus (☎ 456 2045; Plaj; www.sabrinashaus .de; r €47-61, 15% extra May–mid-Nov) Only reachable by boat or a 20-minute walk from the Dolphin Pansiyon, Sabrinas Haus is the ultimate getaway-from-it-all place. There are 20 simple but well-designed rooms in three buildings hidden in a beautiful garden filled with mature trees, hibiscus and bougainvillea. The accommodating German owner offers kayak trips to the many deserted inlets nearby, as well as trekking trips.

EATING & DRINKING
Kandil Restaurant (☎ 456 2227; İskele Mahallesi 3; meze €1.65; ⌚ 7.30am-midnight) The local favourite, this restaurant does good home-style cooking as well as excellent fresh fish. Try the delicious *kalamar tava* (fried squid, €6.40).

Bozburun Restaurant (☎ 456 6943; ⌚ 8.30am-midnight Apr-Sep) Though it looks hideously touristy (and proudly brandishes photos of Bill Gates eating here), it offers some great value two-course fixed meat/fish menus (including 17 types of meze) for €8/€10. Grab a table on the seafront.

Fishermen House (☎ 456 2730; İskele Mahallesi 391; meze €1.40, seafood meze €3.35, fish €10-12 per 500g;

⌚ 8am-midnight Apr-7 Nov) Run by a local fisherman, this place offers fresh fish at unbeatable prices. There are tables on the waterfront.

Sabrinas Haus (☎ 456 2045; ⌚ dinner) Serving traditional Turkish Mediterranean cuisine in a lovely setting, the restaurant (in the hotel of the same name) has a refined reputation. The set menu (including a meze buffet and seasonal fish) costs €22. Note that you can eat here as long as the restaurant's not filled with hotel guests. Call to check and for a boat to pick you up from town.

GETTING THERE & AWAY
Minibuses run between Bozburun and Marmaris (€2.75, 50 to 60 minutes) six times a day via Selimiye year-round.

Datça
☎ 0252 / pop 10,570
Connected only tenuously to the mainland, the little harbour town of Datça seems to have floated away from the big resorts. It has some decent beaches and an easy-going mix of yachties, English and particularly German retirees, as well as trendy İstanbullus and families. A weekly hydrofoil connects the town to Rhodes.

Datça's 'undiscoveredness' may not last long. A big shopping mall is billed to open by the end of 2007, and the road from Marmaris is being improved so that in future it will take just 45 minutes to get to Datça from Marmaris.

Datça has three small beaches: Kumluk Plajı (Sandy Beach), tucked away behind the shops on İskele Caddesi; Taşlık Plajı (Stony Beach), running west from the end of the harbour; and Hastane Altı (Hospital Beach), Datça's biggest beach.

ORIENTATION
The main street, İskele Caddesi, runs downhill from the highway, before arriving at a small roundabout with a big tree. Immediately before the roundabout, Buxerolles Sokak on the right has several small pensions.

After the roundabout İskele Caddesi forks left and runs to Cumhuriyet Meydanı, the main square with a market and otogar. From there it continues to the harbour, with a cluster of small pensions on the left, finally running out at the end of a short peninsula, once an island called Esenada, which features an open air **cinema** (⌚ Jun-Sep).

SLEEPING

Ilıca Camping (☎ 712 3400; www.ilicacamping.com; Taşslik Plajı; per person/campervan €4.45/11, bungalow with/without bathroom €17/11) On the eastern bay and right on the seafront is this pleasant and grassy camping ground shaded by eucalyptus trees. Watch where you camp; the 15 resident ducks leave eggs everywhere!

Tunç Pansiyon (☎ 712 3036; Buxerolles Caddesi; s/d €11/20, apt for up to 5 people €33) Down the second street on the right after the *hükümet* (government) building, the Tunç is family run and very friendly. Rooms are simple but sunny and spotless. The owner also runs one-day car excursions to Knidos and surrounds, charging just for the petrol (€11 for one to three people).

Villa Tokur (☎ 712 8728; r €42, 1-bedroom apt for up to 4 people €61; ✖ mid-Apr–mid-Nov; ✖ ✖) Built and designed by the German-Turkish couple who live here, the Villa Tokur is Datça's best and is situated in a quiet and peaceful location about a five- to 10-minute walk uphill from Taşlık Plajı. Rooms are attractively furnished and have balconies with views over the pool, bay and village.

Villa Carla (☎ 712 2029; www.villacarladatca.com; Kargı Koyu Yolu; s/d high season €36/61, low season €28/50; ✖ ✖) Perched halfway up the hill, the biggest boon of this hotel is its stunning views all the way to Rhodes. All rooms have direct sea views and most have balconies too. The pleasant outdoor pool also boasts a lovely outlook. At 5pm tea and Turkish pastries are served. To get here, follow the road that branches right off the main road at the foot of the mosque in the village centre.

EATING

Emek Restaurant (☎ 712 3375; Yat Limanı; mains €5.50-8); ✖ 9am-1am Mar-Sep) Datça's oldest restaurant boasts delightful views over the bay from its terrace elevated above the waterfront. The owner's son is a fisherman, which guarantees fresh fish at pleasing prices.

Fevzının Yeri (☎ 712 9746; Ambarcı Caddesi 13/A; meals around €7.50; ✖ 7pm-1am) Specialising only in fish, the theme's so nautical here it looks almost like a marine museum, and guests leave their comments too, but on the walls! The fish has an excellent reputation and the prices are unbeatable.

Papatya Restaurant & Bar (☎ 712 2860; Kargı Yolu Caddesi 4; köfte €4.45) This pretty old stone house, with a gorgeous terrace under a vine-covered pergola, is about 60m up the hill from the mosque above the marina. It offers a mouthwatering menu. Try the exquisite *karides güveç şarapli fırında* – shrimps oven-baked in wine.

Zekeriya Sofrası (☎ 712 4303; İskele Caddesi 60; Turkish/English breakfast €2.75/5.25, köfte €3.35) Run by its namesake, the friendly Zekeriya, this place is popular locally for its home-style cooking at decent prices. It's a good place for breakfast and also does a mean *'inegöl köfte'* (mixed meat and lamb meatballs) to Zekeriya's own secret recipe.

DRINKING

Datça's nightlife centres on the harbour, where there are a few small music pubs and bars. The following were among the most popular at the time of writing:

Bolero (☎ 712 9865; Yalı Caddesi 16; beer €1.65; ✖ 8am-2am) Ever popular.

Nurs Gallus Garden (☎ 712 9865; admission incl drink €5.55, beer €2.50; ✖ 11am-4am Jun-Sep) On the hill about 150m from the beach. A new place, it shares the pleasant pool-side bar and the views over the bay with the Sound Dance Club.

Sound Dance Club (admission incl drink €5.55, beer €2.50, ✖ 11am-4am Jun-Sep) Next door to Nurs Gallus, it's the only nightclub in town and sometimes stages live music.

Sun Café Bar (Gallus Bar; ☎ 712 9465; Yat Limani; beer €2.25; ✖ 10am-3am) Another new place about 50m beyond the Bolero.

Sunries Café Bar (☎ 712 9518; Yat Limanı; beer €1.65; ✖ 9.30am-3am) The owner is a colourful character and a local draw.

GETTING THERE & AWAY

Dolmuşes run to Marmaris (€3.85, 1½ hours, 60km) every hour in high season, five times a day in low season. Change here for buses to other destinations. The bus companies have offices along İskele Caddesi between Buxerolles Caddesi and Kargı Yolu and provide a free shuttle service to and from the otogar.

From May to September hydrofoils to Rhodes (single/return €35/70, 45 minutes) and Simi (single/return €30/60, 15 minutes) leave on Saturdays, normally at 4pm. There's also a weekly ferry to Simi (one hour) leaving at the same time as the hydrofoil and for the same price.

A *gület* sails two to three times a week from Datça to Simi (€50, 70 minutes) at 9am. If there are fewer than eight people, it doesn't sail though in high season it almost always does.

Knidos Yachting (☎ 712 9464; www.knidosyachting com; Yalı Caddesi 17) at the marina sells tickets for the hydrofoils, ferries and *gülets*. For Rhodes and Simi, come at 11am on the Saturday of your departure with your passport; for the *gület*, reserve by telephone. Diving trips can also be organised (€30/50 for one/two dives per day).

From mid-June to mid-November regular ferries run daily between Bodrum and Körmen (the name of Karaköy's harbour about 5km from Datça on the Gulf of Gökova). Ferries leave for Bodrum (passenger single/return €11/14, car and driver €28, extra passengers €2.75) on Monday, Wednesday and Friday at 9am, and on Tuesday, Thursday, Saturday and Sunday at 5pm. The trip takes about two hours. From Bodrum they return on Tuesday, Thursday, Saturday and Sunday at 9am, and the rest of the week at 5pm. Tickets are sold in the **Bodrum Ferryboat Association** (☎ 712 2143; fax 712 4239; Turgut Özal Meydanı) next to the town mosque, and there's a free bus shuttle that takes you from Datça to Karaköy.

Boat excursions to Datça often leave from Marmaris and you can sometimes buy a one-way ticket on these. Otherwise, if you can muster a group, you can hire a boat for one day (€139 per day, maximum 10 people) or more. In high season the price can double.

Eski Datça
☎ 0252

Lying 3km from Datça, Eski Datça (Old Datça) is a picturesque hamlet of cobbled streets and old stone houses, most of them lovingly restored. If you're in search of peace and quiet there are a couple of delightful places to stay.

In a 150-year-old stone house with a pool set in a gorgeous walled garden, **Dede Pansiyon** (☎ 712 3951; Can Yücel Sokak; www.dedepansiyon.com; s/d €28/56; ❄ 📶) is a lovely place to stay. The six rooms have individual characters and their own little kitchen. About 350m beyond the village (follow the signs), **Doğa Pansiyon** (☎ 712 2178; www.dogapansiyon.com; Datça Mahallesi 9; s/d low season €17/33, high season €20/39) has simple but spotless rooms with fridge and a little kitchenette that share a veranda overlooking the yard.

There are now two restaurants and two cafés in town, all of them recently opened. With tables under a vine-clad pergola, **Datça Sofrası** (☎ 712 4188; Hurma Sokak 16; mains €3.85-5.55; ❄ 7.30am-midnight) is a picturesque place for lunch or dinner. It specialises in barbecued fish and meat. Occasionally one of the owners, Mehmet, gets out his *ney* (Turkish clarinet) for a tune or two. Cheaper is the **Karya Restoran** (☎ 712 2253; Datça Mahallesi; mains €2.20-3.05; ❄ 10am-midnight) on the main square, with tables inside and outside.

Around 50m before the Dede Pansiyon is the **Antık Café** (☎ 712 9176; Can Yücel Sokak 1; coffee €1.10, mains €2.75-3.85; ❄ 9am-1am) which, with cushioned benches set in a pleasant terrace-garden shaded by almond trees, is a very peaceful place for a coffee, tea or snack.

GETTING THERE & AWAY
From Datça to Eski Datça (€0.85), minibuses run every hour on the hour from May to October. From Eski Datça to Datça, they run every half-hour on the hour. In low season, they run every two hours. From June to August hourly buses run into the village from Datça.

Knidos
At the very tip of the peninsula, 35km west of Datça, are the ruins of the prosperous port city of Knidos dating from about 400 BC. The Dorians who founded it were smart: the winds change as one rounds the peninsula and ships in ancient times often had to wait at Knidos for favourable winds, giving it a prosperous business in ship repairs, hospitality and trading. The ship taking St Paul to Rome for trial was one of the many that had to hole up a while in Knidos.

The ruins aside, Knidos consists of a tiny *jandarma* (police) post with a phone for emergencies, a couple of places to eat and a repository for artefacts found on the site (not open to the public at the time of research). Overnight stays in the village are not allowed, so there are no facilities. You can swim in the bays from wooden piers, but the beaches are several kilometres out of town.

The **ruins of Knidos** are scattered along 3km at the end of a peninsula occupied only by goatherds, their flocks and the occasional wild boar. The setting is dramatic: steep hillsides terraced and planted with groves of olive, almond and fruit trees rise above two picture-perfect bays in which a handful of yachts rest at anchor.

Few of the ancient buildings are easily recognisable, but you can certainly appreciate the importance of the town by exploring the site. Don't miss the **temple of Aphrodite** and the **theatre**, the 4th-century BC **sundial** and the fine carvings in what was once a Byzantine church. The guardian will show you around for a small tip.

GETTING THERE & AWAY
Knidos Taxi, near Cumhuriyet Meydanı in Datça, will take up to three people from Datça to Knidos and return, with up to two hours' waiting time, for €35.

Ask in Datça harbour about excursions to Knidos. Boats tend to leave around 9am or 9.30am and return in the early evening, and cost about €12 per person.

KÖYCEĞIZ
☎ 0252 / pop 7,520

This sleepy little town, set inside a nature reserve, perches at the northern end of a large lake, Köyceğiz Gölü, which is joined to the Mediterranean Sea by the Dalyan River. Except for its small (but growing) tourist trade, Köyceğiz is a farming town producing citrus fruit, olives, honey and cotton. This region is also famous for its liquidambar trees, source of precious amber gum. The only real attraction here is the lake itself – broad, beautiful and serene.

Orientation & Information
The otogar is near the highway turn-off, about 2.5km from the waterfront. The main street, Atatürk Bulvarı, runs from the highway past the police station to the main square. Kordon Boyu, the road skirting the lake, has several pensions and restaurants, and some fine mature eucalyptus trees. The local market, which brings in people from outlying villages, is held every Monday.

The **tourist office** (☎ 262 4703; ☽ 8.30am-7pm Mon-Fri), next to Köyceğiz Öğretmenevi (Teacher's Lodge) on the main square's eastern edge, stocks a simple map.

Sights & Activities
Stroll along the lakeshore promenade past the pleasant town park, shady tea gardens and several restaurants. Several pensions rent out bicycles, so take a ride out to the surrounding orchards and farmland. The road along the western shore of the lake to the Sultaniye mud baths (p351) and Ekincik (opposite) offers superb views of the lake. It's 35km by road to the mud baths or, if you can take a boat excursion

from the promenade, it's eight nautical miles away on the lake's southern shore.

There's a small **waterfall** about 7km west of town, where locals go for a spot of bathing. Take any minibus heading west towards Marmaris and Muğla and tell the driver you want to get off at the şelale (waterfall) – they all seem to know where to drop you (near the 'Arboretum' sign if they miss it). The waterfall is about 800m from the highway.

You can take **boat trips** to Dalyan and the Kaunos ruins for €9 to €12 per person including lunch; the vessels line up on the waterfront.

Sleeping
Most of the accommodation options are off to the west as you approach the mosque when coming into town.

Fulya Pension (☎ 262 2301; fulyapension@myne .com; Ali İhsan Kalamaz Caddesi 100; s/d €8.50/16.50; ⊠ 🖵) Though small and simple, rooms are clean and cheap, all have balconies and there's a roof terrace. The friendly owner offers free use of 24 bikes and boat trips (€5.55) to the local attractions, including lunch.

Flora Hotel (☎ 262 4976; www.florahotel.info; Kordon Boyu 96; s/d/apt €11/22/33; ⊠ 🖵) Around 800m from the centre, this has a peaceful lakeside location, but rooms and balconies have only side views of the lake. Apartments sleep two adults and two children. The manager can arrange treks into the nearby Gölgeli Mountains.

Alila Hotel (☎ 262 1150; Emeksiz Caddesi 13; s/d high season €20/28, low season €14/22; ⊠ 🖵) Uniquely set right by the lakeside, 12 of the Alila's rooms also boast direct views of the water. The friendly owner Ömer, who built the hotel, runs the place professionally and attends to every detail (right down to the swan-folded towels!). It also boasts a pool set in gardens at the lakeside and is by far the best value in town.

Tango Pansiyon (☎ 262 2501; www.tangopension .com; Ali İhsan Kalmaz Caddesi 112; dm/s/d per person €6.50/11/15.50; ⊠ 🖵) Managed by the local school sports teacher, this place is big on activities including day and night boat trips (€6.65 to €8), trekking (€11) and rafting (€22). Prices include lunch and transfers. Rooms are bright, cheerful and well maintained, and there's a pleasant garden. It's popular with tour groups, so you may need to book.

Panorama Plaza (☎ 262 3773; www.panorama-plaza .net; Cengiz Topel Caddesi 69; s/d €22/39; ⊠ 🖵) Lying almost 1km west of the mosque, this rather ugly-looking building has a pleasant pool in peaceful gardens with lake views. Rooms are comfortable and are good value. Bikes, windsurfing and sailing are all free to guests.

Eating
There are lots of cheap and cheerful restaurants off the main square.

Köyeğiz Belediye (☎ 262 4090; Ulucamii Mahallesi; coffee or tea €0.27, cola €0.85; ☼ 8am-10pm) It's actually part of government-owned camping, but the café, 1km out of town on the Ekincik road, serves drinks at rock-bottom prices right on the beach. You can swim and sunbathe here.

Mutlu Kardeşler (☎ 262 2480; Tören Alanı 52; soup €1.10, köfte 2.20, kebap €2.75, pide €1.10-2; ☼ 7am-1am) A simple but charming place off the main square, it is much-loved locally and has tables on a little green and shaded terrace out the back. The prices are unbeatable.

Colıba (☎ 262 2987; Cengiz Topel Caddesi 64; köfte €3.35; ☼ 10am-1am) Its name means 'sweet little house', and that's what this is. Whitewashed and wooden, it has a shaded terrace with views of the lake front. The locals love it for grills at good prices. Try the delicious *ordövr* (mixed meze platter) or the house speciality *alabalık* (trout, €5.55). It's about 100m from the Alila Hotel.

Thera Fish Restaurant (☎ 262 3514; Cengiz Topel Caddesi 1; 350g fish €6.65-11; ☼ 9am-midnight) Close to the Colıba and a favourite locally for its fish, the Thera also has a waterfront terrace. It offers a good range of fresh fish, and prices are not bad. If you haven't yet tasted Turkey's fish, now might be the time.

Getting There & Away
Most buses will drop you at the Köyceğiz otogar on the outskirts of town, 2km from the lake. Dolmuşes (€0.42) run every 15 minutes between the otogar and town.

Dolmuşes run to Dalaman (€2, 30 minutes, 34km), Marmaris (€2.75, one hour, 60km) and Ortaca (€1.40, 25 minutes, 20km) every half-hour. Buses run to Fethiye (€3.35, 1¾ hour, 95km) every half-hour.

EKİNCİK
☎ 0252 / pop 860
This isolated beach village, 36km south of Köyceğiz, is surrounded by high pine-clad hills pitching down to a crescent beach. The

scenery is marred only by the half-built shell of a hotel near the beach, construction of which was halted after legal complications.

Sights & Activities
Ekincik has some great trekking possibilities. Ahmed at Hotel Akdeniz is a good source of information. You can also hire boats from the **Ekincik Boat Cooperation** (☎ 266 0192; ☼ 9am-7pm May-Oct) on the southern side of the beachfront. Trips are for three hours (to Kaunos, €100 for up to 12 people), six hours (Kaunos and Dalyan, €133) and a full day (Kaunos, hot springs, turtle beach etc, €166). If you fancy a swim or some sun-soaking, head for the municipality-run **Köyceğiz Belediyesi Restaurant ve Halk Plaji** (☎ 266 0001; Ekincik Köyü Bulvarı; meals €3.35-7; ☼ mid-Apr–mid-Sep) which has showers, sunlounges and tables, as well as cheap drinks and meals.

Sleeping & Eating
The first two options offer *yarım pension* (half board).

Ekincik Pansiyon (☎ 266 0179; fax 266 0003; s/d half board €17/33; ☒) About 350m from the beach just to the right of the main road is this bright, light and spotless, family-run pension. There's a pleasant shaded area outside under trees, with tables and hammocks.

Hotel Akdeniz (☎ 266 0255; www.akdenizotel.com; s/d €11/22, half board €22/44; ☒) Just uphill from the Ekincik Pansiyon, the Akdeniz has simple but spotless rooms with balconies. Ahmed, the friendly owner, can guide you on treks in the mountain pine forests or organise picnics. There's also a roof terrace with sweeping views of the sea and surrounding landscape.

Ekincik Hotel (☎ 266-0203; www.hotelekincik .com; Ekincik Köyü; per person €19-28 depending on season; ☼ May-Oct; ☒) Set on the seafront and with a garden, the Ekincik is quite nicely designed and maintained. All rooms have balconies and nine have direct sea views.

Ship A Hoy (☎ 266-0045; Ekincik Köyü; meze from €2.20; mains €10-14; ☼ 8am-midnight Apr-Oct) Next to the Ekincik Pansiyon right on the beach, this brand new place has pleasant tables set under giant white parasols and grass-roofed huts and serves good-quality Ottoman-inspired dishes as well as fish fresh from the sea (€10 to €14 for 500g).

For cheap eats, there are plenty of cafés and stalls selling snacks and *tost* (toasted sandwiches, €1) along the seafront in summer.

Getting There & Away

During the school holidays (mid-June to early September), one to two buses run daily between Ekincik and Köyceğiz (€2.20, one hour). The bus leaves the main square (not the otogar) at 9.30am and returns from Ekincik at 6pm.

Unfortunately, at the time of writing the completion of the new road linking Ekincik to Marmaris had been halted by the military, who are concerned about security.

DALYAN

☎ 0252

Once a somnolent farming town and now increasingly a package-tour colony, Dalyan has so far managed to keep some of its peaceful atmosphere. On top of those who choose to stay here, summer afternoons bring an armada of excursion boats from Marmaris and Fethiye carving a path through the reed beds of the Dalyan River (Dalyan Çayı) on their way to the ruins of ancient Kaunos (Caunos) and İztuzu beach. Above the river the façades of Lycian rock tombs gaze silently down on all this activity. Dalyan may be filling up with identical restaurants and the town centre has become another bland concrete agglomeration, but it only takes a few minutes' walk to reach the charming old Dalyan of gardens and willow trees.

Orientation

It's about 10km from the highway at Ortaca to Dalyan's Cumhuriyet Meydanı (the main square) between the mosque and the PTT. Minibuses stop behind the square, which features a statue of Atatürk and another of a pair of turtles.

Most of the village's better hotels and pensions are along Maraş Caddesi, which runs for 1km south and ends near the riverbank.

Information

There's an ATM on the southeastern side of the PTT building in the centre.

Tourist office (☎ 284 4235; Maraş Caddesi 2/C; ☽ 8am-noon & 1-5pm Mon-Fri winter, 8am-7pm summer)

Ünsal Internet Café (Karakol Sokak 23/A; per hr €1.10; ☽ 8.30am-midnight) East of the tourist office on the left.

Sights & Activities

KAUNOS

Founded around the 9th century BC, **Kaunos** (admission €2.50; ☽ 8.30am-5.30pm) became an im-

portant Carian city by 400 BC. Right on the border with the Kingdom of Lycia, its culture reflected aspects of both kingdoms. The **tombs**, for instance, are in Lycian style (you'll see many more of them at Fethiye, Kaş and other points east). If you don't take a river cruise, walk south from town along Maraş Caddesi for about 15 minutes to get a good view of the tombs.

When Mausolus of Halicarnassus was ruler of Caria, his Hellenising influence reached the Kaunians, who eagerly adopted that culture. Kaunos suffered from endemic malaria; according to Herodotus, its people were famous for their yellowish skin and eyes. The Kaunians' prosperity was also threatened by the silting of their harbour. The Mediterranean Sea, which once surrounded the hill on which the archaeological site stands, has now retreated 5km to the south, pushed back by silt from the Dalyan River.

Apart from the tombs, the **theatre** is very well preserved; nearby there are parts of an **acropolis** and other structures, such as baths, a basilica and defensive walls.

Your boat will pull up to the western bank; then it's a five-minute walk to the site. The curious wooden structures in the river are *dalyanlar* (fishing weirs). No doubt the ancient Kaunians also benefited from such an industry.

BOAT TRIPS

Every day in summer, excursion boats leave the quayside at 10am to cruise to Köyceğiz Gölü and the Sultaniye hot springs and mud baths (p351), the ruins of Kaunos (left) and İztuzu beach (p351) on the Mediterranean coast. You can save yourself a lot of money by taking boats run by the local cooperative, **Dalyan Kooperatifi** (☎ 284 7843), for €11 per person including lunch; various pirates charge considerably more.

If you can organise a small group, it may be more economical to hire an entire passenger boat that holds from eight to 12 people. Haggle to get the best price, particularly if it's early or late in the season and many boats are standing idle. A two-hour tour just to Kaunos costs €29 for the entire boat; if you want to visit the Sultaniye hot springs as well, figure on three hours and €45 for the boat.

Boats belonging to the boat cooperative operate a 'river dolmuş' service between the town and İztuzu beach (called 'Turtle Beach by local tour operators), charging €2.75 for the return trip. In high summer boats head out around every 20 minutes from 10am to 2pm and return between 1pm and 6pm. (In high summer minibuses make the 13km run to İztuzu by land as well and drop you at the other, less crowded end of the beach). Take some food as you might not like the kebap stands on the beach.

The boat cooperative also offers a two-hour early morning turtle-spotting tour, which leaves at 6.30am every day (€8.50). Dolmuş boats also go to Kaunos three times a day (€8.50 return), and to the mud baths in the early evening (€8.50). The cooperatives can also pick you up from your hotel if it's on the water.

Evening sunset cruises (€14 per person including dinner) are also offered twice a week (usually on Wednesday and Friday) from June to September.

Sleeping
BUDGET

Dalyan Camping (☎ /fax 284 4157; Maraş Caddesi 144; per tent/caravan €8/14, 2-/3-/4- person bungalows €14/20/28; ☾ Apr-Oct) Though not very large, rather ramshackle and unkempt, the camping has a nice location by the river opposite the tombs. The eight pinewood bungalows are simple, clean and quite attractive.

Aktaş Pansiyon (☎ 284 2042; aktaspension@hotmail .com; Maraş Caddesi 116; s/d €17/22; ☒) Though the rooms are simple and small (with even smaller

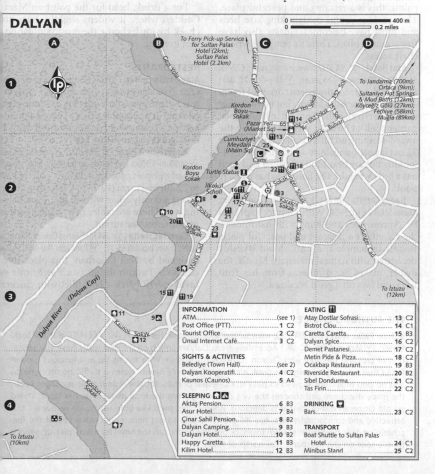

DALYAN

0 — 400 m
0 — 0.2 miles

INFORMATION		EATING 🍴	
ATM	(see 1)	Atay Dostlar Sofrasi	13 C2
Post Office (PTT)	1 C2	Bistrot Clou	14 C1
Tourist Office	2 C2	Caretta Caretta	15 B3
Ünsal Internet Café	3 C2	Dalyan Spice	16 C2
		Demet Pastanesi	17 C2
SIGHTS & ACTIVITIES		Metin Pide & Pizza	18 C2
Belediye (Town Hall)	(see 2)	Ocakbaşı Restaurant	19 B3
Dalyan Kooperatifi	4 C2	Riverside Restaurant	20 B2
Kaunos (Caunos)	5 A4	Sibel Dondurma	21 C2
		Tas Firin	22 C2
SLEEPING 🛏️			
Aktaş Pension	6 B3	DRINKING 🍷	
Asur Hotel	7 B4	Bars	23 C2
Çinar Sahil Pension	8 B2		
Dalyan Camping	9 B3	TRANSPORT	
Dalyan Hotel	10 B2	Boat Shuttle to Sultan Palas	
Happy Caretta	11 B3	Hotel	24 C1
Kilim Hotel	12 B3	Minibus Stand	25 C2

bathrooms), seven have river views and there's a terrace right on the riverbank. It's good value.

Çınar Sahil Pension (☎ 284 2402; www.cinarsahil pansiyon.com; Yalı Sokak 14; s/d €17/28) Rooms are simple and spotless, but the big boon here is its central location and its roof terrace with possibly the best views in Dalyan. Ask for one of the four rooms with balconies and river views. BBQs are organised in season and a boat is rented out for €33 per day (for up to four people).

MIDRANGE & TOP END

Kilim Hotel (☎ 284 2253; www.kilimhotel.com; Kaunos Sokak 7; s/d €22/33; ⊙ Apr-Nov; ✖ ☎) With a pool and seating area set in a terrace shaded by old palms, this is a relaxing and peaceful place. The spacious rooms contain king-size beds and most have balconies. Guests also have free access to bikes. There's a ramp for wheelchair access.

Asur Hotel (☎ 284 3232; www.asurotel.com; s €27-35, d €40.50-49.50 depending on season; ⊙ May-Oct; ✖ ☎) Lying in the far southwestern corner of town, diagonally opposite Kaunos (but on the other side of the river), is the Asur. Set in landscaped gardens full of birds, it was designed by the award-winning architect Nail Çakırhan. The 32 octagonal bungalows are rather oriental-looking but are beautifully finished and each has a little veranda. The hotel also has a lovely pool.

Happy Caretta (☎ 284 2109; www.happycaretta.com; Kaunos Sokak 26; s/d 39/50) With a terrace kept cool by cypress trees and hung with hammocks, the Caretta is a pleasant and peaceful place. Rooms are simple and smallish but stylishly decorated with natural materials. Munir, the owner, makes her own jams from her fruit trees and lays on a good breakfast.

Dalyan Hotel (☎ 284 2239; www.hoteldalyan.com; Kordon Boyu Sokak; s €39-47, d €53-72 depending on season; ⊙ May-Oct; ✖ ☎) Attractively designed in a series of semicircles, the Dalyan is stunningly set right above the river opposite the Lycian tombs. Rooms, simple but stylish, surround the pool in a semicircle and have attractive bougainvillea-clad verandas with Spanish arches. Ten have river views, ten pool views. The hotel has a free boat service to İztuzu Beach.

Eating & Drinking

Several readers have complained of overcharging in Dalyan's restaurants. Be sure to check prices before ordering (particularly fish), as well as your bill afterwards.

For a drink, head for the point on Maraş Caddesi where it widens slightly. Bars are cheek-by-jowl; choose the most popular one that evening.

RESTAURANTS

Atay Dostlar Sofrası (☎ 284 2156; Camı Karşısı 69; main €2.20; ⊙ 6.30am-midnight) Opposite the mosque, this is firm favourite locally for its home-style cooking at unbeatable prices. There's a point and-pick counter and dishes are fresh daily. It does good veggie dishes too (€1.65).

Metin Pide & Pizza (☎ 284 2877; Sulunger Sokak 3/B; ⊙ 8.30am-9.30pm low season, to midnight high season) Hugely popular for its delicious pide (€1.40 to €2.20) and pizza (€2.75 to €5) freshly made, this is a family affair with all members helping out. There are tables in a shaded garden opposite the restaurant.

Caretta Caretta (☎ 284 3039; Maraş Caddesi 124; mez €2.20, mains incl fish €5-11; ⊙ 8am-1am Mar-Nov) Also designed by Nail Çakırhan, this place does delicious Turkish dishes (such as *bonfile v tavuk cığerli börek* – beef fillet with chicken

---

THE AUTHOR'S CHOICE

Sultan Palas Hotel (☎ 284 2103; www.sultanpalasdalyan.co.uk; Horozlar Mevkii; s/d €44/73, with half board €51/87; ⊙ May–mid-Oct; ✖ ☎) Accessible from Dalyan only by ferry, you really have the sensation of crossing the Styx with Charon to reach the Sultan. With rooms set in a luscious garden full of fruit trees and a gorgeous pool, it's truly a heavenly haven. Here no traffic, no tour groups and no pop music are allowed to pass the celestial portals. Nil, the redoubtable manager keeps the place shipshape and chooses the veg personally from the local markets for her table. Styled on old Ottoman dishes, dinner is delicious. Rooms, designed like little suites, are restrained but attractive and comfortable; each has its own veranda. To get here, either catch one of the five scheduled daily boat shuttles from town, or outside hours, call the hotel for a ferry pick-up service from a spot on the riverbank 2km north of town.

ivers baked in puff pastry) at pleasing prices. With a number of tables on the riverbank and the wooden platform above the water, you have a fair chance of bagging one. It's a great place also for a beer (€1.95).

Bistrot Clou (☎ 284 3452; Pazar Yeri Sokak; meze €1.65-2.50; ❂ 9am-midnight Apr–mid-Oct) Just off Market Sq, this delightful little place offers home-style cooking at fair prices. The family who runs it makes everything – from the house special-ty, the delicious *güvec* (casseroles, €4.75 to €11) to the crocheted tablecloths and gourd lamps. There's jazz and traditional music most nights.

Okakbaşı Restaurant (☎ 284 5294; Maraş Caddesi 27; meze €2.20; ❂ 9.30am-midnight Apr-Sep) With ta-bles in a lovely garden with a pool and orange, plum and pomegranate trees, this place is known for its scrumptious kebaps (€6.50).

Riverside Restaurant (☎ 284 3166; Sağlık Sokak 7; meze €3-8, 450g fish €9-11; ❂ 8.30am-midnight) Consid-ered Dalyan's best fish restaurant, the Riverside also boasts a gorgeous and breezy terrace where you can dine under mulberry trees while ad-miring the Lycian tombs and listening to the quack of ducks. The owner, an ex–head chef who still does his own cooking, offers exquisite seafood and fish accompanied by his own spe-cial sauces. The stuffed fish is a speciality.

CAFÉS & QUICK EATS
Tas Firin (☎ 284 3839; Sulunger Sokak 2; ❂ 7am-6pm low season, to 10pm high season) Diagonally opposite the Metin, it sells good fresh bread.

Demet Pastanesi (☎ 284 4124; Maraş Caddesi 39; coffee €0.85; ❂ 7.30am-6pm low season, to midnight high season) With priceless pastries and tantalising Turkish puds (€1.65) it's a great place for brekie or for picnic preparations. The hazel-nut and walnut tart (€1.95) is to die for.

Dalyan Spice (☎ 284 4397; Maraş Caddesi 37; ❂ 8.30am-midnight Apr-Oct) Sells gorgeous Turk-ish delight (box €2.75 to €5), as well as local spices and honey. For ice cream, head for **Sibel Dondurma** (☎ 284 4363; Maraş Caddesi 43/A; 1 scoop €0.55; ❂ 7am-midnight May-Oct), which sells 20 flavours, all locally made.

Getting There & Away
There are no direct minibuses from here to Dalaman. First take a minibus to Ortaca (€0.85, every 30 minutes in high season, every hour in low season) and change there. At Ortaca otogar buses go to Köyceğiz (€1.40, 25 minutes, 20km) and Dalaman (€0.40, 15

minutes, 5km). Dalyan's minibuses leave from the stop west of the PTT.

AROUND DALYAN
Sultaniye Hot Springs & Mud Baths
Southwest of Köyceğiz Gölü, the **Sultaniye Hot Springs** (Sultaniye Kaplıcaları; admission €1.95) contain mildly radioactive mineral waters that are rich in calcium, sulphur, iron, nitrates, potassium and other mineral salts, and are said to be good for skin complaints and rheumatism. Temperatures sometimes reach 40°C. At the smaller mud baths just before Dalyan River joins the lake, you can give yourself a body-pack of mud in a sulphur pool with tempera-tures as hot as in the Sultaniye baths.

To get here, you can get a 'dolmuş boat' (€2.75, 30 minutes), which leave when full (around every half-hour in summer, every hour outside the high season). You can also contract a private boat, though you'll need to negotiate hard.

İztuzu Beach
About 13km south of town, this 4.5km sand-bar separating the sea from the mouth of the Dalyan River is an excellent swimming beach. Developers have been itching to get their paws on it for years, but the government has resolutely forbidden the sort of hotel develop-ment you find between Kuşadası and Alanya. The beach has a few snack bars and ranks of sunbeds but you don't have to walk far to escape the crowds. İztuzu is important as one of the last nesting sites in the Mediterranean of the loggerhead turtle (see the boxed text, above) and special rules to protect the turtles are strictly enforced. To get here, minibuses (€2.20, 15 minutes) run from Dalyan every half-hour in high season.

DALAMAN
☎ 0252 / pop 19,600
This agricultural town was fairly dozy until the regional airport was built on the neigh-bouring river delta. Now it stirs (but doesn't wake) whenever a jet arrives. Most visitors pass straight through and bus connections are good.

It's 5.5km from the airport to the town, and another 5.5km from the town to the east–west highway. Besides flights to many European cities during the tourist season, there are about five daily flights from Dala-man to İstanbul year-round, costing €78 one

TURTLE ALERT

Some years ago Dalyan's İztuzu Beach shot to world fame when a serious threat to one of the last Mediterranean nesting sites of *Caretta caretta*, the loggerhead turtle, was identified.

The loggerhead turtle (*deniz kaplumbağa* in Turkish) is a large flat-headed reptile, reddish brown on top and yellow-orange below. An adult can weigh up to 130kg.

Between May and September the female turtles come ashore at night to lay their eggs in the sand. Using their back flippers they scoop out a nest about 40cm deep, lay between 70 and 120 soft-shelled white eggs the size of ping-pong balls, then cover them over. If disturbed, the females may abandon the nests and return to the sea.

The eggs incubate in the sand for 50 to 65 days and the temperature at which they do so determines the gender of the ensuing young: below 30°C all the young will be male; above 30°C they will be female. At a steady 30°C an even mix of the genders will hatch.

As soon as they're born (at night when it's cool and fewer predators are about), the young turtles make their way towards the sea, drawn by the reflected light. If hotels and restaurants are built too close to the beach, their lights can confuse the youngsters, leading them to move up the beach towards danger instead of down to the sea and safety. So when it was discovered that developers wanted to build a hotel right on the beach there was an outcry that eventually led to the plans being abandoned.

At the same time, rules were introduced to protect the turtles. Although the beach is still open to the public during the day, night-time visits are prohibited from May to September. A line of wooden stakes on the beach indicates the nest sites and visitors are asked to sunbathe behind the stakes to avoid disturbing the nests. It's particularly important not to leave any litter on the beach that could hamper the turtles' struggle for survival.

The loggerhead turtle also nests on the beaches at Dalaman, Fethiye, Patara, Kale, Kumluca, Tekirova, Belek, Kızılot, Demirtaş, Gazipaşa and Anamur and in the Göksu Delta. See p348 for details of turtle-spotting boat tours.

way. In high season, several bus companies pick up passengers outside the airport. At other times you may need to get a taxi into Dalaman for €7 to €9.

At Dalaman's otogar, near the junction of Kenan Evren Bulvarı and Atatürk Caddesi, you can buy tickets to many destinations, such as Antalya (€8, 5½ hours, 272km), Köyceğiz (€1.50, 45 minutes, 34km) and Marmaris (€5, two hours, 120km). All routes north and east pass through either Muğla or Fethiye.

GÖCEK
☎ 0252

This small-scale holiday village is halfway between Köyceğiz and Fethiye on an attractive bay almost enclosed by dry, pine-speckled mountains. It first came to prominence in the 1980s as the favoured holiday retreat of Turgut Özal, Turkey's go-getting prime minister and later president.

Buses drop you at a petrol station on the main road, from where it's a 1km walk to the centre. Minibuses drive down to the main square, which has a bust of Atatürk, a collection of small restaurants, a PTT and ATMs.

Göcek is a place for relaxing. There's only a fairly scrappy **beach** at the western end of the quay, although you can take a '**12-island cruise**' (see p354) to beaches on nearby islands.

Sleeping
CAMPING
About 10km east of Göcek, **Küçük Kargı Orman İç Dinlenme Yeri** (per tent €2.75) has camping facilities in woodland overlooking a lovely bay. About 2km further east, at Katrancı, there's another picnic and camping ground with a small restaurant on a beautiful little cove with a beach.

PENSIONS & HOTELS
Tufan Pansiyon (☎ 645 1334; Marina; s/d high season €14/17, low season €11/14) Just 25m from the sea, the family-run Tufan has small but spotless and rather sweet rooms, four of which have a shared balcony with sea views.

Başak Pansiyon (☎ 645 1024; fax 645 1862; Skopea Marina; s/d €22/33) At the western end of the harbour, it has simple but spotless rooms with a nice veranda.

Dım Pansiyon (☎ 645 1294; www.dimhotel.com; Sokak 14; s/d high season €28/44, low season €28/33;

With simple but well-furnished rooms and a pleasant terrace, medium-sized pool and a location 30m from the beach, this is great value.

A&B Home Hotel (☎ 645 1820; www.abhomehotel.com; Turgut Özal Caddesi; s/d high season €67/83, low season €56/67; ⛄ ☒) The smallish rooms are dolled up a bit with wallpaper and furnishings, but the real boon is the medium-sized pool on the attractive terrace. A good breakfast buffet is served.

Eating

Can Restaurant (☎ 645 1507; Skopea Marina; meze €1.65, seafood meze €3-8; ⛄ 7am-midnight) Set back from the seafront but with a lovely terrace shaded by an old yucca tree, this is an old local favourite that serves a great selection of mezes. The speciality is *tuzda balık* (fish baked in salt, €42 for two to three people).

West Café & Bar (☎ 645 2794; Turgut Özal Caddesi; breakfast €5, mains €4.50-12.50; ⛄ 9am-midnight low season, to 12.30am high season) Well-named, it's Western in cuisine and Western in feel with wireless internet connection, bacon for breakfast and tarts for tea. If you're kebaped-out, it's good for a change but it's not cheap.

Anatolia (☎ 645 6941; Marina; meze €2.20-8; mains €11-17; ⛄ 7am-midnight) Has a pleasant terrace at the back of its cavernous interior and specialises in Anatolian dishes.

Getting There & Away

Minibuses depart every half-hour to Fethiye (€1.95, 30 minutes, 30km). For Dalyan, change at Otacer (€2.75, 25 minutes, 25km, every hour) first.

FETHİYE

☎ 0252 / pop 50,700

Tucked into the southern reaches of an appealing broad bay, Fethiye is a very old town with few old buildings. An earthquake in 1958 levelled it and left only tombs from the time when Fethiye was called Telmessos (400 BC). It's an incredibly relaxed place despite its size, often visited at the beginning or end of a *gület* cruise.

Fethiye's inner bay is an excellent natural harbour, protected from storms by an island, Şövalye Adası; the much larger outer bay has 11 more islands. About 15km south is Ölüdeniz (p359), one of Turkey's seaside hot spots, and the Fethiye region has many interesting sites to explore, including the ghost town of Kayaköy (Karmylassos, p361), just over the hill.

Orientation

Fethiye's busy otogar is 2.5km east of the town centre, with a separate station for minibuses 1km east of the centre. Midrange and top-end hotels are near the centre, but many of the inexpensive pensions are west of it past the marina. Dolmuşes run along the main street, Atatürk Caddesi. The *belediye* seems to enjoy renaming streets, so the smaller streets can be known by several names. The town's Tuesday market takes place along the canal between Atatürk Caddesi and the stadium (Pürşabey Caddesi). Yachting agencies are clustered around the marina.

Information

Atatürk Caddesi has banks with ATMs and foreign exchange offices.

Imagine Bookshop (☎ 614 8465; Atatürk Caddesi 18; ⛄ 9am-6pm) Sells foreign newspapers and magazines, English-Turkish dictionaries and books and maps on Turkey, and Turkish CDs.

Tourist Office (☎ 614 1527; İskele Meydanı; ⛄ 8.30am-noon & 1-5.30pm daily May-Sep, Mon-Fri Oct-Apr) Next to the marina, just past the Roman theatre.

Sights & Activities
ANCIENT TELMESSOS

Throughout the town you will notice curious Lycian stone *sarcophagi* dating from around 450 BC. There's one north of the *belediye* and others in the middle of streets or in private gardens – the town was built around them. All were broken into by tomb robbers centuries ago.

Behind the town is the **Tomb of Amyntas** (admission €2.50; ⛄ 8am-7pm), an Ionic temple façade carved in the sheer rock face in 350 BC. It gets crowded at sunset in summer, the most pleasant time to visit. It's a steep climb up steps to get there; on a hot day it's worth first considering how much Lycian funerary monuments really mean to you. Other smaller tombs lie about 500m to the east.

Behind the harbour you'll see the excavated remains of a **theatre** dating from Roman times.

On the hillside behind the town, just north of the road to Kayaköy, notice the ruined tower of a **Crusader fortress** built by the Knights of St John on earlier foundations dating back to perhaps 400 BC.

FETHİYE

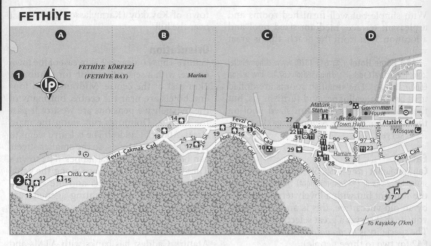

To Kayaköy (7km)

INFORMATION		SLEEPING		Meğri Restaurant.....................25 C2
Hospital.....................1 E1		Artemis Hotel.....................12 A2		Nefis Pide.....................26 D2
Imagine Bookshop.....................2 C2		Duygu Pension.....................13 A2		Özsüt.....................27 C1
Jandarma (Police).....................3 A2		Ece Saray Marina & Resort.....14 B1		Paşa Kebab.....................28 D2
Ocean Turizm & Travel		Ferah Pension.....................15 A2		
Agency.....................(see 6)		Horizon Hotel.....................16 C2		DRINKING
Post Office (PTT).....................4 D1		Ideal Pension.....................17 B2		Car Cemetery.....................29 C2
Toilets.....................5 E2		İrem Hotel.....................18 B2		Ottoman Dancing Bar.............30 D2
Tourist Office.....................6 C2		Tan Pansiyon.....................19 C2		
		V-Go's Hotel & Guesthouse.....(see 13)		ENTERTAINMENT
SIGHTS & ACTIVITIES		Villa Daffodil.....................20 A2		Club Bananas.....................31 C2
Crusader Fortress.....................7 D2				
Lycian Rock Tombs.....................8 F2		EATING		TRANSPORT
Lycian Stone Sarcophagi.....................9 D1		Café Oley.....................22 C2		Boat Tour Companies.............(see 6)
Roman Theatre Ruins.....................10 C2		Hilmi et Balık Restaurant.....................23 D2		Minibus Station.....................32 E2
Tomb of Amyntas.....................11 E2		Meğri Lokantası.....................24 D2		Minibuses to Ölüdeniz.............33 E2

FETHİYE MUSEUM

Among its most interesting exhibits, **Fethiye Museum** (Fethiye Müzesi; 505 Sokak; admission €2.75; 8.30am-5pm Tue-Sun) has some small statues and votive stones (the Stelae of Graves and Stelae of Promise) and the trilingual stele (Lycian-Greek-Aramaic) from the Letoön (see p365), which was used to decipher the Lycian language. It describes how King Kaunos gave money to do some good work in honour of the gods. The ethnography section has some interesting Ottoman-era exhibits although it's sometimes closed.

BEACHES & WATER SPORTS

Ocean Turizm & Travel Agency (612 4807; www.oceantravelagency.com; İskele Meydanı 1; 9am-9pm) sells boat tickets and can also organise diving (per person including two dives, all equipment and lunch €45) and parasailing (per person for 30 minutes including all equipment €75).

About 5km northeast of the centre is **Çalış**, a narrow stretch of gravelly beach lined with mass-produced hotels. Once very popular, it's now overshadowed by Ölüdeniz. Dolmuşes depart for Çalış (€0.85, 10 minutes) from the minibus station every five to 10 minutes throughout the day.

Tours

Many travellers sign up for the **12-Island Tour** (per person incl lunch high season €11, low season €14-17; 9am-6pm or 6.30pm, mid-Apr–Oct), a boat trip around Fethiye Bay (Fethiye Körfezi). The boats usually stop at six islands and cruise by the rest. Some are booze-cruise-style tours so check you're getting what you want. Hotels and agencies sell tickets or you can negotiate a price with the boat companies around the tourist office at the marina.

The normal tour (Fethiye Körfezi) visits **Yassıcalar** (Flat Island) for a stop and a swim,

then **Tersane Island** for a dip in the turquoise waters and a visit to the ruins, followed by **Akvaryum** (Aquarium) for lunch, a swim and a snorkel. **Cennet Köü** (Paradise Bay) is next for a dip, followed by **Klopatra Hamamı** (Cleopatra's Bath), and finally **Kızıl Ada** (Red Island) with its beach and mud baths.

If there are too many boats at an island at the same time, itineraries may change and you may visit some of the other islands.

Highly recommended are the boat tours that go to or include **Butterfly Valley** (per person €11; ⌚ 9.30am-6.30pm mid-Apr–Oct) via Ölüdeniz and include walking, swimming and ruin-visiting; as well as the **Saklıkent Gorge Tour** (per person €22; ⌚ 9am-6.30pm), which includes the ruins at Tlos and walking, trout tickling and a trout lunch; and the **Dalyan Tour** (per person €22; ⌚ 9am-5.30pm), which includes a shuttle to Dalyan, a tour of the lake, Sultaniye mud baths, Dalyan, the tombs at Kaunos and beach at İztusu.

Other options include beach or archaeological tours. Going by minibus will be cheaper, but is usually more time-consuming and a lot less fun.

Sleeping

Fethiye has a good selection of budget and midrange accommodation, but little in the way of luxury.

BUDGET

Dolmuşes marked 'Karagözler' run along Fevzi Çakmak Caddesi towards the pensions every five to 10 minutes. Most budget places

will pick you up from the bus station if you give them a call on arrival.

Ideal Pension (☎ 614 1981; www.idealpension.net; 26 Sokak 1; dm/s/d from €7/8/14; 🄭 💻) The cheapest option, yet still offering clean (albeit small) rooms, a large terrace with bay views and a choice of breakfast, it's very good value. The owner, a retired teacher, is keen to please and offers various services and long-stay incentives (such as a free boat trip for more than three days' stay).

Tan Pansiyon (☎ 614 1584; fax 614 1676; 30 Sokak 43; s/d €11/14) If you'd rather swap backpacker banter for traditional Turkish hospitality and a firm family feel, here's your place. Rooms are small (the bathrooms smaller), but it's sparkling clean and quiet. Guests can use the kitchen and there's a large terrace with bay views.

Artemis Hotel (☎ 612 4980; www.artemishotelfethiye .com; Ordu Caddesi 48; s/d €11/14; 💻 🄭) Try this one if the others listed are full; with pool and bay views, it's a good choice.

Ferah Pension (Monica's Place; ☎ 614 2816; www .ferahpension.com; 2 Ordu Caddesi 21; dm/s/d €5.50/14/20; 🄭 💻) Monika, the manager, 'likes clean' and the rooms, though small and simple, are certainly that. Those with air-con cost an extra €4.45 per day. The 'dormitory' (a glass-enclosed roof terrace) has beautiful views as do two of the rooms. The hotel 'lobby' is so verdant it's like entering a clearing in a forest and is a popular hang-out for backpackers. It's a good source of local information and there's a free shuttle to/from the otogar.

Duygu Pension (☎ 614 3563; www.duygupension .com; Ordu Caddesi 54; s/d €14/20; 🄭 🄭) It may look unpromising, but the Duygu's a homely little place with a lovely position on the bay. It boasts a roof top with blinding bay views and a small pool. Rooms are simple but spotless.

V-Go's Hotel & Guesthouse (☎ 614 5904; www .boatcruisesturkey.com; Ordu Caddesi 66; dm/s/d €8/11/22; 🄭 🄭) Brand new when we visited and bristling to bring in the backpackers, V-Go's offers 14 spotless, pleasant rooms, as well a medium-sized pool and a small roof terrace. Six rooms have direct sea views and small balconies. Good value, well-run and dynamic, it also does BBQs (€5.55 per person).

MIDRANGE & TOP END

Horizon Hotel (☎ 612 3153; www.otelhorizon.net; Abdi İpekçi Caddesi 1; dm €6-11, s €8-22, d €17-39 depending on season; 🄭 🄭) Aptly named, the Horizon easily

BLUE VOYAGES

Between the wars, writer and painter Cevat Şakir Kabaağaç lived in Bodrum and wrote an account of his idyllic sailing excursions along Turkey's southern Aegean and western Mediterranean coasts, an area completely untouched by tourism at the time. Kabaağaç called his book *Mavi Yolculuk (Blue Voyage)*, a name now coopted for any cruise along these shores.

For many travellers a four-day, three-night cruise on a *gület* (wooden yacht) between Fethiye and Kale (Demre) is the highlight of their trip to Turkey. Usually advertised as a Fethiye to Olympos voyage, the boats actually start or stop at Kale and the trip to/from Olympos (1¼ hours) is by bus. From Fethiye, boats call in at Ölüdeniz and Butterfly Valley and stop at Kaş, Kalkan and Kekova, with the final night at Gökkaya Bay where you have the option of partying at the cheesy but fun Smugglers Inn (Pirates Disco). A less common route is between Marmaris and Fethiye, also taking four days and three nights. Aficionados say this is a much prettier route but for some reason it's not as popular.

Food and water is usually included in the price, but you have to buy your booze on the boat. All boats are equipped with showers, toilets and smallish but comfortable double cabins (usually six to eight of them). This might make a single person uneasy if they have to share with a stranger, but in practice most people sleep on mattresses on deck as it's so hot (the boats are without air-conditioning).

Backpacker cruises are usually quoted in pounds sterling. Depending on the season the price is usually €84 to €150 for Fethiye and €150 for Marmaris per person, not at all cheap, so it makes sense to look around. Be savvy and demanding – there are many shoddy operators working the waters and your wallet. Here are some of our suggestions to avoid getting fleeced:

- Ask for recommendations from other travellers.
- Bargain, but don't necessarily go for the cheapest option because the crew will skimp on food and alcohol.
- Check out your boat (if you are in Fethiye) and ask to see the guest list.
- Ask whether your captain and crew speak English.
- Don't go for gimmicks such as free water sports. They often prove to be empty promises and boats rarely have insurance for them in case of accidents.
- Don't buy your ticket in İstanbul, as pensions and commission agents take a healthy cut.
- Don't take a boat just because it is leaving today.
- Book well ahead for July and August in order to be sure of getting on a cruise.

See also the boxed text, opposite for more tips from a classic cautionary tale.

We recommend the owner-operated outfits because they run a much tighter ship. During summer the larger companies often farm out unknowing tourists to lazy captains with suspect boats. Boats come and go just about every day of the week between late April and October (the Marmaris boats usually run twice a week from mid-May to the end of September). Competition is stiff between the following:

Almila Boat Cruise (☎ 0535-636 0076; www.beforelunch.com) Run by a Turkish-Australian couple, who own two superior boats and offer the popular 12-islands cruise (see p354). Numbers are limited to 10 people and the food has garnered good reports.

Big Backpackers (☎ 0252-614 9312; www.bluecruisefethiye.com) A newish venture run from Ideal Pension in Fethiye and offers the Fethiye–Kale cruise.

Interyouth Hostel (☎ 0252-412 3687; interyouth@turk.net) In Marmaris, organises high-quality cruises on its own boat to Fethiye, stopping at the Dalyan mud baths and visiting the 12 islands. Numbers are limited to 12 people.

Olympos Yachting (☎ 0242-892 1145; www.olymposyachting.com) Offers a four-day/three-night cruise direct from Olympos beach to Kaş, run in conjunction with Türkmen's at Olympos (p380).

Yeşil Marmaris Travel & Yachting (☎ 412 2290; www.yesilmarmaris.com) In Marmaris, ask for the helpful Tolunay Bükülmez.

steals the best-view-in-Fethiye crown. Views from the pool, terrace and 17 rooms are stunning. Ibrahim, the new manager, has ambitious plans for the place. 'Extras' currently include free internet use, free city shuttle every hour, free otogar pick up and a good-value set menu (€4).

İrem Hotel (☎ 614 3006; tutantur@yahoo.com; Fevzi Çakmak Caddesi 38; s/d high season €22/33, low season €20/28; ❄ ⬛) Quieter and more private than many, this hotel is good value and has a well-maintained medium-sized pool. Three rooms have balconies overlooking the bay.

Villa Daffodil (☎ 614 9595; www.villadaffodil.com; Fevzi Çakmak Caddesi 115; s/d low season €20/33, high season €25/42; ❄ ⬛) This large Ottoman-designed guesthouse boasts a decent-sized pool, a dining terrace with gorgeous views, and comfortable and homely rooms (all with balcony; eight with direct sea views). Hussein, a retired colonel, keeps the place shipshape. Be

sure to book in high season as tour groups gather here.

Ece Saray Marina & Resort (☎ 612 5005; www.ecesaray.net; Karagözler Mevkii 1; s €100-165, d €125-195 depending on season; ❄ ⬛ ⬛) Despite lacking much character, the Ece boasts good facilities including well-furnished rooms, a large pool, fitness centre, large landscaped gardens, a *hamam*, its own supermarket, and a Wellness Centre.

Eating
RESTAURANTS
Yakamoz Restaurant (☎ 612 4226; Yeni Kordon Dolgu Sahası; meals €8) A pleasant 1km walk from town along the promenade, this is a great place to head for a sunset drink and dinner. It's a traditional Turkish menu and the fish can be pricey, but there's plenty of atmosphere and an attractive outdoor area with big cushions down by the water.

THE CRUISE FROM HELL *Virginia Maxwell*

It was late June, supposedly the perfect time of the year to take a *gület* cruise on the Turkish Mediterranean. Arriving in Fethiye, we went straight to the harbour, keen to check out the boats and sign up for a cruise leaving on the next day. Prices seemed to vary very little (was there a cartel at work?), but what we wanted was a quiet and relaxing time soaking up the sun and swimming in the famous blue waters. One company looked good – it promised everything we were looking for and seemed professional – so we asked to have a look at the boat that was leaving on the following day. Alas, we were told, that particular boat wasn't in the harbour today. We could have a look at another, very similar, boat, though…

Deep down, warning bells were ringing, but we liked the guy we were dealing with and we decided to do as he suggested. The *gület* he showed us was fabulous, with spacious, comfortable cabins and an enormous, well set-up deck. Assured that the following day was going to offer perfect sailing conditions, we decided to sign up (which involved paying in full).

How stupid of us. The next morning brought with it gale-force winds. Making our way down to the harbour, we entered the company office and asked if it was possible to delay our departure until a calm day. The answer was a flat 'no' – all tickets were nontransferable, as we would have noted when we read the (miniscule) conditions on the back of our tickets. And worse was to come – our *gület* was half the size and twice the age of the boat we had been shown on the previous day. Outraged, we made our feelings known. The response? A shrug of the shoulders.

Needless to say, the trip was a disaster. The conditions were so rough that everyone (including members of the crew) spent hour upon hour being violently ill over the side. The meals (for those who could bring themselves to eat) were meagre in size and dubious in quality. There were cockroaches and grubby linen in all of the cabins. And the last shreds of our romantic vision of a traditional Blue Voyage were destroyed when we were told that hardly any modern *gülets* use their sails (in fact, these are often purely ornamental). Instead, the boat's unbelievably noisy diesel engine would be used, and we would have to live with the vile diesel fumes for the entire trip.

The moral? Don't pay until you have confirmed on the day that the weather conditions are favourable, made 100% sure that you are happy with the boat you will be leaving on, and spoken with the captain about meals and whether the diesel engine will be used for the whole cruise.

Hilmi et Balık Restaurant (☎ 612 6242; Hal ve Pazar Yeri 53; meze €2.20, 400g fish €8-11; ☼ 10am-midnight) Set inside the fish market building, this place does meat dishes as well as fish (its speciality) and is a firm favourite locally. You can also bring-your-own (see the boxed text, right).

Meğri Restaurant (☎ 614 4040; Lika Sokak 8-9; meals €10-15; ☼ 9am-midnight) In a beautiful old stone house decorated with traditional artefacts, this place serves a varied menu in a nice atmosphere. With Turkish, Italian and French food all on offer, it might suit bickering couples who can't agree on where to go.

CAFÉS
Café Oley (☎ 612 9532; 38 Sokak 4; breakfast €3.35-6, meals €4-7; ☼ 8am-midnight; ▣) Run by the dynamic Atilla, the Oley offers the best breakfast in town serving everything from bacon and Cornflakes to Vegemite and pancakes. It also does good salads and sandwiches (€2.75 to €4.45). Customers have free internet access and there's a book exchange.

Özsüt (☎ 612 9989; Atatürk Caddesi; ☼ 8am-1am) Serving the usual tantalising Turkish puds and pastries, this excellent chain also sells good ice cream (€0.55 per scoop).

QUICK EATS
Meğri Lokantasi (☎ 614 4047; Çarşı Caddesi 26; mains €5.55-14; ☼ 8am-2am low season, 8am-4am high season) Packed with locals who spill onto the streets, the Meğri does excellent and hearty home-style cooking at very palatable prices. The *güveç* (casseroles, €5.55 to €11) are something of a speciality.

Nefis Pide (☎ 614 5504; Eski Cami Sokak 9; meals €2; ☼ 9am-9pm low season, to midnight high season) Stark and simple but sparkling clean, this popular place does delicious pides (€1.40 to €2.75). It's right next to the mosque – and doesn't sell alcohol!

Paşa Kebab (☎ 614 9807; Çarşı Caddesi 42; meze €1.65-2.20, pide €1.10-3.35, pizza €4-5; ☼ 9am-midnight) Considered locally to offer the 'best kebaps in town', this honest and unpretentious place has a well-priced menu (with useful little photos of dishes!). Try the Paşa special (€4.70) – a delicious oven-baked beef, tomato and cheese concoction.

Drinking & Entertainment
Fethiye's bars and nightclubs are mostly cheek-by-jowl on one little street, Hamam Sokak, just off İskele Meydanı.

BYOF – BRING YOUR OWN FISH

One way to taste Fethiye's fabulous fish without losing too many Turkish lira is to bring your own! Follow fishy smells to find the market, browse what's on offer, check the day's prices chalked up on the boards, then take your time choosing. Next, ferry the fish to one of the rows of restaurants that surround the market – pick the most popular – and ask them to cook it. A nominal cover charge of just €2.75 is levied, but this will procure you a green salad, bread with garlic butter, a sauce to accompany the fish, and fruit and coffee; it's a bargain fit for a king.

Ottoman Dancing Bar (☎ 612 9491; beer €2.20; ☼ noon-4am) Decorated to the extreme *à l'Ottoman*, this is a long-time favourite with both locals and travellers who come to drink or smoke a nargileh (water pipe, €5.55) on the comfy outdoor seating.

Car Cemetery (☎ 612 7872; Haman Sokak 25; beer €2, ☼ 5pm-3am low season, 10am-3am high season) British-pub-meets-club, this place is particularly popular with locals and rarely reports a dull night.

Club Bananas (☎ 612 8441; beer €2.75; ☼ 10pm-5am daily high season, Fri & Sat only low season) The only true club in town (as opposed to pub-club), Bananas is styled like a big barn and plays a mixture of local and Western music. There's usually at least one 'party night' (admission €5.55 including one drink) every week. It lies one block north of Hamam Sokak.

Getting There & Away
The mountains behind Fethiye force transport to go east or west and for many destinations you must change buses at Antalya or Muğla. Buses from the otogar to Antalya (€10, 7½ hours, 295km) head east along the coast at least every hour in high season, stopping at Kalkan (€2.50, two hours, 81km), Kaş (€3, 2½ hours, 110km) and Olympos (€7.50, five hours, 219km). The inland road to Antalya (€9, four hours, 222km) is much quicker.

For intermediate destinations, go to the minibus station off Atatürk Caddesi, around 0.5km east of the centre. Destinations served by minibuses include Faralya, Göcek, Hisarönü, Kabak, Kayaköy (Kaya), Kemer, Kumluova, Ovacık, Ölüdeniz (stops at main otogar as well), Saklıkent and Tlos.

Getting Around

Minibuses ply the one-way system along Atatürk Caddesi and up Çarşı Caddesi to the otogar all day. Take a minibus with a 'Karagözler' sign in the window to get to the pensions west of the centre. There's a fixed charge of €0.85 no matter how far you go. A taxi from the otogar to the pensions east of the centre costs about €5.55.

A couple of agencies along Atatürk Caddesi hire out scooters for €14 per day (or €11 per day for three days or more).

ÖLÜDENIZ

☎ 0252

Ölüdeniz (Dead Sea), about 15km southeast of Fethiye, is not devoid of life like its biblical namesake. Rather, it's a sheltered lagoon hidden from the open sea. The scene as you come down from the pine-clad hills is absolutely beautiful: in the distance open sea, in the foreground a long spit of sandy beach.

Unfortunately the paradise that many past travellers fondly recall has all but been ruined by the tightly packed belt of hotels behind the beach. Ölüdeniz (the lagoon) and Belcekız (the adjacent beach resort) used to be one of the highlights of independent travel in Turkey but the development of identical air-conditioned hotels, loud bars and overpriced restaurants has hardly bolstered its appeal. Many travellers may prefer to shoot straight through. Note that the name of the lagoon (Ölüdeniz) is becoming synonymous with the town and that asking for Belcekız may draw a blank.

Orientation & Information

As you approach Ölüdeniz, the road passes through the hilariously awful package-tour colonies of Ovacık and Hisarönü. It then descends steeply from Hisarönü another 3km to a beautiful beach backed by hotels.

The beach is very much the centre of things. Near the junction of the roads to Fethiye, Belcekız and to Ölüdeniz, you will find a *jandarma* post, a PTT and the entrance to the lagoon. The road continues behind the park to several camping grounds.

To your left as you arrive, the beach promenade is closed to traffic and backed with restaurants and a tight cluster of hotels.

The **Ölüdeniz Tourism Development Co-operative** (Ölüdeniz Turizm Geliştirme Kooperatifi; ☎ 617 0438; Ölüdeniz Caddesi) has an information booth on the access road just inland from the beach.

Sights & Activities

LAGOON

The **Ölüdeniz Tabiat Parkı** (Ölüdeniz Caddesi; adult/student €1.40/0.55; ⏱ 8am-8pm) is a lovely place to while away a few hours on the beach with mountains soaring above you. It has been laid out with paths, showers, toilets and makeshift cafés.

BOAT TRIPS

Throughout summer, boats set out to explore the coast, charging about €14 for a day trip (including lunch). A typical cruise might take in Gemile Beach, the Blue Cave, Butterfly Valley (see p362) and St Nicholas Island, with time for swimming. Boats to Butterfly Valley leave from the beach around 11am and return around 5pm.

PARAGLIDING

With 1960m-high Baba Dağ (Mt Baba) on the doorstep, Ölüdeniz is the perfect place for paragliding. Indeed it now hosts the International Air Games each October.

The descent from the mountain can take up to 45 minutes, with amazing views over the Blue Lagoon, Butterfly Valley and, on a clear day, out to Rhodes.

Various companies offer tandem paragliding flights, but prices vary greatly according to the reputation of the company and the experience of the pilot (usually around €78 to €111). Ensure the company has insurance and the pilot has appropriate qualifications and experience. Parasailing is also possible (€50).

Sleeping

Camping grounds are the only budget options currently in Ölüdeniz, but some offer bungalows or cabins too.

Sugar Beach Club (☎ 617 0048; www.thesugarbeachclub.com; Ölüdeniz Caddesi 20; camp site per person, car and caravan €3.90; bungalows per person with bathroom €17-22, without bathroom €8; ⏱ Apr-Oct; 🖥) Recently renovated, the Sugar Beach is well designed, well run and fun. With its own pleasant strip of beach shaded by palms, it's a chilled out place, with lots of shaded lounging areas, a funky beach bar and a great café. The bungalows range from basic to air-conditioned and comfortable but they're all spotless. Future plans include tree houses, a dorm, bike hire, trekking, beach parties, DJ concerts and BBQs. If you're not staying here but want to hang out, it costs €2.20 to use the sunlounges, parasols and showers. It's about 600m from Ölüdeniz;

follow the signs to the Hotel Meri. Dolmuşes pass back and forth along the road beside the camping.

Nicholas Genç Beach (☎ 617 0088; www.nicholas -homes.com; Ölüdeniz Caddesi; s/d low season €17/28, high season €20/33) If you've ever wondered what it was like to be a caravaner, here's your chance. This new place rents out 10 small but comfortable air-conditioned caravans with fridge, satellite TV, private bathroom and even a table and a couple of chairs! It's a well run, well maintained place with a pleasant beach. It also rents out canoes (€2.75 per hour) and pedalos (€5.55 per hour) and has beach parties and BBQs, though most of its visitors come through agencies. It lies around 1km from the town centre, past the Sugar Beach Club.

MIDRANGE & TOP END

Sultan Motel (Lycian Lodge; ☎ 616 6139; www.sultanmotel .com; s/d incl breakfast €14/28; 🖭 🔊) Just off the road down to Ölüdeniz, on the left as you descend from Hisarönü (2.5km from Ölüdeniz), the Sultan acts as a starting point for the Lycian Way and rooms are in simple but spotless stone chalets, some with good views.

Blue Star Hotel (☎ 617 0069; www.hotelbluestar oludeniz.com; Mimar Sınan Caddesi 8; s €22-39, d €28-47 depending on season; 🖭 🖳 🔊) Quite attractively designed and well maintained, this two-star place is 60m from the beach. Though they're not large, the rooms are light, bright and airy and have balconies overlooking the pool.

Paradise Garden (☎ 617 0545; www.paradisegarden hotel.com; Ölüdeniz Yolu; s €47-72, d €62-122 depending on season; 🖭 🔊) Situated up the hill to the right just before you enter Ölüdeniz village, around 2.5km from the centre, this Eden-like place is well named. Set in a 6-hectare garden, it boasts spectacular views, three pools, a menagerie, and a gourmet restaurant. Rooms are attractively furnished with authentic arts and crafts.

Eating & Drinking

Oba Restaurant (☎ 617 0158; Mimar Sınan Caddesi; mains €3.60-15; ⏰ 8am-midnight May-Oct) Built like a log cabin, the restaurant of the Oba Hostel has a great reputation for home-style food at a palatable price. It also does great Turkish/European breakfasts (€2.75/€3.60) including homemade muesli with mountain yogurt and

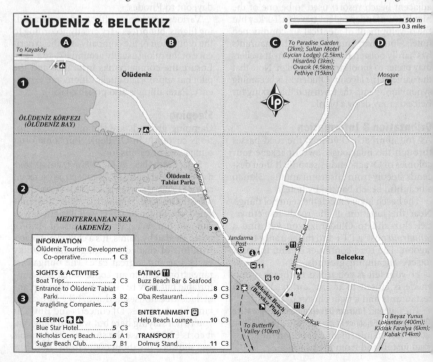

ÖLÜDENİZ & BELCEKIZ

local pine honey. Ranging from snacks to full-on mains, the menu also offers 12 veggie dishes.

Buzz Beach Bar & Seafood Grill (☎ 617 0526; 1 Sokak 1; beer €2, mains €4-14; ☺ restaurant 8am-midnight, bar noon-2am mid-Apr–Oct) With a nice situation on the waterfront, this place offers a wide menu from pizza and pasta to kebabs, fillet steak and seafood. At lunch time you can watch the paragliders plop down on the landing point outside. It's also a very popular nightspot.

Beyaz Yunus Lokantası (White Dolphin; ☎ 617 0068; Likya Yolu; beer €2.75, fish per 450g €22; ☺ 11am-midnight May–mid-Oct) Set on a stunning terrace overlooking the bay, the Beyaz is famous for its fresh fish and seafood. Sample some of the exquisite seafood mezes (€7.75) such as calamari stuffed with feta, or octopus slow-cooked in red wine. Down some steps is a delightful Sunset Bar'–perfect for a pre-dinner apéritif! It's on the Faralya road about 1km from the town centre.

Entertainment
Help Beach Lounge (Sugar Shack; ☎ 617 0650; 1 Sokak; beer €2.50; ☺ 9am-4am May-Oct) The most happening place in town, this funky joint has a large terrace with a beach bar right on the seafront with comfy cushioned benches. Happy 'hour' (cocktails €5.55) is from 6pm to 8pm.

Getting There & Away
In high season, minibuses leave Fethiye for Ölüdeniz roughly every 10 minutes during the day (€1.65, 25 minutes, 15km), passing through Ovacık and Hisarönü; in low season they go every 30 to 45 minutes.

KAYAKÖY (KARMYLASSOS)
☎ 0252
Called Levissi for much of its history, this ghost town of 2000 **stone houses** (admission €2.75; ☺ 9am-7pm), about 5km west of Hisarönü, was deserted by its mostly Ottoman–Greek inhabitants after WWI and the Turkish War of Independence. The League of Nations supervised an exchange of populations between Turkey and Greece (see p41), with most Greek Muslims coming from Greece to Turkey and most Ottoman Christians moving to Greece. The people of Levissi, most of whom were Orthodox Christians, moved to the outskirts of Athens and founded Nea Levissi there.

As there were far more Ottoman Greeks than Greek Muslims, many of the Turkish towns were left unoccupied after the exchange of populations. Kayaköy, as it is called now, has only a handful of Turkish inhabitants.

With the tourism boom of the 1980s, a development company wanted to restore Kayaköy's stone houses and turn the town into a holiday village. Scenting money, the local inhabitants were delighted, but Turkish artists and architects were alarmed and saw to it that the Ministry of Culture declared Kayaköy (or Kaya as it's called locally) a historic monument, safe from unregulated development. Recently it provided the inspiration for Eskibahçe, the village in Louis de Bernieres' latest blockbuster novel, *Birds Without Wings*.

Two **churches** are still prominent: the Kataponagia in the lower part of the town and the Taxiarkis further up the slope. Both retain some of their painted decoration and black-and-white pebble mosaic floors.

Sleeping & Eating
Villa Rhapsody (☎ 618 0042; www.villarhapsody.com; s/d €25/33.50; ☺ mid-Apr–Oct; ⊠) With a swimming pool set in a rather grand walled garden, this place is friendly and welcoming. Comfortable rooms have balconies overlooking the garden. Atilla and Jeanne, the Dutch-Turkish owners, can also offer advice and sketch maps on walking in the area, as well as organising bike hire. Out of season, call first.

Selçuk Pension (☎ 618 0075; enginselcuk48@hotmail .com; s/d €8/14) Set in flower and veg gardens, the Selçuk has rooms that are spotless, quite spacious and homely; four have lovely views of Kaya. Guests can use the swimming pool of the restaurant next door. You'll pay an additional €2.80 in high season.

Sarniç Café & Restaurant (☎ 618 0118; large meze plate €2.20, mains €6.70-11; ☺ 10am-midnight, closed Mon low season) At the foot of the ruins off the main road about 100m beyond the Selçuk Pension, this is a real find. Located in a characterful 300-year-old stone house, its menu is select, more interesting than most and superb, offering regional dishes made with the freshest local ingredients. Prices are extremely reasonable.

Kaya Wine House (☎ 618 0454; www.kayawinehouse .com; Keçiler Mahallesi; meals around €15; ☺ 11am-midnight) Set in a shaded courtyard within a beautiful old stone house, this is a delightful place for dinner, and the traditional Turkish dishes are delicious.

Getting There & Away

Minibuses run to Fethiye (€1.65, 20 to 30 minutes) every half-hour from mid-June to September, every hour in low season. A taxi costs €14.

To Ölüdeniz, two to three minibuses run daily in high season, or you go to Hisaränü (€1.40, 20 mins) from where minibuses go every 10 minutes to Ölüdeniz. A taxi there costs €14.

You can also walk here from Fethiye in 1½ to 2½ hours, depending on your route. The simplest is following the road that winds up behind Fethiye's fortress.

Alternatively it's about a one-hour walk downhill through pine forest from Hisarönü. For a walk, try the very pretty trail to Ölüdeniz that takes two to 2½ hours (8km).

BUTTERFLY VALLEY & FARALYA

As well as being home to the unique Jersey tiger butterfly, beautiful **Butterfly Valley** (☎ 614 2619; www.butterflyvalley.com) also boasts a 60m-high waterfall (admission €1.25 for day-trippers) a beach, and some lovely walks.

A rocky path that's steep in places winds up a cliff to the village of Faralya, on a terrace above the canyon on the right-hand (south) side of the valley. If you take this, be sure to wear proper shoes and keep to the marked trail (indicated with painted red dots) – an Australian backpacker died here after taking a wrong turn. It usually takes an hour to ascend from the valley, 30 to 40 minutes to descend. There are fixed ropes along the path in the steepest or most dangerous parts. Faralya is on a stage of the Lycian Way walk, which is described on p78.

Faralya is the first village south of Ölüdeniz (12km away) on the Yedi Burun (Seven Capes) coast, one of the last undeveloped stretches of the Turkish Mediterranean – the views across to the sea won't soon be forgotten. Until a road was bulldozed along the steep side of Baba Dağ, the village was largely cut off from the world and the residents had to be self-sufficient.

Sleeping

In Butterfly Valley you can stay at the aptly named **Butterfly Valley** (☎ 0538 511 6454; bungalow with half-board per person €17, tent with half-board per person €14, mattress on beach with half-board per person €11). There are currently five bungalows though another 16 are planned.

The following places are all in Faralya above the valley.

Gül Pansiyon (☎ 642 1145; s/d €11/22) With its firm family feel, here you can join the old ladies for a gossip on the attractive terrace knitting and podding peas. Though the eight rooms are simple, they're very clean and some share a veranda overlooking the valley. A bubbling pond contains trout which can be cooked up for you fast (€7). It's the first pension you come to on the road from Ölüdeniz.

George House (☎ 642 1102; www.georgehouse.net; s/d €11/22; 🖥) Run by a charming family, the George offers mattresses in the family house, in tree houses (tented platforms) or in basic bungalows (at the same price). The home cooking is delicious and ingredients come fresh from the family's organic garden, cows or hives! It has a spring water source and a natural pool and the views are ethereal.

Melisa Pansiyon (☎ 642 1012; melisapan@hotmail .com; s/d €17/28) Next door to the Gül, the Melisa has four well-maintained and cheerful rooms and a pretty terrace overlooking the valley. Mehmet speaks English and is a good source of information. Home-cooked set menus are available for €5.50 to €8.

Die Wassermühle (The Watermill; ☎ 642 1245; www .natur-reisen.de; d per person with half-board €43, ste €65 🖥) This beautiful 150-year-old former wheat mill boasts a hillside setting that commands gorgeous views from its restaurant and pool terraces. The seven 'suites' are spacious and have kitchenettes. The gourmet kitchen serves six courses for dinner. To find it, take the small road heading uphill to the left immediately before the Gül Pansiyon.

Getting There & Away

You can either take a tour to Butterfly Valley from Fethiye (see p355) or Ölüdeniz (p359) or – and particularly if you want to spend the night – you can take the 'water dolmuş' (€2.75 each way), which departs daily from Ölüdeniz May to September at 11am, 2pm and 6pm. From Butterfly Valley to Ölüdeniz, they leave at 10am, 1pm and 5pm.

Besides the rocky path connecting Faralya to Butterfly Valley, there are six minibuses daily (€2.20, 25 minutes, 8km) in summer (three in spring and two in winter) between Faralya and Fethiye. Coming from Fethiye, they call in at the minibus stand in Ölüdeniz 30 minutes later.

TOP FIVE SPOTS SANS SUNBEDS

In the middle of summer it can seem like there isn't an inch of coast not filled with gleaming bodies and beach umbrellas. But if you are discerning and a bit adventurous the following will let you tan without feeling as if you're a sardine:

- **Selimiye** (p341) The yachting set has kept this remote village on the Marmaris Peninsula a secret for far too long.
- **Kabak** (below) Where a mule ride takes on a whole new meaning.
- **Patara Beach** (p366) The world-famous 20km stretch of gorgeous white sand has room enough for most.
- **Kaleköy** (p377) A delightfully secluded hideout with ruins.
- **Çıralı** (p379) The grown-up's Olympos – the same beach, the same mountains, a million miles away.

If you miss the bus, you can take a taxi from either Ölüdeniz or Faralya (€14). You can also get to Faralya by scooter, though the road is steep, twisting and not quite fully asphalted yet.

KABAK
☎ 0252

If you are in search of the Turkey that hasn't been lost to the package-holidaymakers, try Kabak, a remote beach community 8km south of Faralya frequented by a curious mix of expats, trekkers and yoga devotees. The twisting road dug into the steep side of Baba Dağ (Mt Baba) is as memorable for its views as for its knuckle-whitening corners. The beach and almost all of the accommodation is a 25-minute walk from Faralya, which begins about 30m down from the minibus stop. However, most of the camps will send a mule to carry your luggage down.

Kabak is on a section of the Lycian Way walk, described on p78.

Sleeping
All accommodation in Kabak includes half-board and is in tented platforms sometimes misleadingly called 'tree houses' (translated from the Turkish 'wood house'). Most open only from May to October.

Full Moon (☎ 642 1081; platform per person €14; 🛋) Halfway up the hill, the Full Moon boasts a natural swimming pool (fed with mountain spring water) and pleasant platforms that have delightful little cushioned 'verandas' that give glorious views over the bay below. They're also nicely spread out from one another and there's a platformed *köşk* (chill-out area).

Turan Camping (☎ 642 1227; www.turancamping .com; platform with/without balcony €20/17; 🕑 Apr-Oct; 🛋) Run by the dynamic Ece and Ahmet, a young Turkish couple who fell for the place following a holiday here, the Turan has platforms with individuality (one with a tree growing inside!), lovely views and lots of mellow lounging areas. Three-week yoga courses are regularly held here, which guests are welcome to join. Meals (mainly vegetarian) are good too.

Sultan Camp (☎ 642 1238; www.sultancamp.com; platform per person €17) Run by a friendly local family, it offers 12 platforms as well as a tiny bathing pool, veg from its own garden and freshly baked bread daily. Metin, the son, can also take you trekking.

Reflections (☎ 642 1020; www.reflectionscamp.com; own tent/camp tent/platform per person €8/11/14) Built from scratch and an 'ongoing project' for American Chris and his Turkish girlfriend, this characterful place has views of the surrounding forest. The toilet, with ferns and ginger plants for decoration, boast the best views in Turkey!

Eating
Lying at the top of the valley, near the dolmuş stop (and the end of the main road) are a couple of simple restaurants.

Mamma's Restaurant (☎ 642 1071; mains €3.40) Mamma's offers a couple of simple but hearty dishes as well as *gözleme* (€1.10) and its own deliciously refreshing home-brewed *ayran* (yogurt drink, €1.10).

Olive Garden (☎ 642 1083; meze €2.75-4.50; mains €6-7; 🕑 mid-Apr–Oct) You'll find it down a side road 100m beyond Mamma (though she may swear it's closed!). With a heavenly and peaceful setting and gorgeous views from the cosy hillside platforms, it's a wonderful place for a meal. It's run by the friendly Fatih, an ex-chef, and many ingredients come from his family's 15 hectares of fruit trees, olive groves and vegetable gardens. If you can't tear yourself away, it has four wooden cabins (€17 per person with half-board).

Getting There & Away

There are minibuses from Fethiye to Kabak. For more information see Getting There & Away under Butterfly Valley & Faralya, p362.

TLOS

☎ 0252

As one of the oldest and most important cities in ancient Lycia, Tlos' prominence was matched by its promontory: the ancient city had a dramatic setting high on a rocky outcrop. As you climb the winding road to the **ruins** (admission €2.75/free Apr-Oct/Nov-Mar; ☯ 8am-6pm), look for the fortress-topped **acropolis** on the right. What you see is Ottoman-era work but the Lycians had a fort in the same place. Beneath it, reached by narrow paths, are the familiar **rock-cut tombs**, including that of Bellerophon, a pseudo-temple façade carved into the rock face that has a fine bas-relief of the hero riding Pegasus, the winged horse. You can reach the tomb by walking along a streambed, then turning left and climbing a crude ladder.

The **theatre** is 100m further up the road from the ticket kiosk. It's in excellent condition, with most of its marble seating intact, although the stage wall is gone. There's a fine view of the **acropolis** from here. Off to the right of the theatre (as you sit in the centre rows) is an ancient **Lycian sarcophagus** in a farmer's field. The **necropolis** on the path up to the fortress has many stone sarcophagi.

One of the men at the ticket kiosk will offer to guide you (for a tip) – a good idea if you want to see all the rock-cut tombs.

Set in a pretty garden with a stream, a pool, lots of shade, seating areas and birdsong, **Mountain Lodge** (☎ 638 2515; www.themountainlodge.co.uk; r per person €20-31; ☯ Feb-Dec; ☒ ☒) is a peaceful and attractive place designed like an old stone house. Rooms are comfy and homely (rates vary according to size) and there a pool set on a terrace with views. Melahat (Mel) offers home-cooked set menus

(€11). From the theatre, it lies 2km back down the road to the highway and another 2km up a side road; coming by minibus, get off at the village of Güneşli, and walk or hitch the 2km up the road to Yaka Köyü.

Getting There & Away

From Fethiye, minibuses travel to Saklıkent (€1.65) every 20 minutes via Güneşli (Tlos).

If you are driving, follow the signs to Saklıkent from Kayadibi and watch for the yellow ancient monument sign on the left.

SAKLIKENT GORGE

Another 12km after the turn-off to Tlos you will come to the spectacular **Saklıkent Gorge** (adult/student €1.40/0.90 high season, free low season; ☯ 8am-8pm) cut into the Akdağlar Mountains. The gorge is 18km long and so steep and narrow that the sun doesn't penetrate, so the water is icy-cold even in summer.

You approach the gorge along a wooden boardwalk above the river that opens out into a series of wooden platforms suspended above the water, where you can buy and eat trout. From there you wade across the river, hanging onto a rope, and then continue into the gorge proper, sometimes walking in mud, sometimes in the water. Plastic shoes can be hired for €0.85, but you're better off bringing your own shoes with good grip.

Guides can be hired and it's a good place for outdoor activities including canyoning.

Sleeping

Across the river from the car park is **Saklıkent Gorge Camp** (☎ 659 0074; www.saklikentgorge.net; tree house with shared bathroom s/d €11/22, camping per tent €2.75, dm on platform by river half-board €5.55; ☯ Jan-Nov; ☒ ☒), a rustic backpacker-oriented camp

---

SAKLIKENT'S SCAM

Reports have reached us recently of touts hanging around Fethiye's dolmuş station (near the bazaar). They intercept travellers heading to the Saklıkent Camp and, after bundling them into a dolmuş, take the travellers to an expensive restaurant or Yuka Park before returning them again to Fethiye. To prevent this, upon arrival at Fethiye head straight for the dolmuş station and ask the driver of the Saklıkent dolmuş to take you directly to the Camp.

with basic but clean tree houses that have little fridges, as well as a natural pool, bar and restaurant (fresh trout €4.45, *köfte* €5.55).

The camp can organise various activities (which include transport and drinks), including tubing (€11 per person, 45 to 60 minutes), rafting (€11/25 for 45 to 60 minutes/three hours), canyoning (€20/50/100 for trips of six hours/one day/two days and one night, minimum four people), fishing (€8 including guide and equipment, half a day), and trekking (€11, five hours). Also offered are jeep safaris (€28 including lunch and guide) and tours of Tlos (€8) and Patara (€8).

Getting There & Away
Minibuses leave every 15 minutes between Fethiye and Saklıkent (€2.75, 45 minutes).

PINARA
Some 46km southeast of Fethiye, near the village of Eşen, is a turn-off (to the right) for the **Pınara ruins** (admission €1.40), which lie another 6km up in the mountains. Infrequent minibuses from Fethiye (€1.70, one hour) drop you at the start of the Pınara road and you can walk to the site or bargain with the driver to take you all the way.

The road winds through tobacco and corn fields and across irrigation channels for more than 3km to the village of Minare, then takes a sharp left turn to climb the slope. The last 2km or so are extremely steep. If you decide to walk make sure you stock up on water first. There's a café at the foot of the slope and nothing after that.

At the top of the slope is an open parking area and near it a cool, shady, refreshing spring. The guardian will probably appear and offer to show you around the ruins – a good idea as the path around the site (which is always open) is not easy to follow. You should probably tip the guardian.

Pınara was among the most important cities in ancient Lycia, but although the site is vast the actual ruins are not Turkey's most impressive. Instead it's the sheer splendour of the isolated setting that makes the journey so worthwhile.

The sheer column of rock behind the site and the rock walls to its left are honeycombed with **rock-cut tombs**; to reach any of them would take several hours. Other **tombs** are within the ruined city itself. The one called the Royal (or King's) Tomb has particularly fine re-

liefs, including several showing walled cities. Pınara's **theatre** is in good condition, but its **odeum** and **temples** of Apollo, Aphrodite and Athena (with heart-shaped columns) are badly ruined.

The village at Eşen, 3km southeast of the Pınara turn-off, has a few basic restaurants.

SİDYMA
About 4km south of Eşen, a rough dirt road to the left goes 12km to Sidyma, where there are some minor Lycian ruins. The village of Dodurga sits in the centre of the site, with the **acropolis** and a badly damaged **theatre** above it. Many of the old stone houses in the village incorporate building materials from the ancient city. In the village outskirts you'll find the **necropolis**, which has an interesting collection of tombs from the Roman era.

LETOÖN
About 17km south of the Pınara turn-off is the road to Letoön, which, with Xanthos (p366), is a Unesco-designated World Heritage site.

When you get to the **ruins** (admission €1.40; ☉ 8.30am-5pm) a person selling soft drinks and admission tickets will greet you.

Letoön takes its name and importance from a large shrine to Leto, who, according to legend, was loved by Zeus and became the mother of Apollo and Artemis. Unimpressed, Zeus's wife Hera commanded that Leto spend an eternity wandering from country to country. According to local folklore she spent much of this time in Lycia, becoming the Lycian national deity. The federation of Lycian cities then built this very impressive religious sanctuary to worship her. It's possible that the shrine was originally dedicated to the Anatolian Mother Goddess.

The site consists of three **temples** side by side: to Apollo (on the left), Artemis (in the middle) and Leto (on the right). The Temple of Apollo has a fine mosaic showing a lyre and a bow and arrow. The **nymphaeum** is permanently flooded (and inhabited by frogs), which is appropriate as worship of Leto was somehow associated with water. Nearby is a large Hellenistic **theatre** in excellent condition.

Getting There & Away
Driving from Patara, the turn-off is on the right-hand (southwest) side near the village of Kumluova. Turn right off the highway, go 3.2km to a T junction, turn left, then right

after 100m (this turn-off is easy to miss) and proceed 1km to the site through fertile fields and orchards, and past greenhouses full of tomato plants. If you miss the second turn you'll end up in the village's main square.

Minibuses run from Fethiye via Eşen to Kumluova. Get out at the Letoön turn-off.

XANTHOS

At Kınık, 63km from Fethiye, the road crosses a river. Up to the left on a rock outcrop is the ruined city of **Xanthos** (admission €1.40; 8.30am-5pm), once the capital and grandest city of Lycia, with a fine **Roman theatre** and pillar **tombs** with Lycian inscriptions.

It's a short uphill walk to the site. For all its grandeur, Xanthos had a chequered history of wars and destruction. Several times, when besieged by clearly superior enemy forces, the city was destroyed by its own inhabitants. You'll see the theatre with the **agora** opposite but the **acropolis** is badly ruined. As many of the finest sculptures and inscriptions were carted off to the British Museum in 1842, most of the inscriptions and decorations you see today are copies of the originals. However, French excavations in the 1950s have made Xanthos well worth seeing.

Follow the road round to the right to find more attractive **Lycian tombs** cut into the rock face.

Minibuses run to Xanthos from Fethiye and Kaş, and some long-distance buses will stop here if you ask.

PATARA
☎ 0242

The slightly scruffy, rambling village of Patara (Gelemiş) attracts an interesting mix of Turkish and foreign eccentrics. Its ruins come with a bonus in the form of a wonderful white-sand beach some 50m wide and 20km long. While there are plenty of pensions and a few mid-range hotels, traditional village life still goes on here. Transport can be irregular, so hopefully this means it will stay the way it is.

Patara was the birthplace of St Nicholas, the 4th-century Byzantine bishop who later passed into legend as Santa Claus. Before that, Patara was famous for its temple and oracle of Apollo, of which little remains. It was once the major port for eastern Lycia and the Eşen valley, but the harbour silted up in medieval times and became a reedy wetland. St Paul and St Luke once changed boats here.

About 95 of the 110 buildings in the village have been served with a court demolition order, which has put a stop to further development. There are ambitious plans to reconstruct the ruins into a spectacle to rival Ephesus, but don't hold your breath.

Orientation

The Patara turn-off is just east of the village of Ovaköy; from here it's 2km to the village and another 1.5km to the Patara ruins. The beach is a further 1km past the ruins. Between June and October local minibuses trundle down to the beach from the village.

As you come into the village, on your left is a hillside holding various hotels and pensions. A turn to the right at Golden Pension takes you to the village centre, across the valley and up the other side to more pensions and the three-star Hotel Beyhan Patara; go straight on for the beach and ruins.

Sights & Activities
RUINS

Admission to the ruins and beach costs €8, valid for over a week, possibly longer if you remember to wave to the man at the ticket gate every day. Patara's ruins include a triple-arched **triumphal gate** at the entrance to the site with a **necropolis** containing several **Lycian tombs** nearby. Next are the **baths** and much later, a **basilica**.

You can climb to the top of the **theatre**, which backs onto a small hill, for a view of the whole site. On top of the hill are the foundations of a **Temple of Athena** and an unusual circular **cistern**, cut into the rock with a pillar in the middle.

There are also several other **baths**, two **temples** and a **Corinthian temple** by the lake, although the swampy ground may mean they are difficult to approach. Across the lake is a **granary**.

PATARA BEACH

The beach is simply splendid. You can get there by following the road past the ruins, or by turning right at Golden Pension and following the track, which heads for the sand dunes and mimosa bushes along the western side of the archaeological zone. It's about a 30-minute walk, or minibuses run to the beach from the village dolmuş stop (€0.55).

Be sure to bring footwear for crossing the 50m of scorching sand to the water's edge.

and also something for shelter as there are few places to escape the sun. You can rent an umbrella on the beach for €2.75.

Behind the beach, Patara Restaurant provides shade and sustenance. There's also a wooden shack on the sand selling kebaps. The beach closes at dusk as it's a nesting ground for sea turtles. Camping is prohibited.

ÇAYAĞZI BEACH

On the western side of the stream by the access road from the highway to Patara, a sign points the way to Çayağzı Beach 5km away. There are basic beach services and camping facilities.

Tours

Dardanos Travel (☎ 843 5151; www.dardanostravel.com; ⏰ 9am-6pm) offers three-hour horse-riding trips through the Patara dunes (€42) and full-day canoeing trips (with BBQ lunch €25) along the Eşen Stream, ending at Patara Beach.

Sleeping

Zeybek 2 Pension (☎ 843 5141; zeybekpension2@hotmail.com; s/d €11/17; ❄) Rooms, clean, homely and hung with traditional rugs, have lovely views from their balcony, as does the attractive roof terrace that boasts 360-degree vistas of the hills. To get here, follow the road past Dardanos Travel up the hill.

Flower Pension (☎ 843 5164; www.pataraflowerpension.com; s/d €10/17, 2-/3-person apt €22/28; ❄) On the road into town, the Flower is well named with simple, sparkling and well-maintained rooms with balconies overlooking the garden. There's a free shuttle to the beach.

Akay Pension (☎ 843 5055; www.pataraakaypension.com; s/d €9.50/17.50, 4-person apt €33; ❄ 🖳) Run by super-keen-to-please Kazım and family, the pension has well-maintained little rooms and comfortable beds with balconies overlooking orange trees. You pay an extra €2.75 per room for air-con. Mrs Akay does a good breakfast.

Golden Pension (☎ 843 5162; www.goldenpension.com; s/d €14/20; ❄ 🖳) With homely rooms with balconies, a pretty shaded terrace and a friendly family that's not overeager to please, it's peaceful and private. There are also plans for a pool. Arif, the village mayor and owner, can take guests canoeing (€14 per day) or on boat trips (€17) including lunch, and also owns a travel agency.

Mehmet Hotel (☎ 843 5032; www.kircatravel.com; s/d €14/22, 4-/6-person apt €33/67; ❄) Though popular with groups, it lies off the main road, has a

pleasant pool and is good value. It's about 100m beyond the Patara View Point.

Patara View Point Hotel (☎ 843 5184; www.pataraviewpoint.com; s/d €20/33; ⏰ Apr-Oct; ❄ 🖳 🔲) Off the main road, so more tranquil than most, it has a nice swimming pool, an Ottoman-style cushioned terrace and rooms with balconies that have views over the valley. The characterful interior is hung with old farm implements – heirlooms from the owner's grandmother. There's a tractor-shuttle twice a day to and from the beach.

Eating

Lazy Frog (☎ 843 5160; mains €6-9; ⏰ 8am-midnight) With its own kitchen garden, this place offers various veggie options, as well as *gözleme* on its relaxing terrace.

Bread & Water (☎ 843 5080; mains €7-9; ⏰ 8am-midnight May-Sep) Styled like a wood cabin with an attractive terrace, the restaurant's reputable İstanbullu chef creates 'Turkish fare with a modern European twist'. It's fairly upmarket for Patara, but the food is excellent.

Tlos Restaurant (☎ 843 5135; meze €2, mains €4.45-10; ⏰ 8am-midnight Apr-Oct) The Tlos is run by the moustached and smiling Osman, the chef-owner who takes great pride in his kitchen ('fresh, *no* frozen'). The Turkish goulash (€5.55) is particularly recommended. Alcohol is not served. About 50m north of the Golden Pension on the main road into the village.

Drinking

Medusa Bar (☎ 843 5193; beer €1.95; ⏰ 9am-3am Apr-Sep) Styled like an old pub with cushioned benches and walls hung with old photos and posters, it has a fairly eclectic CD collection.

Gypsy Bar (beer €1.95; ⏰ 9am-3am) Tiny but traditional and much loved locally, it has live Turkish music from 10pm to 3am every Monday, Wednesday and Saturday.

Tropic Bar (beer €1.65, ⏰ 11am-3am May-Sep) Patara's sole bar-cum-club, the Tropic has cosy cushions on stone benches around a pleasant open terrace. Happy 'hour' (cocktails €2.75) is from 8pm to 11pm nightly.

Getting There & Away

Buses on the Fethiye–Kaş route drop you on the highway 4km from the village. From here dolmuşes run to the village every 45 minutes.

Three to four minibuses a day run to Fethiye (€3.35) as well as Kalkan (€2.75, 20 minutes, 15km) and Kaş (€4.15, 45 mins, 41km).

KALKAN

☎ 0242

Although it was once an Ottoman-Greek fishing village called Kalamaki, Kalkan is now completely devoted to tourism. Discovered by travellers in the 1980s in search of the simple, cheap, quiet life, this perfect Mediterranean village with its Bohemian air soon boasted a yacht marina, then some modern hotels and finally holiday complexes on the outskirts of town.

Most visitors to Kalkan would describe themselves as 'comfortable'; it is not a haven for backpackers or lager lovers. For independent travellers there are some excellent pensions and hotels to suit all budgets, with an excellent restaurant scene. In winter it turns into a ghost town.

Orientation & Information

Kalkan is built on a steep hillside sloping down to a bay. Coming in from the highway the road zigzags down past a taxi rank, with the PTT, municipality building and banks, to a central car park. It then enters the main commercial area and descends the hill as Hasan Altan Caddesi (also called 6 Sokak).

The local **Internet café** (☎ 844 1670; Hasan Altan Caddesi; ☼ 9am-5pm) is really just a stationery shop with two computer terminals perched outside. It's up the hill diagonally opposite the bus and dolmuş stops. Kalkan has a **website** (www.kalkan.org.tr) instead of a tourist office.

Sleeping

BUDGET

Çelik Pansiyon (☎ 844 2126; Süleyman Yılmaz Caddesi 9; s/d €17/20; 🗙) Though rooms are simple and rather Spartan, they're quite spacious and spotless. Two, attic-like, have a balcony overlooking the rooftops and marina, as does the roof terrace. It's also centrally located.

Holiday Pension (☎ 844 3777; Süleyman Yılmaz Caddesi; d with/without breakfast €22/17) Though rooms are simple, they're spotless and charming, some with old wooden beams, antique lace curtains and delightful balconies with good views. It's run by the charming Ahmet and Şefika, who make delicious breakfast jams.

Türk Evi (☎ 844 3129; www.kalkanturkevi.com; Hasan Altan Caddesi; s €14-25, d €22-33) At the upper end of town this tranquil and charming restored stone house has much atmosphere and character including creaky floorboards, antique furniture and walls hung with pictures painted

by enamoured guests. There's also a stepped terrace shaded by vines and oleander trees and rooms are beautifully furnished. It's great value.

MIDRANGE & TOP END

Zinbad Hotel (☎ 844 3404; www.zinbadhotel.com; Yalıboyu Mahallesi 18; s/d €28/33; ☼ mid-Apr–Nov; 🗙) Around the corner from the Daphne, the Zinbad has cheerful and comfortable rooms sponged Mediterranean blue, some with balconies and sea views. Close to the beach, central and with a large terrace, it's a good choice. Prices rise by €8 per person in high season. Renate, the German manager, offers guests archaeological tours (you pay just for the petrol).

Daphne Pansiyon (☎ 844 2788; daphne_kalkan@hotmail.com; Kocakaya Caddesi; r for 2 or 3 persons €45; 🗙) Near the mosque on the road to the harbour, the Daphne boasts a pleasant roof terrace with a restaurant and lovely views, and rooms attractively decorated with traditional touches and furniture.

Patara Stone House (☎ 844 3622; www.korsankalkan.com; Atatürk Caddesi; d €36-50 depending on season; 🗙) On the waterfront opposite the harbour entrance, it offers just two rooms in a lovely old stone house. Spacious, elegantly decorated and right on the waterfront, they're a great choice.

Villa Mahal (☎ 844 3268; www.villamahal.com; d €120-220; 🗙 🗷) One of the most elegant hotels in Turkey lies on a steep hillside on the western side of Kalkan bay, about 2km from town. The 13 rooms, all individually designed in Mediterranean minimalist fashion, are unspeakably tasteful. All have superb views from the walls of windows that open onto private terraces. The pool suite has its own swimming pool, spectacularly suspended on the edge of the hill. There's a bathing platform by the sea. A taxi from Kalkan costs about €3.

Eating

RESTAURANTS

Belgin's (☎ 844 3614; Hasan Altan Caddesi; mains €6.50-8; ☼ 10am-midnight Apr-Oct) A 150-year-old former olive-oil press, it serves traditional Turkish food at very palatable prices. The speciality is *manti* (Turkish ravioli, €6.65). Despite the faux Ottoman artefacts and stuffed sheep, the roof terrace is very pleasant. There's usually live Turkish music nightly from 8pm to 1am.

Zeki's Restaurant (☎ 844 3884; Kocakaya Caddesi; starters €3-5, mains €9-11; ☼ 10am-midnight May-Nov) Small but chicly decked out right down to the

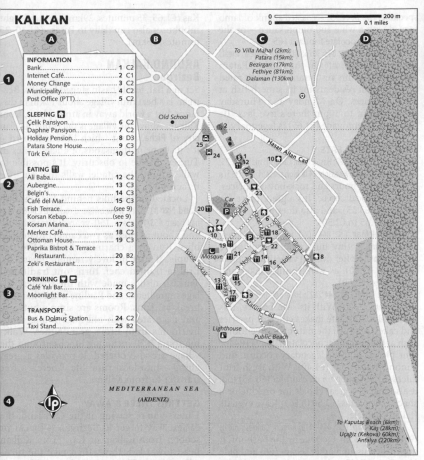

KALKAN

0	200 m
0	0.1 miles

INFORMATION
Bank	1	C2
Internet Café	2	C1
Money Change	3	C2
Municipality	4	C2
Post Office (PTT)	5	C2

SLEEPING
Çelik Pansiyon	6	C2
Daphne Pansiyon	7	C2
Holiday Pension	8	D3
Patara Stone House	9	C3
Türk Evi	10	C2

EATING
Ali Baba	12	C2
Aubergine	13	C3
Belgin's	14	C3
Café del Mar	15	C3
Fish Terrace	(see 9)	
Korsan Kebap	(see 9)	
Korsan Marina	17	C2
Merkez Café	18	C2
Ottoman House	19	C3
Paprika Bistrot & Terrace Restaurant	20	B2
Zeki's Restaurant	21	C3

DRINKING
Café Yalı Bar	22	C3
Moonlight Bar	23	C2

TRANSPORT
Bus & Dolmuş Station	24	C2
Taxi Stand	25	B2

To Villa Mahal (2km);
Patara (15km);
Bezirgan (17km);
Fethiye (81km);
Dalaman (130km)

Old School

Hasan Altan Cad

Car Park

Süleyman Yılmaz Cad

İskele Sokak

Mosque

3 Nolu Sk

4 Nolu Sk

Kocakaya Cad

Atatürk Cad

Lighthouse

Public Beach

MEDITERRANEAN SEA
(AKDENIZ)

To Kaputaş Beach (6km);
Kaş (28km);
Uçağiz (Kekova) 60km);
Antalya (220km)

---

fresh oleander flowers and crisp linen table-cloths, Zeki's does excellent French-Turkish cuisine. It claims to serve 'the best steaks in Kalkan' and its *tarte au chocolat* is much sought-after.

Ottoman House (☎ 844 3667; Kocakaya Caddesi 35; ⏱ 9am-1am) Carpet- and cushion-clad *à l'Ottoman*, this traditional-style restaurant serves excellent Turkish classics such as *testi kebap* (Cappadocean pots containing beef or chicken, broken at your table, €11.50). The attractive roof terrace has good views.

Coast (☎ 844 2971; Yalıboyu 3; ⏱ 9am-midnight Apr-Oct) This new, modern and minimalist place offers superb Turkish dishes with a European twist. Try the speciality, the steak served flaming on a block of hot marble (€14).

Korsan Marina (☎ 844 3622; Kocakaya Caddesi; meze €3-7, mains €9.50-14.50; ⏱ 9.30am-midnight May-Oct) Neighbouring the town beach is one of the oldest (1979) and most consistent restaurants in Kalkan. Its mezes are a speciality (try the mouthwatering *mücver* – courgette fritters), as is the Korsan paella (€11.50).

Aubergine (☎ 844 3332; İskele Sokak; ⏱ 9am-midnight) With tables right on the yacht marina, as well as cosy seats inside, the restaurant is famous for its slow-roasted wild boar (€13), as well as its swordfish fillet served in a creamy vegetable sauce (€13).

Paprika Bistrot & Terrace Restaurant (☎ 844 1136; Yalıboyu 12/B; mains €11-15) Lying opposite the municipal car park, it specialises in meat dishes, which you can eat on its terraces. Try the sumptuous speciality, *incik* (€15) – roasted shank of lamb served with a wine and onion sauce – or the famous hot chocolate fondant (€5.50).

Fish Terrace (☎ 844 3076; Atatürk Caddesi; meals €15; ☷ 9.30am-midnight) On the roof of Patara Stone House, this restaurant is highly rated by long-term residents for its superb fish at pleasing prices. On Monday and Thursday from 8.30pm to 10pm there's live jazz. Its homemade lemonade (€1.65) is legendary.

CAFÉS & QUICK EATS

Ali Baba (☎ 844 3627; Hasan Altan Caddesi; mains €2.75; ☷ 5am-midnight low season, 24 hr high season) With its long opening hours and rock-bottom prices, this is the local choice. It's a great place for breakfast (€3.35), and also does good veggie dishes (€1.65 to €2.50).

Café Del Mar (☎ 844 1068; Hasan Altan Caddesi; ☷ 8am-1am) A tiny but rather sweet place that claims to offer over 70 varieties of coffee (€1.70 to €2.80), as well as milkshakes and smoothies (€2.50).

Merkez Cafe (☎ 844 2823; Hasan Altan Caddesi 17; ☷ 8am-1am May-Oct) With its own bakery, this modest-looking café makes ethereal pastries and cakes, many of them its own inventions, such as the gorgeous chocolate baklava (€4 for four pieces) and the legendary coconut and almond macaroons (€1.40)! With fresh fruit juices (€1.95) and *pain au chocolat* (€0.55) too, it also makes a great choice for brekkie or a snack. The pizzas (€3.50 to €6) please even its Italian clientele.

Korsan Kebap (☎ 844 2116; Atatürk Caddesi; meals €9) With tables on a terrace by the harbour, it does delicious, upmarket kebaps (€6) and pide (€3.85 to €5). Try the speciality, the *dürüm kebap* made with spicy tender steak.

Drinking

Moonlight Bar (☎ 844 3043; Süleyman Yılmaz Caddesi 17; beer €2; ☷ 10am-4am or later mid-Apr–Oct) Kalkan's oldest bar and still its most 'happening', though 95% of people sitting at the tables outside, or on the small dance floor inside, are tourists.

Café Yalı Bar (☎ 844 2417; Hasan Altan Caddesi 19; beer €2; ☷ 1pm-midnight May-Oct) Positioned as it is on a three-road junction, this is a popular place for people-watching.

Getting There & Away

In high season, minibuses connect Kalkan with Fethiye (€3.35, 1½ hours, 81km) and Kaş (€1.65, 35 minutes, 29km). Around eight minibuses also run daily to Patara (€1.40, 25 minutes, 15km).

AROUND KALKAN
Bezirgan

Set in a flat, fertile basin ringed by hills, Bezirgan is a beautiful village about 17km in distance, but a world away in atmosphere, from Kalkan. Above the village is the ruined Lycian city of **Pirha**, about which little is known – it's just one of thousands of ancient sites in Turkey that lie in obscurity. It's possible to walk around the citadel walls that encircle its acropolis.

Located in the hills behind Kalkan, **Owlsland** (☎ 837 5214; www.owlsland.com; s/d €34/68, with half board €53/106) is a 150-year-old farmhouse and about as close as you can get to bucolic bliss. Run by a charming Turkish-Scottish couple, it's set in lovely rambling gardens. Erol, a trained chef, turns out traditional Turkish dishes made with the freshest village ingredients, and Pauline makes her own breakfast jams. Rooms are simple but cosy and decorated with old farm implements, heirlooms from Erol's grandfather. Walking tours (€30 including lunch) around the village are also offered. It provides a great glimpse into local rural life. There's a free transfer to/from Kalkan.

GETTING THERE & AWAY

Unless you're staying at the Owlsland, the easiest way to get to Bezirgan is by car or scooter from Kalkan or Kaş. From Kalkan head towards Fethiye, then take the turn-off to Elmalı. The road climbs steadily, with stunning views across the sea. Eventually you enter the gorge that runs down to the sea at Kaputaş, then at a T-junction turn left and head further up the mountain. Once the road crests the pass you can see Bezirgan below you. Where the road descends to the basin floor there is a turn-off to the left that leads into the village.

Kaputaş

About 7km east of Kalkan and just over 20km west of Kaş, Kaputaş is a striking mountain gorge crossed by a small highway bridge. Below the bridge is a perfect little sandy cove and **beach**, accessible by a long flight of stairs. A dolmuş from Kalkan will take you there in high season for €0.55.

KAŞ

☎ 0242 / pop 7700

Once a place to which political dissidents were sent, the seaside town of Kaş must have been a rather pleasant place of exile. Fishermen bring their catch into the harbour, the locals gather in the shady tea gardens to discuss politics, and wealthy retired Turks, along with the tourists, investigate the shops and boutiques. Watched over by a 500m-high mountain shaped like a human figure lying on its side (Yatan Adam, 'Sleeping Man'), and with the geopolitical oddity of the Greek island of Meis (Kastellorizo) lying offshore, Kaş manages to cling to its distinctive character even today.

The town's appeal doesn't lie in its beaches – the local bays are small and pebbly – but in its excellent array of pensions, restaurants and bars, and its wonderfully mellow atmosphere. For such a relaxed place it is ironic that Kaş is now styling itself the 'Adventure Capital of the Med', but with paragliding, scuba diving and hiking all readily available, as well as fascinating coastal excursions, it makes an ideal base for a few days' strenuous activity.

A well-preserved ancient theatre is about all that's left of ancient Antiphellos, which was the Lycian town here. Above the town several Lycian rock tombs in the sheer rock mountain wall are illuminated at night.

Orientation

The otogar is a few hundred metres uphill north of the town centre; descend the hill along Ataturk Bulvarı to get into the town centre. Cheap pensions are mostly to your right (west), the more expensive hotels to the left (east). At the Merkez Süleyman Çavuş Camii (mosque), turn left to reach the main square, Cumhuriyet Meydanı. İbrahim Serin Caddesi strikes north to the PTT and a bank with an ATM. From the mosque, Likya Caddesi cuts east past lovely shops in restored wooden houses and on past some Lycian rock tombs. Beyond the main square over the hill are more hotels and a small pebble beach.

Turning right at the mosque onto Necip Bey Caddesi and Yaşar Yazici Caddesi takes you to the ancient theatre and a camping ground. Beyond lies the Çukurbağ Peninsula and the narrow stretch of sea to Meis.

Information

There are several banks with ATMs along Atatürk Bulvarı.

Net-C@fé (☎ 836 4505; İbrahim Serin Caddesi 16/B; per hr €0.80; ☺ 9am-1am)

Tourist office (☎ 836 1238; ☺ 8am-noon & 1-7pm May-Oct, to 5pm Nov-Apr) On the main square.

Sights & Activities

ANTIPHELLOS RUINS

Walk up the hill on the street behind (to the east of) the tourist office to reach the **Monument Tomb**, a Lycian sarcophagus mounted on a high base. Kaş was once littered with such sarcophagi but over the years most were broken apart to provide building materials.

The **theatre**, 500m west of the main square, is in very good condition and was restored some time ago. You can walk to the rock tombs in the cliffs above the town. The walk is strenuous so go at a cool time of day.

SWIMMING

For swimming, head for pretty Büyük Çakıl beach. It's clean and just 1.3km from the town centre. Although it's largely pebble-based, there's a few metres of sand at one end where there is free use of parasols and sun beds, as well as a shaded café.

HAMAM

It's small and part of a resort (Hotel Club Phellos), but the mixed bath at the **Phellos Health Club** (☎ 836 1953; Doğrunyol Sokak 4; massage €25) is well worth a visit.

Tours

Several excursions will take you along the coast for cruising and swimming.

The popular three-hour **boat trip** (€12 to €14) to Kekova and Üçağız (see p377 and p376) includes time to see several interesting ruins as well as swimming stops.

Other standard tours go to the Mavi Mağara (Blue Cave), Patara and Kalkan or to Liman Ağzı, Longos and several small nearby islands. There are also overland excursions to Saklıkent Gorge.

You can also charter a boat from the marina in Kaş. A whole day spent around the islands of Kaş should cost between €75 and €100 for the whole boat (for up to eight people).

Good tour companies in Kaş include the following:

Amber Travel (☎ 0242-836 1630; www.ambertravel .com) Run by a British couple, Amber specialises in country-wide itineraries with an intrepid focus. Good option for activities too.

KAŞ

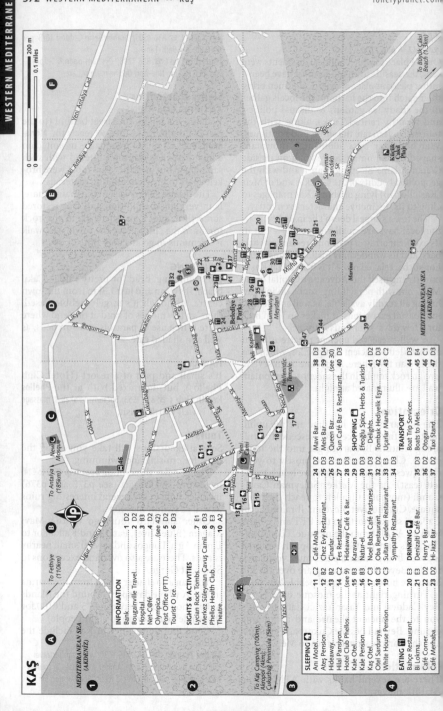

INFORMATION

Bank	1	D2
Bougainville Travel	2	D2
Hospital	3	B3
Net-C@fe	4	D2
Olympica	(see 42)	
Post Office (PTT)	5	D2
Tourist O Ice	6	D3

SIGHTS & ACTIVITIES

Lycian Rock Tombs	7	E1
Merkez Süleyman Çavuş Camii	8	D3
Phellos Health Club	9	E3
Theatre	10	A2

SLEEPING

Anı Motel	11	C2
Ateş Pension	12	B2
Hideaway	13	B2
Hilal Pansiyon	14	C2
Hotel Club Phellos	(see 9)	
Kale Otel	15	B3
Kale Pension	16	B3
Kaş Otel	17	C3
Otel Sardunya	18	C3
White House Pension	19	C3

EATING

Bahçe Restaurant	20	E3
Bi Lokma	21	E3
Café Corner	22	D2
Café Merhaba	23	D2
Café Mola	24	D2
Chez Evy Restaurant	25	D3
Çınarlar	26	D3
Fes Restaurant	27	E3
Hideaway Café & Bar	28	D3
Karavan	29	E3
Natur-el	30	D3
Noel Baba Café Pastanesi	31	D3
Oba Restaurant	32	D2
Sultan Garden Restaurant	33	C2
Sympathy Restaurant	34	D3
Mavi Bar	38	D3
Meis Bar	39	D4
Queen Bar	(see 30)	
Sun Café Bar & Restaurant	40	D3

SHOPPING

Efeoğlu Spice, Herbs & Turkish Delights	41	D2
Tombak Hediyelik Eşya	42	D3
Uçarlar Manar	43	C2

TRANSPORT

Boat Trip Services	44	D3
Boats to Meis	45	E4
Otogar	46	C1
Taxi Stand	47	D3

DRINKING

Denizaltı Café Bar	35	D3
Harry's Bar	36	D2
Hi-Jazz Bar	37	D2

Bougainville Travel (☎ 836 3737; www.bougainville
-turkey.com; İbrahim Serin Caddesi 10) A long-established
English-Turkish tour operator with a good reputation and
much experience in organising activities for travellers; see
below for what is on offer.

Olympica (☎ 836 2049; www.olympicatravel.com;
Ortaokul Sokak 1; ☒ 8.30am-5.30pm) Run by an Austrian-
Turkish team who combine Teutonic efficiency with local
know-how, it specialises in 'build your own activity packages'
according to client's time, interests and budget. The more
activities you book, the cheaper the package.

Festivals & Events

The annual **Kaş Lycia Festival** runs for three days
at the end of June. It features folk-dancing
troupes from around the country and sometimes international acts as well.

Sleeping

BUDGET

Kaş Camping (☎ 836 1050; Yaşar Yazici Caddesi; 2-person
camp sites €11) Situated on an attractive rocky
site 800m west of town, this has long been the
most popular place for camping. The main
draw is the lovely swimming area and bar.

Ateş Pension (☎ 836 1393; www.atespension.com;
Amfi Tiyatro Sokak 3; s/d €11/12.50; ☒ ☐) Well run by
Ahmed and his family, this is a friendly place
with a pleasant roof terrace where BBQs are
sometimes held. Guests also have free use of
the kitchen and internet.

Anı Motel (☎ 836 1791; www.motelani.com; Süleyman Çavuş Caddesi; dm/s/d €5.50/8/14; ☒ ☐) Though
rooms are rather small and Spartan, they're
spotless and have been lent a little charm
with personal touches such as towels folded
to look like bows! All rooms have balconies,
there's a book exchange, and a relaxing roof

terrace with DVD player. Guests can also use
the kitchen.

Hilal Pansiyon (☎ 836 1207; www.korsan-kas.com;
Süleyman Çavuş Caddesi; dm/s/d €5.50/8/17; ☒ ☐) Run
by the friendly Süleyman and family, it offers
similar rooms to the Anı. It also has a plant-
potted terrace where BBQs (€6.65) sometimes
take place. The travel agency below it offers
guests 10% discounts on activities including
kayaking, diving and trips to Saklıkent.

White House Pension (☎ 836 1513; fazisevenz@
hotmail.com; Yeni Cami Caddesi 16; s/d €25/33; ☒ May-Sep)
Decked out in wood, wrought iron, marble
and terracotta paint, this is a stylish little gem
with attractive rooms and a pretty little terrace. Ask for one of the attic rooms with a
balcony.

MIDRANGE

Hideaway (☎ 836 1887; www.kasturkey.com; Amfi Tiyatro
Sokak; s €22, d €28-33; ☒ ☒) Aptly named, the
Hideaway is located at the far end of town and
so is quieter than many. Rooms are simple but
in good order and all have a balcony. There's
a roof terrace with sea views over the water
and amphitheatre, and a pool.

Otel Sardunya (☎ 836 3080; www.sardunyaotel
.com; Necip Bey Caddesi 56; s/d €22/30.50; ☒) Set in a
modern white building, rooms are reasonably
spacious and all have balconies; eight have
direct sea views. The big boon is the verdant
and peaceful seashell-clad restaurant across
the road, where breakfast is served under
mulberry and orange trees a few metres from
the water. Just below, there's a sunbathing
terrace and swimming platform.

Kaş Otel (☎ 836 1271; fax 836 2170; Necip Bey Caddesi
15; s/d €28/34; ☒) One of the best locations,

ALIVE & KAYAKING IN KAŞ

Kaş is a great place for adventure and activities. The sea-kayaking day trips over the Kekova
sunken city are particularly recommended (see the boxed text, p377). All prices include transfers,
guides and lunch. Ask any of the agencies listed (p371) to book you on a trip.

Canoeing €30 per person full day on Patara River. Scheduled trips three times a week.

Canyoning €50 per person for full day.

Mountain biking €36 per person for full day.

Paragliding €100 per person. Flights last 20 to 30 minutes depending on weather.

Scuba diving for qualified divers, €30 per dive including all equipment. For beginners keen to qualify, a three-day
PADI open-water course costs €340 all-inclusive.

Sea kayaking €30 per person for full day all-inclusive.

Bougainville Travel also hires out mountain bikes for €14 per day and canoes (though you'll need
to be qualified) for €20/35 for a single/double.

right above the water: the sea's so close you can hear it lapping from the pleasant terrace or the balconies of the eight simple rooms. The sea views are great too and it's not as noisy as many.

Kale Otel & Pension (☎ 836 4074; hotelkale@hotmail .com; Yeni Cami Caddesi 8; info@guletturkey.com; s/d pension €39/56, s/d hotel €56/77; ❷) Close to the amphitheatre, this well-run hotel offers simple but pleasantly furnished rooms with balconies, many with gorgeous views over the water. Breakfast is an excellent open buffet (the chef cooks omelettes to order in front of you), and you can eat it in the garden overlooking the water. The rooms of the pension are more basic with views set back but are still good value.

Hotel Club Phellos (☎ 836 1953; Doğrunyol Sokak 4; s/d/tr €50/65/85; ❷ ❷) Though something of an eyesore sprawling down the hillside, it's got a great pool overlooking the sea and three-star comfort.

Eating

Kaş has a thriving restaurant scene.

RESTAURANTS

Bi Lokma (☎ 836 3942; Hukumet Caddesi 2; ❷ 9am-midnight) The Bi Lokama has tables meandering around a terraced garden overlooking the harbour. Sabo (Mama) turns out great traditional dishes including *mantı* (€3.90 to €4.40) for which she's well known and Mama's pastries (€3.60). The wine list is also reasonably priced.

Sultan Garden Restaurant (☎ 836 3762; Hükümet Caddesi; meze €1.65-3.35, mains €4.45-6.65; ❷ 10am-midnight) Not yet tried-and-tested but promising much is this restaurant. Specialising in Anatolian-Ottoman cuisine, its dishes are delicious but not at all dear. Try the *içli köfte* (mother-in-law's meatballs) for €3.

Natur-el (☎ 836 2834; Gürsöy Sokak 6; meals €7-10) With its dishes cooked to old Ottoman recipes passed down from generation to generation, Natur-el and the family who run it provides a chance to sample Turkish cuisine at its brilliant best. If you haven't yet eaten *mantı* (Turkish ravioli), then chose from the three varieties (€4.75) here. The Ottoman *hünkar beğendı* (spiced lamb cubes on a bed of smoked aubergine purée) is wonderful.

Sympathy Restaurant (☎ 836 2418; Uzun Çarşı Gürsöy Sokak 11; meals €5-10) Mrs Sevim's cooking is well known locally and attracts a loyal and regular following. Try the delicious aubergine fritters.

Fes Restaurant (☎ 836 3759; Sandıkçı Sokak 3; meze €2.20; ❷ 10am-midnight Apr-Oct) With tables on a peaceful terrace overlooking the harbour, steak (served with enticing sauces) is the speciality (€10) but ask about the daily specials, which are usually superb.

Karavan (☎ 836 3991; Sandıkçı Sokak; ❷ 10.30am-midnight) For something a little different, this place is creative in both its cuisine and presentation.

Bahçe Restaurant (☎ 836 2370; Likya Caddesi 31, meals around €12; ❷ dinner) Up behind the Lycian sarcophagus, it has a pretty garden and serves excellent dishes at decent prices, including a terrific range of mezes (€1.94). The fish in paper (€8.35) has received rave reviews.

Chez Evy Restaurant (☎ 836 1253; Terzi Sokak 2, ❷ 7pm-midnight mid-Apr–Oct) Run by Evy, the restaurant's French namesake, and ex-head chef for a private yacht, this place is unabashedly French *haute cuisine*. It serves superb classics such as *gigot d'agneau* (€17) or *filet de boeuf sauce béarnaise* (€18). If you can, opt to sit in the beautiful and verdant courtyard and listen out for Şahin the parrot, which can be heard whistling for Evy and usually makes a nightly appearance himself!

CAFÉS

Café Mola (☎ 836 7826; Halk Pazan Sokak; ❷ 8am-10pm, A great and inexpensive place for a Turkish breakfast (€3.40) or a snack such as a crêpe or sandwich (€1.70) with coffee or juice.

Noel Baba Café Pastanesi (☎ 836 1225; Cumhuriye Meydanı 1; beer or cappuccino €2, tea €0.60; ❷ 7am-6pm low season, to midnight high season) On the main square, yet not overpriced, this is a favourite local meeting point. With its shaded terrace it also makes a welcome escape from the midday sun.

Café Merhaba (☎ 836 1883; İbrahim Serin Caddes 19; coffee €1.65-2.50; ❷ 9.30am-midnight Mon-Sat mid-April–Oct) Claiming to make the 'best cakes in Kaş', the mellow Merhaba sells delicious confections cooked from natural products. It's not the cheapest place (slices €2.25 to €2.50) but it's the atmosphere you come for. It also stocks one-day-old European and American magazines.

Café Corner (☎ 836 1409; İbrahim Serin Caddesi 20 Long loved by locals and travellers alike, it's the range of food at feasible prices that's the draw, ranging from casseroles (€5 to €7) and salads (€3 to €5) to chips (€2) and omelettes (€3). It's a good place for breakfast (€3.60).

Hideaway Café & Bar (☎ 836 3369; Cumhuriyet Caddesi 16/A; meals around €6-11; 8.30am-3am Apr-Oct) Well named, this enchanting café-garden is hidden from the street and a whole world away from it. Charming owners, Nur and Erdem, are proud of their fresh fare all made with the highest quality local ingredients. On Sunday there's a fabulous eat-all-you-can buffet. At night, lit up with lanterns, it seems truly magical.

QUICK EATS

Oba Restaurant (☎ 836 1687; İbrahim Serin Caddesi 26; meze €1.95, köfte €2.75-3.35, moussaka €2.75) With a pleasant walled terrace under bitter orange trees, the Oba offers tasty Turkish dishes cooked daily by Nuran, the owner's mother. Hearty, tasty and great value, it's simple Turkish home cooking at its best. Try the speciality, köfte – oven-baked or sautéed – or chicken or beef güveç (casserole).

Çinarlar (☎ 836 2860; Mütfü Efendi Sokak 4; pide €2.50-3.35, pizza €3.85-5.55; 8am-1am) Perennially popular among Kaş' young, who come for the affordable pide and pop music, it also has a pleasant courtyard tucked away off the street.

Drinking

Hi-Jazz Bar (☎ 836 1165; Zümrüt Sokak 3; 5pm-3am May-Oct) Run by Yılmaz, a retired New York City taxi driver who has a story or two to tell, this is a mellow little bar with seating inside and out. From mid-June to the end of September, there's live jazz daily from 10pm to 2am.

Mavi Bar (☎ 836 1834; Mütfü Efendi Sokak; 5pm-3am Apr-Oct) Conveniently sited at the far end of the main square the Mavi's permanently packed with people – it was Kaş' favourite when we visited. It plays a good mix of music and has tables outside.

Meis Bar (Liman Sokak 20; 7pm-3am) Newly opened in a lovely old stone house, this place functions as a bar (7pm to 10pm), venue for live music (10pm to 2am) and full-blown nightclub. It's *the* place to be seen currently.

Sun Café Bar Restaurant (☎ 836 1053; Hükümet Caddesi; 9am-3am) With its garden setting next to the Lycian sarcophagus, its décor and lighting, this is a civilised and rather glamorous place for a drink. There's live music nightly (9pm

to midnight in low season, 11pm to 2am in high season).

Queen Bar (☎ 836 1403; Orta Sokak; 4pm-3am) Popular with travellers and locals alike, this place has a lively dance floor on the 1st floor and a more sedentary bar on the second. The friendly DJ, Emin, encourages musical requests!

Denizalti Café Bar ('Submarine'; ☎ 836 1315; Deniz Sokak; beer €1.65; 4.30pm-3am Apr-Oct) Another place for jazz and a 'mean martini' according to one local, it has tables outside, as well as a pleasant terrace that looks out over Atatürk's shoulders across the whole square.

Harry's Bar (☎ 836 1379; İbrahim Serin Caddesi 13; 4pm-2am) English-owned and English-looking, this pub-like place is unashamedly expat, but it gets some traveller traffic too.

Shopping

Kaş has a good selection of little shops selling traditional wares that range from carpets and ceramics to wood-carved furniture and jewellery. Every Friday, there's a market on the Kaş to Fethiye road opposite the marina.

Tombak Hediyelik Eşya (☎ 836 1820; Ortaokul Sokak 1; 8.30am-midnight Apr-Sep) Run by the charming İsmail, who will happily tell you about his wares, the shop sells high-quality Turkish artefacts including İstanbullu coloured-glass lanterns (€14 to €194), intricate inlay work, and good-quality backgammon sets (€11 to €278).

Efeoğlu Spice, Herbs & Turkish Delights (☎ 836 7429; İbrahim Serin Caddesi 16; 9am-8.30pm) If you're keen on culinary keepsakes or looking for a pressie for mamma, then this shop sells all sorts, from mountain tea and strings of dried chillies (*so* urban-chic) to wonderful spices and delicious Turkish delight (€11 per kg).

Uçarlar Manav (☎ 836 3096; 7am-midnight) Come to this place, about 100m northwest of the Belediye Parkı, for gorgeous local honey as well as high-quality fresh fruit.

Getting There & Away

BOAT

Regulations regarding travel to and from Greece change frequently. Be sure to get the latest information from one of Kaş' travel agencies before making plans.

At the time of writing there were no ferries to Rhodes (though they do sail from Marmaris; see p340). You can book tickets here then make your way over.

Ferries do sail daily throughout the year for the Greek island of Meis (Kastellorizo) – though, as it consists of little more than a tiny fishing village and a sprinkle of restaurants, it's not, frankly, a must-do.

Boats leave Kaş daily at 10am (€35 per person return, 30 minutes) and return from Meis at 4pm the same day. Tickets can be bought from any travel agency. When booking with an agency, you'll need to take in your passport 24 hours prior to departure. If you charter your own boat (around €27 per person), you can usually supply passports two hours before the trip. Note also that you can't currently overnight in Meis, nor enter Greece here (go to Rhodes instead). Bizarrely you can enter Turkey through Kaş if coming from Meis. Alternatively, if you can get a group of four or five people together, go for a four- to five-hour day trip with a local boat. Ask the boat captains at the harbour and be prepared to negotiate hard.

If you don't have a multiple-entry visa, you'll need to renew your Turkish visa even for the day trip to Meis. You can usually pick these up at an immigration desk near Customs at Meis.

Note that you can no longer travel to Rhodes from Meis.

BUS
There are daily buses from the Kaş otogar to İstanbul (€30.50, 15 hours) at 6.30am, a nightly one to Ankara (€23.40, 11 hours) at 8.30pm, and two a day to İzmir (€13.35; 8½ hours), at 9.15am and 9pm.

There are also dolmuşes every half-hour to Kalkan (€1.40, 30 minutes, 29km), Olympos (€5, 2½ hours, 109km) and Antalya (€5.55, 3½ hours, 185km) and every hour to Fethiye (€3.90, 2 hours 50 minutes, 110km). Services to Patara (€2.20, 45 minutes, 42km) run every half-hour in high season, hourly in low season.

ÜÇAĞIZ (KEKOVA)
☎ 0242

About 14km east of Kaş, a road leads south for 19km through the scrubby maquis and past farming villages to the tiny outpost of Üçağiz (Three Mouths). This area is regularly visited by day-trippers on boats and yachts from Kaş and Kalkan but you can also stay overnight.

Declared off-limits to development, Üçağiz was until recently an unspoilt Turkish fishing and farming village in an absolutely idyllic setting on a bay amid islands and peninsulas. Nowadays it's becoming an upmarket 'undiscovered hideaway', with prices to match.

Here and there are remnants of ancient Lycian tombs. The little bay is shallow and almost enclosed, but locals don't recommend swimming here as it's not overly clean.

Orientation & Information
The village you enter is Üçağiz, the ancient Teimiussa. Across the water to the east is Kaleköy (Kale), a village on the site of the ancient city of Simena, which is accessible by boat.

South of the villages is a harbour (called Ölüdeniz) and south of that is the channel entrance, shielded from the Mediterranean's occasional fury by a long island named Kekova.

There's a small shop selling groceries in the village centre, opposite an information booth that is open in high summer.

Sleeping
Ekin Hotel Pension (☎ 874 2064; www.ekinhotel.tr.gs; s €11-22, d €19.50-28; ⌘) Run by two brothers, the newer block of the Ekin is the better option, with its pretty roof terrace with panoramic views, and attractive rooms with balconies and sea views. The rooms in the old wing are rather Spartan and dusty.

Onur Pension (☎ 874 2071; www.onurpension.com; s/d €17/22; ⌘ ⌨) With a picturesque setting right above the sea, this well-run pension combines charm with attentive service. It offers free internet access, a free boat service to reach the beaches and a book exchange. Locally born Onur can give great trekking advice and also act as guide. Four of the rooms, kept shipshape by Onur's Dutch wife, Jacqueline, have full sea views.

Kekova Pension (☎ 874 2259; kekovatour@hotmail .com; d €28-33; ⌘) Set on the far end of the waterfront, this is a peaceful and handsome old stone building with a terrace dotted with flowerpots. Rooms are comfortable and share a lovely veranda with views over the water and comfy cushioned benches. There's a free boat service to beaches. Louise is the helpful English manager.

Kordon Restaurant (☎ 874 2067; Üçağiz Köyü; mixed plate meze €3.90, fish per 500g €14; ⌚ 9am-midnight 20 Apr–25 Oct) With an attractive and cool terrace overlooking the marina, and fresh fish served daily, the Kordon is considered the

UNRAVELLING ÜÇAĞIZ (KEKOVA) & KALEKÖY

Given the difficulty of getting to Üçağız (Kekova) and Kaleköy/Simena by public transport, most people end up taking a boat tour of the area from Kaş or Kalkan. A standard boat excursion might start by passing Kekova Island (Kekova Adası).

Along the shore of the island are Byzantine ruins, partly submerged 6m below the sea and called the Sunken City (Batık Şehir). The result of a series of terrible earthquakes during the 2nd century AD, most of what you can still see is said to be the residential part of ancient Simena. Foundations of buildings, staircases and the old harbour can be viewed. Some tour operators have become slack in recent years and cruise rather fast over the most interesting parts. Note, however, that it is now forbidden to stop, photograph or swim around or near the Sunken City (though you can swim around Kekova Island).

Afterwards you have lunch on the boat and then head on to Kaleköy, passing sunken Lycian tombs just offshore. There's usually about an hour to explore Kaleköy and climb up to the eponymous castle. On the way back to Kaş there should be time for another swim. Tours generally leave at 10am and charge around €22 to €25 per person.

The closest you can get to the underwater walls and mosaics is to take a sea-kayaking tour run by one of the travel agencies in Kaş (p371). This superb day excursion, suitable for all fitness levels, also ensures you beat the rush of large tour cruises. A sea-kayaking tour including transfers from Kaş and lunch in Üçağız is €30 per person.

best restaurant in town and its prices are reasonable.

Getting There & Away

Kekova is a tricky place to get to. One dolmuş leaves Antalya for Üçağız daily at 2pm (€5.55). Dolmuşes also run every 40 minutes from Antalya to Demre (€4.44, three hours), from where you can get a taxi (€16.50) to Üçağız. Dolmuşes no longer run from Demre to Üçağız and taking a boat is very expensive.

From Kaş, no dolmuşes run to Üçağız. A taxi (€22) is the only option. However, in summer, you can hitch a lift (€8.35 one way, two hours) with the boat company 'Aquarium' which makes daily tours to Üçağız.

From Kale (Demre), one dolmuş runs daily to Üçağız at 5pm (€2.20, 30 minutes). From Üçağız, dolmuşes leave at 8am.

If you find yourself stuck at Demre, call one of the pensions to see if they can pick you up.

Perhaps the most adventurous – and the simplest – way to get here is by hired scooter from Kaş on a day trip.

KALEKÖY

☎ 0242

Tours from Kaş normally head for the postcard-perfect Kaleköy to see the ruins of ancient **Simena** and the Crusader **fortress** perched above the lovely hamlet. Within the fortress a little theatre is cut into the rock and

nearby are ruins of several temples and public baths, several sarcophagi and Lycian tombs; the **city walls** are visible on the outskirts. It's a delightful spot, also accessible by motorboat from Üçağız (10 minutes) or on foot (45 minutes) along a rough track. There are also several sandy and peaceful spots from where you can swim.

Kaleköy has a couple of pensions, including the well-run **Kale Pansiyon** (☎ 874 2111; kale pansiyon@superonline.com; s/d €33/50; 🏊), closest to the harbour, which has eight homely little rooms all with balconies (with direct views) that are so close to the sea you can hear the water lapping, as well as a nice swimming area. The family also owns the restaurant (set menu with meze, main and beer €14) next door with tables sitting prettily on the pier.

Near the Kale Pansiyon (and owned by the same family) but set back from the harbour is the **Olive Grove** (☎ 874 2234; kalepansiyon@superonline .com; s/d €33/50), freshly christened with the author's help! It's a gorgeous 150-year-old Greek stone house (look out for the lovely mosaic on the veranda) that's almost boutiquey. The four rooms are simple but elegant and share a large veranda with sea views. Amid the cooing doves and ancient olive trees, it's a blissfully peaceful place.

Higher on the hill is the **Mehtap Pansiyon** (☎ 874 2146; www.mehtappansiyon.com; camping per tent €11, s/d €44.50/55.50; 🏊), with spectacular views over the harbour and the Lycian tombs below.

The 200-year-old stone house has a firm family feel (complete with Granny snoozing on the terrace) and is quiet and tranquil. You can either eat at your pension or there are a couple of restaurants on the seafront, all offering similar fare for similar prices. Check out what's currently in favour when you get there.

KALE (DEMRE)

☎ 0242 / pop 14,560

Winding past rocky, scrubby terrain from Kaş, the road descends from the mountains to a fertile river delta, much of it covered in greenhouses, to Kale. Kale was the Roman city of Myra and by the 4th century was important enough to have its own bishop (one of them being St Nicholas of Santa Claus fame). Several centuries before that, St Paul stopped here on his voyage to Rome.

Though Myra had a long history as a religious, commercial and administrative town, Arab raids in the 7th century and the silting of the harbour led to its decline. Today that same silting is the foundation of the town's wealth. The rich alluvial soil supports the intensive greenhouse production of flowers and vegetables – there is even a tomato on the town's coat of arms!

Orientation & Information

Kale sprawls over an alluvial plain. At the centre is the main square, near which are several cheap hotels and restaurants. The street going west from the square to the Church of St Nicholas is Müze Caddesi (also called St Nicholas Caddesi). Going north is Alakent Caddesi, which leads 2km to the Lycian rock tombs of Myra (right). PTT Caddesi (also called Ortaokul Caddesi) heads east to the PTT. The street going south from the square passes the otogar (100m).

Looming above the town on a hilltop to the north is the huge *kale*.

Sights

CHURCH OF ST NICHOLAS

A block west of the main square, the **Church of St Nicholas** (admission €2.75; ☒ 8.30am-7pm May-Oct, to 5.30pm Nov-Apr) was first built in the 3rd century and held the saint's remains after he died in 343. It became a Byzantine basilica when it was restored in 1043. Italian merchants smashed open the sarcophagus in 1087 and carted St Nicholas' bones off to Bari.

Restorations sponsored by Tsar Nicholas I of Russia in 1862 changed the church by building a vaulted ceiling and a belfry. More recent work by Turkish archaeologists was designed to protect it from deterioration.

Not vast like Aya Sofya or brilliant with mosaics like İstanbul's Chora Church (Kariye Museum), the Church of St Nicholas at Kale is, at first, a disappointment, though the remains of Byzantine frescoes and mosaic floors are interesting. What redeems it is the dignity lent it by its age and history.

MYRA

About 2km inland from Kale's main square lie the ruins of **Myra** (admission €2.75; ☒ 7.30am-7pm May-Oct, 8am-5.30pm Nov-Apr), with a striking honeycomb of rock-hewn **Lycian tombs** and a well-preserved **Greco-Roman theatre**, which includes several carved theatrical masks lying in the nearby area. St Nicholas was one of Myra's early bishops and after his death Myra became a popular place of pilgrimage.

A section of the Lycian Way walk begins at Myra. See p80 for more details.

Taxi drivers in town will offer to take you on a tour, but the walk from the main square takes only about 20 minutes and the site is fairly self-explanatory.

ÇAYAĞZI (ANDRIAKE)

About 5km west of Kale's centre is Çayağzı (Stream Mouth), called Andriake by the Romans at a time when the port was an important entrepôt for grain on the sea route between the eastern Mediterranean and Rome.

The **ruins** of the ancient town cover a wide area around the present settlement, which is little more than a dozen boat yards and a beachfront restaurant with decent food and sea views. Some of the land is swampy, so the great **granary** built by Hadrian (finished in AD 139), to the south of the beach access road, can be difficult to reach in wet weather.

Besides the ruins and the 1km-long **beach**, it's interesting to watch the boat builders at work. You can usually find an excursion boat or a taxi boat to Üçağız from here, too.

Occasional dolmuşes run out to Çayağzı from the centre of Kale, but you'll probably have to take a taxi (€5).

Sleeping & Eating

Despite its attractions, Kale doesn't have much accommodation.

Şahin Otel (☎ 871 5687; yusufkamilkolcu@hotmail
.com; Müze Caddesi 2; s/d €14/19.50; ✗) Lying 20m
from the clock tower off the main square, the
hotel is conveniently located even if its rooms
are rather small. It has an enormous shaded
terrace outside.

Hotel Andriake (☎ 871 4640; antriakehotel@hotmail
.com; Finike Caddesi 62; s/d €17/33; ☲) On the main road
at the junction into town stands this standard
provincial three-star. It's rather '70s and impersonal but comfortable enough and has a pool –
albeit not especially clean-looking.

Akdeniz Restaurant (☎ 871 5466; Müze Caddesi;
pide €1.40, köfte €2.75; ☾ 7am-midnight) On the main
square in front of the clock tower, this simple
but spotless place is a local favourite for its
home-style dishes made daily.

Sabancı Pastaneleri (☎ 871 2188; PTT Caddesi 12;
fresh orange juice €0.85, pastries €1.40; ☾ 7am-1am; ✗)
Fabulous for breakfast or a snack. It also does
ice cream (€0.55 per scoop).

Getting There & Away
Buses and dolmuşes travel to Kaş (€1.65,
one hour, 45km) every hour, and to Antalya
(€4.45, 2½ to three hours).

FİNİKE TO OLYMPOS
East of Finike the highway skirts a sand and
pebble **beach** that runs for about 15km. Once
past the long beach, 19km from Finike, the
road transits **Kumluca**, a farming town surrounded by citrus orchards and plastic-roofed
greenhouses, worth visiting on Friday for its
lively market. Kumluca is the nearest town to
Olympos/Çıralı that has banking facilities.

After Kumluca the highway winds back up
into the mountains with an especially good
panorama about 28km from Finike. About
3km later you enter the **Beydağları Sahil National
Park** (Beydağları Sahil Milli Parkı).

OLYMPOS, ÇIRALI & CHIMAERA
☎ 0242
Midway between Kumluca and Tekirova a
roads leads southeast from the main highway
towards Çavuşköy, Olympos and Çıralı, to
Adrasan beach, and to the ruins of ancient
Olympos and the site of the Chimaera, all set
within the glorious Beydağları Sahil Milli Parkı
(Bey Mountains Coastal National Park).

Olympos
The early history of Olympos is shrouded in
mystery. We know that it was an important
Lycian city by the 2nd century BC and that
the Olympians worshipped Hephaestus (Vul-
can), the god of fire. No doubt this veneration
sprang from reverence for the mysterious Chimaera, an eternal flame that still springs from
the earth not far from the city. Along with
the other Lycian coastal cities, Olympos went
into a decline in the 1st century BC. With
the coming of the Romans in the 1st century
AD, things improved, but in the 3rd century
pirate attacks brought impoverishment. In
the Middle Ages, the Venetians, Genoese and
Rhodians built fortresses along the coast (bits
of which still remain) but by the 15th century
the site had been abandoned.

Olympos (admission per day €1.10) is fascinating
not just for its ruins (which are fragmentary
and widely scattered among wild grapevines,
flowering oleander, bay trees, wild figs and
pines), but also for its location, just inland
from a beautiful beach, alongside a stream
that runs through a rocky gorge. The stream
dries to a rivulet in high summer and a ramble
along it, listening to the wind in the trees and
the songs of innumerable birds, is a rare treat,
with never a tour bus in sight.

The site is open all the time but during
daylight hours a custodian collects the fee.

Çıralı
As Ölüdeniz once was, Çıralı still is – a beautiful beach backed by mountains, with an array
of high-quality pensions. Just down the beach
from Olympos, it's an acceptable alternative if you've had your fill of the backpacker
fraternity.

Chimaera
Also known as Yanartaş or Burning Rock,
the Chimaera is a cluster of flames that blaze
spontaneously from crevices on the rocky
slopes of Mt Olympos. This site is the stuff of
legend and it's not difficult to see why ancient
peoples attributed these extraordinary flames
to the breath of a monster – part lion, part
goat and part dragon.

In mythology, Chimaera was the son of
Typhon, himself the fierce and monstrous son
of Gaia, the earth goddess; he was so frightening that Zeus set him on fire and buried
him alive under Mt Etna, thereby creating
the volcano. Chimaera was killed by the hero
Bellerophon on the orders of King Iobates
of Lycia. Bellerophon killed the monster by
aerial bombardment – mounting Pegasus, the

ACTIVE IN OLYMPOS

If all that chilling gets too much, Kadir's Yörük Top Treehouse (below) has an **Adventure Centre** (☎ 892 1316; ⏰ 8.30am-7pm), which offers the following activities (prices are per person):

Boat cruises Full-day trip €20. Minimum eight to 10 people. Includes snorkelling gear and lunch.
Canyoning Full-day trip €28. Includes lunch at trout farm in mountains.
Chimaera Flame Tours €8 for three hours. Departures after dinner at 9pm.
Jeep safaris Full-day trip €22. Includes lunch and transport.
Mountain biking €20 for four hours.
Rock climbing On their natural wall, €14 for two climbs.
Scuba diving €33 for two dives. Qualified divers only. Full-day trip. Includes all equipment and lunch.
Sea-kayaking Half-day trip (noon to 4pm) €17. Includes lunch on beach.
Trekking €17, five hours. Includes lunch.

winged horse, and pouring molten lead into Chimaera's mouth.

Today gas still seeps from the earth and bursts into flame upon contact with the air. The exact composition of the gas is unknown, though it is thought to contain some methane. Although the flames can be extinguished by covering them, they will reignite when uncovered again. In ancient times they were much more vigorous and easily recognised at night by coastal mariners.

These days there are 20 or 30 flames in the main area and a less impressive collection at the top of the hill. The best time to visit is after dark. Various pensions in Olympos run tours here for a modest fee in the evening, but it's worth making the journey in a smaller group to appreciate it in peace and quiet. It's about a 7km walk from Olympos. From Çıralı, follow the road along the hillside marked for the Chimaera until you reach a valley and walk up to a car park. From there it's another 20- to 30-minute climb up a dirt track through the forest (bring a torch) to the site.

Sleeping & Eating

OLYMPOS

Staying in a rustic tree-house camp at Olympos has become one of the most popular backpacker stops in Turkey. Some people love it and stay far longer than they'd anticipated, others feel they're back at school camp and move on. Regardless, the camps have a fine beach, interesting ruins, a fabulous setting in a steep forested valley and, above all, an atmosphere so mellow you may not want to leave.

All the tree-house camps include breakfast and dinner in the price, although drinks are extra. Bathrooms are generally shared,

but many bungalows have their own bathroom and some have air-conditioning. Few tree houses have locks, so store valuables at reception.

Note that it's worth being extra attentive with personal hygiene while staying here. Every year some travellers wind up ill. Unfortunately the huge numbers of visitors, over the summer in particular, can overwhelm the camps' capacity for proper waste disposal, so be vigilant in particular about when, what, where and how you eat.

A dozen or so camps line the track along the valley down to the ruins.

Türkmen Tree Houses (☎ 892 1249; www.turkmen treehouses.com; tree house €10, bungalow with/without bathroom €17/14; ☒ ▣) With a capacity for up to 420 people, this is the biggest camp in Olympos and the only real rival to Kadir regarding party reputations. The tree houses and bungalows are comfortable and the camp claims to serve the best dinner in Olympos. Yacht trips to Kaş can be organised from here.

Kadir's Yörük Top Treehouse (☎ 892 1250; www .kadirstreehouses.com; dm/tree house €8/11, bungalows €17; ☒ ▣) The original tree-house camp that began it all, it just gets ever larger, ever quirkier and ever more fun, with a capacity now for 300. There are three bars (including the very popular Bull Bar) and a new rock-climbing wall. It veritably buzzes with backpackers, but is well managed. It's Adventure Centre (see above) offers a range of activities.

Şaban (☎ 892 1265; www.sabanpansion.com; dm/tree house €8/11, bungalows €14-17; ☒ ▣) The sight of travellers laid out in hammocks snoozing in the shade soon confirms the local lore: that you come here to chill. In the words of the charming manager Meral, 'It's not a party place' and instead sells itself on tranquility.

space, a family feel, and great home cooking. It's an excellent choice for single women (but keep in mind the boxed text, below).

Bayram's (☎ 892 1243; www.bayrams.com; tree house €11, bungalow with/without air-con €17/14; ☒ ☐) Close to the beach, this large camp is run by the friendly Bayram, whose mantra 'Take it easy' about sums up the place. Travellers sit on cushioned benches under orange trees playing backgammon or reading, and the camp has a tangible chilled-out feel.

Caretta Caretta (☎ 892 1292; carettaolympos@hotmail .com; dm/tree house €11/14; bungalow with bathroom €17) Pretty and peaceful with wooden benches under shady orange trees, it also prides itself on its food, which is home-cooked by the family's mother.

Varuna (☎ 892 1347; beer €1.65, mains €3.90-7; ☺ 8am-2.30am) Next to Bayram's, this popular restaurant serves a fair range of snacks and mains including fresh trout (€3.90), *gözleme* (€1.65) and *şiş* kebaps (roast skewered meat, €3 to €4) in some attractive open cabins.

ÇIRALI

Arriving in Çıralı, you cross a small bridge where a few taxis wait to run people back up to the main road. Continue across the bridge and you'll come to a junction in the road disfigured with innumerable signboards – there are about 60 pensions here. Go straight on for the pensions nearest to the path up to the Chimaera. Turn right for the pensions closest to the beach and the Olympos ruins.

Olympia Treehouse & Camping (☎ 8257 311; camp site/tree house per person incl breakfast €5/10) Copying the tree house experience of its namesake, Olympia, but lacking the party atmosphere, this is a pleasant, peaceful place set by the beach amid fruit trees. Boat and snorkelling excursions can be organised.

Myland Nature (☎ 825 7044; www.mylandnature .com; s/d/tr €42/55.50/72; ☒ ☐) Run by a photographer, this is an arty, holistic and laid-back place with 'great vibes' according to some travellers. The spotless bungalows are set around a pretty garden and the food garners high praise. Bikes are available and there are daily boat trips.

Arcadia Hotel (☎ 825 7340; www.arcadiaholiday.com; d with half-board €99; ☒) Escaping over-developing Ölüdeniz, the Canadian-Turkish owners of these four luxury bungalows have established a lovely escape amid verdant gardens at the northern end of the beach, across the road from Myland Nature. The place is well laid out and well managed, and the friendly owners are keen to please. The food at the restaurant is also of a high standard.

Olympos Lodge (☎ 825 7171; www.olymposlodge.com .tr; s/d with half-board €140/175; ☒) Not only situated right on the beach, it also boasts over 1.5 hectares of cool citrus orchards and verdant, manicured gardens. It's professionally managed and the private villas are very peaceful and comfortable. Find it by walking along the beach towards the Olympos ruins.

Getting There & Away

Buses plying the main road between Antalya and Fethiye will drop you or pick you up about 1km further uphill from the turn-off at a roadside restaurant, from where minibuses leave for Çıralı and Olympos.

The first minibus (€1.65, 20 minutes) leaves the restaurant at 8.30am, then they depart every hour on the half-hour until 6.30pm. Returning, minibuses leave Olympos at 9am, then every hour until 7pm. They pick up all along the road, so just stick out your hand to hail one.

Starting from late May, Olympos dolmuşes (€1.25) leave every hour from 9am to 7pm. After October they wait until enough passengers arrive, which can sometimes take a while. Assuming enough people show up, the dolmuş passes all the camps until it reaches the one the driver is paid to stop at.

To Çıralı there are six daily minibuses (€1.25) from May to November, leaving at 9am, 11am, 1pm, 3pm, 5pm and 6pm. Minibuses do a loop along the beach road, then pass the turn-off to the Chimaera and head back along the edge of the hillside.

On Friday there are dolmuşes from Çıralı to Kumluca market.

ADRASAN

☎ 0242

About 10km south along the coast from Olympos is Adrasan, a tiny, little-known coastal resort with a rambling collection of beachfront hotels and pensions. The road runs through the farming village of Çavuşköy, from where it is about 2km to Adrasan. The beach is stark, flanked on two sides by rugged mountains, and seemingly postapocalyptic – remote and exposed – with a row of little restaurants and hotels set back from the water.

The **Ön Otel** (☎ 883 1099; www.onotel.com; s/d €22/33; ⊠ ⊇), an attractive whitewashed building with a lovely pool and a tennis court set amid gorgeous grounds, is a family-run and friendly sort of place. Rooms are simple, but spacious and attractive and all have balcony. There's also a good book collection, and bikes are available.

About 1km back from the beach on the road between Adrasan and Çavuşköy, **Eviniz Pension** (☎ 883 1110; www.eviniz.de; r per person €31; ⊠ May-Nov; ⊠ ⊇) is a boutique hotel that boasts a beautiful pool on a terrace with comfortable, attractive rooms with balconies and distant sea views.

North of the beach along the delightful tree-lined river is a string of restaurants where you eat on wooden platforms set on the water. **Paradise Café Inn** (☎ 883 1267; meals €10-15; ⊠) is an attractive place with a reputation for good food and service and a pleasant atmosphere.

Getting There & Away

To Antalya (€3.90, two hours) three buses leave daily in high season at 7.30am, 11am and 5pm; in low season at 7.30am only. From Antalya two buses leave daily at 9am and 3.30pm in high season; in low season at 3.30pm only.

In high season, boats run from Adrasan beach to Kale and Kaş.

PHASELIS

About 3km north of the Tekirova turn-off, 12km before the turn-off to Kemer and about 56km from Antalya, there is a road marked for Phaselis, a ruined Lycian city on the shore 2km off the highway.

Phaselis was apparently founded by Greek colonists on the border between Lycia and Pamphylia around 334 BC. Its wealth came from being a port for the shipment of timber, rose oil and perfume.

Shaded by pines, the **ruins of Phaselis** (admission €6.25; ⊠ 8am-7pm May-Oct, 9am-5.30pm Nov-Apr) are arranged around three small, perfect bays, each with its own diminutive beach. The ruins are not particularly exciting, and are all from Roman and Byzantine times, but the setting is incomparably romantic.

About 1km from the highway is the site entrance, with a small building where you can buy soft drinks, snacks and souvenirs, use the toilet and visit a one-room museum. The ruins and the shore are another 1km further on.

At the opposite end of the bay to the Phaselis archaeological site, **Sundance Nature Village** (Sundance Camp; ☎ 821 4165; www.sundancecamp .com; camp site/s/d/tr tree houses per person €7/14/12/10, bungalows €20-30) is well named. It's sublimely peaceful with charming bungalows and tree houses shaded under fragrant pine trees. The restaurant offers excellent organic food. BBQs and camp fires are often set up for guests and horses are available for rides (€22 per person for up to three hours).

Getting There & Away

Frequent buses between Kaş and Antalya pass the Phaselis turn-off. To get to Sundance Camp from Antalya, alight at the Tekirova junction, turn left and follow the signs. It's a 20-minute walk from the junction or you can get a taxi.

ANTALYA

☎ 0242 / pop 603,200

Situated directly on the Gulf of Antalya (Antalya Körfezi), this quickly growing epicentre of both ancient history and thoroughly modern Turkish culture has, since the 1960s, become known as a gateway city for the country's so-called 'Turkish Riviera'. Over the past decade sun-worshippers heading to nearby Mediterranean resorts have been laying over in Antalya in such great numbers that the guesthouse industry has experienced astounding growth of its own – by more than 200%, according to tourism officials.

It isn't difficult to discern why: The preserved Roman-Ottoman quarter of Kaleiçi commands a heart-stopping view of the Beydağları (Bey Mountains), as well as the Roman harbour at Kaleiçi's base and the refreshingly clean body of water in between. And although its populace hasn't yet reached the level of urban sophistication found in

İstanbul or Ankara, life here nonetheless pushes forward at a remarkably modern clip. Antalya lays claim to some of Turkey's finest restaurants, one of its most impressive archaeological museums, and some of its best-preserved Ottoman architecture.

History

This area has been inhabited since the earliest times. The oldest artefacts, found in the Karain Cave (Karain Mağarası; p394) 2km inland from Antalya, date back to the Palaeolithic period. As a city, Antalya is not as old as many others that once lined this coast, but it is still prospering while the older ones are dead.

Founded by Attalus II of Pergamum in the 1st century BC, the city was named Attaleia after its founder. When the Pergamene kingdom was bequeathed to Rome, Attaleia became a Roman city. Emperor Hadrian visited here in AD 130 and a triumphal arch (now known as Hadrian's Gate) was built in his honour.

The Byzantines took over from the Romans but in 1207 the Seljuk Turks based in Konya snatched the city from them and gave Antalya a new version of its name, and also its symbol, the Yivle Minare (Grooved Minaret). After the Mongols broke the Seljuk grip on power, Antalya was held for a while by the Turkish Hamidoğulları emirs. It was taken by the Ottomans in 1391.

After WWI the Allies divided up the Ottoman Empire. Italy got Antalya in 1918, but by 1921 Atatürk's armies had put an end to all such foreign holdings.

Orientation

At the centre of the historic city is the Roman harbour, now the yacht marina. Around it is the peaceful historic district called Kaleiçi, which features Ottoman houses sprinkled with Roman ruins. Around Kaleiçi, beyond the ivy-decked Roman walls, is the commercial centre of the city.

Antalya's central landmark and symbol is the Yivli Minare. It stands near the main square, called Kale Kapısı (Fortress Gate), which is marked by an old stone *saat kalesi* (clock tower). The broad plaza with the bombastic equestrian statue of Atatürk is Cumhuriyet Meydanı (Republic Sq).

From Kale Kapısı, Cumhuriyet Caddesi goes west past the tourist office and Turkish Airlines office, then becomes Kenan Evren Bulvarı, which continues for several kilometres to the Antalya Museum and Konyaaltı Plajı, a 10km-long pebble beach.

Northwest from Kale Kapısı, Kazım Özalp Caddesi, formerly Şarampol Caddesi, is a pedestrian way. Antalya's small bazaar is east of Kazım Özalp Caddesi.

East from Kale Kapısı, Ali Cetinkaya Caddesi goes to the airport (10km).

The Gazi Bulvarı *çevreyolu* (ring road) carries long-distance traffic around the city centre. Antalya otogar (Yeni Garaj) is 4km north of the centre on the D650 Hwy.

Information

BOOKSHOPS

Joy Bookstore (Map p386; Fevzi Çakmak Caddesi; ☾ 9am-midnight) Head downstairs to find a limited selection of English-language novels, travel guides and cookbooks. There's a small café selling ice cream and sandwiches on the top-floor balcony.

Owl Bookshop (Map p386; Barbaros Mahallesi, Akarçeşme Sokak 21; ☾ 10am-1pm & 3-7pm Mon-Sat) A small but well-edited selection of new and used English-language books. The owner, Kemal Özkurt, keeps odd hours. Knock with persistence if the shop appears to be closed.

INTERNET ACCESS

There are numerous internet cafés in the alleys and arcades off Atatürk Caddesi, most within easy walking distance of Hadrian's Gate.

Cevher Internet (Map p386; ☾ 9am-midnight) This tiny café offers high-speed access in an alley across the street from Hadrian's Gate.

Natural Internet Cafe (Map p386; ☾ 8am-11pm) Possibly the city's most atmospheric internet café, located within the maze of eateries down the steps behind the Atatürk statue. Next door is the Natural Nargile Café, a cosy spot offering decent food and nargilehs.

INTERNET RESOURCES

About Antalya (www.aboutantalya.net) Historical information about the region and its preserved ancient cities.
Antalya Guide (www.antalyaguide.org) A comprehensive site for visitors with info on everything from climate to TV channels.

MONEY

A number of banks are located on Kazım Özalp Caddesi (Map p384) as are several *döviz* (currency exchange) offices.

POST

There are several post offices within walking distance of Kaleiçi.

Merkez PTT (Map p384; Kenan Evren Buvarı) A few hundred metres past the tourist office and across the street. Use the Seleker tram stop.

TELEPHONES

Turk Telecom (Map p386; Recep Peker Caddesi 4; 8.30am-10.30pm) Call centre near Hadrian's Gate. International calls placed here are generally cheaper than those made with a Turkish calling card.

TOURIST INFORMATION

Tourist office (Map p384; ☎ 241 1747; Yavuz Ozcan Parkı; 8am-7pm) In a small wooden shack tucked behind the souvenir vendors of Yavuz Ozcan Parkı. Ask around if the office is unattended; a staff member is probably nearby. Some employees speak fluent English, German and French.

Sights & Activities

YIVLI MINARE & THE BAZAAR

The **Yivli Minare** (Map p386), downhill from the **clock tower** is a handsome and unique minaret erected by the Seljuk sultan Alaeddin Keykubad I in the early 13th century, next to a church that the sultan had converted to a mosque. It is now the **Güzel Sanatlar Galerisi** (Fine Arts Gallery) with changing exhibits. To its northwest is a **Mevlevi tekke** (whirling dervish monastery), which probably dates from the 13th century; nearby are two **tombs**, those of Zincirkıran Mehmet Bey (built 1377) and the lady Nigar Hatun.

KALEIÇI (OLD ANTALYA)

Go down Uzun Çarşı Sokak, the street opposite the clock tower. On the left is the **Tekeli**

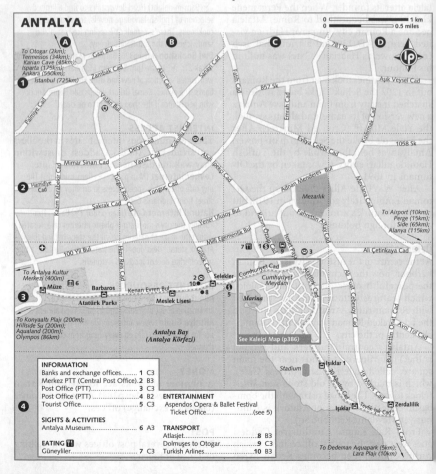

ANTALYA

Mehmet Paşa Camii (Map p386), built by the Beylerbey (Governor of Governors) Tekeli Mehmet Paşa. The building was repaired extensively in 1886 and 1926. Note the beautiful Arabic inscriptions in the coloured tiles above the windows.

Wander further into Kaleiçi, now a historical zone protected from modern development. Many of the gracious old **Ottoman houses** have been restored, then converted to pensions, hotels, or, inevitably, carpet and souvenir shops. The northern part of Kaleiçi is the most touristy; persevere and explore the quieter backstreets abutting Karaalioğlu Parkı.

The **Roman harbour** at the base of the slope was restored during the 1980s and is now a marina for yachts and excursion boats. It was Antalya's lifeline from the 2nd century BC until late in the 20th century, when a new port was constructed about 12km west of the city, at the far end of Konyaaltı Plajı.

In the southern reaches of Kaleiçi is the **Kesik Minare** (Cut Minaret; Map p386; Hesapçı Sokak), a stump of a minaret which marks the ruins of a substantial building. Built originally as a 2nd-century Roman temple, it was converted in the 6th century to the Byzantine Church of the Virgin Mary.

Korkut Camii (Map p386) nearby served the neighborhood's Muslim population until 1896, when it was mostly destroyed by fire. Gates and walls prevent fire now, but it's possible to see bits of Roman and Byzantine marble from outside.

At the southwestern edge of Kaleiçi, on the corner with Karaalioğlu Parkı, rises the **Hıdırlık Kalesi** (Map p386), a 14m-high tower in the ancient walls, which dates from the 1st century AD.

Down Atatürk Caddesi is the monumental marble **Hadriyanüs Kapısı** (Hadrian's Gate, Üçkapılar or the Three Gates, Map p386), erected during the Roman emperor Hadrian's reign (AD 117–38). It leads into Kaleiçi.

Further along Atatürk Caddesi towards the sea is **Karaalioğlu Parkı** (Map p386), a large, attractive, flower-filled park good for a stroll, particularly at sunset.

SUNA & İNAN KIRAÇ KALEIÇI MUSEUM
In the heart of Kaleiçi, just off Hesapçı Sokak, you'll find a **museum** (Map p386; Kocatepe Sokak 25; admission €0.85; ☼ 9am-noon & 1-6pm Thu-Tue). The main building is a lovingly restored Antalya mansion; the 2nd floor contains a very well

done but still somewhat hokey series of life-size dioramas depicting some of the most important rituals and milestones in typical Ottoman lives.

Much more impressive is the collection of Turkish ceramics found in the museum's next building – the former Greek Orthodox church of Aya Yorgo (St George) – which has been so well restored that it's worth seeing in itself.

ANTALYA MUSEUM
Roughly 2km west of the centre and easily reachable by tram (Müze stop) is the **Antalya Museum** (Map p384; Cumhuriyet Caddesi; admission €6; ☼ 9am-7.30pm Tue-Sun), generally regarded as one of the country's most important archaeological collections. Founded in 1919, the museum has only been in its present location since 1972; it was formerly housed in a mosque near the Yivli Minare.

In the first hall is a collection of small works, including finely detailed figurines, which are arranged chronologically from the Stone and Bronze Ages, and then through to the Mycenaean, Classical and Hellenistic periods. Yet while the impressively ancient collection is in an impressively preserved state, visitors approaching museum burnout may not be duly impressed by the displays at first glance. But not to worry: the museum's simply phenomenal collection of priceless treasures lies just ahead, in the Hall of Gods.

Even those not particularly fascinated by Greek mythology will surely be moved by the collection, which includes numerous representations of 16 gods, some in near-perfect condition, and all awe-inspiring. Adding to the experience is a motion detection system that casts a dramatic light upon each statue as a visitor approaches. The vast majority of the statues were found during excavations of the nearby city of Perge in the 1970s; some were uncovered at Aspendos. Viewing the gods either before or after a visit to Perge will certainly enhance your experience there.

The shaded back garden features a collection of artefacts in somewhat deteriorating condition; look out for the curious row of displaced legs and feet.

BEACHES & WATER PARK
Alas, neither of Antalya's two beaches have much to recommend them – at least not as far as silken sand nor paradise views are concerned. **Lara Plajı** is your best bet for

KALEİÇİ

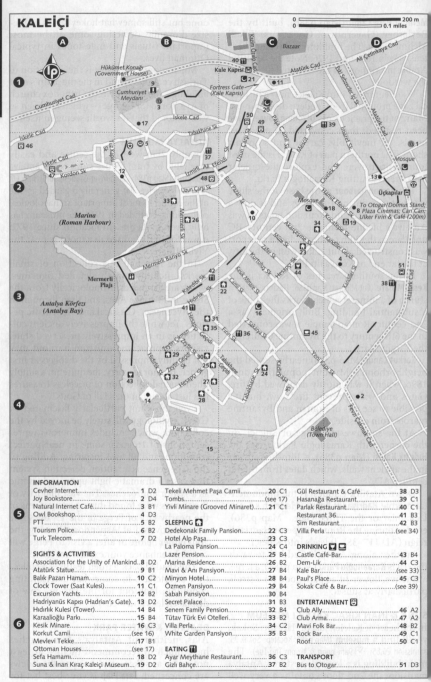

swimming; it's about 12km southeast of the centre. But for a good dose of well-rounded beach culture amusement, head to the much nearer **Konyaaltı Plajı**; it can be accessed by taking the tram to its final stop (Müze), and then walking further west and down the snaking road.

Continue west and you'll come to the **Aqualand** (☎ 249 0900; www.beachpark.com.tr) water park, complete with slides and, yes, live dolphins. Also 6km south of Antalya is the **Dedeman Aquapark** (☎ 316 4400; Dedeman Hotel; Lara Yolu; admission €15; ⏰ 10am-6pm), said to be the largest water park in the Middle East.

Dolmuşes run from Fevzi Çakmak Caddesi to Lara Plajı, passing the aquapark (€0.50).

HAMAMS
The 700-year-old **Balık Pazarı Hamam** (Map p386; ☎ 243 6175; cnr Balık Pazarı Sokak & Paşa Camii Sokak; ⏰ 8am-midnight for men, 8am-9pm for women) saw its latest restoration just four years ago. A bath, a peeling, and a soap and oil massage cost €16, or it's €5 for a bath only. Slightly more atmospheric is the **Sefa Hamam** (Map p386; Kocatepe Sokak 32; ⏰ 9am-11pm). Also restored recently, it boasts 13th-century Seljuk architecture. A bath here costs €6, or €18 for the works.

BOAT & RAFTING TRIPS
Excursion yachts (Map p386) tie up in the Roman harbour in Kaleiçi. Some trips go as far as Kemer, Phaselis, Olympos, Kale (Demre) and Kaş. You can take one-hour (€20) or two-hour (€35) trips or a six-hour voyage (€55 with lunch) which visits the Lower Düden Falls (p392), Gülf of Antalya islands and some beaches for a swim. It's a good idea to ask about lunch when comparing prices; there's a big difference between a sandwich and a three-course seafood feast. Also ask if alcoholic beverages are included.

Many travel agencies in town offer whitewater rafting in the Köprülu Kanyon (see p396).

YOGA SCHOOLS & INSTRUCTION
The **Association for the Unity of Mankind** (Map p386; ☎ 244 5807; Hesapçı Sokak 7) is a yoga, meditation and aerobics studio offering different morning and evening classes daily, as well as classes in group meditation and arts and crafts. A weekly schedule is posted outside the front door. Yoga takes place on Thursdays only, from 10.30am to 11.30am.

Festivals & Events
Antalya is famous for its **Golden Orange Film Festival** (Altın Portakal Film Festivali; http://altinportakal .tursak.org.tr/indexen.php), held in late September or early October.

Sleeping
Although sleeping options are scattered throughout the city, the most welcoming pensions and small hotels are found in the old town of Kaleiçi, an almost vehicle-free district which is also the perfect base from which to explore Antalya's restaurants, nightlife and sights.

BUDGET
To reach Kaleiçi, pass through Hadrian's Gate and walk along Hesapçı Sokak. Kaleiçi's winding streets can be confusing to navigate, although signs pointing the way to most pensions are posted in alleys and on street corners.

Lazer Pension (Map p386; ☎ 242 7194; www.geoci ties.com/lazerpension; Tabakhane Sokak 30; s/d €11/17; ⏰) Right across the street from Sabah, this is one of the cheaper pensions in town. The shaded outdoor garden is comfortably homely, although some of the rooms are a bit shabby around the edges. It's especially popular with Japanese backpackers.

Sabah Pansiyon (Map p386; ☎ 247 5345; www .sabahpansiyon.8m.com; Hesapçı Sokak 60/A; dm/s/d without shower €11/14/19, s/d with shower €14/22; ⏰ ▣) Certainly the most popular backpackers' destination in Kaleiçi, and for good reason: the English-speaking family who operates the place consistently goes out of its way to make guests feel comfortably at home. The shaded courtyard is a perfect spot for hooking up with other travellers, and a wide variety of clean, cosy rooms is available in numerous price ranges. Free wireless internet access is available, and the home-cooked meals are superior to much of what you'll find in local restaurants. Competitive prices on tours and car hire are offered.

Özmen Pansiyon (Map p386; ☎ 241 6505; www.ozmen pension.com; Zeytin Çıkmazı 5; dm/s/d €9/14/22; ⏰ ▣) Not necessarily the cleanest or most comfortable place in town; cheap rates and the massive rooftop patio are the main draws at this backpacker standby, which maintains a decidedly hostel-like vibe. Other plusses: dorm rooms here aren't bunk-bed style, the patio bar frequently fills up after dark, and the enthusiastic, German-speaking owner is quick to share local travel tips.

Senem Family Pension (Map p386; ☎ 247 1752; fax 247 0615; Zeytin Geçidi Sokak 9; s/d €20/25; 🞮) Climb two flights of stairs to reach the outdoor patio and reception area, which has an absolutely stunning view of the bay and often mist-shrouded mountains beyond. Homesick backpackers will feel immediately comfortable here, as Mrs Seval Ünsal (call her 'mama') clearly enjoys doting on guests. Some of the spotless but simple rooms have bay views; rooms without air-conditioning or a view are cheaper.

Dedekonak Family Pansion (Map p386; ☎ 248 5264; Hıdırlık Sokak 13; s/d €14/25) An affordable, super-clean and more upscale alternative to the nearby Özmen Pansiyon. The rooms, with retro French advertising on the walls and satellite TV, aren't terribly impressive, although the outdoor patio with built-in bar more than picks up the slack. Definitely stick around for the evening feast, created nightly by the French-Turkish owners.

Mavi & Ani Pansiyon (Map p386; ☎ 247 0056; www .maviani.com; Tabakhane Sokak 26; s/d €19/28) Something of an odd cross between a restored Ottoman house and Japanese *ryokan*, some rooms sport a mattress laid directly atop raised wooden floors, and the common areas are decorated in Anatolian style. Ask for the single or double rooms with the attached terrace and sea view; they also have a shared refrigerator. Discounts are available for stays longer than three days, and guests can swim free at the nearby Backside Hotel.

MIDRANGE

La Paloma Pansion (Map p386; ☎ 244 8497; www.lapaloma pansion.com; Tabakhane Sokak 3; s/d €35/40; 🞮 🖳 🖵) A somewhat cramped but creatively laid out retreat in a restored Ottoman house. Free wireless access was recently installed, and the rooms – some with Jacuzzi, all with satellite TV – are surprisingly roomy. A few sunken rooms have a pleasing pool view.

Secret Palace (Map p386; ☎ 244 1060; Fırın Sokak 10A; s/d €33/44; 🞮 🖳) It's not really much of a secret – you'll find the back entrance next door to White Garden Pansiyon. What this restored and traditional Turkish house does have is an outdoor garden with orange and tangerine trees, and a kidney-shaped pool. Particularly classy is the outdoor bar complete with marble countertop, and a delightfully

decorated 'oriental corner', ideal for Turkish tea–sipping.

Tütav Turk Evi Otelleri (Map p386; ☎ 248 6591; www .turkeviotelleri.com; Mermerli Sokak 2; s/d €25/45; 🞮 🖳) Because it is comprised of three restored Ottoman guesthouses, this is easily the largest hotel of its type in the area. The pool area, surrounded by the towering harbour wall, is especially charming. Don't be fooled by the rococo lobby detail; the 20 Turkish- and Ottoman-themed rooms are detailed with particularly impressive taste.

Minyon Hotel (Map p386; ☎ 247 1147; www.minyon hotel.com; Tabakhane Sokak 31; s/d €45/55; 🞮 🖳) Staying at this self-described private town house is meant to feel something like staying at the residence of a wealthy and cultured local: heart-stopping antiques and a lobby and pool ringed with tiles are just a few of the artful touches that make life here so decidedly grand. The attention to precise detail extends to the rooms although, for an especially unique stay, request a sea view.

Villa Perla (Map p386; ☎ 248 9793; www.villaperla.com; Hesapçı Sokak 26; s/d €45/60; 🞮 🖳) A wonderfully restored Ottoman house with an atmospheric vibe that feels much more homely and lived-in than upscale. The common areas and 12 rooms (some with Jacuzzi) are outfitted with Turkish carpets, wooden furniture and nargileh pipes. The outdoor garden dining area (see p390) is home to a small pool and bar.

TOP END

Marina Residence (Map p386; ☎ 247 5490; www.marina residence.net; Mermerli Sokak 15; s/d €75/95; 🞮 🖳) An absolute bastion of class, this is clearly one of Antalya's smartest and most modestly posh Ottoman house renovations. The Marina's oddest touch is its outdoor pool; a glass wall on one side allows café patrons a view of the underwater goings-on. All rooms come complete with Jacuzzi and the usual top-end accoutrements. A health centre and sauna are on site.

Hotel Alp Paşa (Map p386; ☎ 247 5676; www.alpPaşa .com; Hesapçı Sokak 30-32; s/d €90/120, with Jacuzzi €120/150; 🞮 🖳) Although it's often packed full with tour groups, a room in this carefully restored 18th-century mansion is well worth booking in advance. The 60 individually designed rooms are fitted out with tasteful Ottoman detail, and the outdoor courtyard, where swimming and dining takes place, displays Roman columns and other artefacts unearthed during the hotel's construction. An on-site *hamam* and an atmospheric stone-walled restaurant featuring an impressive list of French and Turkish wines, round out the amenities.

Hillside Su (☎ 249 0700; www.hillsidesu.com; s/d €160/225; P ⊠ ⊠) One of only three officially designated design hotels in Turkey (the others are in İstanbul and Bodrum), architect Eren Talu's jaw-dropping peon to 1960s minimalism is equal parts modern-art brilliance and pure over-the-top ridiculousness: the entire structure and every last room is a blinding wash of clean white. A sushi bar, a Mediterranean eatery, a health club and a luxurious spa serve beautiful Euro-tourists (and the occasional celebrity).

Eating

A nearly endless assortment of cafés and eateries are tucked in and around the harbour area; those perched over the bay command the highest prices, although the quality of food and service won't necessarily be any better or worse than at restaurants found further inland. For cheap eating, cross over Atatürk Caddesi and poke around deep in the commercial district.

Ulker Fırın & Café (☎ 247 0324; Recep Perker Caddesi 21A; baklava €1.50) Take care not to over-order at this thoroughly modern bakery, which is packed with both traditional and nontraditional Turkish sweets – the tiny pieces of *şöbiyet* (walnut curd) and *fıstıklı* (pistachio) baklava are significantly more filling than they first appear. It's close to Plaza Cinemas.

Can Can Pide Yemek Salonu (☎ 243 2548; Hasim İscan Mahallesi, Arik Caddesi 4A; Adana durum €3; ☻ 9am-11pm Mon-Sat) Dig into fantastically prepared *çorba* (soup), pide and Adana *durum* at prices much lower than you've no doubt encountered in Kaleiçi. With barely enough room inside to bend your elbows, you might want to grab a seat on the pavement. Located diagonally across the street from Plaza Cinemas.

Güneyliler (Map p384; ☎ 241 1117; Elmali Mahallesi 4 No 12; meals €5) With its spare, cafeteria-style interior, this *very* reasonably priced locals-only joint isn't much to look at. But the wood-fired *lahmacun* (Arabic-style pizza) and expertly grilled kebaps are served with so many complimentary extras, you'll likely find yourself returning again and again. If you get lost on the way, ask for directions at the Best Western on Kazım Özlap Caddesi.

Parlak Restaurant (Map p386; ☎ 241 6553; Kazım Özlap Qvenue Zincirlihan 7; meals €5-10) A massive open-air patio favoured by locals and legendary for its grills and skewered fish, Parlak is something of a meat-eater's Mecca. And while hardly a white-tablecloth locale, the restaurant's mighty grill pit is indeed a thing of true beauty, as are the evenly cooked entrées it's been proudly serving for eons. A good choice if you're looking to relax for a while, and just steps away from Kale Kapısı.

Hasanağa Restaurant (Map p386; ☎ 242 8105; Mescit Sokak 15; meals €5-10) Expect to find the garden dining area here absolutely packed on Friday and Saturday nights, when traditional Turkish musicians and folk dancers entertain. Entrées are predictable – *köfte* and mixed grills and such – although the chefs seem to regularly work wonders, and all veggie dishes clock in at around €5.

Restaurant 36 (Map p386; ☎ 244 8661; Hıdırlık Sokak 36; meals around €6) Popular with the backpacker crowd, in part because of its location near to the cheaper pensions, yet also because of its distinctively laid-back vibe. The somewhat international menu offers items like tuna fish salads and omelettes along with the usual mix of mezes, kebaps and grills. Because indoor dining area appears to also be the living room of the owner's home, front patio noshing is recommended.

Gül Restaurant & Café (Map p386; ☎ 247 5126; Kocatepe Sokak 1; meals €5-10) Especially prized by German tourists and love-struck couples, the backyard garden at this intimate eatery is particularly cosy, and shaded by a crop of Antalya's famous orange trees. Portions are small but affordable. Octopus with baked veggies and cheese is €5; an entrée of mushrooms and veggies is €4.

Sim Restaurant (Map p386; ☎ 248 0107; Kaledibi Sokak 7; meals €5-10) A restored and eclectically decorated wood-and-stone house with seating on the second floor. Sure bets here include the *köfte*, *çorba* or *şiş* kebap. When the weather's balmy, leave the Turkish antiques to their own devices and dine underneath the canopy in the narrow passageway at the front.

Ayar Meyhane Restaurant (Map p386; ☎ 244 5203; Hesapçı Sokak 51; meals about €10) With a wide selection of mostly seafood and grilled meat entrées, not to mention a very satisfying wine and liquor list, this is an ideal spot for dining out in large groups. Live classic Ottoman music is performed nightly.

7 Mehmet Restaurant (☎ 238 5200; www.7mehmet .com; Atatürk Kültür Parkı 333; meals €11; ☽ 11am-midnight) One of Antalya's most legendary and highly regarded eateries, 7 Mehmet's spacious indoor and outdoor dining areas sit on the hillside overlooking Konyaaltı Plajı, the city and the bay. The menu of mostly standard grilled entrées and mezes contains some of the most creatively prepared and toothsome food you're likely to encounter anywhere in Turkey.

Gizlı Bahçe (Map p386; ☎ 244 8010; Dizdar Hasan Bey Sokak 1; meals €10-15) A sort of luxury compound featuring two separate restaurants – one Turkish and one Italian – as well as a bar, this is undoubtedly one of Kaleiçi's most dramatically located dining and entertainment spots. The restaurant is almost as lovely to gaze at as the view, and the food (traditional grills, mezes and pasta) and service are equally supreme. Smart dress is encouraged, although prices are kept relatively low.

Villa Perla (Map p386; ☎ 248 9793; Hesapçı Sokak 26; meals €10-15) A small garden restaurant attached to the Villa Perla pension, this relaxing spot comes highly recommended by locals. Try the uniquely prepared meze plate (€8) or any of the surprisingly tasty rabbit-based dishes.

Drinking

Kaleiçi is full to overflowing with options for evening or late-night drinking – everything from cafés with harbour views and affordable cocktails to quaintly modest beer gardens. But beware the quarter's over-the-top discotheques, where drinks are outrageously expensive and Russian and Turkish prostitutes are in full effect.

Castle Café-Bar (Map p386; ☎ 242 3188; beer €1.50; ☽ 10am-midnight) Low-key, affordable, and located close to Kaleiçi's backpacker guesthouses, this is a good place to mix with a younger crowd of Turks than those generally found at bars along the cliff's edge.

Kale Bar (Map p386; ☎ 248 6591; beer €3; ☽ 11am-2am) Attached to the Tütav Turk Evi Hotel and artfully constructed around the old city wall, this is a wonderful choice for quiet evening conversation. But much better is the rooftop patio bar, which may very well own the most spectacular harbour and sea view in all of Antalya.

Dem-Lik (Map p386; ☎ 247 1930; Zafer Sokak 16; beer €2, coffee €1.50; ☽ noon-midnight) Eat and drink with Antalya's hipster contingency here, a pleasant outdoor garden café where rock and blues bands perform on weekends. Conveniently located on one of Kaleiçi's main drags and somewhat hidden by a high wall, this is also a popular meeting place for local students. Meals are about €4.

Paul's Place (Map p386; ☎ 244 6894; www.stpaulcc -turkey.com; Yeni kapı Sokak 24; latte €2.50, smoothie €3; ☽ 10am-6pm Mon-Fri) Because of its location inside the St Paul Cultural Center – ground zero for Antalya's Christian community – some might find an afternoon here tough to stomach. But religious dogma aside, this is an absolute godsend for the homesick: espresso coffee, real filter coffee and home-baked pastries are on offer, as is a fairly well-stocked lending library. And because Turkish language classes and conversation groups happen weekly, this a good place to mix with Antalya's expat community.

Sokak Café & Bar (Map p386; ☎ 243 8041; Mescit Sokak 17; beer €2.50) Like its next-door neighbour, Hasanaga Restaurant (a low stone wall separates the two), every square inch of this café's back garden is covered in a delightful canopy of light-strung trees. Literally. But since Sokak is still the new kid on the block, crowds are generally light. (Might have something to do with the music being *way* too loud.) Otherwise, an acceptable place to kill an evening over cups of çay or, more realistically, glasses of Efes (local beer).

Entertainment
NIGHTCLUBS

Antalya's nightlife seems to revolve largely around its enormous outdoor dance clubs featuring mostly house music and overpriced cocktails. In Kaleiçi there are some bars offering rock music and flavour-of-the-month DJs, as well as restaurants with traditional Turkish and Ottoman musicians.

Club Ally (Map p386; ☎ 244 3000; Selçuk Mahallesi, Musalla Sokak; admission €11) A massive outdoor discotheque complete with seven bars, laser lights, and an eardrum-shattering sound system featuring Top 40 and hip-hop. Club Ally is best experienced late at night, when a sea of beautiful bodies can be found dramatically gyrating around the dance floor's circular bar. An on-site restaurant offers seafood and meat entrées (€8 to €17) with a gorgeous sea view.

Club Arma (Map p386; ☎ 244 9710; www.clubarma .com; Yatlimani 42; admission €6) Formerly known as Club 29, this fantastically garish outdoor disco is built right into the cliffside above the harbour. This may in fact be Antalya's sexiest club in which to watch *gülets* float by while sipping a gin and tonic, but do take care not to fall over the railing or you'll literally end up in the drink.

Mavi Folk Bar (Map p386; ☎ 244 2825; Uzun Çarşi Sokak 58) A laid-back audience of mostly young Turks gathers around the candlelit tables here – a multi-tiered, outdoor bar where Turkish folk musicians take to the stage nightly. The vibe is decidedly low-key, and the bands set up on a stage cut right out of the old stone wall.

Rock Bar (Map p386; Uzun Çarşi) Something of a nonironic throwback to the grunge era, this dark and slightly seedy tavern features local guitar bands playing covers of alt-rock classics. Located down the long alley directly across the street from Mevlana Tours on Uzun Çarşi Sokak; look for the ad-hoc motorcycle parking lot.

Roof (Map p386; Uzun Çarşi Sokak 36; admission €3) The strobe lights inside this cramped 2nd-floor dance club are enough to give you a brain aneurysm, but the music – banging techno and jungle – more than makes up for it. The crowds here are generally small and, although the music is played at a ridiculously high volume, there's an outdoor balcony well suited to conversation.

CINEMA
Plaza Cinemas (☎ 312 6296; Sinan Quarter, Recep Peker Caddesi 22; admission €5) First-run Hollywood blockbusters and the occasional Turkish film are shown at this four-screen cinema, located on the ground floor of a modest shopping centre. Exit Kaleiçi from Hadrian's Gate, walk straight ahead, and look for the large building with 'Antalya 2000' posted across the façade.

THEATRE
Antalya Kültür Merkezi (☎ 238 5444; www.altimpor takal.org.tr; 100 Yıl Bulvarı Atatürk Kültür Parkı İci) West of the city centre, by the Sheraton Hotel, this theatre has an interesting program of cultural events, from opera and ballet to folk dancing and performances by the university choir. Tickets are cheap – never more than €5.

Getting There & Away
AIR
Antalya's small but busy airport is 10km east of the city centre on the Alanya highway. A helpful tourist information desk is located in the lobby; a number of car-hire agencies have counters here as well. **Turkish Airlines** (Map p384; ☎ 243 4383; Cumhuriyet Caddesi 91) has at least eight nonstop daily flights in high season to/from İstanbul and at least two from Ankara. Its office is across the street and two blocks west from the recently relocated tourist office. Across the street is the office of the more affordable **Atlas Jet** (Map p384; ☎ 330 3900, Cumhuriyet Caddesi), which also has daily nonstop flights to/from İstanbul.

SERVICES FROM ANTALYA'S OTOGAR				
Destination	**Fare**	**Duration**	**Distance**	**Frequency (per day)**
Adana	€17	11hr	555km	several buses
Alanya	€5	2hr	115km	every 20 mins in high season
Ankara	€14	8hr	550km	frequent
Bodrum	€16	11hr	600km	once
Denizli (Pamukkale)	€8	4½hr	300km	several
Eğirdir	€6	2½hr	186km	every hr
Fethiye (coastal)	€8	7½hr	295km	several
Fethiye (inland)	€7	4hr	222km	several
Göreme/Ürgüp	€17	10hr	485km	frequent
İzmir	€13	9hr	550km	several
Kaş	€6	4hr	185km	frequent in high season
Kemer	€2	1½hr	35km	every 10 mins
Konya (via Isparta)	€7	6hr	365km	several
Konya (via Akseki)	€6	5hr	349km	several
Marmaris	€15	7hr	590km	a few
Olympos/Çıralı	€3	1½hr	79km	several minibuses & buses
Side/Manavgat	€3	1½hr	65km	every 20 mins in high season

BUS

Antalya's otogar (Yeni Garaj), about 4km north of the city centre, consists of two large terminals fronted by a park. Looking at the otogar from the main highway or its parking lot, the Şehirlerarası Terminalı (Intercity Terminal), which serves long-distance destinations, is on the right. The Provincial Terminal, serving nearby destinations such as Side and Alanya, is on the left. Buses heading to Olympus and Kaş depart from a stop directly across the street from the Sheraton Voyager Hotel.

Getting Around

Antalya's *tramvay* (€0.50) has 10 stops, and provides the simplest way to travel from one end of town to the other. You pay as you board, and exit through the rear door. The tram runs from the Antalya Museum (the stop nearest to Konyaaltı Plajı) along Cumhuriyet Caddesi, Atatürk Caddesi and Isiklar Caddesi.

TO/FROM THE AIRPORT

Havas buses (€5) depart from the Antalya airport every 30 minutes or so. Passengers are conveniently dropped off at Kale Kapısı, just outside Kaleiçi. But to return to the airport, you'll have to get the shuttle outside the Turkish Airlines office on Cumhuriyet Caddesi. (Take the tram to the Selekler stop.)

TO/FROM THE OTOGAR

The blue-and-white Terminal Otobusu 93 (€0.50) heads for Atatürk Caddesi in the town centre every 20 minutes or so from the bus shelter near the taxi stand. To get from Kaleiçi to the otogar, go out of Hadrian's Gate, turn right, and wait at any of the bus stops along Atatürk Caddesi. Look for 'No 93' on the bus stop's marker.

If you're in a hurry, take a dolmuş: go out of Hadrian's Gate, cross Atatürk Caddesi and walk one block towards the large Antalya 2000 building. Follow the constant stream of dolmuş traffic to the nearby glass shelter; most drivers pass the otogar on the highway (just ask). Be sure the driver knows to let you off at the otogar, and be forewarned that you'll need to dart across a wide and busy highway to reach your destination.

Too complicated? A taxi between the otogar and Kaleiçi should cost approximately €7 during the day and €10 at night.

AROUND ANTALYA

Antalya is regularly used as a base for excursions to Phaselis, Termessos, Perge, Aspendos and Side. If you're travelling strictly along the coast, however, substantial time can be saved by visiting Phaselis on your way to or from Olympos or Kaş. Likewise, visiting Perge and Aspendos is easiest when travelling to or from Side or Alanya.

There's a huge array of travel agencies in Antalya's Kaleiçi area, although it's often simpler to book tours at your pension or guesthouse; the vast majority of sleeping options also have agencies attached. Most operate tours to all major sites. The following rates were from Sabah Pensiyon, which seemed to be the most competitive. A half-day tour to the Düden Selalesi (Düden Falls) and Termessos costs €30 per carload. A full-day tour to Perge and Aspendos with side trips to Side and the Manavgat waterfall costs €39. There are plenty of agencies in Antalya hiring out cars for €20 to €30 per day.

Düden Selalesi (Düden Falls)

Less than 10km north of the city centre, the **Yukari Düden Selalesi** (Upper Düden Falls) can be reached by dolmuş from the Antalya dolmuş stand. Within view of the falls is a pleasant park and teahouse. This can be a relaxing spot on a hot summer afternoon, but avoid it on summer weekends when the park is crowded.

Asagi Düden Selalesi (Lower Düden Falls) are down where the Düden Creek meets the Mediterranean at Lara Plajı, southeast of Antalya. Excursion boats (p387) include a visit to the Lower Düden Falls on their rounds of the Gulf of Antalya.

Termessos

Hidden high and deep in a rugged mountain valley, 34km inland from Antalya, lies the ruined but still massive city of **Termessos** (admission €5; 8am-5.30pm). It is believed that the Termessians, a Pisidian people, were fierce and prone to battling. It's known that they successfully fought off Alexander the Great in 333 BC, and that the Romans (perhaps wisely accepted the Termessos' wishes to remain an independent ally in 70 BC.

Certainly one of the best preserved archeological sites in Turkey, Termessos is also magnificently situated: the backdrop of forested mountains against bits and pieces of the ru

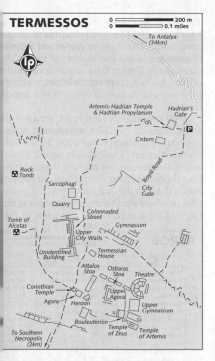

TERMESSOS

To Antalya (34km)

Artemis-Hadrian Temple & Hadrian Propylaeum

Hadrian's Gate

Cistern

Rock Tomb

Sarcophagi

City Gate

Quarry

Colonnaded Street

Tomb of Alcetas

Gymnasium

Upper City Walls

Unidentified Building

Termessian House

Attalos Stoa

Osbaras Stoa

Theatre

Corinthian Temple

Agora

Heroon

Upper Agora

Upper Gymnasium

Bouleuterion

Temple of Zeus

Temple of Artemis

To Southern Necropolis (2km)

---

ined city, especially the somewhat difficult-to-reach theatre, is absolutely majestic. Yet to reach many parts of the city requires much scrambling over loose rocks and up steep paths. Do allow a minimum of two hours to explore; you need closer to four hours if you plan to see everything. Also keep in mind that, on a hot day, Termessos boils over. There's nowhere to buy refreshments, so pack your own water.

The first remains you'll come across are, conveniently enough, located within the car park. The portal on the elevated surface was once the entrance to the **Artemis-Hadrian Temple** and **Hadrian Propyleum**. Next, follow the steep path and glance occasionally to your left, where you see remains of the lower city walls and the city gate before reaching the **lower gymnasium** and **colonnaded street**, which leads to the **quarry** and some **sarcophagi**. It's a full hour's walk all the way to the southern necropolis with a detour to the **upper agora** and its five large partitions. The upper agora is an ideal spot to explore slowly, and in which to catch a bit of shade. Next, push on to the nearby **theatre**, which sits in an absolutely

jaw-dropping locale atop a peak, surrounded by a mountain range that seems remarkably closer than it actually is. Return from the temple to view the cut-limestone **bouleuterion**, but use caution when scrambling across the crumbled **Temple of Artemis** and **Temple of Zeus** south of it. Both are in a fairly sorry state of disrepair, although the Temple of Zeus does offer a rather pleasant view.

The **southern necropolis** (*mezarlik*) is at the very top of the valley, 3km up from the car park. Viewed from afar, it's a rather disturbing scene of still-intact sarcophagi that seem to have been tossed intermittently from the mountainside by angry gods. In reality, earthquakes and grave robbers created the mess. There isn't much to see at the nearby **tomb of Alcetas** (head back to the main path, take a left and follow the signs), but continue on to encounter a magnificent set of **rock-hewn tombs** before returning to the car park. Free Termessos city plan maps are available for the asking at the ticket booth.

The **Güllük Dağı National Park** is also quite nice to drive through. While hiking through the steep canyon walls, some of as high as 600m, keep a lookout for mountain goats, fallow deer, golden eagles, and other wild and endangered animals. You'll need to pay a separate park admission fee (€4) at the entrance, which is also where you'll find the Flora & Fauna Museum, which contains a bit of information about the ruined city, as well as about the botany and zoology of the immediate area.

GETTING THERE & AWAY

Taxi tours from Antalya cost around €35. A cheaper option is to catch a Korkuteli-bound bus to the entrance of Güllük Dağı National Park where, in summer, taxis wait to run you up the Termessos road and back for €10.

If you're driving, leave Antalya by the highway towards Burdur and Isparta, turning left after about 11km onto E87/D350, the road marked for Korkuteli, Denizli and Muğla. About 25km from Antalya, look for a road on the right marked for Karian.

Just after the Karian road, look on the left for the entrance to the national park. Continue another 9km up the road to the ruins. The road winds up through several gates in the city walls to the lower agora and car park, the largest flat space in this steep valley. From here on you must explore the ruins on foot.

Karain Cave

A simply astounding site and one of the more unusual locales in this region of the Turkish Mediterranean, the Karain Mağarası (Karain Cave) is believed by archaeologists (who first excavated the site between 1946 and 1973) to have been continuously occupied for 25,000 years. Much of what was discovered, including stone hand-axes and arrowheads, now resides in Antalya's archaeology museum and in the Museum of Anatolian Civilizations in Ankara. Bone fragments of Neanderthal man were also found. The largest fragment found belonged to the skull of a child. An on-site **museum** (admission €1, ☻ 8am-6pm) has an interesting collection of animal bones and teeth that were found in the cave.

Expect to spend about 15 minutes trekking from the museum to the cave. Once you've arrived, look for the somewhat disturbing relief mask of a human face, which is carved on the central pillar of the main inner room.

GETTING THERE & AWAY

Karain is difficult to reach by public transport. With your own car you can visit Termessos and Karain in the same day; a taxi tour combining the two costs around €40. Descending from Termessos, take the Karain road just outside the national park. After 1.4km the road forks; take either road – they rejoin at 4km. At 8km, turn left (there's a sign) and continue 3km to Karain.

Coming from Antalya by car the highway to Burdur and Isparta, pass the road on the left to Korkuteli, Denizli and Muğla, and take the next road on the left marked for Yeşilbayır, Yenikoy and Karain.

Perge

Now little more than a ruined site that can easily be explored in an hour, **Perge** (admission €6; ☻ 9am-7.30pm), 15km east of Antalya and 2km north of Aksu, was one of the most important towns of ancient Pamphylia. Perge experienced its Golden Age during the 2nd and 3rd centuries BC, under the Romans; the town surrendered to Alexander the Great in 334 BC. Turkish archaeologists first began a series of excavations here in 1947, and a selection of the statues uncovered – many in magnificent condition – can be seen at the Antalya Museum.

Before approaching the site proper, the **theatre** (capacity 15,000) and **stadium** (capacity 12,000) appear along the access road. Both have been closed for some time due to unsafe conditions. The massive **Roman and Hellinistic gates** are found just inside the site. Walk through the Roman Gate, which is curiously off axis, to reach the **colonnaded street**, where an impressive collection of columns still stands erect.

Stroll the length of the street, which ends at the fantastic northern **nymphaeum**; it was responsible for supplying water to the colonnaded street. Look closely at the street, and notice the narrow concave channel running down the centre. From the nymphaeum, which dates to the 2nd century AD, it's possible to follow a path through the brush to the ridge of the acropolis hill. The ruins in this

PERGE

0 — 200 m
0 — 0.1 miles

SIGHTS & ACTIVITIES		
Ticket Booth	1	B4
Later Southern City Wall	2	A4
Stadium	3	A4
Theatre	4	A4
Tomb of Plancia Magna	5	B4
Later City Gate	6	B4
Southern Nyphaeum	7	A4
Eastern Basilica	8	B4
Agora	9	B3
Hellenistic Triumphal Gate	10	B3
Propylaeum & Southern Baths	11	A3
Colonnaded Street	12	B3
City Wall	13	A3
Colonnaded Street	14	A3
Northern Basilica	15	A3
Northern Baths	16	A3
Colonnaded Street	17	B3
Palaestra	18	A2
Colonnaded Street	19	A2
Northern Nymphaeum	20	B2
Water Canal	21	B2
Acropolis	22	B2

To Highway (2km);
Aksu (2km)

part of the city date from the Byzantine era, when many of the city's inhabitants relocated here after attacks from invaders on the flat land below.

GETTING THERE & AWAY

A visit to Perge can be included in the trip eastwards to Aspendos and Side, doing it all in a day if you're pressed for time. Leave early in the morning.

Dolmuşes leave for Aksu from the Antalya otogar. Ride the 13km east from Antalya to Aksu and the turn-off for Perge, then walk (20 to 25 minutes) or hitch the remaining 2km to the ruins. You can include Perge in a taxi tour to Aspendos for €50.

Silyon

About 7km east of Perge are the remains of Silyon, a thriving city when Alexander the Great came through in the 4th century BC. Unable to take the city, the conqueror left it and passed on. The greatest curiosity here is an inscription in the Pamphylian dialect of ancient Greek, a unique example of this little-seen language.

The ruins are difficult to reach without your own vehicle. Despite the sign saying 'Silyon 8km' on the highway, it is further: 7.2km to another right turn (unmarked); go 900m and bear left, then another 100m and turn left at a farm. The ruins are visible 1km further along.

Aspendos

With the possible exception of the serious student of archaeology, visitors largely journey to **Aspendos** (Belkis; admission €6, parking €2; ☯ 8am-7pm) with one solitary objective in mind: to view the ancient city's awe-inspiring **theatre**, generally agreed to be the finest structure of its type in all of Anatolia, and the best-preserved Roman theatre of the ancient world.

The structure was constructed by the Romans during the reign of Emperor Marcus Aurelius (AD 161–80), and restored during the 13th century. Yet while the Golden Age of Aspendos stretched only from the 2nd to 3rd centuries AD, the history of the city goes all the way back to the Hittite Empire (800 BC). In 486 BC a battle took place here between the Greeks and the Persians in which the Greeks were victorious.

The theatre, which had rested in a state of ruin for eons, was brought back to life by none other than Atatürk himself. After a tour of the region in the early 1930s, he declared it too fine an example of historical architecture to not be in use. Following a restoration that many purists weren't entirely pleased with (some questioned the authenticity of the project) the theatre continues to stage operas, concerts and folklore festivals even today.

Should your schedule allow a visit to any event happening at Aspendos, take advantage of the opportunity. What with the stadium's unique acoustics and lighting that radically changes the atmosphere of the stadium once night falls, the experience of listening to live music here must be remarkably similar to the experience one might have had 2000 years ago.

When leaving the theatre, follow the path on the left marked for Theatre Hill. If you're willing to hack through overgrown thornbushes, you'll be rewarded with a phenomenal view of the theatre, the surrounding farm land and the Taurus Mountains. Follow the 'Aqueduct' fork in the trail for a good look at the remains of the city's **aqueduct** and of the modern village to the left of it. You can also follow the unpaved road north for 1km for fine views of the aqueduct.

The ruins of the ancient city are extensive and include a stadium, agora and basilica, but they offer little to look at. Follow the aqueduct trail along the ridge to reach them.

FESTIVALS & EVENTS

The internationally regarded **Aspendos Opera & Ballet Festival** is held in the Roman theatre from mid-June to early July. Tickets can be bought at the office near to the tourist office in Antalya, from the office at the theatre in Side and from the Side museum (see p399).

GETTING THERE & AWAY

Aspendos lies 47km east of Antalya. If you are driving, go as far as the Köprü Creek, and notice the old Seljuk humpback bridge. Turn left (north) along the western bank of the creek, following the signs to Aspendos.

Minibuses to Manavgat drop you at the Aspendos turn-off, from where you can walk (45 minutes) or hitch the remaining 4km to the site. Taxis waiting at the highway junction will take you to the theatre for an outrageous €6, or you can take a taxi tour from Antalya for €45, perhaps stopping in Perge along the way.

Selge (Zerk) & Köprülü Kanyon

Perhaps one of the most exciting surprises offered by a visit to the ruined Roman city of Selge takes place about 12km before the town itself has even been reached. This is where you'll discover a dramatically arched Roman bridge spanning a deep canyon with the Köprü Irmağı (Bridge River) at its base; the bridge has been in service for close to 2000 years.

The ruins of Selge are scattered about the village of Altınkaya, and with the Taurus Mountains acting as a backdrop, the setting is particularly powerful.

As you wander through the village and its ruins, consider that Selge once boasted a population as large as 20,000. This may have had something to do with the fact that, for the majority of its existence, Selge was never sacked by any invader and the Selgians were never made the subjects of any other nation. Because of the city's mountain-top location, an enclosed wall, and its surrounding ravines and bridges, approaching undetected wasn't a simple task. Nevertheless, the Romans eventually took hold of the territory, which survived into the Byzantine era.

About 350m of the wall still exists, and along with it a tower and a small building that is thought to be a customs house.

ACTIVITIES

Villagers can guide you on **hikes** up from Köprülü Kanyon (Bridge Canyon) along the original Roman road, about two hours up (1½ hours down), for about €11 each way. They can also arrange mountain treks for groups to Mt Bozburun (2504m) and other points in the Kuyucuk Dağları (Kuyucuk Range), with a guide *katırcı* (muleteer) and *yemekçi* (cook)

for about €60 per day. Details of a three-day walk through the Köprülü Kanyon on the St Paul's Trail are featured on p81.

Numerous agencies in Antalya offer **rafting trips** in the canyon. The best-value deals are about €20 to €25 per person for a four-to five-hour ride on the river, plus time for swimming.

GETTING THERE & AWAY

Köprülü Kanyon Milli Parkı and Selge are included in tours from Antalya, Side and Alanya for about €30 per person. If you'd rather do it independently, the one daily minibus departs from Antalya's otogar in the morning for Altınkaya (two hours, €6), returning to Antalya in the evening.

With your own vehicle, you can visit in half a day, though it deserves a lot more time. The turn-off to Selge and Köprülü Kanyon is about 5km east of the Aspendos road (48km east of Antalya) along the main highway.

The road is paved for the first 33km. Then about 4km before the town of Beşkonak, the road divides, with the left fork marked for Altınkaya, the right for Beşkonak. If you take the Altınkaya road along the river's western bank, you'll pass Medraft Outdoor Camp, Oncu Turizm Air Raft camp, Selge Restaurant & Pension and Kanyon Restaurant & Pension, at the river's edge. About 11km from the turn-off is the graceful old Ottoman Oluk bridge.

If instead you follow the road through Beşkonak, it's 6.5km from that village to the canyon and the bridge. The unpaved road on the western bank of the river marked for Altınkaya or Zerk (the Turkish name for Selge) climbs 12km from the bridge to the village through ever more dramatic scenery.

Eastern Mediterranean

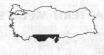

Turkey's Eastern Mediterranean means different things to different people. For holidaying Europeans, it's a radiant and razzle-dazzle beach paradise, with the calm ocean and high-rise resorts around Side and Alanya stretching further than the eye can see. Sometimes referred to as the Turkish Riviera, this part of the Eastern Med tends to fill up to an almost unbearable degree during the high season. But arrive just before or after the crowds, and you'll find largely empty beaches and discounted guesthouses. To get a feel for how the Turks themselves holiday, make your way through the rugged and twisting mountain range to the east and head towards the resort areas of Anamur and Kızkalesi. Visiting Turks – and Western archaeology students – treat this part of the country as an open-air museum, because of the massive amount of impressive ruins scattered about.

Once the craggy mountain range flattens out into the wide-open Cukurova Plain to the east, the cities become much larger, more metropolitan and more imposing. Tourists are almost nonexistent in the large industrial cities of Merlin, Adana and İskenderun. However, those who do choose to brave the urban hustle are rewarded with rarely visited nearby sites, such as the Roman fortress city of Anazarbus, just northeast of Adana. The Armenian retreat of Yılankale is also close, as are a number of important Hittite and Christian sites.

The vibe and energy of the Eastern Mediterranean takes on a considerable change south of İskenderun, due to the area's proximity to the Syrian border. Here is one of Turkey's most fascinating mixes of cultures, religions and languages. In towns such as Antakya you'll find Sunnis, Alevis and Orthodox Christians living side by side, and spoken Arabic can still be heard on the streets.

HIGHLIGHTS

- Visit Side's romantic **Temple of Apollo** (p399) at sunset
- Descend the 452 steps into the massive **Chasm of Heaven** (p421), where the monster Typhon was said to have held Zeus captive
- Swim or take a ferry ride out to **Maiden's Castle** (p422) at Kızkalesi
- Visit Adana's extravagantly beautiful **Sabancı Merkez Cami** (p427), the country's second-largest mosque
- Enjoy the first syrupy bite of an oven-hot piece of *künefe* with a *çay* (tea) and a chat with the locals in **Antakya** (p436)

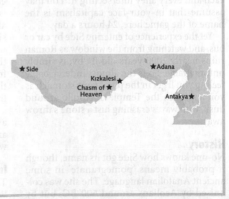

EASTERN MEDITERRANEAN

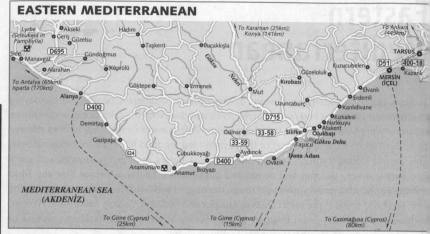

EASTERN MEDITERRANEAN

SİDE

☎ 0242 / pop 18,000

If it were possible for a town to have an identity crisis, the small city of Side (*see*-deh) would undoubtedly be among the afflicted. After all, it wasn't long ago that Side was essentially thought of as a worn-out fishing village, with little more to boast about than a passable stretch of beach and a decent collection of Hellenistic ruins. But things have changed, big-time. Side today is the sort of flash Mediterranean resort town that many intrepid travellers love to hate.

Having long ago deserted its principle industry, fishing, Side has embraced tourist harvesting with a vengeance. An astoundingly large number of souvenir shops have monopolised the city's main drag, as well as each and every alley intersecting it. You may assume that in-your-face capitalism is the name of the game here, 24 hours a day.

Yet the experience of entering Side by car or bus, and watching from the window as Roman ruins nearly 2000 years old fly by, is simply unforgettable. So is the almost indescribable feeling you'll get in the pit of your stomach as you approach the Temple of Apollo around dusk, with waves crashing just a stone's throw away.

History

No-one knows how Side got its name, though it probably means 'pomegranate' in some ancient Anatolian language. The site was colonised by Aeolians around 600 BC, but by the time Alexander the Great swept through, the inhabitants had abandoned much of their Greek culture and language.

Many of Side's great buildings were built from the profits of piracy and slavery, which flourished under the Greeks, only to be stopped when the city came under Roman control. After that, Side managed to prosper from legitimate commerce; under the Byzantines it was still large enough to rate a bishop. The 7th-century Arab raids diminished the town, which was dead within two centuries. During the late 19th century it had a brief flowering under Ottoman rule when it was settled by Muslims from Crete.

Orientation

Side is set on a promontory, 3km south of the east–west coastal highway. Vehicular access is tightly controlled; if you're driving you'll almost certainly have to use the car park outside the village.

The main street, Liman Caddesi, cuts through the village to the harbour, which is fronted by a bust of Atatürk. On either side of the promontory are small beaches, although the main beach is in the north of town.

The otogar (bus station) is east of the archaeological zone. Follow signs for the tramway and you'll find the main road. Turn left if you want to walk, or board the tram (€0.30).

Information

The **tourist office** (☎ 753 1265; ⏰ 8am-noon & 1-5pm Mon-Fri) is about 800m from the village centre,

EASTERN MEDITERRANEAN

on the road in from Manavgat. The **Side Internet C@fé** (€2 per half-hour) is located on Nergis Caddesi. Much better is the **Internet café** (Zambak Caddesi) located upstairs in Ömür Restaurant & Bar. There are ATMs on Liman Caddesi.

Sights

The town's most impressive site is easily its **theatre** (admission €6; 8am-7pm). Built in the 2nd century AD and Roman in design (with the exception of a few barely noticeable Greek details), it's one of the largest Greco-Roman ruins in Asia Minor, and can seat well over 15,000 spectators.

Next to the theatre and across the road from the museum are the remains of an **agora**. You'll find a good number of columns, although a chain-link fence restricts access. The **museum** (admission €3; 9am-7pm) is a ruin itself; its rather impressive, if small, collection of statues and sarcophagi resides inside the old Roman baths.

Take a left as you exit the museum for Side's spectacular field of ruins, among them a **library**, an **agora** and a **Byzantine basilica**. All warrant some exploration, but be forewarned that this area gets scorching hot during the height of summer.

At the southwestern tip of Side Harbour are the ruins of the **Temples of Apollo and Athena**, which date from the 2nd century. A number of columns from the Temple of Apollo have been preserved and placed upright in their original locations, and after dark a spotlight outlines their form dramatically against the night sky. Although the site is relatively small, it's also one of the most romantic and moving ruined sites you're likely to encounter in Turkey.

Festivals & Events

Tickets for the **Aspendos Opera & Ballet Festival** (753 4061) can be bought at the Side museum or at the **ticket office** (753 4061) outside the Roman theatre. For more information see p395.

Sleeping

Many of the hotels and pensions in Side are not operated and managed by their actual owners, but rather are sublet for the tourist season. You can probably guess what effect this has on customer service. Try to find a place where the employees have been around for a while. Also note that if you're staying in a hotel some distance from town, you'll need to round up transport in order to reach Side's ruins.

Pettino's Pansiyon (753 3608; pettino@superonline .com; Cami Sokak 9; s/d €17/23;) Aside from its intimate outdoor courtyard where travellers often congregate around a small fire at night, Pettino's doesn't have a whole lot going for it. The common areas are something of a shabby mess; the same could be said for the pension's dog-eared rooms. Backpackers do flock here during the high season however, so book ahead.

Beach House Hotel (753 1607; www.beachhouse -hotel.com; Barbaros Caddesi; s/d €17/36; P) Unless you're dead-set on staying in a smaller and slightly more intimate pension, this is without a doubt the most relaxing and atmospheric budget hotel in Side. Readers consistently sing its praises: a perfect location right on the beach, ocean-front rooms (some with decent-sized balconies), and free sun-beds for guests.

Yıldırım Pansiyon (753 3209; yildirimpansiyon@ yahoo.com; Lale Sokak; s & d €19) Located just steps from the theatre, this exceptionally laid-back pension is conveniently located across the street from a car park. Expect plain but ship-shape rooms, and a beautiful silence after dark.

Yükser Pansiyon (753 2010; www.yukser-pansiyon .com; Sumbul Sokak 8; s/d €19/25;) Tucked away from the noise of the main drag but still just steps from the beach, this traditional stone-and-timber house offers average but

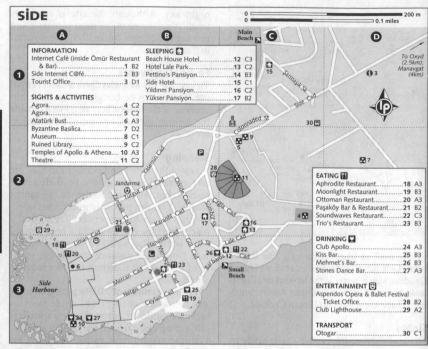

SİDE

EASTERN MEDITERRANEAN

well-maintained rooms and a rather large back patio and garden.

Hotel Lale Park (☎ 753 1131; www.hotellalepark .com; Lale Caddesi 17; s/d €30/45; ☒ ☒) One of Side's largest gardens acts as a sort of commons area here. Roman columns and stone walkways are scattered about; there's also an abundance of conversation areas and an outdoor bar.

Side Hotel (☎ 753 3824; Sarmasik Sokak 25; s/d €31/39; ☒ ☒ P) With over 80 rooms, this concrete block of a hotel is definitely lacking in atmosphere, although many rooms boast spacious balconies overlooking a pristine stretch of beach. Skip the indoor restaurant and instead dine downstairs on the sand.

Eating

Regulars recommend taking care when ordering at the harbourside restaurants. Things such as vegetables or chips that you might have thought were included turn out to come with steep price tags. A portion of grilled fish should cost between €9 and €12.

Trio's Restaurant (☎ 753 1309; Cami Sokak; meals €9) Directly across the street from Pettino's Pension, this is a good choice for standard Turkish fare. International fast foods, such as spaghetti and American-style pizza, are also available. Show up any Friday evening throughout the summer for Turkish folk dancing.

Ottoman Restaurant (☎ 753 1434; Liman Caddesi; meals €12) A decent selection of typical Indian dishes are among the offerings at this otherwise traditional seafood and grilled meat spot. There's no harbour view, but locals contend that this is one of the very few good-value eateries in the area.

Soundwaves Restaurant (☎ 753 1059; Barbaros Caddesi; meals about €16) Owned by the same folks who operate the adjacent Beach House Hotel, this eatery offers the standard seafood and grilled meat menu. Presumably in homage to Side's looting and pillaging past, the servers here are attired in pirate costumes; the restaurant itself is designed to resemble a life-size ship.

Aphrodite Restaurant (☎ 753 1171; İskele Caddesi; meals €15-20) Dozens of tables sit outdoors – mere steps from the water – at this meat and seafood standby. Not only is this an ideal spot to soak in the harbourside drama at eye level, it's also a recommended location for grills and *köfte* (meatballs).

Paşakoy Bar & Restaurant (☎ 753 3622; Liman Caddesi 98; meals €15-20) Essentially Side's interpretation of a theme restaurant, stepping into this curious place feels not unlike entering a plastic rainforest with not-so-subtle Palaeolithic undertones. Plants and massive tree leaves droop every which way, and a stream flowing with real water runs through the centre of the restaurant. The relatively sizeable menu contains standard Turkish grills and seafood, most of acceptable quality.

Moonlight Restaurant (☎ 753 1400; Barbaros Caddesi 49; meals €15-20) With its decidedly romantic setting and mood-enhancing soft rock – not to mention the lapping sounds of the sea, which sits just feet away from the back patio – you can expect to see happy couples dining here *en masse*. The menu is fairly standard stuff, with passable seafood and some international dishes. Fittingly, there's a wonderfully long list of Turkish wines.

Drinking

Kiss Bar (☎ 753 3482; Barbaros Caddesi 23) Expect the fun-loving staff to join your group for at least one round of drinks at this small shack of a bar, which looks as if it might have recently escaped from a forgotten Caribbean cay.

Stones Dance Bar (☎ 512 1498; Barbaros Caddesi 67) Brit culture and karaoke are both celebrated with equal fervour at this seaside bar.

Mehmet's Bar (Barbaros Caddesi) Ideal for quietly sipping a beer while listening to the crashing waves nearby.

Entertainment

Oxyd (☎ 753 4040; Denizbuku Mevkii; cover charge €8) Located about 3km outside the city, this open-air club is well worth a visit for the gawking opportunities alone. With its stately mosque-like façade and futuristic interior (swimming pool included), the level of extravagance at Oxyd is on par with some of the clubs you'll find in Turkey's biggest cities.

Club Lighthouse (☎ 753 3588; Liman Caddesi) Fishing boats docked alongside the outdoor patio here lend a much-needed aura of elegance to an otherwise Bacchanalian discotheque. House and techno DJs are among the usual offerings here, as is the occasional bubble party.

Club Apollo (☎ 753 4092) The entrance to this open-air club sits just a few metres from the Temples of Apollo and Athena. Expensive cocktails, a killer light show and packs of

beautiful people are some of what you'll find here. Women get discounted drinks every Sunday night.

Getting There & Away

In summer, Side has direct bus services to Ankara, İzmir and İstanbul. Otherwise, frequent minibuses connect Side otogar with the Manavgat otogar (€0.80), 4km away, from where buses go to Antalya (€4, 1¼ hours, 65km), Alanya (€4, 1¼ hours, 63km) and Konya (€14, 5½ hours, 296km). Coming into Side, most buses either drop you at the Manavgat otogar, or stop on the highway so you can transfer onto a free *servis* (shuttle bus) into Side.

AROUND SİDE

About 12km east of Manavgat (50km west of Alanya) the excellent D695 highway heads northwest up to the Anatolian plateau and Konya (280km) via Akseki, curving through some beautiful mountain scenery. The road is the preferred route to Konya from this part of the coast. Along the coastal road, it's a seven hour drive from Side to Isparta (via Antalya).

Manavgat

If your beach holiday in Side has you suspecting you're not getting a true taste of the 'real' Turkey, consider hopping on a dolmuş to Manavgat (€0.80), a commercial town with a large covered bazaar. It sits about 4km to the north and east of Side.

The otogar is on the outskirts of town, on the bypass. Except at the height of summer, you'll have to come here from Side to connect with bus services to Antalya, Alanya, Konya and the lakes.

GETTING THERE & AWAY

Frequent *servises* connect Side with Manavgat otogar (€0.50), where there are onward buses to Antalya (€4, 1¾ hours, 65km) and Alanya (€4, one hour, 63km). 'Şehiriçi' dolmuşes from outside the otogar will run you into the town centre (€0.80). A taxi from Side to Manavgat otogar costs €8.

Manavgat Waterfall

About 4km north of Manavgat on the Manavgat River is the appropriately named **Manavgat Waterfall** (Manavgat Şelalesi; admission €1), a colossally popular tourist attraction filled with souvenir vendors and restaurants, some of which sit mere metres from the falls. Manavgat is well known for its trout, which is on the menu at some of the eateries here.

GETTING THERE & AWAY
A dolmuş from Manavgat costs €0.90. In the town centre you'll find boats waiting to run you upriver to the waterfalls. An 80-minute round trip costs €9 per person, providing there are at least four people.

Lyrbe (Seleukeia in Pamphylia)
Shortly after passing the Roman aqueduct, look for a sign on the left marked 'Lyrbe (Seleukeia'; 7km). Continue on through the village of Şıhlar, and note the small bits of columns built into the walls of the village's stone houses. Take the road to the right opposite the minaret, which winds another 3km uphill to the ruins.

The **ruins**, some quite crumbled and others in rather well-preserved condition, are particularly appealing due to their hilltop location. Situated among an expanse of pine trees, the site is shaded and somewhat forested, and can be cool even on hot summer days. Many of the buildings are difficult to identify, although you can clearly make out a bathhouse, an agora and a necropolis.

For years, archaeologists believed this site to be the Seleukeia in Pamphylia, founded by Seleucus I Nicator, a presumably egocentric officer of Alexander the Great who founded a total of nine cities in his own honour. However a fairly recent discovery of an inscription found in the city, written in the language of ancient Side, has convinced researchers that this site is more likely the ruined city of Lyrbe.

GETTING THERE & AWAY
If you don't have your own transport, taxi drivers wait across the bridge in Manavgat to run you to Seleukeia, with a stop at Manavgat waterfall thrown in (€18 return).

ALANYA
☎ 0242 / pop 110,100
Much like Side, its smaller cousin to the west, Alanya has, in the past couple of decades, been discovered – and subsequently conquered – by European package tourism, especially from Germany and Scandinavia. There's good reason for this, of course: Alanya's silky sand beach stretches for more than 20km to the

east, where a parade of all-inclusive five-star resorts now sit practically side-by-side.

Understandably, most of those staying within the city limits seem to have arrived with relatively simple to-do lists: sunbathe during the day, dine in the evening and party well into the night. Should you happen to be interested in exploring the ancient culture of this newly modern town, pay a visit to the fascinating fortress district, which sits high above the harbour. There you'll find a number of hillside cafés and a wonderful mess of ruins, all well worth investigating.

If you want to stay for more than a day or so, check the package-holiday brochures first, since tours inclusive of flights and transfers may well be cheaper than booking privately.

Orientation
Having gone from a small town to a 20km-long city almost overnight, Alanya has no real main square or civic centre. The centre – such as it is – lies inland (north) from the promontory on which the fortress walls sit. The closet thing to a main square is Hürriyet Meydanı, a nondescript traffic junction at the northern end of İskele Caddesi.

Information
The **tourist office** (☎ 513 1240; Kalearkası Caddesi; ⏱ 8.30am-5.30pm) is opposite the Alanya Museum. **C@fé Pruva Internet** (☎ 519 2306; ⏱ 8am-midnight) is off Müftüler Caddesi, just south of Atatürk Caddesi.

Sights
FORTRESS
Alanya's most popular ancient site by far is its Seljuk **fortress** (*kale*), which overlooks the city as well as the Pamphylian plain and the Cilician mountains. The winding road to the fortress is 3km. If you don't want to walk, catch a city bus from Hürriyet Meydanı (€0.50, hourly from 9am to 7pm) or opposite the tourist office (10 minutes past the hour). Taxis wait at the bottom of the hill (€8).

Before reaching the entrance to the fort, the road passes through the old inner citadel; this was the Turkish quarter during Ottoman and Seljuk times, and a number of old wooden houses are still standing. At the top is the **Ehmedek Kapısı**, the gateway to the fort. Enter the **İç Kale** (Inner Fortress; admission €3; ⏱ 9am-7.15pm), where you'll find poorly preserved ruins including cisterns and an 11th-century

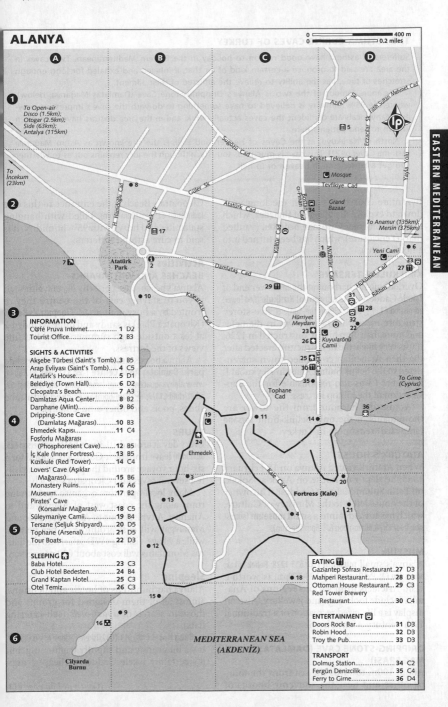

ALANYA

0 — 400 m
0 — 0.2 miles

To Open-air
Disco (1.5km);
Otogar (2.5km);
Side (63km);
Antalya (115km)

To
Incekum
(23km)

To Anamur (135km);
Mersin (375km)

To Girne
(Cyprus)

Şevket Tekoş Cad
Tevfikiye Cad
Mosque
Grand
Bazaar
Atatürk Cad
Güler Sk
Sugözü Cad
Azaklar Sk
Eczacılar Sk
Fatih Sultan Mehmet Cad
Yayla Yolu

Atatürk Park
Damlataş Cad
Kalearkası Cad
H. Hamdioğlu Cad
Bebek Sk
Kültür Cad
Bostan Pınarı Cad
Müftüler Cad
Hükümet Cad
Rıhtım Cad

Yeni Cami
Hürriyet Meydanı
Kuyularönü Camii
İskele Cad

Tophane Cad

Ehmedek
Kale Cad

Fortress (Kale)

MEDITERRANEAN SEA
(AKDENİZ)

Cilyarda
Burnu

INFORMATION
C@fé Pruva Internet................. **1** D2
Tourist Office............................ **2** B3

SIGHTS & ACTIVITIES
Akşebe Türbesi (Saint's Tomb).**3** B5
Arap Evliyası (Saint's Tomb)....**4** C5
Atatürk's House.........................**5** D1
Belediye (Town Hall).................**6** D2
Cleopatra's Beach......................**7** A3
Damlataş Aqua Center...............**8** B2
Darphane (Mint).........................**9** B6
Dripping-Stone Cave
  (Damlataş Mağarası)...............**10** B3
Ehmedek Kapısı.........................**11** C4
Fosforlu Mağarası
  (Phosphoresent Cave)............**12** B5
İç Kale (Inner Fortress)..............**13** B5
Kızılkule (Red Tower).................**14** C4
Lovers' Cave (Aşıklar
  Mağarası)................................**15** B6
Monastery Ruins........................**16** A6
Museum.....................................**17** B2
Pirates' Cave
  (Korsanlar Mağarası)..............**18** C5
Süleymaniye Camii.....................**19** B4
Tersane (Seljuk Shipyard)..........**20** D5
Tophane (Arsenal)......................**21** D5
Tour Boats..................................**22** D3

SLEEPING
Baba Hotel..................................**23** C3
Club Hotel Bedesten...................**24** B4
Grand Kaptan Hotel....................**25** C3
Otel Temiz...................................**26** C3

EATING
Gaziantep Sofrası Restaurant.....**27** D3
Mahperi Restaurant....................**28** D3
Ottoman House Restaurant....**29** C3
Red Tower Brewery
  Restaurant...............................**30** C4

ENTERTAINMENT
Doors Rock Bar...........................**31** D3
Robin Hood.................................**32** D3
Troy the Pub...............................**33** D3

TRANSPORT
Dolmuş Station...........................**34** C2
Fergün Denizcilik........................**35** C4
Ferry to Girne.............................**36** D4

THE ASTHMA-CURING CAVES OF TURKEY

Sufferers of asthma have good reason to holiday in the Eastern Mediterranean. Two caves in the area are said to produce a certain kind of air that, if inhaled and exhaled for long enough stretches of time, has the ability to relieve the afflicted of their ailment.

The more famous of the two is Alanya's Dripping-Stone Cave (Damlataş Mağarası; below), where the 95% humidity is believed to have something to do with the cave's impressive powers. Many locals are confident the caves actually work, and in the area doctors have even been known to send patients here.

North of Narlıkuyu, at the Caves of Heaven and Hell, is the site known as Astım Mağarası (Asthma Cave; p421). This cave is much less touristy, although the jury remains out as to whether you get a better cure in heaven or in hell.

Byzantine church. It's worth the long walk down to explore the village of **Ehmedek**, which includes a former Ottoman **bedesten** (vaulted market enclosure), which has been turned into a hotel (right).

KIZILKULE & TERSANE

Overlooking the harbour at the far lower end of İskele Caddesi is the octagonal **Kızılkule** (Red Tower; admission €1; 9am-7.30pm Tue-Sun), a five-storey structure measuring nearly 30m in diameter and more than 30m high. Constructed in 1226, it was very likely the first structure erected after the then-Armenian controlled town surrendered to the Seljuk Sultan Alaettin Keykubat I. Keykubat I was also responsible for the construction of the hilltop fortress.

Across the harbour from the tower are the remains of the only Seljuk-built **tersane** (shipyard) remaining in Turkey.

ATATÜRK'S HOUSE

When Atatürk visited Alanya on 18 February 1935, he slept in a house on Azaklar Sokak, off Fatih Sultan Mehmet Caddesi. The owner of the house left it to the Ministry of Culture, which has turned it into a small **museum** (admission free; 8.30am-noon & 1-5pm Tue-Sun).

MUSEUM

Alanya's small **museum** (513 1228; Bebek Sokak; admission €1; 9am-noon & 1.30-7.30pm) is worth a visit. Artefacts from various regions of Anatolia include tools, jugs and jewellery. Also on display is a life-sized recreation of a traditional 19th-century Alanya home.

DRIPPING-STONE CAVE (DAMLATAŞ MAĞARASI)

About 100m towards the sea from the tourist office and near the souvenir booths of

Cleopatra's Beach is the entrance to this **cave** (admission €2; 10am-7pm). Filled with hanging stalactites and heavy with 95% humidity, it is said to cure asthma sufferers.

Activities

BEACHES AND WATERPARKS

Alanya's beaches are perfectly decent, although if you're staying east of the centre they're fronted by a busy main road. **Cleopatra's Beach** (Kleopatra Plajı) is sandy and quite secluded – at least outside high summer – and has fine views of the fortress.

Alanya boasts a rather impressive waterslide park. **Damlataş Aqua Centre** (512 5944, 512 6044; www.alanyaaquacenter.com; İsmet Hilmi Balcı Caddesi 62; adult/child €11/7; 9am-6pm) is packed with tube slides, pools and other amusements.

TOURS

Every day at around 10.30am **boats** (per person €25, incl lunch) leave from near Gazipaşa Caddesi for a six-hour voyage around the promontory, visiting several caves and Cleopatra's Beach.

Many local operators organise tours to the ruins along the coast west of Alanya and to Anamur. A typical tour to Aspendos, Side and Manavgat will cost around €28 per person, while a village-visiting 4WD safari into the Taurus Mountains will cost about €20 per person.

Sleeping

Alanya has hundreds of hotels and pensions, almost all of them designed for groups and those in search of *apart-otels* (self-catering flats).

Baba Hotel (513 1032; İskele Caddesi 6; s/d €17/19) It's a bit grungy and slightly frightening, but it's certainly İskele Caddesi's cheapest digs.

(Continued on page 413)

JOHN

Holidaymakers on Cleopatra Beach with a *kale* (fortress) looming above, Alanya (p402)

Overleaf:
A trip in a hot-air balloon (p512) reveals the panorama of an unique landscape, Cappadocia

JOHN ELK III

Moored yachts in the harbour, Fethiye (p353)

JOHN ELK III

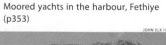

MARTIN MOOS

The imposing columns of the Temples of Apollo and Athena (p399), Side

The Maiden's Castle (p422) seems to float on the sea, Kızkalesi

CHRIS BARTON

City and bay at dusk, Fethiye (p353)

NEIL WILSON

A ruin stands amid wildflowers in a city
long abandoned, Ani (p581)

JEAN-BERNARD CARILLET

IZZET KERIBAR

Rızvaniye Vakfı Camii & Medresesi (p602) with its
enormous fish pond (Balıklı Göl), Şanlıurfa

The sentinel tombs of King Antiochus IV, Nemrut Dağı National Park (p610)

JERRY

The Armenian Akdamar Kilisesi (Church of the Holy Cross; p636) is reachable only by boat, Lake Van

A view of mighty Mt Ararat (Ağrı Dağı; p589), Doğubayazıt area

The contours of Hoşap Castle (p643) are almost indistinguishable from its rocky-outcrop base, Hoşap

ANDERS BLO

Kayakers sweep down the currents of the Çoruh River (p572), Erzurum area

JOHN ELK III

Time to relax with a yacht cruise (p356), Fethiye area

A paraglider soars over the mountains, Ölüdeniz (p359)

JENNY

Overleaf:
Sunset descends over the ancient harbour,
Antalya (p382)
JOHN ELK III

Hikers weave along a valley in the Kaçkar
Mountains (p558), Yukarı Kavron area

JEAN-BERNARD CARILLET

ANDERS BLOMQVIST

A tourist utilises old footholds to reach an
abandoned dwelling, Cappadocia (p492)

(Continued from page 404)

The front entrance is located on the left side of a cement stairway just off the street.

Otel Temiz (☎ 513 1016; fax 519 1560; İskele Caddesi 12; s/d €28/44; 🛠) Rooms here have TVs, minibars and perfectly clean bathrooms, but the real draw are the balconies, which offer a bird's–eye view of the thumping club and bar action down below.

Club Hotel Bedesten (☎ 512 1234; bedestenhotel@ hotmail.com; s/d €36/61; 🛠 🛎) Located high above the city in the old Turkish village of Ehmedek, and just down the road from the fortress, this creatively designed hotel was built right on the site of an old Ottoman *bedesten* (covered market). The cavern-like rooms are comfortable and smartly detailed. You'll need transportation to get to and from the main township.

Grand Kaptan Hotel (☎ 513 4900; www.kaptanhotels .com; İskele Caddesi 70; s/d €39/67; 🛠 🛎) This three-star hotel has a large and somewhat opulent lobby with a nautical theme and a bar. The perfectly clean and tidy rooms have all mod cons but are rather characterless.

Eating

Although they're vanishing fast, there are still a few cheap places to eat in the narrow streets of Alanya's bazaar, in the town centre. Look for signs saying 'İnegöl köftecisi', and snap up *köfte* (meatballs) and salad for around €5.

Gaziantep Sofrası Restaurant (☎ 513 4570; İzzet Azakoğlu Caddesi; meals €8) For something more adventurous than the standard grills and seafood, this is one of central Alanya's best options. Traditional food from Gaziantep is on offer; try the *patlican* kebap (fried egg-

plants) or the *beyti sarma* (spicy meatballs and flat bread).

Mahperi Restaurant (☎ 512 5491; www.mahperi .com; Rıhtım Caddesi; meals €15-25) A much-loved fish and steak restaurant that's been in operation since 1947 (a fairly astonishing feat in Alanya), this place is quite the class act, offering a good selection of international dishes. If you're feeling the need to escape the tourism glitz, this is certainly your best choice in the town centre.

Red Tower Brewery Restaurant (☎ 513 6664; info@ redtowerbrewery.com; İskele Caddesi 80; meals €10-15) An honest-to-goodness brewpub in Alanya? Believe it. In fact, this is the first on the entire so-called Turkish Riviera. The majority of patrons show up for the food, however. International dishes and fish specialities are offered on the restaurant's 1st floor, where the massive beer tanks are stored. There's also seating across the street that overlooks the harbour; this is the perfect place to try Turkish-brewed Marzen, Weizen, Helles and Pilsen.

Entertainment

Although the widespread city of Alanya is home to an enormous parade of bars and clubs, the most popular are those found smack dab in the centre. You won't have any trouble finding the most popular – some discos are three and four storeys high, others have laser lights flashing from their rooftops, and nearly all crank rock or pop music so loud it can easily be heard from blocks away.

Robin Hood (☎ 535 7923; Rıhtım Caddesi 24; 🕐 9pm-3am) Supposedly the biggest club in Alanya, the first two floors of this monstrosity are decked out in (you guessed it) a Sherwood Forest theme. The Hawaiian Beach Club is on the

---

AUTHOR'S CHOICE

Ottoman House Restaurant (☎ 511 1421; Damlataş Caddesi 31; €15-20) Constructed inside what was once Alanya's very first hotel, built over a century ago, the Ottoman House Restaurant is known nationally as being one of Turkey's finest eateries. It's also well-regarded internationally: just take a look at the restaurant's wall of fame, where kind words from scores of guidebooks and periodicals are posted. But don't take their word for it (or ours, for that matter). Settle into a chair on the 2nd floor of this traditional Mediterranean-style stone-and-timber structure, where the house specialities are an expertly prepared blend of standard Turkish grills, seafood and Ottoman dishes.

Especially popular is the *beğendili* kebap, a traditional Ottoman entrée of lamb with aubergine puree. During the busy summer season, live musicians perform nightly in the front garden, while diners are seated underneath a canopy of trees. Outdoor barbeques happen occasionally, and if you happen to be in town during one of the restaurant's fresh tuna barbeques (€14 per person), don't miss out on the rare opportunity to see a carving in action. Call to request a free bus pickup from your hotel.

third floor, and above that is the Latino Club. Beers are around €5.

Troy the Pub (☎ 511 4718; Ziraat Bankaşi Karşişi 67; ☼ 24hr) A restaurant during the day and a bar at night, this pub changes its attitude drastically as the clock slowly turns. Breakfasts here are quiet and relaxing; show up in the afternoon or evening to hear reggae, jazz and hip-hop.

Doors Rock Bar (☎ 519 2573; www.thedoorsrockbar .com; Karakol Karşişi 9; ☼ 7pm-4am) Celebrate the memory of the Lizard King at this rather rough-around-the-edges club, which seems to play more oldies than actual classic rock.

Alanya is also home to a number of large open-air discos that are relatively far from the centre. During the summer, free buses drive down İskele Caddesi about every half-hour; they depart from the harbour. Should you miss the bus back, a taxi will cost about €10.

Getting There & Away
BOAT
There are services to Girne (Kyrenia) in Northern Cyprus from Alanya harbour, operated by **Fergün Denizcilik** (☎ 511 5565, 511 5358; www.fergun.net; İskele Caddesi 84). Boats leave at noon on Mondays and Thursdays. They return to Alanya at 11am on Wednesdays and Sundays.

You must buy a ticket and present your passport a day before departure so they can handle the immigration formalities. Not included in the €32/64 one-way/return ticket prices is a €6 Alanya harbour tax. Returning from Girne, there is a €9 departure tax.

BUS
The otogar is on the coastal highway (Atatürk Caddesi), 3km west of the centre. It is served by city buses (€0.20, every half-hour). Most services are less frequent outside summer, but buses generally leave hourly for Antalya (€5, two hours, 115km) and eight times daily to Adana (€12, 10 hours, 440km), stopping at a number of towns along the way. Buses to Konya (€9.50, 6½ hours, 320km) take the Akseki–Beyşehir route.

Getting Around
Frequent dolmuşes shuttle along the coast, transporting passengers from the outlying hotel areas to the centre.

Dolmuşes to the otogar (€0.60) can be picked up in the bazaar, north of Atatürk Caddesi. From the otogar, you walk out towards the coast road and the dolmuş stand is on the right.

AROUND ALANYA
About 23km west of Alanya is **İncekum** and **Avsallar**, these days virtual extensions of Alanya with little to recommend them. At İncekum the **İncekum Orman İci Dinlenme Yeri** (Fine Sand Forest Rest Area; ☎ 345 1448) has a camping ground (no facilities) in a pine grove near the beach.

About 13km west of Alanya, notice the **Şarapsa Hanı**, a Seljuk *han* (caravanserai) built in the mid-12th century, which is occasionally reinvented as a function centre. Further west towards Side, there's another *han*, the **Alarahan**, accessible by a side road heading north for 9km.

Heading east towards Silifke (275km), the twisting road is cut into the cliffs. Every now and then it passes through the fertile delta of a stream, planted with bananas (as at Demirtaş) or crowded with greenhouses. It's a long drive

---

BEHOLD THE ANAMUR BANANA

Nearly every city and town along Turkey's eastern Mediterranean coast seems to be known for its proficiency in growing a certain type of fruit, and Anamur is no different. Here, the banana reigns supreme.

Until the mid-1980s, Anamur bananas were the only sort of banana available anywhere in the country. That certainly wasn't a bad thing. It's true the bananas are especially small, but their smell, and especially their taste, is outstanding. Anamur bananas are much sweeter and more flavourful than those common in Europe and North America. Unfortunately for local growers though, Turkey began importing cheaper (but less tasty) bananas from other countries; large numbers of Anamur banana growers were driven out of business.

Happily, if you're in Anamur the local bananas can still be bought more cheaply than imported varieties. Keep your eyes peeled when driving through the mountainous regions surrounding town, where you're certain to spot dozens of farmers along the highway hawking great bunches of bananas from wooden fruit stands.

EASTERN MEDITERRANEAN

with few places to stop until you get to Anamur, but the sea views and the cool pine forests are extremely beautiful. On a clear day you can see the mountains of Cyprus across the sea.

This region was ancient Cilicia Tracheia ('Rough' Cilicia), a somewhat forbidding part of the world because of the mountains. Pirates preyed on ships from the hidden coves along this stretch of the coast. In the late 1960s the government completed the good road running east from Alanya, and since then tourism has grown rapidly.

ANAMUR
☎ 0324 / pop 50,000

If ruins are your bag, this is a convenient (if unexciting) base for exploring the massive Byzantine city of Anamurium (right), just west of Anamur. It's also close to the impressive Mamure Castle (Mamure Kalesi; p416), a must-see site that sits directly on the highway to the east.

Orientation & Information
Anamur town centre lies to the north of the highway, 1km from the main square. Mamure

Kalesi is 7km east of the town centre, the ruins of Anamurium 8.5km west of the centre. The otogar is on the intersection of the highway and Anamur's main street (see p417 for information about getting around). The **tourist office** (☎ 814 3529; ☯ 8am-noon & 1-5pm Mon-Fri) is in the otogar complex behind the police station; note though that it keeps irregular hours.

Around 2.5km from the otogar, the waterfront district, İskele, is where most of Anamur's hotels and restaurants are located.

Anamurium
Approaching Anamur from the west or down from the Cilician mountains, just before you reach Anamur itself, a sign on the right points south towards the **ruins** (admission €1; ☯ 8am-8pm). This road bumps 3km past fields – when you reach a fork in the road go to the right – and through the ruins to a dead end at the beach. A good way of exploring the area is on bicycle, which can be arranged at Hotel Dedehan (p416).

Although founded by the Phoenicians, the ruins visible at Anamurium today date from the tail end of the Roman period through to

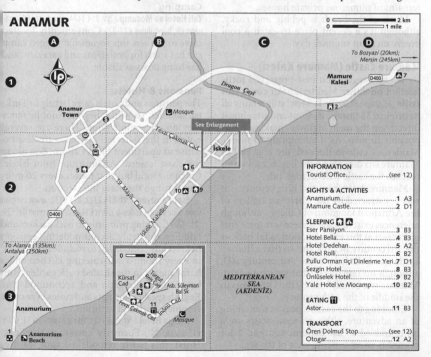

the medieval Byzantine era. The site is both sprawling and inspiring, with ruined structures stretching from the beach to the peak of the mountainside. It's primarily the sheer size of the city, rather than simply the ruins themselves, that impress.

Historians and archaeologists are still debating exactly how and why Anamurium eventually fell. The city suffered a number of devastating setbacks throughout its active existence, including an attack in AD 52 by a Cilician tribe known as the Cetae. However it was long believed that corsairs from Arabia were the last straw for Anamurium, plundering and pillaging it to the point of no return sometime in the mid-7th century. Recently, however, archaeologists working at Anamurium claim to have uncovered evidence suggesting that a massive earthquake destroyed the city sometime in the late 6th century.

The best-preserved structure here is the **public bath**; look for the coloured mosaic tiles that still decorate portions of the floor. Other ruins of interest include a 900-seat **theatre** dating from the 2nd century AD, a **stadium**, and a rather large **necropolis**. There are also the remains of numerous private houses.

Much of the beach is pebbly and rocky, although it's a decent place to catch a cool breeze on a hot summer day.

Mamure Castle (Mamure Kalesi)

By far the biggest and best-preserved fortification on either Mediterranean coast, this **castle** (admission €1.50; ⏲ 8am-6pm) still retains all its original 36 towers. Its front end sits almost directly on the main highway, making it impossible to miss. As if attempting to mimic Maiden's Castle to the east, the rear end of Mamure sits directly on the beach, and water reaches the castle walls at high tide.

Mamure dates from the 12th century – it was constructed by the Christian leaders of the Armenian kingdom of Cilicia – although references exist to suggest there was some sort of fortress at this exact location as far back as the 3rd century BC. It's known that a Roman castle was built here in the 3rd century AD, although no remains of that structure exist. Mamure was briefly held by the Ottomans in the middle of the 14th century.

Climbing to the castle's peak is something of an adventure, although some stairs are a bit crumbled so use extreme caution. Your reward is an astounding view of the sea.

Sleeping

ANAMUR

Pullu Orman İçi Dinlenme Yeri (☎ 827 1151; camp sites or caravans €5) Just under 2km east of Mamure Castle is this large, hilly and forested camp ground. It's especially popular with Turkish families and school groups who arrive for picnics by the sea (where pious Muslim women swim fully clothed).

Hotel Dedehan (☎ 814 7522; D400 Hwy; s/d €11/22; ⌘) This rather pleasant place can be found next to the otogar. With its friendly owner and clean, decent-sized rooms, it's a good choice if you're stuck in town overnight. It's also a good base for excursions to Anamurium or Mamure Castle, as guests are allowed free use of a bicycle. Motorbikes can be rented for about €14 a day.

İSKELE

In the fast-growing İskele (harbour) district, there are numerous pensions and hotels along İnönü Caddesi, the main waterfront street. The dolmuş drops you off at the main intersection.

Camping

Yali Hotel ve Mocamp (☎ 814 3474; camp sites €4, caravans €8, bungalows €17-22) Conveniently located close to the sea, this somewhat rugged camp site has spots for both tents and caravans, and has bungalows available.

Pensions & Hotels

The pensions and hotels cater largely to Turkish families, so while they may not be fancy they do offer good value. There are several hotels in the Yalıevleri district, a treeless expanse of apartment blocks about 2km along the coast towards Anamurium from İskele. Catch the local bus that passes every 20 minutes through the main intersection.

Eser Pansiyon (☎ 814 2322, 814 9130; www.eserpansiyon.com; İnönü Caddesi 6; s/d/tr €14/22/28, 5-person flat €39; ⌘ 🖳) Catering primarily to backpackers and families, this truly accommodating pension has recently remodelled to include satellite TV in every room, a self-catering kitchen and a barbeque pit in the shaded back garden. Run by an ultra-energetic and accommodating English speaker, the flats and suites here come complete with real bathtubs.

Sezgin Hotel (☎ 814 9421; İskele Mahallesi 11; s/d/tr €17/28/36; ⌘) Formerly known as the Sevgi Hotel, this newly remodelled spot features an interesting collection of kilims on its lobby walls. The rooms are quite sparse but clean; 10 out of the 24 have sea-views, and all have TVs.

Hotel Bella (☎ 816 4751; bilgi@eserpansiyon.com; Kursat Caddesi 5; s/d/tr €17/28/36; ✹) Operated by the same owner as Eser Pansiyon, this more upscale locale features perfectly tidy rooms – all with satellite TV – and a tastefully decorated dining area. By no means should you miss trying a meal here; ask for one of their authentic Turkish specials.

Ünlüselek Hotel (☎ 814 1973; www.hotelunluselek .com; Fahri Görülü Caddesi; s/d €19/33; P ✹ ▢) This family-oriented hotel has proved so popular that a new wing was recently constructed. Along with live music at night and free wi-fi, films are occasionally screened on a projector outside, where there's also a playground area for kids. Located just steps from the sea, a beach-volleyball court is usually set up in the summer. The owner also loans his small boat to guests.

Hotel Rolli (☎ 814 4978; www.hotel-rolli.de; Yahevleri Mahallesi; s or d €33; ✹ ▣) Specially designed for wheelchair-bound tourists, this recently renovated hotel has wheelchair-accessible rooms, a wheelchair-accessible lift, and a device that gingerly moves guests from their chair to the hotel pool. The majority of guests here are German, and the very polite staff all speak the language. And talk about astounding customer service: guests can request a free pickup from as far away as the Antalya airport.

Eating

In the warmer months the İskele waterfront is filled with large open-air cafés, serving kebaps, *gözleme* (savoury pancake) and other snacks.

Astor (☎ 816 8016; İnönü Caddesi; meals €11) A fish and steak house on İskele's main intersection, this is one of Anamur's most atmospheric restaurants.

Getting There & Away

There are several buses daily to Alanya (€8, three hours, 135km) and Silifke (€8, 3½ hours, 160km).

Getting Around

Anamur is quite spread out, but easy to get around on public transport. Buses and dolmuşes to İskele depart from next to the mosque, over the road from the otogar (€0.60,

every 30 minutes). A taxi between İskele and the otogar costs about €6.

Dolmuşes to Ören also leave from next to the mosque, over the road from the otogar, and can drop you off at the Anamurium turn-off on the main highway. Alternatively, you'll need to take a taxi from Anamur otogar or from İskele. Expect to pay about €15 to go there and back, with an hour's waiting time – but this is barely enough time to see the highlights.

Frequent dolmuşes to Bozyazı (€0.50) travel past Mamure Kalesi.

AROUND ANAMUR

About 20km east of Anamur, you'll come to the town of **Bozyazı**, spread across a fertile plain backed by rugged mountains. East across the plain, and clearly visible for miles around, is **Softa Castle** (Softa Kalesi), impossibly perched on the rocks above the hamlet of Çubukköy yağı. Like Mamure Castle (opposite) to the west, Softa was built by the Armenian kings who ruled Cilicia for a short while during the Crusades. It is now pretty ruinous, but the walls and location are mightily impressive. As you leave Bozyazı, a sign on the left points inland to the castle, but the road doesn't go all the way to the top.

If you'd like to climb into the mountains and see yet another medieval castle, turn left at Sipahili 3km southwest of Aydıncık and head up towards Gülnar (25km) for a look at **Meydancık Castle** (Meydancık Kalesı), which has stood here in one form or another since Hittite times.

TAŞUCU

☎ 0324

Taşucu, the port of Silifke, is a pleasant mix of working port and low-key tourist resort with a quiet beach. The town lives for the ferries to Girne (Kyrenia) in Northern Cyprus. Hotels put up travellers, while car ferries and hydrofoils take them across the sea.

Orientation & Information

The main square by the ferry dock, one block south of the highway, has a PTT, banks, a customs house, assorted shipping offices and several restaurants. The beach is fronted by Sahil Yolu, which stretches out east of the docks and has several good pensions. There is an internet café in the plaza opposite the pier.

Sleeping

Meltem Pansiyon (☎ 741 4391; Sahil Caddesi 75; s/d €14/19; P) Sitting just a few steps from the small, sandy beach, this family-run pension has a few sea-facing rooms; breakfast is served on the back patio. Rooms are modest but clean. If you're looking for small, intimate and affordable, this is it.

Holmi Pansiyon (☎ 741 5378; holmi.pansiyon .kafeterya@hotmail.com; Sahil Caddesi 23; s/d €16/21;) The covered front porch here is particularly nice for relaxing on a hot day. The rooms have small desks and balconies, although not much of a sea view.

Olba Otel (☎ 741 4222; Sahil Caddesi; s/d €25/44; P) Next door to Meltem Pansiyon and directly on the sea, Olba is tidy, professional and well run. The 2nd-floor balcony (where breakfast is served) offers wonderful sea views. The rooms are clad in cosy, kitschy wood-panelling.

Lades Motel (☎ 741 4008; www.ladesmotel.com; Atatürk Caddesi 89; s/d €31/44; P) One of the prettiest hotels in town, the rather large Lades boasts an Olympic-sized pool and wonderful harbour views from the bedroom balconies. The lobby and sitting areas are tastefully decorated. The hotel is a favourite of bird watchers who come to visit the nearby Göksu Delta (p420).

Taşucu Best Resort Hotel (☎ 741 6300; www.best -resorthotel.com; Atatürk Caddesi 97; s/d €47/72; P) A five-star hotel that has absolutely earned its ranking. A restaurant, hairdresser and *hamam* are all onsite, as is a lovely pool featuring a bridge and waterslide. Some of the (large) rooms even come with portholes!

Eating & Drinking

Alo Dürüm (☎ 741 2464, 741 2463; Atatürk Caddesi 17; meals about €3) Right in the middle of the main drag and close to the ferry terminal, this is an open-air *döner* (spit roast) and pide (Turkish pizza) place popular with locals and travellers coming from – or going to – the Cyprus ferry. A 24-hour delivery service is available, should you get a hankering for *lahmacun* (Arabic pizza) at 3am.

Baba Restaurant (☎ 741 5991; Atatürk Caddesi 87; meals €5-10) Locals regard it as Silifke's best eatery, and for good reason. Portions are generous and artfully prepared, as is the meze cart, which will tempt you from its perch on the veranda all evening long. Cool breezes blowing in from the harbour complete the picture

perfectly. Don't miss the updated selection of fresh fish on the chalkboard.

Getting There & Away

Akgünler Denizcilik (☎ 741 4033; fax 741 4324; www .akgunler.com.tr; Taşucu Atatürk Caddesi) runs *feribotlar* (car ferries) and/or *ekspresler* (hydrofoils) between Taşucu and Girne (Kyrenia) in Northern Cyprus. It has a daily hydrofoil at 11.30am (one way/return €32/56) and a car ferry (one way/return €33/56; car one way/return €56/100) leaving at midnight (although they don't actually sail until 2am), Sunday to Thursday. The hydrofoil leaves Girne at 9.30am daily while the car ferry leaves at noon Monday to Friday.

Hydrofoils are faster (two hours) but the ride can be stomach-churning on choppy seas. Passenger tickets cost less on the car ferry, but the trip is longer (anything from four to 10 hours depending on the weather). Provided your visa allows for multiple entries within its period of validity, you shouldn't have to pay for a new one when you come back into Turkey.

There are frequent dolmuşes between Taşucu and Silifke (€0.50), where you can connect with long-distance services to major destinations.

SİLİFKE

☎ 0324 / pop 85,100

Silifke is a down-to-earth country town with some handsome parks along the Göksu River. A striking castle dominates the town, and there are some fascinating archaeological relics in the vicinity.

Seleucia, as it was known, was founded by Seleucus I Nicator in the 3rd century BC. Seleucus was one of Alexander the Great's most able generals and founder of the Seleucid dynasty that ruled Syria after Alexander's death.

The town's other claim to fame is that Emperor Frederick Barbarossa (r 1152–90) drowned in the river near here while leading his troops on the Third Crusade.

Orientation & Information

The otogar is near the junction of the highways to Alanya, Mersin and Konya, 800m along İnönü Caddesi from the town centre. Halfway between the otogar and the town centre you pass the ruins of the Temple of Jupiter.

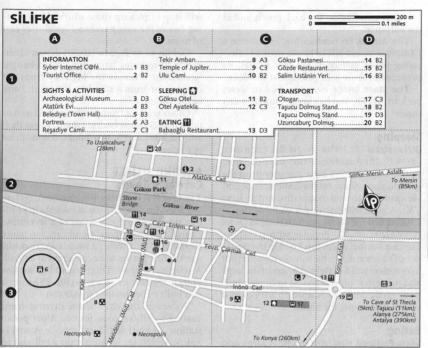

SİLİFKE

0 — 200 m
0 — 0.1 miles

INFORMATION
Syber Internet C@fé.................1 B3
Tourist Office.............................2 B3

SIGHTS & ACTIVITIES
Archaeological Museum..........3 D3
Atatürk Evi..............................4 B3
Belediye (Town Hall)..............5 B3
Fortress...................................6 A3
Reşadiye Camii.......................7 C3

Tekir Amban............................8 A3
Temple of Jupiter....................9 C3
Ulu Cami.................................10 B2

SLEEPING
Göksu Otel..............................11 B2
Otel Ayatekla..........................12 C3

EATING
Babaoğlu Restaurant.............13 D3

Göksu Pastanesi.....................14 B2
Gözde Restaurant...................15 B2
Salim Ustànin Yeri..................16 B3

TRANSPORT
Otogar...................................17 C3
Taşucu Dolmuş Stand.............18 B2
Taşucu Dolmuş Stand.............19 D3
Uzuncaburç Dolmuş...............20 B2

To Uzuncaburç (28km)
To Mersin (85km)
Silifke-Mersin Asfaltı
Göksu Park
Stone Bridge
Göksu River
Atatürk Cad
Cavit Erdem Cad
Fevzi Çakmak Cad
Menderes (Mut) Cad
Kale Yolu
Konya Asfaltı
İnönü Cad
Necropolis
Necropolis
To Konya (260km)
To Cave of St Thecla (5km); Taşucu (11km); Alanya (275km); Antalya (390km)

EASTERN MEDITERRANEAN

The town is divided by the Göksu River, called the Calycadnus in ancient times. Most of the services, including the otogar, are on the southern bank of the river. Exceptions are the tourist office and the dolmuş stop for Uzuncaburç.

The **tourist office** (☎ 714 1151; Veli Gürten Bozbey Caddesi 6; ☽ 8am-noon & 1-5pm Mon-Fri), just north of Atatürk Caddesi, sells an excellent guidebook, *Silifke (Seleucia on Calycadnus) and Environs*, for €10.

The **Syber Internet C@fé** (☎ 714 6884; Sanatcilar 2 Sokak 10; per hr €0.50; ☽ 10am-10:30pm) is around the corner from Salim Ustànin Yeri.

Sights & Activities

Silifke's most impressive sight is the medieval **fortress** that overlooks the city from a high hill. The Byzantine castle, which has 23 towers and underground storage rooms that can still be seen, was used by both the Byzantines and the Knights of St John. From the fortress it's possible to see the **Tekir Ambarı** down below, an ancient cistern carved from rock. To reach the cistern, first head to the junction of İnönü and Menderes Caddesi, then walk up the steep

road to the left of the Küçük Hacı Kaşaplar supermarket. Providing a very pleasant alternative to a dreadful walk up the hill to the castle are the motorcycle drivers who wait at this corner. Expect to pay around €5.50 per person for a round-trip journey; you'll be riding in the small wooden box up front.

The Roman **Temple of Jupiter** is especially striking if you're not expecting to see it; it literally sits right along the side of the very busy İnönü Caddesi. The temple dates from the 2nd century AD, but was turned into a Christian Basilica sometime in the 5th century.

The **Archaeological Museum** (Arkeoloji Müzesi; İnönü Caddesi; admission €1; ☽ 8am-noon & 1-5pm Tue-Sun) located about halfway between the otogar and Taşucu proper, has a decent collection of Roman statues and busts, as well as an archaeological hall filled with pottery, tools and weapons from the Roman and Hellenistic eras.

The **Ulu Cami** (Great Mosque; Fevzi Çakmak Caddesi) is a Seljuk-built mosque, although it's seen renovations over the years. At the **Reşadiye Camii** (İnönü Caddesi), take note of the Roman columns standing on the back porch and at the entrance.

The **Atatürk Evi** (admission free; ♥ 9am-noon & 1-4.30pm) is an old Silifke house with an interesting photo gallery of Mustafa Kemal. Be prepared to show your passport at the door.

The **stone bridge** over the Göksu dates back to AD 78, and has been restored many times.

Sleeping

Otel Ayatekal (☎ 715 1081; fax 715 1085; Otogar Civari; s/d €14/25; 🕸) A quite nice two-star hotel next to the otogar with a large restaurant on the ground floor. Some rooms come with decent views of the city and mountains, and all have TVs. A suite with balcony is available.

Göksu Otel (☎ 712 1021; fax 712 1024; Atatürk Caddesi 20; s/d €22/33; P 🕸) Popular with travelling Turkish businessmen, this hotel in the centre doesn't have much in the way of character, but Westerners will feel right at home in the large and modern rooms, as well as in the ground-floor restaurant, which is worth a try even if you're not staying the night.

Eating

Göksu Pastanesi (Cavit Erdem Caddesi) A large and shaded terrace perched atop the rumbling river below. Close to the stone bridge, this modest eatery sells *çay* and snacks.

Salim Ustànin Yeri (☎ 712 1121; Adliye Karşişi Caddesi 72; meals €3) Turkish fast food – mostly kebaps, *çorba* (soup) and fish – served in an antiseptic setting.

Babaoğlu Restaurant (☎ 714 2041; meals €5) The 2nd-floor seating here overlooks the traffic roundabout near the otogar. Along with the expertly-done kebaps and *pide*, there's a decent selection of fish, lamb and grilled chicken. A touch on the upscale side, at least by Silifke standards.

Gozde Restaurant (☎ 714 2764; Menderes (Mut) Caddesi; meals €5) A *döner* kebap and *lahmacun* joint with a shaded outdoor dining area and English-speaking waitstaff. Surprisingly delicious food, considering the price.

Getting There & Away

At the junction of the coastal highway and the road into the mountains, Silifke is an important transit point with good bus services.

Buses depart for Adana along the highway east of Silifke (€7, two hours, 155km, hourly) throughout the morning and afternoon, and

will stop to pick up those who've been visiting one of the many archaeological sites east of town.

Dolmuşes to Taşucu (€0.50) depart about every 20 minutes from opposite Babaoğlu Restaurant – across the highway from the otogar – or from a stand on the south bank of the Göksu.

Other services from Silifke include to Antalya (€16.50, nine hours, 390km, 10 per day) and to Mersin (€3, two hours, 85km, three per hour).

AROUND SİLİFKE
Cave of St Thecla

The **Cave of St Thecla** (Ayatekla; admission €1; ♥ 9am-noon & 1.30-6pm Mon-Fri), a small rock shelter hidden underneath the remains of a Byzantine church, is a site of great significance to many Christians. St Thecla (Ayatekla in Turkish) was the first person to be converted by St Paul. A religious outcast, Thecla spent her last few years in the cave living a pious life. The church was built in her honour in AD 480.

To reach the cave when driving from Taşucu to Silifke, look for the Alpet petrol station on your left. Next to it is Ayatekla Sokak, which leads directly up a hill and to the site. The entrance to the cave is directly behind the basilica ruins.

GETTING THERE & AWAY

To get to the cave from Silifke take a Taşucu Dolmuş (€0.50) and ask to be dropped off at the Ayatekla junction, 1km from the site.

Göksu Delta & Around

Immediately south of Silifke is the Göksu Delta (above), a renowned wetland area that is rich in birdlife.

East of Silifke, the slopes of the maquis-covered Olbian Plateau, one of Turkey's richest areas for archaeological sites, stretch along the coast for about 60km before the Cilician Plain opens into an ever-widening swathe of fertile land.

Narlıkuyu

About 3km east of Atakent, Narlıkuyu is a pretty village set around a rocky harbour ringed with fish restaurants. An underground stream flows into the little cove, making some areas of the sea refreshingly cool.

Inside the village's tiny **museum** (admission €1), which is actually a 4th-century Roman bath, you'll find a wonderful mosaic of the goddesses of fertility, also known as the Three Graces – Aglaia, Thalia and Euphrosyne.

Although all the eateries wrapped around the cove here are highly regarded (and offer essentially the same menu), a perennial favourite is **Kerim Restaurant** (☎ 723 3295; meals about €10), which is just across the street from the museum. The sea bass is recommended.

Frequent dolmuşes run between Narlıkuyu, Ertur, Kızkalesi and Silifke (€0.50).

Caves of Heaven & Hell (Cennet ve Cehennum)

In the mountainous area above Narlıkuyu, the road winds 2km up to these fascinating **caves** (admission €1; ☾ 8am-5pm).

To enter the **Chasm of Heaven** (Cennet Cöküğü), which is 250m across, make your way down its 452 steps. Along the way you'll pass through a gorgeously leafy expanse where the faithful have tied hundreds of small strips cloth to various tree branches, a ritual somewhat similar to the lighting of candles in a Catholic church.

At the mouth of the cave is the 5th-century Byzantine **Chapel of Virgin Mary**, which for a short time in the 19th century was used as a mosque.

Continue following the path down and into the cave itself, where you'll find the **Cave-Gorge to Hell** (Cehennem Çukuru) which does in fact look frighteningly similar to the image of hell we're given in popular culture. Indeed, locals believe this cave to be one of the entrances to the infernal regions. Should you hear a certain roaring sound, though, fear not: it's simply the sound of an underground stream (which can be seen in the winter but not summer). Legend had it that the roaring stream connects at some point with Styx, the river which in Greek mythology is the border between our world and the underworld.

You'll need a separate ticket to view the nearby **Pit of Hell** (Cehennem Çukuru; €1), which can only be seen from a small viewing platform above. There's not much to see in the charred-looking pit, though it's accounted to be the spot where Zeus imprisoned the hundred-headed monster Typhon after defeating him in battle.

When leaving the car park, turn right and then make a quick left into another car park, where you'll find the **Astim Mağarası** (Asthma Cave). Sufferers of asthma who spend time here are said to be able to find relief from their affliction.

Uzuncaburç

About 30km north of Silifke, the mountain village of **Uzuncaburç** (admission €1; ☾ 8am-noon & 1-5pm Mon-Fri) sits within the ancient Roman city of Diocaesarea, originally a Hellenistic city known as Olbia. This area is thought to have been home to a zealous cult that worshipped Zeus Olbius.

The **Temple of Zeus Olbius** is just inside the site and on the left, but first visit the Roman **theatre** which can be found before the car park, also on the left. The theatre is easy to miss; it's half-sunken into the ground, and is covered with a beautiful bed of wildflowers. Some of the sight's most important structures were Roman-built, including the **fountain** (2nd or 3rd century), the **Temple of Tyche** (1st century), and the **city gate**.

To view a Hellenistic structure built before the Romans sacked Olbia, leave the site and turn left through the village. On the right, a road leads to a massive *burç* (tower), which seems to pop out of the roadside. Continue on and you'll discover a path to the left that winds down 500m to a **necropolis**.

GETTING THERE & AWAY

Minibuses to Uzuncaburç (€2) leave from a side street near the tourist office. Look for the parked minibus with an 'Uzuncaburç' sign in the front window. They leave Silifke at 9am, 11am, 1pm and 3pm, and return an hour later.

Hiring a taxi costs about €24 return, waiting time included, which would allow you to inspect some tombs along the way.

Göksu Valley

From Uzuncaburç the road continues via Kirobasi to Mut and then to Karaman and Konya. Winding up into the forests you may pass huge stacks of logs cut by the Tahtacılar, the Alevi mountain woodcutters who live a secluded life in the forest.

About 40km before Mut the road skirts a fantastic limestone **canyon** that extends for several kilometres. High above in the limestone cliffs are **caves**, which were probably once inhabited. The land in the valleys is rich and well watered. About 20km north of Mut a turn-off on the right leads 5km to the ruins of another **medieval castle** at Alahan.

KIZKALESİ

☎ 0324

Kızkalesi, which pushes right up against the main D400 highway, is the sort of place that seems garish and crude upon arrival. But stick around for a while, and this small village, which today is part open-air museum of antiquated ruins and part tacky tourism epicentre, will almost certainly grow on you.

It's no secret how this very small town, 26km east of Silifke, became so popular. The impressively long beach here is one of the loveliest in this region, and that's to say nothing of the fact that a medieval fortress – the eponymous Kızkalesi – sits 200m out in the sea.

The presence of so many American archaeology students in Kızkalesi should tell you something about the importance and abundance of the nearby ruins, and the frequent sight of American soldiers from the nearby military base speaks volumes – quite often it shouts volumes – about the fun to be had here.

Undoubtedly because of the presence of so many Americans, the locals seem adept at dealing with foreigners. For a visitor, the scene here is more inclusive and relaxed than you'd expect of a typical Turkish village of this size.

Information

There is an ATM in the municipality building, and several internet cafés.

Sights & Activities

Not much can prepare you for the astounding sight of **Kızkalesi** (Maiden's Castle), which lies 200m in the sea, and looks from a distance as if it's literally suspended on top of the water, or possibly floating on air. It is possible to swim to the castle; however, most people choose to pay around €3 for a lift on a boat.

To its left and on the shore is **Korykos Castle** (admission €1), an antiquated fortress that was either built or rebuilt by the Byzantines, and was briefly occupied by the kings of Lesser Armenia. It's a bit of a rough-and-ready site, so be sure to wear proper footwear.

Across the highway from Korykos Castle is a **necropolis** that's well worth exploring. There are sarcophagi and rock carvings scattered about as well.

Sleeping

Hotel Hantur (☎ 523 2367; hotelhantur@tnn.net.tr; s/d €22/33; 🔀) Located right on the beach, you'll be surprised by the large size of the rooms. And while all rooms have balconies, not all face the sea – so be sure to speak up if that's what you want. Room 201 is probably the hotel's best – it has a gorgeous view of the castle. The sea-facing front garden is another plus.

Hotel Rain (☎ 523 2782; www.rainhotel.com; s/d €25/39; 🔀) Family-owned and family-friendly, this relaxing hotel is only 60m from the beach, and is run by the same folks responsible for the popular Café Rain. The owners shuttle guests to local archaeological sites for rates much lower than that of a taxi tour, and the lounge here, complete with satellite TV, is a perfect place to kick back and meet other travellers in the evening. Scuba-diving trips can be arranged for about €33.

Club Hotel Barbarossa (☎ 523 2364; info@hotel barbarossa.com.tr; s/d €33/50; 🔀 🖭) If it's luxury and pampering you're after, this is the place to find it. Spotless rooms have all the usual

---

AUTHOR'S CHOICE:

Yaka Hotel (☎ 523 2444; yakahotel@yakahotel.com; s/d €17/28; 🔀) Of all the possible explanations as to why this two-star hotel is such a wonderfully relaxing place to stay, at the top of the list would have to be Yakup Kahveci, the Yaka Hotel's multilingual and quick-witted owner.

Yakup has worked in the hospitality business for ages, and it's clear he enjoys his profession; he dotes upon guests as if they were members of his own family. Lodgers can dine in the attractive garden area, where the hotel mascot – a scruffy little dog belonging to Yakup's daughter – can often be found lounging about.

Rooms are impeccably tidy, and while there's no official car park, you can safely leave your car outside the front entrance.

Should you care to take a tour of the nearby archaeological wonders, that can be arranged as well. In fact, the Yaka Hotel is one of Kızkalesi's favourite resting spots for archaeology students completing research in this area during their summer break.

amenities, including minibar and TV, but the real treat is the sprawling back garden, where bits of Roman columns – illuminated at night – are scattered about. Swimmers can choose to be out-of-doors or in, and massages are available.

Eating & Drinking
Many pensions have their own restaurants and there are some decent pide and *lahmacun* salons on the highway, but unfortunately there is nowhere spectacular to eat in Kızkalesi. For a more atmospheric dinner, pay a €0.50 bus fare for the 10-minute hop to Narlıkuyu (p420) and eat at one of the fish restaurants there.

Honey Restaurant & Bar (☎ 523 2430; Inci Plaj Yolu 1; meals around €3) Right on the highway, this cosy little place nevertheless manages to give off a rather pleasant vibe; it's not unlike a dim-lit British pub. Try the *saç kavurma* (€3), an Anatolian speciality of meat and veggies, or the *patlıcan* kebap (€3), which is meat wrapped in eggplant.

Café Rain (☎ 523 2234; meals around €5) Featuring an extensive cocktail menu and snack foods geared towards travellers, such as burgers, omelettes and vegetarian dishes.

Paşa Restaurant (☎ 523 1389; Inci Plaj Yolu; meals around €5) A large open-air spot for grills, mezes, and light Turkish snacks with agreeable prices.

Getting There & Away
There are frequent buses to Silifke (€1, 30 minutes) and to Mersin.

AROUND KIZKALESI
The limestone coast of the Olbian Plateau is littered with ruins. From Kızkalesi a sign points 7km north to the **Adamkayalar** (Men's Rocks). The 17 reliefs from the Roman era immortalise warriors wielding axes, swords and lances, sometimes accompanied by their wives and children. There are more ruins and tombs scattered around at the top of the cliff.

These tombs are cut into a rather perilous cliff-face in a gorge, so we advise you to take a guide (which can be arranged from a tourist agency in Kızkalesi).

About 25km further along the road (which deteriorates rapidly and makes for a slow, rattling journey) are the ruins of **Çambazlı**, which feature a necropolis and a Byzantine-era church in remarkably good condition.

About 3km east of Kızkalesi are the extensive but badly ruined remains of ancient **Elaiussa-Sebaste**, a city with foundations dating back to at least the early Roman period, and perhaps even to the Hittite era.

About 8.5km east of Kızkalesi at Kumkuyu is the road to **Kanlıdivane** (admission €1; ☻ 8am-7pm), the ancient city of Kanytelis. The site lies about 4km north of Kumkuyu. The first structure to come into view upon entering the car park is a **Hellenistic Tower**, which was built by the son of a priest-king in Olba (today known as Uzuncaburç) to honour Zeus. It became the location of an ancient Zeus-worshipping cult (see p421).

The name Kanlıdivane translates to 'Bloodstained Place of Madness'. Take a stroll around the 90m-deep chasm; this is where condemned criminals were said to have been tossed to their deaths. Indeed, the charred-looking pit has all the appearance of an evil place; rather resembling the Pit of Hell site north of Narlıkuyu (p421). Various ruins dramatically ring the pit – most from the Roman and Byzantine eras.

Follow the footpath behind the Roman road to discover the splendidly preserved mausoleum perched atop the hill.

MERSIN (İÇEL)
☎ 0324 / pop 750,000
Although this port city has been officially renamed İçel, everyone seems to be sticking with Mersin. The capital of the province of İçel, Mersin is a sprawling modern city built half a century ago to give Anatolia a port close to Adana and its rich agricultural hinterland. Until the 1991 Gulf War, the city was a major port for goods going to and from Iraq. It has several good hotels and makes a decent stopping point on your way through to Kızkalesi, Anamur or Antakya.

Orientation
The town centre is Gümrük Meydanı, the plaza occupied by the Ulu Cami. On the western side is Atatürk Caddesi, a pedestrianised shopping street, while two blocks north is İstiklal Caddesi, the main thoroughfare.

To get to the centre from the otogar, leave by the main exit, turn right and walk up to the main road. Cross to the far side and catch a bus travelling west (€0.50). Make sure you ask if it is going to the train station or you will have a fine tour of Mersin's suburbs.

Information

INTERNET ACCESS

Bilgi Internet (Soğuksu Caddesi 30) Large place with super-fast connections and computer stations with privacy shields.

MONEY

Exchange offices and ATMs are clustered around Gümrük Meydanı and the Ulu Cami. Look for signs for Kanarya Döviz, Kiraz Döviz and many others, all keen to change dollars and euros. Many ATMs in the commercial district behind the Ulu Cami run out of money on weekends and other busy shopping days, so you may be forced to try several before securing your cash.

POST

PTT (☎ 237 3237; İsmet İnönü Bulvarı)

TOURIST INFORMATION

Tourist office (☎ 238 3271; fax 238 3272; İsmet İnönü Bulvarı; ⏰ 8am-noon & 1-5pm)

Sights

Much of the attraction of Mersin comes from wandering through the pedestrian streets between Uray Caddesi and İstiklal Caddesi. There is a small fish market and a covered bazaar with stores selling dried goods and piles of spices. At the eastern end of Atatürk Caddesi is the fine stone **Atatürk Evi** (admission free; ⏰ 9am-noon & 1-4.30pm Mon-Sat), a museum in a house where Atatürk once stayed.

A little further west, beside the Kültür Merkezi (Cultural Centre; not open for tourists), is Mersin's small **museum** (admission €1; ⏰ 8am-noon & 1-5pm). This has a reasonably good archaeological collection with many Roman artefacts on the ground floor, including a small, headless statue of Eros, and the usual ethnographical bibs and bobs on the 1st floor.

Next to the museum, the modest **Orthodox church** has some fine icons. To gain entry, go to the left side of the church, on 4302 Sokak, and look for the entry door. You may have to shout for the caretaker (who will expect a tip to show you around) if no-one is in sight.

A possibly inspiring activity for early morning risers is a stroll on the 12km-long **pathway** that runs parallel to the sea. The path starts behind the Mersin Hilton, and continues west.

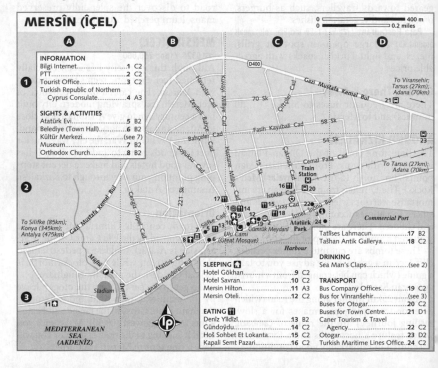

MERSÎN (İÇEL)

INFORMATION
Bilgi Internet.........................1 C2
PTT....................................2 C2
Tourist Office.........................3 C2
Turkish Republic of Northern
    Cyprus Consulate................4 A3

SIGHTS & ACTIVITIES
Atatürk Evi...........................5 B2
Belediye (Town Hall)................6 B2
Kültür Merkezi....................(see 7)
Museum...............................7 B2
Orthodox Church....................8 B2

SLEEPING
Hotel Gökhan........................9 C2
Hotel Savran........................10 C2
Mersin Hilton.......................11 A3
Mersin Oteli........................12 C2

EATING
Deniz Yıldızı.......................13 B2
Gündoğdu...........................14 C2
Hoş Sohbet Et Lokanta............15 C2
Kapali Semt Pazari.................16 C2

Tatlıses Lahmacun..................17 B2
Taşhan Antik Galleryа.............18 C2

DRINKING
Sea Man's Claps..................(see 2)

TRANSPORT
Bus Company Offices...............19 C2
Bus for Vinranşehir..............(see 3)
Buses for Otogar...................20 C2
Buses for Town Centre.............21 D1
Caner Tourism & Travel
    Agency..........................22 C2
Otogar..............................23 D2
Turkish Maritime Lines Office..24 C2

Or, to discover a working-class neighbourhood where *döner* kebaps can be had for €0.50 and vendors sell strawberries and nuts from wooden carts, leave the guidebook at your hotel and stroll the length of **Çakmak Caddesi**.

Archaeology buffs might want to check out **Viranşehir**, the ancient Soles or Pompeiopolis. Buses depart from outside the tourist office.

Sleeping

Many cheap and medium-priced hotels are in Soğuksu Caddesi, just north of the Ulu Cami. If you arrive late at night and are leaving again early in the morning, it's worth noting that there are a number of hotels immediately facing the otogar, some of them decent.

Hotel Savran (☎ 232 4472; Soğuksu Caddesi 14; s/d €14/22; 🗙) The staff at this rugged hotel don't seem the least bit ashamed of their torn hallway carpets and stained bathroom floors, although that may be because you can't easily find prices this cheap anywhere else in the centre. What's more, the management here is happy to consider discounts.

Hotel Gökhan (☎ 232 4665; fax 237 4462; Soğuksu Caddesi 22; s/d €19.50/33; 🅿 🗙) This two-star hotel in the centre offers satellite TV and minibars in the rooms, which look a bit ragged but are certainly clean enough. Guests can leave their cars in the car park across the street at no charge.

Mersin Hilton (☎ 326 5000; www.mersin.hilton.com; Adnan Menderes Bulvarı; s/d €137/152; 🅿 🗙 🖳 🍸) Not just the rooms, but even the hallways at this luxury hotel have amazing views, with the sea on one side and the city on the other. Enjoying two Asian-fusion restaurants, guests here are rather well taken care of. Tennis courts and a health club are both onsite.

Mersin Oteli (☎ 238 1040; www.mersinoteli.com.tr; Gümruk Meydanı 112; s/d €39/60; 🗙) This relatively fancy if not entirely up-to-date four-star hotel in the centre offers bland but nice-enough rooms, some with sea-view balconies. Prices are a touch steep, but discounts are possible.

Eating & Drinking

Gündoğdu (☎ 231 9677; Silifke Caddesi 22; meals €3) This especially toothsome fast-food joint seems to be permanently heaving. It has no menu, so simply order one of the house specialities: *İskender* döner, *börek* (flaky pastry with cheese or meat) or *salata* (salad).

Hoş Sohbet Et Lokanta (☎ 237 0077; Uray Caddesi 34/D; meals €5-10) Popular with besuited businessmen and families, expect the usual grills and seafood here, yet prepared according to a much-higher-than-street-food standard, and with agreeable portions to boot.

Taşhan Antik Gallerya is a collection of bars and outdoor cafés set around a courtyard, popular with young locals. Also popular with locals, and Greek sailors who've arrived from the nearby port, is the unfortunately named **Sea Man's Claps** (☎ 407 3586; Antikhan Sokak), where you'll get live music most nights, but hopefully nothing else.

Soğuksu Caddesi boasts several small fish restaurants, such as **Deniz Yıldızı** (meals €3). These are popular places, although portions won't go far if you're very hungry.

If you're just passing through, there are lots of restaurants mixed in with the hotels outside the otogar. There's something to suit most budgets, and several beer halls. The western reaches of İstiklal Caddesi have a number of *lahmacun* places, including a branch of Tatlises Lahmacun where people queue up for *ayran* (yogurt drink) and *lahmacun*. Self-caterers can try **Kapalı Semt Pazarı** (Çakmak Caddesi), a small fruit and vegetable market.

Getting There & Away

BOAT

The **Turkish Maritime Lines** (☎ 231 2688, 237 0726) ticket office can be found on the 2nd floor of a seemingly empty building right next to the dock entrance, where the ferries depart. Ferries travel from Mersin to Gazimağusa (Famagusta) on the east coast of Northern Cyprus every Monday, Wednesday and Friday at 8pm. The ferry travels from Gazimağusa to Mersin every Tuesday, Thursday and Sunday at 8pm. Tickets (one way/return €25.50/47, per car one way/return €50/100, 10 hours) must be bought a day in advance.

BUS

From Mersin's otogar, on the city's eastern outskirts, buses depart for all points, including up to the Anatolian plateau through the Cilician Gates (p428). Distances, travel times and prices are similar to those from Adana, 70km to the east on a fast, four-lane highway – see p430. From Mersin to Alanya costs €11 (8½ hours, 375km, eight per day) and to Silifke €4 (two hours, 85km, three per hour). Several of the main companies serving İstanbul, Ankara and İzmir have offices on İsmet İnönü Bulvarı.

Buses from town to the otogar (€0.50) leave regularly from outside the train station, as well as from the stop opposite the Mersin Oteli.

CAR
If you want to explore the coast by car, rentals can be arranged at **Caner Tourism & Travel Agency** (Ismet İnönü Bulvarı 88A), opposite the tourist office.

TRAIN
There are frequent services to Tarsus (€0.90), Adana (€1.50) and İskenderun (€3).

TARSUS
☎ 0324 / pop 216,000
Tarsus is one of those towns with a name inextricably linked with one man: St Paul, born here 2000 years ago. One reader wrote that Tarsus 'might have done for Saul/Paul, but it's down in the world since then', and at first sight, few people would disagree with that assessment. Much of the city is a sprawl of concrete apartment blocks. However, this is also one of those towns that repays perseverance.

Information
The new otogar is some way out of town. A taxi from there will cost you €4 to the city centre; or you can walk out the front exit and hop on a bus (€0.50) on the same side of the street. Detailed maps of Tarsus and its attractions are available at the tourist information booth in the town centre.

Sights & Activities
Buses drop you off beside **Cleopatra's Gate**, a Roman city gate that has little to do with the famous lady, although she is thought to have met Mark Antony in Tarsus. In any case, restoration carried out in 1994 has robbed it of any sense of antiquity.

Walk straight ahead, and just before the *hükümet konağı* (government house) you'll see a sign pointing left to **St Paul's Well** (Senpol Kuyusu; see boxed text right). The ruins of Paul's house can be viewed underneath plates of glass.

At the same road junction a second sign to the left points to the **Old City** (Antik Şehir). Follow it and you'll come to Cumhuriyet Alanı, where excavations have uncovered a wonderful stretch of **Roman road**, with heavy basalt paving slabs covering a lengthy drain.

BIRTHPLACE OF ST PAUL

Jewish by birth, Paul (born Saul) was one of Christianity's most zealous proselytisers; during his lifetime he converted scores of pagans and Jews to Christianity throughout much of the ancient world. After dying in Rome, sometime after AD 60, the location of his birthplace became sacred to his followers. Today pilgrims still flock to the site of his ruined house in Tarsus to take a small drink from the well (note that we can't vouch for its cleanliness!).

Return to the *hükümet konağı* and continue northwards until you come to the 19th-century **Makam Camii** on the right. Directly across the street is **Eski Cami** (Old Mosque), a medieval structure which may originally have been a church dedicated to St Paul. Right beside it looms the barely recognisable brickwork of a huge old **Roman bath**.

Beside the Eski Cami you can catch a dolmuş (€0.50) to Tarsus' other main sight, the **waterfall** (*şelale*) on the Tarsus Nehri (Cydnus River) which cascades over the rocks right inside the town, providing the perfect setting for tea gardens and restaurants.

To reach the 16th-century **Ulu Cami** (Great Mosque), which sports a curious 19th-century clock tower, turn right beside the Makam Camii and continue along the side street. Behind it and one street over on the right are the ruins of **St Paul's Church**.

The **Tarsus Museum** (Tarsus Müzesi; admission €1; ◷ 8am-noon & 1-5pm Mon-Fri) has recently moved. It's now located near the corner of Muvaffak Uygur and Cumhuriyet Caddesi, close to the stadium.

Sleeping & Eating
Cihan Palas Oteli (☎ 624 1623; fax 624 7334; Mersin Caddesi 21; s/d €11/16.50; ✷) Very spartan rooms in a rather frightening hotel, although the price is right, and the location – within walking distance of Cleopatra's Gate – is convenient. Acceptable in a pinch, but if you can manage it, sleep in Adana instead.

Tarsus Mersin Oteli (☎ 614 0600; fax 614 0033; Şelale Mevkii; s/d €33/50; P ✷) This four-star hotel looms above the waterfall, and although the rooms are rather lovely and most conveniences are available, the décor and interior design could have used an update some 30 years ago.

Getting There & Away

There are plenty of buses and dolmuşes connecting Tarsus with Mersin (27km) and Adana (43km), so you could take a break here while travelling between the two.

ADANA

☎ 0322 / pop 1.1 million

Turkey's fourth-largest city, Adana, is a big, brash commercial city with a distinct social and physical divide. North of the D400 (also called the Turan Cemal Beriker Bulvarı) new cars cruise the leafy streets, lined with upmarket apartment blocks. The further south of the highway you go, the poorer the city becomes, until the modern city dissolves into a sprawl of unplanned houses crammed together, with lottery-ticket sellers on every corner.

Adana's wealth comes from three sources: local industry (especially the Sabancı conglomerate, Turkey's second-largest); from the traffic passing through the Cilician Gates (p428); and from the intensely fertile Çukurova, the ancient Cilician plain deposited as silt by the Seyhan and Ceyhan Rivers.

Most likely you'll only wind up in Adana because it has an airport, a train station, a large otogar and hotels. There may be few sights, but there are lots of bars and some great restaurants. A night here will give you a glimpse into a real Turkish city that's young, secular and thoroughly modern.

Orientation

The Seyhan River skirts the city centre to the east. Adana's airport (Şakirpaşa Havaalanı) is 4km west of the centre on the D400. The otogar is 2km further west on the north side of the D400. The train station is at the northern end of Ziyapaşa Bulvarı, 1.5km north of İnönü Caddesi, the main commercial and hotel street.

The E90 expressway skirts the city to the north. If you approach by car from the north or west, take the Adana Küzey (Adana North) exit to reach the city centre.

At the western end of İnönü Caddesi is Kuruköprü Meydanı, marked by the highrise Çetinkaya shopping centre. There are several hotels on Özler Caddesi between Kuruköprü Meydanı and Küçüksaat Meydanı to the southeast.

Information

There's a **tourist office** (☎ 359 1994; Atatürk Caddesi 13) one block north of İnönü Caddesi, in the town centre, and a smaller **office** (☎ 436 9214) at the airport. Internet cafés are on İnönü Caddesi north of the hotels.

Sights
MOSQUES

The attractive 16th-century **Ulu Cami** (Great Mosque; Abidin Paşa Caddesi) is reminiscent of the Mamluk mosques of Cairo, with black-and-white banded marble and elaborate window surrounds. The tiles in the *mihrab* (niche indicating the direction of Mecca) came from Kütahya and İznik.

The 1724 **Yeni Cami** (New Mosque) follows the general square plan of the Ulu Cami, with 10 domes, while the **Yağ Camii** (1501), with its imposing portal, started life as the church of St James. Both are on Özler Caddesi.

More conspicuous than either of these is the six-minaret **Sabancı Merkez Cami**, right beside the Girne Bridge and the bank of Ceyhan River. The biggest mosque between İstanbul and Saudi Arabia, it was built by the late industrial magnate Sakıp Sabancı, a wildly successful businessman, generous philanthropist, and, when he passed away in 2004 at the age of 71, the richest man in all of Turkey. Take one look at the mosque he left behind, and it's very obvious that Sabancı was also a devoutly religious man. Which isn't to say he was unapproachable: having grown up

---

TURNIP JUICE, ANYONE?

A once-tried, never-forgotten local drink made by boiling turnips and carrots and adding vinegar, is the crimson-coloured *şalgam*, sold at stalls around town. It's often drunk with a kebap meal or as an accompaniment to rakı (aniseed-flavoured grape brandy). The juice carries an especially strong tang, and tastes as if it were freshly squeezed. You'll probably do a good bit of puckering and funny-face making while you drink your first glass – as with coffee, cigarettes and beer, *şalgam* is an acquired taste. However you may find yourself hankering for more after the initial shock has worn off. Locals drink the juice to relieve an upset stomach, so you might give it a shot the next time you experience a particularly painful dose of Traveller's D.

in the central Anatolian village of Akcakaya, it's said he purposely spoke in a country accent so as to assure his fellow Turks – and certainly his shareholders – that big business hadn't ruined him. Nonetheless, the Sabancı Merkez Cami is certainly a conspicuous monument. Roughly 20,000 worshippers can fit inside, and one of the minarets even conceals a small elevator. Fittingly, the marble and gold-leaf inlaid mosque has quite an influence in the surrounding areas: Prayers originating here are broadcast to nearly 300 other mosques within a 60km radius.

MUSEUMS

Adana's two main museums are a cut above most of Turkey's provincial museums. The

Adana Ethnography Museum (Adana Etnografya Müzesi; admission €1; 8.30am-noon & 1-4.30pm Tue-Sun), on a side street off İnönü Caddesi, is housed in a nicely restored Crusader church. It now holds a display of carpets and kilims, weapons, manuscripts and funeral monuments.

The **Adana Regional Museum** (Adana Bölge Müze; admission €1; 8.30am-noon & 1-4.30pm Tue-Sun) is rich in Roman statuary from the **Cilician Gates**, north of Tarsus. The 'Gates', the main passage through the Taurus Mountains, were an important transit point as far back as Roman times. Note especially the 2nd-century Achilles sarcophagus, decorated with scenes from the *Iliad*. Hittite and Urartian artefacts are also on display.

The small **Atatürk Museum** (Atatürk Müze; Seyhan Caddesi; admission free; 8am-noon & 1.30-5pm), on a

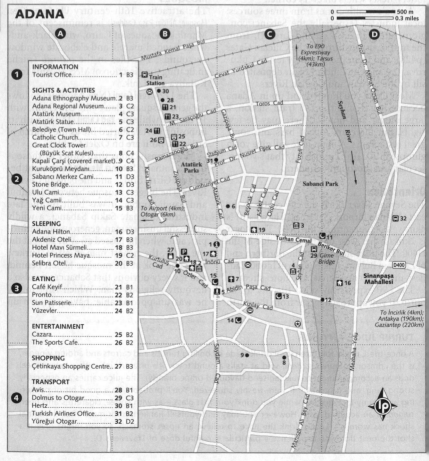

To E90
Expressway
(4km); Tarsus
(43km)

Train
Station

Mustafa Kemal Paşa Bul
Cevat Yurdakut Cad
Toros Cad
N. Saraçoğlu Cad
Çakmak Bul
Ramazanoğlu Bul
Stadyum Cad
Prof. Dr. Nusret Fişek Cad
Fuzuli Cad
Prof. Dr. Mithat Özan Bul
Seyhan River
Sabancı Park
Atatürk
Parkı
Kara İsalı
Zıyapaşa Bul
Cumhuriyet Cad
Atatürk Cad
Beşyok Cad
Adalet Cad
Ordu Cad

Turhan Cemal
Beriker Bul
Girne
Bridge
Sinanpaşa
Mahallesi

To Airport (4km);
Otogar (6km)

Kurtuluş Cad
İnönü Cad
Özler Cad
Abidin Paşa Cad
Kızılay Cad

Seyhan Cad
Mehmet Ali Bey Cad
Mahatma Ali Bey Cad
Seydani Cad
Mezhaha Yolu

D400

To İncirlik (4km);
Antakya (190km);
Gaziantep (220km)

riverside street, is one of the city's few remaining traditional houses. It is a mansion that once belonged to the Ramazanoğulları family. Atatürk stayed here for a few nights in 1923.

OTHER SIGHTS

Have a look at the 16-arched Roman **stone bridge** (taş köprü) over the Seyhan, at the eastern end of Abidin Paşa Caddesi. Built by Hadrian (r 117–138), repaired by Justinian (r 527–565), and now sullied by modern traffic, it's still an impressive sight.

The **Great Clock Tower** (Büyük Saat Kulesi) dates back to 1881. Around it you'll find Adana's **kapalı çarşı** (covered market).

Sleeping

Though Adana has lodgings in all price ranges, there are no hotels near the airport, otogar or train station. All but the cheapest places post high prices as required by the city council, and slash them to far more manageable levels at the first sign of interest.

Selibra Otel (☎ 363 3676; fax 363 4283; İnönü Caddesi 50; s/d € 19.50/28; 🔀) A two-star hotel with fairly uninspiring rooms and tacky 1970's décor, but certainly clean and welcoming enough for the price. The rooms are agreeably decent-sized, and should you need to call home during your morning constitutional, there's even a phone next to the toilet.

Akdeniz Oteli (☎ 363 1510; fax 363 0905; İnönü Caddesi 14/1, s/d €35/61; 🔀) This is a clean and smartly-decorated two-star place with glassed-in shower stalls. Don't miss the psychedelic mirrored staircase leading from the lobby to the 2nd-floor bar, which we don't recommend for a nightcap, as prostitutes generally outnumber actual guests by a ratio of two-to-one.

Hotel Mavi Sürmeli (☎ 363 3437; www.mavisurmeli .com.tr; Inonu Caddesi 109; s/d €55.50/83; 🔀) The main reason to lodge here instead of at the Hilton is the hotel's central location; unless they actually want to, guests at the Mavi won't need to hop in a cab every time they feel the need to grab a quick bite. That said, this is a truly luxurious four-star choice.

Hotel Princess Maya (☎ 459 0966; fax 459 7710; Turhan Cemal Beriker Bulvarı; s/d €58/75; P 🔀) The rooms here aren't terribly exciting – nor is the overall aura – but you will be within easy walking distance of the Sabancı Mosque and the Hilton. Bathrooms are absolutely spotless, and management seems eager to knock about 25% off the price of a room.

Adana Hilton (☎ 355 5000; www.adana.hilton.com; 1 Sokak; Sinanpaşa Mahallesi; s/d €110/185; 🔀 🖳 🖳) Everything you could possibly hope for in one of the region's finest hotels, and probably quite a bit more. Imagine a riverside location with an unreal view of the Sabancı Mosque, out-of-this-world dining options, a fitness centre, and rock-star sized rooms. A little FYI: you'd be wise not to let inquiring locals on the opposite side of the river know that you're staying here.

Eating & Drinking

Adana is famous Turkey-wide for its kebap: minced lamb mixed with hot pepper, squeezed on a flat skewer then charcoal-grilled. It's served with sliced purple onions dusted with fiery paprika, handfuls of parsley, a lemon wedge and flat bread.

Yüzevler (☎ 454 7513; Ziyapaşa Bulvarı, Yüzevler Apt Zemin Kat 25/A; meals €5) If the restaurant's framed photos of Turkish celebs dining here doesn't convince you that this is some of the best Adana kebap the country has to offer, the food itself certainly will.

Sun Patisserie (☎ 458 2134; Ziyapaşa Bulvarı 15/A; 🕙 9am-midnight) Cakes, puddings and a delightfully delicious assortments of chocolates and ice cream have been served up at this Adana standby for over three decades. Don't have a sweet tooth? Come anyway, and join the city's trendiest sidewalk seating scene.

Pronto (☎ 458 4748; Ziyapaşa Bulvarı 27/A; meals €5; 🕙 11am-3am) Tuck into chicken, steak, pasta even cheesecake – at this intimate restaurant and bar with an extensive wine list. Live music nightly, with the exception of Sunday and Monday.

Café Keyif (☎ 457 7820; Ziyapaşa Bulvarı 17/A; meals €5) You might think Turkey had finally joined the EU after spending an hour or two at this wood-panelled, faux-British pub, where nine-to-fivers politely munch on the chef's salads and quietly sip glasses of Efes Pilsen. Sidewalk booths are available for prime people-watching.

Entertainment

Sports Café (☎ 457 3281; Zipaşa Bulvarı 26/C) Just like a Western sports bar, but cleaner, less smoky, and way classier. Extreme sports are shown on five TVs above the bar, and snack foods are of the pizza and burger variety.

Cazara (☎ 459 3305; Ziyapaşa Bulvarı 27/B; 🕙 11am-3am Mon-Sat) Something like a clubhouse for fans of late-80s metal bands and alternative rock. Guitar bands jam every Saturday night; burnouts pound Efes and nod their heads to Skid Row throughout the remainder of the week.

Getting There & Away

AIR

Turkish Airlines (☎ 457 0222; Prof Dr Nusret Fisek Caddesi 22) has daily nonstop flights between Adana and Ankara (one hour), İzmir (1½ hours) and İstanbul (1½ hours). **Onur Air** (☎ 436 6766) flies between Adana and İstanbul.

BUS

Adana's large otogar offers direct buses or dolmuşes to pretty well anywhere. Some useful daily services are listed in the table below. Dolmuşes to Kadirli (€3, one hour, 75km) and Kozan (€3, one hour, 72km) leave from the Yüreği otogar, on the west bank of the Seyhan River.

SERVICES FROM ADANA'S OTOGAR

Destination	Fare	Duration	Distance	Frequency (per day)
Adıyaman (for Nemrut Dağı)	€14	6hr	370km	7 buses
Alanya	€19.50	10hr	440km	8 buses (in summer)
Ankara	€14	10hr	490km	hourly
Antakya	€5.50	3½hr	190km	hourly
Antalya	€16.50	10hr	555km	2 or 3
Diyarbakır	€19.50	10hr	550km	several
Gaziantep	€8	4hr	220km	several
Kayseri	€14	6½hr	335km	several
Konya	€16.50	6½hr	350km	frequent
Şanlıurfa	€16.50	6hr	365km	several
Silifke	€11	2hr	155km	14 buses
Van	€22	18hr	950km	at least one

CAR

Avis city (☎ 453 3045; Ziyapaşa Bulvarı); airport (☎ 453 0476)

Hertz (☎ 458 5062; Ziyapaşa Bulvarı 9)

TRAIN

The façade of the Adana **train station** (☎ 453 3172), at the northern end of Ziyapaşa Bulvarı, is decorated with lovely tiles. The *Toros Ekspres* and the *İçanadolu Mavi* train both travel to İstanbul's Haydarpaşa Station (€18, 19 hours) via Konya (€8, seven hours). Departures are at 2.10pm daily and at 9.10pm on Tuesday, Thursday and Sunday. The *Toros Ekspres* departs for Gaziantep (€5.50, 5½ hours) at 5.05am every Wednesday, Friday and Monday. There are many trains to Mersin via Taurus.

Getting Around

A taxi from the airport into town costs about €5; it's about €7 to the main otogar. Make sure the meter is switched on. A taxi from the city centre to the Yüreği otogar will cost €4.

AROUND ADANA

The far eastern end of the Turkish Mediterranean coast swoops around the Bay of İskenderun (İskenderun Körfezi) to the cities of İskenderun and Antakya, in the province of Hatay. Inland from the bay are ruins of an ancient Hittite city at Karatepe (p432), and of a later Roman one, Anazarbus (Anavarza; opposite). Along the road stand assorted medieval fortresses. The cotton-growing Çukurova plain south of Adana is the landscape used by Turkey's famous author Yaşar Kemal (p55) in his powerful novels about working-class and rural people.

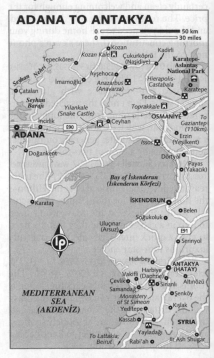

ADANA TO ANTAKYA

Yılankale

If you're driving, keep an eye out for the hilltop **Yılankale** (Snake Castle), 35km east of Adana and 2.5km south of the highway. Built when this area was part of the Armenian kingdom of Cilicia, it's said to have taken its name from a serpent that was once entwined in the coat of arms above the main entrance. It's about a 10-minute climb over the rocks to the fort's highest point.

To continue on to Anazarbus (Anavarza) and Karatepe, head north and east just after the Yılankale turn-off. About 37km east of Adana an intersection is signed on the left (north) for Kozan and Kadirli, on the right (south) for Ceyhan. Take the Kozan–Kadirli road.

Anazarbus (Anavarza)

When the Romans moved into this area in 19 BC they built this fortress city on top of a hill dominating the fertile plain and called it Caesarea-ad-Anazarbus. Later, when Cilicia was divided in two, Tarsus remained the capital of the west and Anazarbus became capital of the east. In the 3rd century AD, Persian invaders destroyed the city. The Byzantine emperors rebuilt it, as they were to do over and over again when later earthquakes destroyed it.

The Arab raids of the 8th century gave Anazarbus new rulers and a new Arabic name, Ain Zarba. The Byzantines reconquered and held it for a brief period, but Anazarbus was an important city at a strategic nexus, and other armies came and snatched it away, including those of the Hamdanid princes of Aleppo, the Crusaders, a local Armenian king, the Byzantines again, the Turks and the Mamluks. The last owners didn't care about it much and it fell into decline in the 15th century. Today it's called Anavarza.

After 5km you reach a road junction and a large **gateway** set in the city walls. Through this gate was the ancient city, now given over to crops and pasture but strewn with ancient stones. Turn left through a village where every other gatepost reuses a Roman column and, after walking 650m, you'll reach the remains of an **aqueduct** with several arches that are still standing.

The village of Anavarza has a couple of simple tea houses and a shop with cold drinks, but that's it. If you have camping equipment you'll probably find a place to pitch a tent.

GETTING THERE & AWAY

From the D400 highway follow the Kozan/Kadirli road north to the village of Ayşehoca, where a road on the right is marked for Anavarza/Anazarbus, 5km to the east. If you're in a dolmuş or bus you can get out here and hitch a ride pretty easily in the morning. Heading on towards Kadirli, hitch back the 5km to Ayşehoca and take the 817 road north

---

ARMENIAN CILICIA

During the early 10th century the Seljuk Turks from Central Asia came hurtling through the continent. Meeting with little resistance from a weak Byzantium, they invaded Asia Minor as well as the Armenian highlands. Thousands of Armenians fled south, taking refuge in the rugged Taurus Mountains and along the Mediterranean coast, where in 1080 they founded the kingdom of Cilicia (or Lesser Armenia) under the young Prince Reuben. The town of Sis (now Kozan; p432) became their capital.

While Greater Armenia struggled against foreign invaders and the subsequent loss of their statehood, the Cilician Armenians lived in wealth and prosperity. Geographically, they were in the ideal place for trade and they quickly embraced Western European ideas, including its feudal class structure. Cilicia became a country of barons, knights and serfs, the court at Sis even adopting European clothes. Latin and French became the national languages. During the Crusades the Christian armies used the kingdom as a safe haven on their way to Jerusalem.

This period of Armenian history is regarded as the most exciting for science and culture, as schools and monasteries flourished, teaching theology, philosophy, medicine and mathematics. It was also the golden age of Armenian ecclesiastical manuscript painting, noted for its lavish decoration and Western influences.

The Cilician kingdom thrived for nearly 300 years before if fell to the Mamluks of Egypt. The last Armenian ruler, Leo IV, spent his final years wandering Europe trying to raise support to recapture his kingdom, before dying in Paris in 1393.

to Naşidiye/Çukurköprü, where the road divides. The left fork is marked for Kozan and Feke, the right for Kadirli.

Kozan

The market town of Kozan (formerly Sis; see p431) was the capital of the kingdom of Cilicia, and the lynchpin of a series of castles overlooking the Çukurova plain. A stunning fortress built by Leo II (r 1187–1219) stretches along a narrow ridge 300m above the town. The view from the top has to be seen to be believed.

Climbing up the road to the castle you pass a pair of towers and then the main gate itself. Inside is a mess of ruined buildings, but if you climb up a narrow ridge (not good if you don't like heights) you can see a many-towered keep on your right, and on your left a massive tower, which once held the royal apartments.

Between the first set of towers and the main gates are the ruins of a church, locally called the *manastir* (monastery). Up until 1921 this was the cathedral of the Catholicos of Sis, one of the two senior patriarchs of the Armenian Church.

Kozan itself has some fine old houses and several cheap eateries and tea houses, and makes a good day trip. There are frequent buses between it and Adana (€1.80, one hour).

OSMANİYE

☎ 0322

Osmaniye lies on the E90, linking Adana and Gaziantep. An uninspiring town, it nevertheless makes a useful base for getting to Hierapolis-Castabala and Karatepe-Aslantaş National Park.

Sleeping & Eating

Hotel Kervansaray (☎ 814 1310; Palalı Süleyman Caddesi; s/d €5/10) This is a basic place – and we do mean basic – with decent rooms. To find it, turn left from the otogar. When you reach the BP garage turn right and the hotel is on the left past the mosque.

Şahin Otel (☎ 812 4444; Dr. Ahmet Alkan Caddesi 27; s/d €22/33) This new hotel, opposite the park on the main street, is the best place to stay in town. The rooms are large and inviting with everything you would expect in a three-star hotel.

This is a town where people eat early. **Uğrak Lokantası** (☎ 813 4990; meals around €2), a few doors down from the Şahin Otel, is a bustling joint

serving up delicious *pilav* (rice) meals as well as hearty *şiş* (spit roast) for around €1.80.

Getting There & Away

Without your own transport your best bet for seeing Hierapolis-Castabala and Karatepe in one day is to organise a taxi. There's a handy taxi rank beside the otogar; to go to Hierapolis for an hour, then to Karatepe for two hours, and either on to Kadirli or back to Osmaniye, should cost about €18.

From the centre of Osmaniye, road 01-08 is signposted northwest for both Hierapolis-Castabala and the Karatepe-Aslantaş Museum. Follow the road until you come to a sign on the right for Hierapolis-Castabala which is 6km along a bumpy road. About 10km beyond Hierapolis-Castabala, a road on the left is marked for Karatepe (9km).

Heading south, there are dolmuşes from Osmaniye to İskenderun (€1.40, one hour). There are also frequent connections west to Adana and east to Gaziantep.

AROUND OSMANİYE
Karatepe-Aslantaş National Park

The **Karatepe-Aslantaş National Park** (Karatepe-Aslantaş Milli Parkı; admission per person/car €0.75/1) incorporates the open-air **Karatepe-Aslantaş Museum**, a site which has been inhabited for almost 4000 years. The ruins date from the 13th century BC, when this was a summer retreat for the neo-Hittite kings of Kizzuwatna (Cilicia), the greatest of whom was named Azitawatas.

From its beautiful, forested hilltop site, the park overlooks **Lake Ceyhan** (Ceyhan Gölü), an artificial lake used for hydroelectric power and recreation.

There is a charge for entrance to the **Hittite ruins** (admission €0.65; ☷ 8am-noon & 1-5pm) in addition to the park admission fee. Be warned that on top of the difficulty of getting to Karatepe without your own transport, the opening hours are rigorously adhered to, and the custodians will only take you around in a group, which can involve hanging about waiting for other people to arrive. Nor are you allowed to take any photographs.

The Hittite remains here are certainly significant, although you shouldn't come expecting something on the scale of Hattuşa (p464). The city was defended by 1km-long **walls**, traces of which are still evident. Its **southern entrance** is protected by four lions and two sphinxes, and lined with fine reliefs showing a coronation or feast complete with sacrificial bull, musicians and chariots.

Hierapolis-Castabala

Set in the midst of cotton fields about 19km south of Karatepe and 15km north of Osmaniye are the ruinss of **Hierapolis-Castabala** (admission €1.25; ☾ 8am-7pm). A *kale* (castle) tops a rocky outcrop above the plain about 1km east of the road. The ticket seller will lend you a leaflet in English, and you can see everything in about an hour.

From the ticket-seller's shed, walk along a **colonnaded street** that once boasted 78 paired columns; some still bear their fine Corinthian capitals. You pass a badly ruined **temple** and **baths** on the right. Keeping the castle on your left, walk past the rock outcrop to the theatre, also badly ruined. Beyond it to the south in the fields is a ruined Byzantine **basilica**. Further along the same path is a *çeşme* (spring) and, in the ridge of rocks further on, some **rock-cut tombs**.

For information on getting to Hierapolis-Castabala, see opposite.

İSKENDERUN

☎ 0326 / pop 160,000

İskenderun, 130km east of Adana, was founded by Alexander the Great in 333 BC; İskenderun is a translation of its original name, Alexandretta.

İskenderun was occupied by the English in 1918, turned over to the French in 1919, and incorporated into the French Protectorate of Syria as the Sanjak of Alexandretta. In 1938 Atatürk reclaimed it for the Turkish Republic. There's nothing to detain you in this modern shipping town but if you have to stop, there are several places to stay near the waterfront, the one attractive area.

Orientation & Information

Assuming you arrive by bus, come out of the otogar and head due south, passing the minibus station before you reach the main highway. To find the sea you'll need to cross the highway and take a right turn towards Şehit Pamir Caddesi. Once on this road, head north until you come to Atatürk Bulvarı and the sea. The main square at the top of Şehit Pamir Caddcsi is marked by a huge monument on the waterfront. Most hotels are within a few blocks of this monument.

The helpful **tourist office** (☎ 614 1620; 49 Atatürk Bulvarı; ☾ 8am-noon & 1.30-5pm Mon-Fri) has local maps and information on the Adana to Antakya region.

Sleeping

Hotel Altındış (☎ 617 1011; hotelaltindis@mynet.com; Şehir Pamir Caddesi 11; s/d €19.50/25; 🗶) The unintentional kitsch factor has been cranked up to 10 at this otherwise unexciting hotel, save for its 2nd-floor lobby, which is ideal for spying on the activity below.

Hotel İmrenay (☎ 613 2117; fax 613 5984; Şehir Pamir Caddesi 5; s/d €22/33; 🗶) A pinch rugged and rundown, although the lobby is rather classy and complete with a flat-screen TV. The owner and his father enjoy having a chat with guests.

Grand Hotel Ontur (☎ 616 2400; Dr Muammer Aksoy Caddesi 8; s/d €76/97; 🗶) İskenderun's poshest hotel has spacious if somewhat dully decorated rooms. Bathrooms are spotless, but considering the outdated state of the place, discounts are definitely in order.

Eating

Saray Restaurant (☎ 617 1383; Atatürk Bulvarı 53) A few doors down from the tourist office, this wonderfully satisfying restaurant has an almost endless menu of mezes, grills and vegetable dishes.

Hasan Baba (☎ 613 2725; Ulucami Caddesi 35; meals around €5) This pide and *lahmacun* joint is sprawling and consistently packed with satisfied diners. Sit in the backyard and enjoy the fountain. City maps are generally available at the front counter.

Getting There & Away

There are frequent minibus and dolmuş connections to Adana (€2.80, 2½ hours, 135km), Antakya (€1, one hour, 58km) and Osmaniye (€1.40, one hour, 63km). Regular dolmuşes scoot down the coast to Uluçınar (Arsuz; €0.80, 30 minutes, 33km).

ANTAKYA (HATAY)

☎ 0326 / pop 140,700

Until its unification with Turkey in 1939, Antakya (Hatay) was Arabic in culture and language. Indeed, many locals still speak Arabic, and the city boasts a mix of Sunni, Alevi and Orthodox Christian faiths.

Modern Antakya is hardly a beautiful place, but its museum is one of Turkey's finest, justifying a lengthy detour. In the cave-church

EASTERN MEDITERRANEAN

ANTAKYA (HATAY)

INFORMATION
Ferah Kırtasiye ve Kitabevi......... **1** C3
Moda-Net Internet Café............ **2** C3
Tourist Office............................ **3** B1
Türk Telecom Phone & Internet.. **4** C2
Yapı Kredi ATM........................ **5** C2

SIGHTS & ACTIVITIES
Antakya Archaeology Museum.. **6** B3
Bazaar...................................... **7** C3
Belediye (Town Hall)................. **8** B3
Catholic Church........................ **9** C4
Habibi Naccar Camii................. **10** C3
Orthodox Church...................... **11** B4
Sermaye Camii.......................... **12** C4
Synagogue................................ **13** C4
Ulu Cami.................................. **14** C3

SLEEPING
Antik Beyazıt Otel..................... **15** B4
Antik Grand Hotel..................... **16** B3
Büyük Antakya Oteli.................. **17** B2
Catholic Church Guesthouse.....(see 9)
Divan Oteli............................... **18** C2
Grand Kavak Otel...................... **19** C2
Hotel Orontes........................... **20** C2
Hotel Saray............................... **21** C3
Mozaik Otel.............................. **22** C3
Onur Hotel............................... **23** C2
Şeker Palas Oteli....................... **24** C2

EATING
Antakya Evi.............................. **25** B4
Han Restaurant......................... **26** B4
Kral Künefe.............................. **27** C3
Sultan Sofrası........................... **28** C3
Süper 96.................................. **29** C3

DRINKING
Sarmaşık Çay Bahçesi.............. **30** A4

ENTERTAINMENT
Konak Sinema.......................... **31** B3

TRANSPORT
İskenderun Dolmuş Stand........ **32** D2
Otogar..................................... **33** C2
Reyhanlı Dolmuş Stand............ **34** D1
Samandağ Dolmuş Stand.......... **35** D1
Taxi Stand................................ (see 36)
Yayladağı Dolmuş Stand.......... **36** D2

of St Peter, Antakya can also lay claim to possessing 'the world's first cathedral', where the apostle is said to have preached and where the term 'Christian' was first used (Acts 11, verse 26). The city is still the titular seat of five Christian Patriarchs – three Catholic (Syrian Catholic, Maronite and Greco-Melchite), one Greek Orthodox and one Syrian-Tacobite – although none are based here any longer.

Throughout Antakya's long history, violent earthquakes have repeatedly shattered the town, most notably in AD 526 when around 250,000 people were killed. This explains why so little remains of the old city.

Antakya is backed by the Altınözü Mountains, with the peak of Mt Silpius dominating the area.

History

Antakya is the ancient Antioch-ad-Orontes, which was founded by Seleucus I Nicator in 300 BC and soon became a city of half a million people. Under the Romans an important Christian community developed out of the already large Jewish one. At one time this was headed by St Paul.

Persians, Byzantines, Arabs, Armenians and Seljuks all fought over Antioch, as did the Crusaders and Saracens. In 1268 the Mamluks of Egypt sacked the city. The Ottomans held onto it until Mohammed Ali of Egypt captured it in 1831, but with European help they eventually drove their rebellious vassal back.

Antakya was part of the French protectorate of Syria until 1938, after which it enjoyed a brief existence as the independent Republic of Hatay. But when Atatürk saw WWII approaching, he wanted the city rejoined to the republic as a defensive measure. Parliament voted for union with Turkey, and on 23 July 1939 Hatay became Turkish. The Syrian government never accepted this, and some Syrian maps still show it as part of Syria.

Orientation

The Asi (Orontes) River divides the town. The modern district is on the west bank, with the PTT, government buildings and museum circling the Cumhuriyet Alanı traffic roundabout.

The older Ottoman town on the east bank is the commercial centre, with most of the hotels, restaurants and services, especially along Hürriyet Caddesi. The otogar is a few blocks northeast of the centre. Continue northeast along İstiklal Caddesi for dolmuşes to Samandağ.

Information

The **tourist office** (☎ 216 0610; ☼ 8am-noon & 1-5pm) is adept at changing homes. It was last sited on a roundabout on Atatürk Caddesi, a good 10-minute walk from town.

There are several ATMs close to the otogar as well as across the Asi River next to the Büyük Antakya Oteli. The **Ferah Kırtasiye ve Kitabevi** (Hürriyet Caddesi 17/D) stocks English-language newspapers.

The Moda-Net Internet C@fé is upstairs in an arcade off Hürriyet Caddesi, between the Saray Hotel and the Ferah Kırtasiye ve Kitabevi.

Sights

ANTAKYA ARCHAEOLOGY MUSEUM

The prime reason for journeying all the way to Antakya is this **museum** (Antakya Arkeoloji Muzesi; ☎ 214 6168; Gündüz Caddesi; admission €3; ☼ 8.30am-noon & 1.30-5pm Tue-Sun). Here you'll see as fine a collection of Roman/Byzantine mosaics as graces any museum in the world, covering a period from the 1st century AD to the 5th century. While some are inevitably fragmentary, others were recovered almost intact. Most labels are in English and Turkish.

Salons I to IV are tall, naturally lit rooms, perfect for displaying mosaics so fine that at first glance you may mistake some of them for paintings. Be sure to see the **Oceanus and Thetis mosaic** (2nd century) and the **Buffet Mosaic**

(3rd century). As well as the standard scenes of hunting and fishing there are stories from mythology. Other mosaics have quirkier subjects: Don't miss the happy hunchback, the black fisherman or the mysterious portrayal of a raven, a scorpion and a pitchfork attacking the 'evil eye'. Many of the mosaics came from Roman seaside villas or from the suburban resort of Daphne (Harbiye), although some are from Tarsus.

BAZAAR DISTRICT

A sprawling **bazaar** fills the back streets between the otogar, Kemal Paşa Caddesi and Kurtulus Caddesi. Around Habibi Naccar Camii you'll find most of Antakya's remaining **old houses**, with carved stone lintels or wooden overhangs. It's one of the most interesting old neighbourhoods in Turkey to wander around; you might catch a glimpse of the courtyards within the compounds. The Italian priests at the Catholic Church believe St Peter would have lived in this area between 42 and 48 AD, as it was then the Jewish neighbourhood.

CAVE-CHURCH OF ST PETER

About 3km from the centre in the northeastern outskirts of town, you'll find this **cave-church** (St Pierre Kilisesi; admission €3; ☼ 8.30am-noon & 1.30-4.30pm Tue-Sun) cut into the slopes of Mt Staurin (Mountain of the Cross). This is said to be the earliest place where Christians met and prayed secretly. Tradition has it that this cave was the property of St Luke the Evangelist, who was from Antioch, and that he donated it to the burgeoning Christian congregation as a place of worship. Peter and Paul lived in Antioch for a few years and are thought to have preached here. When the Crusaders marched through in 1098, they constructed the wall at the front and a narthex.

To the right of the altar faint traces of fresco can still be seen, and some of the simple mosaic floor survives. The water dripping in the corner is said to cure sickness.

You can easily walk to the church in about half an hour, heading northeast along Kurtuluş Caddesi.

RELIGIOUS BUILDINGS

Most of Antakya's 1200-odd Christians worship at the fine **Orthodox Church** (Hürriyet Caddesi; ☼ prayers 8.15am & 6pm). Rebuilt in the 19th century with Russian assistance, the church contains some beautiful icons.

The **Catholic Church** (Kurtuluş Caddesi, Kutlu Sokak 6; ☾ mass 8.30am daily & 6pm Sun) occupies two houses in the city's old quarter, with the chapel in the former living room of one house. Next door is the **Sermaye Cami**, with a wonderfully ornate minaret (you'll see it on posters of Antakya), and nearby at Kurtuluş 56 is a **synagogue**.

Sleeping

BUDGET

Şeker Palas Oteli (☎ 215 1603; İstiklal Caddesi 79; s/d €10/16.50) If you're looking for scary, you've found it. This hotel across from the otogar is the true epitome of rugged lodging. Squatter toilets down the hall, a curious smell throughout, and no breakfast included. But take the manager up on his offer to discount a room rate, and you've got one of the cheapest sleeps in town.

Divan Oteli (☎ 215 1518; İstiklal Caddesi 62; s/d €11/16.50; ✗) Certainly the best of Antakya's budget options, some rooms here have balconies and small desks. There's also a quite comfortable lobby.

Hotel Saray (☎ 214 9001; fax 214 9002; Hürriyet Caddesi; s/d €16.50/25; ✗) Definitely a little rugged and musty, although the rooms (with TV included) are certainly large enough, and some have decent mountain views.

Assuming a tour group hasn't already beat you to it, you may be able to stay at one of the eight rooms of the Catholic Church's **guesthouse** (domenicobertogli@hotmail.com; Kurtuluş Caddesi; Kutlu Sokak 6; per person €8). Note though that you will be expected to attend daily mass.

MIDRANGE

Grand Kavak Otel (☎ 214 3530; www.kavakotel.com; İstiklal Caddesi 16; s/d €20/31; ✗ 🖳) A fantastic choice with plain but very comfortable and clean rooms with satellite TV included. This place also gets good marks for its free wi-fi, free use of an internet terminal, impressive breakfast spread, and especially helpful staff.

Hotel Orontes (☎ 214 5931; fax 214 5933; İstiklal Caddesi 58; s/d €25/39; ✗) This two-star hotel near the otogar is somewhat plainly decorated, although rooms are quite large and satellite TV is included.

Onur Hotel (☎ 216 2210; onurhotel@hotmail.com; İstiklal Caddesi 16; s/d €28/39; ✗) The rooms are a bit shabby and the showers are due for a serious scrubbing, but management is willing to cut rates by about €10. Rooms, such as they are, come complete with TV and minibar.

Antik Grand Hotel (☎ 215 7575; www.antikgrand.com; Hürriyet Caddesi 18; s/d €33/50; ✗) Attached to the Antik Grand Restaurant next door, this new hotel offers tasteful rooms in a beautiful faux-antique style. All rooms have TV and minibar, and discounts are available for the asking.

TOP END

Büyük Antakya Oteli (☎ 213 5858; fax 213 5869; Atatürk Caddesi 8; s/d €54.50/78; ✗) A fairly standard four-star spot with a hairdresser and travel agent onsite. Morning breakfast spreads are lavish, and some rooms have decent city and river views. Certainly large and comfortable enough, yet slightly overpriced.

Antik Beyazıt Otel (☎ 216 2900; beyazit@antikbeyazitoteli.com; Hükümet Caddesi 4; s/d €69.50/86; ✗) A warmly decorated French colonial structure filled with antique furniture and antique details. Expect Turkish carpets on the floors, European paintings and prints in the rooms, and an elegant lobby complete with drapery and an ornate chandelier.

Eating & Drinking

Syrian influences permeate Antakya's cuisine. Handfuls of mint and wedges of lemon accompany many kebaps. Hummus, rare elsewhere in Turkey, is readily available here. Many main courses and salads are dusted with fiery pepper; if this isn't to your taste, ask for yours *acısız* (without hot pepper).

For dessert, try the local speciality, *künefe,* a cake of fine shredded wheat laid over a dollop of fresh, mild cheese, on a layer of sugar syrup, topped with chopped walnuts and baked. Try and get it hot, straight from the oven. Shops at the northern end of Hürriyet Caddesi sell it. Kral Künefe near the Ulu Cami is the most popular of these, and has seating upstairs and outside.

A good place to hang out is the riverside Antakya Belediyesi Park, a few blocks southwest of the museum. Here you'll find tea gardens, such as the Sarmaşık Çay Bahçesi, as well as shady promenades.

Süper 96 (Kutlu Sokak; meals €2-3) A fast-food and *lahmacun* joint popular with teenagers.

Sultan Sofrası (☎ 213 8759; İstiklal Caddesi 20; meals around €5) Right next door to the Mosaic Hotel, this is a cheap eatery that packs in the locals at lunchtime. Try the *İskender* döner or a kebap. The *sütlaç* (rice pudding) is also quite good.

Han Restaurant (☎ 215 8538; Hürriyet Caddesi 17/1; meals €5-7) One of the city's most enjoyable eateries, with a fantastic İskender *döner*, wonderful *künefe*, and an almost comically attentive staff. The outdoor terrace is an absolute delight on a cool evening.

Antakya Evi (☎ 214 1350; Silahlı Kuvvetler Caddesi 3; meals €6-9) With a name like Antakya Evi (*evi* means home), it's little wonder that dining here feels much like eating at a friend's place. Tastefully decorated with photos and antique furniture, and serving toothsome kebaps and standard grills.

Entertainment
Konak Sinema (Karaoğlanoğlu Caddesi; admission €2.50) English-language blockbusters subtitled in Turkish are screened here.

Getting There & Away
BUS
To & From Syria
Everyone needs a visa to enter Syria (see the boxed text p674).

The Jet bus company at Antakya otogar has direct buses to Aleppo (€3, four hours, 105km) at 9am and noon daily, and to Damascus (€5.50, eight hours) at noon daily. These buses follow the route that all cross-border buses and trucks take, the Reyhanlı–Bab al-Hawa border, so you'll need to brace yourself for waits of two to four hours. To avoid hanging about at the border, ensure you are passing through before 8am or take a shared or private taxi, which can negotiate a path through the stationary buses and trucks. A taxi from Antakya (Turkey) to Aleppo (Syria) costs around €25.

If you want to tackle the border in stages, local buses to Reyhanlı (€1, 45 minutes) leave from in front of the petrol station on the corner of Yavuz Sultan Selim and İstiklal Caddesi. From Reyhanlı you can catch a dolmuş to the Turkish border. Then you have to walk a couple of kilometres to the Syrian border.

Alternatively, catch a dolmuş south to Yayladağı (from behind the taxi rank across the road from the entrance to the otogar), from where you pick up a taxi or hitch a few kilometres further to the border. Once across (and crossing takes all of 15 minutes here), you're just 2km from the Syrian mountain village of Kassab, from where regular microbuses make the 45-minute run to Lattakia (S£25).

Within Turkey
The otogar has direct buses to most western and northern points (Ankara, Antalya, İstanbul,

İzmir, Kayseri and Konya), usually travelling via Adana (€5.50, 3½ hours) and through the Cilician Gates (p428). There are frequent services to Gaziantep (€6.50, four hours) and Şanlıurfa (€11, seven hours, 345km), either direct or via Gaziantep. Minibuses and dolmuşes for İskenderun (€1.50, one hour) leave from a stand just north of the otogar.

AROUND ANTAKYA
Harbiye (Daphne)
The hill suburb of Harbiye, 9km to the south of Antakya, is the ancient Daphne where, according to classical mythology, the virgin Daphne prayed to be rescued from the attentions of the god Apollo and was turned into a laurel tree. There are no laurels to be seen nowadays, although pine trees ring a large pool of water, very popular as a picnic place. The best approach is to get off the dolmuş opposite Hotel Çağlayan and walk down into the wooded valley on the left, which is usually full of Antakyalı holidaymakers enjoying the tea gardens and the pools and rivulets of cooling water.

GETTING THERE & AWAY
From Antakya, frequent dolmuşes and city buses run along Kurtuluş Caddesi to Harbiye (€0.50, 15 minutes), where they stop (briefly) to pick up passengers.

Monastery of St Simeon
The remains of this 6th century monastery sit on a mountain 7km from the village of Karaçay, about 18km from Antakya, on the way to Samandağ. There was no ticket office when we visited.

The cross-shaped monastery contains the ruins of three churches. The remains of mosaics can be seen in the first, but the central church is the most beautiful, with rich carvings. The third church is more austere and was probably once used by the monks. The monastery and pillar were carved out of the mountain with an octagonal area around the pillar (the base of it remains) where pilgrims could listen to St Simeon preaching against the iniquities of Antioch. There are also the remains of a stepped structure next to the pillar, which pilgrims might have been able to climb to address the saint personally.

GETTING THERE & AWAY
The turn-off to the monastery is just past the village of Karaçay, reachable by a Samandağ

dolmuş (€0.50, 20 minutes) from Antakya. The dolmuş stand is on İstiklal Caddesi at the junction with Yavuz Sultan Selim Caddesi.

You can take a taxi from the monastery for about €17 return, plus an hour at the site, or you could walk. A sign points up a road just past Karaçay. After 4km the road branches. The monastery lies about 2.5km down the track leading to the right.

Vakıflı

About 35km west of Antakya, on the slopes of Mt Musa, is Vakıflı, the last ethnic Armenian village in Turkey, home to a community of about 130 Turkish-Armenians. Until 1939 there were six Armenian villages in the vicinity, but when the Hatay joined Turkey most of the local Armenians were resettled in Lebanon. The residents of Vakıfli are mostly elderly, but the village seems to be fairly prosperous, making a living from the attractive orchards around it. Turkish Armenians from İstanbul visit in summer. The local church is worth visiting, if it's open.

GETTING THERE & AWAY

Dolmuşes from Antakya to Samandağ (€0.50, 35 minutes, 29km) leave from an unmarked stand on Yavuz Sultan Selim Caddesi, near the corner with İstiklal Caddesi. From Samandağ a few dolmuşes journey to Vakıfli every day, but you might have better luck hitching.

Çevlik

If you continue 6km west towards the sea from Samandağ you'll come to Çevlik and the scant ruins of **Seleuceia-in-Pieria**, the port of Antioch in ancient times. Çevlik itself is pretty dejected, but what you come here for is the **Titus & Vespasian Tunnel** (Titüs ve Vespasiyanüs Tüneli; admission €1), an astonishing feat of Roman engineering. During its heyday, Seleucia lived with the constant threat of inundation from a stream that descended from the mountains and flowed through the town. To counter this threat, the Roman emperors Titus and Vespasian ordered their engineers to dig a diversion channel around the town.

From the Çevlik car park, ascend the steps to the gate. If there's somebody in the booth you'll have to pay the admission fee, after which a guide will accompany you up the hillside, along the channel and through a great gorge. The walk is over rocks – definitely sturdy-shoe rather than sandal terrain.

If you're not up to it, follow the channel until you come to a metal arch on the right. Then take the path behind the arch (right fork) which follows an irrigation canal past some rock-cut shelters, finally arriving at a humpback Roman bridge across the gorge. Here, steps lead down to the tunnel. Bring a torch since the path is still pretty treacherous. At the far end of the channel an inscription provides a date for the work.

The slopes above the Roman bridge provide a perfect picnic spot.

GETTING THERE & AWAY

Dolmuşes run between Samandağ and Çevlik (€0.50) every 30 minutes or so during daylight hours.

Central Anatolia

Central Anatolia is the heartland of Turkey, both geographically and culturally. Tribes, races and empires have been fighting over these dusty steppes and hills for centuries, dragging cities from obscurity to prominence, or from prosperity to destruction, sometimes spending decades battling over the same patch of ground. Civilisations were made or broken in the crucible of the Anatolian summer, leaving tantalising glimpses of themselves behind.

Today the evidence of history's ebbs and flows is laid out all across the region like a giant crime scene, just waiting for the keen-eyed traveller to play detective. Follow the right traces and you'll find Neolithic settlements rubbing shoulders with Hittite cities, and Seljuk pomp vying with Ottoman glamour, all founded on the forgotten ashes of a hundred more failed invaders.

Ultimately, the result of this constant fuss and flux is the characteristic Turkish culture we see today, exemplified above all by the modern cities of Ankara and Konya, which embrace their past but move beyond it, fixing their sights firmly on a prosperous tomorrow. Trends may be set in İstanbul, but it's here that they become fashion, and without its heartland Turkey could never follow its true beat.

One thing's for sure: this is one region where you'll have to work for your experience, and you'll never discover the real heart of Anatolia through a bus window. So whether it's schnitzel in Sivas, chickpeas in Çorum or tea in Tokat, get out, eat the kebaps, sample the sweets, drink the beer, have the massages, visit the mosques, talk to the students, browse the shops and get involved!

HIGHLIGHTS

- Explore millennia of antiquity in Ankara's **citadel** (p445) and **Museum of Anatolian Civilisations** (p443)
- Kip down on a *şedir* (divan) in an Ottoman mansion at **Safranbolu** (p455)
- Decode cuneiform and appreciate hilly Hittite culture amid the ruins of **Hattuşa** (p463)
- Marvel at the surreal beauty of riverside **Amasya** (p468)
- Sample the best kebap in the land in between massages in **Tokat** (p476)
- Inspire own your creative carving at the mighty Ulu Cami portals of **Divriği** (p481)
- Bow down with pilgrims to the memory of a dervish at Konya's **Mevlâna Museum** (p483)

★ Safranbolu
★ Amasya
★ Tokat
★ Ankara
★ Hattuşa
★ Divriği
★ Konya

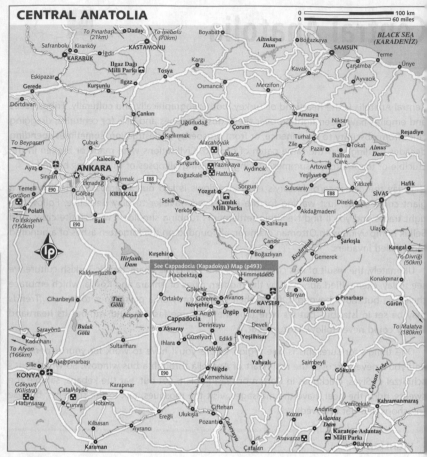

CENTRAL ANATOLIA

ANKARA

☎ 0312 / pop 4.3 million

These days just about everyone could name the capital of Turkey correctly in a pub quiz, which goes to show how far Ankara has come in the public consciousness since the days when 'İstanbul' seemed like the only possible answer. In the 80 years since independence the once anonymous provincial capital has really grown into its role as an international city, assuming a very modern air of sophistication. Café culture in particular has transformed the city, breathing full-on life into its wide, open streets.

As the city expands, everything that's new and now tends to pop up at random points across the lattice of suburbs, making it tricky for short-term visitors to track down the latest hotspots. If you really want to keep up with the thriving city scene, get used to asking locals for tips and taking taxis to find them.

History

Although Hittite remains dating back to before 1200 BC have been found in Ankara, the town really began as a Phrygian settlement that prospered at the intersection of the north–south and east–west trade routes. Later it was taken by Alexander the Great, claimed by the Seleucids and finally occupied by the Galatians, who invaded Anatolia around 250 BC. Augustus Caesar annexed it to Rome in 25 BC as Ankyra.

The Byzantines held the town for centuries, with intermittent raids by the Persians and

Arabs. When the Seljuk Turks came to Anatolia after 1071, they grabbed the city but held it only with difficulty. The Ottomans, too, had problems: Sultan Yıldırım Beyazıt was captured by Tamerlane near here, and subsequently died in captivity. Spurned as a jinxed endeavour, the city slowly slumped into a backwater, prized for nothing but its goats.

That all changed, of course, when Atatürk picked Angora as his base of operations in the struggle for independence. When he set up his provisional government here in 1920, the city was just a small, dusty settlement of some 30,000 people – but after his victory in the War of Independence, Atatürk declared it the new Turkish capital (October 1923), and set about developing it. European urban planners were consulted, and the result is a city boasting long, wide boulevards, a forested park with an artificial lake, and numerous residential and diplomatic neighbourhoods. The city's position in the centre of Turkey made it more suitable than İstanbul, both physically and symbolically, as a capital for the new republic. From 1919 to 1927, Atatürk never set foot in İstanbul, preferring to work at making Ankara top dog in fact as well as on paper.

Orientation

The main street is Atatürk Bulvarı, which runs 5.5km from the old part of town, Ulus, in the north, through Kızılay and Kavaklıdere, to Çankaya in the south.

Ulus is marked by a large equestrian statue of Atatürk in Ulus Meydanı. The most important museums and sights are nearby, as are dozens of budget and midrange hotels and restaurants. The train station, near the terminus for the Havaş airport buses, is 1400m southwest of Ulus Meydanı along Cumhuriyet Bulvarı.

Kızılay, the area around the intersection of Atatürk Bulvarı and Gazi Mustafa Kemal Bulvarı/Ziya Gökalp Caddesi, is the centre of buzzy 'new' Ankara, with midrange and top-end hotels, bars, café-restaurants and bus ticket offices.

Kavaklıdere, 2km south along Atatürk Bulvarı, is a fashionable district with embassies, airline and car rental offices, trendy bars, smart shops, and the Hilton and Sheraton hotels.

Up in the hills south of Kavaklıdere is Çankaya, the residential neighbourhood that hosts the presidential mansion and many of the ambassadorial residences. Its most prominent landmark is the Atakule, a tall tower with a revolving restaurant, visible throughout the city.

The AŞTİ, Ankara's otogar (bus station), is 5.5km southwest of Ulus and 4.5km west of Kızılay.

Information

BOOKSHOPS

Dost Kitabevi (Map p444; ☎ 418 8327; Konur Sokak 4, Kızılay) Some foreign-language novels and local-interest titles.

Turhan Kitabevi (Map p444; ☎ 418 8259; Yüksel Caddesi 8/32, Kızılay) Coffee table books, guidebooks, maps, fiction and a lot of newspapers and magazines.

INTERNET ACCESS

The densest concentration of internet cafés can be found in Kızılay, around Konur Sokak. Wi-fi access is available in many hotels, cafés and bars.

Internet Club (Map p444; Karanfil Sokak 47/A; per hr €1; ☼ 9-1am) Fast access and some outdoor (!) terminals.

Makronet (Map p444; Selanik Caddesi 52; per hr €0.70; ☼ 9-1am) Internet and gamers' café with 100 terminals.

MEDICAL SERVICES

Bayındır Hospital (Map p442; ☎ 428 0808; Atatürk Bulvarı 201, Kavaklıdere) The city's most up-to-date private hospital.

City Hospital (Map p442; ☎ 466 3346; Büklüm Sokak 53) Near Tunalı Hilmi Caddesi, with a modern Women's Health Centre (Kadın Sağlığı Merkezi).

MONEY

There are lots of banks with ATMs in Ulus, Kızılay and Kavaklıdere.

Sakarya Döviz (Map p444; Sakarya Caddesi 6-A, Kızılay) Changes cash quickly and easily.

POST & COMMUNICATIONS

There are PTT branches in the train station, at the AŞTİ otogar and on Atatürk Bulvarı in Ulus. All have public phone booths nearby.

Türk Telekom (Map p442; Gazi Mustafa Kemal Bulvarı, Maltepe; 🖳) Near the tourist office.

TOURIST INFORMATION

Tourist office (Map p442; ☎ 231 5572; Gazi Mustafa Kemal Bulvarı 121, Maltepe; ☼ 9am-5pm Mon-Fri, 10am-5pm Sat) Opposite Maltepe Ankaray station. Offers the usual glossy handouts and free maps; English and some French spoken.

CENTRAL ANATOLIA

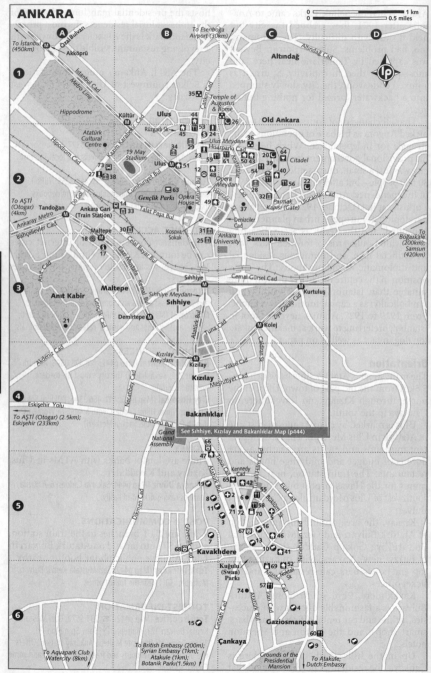

ANKARA

See Sıhhiye, Kızılay and Bakanlıklar Map (p444)

CENTRAL ANATOLIA

TRAVEL AGENCIES

Raytur (Map p442; ☎ 311 4200; www.raytur.com.tr; TCDD Gar Binası İçi, Ulus) Operated by Turkish Railways, in Ankara station. Sells rail and air tickets, jeep safaris, domestic and outbound tours.

Saltur (Map p442; ☎ 425 1333; www.saltur.com.tr; Tunus Caddesi 14/3, Kavaklıdere) Airline and international tour agent.

Sights & Activities

MUSEUM OF ANATOLIAN CIVILISATIONS

Still proudly displaying its 1997 Best European Museum award, Ankara's superb **Museum of Anatolian Civilisations** (Anadolu Medeniyetleri Müzesi; Map p442; ☎ 324 3160; admission €5.60; ☉ 8.30am-5.15pm) is the perfect introduction to the complex weave of Turkey's chequered ancient past, housing artefacts cherrypicked from just about every significant archaeological site in Anatolia.

The museum is housed in a beautifully restored 15th-century *bedesten* (market vault). The 10-domed central marketplace houses reliefs and statuary, while the surrounding hall displays exhibits from the earlier Anatolian civilisations: Palaeolithic, Neolithic, Chalcolithic, Bronze Age, Assyrian, Hittite, Phrygian,

Urartian and Lydian. The downstairs sections hold classical Greek and Roman artefacts and a display on Ankara's history.

You may be approached by would-be guides outside the museum; if you want to use their services, agree a price in advance and be sure that it's for your entire group, not per person. You can buy drinks in the museum.

If it's not too hot, you can climb the hill from Ulus to the museum (1km); from Ulus head east up Hisarparkı Caddesi and turn right into Anafartalar Caddesi, then bear left along Çıkrıkçılar Sokak to reach the museum. A taxi from Ulus should cost about €2.

Touring the Museum

The exhibits here are arranged in a basic spiral: start at the Palaeolithic displays to the right of the entrance, then continue in an anticlockwise direction, visiting the central room last.

Most of the Palaeolithic finds (three million years ago through to 8000 BC) were found in the Karain Cave (p394), near Antalya, and suggest a nomadic hunter-gatherer lifestyle and the development of stone and, later, bone tools. Also here are finds from the Neolithic era (8000-5500 BC), when people started to settle in villages, cultivating crops, raising livestock, and producing storage and cooking vessels. Çatalhöyük (p489), 50km southeast of Konya, is one of the most important Neolithic sites in the world. Here you can see a mock-up of the inside of a dwelling typical of those uncovered at the site; the clay bull-head icons were a feature of the cult of the time.

The Chalcolithic age saw the introduction of copper work, and the refinement of pottery, statuary and painted decoration. The finds on display here are mainly from Turkey's most important Chalcolithic site at Hacılar, near Burdur.

Many of the Bronze Age artefacts on display came from the ancient site of Alacahöyük (p467) and show the proficiency that had been achieved with metalwork. The gold jewellery, idols and various bronze standards would have been used for cult worship and were often buried with the dead.

Also on show are many finds from Kültepe, an Assyrian trading colony near Kayseri, and one of the oldest and wealthiest bazaars in the world. Many of the baked-clay tablets found at the site are on display here.

One of the striking Hittite figures of bulls and stags in the next room used to be the emblem of Ankara. The Hittites were known for their relief work, and some mighty slabs representing the best pieces found in the country,

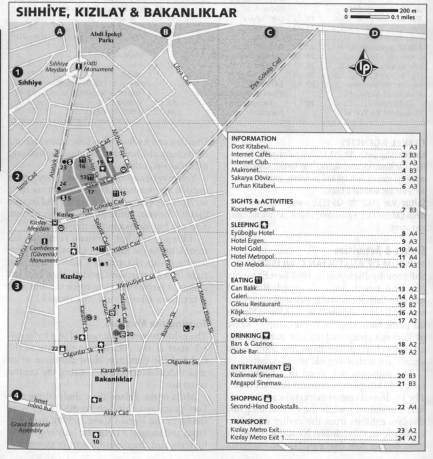

CENTRAL ANATOLIA

SIHHIYE, KIZILAY & BAKANLIKLAR

usually from around Hattuşa (p463), are on display in the museum's central room.

Most of the finds from the Phrygian capital Gordion (p454), including incredible inlaid wooden furniture, are on display in the museum's last rooms.

The best artefacts from the Urartian empire are on display in the Van and Elazığ museums, but Ankara still has a representative collection of works from this lesser known civilisation, including bronze armour indented with figurative decorations, and ivory statues and seals.

Downstairs, the classical-period finds and regional history displays aren't as epoch-defining as the main attractions, but it's good to get the local picture. After all, who knew that Ankara has its own 'missing link', the *Ancarapithecus*, a mere 9.8 million years old?

CITADEL

When you're done with the museum, it would be smart to make the most of its location by wandering to the imposing **hisar** (citadel or Ankara Kalesi; Map p442) just up the hill. By far the most interesting part of Ankara to poke about in, this well-preserved quarter of thick walls and intriguing winding streets took its present shape in the 9th century AD, when the Byzantine emperor Michael II constructed the outer ramparts. The inner walls, which the local authority is slowly rebuilding, date from the 7th century.

To find it, head around the back of the museum up Gözcü Sokak, past the octagonal tower, then turn left to enter through the **Parmak Kapısı** (Finger Gate), also called the Saatli Kapı (Clock Gate).

Just opposite this gate, in the old Çengelhan, the new **Rahmi M Koç Industrial Museum** Rahmi M Koç Müzesi; www.rmk-museum.org.tr; adult/child 1.70/0.70; ⊗ 10am-5pm Tue-Fri, 10am-7pm Sat & Sun) is perfect for kids (and adults) who prefer a hands-on approach to staring at a bunch of pots behind glass, and has slightly less emphasis on transport than its original branch in İstanbul (p123).

Walk straight ahead once you've entered the gate and you'll see, on your left, the citadel mosque, the **Alaettin Camii**, which dates from the 12th century but has been extensively rebuilt. To your right a steep road leads to a flight of stairs taking you up to the **Şark Kulesi** (Eastern Tower), with panoramic city views. Although it's much harder to find, the tower

at the north, **Ak Kale** (White Fort), also offers fine views. If you're coming up to the citadel along Hisarparkı Caddesi, look left about halfway up to see the remains of a **Roman theatre** from around 200 to 100 BC.

Inside the citadel local people still live as in a traditional Turkish village, and you'll see women beating and sorting skeins of wool in the gaps between the inevitable carpet shops. As you wander about, you'll notice broken column drums, bits of marble statuary and inscribed lintels all incorporated into the mighty walls.

There are no fewer than 14 restaurants inside the citadel, most done out in traditional Ottoman style; see p449 for more details. The streets just outside the Parmak Kapısı are also great places to browse for antiques – see p451.

ANIT KABIR

Even if you've never taken much interest in the founder of modern Turkey, Mustafa Kemal (Atatürk)'s monumental mausoleum, the **Anıt Kabir** (Monumental Tomb; Map p442; admission free; ⊗ 9am-5pm Apr-Sep, to 4pm Oct-Mar), is well worth a look to try to grasp just how much sway the man held over his adoring republic.

As you approach the tomb there are two small towers. The **Hurriyet Kulesi** (Independence Tower) contains information about the building of the tomb and photos of Atatürk's funeral, while the **İstiklal Kulesi** (Freedom Tower) explains the iconography of the site.

From the towers a paved walkway is guarded by bored soldiers and paired stone lions – Hittite symbols of power and strength. Sitting on the lions is strictly prohibited (and we wouldn't recommend sitting on the guards either). This path leads to a massive courtyard, framed by colonnaded walkways, with the huge tomb at its southern end.

Within the colonnade, the **museum** rooms display Atatürk memorabilia, personal effects, official automobiles and catafalque (funereal platform), though all the rich artefacts reveal far less about the man than his simple rowing machine and huge multilingual library. On the downstairs level are extensive exhibits about the War of Independence and the formation of the republic, moving from battlefield murals with sound effects to rather overdetailed explanations of the various post-1923 reforms. At the end, a gift shop sells items such as Atatürk posters, plates, ties and height charts, perfect for those 'just what I always wanted' moments.

As you approach the tomb itself, look left and right at the gilded inscriptions, which are quotations from Atatürk's speech celebrating the republic's 10th anniversary in 1932. Remove your hat as you enter, and crick your neck up at the lofty hall, lined in marble and sparingly decorated with mosaics. At the northern end stands an immense marble **cenotaph**, cut from a single piece of stone weighing 40 tons. The actual tomb is in a chamber beneath it.

It should take around 1½ hours to see the whole site, assuming it's not too busy: school groups frequently drop by in midweek, especially in May, June and September.

The memorial stands on top of a small hill in a park about 2km west of Kızılay. The nearest Ankaray station to the entrance is Tandoğan, 1.2km north. It's a pleasant uphill walk to the mausoleum (about 20 minutes), or you can take a taxi (€1.10); if you drive up you will need to leave your licence at the gate. Note that security checks are carried out on entry, including a bag scan, and guns, pets and balloons are not permitted.

OTHER MUSEUMS
Ethnography Museum

South of Ulus, the **Ethnography Museum** (Etnografya Müzesi; Map p442; Talat Paşa Bulvarı; admission €1.25; 8.30am-12.30pm & 1.30-5.30pm) is a real treasure. It's housed inside a white marble post-Ottoman building (1925) that once served as Atatürk's offices (hence the equestrian statue out the front). Around the walls are photographs of Atatürk's funeral, which illustrate a level of genuine national mourning seldom seen in Western cultures.

The museum contains wonderful collections of embroidery, porcelain (the İznik tiles are especially fine) and woodwork, including a stunning 13th-century *mihrab* (niche indicating the direction of Mecca) from Damsa, near Ürgüp. You'll be driven mad by the automatic lighting system and the lack of labelling, but the tableaux of a wedding party and circumcision celebration are pretty self-explanatory.

Just next door, the **Painting & Sculpture Museum** (Resim ve Heykel Müzesi; admission €1.10; 9am-noon & 1-5pm) occupies an equally elaborate building and showcases mainly modern and contemporary Turkish works.

Museum of the War of Independence

This **museum** (Kurtuluş Savaşı Müzesi; Map p442; Cumhuriyet Bulvarı; admission €1.10; 8.45am-12.15pm & 1.30-5.15pm Tue-Sun) is where the republican grand national assembly held its early sessions up until 1925. Before it was Turkey's first parliament, the building was the Ankara headquarters of the Committee of Union & Progress, the party of 'Young Turks' that overthrew Sultan Abdül Hamit II in 1909 and attempted to bring democracy to the Ottoman Empire. Today you'll see numerous photographs, documents and a throng of soldiers, here to learn about the campaigns. You can also see the chambers where delegates met.

Republic Museum

Just down the hill from Ulus Meydanı, the **Republic Museum** (Cumhuriyet Müzesi; p442; Cumhuriyet Bulvarı; admission €1.10; 8.45am-12.30pm & 1.30-5.30pm Tue-Sun) was the second headquarters of the grand national assembly, and its early history appears in photographs and documents. The captions are in Turkish but you don't need to read anything to get a sense of the republic's modest beginnings. The assembly itself is now housed in a rather more imposing building in Bakanlıklar.

Transport Museums

While waiting for a train at Ankara station you may want to take a look at the **Railway Museum & Art Gallery** (Demiryolları Müzesi ve Sanat Galerisi; Map p442; admission free; 9am-12.30pm & 1.30-5pm Sep-Jun), a small building on platform 1 that served as Atatürk's residence during the War of Independence. Right beside it is Atatürk's private rail coach, a gift from one Adolf Hitler.

Slightly further away, the **Open-Air Steam Locomotive Museum** (Açık Hava Buharlı Lokomotif Müzesi; Celal Bayar Bulvarı; admission free) is a collection of slowly rusting vintage engines on the south western side of the station. To find it, descend the underpass as though you were going to the train platforms, but keep walking straight on. Just before entering the Tandoğan Kapalı Çarşı shopping area, climb the steps to your left, then turn right and continue for around 800m.

Back opposite the station, the **Turkish Aeronautical Association Museum** (Talat Paşa Bulvarı; Map p442; admission free) has a collection of old planes and some aviation displays in the shadow of its landmark parachute tower.

ATAKULE

Down south in Çankaya is the **Atakule** (admission €0.85; ☺ 9am-3am), Ankara's landmark tower, with a revolving restaurant on top for 360-degree views of the city; making a reservation exempts you from the admission fee. A glass lift – not for the faint-hearted – whisks you to the top. There is also a cinema here. Get here from Ulus or Kızılay on any Çankaya-bound bus.

MOSQUES

The outline of the huge **Kocatepe Camii** (Map p444) in Kızılay is now the symbol of Ankara. It may be one of the largest mosques in the world but it is also very new. However, Ankara does still have one or two older mosques, and the relics in the Ethnography Museums are poignant reminders of others that have long since disappeared.

Ankara's most revered mosque is **Hacı Bayram Camii** (Map p442), near the Temple of Augustus & Rome. Hacı Bayram Veli was a Muslim 'saint' who founded the Bayramiye dervish order around 1400. Ankara was the order's centre, and Hacı Bayram Veli is still revered by pious Muslims. The mosque precincts are ringed with shops selling religious paraphernalia (including wooden tooth-brushes as used, supposedly, by the Prophet Mohammed). You can buy food to feed the pigeons in the nearby pigeon feeding area (Güvercin Yemleme Alanı).

If you turn left on leaving the *hisar* and walk downhill past the antique shops you will come to the **Arslanhane Camii** (Map p442), which dates back to 1290 and incorporates pieces of old Roman masonry in its walls.

HAMAMS

If you're staying in Opera Meydanı and your bathroom isn't up to much, never fear because there are several *hamams* (bathhouses) in the streets immediately east of the square. The best is **Şengül Merkez Hamamı** (Map p442; wash & massage €8.50; ☺ 5am-11pm for men, 7am-7pm for women).

PARKS

Walk south from Ulus Meydanı along Atatürk Bulvarı and you'll soon reach the entrance to **Gençlik Parkı** (Youth Park; Map p442), where Atatürk had a swamp converted into an artificial lake. The Luna Park funfair provides amusement for children and several pleasant *çay bahçesi* (tea gardens); single women should go for

those with the word *aile* (family) in their name.

Other oases in an often wearing city are **Kuğulu Parkı** (Swan Park; Map p442), at the southern end of Tunalı Hilmi Caddesi, and the **Botanik Parkı** (Botanical Park), spilling into a valley beneath the Atakule in Çankaya.

Further out of town in Gölbaşı, **Aquapark Club Watercity** (☎ 498 2100; www.clubwatercity.com in Turkish; Haymana Yolu 6, Gölbaşı; adult/child €14/7; ☺ 10am-7pm) has a range of outdoor, indoor and children's pools, sports facilities, water slides and restaurants. Dolmuşes run here from Opera Meydanı.

OTHER SIGHTS

Right on Cankırı Caddesi you'll discover the sprawling ruins of the 3rd-century **Roman Baths** (Roma Hamaları; Map p442); admission €1.10; ☺ 8.30am-12.30pm & 1.30-5.30pm Tue-Sun), about 500m north of Ulus Meydanı. The layout of the baths and the system for heating them are clearly visible; look for the standard Roman facilities: an *apoditerium* (dressing room), *frigidarium* (cold room), *tepidarium* (warm room) and *caldarium* (hot room). Remains dating back to Phrygian times (8th to 6th centuries BC) have been found beneath the baths.

To find the **Column of Julian** (Jülyanus Sütunu; Map p442) head north along Cankırı Caddesi from Ulus Meydanı and turn right beside the beautiful old Türkiye İş Bankası. The column stands in a square that is ringed by government buildings – there's usually a stork's nest on top of the column. The Roman Emperor Julian the Apostate (r AD 361–63) visited Ankara in the middle of his short reign and the column was erected in his honour.

Festivals & Events

It's usually İstanbul that gets the wildest events, but the new **AnkiRockFest** (www.ankirockfest.com) has done a lot to build the capital's cred, supplying a full weekend of bands around the end of May. Tickets for the whole event cost around €35.

Sleeping

Ankara hotels are numerous and functional, but very rarely exciting. On a tight budget you will have to stick with Ulus, which is convenient for the main attractions but not the nicest area to stay in. Most of the good midrange hotels are in Kızılay, while the top end roosts in Kavaklıdere.

ULUS

Despite its general seediness, Ulus is undoubtedly handy if you want to visit the Museum of Anatolian Civilisations and then move speedily on again. Several cheap hotels face onto Opera Meydanı; after dark this area is creepily quiet and dimly lit, and even in daytime it's pretty seedy. There are lots of two- and three-star hotels north of Ulus, but most are hopelessly noisy. Lone women and those after quieter digs would be better off staying around Rüzgarlı Sokak, on the northern side of Ulus Meydanı.

Otel Pınar (Map p442; ☎ 311 8951; Hisarparkı Caddesi 14; s/d €15/20) Up towards the citadel, this is the best corner of Ulus for lone, female or nervous travellers, and the Pınar supplies just the right kind of simple budget accommodation you need for a short stay. Breakfast costs €2.80.

Otel Mithat (Map p442; ☎ 311 5410; www.otelmithat .com.tr; Tavus Sokak 2; s/d/tr €14/23/25) Overlooking the busy mobile phone market on Opera Meydanı, this seven-storey block looks good from its Ottoman-styled lobby, though it's back to tatty lino upstairs. Some slightly cheaper rooms with shower and shared toilet are available; breakfast costs €2. Has wi-fi access.

Otel Buhara (Map p442; ☎ 310 7999; Sanayi Caddesi 13; s/d/tr €17/25/34) A block back from Atatürk Bulvarı, the Buhara dodges some of the worst street noise and provides reasonable standards for the price, with the benefit of a smart kebap shop next door. Breakfast costs €2.80.

Hotel Spor (Map p442; ☎ 324 2165; www.hotelspor .com; Rüzgarlı Plevne Sokak 6; s/d/tr €31/39/50; ❄) Despite the rowdy betting shop two doors down, the 'Hotel Sport' bills itself as a family hotel,

---

AUTHOR'S CHOICE

Angora House Hotel (Map p442; ☎ 309 8380; Kalekapısı Sokak 16; s/d €36/56; ◷ Mar-Oct) Sometimes a good thing can be slow to catch on – this is still Ankara's only boutique hotel, run by a friendly Turkish couple who used to sell carpets to the same tourists they now feed and water. It's in a great location inside the citadel and offers beautiful, individually decorated rooms in a restored house, benefiting from some fine half-timbering and a walled courtyard. With only six rooms, advance reservation is recommended.

---

and sure enough the slightly ageing wood mellows the compact rooms.

Hitit Oteli (Map p442; ☎ 310 8617; Hisarparkı Caddesi 12; s/d/tr €27.50/39/59) On the citadel ascent, this is a small but noticeable step up from the budget places in quality, though sadly not in style or taste (even the 'guests' on the brochure look like mourners at a 1970s Mafia funeral) You may get snatches of view through the trees in front.

Hotel Oğultürk (Map p442; ☎ 309 2900; www.ogu turk.com; Rüzgarlı Eşdost Sokak 6; s/d/tr €31/42/56; ❄) Just off Rüzgarlı Sokak; standards here are no far off the lower-end Kızılay options, though there's more mosque noise. It's professionally managed and good for lone women.

Radisson Hotel (Map p442; ☎ 310 4848; info.ankara@ radissonsas.com; İstiklal Caddesi 20; s/d from €72/82 ❄ ❄ ▯) Sixteen floors of international-standard luxury across from Gençlik Parkı.

KIZILAY & BAKANLIKLAR

The tree-shaded streets of Kızılay and Bakanlıklar to the south make much nicer places to stay than those of Ulus, and you'l be close to lots of amenities. Most of the hotels offer air-con, minibars, IDD phones and digital TV; advertised prices can be twice what we quote here, but you'll rarely have to pay them.

Hotel Metropol (Map p444; ☎ 417 3060; www.hotel metropol.com.tr; Olgunlar Sokak 5; s/d from €31/45; ❄) Quite a snip at these rates: the Metropol lives up to its cosmopolitan name with some fair attempts at Art Deco touches, providing quality and character across the board.

Eyüboğlu Hotel (Map p444; ☎ 417 6400; Karanfil Sokak 73; s/d €34/45) One suspects design wasn't a priority here, given the unprepossessing brown facade, rucked carpets and plain white sheets but you can't argue with the restaurant, barbe salon and American-style café-pool hall. It' popular with Turkish groups.

Otel Melodi (Map p444; ☎ 417 6414; www.melodihotel .com; Karanfil Sokak 10; s/d €36/48; ❄) A well-run hotel with a great corner location at the hear of Kızılay's pedestrian café zone, the Melod strikes a chord thanks to spacious, comfy rooms in varied brown tones. It also seems to inspire local cartoonists, whose works adorn the lobby.

Midas Hotel (Map p442; ☎ 424 0110; www.hotelmida .com; Tunus Caddesi 20; s/d €50/62; ❄ ▯) The rate quoted for this brand-new luxury four-sta are promotional prices for quiet periods and will doubtless double as soon as a proper client base is established, but for now it's an irresistible bargain. All facilities, from the spa and fitness centre to the in-room wi-fi, are free for guests.

Hotel Gold (Map p444; ☎ 419 4868; www.ankara goldhotel.com; Güfte Sokak 4; s/d/tr €75/92/100; ⊠) Whatever the 'Gold' refers to, it isn't the fiery orange shades in the rooms, the red carpets on the floors or the marble of the terrace café. Still, the class pervades, and you can't fault a place that gives you free samples of an anti-hangover drink.

KAVAKLIDERE

Gordion Hotel (Map p442; ☎ 427 8080; www.gordionhotel .com; Büklüm Sokak 59; s/d €94/113; ⊠ ▣ ⊠) If you could smell class, this place would reek to high heaven, and quite possibly overpower a lot of European competition to boot. It's the epitome of a refined townhouse hotel, revelling quietly in deep red fabrics, silver tea sets, a conservatory restaurant and full set of spa facilities; even the soap is handmade, doubtless at great expense. Breathe it all in and enjoy.

mega residence (Map p442; ☎ 468 5400; www.mega residence.com; s/d from €147/167, ste €200; ⊠) Targeting the German market, the pine facade of this smart establishment evokes the Austrian Alps, and the Schnitzel restaurant is even more of a giveaway. There's not much Tirolean flavour on the inside, but the rooms are very good indeed, especially the Jacuzzi doubles and kitchenette suite.

Also recommended:

Ankara Hilton (Map p442; ☎ 455 0000; www.hilton .com; Tahran Caddesi 12; s/d €297/315; ⊠) Plush rooms and suites on 16 floors; weekend discounts available.

Sheraton Ankara Hotel & Towers (Map p442; ☎ 468 5454; www.sheraton.com/ankara; Noktalı Sokak; s/d €254/297; ⊠ ▣) Landmark cylindrical luxury high-rise; weekend discounts available.

Eating

ULUS

Like accommodation, most Ulus options are cheap and basic, often serving beer to a purely male clientele. If self-catering suddenly seems like a good option, the colourful Yeni Haller vegetable market (Map p442) is ideal.

Inside the citadel, over a dozen old wood-and-stone houses have been converted into inviting, atmospheric licensed restaurants. Summer opening hours are around 11am to midnight; most places have live music in the evening, but close or cut back their hours in winter. Just outside the walls, on Can Sokak, you'll also find several cafés lurking amid the antique shops.

Zenger Paşa Konağı (Map p442; ☎ 311 7070; www .zengerpasa.com; Doyran Sokak 13; mains €2.80-9.50; ⊠) Built in 1721 for governor Mehmet Fuat Paşa, the Zenger Paşa was the first restaurant of its kind in Ankara, restored and masterminded by a TV executive with a keen eye for the tourist market. Meals are still cooked in the original oven, and the whole place is crammed with Ottoman ephemera. There's live music every evening to complement the perfect citadel views.

Boyacızâde Konağı (Map p442; ☎ 310 2525; Berrak Sokak 7/9; mains €3.50-16) Not far from the museum, the Boyacızâde is another wonderfully converted mansion-restaurant with great views, typical Ottoman-stalgic décor and a good line in fish dishes. Turkish classical, or *fasıl*, music provides the entertainment.

Kale Washington (Map p442; ☎ 311 4344; Doyran Sokak 5/7; mains €10-20; ⊠ from 9.30am) Spliced together from two 17th-century houses, the Washington is a favourite with visiting dignitaries (Hillary Clinton reportedly ate here once) and other aspirational types, who come to chow down on Turkish-international food. Staff sometimes give as much attitude as they get, but as long as you're not a complete scruffbag it's not over-snobby.

Hatipoğlu Konağı (Map p442; ☎ 311 3696; Sevinç Sokak 3; set menus €15-20; ⊠ 7pm-1am) The touristy set menus here are good value, but watch those steps if you go for the unlimited-alcohol option! Acoustic groups play here every day except Sunday. To find it, come out of the citadel through the Parmak Kapısı and turn left.

The next two are closer to Atatürk Bulvarı.

Bosna İşkembe Lokanta ve Kebap Salonu (Map p442; ☎ 310 8701; Çankırı Caddesi 11; mains €2-3.70; ⊠ 24hr) This all-hours place is scarily popular and, thankfully, not as grim as some of its rivals.

Urfalı Hacı Mehmet (Map p442; ☎ 311 2008; Kızılay Sokak 3/A; mains €2.50-3.70; ⊠ 9am-10pm) A welcome haven for family and female diners, kept clean and bright for maximum enjoyment of an extensive fast-food menu.

KIZILAY

This is undoubtedly the best area for a casual meal, particularly in the pedestrian zone north of Ziya Gökalp Caddesi, where pavement eateries and stalls serve everything from *döner* to *kumpir* (baked potatoes).

Kızılay is also Ankara's café central, with terraces lining virtually every inch of space south of Ziya Gökalp Caddesi and the sound of students playing backgammon echoing for miles.

Can Balık (Map p444; ☎ 432 4862; Sakarya Caddesi 8/4; mains €1.70-4.50; ☯ 10am-10pm) A popular alternative to pricey fish restaurants, the classiest thing here are the Coke ads, but the Piscean menu works perfectly.

Galeri (Map p444; ☎ 418 9950; Selanik Caddesi 40/2; mains €1.70-5.50; ☯ 9am-11pm) The breezy booths above street level here are popular with couples, while the mixed brasserie-style menu has treats from breakfasts and salads to cheesecake, all ambitiously presented.

Göksu Restaurant (Map p444; ☎ 431 2219; Bayındır Sokak 22/A; meals €3.10-7.50; ☯ 11am-11pm) Fine dining with uniformed staff and a terrace discreetly shielded from the street by glass and vines. It's popular with besuited blokes guzzling mezes and rakı (aniseed-flavoured grape brandy).

Köşk (Map p444; ☎ 432 1300; İnkılap Sokak 2, Kı; mains €4-11; ☯ 11am-11pm Mon-Sat) Specialising in fish, the Köşk cultivates a slightly staid air to please the decorum-minded older diners who form its core demographic, though at €1.40 the beer's cheap enough to enthuse the younger crowd as well.

KAVAKLIDERE

The scene here is more European and sophisticated, catering primarily to the embassy set, and offers some opportunities to dabble in cuisine beyond the usual Turkish staples.

Tapa Tapa Tapas (Map p442; ☎ 428 3562, Tunalı Hilmi Caddesi 87; dishes €1.40-8.50; ☯ 8.30am-midnight) The chef plays it a bit safe with the chilli and with the booze level of the sangria (€3.50), but the sheer novelty of finding *albondigas* and *patatas bravas* in Turkey doesn't wear off fast. Pasta, crêpes and grills round out the menu.

Café des Cafés (Map p442; ☎ 428 0176; Tunalı Hilmi Caddesi 83; mains €3.60-11; ☯ 8.30am-midnight) Another dash of culinary flair from foreign parts of the Med, the CdC offers ambitious bistro dishes from *quesadilla* to salmon and *arugula*.

Mezzaluna (Map p442; ☎ 467 5818; Turan Emeksiz Sokak 1; meals €20-30; ☯ noon-midnight) The capital's classiest Italian restaurant impresses as soon as you walk in the door, with interior design by Roberto Magris and a real Italian chef at the pass. There's a second branch in the suburb of Bilkent.

Wok (Map p442; ☎ 446 1992; Borusan Bldg, Uğur Mumcu Caddesi 8/2; meals from €20; ☯ noon-midnight, to 2am Sat & Sun) Achingly fashionable, this mixed Oriental bar-restaurant above a BMW showroom supplements its pan-Asian menu with sophisticated European dishes and electronic music. For added entertainment, certain tables have a view of the kitchen action.

Drinking

The best place for a tea is Genclik Parkı, across the road from Opera Meydanı. Head straight for the **Ada Aile Çay Bahçesi** (Map p442), which juts out into the lake, to watch the world go by over a samovar (€1.10).

For a night out with Ankara's student population, head for Bayındır Sokak, between Sakarya and Tuna Caddesis in Kızılay, where Turkish *gazinos* (nightclubs) are packed sometimes three deep per building! Many of these offer live Turkish pop music, and women travellers should feel OK in most.

And Evi (Map p442; ☎ 312 7978; İçkale Kapısı, Ulus) Right on top of the walls inside the citadel, even Hobson would have trouble choosing the panoramic terrace or the sumptuous indoor lounge at this Ottoman-styled café.

Qube Bar (Map p444; ☎ 432 3079; Bayındır Sokak 16/B) Slightly more sophisticated than its neighbours, Qube has an unusually wide range of draught beer, including the slightly appley Pera Pilsener from Tekirdağ.

Locus Solus (Map p442; ☎ 468 6788; Bestekar Sokak 60) A funky orange terrace-lounge sucking in a young, unpretentious crowd for beers, cocktails, smoothies or snacks. The MP3 jukebox covers all kinds of electrica (French ska, sir?), and high-cred DJs play regularly, including occasional international names. Even the barmen reckon it's 'something special'.

Entertainment

CINEMAS

Some of Ankara's cinemas may occasionally show Western films in the original language; the *Turkish Daily News* gives programme details.

Screens include the following:

Kavaklıdere Sineması (Map p444; ☎ 468 7193; Tunalı Hilmi Caddesi 105; tickets €3.50-5)

Kızılırmak Sineması (Map p444; ☎ 425 5393; Kızılırmak Caddesi 21/B; tickets €3.50-5)

Megapol Sineması (Map p444; ☎ 419 4492; Konur Sokak 33; tickets €3.50-4.50)

NIGHTCLUBS & LIVE MUSIC

Most visitors don't hang around Ankara long enough to get to grips with the nightlife, but believe us, it's there – with a whole spectrum of venues from student dives to recherché nightspots. Consult fellow drinkers, bar staff, flyers or local listings to get the latest tips.

IF Performance Hall (Map p442; ☎ 418 9506; Tunus Caddesi 14/A, Kavaklıdere) It's a pretty grand name for what's essentially a basement bar venue, but there's something going on here most nights, and plenty of biggish bands come through. As Kipling might have said, IF you can keep your head when all about are getting off theirs…

OverAll (Map p442; ☎ 468 5785; www.overall.web .tr; Güvenlik Caddesi 97; ✆ Tue-Sat) Another popular dancefloor venue with a mixed bag of nights, from bands to hip-hop, dance and, um, karaoke.

Jazz Time (Map p442; ☎ 463 4348; Bilir Sokak 4/1, Kavaklıdere) A low-key jazz club, with tables, usually hosting live Turkish pop or folk artists. The attached Gitanes Bar has a garden terrace.

Shopping

It's cheapest to shop in Ulus, but to see what fashionable Turkey likes to spend its money on, you'll need to head south to Kızılay and Kavaklıdere. Tunalı Hilmi Caddesi is a great place to watch wealthier Ankaralıs shopping, with lots of local stores alongside more familiar names such as the British department store **Marks & Spencer** (Map p442). Nearby, just below the Sheraton Hotel, is **Karum** (Map p442; İran Caddesi), a flashy shopping mall that could outdo its London cousins.

Behind the Ulus vegetable market, on Konya Caddesi, is the **Vakıf Suluhan Çarşısı** (Map p442), a restored *han* (caravanserai) with clothes shops, a café, toilets and a small free-standing mosque in its courtyard.

The area around the Parmak Kapısı entrance to the citadel was traditionally a centre for trading in Angora wool. In front of the gate is a row of dried-fruit stalls. Walk downhill along Gözcü Sokak to inspect the carpet and antique shops. You're unlikely to find many bargains but you'll come across copperbeaters and other assorted craftsworkers still carrying on their age-old trades.

Cutting across Karanfil Sokak is tree- and café-lined Olgunlar Sokak, with its row of **second-hand bookstalls** (Map p444).

The tourist office (p441) sells good-quality Turkish arts and crafts items.

Getting There & Away

AIR

Ankara's Esenboğa airport, 33km north of the city centre, is the hub for Turkish Airlines' domestic flight network. Of the budget carriers, only Atlasjet and Pegasus Airlines serve Ankara, so you may have more options going via İstanbul.

The table below shows *direct* flights from Ankara only. All schedules are subject to change.

Other international airlines sometimes have flights to Ankara, or connections with Turkish Airlines' flights from İstanbul.

FLIGHTS FROM ANKARA'S AIRPORT

Destination	Frequency (per day)
Adana	2
Antalya	2
Bodrum	4 weekly
Cyprus	up to 2
Diyarbakır	3
Erzurum	1
İstanbul (IST)	at least 14
İstanbul (SAW)	4 or 5
İzmir	3
Kars	1
Malatya	1
Şanlıurfa	1
Trabzon	2 or 3
Van	2

Airline Offices

Air France (Map p442; ☎ 467 4404; Atatürk Bulvarı 231/7, Kavaklıdere)

Atlasjet (Map p444; ☎ 425 4832; Atatürk Bulvarı 109/6, Kızılay)

British Airways (Map p442; ☎ 467 5557; Atatürk Bulvarı 237/2, Kavaklıdere)

KLM (Map p442; ☎ 417 5616; Atatürk Bulvarı 199, Kavaklıdere)

Lufthansa (☎ 442 0580; Cinnah Caddesi 102/5, Çankaya)

Turkish Airlines Kavaklıdere (THY; Map p442; ☎ 428 0200; Atatürk Bulvarı 154) airport (☎ 398 0100)

BUS

Every Turkish city or town of any size has direct buses to Ankara. The gigantic otogar or AŞTİ (Ankara Şehirlerarası Terminali İşletmesi) is at the western end of the Ankaray underground train line, 4.5km west of Kızılay.

The terminal has departure gates on the upper level and arrivals on the lower. There are restaurants, a first-aid post, ATMs, phones and newsstands. The *emanet* (left-luggage room) on the lower level charges €1.10 per item stored; you'll need to show your passport.

As Ankara has many buses to all parts of the country, you can often turn up, buy a ticket and be on your way within the hour. Don't try this during public holidays, though.

AŞTİ has 80 *gişe* (ticket counters) and a central information booth to point you in the right direction. Major companies include:

Bus Company	Counter
Kamil Koç	17, 18
Metro	16, 41
Nilüfer	25
Pamukkale	58, 59
Uludağ/Çanakkale Truva	71
Ulusoy	13
Varan	12

Many bus companies also maintain city-centre ticket offices near Kızılay on Ziya Gökalp Caddesi, Gazi Mustafa Kemal Bulvarı, İzmir Caddesi and Menekşe Sokak. Several premium bus companies, including Varan and Ulusoy, have their own terminal facilities near the otogar. The table below lists details of some useful daily routes from Ankara.

TRAIN

Train services between İstanbul and Ankara are the best in the country, and work is under-way to develop an even faster rail link, though concerns were raised by some accidents in 2004. **Ankara Garı** (Map p442; ☎ 311 0620) has a

SERVICES FROM ANKARA'S OTOGAR

Destination	Fare	Duration	Distance	Frequency (per day)	Counter
Adana	€14	10hr	490km	frequent	57
Amasya	€8.50	5hr	335km	frequent	31
Antalya	€14	8hr	550km	frequent	32
Bodrum	€19.50	13hr	785km	12	41
Bursa	€11.50	6hr	400km	hourly	71
Denizli (for Pamukkale)	€14	7hr	480km	frequent	58, 78
Diyarbakır	€28	13hr	945km	several	34
Erzurum	€22.50	13hr	925km	several	36
Gaziantep	€19.50	10hr	705km	frequent	36, 42
İstanbul	€14	5-6hr	450km	every 15 min	29
İzmir	€8.50	8hr	600km	hourly	25, 35
Kayseri	€7.50	4½hr	330km	frequent	45, 54
Konya	€5.60	3hr	260km	frequent	50, 75
Marmaris	€19.50	10hr	780km	12	17, 41
Nevşehir (for Cappadocia)	€8.50	5hr	285km	frequent	50
Samsun	€11.50	7hr	420km	frequent	52
Sivas	€14	6hr	450km	frequent	27, 32
Sungurlu (for Boğazkale)	€5.60	3hr	177km	hourly	30
Trabzon	€19.50	13hr	780km	several	31, 52

EXPRESS SERVICES FROM ANKARA'S TRAIN STATION				
Destination	Fare	Via	Frequency	Duration
Adana	€9, sleeper €30	Niğde	daily	12hr
Diyarbakır	€12.50, sleeper €31-39	Kayseri, Sivas, Malatya	4 weekly	35hr
İstanbul	from €7, sleeper from €15	Eskişehir, İzmit	up to 10 daily	6½-9½hr
İzmir	€12.50, sleeper €27-36	Kütahya, Balıkesir	3 daily	13hr
Kars	€19.50, sleeper €32-40	Kayseri, Sivas, Erzurum	2 daily	28hr
Tatvan	€18.50, sleeper €31-39	Kayseri, Sivas, Malatya	2 weekly	41hr
Zonguldak	€6.70	Karabük	3 weekly	9½hr

PTT, a restaurant, snack shops, kiosks, ATMs, telephones and a left-luggage room.

The table above summarises the main express routes out of Ankara; returning, most trains continue on to İstanbul. Slower standard trains serve many intermediate destinations.

Getting Around

TO/FROM THE AIRPORT

Esenboğa airport is 33km north of the city. **Havaş** (Map p442; ☎ 444 0487; Kazım Karabekir Caddesi) buses depart from the Havaş Terminal every half-hour between 3.30am and 9.30pm daily, with further night services timed according to flight schedules, and travel directly to the airport (€5.30, 40 minutes). They may leave sooner if they fill up, so claim your seat at least two hours before flight time. Buses stop at the AŞTİ otogar in both directions.

Taxis between the airport and the city cost about €20.

TO/FROM THE AŞTİ OTOGAR

The easiest way to get into town is on the Ankaray metro line, which has a station right next to the AŞTİ otogar. Go to Maltepe station for the tourist office or the train station (a 10-minute walk), or to Kızılay for the midrange hotels in Kızılay and Bakanlıklar. Change at Kızılay (to the Metro line) for Ulus and the cheap hotels.

For a dolmuş to Ulus (€0.85), cross the main road in front of the otogar and catch an 'Ulus–Balgat' or 'Gölbaşı–Opera Meydanı' dolmuş.

A taxi costs about €4 to the train station and €5 to Ulus or Kızılay.

TO/FROM ANKARA GARI (TRAIN STATION)

The train station (see opposite) is about 1.4km southwest of Ulus Meydanı and 2.5km north-west of Kızılay. Any bus or dolmuş heading northeast along Cumhuriyet Bulvarı will take you to Ulus. Many buses heading east along Talat Paşa Bulvarı go to Kızılay and/or Kavaklıdere.

It's a bit over 1km from the station to Opera Meydanı; any bus heading east along Talat Paşa Bulvarı will drop you within a few hundred metres if you ask for Gazi Lisesi.

To go from the train station to the AŞTİ otogar, follow the underpass in the train station through a dingy shopping area and eventually you'll end up at the Maltepe Ankaray station, where you can take the metro to the otogar.

BUS

Ankara has a good bus, dolmuş and minibus network. Signs on the front and side of the vehicles are better guides than route numbers. Buses marked 'Ulus' and 'Çankaya' run the length of Atatürk Bulvarı. Those marked 'Gar' go to the train station, those marked 'AŞTİ' to the otogar.

City buses (€0.70) run on the same prepay system as the metro: tickets can be bought from kiosks at major bus stops or from shops and vendors displaying an EGO Bilet sign. Cards for five/10/20 journeys cost €3.50/7/11.

CAR

Driving within Ankara is chaotic and signs are woefully inadequate, so even if you have a car it's better to ditch it and use public transport instead.

If you plan to hire a car to drive out of Ankara, there are many small local companies alongside the major international firms; most have offices in Kavaklıdere along Tunus Caddesi, and/or at Esenboğa airport. Reliable operators include:

Avis (Map p442; ☎ 467 2313; Tunus Caddesi 68/2)
Budget (Map p442; ☎ 468 5888; Tunus Caddesi 79/1)
National (Map p442; ☎ 426 4565; Tunus Caddesi 73/1)

METRO
Ankara's underground train network currently has two lines: the Ankaray line running between AŞTİ otogar in the west through Kızılay to Dikimevi in the east (see p453); and the Metro line running from Kızılay northwest via Sıhhiye and Ulus to Batıkent. The two lines interconnect at Kızılay. Trains run from 6.15am to 11.45pm daily.

Single-journey tickets for the whole transport system cost €0.70. Note that there are separate barriers for adult and child/student tickets at some stations, so if your ticket doesn't seem to work, check that you're using the right lane.

TAXI
Every second vehicle on the road seems to be a taxi and they all have meters. The drop rate is €0.50; an average trip costs around €3 during daylight hours, 50% more at night.

AROUND ANKARA
You don't have to go too far from Ankara to hit some major pieces of Anatolian history, bit if it's a leisurely day trip you're after rather than an overnight, your options are more limited. The Phrygian archaeological site at Gordion and the small Ottoman town of Beypazarı are the strongest candidates for your time.

Gordion
The capital of ancient Phrygia, with some 3000 years of settlement behind it, Gordion lies 106km west of Ankara in the village of Yassıhöyük.

Gordion was occupied by the Phrygians as early as the 9th century BC, and soon afterwards became their capital. Although destroyed during the Cimmerian invasion, it was later rebuilt, only to be conquered first by the Lydians and then by the Persians. Alexander the Great came through and famously cut the Gordian Knot in 333 BC, but by 278 BC the Galatian occupation had effectively destroyed the city.

The landscape around Yassıhöyük is dotted with tumuli (burial mounds) marking the graves of the Phrygian kings. Of 100 identified tumuli, less than half have been excavated;

you can enter the largest tomb, and also view the site of the Gordion acropolis, where digs revealed 18 different levels of civilisation from the Bronze Age to Roman times.

MIDAS TÜMÜLÜS & GORDION MUSEUM
In 1957 the Austrian archaeologist Alfred Koerte discovered Gordion, and with it the intact **tomb** (admission to tomb & museum €2.80; ☯ 8.30am-5pm) of a Phrygian king, probably buried some time between 740 and 718 BC. The tomb is actually a gabled 'cottage' of cedar surrounded by juniper logs, buried beneath a tumulus 53m high and 300m in diameter. It's the oldest wooden structure ever found in Anatolia, and perhaps even in the world. The tunnel and tomb entrance are modern additions to ease access for visitors; the tomb itself is fenced off, but diagrams and photos give you an idea of what it was like.

Inside the tomb archaeologists found the body of a man between 61 and 65 years of age, 1.59m tall, surrounded by burial objects, including tables, bronze *situlas* (containers) and bowls said to be part of the funerary burial feast. The occupant's name remains unknown, although both 'Gordius' and 'Midas' are good bets – most Phrygian kings seem to have been called one or the other.

Across the road, the **museum** houses finds from the Bronze Age to Phrygian and Hellenistic times. Note the Hellenistic terracotta roof tiles and the many Phrygian bronze fibulae (brooches). The finest examples of Phrygian art, including the intricate inlaid wooden tables found in the tomb, were removed to Ankara's Museum of Anatolian Civilisations.

In the grounds are several simple 8th-century BC mosaics from the Acropolis and a reconstructed Galatian tomb.

ACROPOLIS
Excavations at the 8th-century BC acropolis yielded a wealth of data on Gordion's many civilisations.

The lofty main gate on the city's western side was approached by a 6m-wide ramp. Within the fortified enclosure were four *megara* (square halls) from which the king and his priests and ministers ruled the empire. The mosaics found in one of these halls, the so-called Citadel of Midas, are on display outside the museum.

Today the site is a fenced-off collection of foundations with explanatory signs, which are of small appeal to the casual visitor. It's some 3km from the museum on the far side of the village (follow the main road through).

GETTING THERE & AWAY
Baysal Turizm buses connect Ankara's otogar (ticket counter 28) with Polatlı every half-hour (€2.80, one hour). Once in Polatlı, you'll have to take a taxi the 18km to Gordion and back; negotiate a price in advance, as it could run as high as €50 on the meter if you include the acropolis.

Beypazarı
☎ 0312 / pop 34,500
If you prefer traditional life to ancient remains, Beypazarı, set high above the picturesque İnözü Vadisi, makes a great place for a day trip. Explore the winding back streets and the fascinating old market, and you'll soon come across row upon row of tastefully restored old Ottoman houses. Several of these have been turned into cafés or pensions with inviting courtyards, and one is also open to the public as a **museum** (admission €0.55; ☽ 10am-6pm Tue-Sun) – note in particular the original bathrooms inside cupboards and the magnificent 1894 map of the eastern Mediterranean in the hall.

In June the **Beypazarı Festival** swells the ranks of market traders and introduces a carnival atmosphere, while a quirkier **harvest festival** in October celebrates that crucial crop, the carrot.

While you're here it'd be rude not to try the local delicacies, which include *havuç lokum* (carrot-flavoured Turkish delight), *cevizli sucuğu* (walnuts coated in grape jelly) and Beypazarı's own local mineral water, bottled here and marketed throughout the country.

GETTING THERE & AWAY
To get to Beypazarı you need to take a bus from Ankara's Etlik bus station rather than AŞTİ; to get there take a dolmuş (€0.45, 15 minutes) from beside Hacı Bayram Camii. Sporadic dolmuşes and more comfortable buses travel back and forth to Beypazarı every day (€1.75, 1½ hours). Check the time of the last bus back to Ankara as soon as you arrive.

SAFRANBOLU
☎ 0370 / pop 32,200
Every town in Turkey has its old Ottoman houses, but Safranbolu, the valley town at the heart of the new restoration movement, takes it to a different level: virtually the entire old Ottoman town has been preserved and now spruced up to such good effect that it made it onto the Unesco World Heritage list. This is as close as you'll ever come to historical Turkey, and the town's popularity with domestic tourists reinforces just what a rare treat this is.

The weather, too, can play a part in this unique experience: summer thunderstorms periodically close over the sunken valley like a heavy black lid, and you can watch the lightning-pierced darkness drawing on inch by inch until finally the light is gone and the rain bursts down onto the tiled roofs. Simply magic.

History
During the 17th century, the main Ottoman trade route between Gerede and the Black Sea coast passed through Safranbolu, bringing commerce, prominence and money to the town. During the 18th and 19th centuries Safranbolu's wealthy inhabitants built mansions of sun-dried mud bricks, wood and stucco, while the larger population of prosperous artisans built less impressive but similarly sturdy homes. Safranbolu owes its fame to the large numbers of these dwellings that have survived.

The most prosperous Safranbolulus maintained two households. In winter they occupied town houses in the Çarşı (Market) district, which is situated at the meeting point of three valleys and so protected from the winter winds. During the warm months they moved to summer houses at the garden suburb of Bağlar (Vineyards). When the iron and steel works at Karabük were established in 1938, modern factory houses started to encroach on Bağlar, although Çarşı has remained virtually untouched.

During the 19th century about 20% of Safranbolu's inhabitants were Ottoman Greeks, but most of their descendants moved to Greece during the population exchange after WWI. Their principal church, dedicated to St Stephen, was converted into Kıranköy's Ulu Cami (Great Mosque).

Orientation
Safranbolu falls into three distinct parts: Kıranköy, Bağlar and Çarşı. Approaching from the steel town of Karabük, you arrive first in Kıranköy, the former Greek quarter

CENTRAL ANATOLIA

and now the most modern part of Safranbolu, with plenty of banks, shops and bus offices. Continuing uphill (northeast) along Sadrı Artuç Caddesi, you'll reach Bağlar, with its centre at Köyiçi, which has many fine old houses.

However, most of what you've come to see lies downhill in Çarşı (Market). To get there from Kıranköy, take Kaya Erdem Caddesi at the roundabout, and go 1.7km southeast, down the hill and over the next one. Buses ply this route roughly every half hour.

Information

Batuta Turizm (☎ 725 4533; www.batuta.com.tr; Hilmi Bayaramgil Caddesi 3) Local trekking, cultural and nature tours.

Paşa Internet (per hr €0.55; ☺ 10am-midnight) Slow access near the İzzet Paşa Camii.

Tourist office (☎ 712 3863; www.safranbolu.gov.tr; ☺ 9am-12.30pm, 1.30-6pm) Off the main square.

Türkiye İş Bankası (Kapuçioğlu Sokak 12A) Çarşı's only bank; no ATM.

Sights

OTTOMAN HOUSES

Just walking the streets of Çarşı is a feast for the eyes – virtually every house in the district is an original, whether freshly whitewashed or gently neglected, and what little modern development there is has been held carefully in check. Many of the finest historic houses have been restored, and as time goes on, more and more are being saved from

SAFRANBOLU

0 _____ 200 m
0 _____ 0.1 miles

INFORMATION	
Batuta Turizm	1 C1
Paşa Internet	2 C3
Tourist Office	3 B2
Türkiye İş Bankası	4 C1

SIGHTS & ACTIVITIES	
Cinci Hamam	5 C2
Clock Tower	6 A2
Eski Hükümet Konağı	7 A2
İzzet Paşa Camii	8 C4
Kaymakamlar Müze Evi	9 D3
Kileciler Evi	10 C4
Köprülü Mehmet Paşa Camii	11 C3
Mümtazlar Konağı	12 A2

SLEEPING	
Arasna Pension	13 C2
Bastoncu Pansiyon	14 D3
Cinci Hanı	15 C3
Ev Pansiyonculuğu Geliştirme Merkezi	16 B2
Gül Evi	17 B2
Kadıoğlu Şehzade Konakları	18 C1
Otel Asmalı Konak	19 C1
Otel Hatice Hanım Konağı	20 D2
Paşa Konağı	21 A2
Selvili Köşk	22 B1

EATING	
Arasta Lonca Kahvesi	23 B2
Asmaaltı Café-Bar	24 C2
Çevikköprü 2	25 C2
İmren Lokumları	26 C1
Kadıoğlu Şehzade Sofrası	27 B2
Kazan Ocağı	28 B3
Merkez Lokantası	29 C2

SHOPPING	
Safrantat	30 C2
Yemeniciler Arastası	31 B2

TRANSPORT	
Karabük Minibüs Stop	32 C2
Kıranköy Bus Stop	33 C2
Konarı (Yörük Köyü) Minibus Stop	34 D2
Taxis	35 C2

To Otel Yedekçioğlu Konağı (200m); Bulak Mencilis Mağarası (10km)

To Havuzlu Asmazlar Konağı (400m); Kıranköy (1.7km); Şavaş Turizm (1.7km); Bağlar (3km); Raşitler Bağ Evi (3km); Tokatlı Gorge (3km); İncekaya Aqueduct (7.5km)

To Yörük Köyü (11km)

Kazdağlıoğlu Meydanı

Kazdağlı oğlu Camii

Çarşı

Belediye (Town Hall)

Pazar Yeri

Akçasu Canyon

Demirciler (Metalworks)

Hayvan Pazarı (Livestock Market)

Hıdırlık Parkı

OTTOMAN STYLE

Looking at the concrete cityscapes synonymous with Turkish modernity, it's hard to imagine being back in the 19th century, when fine wooden houses were the rule. Luckily growing tourism has encouraged a virtual Ottoman revival, and restoration has become a boom trade. Excellent examples can be found in Afyon, Amasya and Tokat, but Safranbolu is universally acknowledged to contain the country's single finest collection of pre-independence domestic architecture.

Ottoman wooden houses generally had two or three storeys, the upper storeys jutting out over the lower ones on carved corbels (brackets). Their timber frames were filled with adobe and then plastered with a mixture of mud and straw. Sometimes the houses were left unsealed, but in towns they were usually given a finish of plaster or whitewash, with decorative flourishes in plaster or wood. The wealthier the owner, the fancier the decoration.

Inside, the larger houses had 10 to 12 rooms, divided into *selamlık* (men's quarters) and *haremlik* (women's quarters). Rooms were often decorated with built-in niches and cupboards, and had fine plaster fireplaces with *yaşmaks* (conical hoods). Sometimes the ceilings were very elaborate; that of the Paşa Odası of Tokat's Latifoğlu Konağı, for example, is thought to emulate a chandelier in wood.

Details to look out for inside the Safranbolu houses include their *hayats* (courtyard areas where the animals lived and tools were stored); ingenious *dönme dolaplar* (revolving cupboards that made it possible to prepare food in one room and pass it to another without being seen); bathrooms hidden inside cupboards; and central heating systems that relied on huge fireplaces. *Sedirs* (bench seating that ran round the walls) doubled up as beds, with the bedding being stored in the toilets, which converted neatly into cupboards during the day. Space-efficient, certainly, but sometimes you wonder how anyone ever found anything!

deterioration and turned into hotels, shops or museums.

At time of research the following old houses were open to the public: the **Kaymakamlar Müze Evi**, arguably the most interesting, with recreated tableaux of everyday life; the **Mümtazlar Konağı** (1888), former home of the head mufti at Safranbolu's *medrese;* and the **Kileciler Evi**, built in 1884. The exhibition rooms in each house are open daily from 9am to sunset, charging €1.10 for admission, and tea is served in their gardens. Houses may close in winter.

Some of the largest houses had indoor pools, which, although big enough for swimming, were used instead to cool the room with running water, which also provided pleasing background noise. The best and most accessible example in Çarşı is the **Havuzlu Asmazlar Konağı** (Mansion with Pool), now run as a hotel (p458).

OTHER HISTORIC BUILDINGS

Çarşı's most famous and imposing structure is the brooding **Cinci Hanı** caravanserai (admission €0.55) dating back to 1645, which is now an upmarket hotel (p459). On Satur-

day a busy market takes place in the square behind it.

Beside Çarşı's main square, Kazdağlıoğlu Meydanı, is the **Cinci Hamam** (☎ 712 2103; ☼ 6am-midnight for men, 9am-10pm for women), built at the same time as the Cinci Hanı and still a great place to clean up your act; a wash and massage should cost you around €6. There are separate baths for men and women.

The beefy **Köprülü Mehmet Paşa Camii**, beside the *arasta* (row of shops beside a mosque), was built in 1661; the solar clock in the courtyard used to have its own custodian, whose house is now a research and tourist information centre. The **İzzet Paşa Camii**, on the main square, was built in 1796.

Uphill past the Kaymakamlar Müze Evi you reach **Hıdırlık Parkı**, which offers panoramic views. Peek through the windows of the locked Tomb of Ahmet Lütfi and you'll see a heap of coins left by the faithful.

On the other side of town, Safranbolu's castle was demolished early in the last century to make way for the attractive **Eski Hükümet Konağı** (old government building) on the hilltop near an old clock tower. You can wander round, but don't loiter too long near the police post!

FESTIVALS & EVENTS

September is a great time to visit Safranbolu, with two festivals, the **Altın Safran Documentary Film Festival** and the **Safranbolu Architectural Treasures & Folklore Week**, falling in the same month. Be sure to book accommodation ahead of time, though.

Sleeping

Safranbolu is very popular with Turkish tourists at weekends and over holidays. Prices may rise at particularly busy times, and it can be worth booking ahead outside midweek.

Whatever your budget, splashing out a bit in Safranbolu is virtually an obligation, as you may never get another chance to sleep anywhere so authentically restored. Facilities vary across the spectrum; look out for places that have been renovated rather than sanitised, so you can appreciate some of the building's original character.

If you'd rather stay in a family home than a hotel, the **Ev Pansiyonculuğu Geliştirme Merkezi** (Home Pension Development Centre; ☎ 712 7236; Yemeniciler Arastası 6), inside the *arasta* bazaar, makes reservations for overnight stays in restored houses that are not regular hotels. Use their scrapbook of photos to help you choose.

BUDGET

Bastoncu Pansiyon (☎ 712 3411; a_bastoncu@yahoo .com; Hıdırlık Yokusu Sokak, Bağlar; dm €11, s/d/tr 17/25/34; 🖵) Easily the best cheap choice in town, the Bastoncu still has all its original wood and some closet toilets. It's run by a friendly Turkish couple who speak English and Japanese and clearly appreciate backpacker needs. Aldous Huxley might not like it, but room 101 is the place to be. A second house with mainly three-bed rooms should be open by the time you read this.

Arasna Pension (☎ 712 4170; Arasta Arkası Sokak 5, Bağlar; s/d €23/36) This less personable pension opposite the main mosque and tourist office has a restaurant with regular live music, not good for light sleepers. Most of the rooms are invitingly decorated with old artefacts, but rooms 5 and 7 are best.

Kadıoğlu Şehzade Konakları (☎ 712 5657; www .kadioglusehzade.com; Mescit Sokak 24, Bağlar; s/d €20/34/45) This central branch administers six converted houses of the same name, scattered about various corners of Safranbolu. For that extra agony of choice you can see pictures before making your mind up.

Selvili Köşk (☎ 712 8646; www.hotelselvilikosk.com Mescit Sokak 23, Bağlar; s/d/tr €20/39/56) One of our favourites for authentic original character, the Selvili has a particularly beautiful salon and lovely large rooms with bathtubs. There's a pretty garden too. The same owners run two more properties with the same name, but for our money the original has the most charm and just edges into the budget category.

MIDRANGE

Otel Asmalı Konak (☎ 712 7474; Bayramgil Caddesi 13 Çarşı; s/d €23/42) It's nowhere near Cappadocia but someone obviously thinks naming their hotel after Anatolia's most popular soap opera will bring in the punters. The newly renovated rooms are slightly too modern in feel, but the ceiling in 22 is fantastic and there's little lacking in the overall vibe.

Otel Hatice Hanım Konağı (☎ 712 7545; www.hotel haticehanim.com; Hamamönü Sokak 4, Çarşı; s/d/tr €23/45/67 Another top choice for atmosphere; rooms at this former governor's residence come with marble basins, original fittings and plenty of quirks. The public rooms are also nicely decorated. Four further branches ply their trade around town, including the multistorey Hatice Hanim III right opposite.

Otel Yedekçioğlu Konağı (☎ 712 6597; www.yede cioglu.com; Mescit Sokak, Çarşı; s/d €28/42) Proclaiming itself one of the most beautiful mansions in Safranbolu may seem like faint self-praise amid so much worthy competition, but flag stone floors and a big garden do lend instant appeal. The house itself wears its 200 years well, even if the mod cons (TVs, hot water patio furniture) are distinctly this century.

Havuzlu Asmazlar Konağı (☎ 725 2883; www.tu ing.org.tr; Çelik Gülersoy Caddesi 18, Çarşı; s/d €42/56, st €67; 🕑 Apr-Oct) Halfway towards Kiranköy, the HAK is worth a detour just to glimpse the fine pool that gives the house its name. The 11 guest rooms are beautifully furnished with brass beds, *sedirs* and kilims, and the restaurant comes recommended. Bathrooms are minuscule and soundproofing minimal, but these are minor inconveniences. Two annexes provide cheaper but less atmospheric digs.

Paşa Konağı (☎ 712 8153; www.safranboluturizm .com.tr; Çarşı Kalealtı; s/d €47/57) Izzet Mehmet Paşa prime minister to the Ottoman sultan Selim III, probably would have preferred it here to the mosque that's also named after him – the spacious rooms and secluded garden foster a romantic nostalgia. Certain bathrooms are inside cupboards with high steps, which might be tricky for some guests.

Raşitler Bağ Evi (☎ 725 1345; Değirmenbaşı 65, Bağlar; s €28, d €50-56) This former summer dwelling offers five attractive rooms, an inviting sitting area and a family atmosphere in a good location right behind the remains of an old watermill.

Gökçuoğlu Konağı (☎ 712 6372; www.safranbolu turizm.com.tr; Bağlar; d €62) The Gökçuoğlu is another fine old house with an inviting garden and even more design quirks than most (ask about the 'cat corridor'). Rooms vary in style: in some you sleep Ottoman-style on a *sedir*, but others just have standard beds. The Güneş Odası, with its spectacular wooden ceiling and stone fireplace, would be the den of choice. Book ahead, as reception isn't always staffed.

Gül Evi (gulevi@canbulat.com.tr; Hükümet Sokak 46, Çarşı) Look out for this next new arrival on the scene, due to open soon.

TOP END

Cinci Hanı (☎ 712 0680; www.cincihan.com; Bağlar; s/d/tr €50/78/106, ste from €89) And now for something completely different. Safranbolu's ancient stone caravanserai has a couple of centuries over most of the famed Ottoman houses, though rooms are limited on space and décor compared to their wooden equivalents. If you can handle the price tag, the huge Han Ağası Odası suite is a gem, with kitchen, sitting room, and bathroom with old stone *hamam* basin.

Eating

As food is available at most hotels, Safranbolu is not overly endowed with great places to eat, and some require a bit of a journey to reach them.

RESTAURANTS

Kadıoğlu Şehzade Sofrası (☎ 712 5091; Arasta Sokak 8; mains €2.50-4.50; 🕙 11am-midnight) Near the *arasta* and just behind the Arasna, a jovial plastic chef ushers you into his courtyard domain, complete with adjoining dining room in case of inclement weather. Pide is the speciality here, served in as many different ways as the kitchen has ingredients, with grills as back-up.

Çevrikköprü 2 (☎ 725 2586; Hamamönü Sokak 1; mains €2.50-5; 🕙 11am-10pm) Just off the main square, overlooking the lower part of town, this is a neat old-style restaurant with plenty on the menu. There's another branch next door, and the original is on the way to Yörük Köyü (p460).

Havuzlu Köşk Et Lokantası (☎ 725 2168; Dibekönü Caddesi 32, Bağlar; mains from €2.80; 🕙 noon-11pm) For an enchanted evening, direct your designated driver straight to this attractive licensed restaurant, where you can dine at tables set around an upstairs pool or in a pleasant garden. The menu runs the gamut of Turkish standards: kebaps, *köfte* (meatballs), salads etc.

CAFÉS

Arasta Lonca Kahvesi (Boncuk Café; Yemeniciler Arastası) This is one of the town's most congenial places for a coffee, but it's right in the thick of the *arasta* action, so you pay more for the atmosphere – head to the backstreets for a quieter, cheaper cuppa.

İmren Lokumları (☎ 712 8281; Kazdağlı Meydanı 2) Overlooking the main square in Çarşı, this flagship sweet shop has a sprawling first-floor café complete with fountain and mannequins showing off Ottoman-style costumes. Try the *safranlı zerde*, a gelatinous dessert flavoured with saffron.

QUICK EATS

Kazan Ocağı (Kasaplar Sokak 19; mains €1.10-2.80; 🕙 10am-10pm) The Kazan is a friendly little family place which serves real home-cooked meals at dainty tables with cute little Ottoman-house serviette dispensers.

Merkez Lokantası (☎ 725 1478; Yukarı Çarşı 1; mains €1.10-3; 🕙 10am-10pm) This quaint, clean and friendly place opposite the Köprülü Mehmet Paşa mosque still uses a real wood fire to cook its tasty basic staples.

Asmaaltı Café-Bar (☎ 712 3405; mains €2.50-3.50) Displaying enough dark wood to recreate a rainforest, live music helps the food go down here – or vice versa.

Shopping

Safranbolu is a great place to pick up all sorts of handicrafts – especially textiles, metalwork, shoes and wooden artefacts – whether locally made or shipped in from elsewhere to supply browsing coach tourists. The restored Yemeniciler Arastası (Peasant Shoe-Makers' Bazaar) is the best place to start looking, although the makers of the light, flat-heeled shoes who used to work here have long since moved out. The further you go from the *arasta* the more likely you are to come across shops occupied by authentic working saddle-makers, felt-makers and other artisans.

Safranbolu originally derived its name from saffron, the precious spice used to flavour the local *lokum* (Turkish delight), and the town is still so packed with sweets shops that you half expect the houses to be made out of gingerbread, or at least *lokum*. One regional speciality is *yaprak helvası*, delicious chewy layers of white *helva* (halva) spotted with ground walnuts. Buy it at any branch of İmren or Safrantat. You can also visit the Safrantat factory behind the petrol station in Kıranköy to see how *lokum* is made.

Getting There & Away

There are a few direct buses to Safranbolu, although you will usually be dropped off at nearby Karabük, from where minibuses (€0.40) run the last 8km to Kıranköy. Note that direct buses to Safranbolu from Ankara leave from *peron* (gate) 35 at AŞTİ

There are several bus ticket offices along Sadrı Artuc Caddesi in Kıranköy from where you can catch regular daily services to Ankara (€6.70, four hours) and İstanbul (€11, 6½ hours). **Şavaş Turizm** (☎ 712 7480; Kaya Çarşısı), just off Sadrı Artuc Caddesi, has five daily services to Bartın (€5, 1½ hours), where you change for Amasra; start early in the day to make the onward connection.

There are many other services from Karabük, including buses to Kastamonu (€4.50, two hours) and a direct train to Ankara.

Driving, exit the Ankara–İstanbul highway at Gerede and head north, following the signs for Karabük/Safranbolu.

Getting Around

Every 30 minutes or so until 10pm, local buses (€0.15) ply the route from Çarşı's main square over the hills past the main roundabout at Kıranköy and up to the Köyiçi stop in Bağlar.

A taxi to Kiranköy will cost you €2.50, to the otogar €4. Taxis can also offer tours of all the local attractions (see below) for around €34, including waiting time.

AROUND SAFRANBOLU

Yörük Köyü

Along the Kastamonu road, 11km east of Safranbolu, Yörük Köyü (Nomad Village) is a beautiful settlement of crumbling old houses

once inhabited by the dervish Bektaşi sec (see p517). As if to prove that man *can* live by bread alone, the villagers here grew rich from their baking prowess, and some of the houses are truly enormous.

In fact, the **Sipahioğlu Konağı Gezi Evi** (admission €1.10; ☉ daylight) is so vast that the guided tour comes in two separate parts. Unfortunately it's only in Turkish but look out for: the incredible early central heating system that used the fire to heat running water and behind-the-wall heating; wall paintings in which groups of 12 carnations are symbolic of the Bektaşis; and the delightful gazebo at the top of the house with its stand for the owner's fez.

Nearby in Cemil İpekçi Sokağı is the old village *çamaşırhane* (laundry), with arched hearths where the water was heated in cauldrons, and a huge stone table that was used for the actual scrubbing; taller women worked at one end, shorter ones at the other. The table's 12 sides are another clue to the village's Bektaşi origins (like modern Shi'a Muslims the Bektaşis believed in 12 imams, the last of whom had been hidden by Allah). You may need to ask around for the key.

SLEEPING & EATING

Tarihi Yörük Pansiyon (☎ 737 2153; s/d with share bathroom €17/34) A lovely old wood-and-stone house with an inviting garden. Accommodation is simple but comfortable, although there is just one squat toilet between the four rooms. In one room you sleep on the *sedir* Ottoman-style.

Yörük Sofrası serves *ayran* (yogurt drink) baklava and *gözleme* at indoor and outdoor tables. There's also a **Kahvehanesi** (coffee house), beside the mosque.

GETTING THERE & AWAY

There is no direct bus service from Safranbolu to Yörük Köyü, but dolmuşes depart for the nearby village of Konarı three times daily (times vary). If you ask the driver he may drop you at Yörük Köyü (€0.55). Getting back you'll have to walk the 1km to the main road and hitchhike.

It's much less hassle to get a taxi in Safranbolu for the whole return trip – expect to pay around €15.

Bulak Mencilis Mağarası

Ten kilometres northwest of Safranbolu, thi impressive cave network has only opened t the public in the last few years. So far you can walk through only 400m of it, but that's enough to reveal a fine array of stalactites and stalagmites. There are steps up to the **cave** (admission €1.10; 🕙 8am-dusk) and you should wear sturdy shoes as the metal walkway inside can be slippery and wet.

İncekaya Aqueduct

Just over 7km north of Safranbolu you can visit this **aqueduct** (Su Kemeri), which was originally built in Byzantine times but restored in the 1790s by İzzet Mehmet Paşa, the man responsible for one of Safranbolu's finest mosques. The aqueduct spans the beautiful **Tokatlı Gorge**, and the drive out to it is through lovely, unspoilt countryside. Taxi drivers in Safranbolu will take you there.

KASTAMONU

☎ 0366 / pop 64,700

Any town where the shops are full of chainsaws and milking machines doesn't seem immediately promising, but the cheery murals all over town hint at the conservative yet positive atmosphere here, and Kastamonu has plenty to offer as a stopover between Anatolia and the Black Sea. Potential distractions include several museums, a castle, several old mosques and many fine old Ottoman houses, while if you stay over you could visit an ancient wooden mosque at Kasaba or explore the outdoors around Pınarbaşı.

History

Kastamonu's history has been as chequered as that of most central Turkish towns. Archaeological evidence suggests there was a settlement here as far back as 2000 BC, but the Hittites, Persians, Macedonians and Pontic (Black Sea) kings all left their mark. In the 11th century the Seljuks descended, followed by the Danışmends. In the late 13th century the Byzantine emperor John Comnenus tried to hold out here, but the Mongols and the Ottomans soon swept in, and by 1459 Kastamonu was secured as an Ottoman town.

Bizarrely, Kastamonu's modern history is inextricably linked to headgear: Atatürk launched his hat reforms here in 1925, banning the fez due to its religious connotations and insisting on the adoption of European-style titfers. You have to wonder how the great leader would have reacted to the rise of the baseball cap...

Orientation & Information

Kastamonu's otogar is 7km north of the city centre, reachable by dolmuş or taxi (€6). If you're coming in from Ankara get the bus to drop you in the centre near the old Nasrullah Köprüsü (Nasrullah Bridge).

The centre of town is Cumhuriyet Meydanı, with an imposing *valilik* (government building), a statue of Atatürk, the PTT and local bus stops. Despite the signs, there's no longer a tourist office here – ask around to see if a new one has opened yet.

Just to the north of Cumhuriyet Meydanı a stream passes under the Nasrullah Köprüsü. Most of the hotels are clustered around this bridge.

Sights
MUSEUMS

About 50m south of Cumhuriyet Meydanı, just off Cumhuriyet Caddesi, the **Ethnography Museum** (Liva Paşa Konağı Etnografya Müzesi; admission €1.10; 🕙 8.30am-5pm Tue-Sun) occupies the restored 1870 Liva Paşa Konağı. It's fully furnished as it would have been in Ottoman times and well worth a visit.

Nearby is the **Archaeology Museum** (☎ 214 1070; Cumhuriyet Caddesi; admission €1.10; 🕙 8.30am-4.30pm Tue-Sun), with predominantly Hellenistic and Roman finds from the area.

OTHER HISTORIC BUILDINGS

It may take a little while to notice Kastamonu's **castle** (kale; admission free; 🕙 daylight hr), built on a tall rock behind the town, but once you do you'll want to take a look. Parts of it date from Byzantine times, but most of what you see belongs to the later Seljuk and Ottoman reconstructions. It's a steep 1km climb up through the streets of the old town.

Nasrullah Meydanı centres on the Ottoman **Nasrullah Camii** (1506) and the fine double fountain in front of it; the former **Munire Medresesi** at the rear now houses a cluster of craft shops. The area immediately west of Nasrullah Meydanı is filled with old market buildings, including the **Aşirefendi Hanı** and the **İsmail Bey Hanı**, built in 1466 and restored in 1972. Wander down any of the side streets in this area and you'll come across old *hamams*, fountains and other historic buildings. Look out in particular for the one gateway from the Seljuk **Yılanlı Külliye** (1272), a mosque complex that survived a fire in 1837.

Sleeping

Otel Selvi (☎ 214 1763; www.selviotel.com; Banka Sokak 10; s/d €14/25) Just north of Nasrullah Meydanı, the Selvi has a range of basic but serviceable rooms, some with castle views, and a tatty roof terrace. Breakfast is €1.10; you can save €5.60 per person by settling for a shared bathroom.

Otel İdrisoğlu (☎ 214 1757; Cumhuriyet Caddesi 21; s/d from €20/34) Right on the main road, the brown-toned reception here is the gateway to a selection of minutely differentiated rooms, all of which are quite adequate for an overnighter.

Otel Mütevelli (☎ 212 2018; www.mutevelli.com.tr; Cumhuriyet Caddesi 10; s/d €25/45) Across the road from Cumhuriyet Meydanı, this hotel is Kastamonu's best (or, um, only) decent central business hotel, with well-serviced rooms and a licensed rooftop restaurant.

Osmanlı Sarayı (Ottoman Palace; ☎ 214 8408; www .ottomanpalace.4t.com; Belediye Caddesi 81; s/d/tr €28/50/67) This former town hall (1898) is a historical attraction in itself, so it's great to see it so beautifully restored, and even better to get the chance to stay here. The 18 bedrooms have soaring wooden ceilings and bathrooms in authentic but newly fitted wooden closets. There's a basement restaurant and a rear tea garden.

Toprakçılar Konakları (☎ 212 1812; www.toprak cilar.com; Alemdar Sokak 2; s/d €45/67, ste €111) More restored Ottoman splendour, this time in a pair of old townhouses across the road from İsfendiyorbey Parkı. The owners are so protective of the original flooring that you're required to put plastic galoshes over your shoes. The courtyard restaurant has live music at weekends, when you'd probably be better off in the quieter second building.

Eating

Frenkşah Sultan Sofrası (☎ 212 1905; Nasrullah Meydanı; mains €1.10-2.80; ⌚ 9am-10pm) Housed in Kastamonu's first Seljuk *hamam* (1262), this place quite literally sank over the years, until it was recovered and restored in 1965. You can dine on homemade *gözleme* in an alcove surrounded by handicrafts or sit outside on the square.

Ulugöl Kebap ve Pide Salonu (☎ 214 1196; Cumhuriyet Caddesi 19; mains €1.10-2.80; ⌚ 9am-10pm) Local women and families seem besotted with this brown wood-clad corner eatery, which serves up pide, kebaps and *kiremit* (baked in earthenware) dishes.

Canoğlu (☎ 213 5583; Cumhuriyet Caddesi 18/F; mains €1.10-3.50; ⌚ 9am-10pm) Towards the eastern end of the main street, Canoğlu is a *pastane* (patisserie), restaurant and fast-food joint in one, or in other words a pig-out waiting to happen.

Drinking

Kastamonu has two great **çay bahçesi** (tea gardens): one in the courtyard of the Munire Medresesi, surrounded by craft shops, and a second on the hillside just beneath the old clock tower, looking down over Cumhuriyet Meydanı and the old town. A taxi up the hill will cost you about €1.10; you can easily walk back down again.

Sevgi Çayevi (cnr İnebolu Caddesi & Izbeli Sokak) On the other side of the park from the Toprakçılar houses, this is a cosy teahouse in a perfectly restored building.

Getting There & Away

Kastamonu's otogar offers regular departures for Ankara (€11, four hours), İstanbul (€19.50, nine hours) and Samsun (€11, six hours). To get to Sinop (€8.50) you may have to change buses at Boyabat (€5.60, 1½ hours). There are hourly departures for Karabük (€5.60, 2½ hours), with some buses continuing to Safranbolu.

Minibuses for İnebolu (€4.50, two hours) also leave from the otogar.

AROUND KASTAMONU

Kasaba

The tiny village of Kasaba, 17km northwest of Kastamonu, is a pretty but unlikely place to find one of Turkey's finest surviving wooden mosques. The **Mahmud Bey Camii** was built in 1366; externally, only the lovely wooden doors stand out, but get the *imam* to unlock it and you'll find a stunning, recently restored interior with four painted wooden columns, a wooden gallery and fine painted ceiling rafters.

To get to Kasaba, take a minibus from Kastamonu otogar to Daday and ask to be let off at the road to Kasaba, just past Subaşı (€0.55). From there it's a 5km walk to Kasaba, where you'll have to ask around the village for the *imam*. A return taxi from Kastamonu, with waiting time, should cost €8.50, and the driver should know exactly where the *imam* lives.

Pınarbaşı

Pınarbaşı, a little hill town 73km from Kastamonu, is the main access town for the new

THE HITTITES

While the name may evoke images of skin-clad barbarians, the Hittites, like the Phrygians, were actually a sophisticated people who commanded a vast Middle Eastern empire, conquered Babylon and challenged the Egyptian pharaohs over 3000 years ago. Apart from a few written references in the Bible and Egyptian chronicles, there were few clues to their existence until 1834 when a French traveller, Charles Texier, stumbled on the ruins of the Hittite capital of Hattuşa, next to Boğazkale.

In 1905 excavations turned up notable works of art, most of them now in Ankara's Museum of Anatolian Civilisations. Also brought to light were the Hittite state archives, written in cuneiform on thousands of clay tablets. From these tablets, historians and archaeologists were able to construct a history of the Hittite empire.

The original Indo-European Hittites swept into Anatolia around 2000 BC, conquering the local Hatti, from whom they borrowed their culture and name. They established themselves at Hattuşa, the Hatti capital, and in the course of a millennium enlarged and beautified the city. From about 1375 to 1200 BC Hattuşa was the capital of a Hittite Empire that, at its height, even incorporated parts of Syria.

Never ones to skimp on religion, the Hittites worshipped over a thousand different deities; the most important were Teshub, the storm or weather god, and Hepatu, the sun goddess. The cuneiform tablets revealed a well-ordered society with more than 200 laws. The death sentence was prescribed for bestiality, while thieves got off more lightly provided they paid their victims compensation.

From about 1250 BC the Hittite empire seems to have gone into a decline, its demise hastened by the arrival of the Phrygians. Only the city-states of Syria survived until they, too, were swallowed by the Assyrians.

Küre Dağları National Park (Küre Dağları Milli Parkı; ☎ 0366-214 8663), a 37,000-hectare plateau that was gazetted in 2000. The local government is currently putting a lot of effort into marketing the 'Kure Mountains' as a tourist destination, and there are plenty of attractions for outdoors types who can take the time to explore under their own steam. Spots worth seeking out include the Ilıca waterfall, Horma Canyon, and the Ilgarini 'Inn' and Ilıca 'Hamam' caves. The spectacular 20km Valla Canyon, reached by walking through the forest 26km north of Pınarbaşı, is a great spot for rafting and trekking, but shouldn't be attempted without local assistance.

BOĞAZKALE, HATTUŞA & YAZILIKAYA

Out in the centre of the Anatolian plains, these intriguing sites were crucial to the whole development of the region, and now encapsulate a vital historical moment at the height of Hittite civilisation (see above). Hattuşa was the Hittite capital, while Yazılıkaya was a religious sanctuary with fine rock carvings. Both are now designated Unesco World Heritage sites.

The best base for visiting Hattuşa and Yazılıkaya is Boğazkale, a farming village 200km east of Ankara. Boğazkale has simple travellers' services; if you want something fancier you'll need to stay in Çorum, the uninspiring provincial capital. Alternatively if you start early enough in the morning you could visit the sites on a day trip out of Ankara.

Boğazkale

☎ 0364 / pop 2000

Base camp for the sites, Boğazkale trades on a spot of rural village charm, though it can get dusty in summer. If it's not too hot, you could happily visit the Hattuşa ruins on foot from here. Apart from the accommodation options, the only facilities are a couple of small shops, post office and bank (no ATM).

Boğazkale's small **museum** (admission €1.10; ☺ 8am-5pm) is on the left as you come into the village. Despite the listed hours it's sometimes closed on Monday. Unsurprisingly, Hittite artefacts dominate the collection, with examples of cuneiform tablets (including a state treaty between kings), signature seals, arrow and axe heads, and whimsically shaped vessels, though if you look closely at the Turkish/German labels you'll find that many items are actually copies, the originals having been spirited away to Ankara.

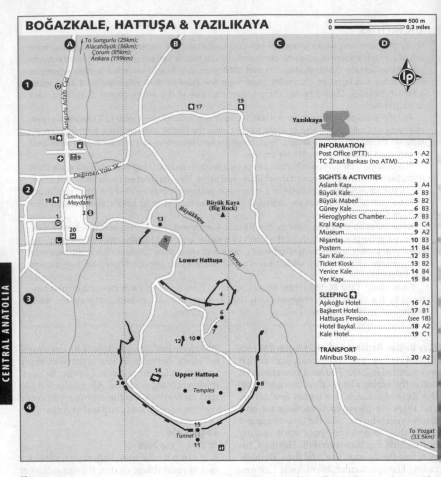

BOĞAZKALE, HATTUŞA & YAZILIKAYA

0 ____ 500 m
0 ____ 0.3 miles

INFORMATION
Post Office (PTT)...........................**1** A2
TC Ziraat Bankası (no ATM)........**2** A2

SIGHTS & ACTIVITIES
Aslanlı Kapı................................**3** A4
Büyük Kale.................................**4** B3
Büyük Mabed..............................**5** B2
Güney Kale.................................**6** B3
Hieroglyphics Chamber.................**7** B3
Kral Kapı...................................**8** C4
Museum.....................................**9** A2
Nişantaş...................................**10** B3
Postern....................................**11** B4
Sarı Kale..................................**12** B3
Ticket Kiosk..............................**13** A2
Yenice Kale...............................**14** B4
Yer Kapı...................................**15** B4

SLEEPING
Aşıkoğlu Hotel...........................**16** A2
Başkent Hotel.............................**17** B1
Hattuşaş Pension.................(see **18**)
Hotel Baykal..............................**18** A2
Kale Hotel.................................**19** C1

TRANSPORT
Minibus Stop..............................**20** A2

Hattuşa

It may be a bare hill now, but **Hattuşa** (admission €2; ☯ 8am-noon & 1-5pm) was once a busy and impressive city, defended by stone walls over 6km in length. Today the ruins consist mostly of reconstructed foundations, walls and a few rock carvings, but there are several interesting features preserved in situ, including a tunnel and some fine hieroglyphic inscriptions. Coach tours do pass through here, and weathered souvenir sellers pop up seemingly from nowhere, but often enough you'll be on your own. The rugged isolation somehow makes the site more atmospheric.

The site is theoretically closed for lunch, but in practice you can enter when you like and let the ticket-seller catch up with you. The admission ticket is also valid for Yazılıkaya.

BÜYÜK MABET

The first site you come to, just past the ticket kiosk, is the vast complex of the **Büyük Mabet** (Great Temple), dating from the 14th century BC and destroyed around 1200 BC. It is the best preserved of the Hittite temples, but you'll need plenty of imagination.

Enter via the wide processional street; to your left (southwest) are the administrative quarters of the temple and a well-worn green cubic rock, supposedly one of only two in the world and a present from Ramses II after the signing of the Kadesh peace treaty (see opposite).

The main temple, to your right, was surrounded by storerooms, thought to be several storeys high. In the early 20th century, huge clay storage jars and thousands of cuneiform tables were found in these rooms. Look for the threshold stones at the base of some of the doorways to see the hole for the hinge-post and the arc worn by the door's movement. The temple is believed to have served as a ritual altar for Teshub, the storm god, and Hepatu, the sun goddess; the large stone base of one of their statues remains.

SARI KALE

About 250m south, past the Büyük Mabed, the road forks; take the right (west) fork and follow the winding road up the hillside. On your left in the midst of the old city you can see several ruined structures fenced off from the road, including the **Sarı Kale** (Yellow Castle), which may be a Phrygian fort on Hittite foundations.

CASTLE WALLS & GATES

From the fork in the road it's about 750m uphill to the **Aslanlı Kapı** (Lion Gate), where two stone lions (one badly defaced) protect the city from evil spirits. This is one of at least six gates in the city's defensive walls, though it may never have been competed. You can see the best preserved parts of the fortifications from here, stretching up the ridge south to Yer Kapı and east to Kral Kapı. These walls, built almost 4000 years ago, illustrate the Hittites' engineering ingenuity: their ability to build in sympathy with the terrain coupled with their ability to transform the landscape. Natural outcrops were appropriated as part of the walls, and massive ramparts were built to create artificial fortresses.

Just east of Aslanlı Kapı is **Yenice Kale**, where you can see how the Hittite engineers transformed a 30m-high rocky peak into a smooth terraced fortress.

From Aslanlı Kapı continue another 600m to the **Yer Kapı** or **Sfenksli Kapı** (Earth or Sphinx Gate), once defended by four great sphinxes, who are now watched over themselves in the museums of İstanbul and Berlin. The hill here is artificial, and a 70m-long **tunnel** runs through the walls to a **postern** on the southern side. As the 'true' arch was not invented until much later, the Hittites used a corbelled arch, two flat faces of stones leaning towards one another. Primitive or not, the arch has done

its job for millennia, and you can still pass down the stony tunnel as Hittite soldiers did, emerging from the postern. Afterwards you can climb back up via one of the **monumental stairways** on either side of the wide stone glacis, and enjoy the wonderful views over the site and its surroundings.

Head northeast down the slope from the Yer Kapı, past some of the upper city's 28 **temples** on the left, and you'll reach the **Kral Kapı** (King's Gate), named after the regal-looking figure in the relief carving. The one here is an obvious copy; the original was removed for safekeeping to the Ankara museum. For the record, the figure is not a king at all, but a Hittite warrior god protecting the city.

NİŞANTAŞ & GÜNEY KALE

Heading downhill again you'll come to the **Nişantaş**, a rock with a long Hittite inscription cut into it, which dates it to the time of Suppiluliuma II (1215–1200 BC), the last Hittite king.

Immediately opposite, a path leads up to the excavated **Güney Kale** (Southern Fortress) and to what may have been a royal tomb, with a fine (fenced off) **hieroglyphics chamber** with human figure reliefs.

BÜYÜK KALE

The ruins of the **Büyük Kale** (Great Fortress) are 200m downhill from the Nişantaş. Although most of the site has been excavated, many of the older layers of development have been re-covered to protect them, so what you see today can be hard to decipher. This elaborate fortress held the royal palace and the Hittite state archives. The archives, discovered in 1906, contained about 2500 pieces, including the Kadesh peace treaty between the Hittite monarch Hattusili III and the Egyptian pharaoh Ramses II, written in cuneiform on a clay tablet.

From the fortress it's about 1km back to the ticket kiosk.

Yazılıkaya

Yazılıkaya means 'Inscribed Rock', and that's exactly what you'll find in these outdoor art galleries, just under 3km from Hattuşa. Yazılıkaya was a Hittite religious sanctuary for years; in later Hittite times (13th century BC) a monumental gateway and temple structure were built out the front, and it's these foundations that you see as you approach from the car park.

There are two natural **rock galleries**: the larger one to the left, which was the empire's holiest religious sanctuary; and a narrower one, with the best preserved carvings, to the right. This latter gallery is thought to be the burial place of King Tudhaliya IV (r 1250–1220 BC), possibly the founder of this gallery, and his family. Together they form the largest known Hittite rock sanctuary anywhere, well enough preserved to make you wish you could have seen the carvings when they were new.

In the large gallery, Chamber A, there are fast-fading reliefs of numerous goddesses and pointy-hatted gods marching in procession. Heads and feet are shown in profile but the torso is shown front on, a common feature of Hittite relief art. In this gallery you'll see the superb large relief of Tudhaliya IV, with a cap and long cape, standing on two mountains. On the far wall look out for another large, worn relief, that of Teshub, the storm god, standing on two deified mountains (depicted as men). Beside him is his (better preserved) wife Hepatu, the sun goddess, standing on the back of a panther; their son, Sharruma, and possibly her two daughters, follow behind her. The rock ledges were probably used for offerings or sacrifices and the basins for libations.

Leave the large gallery and head to the narrow gallery of Chamber B, where the carvings are better protected from the elements; supposedly you should ask permission of the winged lion-headed guard depicted by the entrance before penetrating his lair. Here you'll see another procession of scimitar-wielding gods and a detailed relief of the sword god, the sword's handle consisting of four lion's heads (two pointing towards the blade, one to the left and the other to the right); the central figure at the top of the handle depicts the god himself. Nearby is another relief of Sharruma with his arm protectively around Tudhaliya IV. The rock-cut ledges presumably held crematory urns.

Sleeping & Eating

Hotel Baykal/Hattuşas Pension (☎ 452 2013; www .hattusha.com; Cumhuriyet Meydanı 22; pension s/d/tr from €7/12/18, hotel d/tr €30/45). This friendly dual-identity establishment is right in the heart of the village, overlooking the square. The hotel rooms don't offer much in the way of extras but are neat and comfortable. The pension is scrappier, with shared bathrooms and rural artefacts all over the place, but has that much more character. Breakfast costs €2. Ahmet, the proprietor, speaks good English and knows all there is to know about the area.

Başkent Hotel (☎ 452 2037; www.baskenthattusa .com; Yazılıkaya Yolu Üzeri 45; camping per tent €8.50, s/d €10/20; ☽ Apr-Oct) Up the hill on the road to Yazılıkaya, the Başkent goes for a modern motel style, complete with long porch to take in the views. Bathrooms are variable but the rooms are decent enough. The terraced camp site can sleep up to 60 and accommodate 50 campervans.

Kale Hotel (☎ 452 3126; www.bogazkoyhattusa.com; Yazılıkaya Yolu Üzeri; d/tr €17/28; ☽ Apr-Oct) The Kale, occupying a perfect spot 400m further along the Yazılıkaya road, has big, light rooms with cheerful floral linen; the top ones at the front have good views and some have small balconies. The leafy **camp site** (per site €5.60) has OK views, and the restaurant mainly caters for groups.

Aşıkoğlu Hotel (☎ 452 2004; www.hattusas.com; r from €20, ste €50; ☐) Just outside the village, the Aşıkoğlu offers a great variety of accommodation: plump for a three-star room with spotless bathroom and TV; a two-star room in the yellow pension section, without TV; or the big 'Marilyn Monroe' suite. Three basic **camping areas** (per site €5.60) are also available. English and German are spoken. In summer, the hotel may fill up with tour groups.

Getting There & Away

To get to Boğazkale by public transport, you'll need to go via Sungurlu. Buses from Ankara to Sungurlu (€5.60, three hours, hourly) sometimes drop their passengers on the highway rather than at Sungurlu otogar; lurking taxi drivers will then deny the existence of any dolmuşes to Boğazkale. To be sure of making a connection, travel from Ankara with Hattusus buses (ticket counter 37 at the otogar); they run a beat-up *servis* into Sungurlu that drops you right by the Boğazkale dolmuş stand.

During the week minibuses run from Sungurlu to Boğazkale whenever they fill up (€1.10, 30 minutes); at weekends you may have to hitch or take a taxi for around €8 to €10.

Travellers coming from Cappadocia should note that direct minibuses from Yozgat to Boğazkale are thin on the ground; you're probably better off going to Kırıkkale (east of Ankara) and changing.

Getting Around

To get around Hattuşa and Yazılıkaya without your own transport you'll need to walk or hire a taxi. It's 1km from the Aşıkoğlu Hotel to the Hattuşa ticket kiosk. From there the road looping around the site from the ticket kiosk (not including Yazılıkaya) is another 5km. The walk itself takes at least an hour, plus time spent exploring the ruins, so figure on spending a good three hours here. Take drinking water and start early in the day before the sun is too hot, as there's little shade.

Local taxis from Hattuşa will take you all the way around for about €12. You may want to haggle for an all-day tour including Hattuşa, Yazılıkaya and Alacahöyük.

Yazılıkaya is just under 3km from Hattuşa and about the same distance back to Boğazkale.

ALACAHÖYÜK

The tiny farming hamlet of Alacahöyük is 36km north of Boğazkale and 52km south of Çorum. It's a very old site, settled from about 4000 BC, but so little remains that it's really only worth the effort if you've got your own transport and have some time spare after Hattuşa. As at the other Hittite sites, movable monuments have been taken to the museum in Ankara, although there is a small site museum and a few worn sphinxes have been left in place.

The **museum** (admission €1.10; ⊗ 8am-noon & 1.30-5.30pm) is right by the ruins, displaying artists' impressions of the site at various points in its history and finds from the Chalcolithic and Old Bronze ages. A glass case shows the 15 layers of Alacahöyük's buried history, from 5500 to 600 BC.

At the ruins, the **monumental gate** has two eyeless sphinxes guarding the door. The detailed reliefs (copies, of course) show musicians, acrobats, animals for sacrifice and the Hittite king and queen – all part of festivities and ceremonies dedicated to Teshub, shown here as a bull. The rest of the site is pretty extensive but there's not much to see apart from foundations, and all the detailed signage is in Turkish only.

There's a small **café** with hay-bale seats at the site entrance, perfect for a post-ruins drink or snack.

Getting There & Away

There's no public transport between Alacahöyük and Boğazkale. If you're really keen, you could take a bus or dolmuş from Çorum to Alaca and another from Alaca to Alacahöyük (one or two services per day, none at weekends). Taxis can take you from Boğazkale to Alacahöyük, wait for an hour and then run you to Alaca or the busy Sungurlu–Çorum highway for around €20.

ÇORUM
☎ 0364 / pop 161,400

Set on an alluvial plain on a branch of the Çorum River, Çorum is an unremarkable provincial capital, resting on its modest fame as the chickpea capital of Turkey – proof, perhaps, that pride comes before a felafel. The town's market is crammed with *leblebiciler* (chickpea roasters) and sacks upon sacks of the chalky little pulses, all sorted according to fine distinctions obvious only to a chickpea dealer.

If you're travelling north or east from Boğazkale you may have to change buses in Çorum, and the town can also be a handy base for seeing the Hittite sites.

Orientation & Information

The clock tower (1894) marks the centre of Çorum, with the PTT and *belediye* close by. The otogar is 1.5km southwest of the clock tower along the main drag, İnönü Caddesi, where there are a few banks with ATMs.

Çorum Museum

Close to the otogar is the **Çorum Museum** (admission €1.10; ⊗ 8am-5.30pm Tue-Sun), which has a typical collection of Hittite, Byzantine–Roman and Ottoman exhibits and ethnography. To find it, leave the otogar's main entrance, turn left, then left again at the traffic roundabout and walk a few hundred metres; it's just south of the Ticaret Meslek Lisesi.

Sleeping & Eating

Most hotels are along İnönü Caddesi, either near the otogar or the clock tower.

Otel Konfor Palas (☎ 224 2744; Kubbeli Camii Karşısı; s/d/tr/q with shared bathroom €9/16/23/30, s/d/tr €12.50/19/28) Calling your budget hotel the 'Comfort Palace' may be stretching it a little, but for a bright, cheap bed off the central pedestrian zone we're quite prepared to let it go.

Hotel Sarıgül (☎ 224 2012; Azap Ahmet Sokak 18; s/d/tr €22/34/45) Despite some frankly inhumane deployment of greens, limes and mauves, this smart hotel behind the post office is good for a night or two, with bar, disco and live music in the restaurant.

Anitta Otel (☎ 213 8515; www.anittahotel.com; İnönü Caddesi 30; s/d €35/55; ⚇) A terracotta three-star block standing on its own opposite the otogar, the Anitta has an inflated sense of its own worth (you may have to haggle), but at least this means its standards stay high.

Katipler Konağı (☎ 224 9651; Karakeçili Mahallesi, 2 Sokak 20; mains €2-6; ⏱ 11am-10pm) The best eating experience for miles, spread across two floors of a restored Ottoman house. The highlight is the selection of local dishes such as *çatal asi* (lentil and barley) soup and *keşkek* (mutton and coarse-grained wheat), washed down with delicious black mulberry juice. To find it from the Sarıgül, turn left, cross the road and turn right; take the side street behind the mosque straight ahead, turn left at the end and it's on the right.

Getting There & Away

Being on the main Ankara–Samsun highway, Çorum has good bus connections. Regular buses go to Alaca (€2.50, 45 minutes), Amasya (€4, two hours), Ankara (€6.70, four hours), Kayseri (€9.50, 4¾ hours), Samsun (€6.70, three hours) and Sungurlu (€2.50, 1¼ hours).

AMASYA

☎ 0358 / pop 74,400

Set in a ravine hemmed in between two great ridges of rock, bisected by the Yeşilırmak River, lined with fairytale Ottoman houses, Amasya has a certain fantasy air about it, an ethereal quality to the organic loveliness of the location that makes it feel almost as if it shouldn't exist at all. Luckily, though, it does.

Locals show great pride in their town, which they are anxious to share with any visitors fortunate enough to come this way.

Capital of the modern province of the same name, Amasya was once the capital of a great Pontic kingdom. Its dramatic setting complements its numerous historic buildings, especially the rock-hewn tombs of the kings of Pontus and some fine old mosques and *medreses*. Against this rugged backdrop, the sensitively restored half-timbered houses

seem even more attractive, whether lit by sunlight or shrouded in snow.

Amasya is also famed for its apples, which give autumn visitors just one more thing to sink their teeth into. A walk along the river can be all you need to fall in love with the place.

History

Originally known as Hakmış under the Hittites, the Amasya area has been inhabited continuously since around 5500 BC. The city was conquered by Alexander the Great in the 4th century BC, then became the capital of a successor kingdom ruled by a family of Persian satraps (provincial governors). By the time of King Mithridates II (281 BC), the Kingdom of Pontus was entering its golden age and dominated a large part of Anatolia.

During the latter part of Pontus' flowering, Amasya was the birthplace of Strabo (c 63 BC to AD 25), the world's first geographer. Perhaps feeling restricted by the surrounding mountains, Strabo left home to travel in Europe, west Asia and north Africa, writing 47 history and 17 geography books as a result of his journeys. Though most of his history books have been lost, we know something of their content because many other classical writers chose to quote him.

Amasya's golden age ended when the Romans decided to take control of Anatolia (47 BC); it was supposedly the conquest of Amasya that prompted Julius Caesar's immortal words *Veni, vidi, vici* – 'I came, I saw, I conquered'. After Rome came the Byzantines, the Seljuks (1075), the Mongols (mid-13th century) and the notional republic of Abazhistan. In Ottoman times, Amasya was an important military base and testing ground for the sultans' heirs; it also became a centre of Islamic study, with as many as 18 *medreses* and 2000 theological students by the 19th century.

After WWI, Mustafa Kemal (Atatürk) escaped occupied İstanbul and came to Amasya, where he secretly met with friends on 12 June 1919 and hammered out the basic principles of the Turkish struggle for independence. The monument in the main square commemorates the meeting and depicts the unhappy state of Anatolian Turks before the revolution. Each year, Amasyalıs commemorate the meeting with a week-long art and culture festival.

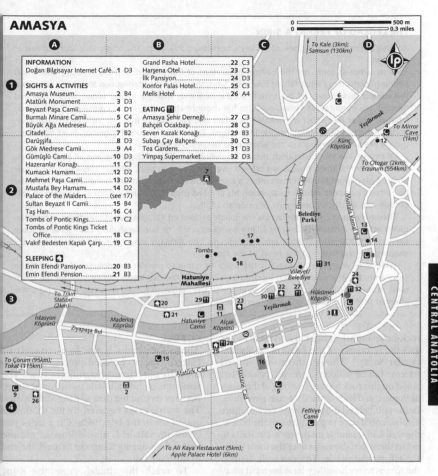

AMASYA

0 ———————————— 500 m
0 ———————————— 0.3 miles

INFORMATION
Doğan Bilgisayar Internet Café...1 D3

SIGHTS & ACTIVITIES
Amasya Museum......................2 B4
Atatürk Monument.................. 3 D3
Beyazıt Paşa Camii...................4 D1
Burmalı Minare Camii.............. 5 C4
Büyük Ağa Medresesi...............6 D1
Citadel...................................7 B2
Darüşşifa................................8 D3
Gök Medrese Camii..................9 A4
Gümüşlü Camii.......................10 D3
Hazeranlar Konağı..................11 C3
Kumacık Hamamı....................12 D2
Mehmet Paşa Camii................13 D2
Mustafa Bey Hamamı.............. 14 D2
Palace of the Maiders..........(see 17)
Sultan Beyazıt II Camii............15 B4
Taş Han.................................16 C4
Tombs of Pontic Kings............17 C2
Tombs of Pontic Kings
  Office................................18 C3
Vakıf Bedesten Kapalı Çarşı.....19 C3

SLEEPING
Emin Efendi Pansiyon..............20 B3
Emin Efendi Pension................21 B3

Grand Pasha Hotel...................22 C3
Harşena Otel..........................23 C3
İlk Pansiyon...........................24 D3
Konfor Palas Hotel..................25 C3
Melis Hotel............................26 A4

EATING
Amasya Şehir Derneği..............27 C3
Bahçeli Ocakbaşı....................28 C3
Seven Kazak Konağı................29 B3
Subaşı Çay Bahçesi..................30 C3
Tea Gardens..........................31 D3
Yimpaş Supermarket...............32 D3

Orientation & Information

The otogar is at the northeastern edge of town and the train station at the northwestern edge. It's 2km from either to the main square, marked by the statue of Atatürk and a bridge across the river. The majority of everyday amenities are on the south bank of the river, but the north bank is the prettiest part of town, with the tombs of the Pontic kings, most of the Ottoman half-timbered houses and the castle. You may want to take a minibus or taxi to and from the otogar and train station; otherwise everything is within walking distance.

Despite all the signs, there's currently no tourist office, though it's hoped one will open soon. The serviceable **Doğan Bilgisayar Internet**

Café (Mustafa Kemal Bulvarı 10) is just north of the main square.

Sights & Activities
PONTIC TOMBS

Looming above the northern bank of the river is a sheer rock face with the conspicuous rock-cut **Tombs of the Pontic Kings** (Kral Kaya Mezarları; admission €1.10; 8am-8pm Apr-Oct, 8.30am-5.30pm Nov-Mar). The tombs, cut deep into the rock as early as the 4th century BC, were used for cult worship of the deified rulers. There are 18 tombs in these valleys, all of them empty.

Climb the well-marked steps to the ticket office. Just past the office the path divides: turn left to find a couple of tombs reached via a

THE LEGEND OF FERHAT & ŞIRIN

Amasya is the setting for one of Turkey's best-loved folk tales, the tragic love story of Ferhat and Şirin.

In its simplest form, it's the Eastern equivalent of Romeo and Juliet: the young *nakış* (wall painting) craftsman Ferhat falls in love with Şirin, the sister of sultan-queen Mehmene Banu, but the sultana disapproves of the match, so she demands that the young suitor carve a channel through the mountains to bring water to her drought-struck city. In the course of his Herculean labours, Ferhat hears that his beloved has died and kills himself in grief; Şirin, very much alive, finds his body and commits suicide in her turn. When they're buried together, tears flow from the graves and bring Amasya the water it so desperately needs.

Of course, like all true legends there's no definitive telling of the story, and all kinds of interpretations of the myth have been offered over the years, in print and on stage or screen. Celebrated playwright Nazım Hikmet offers a more complex reading in which the lovers are undone by Ferhat's stubborn refusal to abandon his ill-fated project, turning it from a superhuman feat of love into an all-consuming act of pride and folly.

Elsewhere you might come across the much-performed Karagöz puppet rendition, where the lovers achieve a happy ending by killing a wicked witch, or Jale Karabekir's 2001 feminist stage version, which removes Ferhat entirely, defining him through absence in the fears and desires shaping the two sisters at the heart of the story.

Whichever you prefer, Amasya is the place to come to ponder the poignant lessons of the story amid the epic scenery that inspired it. A statue of the two lovers can be seen on the south bank of the river in town, and you can also visit the Ferhat Su Kanalı, an actual 6km-long water channel that feeds the imagination perfectly.

rock-hewn tunnel, or right to find more tombs and the remnants of the **Palace of the Maidens** (Kızlar Sarayı). Though there were indeed harems full of maidens here, the palace that stood on this rock terrace was that of the kings of Pontus, and later of the Ottoman governors. In the cliff behind the terrace are several more tombs. You'll have to pass through the hole in the wall and scramble up the rock-cut stairs to get to them, but the views over the town make the effort worthwhile. You can walk around the tombs to see how they have been cut away from the rock face, but beware of couples in dark corners!

Another Pontic tomb, the **Mirror Cave** (Aynalı Mağara), is apart from the others on the road in from Samsun. It's worth visiting if you have time and is a pleasant 4km walk from the main square; follow the river north until you cross the Yeşilırmak Bridge, then look for the signpost on your right.

Although built during Pontic times, it's likely that this tomb was later used as a chapel by the Byzantines who painted the fast-fading frescoes inside. With a Greek inscription high on the façade, this is one of the few tombs to have any type of adornment. If you're feeling lazy, a taxi will run you there and back from the centre for about €5.

CITADEL

Above the tombs is the *kale* (citadel) or Harşena castle, perched precariously atop the cliffs and offering magnificent views. The remnants of the walls date from Pontic times, perhaps around the time of King Mithridates. The fortress was repaired by the Ottomans and again in the late 1980s. On a ledge just below the citadel is an old Russian cannon that is fired during Ramazan to mark the end of the daily fast.

To reach the citadel, cross the Künç Köprüsü and follow the Samsun road for about 1km to a street on the left marked 'Kale'. It's 1.7km up the mountainside to a small car park, then another steep 15-minute climb to the summit, marked by a flagpole. Travellers of either sex are advised not to go up unaccompanied.

AMASYA MUSEUM

Amasya's **museum** (☎ 218 4513; Atatürk Caddesi, admission €1.10; ☽ 8-11.45am & 1-4.45pm Tue-Sun) is well worth a visit. Notable exhibits include the famous Statuette of Amasya, a bronze figure of the Hittite god Teshub, with pointed cap and huge almond-shaped eyes; wooden doors taken from the Gök Medrese Camii, showing the progression between Seljuk and

Ottoman carving; and displays on Ottoman crafts such as rope-making. English signage is good throughout.

The highlight, though, is the tiled Seljuk tomb in the garden, which contains a unique collection of gruesome mummies dating from the İlkhan period. The bodies, mummified without removing the organs, were discovered beneath the Burmalı Minare Cami. None of it's for squeamish or young eyes, but the remains of a baby girl, disintegrated into three pieces, are particularly hard to look at.

HATUNİYE MAHALLESİ

Immediately north of the river, the Hatuniye Mahallesi is Amasya's wonderful neighbourhood of restored old Ottoman houses, interspersed with good modern reproductions to make a harmonious whole.

Just past the steps up to the Pontic Tombs is the **Hazeranlar Konağı** (☎ 218 4018; admission €1.10; ⏱ 8.30-11.45am & 1.15-4.45pm Tue-Sun), constructed in 1865 and restored in 1979. The restored rooms are fully furnished in period style and have models to illustrate their use. Whether you'll enjoy the Directorate of Fine Arts gallery in the basement probably depends on what's showing (historical photos at time of research).

HAMAMS

Amasya has several venerable *hamams* that are still in operation. On the northern side of the Darüşşifa is the 1436 Ottoman **Mustafa Bey Hamamı** (⏱ 6-10am & 4-11pm for men, 10am-4pm for women; full wash €6), while not far away is the 1495 **Kumacık Hamamı** (⏱ 6-10am & 4-11pm for men, 10am-4pm for women; full wash €6).

OTHER SIGHTS

You could spend a very pleasant couple of hours exploring the minor sights of Amasya, which are spread out along both banks of the river. The advantage of the south bank is that you can see the north bank from it, essential for the best views during the day and especially at night, when the castle and rock tombs are artily lit in neon. The bulk of Amasya's old religious buildings are also on this side of the river.

South of the River

At the eastern end of the south bank, near the Künç Köprüsü, is the **Beyazıt Paşa Camii**, an early Ottoman mosque (1419), following a twin-domed plan that was a forebear in style to the famous Yeşil Cami in Bursa. It's closed except at prayer times, but its most interesting features are external anyway.

Follow the riverbank west along and you'll come to the pretty **Mehmet Paşa Camii**, built in 1486 by Lala Mehmet Paşa, tutor to Şehzade Ahmet, the son of Sultan Beyazıt II. Don't miss the beautiful marble *mimber* (pulpit). The complex originally included the builder's tomb, an *imaret* (soup kitchen), *tabhane* (hospital), *hamam* and *handan* (inn).

Continue west and on the left you'll see the **Darüşşifa** (Mustafa Kemal Bulvarı) or Bimarhane, which was built as a mental hospital by Ilduş Hatun, wife of the İlkhanid Sultan Olcaytu, in 1309 and may have been the first place to try to treat mental disorders with music. The İlkhans were the successors to Ghengis Khan's Mongols, who had defeated the Anatolian Seljuks. Their architecture reflects motifs borrowed from many conquered peoples, and the building is based on the plan of a Seljuk *medrese*. Today the building is often used for exhibitions, concerts and events.

A bit further along the river is Amasya's main square with its imposing memorial to the War of Independence. Perched on a rise to the eastern side of the main square is the **Gümüşlü Cami** (Silvery Mosque; 1326), the earliest Ottoman mosque in the town. It was rebuilt in 1491 after an earthquake, in 1612 after a fire, and again in 1688, then added to in 1903 and restored yet again in 1988.

If you keep walking west and head inland from the river you'll come to the **Vakıf Bedesten Kapalı Çarşı** (Covered Market), built in 1483 and still in use today. Keep heading west along Atatürk Caddesi and on the left you'll see the partly ruined **Taş Han** (1758), an Ottoman caravanserai. Behind it is the **Burmalı Minare Camii** (Spiral Minaret Mosque), built by the Seljuks between 1237 and 1247, with elegant spiral carving on the minaret.

Keep walking west and you'll come to the graceful **Sultan Beyazıt II Camii** (1486), Amasya's largest *külliye* (mosque complex), with a *medrese*, fountain, *imaret* and *kütüphane* (library). Finally, you'll reach the **Gök Medrese Camii** (Mosque of the Sky-Blue Seminary), which was built from 1266 to 1267 for Seyfettin Torumtay, the Seljuk governor of Amasya. The *eyvan* (vaulted recess) serving as its main portal is unique in Anatolia, while the *kümbet* (domed tomb) was once covered in *gök* (sky-blue) tiles, hence the name.

North of the River

Across the Künç Köprüsü on the north bank of the river is the impressive octagonal **Büyük Ağa Medresesi**, built in 1488 by Sultan Beyazıt II's chief white eunuch Hüseyin Ağa. It still serves as a seminary for boys who are training to be *hafız* (theologians who have memorised the entire Koran) and is not open to the public.

Sleeping

BUDGET

Like Safranbolu, Amasya is one of those places where it's worth paying a bit more to be able to stay in a real Ottoman house, but at least one budget option is far from terrible.

Konfor Palas Hotel (☎ 218 1260; Ziyapaşa Bulvarı 2/B; s/d/tr €11/20/25) If you can overlook stained carpets and minor design flaws, these small rooms are comfortable enough, and the caretaker may somehow remind you of your dad... Back and side rooms avoid the noise from the cafés outside. Breakfast is not included.

İlk Pansiyon (☎ 218 1689; Hitit Sokak 1; r €17-50) Who says you have to pay imperial measures to stay in an Ottoman house? This restored mansion is one of the best in Turkey, eschewing false luxury in favour of authentic-feeling, characterful rooms. The five airy, spacious salons have low-lying beds and simple bathrooms (one hidden Tardis-style in a closet), while the solitary box room off the leafy courtyard is perfect for couples.

MIDRANGE

Emin Efendi Konakları (☎ 212 0852; www.eminefendi.com.tr; Hazeranlar Sokak 73; pension s/d €20/31, hotel s/d €34/50; ⌘) Whatever your taste, the two Emin Efendi properties seem determined to cater for it – the new hotel building (Emin Efendi Pension) offers an intelligent interpretation of traditional style with modern comforts, while the original pension down the road (Emin Efendi Pansiyon) has exactly the right amount of clutter and Ottoman features, plus a perfect courtyard.

Grand Pasha Hotel (☎ 212 4158; www.grandpashahotel.com; Tevfik Hafız Çıkmazı 5; r €20-67) With 120 years of history behind it, this high-ceilinged house on the river has more than enough Ottoman quirks to keep a stay interesting. If the novelty

wears off, there's always the live music in the courtyard restaurant.

Melis Hotel (☎ 212 3650; www.melishotel.net; Torumtay Sokak 135; s/d €28/42; ⌘ ⌨) Away from the river but near the museum, this tall, narrow hotel-guesthouse is crammed from top to bottom with rustic artefacts. The individually decorated rooms are colourful and clean, there are wood floors and furniture throughout, and the rooftop terrace makes the perfect spot for an evening wind-down.

Harşena Otel (☎ 218 3979; www.harsena.com; PTT Karşısı; s/d €30/55; ⌘) Some choices are harder than others. Will you go for the smart but unexceptional modern building, or the creakingly authentic old Amasya house overhanging the river? Well, duh. In case you're undecided, there's a courtyard and café-bar-restaurant on the old side, too.

TOP END

Apple Palace Hotel (☎ 219 0019; www.theapplepalace.com.tr; Vermiş Sokak 7; s/d €50/80; ⌘ ⌨ ⌘) Amasya's solitary four-star hotel lives in splendid isolation on the hillside south of the river, overlooking the town and the Pontic tombs. Rooms are swish and comfortable, while the facilities are constantly improving and the disco is one of Amasya's only major nightspots. Shuttle buses ferry guests to and from town.

Eating & Drinking

Apart from the hotel restaurants listed above, there are several good cafés and restaurants in Hatuniye Mahallesi and a smattering of more basic options around town.

Bahçeli Ocakbaşı (☎ 218 5692; Ziyapaşa Bulvarı; mains €1.40-3.50; ⏱ 8am-10pm) This is one of half a dozen cafés competing amiably for business on the lively, crowded courtyard outside the Konfor Palas. It also has the biggest sign, which must mean something.

Yimpaş Supermarket (☎ 212 7184; Ziyapaşa Bulvarı 16; meals €3; ⏱ 9am-8pm) More than just a place to get your groceries, the big new Yimpaş has its own rooftop café for light meals and ravine views. Oh, and of course you can get your groceries there.

Seven-Kazak Konağı (Figani Sokak 1; drinks from €0.30; ⏱ 11am-10pm; ⌨) It's not on the river and the basement can get almost rowdy without the calming influence of daylight, but one look at the walled courtyard and you won't want to sip tea anywhere else.

Ali Kaya Restaurant (☎ 218 1505; Çakallar Mevkii; mains €1.70-4; ☺ 11am-10pm) This simple licensed restaurant, up near the Apple Palace, offers breathtaking views of Amasya. Come during the day or just before sunset to do them justice. If there's a group of you, ring ahead for a free pick-up; otherwise a taxi will set you back €3 each way.

Amasya Şehir Derneği (☎ 218 1013; mains €2.50-6; ☺ 11am-11pm) Overlooking the river next to the chunky clock tower by the Hükümet Köprüsü, this three-tiered clubhouse has the best balconies in town, mostly reserved for Amasya's movers and shakers (ie men in suits). Foreign tourists also get a free pass to enjoy the grill menu, live music and frog chorus.

The **Subaşı Çay Bahçesi** (☎ 212 0852; Tevfik Hafız Çıkmazı), opposite the Grand Pasha Hotel, is the north bank's most popular café garden. Several more tea gardens line the river north of Belediye Parkı.

Getting There & Away

Amasya is not far off the busy route between Ankara and Samsun, so buses are frequent. Some bus companies maintain ticket offices on the main square; a dolmuş to the otogar costs €0.40.

To get to Safranbolu (€17, nine hours), take an early morning minibus to Gerede, alight at the Karabük junction and flag down a bus to Karabük. From Karabük take another minibus to Safranbolu – a long day!

Otherwise there are daily buses to Adıyaman (for Nemrut Dağı; €25, 10 hours), Ankara (€14, five hours), Çorum (€5.60, two hours), İstanbul (€20, 10 hours), Kayseri (€17, eight hours), Malatya (€17, eight hours), Nevşehir (€20, nine hours), Samsun (€5.60, two hours), Sivas (€11, 3½ hours) and Tokat (€5.60, two hours).

Amasya **train station** (☎ 218 1239) is served by two daily trains between Samsun (€2.80, 5½ hours) and Sivas (three hours).

TOKAT
☎ 0356 / pop 114,000

Like Amasya, Tokat is essentially laid out in a straight line, backed by some rugged grey rocks, though the busy main street is never going to live up to Amasya's riverside charm. On the plus side, Tokat is still liberally sprinkled with crumbling ruins, many of them below ground level – the whole town is thought to have risen by up to 5m between

the 13th and 20th centuries, as local silt and earthquake debris were carried down into the valley by rain and floods.

As well as these architectural treats, which include the Gök Medrese and the wonderful Latifoğlu Konağı, kebap fetishists should stop here to sample the amazing local rendition of the Turkish classic.

History

Tokat's history, as you'd expect, is a rollcall of Anatolian conquerors: the Hittites and Phrygians, the Medes and the Persians, the empire of Alexander the Great, the Kingdom of Pontus, the Romans, the Byzantines, the Danışmend Turks, the Seljuks and the Mongol İlkhanids all marched through here at some point.

By the time of the Seljuk Sultanate of Rum, Tokat was Anatolia's sixth-largest city and on important trade routes; the approach roads are littered with Seljuk bridges and caravanserais testifying to its importance. However, the Mongols and İlkhanid sultans reversed the trend around the mid-13th century, leaving the city disinherited.

Only in 1402, when the Ottomans took the area, did Tokat resume its role as an important trading entrepot, agricultural town and copper-mining centre. In the 19th century a local boy, Gazi Osman Paşa, even rose from a poor background to become one of the Empire's greatest generals, and Tokat's main street still bears his name.

Significant non-Muslim populations (Armenian, Greek, Jewish) were in charge of Tokat's commerce until the cataclysm of WWI, and there's still a small but active Jewish community.

Orientation

The town centre is Cumhuriyet Meydanı, a large square where you'll find the *vilayet* (provincial government headquarters), *belediye*, PTT and Tarihi Ali Paşa Hamam. There's a shopping centre underneath.

Looming above the town is a rocky promontory crowned by the obligatory ancient fortress. Beneath it cluster the bazaar and many of the town's old Ottoman houses.

The main street, Gazi Osman Paşa (universally abbreviated to GOP) Bulvarı, runs north from the main square past the Gök Medrese to a traffic roundabout. The otogar is 1.7km from Cumhuriyet Meydanı. Local minibuses

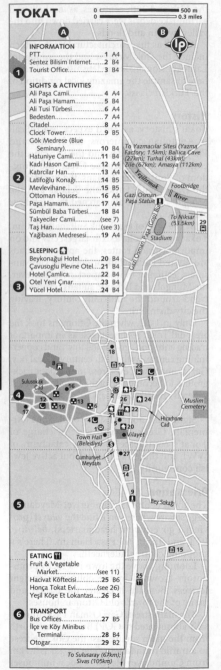

To Yazmacılar Sitesi (Yazma Factory; 1.5km); Ballica Cave (27km); Turhal (43km); Zile (67km); Amasya (112km)

Gazi Osman Paşa Statue

To Niksar (53.5km)

Muslim Cemetery

To Sulusaray (67km); Sivas (105km)

leave from the İlçe ve Köy minibus terminal two blocks east of GOP Bulvarı.

Information

Sentez Bilisim Internet (GOP Bulvarı 148/B; per hr €0.45; ⏰ 9am-midnight) Above Safi Döviz.

Tourist office (☎ 211 8252; Taş Han, GOP Bulvarı 138/I; ⏰ 9am-5pm Mon-Fri May-Nov) No maps, no brochures, no English spoken!

Sights & Activities

GÖK MEDRESE

Constructed in 1277 by Pervane Muhinedin Süleyman, a local potentate, after the fall of the Seljuks and the coming of the Mongols, the **Gök Medrese** (Blue Seminary; GOP Bulvarı; admission €1.10; ⏰ 8am-noon & 1-5pm Tue-Sun) was used as a hospital until 1811; it's now the town's small museum. A number of informative signs are translated into respectably intelligible English.

Gök is an old Turkic word for sky-blue, and the building's blue tiles occasioned its name. Very few of these are left on the façade, now well below street level, but there are enough on the interior courtyard walls to give an idea of what it must have looked like in its glory days. Museum exhibits include Stone and Bronze Age artefacts from excavations at Maşat Höyük, icons and relics from Tokat's churches (look out for John the Baptist carrying his own head on a platter), dervish ceremonial tools and weapons (fancy a 'mystic awl' or 'stones of submission'?), Korans and Islamic calligraphy. An ethnographic section on costume and textiles explains the local art of *yazma* (headscarf) making.

The seminary contains the **Tomb of 40 Maidens** (Kırkkızlar Türbesi), actually an assembly of 20 tombs, probably of the seminary's founders, though popular belief would have it that they are the tombs of 40 girls.

TAŞ HAN & AROUND

Virtually next door to the Gök Medrese is the **Taş Han** (1614-30; GOP Bulvarı; ⏰ 8am-7pm), an Ottoman caravanserai and workshop. The street-facing shops are all fully occupied, but the courtyard units are empty, which seems a waste of such prime real estate.

Behind the Taş Han are streets lined with old half-timbered **Ottoman houses**. Shops offer copperware, *yazmalar* (headscarves), and local kilims and carpets, some with Afghani designs assimilated from the many refugees who settled here during the Soviet invasion of Afghanistan in the 1980s.

In the fruit and vegetable market, across GOP Bulvarı from the Taş Han, stands the **Hatuniye Camii** and *medrese*, dating from 1485 and the reign of Sultan Beyazıt II.

A few hundred metres north of the Taş Han, on the same side of the street, look out for the octagonal **Sümbül Baba Türbesi**, a Seljuk-style tomb dating from 1251. Beside it a road leads up around 1km to the **citadel**, of which little remains but the fine view. Solo women travellers should not go up there alone.

ALİ PAŞA HAMAM

Ask around the steam rooms of Turkey's thousands of *hamams*, and you'll probably find that one of Tokat's biggest exports is its expert masseurs, who seem to get just about everywhere. Assuming there are actually any left in town, it seems like the perfect excuse to go for a scrub'n'rub at the wonderful **Ali Paşa Hamam** (☎ 214 4453; GOP Bulvarı; ☒ 5am-11pm for men, 9am-5pm for women). These baths, under domes studded with glass bulbs to admit natural light, were built in 1572 for Ali Paşa, one of the sons of Süleyman the Magnificent. They have separate bathing areas for men and women, and the full works should cost around €8.

LATİFOĞLU KONAĞI

South of Cumhuriyet Meydanı, don't miss the **Latifoğlu Konağı** (☎ 214 3684; GOP Bulvarı; admission €0.55; ☒ 8.30am-noon & 1.30-5.30pm Tue-Sun), one of the most splendid 19th-century houses on show in Turkey. Its large, gracious rooms are surrounded with low *sedirs* (bench seating that doubles as beds); in the bedrooms, bedding was taken up and stored in cabinets during the day, Ottoman-style. The most spectacular rooms are upstairs: the Paşa Odası (Pasha's Room), for the men of the house, and the Havuzbaşı for the women. The light, airy upstairs hall would have been used in summer only.

SULUSOKAK CADDESİ

Modern Tokat has spun round on its axis and now runs north–south where once it used to run east–west. A happy consequence of this is that many of its old buildings still survive, though abandoned and in ruins, along Sulusokak Caddesi, which was the main thoroughfare before the Samsun–Sivas road was improved in the 1960s.

Sulusokak Caddesi runs west from the north side of Cumhuriyet Meydanı, past the grand **Ali Paşa Camii**, which dates back to 1566. Continue along the road and on the right you'll see the tiny **Ali Tusi Türbesi**, a Seljuk work dating back to 1233 and incorporating some fine blue tiles. Next up, also on the right, is the crumbling wooden **Katırcılar Han**, with some vast pots lying in its courtyard.

On the left you'll then see the locked remains of the **Yağibasın Medresesi**, a Danışmend work dating back to 1145–47; the workshops behind it are full of antique dealers. Directly across the road are the extensive remains of the old *bedesten* (covered market) with, beside it, the 16th-century **Takyeciler Camii**.

A little further west and you'll see the 14th-century **Kadı Hasan Camii** and, nearby, the **Paşa Hamamı**.

OTHER SIGHTS

To the south of the centre don't miss the 19th-century **clock tower** with the numerals on its faces still in Arabic, and a watch-repair shop (what else?) at the bottom.

Just across the road from here is the **Mevlevihane** (Bey Sokak; ☒ Tue-Sun), a rather splendid 19th-century building built as a dervish lodge and dancing hall. After painstaking renovations it was opened as a tourist attraction in 2006; the displays consist only of a few old photos and some slightly laughable model dervish figures that rotate mechanically to music, but the house itself is stunning, particularly in the evening, when the reddish wood of the exterior practically glows in the dimming light.

Sleeping

Hotel Çamlica (☎ 214 1269; GOP Bulvarı 179; s/d €17/23) About the nearest Tokat has to a low-end budget option, though it's hardly worth the slide in quality just to save €3. It's well scrubbed but dim and a bit blokey.

Yücel Hotel (☎ 212 5235; Çekenli Caddesi 20; s/d €20/25; ☐ ☒) Still cheap, but with two major advantages – the quiet location and the *hamam* facilities in the basement, both of which are included in the price. Rooms are small but neat, and there's a bar with digital TV in the marble lobby.

Otel Yeni Çınar (☎ 214 0066; GOP Bulvarı İş Bankası Yanı 2; s/d/tr/q €20/31/39/45) A good range of rooms with nice bathrooms and vistas over the hills from the back; triples even come with their own balcony patio. The first-floor restaurant (mains €2.50 to €5) does a good line in grills, including the famous Tokat kebap (see below).

Çavuşoğlu Plevne Otel (☎ 214 2207; GOP Bulvarı 83; s/d €23/31) You can't fault the renovation job they've done on this place, which has transformed a mediocre budget joint into a smart, central bargain. Pistachio bathrooms, TV, hairdryer and breakfast buffet just reinforce the point.

Beykonaği Hotel (☎ 214 3399; www.otelbeykonagi.com; Cumhuriyet Meydanı; s/d €42/56; 🖥) Fresh on the scene, this 40-room three-star curries favour with compact but smart rooms in light shades and orchid art, plus bar and restaurant. While it's new you can get away with paying half these prices, or a minute €50 for a suite.

Eating

Kebaps and *köfte* are the usual fare here, with shops clustered around the fruit and vegetable market near the Hatuniye Camii.

Hacivat Köftecisi (☎ 212 9418; GOP Bulvarı; mains €0.55-2; 🕑 9am-11pm) South of the centre, Hacivat is an appealing café-restaurant with top-value daily set menus (€1.40). You can even tank up on traditional culture at the same time, as there are Karagöz shadow-puppet performances every Saturday at 7pm; see p297 for more on the Karagöz tradition.

Yeşil Köşe Et Lokantası (GOP Bulvarı 1; mains €1-4; 🕑 9am-10pm) Along with the Yeni Çınar, this cafeteria restaurant does arguably the best

Tokat kebap in town (€4), as well as decent ready-made meals.

Honça Tokat Evi (☎ 213 3818; Ali Paşa Hamam Sokak 5; mains €2.50-6; 🕑 noon-10pm) A magic slice of authentic Ottoman dining. If your Turkish is up to it, the menu's a mini-guidebook on Tokat, and includes lots of non-mainstream traditional dishes; if it's not, just go into the kitchen and let the jovial chef show you what's on offer.

Shopping

At one time Tokat had a monopoly on the right to make *yazmas*, the printed headscarves traditionally worn by many Turkish women. The monopoly may be long gone, but Tokat is still a good place to buy souvenir scarves or printed tablecloths. For decades the scarves were made in a vast building near the Gök Medrese. However, these days the materials are prepared in a modern **factory** (Yazmacılar Sitesi; ☎ 232 0500; Rodi Halısaha; 🕑 9am-5pm Mon-Sat), which you can visit to see the cloths being made. The site is about 4km northwest of the town centre; a taxi will charge around €6 for the return trip, including waiting time.

Getting There & Away

Tokat's small otogar is about 1.7km from the main square. The better bus companies provide a *servis* to ferry you to and from town. Otherwise, if you don't want to wait for the infrequent city buses, a taxi will cost about €2.50.

The otogar is not as busy as some, especially in the morning (there are, for example, fewer buses to Sivas than you might expect), so it's a good idea to book ongoing tickets well ahead, especially on Friday. Several bus companies have ticket offices on GOP Bulvarı.

There are regular buses to Amasya (€5.60, two hours), Ankara (€23, 6½ hours), Erzurum (€20, 8½ hours), İstanbul (€25, 12 hours), Samsun (€11, four hours) and Sivas (€5.60, 1¾ hours).

Local minibuses leave from the separate İlçe ve Köy Terminali.

AROUND TOKAT
Ballıca Cave

If you're interested in the underground, the **Ballıca Cave** (Ballıca Mağarası; ☎ 356-261 4236; admission €0.55; 🕑 daylight), 26km southwest of Tokat, is probably the best one open to the public in Turkey. It's a vast limestone labyrinth, 680m long and 95m high at its tallest point, filled

---

AUBERGINE DREAM

The Tokat kebap is made up of skewers of lamb and sliced eggplant (aubergine) hung vertically, then baked in a wood-fired oven. Tomatoes and peppers, which take less time to cook, are baked on separate skewers. As the lamb cooks, it releases juices that baste the aubergine. All these goodies are then served together with a huge fist of roasted garlic, adding an extra punch to the mix.

It's almost worth coming to Tokat just to sample the dish, and in fact you might have to – it's inexplicably failed to catch on in menus much further afield than Sivas or Amasya, and the standard aubergine *döners* that do crop up are a far cry from the glorious blow-out of the original.

with stalagmites and dripping stalactites and with patterns like marbling on the walls. You'll certainly hear and smell the colony of dwarf bats that live inside, even if you don't get to see them.

There are a lot of steps both inside and outside the cave, although many elderly Turkish matrons in şalwar and slippers manage perfectly well. The views from the Ballıca Café at the entrance are stunning.

Returning, pause in Pazar to inspect the beautiful but graffitied remains of a Seljuk *han* just before you leave town on the Tokat road.

GETTING THERE & AWAY

To get to Ballıca take a minibus to Pazar from Tokat's İlçe ve Köy minibus terminal (€0.85, 40 minutes). In Pazar there will probably be a taxi waiting to run you up the winding country road to the cave (8km); the driver will want at least €7 to run you there and back, with one hour's waiting time.

SİVAS

☎ 0346 / pop 252,000

Here is where we laid the foundations of our republic.

Atatürk

Grand words, but then, like Amasya, Sivas is assured a place in Turkish hearts thanks to the role it played in the run-up to the War of Independence, when the halls of the Congress building resounded with plans, strategies and principles as Atatürk and his adherents discussed their great goal of liberation.

Now that the days of struggle are over, though, you get the impression Sivas isn't quite sure what to do with itself. Modernity has been embraced wholesale in the bustling centre, giving the town a slightly unfocused energy. Sivas has a colourful, sometimes tragic history and some of the finest Seljuk buildings ever erected, but otherwise there's not a huge amount left to engage tourists for more than a day. It's best seen as an enjoyable but non-essential stopover on the way to the real wild east.

Sivas also makes the best base for visiting the marvellous World Heritage mosque-*medrese* complex at Divriği (p481).

History

The tumulus at nearby Maltepe shows evidence of settlement as early as 2600 BC, but

Sivas itself was probably founded by the Hittite king Hattushilish I in around 1500 BC. It was ruled in turn by the Assyrians, Medes and Persians, before coming under the sway of the kings of Cappadocia and Pontus. Eventually the city fell to the Romans, who called it Megalopolis; this was later changed to Sebastea (presumably when someone realised how ridiculous Megalopolis was) and then shortened to Sivas by the Turks.

Byzantine rule lasted from AD 395 to 1075, when the city was seized by the Danışmend emirs. The Seljuks and the Danışmends slogged it out for supremacy between 1152 and 1175 until the Seljuks finally prevailed, only to be dispossessed by the Mongol invasion of 1243. The İlkhanids succeeded the Mongols, but in 1400 lost the city to Tamerlane, who in turn lost it to the Ottomans in 1408.

More recently Sivas was the location for the famous Sivas Congress, which opened on 4 September 1919. Seeking to consolidate Turkish resistance to the Allied occupation and partition of his country, Atatürk arrived here from Samsun and Amasya. He gathered delegates from as many parts of the country as possible to confirm decisions made at the earlier Erzurum Congress. These two congresses heralded the War of Independence.

Orientation

The centre of town is Hükümet Meydanı (or Konak Meydanı), just in front of the attractive *valılık*. The main sights, hotels and restaurants are all within walking distance.

The train station, Sivas Garı, is about 1.5km southwest of Hükümet Meydanı along İnönü Bulvarı/İstasyon Caddesi. The otogar and local bus station are 2km south of the centre. Bus offices and banks with ATMs are just east of Hükümet Meydanı, along Atatürk Caddesi.

Information

Sivas Turizm (☎ 224 4624; www.sivasturizm.com.tr; İstasyon Caddesi 50, Sivas) Car rental, tours and airline tickets.

Tolaman Internet Café (İstasyon Caddesi 52; per hr €0.35; ☯ 9am-midnight)

Tourist office (☎ 221 3135; ☯ 9am-5pm Mon-Fri) On the ground floor of the *valılık*.

Sights

KALE CAMİİ & BÜRÜCİYE MEDRESESİ

Most of Sivas' Seljuk buildings are, conveniently, in the parkland just south of Hükümet

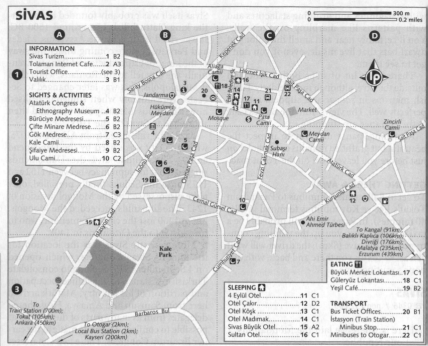

SİVAS

INFORMATION	
Sivas Turizm.............................1	B2
Tolaman Internet Cafe.........2	A3
Tourist Office.................(see 3)	
Valılık.......................................3	B1

SIGHTS & ACTIVITIES	
Atatürk Congress &	
Ethnography Museum ..4	B2
Bürüciye Medresesi............5	B2
Çifte Minare Medrese......6	B2
Gök Medrese......................7	C3
Kale Camii..........................8	B2
Şifaiye Medresesi.............9	B2
Ulu Cami...........................10	C2

SLEEPING	
4 Eylül Otel...........................11	C1
Otel Çakır.............................12	D2
Otel Köşk..............................13	C1
Otel Madımak........................14	C1
Sivas Büyük Otel...................15	A2
Sultan Otel...........................16	C1

EATING	
Büyük Merkez Lokantası..17	C1
Güleryüz Lokantası.........18	C1
Yeşil Café.........................19	B2

TRANSPORT	
Bus Ticket Offices...........20	C1
İstasyon (Train Station)	
Minibus Stop.................21	C1
Minibuses to Otogar......22	C1

To Train Station (700m);
Tokat (105km);
Ankara (450km)

To Otogar (2km);
Local Bus Station (2km);
Kayseri (200km)

To Kangal (91km);
Balıklı Kaplıca (106km);
Divriği (176km);
Malatya (235km);
Erzurum (439km)

Meydanı. Here you'll also find the **Kale Camii** (1580), a squat Ottoman work constructed by Sultan Murat III's grand vizier Mahmut Paşa.

Just east of the Kale Camii, reached through a monumental Seljuk gateway, is the **Bürüciye Medresesi**, built to teach 'positive sciences' in 1271 by the Iranian businessman Muzaffer Bürücerdi, whose tiled tomb is inside. A tea garden currently occupies the courtyard, where regular exhibitions are held.

ŞİFAİYE MEDRESESİ
Across the park from the Bürüciye Medresesi is the **Şifaiye Medresesi**, a medieval medical school and healing centre that ranks as one of the city's oldest buildings. It dates from 1217, when it was built for the Seljuk sultan İzzettin Keykavus I, whose architect used stylised sun/lion and moon/bull motifs in the decoration.

Look to the right as you enter the courtyard to see the porch that was walled up as a tomb for İzzettin when he died of TB in 1220. Note the beautiful blue Azeri tilework and the poignant poem in Arabic, composed by the sultan himself.

The main courtyard has four *eyvans*, with sun and moon symbols on either side of the eastern one. It now boasts a lovely rose garden and is surrounded by cafés and craft shops of variable quality.

ÇİFTE MİNARE MEDRESE
Commissioned by the Mongol–İlkhanid vizier Şemsettin Güveyni after defeating the Seljuks at the battle of Kosedağ, the **Çifte Minare Medrese** (Seminary of the Twin Minarets; 1271) has, as you might guess, a *çifte* (pair) of mighty minarets. In fact, that's about all it has, as the *medrese* behind the elaborate portal was destroyed when the Seljuks retook the city, and the façade has outlived subsequent incarnations. Stand on the path between the Çifte and Şifaiye *medreses* to see the difference half a century made to the extravagance of Seljuk architecture.

ULU CAMİ
The town's other sights are southeast of Hükümet Meydanı along Cemal Gürsel and Cumhuriyet Caddesis. To find them, walk to the southern end of the park and turn left (east) onto Cemal Gürsel Caddesi.

The **Ulu Cami** (Great Mosque; 1197) is Sivas' oldest significant building. Built during the reign of the Danışmend leader Kubbettin Melik Şah, it's a large, low room with a forest of 50 columns. The super-fat leaning brick minaret was added in 1213. It's not as grand as the more imposing Seljuk buildings but has a certain old-Anatolian charm, slightly marred by modern additions.

GÖK MEDRESE

From the Ulu Cami, turn right (south) on Cumhuriyet Caddesi to make your way to the glorious **Gök Medrese** (Sky-Blue Seminary). This was built in 1271 at the behest of Sahip Ata, the grand vizier of Sultan Gıyasettin II Keyhüsrev, who funded the grand Sahip Ata mosque complex in Konya. The façade was decorated with exuberant with tiles, brickwork designs and carving, covering not just the usual inlaid portal but the walls as well. The blue tilework still visible on the twin minarets gave the school its name.

The whole area was fenced off for restoration work at the time of research, but if you can get in the interior is equally worth a look.

ATATÜRK CONGRESS & ETHNOGRAPHY MUSEUM

Opposite the Kale Camii is the imposing Ottoman school building that hosted the Sivas Congress on 4 September 1919. Today it's the **Atatürk Congress & Ethnography Museum** (Atatürk Kongre ve Etnografya Müzesi; İnönü Bulvarı; admission €1.10; 🕅 8.30am-noon & 1.30-5.30pm Tue-Sun). The entrance is around the back, opposite an army barracks, whose occupants are regularly marched in to pay their respects to history.

The Ottoman ethnographical collection, displayed on the ground floor, includes a fine selection of kilims and carpets, some magnificent embroidery, a 12th-century wooden *mimber* from the Kale Camii in Divriği, two huge carved ceiling roses, and relics collected from dervish *tekkes* (monasteries) closed in 1925.

Upstairs, the Congress Hall is preserved as it was when the Sivas Congress met, with photos of the delegates displayed on old school desks as if awaiting a reunion. You can also see Atatürk's bedroom and the cable room that played an important role in developments. The other displays (mainly photographs and documents) are captioned in Turkish and a bit of French.

Sleeping

Otel Çakır (☎ 222 4526; Kurşunlu Caddesi 20; s/d €14/23) The best option in the cheap hotel district around Kurşunlu Caddesi, offering respectable rooms and random poster art. There's no catering, but breakfast is provided in the little café a couple of doors down.

   Otel Madımak (☎ 221 8027; Eski Belediye Sokak 2; s/d/tr €25/39/50) This rebuilt 1st-floor hotel has comfortable digs with a burgundy theme. Be aware, however, that the name has very sad resonances (see boxed text, below).

   Sultan Otel (☎ 221 2986; www.sultanotel.com.tr; Eski Belediye Sokak 18; s/d/tr €36/56/67) The perfect mix of quality and price, with ample extras including a roof bar with live music, safes built into the TV cabinets, extensive breakfast buffets and free hot drinks. Oh, and the bathrooms are virtually as big as the rooms themselves. Popular with business travellers midweek.

MADIMAK MEMORIAL

You won't see it mentioned in the brochure, but the original Madımak Hotel was the site of one of modern Turkey's worst hate crimes, on 2 July 1993, when 37 Alevi intellectuals and artists were burned alive in a mob arson attack. The victims, who had come for a cultural festival, included Aziz Nesin, the Turkish publisher of Salman Rushdie's *Satanic Verses*. A crowd of 1000 extreme Islamist demonstrators gathered outside the hotel after prayer time to protest about the book's publication, and in the ensuing chaos the hotel was set alight and burned to the ground.

   The Madımak has since reopened (with a kebap shop in the foyer!), although many human rights groups are calling for the site to be declared a memorial. The government has already rejected this plan once, sparking accusations that some ministers were directly involved or at least sympathetic to the arsonists.

   As well as a memorial, many protesters want to see the trial of the Madımak suspects reopened, believing they were let off too lightly. Whatever the outcome, the scars from the whole tragedy show no signs of fading fast.

Otel Köşk (☎ 225 1724; www.koskotel.com; Atatürk Caddesi 7; s/d/tr €45/67/73; 🖧) You can't get much more modern than this towering glass block, with its orange highlights and minimalist lobby. Laminate floors and slick design rule, and pillow fans are inundated with the things.

4 Eylül Otel (☎ 222 3799; www.dorteyulotel.com; Atatürk Caddesi 15; s/d/tr €48/78/89, ste €111; 🖧) Oh wait, it turns out you *can* get more modern than the Köşk – Sivas's newest hotel is an even sleeker glass tower… but then changes its mind inside and goes for dark wood, satiny sheets and an understated interpretation of traditional style. Suffice to say it's really rather good.

Sivas Büyük Otel (☎ 225 4767; www.sivasbuyukotel .com; İstasyon Caddesi; s/d/tr €67/106/125; 🖭) Plain corridors and stately rooms characterise the city's original luxury hotel, a chunky seven-storey block laced with marble and mosaics. Refreshingly, one thing it's not short on is space.

Eating

Apart from the hotel restaurants, the Sivas eating scene doesn't show much sense of adventure. On summer evenings everyone promenades along İnönü Bulvarı, where stalls sell everything from *gözleme* to corn cobs.

Güleryüz Lokantası (☎ 224 2061; mains €1.10-4) The tiniest but most characterful of the row of cheap eateries down the street next to the PTT, with pictures for anyone having menu difficulties.

Yeşil Café (☎ 222 2638; Belçuklu Sokak; mains €1.70-4; 🕙 9am-10pm) This friendly apple-green café-restaurant might not look like much until you get out onto the tiny balcony and realise you have the best views of the neon-lit twin minarets, like, ever. What's more, the menu's even enough to distract you from them, with pasta, schnitzel, grills and an actual choice of milkshakes.

Büyük Merkez Lokantası (☎ 223 6434; Atatürk Caddesi 13; mains €1.70-6) Three busy floors of fast food, ready-made meals and kebaps. Its speciality, the *sebzeli Sivas kebapı,* is actually the delicious Tokat kebap (see p476).

Getting There & Away

BUS

Bus services from Sivas aren't all that frequent, so you may want to book ahead at one of the ticket offices in town. There are fairly regular services to Amasya (€11, 3½ hours), Ankara

(€17, six hours), Diyarbakır (€17, eight hours), Erzurum (€17, seven hours), İstanbul (€28, 13 hours), Kayseri (€8.50, three hours), Malatya (€11, four hours), Samsun (€14, six hours) and Tokat (€5.60, 1½ hours).

'Yenişehir–Terminal' dolmuşes (€0.30) pass the otogar and end their run just uphill from the Paşa Camii, a five-minute walk from Hükümet Meydanı or the budget hotels on Kurşunlu Caddesi.

TRAIN

Sivas **station** (☎ 221 7000) is a major rail junction for both east–west and north–south lines. The main east–west express, the *Doğu Ekspresi,* goes through Sivas to Erzurum and Kars (16 hours) or back to Ankara and İstanbul (22 hours) daily; the *Güney Ekspresi* (from İstanbul to Diyarbakır) and the *Vangölü Ekspresi* (from İstanbul to Tatvan) run five times a week. There are also local services to Kangal, Divriği and Amasya.

'İstasyon' dolmuşes run from the station to Hükümet Meydanı and the Paşa Camii.

AROUND SİVAS

Balıklı Kaplıca

The tiny service town of Kangal, known for its famous white sheepdogs (see p63), has one more strange claim to fame: the unique health spa at **Balıklı Kaplıca** (Hot Spring with Fish; ☎ 469 1151; www.balikli.org; admission visitor/patient €2.80/17, car €0.55; 🕙 8am-noon & 2-6pm), a haven for sufferers of psoriasis 14km northeast of town. A shepherd boy is said to have discovered the healing qualities of the local warm mineral water, especially when combined with the action of the 'doctor fish' that nibble at sufferers' scaly skin. These fish are supposed to be able to favour psoriasis over any other type of defect, but they generally seem happy to suck on anything you stick in the water!

The spa complex has several sex-segregated pools set amid trees, together with an efficient **hotel** (r €39-70; 🖭), a restaurant, games room, tea garden, barber and small shop. Room rates can depend on whether you define yourself as 'normal' or 'ill' – the recommended course for genuine patients is eight hours a day in the pool for three weeks! Budget €17 per person for full board if you are planning to stay over.

GETTING THERE & AWAY

Minibuses from the terminal beside Sivas otogar run to Kangal (€3.50, one hour) from where you can take a taxi to the resort (€12 return). From June to the end of September the minibuses come all the way here. The spa also offers its own group transfers from regional towns (Sivas €98, Ankara €470).

DİVRİĞİ
☎ 0346 / pop 14,500

For a building that's been around nearly 800 years, the stunning mosque-*medrese* complex at Divriği is remarkably undervisited, especially given its prestigious inclusion on the Unesco World Heritage list. Still, tourism's loss is the independent traveller's gain, and it's well worth penetrating the 1970m mountain curtain to view one of Turkey's finest old religious structures.

Divriği village occupies a fertile valley and still has an agricultural economy. Its population is mostly made up of Alevis, Muslims whose traditions are very different from those of the majority Sunni Muslims (see p54). The narrow streets conceal a busy market, PTT, Internet café, some simple restaurants and a couple of banks with ATMs.

ULU CAMİ & DARÜŞŞİFA

Uphill from the town centre stands the beautifully restored **Ulu Cami & Darüşşifa** (Grand Mosque & Mental Hospital; admission free; ☉ 8am-5pm Tue-Sat), adjoining institutions founded in 1228 by the local emir Ahmet Şah and his wife, the lady Fatma Turan Melik.

It's almost a shame you can't see the interiors first, as they're totally anticlimactic – it's the ornamental gateways on the building's northern façade that put Divriği on the map (and the Heritage list). The entrances to both the Ulu Cami and the Darüşşifa are truly stupendous, their reliefs densely carved with a wealth of geometric patterns, stars, medallions, textured effects and intricate Arabic inscriptions, all rendered in such minute detail that it's hard to imagine the stone ever started out flat. It's the tasteful Ottoman equivalent of having a cinema in your house, the sort of thing only a provincial emir with more money than sense could have dreamt of building.

The western entrance has some fine work as well, but nothing to compare with the front. If you manage to tear your eyes away from the façade, there are some pretty good valley views in the other direction as well.

Inside, the mosque is very simple, with 16 columns, carpets, some fresco fragments and a plain *mihrab*. The hospital next door, built on an asymmetrical floor plan, is even more basic, its stone walls and uneven columns left entirely unadorned. The octagonal pool in the court has a spiral run-off, similar to the one in Konya's Karatay Medresesi (see p485), which allowed the tinkle of running water to break the silence of the room and soothe patients' nerves. A platform raised above the main floor may have been for musicians who likewise soothed the patients with their music.

As long as local coach parties keep coming through the Darüşşifa is open during the listed hours, but at quieter times you may find it locked. If so, ask around and someone will probably find the key. Friday lunchtime is a good time to come, as you should be able to visit the mosque and *medrese* when prayers are over.

OTHER ATTRACTIONS

As this was once an important provincial capital you will notice several **kümbets** (Seljuk tombs) scattered about town. Ahmet Şah's tomb is near the Ulu Cami, so you might want to go and thank him for his profligacy.

Trailing down the sides of the hill dominating Divriği are the ruined walls of a vast medieval **castle**, with the Kale Camii a solid but equally ruinous structure on the summit. The road heading behind the Ulu Cami and Darüşşifa leads up to the castle.

GETTING THERE & AWAY

Minibuses from Sivas to Divriği (€5.60, three hours) depart from the minibus terminal seven times a day. If you catch the first service you'll have more than enough time to look round and catch the last bus back.

The train station is about 1.5km north of the Ulu Cami, served by the *Doğu Ekspresi* and *Erzurum Ekspresi* between Sivas (€2.80, four hours) and Erzurum (€5.50, 7½ hours).

Both buses and trains serve Istanbul and Ankara, though it's a long way to come for a day trip!

Drivers should note that there's no through road to Erzincan from Divriği, forcing you to backtrack to Kangal before you can start heading east.

KONYA
☎ 0332 / pop 762,000

Turkey's equivalent of the 'Bible Belt', conservative Konya treads a delicate path between its historical significance as the home town of the whirling dervish orders and a bastion of Seljuk culture on the one hand, and its modern importance as an economic boom town on the other.

Luckily the city derives considerable charm from this juxtaposition of old and new. Ancient mosques and the mazey market district, awash with Eastern smells, eager shopkeepers and Muslim pilgrims, rub up against contemporary Konya around Alaaddin Tepesi, where hip-looking university students talk religion and politics freely in the tea gardens.

Many travellers don't even consider stopping in Konya, but if you are passing through this region, say from the coast to Cappadocia, bear in mind that the wonderful shrine of the Mevlâna here is one of Turkey's finest and most characteristic sights. The city's collection of imposing Seljuk buildings should also keep building buffs happy, and at the very least you can get a good dinner here.

History

Almost 4000 years ago the Hittites called this city 'Kuwanna'. It was Kowania to the Phrygians, Iconium to the Romans and then Konya to the Turks. Iconium was an important provincial town visited several times by Saints Paul and Barnabas. There are few remains of its early Christian community, but Sille (p490) has several ruined churches.

From about 1150 to 1300 Konya was capital of the Seljuk Sultanate of Rum, one of the

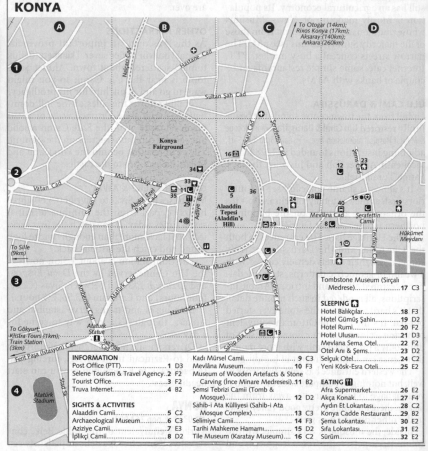

KONYA

INFORMATION	
Post Office (PTT)....................... 1 D3
Selene Tourism & Travel Agency..2 F2
Tourist Office.............................3 F2
Truva Internet............................4 B2

SIGHTS & ACTIVITIES	
Alaaddin Camii.........................5 C2
Archaeological Museum............6 C3
Aziziye Camii...........................7 E3
İplikçi Camii............................8 D2

Kadı Mürsel Camii.....................9 C3
Mevlâna Museum.....................10 F3
Museum of Wooden Artefacts & Stone Carving (İnce Minare Medresesi)..11 B2
Şemsi Tebrizi Camii (Tomb & Mosque)...........................12 C2
Sahib-i Ata Külliyesi (Sahib-i Ata Mosque Complex)...................13 C3
Selimiye Camii.......................14 F3
Tarihi Mahkeme Hamamı.........15 D2
Tile Museum (Karatay Museum)....16 C2

Tombstone Museum (Sırçalı Medrese)...........................17 C3

SLEEPING	
Hotel Balıkçılar.......................18 F3
Hotel Gümüş Şahin..................19 D2
Hotel Rumi............................20 F2
Hotel Ulusan.........................21 D3
Mevlana Sema Otel...................22 F2
Otel Anı & Şems.....................23 D2
Selçuk Otel............................24 C2
Yeni Kösk-Esra Oteli...............25 E2

EATING	
Afra Supermarket....................26 E2
Akça Konak...........................27 F4
Aydın Et Lokantası..................28 C2
Konya Cadde Restaurant...........29 B2
Şema Lokantası......................30 E2
Sifa Lokantası........................31 E2
Sürüm..................................32 E2

successor states to the Great Seljuk Turkish empire of the 11th century. The Sultanate of Rum encompassed most of Anatolia, and the Seljuk sultans endowed its capital with dozens of fine buildings in an architectural style that was decidedly Turkish, but had its roots in Persia and Byzantium.

Traditionally Konya lay at the heart of Turkey's very rich 'bread basket', but these days light industry is at least as important as farming, and pilgrimage tourism is also a big earner.

Orientation

The city centre is Alaaddin Tepesi (Aladdin's Hill), encircled by a ring road. From the hill, Mevlâna Caddesi goes east 700m to Hükümet

Meydanı (Government Plaza), where you'll find the provincial and city government buildings, the main PTT, several banks with ATMs and a vast underground jewellery market. From here the boulevard continues east to the tourist office and the Mevlâna Museum.

The otogar, connected by regular trams, is 14km due north of the centre; the local bus terminal (*Eski Garaj*; Karatay Terminal) is 1km to the south.

Information

Klistra Tours (☎ 238 1421; www.klistratours.com; Gürağaç Sokak 8) City and local tours.
Selene Tourism & Travel Agency (☎ 353 6745; www.selene.com.tr; Ayanbey Sokak 22B) Organises dervish performances, tours and hunting trips.
Tourist office (☎ 351 1074; Mevlâna Caddesi 21; 🕙 8.30am-5pm Mon-Sat),
Truva Internet (Adliye Bulvarı; per hr €0.55; 🕙 9am-midnight)

Dangers & Annoyances

Konya has a long-standing reputation for religious conservatism; you'll see more women in religious headscarves here than in many other towns, and you'll find Friday observed as a day of rest in a way it rarely is elsewhere. None of this should inconvenience you, but take special care not to upset the pious and make sure *you're* not an annoyance! If you visit during Ramazan (see p659) don't eat or drink in public during the day, as a courtesy to those who are fasting.

Ironically, non-Muslim women seem to encounter more hassle in this bastion of propriety than in many other Turkish cities. You can also quickly tire of the touts hanging about Mevlâna Caddesi and the Mevlâna Museum.

Sights & Activities
MEVLÂNA MUSEUM

For Muslims and non-Muslims alike, the main reason to come to Konya is to visit the **Mevlâna Museum** (☎ 351 1215; admission €2.80; 🕙 9am-6pm Tue-Sun, 10am-6pm Mon), the former lodge of the whirling dervishes. On religious holidays the museum (really a shrine) may keep longer hours.

In Celaleddin Rumi, the Seljuk Sultanate of Rum produced one of the world's great mystic philosophers. His poetry and religious writings, mostly in Persian, the literary language of the day, are among the most beloved and

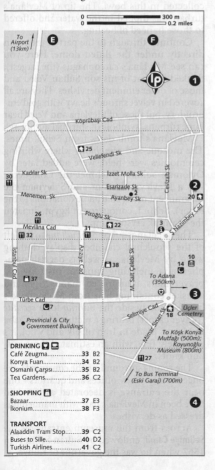

DRINKING 🍺 🍵	
Café Zeugma	33 B2
Konya Fuarı	34 B2
Osmanlı Çarşısı	35 B2
Tea Gardens	36 C2

SHOPPING 🛍	
Bazaar	37 E3
İkonium	38 F3

TRANSPORT	
Alaaddin Tram Stop	39 C2
Buses to Sille	40 D2
Turkish Airlines	41 C2

Map labels: To Airport (13km); Köprübaşı Cad; 25; Veliefendi Sk; 30; Kadılar Sk; İzzet Molla Sk; Esarizade Sk; 26; Ayanbey Sk; 2; Cevizaltı Sk; 20; Menemen Sk; Piroğlu Sk; Mevlâna Cad; 31; 22; 32; 3; S Nazımbey Cad; İstanbul Cad; Azizye Cad; M. Sait Çelebi Sk; 38; 10; 14; To Adana (350km); 37; Türbe Cad; 7; Selimiye Cad; Mamar Sinart Sk; 18; Üçler Cemetery; Provincial & City Government Buildings; To Köşk Konya Mutfağı (500m); Koyunoğlu Müzesi (800m); 27; To Bus Terminal (Eski Garaj) (700m)

respected in the Islamic world. Rumi later became known as Mevlâna (Our Guide) to his followers.

Rumi was born in 1207 in Balkh (Afghanistan). His family fled the impending Mongol invasion by moving to Mecca and then to the Sultanate of Rum, reaching Konya by 1228. His father was a noted preacher, and Rumi became a brilliant student of Islamic theology. After his father's death in 1231, he studied in Aleppo and Damascus, returning to live in Konya by 1240.

In 1244 he met Mehmet Şemseddin Tebrizi (Şemsi Tebrizi or Şems of Tabriz), one of his father's Sufi (Muslim mystic) disciples. Tebrizi had a profound influence on Rumi but, jealous of his overwhelming influence on their master, an angry crowd of Rumi's disciples put Tebrizi to death in 1247. Stunned by the loss, Rumi withdrew from the world to meditate, and wrote his greatest poetic work, the *Mathnawi* (*Mesnevi* in Turkish). He also wrote many aphorisms, *ruba'i* and *ghazal* poems, collected into his 'Great Opus', the *Divan-i Kebir*.

His teachings are summed up in this beautiful verse:

Come, whoever you may be,
Even if you may be
An infidel, a pagan, or a fire-
worshipper, come.
Ours is not a brotherhood of despair.
Even if you have broken
Your vows of repentance a hundred
times, come.

Rumi died on 17 December 1273, the date now known as his 'wedding night' with Allah. His son, Sultan Veled, organised his followers into the brotherhood called the Mevlevi, or whirling dervishes.

In the centuries following Mevlâna's death, over 100 dervish lodges were founded throughout the Ottoman domains. Dervish orders exerted considerable conservative influence on the country's political, social and economic life, and numerous Ottoman sultans were Mevlevi Sufis (mystics). Atatürk saw the dervishes as an obstacle to advancement for the Turkish people and banned them in 1925, but several orders survived on a technicality as religious fraternities. The Konya lodge was revived in 1957 as a 'cultural association' intended to preserve a historical tradition.

For Muslims, this is a very holy place, and more than 1.5 million people visit it a year, most of them Turkish. You will see many people praying for Rumi's help. When entering, women should cover their heads and shoulders, and no one should wear shorts.

Visiting the Museum

The lodge is visible from some distance, its fluted dome of turquoise tiles one of Turkey's most distinctive sights. After walking through a pretty courtyard with an ablutions fountain and several tombs, you remove your shoes and pass into the **Mevlâna Tomb**. Look out for the big bronze *Nisan tası* (April bowl) on the left as you enter. April rainwater, vital to the farmers of this region, was considered sacred and collected in this bowl. The tip of Mevlâna's turban was dipped in the water and offered to those in need of healing.

Continue through to the part of the room directly under the fluted dome. Here you can see Mevlâna's sarcophagus (the largest), flanked by that of his son Sultan Veled and those of other eminent dervishes. They are all covered in velvet shrouds heavy with gold embroidery, but those of Mevlâna and Veled bear huge turbans, symbols of spiritual authority.

Mevlâna's tomb dates from Seljuk times. The mosque and *semahane*, where whirling ceremonies were held, were added later by Ottoman sultans (Mehmet the Conqueror was a Mevlevi adherent and Süleyman the Magnificent made charitable donations to the order). Selim I, conqueror of Egypt, donated the Mamluk crystal lamps.

The small mosque and *semahane* to the left of the sepulchral chamber display clothing worn by Mevlâna, as well as dervish paraphernalia including musical instruments, prayer mats, illuminated manuscripts and a casket containing hair from Mohammed's beard. Look beside the *mihrab* for a *seccade* (prayer carpet) bearing a picture of the Kaaba at Mecca. Made in Iran of silk and wool, it's extremely fine, with an estimated three million knots.

The rooms surrounding the courtyard were once the dervishes' offices and quarters – one near the entrance is decorated as it would have been in Mevlâna's day, with mannequins dressed as dervishes.

Across from the museum entrance is the **Selimiye Camii**, endowed by Sultan Selim II in 1567 when he was the governor of Konya.

OTHER MUSEUMS

Tile Museum (Karatay Müzesi)

Housed in what was once a Seljuk theological school near Alaaddin Tepesi, this **museum** (☎ 351 1914; Alaaddin Meydanı; admission €1.10; ⊙ 9am-noon & 1.30-5.30pm) was constructed in 1251–52 by Emir Celaleddin Karatay, a Seljuk general, vizier and statesman who is buried in one of the corner rooms.

The museum houses an outstanding collection of ceramics, including interesting octagonal tiles from the ruined 13th-century Seljuk palace of Kubadabad by Beyşehir Gölü. At time of research, though, it was closed for major restoration work.

Museum of Wooden Artefacts & Stone Carving

On the western side of the Alaaddin Tepesi ring road is the İnce Minare Medresesi (Seminary of the Slender Minaret), now the **Museum of Wooden Artefacts & Stone Carving** (Tas ve Ahsap Eserler Müzesi; ☎ 351 3204; Adliye Bulvarı; admission €1.10; ⊙ 9am-12.30pm & 1.30-5pm). This religious school was built in 1264 for Sahip Ata, a powerful Seljuk vizier, who may have been trying to outdo the patron of the Karatay Medresesi, built only seven years earlier.

The extraordinarily elaborate doorway, with bands of Arabic inscription running all round it, is far more impressive than the small building behind it. The octagonal minaret in turquoise relief is over 600 years old and gave the seminary its popular name. If it looks a bit short, this is because the top was sliced off by lightning in 1901.

Inside, many of the carvings in wood and stone feature motifs similar to those used in tiles and ceramics. You'll quickly see that the Seljuks didn't heed Islam's traditional prohibition of human and animal images: there are plenty of images of birds (the Seljuk double-headed eagle, for example), men and women, lions and leopards. The *eyvan* in particular contains two delightful carvings of Seljuk angels with distinctly Mongol features. The Ahşap Eserler Bölümü (Carved Wood Section) contains some intricately worked wooden doors.

Tombstone Museum (Sırçalı Medrese)

Several other Seljuk monuments lurk in the narrow warren of streets to the south of Alaaddin Tepesi. Look for the Kadı Mürsel Camii, then walk south along Sırçalı Medrese Caddesi. After a few minutes you'll come to another Seljuk seminary, the Sırçalı Medrese (Glass Seminary), named after its tiled exterior. Sponsored by the Seljuk vizier Bedreddin Muhlis, construction was completed in 1242. It's now a small Tombstone Museum (Mezar Anıtlar Müzesi; ☎ 352 8022; Sırçalı Caddesi; admission €1.10; ⊙ 9am-12.30pm & 1.30-5pm), housing a collection of tombstones with finely carved inscriptions. The main entrance is grand but restrained compared with Konya's other great *medreses*. The *eyvan* on the western side of the courtyard was used for classes; it is decorated with gorgeous blue tiles and its arch has a band of particularly fine calligraphic tile work.

Archaeological Museum

The small but interesting **Archaeological Museum** (☎ 351 3207; Larende Caddesi; admission €1.10; ⊙ 9am-12.30pm & 1.30-5pm Tue-Sun), beside the Sahib-i Ata Külliyesi, houses local Iron Age artefacts, Byzantine mosaics from Sille and Çorum, some bizarre lumpy Assyrian lamps, and several impressive, intact sarcophagi decorated with high-relief carvings. However, the unusually informative displays on Neolithic Çatalhöyük, 50km southeast of Konya (see p489) are the top draw, combining a good explanation of the site with finds including necklaces, rings and a fragment of wall painting.

Koyunoğlu Museum

This **museum** (Kerimler Caddesi 25; admission free; ⊙ 8am-5pm Tue-Sun), sharing the KonTV building 800m from Mevlâna Meydanı, is also well worth visiting.

Founded by a private (and clearly quite compulsive) collector, the displays take a scattergun approach, encompassing everything from fossils, minerals, weapons, stuffed birds, paintings of the sultans and photos of old Konya to kilims, bank notes and bath clogs. The few labels are in Turkish only. Outside, the recreated **Koyunoğlu Konya Evi** is a real highlight, showing how comfortably a well-heeled Konyalı family lived a century ago.

The quickest way to the museum lies through the **Üçler Cemetery**. Use this route only in daylight when other people are about – women are advised not to walk through alone.

MOSQUES

Alaaddin Camii

The Mevlâna shrine aside, Konya's most important **mosque** (⊙ 9.30am-5pm) bestrides

Alaaddin Tepesi at the opposite end of Mevlâna Caddesi. The mosque of Alaeddin Keykubad I, Seljuk Sultan of Rum from 1219 to 1231, it is a great rambling building designed by a Damascene architect in Arab style and finished in 1221. Over the centuries it was embellished, refurbished, ruined and restored.

The grand entrance on the northern side incorporates decoration from earlier Byzantine and Roman buildings. It used to lead through the courtyard and between two huge Seljuk *türbes* (tombs) into the mosque; today a less imposing eastern doorway serves as the main entrance.

While the mosque's exterior is generally plain, the interior is a forest of old marble columns surmounted with recycled Roman and Byzantine capitals. There's also a fine wooden *mimber* and an old marble *mihrab* framed by modern Seljuk-style blue-and-black calligraphy.

Other Mosques

A few blocks south of the Sırçalı Medrese, along Sırçalı Medrese Caddesi, is the **Sahib-i Ata Külliyesi** (Sahib-i Ata Mosque Complex), founded in 1285. Behind its requisite grand entrance with built-in minaret is the Sahib-i Ata Camii, originally constructed during the reign of Alaaddin Keykavus by the Seljuk soldier and statesman Hacı Ebubekirzade Hüseyinoğlu Sahib-i Ata Fahreddin Ali. Destroyed by fire in 1871, it was rebuilt in the same style. The *mihrab* is a fine example of Seljuk light-and-dark blue tile work. Alongside the mosque another grand gateway once led to a dervish lodge.

Dotted about town are other interesting mosques. The **Şemsi Tebrizi Camii**, containing the elegant 14th-century tomb of Rumi's spiritual mentor, is just northwest of Hükümet Meydanı, not far from Alaaddin Bulvarı. The **Aziziye Camii** (1875) in the bazaar was rebuilt in late-Ottoman style after a fire; it's the one with twin minarets bearing little sheltered balconies, and has a sign outside helpfully pointing out its interesting features.

On Mevlâna Caddesi, the **İplikçi Camii**, perhaps Konya's oldest mosque (1202), was built for the Seljuk vizier Şemseddin Altun-Aba in unadorned style: a forest of columns, arches and vaults.

HAMAM

The **Tarihi Mahkeme Hamamı** (Historic Court Hamam; ☎ 353 0093; wash, massage & sauna €12; ☉ 6am-midnight for men, 9am-6pm for women), behind the Şerafettin Camii, is the city's most interesting *hamam*.

Festivals & Events

The **Mevlâna Festival** (☎ 353 6745) runs for a week in early December. The last night com-

---

DANCING WITH DERVISHES

The Mevlevi worship ceremony, or *sema*, is a ritual dance representing union with God; it's what gives the dervishes their famous whirl, and appears on Unesco's third Proclamation of Masterpieces of the Oral and Intangible Heritage of Humanity. Watching a *sema* can be an evocative, romantic, unforgettable experience. There are many dervish orders worldwide who perform similar rituals, but the original Turkish version is the smoothest and purest, more of an elegant trance-like dance than the raw energy seen elsewhere.

The dervishes dress in long white robes with full skirts that represent their shrouds. Their voluminous black cloaks symbolise their worldly tombs, their conical felt hats their tombstones.

The ceremony begins when the *hafız*, a scholar who has committed the entire Quran to memory, intones a prayer for Mevlâna and a verse from the Quran. A kettledrum booms out, followed by the plaintive sound of the *ney* (reed flute). Then the *şeyh* (master) bows and leads the dervishes in a circle around the hall. After three circuits, the dervishes drop their black cloaks to symbolise their deliverance from worldly attachments. Then one by one, arms folded on their breasts, they spin out onto the floor as they relinquish the earthly life to be reborn in mystical union with God.

By holding their right arms up, they receive the blessings of heaven, which are communicated to earth by holding their left arms turned down. As they whirl, they form a 'constellation' of revolving bodies, which itself slowly rotates. The *şeyh* walks among them to check that each dervish is performing the ritual properly.

The dance is repeated over and over again. Finally, the *hafız* again chants passages from the Quran, thus sealing the mystical union with God.

memorates Mevlâna's 'wedding night' with Allah. Tickets (and accommodation) should be booked well in advance; contact Selene Tourism for assistance. A new building specifically to host the *semas* (Mevlevi worship ceremonies) was built in 2003. Don't worry if you can't get a ticket, as other venues around town also host dancers during the festival.

At other times of year visitors can watch whirling dervish ceremonies at the **Cultural Centre** (☎ 351 1215; tickets €15; ☺ Apr-Nov) behind the Mevlâna Museum. The one-hour evening performances usually take place about three times weekly in the season; you can book tickets through travel agencies or your hotel.

Sleeping

Given Konya's character, it's hardly surprising that many hotels boast their own *mescit* (small mosque) rather than minibar. There's no shortage of options but the steady throughput of pilgrims means that even the worst places can get away with prices that would be impossible elsewhere.

BUDGET

Hotel Ulusan (☎ 351 5004; ulusanhotel@mynet.com; Çarşı PTT Arkası; s/d €11/17; ☐) Tucked away behind the PTT, this impeccably renovated gem is as good as many twice the price, with an enthusiastic proprietor and that all-important dash of character (teddy bears!). Some rooms have shared but pristine bathrooms. There's a cosy TV room, with a real fire in winter, and internet access is free.

Yeni Köşk-Esra Oteli (☎ 352 0671; yenikoskoteli@turk .net; Yeni Aziziye Caddesi, Kadılar Sokak 28; s/d from €20/30; ☒) A bizarre subterranean tunnel links two separate buildings here, each with small but well-equipped rooms. It's fairly quiet and a good choice for women travellers. Look for signs pointing the way off Mevlâna Caddesi.

MIDRANGE

Hotel Gümüş Şahin (☎ 352 0422; www.gumussahin.com; Mevlâna Caddesi 39; s/d/tr €25/47/67; ☒) A stylised ceramic hallway provides a dramatic entrance to this decent central choice. The bathrooms are very pink and the balconies overlook the main road, but the 'tree-lined' restaurant should distract you.

Mevlana Sema Otel (☎ 350 4623; Mevlâna Caddesi 59; s/d/tr €35/56/80; ☒) Also on the main road, resplendent in browns, maroons and new laminate floors. Unusually, pets are accepted,

though bringing a dog into a hotel full of Muslims would be like eating bacon in a synagogue.

Otel Anı & Şems (☎ 353 8080; www.hotelani.com; Şems Caddesi 8; s/d/tr €40/60/80; ☒) The location, behind the Şerafettin Cami, may not look promising but the interiors have a distinct charm, particularly the top-floor rooms. There's an in-house travel agent for all your tour and transport requirements.

Hotel Rumi (☎ 353 1121; www.rumihotel.com; Durakfakih Sokak 5; s/d €40/70; ☒ ☐) It's too plain to be really special, but the newly opened Rumi offers immaculate three-star Western standards, with fitness centre, starry lift, alcohol-free minibars and a smart modern lobby.

Selçuk Otel (☎ 353 2525; www.otelselcuk.com.tr; Alaaddin Bulvarı 4; s/d €50/75; ☒) A recent makeover has saturated this refined block hotel in cream tones, giving it an air of the cat who got the beige. The effect works well, especially in the long lounge, and good facilities (including great showers) back up the décor.

Hotel Balıkçılar (☎ 350 9470; www.balikcilar.com; Mevlâna Karşısı 1; s/d €70/90; ☒) Easily the best reception area in town, styled as a cobbled Ottoman street, complete with streetlights. The theme doesn't quite carry through to the rooms, but there are a few nice wooden touches. Facilities include a lobby bar, restaurant, sauna, *hamam* and occasional *sema* performances.

TOP END

Rixos Konya (☎ 221 5000; www.rixos.com; İstanbul Yolu, Selçuklu; d & tw from €120; ☒ ☐ ☒) One of several luxury hotels on the outskirts of the city, about 13km from the airport and 15km from central Konya. Amenities are suitably copious and extravagant, from the bowling alley to the horse-riding centre. Discounts are often available but, if not, rack rates can be double those quoted here.

Eating

Konya's speciality is *fırın* kebap, slices of (hopefully) tender, fairly greasy oven-roasted mutton served on puffy bread. The city bakers also make excellent fresh pide topped with minced lamb, cheese or eggs, but in Konya pide is called *etli ekmek* (bread with meat).

RESTAURANTS

Köşk Konya Mutfağı (☎ 352 8547; Mengüç Caddesi 66; mains €2.80-4.50; ☺ 11am-10pm) Run by the well-known food writer Nevin Halıcı, this excellent traditional restaurant puts her personal twist on classics like kebaps and *ayran*. In summer headscarved women prepare your food in a hut on the lawn. The menu features some unusual dishes like *höşmerim*, a rich, mouth-clogging dessert made from sesame oil, flour and syrup (€1.10). It's southeast of town, towards the Koyunoğlu Museum.

Akça Konak (☎ 350 8108; Mengüç Caddesi 18; mains €2.80-6; ⏰ 11am-10pm) This is a neat restored house near the Hotel Balıkçılar with tables inside and outside, live music and post-prandial nargilehs (water pipes). The menu is pretty standard but does feature a few regional specialities.

Konya Cadde Restaurant (☎ 351 3060; Adliye Bulvarı; mains €2.80-11; ⏰ from noon Mon-Sat) Beside the İnce Minare, this restaurant is a low-lit, 1st-floor place that will do for a night out as well as a meal. On a good night the place is packed with an unconservative slice of the populace seeking beer and live music.

QUICK EATS

Şifa Lokantası (☎ 352 0519; Mevlana Caddesi 56; mains €1.10-4.50) *Tandır kebap* tops the bill of standards at Şifa. Service can be pretty rushed when it's busy, but at least the chandeliers give you something to look at.

Sema Lokantası (☎ 352 3565; İstanbul Caddesi 107; mains €1.10-4.50) In the backstreets north of the centre, the Sema is a cheery place that serves the usual kebaps and stews as well as a good range of desserts – try the *aşure* (Noah's ark pudding).

Aydın Et Lokantası (☎ 351 9183; Şeyh Ziya Sokak 5/E; mains €3-6) Enquiring minds may want to know why there's a giant fake tree in the middle of this grill joint, but really it's easier just to stare at the clay-sculpted walls and concentrate on the comprehensive menu of pide and kebaps.

SELF-CATERING

As ever, the **bazaar** (right) is the most exciting place to shop for fresh fruit, vegetables, cheese etc. Alternatively, there's the **Afra supermarket** (Mevlana Caddesi), and sugar addicts can spoil their sweet teeth at **Sürüm** (İstanbul Caddesi), a chocolate shop established in 1926.

Drinking

In summer few things could be more pleasurable than maxing and relaxing in one of the innumerable **tea gardens** dotting the slopes of Alaaddin Tepesi. In the evening it's also fun to duck into the grounds of the **Konya Fuarı** (Konya Fairground), where you can sip tea while watching the locals navigate pedaloes round an artificial lake.

Osmanlı Çarşısı (☎ 353 3257; İnce Minare Sokak) An early-20th-century house serving *çay*, coffee and nargilehs. It's popular with Turkish students, there's a rustic toast wagon outside and the whole place has more character than a whirlpool full of dervishes.

Café Zeugma (☎ 350 9474; Adliye Bulvarı 33) This self-styled cultural and art centre targets a similar student crowd with live music and 'crazy parties'. Admission costs €3.50 at weekends.

Shopping

Konya's **bazaar** sprawls back from the modern PTT building virtually all the way to the Mevlâna Museum, cramming the narrow streets with stalls, roving vendors and the occasional horse-drawn cart. The streets are divided up in very medieval fashion: here a section for coils of rope, there one for gold jewellery, nearby one for mobile-phone accessories. There's a concentration of shops selling religious paraphernalia and tacky souvenirs at the Mevlâna Museum end.

Ikonium (☎ 350 2895; www.thefeltmaker.com; Bostan Çelebi Sokak 10) The art of felt-making is fast dying out in Turkey, so you might want to pop in here to see a modern take on an old craft.

Getting There & Away

AIR

There are three daily flights to and from İstanbul with **Turkish Airlines** (☎ 351 2000; Mevlâna Caddesi 9) and one with **Onur Air** (☎ 350 6151).

The airport is about 13km northeast of the city centre. An airport service bus (€2) leaves from near the THY office, but you should check the times carefully.

BUS

Konya's otogar is about 14km north of Alaaddin Tepesi, accessible by tram from town (see opposite). Regular buses serve all major destinations, including Afyon (€8.50, 3¾ hours), Ankara (€5.60, three hours), İstanbul (€17, 10 hours), Kayseri (€8.50, four hours) and Sivas (€14, seven hours).

The Eski Garaj (Old Bus Terminal or Karatay Terminal), 1km southwest of the Mevlâna Museum, has services to local villages.

TRAIN

The **train station** (☎ 332 3670) is about 3km southwest. You can get to Konya by train from İstanbul Haydarpaşa (13½ hours) on the *Meram Ekspresi*, the *Toros Ekspresi* (İstanbul to Gaziantep/Damascus, three weekly) or the *İç Anadolu Mavi* (Istanbul to Adana), all via Afyon. Planned new high-speed rail links will add a direct line to Ankara and should knock 9¼ hours off the journey time!

Getting Around

As most of the city centre sights are easily reached on foot, you need public transport only for the otogar or train station. To get to the city centre from the otogar take a tram marked 'Alaadin' from the east side of the otogar to Alaaddin Tepesi (€0.40, 30 minutes). Innumerable minibuses ply Mevlâna Caddesi if you're heading to the far end. A taxi costs around €8 from the otogar.

There are half-hourly minibuses from the train station to the centre (€0.40). A taxi from the station to Hükümet Meydanı costs about €4.

AROUND KONYA

Çatalhöyük

You won't find any towering monuments or reconstructed classical splendour at **Çatalhöyük** (admission free; ☺ 8am-5pm), but the bare, hilly expanse remains one of the world's most famous archaeological sites and one of the oldest town settlements ever discovered. Teams of international archaeologists continue to work away at unearthing its secrets in the summer months (June to August).

The guardian will happily show you the marquees that house the excavations and the preserved remains of the first intact house discovered, Building 5; a tip would probably be appreciated. The site of James Mellaart's 1961–65 excavations, a short way away, shows how the mound turned out to cover the remains of 13 layers of buildings, dating from 6800 to 5700 BC. Another section, the so-called 4040 area, is due to be excavated for public display by the end of 2007.

There may once have been 150 mud-brick dwellings on the site, which was originally a wetland environment. Most seem to have been houses that were accessible via ladders from their roofs, and which were filled in and built over when they started to wear out. Skeletons were found buried under the floors

and most of the houses may have doubled up as shrines. Finds from the site included many layers of murals, bulls' head plaster reliefs, mother-goddess figurines, tools and the earliest known pottery; most are now housed in Ankara's Museum of Anatolian Civilisations (see p443). The settlement was highly organised, with up to 8000 people living here at its peak, but there are no obvious signs of any central government system.

Near the site entrance stands the Experimental House, a reconstructed mud-brick hut used to test various theories about Neolithic culture, along with a small **museum**. The handful of artefacts are accompanied by informative English displays on the site, its houses and the many questions raised by the excavations – such as why many of the human remains found here were missing their heads!

If you're not much interested in archaeology, there would be little point in coming out here. However, the comments in the visitors' book make it clear that many people love the romance of the site, with its echoes of the cult of the mother goddess and reminders of our origins. There's lots of local involvement from schools and individuals, and many of the archaeologists are European volunteers, so if you show up in summer you may find few people to chat to about the site.

GETTING THERE & AWAY

To get here by public transport take one of the hourly minibuses from Konya's Eski Garaj to Çumra (€1.70, 45 minutes) and then hire a taxi from beside the otogar for the last 17km (€14 return). A taxi from Konya to the site and back will cost about €25.

Gökyurt (Kilistra, Lystra)

Konya may be well south of central Cappadocia, but the landscape at Gökyurt (50km to the southwest) is reminiscent of what you'll see in Güzelyurt or Ihlara: a gorge with dwellings and medieval churches cut into the rock face, but without the crowds. There's one particularly fine church cut completely out of the rock, but no frescoes. A trip out here makes a lovely half-day excursion, and the surrounding landscape is simply stunning.

GETTING THERE & AWAY

There are several daily buses from Konya's Eski Garaj to Hatunsaray, from where you could catch a taxi the last 18km (€15 return).

CENTRAL ANATOLIA

A taxi from/to Konya will charge around €25, including one hour's waiting time.

Driving, you should take the Antalya road, then follow signs to Akören. Look for a tiny brown and white sign on the right (marked 'Kilistra-Gökyurt, 16km'), a few kilometres before Hatunsaray. Cyclists need to watch out for sheepdogs roaming about.

Sille

☎ 0332 / pop 2000

If you're looking for an excursion from Konya, the pretty village of Sille, a narrow patch of green on a dry river bed surrounded by sharp rocky hills, is a perfect escape. The traditional village houses, many neglected and crumbling, are mirrored by a rock-face full of cave dwellings and chapels.

The domed Byzantine **St Helen's Church** (Ayaelena Kilisesi; 9am-5pm), near the last bus stop, was reputedly founded by Empress Helena, mother of Constantine the Great. It was completely restored in 1833; the vandalised and fast-fading frescoes date from the 1880s. Despite its use as a mosque from the 1920s until the late 1990s, the church retains some of its old woodwork, including a broken pulpit and an iconostasis stripped of its icons.

On the hill to the north stands a small ruined chapel, the **Küçük Kilese**; it's worth the scramble up for the views over the village alone.

Time your visit to Sille for a mealtime since it has one unexpected gem: the terraced **Sille Konak** (☎ 244 9260; www.sillekonak.com; mains €2-4.50), a restored Greek house lovingly decorated by the family who run it and provide the excellent home cooking.

GETTING THERE & AWAY

Bus 64 from Mevlâna Caddesi (opposite the post office) leaves every half-hour or so (less often on Sunday) for Sille (€0.40, 25 minutes).

KARAMAN

☎ 0338

After the fall of the Seljuk Empire, central Anatolia was split into several different provinces with different governments, and for some time Karaman served as a regional capital. Although little-visited these days, it boasts a selection of fine 13th- and 14th-century buildings and makes a base for excursions to Binbirkilise (right) and Sultanhanı (opposite).

The **Hacıbeyler Camii**, dating from 1358, has a magnificent squared-off entrance, with decoration that looks like a baroque variant on Seljuk art. The **Mader-i Mevlâna (Aktepe) Cami,** dating from 1370, is the burial place of the great Mevlâna's mother and has a dervish-style felt hat carved above its entrance. The adjacent **hamam** is still in use.

The tomb of the great Turkish poet Yunus Emre (1320) is beside the **Yunus Emre Camii**. Extracts from his verses are carved into the walls of a poetry garden to the rear of the mosque.

The slightly disorganised **Karaman Museum** (Turgut Özal Bulvarı; admission €1.10; 8am-noon & 1-5pm Tue-Sun) contains cave finds from nearby Taşkale and Canhasan and has a fine ethnography section. Next door is the magnificent **Hatuniye Medresesi**, built in 1382, whose ornate portal is one of the finest examples of Karaman art. It's now a rather smart restaurant.

Getting There & Away

Frequent buses link Karaman with Konya (€2.80, two hours) and Ereğli (€2.80, two hours). Onward buses from Ereğli to Niğde are few and far between.

BİNBİRKİLİSE

Just before WWI the great British traveller Gertrude Bell travelled 42km northwest of Karaman and recorded the existence of a cluster of Byzantine churches set high up on a lonely hillside and rather generously known as Binbirkilise (One Thousand and One Churches). Later Irfan Orga came here in search of the last remaining nomads, a journey recorded in his book *The Caravan Moves On*. You won't see any nomads around these days, or indeed much to mark the ruins out as churches, but plenty of goats and tortoises graze peacefully and a few curious villagers amble among the low piles of loose stone foundations.

It's easiest to reach the churches with your own transport. Drive out of Karaman on the Karapınar road and follow the yellow signs. The first sizable ruin pops up in the village of Madenşehir, after which the road becomes increasingly rough. There are fantastic views all along the road, which is just as well, as you'll have to come back the same way.

A taxi from Karaman otogar should cost around €40 for the return trip; the drivers know where the churches are.

CENTRAL ANATOLIA

SULTANHANI

☎ 0382

The highway between Konya and Aksaray crosses quintessential Anatolian steppe: flat grasslands as far as the eye can see, with only the occasional tumbleweed and a fist of mountains in the distance breaking the monotony. Along the way, 110km from Konya and 42km from Aksaray, is the dreary village of Sultanhanı, its only redeeming feature being one of several Seljuk *han* bearing that name. This stunning **Sultanhanı** (admission €1.10; ☉ 7am-7pm), 200m from the highway, is apparently the largest in Anatolia, and can be explored in about half an hour.

It was constructed in 1229, during the reign of the Seljuk sultan Alaaddin Keykubad I and restored in 1278 after a fire (when it became Turkey's largest *han*). Note the wonderful carved entrance, the raised central *mescit* and the huge *ahır* (stable) at the back. Other rooms once served as baths, bedrooms and an accounting house.

Getting There & Away

Around 10 buses run to/from Aksaray otogar Monday to Friday (€1.10, 45 minutes); there are only two services at weekends. Alternatively you can flag down a bus heading for Konya or Aksaray from the main highway. If you start out early you can hop off the bus, see the *han* and be on your way again an hour or so later.

> **HAN SWEET HAN**
>
> The Seljuks built a string of *han* (caravan-serais) along the route of the 13th-century Silk Road through Anatolia. These camel caravan staging posts were built roughly a day's travel apart (about 15km to 30km), to facilitate trade. Expenses for construction and maintenance of the *hans* were borne by the sultan, and paid for by the taxes levied on the rich trade in goods.
>
> As well as the Sultanhanı, fine specimens include the Sarıhan, 6km east of Avanos, and the Karatay Han, 48km east of Kayseri. Many other *hans* dot the Anatolian landscape, including the Ağzıkara Hanı, 16km northeast of Aksaray on the Nevşehir highway, and another Sultan Han, 45km northeast of Kayseri off the Sivas highway.

CENTRAL ANATOLIA

Cappadocia

Those troglodytes sure knew what they were doing when they decided to lay down their hats and call Cappadocia home. Deep in the heart of the country, they settled within the lunar-like landscape and burrowed their houses and churches into stone cliffs and their cities underground. In so doing, they provided a still-cogent example of the simplicity and sense of living at one with nature rather than imposing upon it.

These days the cave dwellers are predominantly tourists staying in cave hotels who have been drawn to this part of Turkey by its surreal scenery, wealth of ancient churches and unparalleled opportunities for adventure activities. Where else can you float over the fairy chimneys in a hot-air balloon in the morning, admire Byzantine frescoes in the afternoon and sample fine food and wine at night? Let alone take a spectacular hike through a rose-tinted gorge, indulge in a frenzy of shopping at a covered bazaar dating from Ottoman times and see dervishes whirl in an atmospheric caravanserai. It's this mix of attractions that makes Cappadocia such a compelling tourist destination – there truly is something here for everyone.

Let's be clear, though. The true joy of Cappadocia doesn't come courtesy of its wealth of boutique hotels, its spectacular sunsets, its world-class hiking or its warm and welcoming locals. Instead, it stems from the fact that life still follows a village rhythm here, far removed from the wannabe jet-set lifestyle of the Mediterranean tourist resorts or the marvellous mayhem of İstanbul. This is a place to enjoy at your own pace.

HIGHLIGHTS

- Marvel at the luminous frescoes and rock-hewn churches at **Göreme Open-Air Museum** (p499)
- Sample the boutique hotels and local wines in **Ürgüp** (p519)
- Follow the river and explore the ancient churches in the magnificent **Ihlara Valley** (p529)
- Explore the subterranean wonders of the **underground cities** (p528) at Derinkuyu and Kaymaklı
- Brave the rapids of the Zamantı River in the magnificent **Ala Dağlar National Park** (p526)
- Float over the fairy chimneys in a **hot-air balloon** (p512)
- Spot the old Greek mansions on the streets of **Mustafapaşa** (p524)

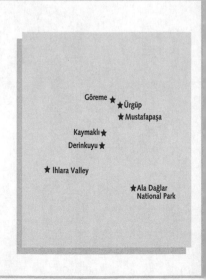

History

The Hittites settled Cappadocia from 1800 BC to 1200 BC, after which smaller kingdoms held power. Then came the Persians, followed by the Romans, who established the capital of Caesarea (today's Kayseri). During the Roman and Byzantine periods, Cappadocia became a refuge for early Christians and, from the 4th to the 11th century, Christianity flourished here; most churches, monasteries and underground cities date from this period. Later, under Seljuk and Ottoman rule, Christians were treated with tolerance.

Cappadocia progressively lost its importance in Anatolia. Its rich past was all but forgotten until a French priest rediscovered the rock-hewn churches in 1907. The tourist boom in the 1980s kick-started a new era, and now Cappadocia is one of Turkey's most famous and popular destinations.

Dangers & Annoyances

A warning is needed about bus services to Cappadocia from other parts of Turkey. Many readers have complained that although they purchased tickets to Göreme, they found themselves instead deposited at Nevşehir otogar (bus station) and were left with no alternative except to catch an overpriced taxi to Göreme. We've even heard of some unscrupulous bus companies abandoning travellers on the highway outside Avanos. In reality, many long-haul buses do terminate in Nevşehir, but the legitimate companies (including Göreme,

CAPPADOCIA

Metro, Nevşehir, Öncü or Kapadokya) always then transfer their passengers from Nevşehir to the surrounding villages on free *servises* (shuttle minibuses).

When you purchase your bus ticket, make absolutely sure that it clearly states that it is for Göreme; having it state 'Cappadocia' is not enough. With this proof, you will be able to insist on a free shuttle transfer (even if it means refusing to get off the bus!). It's also a good idea to confirm your final destination with your driver before you get on the bus at the start of the trip.

For more information about transport from Nevşehir otogar, see p516.

Tours

Cappadocia is overrun with travel agents. In the past, tour prices were agreed among the agencies at the start of each season; these days, the increasingly cut-throat business environment has led to some agencies undercutting others. This means that it's well worth shopping around.

Most tour companies tend to offer the following:

Ihlara Valley trip A full day, including a guided hike and lunch. Costs between €30 and €50.

Full-day tours These often take in one of the underground cities, a stretch of the Ihlara Valley and one of the caravanserais, but others go to Soğanlı and Mustafapaşa. Most cost €50.

Guided day hikes Usually in the Rose, Sun, Red or Pigeon Valleys. Cost anywhere between €20-50, depending on the destination, degree of difficulty and length.

At the start and end of the season, when customers are thin on the ground, local tour companies tend to join forces rather than have a fleet of half-empty minibuses trundling back and forth. Most of the pensions either operate their own tours or work with one of the travel agencies. To save arguments, check whether any visits to carpet shops, pottery factories or onyx factories are scheduled before you sign up for the tour.

We strongly counsel you to avoid booking an expensive package tour upon arrival in İstanbul. If your time is limited and you want to take a tour, you're probably better off booking a tour directly from an agent in Cappadocia.

For listings of tour agencies, see p501 (for Göreme), p519 (Ürgüp), p511 (Çavuşin) and p513 (Avanos).

Getting There & Away

Two airports service central Cappadocia: Kayseri and Nevşehir. For details of flights to/from İstanbul and İzmir see p498 and p516.

Turkish Airlines and Onur Air operate 14-seat transfer buses (tickets €7 to €8.50 per person) for passengers leaving or arriving at Kayseri on mid-morning and early evening flights. There is no shuttle for Sun Express or Pegasus passengers. The buses pick up from and drop off to hotels and pensions in Göreme, Uçhisar, Ortahisar, Avanos, Nevşehir and Ürgüp. If you want to use one of these shuttle services you *must* prebook through **Argeus Tours** (☎ 0384-341 4688; www.argeus.com.tr, www.cappadociaexclusive.com; İstiklal Caddesi 7; ⏰ 8.30am-7pm Nov-Mar, 8.30am-6pm Apr-Oct) in Ürgüp if you fly Turkish Airlines; or through **Peerless Travel Services** (☎ 0384-341 6970; www.peerlessexcursions.com; İstiklal Caddesi 19A; ⏰ 8.30am-8.30pm daily), also in Ürgüp, if you fly Onur Air. Alternatively, you can easily request your hotel or pension in Cappadocia to book a seat for you. If you don't prebook you will either have to make your way to the Kayseri otogar to catch a bus to your final destination (note that this is not an option in the evening) or catch a taxi, which is an expensive proposition (eg €50 to Göreme).

It's very easy to get to Cappadocia by bus from İstanbul or Ankara. Buses from İstanbul to Cappadocia travel overnight (in high summer there may also be day buses) and bring you to Nevşehir, where there should be a *servis* to take you onto Uçhisar, Göreme, Avanos or Ürgüp. From Ankara you can travel more comfortably during the day. It's easy enough to travel back from Cappadocia to İstanbul by day bus via Ankara because there are so many buses between these two cities.

The nearest train stations are at Niğde and Kayseri. See p528 and p498 for information about services.

Getting Around

The most convenient bases for exploring central Cappadocia are Göreme, Ürgüp and Avanos. Bus and minibus services are frequent in high summer, much less so in winter. Belediye Bus Corp minibuses (€0.80 to €1.10 depending on where you get on and off) travel between Ürgüp and Avanos via Ortahisar, the Göreme Open-Air Museum, Göreme village and Çavuşin every two hours, starting in Ürgüp at 8am and operating until 6pm. The bus will also stop in Zelve on request. You can hop on and off anywhere around the loop. Note that Sunday services are less frequent. There's also an hourly *belediye* (municipal council) bus running from Avanos to Nevşehir via Çavuşin (10 minutes), Göreme (15 minutes) and Uçhisar (30 minutes). It operates from 7.10am to 6pm and costs between €0.40 and €1.10 depending on where you get on and off.

The Ihlara Valley in western Cappadocia can be visited on a day trip from Göreme or by bus from Aksaray.

In summer, travelling between these places by public transport is relatively easy, although on Sunday the transport slows right down. In winter, public transport is less frequent.

KAYSERİ

☎ 0352 / pop 603,700 / elevation 1067m

Kayseri is one of Turkey's great modern success stories. Home to a vibrant and ever-expanding manufacturing industry and reaping the economic benefits that flow from this, it's a city that clearly knows its own worth. The locals here are as confident of their city's future as they are proud of its past, which is a rare thing indeed. It's also a city that has no need to rely on the vagaries of international tourism for its economic prosperity. This can be liberating – and just a wee bit frustrating – for the visitor, as the touts, tour operators and tourist infrastructure taken for granted elsewhere in Cappadocia are thin on the ground here.

Most people fly into Kayseri and are transferred by shuttle bus to central Cappadocia, but there's a lot to be said for spending a day exploring its sights and meeting its people.

History

The first Hittite capital, Kaniş, was the chief city of the Hatti people and you can visit the remains at Kültepe, 20km northeast of Kayseri, off the Sivas road. There was probably an early settlement on the site of Kayseri as well.

Under the Roman emperor Tiberius (r AD 14–37), the town was renamed Caesarea. Later it became famous as the birthplace of St Basil the Great, who was responsible for organising the monastic life of Cappadocia. Its early Christian history was interrupted by Arab invasions from the 7th century. The Seljuks took over in 1084 and held the city until the Mongols' arrival in 1243, except for a brief period when the Crusaders captured it on their way to the Holy Land.

After Kayseri had been part of the Mongol Empire for almost 100 years, its Mongol governor set up his own emirate (1335). This lasted a mere 45 years and was succeeded by another emirate, then captured by the Ottomans, taken by the Mamluks, and finally conquered by the Ottomans again in 1515 – all in just over 100 years.

Orientation & Information

The basalt-walled citadel at the centre of the old town, just south of Cumhuriyet Meydanı, the huge main square, is a good landmark. Another convenient point of reference is Düvenönü Meydanı, 350m west of the citadel along Park Caddesi.

The train station is at the northern end of Atatürk Bulvarı, over 500m north of Düvenönü Meydanı. Kayseri's otogar is about 700m northwest of Düvenönü Meydanı, along Osman Kavuncu Caddesi.

The helpful **tourist office** (☉ 8am-5pm Mon-Fri) is on Cumhuriyet Meydanı.

You'll find numerous banks with ATMs in the centre. To collect your email, head to the excellent **Hollywood Internet Café** (Sivas Caddesi 15; per hr €0.55; ☉ 8am-midnight).

Sights

The monumental walls of the **citadel** (*hisar* or *kale*) were constructed out of black volcanic stone by Emperor Justinian in the 6th century and extensively repaired by the Seljuk sultan Keykavus I around 1224. In 1486, Mehmet the Conqueror made further repairs, a practice kept up by the modern city fathers.

Just southeast of the citadel is the wonderful **Güpgüpoğlu Konağı**, a fine stone mansion dating from the 18th century, now housing the city's **Ethnography Museum** (admission €1.10; ☉ 8am-5pm Tue-Sun). Also worth having a look at nearby is the modest but stylish **Atatürk Evi** (admission free; ☉ 8am-5pm Mon-Fri), a small, originally furnished Ottoman-era house where Atatürk stayed when he visited Kayseri.

Among Kayseri's distinctive features are several important building complexes that were founded by Seljuk queens and princesses, including the austere-looking **Mahperi Hunat Hatun Complex**, east of the citadel. It

CAPPADOCIA

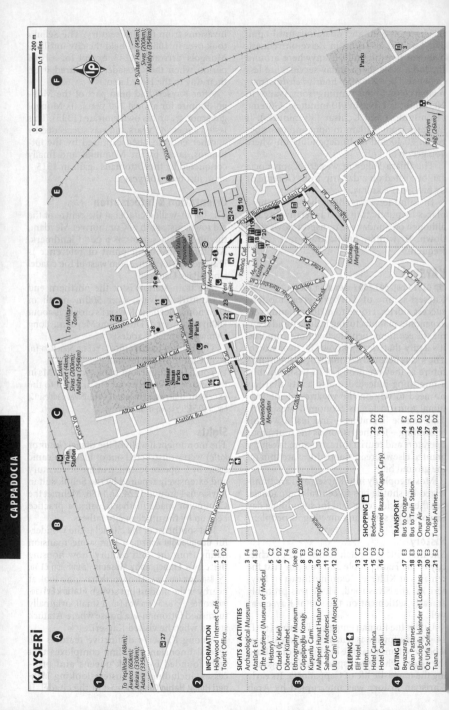

KAYSERİ

CAPPADOCIA

comprises the Mahperi Hunat Hatun Camii (1238), built by the wife of the Seljuk sultan Alaettin Keykubad; the Hunat Hatun Medresesi (1237); and a decent *hamam* (Turkish bathhouse), which is still in use.

Another striking monument is the **Çifte Medrese** (Twin Seminaries). These adjoining religious schools, set in Mimar Sinan Parkı north of Park Caddesi, were founded at the bequest of the Seljuk sultan Gıyasettin I Keyhüsrev and his sister Gevher Nesibe Sultan (1165–1204).

Back towards the citadel, be sure to have a look at the **Sahabiye Medresesi**, an Islamic theological school that dates from 1268 and now functions as a book bazaar. A bit west of Cumhuriyet Meydanı stands the Ottoman-style **Kurşunlu Cami** (Lead-Domed Mosque). Also called the Ahmet Paşa Camii after its founder, it was completed in 1585 possibly following plans drawn up by the great Sinan (who was born in a nearby village).

Another mosque worth inspecting is Kayseri's **Ulu Cami** (Great Mosque), immediately to the south. It was begun in 1142 by the Danışmend Turkish emirs and finished by the Seljuks in 1205. Despite all the 'restoration' over the centuries, it's still a good example of early Seljuk style.

If you have half an hour to spare, consider visiting the city's small **Archaeological Museum** (admission €1.10; ☼ 8am-5pm Tue-Sun), 800m southeast of the citadel. It houses finds from Kültepe (ancient Kaniş) including baked cuneiform tablets that told historians much about the Hittite Empire, a stunning sarcophagus illustrating the labours of Hercules, and a noteworthy collection of Roman jewellery.

Scattered about Kayseri are several conical **Seljuk tombs** dating from Seljuk times. Most famous is the so-called **Döner Kümbet** (Revolving Tomb), about 600m southeast of the citadel along Talas Caddesi, but you'll spot many others as you walk around.

Sleeping

It can be hard to find an available hotel room in Kayseri due to the fact that businesspeople from all over Turkey regularly visit the city.

Hotel Çamlıca (☎ 231 4344; cnr Bankalar Caddesi, Gürcü Sokak 14; s/d incl breakfast €14/25) This grubby and depressing place is only mentioned here due to the dearth of budget options in the city. Rooms have hard beds and impossible

bathrooms; if you can possibly afford to, we'd suggest sleeping elsewhere.

Elif Hotel (☎ 336 1826; fax 336 5478; Osman Kavuncu Caddesi 2; s/d incl breakfast €19.50/34) This modern place has conservative Islamic management, so it frowns upon alcohol in the rooms or any other forms of hanky-panky. If you can rein yourself in, the rooms are clean and cheerful and the prices are a bargain. Ask for a room at the rear, as they are much quieter.

Hotel Çapari (☎ 222 5278; fax 222 5282; Gevher Nesibe Mahellesi Donanma Caddesi 12; s/d/ste incl breakfast €28/48/67; 🗙) This three-star hotel in a quiet street off Atatürk Bulvarı may be old fashioned, but it's one of the best options available. Charging extremely reasonable prices (something unusual in Kayseri), it offers well-equipped rooms with satellite TV and minibar.

Hilton (☎ 207 5000; www.hilton.com; Cumhuriyet Meydanı; d €115-131; 🅿 🗙 🐾) Slap bang in the town centre, this is Kayseri's only five-star hotel. Its futuristic design is a striking contrast to the surrounding mosques and historical buildings. Inside it's swanky, with an atrium as vast as a station, luxurious rooms and all the requisite amenities, including a fitness centre. The views from upper floors are great.

Eating

Kayseri boasts a few special dishes, among them *pastırma* (salted, sun-dried veal coated with *çemen*, a spicy concoction of garlic, red peppers, parsley and water), the original pastrami. Few of the town's restaurants serve alcohol – if you want a drink with your meal you'll probably have to eat at the Hilton.

Tuana (☎ 222 0565; 2nd fl, Sivas Caddesi; mains €2.50-5) Behind the PTT, Tuana offers well-cooked dishes and wonderful views of Erciyes Dağı (Mt Erciyes). If you're on a budget, the open buffet (€4.50) is an attractive proposition; otherwise, you can opt for pides, *köfte* (meatballs), steaks or kebaps.

Beyazsaray (☎ 221 0444; Millet Caddesi 8; mains €3-5) Across the road from Öz Urfa Sofrası, this frantically busy place serves İskender kebaps that are nearly as good as those served at Elmacıoğlu İskender et Lokantası. Best of all, it has a takeaway counter at the front where you can grab an absolutely delicious chicken döner sandwich for a mere €0.55.

Elmacıoğlu İskender et Lokantası (☎ 222 6965; 1st & 2nd fls, Millet Caddesi 5; mains €3-5) Just near the citadel, this busy eatery has been churning out *İskender* kebaps and other Turkish classics for several decades. It's glitzy, but the meat dishes are quite wonderful. If you don't opt for the house speciality (€7) you may want to try the enormous *karışık ızgara* (mixed grill, €7). Even the pide is good here.

Öz Urfa Sofrası (☎ 232 7777; 1st fl, Millet Caddesi 11) Another safe choice for a kebap feast, this busy place is always full of locals. The Öz Urfa serves local specialities such as pide with *pastırma* (€3) and the usual line-up of meat on sticks.

Divan Pastanesi (☎ 222 3974; Millet Caddesi) Opposite the Elmacıoğlu İskender et Lokantası, this modern pastry shop is a favourite among Kayseri's sweet tooths.

The western end of Sivas Caddesi has a strip of fast-food joints that still seem to be pumping when everything else in town is quiet.

Shopping

Set at the intersection of age-old trade routes, Kayseri has been an important commercial centre for millennia and its Ottoman covered markets beside the citadel have been beautifully restored. Don't leave without a stroll in the small and lovely *bedesten* (vaulted market place), built in 1497. It was first dedicated to the sale of textiles, and still sells carpets and kilims. The *kapalı çarşı* (vaulted bazaar) was built in 1859, restored in 1988, and now sells mainly gold jewellery.

Getting There & Away

AIR

Turkish Airlines (☎ 222 3858; Tekin Sokak Hukuk Plaza 6C; ☻ 8.30am-5.30pm Mon-Fri, 8.30am-1pm Sat) has three daily flights (€44 to €94 one way, 1¼ hours) to/from İstanbul. Sun Express, a Turkish Airlines subsidiary, offers twice-weekly morning flights from İzmir on Thursdays and Sundays (€39 to €72 one way).

There is no shuttle bus to meet Turkish Airlines or Sun Express passengers and take them into the centre of town.

Onur Air (☎ 231 5551; Ahmetpaşa Caddesi) has two daily flights to/from İstanbul (€38 to €77 one way). A free shuttle bus meets both flights and brings Onur Air passengers into the centre of town.

To get to the airport, a shuttle leaves from a stop near the Sahabiye Medresesi at 7.30am and 8.30pm (€2). At all other times you'll need to grab a taxi (around €8.50).

BUS

On an important north–south and east–west crossroads, Kayseri has lots of bus services. If there's no *servis*, walk out the front of the otogar, cross the avenue and board any bus marked 'Merkez' (Centre). A ticket will cost €0.55. A taxi to the citadel should cost less than €3.

For details of some useful services from Kayseri's otogar see the table, below.

SERVICES FROM KAYSERİ'S OTOGAR

Destination	Fare	Duration	Frequency (per day)
Adana	€8.50-11.50	5hr	frequent morning
Ankara	€8.50	5hr	frequent
Erzurum	€11.50-17	10hr	2 morning & evening
Gaziantep	€10	6hr	several morning, afternoon & evening
Göreme	€3	1½hr	hourly to 6pm, 6.30pm & 8pm
Kahramanmaraş	€8.50	5½hr	frequent
Malatya	€8.50	5hr	several morning, afternoon & evening
Nevşehir via Ürgüp	€3.50-4	1½hr	frequent to 6pm, 6.30pm & 8pm
Sivas	€7.50	3hr	frequent morning
Van	€17	14hr	1 afternoon & evening

TRAIN

The *Vangölü/Güney Ekspresi* (between İstanbul and Tatvan or Diyarbakır, depending on the day), the *Doğu Ekspresi* (between İstanbul and Kars), the *Erzurum Ekspresi* (between Ankara and Kars) and the *4 Eylül Mavi Train* (between Ankara and Malatya) all stop at Kayseri. Departures for İstanbul (€10, 18 hours) are at 4am and 4.40am daily; departures for Kars (€12, 21 hours) are at 1.30am and 8.20pm daily; departures for Ankara (€10, 6½ hours) are at midnight and 4.19am daily; departures for Tatvan (€13, 22 hours) are at 2.48pm on Monday and Friday; departures to Kurtalan (€12, 20 hours) are at 2.48pm on Tuesday, Friday and Sunday; departures to

Diyarbakır (€12, 20 hours) are at 2.48am on Thursday; and departures to Malatya (€6, 8½ hours) are at 2.52am daily.

To reach the centre from the train station, walk out of the station, cross the big avenue (Çevre Yol) and board any bus heading down Atatürk Bulvarı to Düvenönü Meydanı.

AROUND KAYSERI
Sultan Han

Built in the 1230s, the **Sultan Han** (admission €1.50; ⏰ 9am-1pm & 2-6pm) is a striking old Seljuk caravanserai on the old Kayseri–Sivas highway, 45km northeast of Kayseri and visible from the new highway. Besides being a fine example of a Seljuk royal caravan lodging and the second largest in Anatolia (after the Sultanhanı near Aksaray), it has been beautifully restored.

You may arrive to find it closed even during official opening hours, but a boy will soon come running with the key and a ticket.

GÖREME
☎ 0384 / pop 2100

Some places are magical – and Göreme is one of them. Located 70km west of Kayseri, this small village is set amid towering fairy chimneys and majestic honeycomb cliffs, with the stunning backdrops of the Rose, Honey and Pigeon Valleys surrounding it. Guidebook-speak really can't do the place justice, as its overall package is much, much greater than the sum of its parts (and those parts are all pretty damn impressive in their own right). Though some jaded travellers whinge that it 'isn't what it used to be', we think they're full of tuff: Göreme is one of Turkey's unspoiled treasures, where traditional village life manages to happily coexist with a thriving modern tourism industry and where visitors are – and always have been – made welcome by a local community as friendly as it is close-knit.

Orientation & Information

Most of Göreme's shops and restaurants are in the streets surrounding the otogar. The Open-Air Museum is an easy walk 1km to the east of town.

INTERNET ACCESS

Mor-tel Telekom Call Shop/Internet Café (per hr €1.50; ⏰ 9am-midnight)
Nese Internet Café (per hr €1.50; ⏰ 8.30am-10pm)

MONEY

There are three ATMs in town: two in booths at the otogar (Vakif Bank and Türkıye Bankası) and one at the Deniz Bank branch on Müze Caddesi. Some of the town's travel agencies will exchange money, although you're probably better off going to the PTT.

POST

The **PTT** (just off Bilal Eroğlu Caddesi) has phone, fax and money-changing services.

TOURIST INFORMATION

Considering the fact that Göreme is the centre of the Cappadocian tourist industry, it never ceases to amaze us that it has no real tourist office. There's an information booth at the otogar that is open when most long-distance buses arrive, but it's run by the **Göreme Turizmciler Derneği** (Göreme Tourism Society; ☎ 271 2558; www.goreme.org), a coalition of hotel-, restaurant- and carpet-shop owners, and is solely aimed at directing travellers to accommodation in the village. Its staff speak little English and can't supply any meaningful information about the village or surrounding areas.

Sights
GÖREME OPEN-AIR MUSEUM

One of Turkey's World Heritage sites, the **Göreme Open-Air Museum** (Göreme Açık Hava Müzesi; admission €5.50, parking €1.25; ⏰ 8.30am-7pm Apr-Oct, 8am-5pm Nov-Mar) is an essential stop on any Cappadocian itinerary. A cluster of rock-cut Byzantine churches, chapels and monasteries 1km uphill from the centre of the village, it deserves at least a two-hour visit.

Try to arrive early in the morning in summer and space yourself between tour groups – apart from the crowds, when lots of people crowd into one of these little churches they block the doorway, which is often the only source of light. And if at all possible, avoid visiting on weekends, when the site is packed with domestic tourists.

To the left, after you enter, is the **Rahibeler Manastırı** (Nun's Convent). Although this was originally several storeys high, today you can only see what is thought to be the large plain dining hall, with steps up to a small chapel (with unremarkable frescoes). To its right is the similar Monk's Monastery.

Follow the cobbled path until you reach **Aziz Basil Şapeli** (Chapel of St Basil). It's rather dark inside because the main room is off to the left,

CAPPADOCIA

GÖREME

0 — 200 m
0 — 0.1 miles

INFORMATION
Alpino Tours.................................**1** C3	
Information Booth...................(see 60)	
Middle Earth Travel................**2** C3	
Mor-Tel Telekom Call Shop/	
Internet....................................**3** C3	
Neşe Tour..................................**4** C3	
Nese Internet Café....................**5** B3	
Post Office (PTT).......................**6** D2	
Rose Tour..................................**7** C3	
Yama Tours...............................**8** C3	

SIGHTS & ACTIVITIES
El Nazar Kilise...........................**9** E4	
Göreme Balloons.....................**10** D3	
Hikmet's Place........................**11** F3	
Kapadokya Balloons................**12** B2	
Roman Castle...........................**13** C3	
Saklı Kilise...............................**14** E4	

SLEEPING
Anatolia Pension.....................**15** D3	
Anatolian Houses Göreme.......**16** D3	
Arch Palace.............................**17** C4	
Canyon View Hotel..................**18** B4	
Cappadocia Cave Suites...........**19** D4	
Cappadocia Dora......................**20** C3	
Elif Star Caves.........................**21** A4	
Fairy Chimney Inn...................**22** A4	
Göreme House..........................**23** C4	
Gültekin Motel........................**24** C3	
Güven Cave Hotel...................**25** B3	
Kelebek Hotel & Cave Pension...**26** B4	
Kemal's Guest House................**27** B3	
Kookaburra Pension................**28** B3	
Köse Pansion..........................**29** C2	
Legend Cave Hotel..................**30** C4	
Local Cave House Hotel...........**31** D3	

Pasahan Hotel.........................**32** C3	
Sarhan Cave Hotel...................**33** D4	
Shoestring Cave Pension..........**34** B4	
Tabiat Pension.........................**35** C4	
The Flintstones Cave...............**36** A3	
Traveller's Cave Pansiyon.........**37** C4	
Village Cave House Hotel.........**38** D4	
Walnut House.........................**39** B3	

EATING
A'lturca..................................**40** C3	
Cappadocia Kebap Center.......**41** C3	
Cappadocia Patisserie.............**42** C3	
Cappadocia Pide Salonu..........**43** B4	
Dibek.....................................**44** C3	
Finn Express............................**45** C3	
Göreme Restaurant..............(see 55)	
Local Restaurant......................**46** D2	
Mercan...................................**47** C3	
Nazar Börek............................**48** C3	
Orient Restaurant....................**49** B2	
Silk Road Restaurant &	
Çavuşin, Zelve & Avanos...**50** C3	
SOS & Sultan Restaurant &	
Café....................................**51** D2	

DRINKING
Fat Boys.................................**52** C3	
Flintstones Cave Bar...............**53** D2	
Pacha Bar...............................**54** C3	
Red Red Wine House..............**55** C3	

ENTERTAINMENT
Club Libra...............................**56** D2	

TRANSPORT
Hitchhiker...............................**57** C3	
Local Bus Stop for Ürgüp,	
Çavuşin, Zelve & Avanos...**58** D2	
Motodocia...............................**59** C3	
Otogar....................................**60** C3	
Öz Cappadocia Tour.............(see 57)	

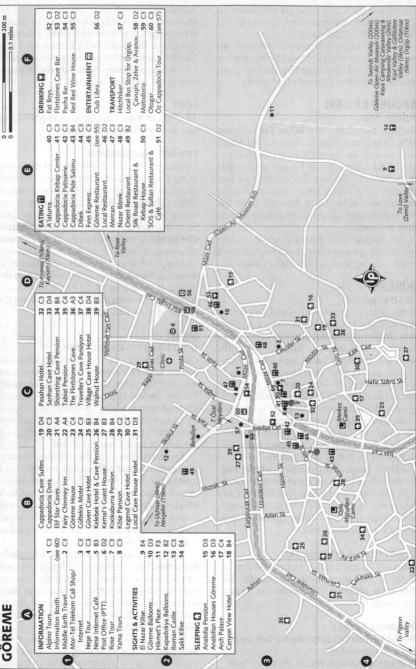

To Swords Valley (200m);
Göreme Open-Air Museum (200m);
Kaya Camping Caravanning (2km);
Meskendir Valley (2km);
Kızıl Valley & Güllüdere
Valley (6km); Ortahisar
(6km); Ürgüp (10km)

To Avanos (10km);
Kayseri (70km)

To Rose
Valley

To Love
(Zemi) Valley

To Uçhisar (4km);
Nevşehir (15km)

To Pigeon
Valley

away from the door. The grate-covered holes in the floor were graves.

Back on the path, the first place you'll come to is the **Elmalı Kilise** (Apple Church), with a stunning display of frescoes, eight small domes and one large dome. Where's the apple? Some say the Angel Gabriel, above the central nave, is holding it. There's also some decoration typical of the iconoclastic period (725–842) when images were outlawed – red ochre painted on the stone without any images of people or animals.

The **Azize Barbara Şapeli** (Chapel of St Barbara) has iconoclastic decoration, beautiful in its simplicity. There's also a fairly worn fresco of Christ the Pantocrator in the apse, and frescoes of the Virgin Mary and St Barbara.

The **Yılanlı Kilise** (Snake Church or Church of St Onuphrius) has 11th-century frescoes on part of the vault. On the left wall, St George and St Theodore attack the dragon, while Constantine the Great and his mother Helena hold the True Cross. On the right wall, the naked St Onuphrius, a hermit from Egypt, hides his nudity behind a date palm frond.

A few steps from the Yılanlı Kilise, don't miss the **refectory**, with its long dining table and benches cut from the rock. At the end of the table is a trough in the floor that was probably used for pressing grapes. Attached to the refectory is a larder, where you can see storage shelves carved into the walls, and a kitchen. Another smaller, nameless church here retains a rock-cut iconostasis.

The stunning fresco-filled **Karanlık Kilise** (Dark Church; admission €3) is the most famous of the Open-Air Museum's churches. It took its name from the fact that it originally had very few windows. Luckily this lack of light preserved the vivid colour of the frescoes, which show, among other things, Christ as Pantocrator, Christ on the Cross and the Betrayal by Judas. The church was restored at great expense, which partly explains the extra fee to visit it. However, the charge is also intended to keep numbers down in an attempt to preserve the frescoes. It's worth every lira.

Just past the Karanlık Kilise, the **Azize Katarina Şapeli** (Chapel of St Catherine) has frescoes of St George, St Catherine and the Deesis.

The **Çarıklı Kilise** (Sandal Church) is named for the footprints marked in the floor opposite the doorway. One of the best frescoes (in the arch over the door to the left) shows the Betrayal by Judas.

When you exit the museum, don't forget to cross the road and visit the **Tokalı Kilise** (Buckle Church), 50m back down the hill towards Göreme on the right. This is among the biggest and finest of the Göreme churches, with fabulous frescoes in the two main chambers, and two smaller chapels (one underground). Entry is via the 10th-century 'old' Tokalı Kilise, through the barrel-vaulted chamber covered with frescoes portraying the life of Christ. The 'new' church, built less than a hundred years later, is also alive with frescoes on a similar theme.

OTHER CHURCHES

On the road between Göreme and the Open-Air Museum, a sign points to the **El Nazar Kilise** (Church of the Evil Eye; admission €3; ☯ 8am-5pm Apr-Oct, 8am-6.30pm Nov-Mar). Carved out of a fairy chimney, the church has been restored but is of marginal interest. It's a pretty 10-minute walk from the main road.

Back towards the Open-Air Museum is another sign pointing to the **Saklı Kilise** (Hidden Church), tucked away behind the small shop Hikmet's Place. You'll have to ask Hikmet not just for the key but also to help you find it.

GÖREME VILLAGE

Göreme village, set amid cones and pinnacles of volcanic tuff, is its own biggest attraction. At its centre is the so-called **Roman Castle** (Roma Kalesi), a fairy chimney with a rock-cut Roman tomb; you can see the remains of the column tops on the temple façade. Some think Göreme may have been a burial ground for the Romans of Venasa (now Avanos).

Tours

See p494 for details of the types of tours offered by all of these agencies.

The following businesses have been recommended by readers or can be vouched for by us. However, the list is by no means exhaustive.

Alpino Tours (☎ 271 2727; www.alpino.com; Müze Caddesi 5)

Heritage Travel (☎ 271 2687; www.goreme.com; Aydinli Mahallesi, Yavuz Sokak 1) Based at the Kelebek Hotel & Cave Pension. Runs all of the usual tours but also one-week cuisine tours (€1050) and 15-day kilim weaving tours where you stay in a nomad village and learn all about carpet-making (€1600). Highly recommended.

Middle Earth Travel (☎ 271 2528; www.middleearth travel.com; Gaferli Mahallesi Cevizler Sokak 20) Brands

---

WALKS AROUND GÖREME

Göreme village is surrounded by the magnificent Göreme National Park. Valleys with gorgeous scenery and a mixture of ancient pigeon houses and even more ancient rock-cut churches fan out from all around the village.

A handful of valleys are easily explored on foot; each needs about one to three hours. Most are interconnected, so you could easily combine several in a day.

These are some of the most interesting and accessible valleys:

Bağlıdere (White Valley) From Uçhisar to Çavuşin.

Ballıdere (Honey Valley) Behind Göreme village.

Güllüdere (Rose Valley) Connecting Göreme and Çavuşin.

Güvercinlik (Pigeon Valley) Connecting Göreme and Uçhisar; colourful dovecotes.

Kılıçlar Vadısı (Swords Valley) Running off the Göreme Open-Air Museum road.

Kızıl Valley (Red Valley) Superb dovecotes, churches with frescoes.

Meskendir Valley Trail head next to Kaya Camping; tunnels and dovecotes.

Zemi Valley (Love Valley) West of the Göreme Open-Air Museum, with some particularly spectacular rock formations.

A word of warning: most of the valleys have signposts directing you to them, but nothing to keep you on the straight and narrow once you get there. Nor are they all particularly easy to walk. On top of that, there's no detailed map available – you'll have to rely on very basic print-outs. **Mehmet Güngör** (☎ 0532 382 2069) is one local guide with an encyclopaedic knowledge of Göreme's highways and byways; for €38 (up to four people) he will lead you through any of the local valleys. Most pension owners will also be happy to guide you on these trails for a minimal fee (it may even be complimentary).

---

itself as an 'adventure travel specialist' and offers activities such as abseiling at Ortahisar (€40), climbing and treks.

Neşe Tour (☎ 271 2525; www.nesetour.com; Avanos Yolu 54) All the usual tours, plus 2-night, 3-day trips to Nemrut Dağı (Mt Nemrut; €159), leaving on Monday and Thursday.

Rose Tour (☎ 271 2708; www.rosetour.com; Müze Caddesi 11)

Yama Tours (☎ 271 2508; www.yamatours.com; Müze Caddesi 2) Also offers 3-day trips to Nemrut Dağı (€159).

Sleeping

Göreme has a wealth – some might say an overindulgence – of places to stay and most of them offer extremely good value for money.

If you're visiting between October and May, be sure to pack warm clothes as it gets very cold at night and pension owners may delay putting the heating on. Ring ahead, too, to check that your choice is open. Those that do open in winter sometimes offer a low-season discount, but the prohibitive cost of heating means that this is relatively unusual.

BUDGET
Camping

Kaya Camping Caravaning (☎ 343 3983; kayacamp ing@www.com; camp sites per person/tent/campervan €4.50/1.75/4.50; ☐ ☒) This impressive camping ground is 2.5km from the centre of Göreme town, uphill from the Göreme Open-Air Museum. Set among fields of vines and a good sprinkling of trees, it has magnificent views and top-notch facilities such as clean bathrooms, plentiful hot water, a restaurant, supermarket, communal kitchen and washing machines. It's an excellent place for a family holiday, particularly as it has a large swimming pool complete with kiddie pool and sun lounges.

Pensions

Köse Pansion (☎ 271 2294; www.kosepension.com; dm/hut per person €5/7, s with shared bathroom €6, d with private bathroom €12.50; ☒ ☒) In a slightly isolated position close to the PTT, this is – and ever has been – a popular backpacker option thanks to the tender loving care of owners Dawn and Mehmet Köse. The rooftop is home to an enormous, light-filled dorm and two simple wooden huts (mattresses on the floor, BYO sleeping bag), and there is an array of clean and neat rooms, most of which have balconies, bathrooms and uncomfortable beds. Our readers adore this place, particularly its lovely swimming pool, convivial communal meals (three-course dinner €7) and attractive garden. Breakfast costs €2 and nonguests can use the pool for €4.

Shoestring Cave Pension (☎ 271 2450; www.shoe stringcave.com; dm €3.30, d with/without bathroom €13.50/10; ☑ ☑) One of the longest-running pensions in Göreme, the Shoestring Cave isn't content to rest on its laurels. When we last visited, its owners were in the process of building a swimming pool on the roof terrace, as well as four attractive new double rooms complete with marble bathrooms. Downstairs there are musty and somewhat claustrophobic rock-cut rooms and a dorm set around a courtyard. There's a pleasant restaurant where tasty breakfasts (€2.20) and snacks such as *gözleme* (savoury pancake) and *menemen* (eggs with green peppers, tomatoes and white cheese) are served.

Rock Valley Pension (☎ 271 2153; www.rockval leycappadocia.com; camping €3, dm incl breakfast €5, s/d incl breakfast €14/16; ☑) At the edge of the village just past the main mosque, Rock Valley has been around for years and its new owner is currently undertaking a staged renovation. Rooms are brightly painted, with worn carpets and scattered rugs; most have simple tiled bathrooms. Although we were impressed with how light the upstairs rooms were, the standard of cleanliness throughout the building was disappointing. The atmospheric pavilion restaurant in the rear garden overlooks the hotel's best feature, its very large swimming pool.

Kookaburra Pension (☎ 271 2549; konakgoreme@ hotmail.com; Konak Sokak 10; dm €4.50, s/d with bathroom & breakfast €8.50/16.50; ☑) This small pension has a lot going in its favour. The five light and airy upstairs rooms have polished boards, rugs, cheerful bedcovers and tiny but clean bathrooms. There's also a slightly musty downstairs dorm in an old cave kitchen that benefits from its own bathroom. The stand-out feature here is the roof terrace, which has loads of pot plants, wonderful views and a bar/restaurant with satellite TV.

Tabiat Pension (☎ 271 2267; tabiatpension@yahoo .com; s/d with shared bathroom & breakfast per person €7/14, with bathroom & breakfast €8.50/16.50; ☒) Run by the friendly İbrahim, this unassuming place near the main mosque has basic rooms arranged around a tidy central courtyard. The good news is that everything here is immaculately clean; the bad news is that the beds are so uncomfortable that they are likely to lead to the start of a prolonged relationship between you and a chiropractor.

Traveller's Cave Pansiyon (☎ 271 2707; www.travel lerscave.com; Aydınkırağı Mevkii 28; dm €3.50, s/d with shared bathroom & breakfast €8.50/12.50, s/d with bathroom & breakfast €13.50/16.50; ☒ ☑) One of the best budget choices in town, the Traveller's Cave offers small but serviceable cave rooms that are blessedly free of the musty aroma that afflicts similar rooms in other establishments. If you can score double room number 11 or the top-floor triple, both of which have private bathrooms and terraces with great views, you'll be happy indeed. There are two dorms (one mixed, one female only) that share a very clean bathroom and there's also a roof terrace lounge-restaurant with excellent views and a satellite TV.

Anatolia Pension (☎ 271 2221; www.anatoliacave .com; Müze Caddesi; dm €3.50, r with shared bathroom & breakfast per person €8.50, s/d with bathroom & breakfast €11/19; ☑) At the start of the road to the Open-Air Museum, this simple place has rooms (some cave) with spectacularly ugly furniture and fittings, complete with garish plaid carpet, stalactite ceilings and bizarre toilet seats, but offset by friendly owners, a decent view and pleasant garden.

Walnut House (☎ 271 2235; www.cevizliev.com; Zeybek Sokak; s/d incl breakfast €14/19.50; ☑) A few steps away from the otogar, this hotel in an Ottoman mansion offers one of the best deals in this price range. In fact, the place is so popular that the owners are building a new extension in the rear garden so as to meet demand for rooms. The main building offers six upstairs rooms with traditional arched stone ceilings, hard beds and small but clean bathrooms. Downstairs there's an attractive, kilim-filled lobby-lounge that overlooks the gorgeous rose garden at the front of the building. Don't stay here if cigarette smoke bothers you, as the downstairs area absolutely reeks.

Cappadocia Dora (☎ 271 2874; www.doramotel.com; s/d incl breakfast €11/22; ☑) Sometimes it pays to trade atmosphere for comfort and value. Göreme is full of pensions with fairy chimney rooms full of rugs and Anatolian textiles, but all too often this goes hand in hand with grubby bathrooms and uncomfortable beds. Here at the Dora, the décor is no-nonsense and the building is functional rather than whimsical, but its light-drenched rooms are impeccably clean and exceptionally comfortable. The roof terrace has fabulous views and there's a cave lounge with satellite TV and a blizzard of floor cushions.

CAPPADOCIA

Gültekin Motel (☎ 271 2584; gultekinmotel@hotmail.com; Müdür Sokak 3; dm/s/d €5.50/14/22; 🖳) A somewhat odd place that doesn't overplay the cave or chimney-rooms card but isn't quite sure what to offer up instead, the Gültekin has three depressing cave rooms and seven much nicer upstairs rooms. These are very light and come complete with hard beds and small bathrooms. There's a comfortable and clean upstairs six-bed dorm with its own bathroom, and a roof terrace with excellent views.

Flintstones Cave (☎ 271 2555; www.theflintstones cavehotel.com; camp site €2.50, dm/s/d incl breakfast €5.50/11/22; 🖳 🍷) Among the fields on the edge of the village but only a short walk from the otogar, this long-standing backpackers' haunt has recently been given a well-needed facelift. The four clean dorms have decent beds and good linen; unfortunately there are only three showers and two toilets to share among the 24 beds. The clean and well-kept private rooms have a variety of features; some have sitting areas, others have balconies and one even has a Jacuzzi. With the best swimming pool in Göreme, a bar-restaurant with pool table and very friendly staff, this place is very hard to beat.

Sarıhan Cave Hotel (☎ 271 2216; www.sarihancave hotel.com; Gafferli Mahallesi Ünlü Sokak 20; s €16.50-19.50, d €22-33.50 all incl breakfast; 🖳) The terraces outside all rooms in this large family-run place have fabulous views over the village. Though characterless, rooms are clean and comfortable and some have satellite TVs. It's a safe if uninspired choice.

Kemal's Guest House (☎ 271 2234; www.kemals guesthouse.com; Zeybek Sokak 3; dm €5.50, s/d with bathroom & breakfast €11/25) A few steps away from Walnut House, this guesthouse is run by an extremely friendly and knowledgeable Turkish-Dutch couple and has many fans. Though the flower-filled garden, laid-back atmosphere and restaurant (three-course meals €10) are strong features, the lack of views, spartan rooms and characterless décor are a bit disappointing.

Pashahan Hotel (☎ 271 2283; www.pashahan.com; Roma Kalesi Arkası 7; s/d incl breakfast €14/25; ☒ 🖳) What a find! This relatively new hotel is in an attractive old building just off the main strip. The owners run a nearby carpet shop, which explains the hotel's profusion of carpets, rugs and textiles. The overall impression is classy and atmospheric at the same time and the prices are so reasonable that we checked them three times just to make sure they

were correct. All eight rooms have polished floorboards, comfortable beds and excellent bathrooms – they're pretty much three-star standard. And as if this wasn't enough, there's also a fabulous roof terrace and restaurant with an excellent view.

Güven Cave Hotel (☎ 271 2374; www.guvencavehotel .com; Çakmaklı Sokak; dm/s/d incl breakfast €8.50/16.50/27.50; ☒ 🖳) The 10 standard rooms here are extremely attractive, with arched ceilings, plenty of light, polished boards, great views and tasteful modern décor. There are also three dorms in dark cave rooms. If the owners gave the same level of attention to the rooftop restaurant and terrace as they have to the rooms, this place would be one of Göreme's best budget options. As it is, it's still a good choice.

Elif Star Caves (☎ 271 2479; www.elifstar.com; Uzundere Caddesi; s €19.50-22, d €28-33.50 incl breakfast; 🖳) This homey place is run by a Turkish-English couple and offers excellent value for money. The seven cave rooms are attractive and comfortable in equal measure; they also get our vote for having the cleanest bathrooms in Cappadocia! Jacky was a chef in the UK and is known for her set three-course dinners (€8.50 to €11), which change according to guest requests and the availability of local produce. These are enjoyed in the tree-filled garden or in the downstairs lounge-restaurant.

Arch Palace (☎ 271 2575; www.archpalace.com; Gafferli Mahallesi Ünlü Sokak 14; s/d incl breakfast €16.50/33.50; ☒ 🖳) The Arch Palace has many fans, largely because owner Mustafa Yelkalan has a reputation for being a helpful and knowledgeable host, everything is squeaky clean and the rooftop terrace restaurant has sensational views. Unfortunately, carpets are worn, some rooms are cramped and there's not a lot of atmosphere. If prices were lower we'd be more enthusiastic in our recommendation.

Village Cave House Hotel (☎ 271 2182; www .villagecavehouse.com; Gafferli Mahallesi Ünlü Sokak; s/d €16.50/36.50; 🖳) Another hotel that seems to be pricing itself out of the competitive local market, the Village House offers nine impeccably clean rooms carved into the cliff. All have extremely comfortable beds and basic bathrooms (Rooms 2 and 3 are particularly attractive). There are impressive views from the terraces.

MIDRANGE
Kelebek Hotel & Cave Pension (☎ 271 2531; www .kelebekhotel.com; Aydınlı Mahallesi, Yavuz Sokak 1; standard

s/d €25/30 incl breakfast, deluxe s/d €35/40, ste €60-100; 🖳)
Ali Yavuz started a trend when he opened the Kelebek back in 1993. At that time Göreme was full of basic backpacker joints and had no boutique-style hotels. Setting out to change this, he adopted a winning formula that has since been copied by rivals throughout Cappadocia. It sounds simple: sympathetically restore a traditional local building (preferably with a fairy chimney or two), decorate the rooms in an attractive Anatolian style and make sure you have a roof terrace with view. In fact, it's not that simple – the reason why the Kelebek is the most successful hostelry in Göreme has more to do with its owner's local knowledge, professionalism and drive than its physical form. The rooms here are in two adjoining buildings: the attractive purpose-built hotel is set around a glorious garden and has plush suites; and the pension in the original main building offers a variety of room types and the best roof terrace in the village. Staff are extremely helpful and the prices are a real bargain.

Local Cave House Hotel (☎ 271 2171; www.local cavehouse.com; Gaferli Mahallesi Cevizler Sokak 11; s €25, d €30-40 incl breakfast; ⊠ 🖳 🖳) Another excellent midrange choice, the Local boasts what so many hotels in Göreme cannot: a swimming pool among the fairy chimneys. The 10 good-sized cave rooms are attractively decorated with Anatolian textiles and come with comfortable beds and clean, tiled bathrooms. There are two terraces with wonderful views as well as a glass-fronted lounge-restaurant overlooking the pool.

Canyon View Hotel (☎ 271 2333; www.canyonview hotel.com; s/d/ste €25/35-45/50 incl breakfast, child 6 & over/under 6 half-price/free; ⊠ 🖳) The fact that its views rival (but don't quite match) those at the nearby Kelebek and Fairy Chimneys Inn means that this relatively new hotel is destined for a long and prosperous life. Occupying a converted 9th-century cave church and Byzantine houses, it offers seven rooms with attractive décor; the more expensive of these come complete with balconies and/or Jacuzzis (Rooms 3 and 6 are the nicest). The hotel's multitiered terraces are particularly impressive.

Legend Cave Hotel (☎ 271 2059; www.legendcaveho tel.com; Aydınkırağı Sokak; s/d standard incl breakfast €26/52, s/d deluxe incl breakfast €38.50/77, r with terrace & breakfast €100; 🖳) The 19 rooms in this very comfortable midrange choice are well equipped,

featuring satellite TV, Jacuzzi and tea-and-coffee-making facilities. There are excellent family rooms (€78) and a few rooms with amazing views (ask for number 18, which is in the top of a fairy chimney and has a private terrace).

Fairy Chimney Inn (☎ 271 2655; www.fairychimney .com; Güvercinlik Sokak 3/7; s €36.50-55, d €50-83.50, ste €139; ⊠ 🖳) This fairy chimney high on the Göreme hill has been converted into a comfortable hotel by its owner, a German anthropologist who has ensured that his conversion is as respectful of the original fabric as possible. With his Turkish wife, he has created a wonderfully tranquil retreat on the village's highest point and can rightly claim to have the best views in the village. Rooms are relatively simple, featuring concrete floors covered in a profusion of rugs, lovely bathrooms and comfortable beds adorned with bright textiles. Added extras are the fully functioning *hamam* in a cave, communal lounge, home-cooked meals and glorious garden terrace.

Göreme House (☎ 271 2060; www.goremehouse .com; Eselli Mahallesi Sokak 47; s/d standard €50/60, s/d deluxe €62/72, ste €95 incl breakfast; ⊠ 🖳) We can't gush enough about this recently opened hotel. Owned and managed by a couple who have a long history of working in five-star boutique hotels in Europe, it offers levels of service and professionalism previously unheard of in Göreme. The attractively decorated rooms are blissfully comfortable, with great beds tea-and-coffee-making facilities and well-equipped bathrooms. Some rooms even have satellite TVs and a small sitting area. After a day's walking or sightseeing, guests can relax in the shade of a large mulberry tree in the courtyard or on the roof terrace, which has good views. Though everything here is impressive, it's the extras that make this place so great: breakfasts include fresh orange juice and *börek* (filled pastry) straight from the oven, olive oil soaps are in every bathroom, bottled water is provided at no charge in the rooms and small boutique touches such as a pillow menu have been introduced. Great stuff.

TOP END

Cappadocia Cave Suites (☎ 271 2800; www.cappadocia cavesuites.com; Gafferli Mahallesi Ünlü Sokak 19; s/d deluxe rooms incl breakfast €128/150, s/d ste incl breakfast €178-212/209-250; 🖳) Set high among the fairy chimneys, Göreme's long-established top-end favourite features a range of comfortable rooms, all of which come with satellite TV, large beds, attractive Anatolian-style decoration, tea-and-coffee-making facilities and minibar. Clearly spooked by the opening of the nearby and infinitely sleeker Anatolian Houses, the owners here have plans to build a pool, a *hamam* and 15 extra rooms.

Anatolian Houses Göreme (☎ 271 2463; www.anatolianhouses.com; Gafferli Mahallesi Ünlü Sokak; r standard €170, r deluxe €270-310, ste €390-700, all incl breakfast; ▢ ▣) This recently opened boutique hotel is swish. Very, very swish. Occupying a group of fairy chimneys, it took six years to build and no wonder. If you're not bowled over by features such as the spa, with its indoor/ outdoor swimming pool, *hamam,* sauna and wellness centre, you certainly will be by the hotel's sleek restaurant and extensive wine cellar. It's not just the common areas that are impressive here – all 19 rooms are exquisitely decorated with *objets d'art* and handmade textiles. This is as luxurious as Cappadocia gets, so if your credit card has some leverage we recommend booking the outrageously expensive Ottoman suite and living like a sultan during your stay.

Eating

Cappadocia Kebap Center (☎ 271 2682; Müze Caddesi; mains €2) This tiny and very friendly joint is a great place for a cheap and fast meal. You can enjoy a chicken döner kebap sandwich for a mere €1.50 or a spicy *acılı* kebap sandwich for €2.50. A plate of chips (€2) and a cold beer (€2) or freshly squeezed orange juice (€2) are the perfect accompaniments. There are four outdoor tables under the veranda and a few more inside. Recommended.

Cappadocia Patisserie (Belediye Caddesi; ⊙ 7.30am-midnight) Close to the otogar, this place brings in cakes, pastries, baklava and ice cream from Nevşehir and serves them with cappuccino (€2.50) or fresh orange juice (€2.50).

Nazar Börek (Müze Caddesi; börek €2.50, gözleme €2-3) If you're after a cheap and filling meal, you could do a lot worse than sample the *börek, gözleme* and *sosyete böregi* (stuffed spiral pastries served with yogurt and tomato sauce, €3) served at this simple place. Friendly staff and a pleasant outdoor eating area on the dry canal mean that this is a perennially popular option. There's often a tasty special of the day (eg chicken curry, Persian rice and a large salad, €4.50), but no alcohol is served.

Cappadocia Pide Salonu (☎ 271 2858; Hakki Paşa Meydanı; pide €2.50-4) Ask any local where the best pide in town is served and they will inevitably nominate this cavernous place near the tea shop (well, they will unless a family member owns or runs one of the town's other eateries). You can also get a cold beer here (€2.50).

Fırın Express (☎ 271 2745; Eski Belediye Yani Sokak; pide €2-3, pizza €4-5.50, claypot dishes €3-3.50) Set slightly back from the main strip, this simple place makes the most of its large wood oven. The pides are very good, and the claypot dishes such as *tavuk güvec* (chicken stew, €3) are extremely well priced. There's no alcohol, but customers are usually offered a complimentary tea at the end of their meal.

Silk Road Restaurant & Kebap House (Müze Caddesi; grills €3.50-5) This ramshackle place on the main strip is known for its cheap meals and laidback atmosphere. You can enjoy a set meal of kebap, chips and beer for €5 or grab a chicken kebap sandwich to go (€1.50).

Dibek (☎ 271 2209; Hakki Paşa Meydanı 1) This restaurant in a lovingly restored village house is the only place in Göreme where travellers can sample true home-style village cooking. For instance, although most of the eateries opposite the otogar offer *testi kebap* (meat and vegetables cooked in a sealed terracotta pot, which is broken at the table to serve), this is the only place where you must give the requisite five hours' notice before eating, so that the dish can be authentically slow-cooked in a deep oven. If you can't do this, don't fear – there are other village specialities on the menu, including *kurufasulye* (white beans with sundried lamb and tomato sauce, €3) and *saç tava* (cubed lamb with tomatoes, peppers and garlic, €5.50). Seating is on cushions around brass tables and you can even sample wine made by the owners (€3.50).

Göreme Restaurant (☎ 271 2183; Müze Caddesi 18, meze €2-2.50, mains €4-7) The live Turkish music played here every night tends to lure diners off the comfortable floor cushions and onto the impromptu dance floor around the low brass tables. The food is nothing special, but it's well priced and the menu includes 'world kitchen' items such as green curry chicken (€5.50), stir-fried noodles with vegetables (€4) and felafel sandwiches (€3.50). Beer and rakı (aniseed brandy) flow freely and service is good.

Local Restaurant (☎ 271 2629; Müze Caddesi 38, mains €4.50-9) At the start of the road to the Open-Air Museum, the Local has recently been renovated and now comes close to rivalling A'laturca and the Orient for the tag of Göreme's best eatery. There's an elegant dining room as well as an outdoor terrace with comfortable cane furniture. Vegetarians will be particularly enamoured of the menu here – it features delectable Turkish dishes such as zucchini with garlic yogurt (€4.50) as well as Asian favourites such as stir-fried vegetables (€5.50). All ingredients are fresh, prices are extremely reasonable and service is attentive.

A'laturca (☎ 271 2882; Müze Caddesi; mains €5-10) Style meets substance at this elegant eatery. The menu here has been thoughtfully and creatively designed and the food is exceptionally well prepared. We enjoyed the classic meze selection (€6.50) and were very impressed by the succulent A'laturca-style lamb şiş kebap (€9.50) served on a perfectly cooked ratatouille. Other visits have introduced us to the delights of the chicken şiş kebap and the wickedly rich *Kayseri mantısı* (ravioli with garlic yogurt and spices, €4.50). The restaurant has a number of eating areas, the most popular of which are the upstairs terrace and the quirky downstairs garden with its brightly coloured beanbag seating. Highly recommended.

Orient Restaurant (☎ 271 2346; Adnan Menderes Caddesi; meze €3-7, mains €12.50) One of Göreme's best eating options, the Orient has an attractive terrace and a stylish dining room, both are extremely comfortable and provide the perfect setting in which to sample outstanding meat dishes. Try the marble steak, which is theatrically served on a sizzling marble slab and is wonderfully tender, or the perfectly cooked rack of lamb. Though vegetarians won't find much joy on the mains menu, they'll be happy with the plethora of vegetarian meze on offer. Those on a budget may want to sample the fixed menu, which offers four courses for a bargain basement €8.50.

Most of Göreme's pensions provide good, cheap meals and serve wine and beer; you'll often eat as well in them as in the restaurants around town. If you're after belly fuel and don't really care about the quality, there's a swathe of cheapish restaurants along Müze Cadessi opposite the otogar. These include **SOS & Sultan Restaurant & Café** (☎ 271 2872; Müze Caddesi; pide €3, mains €4.50-7) and **Mercan** (☎ 271 2476; Müze Caddesi; pide €3-3.50, mains €4.50-7). All are geared to the bus-tour trade, but they have pleasant terraces where you can sit and eat while gazing over the town.

Drinking & Entertainment

Most of the village's watering holes are open from noon till late.

Red Red Wine House (☎ 0532 657 7573; Müze Caddesi; beer €3, glass of wine €3-5.50) Göreme's most atmospheric bar is a wonderful place to while away an hour or two. An intimate candlelit space with a low arched ceiling, it has mood lighting, an open fireplace for chilly evenings and an impressive Cappadocian wine list. We guarantee that you'll enjoy relaxing over a drink and a nargileh (water pipe) – free if you've bought a few drinks, €3.50 otherwise – while listening to the sounds of live guitar music.

Flintstones Cave Bar (Müze Caddesi; beer €2.50) At the start of the Open-Air Museum road, this long-time backpackers' favourite is cut right into the rock face and really fires up in season. It has a terrace with impressive views where you can enjoy a nargileh (€3), and hosts occasional live music.

Pacha Bar (Müze Caddesi; beer €2.50) We don't know whether to be amused or disapproving of the Pacha Bar's advertising slogan, which urges customers to 'get their rocks off'. Behind the otogar, it has sultry lighting, the mandatory disco ball and plenty of dark corners. It also has a pool table and big-screen TV.

Fat Boys (☎ 0535 386 4484; beer €2.50; ☾ 24hr) This place labours under the weight of an unfortunate name and equally unfortunate barn-like interior. It's just around the corner from the otogar, proving our theory that places so located are usually rough as guts.

Club Libra (☎ 271 2909; www.librabar.com; beer €2.50; ☒) A glitzy place with three levels of dance floors and bars, Club Libra caters mainly to Turks but tries to get travellers (especially females) in by waiving the usual entrance fee. There are belly dancers on Friday and Saturday nights.

Getting There & Away

For details of shuttle bus services between Kayseri airport and Göreme see p494.

There are daily long-distance buses to all sorts of places from Göreme's otogar, although normally you're ferried to Nevşehir otogar to pick up the main service (which can add nearly an hour to your travelling time). See p494 for the bus services that connect Göreme with nearby villages.

Details of some useful long-distance daily services from Göreme are listed in the table, below. Note that the morning bus to İstanbul goes via Ankara, so takes one hour longer than the evening bus.

SERVICES FROM GÖREME'S OTOGAR

Destination	Fare	Duration	Frequency (per day)
Adana	€7	5hr	several evening only
Aksaray	€4	1½hr	frequent morning & evening
Ankara	€8.50	4½hr	frequent
Antalya	€14-16.50	9hr	a few morning & evening
Çanakkale	€27.50	16hr	2 evening only
Denizli (for Pamukkale)	€14-19.50	11hr	a few evening only
Fethiye	€19.50-25	14hr	2 evening only
İstanbul	€17-22	11-12hr	several morning & evening
İzmir & Selçuk	€19.50-25	11½hr	2 evening only
Kayseri	€4	1½hr	hourly morning, afternoon & evening
Kayseri airport	€11	1½hr	2 late afternoon & early evening
Konya	€8.50	3hr	several morning & evening
Marmaris/ Bodrum	€22	13hr	2 evening only

Getting Around

There are several places to hire mountain bikes, scooters, quads and cars, including **Hitchhiker** (☎ 271 2169; www.cappadociahitchhiker .com; T Ozal Meydanı), **Öz Cappadocia Tour** (☎ 271 2159; www.ozcappadocia.com; T Ozal Meydanı) and **Motodocia** (☎ 271 2517), all of which are located close to the otogar. It pays to shop around, as prices vary quite dramatically. As a rule, mountain bikes cost between €5 and €5.50 for four hours; mopeds and scooters go for €14 to €25 for four hours; and those ridiculous quads cost €55 for four hours (the agencies don't offer insurance for these). A manual Renault Clio car costs €50 per day if hired through Öz Cappadocia and a Ford Fiesta costs €42 per day if hired through Motodocia. Motodocia also has automatic cars (a Fiat Palio costs €47.50 per day). You'll need to leave your passport as a security deposit when hiring all of the bikes, scooters and quads.

Since there are no petrol stations in Göreme and the rental companies will hike petrol prices, fill up your tank in Nevşehir, Avanos or Ürgüp before returning the vehicle.

UÇHİSAR
☎ 0384 / pop 6350

If coming east from Nevşehir, the panorama of Cappadocia begins to unfold: across the sandy landscape, distant fairy chimneys and valleys with undulating walls of soft, volcanic ash appear. In the distance, the gigantic snow-capped summit of volcanic **Erciyes Dağı** (Mt Erciyes; 3916m) floats above a layer of cloud, providing a fantastic backdrop.

After 8km you come to the small village of Uçhisar, which is dominated by its rock castle. Especially popular with French tourists, old Uçhisar is more tranquil than Göreme and is worth considering as an alternative base for exploring Cappadocia.

There's a Türkıye Bankası ATM in a booth on the main square and a PTT close by.

Watching the sun set over the Rose and Pigeon Valleys from the wonderful vantage point of **Uçhisar Castle** (Uçhisar Kalesi; admission €1.50; 8.30am-7pm) is a popular activity. A tall volcanic rock outcrop riddled with tunnels and windows, the castle is visible for miles around. Now a tourist attraction complete with tacky souvenir stands at its entrance, it provides panoramic views of the Cappadocian valleys and countryside. Unfortunately, many of the bus groups who visit here leave their rubbish, which diminishes the experience considerably. The lack of barriers means that you should be very careful when here – a European photographer recently died when he fell over the edge after stepping back to get a good shot.

There are some excellent **hiking** possibilities around Uçhisar; see the boxed text on p502.

Sleeping

Uçhisar has three excellent budget pensions, at least one top-notch midrange choice and a growing number of top-end boutique hotels.

BUDGET
Erciyes Pension (☎ 219 2090; www.erciyespension.com; Ürgüp Caddesi 8; s/d incl breakfast €11/22) This friendly, family-run place is just near the PTT. It offers clean old-fashioned rooms, the best of which are at the front of the house and have balconies. The owners grow fruit and vegetables

in the large garden and use them to prepare home-cooked dinners (€8).

Kilim Pansiyon (☎ 219 2774; www.sisik.com in Turkish; Eski Göreme Yolu; s/d incl breakfast €12.50/25) Though there are three good budget sleeping options in Uçhisar, this is the only one with a view. And oh what a view! You'll really enjoy relaxing on the rooftop terrace here, and you'll be equally happy with the rooms, which are simply but attractively decorated. Ask for one upstairs, as these have more light than the downstairs alternatives. There's also an atmospheric dining room and a vine-shaded courtyard. Great value.

La Maison du Rêve (☎ 219 2199; www.lamaisondureve.com; Tekelli Mahallesi 17; s/d incl breakfast €15-18/25-29; 🖳) Teetering on the edge of a high cliff and enjoying spectacular views as a result, 'Dream House' is a veritable ant colony of a hotel, with 35 simple rooms over three floors. The best of these are on the top floor and have attached terraces. There's a laid-back restaurant (mains €4.50 to €5.50) and the owners rent out scooters (€22 per day) and mountain bikes (€11 per day).

Anatolia Pension (☎ 219 2339; www.anatoliapension.com in French; s/d incl breakfast €20/30; 🗙 🖳) Occupying a sturdy stone house on the main street, this excellent pension has 30 light-filled rooms with comfortable beds, clean linen and extremely clean bathrooms. It's notable for offering midrange facilities for budget prices. Evening meals are available on request (€10).

MIDRANGE

Les Terrasses d'Uçhisar (☎ 219 2792; www.terrassespension.com; Eski Göreme Yolu; s/d/ste incl breakfast €28/32/72; 🖳) The splendid location of this relaxed French-owned place is its best asset. Rooms are arched or in caves and all feature simple but stylish decoration; those upstairs have absolutely fabulous views. There's a great terrace for soaking up the views in the evening, and a well-regarded restaurant. And if that wasn't enough, the owner even offers a free hike in the valley every morning.

Ahbap Konağı (☎ 219 3020; www.ahbapkonagi.com; Karlık Mahallesi; s/d/ste incl breakfast €65/90/120; 🗙 🖳 🕿) Owned by a friendly Turkish-French couple, the Ahbap Konağı has the best view of the citadel in town. The rooms are large and cheerful, but not at all posh; ask for one with a balcony. The terrace bar is a plus.

TOP END

Villa Cappadocia (☎ 219 3133; www.villacappadocia.com; Kayabaşı Sokak 18; s/d €50/65-75 incl breakfast; 🗙) This small and immensely comfortable hotel takes good advantage of its spectacular view of Pigeon Valley. With only 10 rooms, it has a tranquil atmosphere and is designed to give guests as relaxed a holiday as possible. The pick of the rooms is the Honeymoon Room (€105), which has a Jacuzzi and a private terrace with magnificent view. There's a posh restaurant (mains €4.50 to €8.50), a garden and two splendid terraces that are perfect spots for a sunset drink.

Museum Hotel (☎ 219 2220; www.museum-hotel.com; Tekeli Mahallesi 1; d €94-141, ste €180-705, all incl breakfast; 🖳 🕿) Ooh la la! This exquisitely decorated boutique hotel is one of Cappadocia's best, featuring 26 luxe rooms and truly magnificent common areas. Standard rooms come complete with brass beds, rich rugs and attractive textiles, and the opulent suites (some in caves) have to be seen to be believed. The mosaic-adorned infinity pool, stylish restaurant (mains €8.50 to €14) and panoramic rooftop terrace are equally impressive. In all, this is an exceptionally fine hotel that charges reasonable prices for its standard rooms and offers true luxury to those who can afford one of the suites.

Karlık Evi (☎ 219 2995; www.karlikevi.com; Karlık Mahallesi; s/d €100/150; 🕿) Once a former hospital, this retreat offers 20 spacious rooms, some with private balcony or terrace. The atmosphere is of discreet elegance, and the overall style is best described as 'rustic chic'. Facilities are excellent: there's a restaurant, a *hamam*, a garden and a roof terrace; one suite is even set up for disabled access. Guests can also enjoy massages or book into meditation, yoga and cooking courses.

Les Maisons de Cappadoce (☎ 219 2813; www.cappadoce.com; Belediye Meydanı 24; studios €110-150, villas €180-320, all incl breakfast) When French architect Jacques Avizou opened his first two rental villas 14 years ago, he had no inkling that they would be the first in an empire that now numbers 12 and is still expanding. There's no secret as to why Les Maisons de Cappadoce is so successful: it offers stylish and supremely comfortable accommodation that allows maximum independence and privacy while still offering services such as daily cleaning and breakfast. Four of the properties are studios perfect for a romantic getaway, the others are well-equipped houses that can accommodate up to seven people. The reception is in an office in the main square.

Eating

Sakirin Yeri Pide Salonu (☎ 219 2576; pide €2-3) On the main street just before the main square, this simple place is a decent option if you're after a cheap and quick lunch.

House of Memories (☎ 219 2947; Eski Göreme Yolu 41; meze €2, mains €4-5) Despite the name, the food here isn't particularly memorable. Seating is in the kilim-strewn downstairs dining room or on the ramshackle but undeniably welcoming upstairs terrace, which enjoys a good view. The menu features Turkish staples, a beer costs €2.50 and service is very friendly.

Le Mouton Rouge (☎ 219 3000; Belediye Meydanı; mains €4-5.50) Living up to Uçhisar's reputation as Cappadocia's 'Petite France', this large courtyard restaurant-bar on the main square has a menu replete with French dishes and a cheerful bistro ambience.

Center Café & Restaurant (☎ 219 3117; Belediye Meydanı; mains €5.50) Another outdoor eatery on the main square, the Centre has tables dotted around a shady but slightly scruffy garden. Locals enjoy the kebaps and absolutely swear by the *patlican salatası* (eggplant salad, €4.50). A beer costs €3.

Les Terrasses d'Uçhisar (☎ 219 2792; www.terrasses pension.com; Eski Göreme Yolu; dinner €9) This cosy bar-restaurant in the pension of the same name is justly popular for its home-cooked meals. You can order à la carte or sign up for the well-priced set menu, which offers four courses for €9.50. The menu features Turkish dishes such as *saç tava* (€5) and classic French alternatives such as *filet de boeuf avec sauce poivre* (beef fillet with pepper sauce, €8). Nonguests are welcome, but should book ahead.

Elai (☎ 219 3181; www.elairestaurant.com; Eski Göreme Yolu 61; mains €10-12.50) This stylish place is owned and managed by Özge Bozunoğulları, who worked for more than a decade for Club Med resorts around the world, and he has implemented the many secrets he learned about five-star service and dining here. Guests can kick off with a drink enjoyed on the terrace with its magnificent view before moving into the elegant restaurant to sample beautifully prepared dishes such as crispy *köfte* with a thin pastry crust and demiglace sauce (€10). Dishes travel around the world (starters include Thai beef salad, for instance) but really shine when they are Turkish in inspiration.

> ### RUDE BOYS
>
> The *peribacalar* (fairy chimneys) that have made Cappadocia so famous were formed when erosion wiped out the lava covering the tuff (consolidated volcanic ash), leaving behind isolated pinnacles. They can reach a height of up to 40m, have conical shapes and are topped with caps of harder rock resting on pillars of softer rock. Depending on your perspective, they look like giant phalluses or outsized mushrooms. The villagers call them simply *kalelar* (castles).

Getting There & Away

For details of shuttle bus services between Kayseri airport and Uçhisar see p494.

Kapadokya Bus Company has an office in the main square. You'll probably end up being taken to Göreme in a *servis* to pick up onward connections to destinations throughout Turkey. See p508 for details.

Half-hourly buses travel between Nevşehir, Uçhisar (the main highway), Göreme, Çavuşin and Avanos (€0.50, every hour from 7am to 6pm in summer, every two hours in winter). There's also an Uçhisar *belediye* (local council) dolmuş that runs between Nevşehir and a stop behind the Center Café & Restaurant (€0.80, every 30 minutes from 7.30am to 6.30pm Monday to Friday, every hour on weekends).

ÇAVUŞIN
☎ 0384

Midway between Göreme and Avanos is sleepy little Çavuşin. If you're after an authentic village experience, this place could be for you.

On the highway you'll find the **Çavuşin Church** (Big Pigeon House Church; admission €3; ⏰ 8.30am-5pm), which is accessed via a steep and rickety iron stairway. The church is home to some fine frescoes. Once you've visited here, walk up the hill through the new part of the village and continue past the main square to find the old part of Çavuşin (you'll know you've found it when you see the souvenir stands). Here you can explore a steep and labyrinthine complex of abandoned houses cut into a steep rock face, as well as one of the oldest churches in Cappadocia, the **Church of John the Baptist**, which is located towards the top of the cliff here.

Çavuşin is the starting point for **scenic hikes** through the Güllüdere Vadisi (Rose Valley) and Kızılçukur (Red Gulch), to the east of the village. You can even go as far as the Zindanönü viewpoint (6.5km), then walk out to the Ürgüp–Ortahisar road and catch a dolmuş back to your base.

There is no bank or ATM in the village, but there are three internet cafés, including **Cave House Net C@fe** (per hr €0.50, ☯ 8am-midnight) in the main square.

Tours

Mephisto Voyage (☎ 532 7070; www.mephistovoyage .com) is based at the İn Pension and has a very good reputation. It's been operating for over a decade and offers a range of packages including eight-day treks around Cappadocia and 14-day treks around Cappadocia and the Taurus Mountains. It also offers special tours for mobility-impaired people, utilising the Joelette system.

Sleeping & Eating

Although Çavuşin has a growing number of hotels and pensions, there are no restaurants worth recommending – you'll need to eat in your pension, subject yourself to the dodgy-looking cafés around the main square or make your way to Göreme for meals.

Panorama Pansion (☎ 532 7002; ozi_rodi@hotmail .com; s/d incl breakfast €8.50/17) In a family house, this basic option offers neat rooms with hard beds; two have their own (cramped) bathrooms and the others share very clean facilities. It has a *çay bahçesi* (tea garden) in its front garden.

Green Motel (☎ 532 7050; Mehmet@motelgreen.com; camp site €4.50, s/d incl breakfast €11/22) Our favourite of the Çavuşin accommodation options, this friendly place is set amid farmland and offers simple rooms with white walls, comfortable beds, crisp linen and very clean bathrooms. There's a dining room; an extensive garden; a large terrace; and a charming lounge with stone floor, Turkish seating and a profusion of rugs.

İn Pension (☎ 532 7070; www.pensionincappadocia .com; d incl breakfast €15-25; 💻) Right on the main square, this converted village house is nothing flash but it's worth considering solely due to the fact its owner, Ahmet Kılınç, is a mine of local information and one of the most highly regarded trekking guides in Cappadocia. The rooms themselves differ in quality; we suggest

opting for one of the four upstairs rooms with private bathroom. Meals are available for €5.50.

Village Cave Hotel (☎ 532 7197; www.thevillagecave .com; s €40-55, d €70-120, all incl breakfast) Overlooking the old village, this is Çavuşin's only upmarket hotel. It boasts a superb location and extremely attractive rooms, some of which are arched and some rock-cut.

Getting There & Away

See p494 for information about the bus services that connect Çavuşin with nearby villages.

ZELVE

The road between Çavuşin and Avanos passes a turn-off to the **Zelve Open-Air Museum** (admission €3; ☯ 8.30am-7pm Apr-Oct, 8.30am-5.30pm Nov-Mar), where three valleys of abandoned homes and churches converge.

Zelve was a monastic retreat from the 9th to the 13th centuries. It was inhabited until 1952, when the valley was deemed too dangerous to live in any longer and the villagers were resettled a few kilometres away in Aktepe, also known as Yeni Zelve (New Zelve). There's a small, unadorned, rock-cut **mosque** and an old *değirmen* (mill) here, remnants of Zelve village life.

Arguably the two most interesting churches are also the easiest to find – they're on the left soon after the entrance. The **Balıklı Kilise** (Fish Church) has fish figuring in one of its primitive paintings. Adjoining it is the more impressive **Üzümlü Kilise** (Grape Church), with obvious bunches of grapes. What's left of the **Geyikli Kilise** (Church with Deer) and the **Yazılılık Kilise** (Church with Scriptures) is also worth seeing.

In general, Zelve doesn't have as many impressive painted churches as Göreme's Open-Air Museum. Still, you can while away several happy hours exploring tunnels and houses and gazing on gorgeous vistas. Unfortunately, erosion continues to eat into the valley structures and some parts may be closed because of the danger of collapse, while others may require scrambling and ladders.

There are cafés and *çay bahçesi* (tea gardens) in the car park outside.

At **Paşabağı**, halfway along the turn-off road to Zelve, a cluster of fairy chimneys, one of them 'three-headed', stands within a vineyard near a mess of souvenir stalls. This highly photogenic spot is a popular place to come to watch the sunset.

Getting There & Away

The hourly buses running between Ürgüp, Göreme, Çavuşin and Avanos (see p494) will stop at Zelve on request. If you're coming from Ürgüp, Göreme or Çavuşin and tell the driver that you want to go to Zelve, the bus will turn off the highway past Çavuşin, pass Paşabağı, let you off at Zelve and then go up to Aktepe and on to Avanos. If no-one wants Zelve, the bus will not make this detour. Getting a bus from Zelve is more difficult; you may have to walk the 3.5km from the site to the main highway, from where you can flag down a bus going towards either Göreme or Avanos.

DEVRENT VALLEY

From Zelve, go about 200m back down the access road to where the road forks and take the right road marked for Ürgüp. After about 2km you'll come to the village of **Aktepe**

CAPPADOCIA FROM ABOVE

If you've never taken a flight in a hot-air balloon, Cappadocia is one of the best places in the world to try it. Flight conditions are especially favourable here, with balloons operating most mornings from the beginning of April to the end of November. It's a truly magical experience and many travellers judge it to be the highlight of their trip.

Flights take place at dawn. The reputable companies have an unwritten agreement that they will only offer one early flight per day due to the fact that the winds can become unreliable and potentially dangerous later in the morning. Transport to and from your hotel to the balloon launch site is included in the hefty price, as is a champagne toast.

Despite the fact that there is an ever-increasing number of ballooning companies in Cappadocia, increased competition hasn't led to price discounting. This is because the balloon companies offer large commissions to the hotels and tour agencies who sell their flights, and don't want to further erode their profits by discounting flights sold direct to customers. Some companies will give a €10 discount for cash payments or a slightly larger discount for direct online bookings, but that's about as far as the reputable outfits will go.

You'll quickly realise that there's a fair amount of hot air between the operators about who is and isn't inexperienced, ill-equipped, underinsured and underlicensed. Be aware that hot-air ballooning is potentially dangerous. It's your responsibility to check the credentials of your chosen tour operator carefully and make sure that your pilot is experienced and savvy – even if it means asking to see their licences and logbooks. And don't pick the cheapest operator if it means they might be taking short cuts with safety (ie operating two flights per day).

It's important to note that the balloons travel with the wind, and that the companies can't ensure a particular flight path on a particular day. All companies try to fly over the fairy chimneys, but sometimes – albeit rarely – the wind doesn't allow this. Occasionally, unfavourable weather conditions mean that the pilot will cancel the flight for the day for safety reasons; if this happens you'll be offered a flight on the next day or will have your payment refunded.

All passengers should take a warm jumper or jacket and women should wear flat shoes and pants. Children under seven and adults over 70 will not be taken up by most companies.

The following agencies have good credentials:

Göreme Balloons (☎ 0384-341 5662; www.goremeballoons.com; Kayseri Caddesi Altıkapılı Mahallesi 13, Ürgüp) This long-running and highly regarded outfit is based in Ürgüp and offers a deluxe flight (€230, 1½ hours, eight to 11 passengers) and a standard flight (€160, one hour, 16 to 21 passengers).

Kapadokya Balloons (☎ 0384-271 2442; www.kapadokyaballoons.com; Adnan Menderes Caddesi, Göreme) The most respected company in the region, Kapadokya is run by Kaili and Lars, who have been operating hot-air balloons for over 20 years. They speak English, French, Swedish and German, and their pilots are excellent. On offer are a classic flight (€230, 1¾ hours, 10 passengers) and a sponsored balloon flight (€160, one hour, 20 passengers).

Sultan Balloons (☎ 0533 239 3788; www.sultanballoons.com) This new company is run by Ismail Keremoglu, who is a former chief pilot of Göreme Balloons. It offers a standard flight (€160, one hour, 12 to 18 passengers) and will discount this to €135 if you book online. Sultan is the only company to offer VIP flights for two passengers in a small balloon (€600 for two, 1¼ hours).

(Yeni Zelve). Bear right, follow the Ürgüp road uphill and, after less than 2km, you'll find yourself in the stunning Devrent Valley, sometimes known as the Valley of Fairy Chimneys.

Though many Cappadocian valleys boast collections of strange volcanic cones, these are the best formed and most thickly clustered. Most of the rosy rock cones are topped by flattish, darker stones of harder rock that sheltered the cones from the rain until all the surrounding rock was eaten away, a process known as differential erosion.

If you continue to the top of the ridge, you'll reach the Avanos–Ürgüp road, with Avanos to the left and Ürgüp to the right.

AVANOS

☎ 0384 / pop 13,000 / elevation 910m

The red clay for which Avanos is famed comes from the Kızılırmak (Red River), which runs through its centre. For centuries, local potters have used it to make the simple pots that today still form the backbone of the local economy. Visitors have been coming here since Roman times (Avanos was once the Roman city of Venasa), but quite frankly we don't see the attraction of this place. Its setting is bland indeed when compared with those of Ürgüp, Göreme and Uçhisar, and it doesn't have any attractions other than the pottery workshops to distract attention from this fact. Some may choose to stay in Avanos as it is a convenient base for exploration.

Orientation & Information

Most of the town is on the northern bank of the river, with Atatürk Caddesi providing the main thoroughfare. Although there is an otogar south of the river, all dolmuşes for the local area stop outside the PTT, on Atatürk Caddesi across from the main square. The **tourist office** (☎ 511 4360; Atatürk Caddesi; ☯ 8am-5.30pm Apr-Oct, 8am-5pm Nov-Mar) is on the main street. It can supply a basic map of the town, but its staff members don't speak English. You'll find several banks with ATMs on or around the main square.

To check your email head to the **Hemi Internet Café** (Uğur Mumcu Caddesi; per hr €1; ☯ 8am-midnight).

Be warned that Avanos has one of the loudest (and least tuneful) muezzins we have ever heard. Early mornings can be traumatic as a result.

Sights & Activities

Tour groups tend to find themselves shopping for pots in vast warehouses on the outskirts of town. It's much more enjoyable (and infinitely cheaper) to patronise one of the smaller **pottery workshops** right in town, most of which will happily show you how to throw a pot or two. These are located in the small streets around the main square and in the group of shops opposite the PTT.

If you fancy horse-riding, **Akhal-Teke** (☎ 511 5171; www.akhal-tekehorsecenter.com; Camikebir Mahallesi, Kadı Sokak 1) and Kirkit Voyage (below) organise guided half-day horse-riding treks in the area. These range in price from €30 per person for two hours to €40 for a full day.

Avanos is a base for rafting trips in Cappadocia. **Medraft** (☎ 213 3948; www.cappadociarafting .com) offers a variety of one-, two-, three- or four-day trips on the Kızılırmak and Zamantı Rivers (Grades 2 to 5) ranging in price from €65 to €585 per person including all equipment, guides, meals and camping.

Tours

Kirkit Voyage (☎ 511 3259; www.kirkit.com; Atatürk Caddesi 50) has an excellent reputation. It can arrange walking, biking, canoeing, horse-riding and snowshoe trips, as well as the more-usual guided tours around Cappadocia. It's also an agency for Onur Air and Pegasus Airlines.

Sleeping

Ada Camping (☎ 511 2429; www.adacampingavanos.com; Jan Zakari Caddesi 20; camp sites €5.50 per person incl electri city; ☒) This large camping ground, 1km west of the otogar, boasts a superb setting close to the river. There's lots of shade and grass, clean bathrooms, a restaurant and an enormous swimming pool.

Kirkit Pension (☎ 511 3148; www.kirkit.com; Atatürk Caddesi; s/d incl breakfast €19/25; ☐) Set in converted old stone houses, this long-running pension is known throughout Cappadocia for its congenial, laidback atmosphere. The simple rooms are decorated with kilims, historical photographs of the region and *suzani* (Uzbek bedspreads) – some are a bit cramped, so ask to see a few before checking in. Guests can enjoy a home-cooked local meal (€5 for dinner) in the vaulted restaurant or pleasant courtyard. Good value.

Duru Motel (☎ 511 2402; www.duruhotel.com; Yukarı Mahallesi; s/d incl breakfast €17/28; ☐) Perched high above the town (it's one hell of a walk), this

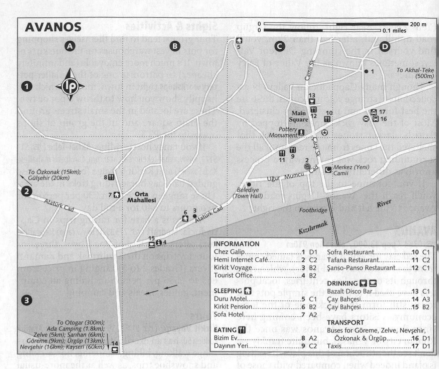

AVANOS

0 — 200 m
0 — 0.1 miles

INFORMATION	
Chez Galip	1 D1
Hemi Internet Café	2 C2
Kirkit Voyage	3 B2
Tourist Office	4 B2

SLEEPING	
Duru Motel	5 C1
Kirkit Pension	6 B2
Sofa Hotel	7 A2

EATING	
Bizim Ev	8 A2
Dayının Yeri	9 C2

Sofra Restaurant	10 C1
Tafana Restaurant	11 C2
Şanso-Panso Restaurant	12 C1

DRINKING	
Bazalt Disco Bar	13 C1
Çay Bahçesi	14 A3
Çay Bahçesi	15 B2

TRANSPORT	
Buses for Göreme, Zelve, Nevşehir,	
Özkonak & Ürgüp	16 D1
Taxis	17 D1

clean and simple place offers two types of rooms. Those in the new wing are light and comfortable, but lack atmosphere; the cheaper alternatives in the original (but still modern) building offer dodgy beds, worn carpet and basic bathrooms. The real drawcards here are the grassy terrace and the exceptional views over Avanos.

Sofa Hotel (☎ 511 5186; www.sofa-hotel.com; Orta Mahallesi Baklacı Sokak 13; s/d incl breakfast €25/40; ☒) This excellent midrange choice consists of 35 rooms in 15 stone houses. The best rooms are in the new 'built-to-look-old' wing near the reception area; most of these have large modern bathrooms, satellite TV and tea-and-coffee making facilities. Though comfort is a priority here, the place has more than its fair share of charm courtesy of the many rugs, pictures, ceramics and knick-knacks scattered throughout its rooms, courtyard and restaurants.

Eating

Şanso-Panso Restaurant (mains €2-4) This low-key eatery on the main square is a great spot to have a beer (€2) and people-watch. Given

Avanos' pottery trade, it's hardly surprising that the speciality is *güveç* (beef stew with potatoes, tomatoes, garlic, paprika and cumin, baked in a clay pot; €3.50). Tea costs €0.55 and a fresh orange juice will set you back a mere €1.

Dayının Yeri (☎ 511 6840; Atatürk Caddesi 23; mains €2-5) The shiny and modern Dayının Yeri is one of the best *ocakbaşıs* (grill restaurants) in Cappadocia and should be an essential stop on any visit to Avanos. The kebaps are sensational and the pide is just as good. Don't even *think* of leaving without sampling the freshly prepared *künefe* (strands of cooked batter over a creamy sweet cheese base baked in syrup; €2). No alcohol is served.

Tafana Restaurant (Atatürk Caddesi; mains €2-5) This cluttered but reasonably attractive eatery on the main street is nowhere near as impressive as Dayının Yeri, but is a decent fall-back option if one is needed. It specialises in pide (€3 to €5.50), which is cooked in a wood-fired oven. The beer here is cheap (€2).

Sofra Restaurant (☎ 511 4324; Hükümet Konağı Karşısı; grills €3.50-4.50) A favourite with the tour groups that descend on Avanos every weekend

CAPPADOCIA

during summer, Sofra has a welcoming feel and its cheerful rear dining room is a pleasant place to sample good-quality grills. Best of all, you can order a beer (€2.50) to accompany your kebap.

Bizim Ev (Our House; ☎ 511 5525; Orta Mahallesi Baklacı Sokak 1; meze €1.50-5, mains €4-6) This welcoming family-run restaurant is about as swish as dining gets in Avanos. Local specialities such as fresh trout (€4.50) and *manti* (Turkish ravioli) (€4) are served in the elegant air-conditioned dining room or on the rooftop terrace. A beer costs €3.

Drinking

If you're keen to linger over a tea and nargileh, try the *çay bahçesi* adjoining the tourist office, which is as welcoming to women as it is to men, or the large riverside *çay bahçesi* in front of the pottery workshops on the southwestern side of the bridge.

There are a few bars dotted along Atatürk Caddesi and around the main square, but most are geared towards locals and don't make visitors (particularly females) feel very welcome. The only one we'd really recommend is **Bazalt Disco Bar** (Yukarı Mahallesi; ☽ Tue-Sun), which hosts live music and has a friendly vibe.

Getting There & Around

For details of shuttle bus services between Kayseri airport and Avanos see p494.

There are two bus routes from Avanos to Nevşehir: one leaves every 30 minutes and goes direct and the other leaves every hour and travels via Göreme and Çavuşin. Both services operate from 7am to 7pm and charge €1.50 per ticket. There's also an hourly *belediye* bus running from Avanos to Nevşehir via Çavuşin (10 minutes), Göreme (15 minutes) and Uçhisar (30 minutes). It operates from 7.10am to 6pm and costs between €0.40 and €1.10 depending on where you get on and off.

See p494 for details of the Belediye Bus Corp service between Ürgüp and Avanos.

Kirkit Voyage (p513) hires out mountain bikes for €11 per day.

AROUND AVANOS
Sarıhan

Built in 1249, the Sarıhan (Yellow Caravanserai), 6km east of Avanos, has an elaborate gateway with a small mosque above it –

it's one of the best of the remaining Seljuk caravanserais.

The caravanserai was restored in the late 1980s. These days it serves as a cultural centre, staging a 45-minute **whirling dervish sema** (☎ 511 3795; admission €20-25; ☽ 9.30pm Apr-Oct, 8.30pm Nov-Mar). Though the setting is extremely atmospheric, the *sema* (ceremony) here is nowhere near as impressive as those staged at the Mevlevi Monastery in Istanbul's Beyoğlu (see p119). If you've seen that one you should probably give this one a miss. You must book ahead – most of the pensions in Göreme, Ürgüp, Avanos or Uçhisar will arrange this for you. Note that the price varies according to how much commission your tour agent or pension is skimming off the top.

GETTING THERE & AWAY

Getting to the Sarıhan without your own transport is difficult, as there are no dolmuşes and few vehicles with which to hitch a ride. An Avanos taxi driver will probably want around €11 to take you there and back, including waiting time.

Özkonak Underground City

About 15km north of Avanos, the village of Özkonak hosts a smaller version of the underground cities of Kaymaklı and Derinkuyu (see the boxed text, p528), with the same wine reservoirs, rolling stone doors etc. **Özkonak underground city** (admission €3; ☽ 8.30am-7pm Jun-Sep, 8.30am-5.30pm Oct-May) is neither as dramatic nor as impressive as the larger ones, but is much less crowded.

The easiest way to get there is by dolmuş from Avanos (€1, 30 minutes), but there are few services on weekends. Ask to be let off for the *yeraltı şehri* (underground city); the bus stops at the petrol station, a 500m stroll from the entrance.

NEVŞEHİR
☎ 0384 / pop 77,060 / elevation 1260m

Nevşehir, the provincial capital, is an ugly modern town that offers travellers little incentive to linger. Basically, it's useful as a transport hub but not for much else.

Orientation & Information

The main otogar is 1.5km north of Atatürk Bulvarı, the town's main road. To find it, look for the TC Ziraat Bankası branch on Atatürk Bulvarı and then turn into Lale Sokak, which is directly opposite. This busy street leads to both the otogar and the Gülşehir highway. In reality, locals avoid the otogar, instead catching buses and dolmuşes to most local towns from a more central bus stop on a cross street located a short distance north of the Alibey Cami on Lale Sokak. When you reach the traffic lights a little way on from the mosque, turn right and you'll see people waiting outside a group of arcaded shops. Services to Göreme, Uçhisar and Avanos also stop on the main road outside the museum (on the same side of the road, but a bit further towards Göreme).

Nevşehir's **tourist office** (☎ 213 3659; Atatürk Bulvarı) is in a large government building on the town's main road. Staff here can supply a basic map of Nevşehir, but not much else. To check your email, head to **Step Internet Café** (Atatürk Bulvarı; per hr €0.55; ✆ 8am-midnight), just up from the tourist office. There are also a number of banks with ATMs along here.

Sights

Nevşehir Museum (☎ 213 1447; Türbe Sokak 1; admission €1.10; ✆ 8am-noon & 1-5pm Tue-Sun) is housed in the extremely ugly Kültür Merkezi (City Cultural Centre) 1km from the centre of town, on the road to Göreme. The collection includes a mildly interesting archaeological room with Phrygian, Hittite and Bronze Age pots and implements, as well as Roman, Byzantine and Ottoman articles. The upstairs ethnographic section is dusty, poorly presented and of only marginal interest.

The statue in the small park in front of the cultural centre is of Nevşehir'li Damat İbrahim Paşa (1662–1730), the Ottoman grand vizier after whom the town is named. This local luminary endowed the town's grand mosque complex, which is clearly visible on the hill to the south of Atatürk Caddesi and still has a functioning mosque, medrese (which is now a library), hamam and tea house.

Dangers & Annoyances

The tour companies and taxi drivers based at Nevşehir's otogar have a formidable reputation for pouncing on travellers who arrive on buses from İstanbul and other long-distance destinations as soon as they get off the bus. Once cornered, the unsuspecting and tired victims are often conned into signing up for overpriced tours or agreeing to ridiculously overinflated prices for a taxi trip to their final destination (be it Göreme, Ürgüp, Uçhisar or any of the nearby villages). We suggest that you avoid any dealings with the tour agents here and follow the advice outlined on p493 to ensure that your bus ticket includes a shuttle bus transfer to your final destination from Nevşehir. If you do decide to take a taxi from the otogar, follow the price guidelines included in the Getting There & Away section on below.

Sleeping & Eating

We can't think of a good reason to stay in Nevşehir after checking out its hotels. These fall into two categories: bland four- and five-star places on the city fringe that are geared solely towards package groups; and horrible dingy places in the city centre where Russian prostitutes ply their trade and the sheets certainly don't bear inspection. Even if you arrive here in the middle of the night, we recommend that you make your way to nearby Göreme, where the accommodation is cheaper and infinitely superior.

Öz Hanedan Restaurant (☎ 213 1179; Gazhane Caddesi 18A; kebaps €2.50-3) In our opinion, noshing on the İskender kebaps served at this sleek modern restaurant is the only compelling reason to spend time in Nevşehir. In a side street about 150m off Atatürk Caddesi, Öz Hanedan is impeccably clean, has extremely friendly staff and serves exceptionally fine variations of döner kebap. To find it, turn left at the main crossroads just past the tourist office as you come into town from Göreme, then take the first right, and then the first left.

If you're in need of a tea and baklava stop before or after catching a bus, the Karadeniz Pastanesi just off Atatürk Caddesi on the road to Gülşehir is worth a visit.

Getting There & Away

At the time of writing **Pegasus Airlines** (www .pegasusairlines.com) had just commenced flights between İstanbul and Nevşehir five times per week (€42 to €53 one way).

Nevşehir is the main regional transport hub. There are services to surrounding towns and villages from the otogar and from the dolmuş stop close to the centre (see p515). These go to Göreme (€1, every 30 minutes from 7am to 8pm Monday to Friday in summer and 7am to 6.30pm Monday to Friday in winter, every hour on weekends); Uçhisar (€0.80, every 30 minutes from 7.30am to 6.30pm Monday to Friday, every hour on weekends); Ürgüp (€1, every 15 minutes from 7.30am to midnight); and Niğde (€3.30, every 30 minutes from 6.30am to 7pm). The Niğde bus stops at Kaymaklı and Derinkuyu en route. There are two bus routes from Nevşehir to Avanos: one leaves every 30 minutes and goes direct and the other leaves every hour and travels via Göreme and Çavuşin. Both services operate from 7am to 7pm and charge €1.50 per ticket. To get to Ortahisar (€0.55, every 30 minutes from 7am to 6.30pm Monday to Saturday) you'll need to make your way to the bus stop at the junction of Atatürk Caddesi and the Ürgüp road. Alternatively, you can catch a Nevşehir–Ürgüp dolmuş and ask to get off on the main highway at the turnoff to Ortahisar. It's then a 1km walk into the centre of town.

A taxi should cost no more than €10 to Göreme, €10 to Ortahisar, €15 to Ürgüp, €8 to Uçhisar or €15 to Avanos.

AROUND NEVŞEHİR

If you're heading for Ankara, consider stopping off to see Gülşehir and Hacıbektaş along the way. While this is easily done if you have your own vehicle, it's not too hard by public transport either.

Gülşehir
☎ 0384 / pop 9800

This small town 19km north of Nevşehir has two rocky attractions on its outskirts that are worth visiting if you're passing through.

Four kilometres before Gülşehir's town centre you'll find the **Open Palace** (Açık Saray; admission free; ☺ 7am-7pm), a fine rock-cut monastery dating from the 6th and 7th centuries. It includes churches, refectories, dormitories and a kitchen, all of which are cut into fairy chimneys.

Two kilometres closer to town and a five-minute walk down a signed road on the left of the highway (the sign reads 'Church of St Jean/Karşı Kilise') is the splendid **Church of St John** (admission €2.75; ☺ 8.30am-5pm). This 13th-century church on two levels has marvellous frescoes, including scenes depicting the Annunciation, the Descent from the Cross, the Last Supper and the Betrayal by Judas. The frescoes are particularly well preserved due to the fact that until restoration in 1995 they were covered in a layer of black soot.

Buses and dolmuşes to Gülşehir (€0.55, 15 minutes) depart from the dolmuş and bus stop in the centre of Nevşehir (see p515). Ask to be let off at the Açık Saray or Karşı Kilise to save a walk back from town. Returning, just flag the bus down from the side of the highway. Onward buses to Hacıbektaş leave from Gülşehir's small otogar opposite the Kurşunlu Camii (€0.55, 30 minutes).

Hacıbektaş
☎ 0384 / pop 6781

The town of Hacıbektaş is right on the edge of Cappadocia, 46km from Nevşehir. For most of the year it slumbers undisturbed, but from 16 to 18 August it bursts into life to host the annual festival in memory of Hacı Bektaş Veli (1248–1337), founder and spiritual leader of the Bektaşi order of dervishes. Up to 100,000

HACI BEKTAŞ VELİ & THE BEKTAŞİ SECT

Born in Nishapur in Iran in the 13th century, Hacı Bektaş Veli inspired a religious and political following that blended aspects of Islam (both Sunni and Shiite) with Orthodox Christianity. During his life he is known to have travelled around Anatolia and to have lived in Kayseri, Sivas and Kırşehir, but eventually he settled in the hamlet that is now the small town of Hacıbektaş.

Although not much is known about Hacı Bektaş himself, the book he wrote, the *Makalât*, describes a mystical philosophy less austere than mainstream Islam. In it he laid out a four-stage path to enlightenment (the Four Doors). Though often scorned by mainstream Islamic clerics, Bektaşi dervishes attained considerable political and religious influence in Ottoman times. Along with all the other dervishes, they were outlawed in 1925.

The annual pilgrimage of Bektaşi dervishes is an extremely important event for the modern Alevi community. Politicians tend to hijack the first day's proceedings, but days two and three are given over to music and dance.

In town, you can visit the **Hacıbektaş Museum** (admission €1.10; ☺ 8.30am-noon & 1-5.30pm Tue-Sun), set up around the tomb of the great man. Several rooms are arranged as they might have been when the dervishes lived here.

believers descend on the saint's tomb during this pilgrimage.

There's a **tourist office** (☉ 8.30am-midday & 1-5.30pm Mon-Fri) in the Kültür Merkezi next to the museum. Its staff speak no English, and it is unable to supply any printed information other than a glossy booklet about Hacı Bektaş Veli. You'll find a Vakif Bank ATM in a booth in front of the PTT on the main street.

Hacıbektaş has limited hotel options. Should you want to overnight here, the unremarkable **Hünkar Otel** (☎ 441 3344; www.hunkarotel .com.tr; s/d €11/22), on the *meydanı* (town square) between the shrine and the otogar, offers small rooms that are relatively clean and comfortable. The price should be negotiable except in August, when it's booked solid. Eating options are limited to the basic *lokantas* (restaurants), *pastanes* (patisseries) and *kebapçıs* (kebap eateries) on the main street.

Buses from the centre of Nevşehir to Hacıbektaş (€1.10, 45 minutes, nine daily between 7.45am and 5.45pm on weekdays, fewer services on weekends) depart from the 'Has Hacıbektaş' bus office just down from the Alibey Camii on the road to Gülşehir. The last bus from Hacıbektaş' otogar to Nevşehir leaves at 5pm (4.45pm on weekends).

ORTAHİSAR

☎ 0384 / pop 4800

Mainstream tourism has bypassed Ortahisar, and it remains a quaint farming village with a thriving trade in storing citrus fruits in its caves. But it has a secret or two up its sleeve in the form of charming boutique hotels located in tranquil and extremely scenic spots on the edge of town. These offer the best possible excuse for getting away from it all for a few days.

Staff at the small **tourist office** (☎ 343 3071; Tepebaşı Meydanı; ☉ 8am-5pm) near the castle are friendly, but don't speak English. You can check emails at **Kilim Net C@fe** (Huseyin Galif Efendi Caddesi; per hr €1.10; ☉ 9am-1am) near Hotel Gümüş. If you want a guide to visit Pancarlık Valley, ask 'Crazy Ali', who runs the antique shop next to the tourist office and speaks a bit of English.

Sights

There are no monuments in the village other than the **castle**, an 18m-high rock used as a fortress in Byzantine times and now undergoing a seemingly interminable restoration.

Those keen to grasp the basics of local culture should consider visiting the **Culture Folk Museum** (Kültür Müzesi; Tepebaşı Meydanı; admission €1; ☉ 9am-9pm), on the main square near the castle. Tour groups love its twee dioramas and interpretative panels (in four languages including English).

On the road to the AlkaBris hotel, you'll find **Manzara ve Kültür Parkı**, a pleasant municipal park with grassed areas, playground equipment, fountains and a wonderful view of the castle. It's a great spot for a picnic.

From Ortahisar you can hike to little-known churches in the nearby countryside, especially in the Pancarlık Valley.

In 2006, Ortahisar acquired an unfortunate tourist attraction when the Türkbalon, a ridiculous, permanently tethered hot-air balloon, was moved here from İstanbul. Cappadocian locals were horrified that the wonderful landscape surrounding the Devrent Valley inherited the curse. Hopefully tourists will illustrate their disdain by ignoring this visually intrusive and monumentally tacky attraction.

Sleeping & Eating

Gümüş Hotel (☎ 343 3127; www.gumushotel.com; Huseyin Galif Efendi Caddesi; s/d incl breakfast €8.50/16.50) On the road into the centre of town, the Gümüş is a clean and simple place offering neat rooms (some with balconies) and great views from its roof terrace.

Hisar Evi (☎ 343 3005; www.hisarevi.com; Kale Mahallesi Tahirbey Sokak; s/d/ste incl breakfast €39/67/84; ☒) A perfect spot for a getaway, this friendly retreat is known for its genial host, extremely comfortable rooms and excellent home cooking (dinner €11). There are terraces everywhere and the views over the valley and castle are quite wonderful. Prices are surprisingly reasonable considering the quality of the accommodation on offer.

AlkaBris (☎ 343 3433; www.alkabris.com; Cedidi Mahallesi, Ali Reis Sokak 23; r €110-139, ste €156, all incl breakfast; ☐) An oasis of calm and luxury, this lovingly restored Cappadocian house offers five tastefully furnished rooms. Three of these boast views over the castle, the old village and Erciyes Dağı. There's also a rock-hewn restaurant (dinner €17) and two magnificent terraces where guests can relax over tea. To find it, follow the signs from the centre of town; it's a steep 1.5km walk.

Park Restaurant (☎ 343 3361; Tepebaşı Meydanı; pide €3-3.50, mains €4.50-5.50) The Park overlooks the main square, with the castle as a backdrop. Its attractive garden is a perfect spot to rest over a tea (€0.50), beer (€3) or glass of 'house viagra' (fresh orange juice, €2).

Cultural Museum Restaurant (mains €5.50-8) This restaurant looks great, so it's a shame the food and service aren't better. Clearly gearing itself towards tour groups, its terrace and pretty dining room are a pleasant place for a tea (€0.50), but our experience would indicate that the food is best avoided.

Getting There & Away

For details of shuttle bus services between Kayseri airport and Ortahisar see p494.

Dolmuşes make the 5km run between Ürgüp and Ortahisar every 30 minutes from 8.10am to 4.30pm Monday to Saturday (€0.90). See page p516 for details of the bus services between Ortahisar and Nevşehir. All buses stop in the main square.

ÜRGÜP

☎ 0384 / pop 17,050

If you have a soft spot for upmarket hotels and fine dining, you need look no further – Ürgüp is the place you're looking for. The ever-growing battalion of boutique hotels in the town's honey-coloured stone buildings (left over from the pre-1923 days when the town had a large Greek population) are proving very popular with travellers. With a spectacular natural setting and a wonderful location at the very heart of central Cappadocia, this is one of the most seductive holiday spots in the whole of Turkey.

Orientation & Information

Ürgüp is set within a steep valley about 23km east of Nevşehir and 7km east of Göreme Valley. Most of the action occurs on or around Cumhuriyet Meydanı, which has at its centre a modern shopping plaza complex. The otogar is close to Cumhuriyet Meydanı.

There are several banks with ATMs on or around the main square. The PTT is northeast of the main square.

The **tourist office** (☎ 0384 213 4260; Kayseri Caddesi 37; 🕑 8am-5pm Mon-Fri Oct-Apr, 8am-5.30pm Mon-Fri May-Sep) is helpful and well informed.

You can check your emails at **Club Café Internet** (3rd fl, Suat Hayri Caddesi 42; per hr €1.10; 🕑 9am-1am) or at **Tera@s Internet Café** (3rd fl, Suat Hayri Caddesi 42; per hr €1; 🕑 9am-1am) in the same building. To find both, enter the arcade opposite the plaza

and next to Kardeşler Restaurant and go up the grubby stairs to the 3rd floor.

Sights & Activities

Northwest of the main square is the oldest part of town, with many fine **old houses**, reached through a stone arch. It's well worth a stroll, after which you can head up Ahmet Refik Caddesi and turn right to the **Temenni Wishing Hill** (admission €0.30; 🕑 9am-11pm), home to a saint's tomb, a café and 360-degree views over the town. Back on Ahmet Refik Caddesi, you may want to explore the town's unofficial and underwhelming 'underground city'. If you do so, you'll probably need to tip one of the guides who hang around here.

Right by the main square is the **Tarihi Şehir Hamamı** (€8.50; 🕑 7am-10pm), the local *hamam*. Partly housed in what was once a small church, it offers mixed but respectable bathing (male masseurs only).

There is an uninspiring **museum** (admission €1.10; 🕑 8.30am-noon & 1-5pm Tue-Sun) next to the tourist office.

WINERIES

The abundant sunshine and fertile volcanic soil of Cappadocia produce delicious sweet grapes, and several small local wineries carry on the Ottoman-Greek wine-making tradition. You can sample some of the local produce at the big **Turasan Winery** (Çimenli Mevkii; 🕑 7.30am-7pm).

Tours

Several travel agents based in Ürgüp run tours around Cappadocia. Recommended agents include:

Argeus Tours (☎ 341 4688; www.argeus.com.tr, www.cappadociaexclusive.com; İstiklal Caddesi 7; 🕑 8.30am-7pm Nov-Mar, 8.30am-6pm Apr-Oct) Helps with cycling, walking and horse riding holidays as well as day tours and flights. Ürgüp's Turkish Airlines representative.

Peerless Travel Services (☎ 341 6970; www.peerlessexcursions.com; İstiklal Caddesi 19A; 🕑 8.30am-8.30pm) Also Ürgüp's Onur Air representative.

Sleeping

Ürgüp is blessed with an impressive array of boutique hotels, a few good-quality midrange choices and a couple of budget pensions worth considering. Many of these close down between November and March, when Ürgüp's weather keeps locals indoors and travellers elsewhere.

CAPPADOCIA

ÜRGÜP

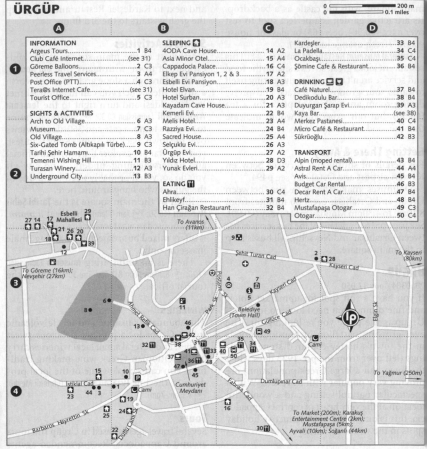

INFORMATION	
Argeus Tours	1 B4
Club Café Internet	(see 31)
Göreme Balloons	2 C3
Peerless Travel Services	3 A4
Post Office (PTT)	4 C3
Tera@s Internet Cafe	(see 31)
Tourist Office	5 C3

SIGHTS & ACTIVITIES	
Arch to Old Village	6 A3
Museum	7 C3
Old Village	8 A3
Six-Gated Tomb (Altıkapılı Türbe)	9 C3
Tarihi Şehir Hamamı	10 B4
Temenni Wishing Hill	11 B3
Turasan Winery	12 A3
Underground City	13 B3

SLEEPING 🏠	
4ODA Cave House	14 A2
Asia Minor Otel	15 A4
Cappadocia Palace	16 C4
Elkep Evi Pansiyon 1, 2 & 3	17 A2
Esbelli Evi Pansiyon	18 A2
Hotel Elvan	19 B4
Hotel Surban	20 A3
Kayadam Cave House	21 A3
Kemerli Evi	22 B4
Melis Hotel	23 A4
Razziya Evi	24 B4
Sacred House	25 A4
Selçuklu Evi	26 A3
Ürgüp Evi	27 A2
Yıldız Hotel	28 D3
Yunak Evleri	29 A2

EATING 🍴	
Ahra	30 C4
Ehlikeyf	31 B4
Han Çirağan Restaurant	32 B4

Kardeşler	33 B4
La Padella	34 C4
Ockbaşı	35 C4
Şömine Cafe & Restaurant	36 B4

DRINKING 🍷 🍸	
Café Naturel	37 B4
Dedikodulu Bar	38 B4
Duyurgan Şarap Evi	39 A3
Kaya Bar	(see 38)
Merkez Pastanesi	40 C4
Micro Café & Restaurant	41 B4
Sükrüoğlu	42 B3

TRANSPORT	
Alpin (moped rental)	43 B4
Astral Rent A Car	44 A4
Avis	45 B4
Budget Car Rental	46 B3
Decar Rent A Car	47 B4
Hertz	48 B4
Mustafapaşa Otogar	49 C3
Otogar	50 C4

BUDGET

Hotel Elvan (☎ 341 4191; hotelelvan@superonline.com; Barbaros Hayrettin Sokak 11; s/d €17/28 incl breakfast; 🖳) A friendly welcome and homely atmosphere awaits you at this unpretentious but immaculate guesthouse. The rooms are arranged around a small courtyard and have midrange amenities such as satellite TVs and hairdryers. There's also a small roof terrace and comfortable dining room. Excellent value.

Yıldız Hotel (☎ 341 4610; www.yildizhotel.com; Kayseri Caddesi; s/d/bungalow incl breakfast €14/28/45) Nowhere near as impressive as the other budget options mentioned here, the Yıldız offers old-fashioned rooms that are clean but desperately in need of a paint job and new carpet. The renovated bungalows in the flowery garden

are much nicer, but carry a slightly ambitious price-tag.

Cappadocia Palace (☎ 341 2510; www.hotel-cappadocia.com; Duayeri Mahallesi Mestan Sokak 2; standard s/d incl breakfast €23/34, ste incl breakfast €45-70) This large and comfortable hotel is housed in a converted Greek house that's conveniently located a stone's throw from Cumhuriyet Meydanı. It has 14 motel-style rooms with satellite TV and small bathrooms, as well as four impressive cave suites. There's a lovely arched restaurant-lounge and an attractive foyer area.

MIDRANGE

Razziya Evi (☎ 341 5089; www.razziyaevi.com; Cingilli Sokak 24; s/d incl breakfast €27/38-43) There aren't many midrange options in Ürgüp, so the existence of this lovingly restored *evi* (house) should be wholeheartedly celebrated. Its seven cheerful rooms (some in slightly musty caves) are comfortable and clean; they're not at all posh, but in a town where posh boutique hotels are a dime a dozen this almost comes as a welcome relief. There's a *hamam* (€5 per person), a salon with satellite TV, a pretty courtyard and a kitchen that guests can use.

Melis Hotel (☎ 341 2495; www.melishotel.com; İstiklal Caddesi 34; dm/s/d incl breakfast €14/25/40; ♨ 🖳) On a main road right next to a mosque (pack those ear-plugs!), the Melis offers arched rooms set around a large and quite lovely swimming pool. The older main building is home to a restaurant, three atmospheric cave rooms and a pleasant four-bed dorm.

Asia Minor Otel (☎ 341 4960; www.cappadociahouse .com; İstiklal Caddesi 38; s/d incl breakfast €28/42; 🖳) The large grassed garden is the knock-out feature of this friendly but slightly shabby hotel. There's a wide choice of room styles, the best of which are the downstairs arched rooms and the light and airy upstairs rooms with balcony.

Hotel Surban (☎ 341 4603; www.hotelsurban.com.tr; Yunak Mahallesi; s/d with half board €35/45; ✕ 🖳) The Surban's simple arched rooms are pleasantly light and have small but very clean bathrooms; all come with satellite TVs and pretty embroidered bed linen. There's a roof terrace with good views and a large restaurant-lounge. It's good value, particularly considering the fact that the price includes breakfast and dinner.

Kemerli Evi (☎ 341 5445; www.kemerliev.com; Dutlu Camii Mahallesi Çıkmaz Sokak 12; s/d incl breakfast €67/90; ✕ 🖳 ♨) The small and stylish Kemerli Evi straddles the dollar divide between midrange and top end. Located in the backstreets southwest of the main square, it has 10 attractively

decorated rooms set in two restored Greek houses. There's a small swimming pool, a cosy upstairs lounge and an unassuming roof terrace.

TOP END
Most top-end lodgings are on the northwestern fringes of Ürgüp, high up on the Esbelli hill.

Kayadam Cave House (☎ 341 6623; www.kayadam .com; Esbelli Mahallesi Sokak 6; s/d €52/72, ste €120 incl breakfast; ✕ 🖳) The six standard rooms at this lovely boutique hotel are directly carved into the tuff cliff and front onto a cascade of terraces. All feature polished floorboards, comfortable beds and decent-sized modern bathrooms. The owners also operate the nearby Villa Bacchus, which has two deluxe rooms and one utterly fabulous suite with its own terrace, equipped kitchen and large living area.

Elkep Evi Pansiyon 1, 2, 3 & 4 (☎ 341 6000; www .elkepevi.com; Esbelli Mahallesi Sokak; s/d incl breakfast €55/75, ste incl breakfast €110-170; ✕ 🖳) The largest of the boutique hotels on Esbelli Mahallesi, Elkep Evi boasts four separate buildings set in an attractive garden. Most of the rooms are in caves, but the newest wing also has arched family rooms on its roof terrace. Space is plentiful here: all rooms are large (some are enormous and even have their own roof terraces), the restaurant is cavernous and there's a sprawling roof terrace with sensational views.

Selçuklu Evi (☎ 341 7460; www.selcukluevi.com; Yunak Mahallesi; r incl breakfast €70-90; ✕ 🖳) Though it's not among our favourite Ürgüp hotels, this imposing mansion hotel still has lots to offer. Its 20 individually decorated and extremely comfortable rooms sport amenities such as satellite TVs and minibars, and its pretty

---

THE AUTHOR'S CHOICE

Esbelli Evi Pansiyon (☎ 341 3395; www.esbelli.com; Esbelli Mahallesi Sokak 8; s/d/ste incl breakfast €80/90/200; ✕ 🛏 🖳) It's not often that we give hotels a 10 out of 10 score, but that's what the Esbelli Evi deserves. The first of Cappadocia's boutique hotels, it has been copied by innumerable competitors but none have been able to fully emulate its unforgettable mix of comfort, style and ambience. Owner Süha Ersöz knows what makes travellers happy – the cave rooms here have comfortable beds, elegant (but never pretentious) décor and excellent bathrooms. Thoughtful touches such as bottled water and a choice of reading matter in each room provide the icing on the cake. We could go on about the fabulous breakfasts, magnificent terrace views and exemplary levels of service, but really, all we need to say is that a stay in this incredibly welcoming place will be a highlight of your trip.

courtyard garden is a perfect spot in which to relax (particularly as it has wine fountains dispensing free-of-charge product!). Our main quibble is that most of its rooms get hot in summer and it has no air-conditioning.

40DA Cave House (☎ 341 6080; www.4oda.com; Esbelli Mahallesi Sokak 46; s/d incl breakfast €70/90; 🖳) It may only have four rooms, but this peaceful new pension has more than its fair share of atmosphere and comfort. The infectiously cheerful and friendly owner lives on site and goes out of her way to make guests feel at home, supplying tea and home-cooked cakes in the afternoon and sharing her personal library and lounge room. The rooms are gorgeous, featuring private terraces, top-quality beds, antique *suzani* (Uzbek bedspreads) and handmade soaps. We highly recommend staying here.

Ürgüp Evi (☎ 341 3173; www.urgupevi.com.tr; Esbelli Mahallesi Sokak 54; s/d incl breakfast €75/100, ste incl breakfast €135-200; 🖳) This long-running favourite has recently been the subject of a chic makeover. Its gorgeous stonework has been left untouched, but its cave rooms now have extremely comfortable beds with luxe linen. The hotels' strongest selling-points are its location right at the top of the hill (the views are quite amazing), its attractive cave restaurant and its terrace garden, which is home to a scattering of gaily coloured beanbag seats.

Sacred House (☎ 341 7102; www.sacred-house.com; Karahandere Mahallesi Barbaros Hayrettin Sokak 25; s incl breakfast €95-125, d incl breakfast €105-145; ☒ 🖳) Hotel owners throughout Cappadocia stood up and took notice when this most boutique of all boutique hotels opened in 2006. Set in an old Greek mansion, it offers seven exquisitely decorated (and dark) rooms with large and very posh bathrooms. Antiques and *objets d'art* are scattered throughout the building, and there's a very stylish rooftop lounge/terrace. You'll either love it or find it unbearably pretentious.

Yunak Evleri (☎ 341 6920; www.yunak.com; Yunak Mahallesi; d €120-145, ste €180; ☒ 🖳) This swish hotel is a combination of six cave houses with 29 rooms. We were superimpressed with the main building, which occupies an old and very attractive Greek house and houses a state-of-the-art DVD room and music lounge, but not quite as taken with the general setting, which suffers from an exposed position and lack of greenery. That said, guest rooms are extremely comfortable and well appointed.

Eating

The range of restaurants in Ürgüp is more limited than in Göreme, but the overall standard is much higher.

Kardeşler (☎ 341 2376; Suat Hayri Caddesi 5; mains €2.50-4) This cheap-and-cheerful place is popular for its *tandır*s (stews cooked in a clay pot with a bread crust). These come with beef and white beans or you can order a vegetarian alternative. A beer to accompany your meal costs €2.

Ocakbaşı (☎ 341 3277; Güllüce Caddesi 44; mains €4-5) Right above the otogar, this long-established place has a cavernous dining room and smaller roof terrace. It's low on atmosphere but has a sound reputation for its grilled meats. A beer costs €2.50 and an *ayran* (yogurt drink) €1.50.

La Padella (☎ 341 2068; Dumlupınar Caddesi 33; mains €4.50-6.50) La Padella's chef-owner previously worked at Göreme's well-regarded A'laturca, and it shows. The menu showcases many of the same dishes, but offers them at prices that are considerably cheaper. We heartily approve! The menu (presented in Turkish and English) includes favourites such as *soğuk salata tabağı* (mixed cold meze plate, €4) and *kapaturco tavuk şiş* (chicken kebap served on a bed of eggplant, tomato, onion and peppers, €5) A beer costs a bargain-basement €2 and service is extremely friendly. Highly recommended.

Ahra (☎ 341 3454; Fabrika Caddesi 66; mains €4-7) This is undoubtedly the most atmospheric restaurant in town. Located on the 1st floor of a beautifully renovated old house on the road to Mustafapaşa, it has an intimate feel and simple but attractive décor. The simplicity extends to the excellent menu, which features home-cooked dishes such as *sulu köfte* (meatball stew, €4) and *Kayseri mantısı* (€4.50). You can celebrate your good fortune at being here by ordering a bottle of local wine (€17).

Han Çirağan Restaurant (☎ 341 2566; Cumhuriyet Meydanı; mains €5-7) The Han Çirağan is a perennial favourite thanks to its atmospheric setting and reasonable prices. In summer, the pleasant vine-shaded courtyard is a lovely spot for dinner; in winter, the intimate arched-ceiling dining room is just as welcoming. Don't expect anything special when it comes to the food – this is stock-standard Turkish fare.

Şömine Cafe & Restaurant (☎ 341 8442; Cumhuriyet Meydanı; salads €2-5, mains €4-7) This popular restaurant on the plaza is as sophisticated as the Ürgüp dining scene gets. Choose a table on the outdoor terrace or in the attractive indoor dining room, sit down and admire the pristine napery and quality tableware, and then make your choice from the large menu. Most people choose a salad to start and then move on to a *kiremit* (meat dish baked on a tile in a traditional oven), accompanied by crisp, freshly baked *lavash* bread. The food is good but doesn't quite live up to the promise of the décor.

Ehlikeyf (☎ 341 6110; Cumhuriyet Meydanı; mains €5-8) Ehlikeyf occupies a sleek, modern dining room overlooking the plaza and is close to overtaking Şömine in the contest for the mantle of the town's best restaurant. Large, well-spaced tables and comfortable leather chairs put diners in the right mood to settle down for a big night sampling the ambitious dishes on offer. These include a fabulous *Ehlikeyf kebap* (steak served on slivered fried potatoes, garlic yogurt and a demiglace sauce; €9). Service can be frustratingly slow.

Drinking

The two most popular bars in town are Kaya Bar and Dedikodulu Bar, which are next to each other on Cumhuriyet Meydanı. For something a bit more restrained, try **Duyurgan Şarap Evi** (Esbelli Mahallesi), a wine house where you can sample a glass of Cappadocian wine (or three!) while listening to live music in the evening.

There are a number of cafés and patisseries on the main square where you can grab an outdoor table, order a drink and watch the world go by. If you're after coffee or alcohol, try Café Naturel or Micro Café & Restaurant. For tea, cakes and ice cream, check out Merkez Pastanesi or Şükrüoğlu. All are on Cumhuriyet Meydanı.

Getting There & Away

For details of shuttle bus services between Kayseri airport and Ürgüp see p494.

Most buses leave from the main otogar. Dolmuşes travel to Nevşehir every 15 minutes from 6.55am to 11.30pm (€1). For details of the Belediye Bus Corp services running between Ürgüp and Avanos via Ortahisar, the Göreme Open-Air Museum, Göreme village and Çavuşin, see p494.

Nine buses per day (but only three on Sunday) travel between Ürgüp and Mustafapaşa between 8.15am and 6.15pm (€0.90). They leave from the Mustafapaşa otogar, which is east of the main otogar.

Details of some useful long-distance daily services from Göreme are listed below:

SERVICES FROM ÜRGÜP'S OTOGAR

Destination	Fare	Duration	Frequency (per day)
Adana	€11.50	5hr	3 morning & afternoon
Aksaray	€4	1½hr	frequent morning & evening
Ankara	€10	4½hr	at least 7 (in summer)
Antalya	€17-22	10hr	2 evening only
Çanakkale	€25-28	16hr	1 afternoon only
İstanbul	€20	11hr	at least 3 morning & evening
İzmir & Selçuk	€20-25	11½hr	1 evening only
Kayseri	€3	1¼hr	hourly 7am to 6pm
Konya	€8.50	3hr	frequent
Marmaris/Bodrum/ Pamukkale	€17-25	11-15hr	1 evening only

Getting Around

Ürgüp is a good base for hiring a car, with most agencies located on or around the main square. Rates hover around €35 to €40 per day for a small manual sedan such as a Fiat Palio and climb to €55 to €60 for a larger automatic. **Decar Rent A Car** (☎ 341 6760) provides good service, but you can also try **Budget Car Rental** (☎ 341 6541), **Astral Rent A Car** (☎ 341 3344), **Hertz** (☎ 341 4906) or **Avis** (☎ 341 2177). If you're planning on dropping the car off in another part of Turkey your best bet is Decar, as it doesn't charge the prohibitively large drop-off fees (eg €100 to drop off in Antalya) that the other companies levy.

Several outlets in town rent mopeds and motorcycles. Try **Alpin** (☎ 341 8008) on the main square or **Astral Rent A Car** (☎ 341 3344). Expect to pay about €25 per day.

The steep walk from the centre of town up to Esbelli Mahallesi is an absolute killer – many people instead opt to catch a taxi from the rank next to Micro Café & Restaurant on the main square (€2.50).

AYVALI

Heading south from Ürgüp to Mustafapaşa look out for a turn-off to Ayvalı, a tiny unspoilt Cappadocian village that boasts a delightful get-away-from-it-all place to stay,

the **Gamırasu Hotel** (☎ 0384-341 7485; www.gamirasu
.com; d €56-104, ste €120-560). Set in a 1000-year-old
monastery, it offers slightly claustrophobic
standard cave rooms and much nicer deluxe
rooms and suites. All are stylish and extremely
comfortable. It has an on-site restaurant, a
church with frescoes and an ancient winery
on the premises.

MUSTAFAPAŞA
☎ 0384 / pop 2500

Until WWI, Mustafapaşa was called Sinasos
and was a predominantly Ottoman Greek settlement. These days it greatly benefits from this
Greek legacy, as its exquisitely decorated stone-
carved houses and minor rock-cut churches
attract the attention of a small but respectable
number of foreign and domestic tourists. It's a
wonderful spot to spend a day or two.

You enter Mustafapaşa at an enlarged
intersection, the Sinasos Meydanı, where a
signboard indicating the whereabouts of the
local rock-cut churches is located. Follow the
road downhill and you'll come to Cumhuriyet Meydanı, the centre of the village, which
sports the ubiquitous bust of Atatürk and
several tea houses.

There's no tourist office in town, and no
ATMs.

Sights
A sign pointing off Sinasos Meydanı leads
1km to the 12th-century **Ayios Vasilios Kilise** (St
Basil Church; admission €3; ☉ variable), perched near
the top of a ravine. Its interior features unimpressive 20th-century frescoes.

Between Sinasos Meydanı and Cumhuriyet
Meydanı is a 19th-century **medrese** with a fine
carved portal. The stone columns on either
side of the doorway are supposed to swivel
when there's movement in the foundations,
thus warning of earthquake damage.

Cumhuriyet Meydanı is home to the im-
posing **Ayios Kostantinos-Eleni Kilise** (Church of SS
Constantine & Helena; admission €3), erected in 1729
and restored in 1850. A fine stone grapevine
runs around the portal but the interior is
falling into ruin and the frescoes, which date
from 1895, are fading fast. You'll need to
pay the admission cost and get the key to the
church from the uniformed council worker
who should be posted outside. If not, enquire
at the nearby *belediye* building.

There are other churches in the **Monastery
Valley**, including **Ayios Stephanos Church** (St

Stephen's), but they're disappointing compared to others in Cappadocia. Nonetheless,
it's a lovely walk.

Sleeping & Eating
Many of Mustafapaşa's accommodation options are closed from November to March.

Monastery Hotel (☎ 353 5005; www.monasteryhotel
.com; Mehmet Şakirpaşa Caddesi; s/d €10/20) On the road
leading to Monastery Valley, this rough-as-
guts place has some squalid downstairs rooms
and a few much-more-bearable upstairs alternatives. We doubt that the hotel's bizarre
disco-bar sees much action.

Hotel Pacha (☎ 353 5331; www.pachahotel.com;
Sinasos Meydanı; s/d incl breakfast €15/24) Lots of Cappadocian hotels boast of the fact that theirs
are family-run businesses that offer a warm
welcome, but in reality this is often not the
case. Fortunately, the Pacha is the real thing.
A restored Ottoman-Greek house off the main
roundabout, it has a great feel about it from
the moment you enter the pretty vine-trellised
courtyard. The rooms have a bright, modern
appearance and are very clean, albeit on the
smallish side. Their size doesn't really matter,
though, because guests seem to spend most
of their time relaxing in the simply wonderful
upstairs restaurant-lounge, which overlooks
the courtyard.

Hotel Cavit (☎ 353 5186; musti_clb@hotmail.com;
Baraj Caddesi; s/d incl breakfast €14/28) On the road to
Soğanlı, the Cavit is another family-run winner. Though not as impressive as the Pacha, it
also has a pleasant garden courtyard and wonderfully light and airy rooms. The owners are
charming, but don't speak any English. Best
of all, it has a great view from its comfortable
terrace-lounge.

Old Greek House (☎ 353 5306; www.oldgreekhouse
.com; Şahin Caddesi; s/d incl breakfast €30/40; 🖳) The
big drawcard here is the historic aura that
shrouds this wonderful old Ottoman-Greek
house. Centred on an internal courtyard that
hosts an excellent restaurant, it still retains
many of its original 19th-century frescoes and
trimmings. The 16 large rooms have polished
floorboards covered in rugs, comfortable beds
with embroidered bedspreads, and simple but
clean bathrooms. Most are arranged around
the courtyard, which means that they can be
noisy during meal times.

Ukabeyn Pansiyon (☎ 353 5533; www.cappadocia
pensiyon.com; s/d €40/55; 🏊) What a surprise! This
boutique hotel high on the hill overlooking

CAPPADOCIA

the town has five arched rooms furnished in an attractive modern style. There's also a swimming pool, a series of terraces and a fully equipped apartment (€75) that would make a fabulous base for an extended visit. From Cumhuriyet Meydanı, head towards Monastery Valley – it's a stiff 1km up the hill on the right.

Lamia Pension (☎ 353 5413; www.lamiapension. tr; s/d €28/56) Run by a Turkish-German artist, this homely pension has five large rooms adorned with an eclectic mix of *objets d'art*, paintings and textiles. Though it's impressively clean and very comfortable, it's overpriced for what it offers. To find the Lamia, follow the instructions for the Ukabeyn Pansiyon, opposite.

Sinasos Gül Konaklari (Rose Mansions; ☎ 353 5486; www.rosemansions.com; Sümer Sokak; s/d incl breakfast & dinner €100/150; ☐) Occupying two heavily restored Greek mansions, this hotel has an impersonal air that no doubt stems from the fact that it is part of the Dinlar hotel chain's national portfolio. Rooms have four-star accoutrements and are extremely comfortable, though their décor won't be to everyone's taste. There's a posh restaurant (dinner €15 for nonguests), a vaguely bizarre 'Ottoman-meets-Holiday-Inn' lounge in a wooden pavilion and a lovely rose garden.

Most of the town's hotels and pensions offer meals and this is fortunate, as the other eateries in town are dreadful. We recommend Old Greek House (opposite), which serves an excellent Turkish set menu to its guests and anyone else seeking a meal (€10 per person); and Hotel Pacha (opposite), which offers a set menu for the slightly cheaper price of €6.

Getting There & Away

Nine buses a day (fewer on Sunday) travel the route between Ürgüp and Mustafapaşa (€0.90, 20 minutes). The first leaves Mustafapaşa at 7.45am and the last leaves Ürgüp at 6.15pm. A taxi costs €5.50.

SOĞANLI

The twin valleys of Soğanlı, about 36km south of Mustafapaşa, are much less visited than Göreme or Zelve. Indeed, in recent years the number of visitors to Soğanlı has actually diminished. Nevertheless, it's a magnificent place to explore, and unless your visit coincides with one of the day tours from Göreme, you may well have the valleys all to yourself.

To reach Soğanlı turn off the main road from Mustafapaşa to Yeşilhisar and proceed 4km to the village. Buy your ticket for the churches (adult/child €1.10/free; ☒ 7am-8.30pm) near the **Kapadokya Restaurant** (☎ 0352-653 1045; set menu €4.50; ☒ lunch only), which boasts tables set under shady trees and serves stodgy but acceptable food. The village square is backed by toilets, the modest **Soğanlı Restaurant** (mains €2-3.50; ☒ lunch only) and a line of women selling the dolls for which Soğanlı is supposedly famous. Facing the square is the village's solitary pension, the family-run **Emek** (☎ /fax 0352 653 1029; d per person with half board €17), which offers clean cave dorms with between five and nine beds. Meals are cooked by the owner's wife and served on a pleasant upstairs terrace.

Sights

The valleys of **Aşağı Soğanlı** and **Yukarı Soğanlı** were first used by the Romans as necropolises and later by the Byzantines for monastic purposes (similar to Göreme and Zelve), with ancient **rock-cut churches**.

At the point where the valleys divide, a billboard indicates all the churches. Most of the interesting ones are in the right-hand valley (to the north), easily reached by foot.

Coming from the main road, about 800m before the ticket office, signs point to the **Tokalı Kilise** (Buckle Church), on the right, reached by a steep flight of worn steps, and the **Gök Kilise** (Sky Church), to the left across the valley floor. The Gök has twin naves separated by columns and ending in apses. The double frieze of saints is badly worn.

One of the most interesting churches is the **Karabaş** (Black Head), further into the valley and covered in paintings showing the life of Christ, with Gabriel and various saints. A pigeon in the fresco reflects the importance of pigeons to the monks, who wooed them with dovecotes cut into the rock.

Also in the right-hand valley, across the valley floor and high on the far hillside, are the **Kubbeli** and **Saklı Kilisesi** (Cupola and Hidden Churches). The Kubbeli is unusual because of its Eastern-style cupola cut clean out of the rock. The Hidden Church is just that: hidden from view until you get close.

Furthest up the right-hand valley is the **Yılanlı Kilese** (Snake Church), its frescoes deliberately painted over with black paint, probably to protect them. You can still make out the serpent to the left as you enter.

CAPPADOCIA

In the left-hand valley, you'll first come across the **Geyikli Kilise**, where the monks' refectory is still clearly visible and, 200m further up, the **Tahtalı Kilise** (Church of Santa Barbara) with well-preserved Byzantine and Seljuk decorative patterns.

Getting There & Away

It's basically impossible to get to Soğanlı by public transport. Your best bet is to make your way to Yeşilhisar from Kayseri (€1.50, every 30 minutes from 7am to 9pm) and then negotiate for a taxi to take you the rest of the way. Alternatively you could sign up for one of the day tours run from Ürgüp or Göreme.

ALA DAĞLAR NATIONAL PARK

The Ala Dağlar National Park (Ala Dağlar Milli Parkı) protects the rugged middle range of the Taurus Mountains between Kayseri, Niğde and Adana. It's famous throughout the country for its extraordinary trekking routes, which make their way through craggy limestone ranges dotted with waterfalls. It's best to trek here between mid-June and late September; at other times weather conditions can be particularly hazardous, especially since the ranges have few villages or other support services. Bring warm gear and be prepared for extreme conditions.

The most popular walks start at the small villages of **Çukurbağ** and **Demirkazık**, which lie beneath Mt Demirkazık (Demirkazık Dağı, 3756m), some 40km east of Niğde.

You can also reach the mountains via Yahyalı, 70km due south of Kayseri, a short drive away from the impressive **Kapuzbaşı Waterfalls** on the Zamantı River. **Medraft** (see p513) can organise rafting trips here.

Although there are a variety of walks in the mountains, many people opt for the two-day minimum walk to the beautiful **Yedigöller** (Seven Lakes, 3100m), which starts and finishes at Demirkazık. An easier three- to four-day walk begins at Çukurbağ and leads through the forested Emli Valley, before finishing at Demirkazık. Although solo trekkers do sometimes venture into the mountains, unless you're experienced and well prepared you should consider paying for a guide or joining a guided tour. A guide should cost around €50 per day, a horse another €30. If you want to do a full trek in the range (about €200 for a week, all inclusive), ask at your pension or contact one of the following trekking agencies in Niğde:

Demavend Travel (☎ 0388-232 7363; www.demavendtravel.com; Şah Sülrymsn Mahallesi Tacıroğlu Sokak Birlik, Apt 5)

Dijon Travel (☎ 0388-232 2112; www.dijontravel.ofisi.com; 3rd fl, Mandacilar Ishanı 5, Ali Paşa Mahallesi, Yeni Çarsi)

Sobek Travel (☎ 0388-232 1507; www.trekkingin turkeys.com; Avanoğlu Apt 70/17, Bor Caddesi)

Sleeping & Eating

Şafak Pension & Camping (☎ 0388-724 7039; www.safaktravel.com; camp sites per person €5.50, d per person with half board €17; ⊠ ▣) This is run by the friendly, English-speaking Hassan, who also works as a guide. The eight rooms are simple but extremely clean, with important features such as plentiful hot water, heating and comfortable beds. The terrace and garden command magnificent views overlooking Mt Demirkazık, and the lounge is equipped with a satellite TV. Camp sites are to the side of the house; they have electricity and their own bathroom facilities.

On the other side of the road, the same family has recently opened another, very similar, pension called Öz Şafak, which charges the same rates. You'll find both pensions off the main road, about 1.5km from the bridge and the signpost marked 'Demirkazık 4, Pinarbaşı 8'.

Çukurbağ has basic shops for supplies.

Getting There & Away

From Niğde, take a Çamardı-bound minibus (€3, 90 minutes, every hour between 7am and 5.30pm) and ask to be let off at the Şafak Pension (it's 5km before Çamardı).

NIĞDE

☎ 0388 / pop 93,760

Backed by the snow-capped Ala Dağlar range, Niğde, 85km south of Nevşehir, was founded by the Seljuks. It's an agricultural centre with a clutch of impressive historic buildings. You won't want to stay, but may have to if you want to visit the fabulous Eski Gümüşler Monastery, 10km to the northeast. Niğde is also a handy base for getting to and from the base-camp villages for trekking in the Ala Dağlar National Park (left).

The **tourist office** (☎ 232 3393; Belediye Sarayı 38/39; ⊙ 8am-noon & 1-5pm Mon-Fri) is located on the 1st floor of the ugly Kültür Merkezi (City

Cultural Centre) on Bor Caddesi. There are a number of internet cafés in a small mall on İstiklal Caddesi, including **Gökkuşaği Internet Café** (Bankalar Caddesi; per hr €0.55; ☻ 8am-11pm). ATMs are dotted along Bankalar/İstiklal/Bor Caddesi.

Sights

The excellent **Niğde Museum** (Niğde Müzesi; admission €1.10; ☻ 8am-noon & 1-5pm Tue-Sun) houses a well-presented selection of finds from the Assyrian city of Acemhöyük near Aksaray, through the Hittite and Phrygian ages to sculptures from Tyana (now Kemerhisar), the Roman town 23km southwest of Niğde. Several mummies are exhibited too, including the 10th-century mummy of a blonde nun discovered in the 1960s in the Yılanlı church in the Ihlara Valley.

The Seljuk **Alaeddin Camii** (1223), on the hill crowned with the fortress, is the town's grandest mosque but the **Süngür Bey Camii**, on a terrace at the end of the marketplace, is more interesting. Built by the Seljuks but restored by the Mongols in 1335, it is a curious blend of architectural styles.

The attractive **Ak Medrese** (1409) houses a cultural centre that may – or may not – be open.

Also take a look at the **Hüdavend Hatun Türbesi** (1312), a fine Seljuk tomb, and the Ottoman **Dış Cami**.

Sleeping & Eating

Niğde has several drab concrete hotels on its main road and numerous cheap and cheerful *lokantas* and *pastanes* in its centre.

Hotel Nahita (☎ 232 3536; fax 232 1526; Emin Erişingil Caddesi 19; s/d €25/34) On the main road into town and close to the otogar, this three-star block is the most convenient accommodation choice if you are forced to stay in town overnight. Though it totally lacks character, it's clean and comfortable.

Damak Lahmacun (☎ 233 7312; İstiklal Caddesi; mains €1.50-3) This bustling place is justly popular for its excellent pide, *lahmacun* (Arabic pizza) and melt-in-the-mouth *İskender* kebap. You can eat in or take away.

Saruhan (☎ 232 2172; Bor Caddesi 13; mains €2-4) Occupying a restored *han* (caravanserai) dating from 1357, Saruhan is heavy on atmosphere

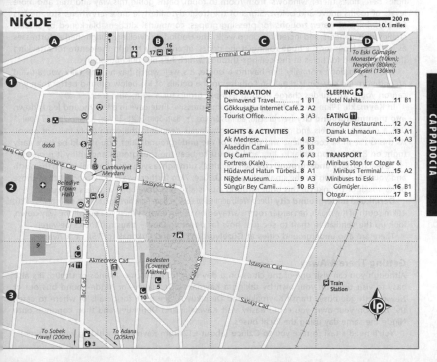

INFORMATION			SLEEPING 🛏		
Demavend Travel	1	B1	Hotel Nahita	11	B1
Gökkuşağu Internet Café	2	A2			
Tourist Office	3	A3	EATING 🍴		
			Arısoylar Restaurant	12	A2
SIGHTS & ACTIVITIES			Damak Lahmacun	13	A1
Ak Medrese	4	B3	Saruhan	14	A3
Alaeddin Camii	5	B3			
Dış Cami	6	A3	TRANSPORT		
Fortress (Kale)	7	B2	Minibus Stop for Otogar &		
Hüdavend Hatun Türbesi	8	A1	Minibus Terminal	15	A2
Niğde Museum	9	A3	Minibuses to Eski		
Süngür Bey Camii	10	B3	Gümüşler	16	B1
			Otogar	17	B1

CAPPADOCIA

and no lightweight when it comes to its food. It serves an array of delicious döner and İskender kebaps as well as rustic dishes such as işkembe çorbası (tripe soup, €1.10). We enjoyed the delicious Adana kebaps (€2) and were blown away by how cheap everything was, but quickly came back to earth when we encountered the utterly filthy toilets. No alcohol is served.

Arısoylar Restaurant (☎ 232 5035; Bor Caddesi 8; mains €3.50-4.50) The menu at this sleek modern eatery focuses on classics such as İskender kebap, çiğ köfte (patties of raw spiced lamb, €1.10 per small serve) and beyti sarma (wrapped lamb with garlic, €4.50). Its air-conditioned dining room is a perfect place to escape the heat and noise of the town.

Getting There & Away

Minibuses to/from the otogar (Terminal; €0.30) trundle up and down Bankalar/İstiklal/Bor and Terminal Caddesis. There are buses to

---

DEEP WITHIN THE EARTH

For sheer fascination and mystery, you can't beat the underground cities of Cappadocia. Make sure you visit one of the estimated 36 underground cities that have been identified (if not always excavated) here, but be prepared for a claustrophobic and sometimes unpleasantly crowded experience. For this reason, it's best to avoid visiting on weekends, when busloads of domestic tourists descend on the cities.

Some archaeologists date the earliest portions of these underground cities back 4000 years to Hittite times, but they were certainly occupied by the 7th century BC. The ancient Greek historian Xenophon mentioned the underground dwellings of Cappadocia in his *Anabasis*.

In times of peace the people of this region lived and farmed above ground, but when invaders threatened they took to their troglodyte dwellings where they could live safely for up to six months at a time.

As you go down inside the cities, it's as if you've entered a huge and very complex Swiss cheese: holes here, holes there, 'windows' from room to room, paths going this way and that and more levels of rooms above and below. Signs of the troglodyte lifestyle are everywhere: storage jars for oil, wine and water; troughs for pressing grapes; communal kitchens blackened by smoke; stables with mangers; and incredibly deep wells. The troglodyte dwellings functioned as fortresses as well – look out for the huge rolling-stone doors, often with a hole in the centre for attacking the enemy, and for holes in the ceilings through which hot oil could be poured.

Even if you don't normally like having a guide, it's well worth having one take you around an underground city, since they can conjure up the details of life below ground better than you can on your own. Guides charge around €13 per group for a 45-minute tour.

In **Kaymaklı**, 19km south of Nevşehir, an unimpressive little cave in a low mound leads down into the **underground city** (yeraltı şehri; admission €6; ⊗ 8am-5pm 2 Oct–16 Apr, 8.30am-7pm 17 April–1 Oct), a maze of tunnels and rooms carved eight levels deep into the earth (only five are open). As this is the most convenient and popular of the underground cities, you should be here early (right on 8.30am if possible) in July and August to beat the tour groups and enjoy it properly.

To reach **Özlüce underground city** (admission free), turn right as you enter Kaymaklı from the north and you'll be heading for the small village of Özlüce, 7km further away. More modest than those of Kaymaklı or Derinkuyu, this underground city is also less developed and less crowded.

Derinkuyu underground city (Deep Well; admission €6; ⊗ 8am-5pm Nov-Apr, 8.30am-6.30pm May-Oct), 10km south of Kaymaklı, has larger rooms arrayed on seven levels. When you get all the way down, look up the ventilation shaft to see just how far down you are – claustrophobics beware!

There are also underground cities at Güzelyurt (p531) and Özkonak (p515), near Avanos.

Getting There & Away

Although you can visit one of the cities on a day tour from Göreme, Avanos or Ürgüp, it's also easy to visit them on your own by taking a Kaymaklı-, Derinkuyu- or Niğde-bound bus out of Nevşehir (Niğde buses transit Kaymaklı and Derinkuyu). See p516 for details of where to catch the bus. On your own, you could easily visit Kaymaklı and Derinkuyu and then continue onto Niğde the same day using the local buses.

You'll need a taxi to take you to Özlüce (about €12 from Kaymaklı, including waiting time).

CAPPADOCIA

Adana (€7.50, 3½ hours, four daily), İstanbul (€14, 11 hours, morning and evening), Ankara (€8.50, five hours, five daily), Aksaray (€3.50, 1½ hour), Kayseri (€4, 1½ hours, every 30 minutes) and Konya (€8.50, 3½ hours, five daily). Buses to Nevşehir (€3.50, one hour, 85km) depart every 30 minutes from 7am to 10.30am and then every hour until 6.30pm.

Niğde is on the Ankara–Adana train line. A daily service leaves for Adana at 4.32am (€5, 3½ hours) and for Ankara at 11.32pm (€12, 8½ hours).

AROUND NIĞDE

Eski Gümüşler Monastery

The ancient rock-hewn **Eski Gümüşler Monastery** (admission €1.10; 9am-noon & 1-6pm Jun-Sep, 8am-noon & 1-5pm Oct-May), about 10km east of Niğde, has some of the best-preserved frescoes in Cappadocia and is well worth a visit.

The monastery was only rediscovered in 1963. You enter via a rock-cut passage that opens onto a large courtyard surrounded by rock-hewn dwellings, crypts, a kitchen and a refectory with deep reservoirs for wine and oil. A small hole in the ground acts as a vent for a mysterious 9m-deep shaft beneath.

The lofty main church has wonderful Byzantine frescoes painted between the 7th and 11th centuries. The charming Nativity looks as if it is set in a rock-caved structure like this one, and the striking Virgin and Child to the left of the apse has the elongated Mary giving a *Mona Lisa* smile – it's said to be the only smiling Mary in existence.

GETTING THERE & AWAY

Gümüşler Belediyesi minibuses (€0.55, 15 minutes) depart on the hour from the minibus terminal beside Niğde's otogar. As you enter the town, don't worry when the bus passes a couple of signs pointing to the monastery – it eventually passes right by it. To catch a bus back to Niğde flag one down on the roundabout outside the monastery.

IHLARA VALLEY (IHLARA VADİSİ)

☎ 0382

About 45km southeast of Aksaray is Ihlara village, at the head of the Ihlara Valley. Once called Peristrema, the valley was a favourite retreat of Byzantine monks. Dozens of painted churches carved from the rock have survived and hikers can follow the course of the stream (Melendiz Suyu) as it flows for 16km from the wide, shallow valley at Selime to a narrow gorge at Ihlara village. It's an unforgettable experience, thanks to the sea of greenery – alive with birds – hugging the banks of the stream at the base of this beautiful canyon. Many people visit on day tours from Göreme, which allow only a few hours to walk the central part of the gorge, but to walk the whole way is likely to be a highlight of your trip to Turkey. Especially good times to visit are midweek in May or September when fewer people are about. Roughly midway along the valley, at Belisırma village, the presence of a swathe of restaurants along the riverbank means that you needn't come weighed down with provisions.

There are no ATMs in Ihlara village, Selime or Belisırma and the valley's only **internet café** (per hr €1; 9am-11pm) is in a modern shopping block opposite Akar Pansion in Ihlara village.

Walking Ihlara Valley

There are four entrances along the **Ihlara Valley** (admission €3; 8am-7pm Apr-Oct, 8.30am-5pm Nov-Mar; parking per car €1.25). If, like most people, you only want to walk the short stretch with most of the churches, then enter via the 360 knee-jarring steps leading down from the **Ihlara Vadisi Turistik Tesisleri**, perched on the rim of the gorge 2km from Ihlara village. Alternatively there are entrances near the Star Otel in Ihlara village (take the path behind it), at Belisırma and at Selime.

It takes about 2½ to three hours to walk from the Ihlara Vadisi Turistik Tesisleri to Belisırma, and about three hours to walk from Belisırma to Selime. You'll need seven to eight hours if you want to walk all the way from Ihlara village to Selime, stopping in Belisırma for lunch along the way.

If you're planning to walk all the way, it's best to start early in the day, particularly in summer, when you'll need to take shelter from the fierce sun.

Churches

Along the valley floor, signs mark the different churches. Although they're all worth visiting if you have the time, the following list includes the real must-sees:

Kokar (Fragrant) Kilise This church has some fabulous frescoes – the Nativity and the Crucifixion for starters – and tombs buried in the floors.

Sümbüllü (Hyacinth) Kilise This church is noteworthy not so much for its frescoes, or what's left of them, but for its well-preserved, simple but elegant façade.

Yılanlı (Serpent) Kilise Many of the frescoes here are badly damaged, but it's still possible to make out the fresco outlining the punishments doled out to sinners, especially the three-headed snake with a sinner in each mouth and the nipple-clamped women (ouch!) who didn't breastfeed their young.

Kırk Dam Altı (St George) Kilise It's a scramble to get to, but the views of the valley make all the puffing worthwhile. The frescoes are quite badly graffitied, but above the entrance you can see St George on a white horse, slaying a three-headed snake.

Bahattın'ın Samanlığı (Bahattin's Granary) Kilise This church has some of the best-preserved frescoes in the valley. It's named after a local who used to store grain here. Frescoes show scenes from the life of Christ, including the Crucifixion, Massacre of the Innocents and Baptism scenes.

Direkli (Columned) Kilise This cross-shaped church has six columns, hence the name. The large adjoining chamber originally had two storeys, as you can see from what's left of the steps and the holes in the walls from the supporting beams. There are burial chambers in the floor.

Selime Monastery

The **monastery** (🕑 dawn-dusk) at Selime is an astonishing rock-cut structure incorporating a vast kitchen with soaring chimney, a church with a gallery all around it, stables with rock-carved feed troughs and other evidence of the troglodyte lifestyle. The admission price is supposedly included in the Ihlara Valley ticket. The entrance is just opposite the Ali Paşa Tomb (1317).

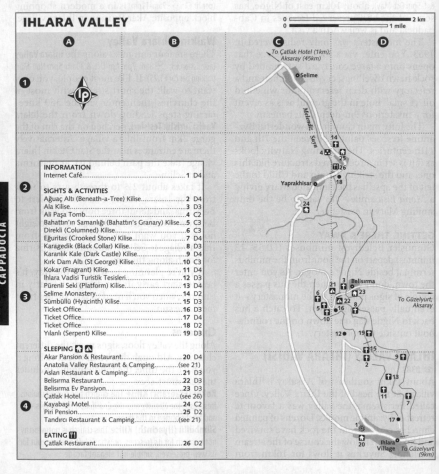

IHLARA VALLEY

0 — 2 km
0 — 1 mile

To Çatlak Hotel (1km);
Aksaray (45km)

Selime

Melendiz Suyu

Yaprakhisar

Belisırma

To Güzelyurt;
Aksaray

To Güzelyurt
(9km)

Ihlara
Village

Tours

Travel agencies in Göreme (p501), Avanos (p513) and Ürgüp (p519) offer full-day tours to Ihlara for between €30 and €50 per day, including lunch.

Sleeping & Eating

If you want to walk all the way along the gorge there are modest pensions handily placed at both ends (Ihlara and Selime). You can also break your journey into two parts with an overnight stay in Belisırma's camping grounds or lone pension. Note that all accommodation is closed out of season (December to March).

IHLARA VILLAGE

Akar Pansion & Restaurant (☎ 453 7018; fax 453 7511; s/d €11.50/23) One of the only places in town, and offering 18 motel-style rooms in two buildings. These are simple, but perfectly acceptable. There's an on-site restaurant serving up local trout (€3) and a small shop that sells picnic ingredients. The owner has a minibus in which he shuttles people to Selime (€5.50) and Belisırma (€3).

BELİSIRMA

Midway along the gorge, beside Belisırma village, there are four low-key but agreeable licensed restaurants. These benefit from their enviable position right by the river, and all serve basic meals of grilled trout, *saç tava*, kebaps, salads and soups. You can camp in the grounds for no charge if you eat in the associated restaurant – all four places have basic ablution blocks.

Anatolia Valley Restaurant & Camping (☎ 457 3040; mains €4-5) A good site, with a couple of vine-covered pergolas for shade. It also has a few ramshackle wooden 'tree houses' that you can sleep in (€5.50 per person). The owner will drive hikers back to Ihlara carpark if they are tired (€11.40 per carload).

Aslan Restaurant & Camping (☎ 457 3033; mains €4-5) The best camp site, set at the base of a cliff and with lots of trees. Its ablution block isn't too clean, though.

Belisırma Restaurant (☎ 457 3057; mains €3.50-4.50) On the opposite bank of the river, this is the most attractive of the four restaurants. The camp site is at the rear and doesn't have much shade.

Tandırcı Restaurant & Camping (☎ 457 3110; mains €3.50) Camp sites are dotted among vegetable gardens and a small orchard.

There's also a small pension in the old village on the hill overlooking these restaurants. To find it, cross the bridge in front of the Aslan Restaurant and ask for directions to **Belisırma Ev Pension** (☎ 457 3037; dm €5.50, r per person incl breakfast €8.50), which offers basic rooms with great views and hard beds. Its bathrooms are shared and slightly grubby.

SELİME

At the northern end of the gorge, there are three decent accommodation options if you want to stay overnight. The cheapest of these are the worn but clean **Piri Pension** (☎ 454 5114; carpet_Mustafa@yahoo.com; s/d incl breakfast €11.50/23), a tranquil and friendly place that overlooks some fairy chimneys; and the newly built **Kayabaşi Motel** (☎ 454 5565; s/d incl breakfast €11.50/23), which is 2km outside the village on the road to Belisırma and offers clean and comfortable rooms with great views. For something a bit more upmarket, try the imposing **Çatlak Hotel** (☎ 454 5006; catlakpansion@hotmail.com; r incl breakfast €25; ✕ 🖳), about 3km from the start of the valley walk, on the Aksaray side of Selime. Its rooms are large and light, with modern fittings and simple bathrooms. The same owners run the eponymous restaurant, a few steps from the start of the walk, and can shuttle you between the two.

Getting There & Away

There are four minibuses per day between Ihlara village and Aksaray, travelling via Selime. The first of these leaves Ihlara at 6.45am and the last at 4pm; there's only one service on Sundays (at 1pm). The fare costs €1.50.

Buses travelling between Aksaray and Güzelyurt (see p533) stop in Selime en route. The fare is €1 from Selime to Güzelyurt and the same from Selime to Aksaray.

If you want to go to Belisırma, catch the Aksaray–Güzelyurt bus or the Ihlara–Aksaray bus and ask to be dropped off in the new part of Belisırma up on the plateau; you'll then have to hike the few hundred metres down into the valley.

You'll need to catch a taxi (€11.50) to get between Ihlara and Güzelyurt.

GÜZELYURT

☎ 0382 / pop 3735 / elevation 1485m

About 9km from Ihlara village is Güzelyurt, a sleepy Cappadocian farming village filled with stone houses, rock-cut churches and its very own underground city. You may run into other tourists in July or August but most of the time this Cappadocian gem is refreshingly undervisited.

In Ottoman times this was the town of Karballa (Gelveri), which was inhabited by 1000 Ottoman-Greek families and 50 Turkish-Muslim families. In the population exchanges between Turkey and Greece in 1924, the Greeks of Gelveri went to Nea Karvali in Greece, while Turkish families from Kozan and Kastoria in Greece moved here. The relationship between the two countries is now celebrated in an annual 'Turks & Greeks Friendship Festival' held in July.

Güzelyurt has a PTT, a branch of the T C Ziraat Bankası (but no ATM) and several shops. The extremely helpful **tourist office** (☉ 8am-5.30pm) is in the main street and can supply a wealth of information about both the town and the Ihlara Valley. The poorly signed **Arikan Internet Café** (per hr €0.55; ☉ 8am-midnight) is on the 1st floor of a *pastane* in a small square behind the bank.

Sights

MONASTERY VALLEY & ANTIQUE CITY

Walk downhill from the main square following the signs to the Monastery Valley & Antique City. About 300m from the square, a sign points left to a small, recently restored **underground city** (yeraltı şehri; admission €3; ☉ 8am-5.30pm), actually more of an underground village.

There are also several churches in the valley, including the **Koç** (Ram) and the **Cafarlar** (Rivulets), with its interesting frescoes. The most striking of all is the **Aşağı** or **Büyük Kilise Camii** (Lower or Big Mosque), built as the Church of St Gregory of Nazianzus in AD 385, and restored and modernised in 1896. St Gregory (AD 330–90) grew up in Güzelyurt and went on to become a theologian, patriarch and one of the Four Fathers of the Greek Church. In the garden, a subterranean stairway leads to an *ayazma* (sacred spring). Plans exist to turn the church into a museum, with the whitewash removed from the frescoes, but they are unlikely to come to fruition during the lifetime of this book.

After your visit, ask the imam to point you in the direction of the nearby **Sivişli Kilise** (Anargyros Church), a much later rock-hewn church with square pillars and an impressive cupola sporting some faded frescoes. Climb the steps behind it for fabulous valley views.

Afterwards you can continue through the **Monastery Valley** (a sort of Ihlara in miniature).

Just walking through this quiet unspoilt valley is pleasant, but there are also more rock-cut churches and dwellings to explore, including the **Kömürlü Kilisesi** (Coal Church), with an elaborate lintel carved above the entrance, and the almost adjoining **Kalburlu Kilisesi** (Church with a Screen), with a superb entrance and a carved Maltese cross inside, but no frescoes.

YÜKSEK KİLİSE & MANASTIR

Perched high on a rock overlooking the Güzelyurt lake is the **Yüksek Kilise & Manastır** (High Church & Monastery), 1km or so west of the town off the road to Ihlara. A walled compound contains the plain church and monastery but it's more impressive when viewed from a distance.

KIZIL KİLİSE

Set in farmland surrounded by rugged mountains, the **Kızıl Kilise** (Red Church) is about 6km east of Güzelyurt, off the road to Gölcük, just past the village of Sivrihisar. Named for the colour of its stone, it's currently undergoing an extensive restoration. Take a taxi from Güzelyurt (about €10, including waiting time).

Sleeping & Eating

Halil Pension (☎ 451 2707; www.halilpension.com; Yukarı Mahallesi Amaç Sokak; s/d with half board €19.50/39; ⬚) The five guest rooms in this family home would make a great base for those intending to explore the area for a few days, particularly as the friendly lady owner is an absolutely sensational cook. Rooms are in a modern extension to the original Greek house and are very pleasant, with loads of natural light, small but spotlessly clean bathrooms and a cheerful modern décor. When we visited, a roof terrace with magnificent views was under construction. As you enter town it's signposted off to the right, a short walk from the centre.

Hotel Karvalli (☎ 451 2736; www.karvalli.com in German; Karvalli Caddesi 4; s/d incl breakfast €22/40; ✕ ⬚) Occupying a sentinel-like position on the outskirts of town and commanding stunning views of Hasan Dağı, the Karvalli is a safe choice. Its large modern rooms are comfortable and it has a convivial bar-restaurant with a pool table and satellite TV. The enthusiastic young management team will ensure that you enjoy your stay.

Hotel Karballa (☎ 451 2104; www.karballahotel.com; s/d standard €34/45, deluxe €45/55, incl breakfast; ✕ ⬚) We bet the monks enjoyed living and working in this 19th-century Greek monastery close to the town centre. Though now converted into a hotel, the building has retained a contemplative atmosphere and is a nice spot for a break. The standard rooms are basic, but the four deluxe rooms are bright and attractive, with cheerful kilims on the walls and elaborate Uzbeki spreads on the beds. There's a hilltop swimming pool and an atmospheric restaurant in the former refectory (dinner €7). Horse-riding, mountain biking and hiking tours can all be arranged here.

Asrav Pansiyon (☎ 451 2501; asravpansiyon@asrav .com.tr; s/d incl breakfast €25/50) A newcomer to Güzelyurt's limited accommodation scene, this pension is housed in an imposing building near the Hotel Karvalli. The owners have done a good job with the fit-out here – it's simple and stylish in equal measure and there has been a sensible emphasis on providing quality where it's most needed, eg excellent mattresses on the beds and hairdryers in the bathrooms.

Gelveri Restaurant (☎ 451 2771; mains €3-4) Nestled in the small square behind the bank, this basic eatery whips up grills, lahmacun, pizza and fish. It has the reputation of being the best place to eat in town, though as there is only one other place to provide competition (the Kalvari Döner Kebap and Pide Salonu on the main street), that's not saying much.

Getting There & Away

Buses from Aksaray travel to Güzelyurt via Selime every two hours starting at 6am; the last bus returns from Güzelyurt at 5.30pm. On Sundays there are fewer services. The fare costs €1.50 from Güzelyurt to Aksaray and €1 from Selime to Güzelyurt.

You'll have to catch a taxi (€11.50) to get between Ihlara and Güzelyurt.

AKSARAY

☎ 0382 / pop 156,900

Like Nevşehir, Aksaray is an ugly modern town with a sprinkling of old buildings and very little to attract the traveller. You may need to transit through here on your way to the Ihlara Valley, but otherwise you're best off avoiding it.

Orientation & Information

Aksaray's main otogar is about 3km out of town. A free servis shuttles between it and the

small eski otogar (old otogar), from where it's a 200m walk to the vilayet (provincial government building) in the centre of town. You'll find banks with ATMs along Bankalar Caddesi, a main thoroughfare running in front of the vilayet. Continue straight along Bankalar Caddesi to find the Ulu Cami.

The **tourist office** (☎ 213 2474; Taşpazar Mahallesi; 8.30am-noon & 1.30-5pm Mon-Fri) occupies a beautifully restored mansion. To find it follow the signs along Ankara Caddesi (which runs west off Bankalar Caddesi near the vilayet), walk past the Zafer Okulu (school) and take the first left. The staff here are very helpful and can supply a map of the town. The grubby but cheap **VIP Net** (Ankara Caddesi 7/A; per hr €0.40; 8am-midnight) is near Kurşunlu Camii on the corner of Bankalar and Ankara Caddesis.

Sights

The **Ulu Cami** (Bankalar Caddesi), near Otel Üçyıldız, has decoration characteristic of the post-Seljuk Beylik period and a little of the original yellow stone remains in the grand doorway. The **Aksaray Museum** (Aksaray Müzesi; admission €1.10; 8.30am-5.30pm) is housed in the Zinciriye Medresesi, which was built in Seljuk style in 1336. Though the collection here is underwhelming, it's worth coming here for the building alone. To find it, walk from the Ulu Cami across the main street to find Vehbibey Caddesi (the paved one with the Vakif Bank on the corner), then head 300m downhill towards the river.

The older part of town, along Nevşehir Caddesi, has the curious **Eğri Minare** (Crooked Minaret), built in 1236 and leaning at an angle of 27°. Inevitably, the locals know it as the 'Turkish Tower of Pisa'.

Sleeping & Eating

Otel Yuvam (☎ 212 0024; fax 213 2875; Eski Sanayi Caddesi Kavşağı; s/d €11/22) The town's best budget option is centrally located next to the Kurşunlu Cami, so be warned that the call to prayer is earsplitting in the morning. The overwhelming feel here is old-fashioned, with rooms sporting lino floor coverings and solid wooden furniture. Bathrooms are spotless and beds are hard but have crisp, clean linen. The friendly owners speak Turkish and German, but no English.

Otel Vadim (☎ 212 8200; fax 212 8232; 818 Vadi Sokak 13; s/d €19/31;) This excellent midrange choice is in a side street off Büyük Kergi Caddesi, the southern extension of Bankalar Caddesi. Blessedly quiet, it has a green-tiled façade and large and very comfortable rooms.

Otel Üçyıldız (☎ 212 0404; fax 212 5003; Bankalar Caddesi 6; s/d €29/38; ❄) A modern glass-fronted high-rise near the Ulu Cami, the Üçyıldız offers rooms with satellite TV and other mod-cons. It's popular with tour groups and business travellers, who appreciate the comfortable beds, rooftop restaurant and excellent service on offer.

Harman (☎ 212 3311; Bankalar Caddesi 16/A) Asked to nominate the best eatery in town, most locals are quick to mention this attractive eatery opposite the *vilayet*. It offers a great selection of *ızgara* (grills, €3), döner kebaps (€4), pide (€1 to €2) and soups (€1). Those who enjoy a sweet at the end of the meal will be impressed by the excellent homemade baklava (€1) and *künefe* (€2).

Merkez Lokantası (☎ 212 8825; Ziraat Bankası Karşısı 37) Another local favourite, this friendly place just down from Harman has three eating areas: an airy roof terrace, a no-nonsense ground-floor *lokanta* and a rear courtyard complete with gently playing fountain. There's an array of daily specials (€2 to €2.50) on display in the *bainmaries*, or you can order specialities such as the *İskender* kebaps (€3.50) to order. Takeaway döner sandwiches are available for €1.10.

Aksaray Pastanesi (Bankalar Caddesi 48) This popular pastry shop opposite Merkez Lokantası has a café upstairs where you can linger over a tea and a plate of honey-drenched *fıstıklı* (pistachio) baklava (about €0.30 per piece). Tuna Pastanesi opposite is an equally pleasant choice for a mid-afternoon stop.

Getting There & Away

From Aksaray, direct buses go to Ankara (€7.80, 3½ hours, 230km), Konya (€5.50, two hours, 140km), Nevşehir (€3.30, one hour, 65km) and Niğde (€3.90 to €4.40, 1½ hours, 115km).

Dolmuşes from the old otogar go to Ihlara (€1.40, one hour, 45km, four daily), Güzelyurt (€1.40, 1¼ hours, 54km, six daily), Sultanhanı (€0.83, 45 minutes, 42km, 10 daily) and Selime (€1.40, 30 minutes, 40km, six daily); there are few Sunday services.

AROUND AKSARAY

The road between Aksaray and Nevşehir followed one of the oldest trade routes in the world, the Uzun Yol (Long Rd). The route linked Konya, the Seljuk capital, with its other great cities (Kayseri, Sivas and Erzurum) and ultimately with Persia (Iran).

The Long Rd was formerly dotted with *han* where the traders would stop for accommodation and business. The remains of three caravanserais can be visited from Aksaray, the best preserved being the impressive **Ağzıkara Hanı** (admission €1.50; ☾ 7.30am-7.30pm), 16km northeast of Aksaray, which was built between 1231 and 1239. From Aksaray a taxi will charge about €15 for the run there and back. If you'd prefer to go by bus, catch one heading to Nevşehir and jump off at the Ağzıkara Hanı. Many of the day tours from Göreme and Ürgüp also call in on the caravanserai.

Further towards Nevşehir you'll pass the scant remains of the 13th-century **Tepesidelik Hanı**, 23km northeast of Aksaray, and the 12th-century **Alay Hanı**, another 10km on.

Black Sea Coast & the Kaçkar Mountains

Admit it – you forgot Turkey has a northern coast. Fair enough, the might of the Med often overshadows the simpler pleasures of the less-popular Black Sea, and if it's just sun, sea and sand you want, you couldn't be blamed for heading south rather than trying to hit the all-too-brief swimming season here. Luckily, there's far more to the Karadeniz (Black Sea) than a tourist industry, and discerning travellers can explore a wealth of sights without a sniff of the crowds that plague the real resort regions.

Of course, the defining feature of this coast is still the sea, but Black Sea dwellers enjoy it in an altogether civilised manner, seeking out the best spots to dig into a catch-fresh fish dinner or sup a cup of local tea amid the crumbing remnants of a past every bit as colourful as central Anatolia's. Fragments of castles and fortifications litter the coastline – legacies of the kings of Pontus, or the Genoese, or the Ottomans, or whoever got hold of them last. Recent history, too, has marked the region, which acted willingly as the flashpoint for Atatürk's republican revolution.

At the far eastern end of the coast, just before you have to turn round or dive into Georgia, lies the Black Sea's other trump card, the scenic Kaçkar Mountains. The trekking season's even shorter than the beach period, but you still have a four-month window around summer to explore isolated mountain villages, field-test hearty mountain food and experience some fading mountain cultures. And trust us, once you've done all that, there's no risk you'll forget Turkey's north coast again.

HIGHLIGHTS

- Admire Byzantine frescoes in an impossible cliff-face setting at the **Sumela Monastery** (p554)

- Trek the peaks to sample local dishes and village hospitality in the **Kaçkar Mountains** (p558)

- Road-test the first wave of mountain eco-tourism in **Çamlıhemşin** (p560)

- Twist and turn scenically on the long and winding coast road between attractive **Amasra** and seductive **Sinop** (p539)

- Hustle, bustle, taste, test, shop, drop and sightsee in busy-busy **Trabzon** (p548)

★ Sinop
Amasra
Kaçkar Mountains; Çamlıhemşin
Trabzon
Sumela Monastery ★

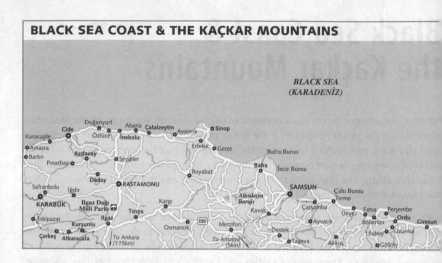

BLACK SEA COAST & THE KAÇKAR MOUNTAINS

BLACK SEA
(KARADENİZ)

History

The coast was colonised in the 8th century BC by Milesians and Arcadians, who founded towns at Sinop, Samsun and Trabzon. Later it became the Kingdom of Pontus. The most famous Pontic king, Mithridates VI Eupator, waged a war against the Romans in 88 to 84 BC and conquered Cappadocia and other Anatolian kingdoms, but was later forced to agree a peace based on pre-war borders.

From 74 to 64 BC he was at it again, this time encouraging his son-in-law, Tigranes I of Armenia, to grab Cappadocia from the Romans. The Roman response was to conquer Pontus, whereupon Mithridates was forced to flee; he later committed suicide. The Romans left a small kingdom of Pontus at the far eastern end of the coast, based in Trebizond (Trabzon).

The coast was subsequently ruled by Byzantium, and Alexius Comnenus, son of Emperor Manuel I, proclaimed himself emperor of Pontus when the crusaders sacked Constantinople and drove him out in AD 1204. His descendants ruled this small empire until 1461, when it was captured by the Ottomans under Mehmet the Conqueror.

While Alexius remained in Trabzon, Samsun was under Seljuk rule and the Genoese had trading privileges. But when the Ottomans came, the Genoese burned Samsun to the ground and sailed away.

After WWI the Ottoman Greek citizens of this region attempted to form a new Pontic state with Allied support. Disarmed by the Allied occupation authorities, Turkish inhabitants were persecuted by ethnic Greek guerrilla bands who had been allowed to keep their arms. In these circumstances, the Turks proved very responsive to calls for revolution. Using a bureaucratic ruse, Mustafa Kemal (Atatürk) escaped the sultan's control in İstanbul and landed at Samsun on 19 May 1919. He soon moved inland to Amasya and began to organise Turkey's battle for independence.

Climate

The Black Sea coast receives the heaviest rainfall in Turkey. The damp climate of this long stretch of land is characterised by warm, showery summers and mild, rainy and foggy winters with moderate temperatures. Spring and autumn bring generally changeable conditions. In the Kaçkars winters are long, harsh and snowy. Be prepared for unpredictable weather because of the altitude.

AMASRA

☎ 0378 / pop 6400

Coming from the west, Amasra is the first town of any real note along the Black Sea coast, and has a good claim to be one of the prettiest, squeezed neatly between two harbours and a sandy beach and overlooked by a thick-walled citadel. It's a popular tourist centre for this region, but has still been spared the kind of overdevelopment it might have suffered were it on the Aegean.

The Byzantines held Amasra as part of the Pontic kingdom, but rented the port to the

small commercial port was known as Sesamos Amastris.

Most of the area inside the citadel is now residential; most of the original walls survive and there are a few old relics such as the 15th-century **Eski Chapel** (Old Chapel), now a cultural centre. Make your way to the northeastern outcrop to sip tea and soak up sunset views of a noisy seagull colony on an offshore islet.

The **Amasra Museum** (Amasra Müzesi; ☎ 315 1006; Dereoğlu Sokak 4; admission €1.10; ☯ 9am-5.30pm Tue-Sun), overlooking Küçük Liman, contains a standard collection of Roman, Byzantine and Hellenistic odds and ends, including some impressive statues from the 2nd century.

Amasra's magnificent location is best admired from the sea. In season, several operators in Büyük Liman offer **boat trips** in the harbour and along the coastline. Expect to pay about €3 for a short tour (45 minutes) and €15 for a longer tour (six hours).

Genoese as a trading station from 1270 until 460, when Mehmet the Conqueror walked in without a fight. Under Ottoman rule, Amasra ost its commercial importance to other Black ea ports, and today it's simply a perfect spot o relax and enjoy some summer waterlife.

Orientation

As you come into Amasra, you'll pass the museum in an old stone building on the left, and couple of pensions. Most of the buses stop at n intersection right by the PTT. Follow the ign to 'Şehir Merkezi' (north) for the Küçük Liman (Small Harbour) with restaurants, pensions and the *belediye* (town hall), or walk traight (east) until you hit the sandy strip of he Büyük Liman (Large Harbour).

The entrance to the citadel lurks amid the ouvenir shops in the Küçük Liman.

Information

Amasra Turizm (☎ 315 1978; www.amasraturizm.com; umhuriyet Caddesi 13) Hotel bookings, car hire and local ourist services.

afé S (Özdemirhan Sokak; per hr €0.75; ☯ 9am-hidnight) Internet access and phone services.

ourist information (☎ 315 1219; Atatürk Kültür arkı; ☯ 11am-7pm) Erratic opening hours, no English poken.

Sights & Activities

North of the two harbours, three massive gate-vays lead to the **kale** (citadel), Amasra's most triking feature. It encompasses the promontory fortified by the Byzantines when this

Sleeping

Rates in Amasra can rise by 10% to 40% on busy summer weekends; prices quoted here are for midweek. If you're planning to visit out of season, be warned that many places close at the end of October and don't open again until May at the earliest.

Amasra is also a good spot for *ev pansiyons* (pensions in private homes), which are worthwhile options for budget travellers. You'll find some along the seafront and a handful within the castle walls; look out for the signposts or 'Pansiyon' notices in individual windows.

Kale Pansiyon (☎ 315 1251; Topyanı Sokak; d €17) A good home pension in the citadel area, *deniz manzaralı* (with sea view) and boasting a shady terrace. Plain rooms come with poky private bathrooms.

Balkaya Pansiyon (☎ 315 1434; İskele Caddesi 35; s/d €10/20) The cheapest formal pension in town, offering small, basic rooms on a side street between the harbours.

Kuşna Pansiyon (☎ 315 1033; Kurşuna Sokak 36; d €24) Run by the same people as the Karadeniz Aile Pide Salonu (see p538), this castle option is that bit nicer than your average *ev pansiyonu*, with six bright, colourful rooms surrounded by a verdant garden. Breakfast not included.

Şahil Otel (☎ 315 2211; Turgut Işık Caddesi 82; s/d €17/34) Opposite the local sailing club on the Büyük Liman, this is a small but smart modern option with sea facing balconies offering some perfect beach views.

Timur Otel (☎ 315 2589; oteltimur@ttnet.net.tr; Çekiciler Caddesi 27; s/d/tr €17/34/42) The Timur, slap-bang in the centre, has bright, pleasantly furnished rooms, double-glazing and 'pathogen-free' bathrooms, though no sea aspect. Unusually, prices actually fall at weekends.

Camcıoğlu Otel Bedesten (☎ 315 1938; Celal Eyiceoğlu Caddesi 8; s/d/tr €17/34/42) A rather bizarre option occupying the top floors of a half-empty shopping centre, with reception shared by the Metro bus office, the Bedesten nevertheless has good-standard rooms with new fittings and an attractive restaurant. Be sure to ask for outside-facing windows.

Hotel Türkili (☎ 315 3750; www.turkili.com.tr; Özdemirhan Sokak 6; s/d €23/36) Behind the wrought-iron balconies and blackcurrant-pink façade, you'll find creature comforts galore at this excellent Amasra favourite. Good English is spoken, the rooftop restaurant gets views across both harbours, and there are some big suite-like corner rooms (€67).

Büyük Liman Otel (☎ 315 3900; Turgut Işık Caddesi; s/d €20/39) In an excellent location on the harbour road, this well-run place offers attractive rooms with lots of front balconies facing the beach. The hotel and its Veneto café-restaurant are both particularly popular at weekends.

Amastris Hotel (☎ 315 3700; www.amastrisotel.com; Cumhuriyet Meydanı; s/d €36/72; 🏊) It's not quite the top-end option it thinks it is, but the pool and palm trees do add a resort flavour and the upper-level rooms are almost worth the money. Views take in the harbour and the military barracks next door, and the Bofe Bar is one of the liveliest nightspots in town.

Eating

Amasra has several pleasant, licensed seafront restaurants serving superb *canlı balık* (fresh fish) by the portion (three-portion deals usually available for groups). In the high season, they're often full of coach parties.

Karadeniz Aile Pide Salonu (☎ 315 1543; Mustafa Cengiz Caddesi 9; mains €1.10-3; 🕒 9am-9pm) One of a row of streetside places south of the *belediye* in Küçük Liman, you can't go wrong with pide (Turkish-style pizza) or *çorba* (soup) here.

Sormagir Café (☎ 315 3404; Küçük Liman Caddesi 24; mains €1.10-3; 🕒 9am-9pm) At the castle entrance, opposite Amasra's tiny 'pub quarter', the family-run Sormagir serves up the best *gözleme* (savoury pancake) in town in its cosy 1st-floor salon.

Hamam Café (☎ 378 3878; Tarihi Sağır Osmanlar Hamam; mains €1.10-4) As you'd expect from the name, this café occupies the historic old *hamam* (bath house) off the seafront, offering a terrace and Ottoman-styled lounge for drinks, traditional meals and nargilehs (water pipes).

Amasra Sofrası (☎ 315 2483; G Mithat Ceylan Caddesi; mains €2-4.50; 🕒 9am-10pm) Right in the centre of town, midway between the two harbours, this is Amasra's prime grill and fast-food spot with plenty of chicken dishes.

Çınar Restaurant (☎ 315 1018; Küçük Liman Caddesi; mains €3-6; 🕒 11am-11pm) One of several places providing the fresh fish dinners that help sell the town to visitors; set your sights on the rear terrace, just above the water. It's right by the Küçük Liman, near the *belediye*.

Çeşm-i Cihan Restaurant (☎ 315 1062; Büyük Liman; mains €3-8; 🕒 11am-11pm) Fulfilling the same role on the busier Büyük Liman, this multistorey traditional-style house hits all the right charm buttons. *Levrek* (bass) and *istavrit* (mackerel) are regulars on the menu, served with copious salad.

Mustafa Amca'nın Yeri (☎ 315 2606; Küçük Liman Caddesi; mains €4-8.50; 🕒 11am-11pm) Amasra's smartest seafood choice, established in 1945, is a favourite with tour groups and locals alike, arguably in spite of the OTT aquatic décor. Go early to bag a waterside table.

Drinking & Entertainment

Amasra Belediyesi Aile Çay Bahçesi (Küçük Liman) The municipality tea garden is a delightfully shady social hub in a prime location.

Ağlayan Ağaç Çay Bahçesi (Nöbethane Sokak) Head up the streets within the *kale* to find this perfect panoramic sipping spot – a handful of signs point the way.

Teras Cafe & Bar (☎ 315 2046; Turgut Işık Caddesi) Right on the beach by the Büyük Liman, Teras makes itself even more indispensable by blocking the views of the rival joints behind it, so it really is hard to beat for a waterfront beer.

Han Bar (☎ 315 2775; Küçük Liman Caddesi 17) This is the main emissary of Amasra's small cluster of pubs, a hut-like wooden building sandwiched between houses opposite the castle walls. There's usually *canlı musik* (live music) at night.

Getting There & Away

If you plan to travel east along the coast from Amasra, start early in the morning. Minibuses

DETOUR TO BARTIN

Strictly speaking it's not on the coast, but as you'll probably have to pass through it anyway on your way to/from Ankara or Safranbolu, you may as well throw in a quick stop at Bartın, 15km southwest of Amasra on Hwy 755. It's a charming town set amid the typically hilly landscape that separates the Black Sea from the plains of Anatolia. Numerous old wooden houses are scattered around the centre; most are pretty rundown but some have been renovated, and you can expect more to follow as the Ottoman revival continues. Who knows, if someone has the vision to open a hotel or two, the town may even start to rival Amasra as an appealing overnight and local base…

…ecome increasingly difficult to find as the day wears on.

Big intercity bus companies don't oper-…te to Amasra. Instead, minibuses to Bartın (€0.15, 30 minutes) leave about every 40 min-…tes from near the intersection by the PTT. …rom Bartın you can catch regular buses to …afranbolu (€5, two hours), Ankara (€14, five …ours) and İstanbul (€20, seven hours).

AMASRA TO SİNOP

Winding round the rugged hills that hug the Black Sea coastline, the wonderfully scenic …oad from Amasra east to Sinop (312km) …hould be on every traveller's itinerary, …vhether you're a driver, cyclist or passenger. The switchback curves afford stunning views …t every turn, and it's not a major route so you …von't often encounter much traffic. The flip-…ide is that it's narrow and slow going (average …peed is 40km/h to 50km/h, taking seven or …ight hours to Sinop), with the road surface …ften broken and the occasional *heyelan* (land-…lide) to hinder progress. If you want to get …bout by public transport, you'll have to pick …p local services between the many tiny towns …long the way – start early in the morning! If …ou're really lucky you may catch one of the …are daily bus services from İstanbul.

Quite a few villages here have camp sites …nd with your own wheels the coast is your …obster: simply stop wherever you like what …ou see. Starting out west to east, a swim at …ozköy beach, west of Çakraz, is a fine start, or …rop in to see the boat-builders at work in the

town of **Kurucaşile**, 45km east of Amasra. Both towns have modest hotels and pensions.

The picturesque village of **Kapısuyu**, with its two beaches, is another good spot to break your journey, and the tiny harbour on the perfect cove at **Gideros** is idyllic.

About 63km east of Amasra the road descends to a broad, sand-and-pebble beach that stretches for several kilometres to the aptly named village of **Kumluca** (Sandy). The beach continues 8km eastward to **Cide**, a small town where many dolmuş (minibus) services terminate. If you're stuck overnight, the **Yalı Otel** (☎ 0366-866 2087; www.yaliotel.com; Liman Yolu; s/d €9/18) is good value and has an on-site restaurant.

Leaving Cide, there's a panoramic view-point by the flagpole on the ridge above town. Around 12km on is **Kuscu Köyü**, a small village that gives access to the **Aydos Canyon**, a steep river ravine leading from the interior.

Further east, as you pass through the village of **Denizkonak**, look out for the semicollapsed mosque, left by subsidence at an angle that would terrify the Leaning Tower of Pisa.

Doğanyurt, 31km before İnebolu, is yet another pleasant harbour town, while **Abana**, 9km further east, is a fast-growing resort with a decent beach.

Over halfway to Sinop, **İnebolu** is another handy stopping point, especially as you may not be able to find onward transport by late afternoon. The **Yakamoz Tatıl Köyü** (☎ 0366-811 3100; www.yakamoztatilkoyu.com, in Turkish; İsmetpaşa Cad-desi; r €25-78; 🏊), a small resort complex about 800m west of the centre, provides varied ac-commodation, a restaurant (mains €3 to €9), bar, café and a pebble beach. In the centre of town, be sure to have a look at the clutch of old Ottoman houses scattered around, and note the big restored mansion where Atatürk slept once in 1925.

About 41km east of İnebolu, near **Çatalzey-tin**, there is a long pebble beach surrounded by beautiful scenery. At **Ayancık** the road divides, with the left (northern) fork offering the more scenic route to Sinop, about 2½ hours from İnebolu. There are numerous lakes and caves around here.

SİNOP

☎ 0368 / pop 101,000

Sinop, on a promontory jutting into the Black Sea, is a natural site for a port and has been one for a thousand years. Today it's a popular destination for holidaymakers from İstanbul

LIKE A VIRGIN

Sinop takes its name from the legend of Sinope, daughter of the river god Asopus. Zeus fell in love with her and, in an attempt to buy her affections, promised to grant her any wish. Sinope, who had no intention of letting herself be seduced even by the king of the gods, promptly asked for eternal virginity. Outwitted, Zeus gave in gracefully, and allowed Sinope to live out her days in happy (and celibate) solitude at the tip of the peninsula.

and Ankara, and apparently for model-ship enthusiasts, who are spoilt for choice in the many model shops. While it has little to offer in terms of sights, it's a great Black Sea base, and most visitors find its laid-back charm, wining and dining options amenable to say the least.

History

Colonised from Miletus in the 8th century BC, Sinop's trade slowly grew, and successive rulers – Cimmerians, Phrygians, Persians, the Pontic kings (who made it their capital), Romans and Byzantines – turned it into a busy trading centre.

The Seljuks used Sinop as a port after taking it in 1214, but the Ottomans preferred to develop Samsun, which had better land communications.

On 30 November 1853, a Russian armada attacked Sinop without any warning, overwhelming the local garrison and inflicting great loss of life. The battle hastened the beginning of the Crimean War, in which the Ottomans allied with the British and French to fight Russian ambitions in the Near East.

Orientation

Sinop is at the narrow point of the peninsula, with the road continuing east beyond the town to beaches and land's end. The otogar (bus station) is at the western entrance to the town by the fortified walls. From here the unattractive main street, Sakarya Caddesi, cuts east through the centre 800m directly to the Sinop *vilayet konağı* (provincial government headquarters).

Information

Hit Café Internet (Gazi Caddesi; per hr €0.55; ✆ 10am-midnight)

Tourist information (☎ 261 5298; Gazi Caddesi; ✆ 8.30am-5pm mid-Jun–mid-Sep) Very friendly, helpful office with English-speaking female staff. There's a secondary booth by the otogar.

Sights & Activities

Sinop's prime attraction is the relatively well preserved **fortifications**. Open to attack from the sea, Sinop seems to have been fortified even since 2000 BC, but the existing walls are developments of those originally erected in 72 BC by Pontic King Mithridates IV. At one time the walls, some 3m thick, were more than 2km long, with seven gates, and towers 25m high. You can still walk along the ramparts in places to look out over the sea or back toward the distant mirage-like hills.

Near the shore on the northern side of the otogar is an ancient bastion called the **Kumkapı** (Sand Gate); on the southern side you can visit the **Tarihi Cezaevi** (Old Jail; admission €0.85; ✆ 9am-6pm), a hulking former prison block with most of its walled complex intact. Another square tower looms above the harbour nearby.

Sinop's **Archaeological Museum** (☎ 261 1975; Okulla Caddesi; admission €1.10; ✆ 8am-noon & 1-5pm Tue-Sun) is one of the better institutions along the coast – after all, how many local museums can boast their own excavation site next door? Apart from the Temple of Serapis dig, displays cover the classical, Byzantine and Ottoman periods, and there's an Ottoman tomb in the open garden.

In the town centre on Sakarya Caddesi stands the **Alaadin Camii** (1267), also called the Ulu Cami, a mosque set in a wide walled courtyard. It was constructed for Muinetti Süleyman Pervane, a powerful Seljuk grand vizier. The mosque has been repaired many times; its marble *mihrab* (the niche indicating the direction of Mecca) and *mimber* (pulpit) were added by the local Candaroğlu emir.

Next to it is the **Pervane Medresesi** (Pervane Seminary), built by Süleyman Pervane in 1262 to commemorate the second conquest of Sinop. It's now full of shops selling craft and local products.

Near the harbour is the **Tersane Hacı Ömer Camii** (1903) with, next to it, a touching monument, the Şehitler Çeşmesi (Martyrs' Fountain), built in memory of the many Turkish soldiers who died in the surprise Russian attack of 1853. The fountain was built using the money recovered from the soldiers' pockets.

Sinope Tours (☎ 261 7900; www.sinopetours.com; Kibris Caddesi 3) runs daily city and local tours.

Sleeping

Yılmaz Aile Pansiyonu (☎ 261 5752; Tersane Çarşısı 11; s/d/tr €8.50/17/23) Great value for a budget price, these plain but neat rooms have TVs and individual boilers for the showers. Quite a few have views, and room 47 in particular is a nice bright triple with balcony. Room 46, on the other hand, appears to be missing entirely! Breakfast not included.

Otel Meral (☎ 261 3100; Kurtuluş Caddesi 19; s/d/tr/q €11/20/22/34) The hearts on the bedspreads merit a quick 'aww', but you might not be so impressed with the bathrooms – some are shared, and even some of the private showers are missing their heads. Still, if it's budget you want this'll do.

Otel 57 (☎ 261 5462; otel57@hotmail.com; Kurtuluş Caddesi 29; s/d €17/22) Amazing what you can get

for those extra few euros: digital TV, in-house bar, balconies and big butch, beefy shower heads. The pink and brown colour scheme may not count as a bonus.

Otel Gönül (☎ 261 1829; gonulltd@superonline.com.tr; Meydankapı Mahallesi 11; s/d €17/25) Away from the waterfront, near the museum, this tall, slightly quirky hotel comes with schoolyard murals in the stairways, statues in the 1st-floor café, pinks and yellows in the rooms and a mosque right next door.

Otel Sarı Kadır (☎ 260 1544; Derinboğazağzı Sokak 22; s/d/tr €17/25/28) Plain but spacious rooms with TV, sofa and fridge make this waterfront establishment a fine value choice. There are sea views from the front balconies, a terrace for breakfast and a tea garden right opposite.

Denizci Otel (☎ 260 5934; Kurtuluş Caddesi 13; s/d/tr €20/28/34) The Denizci goes for an all-round classy impression, and for the most part achieves it, especially in the slick bar-lounge. Rooms are compact but comfortable.

Eating

Sinop has a lively restaurant scene. The waterfront is lined with licensed Mediterranean-style open-air restaurants, right by the boats in the harbour.

Dolunay Pastanesi (☎ 261 8688; Kurtuluş Caddesi 14; desserts from €1.10; ☺ 9am-11pm) A bright and colourful tropical-styled patisserie for those après-fish sweet cravings.

Birhan Café (Atatürk Caddesi; mains €1.50-3; ☺ 9am-10pm) A slick bistro-café with a few modern design touches, pulling in a vaguely trendy young crowd for breakfast, drinks and grills.

Barınak Café (☎ 261 7421; İskele Caddesi 9; mains €2-4; ☺ 11am-11pm) The only waterfront eatery brave enough to skip seafood entirely, with an emphasis on pizzas, burgers and steaks – a welcome break if you're tired of fish and kebaps.

Kardelen Restaurant (☎ 260 3032; İskele Caddesi 4; mains €2.50-5; ☺ 11am-11pm) Just round the corner from the main harbour strip, this brown-toned restaurant has a more laid-back old-time vibe than some of its contemporaries, though it sticks to the same broad menu.

Saray Restaurant (☎ 261 1729; İskele Caddesi 18; fish dishes €4.50-7; ☺ 11am-11pm) Oft tipped as Sinop's top option, with a floating pontoon terrace bobbing right on the water next to the fishing boats in summer. Choose from the harbour-fresh fish on display – *cinekop* (bluefish), *levrek* or *barbun* – and sample it grilled or fried with a salad.

Drinking & Entertainment

Yalı Kahvesi (☎ 261 3996; Derinboğazağzı Sokak 14) A prime waterfront spot for nondiners throughout the day, with plastic tables spilling onto the terrace and pavement for the assorted drinkers and gamers.

Sinop Sofrası (☎ 260 5461; Pervane Medresesi, Batur Sokak) A mercilessly cute little tea room just inside the gate of the old *medrese*, punting plenty of local products.

Burç Café (☎ 260 0420; Sinop Kalesi, Tersane Caddesi) This popular haunt perched in the tower of the fortifications attracts a feisty young crowd for live music, wide views and, of course, cold beer.

Lonca Disco Bar (Cumhuriyet Caddesi) The best of Sinop's handful of bars and discos, set in an enviable location in the city walls themselves, at the old Lonca gate.

Getting There & Away

The table, below, lists some useful daily services from Sinop's small otogar. There are no direct services to Amasra, 312km to the west; you'll need to take point-to-point minibuses or change at İnebolu or Cide.

SERVICES FROM SİNOP'S OTOGAR

Destination	Fare	Duration	Distance	Frequency (per day)
Ankara	€20	9hr	443km	3
İnebolu	€7	3hr	156km	1 at 8am
İstanbul	€25	10½hr	700km	5
Karabük (for Safranbolu)	€14	6hr	340km	5
Samsun	€6	3½hr	168km	roughly hourly
Trabzon	€17	9hr	533km	1 at 8pm

AROUND SİNOP

If you have your own transport or fancy a day tour out of Sinop, there are a few attractions in nearby towns and villages – consult the tourist office or a travel agency for suggestions. The most common excursions are to **Erfelek**, famed for its 28 waterfalls, the historic fishing town of **Gerze** and the area around **Ayancı** (see p539). Walking and canoeing are popular pastimes for the more energetic visitor.

If you just want a dip in the Karadeniz (Black Sea), the black-sand **Karakum Plajı** is about 3km east of Sinop harbour, with a restaurant, camp site and a couple of homestays.

SAMSUN

☎ 0362 / pop 364,000

Samsun is the largest city on the coast, known primarily as a major port and commercial centre. While the local tourist board is trying to market it as a spa town, few travellers stop for more than a bite to eat or a change of bus – even the enterprising Genoese only paused long enough to burn the city to the ground in the 15th century. That said, there are enough facilities here to warrant a convenience break.

Orientation & Information

The city centre is Cumhuriyet Meydanı (Republic Sq), inland, and just west of Atatürk

Park, which lies on the coastal highway (Atatürk Bulvarı). Southeast of the park stands the old *vilayet*. The huge Samsun *valiliği* building is across Atatürk Bulvarı to the north. Cumhuriyet Caddesi runs along the south side of the park.

The **tourist office** (☎ 431 1228; Atatürk Bulvarı; ⏱ 8am-noon & 1-5pm daily Jun-Aug, Mon-Fri Sep-May), across the coastal road from Cumhuriyet Meydanı, gives out decent maps and brochures, including a list of spas, and may also offer to arrange tours.

The train station is 550m southeast of Atatürk Park on the shore road, Atatürk Bulvarı, while the otogar is a further 1.5km southeast, also on the shore road.

Sights

With an hour or so to spare it's well worth visiting the **Archaeology & Ethnography Museum** (Arkeoloji ve Etnoğrafya Müzesi; ☎ 431 6828; Fuar Caddesi; admission €1.10; ⏱ 8.30am-noon & 1-5pm Tue-Sun), west of the Samsun Valiliği building. The most striking exhibit is a huge Romano-Byzantine mosaic depicting Thetis, Achilles and the Four Seasons, found nearby at Karasamsun (Amisos). Other highlights include the elegant gold jewellery found in a cemetery tomb in 1995, thought to date from the time of the legendary Mithridates (VI Eupator, 120 to 130 BC), and a daunting display on ancient skull surgery.

Right next door is the **Atatürk Museum** (Atatürk Müzesi; Fuar Caddesi), commemorating the start of the War of Independence here on 19 May 1919. The museum was closed at time of research.

After the highbrow stuff, you could nip along the coast road and indulge your inner (or outer) child at the **Akyol Luna Park** funfair.

Sleeping & Eating

Hotel Necmi (☎ 432 7164; otelnecmi@hotmail.com; Bedestan Sokak 6; s/d/tr with shared bathroom €11/20/25) Not the best budget option you'll ever come across: breakfast is not included, and when we visited there were some distinctly unpleasant smells. It's the cheapest you'll get, though, and the clothing-bazaar location is fun.

Samsun Park Otel (☎ 435 0095; Cumhuriyet Caddesi 8; s/d/tr €25/34/50) A hieroglyphic lift whisks you up to a full set of compact but perfectly comfortable rooms just south of the city centre. As well as having a house restaurant it's near several good patisseries.

Vidinli Oteli (☎ 431 6050; Kazımpaşa Caddesi 4; s/d €34/50; ⏱ ▯) Rooms here seem a bit plain for the price you pay, even with sea views,

but overall standards are good and there's a smart bar-restaurant to tear you away from the digital TV.

North Point Hotel (☎ 435 9595; www.northpointhotel.com; Atatürk Bulvarı 594; s/d €44/61; ⏱ ▯) Twelve storeys of new conference-class comfort on the coast road. Buses and dolmuşes stop conveniently right outside, and you can look out and chuckle at how much guests in the huge Büyük Samsun Oteli opposite must be paying.

Sıla Restaurant (☎ 432 9515; Vilayet Karşısı 36; mains €1.50-5; ⏱ 9am-9pm) Şiş, İskender and all the usual kebap and pide favourites await your pleasure at this reliable central eatery.

Demircioğlu Balık Restaurant (☎ 435 7550; Kazımpaşa Caddesi 20; mains €3-8; ⏱ 11am-10pm) Samsun's number-one fish pedlar is a neat little brick house wedged between nondescript blocks, dishing up fine fresh sea-dwellers in its quaint 1st-floor dining room.

Getting There & Away

AIR

There are three or four daily direct flights to İstanbul with **Turkish Airlines** (☎ 435 2330; Kazımpaşa Caddesi 18/A) and one with **Onur Air** (☎ 431 6665; 19 Mayıs Bulvarı 35/2). Turkish Airlines also has one daily service to Ankara. Both companies operate a *servis* (shuttle minibus) from their offices to the airport (€3).

BUS

Most major bus companies have offices at the Cumhuriyet Meydanı end of Cumhuriyet Caddesi. Services to major destinations are listed in the table, below; to the otogar costs €0.55.

SERVICES FROM SAMSUN'S OTOGAR

Destination	Fare	Duration	Distance	Frequency (per day)
Amasya	€5	2½hr	130km	frequent
Ankara	€17	7hr	420km	frequent
Artvin	€14	8hr	577km	4
Giresun	€8.50	3½hr	220km	5
İstanbul	€25	11hr	750km	several
Kayseri	€20	9hr	530km	a few
Sinop	€5.60	3hr	168km	several
Trabzon	€11	6hr	355km	several
Ünye	€4	1½hr	95km	every 30 minutes

CAR & MOTORCYCLE

Samsun has a small cluster of car-rental agencies along or around Lise Caddesi, including

TRACING THE AMAZONS

The Samsun–Ünye region, and the small town of Terme in particular, is often associated with one of the most enduring peoples found in Greek mythology: the Amazons. This fierce race of warrior women, famed for cutting off one breast to aid their archery skills, were said to have ruled the coast in pre-Pontic times and picked fights with everyone from the Lycians to the Phrygians. Writers from Homer and Herodotus to Amasya's own Strabo all relate various tales involving these strapping female soldiers, some more credible than others: the greatest relish is reserved for discussion of their supposed reproductive habits, suggesting either annual coitus with a neighbouring tribe or 'breeding colonies' of captive male sex slaves. If you believe some early biographers, Alexander the Great himself may have had a child with the Amazonian queen Thalestris!

Historically speaking, there is little evidence to support any Amazonian presence in the Black Sea area around the purported 1200 BC timeframe, though female warrior burials have been found in central Asia. One theory is that the myth sprang from the role of high priestesses in certain mother-goddess cults, while other historians believe that it arose from travellers encountering Anatolian tribes with matriarchal systems or simply a measure of equality between the sexes, which would have run contrary to their own ingrained sense of gender roles.

Wherever the story came from, it was one of many classical legends to capture public imagination in the following centuries, and eventually provided the name for the world's largest river. Who would have thought coastal Turkey could have something in common with rainforest Brazil?

Avis (☎ 231 6750; Ümraniye Sokak 2) and **Budget** (☎ 231 5300; Lise Caddesi). To find them, head southeast for about 700m from Atatürk Park along Cumhuriyet Caddesi.

TRAIN

Two daily trains run from Samsun **station** (☎ 233 5002) to Sivas (€8.50, 8½ hours) and Amasya (€3, three hours).

ÜNYE

☎ 0452 / pop 70,000

You'd never think it to look at it, but Ünye, a small, pretty holiday town amid hazelnut groves 95km east of Samsun, has one of the longest settlement histories in Anatolia, with evidence of inhabitation going back to the Paleolithic period. The town's position at the junction of the Silk Road and the coastal highway made it an important port during the Ottoman period. The great Turkish mystical poet Yunus Emre, who wrote during the early 14th century, is thought to have been born here, and it's also believed that one St Nicholas lived nearby, in the days before he became known as Santa Claus. Despite all this history, though, most visitors find Ünye little more than a brief and pleasant coastal stopover.

The friendly **tourist office** (☎ 323 2569; ☻ 8am-noon & 1-5pm Mon-Fri), in the pink government Kaymakamliği building on the main square, dispenses a couple of brochures and can dem-

onstrate a fuzzy computer slideshow of the area's main attractions.

Sights & Activities

About 7km inland from the town stands **Ünye Castle**, a ruined fortress founded by the Pontics and rebuilt by the Byzantines, with an ancient tomb cut into the rock face below. To get there catch a minibus heading to Kaleköy or Akkuş (€0.30) from the Niksar road, and ask to be dropped off at the road to the castle. From here you've got at least a half-hour trek to the top.

Another minor excursion is the **Tozkoparan Kay Mezarı** (Tozkoparan Rock Tomb), off the Trabzon road 5km from the centre. Any eastbound minibus can drop you by the cement factory at the turn for the cave.

Back in town, just east of the square, have a look at the **Ali-Namık Soysal Eski Hamam**, which was once a church. It's open to men from early morning to noon and all day Sunday and for women from noon until 4pm. The massive **plane trees** in the centre are also worthy of note – they're reckoned to be around 500 years old.

Sleeping

Otel Çınar (☎ 323 1148; Hükümet Caddesi 18; s/d €8.50/17) A recent lick of paint has spruced up this central budget option, which remains good value. Some bathrooms are shared, and no breakfast is provided.

Otel Lider (☎ 324 9250; Hükümet Caddesi 36; s/d 11/22) Another good pick for the thrifty travel-er, comfortably central, with unfussy rooms, unctional bathrooms, digital TV and a pleas-nt rooftop terrace. Breakfast costs €2.

Hotel Grand Kuşçalı (☎ 324 5200; Devlet Sahilyolu ehir Merkezi 42; s/d/tr €28/48/59; 🌫) The billet of hoice for tour groups, the Kuşçalı isn't *that* rand but there's nothing else in town to ouch it for facilities or contemporary style. 'erks include sauna, *hamam* and sea-facing th-floor restaurant.

Ünye has a generous eight camp sites and a andful of beach pensions, mostly spread out long the Samsun road west of town. **Cafe Gülen laj Camping** (☎ 324 7368; Devlet Sahil Yolu; camp sites €6, ungalows €30) has an excellent setting and cute vooden bungalows. The adjoining **Uzunkum estaurant Plaj & Camping** (☎ 323 2022; Devlet Sahil olu; camp sites €6) is another welcoming spot raced with a beachfront setting and loads of hade. Green-and-white minibuses regularly ·ly the coastal route between these places and he centre of town from early in the morning ntil around 11pm.

ating

afé Vanilya (☎ 324 4106; Cumhuriyet Meydanı 3; snacks 1-3; 🕑 10am-8pm) Set in a rather swish restored illa-style townhouse, the Vanilya is a tenta-vely chic but unpretentious terrace café serv-ıg Ünye's would-be bright young things.

Evim (☎ 324 3341; Hacı Emin Caddesi; dishes €1-3; 🕑 8am-7pm) A genuinely local eatery off the nain square, dishing up homemade baklava, *örek* (filled pastries) and *mantı* (Turkish avioli) to real regulars.

Sofra (☎ 323 4083; Belediye Caddesi 25; mains €1-5; 🕑 9am-11pm) No relation to the international estaurant chain, this Sofra is a square stone ouse facing the sea, with a weighty range of ebabs and Ottoman dishes. The roadside ·rrace is sheathed in plastic, which keeps out ımes but kills the atmosphere a bit.

Çakırtepe (☎ 323 2568; Çakırtepe; mains €2-5; 🕑 11am-10pm) Atop the hill west of the town entre, this picnic site, tea garden and café s a local favourite for long summer lunches. njoy the sublime views and tuck into the ·eservedly revered *pide* or *güveç* (stew in a lay pot). Minibuses leave from the west side f Cumhuriyet Meydanı, and will take you ·ithin steps of the restaurant.

Çamlık Restaurant (☎ 323 1175; Çamlık İçi; mains €2-5; 🕑 11am-10pm) This is another popular picnic place and recreation area, featuring a good selection of fish and meat dishes, along with delicious mezes. In summer, the shady ter-race overlooking the sea is reason enough to come here.

Yunus Emre Çay Bahçesı (☎ 323 3068; Yunus Emre Parkı; dishes €2.50-4; 🕑 9am-9pm) Unusually, this big, well-frequented tea garden beside the pier serves substantial pides and stews as well as the usual drinks, perfect for sunset with sustenance.

Park Restaurant (☎ 323 3053; Devlet Sahil Yolu 6; mains €3-6; 🕑 11am-11pm) Generally rammed with families, tour groups and other voluble table-fuls, the Park is unashamedly outré with its pink exterior and bogus classicism. Luckily the menu is wide-ranging, the open terrace is gorgeous, the booze flows freely and the live music helps things along.

Getting There & Away

Bus companies have offices on the coastal road. Minibuses and midibuses rumble up and down this road to Samsun (€4, 1½ hours) and Ordu (€4, 1¾ hours), via Fatsa, Bolaman and Perşembe, roughly every 20 minutes.

AROUND ÜNYE

About 5km east of Ünye, the road passes the otogar, the cement factory and the **Asarkaya National Park** (🕑 May-Oct), a forested recreation zone with facilities for walkers and picnickers. Another 14km along is the slightly tacky town of **Fatsa**. From here the shore is largely for-ested, and the winding road throws up some lovely vistas, at least until you hit **Bolaman**, which has little going for it except a hand-ful of dilapidated Ottoman wooden houses. Then you'll pass **Çaka Beach**, an unexpectedly delightful strip of white sand, and arguably the best beach on the Black Sea; if you've been smart and packed a picnic, it's worth pausing here in the shade. **Perşembe**, 15km west of Ordu, faces a pretty harbour with two lighthouses. If you need to break up your journey, drop by the modern two-star **Dede Evi** (☎ 0452-517 3802; Atatürk Bulvarı; s/d €18/24), a smart option boasting sea views and high standards, with wrought-iron balconies, par-quet flooring and rooms decorated in warm yellow tones.

You can get to any of these towns by flag-ging down the many minibuses or midibuses going in either direction along the coast road – you shouldn't have to wait too long.

ORDU

☎ 0452 / pop 113,000

An old town with a modern heart, Ordu is about 80km east of Ünye, basing its bustling, well-kept centre around a pleasant seafront boulevard. The city limits sprawl in both directions, but somehow it's easy to feel like you're in a small resort when you're pottering around the narrow central streets.

The **tourist office** (☎ 223 1608; ☽ 8am-5pm Mon-Fri, Mon-Sat Jun-Aug) is conveniently situated on the sea-facing side of the *belediye*, just east of the mosque on the coastal road. It's run by the very friendly and knowledgeable M Gürcan, who speaks good English.

Internet access is available at **Ordu Net** (Fidangör Sokak; per hr €0.55; ☽ 10am-midnight).

Sights

A gem of a place, **Pasha's Palace & Ethnography Museum** (Paşaoğlu Konağı ve Etnoğrafya Müzesi; Taşocak Caddesi; admission €1.10; ☽ 9am-noon & 1.30-5pm Tue-Sun) occupies a late-19th-century house 500m uphill from Cumhuriyet Meydanı. Signs reading 'Müze – Museum' direct you here past the small handicrafts bazaar. The downstairs displays are easily overshadowed by the re-created Ottoman rooms on the 1st floor, furnished with worn original artefacts that only add to the authenticity of the set-up. The tiles and braziers are notable touches, as is the chair where Atatürk himself supposedly had a rest in 1924.

A few other scraps of Ordu's old town survive, centred around the **Tasbaşı Cultural Centre**, an old Greek church about 800m from the main square. A perfectly placed terrace café is due to open here soon.

If you have some more time, catch a dolmuş up the hill to **Boztepe** (6.5km) for breathtaking views over the town and the coast. Bring a picnic, or nibble on snacks in one of the restaurants there.

Sleeping & Eating

The accommodation and eating scene in Ordu is disappointingly limited, but there are a couple of notable exceptions worth considering.

Hotel Turist (☎ 225 3140; Atatürk Bulvarı 134; s/d/tr €23/34/45; ☒) Distinctly unimpressive for the price, these basic rooms in mustard tones aren't always as fragrant as they could be, but sea-facing front balconies and a conservatory breakfast room help redeem them.

Karlıbel Atlıhan Hotel (☎ 225 0565; www.karlibelh tel.com; Kazım Karabekir Caddesi 7; s/d/tr €28/50/67; ☒) A much more professional establishment with spacious rooms in subdued colours and hint at a predilection for horse art. The same firm runs another fine hotel in converted Ottoman buildings just outside town.

Jazz Café (☎ 214 6778; Sımpasa Caddesi 28; mair €2.50-4; ☽ 9am-10pm) A modern, musically themed eatery on Ordu's pedestrian shopping drag, it offers everything from pizz and omelettes to *gözleme* and *kumpir* (bake potatoes). Sadly, it's no relation to the grea London venue.

Ayışığı (☎ 223 2870; Atatürk Bulvarı; mains €3-€ ☽ from 11am) Occupying a bizarre rounded concrete structure on the beach, not unlike bunker, the 'Moonlight' combines a terrace café, restaurant and *meyhane* (Turkish pub to good effect, with a tea terrace on top fo daytime sea-gazing.

Grand Mıdı Restaurant (☎ 214 0340; İskele Üstü 5; mains €3-8; ☽ 11am-11pm) On the shore near th tourist office, a long, covered pontoon lead to a bright, very spacious dining room o stilts. The interior boasts black-and-whit pictures of old Ordu, full colour views of th real thing, and a strong line in fish from th surrounding sea.

Getting There & Around

Buses from behind the *belediye* leave ever half-hour for Giresun (€2, one hour); fo Ünye (€4, 1¾ hours) you must go to the bu stand, 1.5km east of the centre, or flag dow a minibus along the coastal road.

Local dolmuşes regularly loop through th city centre. Line 2 will take you from the cen tre of town past the Karlıbel İkizevler Hote in one direction, and near the otogar in th other. A dolmuş to Boztepe costs €0.85.

GIRESUN

☎ 0454 / pop 84,000

The town of Giresun, 46km east of Ordu, wa founded some 3000 years ago and is steepe in history. Legend has it that Jason and th Argonauts passed by on their voyage to th fabled Kingdom of Colchis (Georgia), o the eastern shores of the Black Sea, in searc of the Golden Fleece. The city is also credite with introducing cherries to Italy, and fror there to the rest of the world; apparently eve the name Giresun comes from the Greek fo cherry.

Today Giresun's wealth still grows on trees, but now it's the humble hazelnut that brings in most revenue – the area is widely reputed to have the best *fındık* plantations in Turkey. Come here to enjoy the edible treats as well as fabulous views over the city and bay from the hillside park near the centre.

Orientation & Information

The centre of Giresun is Atapark on the coastal road. The *belediye* is just inland from the park. The main commercial street is Gazi Caddesi, climbing steeply uphill from the *belediye*.

There is a **tourist office** (☎ 216 4707; Gazi Caddesi 9; ☺ 8am-5pm Mon-Fri) and a more convenient **kiosk** (☺ 8am-5pm) in Atapark, but there's no English spoken at either place. The **PTT** and several internet cafés are a few hundred metres uphill from the *belediye*.

Sights & Activities

Once you've had your fill of hazelnuts, cherries and chocolate bars containing hazelnuts or cherries, burn off the calories by walking the 2km to the **Kalepark** (Castle Park), perched on the steep hillside above the town. This beautiful shady park offers panoramic views of the town and the sea. It also has beer gardens for a sunset brew, groves for lovers and barbecues for grillers. It's busy on weekends.

No public transport serves the park, so you'll need to walk inland and uphill from Atapark on Gazi Caddesi and turn left onto Bekirpaşa Caddesi, 200m or so past the Otel Kit-Tur. A taxi costs around €2.

The **City Museum** (Şehir Müzesi; ☎ 212 1322; Atatürk Bulvarı 62; admission €1.10; ☺ 8am-5pm) is housed in the disused 18th-century Gogora church, .5km around the promontory east of Atapark on the coastal road. The building is more appealing than the museum itself, with well-preserved architectural features outshining the usual archaeological and ethnographic sections.

If you plan on spending a bit more time here, you could explore the old houses in the Zeytinlik district, or head to the **alpine plateaus** about 40km inland, which offer ample walking opportunities and some winter sports.

Festivals & Events

The four-day **International Giresun Aksu Festival**, starting annually on 20 May, hails rebirth, fecundity and the start of the new growing season with concerts, traditional dance performances and other open-air events.

Sleeping & Eating

As Giresun isn't much of a tourist town, most hotels here cater primarily to Turkish businesspeople.

Er-Tur Oteli (☎ 216 1757; otelertur@mynet.com; Çapulacılar Sokak 8; s/d/tr €17/25/36) Unfussy but entirely acceptable one-star standards on a side street east of the Atapark. The 'family' triples can sleep four people on request.

Otel Ormancılar (☎ 212 4391; otelormancilar@hotmail .com; Gazi Caddesi 37; s/d/tr €20/28/34; ⊠ ⊒) Essentially the best midrange deal in town, the Ormancılar tricks its rooms out with starburst doors and brown tones, with TV and phone, and there's even an in-house jeweller. There's a bit of street noise but nothing to lose sleep over.

Otel Çarıkçı (☎ 216 1026; otelcarikci@yahoo.com; Osmanağa Caddesi 6; s/d/tr €25/35/42; ⊠) More excellent value in this price range, flashing laminate floors, shiny new tiled bathrooms and wireless internet access. It's down the first street off Gazi Caddesi,.

Otel Başar (☎ 212 9920; www.hotelbasar.com.tr; Atatürk Bulvarı; s/d/tr €34/56/67; ⊠) Right on the waterfront by the busy coast road, it's far better to be inside this eight-storey eyesore than outside, not least because it's actually surprisingly tasteful and well laid-out. Facilities include a roof café and smart restaurant.

Deniz Lokantası (☎ 216 1158; Alpaslan Caddesi 3; mains €1.10-4; ☺ 10am-10pm) Next to the *belediye*, this modernised cafeteria has been churning out decent meals since 1953. It's very busy at lunch time.

Ellez (☎ 216 1491; Fatih Caddesi 9; mains €1.50-4; ☺ 10am-10pm) One block north of Atapark, this cute little pide-*lahmacun*-pizza joint has an upstairs salon with straggly plants and Turkish flags protruding from the tiny balcony.

Getting There & Away

The bus station is 4km west of the centre, but buses usually drop people at Atapark too. Frequent minibuses shuttle from Giresun to Trabzon (€4, two hours) and to Ordu (€2, one hour). Trabzon services leave from offices on the main road one block east of Atapark; those to Ordu stop on the main highway opposite. Several daily buses head west to Samsun (p543).

GİRESUN TO TRABZON

From Giresun it's another 150km to Trabzon; sadly major roadworks right by the shore have ruined many of the coastal vistas. Along the way, the road passes through several small towns, including the attractive town of **Tirebolu**, with a chirpy small harbour and two castles (St Jean Kalesi and Bedrama Kalesi). The Çaykur tea-processing plant, one of dozens strung out along the coast, signals your arrival in Turkey's tea country.

Görele is the next town eastward. Here your bus might stop for everyone to pile out into one of the many bakeries selling the big round loaves the town is famous for. Soon after Görele is **Akçakale**, where you'll see the ruins of a 13th-century Byzantine castle on a little peninsula. Shortly before reaching Trabzon you pass through **Akçaabat**, a small town known for its *köfte*, with a decent restaurant or two offering samples.

TRABZON

☎ 0462 / pop 215,000

While it retains the slightly seedy character peculiar to port towns, most of Trabzon is far too caught up in its own whirl of activity to worry about visitors, and if there's one impression of the place that people can agree on, it's the crazy-busy bustle of the fast-paced, hectic city centre, packed solid with cars, taxis, minibuses, idlers, police, parents and pedestrians throughout the day. The buzz can be infectious after enough village calm'n'charm, but if you haven't yet had your quota of coastal relaxation Trabzon may well make you feel it's long overdue.

It's not just the streets that are busy, either: Trabzon is the largest port along the eastern coast, handling and dispatching goods for Georgia, Armenia, Azerbaijan and Iran. Russian tourists are also a major import, gradually replacing the swarms of traders and 'natashas' (prostitutes) who arrived after the collapse of the Soviet Union. You'll hear Russian spoken about town and see some shop signs in Cyrillic script.

Most people come to Trabzon to visit the medieval church of Aya Sofya, poke around in the old town, visit Atatürk's lovely villa on the outskirts, and to make an excursion to Sumela (p554), a dramatic Byzantine monastery carved out of a sheer rock cliff. With good transport connections and plenty of life, it's a prime stopover for anyone heading east or west.

History

Trabzon's recorded history begins around 74 BC, when Miletus colonists came from Sino and founded a settlement, Trapezus, with a acropolis on the *trápeza* (table) of land abov the harbour.

The town did reasonably well for 200 years, occupying itself with port activitie until the Christian soldiers of the Fourth Cru sade seized and sacked Constantinople i 1204, forcing its noble families to seek refug in Anatolia. The imperial family of the Com neni established an empire along the Blac Sea coast in 1204, with Alexius Comnenus reigning as the emperor of Trebizond.

The Trapezuntine rulers became skilful a balancing their alliances with the Seljuks, th Mongols, the Genoese and others. Prosper ing through trade with eastern Anatolia an Persia, the empire reached the height of i wealth and culture during the reign of Alexiu II (1297–1330), after which it fell to piece in factional disputes. Even so, the Empire c Trebizond survived until the coming of th Ottomans in 1461, holding out for eight year longer than Constantinople.

When the Ottoman Empire was defeate after WWI, Trabzon's many Greek resident sought to establish a Republic of Trebizon echoing the old Comneni Empire, but th Turks were ultimately victorious, and Atatür himself declared Trabzon 'one of the riches strongest and most sensitive sources of trus for the Turkish Republic'.

Orientation

Modern Trabzon's heart is the Atatürk Alar district around the park of the same name, als known as Meydan Parkı. The port is directl east of Atatürk Alanı, down a steep hill.

There are cafés and restaurants west c Atatürk Alanı along Uzun Sokak (Long Lane and Kahramanmaraş Caddesi (Maraş Cadde for short). West of the centre, past the bazaa is Ortahisar, a picturesque old neighbourhoo straddling a ravine.

Trabzon's otogar is 3km east of the port.

Information

Most banks, ATMs, exchange offices and th PTT are along or around Maraş Caddesi.

Atlas Laundry (Map p550; ☎ 322 4475; Deniz Sokak; 5kg load €4.50)

Tourist office (Map p550; ☎ 326 4760; Camii Sokak; ☼ 8am-5.30pm daily Jun-Sep, 8am-5pm Mon-Fri ct-May) Right by Hotel Nur, this place is very helpful and well used to travellers' needs. English is usually spoken.

Tourist Police (Map p550; ☎ 326 3077; Atatürk Alanı)

Ustatour (Map p550; ☎ 326 9545; Usta Park Hotel, İskenderpaşa Mahallesi) Domestic airline agent.

VIP Internet (Map p550; Gazıpaşa Caddesi 6; per hr 0.55; ☺ 9am-midnight)

World Internet (Map p550; Atatürk Alanı 28; per hr 0.55; ☺ 8am-11.30pm)

Sights & Activities

TRABZON MUSEUM

Just south of Uzun Sokak, a marvellous Italian-designed mansion was built for a Russian merchant in 1912 and inhabited briefly by Atatürk. It now houses the **Trabzon Museum** (Trabzon Müzesi; Map p549; Zeytinlik Caddesi 10; admission €1.10; ☺ 9am-noon

& 1-6pm Tue-Sun). Inside, the fantastic interiors and original furnishings put most Ottoman re-creations to shame, with a series of impressive high-ceilinged living rooms displaying a variety of ethnographic and Islamic artefacts, mostly labelled in English. The archaeological section in the basement also has some significant pieces, including a flattened bronze statue of Hermes from local excavations at Tabakhane and Byzantine finds from around the Sumela Monastery.

AYA SOFYA MUSEUM

One of Trabzon's star attractions, the **Aya Sofya Museum** (Aya Sofya Müzesi; ☎ 223 3033; admission €1.10; ☺ 9am-6pm Tue-Sun Apr-Oct, 9am-5pm Tue-Sun Nov-Mar), originally Hagia Sophia (Church of the Divine

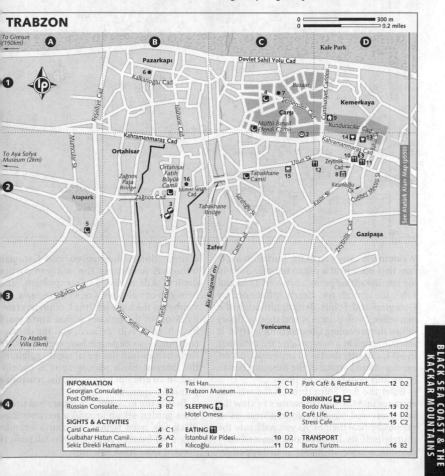

TRABZON

0 — 300 m
0 — 0.2 miles

BLACK SEA COAST & THE KAÇKAR MOUNTAINS

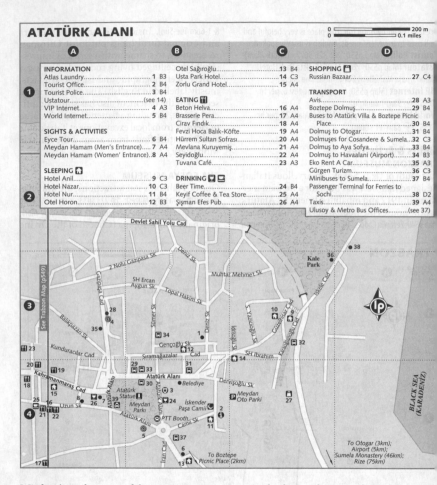

ATATÜRK ALANI

0 ————————— 200 m
0 ————————— 0.1 miles

INFORMATION
Atlas Laundry.................................. 1 B3
Tourist Office.................................. 2 B4
Tourist Police................................. 3 B4
Ustatour.....................................(see 14)
VIP Internet.................................... 4 A3
World Internet................................ 5 B4

SIGHTS & ACTIVITIES
Eyce Tour...................................... 6 B4
Meydan Hamam (Men's Entrance)..... 7 A4
Meydan Hamam (Women' Entrance)..8 A4

SLEEPING
Hotel Anil...................................... 9 C3
Hotel Nazar................................... 10 C3
Hotel Nur...................................... 11 B4
Otel Horon.................................... 12 B3

Otel Sağıroğlu................................13 B4
Usta Park Hotel..............................14 C3
Zorlu Grand Hotel...........................15 A4

EATING
Beton Helva...................................16 A4
Brasserie Pera................................17 A4
Cirav Fındık...................................18 A4
Fevzi Hoca Balık-Köfte....................19 A4
Hürrem Sultan Sofrası.....................20 A4
Mevlana Kuruyemiş.........................21 A4
Seyidoğlu......................................22 A4
Tuvana Café..................................23 A3

DRINKING
Beer Time.....................................24 B4
Keyif Coffee & Tea Store.................25 A4
Şişman Efes Pub.............................26 A4

SHOPPING
Russian Bazaar..............................27 C4

TRANSPORT
Avis..28 A3
Boztepe Dolmuş.............................29 B4
Buses to Atatürk Villa & Boztepe Picnic
    Place.......................................30 B4
Dolmuş to Otogar...........................31 B4
Dolmuşes for Cosandere & Sumela...32 C3
Dolmuş to Aya Sofya.......................33 B4
Dolmuş to Havaalani (Airport)..........34 B3
Eko Rent A Car..............................35 A3
Gürgen Turizm...............................36 C3
Minibuses to Sumela.......................37 B4
Passenger Terminal for Ferries to
    Sochi.......................................38 D2
Taxis..39 A4
Ulusoy & Metro Bus Offices..........(see 37)

Wisdom), is 4km west of the centre on a terrace that once held a pagan temple. Built in the late Byzantine period, between 1238 and 1263, the church was clearly influenced by Georgian and Seljuk design, although the marvellous wall paintings and mosaic floors follow the prevailing Constantinople style. It was converted to a mosque after the conquest in 1461, and later used as an ammunition storage depot and hospital by the Russians, before being fully restored in the 1960s.

Enter the Aya Sofya through the western entrance into the vaulted narthex to view the best-preserved, vividly coloured frescoes of various biblical themes. As you walk into the church itself, its design becomes immediately obvious: a cross-in-square plan topped by

a single dome, showing obvious Georgia₁ influence. A fresco in the southern portic₀ depicts Adam and Eve's expulsion, an₀ here you can also see a relief of an eagle, th₀ symbol of the founders, the Comnenus fam ily. Most of the frescoes within arm's reac₁ have been heavily defaced, and the damag₀ continues – some people have even scratche₀ their names into the metal signs explainin₉ the images! Flash photography is prohib ited, in an attempt to preserve the remainin₉ painted fragments.

Beside the museum is a square bell tower a tea garden set up around a reconstructe₀ Black Sea coast farmhouse, and a *serande* (granary) from Of county, set on tall posts t₀ prevent mice from entering.

The site is above the coastal highway, eachable by dolmuş from the northern side of Atatürk Alanı.

ATATÜRK VILLA

Town life too hectic for you? Head to the Atatürk Villa (Atatürk Köşkü; ☎ 231 0028; admission €1.10; 8am-7pm May-Sep, 8am-5pm Oct-Apr), 5km southwest of Atatürk Alanı. Set above the town, it has a fine view and lovely gardens. The three-storey white villa, designed in a Black Sea style popular in the Crimea, was built between 1890 and 1903 for a wealthy Trabzon banking family, and was given to Atatürk when he visited the city in 1924. It's now a mildly interesting museum of Atatürk memorabilia, but the best reason to come is to see the building and the pretty grounds, or to relax in the pleasant tea garden at the back.

City buses labelled 'Köşk', from the northern side of Atatürk Alanı, will drop you right outside the villa (€0.50). Buses depart about every half-hour.

BAZAAR DISTRICT

The lively bazaar is to the west of Atatürk Alanı, in the Çarşı (Market) quarter, accessible by the pedestrianised Kunduracılar Caddesi from Atatürk Alanı, which cuts through the tightly packed streets of the ancient bazaar. Close to the recently restored Çarşı amii (Market Mosque; Map p549), you'll see the Taş Han (Vakıf Han; Map p549), a single-domed han (caravanserai) thought to have been constructed around 1647, making it the oldest marketplace in Trabzon. It's now full of workshops and stores.

MOSQUE OF THE OTTOMANS

West of the centre, Gülbahar Hatun Camii (Map p549), another mosque worth taking a close look at, was built by Selim the Grim, the great Ottoman conqueror of Syria and Egypt, in honour of his mother, Gülbahar Hatun, in 1514. Next to it, the Atapark (Map p549) has a tea garden for refreshments and a reconstructed wooden serander from a village further along the coast.

BOZTEPE PICNIC PLACE

On the hillside 2km southeast of Atatürk Alanı is the Boztepe Picnic Place (Boztepe Piknik Alanı) with fine views of the city and the sea, tea gardens and restaurants. In ancient times, Boztepe harboured temples to the Persian sun god Mithra. Later the Byzantines built several churches and monasteries here.

To get to Boztepe from Atatürk Alanı, take one of the frequent Boztepe dolmuşes (from a side street on the northern side of Atatürk Alanı). The route goes uphill 2.2km to Boztepe park.

HAMAMS

The Sekiz Direkli Hamamı (Map p549; admission €9; 7am-5pm Fri-Wed for men, 8am-5pm Thu for women), 600m west of the Çarşı Camii, is among the city's most pleasant Turkish baths. The rough-hewn pillars are said to date from Seljuk times, although the rest of the building has been modernised.

The Meydan Hamam (Map p550; Maraş Caddesi; admission €7; 6am-11pm for men, 9am-6pm for women), right in the heart of town, is clean and efficiently run.

Tours

A couple of Trabzon agencies organise tours from June to the end of August. Eyce Tours (Map p550; ☎ 326 7174; www.eycetours.com, in Turkish; Taksim İşhanı Sokak 11), run by the helpful, English-speaking Volkan Kantarcı, offers day trips to Sumela (€6, departing 10am daily), Uzungöl (€8, departing 9am daily) and Ayder (€10, minimum six people), as well as longer walking and camping tours.

Sleeping

BUDGET

There are numerous cheapies off the northeastern corner of Atatürk Alanı and along the coastal road, but many double as brothels, so it's best to stick to the reliable places listed here or seek local recommendations.

Hotel Anıl (Map p550; ☎ 326 7282; Güzelhisar Caddesi 12; s/d €14/20) Built onto the side of the hill, so even the downstairs rooms have views, this is about the only acceptable budget option in this corner of town. The yellow-painted rooms are fairly musty and the French porn channel may raise a few eyebrows, but that's about the worst surprise you'll get.

Hotel Nur (Map p550; ☎ 323 0445; Camii Sokak 15; s/d €20/25;) A long-standing but often over-popular travellers' favourite near the tourist office, with amiable, English-speaking staff and small, brightly painted rooms. The hotel runs its own daily Sumela tours (€8.50). Light sleepers be warned: the mosque opposite doesn't skimp on the 5am call to prayer.

MIDRANGE

Hotel Nazar (Map p550; ☎ 323 0081; www.nazarhotel.net; Güzelhisar Caddesi 5; s/d €28/50; 🅿) If you can forgive the flagrant Photoshopping in the brochure (flower gardens in central Trabzon? Nice try), you'll find the Nazar a slick, smart modern business-class option. The manager speaks English and is keen to dispense tips on his home Kaçkar region.

Otel Horon (Map p550; ☎ 326 6455; www.otelhoron .com; Sıramağazalar Caddesi 125; s/d €36/53; 🅿) The dull grey frontage belies the genuine internal appeal of the Horon's mildly dated décor and unflashy rooms, not to mention the well-stocked minibars and uninterrupted views from the rooftop bar and restaurant. It employs some female reception staff, which is generally a good sign of propriety here.

Hotel Omesa (Map p549; ☎ 323 0151; hotelomesa@ mynet.com; Cumhuriyet Caddesi 22; s/d/tr €39/53/70; 🅿 🖳) Aiming for a business-modern style, the Omesa may not entirely justify its room rates with salmon walls and gold linen, but it's 'purified from environmental problems', the location's a handy five minutes from the airport, and the bar has live music three times a week.

Otel Sağıroğlu (Map p550; ☎ 3323 2899; www.sagir ogluotel.com, in Turkish; Taksim İşhanı Sokak 1; s/d/tr €56/ 80/89; 🅿) This large yellow block offers plenty of amenities but seems to be lacking some of the quality control you'd expect to find at this price: perhaps they're hoping the occasional Impressionist print will distract guests from the stained carpets.

TOP END

Usta Park Hotel (Map p550; ☎ 326 5700; www.usta parkhotel.com; İskenderpaşa Mahallesi 3; s/d/tr €90/115/150; 🅿) The new incarnation of what was once an irredeemably dodgy scum pit is clearly out to impress its intended business clientele, flaunting a tenuously Egyptian-themed lobby, a restaurant, bar, fitness centre, travel agency, *hamam*, understated rooms and staff who are service oriented.

Zorlu Grand Hotel (Map p550; ☎ 326 8400; www .zorlugrand.com; Maraş Caddesi 9; s/d €200/250, ste €287-750; 🅿) Understatement is the last thing on anyone's mind at this ludicrously extravagant five-star. The immense mezzanine atrium is quite staggering, touched by the strains of classical music (the only time you'll ever hear harpsichord in Turkey), and the list of facilities is as long as a sultan's genealogy,

with two restaurants, two cafés, a pub and a *hamam* just for starters. Worthwhile mainly if you can negotiate a substantial *indirim* (discount).

Eating

Trabzon is not the gastronomic capital of the Black Sea, but scores of cheap and cheerful *lokantas* (restaurants) vie for your custom around Atatürk Alanı and in the two main drags to the west.

Seyidoğlu (Map p550; Uzun Sokak 15A; dishes €0.55-2; 🕑 8am-9pm) This small, tiled snack stop has been dishing up succulent, thin-crusted *lah macun* (Arabic pizza) and kebaps for 38 years and regulars still swear by it.

İstanbul Kır Pidesi (Map p549; ☎ 321 2212; Uzun Sokak 48; mains €1-2; 🕑 8am-10pm) A top choice for pide and *börek* aficionados at any time of day.

Tuvana Café (Map p550; ☎ 326 0443; Kunduracılar Caddesi, Sanat Sokak 2; mains €2.50-4.50; 🕑 9.30am-9.30pm) Discreetly mounted on the 1st floor of a restored house, this quietly chic café-restaurant show some ambition in its dishes and some class in its presentation.

Brasserie Pera (Map p550; ☎ 326 4696; Yavuz Selim Bulvarı 173; mains €2.50-4.50; 🕑 8am-11pm) The Pera brings full European bar-bistro style to Trabzon, from the pop art and plasma screens to the eccentric music policy. The menu takes in burgers, salads, pasta, chicken, plenty of lighter grills and a good range of beverages.

Hürrem Sultan Sofrası (Map p550; ☎ 321 8651; Maraş Caddesi 30; mains €2.50-6; 🕑 9am-10pm) An above-average cafeteria restaurant in shade of pistachio, enlivening the usual kebap-grill spectrum with regional specialities such as *muhlama* and *kuymak* (melted cheese dishes; see boxed text, p556).

Park Café & Restaurant (Map p549; ☎ 322 2999; İskerdepaşa İlkolul Karşısı, Uzun Sokak; mains €3.50-5; 🕑 8am-10pm) Tucked away behind a courtyard car park off Uzun Sokak, this 1st-floor family restaurant adds a refined, almost exclusive feel to the kebap experience. The hall underneath is popular for weddings and other big occasions.

Fevzi Hoca Balık-Köfte (Map p550; ☎ 326 5444; İpekyolu İş Merkezi, Maraş Caddesi; meals €7-14; 🕑 noon-9.30pm) The fish dinners at this speciality restaurant opposite the Zorlu Grand are top value, including salad, pickles and even dessert in the meal price. Tightwads and fish haters can opt for the bargain *köfte* (€1.50).

The sweet treats at **Kılıcoğlu** (Map p549; ☎ 321 4525; Uzun Sokak 42; desserts from €1.10; ☺ 9am-10pm) are damn near irresistible, whatever time you wander past the window. Eat in and have your profiteroles with ice cream (€3.50). For more sweetness, **Mevlana Kuruyemiş** (Map p550; ☎ 321 9622; Uzun Sokak 31) is a renowned *kuruyemiş* (dried fruit) vendor, and also sells fattening *lokum* (Turkish delight), *helva* (a traditional sweet made from sesame seeds), *pestil* (sheets of dried fruit) and some excellent *kestane balı* (chestnut honey). Virtually next door, **Beton Helva** (Map p550; ☎ 321 2550; Uzun Sokak 15/B) is an old-fashioned local specialist, selling slabs of *helva* like paving stones at all hours. Also worth investigating is **Cirav Fındık** (Map p550; ☎ 322 2050; Ticaret Mektep Sokak 8/C), off Maraş Caddesi, where you can take your pick from numerous varieties of hazelnut and related confectionery.

Drinking

Trabzon quietens down quite drastically after dark and, while there is certainly a drinking scene, most places close by midnight.

Keyif Coffee & Tea Store (Map p550; ☎ 326 8026; Canbakkal İş Merkezi, Uzun Sokak) Achieving a rare level of hauteur amid its hefty leather armchairs and tartan wallpaper, the Keyif offers no fewer than 200 varieties of hot beverage to tantalise tea-loving tastebuds.

Stress Café (Map p549; ☎ 321 3044; Uzun Sokak) Misnomers don't come more ironic than this: whether you're chilling out with a nargileh on the back terrace or funking it up to live music in the downstairs bar, stress will be the last thing on your mind here.

Bordo Mavi (Map p549; ☎ 326 2077; Halkevi Caddesi 12) This atmospheric bar-café hangout is the clubhouse of Trabzonspor, the beloved local football team. The garden seating is popular with a buzzy young crowd in summer but, rather unsportingly, the whole place closes by 10pm.

Şişman Efes Pub (Map p550; ☎ 326 6083; Maraş Caddesi 5) Now this is a proper pub: wooden tables, doodling barman, music drowned out by the general hubbub and the eponymous Efes beer served in 2.5L towers (€8) on request.

Beer Time (Map p550; Atatürk Alanı) Another hostelry in the same vein as the Şişman, but spread over two whole storeys, with wooden floors and a largely male crowd, just avoiding that spit'n'sawdust feel.

Café Life (Map p549; ☎ 321 2955; Halkevi Caddesi 15) Choose Life: just opposite the Bordo Mavi,

this wood-floored café-bar offers a beguiling mix of fast food and folky live music.

Shopping

Thanks to the influx of cheap goods and materials from the former Soviet territories, Trabzon is a good place to shop for clothes and other essentials, especially from the Russian Bazaar (Map p550) stalls near the port; a T-shirt, complete with designer logo, should set you back just €3.

This is also a prime area for leather goods – half a dozen shops along Sıramağazalar Caddesi sell jackets, bags and other garments, with alterations or made-to-measure fittings available. At the time of research the standard asking price for a basic soft-leather jacket was US$100, maybe half what you'd pay in İstanbul.

Getting There & Away

AIR

Trabzon is well served by all the main carriers, and the centre is peppered with airline agents dealing exclusively in domestic flight tickets.

Turkish Airlines (☎ 321 1680; www.thy.com) has two daily flights to Ankara (1½ hours), three or four daily flights to İstanbul's Atatürk International airport (1¾ hours), two daily flights to İstanbul Sabiha Gökçen (1¾ hours) and four flights a week to İzmir (two hours).

Pegasus Airlines (www.flypgs.com) has two daily direct flights to Sabiha Gökçen and one to Ankara. **Atlasjet** (☎ 444 3387; www.atlasjet.com), **Fly Air** (☎ 326 4707; www.flyair.com.tr) and **Onur Air** (☎ 325 6292; www.onurair.com.tr) each have two daily direct flights to İstanbul Atatürk.

BOAT

Burcu Turizm (Map p549; ☎ 321 9588; Mimar Sinan Caddesi), near the Russian consulate, and **Gürgen Turizm** (Map p550; ☎ 321 4439; İskele Caddesi 61), one of several similar offices down by the harbour, sell tickets for ferries going to Sochi in Russia (€42, twice weekly). Burcu Turizm can also help arrange visas (see boxed text, p674).

BUS

Trabzon's otogar is 3km east of the port, on the landward side of the shore road, Devlet Sahil Yolu Caddesi. It is served by dolmuşes running along the coastal road and up to Atatürk Alanı.

There are no direct buses to Ayder; you'll have to catch a bus heading to Hopa and change at Pazar or Ardeşen. Some useful daily services are listed in the table, below.

SERVICES FROM TRABZON'S OTOGAR

Destination	Fare	Duration	Distance	Frequency
Ankara	€20	12hr	780km	several per day
Artvin	€9	4½hr	255km	frequent
Baku (Azerbaijan)	€28	30hr	-	1 weekly
Erzurum	€11	6hr	325km	several per day
Hopa	€7.50	3½hr	165km	half-hourly
İstanbul	€35	24hr	1110km	several per day
Kars	€20	10hr	525km	1 nightly or change at Erzurum or Artvin
Kayseri	€23	12hr	686km	several per day
Rize	€2.80	1hr	75km	half-hourly
Samsun	€11	6hr	355km	frequent
Sinop	€17	9hr	533km	1 at 8pm
Tiflis (Tbilisi, Georgia)	€14	20hr	-	several per day
Erivan (Armenia, via Tiflis)	€23	25hr	-	2 per day Fri-Sun

CAR & MOTORCYCLE

There are several car-hire agencies in Trabzon, including **Avis** (Map p550; ☎ 322 3740; Gazipaşa Caddesi 20) and smaller companies such as **Eko Rent A Car** (Map p550; ☎ 322 2575; Gazipaşa Caddesi 3/53).

Getting Around
TO/FROM THE AIRPORT

The *havaalanı* (airport) is 5.5km east of Atatürk Alanı. Dolmuşes to the airport (€0.55) leave from a side street on the northern side of Atatürk Alanı, but they drop you on the opposite side of the main coastal road, 500m from the terminal entrance. Alternatively, you can pay €3 extra to be dropped at the door. A taxi costs about €8. Buses bearing the legend 'Park' or 'Meydan' go to Atatürk Alanı from the airport.

BUS & DOLMUŞ

To reach Atatürk Alanı from the otogar, cross the shore road in front of the terminal, turn left, walk to the bus stop and catch any

bus with 'Park' or 'Meydan' in its name; the dolmuş for Atatürk Alanı is marked 'Garajlar-Meydan'. A taxi between the otogar and Atatürk Alanı costs €4.

The easiest way to get to Trabzon's otogar is to catch a dolmuş marked 'Garajlar' or 'KTÜ' from the northeastern side of Atatürk Alanı.

Dolmuşes mainly leave from Atatürk Alanı, although you can flag them down along their routes. Whatever your destination, the fare should be €0.50.

TAXI

There are several taxi stands in the centre, including one on Atatürk Alanı.

AROUND TRABZON
Sumela Monastery

One of the highlights of the Black Sea coast, the Greek Orthodox **Monastery of the Virgin Mary** (admission €2.80; ⏰ 9am-6pm Jun-Aug, 9am-4pm Sep-May) at Sumela, 46km south of Trabzon, was founded in Byzantine times and abandoned in 1923 after the creation of the Turkish Republic put paid to hopes of creating a new Greek state in this region. The setting is absolutely magical. The monastery clings to a sheer rock wall high above evergreen forests and a rushing mountain stream. It can be a mysterious, eerie place, especially when mists swirl among the tops of the trees in the valley below and the weird, ethereal call of an unseen mosque filters strangely through the forest.

To get to Sumela, take the Erzurum road and turn left at Maçka, 29km south of Trabzon. It's also signposted as Meryemana (Virgin Mary), to whom the monastery was dedicated.

The road then winds into dense evergreen forests, following the course of a rushing mountain stream interrupted by commercial trout pools. Village houses reminiscent of those in the alpine areas of central Europe are interspersed with more modern brick blocks.

If you're driving, at the entrance to Altındere Vadısı Milli Parkı (Altındere Valley National Park) you pay €4 per vehicle to visit the monastery.

At the end of the road you'll find a shady park with picnic tables by a roaring brook, a post office, the Sumela Restaurant and several bungalows for rent (no camping is allowed).

The head of the trail up to the monastery begins by the restaurant and is steep but easy to follow. A second trail begins further up the valley. To get to it, follow the concreted road 1km uphill and across two bridges until you come to a wooden footbridge over the stream on the right, marked by a sign reading 'Manastıra gider' (to the monastery). This trail cuts straight up through the trees, past the shell of the Ayavarvara chapel. On busy days it's likely to be much quieter than the main route.

If you drive even further up the road, you reach a small car park, from which it's only a 10-minute walk to the monastery.

As you climb through forests and alpine meadows, catching occasional glimpses of the monastery above you, the air gets noticeably cooler. You'll ascend 250m in about 30 to 45 minutes. In autumn, just before the snow arrives, a beautiful variety of crocus, kar çiçeği (snowflower), blooms in the meadows.

After the ticket office, a steep flight of steps leads up the rock face to the monastery complex, sheltered underneath a hefty outcrop. The main chapel, cut into the rock, is the indisputable highlight, covered both inside and outside with colourful frescoes. The earliest examples date from the 9th century, but most of them are actually 19th-century work. Sadly, bored shepherd boys used the paintings as targets for their catapults, and later needless visitors – from Russian tourists to USAF grunts (1965 vintage) – scratched their names into them, proving that idiocy is indeed international.

In recent years the monastery has been substantially rebuilt in an effort to make sense of the various chapels and rooms for visitors (look out for the old lavatories). You're still likely to find builders at the site as the restoration works continue.

SLEEPING & EATING

Maçkam Hotel (☎ 512 3640; s/d €28/45) In the centre of Maçka, this is a good option offering fine standards across yellow-themed rooms, aided by what must have been a job lot of comfy chairs.

Hotel Büyük Sümela (☎ 512 3540; www.sumelaotel.com in Turkish; s/d/tr €55/70/93; 🖾 🖳) Buying into its own four-star pomp, the BS seems to have its eye on a Sumela monopoly, controlling both the Maçkam and the Sümela Sosyal Tesis-

leri. Facilities in the eight-storey block on the edge of Maçka are generous to say the least, but frankly we'd rather stay in either of its other properties.

Coşandere Tesisleri Restaurant & Pansiyon (☎ 531 1190; www.cosandere.com, in Turkish; Sümela Yolu; r from €17) Located in Coşandere, a tiny stream-fed village 5km out of Maçka, this place has three pine-clad seranders sleeping up to six and a huge new building with motel-like rooms, favoured by tour groups. The owners organise various tours, treks, day trips and even paintballing in the area.

Sümela Sosyal Tesisleri (☎ 531 1207; bungalows from €45) Right by the car park at Sumela itself, this is a row of comfortable A-frame bungalows with full amenities, including kitchenette. The restaurant is just across the road by the stream. It's a bit overpriced, but you're paying for the attractive setting.

GETTING THERE & AWAY

From May to the end of August, Ulusoy and Metro run buses from Trabzon to Sumela, departing at 10am from outside their Atatürk Alanı offices and returning at 3pm. Return tickets cost €8.50.

Dolmuşes for Maçka (€0.85) or Coşandere village (€3) depart all day from the minibus dolmuş ranks by the Russian Bazaar. It'll cost you €5.60 all the way to Sumela, but you'll have to wait until the driver decides enough people are coming.

A couple of Trabzon agencies (see p551) run basic tours to Sumela.

TRABZON TO ERZURUM

Heading south into the mountains, you're in for a long (325km) but scenic ride. Along the highway south, you zoom straight to **Maçka**, 29km inland from Trabzon. About 1.5km north of Maçka look out along the roadside for basaltic rock columns resembling California's Devil's Postpile or Northern Ireland's Giant's Causeway. From Maçka, you begin the gradual climb along a mountain road through active landslide zones towards the **Zigana Geçidi** (Zigana Pass; 2030m).

The dense, humid air of the coast disappears as you rise and becomes light and dry as you reach the southern side of the eastern Black Sea mountains. Along with the landscape, the towns and villages change: Black Sea towns look vaguely Balkan, while places higher up appear much more Central Asian.

FOOD FOR THOUGHT

The eastern Black Sea has a culture very much its own and, as a traveller, chances are that your first experience of the region's unique character will be through your stomach – local cuisine entertains a number of treasured taste sensations you won't come across anywhere else.

For a start, the Black Sea peoples have a reverence for cabbage only surpassed by certain Eastern Europeans, and no trip would be complete without sampling *labana sarması* (stuffed cabbage rolls) or *labana lobia* (cabbage and beans), fibre-rich and surprisingly tasty dishes unique to the coast.

Also very popular are *muhlama* (or *mıhlama*) and *kuymak*, both types of thick molten cheese served in a metal dish, much like a fondue but without the faffy dips. Even if you scoop it up with bread, that much heavy dairy can sit on your stomach – it's best experienced in the mountain villages of the Kaçkars, where it's cooked with egg for a lighter effect.

Whatever you think of these rarefied savoury treats, you can't sniff at *laz böreği*, a delicious flaky pastry layered with confectioner's custard. Like most Turkish desserts, it doesn't take much to be addictive!

Snow can be seen in all months except perhaps July, August and September.

Gümüşhane, about 145km south of Trabzon, is a small town in a mountain valley with a few simple travellers' services but not much to stop for except the scenery.

By the time you reach the provincial capital of **Bayburt**, 195km from Trabzon, you're well into the rolling steppe and low mountains of the high Anatolian plateau. A dry, desolate place, Bayburt has a big medieval fortress.

The road from Bayburt passes through rolling green farm country with poplar trees and flocks of brown-fleeced sheep. In early summer wild flowers are everywhere.

Exactly 33km past Bayburt is the **Kop Geçidi** (Kop Pass) at an altitude of 2370m; if you've got your own vehicle, it's worth stopping for the views. From Kop Geçidi, the open road to Erzurum offers fast, easy travelling.

UZUNGÖL
☎ 0462 / pop 2800

Uzungöl used to be an idyllic lakeside village backed by forested mountains. It still has the idyllic setting, but it has been somewhat spoilt by a handful of tacky hotels to the east and pollution scares in the lake itself. Nevertheless, the place can make a restful day trip or overnight stop; trekkers can also use it as a base for day hikes in the Soğanlı Mountains to the lakes around Demirkapı (Holdizen).

If you do want to stay, try the **Ensar Motel & Restaurant** (☎ 656 6321; www.ensarmotel.com, in Turkish; Fatih Caddesi 18; s/d €25/35), an attractive resort with above-average amenities, good-value rooms

and a lovely setting near the lake. Everything is wood panelled except the roof, and there's traditional decoration throughout.

A couple of minibuses travel daily between Trabzon and Uzungöl; Ulusoy has a daily service at 9am in summer (€8.50 return). Alternatively, take a Rize-bound dolmuş to Of (€2) and then wait for another heading inland. Eyce Tours (p551) runs regular day trips from Trabzon.

RİZE
☎ 0464 / pop 78,000

About 75km east of Trabzon, Rize lies at the heart of Turkey's tea-plantation area. The steep hillsides above the town are thickly planted with tea, which is cured, dried and blended here, then shipped throughout the country. Though lacking any truly significant monuments, it's not short on eating options and you can easily while away a few hours over a cuppa.

Orientation & Information
The main square, Atatürk Anıtı, where you'll find a beautifully reconstructed old PTT and the Şeyh Camii, is 200m inland from the coastal road, Menderes Bulvarı. The hotels are to the east of the main square along or just off Cumhuriyet Caddesi, which runs one block inland and almost parallel to Menderes Bulvarı. The otogar is also along Cumhuriyet Caddesi, about 1km northwest of the main square.

The friendly, helpful **tourist office** (☎ 213 0408; ☺ 9am-5pm Mon-Fri 15 May–15 Sep) is on the main square next to the PTT. **Matrix Internet**

Café (Kamburoğlu Sokak; per hr €0.55; 10am-11pm) is just off Atatürk Caddesi.

Sights

Up the hill behind the tourist office is the **Rize museum** (214 0235; Ulubatlı Sokak; admission €1.10; 9am-noon & 1-4pm Tue-Sun), a fine reconstructed Ottoman house with a lovely *serander* beside it. The rooms upstairs have been decorated in traditional style, with a few artefacts and a huge wireless set to remind you that the later Ottomans were still part of the modern age. Mannequins model Laz costumes from central Rize and Hemşin costumes from around Ayder.

One of Rize's magnets is the magnificent **tea garden** set amid a fragrant flower garden, 900m above town via the steep road behind the Şeyh Camii (it's signposted 'Ziraat Çay ve Botanik Parkı'). Enjoy the smashing views while taking pleasure in a cup of tea (€0.30) – a typical Rizeli experience. A taxi from outside the mosque will drive you here for €2.

The other key feature is the town's ancient **castle**, built by the Genoese on the steep hill at the back of town. Signs point the way up Kale Sokak from Atatürk Caddesi.

Sleeping & Eating

Hotel Milano (213 0028; milano_hotel@hotmail .com; Cumhuriyet Caddesi 169; s/d €23/34, ste €61;) It's no more fashionable or Italian than a döner kebap, but this tiled option east of the centre is comfortable enough to forgive the lack of professional finish.

Otel Kaçkar (213 1490; Cumhuriyet Caddesi 101; s/d/tr €23/39/45;) Just off the main square, look out

for the Kaçkar's mosaic facade, which bids you in to sample the neat, unfussy but adequate rooms. There's a *hamam* round the back.

Dergah Pastaneleri (532 1704; Deniz Caddesi 19; dishes €2-3; 9am-10pm) This popular *pastane* (patisserie) has been tormenting the sweet-toothed and weak-willed since 1985, and does a mean ice cream (€4 for one kilo!). There's also an extensive snack menu covering breakfast, salads, pizza, spaghetti and sandwiches. There's a smaller second branch at Atatürk Caddesi 356. Wireless internet access is available.

Bekiroğlu (217 1380; Cumhuriyet Caddesi 161; mains €2-4; 9am-10pm) One of a number of family terrace restaurants on the pedestrian strip south of the coast road, the Bekiroğlu doesn't do things by halves, with multiple shrubs, breadbaskets piled a foot high and meat spits like elephants' ankles.

Getting There & Away

Although Rize does have an otogar, many of the buses and dolmuşes plying the coastal highway drop passengers off all along the seafront, where you can also flag down one of the frequent minibuses to Hopa (€4, 1½ hours) and Trabzon (€2.80, one hour, every 25 minutes). In summer there are daily direct services to Ayder (€5.50, 1¾ hours), otherwise take an eastbound minibus to Pazar (€1.80) and change.

HOPA

 0466 / pop 24,000

Like many border service towns, Hopa, 165km east of Trabzon and 30km southwest of the

---

ONE OF THE LAZ

Rize is the last major centre of the Laz people (see p48), a loose community numbered at around 250,000, of which 150,000 still speak the Caucasian-based Lazuri language. Known for their colourful traditional costumes and *lazeburi* folk music, you can see Laz cultural performances at any major local festival in the Rize region.

However, calling someone Laz is nowhere near as straightforward as it might seem. The Turkish Laz strenuously dispute any kind of categorisation that would lump them in with their Georgian counterparts; on the other hand, with many Turks using Laz as a simple catch-all term for anyone living east of Samsun, they're just as keen to differentiate themselves from other coastal denizens and shrug off the stereotype of the anchovy-munching 'Laz fisherman', butt of countless local jokes.

To confuse the issue still further, rumours have circulated of a 'Laz Homeland Party' (Lazuri Dobadona Partiya), supposedly founded in 1999 to press claims for autonomy. As the only evidence of this is on the internet, and as even the Laz themselves seem totally divided on who counts as Laz anyway, it's likely this is just another bit of coastal humour!

border into Georgia, is a mildly depressing pit stop, best appreciated on a sweaty grey day with a bad rakı hangover (since that's what it'll feel like anyway). You're only likely to want to stay here if you're heading to or from Georgia and have arrived too late to move on. It has all the standard amenities – a couple of banks with ATMs, internet cafés, a PTT and, of course, the otogar. Note that Hopa's exchange offices give lousy rates for Georgian lari, knowing that you won't be able to change them anywhere else.

Sleeping & Eating

Otel Ustabaş (☎ 351 4507; Ortahopa Caddesi; s/d €11/22; ⊠) The town's best central budget deal, with oppressive carpets and missing shower heads offset by simple comforts and a café downstairs.

Otel Cihan (☎ 351 4897; hotelcihan@ttnet.net.tr; Ortahopa Caddesi 36; s/d €23/28) This towering yellow block offers a bar and roof restaurant along with the small rooms. It's about 300m along the coast road, next to a petrol station.

Peronti Otel (☎ 351 7663; www.peronti-otel.com; Turgay Ciner Caddesi 78; s/d €46/69; ⊠) Easily the fanciest option in town, despite the faintly ridiculous statues outside and abandoned maritime theme within. Facilities include a disco bar, American bar, barber, restaurant and room service.

Green Garden (☎ 351 4277; Cumhuriyet Caddesi; mains €1.10-4; ⊠ 9am-10pm) Does exactly what it says on the tin, with two terraces and a brick dining room dishing up pide and kebaps in the small municipal park.

Getting There & Away

The otogar is on the western side of the Sundura Çayı, on the road to Artvin. Direct buses from Hopa to Erzurum (€14, six hours) leave in the morning. There are also regular buses or minibuses to Artvin (€5.60, 1½ hours), Rize (€4, 1½ hours) and Trabzon (€7.50, 3½ hours). For Kars (€17, 11 hours), there's only one direct bus, leaving in the morning.

Frequent minibuses for Sarp (€2.80) and the Georgian border leave from the petrol station beside the Otel Cihan and the stand at the Sundura Çayı junction north of the otogar. Trabzon–Tiflis buses also pass through Hopa, some going via the Posof border crossing (€17, 10 hours). For more details on crossing to Georgia, see p675.

KAÇKAR MOUNTAINS

The Kaçkar Mountains (Kaçkar Dağları) form a rugged range bordered by the Black Sea coast to the north and the Çoruh River to the south. The range stretches for about 30km, from south of Rize almost to Artvin at its northeastern end. Dense forest covers the lower valleys, but above 2100m grasslands carpet the passes and plateaus, and the jagged ranges are studded with lakes and alpine summer *yayla* (villages).

The Kaçkars are becoming increasingly visited for their trekking opportunities. The highest point, **Mt Kaçkar** (Kaçkar Dağı; 3937m), with a glacier on its northern face, is popular with trekkers, but the northeastern ranges around the peak of **Altıparmak** (3310m) are also popular. You could visit the Kaçkars on a day trip, but you'll get much more from it if you allow at least three days to explore.

ACTIVITIES
Trekking

Trekking is the main reason people come to the Kaçkars, and there are innumerable walks you could do. Talk to locals and the trekking guides to create your own adventure.

Note that the trekking season in this region is very short, and you will only be able to do the higher mountain routes between mid-July and mid-August, when the snowline is highest. From mid-May to mid-September there are still plenty of walks you can do on the lower slopes and dozens of little mountain villages where you can catch a slice of authentic Kaçkar life.

One of the most popular multiday trips is the **Trans-Kaçkar** trek, described in detail in the Trekking chapter, p85. The trek to the **Kaçkar Summit** by its southern face takes an easy three days, but may require specialist snow equipment. The three- to four-day **Trans-Altıparmak** route is similar to the Trans-Kaçkar, except that it crosses the Altıparmak range and doesn't climb the summit. If you stay in **Barhal (Altıparmak)** you could trek for four to five sweaty hours up to **Karagöl**, camp overnight, and return the next day.

Most people base themselves in Ayder or Çamlıhemşin, and start treks from the eastern flanks of the range at Barhal (Altıparmak) Yaylalar (Hevek) or Olgunlar. **Day walks** around the slopes and lakes are possible from Yukarı

KAÇKAR MOUNTAINS

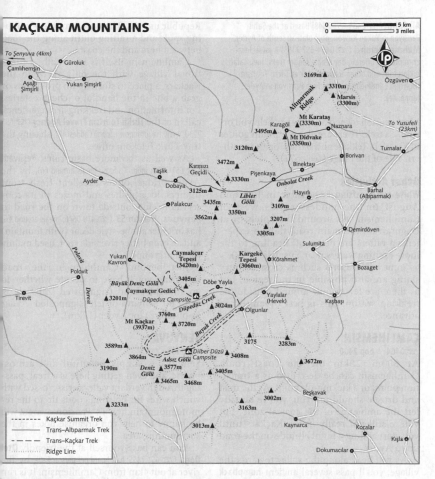

Kavron, Caymakçur and Avusor, all served by dolmuş from Ayder. At Yukarı Kavron, try asking for Mehmet Ali, a guide in his 70s known locally as the 'king of Kaçkar'.

TREKKING GUIDES

Although some people are happy heading off into the mountains alone, it's a good idea to hire a local who knows the tracks. The walks are mostly unsigned, and misty weather conditions can put paid to your schedule, let alone your sense of direction. If you ask around at the pensions you should be able to find someone willing to go with you for around €30 a day. You may also want to hire a mule to carry your luggage (around €20 per day).

You should bring a good tent, stove and sleeping bag, but you could get away with just bringing walking boots and warm clothes provided you're going with one of the all-inclusive trekking operators.

For fully guided tours, including guide fee, tents, bedding, and all transport and food, expect to pay between €30 and €60 per day from Ayder, depending on group size (a minimum number often applies). A one-week trek should cost around €300, all included.

Reliable English-speaking guides include the following:

Adnan Pirikoğlu (☎ 0464-657 2021; adnanpirikoglu@ hotmail.com) Experienced mountain guide who knows the area like the back of his hand, based at the Pirikoğlu Aile Lokantası in Ayder year-round.

Ali Şahin (☎ 0464-651 7348) Based at the Şahin Pansiyon in Yukarı Kavron, on a plateau south of Ayder.
Mehmet Demirci (☎ 0464-657 2153) A jovial local entrepreneur offering day walks, longer treks, Jeep safaris, biking trips and other activities. Ask at Türkü Tourism (right) in Çamlıhemşin or the Fora Pansiyon in Ayder (opposite).

Most pension owners will happily help you organise a trek. There are also mountain guides in Yusufeli, Tekkale and Barhal, on the southern side of the range (see p571).

Other Activities

White-water rafting is possible in July and August on the modest rapids west of Çamlıhemşin; ask around the hotels or at Dağuraft on the main road, though experienced rafters are better off heading to the more exciting waters near Yusufeli (p572).

Some **winter sports** such as cross-country skiing are also possible in the region, but as there are few people around outside the trekking season, this is best organised in advance.

ÇAMLIHEMŞİN

☎ 0464 / pop 2400
At 300m, 20km off the coast road, Çamlıhemşin can be described as a transition point, or a kicking-off point. As the mist and drizzle should tell you, you've already left the ambience of the coastal zone, but you're still not really in the Kaçkars until you start adding a bit of altitude on the road up to Ayder.

As you head along the valley towards the village, you'll pass several ancient **humpback bridges** across the Fırtına Çayı (Storm Stream), some of which were restored for the 75th anniversary of the establishment of the Turkish Republic in 1998. There are a couple of camping spots and a rafting outfit along the road between here and the coast.

Çamlıhemşin itself is essentially a functional village with the only ATM in the Kaçkars, a place to stock up on provisions or grab a bite in the handful of cheap eateries. For information and trekking arrangements, call in at the **Türkü Tourism Travel Agency** (☎ 651 7230; www.turkutour.com; İnönü Caddesi 47), sharing the tiny Türk Telekom office.

As well as the more basic cafés, **Yeşilvadi** (☎ 651 7282; İnönü Caddesi; meals around €6), by the Ayder bridge, offers excellent fresh trout dinners, local dishes and mezes in its conservatory. Just outside town on the road to Şenyuva, **Kervan 53** (☎ 418 0646; meals around €6), has brighter adobe-style décor (with fountain) and an even better riverside spot, used mainly for tour groups.

Just beyond Çamlıhemşin the road forks and you'll have to decide whether to go straight ahead (signposted 'Zil Kale & Çat') for Şenyuva or left (signposted 'Ayder Kaplıcaları') for Ayder (17km).

ŞENYUVA

☎ 0464
Şenyuva is simply beautiful and atmospheric, and even getting here is a treat, passing through verdant valleys crisscrossed with winch wires for hoisting goods up to the remote mountain houses. Pension owners will be happy to help you organise hikes in the surrounding area.

You can base yourself at the friendly **Otel Doğa** (☎ 651 7455; half board per person €20), by the river about 4km from Çamlıhemşin. It is run by the well-travelled İdris Duman who speaks French and English. The rooms are simple but salubrious, mostly with private bathrooms.

THE AUTHOR'S CHOICE

ekodanitap (☎ 651 7230; www.ecodanitap.com, in Turkish) The latest venture from Türkü Tourism, this is a fantastic self-built sustainable eco-camp hidden away up a steep hill off the main road just west of Çamlıhemşin. The four solar-powered wooden cabins are amazingly well turned-out, with TV, fridge and hot showers; owner Mehmet has big plans for the place, intending to base a range of year-round local activities and excursions here, and seemingly half his extended family are involved with the project. It was only just getting up and running at the time of research, so prices are not yet fixed – expect to pay around €30 per person per night, including meals (and, probably, a healthy dose of rakı). The plot is 200m off the road, in a perfectly secluded clearing at the end of an overgrown track; you've got no chance of finding it on your own, so enquire in advance at Türkü Tours or the Fora Pansiyon in Ayder.

Some have balconies overlooking the river and there's a spacious lounge and a restaurant.

Around 2km further on, in Şenyuva village itself, is the leafy **Fırtına Pansiyon** (☎ 653 3111; pansiyon@firtinavadisi.com; half board per person €25), with two cute bungalows near the river and cheerfully painted rooms in former school buildings, all with shared bathrooms. The lounge room is inviting.

A few hundred metres north is the thin, arched **Şenyuva Köprüsü** (Şenyuva Bridge, 1696). From here the road continues for 9km to the spectacularly sited ruins of **Zil Castle** (Zil Kale), a round stone tower on a stark rock base, surrounded by lush rhododendron forests – it's a superb walk, but tough going for cars. Another 15km will lead you to **Çat** (1250m), a mountain hamlet used as a trekking base, where you'll find a shop, a couple of seasonal pensions and the start of the even rougher roads into the heart of the mountains.

Only one minibus a day runs between Şenyuva and Çamlıhemşin, so you may have to walk (6km) or take a taxi for about €6 each way.

AYDER

☎ 0464

The hub of the Kaçkar tourist industry, Ayder is a high-pasture village enjoying a glorious valley-side setting at 1300m, with snow-capped mountains above and waterfalls cascading to the river below. Despite a few painful concrete buildings thrown up to meet visitor demand, the charming alpine-chalet look still predominates, and new buildings must now be in 'traditional style' (ie sheathed in wood).

Ayder really only functions during the trekking season, which runs from mid-May to mid-September. At other times there may only be a few local families living here, and even in early May you might find nothing open and no public transport to get you back out. Conversely, in August the village can hardly cope with the flood of domestic tourists, especially at weekends, when most places will be full by mid-afternoon.

Orientation & Information

About 4.5km below Ayder is the gate marking the entrance to the Kaçkar Dağları Milli Parkı (Kaçkar Mountains National Park), where you must pay an admission fee of €2 per vehicle in season.

The nominal centre of the village has a couple of restaurants, a bakery, supermarket, *tekel bayii* (off-licence), two internet cafés, the minibus office and bus stop, a car-hire office and several gift shops. The hotels are scattered for about 1km along the road either side of the centre. There is nowhere to change money.

Sights & Activities

Most people use Ayder as a base for trekking in the mountains, but even if you don't have time to do that it's still worth popping up here for a day or so to get your fill of the wonderful scenery. Wildlife enthusiasts should note that rare Caucasian black grouse, salamanders and brown bears all live in the national park, though it'd be a miracle to see them anywhere near the village.

Post-trek muscle relief can be had at the spotless **kaplıca** (hot springs; ☎ 657 2102; admission €4.50, private cabin €14; ⏰ 7am-8pm), where the water reaches temperatures of 56°C (133°F); it's said to be good for ulcers, skin complaints, cuts and allergies.

Sleeping

Many of Ayder's pensions are set halfway up the hill next to the road, reached by narrow, slanting paths; bear in mind that getting back up to them can be tricky when the mist rolls in!

Zirve Ahşap Pansiyon (☎ 657 2162; s/d with shared bathroom €8.50/17) One for the budget crowd, this hillside house doesn't have the most stellar standards, but there's a kitchen for guests, it's friendly and English is spoken. Breakfast costs €2.50.

Fora Pansiyon (☎ 657 2153; turku@turkutour.com; s/d half board €20/40) Türkü Tourism's original hillside family pension, provides a homely sitting room, simple pine-clad rooms, shared bathrooms, balconies, laundry and a terrace with good views. Ask here about treks, activities and visits to ekodanitap (see opposite).

Nehirim Pansiyon (☎ 657 2040; adsiz_masal@hotmail .com; s/d/tr €20/40/60) A new addition to the hillside cluster; you can almost smell the pine sap in the pristine rooms. The manager's a former rafting champion turned professional instructor, and can advise on white-water trips across the region.

Kuşpuni Pansiyon (☎ 657 2052; ali_the_conqueror@ hotmail.com; s/d €23/46) Another very appealing family-run chalet-pension, it revels in a stove-heated lounge with decent views and hearty meals. It's run by Buklamania Tours, who

---

HEMŞIN CULTURE

If you visit Ayder over a summer weekend you may get the chance to witness some of the last surviving Hemşin culture (see p48). In the meadows of the town groups of Hemşin holidaymakers often gather to dance the *horon*, a cross between the conga and the hokey-cokey set to the distinctive whining skirl of the *tulum*, a type of goatskin bagpipe. Even if you don't run into one of these parties, you'll see women all around the mountains wearing splendid headdresses, often incongruously matched with cardigans, long skirts and running shoes or woollen boots.

Whether you realise it or not, you'll probably also *hear* some traces of Hemşin heritage: the peculiar Armenian-derived dialect is still commonly spoken in Çamlıhemşin and Ayder. Listen out for Ayderlis softening their g's ('jel' and 'jit' instead of 'gel' and 'git') and aspirating their k's like Scottish ch's ('Amlachit' instead of Amlakit).

---

specialise in trekking and activity tours for the domestic market but can happily cater for foreign visitors.

Yeşil Vadi Otel (☎ 657 2050; www.ayderyesilvadi.com in Turkish; s/d €23/46) Clad in more pine than a Swedish sauna, this is a great central option by the main road with rustic timber rooms, heavy duvets and impeccable bathrooms. Many rooms boast valley views, and the restaurant comes recommended.

Otel Ayder Haşimoğlu (☎ 657 2037; www.hasimogluotel.com; s/d/d €27/54/81) Run by Ayder Turizm, who also operate the hot springs, this big posh pine place is by the river, 100m downhill from the centre (follow the path by the town mosque). It's popular with tour groups, and offers plenty for your buck. AT also rents 'villas' (half board from €85) next to the *kaplıca*, sleeping at least four people.

Eating & Drinking

Many people eat in their pensions, but there are a few other options if you want to venture out.

Nazlı Çiçek (☎ 657 2130; mains €3-6) Right in the centre of the village, this charming old house specialises in freshly caught trout, but also whips up a limited range of standards and Black Sea specialities such as *muhlama*.

Çise Restaurant (☎ 657 2171; mains €3-6) Next door to the Nazlı Çiçek, it plagiarises its rival's menu shamelessly, but adds live music in place of traditional décor.

Horon Bar & Restaurant (☎ 433 5858; mains €2.80-4.50) Back down the hill, this is one of Ayder's few licensed premises, frequented by a predominantly male crowd.

Getting There & Away

From mid-June to mid-September frequent dolmuşes run between Pazar on the coast and Ayder (€3.50, one hour) via Ardeşen and Çamlıhemşin. There are also sometimes direct services from Rize. On summer Sundays the trickle of minibuses up to Ayder turns into a flood. Otherwise, passengers are mostly shoppers from the villages, so dolmuşes descend in the morning and return from Pazar in the early afternoon.

In season, morning dolmuşes also run from Ayder to other mountain villages, including Galer Düzü, Avusor, Yukarı Kavron and Ceymakcur. Check with locals for exact schedules.

Even in the low season there are still four minibus services daily between Pazar and Çamlıhemşin. A taxi between Ayder and Çamlıhemşin costs around €20.

Northeastern Anatolia

If you yearn to explore, push Turkey's back door. Not only is the least-visited corner of the country a secretive world (even for the Turks), it's also a gold mine for wannabe adventurers. You can plan a thorough itinerary, with highlights that cover the most accessible sights, or you can take a more DIY approach, stumbling around in remote villages or wandering in the *yayalar* (highland pastures) without another traveller in sight. Whatever your perspective, the warmth you'll experience is another incentive to discover the region. And there's a distinctly Caucasian flavour, courtesy of the proximity of Armenia and Georgia, which adds to the appeal.

For James Bond action-seekers, there are outdoor adventures galore to gorge on in a variety of mind-boggling playgrounds. Rafting enthusiasts swear that the frothing rapids of the Çoruh are the most thrilling in the world, while snow bunnies will be in seventh heaven at Palandöken ski resort. If hiking is more to your liking, consider scaling Mt Ararat, Turkey's highest summit, or tackling the Kaçkar Mountains.

And culture? The region musters up enough surprises to enthral even the most jaded history buffs. It's like a vast open-air museum, with a gobsmacking portfolio of palaces, castles, mosques and churches dotted around the steppe. The astonishing İshak Paşa Sarayı and the ruins of Ani are must-sees for anyone with an interest in Turkey's ancient flourishing civilisations. There are also hidden treasures that await you, including a bonanza of Georgian churches near Yusufeli and Armenian monuments near Kars, all set against the extraordinary gorges or steppes.

Go on. Break the mould and delve a little deeper into Anatolia.

HIGHLIGHTS

- Piece together eastern Turkey's mysterious past through ancient churches and castles, such as **Şeytan Kalesi** (p585) or **Öşkvank cathedral** (p570)
- Psyche yourself up and join the adrenaline junkies on a white-water run through the **Çoruh Gorge** (p572)
- Dose up on amazement at the ruins of **Ani** (p581), an ancient Armenian capital
- Impress your peers and rip up some powder at the **Palandöken ski resort** (p569)
- Wake to clear skies and astounding views, and search for words atop **Mt Ararat** (p589), Turkey's highest mountain
- Thank the heavens for the sight of **İshak Paşa Palace** (p586) in Doğubayazıt, the castle of every child's imagination
- Cross Turkey's most isolated border at Posof, sup a full-bodied wine in **Georgia** (p585) and re-enter Turkey the next day

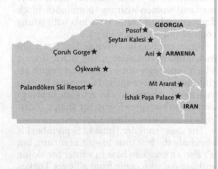

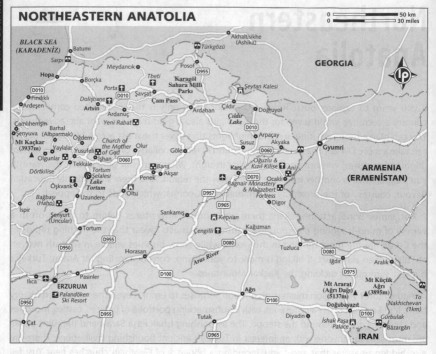

NORTHEASTERN ANATOLIA

ERZURUM

☎ 0442 / pop 362,000 / elevation 1853m

Forget any preconceived notion you have of a cold, austere and overwhelmingly conservative city. Sure, the climate is off-putting much of the year and the city feels much less liberal than its Mediterranean counterparts, but Erzurum is rapidly metamorphosing into a vibrant metropolis and the sizeable student population brings a refreshing touch of modernity. The 'peoplescape' of Erzurum is absorbing its contrasts. Patriotic, conservative men and women wearing voluminous black drapes or at least headscarves mix with young couples and stalwart soldiers.

Ditch your bags on arrival and leg it straight to Cumhuriyet Caddesi, the main artery, which showcases some of the best Seljuk architecture in the country. Then sweat it up to the citadel, where you can get your bearings over the urban sprawl, with the steppe forming a heavenly backdrop.

The short summer (June to September) is obviously the best time to visit Erzurum, but it's also an excellent base in winter for skiing enthusiasts, who come from all over Turkey and abroad to enjoy the nearby Palandöken ski resort.

History

Being in a strategic position at the confluence of roads to Constantinople, Russia and Persia, Erzurum was conquered and lost by armies of Armenians, Persians, Romans, Byzantines, Arabs, Saltuk Turks, Seljuk Turks, Mongols and Russians. As for the Ottomans, it was Selim the Grim who conquered the city in 1515. It was captured by Russian troops in 1882 and again in 1916.

In July 1919 Atatürk came to Erzurum to hold the famous congress that provided the rallying cry for the Turkish independence struggle. The Erzurum Congress is most famous for determining the boundaries of what became known as the territories of the National Pact, the lands that became part of the Turkish Republic.

Orientation

Cumhuriyet Caddesi, which becomes Cemal Gürsel Caddesi along its western reaches, is Erzurum's most sizzling eat-drink-shop-bank street. These streets are divided by the Havuzbaşı traffic roundabout. Most of the city's blockbuster sights and hotels are in this vicinity.

The train station is about 1km north of Cumhuriyet Caddesi. You will need transport to get to the otogar (bus station), 3km west of the centre, and the airport. The minibus

garage, the Gölbaşı Semt Garajı, is northeast of the town centre.

Information

Erzurum has many internet cafés on Erzincan Kapı Caddesi, which runs parallel to Cumhuriyet Caddesi. Most banks have branches with ATMs on or around Cumhuriyet Caddesi.

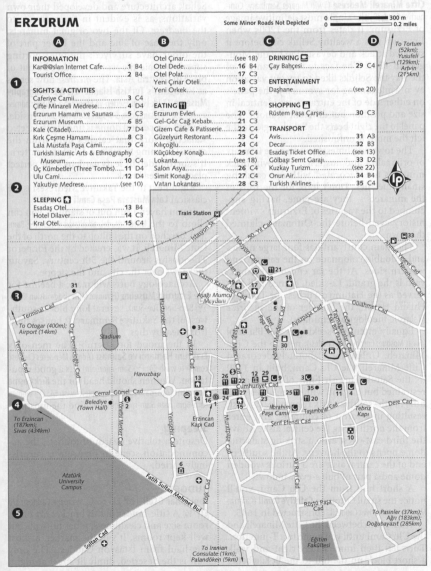

ERZURUM

Some Minor Roads Not Depicted

INFORMATION
Kar@@slan Internet Cafe....1 B4
Tourist Office....2 B4

SIGHTS & ACTIVITIES
Caferiye Camii....3 C4
Çifte Minareli Medrese....4 D4
Erzurum Hamamı ve Saunası....5 C3
Erzurum Museum....6 B5
Kale (Citadel)....7 D4
Kırk Çeşme Hamamı....8 C3
Lala Mustafa Paşa Camii....9 C4
Turkish Islamic Arts & Ethnography Museum....10 D4
Üç Kümbetler (Three Tombs)....11 D4
Ulu Cami....12 D4
Yakutiye Medrese....(see 10)

SLEEPING
Esadaş Otel....13 B4
Hotel Dilaver....14 C3
Kral Otel....15 C4

Otel Çınar....(see 18)
Otel Dede....16 B4
Otel Polat....17 C3
Yeni Çınar Oteli....18 C3
Yeni Orkek....19 C3

EATING
Erzurum Evleri....20 C4
Gel-Gör Cağ Kebabı....21 C4
Gizem Cafe & Patisserie....22 C4
Güzelyurt Restorant....23 C4
Kılıçoğlu....24 C4
Küçükboy Konağı....25 C4
Lokanta....(see 18)
Salon Asya....26 C4
Simit Konağı....27 C4
Vatan Lokantası....28 C3

DRINKING
Çay Bahçesi....29 C4

ENTERTAINMENT
Daşhane....(see 20)

SHOPPING
Rüstem Paşa Çarşısı....30 C3

TRANSPORT
Avis....31 A3
Decar....32 B3
Esadaş Ticket Office....(see 13)
Gölbaşı Semt Garajı....33 D2
Kuzkay Turizm....(see 22)
Onur Air....34 B4
Turkish Airlines....35 C4

Kar@@slan Internet Cafe (Erzincan Kapı Caddesi; per hr €0.60; ☼ 8am-midnight)

Tourist office (☎ 235 0925; Cemal Gürsel Caddesi; ☼ 8am-5pm Mon-Fri) Has some brochures and, if you're lucky, a city map.

Sights & Activities

East of the centre of town is the magnificent **Çifte Minareli Medrese** (Twin Minaret Seminary; Cumhuriyet Caddesi), the single most definitive image of Erzurum. It dates from the 1200s when Erzurum was a wealthy Seljuk city before it suffered attack and devastation by the Mongols in 1242. The façade is an example of the way the Seljuks liked to try out variation even while aiming for symmetry: the panels on either side of the entrance are identical in size and position but different in motif. The panel to the right bears the Seljuk eagle; to the left the motif is unfinished.

The towering limestone entrance is a mix of originality and austerity. The twin brick minarets are decorated with eye-catching small blue tiles. Don't look for the tops of the minarets – they are gone, having succumbed to the vagaries of Erzurum's violent history even before the Ottomans claimed the town.

The main courtyard has four large niches and a double colonnade on the eastern and western sides. At the far end of the courtyard is the grand, 12-sided, domed hall that served as the Hatuniye Türbesi, or Tomb of Huand Hatun, the founder of the *medrese* (Islamic theological seminary).

Equally attention-seeking is the **Ulu Cami** (Great Mosque; Cumhuriyet Caddesi), next to the Çifte Minareli. Unlike the elaborately decorated Çifte Minareli, the Ulu Cami, built in 1179 by the Saltuk Turkish Emir of Erzurum, is restrained but elegant, with seven aisles running north–south and six running east–west, resulting in a forest of columns. You enter from the north along the central aisle. Above the third east–west aisle a striking stalactite dome opens to the heavens. At the southern end of the central aisle are a curious wooden dome and a pair of bull's-eye windows.

A short hop from the Ulu Cami, you'll notice the small Ottoman **Caferiye Camii** (Caferiye Mosque; Cumhuriyet Caddesi), constructed in 1645.

Walk south between the Çifte Minareli and the Ulu Cami until you come to a T-junction. Turn left then immediately right and walk a short block up the hill to the **Üç Kümbetler**

(Three Tombs) in a fenced enclosure to the right. Note the near-conical roofs and the elaborately decorated side panels.

Back on Cumhuriyet Caddesi proceed further west until you reach the **Yakutiye Medrese** (Yakutiye Seminary; Cumhuriyet Caddesi), a Mongol theological seminary dating from 1310. The Mongol governors borrowed the basics of Seljuk architecture and developed their own variations, as is evident in the entrance to the *medrese*. Of the two original minarets, only the base of one and the lower part of the other have survived; the one sporting superb mosaic tile work wouldn't be out of place in Central Asia. The *medrese* now serves as Erzurum's **Turkish-Islamic Arts & Ethnography Museum** (Türk-İslam Eserleri ve Etnoğrafya Müzesi; admission €1.25; ☼ 8am-noon & 1-5pm Tue & Thu-Sun). Inside, the striking central dome is lined with faceted stalactite work that catches light from the central opening to make a delightful pattern. It's surrounded by leafy gardens – the perfect place for a tea break.

Right next to the Yakutiye Medresesi is the classical **Lala Mustafa Paşa Camii** (1562).

If you haven't run out of stamina, you can climb to the **kale** (citadel; admission €1.25; ☼ 8am-5pm), perched on the hilltop to the north of the Çifte Minareli. It was erected by the Emperor Theodosius around the 5th century. Savour the views over the city and the steppe.

Archaeology buffs will make a beeline for the **Erzurum Museum** (Erzurum Müzesi; admission €1.25; ☼ 8am-5pm Tue-Sun), several long blocks southwest of the Yakutiye Seminary. It houses finds from nearby digs.

In the mood for a scrub? The men-only **Erzurum Hamamı ve Saunası** (Adnan Menderes Caddesi; complete wash €4; ☼ 5am-midnight) has a good reputation. Women should head for the **Kırk Çeşme Hamamı** (Ayazpaşa Caddesi; complete wash €4; ☼ women 8am-6pm, men 5am-midnight), behind the mosque.

Sleeping

Despite a relative dearth of tourists, the accommodation scene in Erzurum is surprisingly varied.

BUDGET

Yeni Çınar Oteli (☎ 213 6690; Ayazpaşa Caddesi; s/d €12/16) A title-holder in this bracket for price, room size and cleanliness, it has no-frills but well-kept rooms. It's in the market, a short bag-haul from İstasyon Caddesi. The only flaw is the deserted, dimly lit street at night.

Breakfast is not included. Hungry? There's a *lokanta* next door.

Otel Çınar (☎ 213 5249; Ayazpaşa Caddesi; s/d €12/15) If the Yeni Çınar is full, the adjoining Çınar is an OK runner-up, with greenish, smartish rooms and well-scrubbed bathrooms. No breakfast is served.

Otel Dede (☎ 233 1191; Cumhuriyet Caddesi; s €9-14, d €17-20) The pros of staying here include cheap prices and a brilliant location, smack bang in the centre. The cons include a meagre breakfast (€2 extra), unadorned rooms and a migraine-inducing pinkish colour pattern. True budget-seekers will opt for the passable rooms on the 4th floor, with shared toilets and sinks (but no shower).

Yeni Ornek (☎ 233 0053; Kazım Karakebir Caddesi; s/d €14/20) The Yeni Ornek is a good choice away from the hustle and bustle of the exact centre, but within walking distance of all you need. It has appealing pastel-green rooms and well-kept tiled bathrooms. Note the ancient switchboard in the lobby.

Otel Polat (☎ 235 0363; fax 234 4598; Kazım Karabekir Caddesi; s/d €17/28) One of the best deals in town, without question, though these prices only just scrape into the budget category. Don't be fooled by the greyish exterior. Inside, it's much more appealing, with cosy rooms, good amenities and prim bathrooms, as well as a bright rooftop breakfast room boasting uninterrupted views of the city – splendid on a sunny day!

MIDRANGE

Erzurum also has a couple of comfortable midrange options, but top-end ventures are as scarce as hen's teeth in the centre. If you want full-on luxury you'll need to stay at the Palandöken Ski Resort (p569), 5km southwest of Erzurum.

Esadaş Otel (☎ 233 5425; www.erzurumesadas.com.tr in Turkish; Cumhuriyet Caddesi; s/d €23/39; P □) The best you can say about this nominally three-star middling place is that it's very central, efficiently run, well maintained and serviceable. Oh, and wi-fi is available.

Kral Otel (☎ 234 6400; fax 234 6474; Erzincan Kapı Caddesi; s/d €25/39) Just off Cumhuriyet Caddesi, the Kral is a brave attempt at traditional-meets-modern décor. The façade is a bit off-putting but the rooms make up in visuals what they lack in size. Each floor has a theme – choose from the 'Republic', Seljuk', or 'Palandöken'. It's also handy if you want to be close to the

sights, restaurants and internet cafés in the centre.

Hotel Dilaver (☎ 235 0068; www.dilaverhotel.com.tr; Aşağı Mumcu Caddesi; s/d €25/42; ✕) Sure, there are plenty of cheaper places to stay in Erzurum, but the staff here are professional, the location's ace and the beds are comfortable. Be sure not to skip breakfast in the rooftop breakfast room, which affords smashing views over the city.

Eating & Drinking

Rumbling tummies won't go hungry in Erzurum. You'll find plenty of eateries sprinkled around Cumhuriyet Caddesi.

Simit Konağı (Cumhuriyet Caddesi; simits €0.60; ⊙ 8am-11pm) This humming venue adjoining Kılıçoğlu churns out *simits* (O-shaped bread rings sprinkled with sesame seeds) that are so yummy we guarantee you'll be back for more.

Gel-Gör Cağ Kebabı (☎ 213 3253; İstasyon Caddesi; mains €2-4; ⊙ 10am-11pm) You know those restaurants with menus a mile long, where it takes forever to make up your mind? Well, you won't have that torment at this charismatic Erzurum eatery, for it specialises in *cağ kebap* (mutton grilled on a horizontal spit) served with small plates of salad, onions and yogurt. It's a concept that's been a cult since 1975, so dedicated carnivores can't go wrong here.

Salon Asya (☎ 234 9222; Cumhuriyet Caddesi; mains €2-4; ⊙ 10am-10pm) With its doesn't-get-more-central location, bright dining room and good repertoire of classic dishes, this long-running eatery is one of the essential culinary stops you should make while in town.

Küçükbey Konağı (☎ 214 0381; Cumhuriyet Caddesi, Erzurum Düğün Salonu Karşısı; mains €2-5; ⊙ 8am-10pm) If you need a break from the hurly-burly of Cumhuriyet Caddesi, lug your bags to this welcoming refuge, tucked away in a converted house full of nooks and crannies. The food – consisting mostly of *mantı* (Turkish-style avioli) and other simple dishes – is OK, but not the main reason to come. The Turkish coffee kicks like a mule.

Vatan Lokantası (☎ 234 8191; İstasyon Caddesi; mains €3-5; ⊙ 8am-10pm) Don't expect culinary revelations in this snappy joint, just the usual suspects honestly prepared and served by attentive waiters. Grab a *tavuk şiş* and satisfy the inner self.

Güzelyurt Restorant (☎ 234 5001; Cumhuriyet Caddesi; mains €4-7; ⊙ noon-11pm) After feeding your

---

AUTHOR'S CHOICE

Erzurum Evleri (☎ 213 8372; Cumhuriyet Caddesi, Yüzbaşı Sokak; mains €3-5; ☼ 8am-11pm) This one-of-a-kind Erzurum institution scores a perfect 10 on our 'charm-meter', not for offering particularly gourmet food but for its mind-blowing décor and mellow atmosphere. It feels like half the paraphernalia from six centuries of the Ottoman Empire has ended up here, with an onslaught of kilims, pictures, weapons and other collectibles from floor to ceiling. For the complete *paşa* feel, surrender to the languor of the private alcoves with cushions and low tables and treat yourself to a soup, a cup of tea or a nargileh. A tad too folksy for some tastes, but after so many characterless interiors we found this dash of Ottoman-esque exoticism refreshingly authentic. It's connected to the nearby **Dashane** (☎ 213 7080; ☼ 8am-11pm), which features live music on Friday and Saturday evenings.

---

mind with the artistic beauty of the Çıfte Minareli, retrace your steps on Cumhuriyet Caddesi and feed your belly in this Erzurum dining shrine. Don't be put off by the shrouded windows that give it a look of a Soviet-style Mafia bolthole. Inside it's much more inviting, with soft lighting and black-clad waiters. 'Tavuk Şinitzel', 'Bof Stroganof' and 'Rulo Bif' (no typo) feature on the menu, as well as a host of appetising meze. Feeling provocative? Dare to quaff an incendiary *duble* (glass of rakı) while gazing at the mosque across the street – pure perversity in this God-fearing city.

Gizem Cafe & Patisserie (☎ 235 2200; Cumhuriyet Caddesi; ☼ 7am-11pm) This snazzy pastry shop with polished surrounds is something of a treasure-trove for carb-lovers, with lots of ravishing cakes, baklavas and ice creams. The upstairs salon is a good place to make eye contact (and eye contact *only*) with Turkish students of both sexes, here to enjoy the atmosphere, gossip and giggle. And if you travel with a laptop (and we're guessing you do), you'll be pleased to know that it has free wi-fi access.

Kılıçoğlu (☎ 235 3233; Cumhuriyet Caddesi; ☼ 7am-11pm) This übertrendy pastry shop wows you with its sleek setting and a wide array of tantalising pastries, which have such poetic names as *fıstıklı kıvrım, beyaz saray, prenses* or *dilber dudağı* (look at the playful picture-book format menu). With 27 kinds of baklava and 23 ice-cream flavours, this is a Shangri-la for a sweet tooth. Snacks are also available. It's so popular it's spawned a second place over the road.

Çay Bahçesi (Cumhuriyet Caddesi; ☼ 7am-10pm) Need some hush and a cool place to rest your sightseeing-abused feet? Nothing beats this delightful, leaf-dappled tea garden, just off the Turkish Islamic Arts & Ethnography

Museum. Nurse a (soft) drink and you'll feel happy with life.

Shopping

Erzurum is known for the manufacture of jewellery and other items from *oltutaşı*, the local black amber.

Rüstem Paşa Çarşısı (Adnan Menderes Caddesi) Built between 1540 and 1550 by Süleyman the Magnificent's grand vizier, this two-storey covered *han* (Ottoman tavern), north of Cumhuriyet Caddesi, now serves as a centre for the manufacture and sale of items made from *oltutaşı*. If you've found the souvenir of your dreams, we'll be happy to hear about it!

Getting There & Away

AIR

All airlines provide *servises* to shuttle passengers to the airport (€3).

Kuzkay Turizm (☎ 234 2447; www.sunexpress.com.tr; Cumhuriyet Caddesi; ☼ 8am-8pm) Represents Sun Express. Two weekly flights to İzmir (from €44, two hours).

Onur Air (☎ 235 0280; www.onurair.com.tr; Cumhuriyet Caddesi; ☼ 8am-6.30pm) One daily flight to İstanbul (from €49, two hours).

Turkish Airlines (☎ 213 6717; www.thy.com; Cumhuriyet Caddesi; ☼ 9am-6pm Mon-Fri, 9am-2pm Sat) One daily flight to İstanbul (from €44, 1¾ hours) and a daily flight to Ankara (from €44, 90 minutes).

BUS

The otogar (bus station), 2km from the centre along the airport road, handles most of Erzurum's intercity traffic.

If you're heading to Ankara or İstanbul, Esadaş buses have the best reputation. For Iran (if you already have your visa; see the boxed text, p674), take a bus to Doğubayazıt from where you can catch a minibus to the Iranian frontier.

Details of some daily services from Erzurum's otogar are listed in the table below.

The Gölbaşı Semt Garajı, about 1km northeast of Adnan Menderes Caddesi through the back streets, handles minibuses to towns to the north and east of Erzurum, including Artvin, Hopa, Rize and Yusufeli. Minibuses to Yusufeli leave at 9am, 1.30pm and 4pm daily (€9, three hours, 129km); minibuses to Artvin (€10, four hours, 215km), Hopa and Rize leave at 7.30am, 11.30am, 2pm, 4.30pm and 6pm. The Gölbaşı Semt Garajı can be difficult to find unless you take a taxi (about €3).

SERVICES FROM ERZURUM'S OTOGAR

Destination	Fare	Duration	Distance	Frequency (per day)
Ankara	€23	13hr	925km	about 10
Diyarbakır	€14	8hr	485km	5
Doğubayazıt	€9	4½hr	285km	5
İstanbul	€31	19hr	1275km	7
Kars	€9	3hr	205km	frequent
Kayseri	€20	10hr	628km	several
Trabzon	€10	6hr	325km	several
Van	€12	6½hr	410km	about 3

TRAIN

The *Doğu Ekspresi* leaves daily at noon for İstanbul via Sivas, Kayseri and Ankara (€20); for Kars, it departs at 5.20pm (€5). The *Erzurum Ekspresi* leaves for Ankara, via Sivas and Kayseri, daily at 1.30pm (€17; 24 hours); for Kars, it departs at 11.09am (€5; 4½ hours).

Getting Around

A taxi to/from the airport, about 15km from town, costs around €17. A taxi trip within the city costs €2 to €4.

Minibus and city buses pass the otogar and will take you into town for €0.40; a taxi costs about €4.

Car rental is available through **Avis** (☎ 233 8088; www.avis.com.tr; Terminal Caddesi, Mavi Site 1 Blok 5; ☼ 8am-7pm) and **Decar** (☎ 234 6160; www.decar .com; Milletbahçe Caddesi; ☼ 8am-7pm), off Çaykara Caddesi.

AROUND ERZURUM
Palandöken Ski Resort
☎ 0442

Did you know? A mere 5km south of Erzurum, Palandöken is regarded as the best ski area in the country, with 10 ski lifts, including one telecabin, and 28km of ski runs on three

levels (seven beginner runs, six intermediate and two advanced). At weekends from December to April, be prepared to jostle with other snow-lovers for a spot on the slopes and a place in the ski-lift queues. Rental equipment is available at the hotels (about €20 to €25 per day).

SLEEPING

With the exception of the Dedeman, the places to stay are open all year. All hotels have their own restaurants, bars and discos. The prices quoted here are high-season winter rates (expect discounts of up to 20% off season).

Palan Otel (☎ 317 0707; www.palanotel.com; s/d €50/75; P ✖ ☼) What the Palan lacks in style it makes up for in service and amenities, which include a sauna and gym.

Ski Lodge Dedeman (☎ 317 0500; www.dedeman .com; s/d €55/85; P ✖) Our favourite, by far. Opened in 2006, this stylish abode has somewhat managed to retain a low-key charm and a congenial atmosphere. It's shiny-clean, light-filled and well organised. And did we mention the well-sprung mattresses, which are so bouncy you could use them as trampolines?

Dedeman (☎ 316 2414; www.dedeman.com; s/d €84/109; ☼) This second Dedeman is older than the Ski Lodge but it's right at the foot of the ski runs, at 2450m.

Polat Renaissance (☎ 232 0010; www.polatrenais sance.com; s/d €84/109; P ✖ ☼) Gloating over its shiny five stars, the massive, pyramid-shaped Renaissance is reminiscent of George Orwell's Ministry of Truth, but it has all the bells and whistles you could dream of.

GETTING THERE & AWAY

In theory, there are minibuses from south of central Erzurum to Palandöken during the ski season. Otherwise, you can take a taxi (€8).

GEORGIAN VALLEYS

The mountainous country north of Erzurum towards Artvin is the perfect combination of nature and culture. It was once part of the medieval kingdom of Georgia, and has numerous churches and castles to show for it. The trouble you take to see this region will be amply rewarded. The good news is that you don't need to be an architecture buff to marvel at these buildings. The mountain scenery is spectacular, and the churches, which mix characteristics of Armenian, Seljuk and

Persian styles, are eye-catching and seldom visited. If you happen to be passing in mid-June, the orchards of cherries and apricots should be in bloom – a special treat. If the rains hold off, late September and early October can also be fine times to visit, as the trees will have autumnal colouring.

History

The Persians and Byzantines squabbled over this region from the 4th century. Then it was conquered by the Arabs in the 7th century, recovered by the Byzantines, lost again and so on. It was part of the medieval Georgian kingdom in the 10th century, governed by the Bagratids, from the same lineage as the Armenian Bagratids ruling over the Kars region. A mixture of isolation brought about by the rugged terrain, piety and the support of Byzantium all fostered a flourishing culture that produced the churches you see today.

However, it was the ambitious King Bagrat III who looked outside the sheltered valleys and unified Georgia's warring kingdoms in 1008. Bagrat III shifted the focus of the newly formed kingdom by moving the capital from Tbilisi, nominally under the control of the Arabs, to Kutaisi, and by gradually disengaging from the southwest valleys that had been under the sway of the Byzantines since 1001.

The southwest provinces had been coexisting relatively harmoniously between the Byzantines and Georgians, but the arrival of the Seljuk Turks in 1064 dashed hopes of real stability. King David IV ('The Builder'; 1089–1125) defeated the Seljuks in 1122, and took up where King Bagrat III had left off by reunifying Georgia with Tbilisi and the southwest provinces. So began the 'Golden Age' for Georgian culture, which reached its peak during the rule of Queen Tamar (1184–1213).

Alas, stability was relatively short-lived. With the arrival of the Mongol conqueror Tamerlane in 1386, the kingdom was dealt its most savage blow by the Ottoman capture of Constantinople in 1453 and the ending of the protection the Georgians had enjoyed under quasi-Byzantine rule. The kingdom went into decline, the Ottomans annexed the Georgian Valleys and, later, imperial Russia took care of the rest.

Today many locals have Georgian heritage, but most converted to Islam or left after the troubles in the early 20th century.

Getting There & Away

The small mountain villages in these valleys are a delight to explore, but public transport to and from most of them consists of a single minibus that heads between Erzurum and Artvin early in the morning, returning in the afternoon. Buses run between Erzurum and Yusufeli, though these allow little opportunity for exploration. Hiring a car in Erzurum or Artvin, although relatively expensive, is the best way to get around and needn't be too costly if you assemble a group. From Yusufeli, you could also hire a taxi, but be prepared to cough up at least €100.

Bağbaşı (Haho)

About 16km south of the turn-off to Öşkvank is another turn-off on the right (west), over a humpbacked bridge, to the village called Haho by the Georgians. It's signposted 'Taş Camii, Meryemana Kilisesi'. Go 7km up the partly paved road through orchards and fields to the village. The **monastery complex** is about 800m further up the road. It dates from the late 10th century and is in good condition. Don't miss the conical-topped dome, with its multicoloured tiles, or the fine reliefs, including a stone eagle grasping a doe in his claws. The use of alternating light and dark stones adds to the elegance of the building.

The church is used as a mosque, so some restoration work has taken place here.

Öşkvank & Around

Continuing north on Hwy 950, you'll reach the turn-off to Öşkvank, which is 7km off the highway. Keep on the main road winding up the valley to the village, where you can't miss the impressive **cathedral**, built in the late 10th century. It's the grandest of the Georgian cathedrals in this region with a three-aisled basilica (as in the earlier churches of Dörtkilise or Barhal) topped off by a dome. Marvel at the blind arcades and the reliefs of the archangels.

The central nave has two walled-off aisles on either side. The southwest aisle, like the triple-arched narthex, is still in relatively good shape – notice the intricate carvings on the capitals, with elaborate geometric designs, typical of Georgian church decoration. There are other fine relief carvings, both on the massive capitals that supported the equally majestic dome (it has fallen in) and on the exterior walls. Look for the fine relief of the three wise men and Mary and Joseph, to the right (northeast) of the main entrance.

Much of the roof has fallen in, but there are still well-preserved fragments of frescoes; look in the half-dome on the inside of the main porched portal.

Highway 950 skirts the western shore of **Tortum Gölü** (Lake Tortum), which was formed by a landslide about three centuries ago. Feeling peckish? Stop at the **İskele Alabalık Tesisleri** (☎ 792 2471; fish dishes €4), where you can tuck into well-prepared fish dishes. The décor is nothing flash, but the setting is awesome.

A little further up the road are the impressive **Tortum Şelalesi** (Tortum Waterfalls), about 35km from Yusufeli and signposted 700m off the main road.

İşhan

When Hwy 950 meets the D060, take the road on the right marked for Olur and Kars. Go 7km to the road on the left for İşhan, marked by a sign reading 'İşhan Kilisesi'. The mountain village is spectacularly situated, 6km up a steep, paved road carved out of the mountainside.

Located past the modern white mosque, the wonderful **Church of the Mother of God** (admission €1.50) was built in the 8th century and enlarged in the 11th. There are traces of blue frescoes in the near-conical dome (vanishing fast – 25 years ago whole walls were covered in them), and a superb arcade of horseshoe-shaped arches in the apse, all with different capitals. The four pillars are impressive, as in Öşkvank (see opposite). Unfortunately, a huge dividing wall was built in the nave – half of this church functioned as a mosque until the replacement mosque was built in 1984. The most detailed of the many fine reliefs – above the portal of the small chapel next door – ascribes the founding of the church to King Bagrat III. Also worth admiring are the inscriptions above the bricked-up portal of the main building and an elaborate fretwork around the windows. The drum also sports some fine blind arcades and elegantly carved colonnades.

Bana & Penek

Continuing along the D060 in the Kars direction, after the village of Kalidibi you'll see a **castle** on a mound. It's an eerie sight, in keeping with the surreal landscape, where craggy gorges alternate with reddish bluffs. About 400m further on you'll see a second crumbling **castle** on the left, built on a rocky outcrop and overlooking a river lined with poplars.

From the junction with Highway 955, driving a further 14.5km on the D060 towards Kars will lead you past a bridge crossing the Penek Çayı (it's signposted). About 100m past the bridge, take the side track on the left. It goes uphill for 2km to the village of **Penek**. Continue through the village and turn left about 700m further on. The awesome Armenian **church of Bana** comes into view, standing on a mound with the mountains forming a fantastic backdrop – an unforgettable vision. Its most distinctive architectural feature is its rotunda shape. Beware: in wet weather you could get trapped if the road is muddy.

Oltu

Along the D955, the peaceful town of Oltu is huddled beneath a startling **kalesi** (citadel), painstakingly restored in 2002. Little is known about its history, but it is supposed to have been built by Urartus in 1000 BC. The castle was probably used by Genoese colonies and was of some importance during the Roman and Byzantine periods, before being occupied by the Seljuks and then by the Ottomans in the 16th century.

YUSUFELİ

☎ 0466 / pop 6400 / elevation 560m

Yusufeli's fate is sealed: the foundations of a nearby dam are scheduled to be carried out in the forthcoming years. The whole valley will vanish underwater, and people will be relocated higher in the mountains. Turkish officials have guaranteed that no church will be submerged. Before this happens you should enjoy Yusufeli while you can. And there's a lot to do here if you're an adrenaline junkie. The swift Barhal Çayı rushes noisily through Yusufeli on its way to the nearby Çoruh River, and the town is a popular base for white-water rafting and trekking groups.

But it's not all about nature and outdoor activities: Yusufeli is also a good base for culture vultures. The churches at Barhal and Dörtkilise are definitely worth the trip. There are limited minibus services to these villages, but if you have cash to spare you can hire a taxi to take you to them.

Orientation & Information

A short stroll reveals everything Yusufeli has to offer: Halit Paşa Caddesi and İnönü

WHAT DOES THE FUTURE HOLD FOR YOUNG YUSUFELIANS?

Fatih Şahin is a well-known trekking guide in Yusufeli and an opponent of the construction of a dam that will flood part of the Çoruh valley in a few years: 'Not only will we lose our land and our houses, but we will lose also lose our past, our memories, our traditions. This is the land of our ancestors, they are buried here, and all will vanish under water. That's not acceptable. And any tourism development is now blighted. Activities are doomed to disappear. When the dam is completed, there will no longer be any rafting trips, and certainly less trekking routes. The roads to the churches will be flooded. Young people in the valley feel desperate and are forced to move because they know they have no future here. The government assures us that we will be relocated in this area, but we still don't know where. The bureaucrats in Ankara put pressure on those who are against the dam.'

Caddesi, joining to form the main street; the banks with ATMs; the post office behind the school in the eastern part of town; and the few small hotels and restaurants. A **tourist office** (☎ 811 4008; İnönü Caddesi; ☺ 8am-6pm), near the otogar, was opened in 2006. In principle, it's staffed by English-speaking students. The **Yakamoz Café** (Enver Paşa Caddesi; per hr €0.60; ☺ 9am-11pm), in the small alley opposite Hotel Barhal, has internet facilities.

Activities
WHITE-WATER RAFTING
The Çoruh River is one of the world's best rafting rivers. Die-hard fans love tackling Yusufeli Gorge's very own 'King Kong' rapids, but most of us are exhilarated enough by the other frothing challenges in this class 4 to 5 rafting river. Bobbing down the river you can also enjoy a taste of traditional eastern-Anatolian village life and the tall craggy gorges. It would be interesting to hear about your experience. Rafting is best in May and early June; by the end of July the volume of water is insufficient.

Various local operators run day trips out of Yusufeli for about €25 per person (minimum four people) for 3½ hours of rafting; ask at Hotel Barhal, Otel Barcelona or at Greenpiece Camping. One English-speaking guide who comes recommended is **Necmettin Coşkun** (☎ 0505 541 2522; coruhrafting@hotmail.com). Other companies run longer trips with three nights' camping and four days' rafting culminating at Yusufeli Gorge. Prices start at around €1000 for one week, including food and camping. Travellers have recommended **Water by Nature** (☎ in the UK 0148-872 293; www.waterbynature .com), based in the UK. When we visited, this company used Cemil's Pension in Tekkale as a base. **Alternatif Outdoor** (☎ 0252-417 2720; www .alternatifraft.com) is a Turkish group operating out of Marmaris.

TREKKING
From Yusufeli, guides **Özkan Şahin** (☎ 811 2187, 0532 505 8975; www.way2kacgar.com) and **Fatih Şahin** (☎ 811 2150, 0532-622 9489; www.bukla.com) can lead you on customised treks up into the Kaçkar Mountains; see p558. Both speak good English. Pension owners in Barhal (opposite) and Olgunlar (p574) also arrange treks.

Sleeping
Unfortunately, Yusufeli doesn't have a lot of good accommodation, and it's no wonder – the dam project has blighted tourism development. The cheapies in the centre are best avoided – they look like they might collapse in a cloud of dust before your eyes.

Greenpiece Camping (☎ 811 3620; camping per person €3, tree house per person €6-9, s/d €9/14; ☐) Greenpiece boasts an excellent setting and has various types of accommodation. For shoestringers, the ultra-basic tree houses hiding in the leaves of an orchard can do the trick (one more ablution block wouldn't harm, though), or you can pitch your tent in the grassy grounds; for more comfort, upgrade to one of the three rooms with bathrooms. There's a pleasant restaurant by the riverside (dinner is about €5) and, yes, it's licensed. Rafting trips can be organised. Cross the bouncing suspension footbridge beside Hotel Barhal & Restaurant, and follow the signs to find this place about 700m from the bridge.

Hotel Barhal & Restaurant (☎ 811 3151; Enver Paşa Caddesi; s/d €9/18) Ideally located by the suspension bridge, the Barhal is the most obvious port of call if you don't want to deplete your accommodation budget. The rooms are not going to win a beauty contest but are fresh and luminous, and bathrooms are functional; some rooms overlook the river. The on-site restaurant serves up decent dishes and overlooks the river – if the terrace was any nearer the water you'd have to swim to dinner. The owners can organise various trips in the area, including trekking and rafting. Breakfast is extra.

Hotel River (☎ 824 4345; Bostancı; riverotel@yahoo .com.tr; s/d with half board €25/40) A friendly welcome from a charming family awaits at this newish pension, judiciously positioned right by the Barhal River. Although it's about 12km from Yusufeli on the road to Barhal, it's easily accessible by minibus from Yusufeli (€3). Rooms are sparklingly clean and cosy, with pine cladding, TV, well-sprung mattresses, colourful linen and private bathrooms. Meals are served on a breezy terrace, and the gushing river provides a soothing soundtrack. Rafting and trekking trips can be organised. Warmly recommended.

Otel Barcelona (☎ 811 2627; www.hotelbarcelonanet com; Arikli Mahallesi; s/d €55/70; P ⛱ 🖳 🖵) Almost incongruous in this backpacker territory, this upmarket resort-style abode, under Turkish-Spanish management, flaunts excellent amenities (including free wi-fi and a pool), roomy rooms with scrupulously clean bathrooms, pleasing colourful tones and an attached quality restaurant. The icing on the cake here is that you can take a dip in the big pool. Various trips can be organised in the area, including 4WD tours, as well as hiking and rafting trips.

Eating

Gourmet food in Yusufeli? Dream on! Remember what you're here for: nature and adventure, darlings. Check out also the hotel restaurants (see earlier).

Çoruh Pide ve Lahmacun Salonu (☎ 811 2870; Ersis Caddesi; mains €2-3; ⏰ 10am-8pm) It's all in the name. This is arguably the best place in town for Turkish and Arabic pizzas, served fresh from the oven, with plenty of pizzazz.

Hacıoğlu Cağ Döner (☎ 811 3009; İnönü Caddesi; mains €2-3; ⏰ 8am-10pm) Close to the tourist office. If you want to branch out from the standard kebaps, the *alabalık* (trout) deserves a try. The terrace by the river is an added bonus.

Arzet Lokantasi (☎ 811 2181; İnönü Caddesi; mains €2-4) If your stomach is in knots, this eatery plates up face-filling kebaps and other standards at paupers' prices.

Aile Çay Bahçesi (İnönü Caddesi; ⏰ dawn-dusk) On the main square, it's the most agreeable place in town to relax over a cuppa in the shade and watch the world go by.

Getting There & Away

From Yusufeli there are at least two buses in the morning for Erzurum (€9, three hours), a 9am service to Trabzon (€13) and several minibuses to Artvin (€7). For Kars, you'll have to take a taxi out to the petrol station along the Artvin–Erzurum road and catch the bus from there, at about 1pm (€8).

AROUND YUSUFELİ
Barhal (Altıparmak)
☎ 0466 / pop 1000 / elevation 1300m

Heaven! Picture this: a village nestled in a verdant valley, a rippling stream running through its heart and a lovely mountainscape. It's bucolic to boot. About 28km northwest of Yusufeli, you could be forgiven for thinking you've landed in Switzerland. Well, Switzerland without the crowds, that is. Once this initial euphoria subsides and you've had your fill of the wonderful scenery, you'll want some cultural sustenance. Barhal (officially called Altıparmak) preserves a 10th-century **Georgian church**. Take the walk up to the small ruined **chapel** in a meadowed ridge above the town – it's worth the half-hour pant for the bird's-eye views over the town and the jagged, snowcapped peaks beyond. The (unsigned) walk starts over a plank footbridge near Mehmet Karahan's pension.

Pension owners also arrange two- to four-day treks across the mountains to Çamlıhemşin with horses to carry your baggage. One horse, costing €30, can porter for two trekkers. Add another €40 per day for a guide (flat fee). Other costs are negotiable.

SLEEPING

Once you arrive in Barhal you won't want to leave, especially since the handful of pensions here are far more inviting than those in Yusufeli.

Barhal Pansiyon (☎ 826 2031; www.barhalpansiyon .com; half board per person €16) The first place you'll pass on the road into town. It's congenial, and the 12 rooms (with shared bathroom) are well tended. Enjoy the scenery and the hush from the terrace.

Marsis Village House (☎ 826 2002; www.marsisotel .com; half board per person €20) A few steps further up, just back from the river. It feels like a cosy doll house, with 16 comfy rooms, an agreeable terrace and amiable staff. Three rooms come with private bathrooms. We plumped for rooms 301, 106 and 107, poky yet intimate and cosy, with pine cladding, parquet flooring and river views thrown in for free. The wholesome dinners come in for warm praise.

Karahan Pension (☎ 826 2071; www.karahanpension .com in Turkish; half board per person €17) Run by affable Mehmet Karahan, this idiosyncratic pension on a hill beside the church has everything in spades. No glitz or pomp, just friendly ambience and neat rooms that have been recently refurbished. Angle for a room with private bathroom and a view over the valley. To make matters even more agreeable, food here is a definite plus: feast on fresh village honey and artery-clogging cream with bread at breakfast time. Here, '*Hayat çok güzel*' – you'll certainly agree.

GETTING THERE & AWAY

A couple of minibuses make the run from Yusufeli (€4, two hours), usually at 2pm and 4pm or 5pm. If you have your own vehicle, note that only the first 18km are sealed. If it's dry, the winding, narrow road can be braved in an ordinary car, but it's wise to seek local advice before setting off.

Yaylalar (Hevek) & Olgunlar
☎ 0466 / pop 500

It's a darn tiring ride to get to **Yaylalar**, about 22km further from Barhal, but peace and seclusion have a price. Believe us, this is an ideal retreat to rejuvenate mind and body, with a glorious setting, jagged peaks, babbling brooks, traditional farmhouses and the purest air we've ever breathed in Turkey – not to mention the superb hikes that await you. Recharge the batteries, feast on organic food, explore the surrounding *yaylalar* (highland pastures) and you'll be happy with life. A hint: don't forget your Turkish phrasebook as nobody speaks a single word of English.

Yaylalar boasts an excellent place to stay, **Çamyuva Pension** (☎ 832 2001; www.kackar3937.com; half board per person in old/new room €15/23, bungalow €55), with a variety of sleeping options. You can bunk down either in the plain rooms with shared bathrooms in the first building or, if you seek more privacy and comfort, in one of the four adjoining cabins, which are called, with some exaggeration, bungalows (up to

four persons). A second building resembling a big Swiss chalet was opened in 2006 and features 13 spotless rooms with private bathrooms. The food is fresh, varied and plentiful, with no fewer than 15 *çeşit* (dishes) at breakfast. Your friendly hosts, İsmail and Naim, also run a food shop and a bakery. İsmail is the minibus driver to Yusufeli and can drive you to Olgunlar.

The village of **Olgunlar** is about 3km further up in the mountains. Here you'll find the **Denizgölü Pansion** (☎ 832 2105; half board per person €20), with salubrious rooms and private bathrooms, overlooking the river, and the 15-room **Kaçkar Pansion** (☎ 832 2047; www.kackar.net; half board per person €25), another haven of peace complete with pine cladding and similar in standard to the Denizgölü.

Both these villages can be used as bases for **hikes** over the Kaçkar Mountains (p558). From Olgunlar, it takes about two to three days to reach Ayder, through the Çaymakçur Pass (approximately 3100m). The pension owners will be happy to help you organise a trek. They can provide mules, horses, a guide and camping equipment.

GETTING THERE & AWAY

Minibuses to Barhal usually travel a further 22km to the end of the line at Yaylalar (€9 from Yusufeli). There are no services for Olgunlar, about 3km from Yaylalar.

Tekkale & Dörtkilise
☎ 0466 / pop 2000

Peaceful Tekkale lies 7km southwest of Yusufeli. It's an ideal jumping-off point for exploring Dörtkilise (Four Churches), another ruined 10th-century Georgian church and monastery lying about 6km further upstream. The building is domeless, with a gabled roof and very few frescoes. It's similar to, but older and larger than, the one at Barhal, and takes less time and effort to visit. It's a perfect picturesque ruin, with weeds and vines springing from mossy stones.

On the way to Tekkale you'll pass the ruins of a **castle** almost hanging above the road.

Cemil's Pension (☎ 811 2908, 0536-988 5829; Tekkale camp site/with half board per person €3/17) is a cheerful chalet-like pension, with lots of nooks and crannies as well as a convivial terrace right beside the river and a tank full of trout. You can choose between a bed in a room (aim for a room in the new building) or sleeping on the terrace. Evening meals are also available. Cemil Albayrak, the chirpy owner, can arrange treks into the surrounding countryside, as well as rafting trips. He may also play *saz* (guitar) for his guests in the evening.

GETTING THERE & AWAY
To get to Tekkale take a minibus from the south side of the bridge (along Mustafa Kemal Paşa Caddesi) in Yusufeli towards Kılıçkaya or Köprügören; there are about five services per day (€0.50). A taxi costs about €10. From Tekkale you have to hike 6km to Dörtkilise, bearing in mind that there is no sign for the church, which is high up amid the vegetation on the left-hand side of the road. If you have a car, the road is pretty rough from Tekkale onwards and shouldn't be braved if it's wet.

ARTVİN

☎ 0466 / pop 21,000 / elevation 600m
Artvin's main claim to fame is its spectacular mountain setting – it's precariously perched on a steep hill above the road linking Hopa (on the Black Sea coast) and Kars.

Sadly, in the last few years this has turned into a spectacularly scarred setting, thanks to kilometres of dam and road works. Apart from a couple of ancient houses, the city itself does not have much to captivate you. Despite these minor shortcomings, it's the best launching pad for exploring the mystifying *yaylalar* (high pastures). And if you plan a visit in summer, try to make it coincide with the Kafkasör Kültür ve Sanat Festivalı – a definite must-see.

Orientation & Information
Artvin is perched on a valley side, high above a bend in the Çoruh River. It's little more than one steep street (İnönü Caddesi) and is easily negotiated on foot, except for the trip to and from the otogar, which lies further down the valley, about 500m from the town centre, off a hairpin bend.

For internet access head to **Özle Internet Cafe** (İnönü Caddesi; per hr €0.60; ⏳ 8am-midnight), next door to Karahan Otel. In the same street you'll find the PTT and banks with ATMs. At its western end is a roundabout overlooked by the **tourist office** (☎ 212 3071; İnönü Caddesi; ⏳ 8am-5pm Mon-Fri), where you can pick up a couple of brochures and a useful map of the area. Most hotels are within a block of the *valilik* (provincial government building).

Festivals & Events
Over the last weekend of June, the Kafkasör Yaylası, a pasture 7km southwest of Artvin, becomes the scene of the annual **Kafkasör Kültür ve Sanat Festivalı** (Caucasus Culture & Arts Festival; ☎ 0232-464 0529), with *boğa güreşleri* (bloodless bull-wrestling matches) as the main attraction. It's attended by people from all over the Caucasus.

Sleeping
Many hotels double as brothels, but you should do fine if you stick to the following options.

Otel Uğrak (☎ 212 6505; PTT Arkası, Hamam Sokak; s/d with shared bathroom €9/12) Tucked away in a quiet lane off the main drag, this cheapie is rather ho-hum, but it is central and serviceable, the shared bathrooms are OK and some rooms at the rear boast terrific views. Overall, it's a good deal if you're not too choosy. Breakfast is not included.

Otel Kaçkar (☎ 212 9009; Hamam Sokak; s/d €17/28) The bedroom furniture is a little creaky and the carpets seriously battered, but the bathrooms are good and the bedspreads colourful, and the occasional whiff of hospital-strength disinfectant is testament to the place's spotlessness.

Turistik Otel Genya (☎ 212 3131; Cumhuriyet Meydanı; s/d €17/28; 🗙) Taking a brave step away from the trademark greyish façade scheme, this recent outfit, daubed a camp shade of yellow, has spotless new facilities, including air-con, parquet flooring, luminous rooms, salubrious bathrooms and a rooftop terrace. It's just behind the mosque.

Ağasın Otel (☎ 212 3333; fax 212 8528; İnönü Caddesi; s/d €20/28; Ⓟ 🗙) This modern number is a good alternative to the Karahan, with neat rooms and sparkling bathrooms. Some doubles at the back are blessed with superb views over the valley. Sure, you might find yourself running into the occasional prostitute at the lounge-bar behind the reception, but it's pretty harmless, though lone women travellers are better advised to stay somewhere else.

Karahan Otel (☎ 212 1800; fax 212 2420; İnönü Caddesi; s/d €25/31, with air-con €31/37; Ⓟ 🗙) The Karahan is as sexy as a multistorey car park from the outside – and the grotty entrance doesn't help – but the lift will whisk you up to fancier surrounds. Refurbished, sun-filled and spacious rooms, bathrooms as clean as a whistle and competent staff conspire to make it a recommended option. Breakfasts are served in a vast room (complete with pine-clad walls), that resembles a sauna.

Eating & Drinking

For cheap fare, stroll along İnönü Caddesi and size up the assorted small *kebapçıs* (kebap joints) and *pidecis* (pizza places).

Arses Cafe Bar (☎ 212 3484; Hürriyet Caddesi; snacks €1-3; ☽ 10am-midnight) Sometimes you want the simple things in life: a dangerously cheap beer, inexpensive nibbles, a decent dollop of authentic charm and a few smiles from the waiters. This place has all that, plus live bands most evenings. It's unsurprisingly popular with students. Interesting name, though.

Köşk Pastanesi (☎ 212 1621; İnönü Caddesi, Tekel Sokak; ☽ 7am-9pm) A popular bolthole on the main drag. If you need to re-energise, skip the unexceptional baklavas and stick to inoffensive snacks or sample an ice cream.

Sedir Pastanesi (☎ 212 5960; İnönü Caddesi; ☽ 7am-10pm) This pastry shop has an invigorating *şahlep* (a hot drink made from crushed tapioca root extract, which has aphrodisiac qualities – no, really?) as well as stodgy cakes. It's just opposite the Köşk.

Nazar Restoran (☎ 212 1709; İnönü Caddesi; mains €2-5; ☽ 8am-10pm) At the foot of the main street where it turns to descend the valley, the licensed Nazar won't win any culinary awards, but if you nab a window-side seat you'll enjoy fabulous views of the valley (and the dam construction works, incidentally).

Efkar Restaurant (☎ 212 1134; İnönü Caddesi; mains €2-5; 8am-10pm) In the same building as the Nazar, upstairs. The interior is dull and cramped but from the little balcony you'll be graced with a 'million-dollar view' (as they say).

Getting There & Around

There's one morning bus a day to Kars (€14, five hours, 270km), four to Samsun (€14, eight hours, 577km) and regular buses to Trabzon (€9, 4½ hours, 255km). For Erzurum there are several daily buses and minibuses (€12, four hours, 215km). Some buses coming from Erzurum or Ardahan and heading on to Hopa don't go into the otogar but drop you at the roadside at the bottom of the hill.

There are also frequent minibuses to Hopa (€7, 1½ hours, 70km), about two minibuses to Ardahan (€9, 2½ hours, 115km) and Tortum (€9, 2½ hours, 91km), and at least six minibuses to Yusufeli (€6, 2¼ hours, 75km). There are also regular services to Ardanuç

GETTING LOST IN THE YAYLALAR

In summer, the area that extends to the northeast of Artvin is simply magical. The *yaylalar* (summer pastures) represent the heart and soul of traditional rural eastern Anatolia. There's a tapestry of bucolic ambience, with lakes, rivers, mountains, lush valleys, forests, pastures, traditional wooden houses, villages, grazing cattle and sheep... The landscape is completely unspoiled, and there's virtually no traffic. Amid this pastoral setting stand several ruined churches and castles that are definitely worth a look.

This territory lends itself perfectly to a DIY approach, preferably with your own wheels because public transport is unreliable. Put away your guidebook and follow your nose. All you need is a map (the *Artvin Kent Planı & İl Haritası*, which is available at the tourist office in Artvin, and any good touring map of the country should suffice) and a picnic. Of course, some words in Turkish for directions always help.

From Artvin, you could follow the D010 eastwards – the road to Kars – then head to the 10th-century **Church of Dolişhane**. The 9th-century **Georgian Monastery and Church of Porta**, near Pnarlı, is also worth a peek. If you continue east along the Çoruh, don't miss the turn-off that leads up to **Meydancık**, the quintessential *yaylalar* settlement, near the Georgian border. From there, you could make your way to the old Georgian town of **Şavşat**, on the main road, and take a small detour to the 10th-century **Church of Tbeti**, in ruins but in a beautiful setting. Further east, the **Karagöl Sahara National Park**, a national park blessed with spectacular mountain scenery, beckons. Continuing east, you cross over the **Çam Pass** (2540m), leaving the lush, wooded valleys behind, to reach **Ardahan**.

From Artvin, you could also take a southern route to **Ardanuç**, which boasts the remains of a fortress, and reach the **Church of Yeni Rabat**, near the village of Bulanık.

All we can say is *İyi yolculuklar* (have a nice trip)!

€4, one hour, 30km) and to Şavşat (€6, 1½ hours, 60km).

Artvin Ekspres (İnönü Caddesi), west of the *valilik*, runs a *servis* to the otogar. 'Köprü' minibuses (€0.50) also shuttle passengers between the *valilik* and the otogar. Alternatively, a taxi up will cost you about €3.

KARS

☎ 0474 / pop 76,000 / elevation 1768m

This is the city that provided the setting for Orhan Pamuk's prize-winning novel *Kar Snow)*. Kars always elicits strong reactions – negative or positive, depending on your perspective. Some travellers loathe it ('muddy', 'lethargic', 'stark', 'sad'); others scratch below the surface and realise that Kars is high on personality and atmosphere. All right, it's a bit nibbled around the edges, but when the sun shines, the stately, pastel-coloured stone buildings look almost chirpy, giving the town the look of a Little Russia in Turkey. And the mix of influences – Azeri, Turkmen, Kurdish, Turkish and Russian – adds to the appeal.

The main reason for coming to Kars is usually to visit Ani (p581), but don't forget to enjoy the delicious local *bal* (honey) and *peynir* (cheese); these will certainly keep your spirits high. When the border with Armenia reopens, which is bound to happen one of these days, business with nearby Gyumri will thrive.

History

Dominated by a stark medieval fortress, Kars was once an Armenian stronghold, capital of the Armenian Bagratid kingdom (before Ani) and later a pawn in the imperial land-grabbing tussle played out by Turkey and Russia during the 19th century. The Russians captured Kars in 1878, installed a garrison, and held it until 1920 and the Turkish War of Independence when the republican forces retook it. One of the town's large mosques was obviously built as a Russian Orthodox church, and many of the sturdier stone buildings along the main streets date back to the Russian occupation.

The locals are said to be descended from the Karsaks, a Turkic tribe that came from the Caucasus in the 2nd century BC and gave their name to the town.

Orientation

The Russians obviously had great plans for Kars, which they laid out on a spacious grid plan. Most banks (and ATMs), hotels and restaurants are in or close to Atatürk Caddesi, the main drag. Although the otogar (bus station) is 2km southeast of the centre, off the Artvin–Ardahan road, almost everything else (except the train station and the museum) is within walking distance. Dolmuşes run from the minibus terminal just east of the town centre.

Information

Limited tourist information is available at the **tourist office** (☎ 212 6817; Lise Caddesi; ◷ 8am-noon & 1-5pm Mon-Fri), west of the centre. It can help you organise a taxi to Ani, but maybe a better bet is to contact **Celil Ersoğlu** (☎ 212 6543, 0532 226 3966; celilani@hotmail.com), who acts as a private guide and speaks very good English. He'll probably meet you at your hotel's reception.

Internet access is widely available. The brightest outlet is **Comsis** (Atatürk Caddesi; per hr €0.60; ◷ 8am-11pm), which has flat screens and snacks.

Numerous banks with ATMs can be found in the centre. The **Azerbaijani consulate** (☎ 0474-223 6475, 223 1361; fax 223 8741; Erzurum Caddesi; ◷ 9.30am-12.30pm Mon-Fri) is northwest of the centre (also see the boxed text, p674).

Sights & Activities

Don't even consider missing the prominent **Kars Castle** (Kars Kalesi; admission free; ◷ 8am-5pm), north of the river in the older part of the city. It's worth the knee-jarring climb, if only for the smashing views over the town and the steppe in fine weather. Records show that Saltuk Turks built a fortress here in 1153. It was torn down by the Mongol conqueror, Tamerlane, in 1386 and rebuilt for the Ottoman sultan Murat III by his grand vizier Lala Mustafa Paşa in 1579. The entire complex was rebuilt yet again in 1855. The castle was the scene of bitter fighting during and after WWI. When the Russian armies withdrew in 1920, control of Kars was left in the hands of the Armenian forces, until the republican armies took the *kalesi*.

On the way to the castle, along the riverbanks huddle assorted crumbling reminders of Kars' ancient past, including the **Church of the Apostles** (Kumbet Camii). Built between 932 and 937 for the Bagratid King Abas, it was repaired extensively and turned into a mosque in 1579 when the Ottomans rebuilt much of the city; the Russians added the porches in the 19th century. The 12 relief carvings on the drum are of the apostles. Near the church you'll see the ruins of the **Ulu Cami** and the **Beylerbeyi Sarayı** (Beylerbeyi Palace) nestling beneath the castle.

One of the more attractive – and intact – structures in the area is the 15th-century **Taş Köprü** (Stone Bridge), ruined by an earthquake and rebuilt in 1725.

The **Kars Museum** (Kars Müzesi; Cumhuriyet Caddesi; admission €1.25; ☯ 8am-5pm Tue-Sun), inconveniently located in the eastern fringes of the town, has exhibits from the Old Bronze Age, the Urartian, Roman and Greek periods, and the Seljuk and Ottoman times. Photographs show excavations at Ani and the ruins of some of the Armenian churches in Kars province.

The cleanest *hamam* (bathhouse) in Kars is the modern **Kızılay Hamam** (Faik Bey Caddesi; ☯ women noon-5pm Mon-Fri, men 5am-noon & 5pm-midnight), which charges around €6 for the works.

Sleeping

Kent Otel (☎ 223 1929; Hapan Mevkii; s/d €9/15) Look at the rates! Fear not, it's well maintained, central and secure. Sure, the shared bathroom could do with a more serious deodorising session, but the colourful rooms are more than acceptable for unfussy backpackers. Breakfast is not included.

Güngören Hotel (☎ 212 5630; fax 223 4821; Millet Sokak; s/d €15/24; ℗) Splashes of colour and modern furniture bring the bright, good-sized

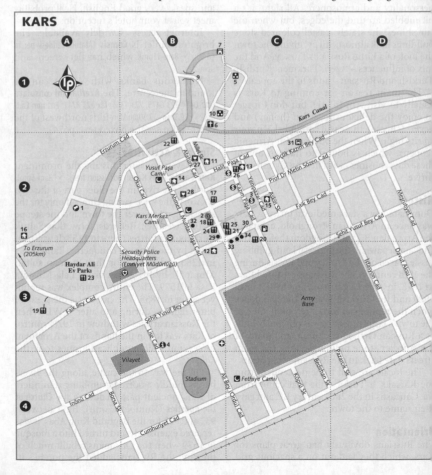

ooms to life. Other perks include an airy *:ahvaltı salonu* (breakfast room), a good resaurant, a men-only *hamam* (€6) and more han the odd smile. It's also a good choice for vomen travellers.

Hotel Temel (☎ 223 1376; fax 223 1323; Yenipazar addesi; s/d €14/25) From the outside the Temel ooks like just another crummy motel, but nside it's one of the best bargains in town – on a par with the Güngören. The rooms are ıeat, the bathrooms sparkle and the bluend-yellow colour scheme brings cheer to the nstitutional setting. Management can be a bit grumpy, though.

Hotel Karabağ (☎ 212 3480; www.hotel-karabag.com; aik Bey Caddesi; s/d €33/50; ❄) There's an imperonal feel to this three-star venture, but it's

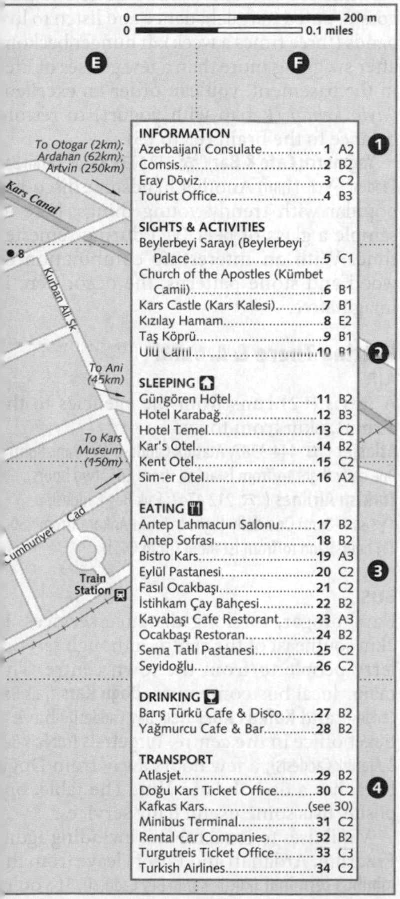
0 200 m
0 0.1 miles
E
F
1
2
3
4
To Otogar (2km); Ardahan (62km); Artvin (250km)
Kars Canal
8
Kurban Ali Sk
To Ani (45km)
To Kars Museum (150m)
Cumhuriyet Cad
Train Station
INFORMATION
Azerbaijani Consulate 1 A2
Comsis 2 B2
Eray Döviz 3 C2
Tourist Office 4 B3
SIGHTS & ACTIVITIES
Beylerbeyi Sarayı (Beylerbeyi Palace) 5 C1
Church of the Apostles (Kümbet Camii) 6 B1
Kars Castle (Kars Kalesi) 7 B1
Kızılay Hamam 8 E2
Taş Köprü 9 B1
Ulu Camii 10 B1
SLEEPING
Güngören Hotel 11 B2
Hotel Karabağ 12 B3
Hotel Temel 13 C2
Kar's Otel 14 B2
Kent Otel 15 C2
Sim-er Otel 16 A2
EATING
Antep Lahmacun Salonu 17 B2
Antep Sofrası 18 B2
Bistro Kars 19 A3
Eylül Pastanesi 20 C2
Fasıl Ocakbaşı 21 C2
İstihkam Çay Bahçesi 22 B2
Kayabaşı Cafe Restorant 23 A3
Ocakbaşı Restoran 24 B2
Sema Tatlı Pastanesi 25 C2
Seyidoğlu 26 C2
DRINKING
Barış Türkü Cafe & Disco 27 B2
Yağmurcu Cafe & Bar 28 B2
TRANSPORT
Atlasjet 29 B2
Doğu Kars Ticket Office 30 C2
Kafkas Kars (see 30)
Minibus Terminal 31 C2
Rental Car Companies 32 B2
Turgutreis Ticket Office 33 C3
Turkish Airlines 34 C2

AUTHOR'S CHOICE

Kar's Otel (☎ 212 1616; www.karsotel.com; Halit Paşa Caddesi; s/d €90/130; ❄ 💻) Beg, borrow and/or steal to stay at this splendid conversion of an old Russian mansion that has just eight rooms. Some might find the white colour scheme a bit hospital-like, but we love the refined yet informal environment, and the cocoon ambience. Added bonuses include free wi-fi, TVs with flat screens, a pleasant courtyard, elegant furnishings and the Ani Restaurant (mains €2 to €8; open 11am to 10pm), easily the slickest eatery in northeastern Anatolia. This is well worth the budgetary blowout, especially if you can bargain the prices down when it's quiet.

ideally positioned right in the heart of things and the rooms are comfortable enough. Like the Sim-er following, it's popular with tour groups. The noise of the street seeps right into the street-facing rooms – light sleepers should ask for a back room. You could probably slash the price by 20% if it's quiet.

Sim-er Otel (☎ 212 7241; fax 212 0168; Eski Erzurum Yolu; s/d €34/59; P ❄) This modern monolith is functional and professionally run, and has many facilities, including a sauna, but it doesn't even register a blip on the traditional charm radar. It's across the river, a tad out of the action, and is popular with tour groups. Posted rates are ridiculously expensive – haggle for a substantial discount if it's slack.

Eating & Drinking

Kars is noted for its excellent honey. It's on sale in several shops along Kazım Paşa Caddesi, which also sell the local *kaşar peyniri* (a mild yellow cheese), *kuruyemiş* (dried fruits) and other sweet treats – the perfect ingredients for a picnic in the steppe!

Antep Lahmacun Salonu (☎ 223 0741; Atatürk Caddesi; mains €1-2; 🕑 11am-9pm) Pide and *lahmacun* (Arabic pizza) aficionados head straight to this humble joint to gobble a flavoursome local-style pizza at paupers' prices any time of the day.

Seyidoğlu (☎ 223 7668; Kazım Paşa Caddesi; mains €1-3; 🕑 7am-11pm) This is the place all heads turn towards when it comes to sampling a heavenly baklava or a sticky *dondurma* (ice cream) in civilised surroundings. You can also chow down on inexpensive snacks. Ah, luscious Seyidoğlu.

Ocakbaşı Restoran (☎ 212 0056; Atatürk Caddesi; mains €2-4; ◷ 11am-10pm) One of Kars' best choices, the Ocakbaşı has two adjoining rooms, including a mock troglodytic one in the Ocakbaşı 2, and does a brisk trade any time of the day. It continues to win plaudits for its excellent *ali nazık* (eggplant puree with yogurt and meat).

Fasıl Ocakbaşı (☎ 212 1714; Faik Bey Caddesi; mains €3-5; ◷ noon-10pm) This place is housed in an unsightly concrete building, at a major intersection. Never mind, the interior is much more elegant, with parquet floors, dark wood furniture, earthy tones and large windows. The menu covers enough territory to please most palates, but results can be patchy.

Antep Sofrası (☎ 212 9093; Atatürk Caddesi; mains €3-5; ◷ 11am-11pm) The pastel-coloured walls of this relative newcomer are only part of its appeal. It's usually the tasty kebaps, pide and other feel-good food that keep the cash register ringing.

Kayabaşı Cafe Restorant (☎ 223 2065; Mesut Yılmaz Parkı; mains €3-5; ◷ 10am-11pm) After a turn around the nearby park, nab a table on the terrace and warm yourself with a kebap, a pide or *balık* (fish) in this well-positioned eatery, about 500m west of the centre. Forget the cold beer in hand – it's not licensed.

Bistro Kars (☎ 212 8050; Resul Yıldız Caddesi; mains €3-8; ◷ 10am-11pm) It didn't take long for the Bistro Kars, opened in 2005, to capture the hearts and tummies of well-heeled locals and visitors alike. The list of meze gallops through *patlıcan* (aubergine), yogurt, pepper, salads and other goodies that are too hard to pronounce – all irresistibly fresh. You can also dig into well-executed meat and fish dishes and wash it all down with a glass of wine or a beer (hallelujah!). The dining room is an enchanting mix of elegance and rustic charm, but on a hot summer's day the breezy terrace is a sure winner.

Sema Tatlı Pastanesi (☎ 212 2323; Atatürk Caddesi; ◷ 8am-10pm) With a remarkable rack of cakes, pastries and puddings from which to choose, plus a mellow atmosphere and a historic setting, this is the ideal spot for capping a meal off.

Eylül Pastanesi (☎ 223 4254; Kazım Paşa Caddesi; ◷ 7am-10pm) If you've got the munchies, this colourful pastry shop has a wide range of treats, best enjoyed at the small tables out the front. It's also a good place to start the morning with a hearty *kahvaltı* (€2).

İstihkam Çay Bahçesi (Atatürk Caddesi; ◷ 8am-9pm) This leafy spot by the canal is the perfect salve after trudging up to the castle. Sip a glass o tea in the shade.

Entertainment

Who said that Kars was an austere city? Sure it ain't Dakar, but you'll find a handful of ven ues for whooping, sweating and jigging.

Barış Türkü Cafe & Disco (☎ 212 8281; Atatürk Cad desi; ◷ 10am-midnight) The Barış was the flavour of the month when we visited, and it's easy to see why. Housed in a historic mansion, thi atmosphere-laden café-bar-disco-restauran has a happening buzz and is a magnet fo students of both sexes who come here to flirt gossip, puff a nargileh, dance and listen to live bands (three times a week). If hunger beckon after swigging more than a few glasses of Efe in the basement, you can order an excellen *yayla kebap* (kebap with yogurt) to restor balance to the brain (€3 to €5).

Yağmurcu Cafe & Bar (☎ 212 6199; Küçük Kazım Be Caddesi; ◷ 6-11pm) Another handsome disco-ba popular with trendy young things, here to sample a glass of beer (€2) during semeste time. With an interesting combination o wood and stone patterns, the décor here i imaginative.

Getting There & Around

AIR

A *servis* (€2) runs from the agencies to th airport, 6km from town.

Atlasjet (☎ 444 3387; Atatürk Caddesi; ◷ 8am-8pm) One daily flight to/from İstanbul (from €55, two hours).

Turkish Airlines (☎ 212 4747; Faik Bey Caddesi; ◷ 8am-8pm) One daily flight to/from Ankara (from €50, 1¾ hours) and to/from İstanbul (from €45).

BUS

Kars' otogar, for long-distance services, i 2km southeast of the centre, although *servise* ferry people to/from the town centre. Th major local bus companies, **Doğu Kars** (Faik Bey Caddesi) and **Kafkas Kars** (Faik Bey Caddesi), have ticket office in the centre. **Turgutreis** (cnr Faik Be & Atatürk Caddesis), a few doors away from Doğu Kars, has a daily bus to Van. The table, op posite, lists some useful daily services.

Minibuses to local towns (including Iğda Erzurum, Ardahan and Posof) leave from th **minibus terminal** (Küçük Kazım Bey Caddesi). If you'r

eading for Doğubayazıt be warned that there
re no direct services. The usual way to get
here is to take a minibus to Iğdır, then another
o Doğubayazıt. For Georgia (see p675), take
. minibus to Posof. Should the border with
Armenia eventually reopen to travellers, you'll
need to get a minibus to Akyaka. For Yusufeli,
ake a bus to Artvin and ask to be dropped at
he nearest junction (about 10km to Yusufeli)
long the Artvin–Erzurum road, from where
'ou'll have to hitch a ride to Yusufeli.

For details of transport to Ani, see p585.

SERVICES FROM KARS' OTOGAR

Destination	Fare	Duration	Distance	Frequency (per day)
nkara	€20	16hr	1100km	a few
rdahan	€5	1hr	80km	frequent minibuses
rtvin	€14	6hr	270km	2
rzurum	€9	3hr	205km	frequent minibuses
jdır	€6	3hr	132km	several
osof	€7	2hr	142km	a few minibuses
rabzon	€20	9-10hr	525km	2 direct, or change at Erzurum or Artvin
an	€17	6hr	370km	1 in the morning

CAR
You'll find several car-rental companies on
Gazi Ahmet Muhtar Paşa Caddesi.

TRAIN
The *Doğu Ekspresi* leaves for İstanbul (€20), via
Erzurum, Kayseri and Ankara, at 7.10am daily.
The *Erzurum Ekspresi* (€17) leaves for Ankara,
via Erzurum and Kayseri, at 9am daily. It's
worth considering these trains for the relatively
short hop to Erzurum (€5, about four hours).

EAST OF KARS
Ani
The ruins of Ani, 45km east of Kars, are an
absolute must-see, even if you're not an architecture buff. Set amid spectacular scenery, the
site exudes an eerie ambience that is unique
and unforgettable.

Once the stately Armenian capital, Ani is
now little more than ruins dotting a windswept
plateau overlooking the Turkish–Armenian

border. Come here to ponder what went
before: the thriving kingdom; the solemn
ceremony of the Armenian liturgy; and the
travellers, merchants and nobles bustling
about their business in this Silk Road entrepôt.
There's a mystique here that transcends its
abandonment and leaves you with a mix of
wonderment and melancholy at Ani's fate.

Given the proximity of the border, the area
is still under military control, but things are
much more relaxed than they were – a permit
is no longer required, and photography is
permitted.

HISTORY
On an important east–west trade route and
well served by its natural defences, Ani was
selected by the Bagratid king Ashot III (r
952–77) as the site of his new capital in 961,
when he moved here from Kars. His successors Smbat II (r 977–89) and Gagik I (r
990–1020) presided over Ani's continued
prosperity, but after Gagik, internecine feuds
and Byzantine encroachment weakened the
Armenian state.

The Byzantines took over the city in 1045,
then in 1064 came the Great Seljuks from
Persia, then the Kingdom of Georgia and, for
a time, local Kurdish emirs. The struggle for
the city went on until the Mongols arrived
in 1239 and cleared everybody else out. The
nomadic Mongols had no use for city life, so
they cared little when the great earthquake
of 1319 toppled much of Ani. The depredations of Tamerlane soon afterwards were the
last blow: trade routes shifted, Ani lost what
revenues it had managed to retain and the city
died. The earthquake-damaged hulks of its
great buildings have been slowly crumbling
away ever since.

INFORMATION
You no longer need permission to visit Ani,
and you can buy your ticket at Ani itself.
Not all the site is open to visitors, though:
some parts are still off-limits. Allow at least
2½ hours at the site, and preferably three
or four.

At the time of writing there were no facilities at the site.

THE RUINS
Enter the ruins of **Ani** (admission €3; ⏱ 8.30am-
5pm) through the sturdy **Arslan Kapısı** (or Aslan
Kapısı), a gate supposedly named after Alp

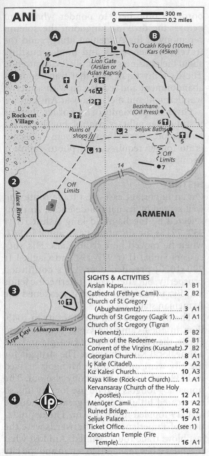

ANİ

0 — 300 m
0 — 0.2 miles

To Ocaklı Köyü (100m);
Kars (45km)

Lion Gate
(Arslan or
Aslan Kapısı)

Bezirhane
(Oil Press)

Rock-cut
Village

Ruins of
shops

Seljuk Baths

Off
Limits

Off
Limits

ARMENIA

Arpa Çayı (Ahuryan River)

SIGHTS & ACTIVITIES

Arslan Kapısı	1	B1
Cathedral (Fethiye Camii)	2	B2
Church of St Gregory (Abughamrentz)	3	A1
Church of St Gregory (Gagik 1)	4	A1
Church of St Gregory (Tigran Honentz)	5	B2
Church of the Redeemer	6	B1
Convent of the Virgins (Kusanatz)	7	B2
Georgian Church	8	A1
İç Kale (Citadel)	9	A2
Kız Kalesi Church	10	A3
Kaya Kilise (Rock-cut Church)	11	A1
Kervansaray (Church of the Holy Apostles)	12	A1
Menüçer Camii	13	A2
Ruined Bridge	14	B2
Seljuk Palace	15	A1
Ticket Office	(see 1)	
Zoroastrian Temple (Fire Temple)	16	A1

was supposedly built to house a portion o
the True Cross brought here from Constan
tinople; Armenian inscriptions on the façad
relay the history.

The architecture is typical of the circular
planned, multi-apsed Armenian churche
built in this era. The round porthole windov
above the ornamental portal is one of the fev
windows the church could withstand.

Church of St Gregory (Tigran Honentz)

Beyond the Church of the Redeemer, down b
the walls separating Ani from the gorge of th
Arpa Çayı and easy to miss, is the Church of S
Gregory the Illuminator (in Turkish, Resiml
Kilise – Church with Pictures). Named afte
the apostle to the Armenians, it was built b
a pious nobleman named Tigran Honentz i
1215, and although exposure and vandalism
have done great damage to the interior, i
is still in better condition than most othe
buildings here. Look for the long Armenia
inscription carved on the exterior walls, a
well as the colourful and lively frescoes de
picting scenes from the Bible and Armenia
church history. It also features well-preserve
relief work, with floral, avian and sinuou
geometric designs.

Convent of the Virgins (Kusanatz)

Return to the plateau and follow the path
down into the Arpa Çayı gorge to visit th
Convent of the Virgins, with its distinctive
serrated-domed chapel enclosed by a defen
sive wall, dramatically perched on the edg
of the gorge. This monument might be off
limits; check at the ticket booth. Scant ruin
of a **bridge** across the river lie to the west in a
area that is definitely off-limits.

Cathedral

Up on the plateau again, the cathedral, re
named the Fethiye Camii (Victory Mosque
by the Seljuk conquerors, is the largest an
most impressive of the buildings. Ani cath
edral was begun by King Smbat II in 987 an
finished under Gagik I in 1010.

Ani was once the seat of the Armenia
Orthodox Patriarchate; the three doorway
served as separate entrances for the patriarc
the king and the people. As the grandest re
ligious edifice in the city, it was transforme
into a mosque whenever Muslims held An
but reverted to a church when the Chris
tians took it back again. Unfortunately, th

Arslan, the Seljuk sultan who conquered Ani
in 1064, but probably also suggested by the
aslan (lion) in relief on the inner wall.

Your first view of Ani is stunning: wrecks of
great stone buildings adrift on a sea of undulating grass, landmarks in a ghost city that was
once home to nearly 100,000 people, rivalling
Constantinople in power and glory.

Follow the path to the left and tour the
churches in clockwise order.

Church of the Redeemer

The Church of the Redeemer soon comes
into view. It's a startling vision – only half
of the ruined structure remains, the other
half having been destroyed by lightning in
1957. This church dates from 1034–36 and

HIDDEN GEMS – ARMENIAN CHURCHES AROUND ANİ

Ani may be the highlight, but there are other impressive Armenian churches and castles in the vicinity that are also worth investigating. These sites usually boast awesome settings, and part of the pleasure lies in getting to them. There are no tourist facilities, so stock up on food and water. There's no public transport to these sites, so you'll have to rely on your own wheels or hire a taxi for the day (it shouldn't cost more than €80). Although the area is still under military control, tourists won't be hassled.

The four monuments described below are relatively easily accessible. No permit was necessary at the time of writing, but it's wise to double-check. A word of warning: village sheepdogs can be seriously nasty; it's best to be accompanied by locals when arriving in a village. If it's wet, the gravel roads may be impassable without 4WD.

Oğuzlu Church

From Kars, take the road to Ani. In Subatan, about 27km from Kars, take the asphalted road marked for Başgedikler, 11km to the northeast. There's a right-angle intersection at the entrance to the village; bear left onto the gravel road for 3km and you'll arrive in Oğuzlu. The monumental 10th-century church rises up from the steppe and dominates the surrounding houses. Unfortunately, it's in a bad state of preservation. An earthquake in 1936 caused the dome and other structures to collapse.

Kızıl Kilise (Karmir Vank)

From Oğuzlu, drive back to the junction in Başgedikler. Turn left and cross the village. As you come out of the village, the asphalt road ends and becomes a gravel road. About 1.6km from the junction, you'll skirt Ayakgedik; a further 3km brings you to Bayraktar. From Bayraktar, it's another 3.7km to Yağkesen where the church stands, visible from some distance. It's an eerie vision, with the building rising up on a small mound, the sole towering element in an otherwise flat, treeless grassland. It's the best-preserved structure in the area. Outstanding features include a conical roof, V-shaped niches on the exterior and slender windows, an inscription in Armenian above the portal and some handsome carvings.

Bagnair Monastery

Back on the main road linking Kars with Ani, drive west until the village of Esenkent comes into view. About 200m before the Esenkent signpost, take the gravel road on the right. Drive 4.5km until you reach a first junction; continue straight ahead for about 1.8km and you'll arrive at a second intersection. Bear right and after 1.5km you'll enter the Kurdish village of Kozluca, where you can admire two Armenian monuments. The larger church, thought to have been constructed in the 11th century, is badly damaged, whereas the minor one, 200m across a small ravine easily negotiated on foot, is still in good shape, with a nice, 12-sided dome-drum adorned with blind arcades. Both are used as cattle pens.

Magazbert Fortress

From Bagnair Monastery, return to the junction, 1.5km downhill. Turn right (south) and carry on a further 3km until another right-angle intersection. Bear left for 1.3km and you'll reach Üçölük village. Continue through the village and stop at the *jandarma* (police) barracks. From here you can see a Turkish flag flying about 1km to the south on a mound. Try to persuade the *jandarma* to let you walk as far as this vantage point (it's wise to be accompanied by a local) and you'll be rewarded by an achingly beautiful view over this pearl of an Armeno-Byzantine fortress standing atop a rock spur and overlooking a bend in the river. It's said to date from the early 11th century and was captured by the Ottomans in 1579. Unfortunately, at the time of writing you were not allowed to walk down into the valley and approach this superb fortress. Even from a distance, you can easily see a row of three semicircular bastions.

spacious dome, once supported by four massive columns, fell down centuries ago.

Seen from a distance, the building looks quite featureless, but a closer inspection reveals eye-catching decorative elements, including several porthole windows, slender windows surrounded by elegant fretwork, several triangular niches, an inscription in Armenian near the main entrance and a blind arcade with slim columns running around the structure.

Walking towards the Menüçer Camii to the west, you'll go past an **excavated area**, supposed to be a former street lined with shops.

Menüçer Camii

The rectangular building with the tall octagonal, truncated minaret, the Menüçer Camii is said to have been the first mosque built by the Seljuk Turks in Anatolia (1072). Six vaults remain, each of them different, as was the Seljuk style, but several others have fallen into ruin. This odd but interesting blend of Armenian and Seljuk design probably resulted from the Seljuks employing Armenian architects, engineers and stonemasons. The alternating red-and-black stonework is a distinctive feature. Look also for the polychrome stone inlays that adorn the ceilings. The structure next to the mosque may have been a Seljuk *medrese* or palace.

Climbing up the minaret is forbidden – the spiral staircase is steep and narrow, and there's no parapet at the top. It's much safer to enjoy the view over the canyon, the ruined bridge and the cathedral from the main gallery.

İç Kale

Across the rolling grass, southwest of the mosque, rises the monumental İç Kale (the Keep), which holds within its extensive ruins half a ruined church. Beyond İç Kale on a pinnacle of rock in a bend of the Arpa Çayı is the small church called the **Kız Kalesi** (Maiden's Castle). You'll have to look from a distance – both these sites are out of bounds.

Church of St Gregory (Abughamrentz)

On the western side of the city, this rotunda-shaped church topped by a conical roof dates from the late 900s. It was built for the wealthy Pahlavuni family by the same architect as the Church of the Redeemer. On the 12-sided exterior you'll see a series of deep niches topped by scallop-shell carvings. Then look up to see the windows of the drum, framed by a double set of blind arcades.

Kervansaray (Church of the Holy Apostles)

The Church of the Holy Apostles dates from 1031, but after their conquest of the city in 1064 the Seljuks added a gateway with a fine dome and used the building as a caravanserai, hence its name.

Seen from a distance you could think it's in ruins, but in fact it's fairly well preserved. Taking a closer look, you'll notice decorative carvings, porthole windows, diagonally intersecting arches in the nave, and ceilings dynamically decorated with geometric patterns made of polychromatic stone inlays, as well as various Armenian inscriptions.

Church of St Gregory (Gagik I)

Northwest from the Kervansaray, the gigantic Church of St Gregory was begun in 998 to plans by the same architect as Ani's cathedral. Its ambitious dome collapsed shortly after being finished, and the rest of the building is now also badly ruined. You can still see the outer walls and a jumble of columns.

Zoroastrian Temple (Fire Temple)

North of the Church of the Holy Apostles are the remains of a Zoroastrian temple, thought to have been built between the early 1st century and the first half of the 4th century AD – therefore the oldest structure in Ani. It might have been converted into a Christian chapel afterwards. The only remains consist of four circular columns, not exceeding 1.5m in height – it's not easy to spot them in the undulating steppe. They lie between the Church of the Holy Apostles and the Georgian Church – proceed about 100m due north from the Church of the Holy Apostles and you should come across the temple.

Georgian Church

You can't miss the only surviving wall of the Georgian Church, north of the Zoroastrian temple, which was probably erected in the 11th century. It used to be a large building, but most of the south wall collapsed around 1840. Of the three arcades left, two sport bas-reliefs, one representing the Annunciation, the other the Visitation.

Seljuk Palace

To the northwest of the Church of St Gregory (Gagik I) is a Seljuk palace built into the city's defensive walls and painstakingly over

GEORGIA, ANYONE?

What about a nice little foray into neighbouring Georgia? It's now pretty straightforward to enter this country as visas are no longer necessary for most Western nations. Fewer things will get your heart pumping faster than crossing the border at Posof, Turkey's smallest and most isolated border crossing. Take a minibus from Kars (€7), then ask the driver to continue to the border, a further 16km ride (€12). Cross the border (no hassles), then take a taxi to Akhaltsikhe, the nearest substantial town. From there, there are buses to Borjomi, where you can find accommodation and, most importantly, some good Georgian wines to sluice – perfect for a night out. The next morning, provided you've recovered from the hangover, you could forge west to Batumi, get an eyeful of the Black Sea and take a minibus to the Turkish border at Sarpi. This is an exhilarating two-day trip, with a guaranteed culture shock (read: women wearing miniskirts and no headscarves) and ever-changing scenery.

This is a suggested route, but there's ample scope for further exploration. For instance, we'd love to hear about the ride from Akhaltsikhe to Batumi, or from any reader who's made this trip by bike/motorbike/horse.

restored so that it looks quite out of place. Nearby is the partly crumbled, rock-cut **Kaya Kilise**.

GETTING THERE & AWAY

Transport to Ani has always been a problem. Most people opt for the taxi minibuses to the site organised by Kars tourist office or Celil Ersoğlu (see p577), for about €12 per person, provided there's a minimum of six persons. If there are no other tourists around, you'll have to pay the full fare of €39 return plus waiting time; the drive takes around 50 minutes. Make sure that your driver understands that you want a minimum of 2½ hours and preferably three hours at the site.

NORTH OF KARS

Very few tourists even suspect **Çıldır Gölü**'s existence. Far less talismanic than Lake Van, this loch-like expanse of water about 60km north of Kars is worth the detour nonetheless, if only for the complete peace and quiet. It's also an important breeding ground for various species of birds, best observed at **Akçekale Island. Doğruyol**, the only significant town on the eastern shore, has an eye-catching hilltop church.

From the town of **Çıldır**, on the northern shore, continue 3.5km until you reach the village of Yıldırımtepe. From there, a path snakes into a gorge and leads up to **Şeytan Kalesi** (Devil's Castle). Standing sentinel on a rocky bluff over a bend of the river, it boasts a sensational setting that will make even the most panorama-weary traveller dewy-eyed. Come and see for yourself!

You'll need your own transport to reach these places.

SOUTH OF KARS

This is what we scribbled on our notepad when we visited the area: 'Çengilli: fantastic'. While you're in Kars, you should definitely take a trip to the Kurdish village of **Çengilli**. It is home to a superb 13th-century **Georgian monastery**, which jabs the skyline. It's similar in many respects to the Armenian churches near Ani, but the views over the Aras mountains are unforgettable. Çengilli is about 20km off the D965-04 (the road that connects Kars with Kağızman). The road that leads up from the D965-04 to Çengilli is not tarred, and some sections are very steep – don't brave it in wet weather.

From Çengilli, backtrack to the main road and drive to the north (towards Kars), until you see a turn-off on the left for Ortaköy. This secondary road leads to the village of **Keçivan**, which boasts superb ruins of a castle, precariously perched on a ridge – another dazzling sight.

These sights are difficult to reach without your own transport. Your best bet is to rent a car in Kars or in Erzurum, or to hire a taxi and a cooperative driver for a day. You can also contact Celil Ersoğlu in Kars (see p577).

KARS TO DOĞUBAYAZIT

To reach Doğubayazıt and Mt Ararat, head south from Kars via Digor, Tuzluca and Iğdır, a distance of 240km. From Tuzluca the road follows the Armenian frontier. The army patrols the area to prevent border violations and smuggling, and if you're on the road at night expect a couple of checkpoints.

If you want to break your journey, **Iğdır** has the best choice of accommodation.

From Iğdır it's possible to take a bus east to the Azerbaijani enclave of **Nakhichevan** (€6, 2½ hours, at least five daily buses), provided you have already obtained a visa (there's an Azerbaijani consulate in Kars). The bus leaves from near Otel Aşar, on the main drag. This enclave is cut off from the rest of Azerbaijan by Armenia, and you'll have to take one of the few daily flights to get to Baku.

Minibuses for Kars (€6, three hours) also leave from near Otel Aşar; cross the street and head to Impaş store.

DOĞUBAYAZIT

☎ 0472 / pop 36,000 / elevation 1950m

Lucky Doğubayazıt (doh-*oo*-bay-yah-zuht) – this dusty frontier town crawling with soldiers has few charms of its own but is blessed with a fabulous backdrop. **Mt Ararat** (Ağrı Dağı, 5137m), a Kilimanjaro-esque snow-capped summit and, incidentally, Turkey's highest mountain, hovers majestically over the horizon. Doğubayazıt's appeal lays also in its proximity to İshak Paşa Palace (İshak Paşa Sarayı), a breathtakingly beautiful fortress-palace-mosque complex 6km southeast of town. And yes, it's a quintessentially Kurdish town that prides itself on its strong Kurdish heritage.

Doğubayazıt is also the main kicking-off point for the overland trail through Iran (the border is a mere 35km away). You'll find traders from neighbouring countries in the streets.

Orientation & Information

Doğubayazıt is small and easily negotiated on foot. For tourist information, various travel agencies, including **East Turkey Expeditions** (☎ 536-702 8060; www.eastturkey.com; Dr İsmail Beşikçi Caddesi; ☼ 8am-8pm) and **Tamzara** (☎ 544 555 3582; www.tamzaratur.com; Emniyet Caddesi; ☼ 8am-8pm), in Hotel Urartu, will be able to help with your queries. Staff usually speak English. They can also help with getting a visa to Iran (allow a week; see also the boxed text, p674).

Most banks have ATMs. There are also several moneychangers, including **Nişantaş Döviz** (Dr İsmail Beşikçi Caddesi; ☼ 7am-7pm Mon-Sat, 7am-noon Sun), which keeps longer hours and happily changes cash, including Iranian rials.

The best place to check your emails is the bright **Elit Cafe** (Dr İsmail Beşikçi Caddesi; per hr €0.60; ☼ 9am-11pm).

Sights

İSHAK PAŞA PALACE

One of eastern Turkey's star attractions, the stalwart and restored **İshak Paşa Palace** (İshak Paşa Sarayı; admission €3; ☼ 8.30am-5.30pm Tue-Sun Apr-Oct, 8.30am-5pm Nov-Mar), 6km uphill southeast of town, is the epitome of the *Thousand and One Nights* castle. Part of its magic derives from its setting – it's perched on a small plateau abutting stark cliffs and overlooking a plain, framed by Mt Ararat.

The palace was begun in 1685 by Çolak Abdi Paşa and completed in 1784 by his son, a Kurdish chieftain named İshak (Isaac). The architecture is a superb amalgam of Seljuk, Ottoman, Georgian, Persian and Armenian styles.

The palace's elaborate main entrance leads into the **first courtyard**, which would have been opened to merchants and guests. Note the ornate fountain just inside the door, here to refresh weary visitors.

Only family and special guests would have been allowed into the **second courtyard**. Here you can see the entrance to the Haremlik, Selamlık, guards' lodgings and granaries to the south, and the tomb in the northwest corner. The tomb is richly decorated with a mix of Seljuk carvings (note the faceted stalactite work) and Persian relief styles, evident in the floral decorations. Steps lead down to the sarcophagi.

From the second court you can pass through the marvellously decorated portal of the **Haremlik** into the living quarters of the palace. You'll notice channels in the floors of the rooms, once part of the unheard-of luxuries of central heating, sewerage and running-water systems built throughout the palace. The harem's highlight is undoubtedly the beautiful dining room, a melange of styles with walls topped by Seljuk triangular stonework, Armenian floral-relief decoration and ornate column capitals betraying Georgian influence.

You'll have to return to the second courtyard to enter the **Selamlık** from the northern side. Entry is via the stately hall where guests would have been greeted before being entertained in the ceremonial hall-courtyard to the right.

Across the valley from the palace are the ruined foundations of **Eski Beyazıt** (Old Beyazıt), which was probably founded in Urartian times c 800 BC. Modern Doğubayazıt is a relative newcomer, the villagers having moved from the hills to the plain only in 1937. You can also spot a well-worn mosque, a tomb and the ruins of a fortress, which may date from Urartian times (13th to 7th centuries BC).

Getting There & Away
Minibuses (€0.70) rattle between the otogar and the palace, but there's no fixed schedule – they leave when they are full; otherwise a taxi driver will want about €12 for a return trip, waiting time included. Walking back down is pleasant, although women in particular might feel rather isolated.

Festivals & Events
Over the last weekend of June, the city hosts the **Kültür Sanat ve Turizm Festival** (Culture and Arts Festival), a great occasion to immerse yourself in Kurdish culture, with singing, dancing and theatre. It usually takes place in the stadium. Kurdish big names, such as singers Ferhat Tunç or Aynur Doğan, sometimes hold concerts during the festival.

Sleeping
BUDGET
Lale Zar Camping (☎ 544 269 1960; site €3) This recent camp site is run by two male friends, Bertil and Mecit – one Dutch, one Kurd. The well-tended property and abundant greenery (but no shade to speak of) make it a peaceful place to pitch your tent. There are only nine camp sites, which ensures intimacy. If hunger beckons, there's an on-site food store and restaurant. It's a fair old walk from the centre (on the road to İshak Paşa Palace), but the outskirts-of-town location does mean a multitude of stars in the night sky and quiet, quiet nights. Note that the camping grounds near İshak Paşa Palace are not recommended for women travellers.

Hotel Erzurum (☎ 312 5080; Dr İsmail Beşikçi Caddesi; s/d with shared bathroom €4/6) This cheapie won't hit any style award, but look at the rates! Rooms are shoebox-sized but presentable, and the shared bathrooms won't have you squirming. The young owner, Metin, can help you

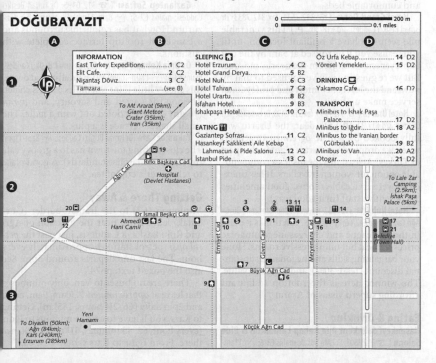

To Mt Ararat (5km); Giant Meteor Crater (35km); Iran (35km)

Ağrı Cad

Rıfkı Başkaya Cad

Hospital (Devlet Hastanesi)

To Lale Zar Camping (2.5km); İshak Paşa Palace (5km)

Dr İsmail Beşikçi Cad

Ahmedi Hani Camii

Emniyet Cad

Güven Cad

Büyük Ağrı Cad

Meydanlana Cad

Belediye (Town Hall)

To Diyadin (50km); Ağrı (84km); Kars (240km); Erzurum (285km)

Yeni Hamamı

Küçük Ağrı Cad

organise a trek to Mt Ararat. No breakfast is served.

Hotel Tahran (☎ 312 0195; www.hoteltahran.com; Büyük Ağrı Caddesi 124; s/d €9/14; 🖳) Many cash-conscious travellers, including solo female travellers, park their grungy backpack in this peaceful outfit, and we can understand why. Although on the small side, the rooms are cheerful enough and come equipped with back-friendly beds and crisp sheets, and the private bathrooms have hygienic red floor tiles. The rooftop terrace is another drawcard. And if you intend to journey on to Iran, Celal, the affable manager, is well clued up on the subject. Breakfast is extra (€1.50).

İshakpaşa Hotel (☎ 312 7036; fax 312 7644; Emniyet Caddesi; s/d €9/14) Ignore the tatty carpets at the entrance – most rooms have benefited from a fresh paint job and will fit the bill for penny-pinchers, with salubrious bathrooms, TVs, balconies and well-sprung mattresses.

MIDRANGE

İsfahan Hotel (☎ 312 4363; Emniyet Caddesi; s/d €14/23; 🅿) A popular option with tour groups. Fairly mundane, it nonetheless offers sizeable rooms and comfortable beds.

Hotel Grand Derya (☎ 312 7531; fax 312 7833; Dr İsmail Beşikçi Caddesi; s/d €18/30; 🅿) This venerable pile seems to have a brilliant location, until you realise you'll be roused at 5am by the call to prayer emanating from the nearby mosque. But we're guessing you've got used to that by now, and the level of comfort and professional service make up for it.

Hotel Urartu (☎ 312 7295; fax 312 2450; Dr İsmail Beşikçi Caddesi; s/d €17/31; 🅿) Oh dear, the Urartu was fully booked by female öğretmen (teachers) when we dropped by – a rare sight in this part of Turkey! At least this means it's a commendable option for women travellers. It has unexciting yet serviceable rooms, good amenities and attentive staff (in a good way).

Hotel Nuh (☎ 312 7232; www.hotelnuh.8m.com; Büyük Ağrı Caddesi; s/d €42/66; 🅿) The Nuh thinks it plays in the top league and charges megalomaniac prices for neat but unimpressive rooms. Hone your bargaining skills and negotiate a substantial discount (read: 30%), and it's good value. The winner here is the rooftop restaurant affording superb vistas of Ararat.

Eating & Drinking

Hasankeyf Saklıkent Aile Kebap Lahmacun & Pide Salonu (☎ 312 8802; Yol Altı Sokak; mains €3-6; ⏱ 11am-11pm) Serious travelling or hiking requires serious nourishment, and this buzzing eatery east of the main drag gets the thumbs up for its invigorating fare – the Saklıkent kebap, with a bit of everything, will assuage all hunger pangs. The décor is a bit kitsch (a mock cavern and walls adorned with cheesy frescoes), but after so many neon-lit establishments you may find it almost stylish.

Yöresel Yemekleri (☎ 312 4026; Dr İsmail Beşikçi Caddesi; mains €2-5; ⏱ noon-8pm) Yes, it's possible: no moustachioed men; only women do the service here – cooool. But they wear headscarves – boo. This establishment is run by an association of Kurdish women whose husbands are imprisoned. They prepare savoury yöresel (traditional) meals at bargain-basement prices. Everything is pretty good, but if you want a recommendation, go for the abdigör köfte (giant meatballs served with rice). The only criticism is that the décor is a bit bland. More feminine touches, please.

İstanbul Pide (☎ 312 2324; Dr İsmail Beşikçi Caddesi; pide €0.50; ⏱ 8am-10pm) Widely considered to serve the best pide and börek (flaky pastry) in town.

Gaziantep Sofrası (☎ 312 0195; Dr İsmail Beşikçi Caddesi; mains €2-5; ⏱ 8am-11pm) Facing the Erzurum Hotel, it has colourful surrounds and a congenial rooftop terrace complete with cushions.

Öz Urfa Kebap (☎ 312 2673; Dr İsmail Beşikçi Caddesi; mains €3-5; ⏱ 11am-10pm) With its all-wood décor, this cheery little joint resembles a Swiss chalet. The food is varied and savoury, and ayran (yogurt drink) is doled out with a ladle. The small shaded terrace is a plus.

Yakamoz Cafe (Dr İsmail Beşikçi Caddesi; ⏱ 8am-11pm) The closest thing the town has to a groovy café (by eastern Anatolia standards). A good place to relax over a cup of tea.

Getting There & Away

Minibuses (€2) to the Iranian border (Gürbulak) leave from near the junction of Ağrı and Rıfkı Başkaya Caddesis, just past the petrol ofisi (petrol station), approximately every hour. The last one departs around 5pm. See also the boxed text, p674.

There are no buses to Van, only minibuses that leave at approximately 7.30am, 9am, noon and 2pm daily (€6, 2½ hours, 185km). Getting to Kars, you'll have to catch a minibus to Iğdır (every hour, €2, 45 minutes, 51km) and change there. From Iğdır to Kars should cost €6.

Go to the main otogar (bus station) for services to other long-distance destinations; often you'll have to travel via Erzurum (€9, four hours, 285km). There are two daily buses to Ankara (€23, 17 hours, 1210km).

AROUND DOĞUBAYAZIT

The travel agencies and most hotels in Doğubayazıt can help you organise a daily excursion to sights around the town. Half-day tours (about €20 per person) take in İshak Paşa Palace, 'Noah's Ark' (an elongated oval shape in stone that is supposed to be Noah's boat), the over-rated 'Meteor Crater' (most probably a geological aberration) and a village at the base of Mt Ararat. Full-day tours (€20 to €45, depending on the number of people) cover the same sites plus a visit to the Diyadin Hot Springs, 51km west of Doğubayazıt.

Mt Ararat (Ağrı Dağı)

A highlight of any trip to eastern Turkey, the twin peaks of Mt Ararat have figured in legends since time began, most notably as the supposed resting place of Noah's Ark. The left-hand peak, called Büyük Ağrı (Great Ararat), is 5137m high, while Küçük Ağrı (Little Ararat) rises to about 3895m.

CLIMBING MT ARARAT

For many years permission to climb Ararat was routinely refused because of security concerns, but this fantastic summit is now back on the trekking map, albeit with restrictions. A permit and a guide are mandatory. At the time of research you needed to apply at least 45 days in advance, your application had to be endorsed by a Turkish travel agency and you had to include a passport photocopy and a letter requesting permission and stating the dates you wish to climb.

You can apply through any reputable agency in Turkey.

Several guides and hotel staff in Doğubayazıt claim they can get the permit in a couple of days. Don't believe them. There's probably some bribery involved or, even worse, a scam, whereby they take your passport and let you think they'd obtained the permit but in reality would be taking you up Ararat unofficially. It's much safer to follow the official procedure, even if you have to endure the excruciatingly slow-turning wheels of bureaucracy. Hopefully things should become more relaxed in future.

The bad news is the price. Whatever agency you use, expect to cough up at least €350 per person for the trek (three days, including guides, camping and food) from Doğubayazıt (a bit less if you're a group).

Despite the extortionate fare, climbing Ararat is a fantastic experience. You'll be rewarded with stupendous views and stunning landscapes. The best months for climbing are July, August and September, but you must come well prepared. You'll need to be comfortable with snow-climbing techniques using crampons past 4800m even in the height of summer.

The usual route is the southern one, starting from Eliköyü, an abandoned village in the foothills, at about 2500m. There's another route starting from the village of Çevirme. The first camp site is at 3200m, and a second one at 4200m.

You can also do daily treks around the mountain. Provided you stay under 2500m you won't have to go through so much official hoohah, but you still need permission from the local *jandarma* – it's best to go with a local agent. Expect to pay around €150 per person.

Southeastern Anatolia

No carpet shops. No bus parties. No tacky resorts. Southeastern Anatolia is another world. Past Gaziantep or Malatya, the gateways to the southeast, opportunities for off-the-beaten-track exploration abound. You'll instantly feel a 'last frontier' ambience and an overpowering sense of exoticism and adventure.

Here's the menu: jagged peaks, scorched plains, extinct volcanoes, vast lakes and historical cities. If one place had to be singled out, it would be pretty Mardin, perched on a hillside dominating Mesopotamia, midway between the Euphrates and Tigris Rivers. The holy city of Şanlıurfa, which is redolent of the Middle East, is making a challenge for that title. Other must-sees are Van, the most sophisticated city in eastern Turkey; Diyarbakır, with its mighty basalt walls; and Hasankeyf, blessed with a delightful setting. Nemrut Dağı (Mt Nemrut), topped with colossal ancient statues, never fails to impress.

This huge territory is also considered 'other' partially as it's the bastion of Kurdish identity and culture. Apart from some Arabic pockets, most towns and villages are predominantly Kurdish. Sure, there's an edgy roughness to the region, but this is part of the appeal. Relax. Gone is the rather sullen, oppressed atmosphere that prevailed several years ago, and very few areas are still off-limits. More often than not you'll be considered as a *misafir* (guest), not an outsider. The southeast has many treasures and few tourists. Dare to open Pandora's Box – it will win your heart, we swear. Come and experience it for yourself.

HIGHLIGHTS

- Lap up gooey pistachio baklavas at **İmam Çağdaş** (p596) in Gaziantep
- Witness the high emotions of pilgrims in **Şanlıurfa** (Urfa; p600), a holy city where prophets Job and Abraham left their imprints
- Feast on fresh trout at **Halfeti** (p600), then take a boat trip to **Rumkale** (p600), a magical place with poignant ruins overlooking the Euphrates
- Delight in the charming atmosphere of **Mardin** (p626) and drink in the views over Mesopotamia
- Hear yourself scream *'Cennet!'* (paradise) in **Savur** (p630), the region's best-kept secret
- Text your friends that you're up on the 'thrones of the gods' – **Nemrut Dağı** (Mt Nemrut; p610) – a glass of wine in hand
- Cross sparsely populated mountainscapes from Van to reach **Bahçesaray** (p643)

Nemrut Dağı ★ (Mt Nemrut)
Halfeti & ★ Rumkale
★ Bahçesaray
Mardin ★★ Savur
★ Goziantep ★ Şanlıurfa

KAHRAMANMARAŞ (MARAŞ)
☎ 0344 / pop 543,900

Mmmm… ice cream! If you're heading to this neck of the woods from Cappadocia or the Mediterranean coast, a stop in Kahramanmaraş is mandatory for all ice-cream lovers. It produces an insanely good *dövme dondurma* (beaten ice cream), which is justly revered throughout Turkey. Its unique elasticity comes from *salep*, a flour made from wild orchid roots. It is made with so much jaw-sticking binder that it can withstand the city's intense summer heat and be displayed hanging on a hook like meat. If you find that it's not reason enough to stop here, there are a handful of cultural treasures that will keep you busy for at least a day, with not a tourist in sight. For a first taste (literally!) of southeastern Anatolia, Kahramanmaraş is ideal.

Sights
The **Ulu Cami** (Atatürk Bulvarı), built in Syrian style in 1502, has a tall and unusual minaret, which has survived the depredations of earthquakes and invaders relatively intact. The hilltop **kale** (fortress) is also worth investigating, if only for the smashing views of the city.

Then head back from here towards Kıbrıs Meydanı. In the streets to your left you'll find Kahramanmaraş' lively **bazaar**. Poke around this ancient labyrinth and you'll encounter men making saddles, beating vast copper vats and manufacturing buckets out of old tyres. Some readers have recommended the sections where Ottoman-style leather shoes are made and wood is carved. Just try to find them!

The passable **Kahramanmaraş Museum** (Azerbaycan Bulvarı; admission €1.25; ⏰ 8am-noon & 1.30-5pm Tue-Sun) is 300m uphill from the otogar. Exhibits include a dozen fine Hittite stellae covered in lively reliefs.

Sleeping & Eating
Hotel Belli (☎ 223 4900; fax 214 8282; Trabzon Caddesi; s/d €25/38; ❄) Ideally located just to the southeast of Kıbrıs Meydanı, the Belli has been refurbished and features spruce rooms and prim bathrooms. Brilliant value.

Yaşar Pastanesi (☎ 225 0808; Trabzon Caddesi; ⏰ 8am-10pm) We start salivating just thinking of Yaşar's truly indulgent *dondurma* (ice cream); you don't want to know what happens when we recall the platter of Turkish sweets. The décor is another draw: while the entrance

is super-slick, there's a cosy lounge decorated with various knick-knacks at the back. It's a skip and a jump from Hotel Belli.

Getting There & Away
From the otogar there are hourly minibuses to Gaziantep (€3, two hours, 80km), while five daily buses ply the stunning route to Kayseri (€9, 5½ hours, 291km).

GAZİANTEP (ANTEP)
☎ 0342 / pop 1,100,000

Believe us: if one day there's a Barcelona-like *movida* (a hedonistic and cultural revolution) in eastern Turkey, it will happen in Gaziantep. A fast-paced and forward-looking city, Antep vibrantly accommodates its traditional Mesopotamian culture with the buzz of thriving industry. One of the most desirable places to live in eastern Anatolia, Antep's beguiling résumé includes clusters of old stone houses sprinkled around the city centre, an imposing fortress, a row of vibrant bazaars, a burgeoning café culture, the biggest city park in eastern Turkey, active pedestrianised streets and taste-bud-tingling cuisine. The old and the new combine to form an attractive, civilised and welcoming confection.

And if all you want is to please your palate, Antep could prove to be your Shangri-la: it is reckoned to harbour more than 180 pastry shops and to produce the best *fıstıklı* (pistachio) baklavas you can gobble down in Turkey, if not in the world.

If you start your eastern Turkey trip in Gaziantep, be sure to make the most of its epicurean potential. Further east it's much more limited.

History
Before the Arabs conquered the town in AD 638, the Persians, Alexander the Great, the Romans and the Byzantines all left their imprints on the region. Proceeding from the east, the Seljuk Turks strolled into the picture around 1070.

Aintab (the former name of Gaziantep) remained a city of Seljuk culture, ruled by petty Turkish lords until the coming of the Ottomans under Selim the Grim in 1516.

During the Ottoman period, Aintab had a sizable Christian population, especially Armenians. You'll see Armenian churches, community buildings and mansions scattered throughout the city's historical core.

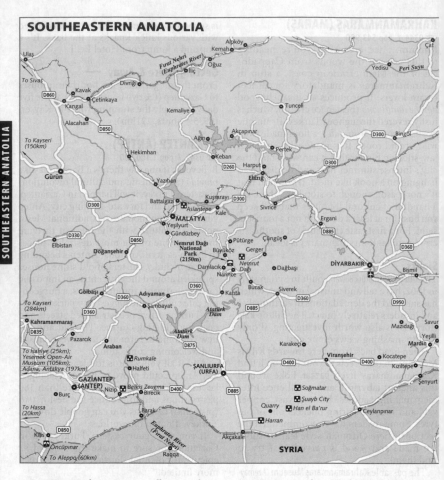

In 1920, as the victorious allies sought to carve up the Ottoman territories, Aintab was besieged by French forces intent on adding Turkish lands to their holdings in Syria and Lebanon. Aintab's fierce nationalist defenders surrendered on 8 February 1921. The epithet *Gazi* (War Hero) was added to Antep in 1973 to pay homage to the tenacious defence of the defenders.

Orientation

The centre of this fast-growing city is the intersection of Atatürk Bulvarı/Suburcu Caddesi and Hürriyet/İstasyon Caddesis, marked by a large equestrian statue of Atatürk and still called *hükümet konağı* (government house) square.

Most essentials are within walking distance of the main intersection, including hotels, banks with ATMs, bureaus de change, restaurants and sights; the train station is 800m north. The otogar is about 6km from the town centre.

Information

The post office, most banks with ATMs and exchange offices are on or around the main square.

Arsan (☎ 220 6464; www.arsan.com.tr; Nolu Sokak; ⏱ 8am-7pm) This reputable travel agency sells tickets for domestic and international companies and can arrange various tours (from €30 per person), including Halfeti, Belkıs-Zeugma and Yesemek. Ayşe, the helpful manager, speaks good English.

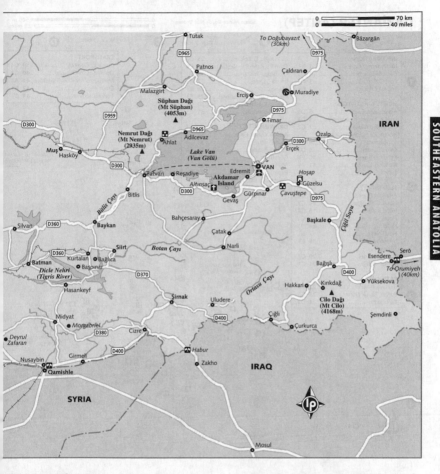

Nil Cybernet Cafe (Atatürk Bulvarı; per hr €0.60; ⏰ 8am-11pm)

Olimpia Internet (Kayacık Sokak; per hr €0.60; ⏰ 8am-11pm) Across the street from Hotel Uğurlu.

Tourist office (☎ 230 5969; 100 Yıl Atatürk Kültür Parkı İçi; ⏰ 8am-noon & 1-5pm Mon-Fri) In a pinkish building standing in the city park, it has well-informed staff, who speak English and German. Brochures and maps available.

Sights
KALE DISTRICT
Get your bearings over the urban sprawl you're going to embrace by climbing up the unmissable **kale** (citadel; admission free; ⏰ 8.30am-4.30pm Tue-Sun). The citadel is thought to have been constructed by the Romans. It was restored by Emperor Justinian in the 6th cen-

tury AD, and rebuilt extensively by the Seljuks in the 12th and 13th centuries.

At the foot of the citadel is an interesting quarter with a fruit and vegetable market, workshops where you can watch men beating copper into coffeepots and shiny bowls, old stone houses and little mosques. You can walk back into town through a partially covered **bazaar** area, looking out for saddle makers and other artisans at work. Coffee break? Try to find **Tahmis** (Buğdaypazarı Sokak), possibly the most atmospheric *kahvehane* (coffeehouse) in Gaziantep. Tell us what you think!

GAZİANTEP MUSEUM
The place to see some of the most magnificent mosaics in the world, the **Gaziantep Museum**

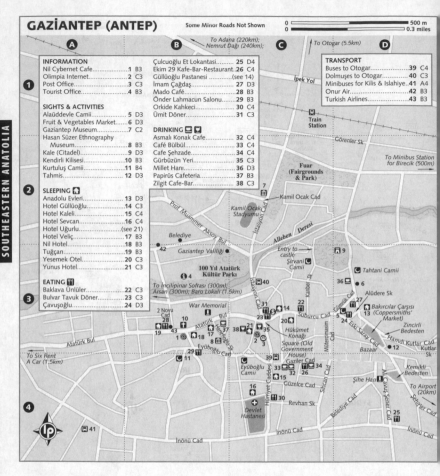

GAZİANTEP (ANTEP)

Some Minor Roads Not Shown

0   500 m
0   0.3 miles

INFORMATION
Nil Cybernet Cafe................1 B3
Olimpia Internet..................2 C3
Post Office...........................3 C3
Tourist Office.......................4 B3

SIGHTS & ACTIVITIES
Alaüddevle Camii................ 5 D3
Fruit & Vegetables Market...6 D3
Gaziantep Museum..............7 C2
Hasan Süzer Ethnography
  Museum...........................8 B3
Kale (Citadel)......................9 D3
Kendirli Kilisesi..................10 B3
Kurtuluş Camii...................11 B4
Tahmis.............................. 12 D3

SLEEPING
Anadolu Evleri...................13 D3
Hotel Güllüoğlu.................14 C3
Hotel Kaleli......................15 C4
Hotel Sevcan.....................16 C4
Hotel Uğurlu.................(see 21)
Hotel Veliç........................17 B3
Nil Hotel...........................18 B3
Tuğcan.............................19 B3
Yesemek Otel.................... 20 C3
Yunus Hotel......................21 C3

EATING
Baklava Ünlüler................. 22 C3
Bulvar Tavuk Döner........... 23 C3
Çavuşoğlu........................24 D3

Çulcuoğlu Et Lokantası......... 25 D4
Ekim 29 Kafe-Bar-Restaurant.26 C4
Güllüoğlu Pastanesi.........(see 14)
İmam Çağdaş.....................27 D3
Mado Café........................ 28 B3
Önder Lahmacun Salonu.....29 B3
Orkide Kahkeci................. 30 C4
Ümit Döner.......................31 C3

DRINKING
Asmalı Konak Cafe.............. 32 C4
Café Bülbül...................... 33 C4
Cafe Şehzade.................... 34 C4
Gürbüzün Yeri................... 35 C3
Millet Hanı....................... 36 D3
Papirüs Cafeteria............... 37 B3
Zilgit Cafe-Bar.................. 38 C3

TRANSPORT
Buses to Otogar...................39 C4
Dolmuşes to Otogar............. 40 C3
Minibuses for Kilis & Islahiye..41 A4
Onur Air............................42 B3
Turkish Airlines...................43 B3

To Adana (220km);
Nemrut Dağı (240km);

İpek Yol

To Otogar (5.5km)

Train Station

Görenler Sk

To Minibus Station
for Birecik (500km)

Fuar
(Fairgrounds
& Park)

Kamil Ocak Cad

Kamil Ocak
Stadyumu

Allehen Deresi

Prof Muammer Aksoy Bul

Belediye

Gaziantep Valiliği

Entry to
castle

Şirvani
Camii

Tahtani Camii

Alüdere Sk

100 Yıl Atatürk
Kültür Parkı

To İncilipınar Sofrası (300m);
Arsan (300m); Baro Lokali (1.5km)

War Memorial

Bakırcılar Çarşısı
(Coppersmiths'
Market)

Zincirli
Bedesten

2 Novu

Atatürk Bul

Suburcu Cad

Günük Cad

Eski Saray Cad

Hamdi Kutlar Cad

Hükümet
Konağı

Hamdi Kutlar
Bazaar

Kutlar
Sk

Eyüboğlu Cad

Square (Old
Government
House)

Gazler Cad

Mütercimasım Cad

Kemikli
Bedesten

Ali Çavuş Şenel Cad

To Airport
(20km)

Atatürk Bul

To Six Rent
A Car (1.5km)

Eyüboğlu
Camii

Hürriyet Caddesi

Güzelce Cad

Silican Cad

Şihe Han

Belediye Cad

Şehitler Cad

Devlet
Hastanesi

Revhan Sk

İnönü Cad

İnönü Cad

(☎ 324 8809; İstasyon Caddesi; admission €1.25; ⏲ 8.30am-noon & 1-5pm Tue-Sun) has been spruced up, expanded and rearranged. Even if the idea of an archeology museum usually sends you to sleep, this place will amaze you with its collection of the many mosaics unearthed at the rich Roman site of Belkıs-Zeugma, just before the new Birecik Dam flooded some of the site forever. It's impossible not to fall in love with the *Gipsy Girl*, from the 2nd century AD, reportedly the museum's highlight – we agree. Make also a beeline for the famous *Scene of Achilles being sent to the Trojan War*.

HASAN SÜZER ETHNOGRAPHY MUSEUM
Occupying a restored two-century-old Gaziantep stone house tucked away in a side street off Atatürk Caddesi, the **Hasan Süzer Ethnography Museum** (admission €1.25; Hanifioğlu Sokak; ⏲ 8.30am-5.30pm Tue-Sun) is well worth a visit. A central *hayat* (courtyard) patterned with light and dark stone provides light and access to the rooms. Those on the ground floor were for service; those on the 1st floor made up the *selamlık*, quarters for male family members and their visitors; and those on the 2nd floor made up the *haremlik*, for female family members and their visitors.

100 YIL ATATÜRK KÜLTÜR PARKI
In search of a respite where you can flake out? Spitting distance from Gaziantep's traffic-snarled main thoroughfares, the **100 Yıl Atatürk Kültür Parkı** (admission free) is a lovely space in the

middle of the city and provides a green haven for nature lovers, families and courting 20-somethings.

KENDİRLİ KİLİSESİ
Wedged between modern buildings smack in the centre, this **church** (Atatürk Bulvarı) is a startling vision. It was constructed by French priests with the help of Napoleon III in 1860. Seen from a distance, the building looks quite featureless, but a closer inspection reveals a number of eye-catching decorative elements, including black-and-white medallions.

MOSQUES
Of Gaziantep's many mosques, the most impressive is the **Kurtuluş Camii**, built on a small hill off the main drag. Initially constructed as a cathedral in 1892, it features alternating black-and-white stone banding. Another mosque worth admiring is the **Alaüddevle Camii**, near the Coppersmith's market.

Sleeping
Gaziantep is rolling in accommodation, much of it on or near Suburcu, Hürriyet and Atatürk Caddesis. Most places to stay are business-oriented.

BUDGET
Yunus Hotel (☎ 221 1722; fax 221 1796; Kayacık Sokak; s/d €18/29; P ⚡) Vying with the Güllüoğlu for the accolade of Gaziantep's best budget hotel, the Yunus is kept in good nick, featuring a fine selection of tidy rooms with salubrious bathrooms and a working lift for easy access. Just one grumble: the breakfast room has no windows. It's in a tranquil side street, but close to the action.

Hotel Uğurlu (☎ 220 9690; fax 220 9627; Kayacık Sokak; s/d €18/29; P ⚡) Almost a carbon copy of the Yunus next door (same architect?), this is another boon if you don't want to stretch your wallet, with a fine selection of hanky-sized but cheerful rooms with all creature comforts.

Hotel Güllüoğlu (☎ 232 4636; fax 220 8689; Suburcu Caddesi; s/d €20/31; ⚡) The Güllüoğlu has been smartened up and is now heralded as one of the best venues in this price bracket. Right in the heart of the action, it offers super clean rooms with double-glazing, the bathrooms are probably the cleanest-smelling this side of the Euphrates and the rooftop breakfast room proffers unabashed views over the citadel. And if you need to sate a sweet tooth, the

eponymous pastry shop is just on the ground floor – lucky you!

Hotel Veliç (☎ 221 2212; www.velicotel.com; Atatürk Bulvarı; s/d €20/31; ⚡) This concrete lump on the main drag is certainly not a paean to design but at least it's serviceable, well maintained and tidy. Some rooms are more spacious than others, so check out a few before committing. Top marks go to the bright top-floor breakfast area, with smashing views over the city.

MIDRANGE
Hotel Kaleli (☎ 230 9690; fax 230 1597; Hürriyet Caddesi; s/d €28/39; P ⚡) Well, the furnishings here are a bit jaded but the bathrooms are kept in fine fettle, so we're not complaining.

Nil Hotel (☎ 220 9452; www.nilhotel.com in Turkish; Atatürk Bulvarı; s/d €25/40; P ⚡) After a complete make-over, this hulking tower on the main drag flaunts its rejuvenated look with pride. Rooms are snug and well appointed ,and it's high on facilities, with satellite TV, air-con, wi-fi, lift and modern furnishings.

Hotel Sevcan (☎ 220 6686; fax 220 8237; Eyüboğlu Mahallesi; s/d €28/42; P ⚡) With its marshmallowesque façade, baby-pink walls as well as bordello-red curtains and bedspreads, one wonders whether a lost designer once wandered into the Sevcan. Mind you, it's a pleasant change from the typical brown Turkish hotel rooms you'll be getting used to by now. Solid amenities complete this rosy picture.

Yesemek Otel (☎ 220 8888; İsmail Sokak; s/d €30/42; P ⚡) Bang in the thick of things, the well-respected Yesemek rightly prides itself on its high level of service and amenities. Its well-equipped, comfortable rooms deliver good value for money if you can bargain a bit on the posted rates. Some rooms have balconies.

TOP END
Anadolu Evleri (☎ 220 9525; www.anadoluevleri.com; Köroğlu Sokak; s/d €60/80, 1-person/2-person ste €80/100; 🖳) Enter here at your own risk: you may never feel like leaving! This bijou boutique hotel, a stone's throw from the bustling bazaar, is set in a splendid, old stone Gaziantep house built around a lovely courtyard. The 10 rooms exude bucketloads of charm, with beamed or painted ceilings, mosaic floors, secret passageways, and antique furniture and artefacts. The three gleaming suites, offering a fine sense of individuality, are designed to spoil you rotten. At the end of the day, treat yourself to a tipple (wine or rakı) and a platter

of cheese in the cosy wine lounge and you'll be in seventh heaven. To top it off, your host, Tim Schindel, speaks excellent English and is a mine of local knowledge.

Tuğçan (☎ 220 4323; fax 220 3242; Atatürk Bulvarı; s/d €68/84; P ⊠ 및 ⚐) After having fallen for the Anadolu Evleri, it's hard to praise the Tuğçan, which pales in comparison, with its massive proportions and lack of charm. That said, this behemoth scores high on amenities, with conference rooms, a brace of bars and restaurants, a swimming pool and a reception area resembling a concourse.

Eating

Gaziantep is a nirvana for food-lovers, with a good selection of eateries and pastry shops to suit all palates and budgets. Along Suburcu Caddesi and Atatürk Bulvarı, banks and mobile-phone shops jostle with a number of shops crammed with a mind-reeling choice of Turkish sweeties. Some recommended treasure troves are listed here, but it's by no means exhaustive – do your own research and let's share our views on the squishiest baklavas in the city!

Bulvar Tavuk Döner (İstasyon Caddesi; mains €1-2; ☉ 11am-10pm) This central hole-in-the-wall would be a mere blip on busy İstasyon Caddesi, were it not for its well-executed chicken sandwiches and melt-in-your-mouth *gözleme* (savoury pancakes). If the weather permits, grab one and walk down the street to the 100 Yıl Kültür Parkı.

Çulcuoğlu Et Lokantasi (☎ 231 0241; Kalender Sokak; mains €2-4; ☉ 11.30am-10pm Mon-Sat) If there were a döner or kebap Oscar, this Gaziantep institution would be a serious contender. It has been whipping up supertasty meat dishes since 1975 to a loyal stream of customers. Business is brisk here, and it's more lively than intimate. It's a bit difficult to find, tucked away down a narrow side street off İnönü Caddesi (about 20m from a little mosque) but worth searching for.

İmam Çağdaş (☎ 231 2678; Kale Civarı Uzun Çarşı; mains €2-5; ☉ 8.30am-9.30pm) We don't mean to spoil it by raving too much. However, baklava purists swear this is the best place in Turkey to sample pistachio baklava – we agree that there's good reason to claim this. It also churns out scrumptious kebaps. The secret? Fresh, carefully chosen ingredients and the inimitable 'Çağdaş touch' (see the boxed text, opposite). Expect queues and occasional groups of tourists (the

word is out). A typical Gaziantep experience at the worst, an orgasm for the palate at the best. Since 2006 the restaurant moved into a new, bigger building across the street. Less authentic? Let us know.

Çavuşoğlu (☎ 231 3069; Eski Saray Caddesi; mains €2-5; ☉ 11am-9pm Mon-Sat) This sprightly outfit rustles up dishes that will fill your tummy without emptying your wallet. The menu roves from the usual kebaps to faultlessly cooked pide. A toothsome baklava will finish you off sweetly. Yum.

Ümit Döner (☎ 231 1790; İstasyon Caddesi; mains €3-5; ☉ 11am-10pm) If you're pining for a yummy *İskender* kebap, Ümit's signature dish, this is the place to go. Portions are copious, the meat is perfectly slivered and the salads are fresh. Sandwiches and rice are also available.

Ekim 29 Kafe-Bar-Restaurant (☎ 230 2766; www.ekim29.com in Turkish; Gaziler Caddesi; mains €3-5; ☉ 9am till late) Set in a converted old house, this mellow place feels light years away from the grinding pace of Gaziler Caddesi and time-warps you back to the past century, with dark wood furniture, cushions and wooden beams. Foodwise, it focuses on simple meals, such as salads, chicken dishes, appetisers and grills. There's live music every evening. Yes, it's licensed!

Mado Café (☎ 221 1500; Atatürk Bulvarı; mains €3-5; ☉ 8am-11pm) It's difficult for even the staunchest dieter to pass by the tantalising display of treats offered by this hip pastry shop and ice-cream parlour. You can also nosh on snacks and sip explosively fruity cocktails. It occupies a classy building with parquet floors and high ceilings, west of the main square.

İncilipinar Sofrası (☎ 231 9816; 100 Yıl Atatürk Kültür Parkı İçi; mains €3-6; ☉ 10am-10pm) Hmm, will it be *çoban salata* (salad), *altı ezmeli* (a stew with tomato sauce served in a clay pot) or *ali nazik* (aubergine puree with yogurt and ground meat)? Set on the edge of a leafy park, this widely acclaimed venue serves savoury fare in seductively cosy rooms complete with cushions, low tables and old artefacts. It's also a good place to puff a nargileh (water pipe). Alas, it's not licensed – there's a mosque nearby.

Baro Lokali (☎ 339 4140; 100 Yıl Atatürk Kültür Parkı; mains €3-6; ☉ 10am-9pm Mon-Sat) It may be off the beaten track, at the western end of the 100 Yıl Kültür Parkı, but you will no doubt be glad you made the pilgrimage. The leaf-dappled outdoor terrace is perfect for escaping sticky

THE ÇAĞDAŞ' (MAGICAL) TOUCH

Oh dear, for any sweet tooth, discussing the qualities of a perfectly crafted baklava with Burhan Çağdaş himself amounts to talking about soccer with Zinedine Zidane in person. Every day more than two tons of the divine stuff is sent throughout the country – even to the presidency!

Burhan Çağdaş is the owner of the eponymous İmam Çağdaş pastry shop and restaurant in Gaziantep, which vies for the title of most iconic eatery in southeastern Anatolia, if not in Turkey. Since 1887 five generations of Çağdaş have been tormenting carb-lovers. In 120 years İmam Çağdaş, the founder, and his descendants have refined the art of making baklava – layered filo pastries with honey and nuts. The pistachio baklava has reached cult status. Any secret, Mr Çağdaş?

'I carefully choose the freshest ingredients imaginable. Everything is organic. I know the best oil and pistachio producers in the Gaziantep area. The nature of the soil here gives a special aroma to pistachio. All my cooks use techniques from days of yore and we use wood for cooking, not electricity. The ovens are built with special stones. And we don't go into mass production. Quality is paramount.'

How can one judge whether a baklava is fresh?

'It's simple: when it's in your mouth, it should make like a *kshhhh* sound.'

He's right. We'll never forget the typical *ksshhh* that characterises a fresh baklava when we gobbled these damn little things. If you want to whet your palate before your trip, check out www .imamcagdas.com – you'll understand why we are hooked forever. So will you be!

Gaziantep on a hot summer day. The kitchen produces fireworks of flavours, from choice meat dishes to lip-smacking mezes. Rejoice! You can order beer, rakı or wine with your meal, and there's live music most evenings in summer. We'll be back.

Other temptations in the centre include:

Baklava Ünlüler (☎ 232 2043; Suburcu Caddesi; 🕙 8am-8pm) Another treasure-trove for cake and sweet lovers with – you guessed it – excellent *fıstıklı* (pistachio) baklavas.

Güllüoğlu Pastanesi (☎ 231 2282; Suburcu Caddesi; 🕙 8am-8.30pm) A perennial fave, with the usual winning tryptich: squidgy pistachio baklava (we can't have enough of these little treats!), flavoursome ice creams and good tea.

Önder Lahmacun Salonu (☎ 231 6455; Eyuboğlu Caddesi; 🕙 8am-9pm) A short bag-haul from Kurtulus Cami. The pide and *lahmacun* (Turkish-style pizza) are healthily prepared right in front of you. Pizza never tasted this good.

Orkide Kahkeci (☎ 231 2277; Hürriyet Caddesi; 🕙 8am-9pm) The tantalising scent of freshly baked cakes and biscuits wafting from the door will perk up even the most jaded proboscis.

Drinking

Cafe Şehzade (☎ 231 0350; Gaziler Caddesi; snacks €1-2; 🕙 8.30am-8pm) The décor alone is worth a gander: the atmospheric Şehzade is housed in an 800-year-old converted *hamam* (bathhouse).

The food, mostly snacks, is so-so, but it's a good place to meet students and sip a cup of tea. Drop by in late afternoon, when there's live music.

Gürbüzün Yeri (Hürriyet Caddesi; juices from €0.70; 🕙 8.30am-11pm) Ultrafresh fruit juices are the deal in this buzzing hole-in-the-wall, so put some bounce in your step with a glass of *atom* (an explosive mixture of milk, honey, banana, hazelnuts and pistachio) or *şalgam*, a bitter but refreshing drink made from root vegetables, garlic and hot peppers. *Lezzetli* (delicious)!

Asmalı Konak Cafe (☎ 231 4105; Gaziler Caddesi; 🕙 8am-8pm) A soothing venue set in a converted house, on a lively pedestrianised street. Nab a table on the balcony and watch the world stroll by with a glass of ayran in hand.

Café Bülbül (☎ 221 2616; Gaziler Caddesi; h8am-8pm) Another peaceful refuge. It lures in students in search of a pleasant spot to flirt and relax over a soft drink.

Zılgıt Cafe-Bar (☎ 230 0490; Kayacık Sokak; 🕙 9am-11pm) This cosy place full of nooks, crannies, carpets and cushions features live music every evening. Soft drinks and alcohol are available. It's near the Yunus Hotel.

Millet Hanı (Uzun Çarşı; snacks €1-3; 🕙 8am-10pm) A pleasant venue. Where else could you sip a cup of tea or sup a soup in a five-century-old converted caravanserai? The whole experience

THE AUTHOR'S CHOICE

Papirüs Cafeteria (☎ 220 3279; Noter Sokak) By far our favourite. Housed in a historic mansion off Atatürk Caddesi, this treasure-trove is perfect for unwinding after a bout of sightseeing. It has bags of character, and features a leafy courtyard and several rooms with ancient frescoes and old furniture. It's a good place to make eye contact with students of both sexes.

is a bit marred by the gaudy beach umbrellas in the courtyard.

Getting There & Away
AIR
Gaziantep's Oğuzeli airport is 20km from the centre. An airport bus departs from outside each airline office 1½ hours before flights (€3).

Cyprus Turkish Airlines (www.kthy.net) Two weekly flights to Ercan (Northern Cyprus), from €50.

Onur Air (☎ 221 0304; www.onurair.com.tr; Kazaz İş Merkezi; ☼ 7am-7pm) Two daily flights to/from İstanbul (from €50; 1¾ hours).

Pegasus (www.flypgs.com) Daily flights to/from İstanbul (from €45) and to/from İzmir (from €45).

Sun Express (www.sunexpress.com.tr) Three weekly flights to/from İzmir (from €45, 1¾ hours).

Turkish Airlines (☎ 230 1563; www.thy.com; Atatürk Bulvarı; ☼ 8.30-5.30pm Mon-Fri & 8.30am-1pm Sat) Two to three daily flights to/from İstanbul (from €50, 1¾ hours).

These airline companies don't have offices in Gaziantep but any travel agency, including Arsan (see p592), can issue tickets in behalf of these companies

BUS
The otogar is 6km from the town centre, although if you arrive by minibus it'll usually weave through the town centre before heading out there. Frequent city buses (€0.60) rattle between the otogar and the town centre. To get to the otogar, catch the bus in Hürriyet Caddesi, north of Gaziler Caddesi, or a dolmuş about 400m further north in İstasyon Caddesi. A taxi costs about €6.

There's no direct bus to Syria; you'll have to go to Kilis first, then take a taxi to the border or to Aleppo. Minibuses to Kilis (€3, 65km) leave every 15 minutes from a separate

minibus terminal on İnönü Caddesi. This terminal also handles minibuses to İslahiye (€3, 95km). Minibuses to Birecik (€3, 46km) have their own terminal on İpek Yolu, east of the centre.

Details of some daily services are listed in the table, below.

SERVICES FROM GAZİANTEP'S OTOGAR

Destination	Fare	Duration	Distance	Frequency (per day)
Adana	€7	4hr	220km	frequent buses
Adıyaman	€5	3hr	162km	frequent minibuses
Ankara	€20	10hr	705km	frequent buses
Antakya	€7	4hr	200km	frequent minibuses
Diyarbakır	€12	5hr	330km	frequent buses
İstanbul	€21	15hr	1136km	several buses
Kahramanmaraş	€4	1½hr	80km	frequent buses & minibuses
Mardin	€12	6hr	330km	several buses
Şanlıurfa	€5	2½hr	145km	frequent buses
Van	€18	12hr	740km	several buses

CAR
You may need a car to see some of the surrounding sights, especially Yesemek Open-Air Museum (opposite). Try Arsan (p592) or **Sixt Rent A Car** (☎ 336 7718; Ordu Caddesi), 1.5km west of town.

TRAIN
The comfortable *Toros Ekspresi* leaves for İstanbul via Adana and Konya at 2.30pm on Tuesday, Thursday and Sunday (€20, 27 hours). To get to Aleppo and Damascus by train, you'll need to go to İslahiye to catch the twice-weekly train to Syria (about five hours from İslahiye, €5)

AROUND GAZİANTEP
Kilis
☎ 0348 / pop 70,700
Go there now! The word is not out – yet. Easily accessible from Gaziantep, Kilis beckons

the savvy with its convivial atmosphere and bristles with splendiferous historical buildings scattered around the city centre: mausoleums, caravanserais, *hamams*, mosques, fountains, *konaks* (old houses)… Most ancient buildings are in the process of being restored, including the Adliye, the Mevlevi Hane, the Tekye Camii, the Paşa Hamamı, the Cuneyne Camii, the Çalik Camii and the Kadı Camii… Mosey around the narrow streets off the main drag and you'll find them, among a number of others.

Take a minibus from Gaziantep and allow a day in this surprising city to do it justice. Should you want to stay overnight here, the **Hotel Arca** (☎ 814 08343; Zekerya Korkmaz Bulvarı; s/d €31/45; P ⊠ ⊠) is the best shut-eye option, with bathrooms so clean you could eat off the floor. If hunger beckons, there's a pastry shop and an ice-cream parlour on the ground floor.

There are frequent minibus services to Gaziantep (€3, 65km, one hour). Minibuses to İslahiye depart every hour (€3, 82km, 1½ hours). For Aleppo in Syria, take a taxi to Öncüpınar at the border (€6, 7km). From the Syrian side of the border, you can pick up a taxi on to Aleppo.

Yesemek Open-Air Museum

One of the star attractions in the Gaziantep area, the **Yesemek Open-Air Museum** (Yesemek Açık Hava Müzesi; admission €1.25; ☼ dawn-dusk) is a vast hillside studded with some 300 Hittite stones and statues. Even if you're not a fan of the Hittites, you will find a visit rewarding, if only for the picturesque setting.

The unique use of the site is intriguing. From around 1375 BC this hillside was a Hittite quarry and sculpture workshop. For over 600 years it churned out basalt blocks, weighing anywhere from 1.5 to eight tonnes, carved into lions, sphinxes and other designs. Today, the pieces are left in various states of completion, abandoned at the end of the Hittite era.

Yesemek is a long 113km haul from Gaziantep. Getting there by public transport is not really convenient. First, you'll need to catch one of the half-hourly minibuses from Gaziantep to İslahiye (€3, 1½ hours), in time for the 1.30pm (no Sunday service) minibus to the site, which is 25km southeast of İslahiye. You'll need to pay for the minibus to bring you back to İslahiye (around €15 to €20) the

same day, since they usually stay overnight in the village.

It's easier to hire a car or a taxi in Gaziantep (about €60). You could do a scenic loop, taking in Kilis, Yesemek and İslahiye. From Kilis, follow the D410 to Hassa/Antakya, then bear right onto the gravel road marked for Yesemek.

Belkıs-Zeugma

The city of Belkıs-Zeugma was once an important city. Founded by one of Alexander the Great's generals around 300 BC, it had its golden age with the Romans, and later became a major trading station along the Silk Road. Unfortunately, it has lost much of its appeal since most of the site disappeared beneath the waters of the Birecik Dam. Despite numerous excavations, all that is left of its former grandeur is a pile of rubble and a couple of dilapidated pillars. Nor are there any explanatory signs. Most interesting mosaics and finds have been transferred to Gaziantep Museum, where some are on display.

The site is about 50km from Gaziantep and 7km off the main road to Şanlıurfa (it's signposted), but there's no minibus service. If you don't have your own vehicle, you may think it's too much effort getting there for too little reward.

Birecik

About 46km east of Gaziantep, right by the Euphrates River (Fırat Nehri), Birecik is one of the few nesting places in the world of the eastern bald ibis *(Geronticus eremita)*, a bird species that, sadly, hovers on the brink of extinction.

The birds are tagged, released into the wild, and supposed to be here only during the breeding season (February to July), but you can usually see at least a few of the home-bodies year-round.

If you've got your own vehicle, getting to the breeding station is reasonably simple. Follow the riverbank north for about 1km looking out on the right for the brown-and-yellow sign marked **Birecik Kelaynak Üretme İstasyonu** (Birecik Ibis Breeding Station; ☼ 7am-7pm).

If feathered creatures are not your thing, you can visit the ruins of the **fortress** that is perched on the hill.

If you get stuck in Birecik, head to the **Mırkelam Otel & Restaurant** (☎ 0414-661 0500; s/d €17/28; P ⊠ ⊠), on the highway just west of the Euphrates, where the coaches stop. This motel-like establishment is not exactly a honeymoon destination but at least it's clean, serviceable and well organised.

The best place for a good meal is **Kıyı Restaurant** (☎ 661 0117; Karşıkaya; mains €3-7; ⏰ 8am-9pm), right by the Euphrates, about 500m from Mırkelam Otel (it's signposted). Picture this: an open-air terrace overlooking the river, great views of the fortress, lots of shade and patently fresh fish. Wash it all down with a glass of beer – this is all the therapy you need after a half-day's sightseeing.

Any of the buses travelling between Şanlıurfa and Gaziantep can drop you at Birecik, so you can easily make a stop-off visit on your way through without having to stay overnight (provided you're ready to leave by early afternoon). At Birecik ask to be let off at the *kale* (fortress), by the river. Then you'll have to walk 1.3km to the breeding station or hire a taxi.

The small otogar is near the vegetable market, by the river, at the foot of the fortress. There are frequent minibuses to Şanlıurfa (€3, 1½ hours) and Gaziantep (€3, one hour). For Halfeti (€2, 45km), there are regular minibuses on weekdays, but very few services at weekends. A taxi ride to Halfeti costs about €26.

Halfeti & Rumkale

Need a break in a secluded place? Then Halfeti is for you. This peaceful village lies about 40km north of Birecik, right on the bank of the Euphrates. It's the perfect spot to unwind before tackling the busy cities of Şanlıurfa to the east or Gaziantep to the west. The setting couldn't be more appealing, with attractive houses that trip down the side of the hillside above the river. Sadly, with the construction of the Birecik Dam, half of the city was inundated, including several archaeological sites, and part of the population had to be resettled.

There are a couple of places to soak up the atmosphere. For a cup of tea or a fresh fish from the lake, the leafy **Siyah Gül Restaurant** (☎ 0414-751 5235; mains €3-5), overlooking the lake, is a sound option and alcohol is served. The licensed **Duba Restaurant** (☎ 0414-751 5704; mains €2-6), further down, at the end of the village (just follow the road that goes along the lake), is even better, with a shady pontoon on the water. Should you decide to stay overnight,

the welcoming **Şelaleli Konak** (☎ 0414-751 5500; d per person €10) fits the bill, but there are only three rooms (one with private bathroom). Breakfast is extra (€2).

From Halfeti, boat trips to nearby **Rumkale** can easily be organised (about €30 for the whole boat) – a definite must-do. This ruined fortress sits atop a rocky bluff overlooking the river and is accessible by a short but steep path. It features a mosque, a church, a monastery, a well and other remains, all in a relatively good state of preservation. And, man-oh-man, the views are just lovely.

Halfeti is relatively easily accessible by public transport on weekdays. Hourly minibuses ply the route between Birecik and Halfeti (€2).

ŞANLIURFA (URFA)

☎ 0414 / pop 463,800 / elevation 518m

Mystical and pious Şanlıurfa (the Prophets' City; also known as Urfa) casts a spell on anyone who visits this great pilgrimage town, one of the greatest religious and historical sites in Turkey – it's light years away from nearby Gaziantep in this respect. It also has a distinctly Middle Eastern flavour, courtesy of its proximity to Syria. Women cloaked in black chadors elbow their way through the odorous crush of the bazaar streets; moustached gents in *şalvar* (traditional baggy Arabic pants) swill tea and click-clack backgammon pieces in a shady courtyard; pilgrims feed sacred carp in the shadows of a medieval fortress… If you're after touches of exoticism, you'll be amply rewarded here. Urfa also has its share of the mundane – out on the highway the traffic is noisy and unruly, and the suburbs are disfigured by the ubiquitous concrete eyesores. Regardless of this, it's a must-see for any visitor to the southeast.

History

The Hittites imposed their rule over the area around 1370 BC. After a period of Assyrian rule, Alexander the Great hit Urfa. He and his Macedonian mates named the town Edessa, after a former capital of Macedonia, and it remained the capital of a Seleucid province until 132 BC, when the local Aramaean population set up an independent kingdom and renamed the town Orhai. Orhai finally succumbed to the Romans, as did everywhere hereabouts.

Edessa pursued its contrary history by speedily adopting Christianity (c 200)

ŞANLIURFA (URFA)

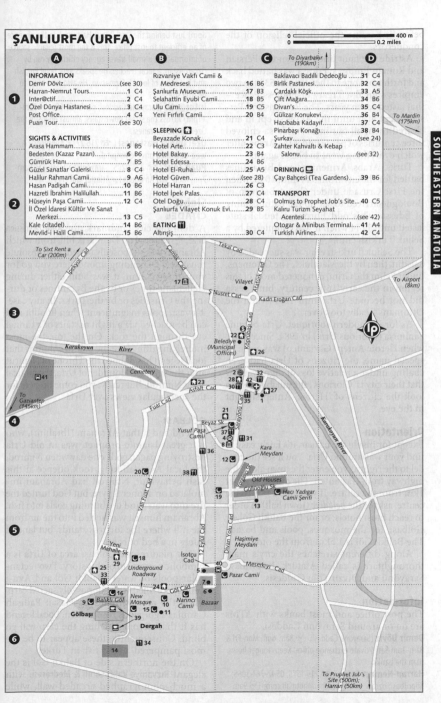

before it became the official religion of the conquerors.

Astride the fault line between the Persian and Roman Empires, Edessa was batted back and forth from one to the other. In 533 the two empires signed a Treaty of Endless Peace – that lasted seven years. The Romans and Persians kept at it until the Arabs swept in and cleared them all out in 637. Edessa enjoyed three centuries of peace under the Arabs, after which everything went to blazes again.

Turks, Arabs, Armenians and Byzantines battled for the city from 944 until 1098, when the First Crusade under Count Baldwin of Boulogne arrived to set up the Latin County of Edessa. This odd European feudal state lasted until 1144 when it was conquered by a Seljuk Turkish emir.

The Seljuk Turkish emir was succeeded by Saladin, then by the Mamluks. The Ottomans, under Selim the Grim, conquered most of this region in the early 16th century, but Edessa did not become Urfa until 1637 when the Ottomans finally took over.

As for its modern sobriquet, Urfa became Şanlıurfa (Glorious Urfa) in 1984. Since 1973, when Heroic Antep (Gaziantep) was given its special name, the citizens of Urfa had been chafing under a relative loss of dignity. Now that their city is 'Glorious', the inhabitants can look the citizens of 'Heroic' Antep straight in the eye.

Orientation

Except for inside the bazaar, it's fairly easy to find your way around Urfa. You'll see the citadel to the right as you enter the town along the highway from Gaziantep. The otogar is about 1km from the centre. If you take a taxi to the centre, ask for the *belediye* (town hall) in order to reach most hotels; or for the Balıklı Göl, or Gölbaşı, for the mosques, pools and bazaar. The Balıklı Göl is 1.5km from the otogar.

Along different stretches the city's main thoroughfare is called Atatürk, Köprübaşı, Sarayönü and Divan Yolu Caddesis.

Information

The post office and most banks with ATMs are on or around Sarayönü Caddesi.

Demir Döviz (Sarayönü Caddesi; 🕙 8am-6pm Mon-Fri & 8am-1pm Sat) Private exchange office. Keeps longer hours than the banks.

Harran-Nemrut Tours (☎ 215 1575, 0542-761 3065; Köprübaşı; ozcan_aslan_teacher@hotmail.com; 🕙 9am-

6pm) Just behind the Özel Dünya Hastanesi. In the absence of an efficient tourist office, this is the most reliable source of information, a small travel agency efficiently run by Özcan Aslan, a local teacher. He speaks very good English and is a mine of local information. He also runs tours to nearby sites.

Inter@ctif (Sarayönü Caddesi; per hr €0.60; 🕙 9am-11pm) Across the street downstairs, almost opposite the Özel Dünya Hastanesi.

Özel Dünya Hastanesi (☎ 216 2772; Köprübaşı) A well-equipped private hospital.

Puan Tour (☎ 216 0295; Sarayönü Caddesi; 🕙 8am-7pm Mon-Sat) An agent for Atlasjet and Fly Air.

Sights

CITADEL

A defining city landmark, the **kale** (admission €1.25; 🕙 8am-8pm) on Damlacık hill, from which Abraham was supposedly tossed, is an absolute must-see. Depending upon where you go for your information, it was built either during Hellenistic times or by the Byzantines or during the Crusades or by the Turks. In any case, it's vast, looks magnificent when floodlit and can be reached via a flight of stairs or a tunnel cut through the rock. On the top, the most interesting things are the pair of columns that local legend has dubbed the Throne of Nemrut after the supposed founder of Urfa, the biblical King Nimrod. But really, you come up here for the spectacular views over Urfa.

GÖLBAŞI

Legend had it that Abraham (İbrahim), who is a great Islamic prophet, was in old Urfa destroying pagan gods one day when Nimrod, the local Assyrian king, took offence at this rash behaviour. Nimrod had Abraham immolated on a funeral pyre, but God turned the fire into water and the burning coals into fish. Abraham himself was hurled into the air from the hill where the fortress stands, but landed safely in a bed of roses.

The picturesque Gölbaşı area of Urfa is a symbolic recreation of this story. Two rectangular pools of water (Balıklı Göl and Ayn-i Zeliha) are filled with supposedly sacred carp, while the area west of the Hasan Padişah Camii is a gorgeous rose garden. Local legend has it that anyone catching the carp will go blind. Consequently, these appear to be the most pampered, portly fish in Turkey.

On the northern side of Balıklı Göl is the elegant **Rızvaniye Vakfı Camii & Medresesi**, with a much-photographed arcaded wall, while

at the western end is the **Halilur Rahman Camii**. This 13th-century building, replacing an earlier Byzantine church, houses the site where Abraham fell to the ground. The two pools are fed by a spring at the base of Damlacık hill, on which the castle is built.

DERGAH

Immediately to the southeast of the pools and the park is the Dergah complex of mosques and parks surrounding the colonnaded **courtyard of the Hazreti İbrahim Halilullah** (Prophet Abraham's Birth Cave), built and rebuilt over the centuries as an active place of pilgrimage. Its western side is marked by the **Mevlid-i Halil Camii**, a large Ottoman-style mosque. At its southern side you'll see the entrance to the **Hazreti İbrahim Halilullah** (Prophet Abraham's Birth Cave; admission €0.40) in which legend has it that the Prophet Abraham was born. He lived here in hiding for his first seven years – King Nimrod, responding to a prophecy he'd received in a dream, feared that a newly born would eventually steal his crown, so he had all babies killed. This is still a place of pilgrimage and prayer, with separate entrances for men and women.

To the north, on Göl Caddesi, is the **Hasan Padişah Camii** (1460), but it's of little interest inside. All of these buildings are open to visitors but, as they are important places of worship, you should be modestly dressed.

MOSQUES

Urfa's Syrian-style **Ulu Cami** (Divan Yolu Caddesi) dates from the period 1170–75. Its 13 *eyvans* (vaulted halls) open onto a spacious forecourt with a tall tower topped by a clock with Ottoman numerals.

At Kara Meydanı, the square midway between the *belediye* and Dergah, is the **Hüseyin Paşa Camii**, a late-Ottoman work built in 1849.

On Vali Fuat Caddesi, which leads up from behind Gölbaşı to the Cevahir Konuk Evi, is the enormous, beautifully restored **Selahattin Eyubi Camii**. It was once St John's church, as you can see by the altar, and is adorned with carvings. Follow Vali Fuat Caddesi north and you'll notice the **Yeni Fırfırlı Camii**, another finely restored building, once the Armenian Church of the Twelve Apostles.

ŞANLIURFA MUSEUM

Up the hill to the west of the *vilayet* (provincial government headquarters) building, off Atatürk Caddesi, the **Şanlıurfa Museum** (Şanlıurfa Müzesi; admission €1.25; 8am-5pm Tue-Sun) captivates visitors with a journey into Eastern Turkey's archeological evolution.

The gardens contain various sculptures, and on the porch as you enter are several mosaics, the most interesting showing assorted wild animals. Inside, noteworthy artefacts include Neolithic implements, Assyrian, Babylonian and Hittite relief stones and other objects from Byzantine, Seljuk and Ottoman times.

BAZAAR

After visiting the museum, ponder on your new-found knowledge with a wander through Urfa's **bazaar** (daylight Mon-Sat). Spreading itself east of the Narıncı Camii, it is a jumble of streets, some covered, some open, selling everything from sheepskins and pigeons to jeans and handmade shoes. It was largely built by Süleyman the Magnificent in the mid-16th century. The best idea is just to dive in and inevitably get lost. Women should be on guard for lustful hands.

One of the most interesting areas is the **bedesten** (*kazaz pazarı*), an ancient caravanserai where silk goods were sold. Today you'll still find silk scarves sold here, as well as gaudy modern carpets and the lovely blue and red scarves worn by local women. Right by the *bedesten* is the **Gümrük Hanı** (customs depot), with a delightful courtyard that is always full of tea- or coffee-swilling moustached gents playing backgammon. A very authentic ambience.

Buried in the lanes of the bazaar are several ancient and very cheap **hamams**, including **Arasa Hamamı**.

OLD HOUSES

Delve into Urfa's back streets and you'll find examples of the city's distinctive limestone houses with protruding bays supported on stone corbels. Although many of these houses are falling into decay (and some are far too large for modern families), a few have been restored, most notably the house of Hacı Hafızlar, near the PTT, which has been turned into an art gallery, the **Güzel Sanatlar Galerisi** (8am-5.30pm Mon-Fri, noon-4pm Sat). The art here is usually pretty ordinary but the courtyards and fine carved stonework are a joy to behold and the cusodians don't mind you wandering through.

SOUTHEASTERN ANATOLIA

You can also pop into the **Şurkav** (Balıklı Göl Mevkii), a local government building near the entrance to Hotel Edessa, where the courtyard is draped with greenery.

In the market area, try to find the **İl Özel İdaresi Kültür Ve Sanat Merkezi**, another splendid house restored in 2002. It was once a church.

PROPHET JOB'S SITE

Although it's not the highlight of a trip, Prophet Job's Site is worth the bus ride for its historic significance. It's about 1km southeast of the Gölbaşı district. Legend holds that Eyyüp (Job) was a prosperous and devout man, thus despised by İblis (Satan). İblis took away Job's health, wealth and family, to force him into a crisis of faith. Instead, Job retreated to the **cave** (Eyyüp Peygamber Makamı) you see here, where he waited patiently in devotion to God. After seven years, God restored his possessions and health, the latter by means of a freshwater spring that Job unleashed by thumping the ground with his heel. Pilgrims come here to wish for the patience of Job and to restore their health with the spring water collected from a **well**.

Entrance is free but a small donation is expected. The nearby mosque features exquisitely tiled archways.

Regular 'Eyyüp Pey' minibuses departing from outside the Urfa bazaar will drop you right by the gate to the compound.

Sleeping

BUDGET

With few foreign tourists passing through, most Urfa hotels cater for pilgrims and businessmen. Unmarried couples can be made to feel unwelcome and solo female travellers even more so. The Hotel Bakay is often recommended as a comfortable place for solo women; unmarried couples should feel welcome at Hotel İpek Palas. Ignore the touts for the pensions who may accost you at the bus station or in the centre – we've had some bad reports about these pensions, especially from women.

Otel Doğu (☎ 215 1228; Sarayönü Caddesi; s/d €9/12) The Doğu is not exactly decked out for honeymooners but the spare rooms are acceptable and the private bathrooms passed the schoolmarm's cleanliness inspection. It's also well positioned for access to cafés and restaurants. Be prepared for a sweaty night in summer for there's no air-con.

Hotel Bakay (☎ 215 8975; fax 215 1156; Asfalt Yol Caddesi; s/d €14/22; 🅿 🖳) One of the best ventures if you're watching the pennies. This jolly good hotel wins no prize for character but sports well-equipped (if smallish) rooms with salubrious bathrooms, some with TV and balcony. Some are brighter than others, so ask to see a few. It's popular with Turkish families – a good sign for female travellers. For your information: 'If you like to have a make-up call please press 9' – this was written on the telephone. Free wi-fi.

Hotel İpek Palas (☎ 215 1546; Köprübaşı Dünya Hastanesi Arkası; s/d €17/25; 🔀) Heave a sigh of relief: there's air-con in this good-value, well-maintained hotel with compact rooms. The fake-painted brick walls in the corridors are a tad cheesy, but who cares? It's tucked away in a side street behind the private *hastane* (hospital).

MIDRANGE

Hotel Güven (☎ 215 1700; www.hotelguven.com; Sarayönü Caddesi; s/d €17/28; 🅿 🔀) All's shipshape at the welcoming Güven, although it's not exactly a home away from home. The rooms are reassuringly Air-Wicked and the bathrooms have been smartened up.

Beyzade Konak (☎ 216 3535; www.beyzadekonak.com in Turkish; Sarayönü Caddesi, Beyaz Sokak; s/d €18/30; 🔀) Another utterly charming 19th-century stone building featuring a soothing courtyard and several comfy Ottoman-style lounges. The Beyzade bills itself as *Urfadaki Eviniz* (your home in Urfa), and rightly so. Bring earplugs, though – the *sıra geceleri* (live music evenings) can be noisy.

Hotel Arte (☎ 314 7060; www.otel-arte.com.tr; Köprübaşı Cad; s/d €28/39; 🔀 🖳) An excellent addition to Urfa's sleeping scene. If you've had your fill of cheesy fixtures and mismatched furniture, the Arte is the perfect salve, with smart rooms, exceedingly clean bathrooms, large double-glazed windows overlooking the main drag, parquet flooring, wi-fi access and contemporary trappings. A winning formula.

Cevahir Konuk Evi (☎ 215 4678; www.cevahir konukevi.com; Yeni Mahalle Sk; s/d €28/50; 🔀) Formerly the Sanliurfac Vilayet Konuk Evi, this nearly-but-not-quite boutique hotel is set in a delightful 19th-century stone building in a peaceful area. It's a smart place to rest your head – staff wear Ottoman costumes, and the central courtyard with fountain offers a delightful café-restaurant – but it's disappointing to find the bedrooms furnished in more or less standard Turkish hotel style.

TOP END

Hotel Edessa (☎ 215 9911; fax 215 5030; Balıklı Göl Mevkii; s/d €34/50; P 🎮) Don't expect a whole lotta lovin' when you're checking in or out – just an ace position overlooking the Gölbaşı and well-organised, if a bit anonymous, rooms with all mod cons. Angle for a room with a view of the Gölbaşı. It's a popular option with tour groups.

Hotel Harran (☎ 313 2860; fax 313 4918; Köprübaşı Cad; s/d €37/56; P 🎮 🏊) If fancy décor is out of the question but hygiene and wide-ranging facilities are high on your list, then the Harran could be worth it. This tower-block hotel features rosy rooms with spick-and-span bathrooms. Added bonuses include an on-site restaurant, a *hamam* (men only) and a swimming-pool.

Hotel El-Ruha (☎ 215 4411; www.hotelelruha.com in Turkish; Balıklı Göl; s/d €63/84, ste €125; 🎮 🖥) Much too massive to be awarded the status of boutique hotel, the five-star El-Ruha is the swankiest hotel in town nonetheless, with shiny-clean rooms and a host of top-notch facilities, including a sauna, a *hamam* and a fitness centre. Alcohol is forbidden on the premises.

Eating & Drinking

It pays to be a bit careful what you eat in Urfa because the heat makes food poisoning more likely. Make sure whatever you choose is hot and freshly cooked. Alcohol is usually not served. Urfa's culinary specialities include: Urfa kebap (skewered chunks of lamb served with tomatoes, sliced onions and hot peppers); *çiğ köfte* (minced uncooked mutton); and *içli köfte* (deep-fried mutton-filled meatballs covered with bulgur).

Baklavacı Badıllı Dedeoğlu (☎ 215 3737; Sarayönü Caddesi; 🕑 8am-9pm; pastries €0.50-1) If there's heaven in this holy city, it just might be Dedeoğlu. Cognoscenti swear it concocts the most flavoursome baklavas in Urfa.

Birlik Pastanesi (☎ 313 1823; Köprübaşı Caddesi; 🕑 8am-10pm; pastries €0.50-1) Come here to re-energise over a bountiful selection of cakes and other goodies.

Hacıbaba Kadayıf (Sarayönü Caddesi; 🕑 8am-9pm; pastries €0.50-1) Near the Yusuf Paşa Camii, this is where you can sample *peynirli kadayıf* (cheese-filled shredded wheat doused in honey).

Zahter Kahvaltı & Kebap Salonu (Köprübaşı Caddesi; mains €2-3) This cute place is a delicious respite from the usual Turkish breakfast. Here you'll enjoy gooey honey and cream on flat bread, washed down with a large glass of *çay* (tea) or *ayran* (yogurt drink) – all for around €2.

Divan's (☎ 215 8552; Sarayönü Caddesi; mains €2-3; 🕑 8am-10pm) Off the main drag, this restaurant-café-fast-food joint is a judiciously laid-out complex, where you can nosh on burgers, pizzas, ready-made meals and kebaps. With its fountain and breezy outdoor seating, it's a great place to loll after a day's sightseeing. For an energy bolt, slug down a freshly squeezed orange juice.

Çift Mağara (☎ 215 9757; Çift Kubbe Altı Balıklıgöl; mains €2-5; 🕑 10am-10pm) The dining room is directly carved into the rocky bluff that overlooks the Gölbaşı, but the lovely terrace for dining alfresco beats the cavernous interior (views!). It's famed for its delicious *içli köfte* and, with prices starting at €2, they are a filling option if you're suffering from wallet stress. If only it served alcohol, life would be perfect.

Pınarbaşı Konağı (☎ 215 3919; 12 Eylül Caddesi; mains €2-5; 🕑 8am-10pm) Almost a carbon copy of Gülizar Konukevi, this eatery has bags of character. It occupies a wonderful old Urfa house where you dine on floor cushions in a series of rooms set around a courtyard. There's live music in the evening.

Altınşiş (☎ 215 4646; Sarayönü Caddesi; mains €3-5; 🕑 11am-10pm) Business is brisk here as the lunchtime punters pile in for their daily fill-up. You'll find all the usual suspects. Judging by the *sarma beyti* (a kind of kebap), the servings are voluminous, so bring an empty tum.

Gülizar Konukevi (☎ 215 0505; www.gulizarkonukevi .com; Karameydanı Camii Yanı; mains €4-5; 🕑 8am-10pm) Good food and traditional surrounds. Use your chance to try its speciality, *şıllık*, a type of walnut pancake. The cosy setting is an added bonus.

Çardaklı Köşk (☎ 217 1080; www.cardaklikosk.com in Turkish; Vali Fuat Caddesi, Tünel Çıkışı; mains €4-6; 🕑 9am-11pm) This also occupies an old house but one that has been so restored it feels almost new. Here too there are several rooms varying in shape and size arranged around the courtyard. But the real wow is the view over Gölbaşı. We wish the food and service were equally impressive.

Cevahir Konuk Evi (☎ 215 9377; www.cevahirkonuk evi.com; Yeni Mahalle Sokak; mains €4-8; 🕑 8am-10pm)

SOUTHEASTERN ANATOLIA

URFA'S WILD NIGHTS *Jean-Bernard Carillet*

Nightlife in Urfa? In the City of Prophets, this may sound a contradiction in terms but, to my great surprise, I found the evenings in Urfa the hottest in eastern Anatolia, with high-octane dancing almost every night. What makes the city tick is the *sıra geceleri* ('traditional nights') that are held in upscale restaurants. Picture *şark odası* (lounges) where guests sit, eat, sing and dance. After the meal, a live band plays old favourites that keep revellers rocking and dancing to their hearts' content. I found myself lured into one of the lounges – *'Gel, gel'* (come, come)! I couldn't decline the invitation to join the dance. Folksy evenings never looked so fun. That evening I thanked my lucky stars that nobody took a picture of my body contortions to the sounds of Kurdish flute on the 'dance floor'… If you want your moment of glory too, the best venues to check out are Beyzade Konak, Gülizar Konukevi, Pınarbaşı Konağı and Cevahir Konuk Evi. Send us the pictures!

Another popular option with Turkish tourists, the Cevahir uses a winning combination: a lovely setting (think: a well-tended garden and an old mansion with several comfy lounges), live music in the evening and tasty dishes. If you think it's time to give your palate some much-needed diversity, opt for the *karışık peynir tabağı* (platter of cheese). A true pleasure.

If all you want is to relax over a cup of tea in leafy surrounds, head for the various *çay bahçesis* in the Gölbaşı park – a great experience any time of the day.

Getting There & Away

AIR

Turkish Airlines (☎ 215 3344; www.thy.com; Kaliru Turizm Seyahat Acentesi, Sarayönü Caddesi; ☒ 8.30am-6.30pm) has five weekly flights to/from Ankara (from €65, 1½ hours). A bus service leaves from outside the office for the airport, 1½ hours before the departure (€2).

Atlasjet (www.atlasjet.com) operates four weekly flights to/from İstanbul (from €44, two hours). **Fly Air** (www.flyair.com.tr) has three weekly flights to/from İstanbul (from €43).

BUS

The otogar, on the main highway serving the southeast, receives plenty of traffic, but most buses are passing through, so you must take whatever seats are available. Buses to the otogar can be caught on Atatürk Bulvarı (€0.40). Taxis usually ask €4 for the short hop between the otogar and the main drag. Details of some daily services are listed in the table, right.

Minibuses to Akçakale, Harran, Birecik, Kahta and Adıyaman (€4, two hours) leave from the minibus terminal beside the otogar. If you're travelling to Syria, you'll need to catch a minibus to Akçakale (€2, one hour), then catch a taxi over the border to Raqqa.

SERVICES FROM ŞANLIURFA'S OTOGAR

Destination	Fare	Duration	Distance	Frequency (per day)
Adana	€10	6hr	365km	frequent
Ankara	€22	13hr	850km	5-6
Diyarbakır	€6	3hr	190km	frequent
Erzurum	€17	12hr	665km	1
Gaziantep	€5	2½hr	145km	frequent
İstanbul	€28	20hr	1290km	a few
Malatya	€8	7hr	395km	1
Mardin	€6	3hr	175km	a few
Van	€18	9hr	585km	2

CAR

For car hire try **Kalıru Turizm Seyahat Acentesi** (☎ 215 3344; fax 216 3245; Sarayönü Caddesi, Köprübaşı; ☒ 8.30am-6.30pm), the Turkish Airlines agency, or **Sixt Rent A Car** (☎ 315 0440; fax 315 0307, ☒ 8am-7pm).

HARRAN

☎ 0414 / pop 6900

Don't skip Harran. It seems certain that this settlement is one of the oldest continuously inhabited spots on Earth. The Book of Genesis mentions Harran and its most famous resident, Abraham, who stayed here for a few years back in 1900 BC. Its ruined walls and Ulu Cami, crumbling fortress and beehive houses are powerful, evocative sights and give the city a feeling of deep antiquity. Traditionally, locals lived by farming and smuggling, but the coming of the Atatürk Dam looks set to change that as cotton fields sprout over what was once desert. Many seemingly poor villagers are actually quite comfortably off, with huge TVs and ghetto-blasters in their houses.

On arrival in Harran you are officially expected to buy a ticket (€1.25), but there may not be anyone in the booth to collect the money. If anyone in the castle tries to charge you, insist on being given the official ticket.

You will probably need to hire a local guide to tour the sites, but also to ward off the flocks of children demanding coins, sweets, cigarettes, ballpoint pens and 'presents'. The guides will want around €5 for their services.

History

Besides being the place of Abraham's sojourn, Harran is famous as a centre of worship of Sin, god of the moon. Worship of the sun, moon and planets was popular in Harran, and at neighbouring Soğmatar, from about 800 BC until AD 830, although Harran's temple to the moon god was destroyed by the Byzantine emperor Theodosius in AD 382. Battles between Arabs and Byzantines occupied the townsfolk until the coming of the Crusaders. The fortress, which some say was built on the ruins of the moon god's temple, was restored when the Crusaders approached. The Crusaders won and maintained it for a while before they too moved on.

Sights

BEEHIVE HOUSES

Harran is famous for its beehive houses, the design of which may date back to the 3rd century BC, although the present examples were mostly constructed within the last 200 years. It's thought that the design evolved partly in response to the lack of wood for making roofs and partly because the ruins provided a ready source of reusable bricks. Although the Harran houses are unique in Turkey, similar buildings can be found in northern Syria.

The **Harran Kültür Evi**, within walking distance of the castle, is set up to allow visitors to see inside one of the houses and then to sip cold drinks in the walled courtyard afterwards. The **Harran Evi** is similar. You can also stay at these places.

KALE

On the far (east) side of the hill, the crumbling *kale* stands right by some beehive houses. Although a castle probably already existed

on the site from Hittite times, what you see now dates mainly from after 1059 when the Fatimids took over and restored it. Originally, there were four multiangular corner towers, but only two remain. Once there were also 150 rooms here, but many of these have caved in or are slowly filling up with silt. Make sure you see the **Eastern Gate** with carvings of chained dogs, here to protect the city.

WALLS & MOSQUE

The crumbling stone **city walls** were once 4km long and studded with 187 towers and four gates; of these only the overly restored **Aleppo Gate**, near the new part of town, remains.

Of the ruins inside the village other than the *kale*, the **Ulu Cami**, built in the 8th century by Marwan II, last of the Umayyad caliphs, is most prominent. You'll recognise it by its tall, square and very un-Turkish minaret. It's said to be the oldest mosque in Anatolia. Near here stood the first Islamic university, and on the hillside above it you'll see the low-level ruins of ancient Harran dating back some 5000 years.

Sleeping

Most people visit from Urfa on a day trip.

Harran Evi (☎ 441 2020; beds with half board €15) and **Harran Kültür Evi** (☎ 441 2477; beds with half board €15) Some people have slept in a beehive dormitory or under the stars on raised *tahtlar* (sleeping thrones) to catch the breeze, but it's ultra-basic and particularly uncomfortable when it's scorching hot.

Bazda Motel (☎ 441 2001; fax 441 2145; s/d/ste €18/35/40; P 😣) On the road as you come into town, this is a reliable option. It has been designed to mimic the beehive houses – a brave but somewhat misdirected attempt. The airy rooms have spotless bathrooms and air-con, but are overpriced.

Getting There & Away

Getting to Harran is straightforward and you don't really need to take a tour. Minibuses (€2, one hour) leave from Urfa's otogar approximately every hour and will drop you at the new part of Harran near the *belediye* and PTT – it's a 10-minute walk to the old part.

If you're driving to Harran, leave Urfa by the Akçakale road at the southeastern end of town and go 40km to a turn-off to the left (east). From there, it's another 10km to Harran.

AROUND HARRAN

Although the sites beyond Harran are miss-able if you're pushed for time, it would be a shame not to see the astonishing transformation wrought on the local scenery by the GAP project (see the boxed text, below) – field upon field of cotton and barley where once there was just desert.

To get around the sites without your own transport is virtually impossible unless you have limitless time. Even with your own car the roads are rough and poorly signed, and it is easy to go astray on the dusty tracks, so the tours offered by Harran-Nemrut Tours (p602) are certainly worth considering. For €25 per person for four or more people you visit Harran, Han el Ba'rur, Şuayb City and Soğmatar, with a chance to take tea with villagers. Expect a simple taxi service. You may need to take a picnic lunch, or you might have a village lunch-stop. It's useful to have a pocketful of change for the tips you'll be expected to give.

Han el Ba'rur

About 10km east of Harran you can visit a deep **quarry**. Locals will tell you the stones quarried here were used to build the walls of Harran. A further 20km east are the remains of the Seljuk **Han el Ba'rur**, a caravanserai built in 1128 to service the local trade caravans. Although some restoration work has been done here, there are not enough visitors to justify any services (or tickets for that matter). The stones in the **Bazda Caves** nearby are also supposed to have been used for the construction of Harran.

Şuayb City

Another 12km northeast of the caravanserai are the extensive remains of Şuayb City, where hefty stone walls and lintels survive above a network of subterranean rooms. One of these contains a mosque on the site of the supposed home of the prophet Jethro. Once again, don't expect to find any services, but it's a good idea to bring a torch (flashlight) and to wear sturdy shoes.

Soğmatar

About 18km north of Şuayb, the isolated village of Soğmatar is a very atmospheric, eerie place, surrounded by a barren landscape with bare rocks and ledges. On one of the ledges there was once an open-air temple, where sacrifices were made to the sun and moon gods, whose effigies can be seen carved into the side. This open-air altar was the central, main temple. On the top of the rock are assorted ancient Assyrian inscriptions. Like Harran, Soğmatar was a centre for the cult worship of Sin, the moon god, from about AD 150 to 200.

Standing on the summit of the structure, you can see remains of other temples on the surrounding hills. There were supposedly seven in all.

Once again there are no services at Soğmatar, although villagers will no doubt be happy to point out the sites.

KAHTA

☎ 0416 / pop 60,700

Dusty Kahta isn't the most atmospheric place to spend your holiday, but it's well set up for

---

GAP – THE SOUTHEASTERN ANATOLIA PROJECT

The character of the landscape in southeastern Anatolia is changing as the Southeastern Anatolia Project (Güneydoğu Anadolu Projesi), better known as GAP or Güneydoğu, comes on line, bringing irrigation waters to large arid regions and generating enormous amounts of hydroelectricity for industry. Parched valleys have become fish-filled lakes, and dusty villages are becoming booming market towns and factory cities.

The scale of the project is awe-inspiring, affecting eight provinces and two huge rivers (the Tigris and the Euphrates). In 2006, 17 dams (out of a planned total of 22) had been completed.

Such a huge, hope-generating project can also generate sizable problems, especially ecological ones. The change from dry agriculture to wet has already caused an explosion of disease. The incidence of malaria has increased tenfold, and it is feared that diarrhoea and dysentery, already on the rise, will follow suit.

The project has also generated political problems, as Syria and Iraq, the countries downriver for whom the waters of the Tigris and Euphrates are also vital, complain bitterly that Turkey is using or keeping a larger share of the water than it should. Innumerable archaeological sites have also disappeared under dam water, or are slated to do so.

visits to Nemrut Dağı, with plenty of tours on offer and a decent selection of hotels. If you'd prefer somewhere more inspiring head straight to Karadut (p613).

A good time to visit would be 25 June when the three-day **International Kahta Kommagene Festival** starts, with music, folk dancing and all sorts of fun and games. All the hotels will be filled with tour groups, so it's wise to book ahead at this time.

You can check your emails at the **Medy@ Bilgisayar Internet Cafe** (Mustafa Kemal Caddesi; per hr €1; 🕙 9am-11pm).

Sleeping

Pension Kommagene (☎ 725 9726; fax 725 5548; Mustafa Kemal Caddesi; camp sites per person €3, s/d with shared bathroom €6/9, s/d €12/17; 🔀) While the no-fuss rooms don't set hearts aflutter, this guesthouse is the most commendable option if the bottom line counts. The more expensive air-con rooms with private bathrooms are markedly better. Self-caterers can use the kitchen, and campers can pitch their tent in the partially shady garden. Add €3 for breakfast and €6 for dinner. It's noted for being a bit pushy with its tours to Nemrut.

Hotel Nemrut (☎ 725 6881; fax 725 6880; Mustafa Kemal Caddesi; s/d €23/39; P 🔀) This high-rise lump with a glass-panelled façade is popular with tour groups, which is not a bad sign. Spruce rooms with iffy toilets and well-sprung mattresses are the order of the day here. A few more smiles at the reception would sweeten the deal.

Zeus Hotel (☎ 725 5694; www.zeushotel.com.tr; Mustafa Kemal Caddesi; camp sites per person €6, s/d €25/45; P 🔀 🍷) All the perks of a three-star, including a licensed bar and a restaurant. The rooms may not be glamorous, but they're spotless, largish and pleasantly appointed. Fancy a dip? There's a well-tended pool to cool off in when it's sweltering. Campers can pitch their tent on the parking lot and have their own ablution block.

Eating

With your own wheels you may prefer to drive along Baraj Yolu, the continuation of Mustafa Kemal Caddesi, to the vast lake formed by the Atatürk Barajı, where there is a handful of licensed restaurants (a taxi would charge about €4 to get there).

Urfalim Lahmacun Salonu (☎ 725 6305; Mustafa Kemal Caddesi; mains €2-3; 🕙 8am-9pm) The lure?

Pizzas fresh from the oven. Get stuffed for minimal coinage at this enticing eatery, about 250m west from the main junction.

Papatya Restaurant (☎ 726 2989; Mustafa Kemal Caddesi; mains €2-3; 🕙 8am-10pm) Don't expect culinary sophistication in this snappy joint next to Hotel Nemrut, just the usual suspects honestly prepared and served by efficient waiters. There's no menu – just point at what you want.

Kahta Sofrası (☎ 726 2055; Mustafa Kemal Caddesi; mains €2-4; 🕙 8am-10pm) Off the main intersection, this is the most obvious place to line the stomach without breaking the bank. Order a tasty kebap or a well-prepared pide, and you'll leave with a smile on your face.

Akropalian (☎ 725 5132; Baraj Yolu; mains €3-6; 🕙 9am-10pm) The perfect place to give your palate some needed diversity. Skip the kebaps and hoe into a faultless grilled *alabalık* (trout), served in a *kiremit* (clay pot) and accompanied by a wonderful loaf of metre-long bread. Sample the whole thing in the leafy garden, from where you can enjoy wonderful views over the lake.

Neşetin Yeri (☎ 725 7675; Baraj Yolu; mains €3-6; 🕙 9am-10pm) Soothingly positioned right by the lakeside, the Neşetin is similar in standard to the Akropalian. The emphasis is also on fresh fish from the lake. Here you can dine overlooking the lake with a background symphony of frogs; come just before sunset. Very atmospheric.

Getting There & Away

Kahta's small otogar is in the town centre with the minibus and taxi stands right beside it. There are regular buses to Adana (€12, six hours, 532km), Adıyaman (€1, 30 minutes, 32km), Ankara (€20, 12 hours, 807km), İstanbul (€29, 20 hours, 1352km), Kayseri (€15, seven hours, 487km), Malatya (€6, 3½ hours, 225km) and Şanlıurfa (€4, 2½ hours, 106km).

A dolmuş leaves Kahta at about 2pm daily (except Sunday) for Karadut (€2), returning from Karadut at 7am the next day.

The road east to Diyarbakır was flooded by the lake formed behind the Atatürk Barajı, and buses from Kahta now travel to Diyarbakır north of the lake (€9, five hours, 174km). A more interesting way is via one of the six daily minibuses to Siverek, which are timed to meet the ferries across the lake. In Siverek you may have to wait half an hour or so for a connection to Diyarbakır, but the bazaar is enough fun to fill in the time.

NEMRUT DAĞI NATIONAL PARK

Nemrut Daği Milli Parkı (Mt Nemrut National Park) is probably the star attraction of eastern Turkey, and rightly so. The enigmatic statues sitting atop the summit have become a symbol of Turkey. The stunning scenery and historical sights and the undeniable sense of mystique and folly that emanates from the site make a visit here essential.

The spellbinding peak of **Nemrut Daği** (*nehm-root dah-uh*) rises to a height of 2150m in the Anti-Taurus Range between the provincial capital of Malatya to the north and Kahta in Adıyaman province to the south. This is not to be confused with the less visited Nemrut Daği (2935m) near Lake Van (see p635).

Nobody knew anything about Nemrut Daği until 1881, when a German engineer, employed by the Ottomans to assess transport routes, was astounded to come across the statues covering this remote mountaintop. Archaeological work didn't begin until 1953, when the American School of Oriental Research undertook the project.

The summit was created when a megalomaniac pre-Roman local king cut two ledges in the rock, filled them with colossal statues of himself and the gods (his relatives – or so he thought), then ordered an artificial mountain peak of crushed rock 50m high to be piled between them. The king's tomb and those of three female relatives may well lie beneath those tonnes of rock. Nobody knows for sure.

Earthquakes have toppled the heads from most of the statues, and now many of the colossal bodies sit silently in rows with the 2m-high heads watching from the ground. Plans exist to replace the heads on the bodies but so far not much has happened.

Although it's relatively easy to get to the summit with your own vehicle, most people take tours, organised in either Kahta or Malatya or, increasingly, from Şanlıurfa or Cappadocia (see the boxed text, p614).

Plan to visit Nemrut between late May and mid-October, preferably in July or August; the road to the summit becomes impassable with snow at other times. Remember that at any time of year, even in high summer, it will be chilly and windy on top of the mountain. This is especially true at sunrise, the coldest time of the day. Take warm clothing on your trek to the top, no matter when you go.

There are various accommodation options actually on the mountain, and it's well worth taking advantage of them since the stunning views and peaceful setting make up for any lack of mod cons. Be sure to check that adequate blankets are provided.

History

From 250 BC onwards, this region straddled the border between the Seleucid Empire (which followed the empire of Alexander the Great in Anatolia) and the Parthian Empire to the east, also occupying a part of Alexander's lands. A small but strategic area, rich, fertile and covered in forests, it had a history of independent thinking ever since the time of King Samos (c 163 BC).

Under the Seleucid Empire, the governor of Commagene declared his kingdom's independence. In 80 BC, with the Seleucids in disarray and Roman power spreading into Anatolia, a Roman ally named Mithridates I Callinicus proclaimed himself king and set up his capital at Arsameia, near the modern village of Eski Kahta. Mithridates prided himself on his royal ancestry, tracing his forebears back to Seleucus I Nicator, founder of the Seleucid Empire to the west, and to Darius the Great, king of ancient Persia to the east. Thus he saw himself as heir to both glorious traditions.

Mithridates died in 64 BC and was succeeded by his son Antiochus I Epiphanes (r 64–38 BC), who consolidated his kingdom's security by immediately signing a nonaggression treaty with Rome, turning his kingdom into a Roman buffer against attack from the Parthians. His good relations with both sides allowed him to grow rich and revel in delusions of grandeur, seeing himself as equal to the great god-kings of the past. It was Antiochus who ordered the building of the fabulous temples and funerary mound on top of Nemrut.

In the third decade of his reign, Antiochus sided with the Parthians in a squabble with Rome, and in 38 BC the Romans deposed him. From then on, Commagene was alternately ruled directly from Rome or by puppet kings until AD 72, when Emperor Vespasian incorporated it into Roman Asia. The great days of Commagene were thus limited to the 26-year reign of Antiochus.

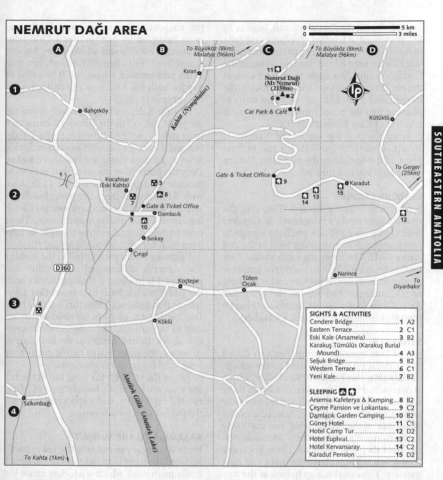

NEMRUT DAĞI AREA

SIGHTS & ACTIVITIES
Cendere Bridge.............................1	A2
Eastern Terrace............................2	C1
Eski Kale (Arsameia)....................3	B2
Karakuş Tümülüs (Karakuş Burial Mound).................................4	A3
Seljuk Bridge...............................5	B2
Western Terrace...........................6	C1
Yeni Kale.....................................7	B2

SLEEPING
Arsemia Kafeterya & Kamping.....8	B2
Çeşme Pansion ve Lokantası......9	C2
Damlacık Garden Camping......10	B2
Güneş Hotel..............................11	C1
Hotel Camp Tur.........................12	D2
Hotel Euphrat............................13	C2
Hotel Kervansaray.....................14	C2
Karadut Pension 15	D2

Orientation

There are three ways of approaching the summit. From the southern side, you will pass through Karadut, a village some 12km from the top, before embarking upon the bone-jolting last few kilometres to the car park. From the southwestern side, you will travel via a secondary road that goes past Eski Kale (Arsameia) and climbs steeply for about 10km until it merges with the Karadut road, some 6km before the car park at the summit. From the northern side, you can start from Malatya – it's a long 98km haul, but it's a very scenic drive and the road is asphalted until the Güneş Hotel, near the summit. If you don't want to backtrack, it's possible to do a loop (see p615).

It costs €3 to enter Mt Nemrut National Park. Coming from the southwest, the entrance gate is just after the turn-off to Eski Kale (Arsameia); from the south, the gate is just past Çeşme Pansion; from the north, the gate is at the Güneş Hotel.

At the car park just below the summit are a café and toilets. To reach the ruins themselves, you'll have to walk for about 600m.

Sights & Activities
KARAKUŞ TÜMÜLÜS

Highway D360, marked for Nemrut Dağı Milli Parkı (9km), starts in Kahta next to the Pension Kommagene. The first site you'll see in the park is **Karakuş Tümülüs**, via a road to the left, 200m off the highway. Like the Nemrut mound, the Karakuş burial mound, built in 36 BC, is artificial. A handful of columns ring the mound – there were more but the limestone blocks were used by the Romans to build the Cendere bridge. An eagle tops a column at the car park, a lion tops another around the mound, and a third has an inscribed slab explaining that the burial mound holds female relatives of King Mithridates II.

From Karakuş the summit of Nemrut is clearly, if distantly, visible; it's the highest point on the horizon to the northeast. Return to the highway and turn left.

CENDERE BRIDGE

Some 10km from the Karakuş Tümülüs, the road crosses a modern bridge over the Cendere river. On the left-hand side, you'll see a magnificent humpback Roman bridge built in the 2nd century AD. The surviving Latin stellae state that the bridge was built in honour of Emperor Septimius Severus and his wife and sons (long after Commagene had become part of Roman Asia). Of the four original Corinthian columns (two at either end), three are still standing.

YENİ KALE

About 5km from the bridge you can take a 1km detour off the main road to the village of **Eski Kahta**, also known as Kocahisar, which is overlooked by castle ruins. Although there was once a palace here, built at the same time as the Commagene capital of Arsameia on the other side of the ravine, what you see today is the ruins of a 13th-century Mamluk castle, **Yeni Kale** (New Fortress). There are some Arabic inscriptions above the main and only gateway. You can climb up to look at the castle, but make sure you're wearing appropriate shoes, and watch your step.

At the base of the path up to the castle is the **Kocahisar Halı Kursu** (Kocahisar Carpet Course), a rudimentary workshop where local women learn carpet-weaving techniques to keep the tradition alive. They don't sell the carpets here but don't usually mind if you poke your head in to have a look.

After Yeni Kale you'll cross the Kahta (Nymphaios) River, where you can see the old road that crossed the river at a graceful **Seljuk Bridge**.

ESKİ KALE (ARSAMEIA)

About 1.5km further along the main road, a road to the left takes you 2km to Eski Kale, the ancient Commagene capital of Arsameia, founded by Mithridates I Callinicus in around 80 BC, and added to by his son Antiochus I. Just after the turn-off, you stop at the **park entrance**, where you'll be asked to pay for both the Arsameia site and access to the summit (€3).

At Eski Kale, walk up the path from the car park. Just off to the left you'll come to a large **stele** depicting Mithras (or Apollo), the sun god, wearing a cap with sunrays radiating from it. Further along are two more **stellae**. Only the bases have survived, but they were thought to depict Mithridates I Callinicus, with Antiochus I, the taller stele, holding a sceptre. Behind them is a cave entrance leading down to an underground room. These cave-temple structures were thought to have been built for Mithras-worshipping rites.

Continue on the path uphill to the striking and virtually undamaged stone relief that portrays Mithridates I shaking hands with the god Heracles. Next to it is another cave-temple that descends 158m through the rock. Don't attempt to go down the steps as they are said to be perilous. The long Greek inscription above the cave describes the founding of Arsameia; the water trough beside it may have been used for religious ablutions.

Above the relief on the level top of the hill are what are left of the foundations of Mithridates' capital city, and a spectacular view – the perfect spot for a picnic.

ARSAMEIA TO THE SUMMIT

From Arsameia you can take the 16km partly surfaced short cut to the summit or backtrack to the main road, which is a longer route but less steep and fully surfaced. The short cut leaves from beside the entrance to Arsameia and slogs up the mountain for about 8km to join the main route about 6km before the summit car park. It's passable only during daytime and in dry weather, and it has precipitous hairpin bends, so drive slowly and very carefully. The last 2km before the junction are unpaved and can be very muddy if it's wet.

Most tours combine the two routes, thus making a loop. Sunrise tours take the longer route (via Narince and Karadut) on the way up and take the short cut to descend back to Kahta. Sunset tours take the short cut on the way up and the longer route to get back to Kahta.

If you take the longer route from Arsameia, return to the main road and turn left. About 3km further is the sleepy village of **Damlacık**. Then you'll pass through various little stone-housed settlements until you reach the larger **Narince**, where a turn-off to the left is marked for Nemrut. North of Karadut, the last half-hour's travel (12km) to the summit is along a steep, bumpy road mostly paved with basalt blocks. The last 3km are particularly horrendous – you'll have to drive in first gear.

Hiking

Travellers staying in Karadut may wish to walk the 12km to the summit. It's a clearly marked road with a steady gradient.

THE SUMMIT

By the time you arrive at the car park and café you're well above the tree line. The **Nemrut Dağı park entrance** (€3; ☼ dawn-dusk) is 200m up from the Çeşme pension and 2.5km before the junction with the short cut to Arsameia.

Beyond the building, hike 600m (about 20 minutes) over the broken rock of the stone pyramid to the **western terrace**. Antiochus I Epiphanes ordered the construction of a combined tomb and temple here. The site was to be approached by a ceremonial road and was to incorporate what Antiochus termed 'the thrones of the gods', which would be based 'on a foundation that will never be demolished'. Antiochus planned this construction to prove his faith in the gods, and in so doing assumed that upon his death his spirit would join that of Zeus-Ahura Mazda in heaven.

As you approach, the first thing you see is the western temple with the conical funerary mound of fist-sized stones behind it. At the western temple, Antiochus and his fellow gods sit in state, although their bodies have partly tumbled down, along with their heads.

From the western terrace it's five minutes' walk to the **eastern terrace**. Here the bodies are largely intact except for the fallen heads, which seem more badly weathered than the western heads. On the backs of the eastern statues are inscriptions in Greek.

Both terraces have similar plans, with the syncretistic gods, the 'ancestors' of Antiochus, seated. From left to right they are Apollo, the sun god (Mithra to the Persians; Helios or Hermes to the Greeks); Fortuna, or Tyche; in the centre Zeus-Ahura Mazda; then King Antiochus; and on the far right Heracles,

also known as Ares or Artagnes. The seated figures are several metres high, their heads alone about 2m tall.

Low walls at the sides of each temple once held carved reliefs showing processions of ancient Persian and Greek royalty, Antiochus' 'predecessors'. Statues of eagles represent Zeus.

Sleeping & Eating

There are several places to stay along the roads to the summit. The pretty village of Karadut has a few small eateries.

Damlacık Garden Camping (☎ 0416-741 2027; camp sites per person €3; ⓢ) At Damlacık, about 2.5km from the junction for the entrance gate, this camp site has very basic facilities but the owners are hospitable and the lovely grassed camping areas are a distinct bonus. In summer you'll probably be offered apricots and prunes from the nearby orchard. Meals are available on request (€4).

Arsemia Kafeterya & Kamping (☎ 0505-320 0882; camp sites per person €3) In Eski Kale, about 1km past the entrance gate, this congenial place is an ideal base for unfussy backpackers. Pitch your tent on a small ridge and soak up the views over the valleys. The catch? There's no shade. On a balmy summer's night you can also drag a mattress out on the rooftop and sleep beneath the star-studded skies. Orhan occasionally plays the Kurdish flute for guests. Meals are available (about €4).

Karadut Pension (☎ 0416-737 2169; www.karadut pansiyon.net; camp sites per person €3, d per person €12; ⓢ) This pension-cum-hostel in Karadut has six pea-sized but neat rooms, cleanish shared bathrooms, a kitchen you can use and three-course meals for €4. It's a bit cramped but perfectly acceptable if you can forgo privacy. Campers can pitch their tent in the pleasant garden at the back, with good views over the mountains and a well-kept ablution block. Two rooms boast air-con.

Çeşme Pansion ve Lokantası (☎ 0416-737 2032; camp sites per person €3, s with half board €12) The best you can say about this pension is that it has yawn-inspiring but acceptable rooms with private bathrooms and boasts a lovely setting, only 6km from the summit. There's also a camping ground with a well-scrubbed ablution block.

Hotel Camp Tur (☎ 0416-737 2061; camp sites €6, s/d with half board €14/28) This family-run outfit is 15km from the summit, on the right, just

ORGANISED TOURS TO NEMRUT DAĞI (MT NEMRUT)

The main tour centres are Kahta and Malatya, but there are also tours from Karadut, Şanlıurfa and Cappadocia.

From Karadut

Several pensions in Karadut offer return trips to the summit, with one hour at the top for about €28 (Karadut Pension) or €34 to €39 (Hotels Euphrat or Kervansaray).

From Kahta

Kahta has always had a reputation as a rip-off town so you need to be wary of what's on offer. Always check exactly what you will be seeing in addition to the heads themselves, and how long you'll be away. The hotels and guesthouses in Kahta run most of the tours.

The majority of tours are timed to capture a dramatic sunrise or sunset. If you opt for the 'sunrise tours', you'll leave Kahta at about 2am via Narince and Karadut, arriving at Nemrut Dağı for sunrise. After an hour or so, you'll go down again following the upgraded direct road to Arsameia. Then you'll stop at Eski Kahta, Yeni Kale, Cendere Bridge and Karakuş Tümülüs. Expect to be back in Kahta at about 10am. If you sign up for the 'sunset tour', you'll do the same loop but in the reverse direction – in other words, you'll leave at 1.30pm and start with the sights around Arsameia, then go up to the summit, before descending via Karadut and Narince. You'll be back in Kahta at 9.30pm.

A third option is the 'small tour', which lasts about three hours. It zips you from Kahta to the summit and back again, allowing about an hour for sightseeing. It's a bit less expensive (a taxi would charge about €35), but it's much less interesting. If you have enough time you really should do the long tour to get the most out of your visit.

Although Kahta hotels and guesthouses advertise these services as 'tours', you'll quickly catch on that they're only taxi services when your driver proffers comments like 'that's an old bridge'. If you want an English-speaking guide who actually knows what they're talking about, go with **Mehmet Akbaba** (☎ 0416-726 1310, 0535 295 4445; akbabamehmet@hotmail.com) or **Nemrut Tours** (☎ 0416-725 6881; Mustafa Kemal Caddesi), based in Hotel Nemrut. Expect to pay around €100 per group for the longer tours with these guides.

From Malatya

Malatya offers an alternative way to approach Nemrut Dağı. However, visiting Nemrut from this northern side means you miss out on the other fascinating sights on the southern flanks (reached

before the turn-off to Nemrut out of Narince. Here you'll find a nondescript building with six recent, modern rooms with private bathrooms, bare camping facilities, a petrol pump, which may or may not be working, and tours to the summit.

Hotel Kervansaray (☎ 0416-737 2190; fax 737 2085; camping per person €4, s/d €23/32, half board €26/44; P 🛱) Same brick walls, same setting and same family, the low-slung Kervansaray is a carbon copy of the Euphrat. What sets it apart, though, is the smaller number of rooms (14), which ensures greater intimacy. It has neat rooms with impeccable bathrooms, a restaurant with a kitschy rustic interior, a swimming pool and a pleasant camping ground. The owners can drive you to the summit (€34 per minibus).

Güneş Hotel (half board per person €23) About 2.5km from the eastern terrace, in the valley below, this place is of use mostly to those coming up from Malatya. The setting is superb, the hush enjoyable and the rooms comfortable, but the meals are disappointing.

Hotel Euphrat (☎ 0416-737 2175; fax 737 2179; s/d with half board €32/44; P 🛱) With 52 rooms, the low-rise Euphrat has the largest room capacity in the area and is popular with tour groups in peak season. The main selling points are the terrace with stupendous views over the valley, and the swimming pool. However, we found the rooms a tad more impersonal than at the Kervansaray. It's just 8km from the summit – the owners can drive you up there (€39 per minibus).

via Kahta). You can get the best of both worlds by traversing the top by foot and hitching a ride to Kahta; if you're travelling by car you'll have to take the long route via Adıyaman.

The Malatya tourist office organises hassle-free minibus tours to Nemrut Daği from early May to the end of September, or to mid-October if the weather is still warm. Tours leave at noon from near the tourist information booth in the tea garden behind the *vilayet*.

The three-hour ride through dramatic scenery to the summit is asphalted all the way up. After enjoying the sunset from the summit for two hours, you descend to the Güneş Hotel (opposite). Here you have dinner and stay the night before taking the minibus back up to the summit for sunrise. After breakfast at the Güneş you return to Malatya at around 10am.

The per person cost of €30 (minimum three people) includes transport, dinner, bed and breakfast, and you pay for admission to the national park and the site. In theory, there are tours every day, but if you turn up alone you have to be prepared to pay substantially more. If you prefer to descend via Kahta, hike across the summit to the car park and café building (30 minutes), and ask around for a minibus with an empty seat; or hitch a ride with someone going down to Kahta.

From Şanlıurfa
Two-day tours (€60, minimum four) or sunrise/sunset tours (€40, minimum four) to Nemrut are also available from Harran-Nemrut Tours (p602) in Şanlıurfa. These tours usually take you to the Atatürk Dam along the way. They're relatively good value, but don't expect more than a driver. At the time of research no other operators were offering these tours from Urfa.

From Cappadocia
Many companies in Cappadocia offer minibus tours to Nemrut from mid-April to mid-November, despite the distance of over 500km each way. Two-day tours cost about €120 and involve many hours of breakneck driving. If you have enough time, it's better to opt for a three-day tour (costing about €140), which allows the journey to be broken into more manageable chunks.

Most three-day tours take in the Karatay Han near Kayseri, and ice cream in Kahramanmaraş, before arriving in Kahta. On the second day you visit Nemrut Daği for sunrise and then take in the sights at Arsameia, Cendere and Karakuş, and Atatürk Dam. Afterwards, you continue to Harran, before stopping for the night in Şanlıurfa. On the last day you drive back via Birecik, Gaziantep and Adana, returning to Göreme over the Taurus Mountains via Niğde.

In Göreme, three-day tours are run by Neşe Tour (see p502) with twice-weekly departures. Other companies in Göreme offer similar packages, but it's worth checking exactly where you'll be stopping.

Getting There & Away
CAR
To ascend the southern slopes of Nemrut from Kahta, you can do one of the following: drive along the old road via Koçtepe and Narince; take the shorter route via Damlacık and Arsameia, then the 15km short cut; or take a longer but more scenic route that includes Karakuş, Cendere, Eski Kahta and Arsameia. Make sure you have fuel for at least 250km of normal driving. Though the trip to the summit and back is at most 160km, you have to drive some of that in low gear, which uses more fuel. Be prepared for the rough, steep last 3km before the summit.

You can also approach the summit from Malatya (98km one way) and drive up to the Güneş Hotel – the road is surfaced and it's a very scenic drive. From there, a rough road leads to the eastern terrace, a further 2.5km – it's OK with a normal car in dry weather. If you don't want to drive all the way back to Malatya, you can backtrack 10km to the village of Büyüköz from the Güneş Hotel. In Büyüköz, villagers will show you the road to Eski Kahta, a further 21km. The first 8km are unsurfaced. This road is passable with a normal vehicle in dry weather, but seek local advice at the Güneş Hotel before setting off.

TAXI & MINIBUS
From Kahta, taxi drivers charge about €35 to run you up to the summit and back, but don't expect anything in the way of guidance.

One dolmuş leaves Kahta at about 2pm daily (except Sunday) to go up the mountain as far as the Çeşme Pansion, about 6km from the summit, stopping at Karadut village (€2) on the way. (It returns to Kahta at around 7am the next morning.) To rent an entire minibus for a trip to the summit and back to Karadut costs from €25.

MALATYA

☎ 0422 / pop 455,000 / elevation 964m

Apricot, apricot, apricot. Malatya is all about *kayısı* (apricot). After the late-June harvest thousands of tonnes of the luscious fruit are shipped from here throughout the world. Among Malatya's other rewards are a bevy of verdant parks, tree-lined boulevards, a lively atmosphere and the weird feeling that you're the only tourist for miles around.

If you think Malatya is short on specific sights, the nearby historic site of Battalgazi offers ample compensation. But if all you want is simply to unwind, the surrounding countryside and villages lend themselves perfectly to a day or two's relaxed pottering around.

History

The Assyrians and Persians conquered the city alternately, and later the kings of Cappadocia and Pontus did the same. In 66 BC Pompey defeated Mithridates and took the town, then known as Melita. The Byzantines, Sassanids, Arabs and Danışmend emirs (Turkic tribal leaders) held it for a time until the coming of the Seljuks in 1105. Then came the Ottomans (1399), the armies of Tamerlane (1401), Mamluks, Dülkadır emirs and the Ottomans again (1515).

When the forces of Egypt's Mohammed Ali invaded Anatolia in 1839, the Ottoman forces garrisoned Malatya, leaving much of it in ruins on their departure. Later the residents returned and established a new city on the present site. You can visit the remains of old Malatya (Eski Malatya), now called Battalgazi, nearby.

Orientation

Malatya stretches for many kilometres along İnönü/Atatürk Caddesi, the main drag, but hotels, restaurants, banks and other services are clustered near the main square with its massive statue of İnönü.

MALATYA

0   0 —— 400 m   0 —— 0.2 miles

To Aslantepe (6km); Battalgazi (11km)

To Train Station (1km); Otogar (3km); Yeşilyurt (9km); Gündüzbey (11km)

INFORMATION	
Akdeniz Bilgisayar & Internet.................. 1	D3
Information Booth...........(see 19)	
Öz Murat Döviz................ 2	D2
Tourist Office................... 3	C2

SIGHTS & ACTIVITIES	
Museum........................... 4	D3

SLEEPING 🛏	
Aygün Hotel..................... 5	C2
Bezginler Hotel................ 6	D1
Hotel Yeni Sinan............. 7	D2
Malatya Büyük Otel......... 8	C2
Yeni Hotel....................... 9	C2

EATING 🍴	
Hacıbey Lahmacun........ 10	D2
Kaşık Restaurant............ 11	D3
Mado.............................. 12	D3
Mangal Vadisi................ 13	D2
Nostalji.......................... 14	C2
Serhent Simit Sarayı...... 15	D2
Sevinç............................ 16	D2
Şelale Kernek Restaurant... 17	D3

DRINKING 🍸	
Semerkant...................... 18	D2
Vilayet Çay Bahçesi....... 19	D2

SHOPPING 🛍	
Armağan......................... 20	D2

TRANSPORT	
Atlasjet........................... 21	D2
Bus Stop for Battalgazi & Aslantepe.................. 22	D1
Bus Stop for Gündüzbey & Yeşilyurt................... 23	C2
Bus Stop for Otogar & Train Station.................... 24	C2
Meydan Rent a Car......... 25	A2
Minibus Terminal............ 26	A1
Onur Air......................... 27	D2
Turkish Airlines.............. 28	D2

The otogar is 4km west of the centre, just off the main highway, Turgut Özal Bulvarı. The train station is also on the outskirts, 2km west of the centre. City buses and minibuses marked 'Vilayet' operate between the station and the centre.

Information

There are branches of the main banks with ATMs on the main street. **Öz Murat Döviz** (Atatürk Caddesi; ☒ 7.30am-7pm Mon-Sat), a private exchange office right in the centre, keeps longer hours than banks.

Malatya's helpful **tourist office** (☎ 323 2942; fax 323 2912; Atatürk Caddesi; ☒ 9am-5pm Mon-Fri) is on the ground floor of the *vilayet* in the heart of town. It distributes a basic town map and a useful brochure on the Malatya area. In the tea garden behind, there's also a private **information booth** (☎ 0535-760 5080; Atatürk Caddesi; ☒ 8am-7pm May-Sep) managed by the Güneş Hotel (p614) – ask for Kemal. Good news: good English is spoken at both the office and the booth.

There is internet access at **Akdeniz Bilgisayar & Internet** (Kanal Boyu; per hr €0.60; ☒ 9am-11pm) and at the information booth in the tea garden.

Sights & Activities

No trip to Malatya would be complete without a stroll through the particularly vibrant **bazaar** that sprawls north from PTT Caddesi and the Malatya Büyük Otel. It's a great place to ramble and get lost – which you will certainly do at least once. The large covered area is fascinating, especially the lively metalworking area, where the air is filled with hammering, sawing and welding. You'll probably be invited for a tea in the workshop in exchange for a few words. Want to buy a bag of apricots? Brush up your Turkish and wind your way to the *kayısı pazarı* or the *şire pazarı* (apricot market). Good luck!

Malatya's **museum** (Fuzuli Caddesi; admission €1.25; ☒ 8am-5pm Tue-Sun), about 750m from the town centre, has finds from the excavations at Aslantepe.

Malatya also offers tours with an alternative way to approach Nemrut Dağı (p610).

Sleeping

Malatya has a smattering of good-value options, conveniently located in the bazaar and in the city centre. They are suitable for female travellers.

Aygün Hotel (☎ 325 5657; fax 3260212; PTT Caddesi; s/d with shared bathroom €12/17) Near the PTT, the Aygün, with uncluttered rooms and OK shared bathrooms, is nothing fancy but will do for a night's kip. Breakfast is optional (€2).

Hotel Yeni Sinan (☎ 321 2907; Atatürk Caddesi; s/d €17/28) We found the rooms fairly unspectacular for the price, the corridors as sexy as a dentist's waiting room and the beds a bit too unkind to our creaky joints, but the Yeni Sinan is an acceptable fallback if the others are full. Its main selling point is its peerless location, smack dab in the centre.

Yeni Hotel (☎ 323 1423; www.yenihotel.com in Turkish; Yeni Cami Karşısı İş Hanı; s/d €23/34; ☒) Just behind the Büyük Otel, this is another excellent deal that won't hurt the hip pocket. Clean-smelling, appealing rooms with modern furnishings, spanking clean bathrooms, colourful bedspreads that provide candy to the eye, copious breakfast and obliging staff.

Malatya Büyük Otel (☎ 325 2828; fax 323 2828; Halep Caddesi, Yeni Cami Karşısı; s/d €17/50; ☒) Sizzling hot value for what you get: light-filled, tidy rooms with TV, well-maintained bathrooms, acceptable breakfast, professional staff and even good views from the upper floors. Some rooms (especially rooms 302 and 303) have plenty of space to really strew your stuff around. It's just opposite the Yeni Cami – be prepared for an early morning wake-up call.

Bezginler Hotel (☎ 324 1252; fax 326 2327; Çevre Yolu Adlige Kavşağı; s/d €40/70; P ☒) A flat 10-minute walk north of the city centre, looking onto the ring road, this stock standard four-star hotel thinks it can impress with its glass-fronted façade and impressive marble lobby. Although the location is not exactly sensational, it's a good base for those with their own wheels. It also boasts all the amenities of a solid midrange option – including satellite TV, conference rooms, a restaurant, a bar and showers with Jacuzzi. You should get substantial discounts during slack times.

Eating & Drinking

Atatürk Caddesi is awash with inexpensive eateries, but there are funkier, more attractive options around. Kanal Boyu is a tree-lined boulevard divided by a canal and is the closest thing Malatya has to a hip area. On balmy summer evenings it fills with promenading, well-groomed 30-somethings.

SOUTHEASTERN ANATOLIA

Sevinç (☎ 321 5188; Atatürk Caddesi; pastries €0.50-1; 7am-10pm) This pastry shop features a sleek, modern interior and a batch of mouthwatering desserts, including baklava and *kadayıf* (shredded wheat and nuts in honey). There's a welcoming *aile salonu* (family dining room) upstairs.

Mado (☎ 323 2346; Kanal Boyu; ice creams €0.50-1.25; 9am-11pm) Is this the sexiest place in the city? Whatever your verdict, it's the best outfit to enjoy a delicious ice cream or a pastry in sleek surrounds.

Serhent Simit Sarayı (İnönü Caddesi; simit €0.60; 7am-10pm) Hmm, those damn little calorie-busting *simits* (O-shaped bread rings sprinkled with sesame seeds) eye-catchingly displayed continue to torment us! The *peynirli* (*simit* with cheese) is a killer. More, please.

Nostalji (☎ 323 42 08; Müçelli Caddesi; snacks €1-3; 8am-11pm) No matter how hectic the day, as soon as you step inside this squeaky-boarded, old Malatya mansion complete with memorabilia, stress evaporates as fast as light drizzle on asphalt in summer. Soak up the cool karma in the light-filled main lounge while listening to the mellow music and sipping a cup of Turkish coffee. Simple dishes are also available. It's also a good place to meet students of both sexes.

Vilayet Çay Bahçesi – VIP Cafe (Vilayet Tea Garden; İnönü Caddesi; snacks €1-4; 7am-11pm) We're suckers for the relaxing atmosphere that prevails in this unexpected oasis of calm, just off the busiest junction in the city. Nab a table at VIP Cafe and chow down on burgers or *gözleme*, or linger over a cuppa – an instant elixir after a hectic bout of sightseeing. No doubt you'll be approached by friendly Kemal, who runs the information booth nearby.

Mangal Vadisi (☎ 326 22 00; Kışla Caddesi; mains €2-5; 11am-10pm) With its big *mangals* (barbecues) on the ground floor, the restaurant will give dedicated meat eaters reason to smile. Unsurprisingly, the emphasis is on grilled meat (chicken, lamb, liver and more). The neon-lit dining room upstairs is less attractive. It's in a little street off Atatürk Caddesi.

Hacıbey Lahmacun (☎ 324 9798; Kışla Caddesi; mains €3-4; 11am-10pm) Our favourite refuelling stop for a hearty pide or a *lahmacun*, washed down with a refreshing *ayran*. The menu is translated into English, and there are photos of each kind of pide. The wood-panelled façade of the building looks like a Swiss chalet – very exotic for Malatya.

Şelale Kernek Restaurant (☎ 323 9313; Kernek Meydanı; mains €3-5; 10am-10pm) The main drawcard of the Kernek is its open-air rooftop overlooking verdant gardens, perfect in summer. Otherwise the dining room doesn't contain one whit of soul or character. The menu focuses on pide and grills.

Kaşık Restaurant (☎ 323 6292; Kanal Boyu; mains €3-5; 8am-11pm) Priding itself on its savoury *kiremit* (meat cooked in a clay pot), the Kaşık also serves comforting grills and pide. Some pictures of the dishes feature prominently above the entrance, so you can't really go wrong. For a splurge, try their *Kaşık special*, which has a bit of everything. Bonuses include the outside terrace and late opening hours.

Semerkant (☎ 325 6031; Kanal Boyu; mains €3-5) If you want a quiet drink, a nargileh or a snack alfresco, you could do worse than occupy a seat on the terrace of this tentatively hip bar-restaurant. The fake stone walls are amusing too.

Shopping

You won't leave Malatya without filling your bags with apricots, the city's delight. There's a handful of dried-fruit shops specialising in apricot baskets, jams and pickles on Atatürk Caddesi. **Armağan** (☎ 325 7005; Atatürk Caddesi; 8am-9pm) has the best selection. More dried-fruit shops can be found in the bazaar (see p617).

Getting There & Away

AIR

All companies operate an airport bus (€3).

Atlasjet (☎ 324 1313; www.atlasjet.com; Müçelli Caddesi; 8.30am-8pm) One daily flight to/from İstanbul (from €44, 1½ hours).

Onur Air (☎ 326 5050; www.onurair.com.tr; İnönü Caddesi; 8am-8pm) One daily flight to/from İstanbul (from €48).

Turkish Airlines (☎ 324 8001; www.thy.com; Kanal Boyu; 8.30am-5.30pm Mon-Fri, 8.30-1.30pm Sat) Two daily flights to/from İstanbul (from €44), and a daily flight to/from Ankara (from €44, one hour).

BUS

Malatya's enormous otogar, MAŞTİ, is 4km out on the western outskirts. Most bus companies operate *servises* (shuttle minibuses) there from the town centre. If not, minibuses from the otogar travel along Turgut Özal Bulvarı Buhara Bulvarı (aka Çevre Yol). However, they aren't allowed into the town centre. Ask to be let off at the corner of Turan Temelli Caddesi and Buhara Caddesi and walk from there. City buses to the otogar leave from near the *vilayet*. A taxi to the otogar costs about €7.

Some daily bus services to major destinations are listed in the table, below.

SERVICES FROM MALATYA'S OTOGAR

Destination	Fare	Duration	Distance	Frequency (per day)
Adana	€12	8hr	425km	a few
Adıyaman	€7	2½hr	144km	frequent
Ankara	€20	11hr	685km	frequent
Diyarbakır	€8	4hr	260km	a few
Elazığ	€4	1¾hr	101km	hourly
Gaziantep	€8	4hr	250km	a few
İstanbul	€25	18hr	1130km	a few
Kayseri	€12	4hr	354km	several
Sivas	€9	5hr	235km	several

CAR

Car-hire agencies are clustered just west of the Tekel Factory on İnönü Caddesi. **Meydan Rent a Car** (☎ 325 6060; www.meydanoto.com.tr in Turkish; İnönü Caddesi, Sıtmapınarı Ziraat Bankası Bitişiği; ☯ 8am-7pm) is a reliable outlet.

TRAIN

Right in the middle of Turkey, Malatya is a major railway hub and is well connected by train to the east of the country (Elazığ, Tatvan, Diyarbakır), the west (İstanbul, Ankara, Sivas, Kayseri) and the south (Adana). A train via here can be a good alternative to tiring bus trips.

The *Vangölü Ekspresi* leaves for İstanbul via Sivas, Kayseri and Ankara at 6.10pm on Tuesday and Thursday (€12); for Elazığ and Tatvan (€6), it leaves at 1.35am on Wednesday and Sunday.

The *Güney Ekspresi* leaves for İstanbul via Sivas, Kayseri and Ankara at 6.10pm on Monday, Wednesday, Friday and Sunday (€12); for Elazığ and Diyarbakır (€6), it departs at 1.35am on Tuesday, Thursday, Saturday and Sunday.

The *4 Eylül Ekspresi* leaves daily for Ankara via Sivas and Kayseri at 2.55pm (€12).

The *Fırat Ekspresi* leaves daily for Adana at 10.20am (€8); for Elazığ, it departs at 5.40pm (€3).

Malatya's train station can be reached by dolmuş (€0.40) or by 'İstasyon' city buses from near the *vilayet*.

AROUND MALATYA
Aslantepe

The scant finds of this archaeological site, located about 6km from Malatya, are not exactly gripping, but if you have an interest in Anatolian archaeology you'll enjoy **Aslantepe** (☯ 8am-5pm) and its pretty village setting.

When the Phrygians invaded the Hittite kingdom at Boğazkale, around 1200 BC, many Hittites fled southeast over the Taurus Mountains to resettle and build walled cities. The city of Milidia, now known as Aslantepe, was one of these neo-Hittite city-states (for more information about the Hittites, see the boxed text, p463).

On-off excavations since the 1930s have so far uncovered seven layers of remains.

To get to Aslantepe from Malatya, catch a bus marked 'Orduzu' (€0.40, 15 minutes) from the southern side of Buhara Bulvarı near the junction with Akpınar Caddesi. Buy an extra ticket for the return trip, and tell the driver where you want to get off; the site is a pleasant 500m stroll from the bus stop.

Old Malatya (Battalgazi)

You don't need to be an archaeology buff to be captivated by the remains of old Malatya, the walled city settled alongside Aslantepe, about 11km north of Malatya at Battalgazi.

As you come into the village you'll see the ruins of the old **city walls** with their 95 towers, built during Roman times and completed in the 6th century. They've lost all their facing stone to other building projects, and apricot orchards now fill what were once city blocks. The village of Battalgazi has grown up in and around the ruins.

The bus from Malatya terminates in the main square. Just off here, beside the mosque boasting the smooth-topped minaret, is the **Silahtar Mustafa Paşa Hanı**, an Ottoman caravanserai dating from the 17th century. Although restored, it's virtually abandoned.

When you've finished at the caravanserai, turn right and follow Osman Ateş Caddesi for about 600m until you see the broken brick minaret of the finely restored 13th-century **Ulu Cami** on the left. This is what you've really come to see. This stunning, if fast-fading, Seljuk building dates from the reign of Alaettin Keykubad I. Note the remaining Seljuk tiles lining the dome over the *mimber* (pulpit) and worked into Arabic inscriptions on the *eyvan* and *medrese* (seminary) walls. Also

SOUTHEASTERN ANATOLIA

BACKROADS: UPPER EUPHRATES

If you really want to get off the beaten track, you could venture into a territory that is still overlooked by travel books (including this one!): the upper valley of the Euphrates, from Elazığ to Erzincan. From Elazığ you could head north to Petek, then follow the shores of the Keban Barajı. There are no primary roads, only secondary roads that serve intriguing towns and villages – it's a wonderful scenic drive. For adventurous types with plenty of time and their own wheels, this region offers an insight into a fascinating world that few Westerners have seen. There aren't many facilities but if you think travel is more about meeting people and discovering new places than swanning around in top-notch accommodation, you might find your nirvana here. Allow three days to cover this suggested route.

---

worthy of interest is the **Ak Minare Camii** (White Minaret Mosque), about 50m from the Ulu Cami. This also dates from the 13th century.

Close by is the 13th-century **Halfetih Minaret**, made completely of bricks, and the **Nezir Gazi Tomb**.

Buses to Battalgazi (€0.40, 15 minutes) leave every 15 minutes or so from the same bus stop as those for Aslantepe.

Yeşilyurt & Gündüzbey

It's a true pleasure to enjoy the refreshingly peaceful atmosphere of Yeşilyurt and Gündüzbey, respectively 9km and 11km from Malatya. Old houses, lots of greenery, pleasing tea gardens, picnic areas… So cool! Take a minibus from Milli Eğemenlik Caddesi in Malatya (€0.40, 20 minutes) and enjoy the hush.

ELAZIĞ

☎ 0424 / pop 305,000 / elevation 1200m

If you're passing through the vibrant city of Elazığ, you must see the Urartian treasures in the **Archaeology & Ethnography Museum** (Arkeoloji ve Etnoğrafya Müzesi; admission €1.25; ☼ 9am-5pm Tue-Sat) on the campus of the Euphrates University, in the western outskirts of the city. You may also want to visit **Harput**, about 6km from Elazığ, which was an important staging post on the Silk Road to and from China and India. The main attraction there is the huge but badly ruined **castle** astride a rocky outcrop – an eerie vision. The Urartians built the first castle on this site way back in the 8th or 9th century BC, but what you see today are the remains of the castle built by Turks in the 11th century AD. Other assorted historic buildings are scattered about, including the **Ulu Cami**, sporting a crooked minaret, and several mausoleums. Harput is a popular place for picnicking families at weekends.

Frequent minibuses (€0.40) run to Harput from a small terminal in the centre of Elazığ.

Sleeping

There's a thicket of hotels 200m or so east of Cumhuriyet Meydanı along Hürriyet Caddesi.

Turistik Otel (☎ 218 1772; Hürriyet Caddesi; s/d €12/17) It won't feature in the pages of the *Condé Nast Traveller* (read: ageing plumbing in the bathrooms and worn curtains), but the prices are competitive, the rooms presentable and the location hard to beat. Enough for a night's kip. You'll have to forgo breakfast.

Hotel Varan (☎ 233 8824; Hürriyet Caddesi; s/d €14/23; ✷) Renovations were in progress when we popped in (you could still smell the paint), which bodes well. It's spitting distance from the Turistik. Luminous rooms with back-friendly beds and pathogen-free bathrooms. No breakfast is served.

Marathon Hotel (☎ 238 8686; www.themarathon hotel.com.tr; Bosna Hersek Bulvarı; s/d €28/40; 🅿 ✷ 🖳) Bump it up a notch in this four-star establishment. A saunter from the main square, it sports 60 cosy rooms with fluffy carpet, five swish suites, two bars, a *hamam*, a sauna, a fitness centre and a panoramic restaurant. And for those aching legs, there is a *masaj salonu* (massage room).

Eating

You'll find scores of cheap eateries and pastry shops along Hürriyet Caddesi and in the side streets.

Hacıoğulları Lahmacun (☎ 212 1996; Hürriyet Caddesi; mains €1-3; ☼ 10am-10pm) *Lahmacun, lahmacun, lahmacun*. Or pide. This hole-in-the-wall on the main drag concocts scrumptious Turkish and Arabic pizzas, cooked before your eyes and served on a wooden plate.

Kilis Kebap Salonu (☎ 236 7572; İşbankası Yanı; mains €2-4; ⏱ 10am-8pm) An easygoing eatery where you can fill your belly without spending a fortune. It's been in business since 1952, so it knows its stuff.

Getting There & Away

Six Turkish Airlines flights a week connect Elazığ with Ankara (from €45, 1¼ hours).

Elazığ's spacious otogar is 3km east of the centre. There are fairly frequent services to and from Diyarbakır (€5, two hours, 151km), Erzurum (€14, seven hours, 324km), Malatya (€4, 1¾ hours, 101km) and Tatvan (€10, six hours, 329km).

Like Malatya, Elazığ is well connected by train to the east of the country (Tatvan, Diyarbakır), the west (İstanbul, Ankara, Sivas, Kayseri, Malatya) and the south (Adana).

DİYARBAKIR

☎ 0412 / pop 665,400 / elevation 660m

Let's get right to the point – Diyarbakır is best known as the town that, since the 1980s, has been the centre of the Kurdish resistance movement. This speaks volumes. Nowhere else in eastern Turkey will you hear people priding themselves so much on being Kurdish. Diyarbakır remains *the* stronghold of Kurdish identity and tenacity. Fortunately, the situation has improved considerably; walking down the streets of this animated city on a sunny day, you wouldn't think it was the centre stage of pitched battles between the rebels of the Kurdistan Workers Party (PKK) and the Turkish army. Sure, it's not entirely stabilised, but this doesn't mean you should give Diyarbakır a miss.

With its narrow alleyways, its countless historical buildings, its Arab-style mosques and its uniquely unforgettable ambience, the old walled city will make you feel like you're floating through another time and space. Some travellers think it's a bit rough around the edges; others regard it as a veiled, self-contained city that doesn't easily bare its soul. Whatever your perspective, Diyarbakır is undisputably filled with character, soul and energy. Be sure to squeeze it into your Anatolian trip.

History

Mesopotamia, the land between the Tigris and Euphrates Valleys, saw the dawn of the world's first great empires. So it's no surprise that

Diyarbakır's history begins with the Hurrian kingdom of Mitanni c 1500 BC and proceeds through domination by the civilisations of Urartu (900 BC), Assyria (1356–612 BC), Persia (600–330 BC) and Alexander the Great and his successors, the Seleucids.

The Romans took over in AD 115, but because of its strategic position the city changed hands numerous times until it was conquered by the Arabs in 639. The Arab tribe of Beni Bakr that settled here named their new home Diyar Bakr, which means the Realm of Bakr.

For the next few centuries the city was occupied by various tribes, until 1497 when the Safavid dynasty founded by Shah İsmail took over Iran, putting an end to more than a century of Turkoman rule in this area. The Ottomans came and conquered in 1515, and even then, Diyarbakır was not to know lasting peace. Because it stood right in the way of invading armies originating from Anatolia, Persia and Syria, it suffered many more tribulations.

Banned until a few years ago, the Nevruz festival takes place on 21 March and is a great occasion to immerse yourself in Kurdish culture. For more details, see p658.

Orientation

Old Diyarbakır is encircled by walls pierced by several main gates. Within the walls the city is a maze of narrow, twisting, mostly unmarked alleys. Most services useful to travellers are in Old Diyarbakır, on or around Gazi Caddesi, including the PTT, internet cafés and banks with ATMs.

KURDISH WAY WITH WORDS

Southeastern Anatolia is predominantly Kurdish territory. Most Kurds speak Turkish, but in remote places you'll hear Kurmancı and Zazakı, the two Kurdish dialects spoken in Turkey. Surprisingly, those who speak Kurmancı won't understand those who speak Zazakı. Kurdish languages don't share any linguistic features with Turkish, but are related to Persian and other Indo-European languages. Instead of the ubiquitous *teşekkür ederim* ('thanks' in Turkish), you'll hear the much more straightforward *spas* in Kurmancı and instead of *merhaba* (hello), you'll hear *rojbas*.

The train station is about 1.5km from the centre, at the western end of İstasyon Caddesi. The otogar is 3.5km northwest of the centre.

New Diyarbakır sprawls to the northwest of the old city, but you'll have no reason to go there.

Information

Most banks have branches with ATMs on İnönü Caddesi.

Nazlı Saray Döviz (Gazi Caddesi; 8am-7pm Mon-Sat) Private exchange office that keeps longer hours than banks.

Şafak Internet Cafe (per hr €0.60; 8am-11pm) Off Kıbrıs Caddesi.

Teknoloji Bilgin (Ali Emiri Caddesi; per hr €0.60; 8am-10pm) Internet café. Just outside the city walls, a few doors from the Selim Amca'nın Sofra Salonu.

Tourist office (☎ 228 1706; Kapısı; 8am-5pm Mon-Fri) Housed in a tower in the wall. Has some brochures and can only help with simple queries.

Sights

CITY WALLS & GATES

Diyarbakır's single most conspicuous feature is its great circuit of basalt walls, probably dating from Roman times, although the present walls date from early Byzantine times (AD 330–500). At almost 6km in length these walls are said to be second in extent only to the Great Wall of China. They make a striking sight whether you're walking along the top or the bottom.

Numerous bastions and towers stand sentinel over the massive black walls. There were four main gates originally: **Harput Kapısı** (north), **Mardin Kapısı** (south), **Yenikapı** (east) and **Urfa Kapısı** (west).

Fortunately, the most easily accessible stretch of walls is also the most interesting in terms of inscriptions and decoration. Start near the Mardin Kapısı close to the Deliller Han, a stone caravanserai now home to the Otel Büyük Kervansaray. Be sure not to miss **Nur Burcu** (Tower Nur), the **Yedi Kardeş Burcu** (Tower of Seven Brothers), with two Seljuk lion bas-reliefs, which you can see only from outside the walls, and the **Malikşah Burcu** (Tower of Malik Şah, also called Ulu Badan), which has some bas-reliefs too.

You can also ascend the walls of the **İç Kale** (fortress or keep) to enjoy the fine views of the Tigris, flanked by a patchwork of market gardens, as it meanders 2km to 3km south to flow under the 11th-century **On Gözlu Köprüsü** (Ten-Eyed Bridge).

At various spots inside the base of the walls you can see brightly painted, open-air **Sufi sarcophagi**, notable for their turbans, their size a symbol of spiritual authority. There's a cluster a few hundred metres northeast of the Urfa Kapısı.

Unfortunately, you must be careful when walking on and along the walls as there have been reports of attempted robberies. Try to go in a group.

MOSQUES

Of Diyarbakır's many mosques, the most impressive is the **Ulu Cami**, built in 1091 by Malik Şah, an early Seljuk sultan. Incorporating elements from an earlier Byzantine church on the site, it was extensively restored in 1155 after a fire. It's rectangular in plan – Arab style, rather than Ottoman. The entrance portal, adorned with two medallions figuring a lion and a bull, leads to a huge courtyard. This is the most elegant section of the building, with two-storey arcades, two cone-shaped *şadırvans* (ritual ablution fountains), elaborate pillars, and friezes figuring fruits and vegetables – a real feast for the eyes.

Across Gazi Caddesi is the **Hasan Paşa Hanı**, a 16th-century caravanserai occupied by jewel and antiques vendors. It was extensively restored in 2006.

Alternating black-and-white stone banding is a characteristic of Diyarbakır's mosques, many of which date from the time of the Akkoyunlu dynasty. One of these is the **Nebi Camii** (1530) at the main intersection of Gazi and İzzet Paşa/İnönü Caddesis, which has a detached minaret sporting a stunning combination of black-and-white stone.

The **Behram Paşa Camii** (1572), in a residential area deep in the maze of narrow streets, is Diyarbakır's largest mosque. More Persian in style, the **Safa Camii** (1532) has a highly decorated minaret with blue tiles incorporated in its design.

The **Şeyh Mutahhar Camii** (1512) is also famous for its minaret, but its engineering is even more interesting – the tower stands on four slender pillars about 2m high, earning it the name **Dört Ayaklı Minare** (Four-Legged Minaret).

The 12th-century **Hazreti Süleyman Camii**, beside the İç Kale, is particularly revered because it houses the tombs of heroes of past Islamic wars. Local people flock here on Thursdays to pay their respects.

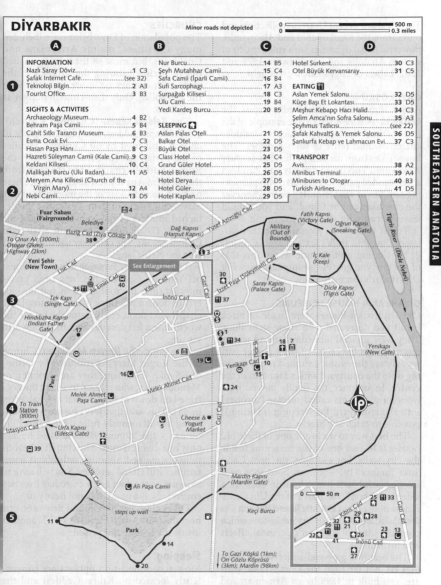

DIYARBAKIR

Minor roads not depicted

0 — 500 m
0 — 0.3 miles

INFORMATION
Nazlı Saray Döviz.........................**1** C3
Şafak Internet Cafe..................(see 32)
Teknoloji Bilgin.........................**2** A3
Tourist Office.............................**3** B3

SIGHTS & ACTIVITIES
Archaeology Museum...................**4** B2
Behram Paşa Camii......................**5** B4
Cahit Sıtkı Tarancı Museum..........**6** B3
Esma Ocak Evi............................**7** C3
Hasan Paşa Hanı.........................**8** C3
Hazreti Süleyman Camii (Kale Camii)..**9** C3
Keldani Kilisesi...........................**10** C4
Malikşah Burcu (Ulu Badan)..........**11** A5
Meryem Ana Kilisesi (Church of the
    Virgin Mary)...........................**12** A4
Nebi Camii.................................**13** D5

Nur Burcu...................................**14** B5
Şeyh Mutahhar Camii...................**15** C4
Safa Camii (İparli Camii)...............**16** B4
Sufi Sarcophagi..........................**17** A3
Surpağab Kilisesi.........................**18** C3
Ulu Cami....................................**19** B4
Yedi Kardeş Burcu.......................**20** B5

SLEEPING
Aslan Palas Oteli........................**21** D5
Balkar Otel.................................**22** D5
Büyük Otel.................................**23** D5
Class Hotel................................**24** C5
Grand Güler Hotel.......................**25** D5
Hotel Birkent..............................**26** D5
Hotel Derya...............................**27** D5
Hotel Güler................................**28** D5
Hotel Kaplan..............................**29** D5

Hotel Surkent.............................**30** C3
Otel Büyük Kervansaray...............**31** C5

EATING
Aslan Yemek Salonu....................**32** D5
Küçe Başı Et Lokantası.................**33** D5
Meşhur Kebapçı Hacı Halid...........**34** C3
Şelim Amca'nın Sofra Salonu.........**35** A3
Şeyhmus Tatlıcısı.....................(see 22)
Şafak Kahvaltı & Yemek Salonu.....**36** D5
Şanlıurfa Kebap ve Lahmacun Evi...**37** C3

TRANSPORT
Avis...**38** A2
Minibüs Terminal.........................**39** A2
Minibuses to Otogar....................**40** B3
Turkish Airlines...........................**41** D5

Note that most of these mosques have more than one name; the alternative names are shown on the map key. When visiting these mosques, you should try to time your visit for 20 to 25 minutes after the call to prayer (when the prayers should be finished), as most of them will be locked outside prayer times.

ARCHAEOLOGY MUSEUM

Diyarbakır's **Archaeology Museum** (Arkeoloji Müzesi; off Elazığ Caddesi; admission €1.25; 8am-5pm Tue-Sun) is near the Fuar Sahası (Fairground), behind the towering Dedeman Hotel.

It has a well-presented collection including finds from the Neolithic site of Çayönü (7500–6500 BC), 65km north of Diyarbakır.

There's also a decent Urartian collection and relics from the Karakoyunlu and Akkoyunlu, powerful tribal dynasties who ruled much of eastern Anatolia and Iran between 1378 and 1502. Labels in English are a great help.

GAZİ KÖŞKÜ

About 1km south of the Mardin Kapısı, the **Gazi Köşkü** (admission €0.60) is a fine example of the sort of Diyarbakır house to which its wealthier citizens would retire in high summer. The house dates from the time of the 15th-century Akkoyunlu Turkoman dynasty and stands in a well-tended park, very popular with picnicking families at weekends. It's open whenever the caretaker can be found, and you should leave him a tip for showing you round.

To get there, it's a pleasant, if rather isolated, downhill walk. Taxis charge a rip-off €12 including waiting time. From this side of the city you get fine, unimpeded views of Diyarbakır's dramatic walls.

DİYARBAKIR HOUSE MUSEUMS

Old Diyarbakır houses were made of black basalt and decorated with stone stencilling. They were divided into summer and winter quarters, and the centre of the summer part was always the *eyvan,* a vaulted room opening onto the courtyard with a fountain in the centre. In summer, the family moved high wooden platforms called *tahtlar* (thrones) into the courtyard for sleeping, making it possible to catch any breeze.

The best way to see inside one of these old houses is to visit one of the museums inside the city walls. For example, the poet Cahit Sıtkı Tarancı (1910–56) was born in a two-storey black basalt house built in 1820, in a side street about 50m north of the Ulu Cami. It now houses the **Cahit Sıtkı Tarancı Museum** (Ziya Gökalp Sokak; admission free; ⊗ 8am-5pm Tue-Sun), which contains some of the poet's personal effects and furnishings.

The beautiful grey-and-white-striped **Esma Ocak Evi**, not far from the Dört Ayaklı Minare, was built in 1899 by an Armenian and restored in 1996 by a female writer, Esma Ocak. You'll need to bang hard on the door to alert the caretaker, who will show you the gracefully furnished living rooms. Admission is by donation, but you'll be encouraged to give at least €1 per person. While you're there ask the caretaker to show you the Armenian Surpağab Kilisesi (right) opposite.

CHURCHES

The population of Diyarbakır once included many Christians, mainly Armenians and Chaldeans, but most of them were pushed out or perished during the troubles in the early 20th century or, more recently, with the Hezbollah. Only their churches linger as reminders.

The **Keldani Kilisesi** (Chaldean Church), off Yenikapı Caddesi, is a plain, brightly lit church, still used by 30 Christian families of the Syrian rite (in communion with the Roman Catholic church). The chaplain from the Meryem Ana Kilisesi holds a service here on the second Sunday of the month. It's fairly easy to find on your own. Walk past the detached minaret of the Nebi Camii, take the first left (Dicle Sokak) then the first right (Şeftali Sokak). The caretaker usually sits outside the Nebi Camii.

The Armenian **Surpağab Kilisesi**, also just off Yenikapı Caddesi, has long been grass-infested since the roof caved in, but the elderly custodian will show you the atmospheric chapel next door, eerily untouched since the worshippers left decades ago. It's well worth visiting.

The wonderful **Meryem Ana Kilisesi** (Church of the Virgin Mary) is still used by Orthodox Syrian Christians; they are Jacobites, or Monophysites, who refused to accept the doctrine laid down at the Council of Chalcedon in 451. This said that Jesus had two natures, being simultaneously fully divine and fully human – the Monophysites insisted he had only one divine nature. The church is beautifully maintained, although only about seven families still attend services. You will have to hammer on the door as the custodian lives two courtyards away and may not hear you.

Other churches have found new uses: one near the Dört Ayaklı Camii as a PTT, another inside the İç Kale as a prison.

Sleeping

Most accommodation options are conveniently located on Kıbrıs Caddesi and the nearby İnönü Caddesi, where there's a range of hotels in all price brackets interspersed with restaurants. In summer it's scorching hot here, something to bear in mind when choosing a room. The best accommodation choices for lone female guests are the Hotel Birkent, the Otel Balkar and the top-end options.

BUDGET

Aslan Palas Oteli (☎ 228 9224; Kıbrıs Caddesi; s/d with shared bathroom €9/14, s/d €12/20; ✖) This long-standing fave is a good haunt for frugal (male) travellers, with a mixed bag of rooms – ask to see a few before you make a decision to stay here, as some are more luminous than others. Air-con in all the rooms. The catch? There's no double-glazing, and prices don't include breakfast.

Hotel Surkent (☎ 228 1014; İzzet Paşa Caddesi; s/d €14/20; ✖) The new kid on the block, the Surkent was just getting a lick of flamingo-pink paint and other final renovations when we visited – a good omen. The Smartie-like façade, with an odd mix of aluminium plates and tangerine frames, is amusingly quirky.

Hotel Güler (☎/fax 224 0294; Yoğurtçu Sokak; s/d €15/20; P ✖) Tucked in an alleyway off Kıbrıs Caddesi, this two-star outfit is a perfect place to rest your head after a long day's sightseeing, with well-looked-after rooms, well-sprung mattresses and prim, if pint-sized, bathrooms.

Hotel Kaplan (☎ 229 3300; fax 224 0187; Kıbrıs Caddesi, Yoğurtçu Sokak; s/d €15/23; P ✖) A short stagger from the Güler, the Kaplan is a pleasant surprise, with spacious and comfortable yet impersonal rooms. Try to snaffle one of the brighter top-floor rooms.

Hotel Birkent (☎ 228 7131; fax 228 7145; İnönü Caddesi; s/d €16/25; P ✖) If you bet the Birkent has air-con, stout bedding and spruce rooms, you'll hit the trifecta! Yes, this is one of the most dependable options in town, with consistently good reviews from travellers. Other pluses include a lift, double-glazing and an ace location.

MIDRANGE

Balkar Otel (☎ 228 1233; fax 224 6936; Kıbrıs Caddesi 38; s/d €19/25; P ✖) This typical middling three-star boasts colourful, well-appointed rooms with TV and minibar. Bathroom-wise, don't even think of gesticulating in the diminutive cubicles in the single rooms. Added bonuses include a lift, a hearty breakfast and a rooftop terrace that proffers stunning views over the walls.

Grand Güler Hotel (☎ 229 2221; fax 224 4509; Kıbrıs Caddesi; s/d €21/31; P ✖) 'Grand' is a very optimistic description but it sports well-furnished rooms and neat bathrooms. The front rooms have double-glazing so it shouldn't be too noisy.

Büyük Otel (☎ 228 1295; fax 221 2444; İnönü Caddesi; s/d €24/34; P ✖) The Balkar's most serious competitor, this reliable player stands its ground with spick-and-span rooms, excellent amenities and bathrooms that you won't dread using. A good choice for women travellers.

Hotel Derya (☎ 224 2555; fax 221 9735; İnönü Caddesi; s/d €25/34; P ✖) Another option worth considering, with an elegant blue mosaic façade, a rooftop restaurant and good facilities. The petite among us will find the rooms intimate, while others may argue for the term 'claustrophobic'.

TOP END

Otel Büyük Kervansaray (☎/fax 228 9606; Gazi Caddesi; s/d/ste €50/80/100; P ✖ ✖) This historic place comes recommended if you need to pamper yourself after a tiring trip. Housed in the 16th-century Deliller Han, a converted caravanserai, it has charm in spades. This is not the height of luxury, but it scores high on amenities, with a restaurant, a bar, a *hamam* and a nifty pool in which to cool off. The standard rooms are itty-bitty, but how much time are you going to spend in your room when the inner courtyard is so agreeable?

Class Hotel (☎ 229 5000; www.diyarbakirclasshotel .com in Turkish; Gazi Caddesi; s/d €90/115; P ✖ ▣ ▣) An angular building right in the heart of the old town, this five-star bigwig won't appeal to fans of minimalism, but it has all the bells and whistles your platinum card will allow for, including a pool, a sauna, a nightclub and a conference room – not to mention the fitness centre to keep off those extra kilos added by a baklava overdose. Or you could linger over a cuppa in the delightful Çizmeci Pavilion, built in 1317 and converted into a cosy lounge.

Eating & Drinking

A stroll along Kıbrıs Caddesi reveals plenty of informal places to eat. They're nothing fancy, but they offer authentic fare at very moderate prices.

Selim Amca'nın Sofra Salonu (☎ 224 4447; Ali Emiri Caddesi; mains €4-7, set menu €9; ⏰ noon-9.30pm) This rather upscale eatery outside the city walls is famous for one thing and one thing only: *kaburga dolması* (lamb or chicken stuffed with rice and almonds). Round it off with a devilish *İrmik helvası* (a gooey dessert) and wash it all down with a soft drink. (Alcohol? Dream on!) Well worth the splurge.

Küçe Başı Et Lokantası (☎ 229 5661; Kıbrıs Caddesi; mains €4-7; 🕑 8am-10pm) A few doors from most hotels, this outfit gets kudos for its wide-ranging menu and its original setting – the room at the back is designed like a rustic barn. Try innovative (read: not kebaps) dishes like *kiremit* or *saç tava* (deep-fried meat in a flat-bottomed pan). There's a picture menu to facilitate your choice.

Şanlıurfa Kebap ve Lahmacun Evi (☎ 228 2312; İzzet Paşa Caddesi; mains €3-5; 🕑 7am-8pm Mon-Sat) Ease a belt hole at this sleek venture and feast on belly-filling kebaps or well-prepared pide at puny prices.

Şafak Kahvaltı & Yemek Salonu (Kıbrıs Caddesi; mains €1-2; 🕑 7am-11pm) Nosh on freshly prepared meat dishes and expertly cooked pide in this brisk Diyarbakır institution, ideally positioned on Kıbrıs Caddesi. It's also a good place to partake in a restorative morning *kahvaltı* (breakfast).

Otel Büyük Kervansaray (☎ 228 9606; Gazi Caddesi; mains €3-6; 🕑 8am-11pm) Even if you're not staying in this historic hotel it's worth popping in just for a cuppa in the delightful courtyard or for a meal in the restaurant, a converted camel stable. There's live music here most nights.

Other recommendations:

Aslan Yemek Salonu (Kıbrıs Caddesi; mains €2-5; 🕑 8am-10pm) An excellent-value stomach-filler, with a wide selection of meat dishes.

Meşhur Kebapçı Hacı Halid (Borsahan Sokak; mains €2-4; 🕑 11am-9pm Mon-Sat) The ideal pit stop if money really matters. Tasty kebaps and ready-made meals served in bright surroundings. It's in a small pedestrianised side street, off Gazi Caddesi.

Şeyhmus Tatlıcısı (Kıbrıs Caddesi; 🕑 7am-8pm) Keep up your strength with a delectable baklava or a sticky *kadayıf*.

Getting There & Away

AIR

There is no airport service; a taxi from the town centre to the airport will cost about €8.

Onur Air (☎ 223 5312; www.onurair.com.tr; Gevran Caddesi, Rızvan Ağa Sokak; 🕑 8am-7pm) Has two daily flights to/from İstanbul (from €50, 1¾ hours).

Sun Express (www.sunexpress.com.tr) Is represented by Turkish Airlines. Has three weekly flights to İzmir (from €60, two hours).

Turkish Airlines (☎ 228 8401; www.thy.com; İnönü Caddesi; 🕑 8am-7pm) Has three daily flights to/from İstanbul (from €55) and two daily flights to/from Ankara (from €44, 1½ hours).

BUS

Many bus companies have ticket offices on İnönü Caddesi or along Gazi Caddesi near the Dağ Kapısı. A free *servis* will ferry you to the otogar.

There's a separate minibus terminal (İlçeler Minibüs Terminalı) outside Urfa Kapısı, with services to Batman (€3, 1½ hours), Elazığ (€6, two hours), Hasankeyf (€2), Mardin (€4, 1¼ hours), Malatya (€9, 5 hours), Midyat (€3) and Siverek (to get to Kahta without going right round the lake via Adıyaman).

Details of some daily services on the main routes are listed in the table, below.

SERVICES FROM DİYARBAKIR'S OTOGAR

Destination	Fare	Duration	Distance	Frequency (per day)
Adana	€17	8hr	550km	several
Ankara	€27	13hr	945km	several
Batman	€3	1½hr	85km	frequent minibuses
Erzurum	€12	8hr	485km	several
Malatya	€8	5hr	260km	frequent
Mardin	€3	1½hr	95km	hourly
Şanlıurfa	€6	3hr	190km	frequent
Sivas	€13	10hr	500km	several
Tatvan	€8	4hr	264km	several
Van	€13	7hr	410km	several

CAR

There is an **Avis** (☎ 236 1324, 229 0275; www.avis.com.tr; Elazığ Caddesi; 🕑 8am-7pm) office across the street from the *belediye* and at the airport.

TRAIN

The *Güney Ekspresi* leaves for İstanbul via Malatya, Sivas and Kayseri at 11.36am on Monday, Wednesday, Friday and Sunday (€18).

MARDİN

☎ 0482 / pop 55,000 / elevation 1325m

Everyone loves Mardin, and it's immediately apparent why: this ancient town crowned with a castle overlooks the vast, roasted Mesopotamian plains extending to Syria, and the honey-coloured stone houses that trip down the side of the hillside give it something of the feel of old Jerusalem. Whatever the time of the year, the interplay of light and stone is enchanting. Another draw is the mosaic of people. Sizeable Yezidi, Christian and Syrian settlements, among others, add to the popu-

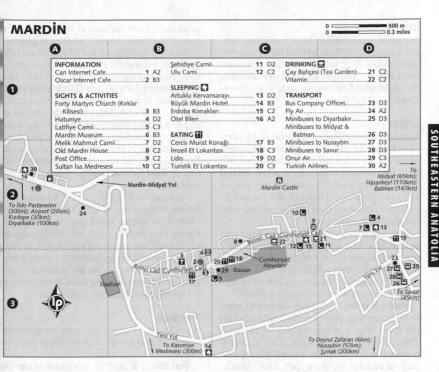

MARDİN

0 ————— 500 m
0 ————— 0.3 miles

INFORMATION			
Can Internet Cafe	1 A2	Şehidiye Camii	11 D2
Oscar Internet Cafe	2 B3	Ulu Cami	12 C2

SIGHTS & ACTIVITIES		SLEEPING	
Forty Martyrs Church (Kırklar		Artuklu Kervansarayı	13 D2
Kilisesi)	3 B3	Büyük Mardin Hotel	14 B3
Hatuniye	4 D2	Erdoba Konakları	15 C2
Latifiye Camii	5 C3	Otel Bilen	16 A2
Mardin Museum	6 B3		
Melik Mahmut Camii	7 D2	EATING	
Old Mardin House	8 C2	Cercis Murat Konağı	17 B3
Post Office	9 C2	İmzeil Et Lokantası	18 C2
Sultan İsa Medresesi	10 C2	Lido	19 D2
		Turistik Et Lokantası	20 C3

DRINKING	
Çay Bahçesi (Tea Garden)	21 C2
Vitamin	22 C2

TRANSPORT	
Bus Company Offices	23 D3
Fly Air	24 A2
Minibuses to Diyarbakır	25 D3
Minibuses to Midyat &	
Batman	26 D3
Minibuses to Nusaybin	27 D3
Minibuses to Savur	28 D3
Onur Air	29 C3
Turkish Airlines	30 A2

lation mix, giving the area a refreshing burst of multiculturalism.

This region was particularly hard-hit by the troubles of the 1980s and '90s and has really reopened to tourism only in the last few years. It's now a completely safe place to travel, and Mardin has started to become popular with Turkish travellers. Get there before the crowds do.

History

As with Diyarbakır, Mardin's history is one of disputes between rival armies over millennia, though in recent years the only dispute that anyone really cared about was the one between the PKK and the government. A castle has stood on this hill from time immemorial, and the Turkish army still finds the site useful.

Assyrian Christians settled here during the 5th century, and the Arabs occupied Mardin between 640 and 1104. After that, it had a succession of Seljuk Turkish, Kurdish, Mongol and Persian overlords, until the Ottomans under Sultan Selim the Grim took it in 1517. In the early 20th century many of the Assyr-

ian Christians were pushed out or perished during the troubles, and in the last few decades many have emigrated. An estimated 600 Christians remain, with 11 churches still in use on a rotational basis.

Orientation

Coming from Diyarbakır, you first pass through the new part of Mardin, where you'll find the Otel Bilen (Bilen Hotel). From here the main road winds up a hill. Continue up the hill to the roundabout where the road forks. Go uphill to the main drag, Cumhuriyet Caddesi (still called by its former name, Birinci Caddesi), to find the hotels and the main square, Cumhuriyet Meydanı, with the statue of Atatürk. The right-hand road from the roundabout, Yeni Yol, curves round the hillside on a lower latitude to rejoin Cumhuriyet Caddesi, just north of the bus company offices.

Everything you'll need is along or just off Cumhuriyet Caddesi, a one-way street with dolmuşes running along it. If you're driving your own car, you can park in Cumhuriyet Meydanı.

Information

All major banks with ATMs are on Cumhuriyet Caddesi. The **Oscar Internet Cafe** (Cumhuriyet Caddesi; per hr €0.60; ☺ 9am-11pm) is across the street from **Akbank** (Cumhuriyet Caddesi). In new Mardin, try **Can Internet Cafe** (Yenişehir; per hr €0.60; ☺ 9am-11pm), near Otel Bilen.

Sights

Mardin's most obvious attraction is the rambling **bazaar** that parallels Cumhuriyet Caddesi one block down the hill. Here donkeys are still the main form of transport, and are decked out in all the finery you sometimes see on sale in carpet shops. Look out also for saddle repairers who seem to be able to restore even the shabbiest examples.

Strolling through the bazaar, keep your eyes open for the secluded **Ulu Cami**, a 12th-century Iraqi Seljuk structure, which suffered badly during the Kurdish rebellion of 1832. Inside it's fairly plain, but the delicate reliefs adorning the minaret make a visit worthwhile.

Mardin Museum (Mardin Müzesi; Cumhuriyet Caddesi; €1.25; ☺ 8am-5pm), prominently positioned on the main drag, is worth visiting for the late-19th-century building alone. This superbly restored mansion sports carved pillars and elegant arcades on the upper floor. Inside, it has a small but well-displayed collection including everything from a finely detailed 7th-century BC Assyrian vase to finds from Girnavaz, a Bronze Age site 4km north of Nusaybin. Afterwards, head east along Cumhuriyet Caddesi, keeping your eye out for a fabulous example of Mardin's domestic architecture on your left – the three-arched façade of an ornately carved **house**.

Continue east, looking for steps on the left (north) that lead to the **Sultan İsa Medresesi** (☺ daylight hr), dating from 1385 and the town's prime architectural attraction. The highlight is the imposing recessed doorway, but make sure you wander through the pretty courtyards, lovingly tended by the caretaker, and onto the roof to enjoy the cityscape.

Further east is what surely must be Turkey's most gorgeous **post office**, housed in a 17th-century caravanserai with carvings such as frills around the windows and teardrops in stone dripping down the walls – shame they added the clunky staircase! Across the street you can't miss the elegant, slender minaret of the 14th-century **Şehidiye Camii**. It's superbly carved, with colonnades all around, and three small bulbs superimposed at the summit. The base of the minaret sports a series of pillars.

Also worth visiting is the 14th-century **Latifiye Camii**, behind the Akbank, where a shady courtyard has a şadırvan in the middle. The 15th-century **Forty Martyrs Church** (Kırklar Kilisesi; Sağlık Sokak) is to the west, with the martyrs depicted above the doorway of the church as you enter. If it's closed, bang hard on the door to alert the caretaker. Services are held here each Sunday. In the vicinity of the Artuklu Kervansarayı, the eye-catching **Hatuniye** and nearby **Melik Mahmut Camii** have been recently restored.

Another striking sight, the **Kasımiye Medresesi**, 800m south of Yeni Yol, was built in 1469. Two domes stand over the tombs of Kasım Paşa and his sister, but the highlights are the sublime courtyard walled with arched colonnades and the magnificent, carved doorway. Upstairs, you can see the students' quarters, before ascending the stairs to the rooftop for another great Mardin panorama.

Sleeping

If you're on a budget, grit your teeth: cheap hotels are annoyingly thin on the ground in Mardin.

Otel Bilen (☎ 213 0315; www.bilemhotel.com; s/d €25/45; Ⓟ ⓧ) In the new part of Mardin (Yenişehir), 2km northwest of Cumhuriyet Meydanı, this mundane three-star hotel won't bowl you over with charm, but it has spacious rooms with TV and well-scrubbed, tiled bathrooms. It's a bit overpriced, but there's room for negotiation if it's quiet. To get to the town centre from here, cross the road and flag down any dolmuş.

Erdoba Konakları (☎ 212 7677; fax 212 8821; www .erdoba.com.tr; Cumhuriyet Caddesi; s/d €48/72; ⓧ) Pomp it up in this stylish 'boutique hotel' – the first of its kind in Mardin – right in the heart of the old town. It comprises two historic mansions finely restored, with graciously decorated rooms and several terraces offering unimpeded views over the Mesopotamia plain. The catch? Only five rooms come with a view. It also houses a vaulted restaurant.

Artuklu Kervansarayı (☎ 213 7353; www.artuklu .com in Turkish; Cumhuriyet Caddesi; s/d €45/73; Ⓟ ⓧ ▯) This new kid in town wows you with a wide range of amenities but rates zero on the view scale. The décor is all borders and valances, and the rooms are above average, with dark furniture, parquet flooring and brick walls.

A SUCCESS STORY

Ebru Baydemir is what you would call a 'local character'. Aged 30, she is the dynamic owner of Cercis Murat Konağı in Mardin (see below) and the head of the Mardin tourism association. A rare example of a female entrepreneur in eastern Anatolia, she has managed, against all odds, to foster a new mindset among many Mardin women and has somewhat paved the way for the changing roles of women in a predominantly male-oriented society. 'When I opened my restaurant in 2001, I wanted to offer jobs to women but this was difficult because of the prevailing women-should-stay-at-home mentality. I started with a few female cooks who knew tried-and-true recipes, but I was obliged to set up partition walls so that they could not be visible in the kitchen. Little by little, I gained the confidence of their husbands. At present 15 female employees work here and they don't have to conceal themselves any longer. In Mardin it's now accepted that women can work outside.' Any other achievement, Mrs Ebru? 'Cercis is the first licensed restaurant in southeastern Anatolia' – something for which travellers will be eternally grateful.

Best of all, cooking courses are available for tourists. The cooks are ready to impart some of their secrets – a wonderfully authentic experience. Check out www.cercismurat.com for more details.

Büyük Mardin Hotel (☎ 213 10 47; fax 213 1447; Yeni Yol Caddesi; s/d €67/84; P ❂ 🖳) This massive structure is not a triumph of harmony and proportion but features all mod-cons, including a sauna and *hamam*, and the views over old Mardin and the Mesopotamia plain are just sensational. It caters predominantly to groups and is often booked solid, so reservations are advised.

Eating & Drinking

İmzeil Et Lokantası (☎ 212 1062; Cumhuriyet Meydanı; mains €2-4; ❂ 10am-7pm) A hanky-sized, bright little spot where you can get a protein fix without depleting your travel budget.

Turistik Et Lokantası (☎ 212 1647; Cumhuriyet Meydanı; mains €3-6; ❂ 9am-10pm) Judging by the awkward greeting ('Hallo'), 'Touristy Et Lokantası' would sound more appropriate. The food is predictable and the décor nothing flash, but it stays open late. It's right next door to the İmzeil.

Cercis Murat Konağı (☎ 213 6841; Cumhuriyet Caddesi; mains €4-7; ❂ 11am-11pm) Send your tastebuds on a tailspin at this innovative restaurant serving authentic village food with a creative twist (not a kebap in sight). Sink your teeth into a *közlenmiş peynir* (grilled cheese) or the *ayvalı kavurma* (lamb meat with quince), and you'll quickly discover the reason for its cult status (see boxed text, above). All dishes are prepared by women from Mardin, with recipes from the days of yore. There's a TV screen where you can watch them working their magic in the kitchen. The Cercis occupies a traditional Syrian Christian home with two

finely decorated rooms and a terrace affording simply stunning views. A respectable wine list and exemplary service complete the perfect equation. *Afiyet olsun* (enjoy your meal)!

Lido (Cumhuriyet Caddesi; pastries €0.40-1 ❂ 8am-8pm) Near the Artuklu, this small pastry shop has its fair share of sinful pleasures. There's a pleasant terrace.

İldo Pastaneleri (☎ 213 7288; Hükümet Konağü Arkası; pastries €0.50-1 ❂ 8am-11pm) A lighthouse for sybarites, with a wide array of pastries and ice creams served in sleek surrounds. The *fıstıklı dondurma* (pistachio ice cream) is worthy of an Oscar.

Vitamin (Cumhuriyet Caddesi; ❂ 8am-7pm) This unassuming place is the size of a postage stamp but is a victory for humanity when it comes to freshly squeezed fruit juices (from €0.50).

Çay bahçesi (Cumhuriyet Caddesi) The best tea garden in town is across the road from the PTT. It's the perfect place to soak up the atmosphere and be hypnotised by the terrific views over the old city and the scorching plains.

Getting There & Away

AIR

Mardin airport is 20km south of Mardin. There's no airport shuttle, but any minibus to Kızıltepe can drop you at the entrance (€0.70).

Fly Air (☎ 444 4359; www.flyair.com.tr; Yenişehir; ❂ 8.30am-7pm Mon-Sat) Has three weekly flights to/from İstanbul (from €43, two hours).

Onur Air (☎ 212 4141; www.onurair.com.tr; Cumhuriyet Meydanı; ❂ 8am-8pm) Has six weekly flights to/from İstanbul (from €48).

Turkish Airlines (Bilem Turizm ve Seyahat Acentası; ☎ 213 3773; www.thy.com; Karayolları Karşısı Yenişehir; 8am-6pm) Near the Bilen Hotel. Has three weekly flights to/from Ankara (from €44).

BUS

Most buses leave from outside the bus company ticket offices east of the centre. From around 4pm services start to dry up so it's best to make an early start. Minibuses depart every hour or so for Diyarbakır (€4, 1¼ hours), and for Midyat (€3, 1¼ hours) and Nusaybin (the Syrian border; €2). There are also four to five daily minibuses to Savur (€2, 45 minutes). Several daily buses connect Mardin with Urfa (€6, three hours) but, heading west, they're often already full when they arrive in Mardin; you'd be well advised to book a ticket as soon as you arrive. Other useful services for travellers include to Cizre (€4, three hours), the major hub for northern Iraq (see the boxed text, opposite); to Şirnak (€8, 3½ hours); and to Batman (€4).

AROUND MARDİN

Deyrul Zafaran

The magnificent **monastery of Mar Hanania (Deyrul Zafaran)** (9-11.30am & 1-3.30pm) stands about 6km along a good but narrow road in the rocky hills east of Mardin. The monastery was once the seat of the Syrian Orthodox patriarchate and, although this has now moved to Damascus, the site continues to act as a local boarding school.

In AD 495 the first monastery was built on a site previously dedicated to the worship of the sun. Destroyed by the Persians in 607, it was rebuilt, only to be looted by Tamerlane six centuries later.

Shortly after you enter the walled enclosure via a portal bearing a Syriac (a dialect of Aramaic) inscription, one of the school kids will volunteer their services as a guide. First they'll show you the **original sanctuary**, an eerie underground chamber with a ceiling of huge, closely fitted stones held up as if by magic, without the aid of mortar. This room was allegedly used by sun worshippers, who viewed their god rising through a window at the eastern end. A niche on the southern wall is said to have been for sacrifices.

The guide then leads you through a pair of 300-year-old doors to the **tombs** of the patriarchs and metropolitans who have served here.

In the chapel, the **patriarch's throne** to the left of the altar bears the names of all the patriarchs who have served the monastery since it was refounded in 792. To the right of the altar is the **throne of the metropolitan**. The present **stone altar** replaces a wooden one that burnt down about half a century ago. The walls are adorned with wonderful paintings and wall hangings. Services in Aramaic are held here.

In the next rooms you'll see **litters** used to transport the church dignitaries, and a **baptismal font**. In a small side room is a 300-year-old **wooden throne**. The floor **mosaic** is about 1500 years old.

A flight of stairs leads to very simple guest rooms for travellers and those coming for worship. The patriarch's small, simple bedroom and parlour are also up here.

There's no public transport here so you must take a taxi or walk. Hopeful drivers wait outside the bus company offices in Mardin and will ask €14 to run you there and back and to wait while you look round.

Savur

Ah, Savur. Come here on a clear day, and you'll fall in love with this diamond of a town – at least we did. About an hour's minibus ride from Mardin, Savur is clearly special. If you're looking for some hush and seclusion, this is

THE AUTHOR'S CHOICE

Hacı Abdullah Bey Konagü (☎ 0482-571 2127, 0533 239 7807; r per person with shared bathroom & half board €34) Step through the door into this cocoon-like *konak* (mansion) perched on the hilltop and you may never feel like leaving again. Staying at this peach of a place is arguably the best hotel experience you'll have in southeastern Anatolia. The seven rooms are impeccable, and the common areas are attractively decked out, with judiciously positioned artefacts. It's full of nooks and crannies, and no two rooms are identical. Homemade meals come in for warm praise and can be served on the rooftop terrace, with lovely views over Savur. Throw in the warm welcome of the Öztürk family, and you have a winner. Simply *cennet* (paradise).

the perfect place to decompress. The atmosphere is charmingly lethargic and the setting is enchanting, with honey-coloured old houses that are huddled beneath a citadel, lots of greenery and a gushing river running in the valley. Another pull is the warm welcome you'll receive.

The time to visit is now, before this haven of serenity is let out of the bag and becomes the new Mardin, a place on everyone's itinerary.

Should you decide to stay overnight, there's the wonderful Hacı Abdullah Bey Konagü (see boxed text, opposite), which is reason enough to come here. If you want to eat out, the **Perili Bahçe – Alabalık Tesisi** (☎ 0482-571 2832; Gazi Mahallesi; mains €3-4; ☽ 8am-9pm), off the Mardin road, is a killer, with a large open-air area overlooking the gushing river and shade in abundance. As the cook puts it, '*herşey natural*' (everything is natural here) – we agree. Relish fresh trout, salads, potatoes or *içli köfte* and sluice it all down with a glass of *kıllıt* (local wine) or rakı. So cool!

Reaching Savur by public transport is a doddle. From Mardin there are regular minibus services (€2, one hour).

MIDYAT

☎ 0482 / pop 61,600

About 65km east of Mardin lies sprawling Midyat, with a drab new section, Estel, linked by 3km of potholed Hükümet Caddesi to the inviting old town. Midyat has lots of potential but is not as touristy as Mardin, mostly because it lacks Mardin's hillside setting. It's definitely worth a visit nonetheless.

The centrepiece of the old part of town is merely a traffic roundabout. Close by, **honey-coloured houses** are tucked away behind a row of jewellery shops. Here, the alleyways are lined with houses whose demure doorways open onto huge courtyards surrounded by intricately carved walls, windows and recesses. Watch out for the many curved *fırın* (ovens) in the streets shared by neighbouring families.

Like that of Mardin, Midyat's Christian population suffered in the early 20th century and during the last few decades, and much of the community has emigrated. There are nine Syrian Orthodox **churches** still in use in the town, though only four regularly hold services. Although you can see the steeples, it's hard to find the churches in the maze of streets so the best option is to accept one of the local guides, who are likely to be hot on your heels.

There are a couple of hotels and the modern **Saray Lokantası** (☎ 462 3436; Mardin Caddesi; mains €2-3; ☽ 10am-10pm) with good-value meals, in new Midyat where the Mardin minibuses first stop. Close by, the **Hotel Demirdağ** (☎ 462 2000; fax 462 1482; Mardin Caddesi; s/d €15/23; ☒) is the best option in town and has colourful, decent-value rooms.

Rattly minibuses regularly ply the bumpy route from outside the Saray Lokantası to old Midyat to save you the charmless walk. Most services leave from old Midyat, some 100m north of the roundabout along the road to

---

WELCOME TO IRAQ *Tony Wheeler*

At the Habur border post, we'd spent over an hour wandering from office to office in the pouring rain. At one of them my taxi driver reluctantly slipped a banknote into the pages of my passport before handing it over the counter. It seemed to work; the passport came back within minutes with a stamp inside. I was finally out of Turkey. We drove over the bridge and stopped in a car park just beyond the sign announcing: 'Welcome to Iraq'.

Crazy? Suicidal? No. Most of Iraq may be a death zone, but the northern region, which local Kurds hope to establish as an autonomous state of Kurdistan, has been fairly safe and it's easy to enter via the Habur border crossing, south of Cizre and Silopi. Just don't mention the name 'Kurdistan' to Turks; on the Turkish side of the border 'Iraq' is the diplomatically safe place to talk about.

In Iraq, I took a taxi on to Zakho and then to Dohuk where I spent the night. From there I explored north to the mountain town of Amadiya and then continued east to Arbil (aka Erbil or Hawler), which huddles around a magnificent hilltop citadel. Although I travelled on to Sulaymaniyah, the other major city in the region, I didn't head further south to Iraq's ancient centres such as Nineveh, Nimrud or Ur.

Well, I'm not completely mad.

Batman. Minibuses from here leave at least hourly for Hasankeyf and Batman (€3, 1½ hours, 82km) and Mardin (€3, 1¼ hours). Minibuses for Cizre leave from just south of the roundabout on the Cizre road.

Minibuses from Mardin will pass through the new town, then drop you off at the roundabout in the old town. You could easily base yourself in Midyat and make a day trip to Mardin or Hasankeyf.

AROUND MİDYAT

Morgabriel

About 18km east of Midyat, **Morgabriel (Deyrul Umur) Monastery** (9-11.30am & 1-4.30pm) rises like a mirage from its desert-like surroundings. Though much restored, the monastery dates back to AD 397. St Gabriel, the namesake of the monastery, is buried here – the sand beside his tomb is said to cure illness. You'll see various frescoes and the immense ancient dome built by Theodora, wife of Byzantine emperor Justinian, and a more recent bell tower.

Morgabriel is home to the archbishop of Tür Abdin (Mountain of the Servants of God), the surrounding plateau. These days he presides over a much diminished flock of around 80 people, the majority students. Fortunately, life for the residents seems to be looking up after the recent troubles, and there should be no problem about visiting.

You could ask here about visiting some of the other churches in the region, such as the Meryem Ana Kilisesi at Anıttepe (Hah).

To get to the monastery from Midyat take a minibus (€2) heading along the Cizre road and ask to be dropped at the signposted road junction, from where it's a 2.5km walk uphill to the gate. Start early in the morning as minibuses become increasingly difficult to find as the day wears on. If you don't feel like walking you can charter one of the minibuses for about €20 return, including waiting time.

Hasankeyf

☎ 0488 / pop 5500

Hasankeyf, a gorgeous honey-coloured village clinging to the rocks of a gorge above the Tigris River, is a sort of Cappadocia in miniature where some people still live a troglodyte lifestyle. It's a definite must-see.

SIGHTS

Arriving in Hasankeyf from Batman, you'll see on the right-hand side of the road the conical **Zeynel Bey Türbesi**, isolated in a field near the river. This turquoise-tiled tomb was built in the mid-15th century for Zeynel, son of the Akkoyunlu governor, and it's a rare survivor from this period.

A modern bridge now spans the Tigris, but as you cross you'll see, to the right, the broken arches and pylons of the **Eski Köprüsü** (Old Bridge), their size giving some idea of the importance of Hasankeyf in the period immediately before the arrival of the Ottomans.

Across the bridge a sign to the right points to the **Kale** (Fortress) and **Mağaralar** (Caves). As you walk along the road you'll see the **El-Rizk Cami** (1409), sporting a beautiful, slender minaret similar to those in Mardin and topped with a stork's nest. Just past the mosque, the road forks. The right fork leads down to the banks of the river with a great wall of rock soaring up on the left. The left fork cuts through a rocky defile, the rockfaces pitted with caves. Take the slippery stone steps leading up on the right to the castle.

You quickly come to the finely decorated main gate to the castle. This strategic site has been occupied since Byzantine times, but most of the relics you see today were built during the reign of the 14th-century Ayyubids.

HASANKEYF UNDER THREAT

Hasankeyf is a gem of a place, but has the cloud of a giant engineering project hanging over it. Despite its beauty and history, the town is slated to vanish beneath the waters of the İlisu Dam, part of the GAP project – see the boxed text, p608. The proposed dam will flood a region from Batman to Midyat, drowning this historic site and several other archaeological treasures, and displacing over 37 villages. In 2002, several foreign investors pulled out amid the controversy provoked by the dam, but it seems that the works won't be delayed indefinitely, and the construction works should start sooner or later, in spite of mounting local resistance. The mayor of Hasankeyf tries to gain international support to protect the sites and would like to take legal action, but the battle is virtually almost lost. So a visit to Hasankeyf is a must. Now!

Beyond the gate are caves, which youthful guides will describe as shops and houses. At the top of the rock you face the ruins of the 14th-century **Küçük Saray** (Small Palace), with pots built into the ceiling and walls for sound insulation and superb views over the river.

You will then be led past a small **mosque**, which was obviously once a Byzantine church, to the **Büyük Saray** (Big Palace), with a creepy gaol underneath, right by a tower teetering on the edge of the cliff. It was probably built as a watchtower. The 14th-century **Ulu Cami** was built on the site of a church.

SLEEPING & EATING

There's only one shut-eye option in Hasankeyf. If it's full, you can base yourself in Batman, about 35km to the north. Batman is a charmless modern town.

Hasankeyf Motel (☎ 381 2005; Dicle Sokak; s/d €9/17) By the Tigris bridge, this no-nonsense motel offers unadorned rooms with shared bathrooms. Some rooms overlook the river. No towels are provided, and no breakfast is served. There are only seven rooms, so it's wise to book ahead.

Few things could be more pleasurable than lunching where a series of *çardaks* (leafy-roofed shelters) have been set up along the riverbank. Tables stand in the river, so while you tuck into your fish you can soak your lower limbs in the icy clear water of the Tigris. A normal meal of grilled meat with salad and a cold drink is unlikely to come to more than €4. Try the following options.

Yolgeçen Hanı (☎ 381 2287; Dicle Kıyısı; mains €2-5; ☾ 8am-10pm) One of the most atmospheric restaurants, with a series of rock-hewn dining rooms overlooking the river. Sit on lumpy cushions, hoe into a kebap or a grilled fish, knock it all down with a glass of rakı (yes, it's licensed!) and you should depart happy and buzzing.

Hasankeyf Fırınlı Et Lokantası (☎ 381 2270; mains €1-3; ☾ 8am-10pm) Near the Hasankeyf Motel, this unpretentious yet welcoming joint dishes up fresh pide.

Has Bahçe (☎ 381 2609; Dicle Sokak; mains €2-4; ☾ 8am-10pm) Along the river (but no views to speak of), this eatery occupies a shady garden and serves up fresh fish, chicken and lamb.

GETTING THERE & AWAY

Frequent minibuses run from Batman to Midyat, transiting Hasankeyf (€2, 40 minutes, 37km). There's also a daily service to Van (€12, 310km).

ŞIRNAK

Şirnak boasts a stunning location, with jagged mountains as a backdrop. There's not much to do, but it's a convenient staging post if you plan to explore the deep southeast. From there, you can take the long but highly scenic haul to Hakkari in the one daily minibus (€9, 181km, five to six hours depending on waits at checkpoints). The landscape is sublime, with a mix of canyons, passes, gorges and mountains; at times the road skirts the border with neighbouring Iraq.

Although the accommodation scene is nothing to write home about, you can stay overnight there. The best we can say about the **Hotel Menekşe** (☎ 0486-216 1902; Uludere Caddesi; s/d €20/30) is that it's an acceptable choice despite its greyish exterior, peeling walls and battered carpets. At least it has clean sheets and good views at the back. If it's full, try the nearby **Otel Murat** (☎ 0486-216 2857; Uludere Caddesi; r with/without bathroom €17/8), which features hanky-sized rooms and mattresses that sink like hammocks, but at this price we're not complaining. The gloomy **Hotel Ilkar** (☎ 0486-216 6464; Uludere Caddesi; s/d €14/25), frequented by prostitutes, is best avoided.

If you want to fill your grumbling belly at wallet-friendly prices, head to the busy **Diyarbakır Faysal Ustanin Evi** (Cumhuriyet Caddesi; mains €2-3; ☾ 8am-10pm), opposite the Ilkar, which tosses up generous plates of meat and mezes. It features a cosy Turkish corner at the back. There's even a pleasant **Aile Çay Bahçesi** (Aile Tea Garden; Cumhuriyet Caddesi; ☾ dawn-dusk) right in the centre. It's great for relaxing over a cuppa while soaking up the lovely views over the mountains.

From Şirnak onward to the west, there are at least two daily minibuses to Siirt (€5, two hours, 96km) and two bus services to Diyarbakır (€9, five hours, 340km). You can stay overnight in Siirt, but the city is quite dull; **Otel Erdef** (☎ 0484-223 1081; Cumhuriyet Caddesi; s/d €25/42) is serviceable but pricey for what you get.

BITLIS

☎ 0434 / pop 220,400
Bitlis has lopsided charm. While the city centre is an obvious nomination for the muddiest-pavements-in-the-Van-area award,

overall it's a beguiling city with a smorgasbord of monuments that testify to rich ancient origins. The contrast with neighbouring Tatvan is striking. While modern Tatvan boasts an orderly street plan, Bitlis is a somewhat chaotic old town squeezed into the narrow valley of a stream. Women travellers, come prepared: Bitlis feels overwhelmingly male.

A **castle** dominates the town, and two ancient bridges span the stream. Make a beeline for the **Ulu Cami**, which was built in 1126, while the **Şerefiye Camii** dates from the 16th century. Other must-sees include the splendid **İhlasiye Medrese** (Quranic school), the most significant building in Bitlis, and the **Gökmeydan Camii**, which has a detached minaret.

The main problem in Bitlis is the lack of facilities, which means you'll have to base yourself in Tatvan. Regular minibuses travel from Tatvan to Bitlis (€2, 30 minutes).

TATVAN

☎ 0434 / pop 54,000

While Tatvan doesn't set the heart aflutter, it's ideally positioned if you plan a trip to spectacular Nemrut Dağı (Mt Nemrut; opposite) – not to be confused with the higher-profile, iconic and volcanic (inactive) Nemrut Dağı south of Malatya, Ahlat (opposite) and Bitlis (p633). Several kilometres long and just a few blocks wide, it is not much to look at, but its setting on the shores of Lake Van (backed by bare mountains streaked with snow) is magnificent. It is also the western port for Lake Van steamers.

Information

Everything you'll need (hotels, restaurants, banks, the PTT and the bus company offices) huddles together in the town centre.

Sleeping & Eating

Tatvan has a handful of hotels that are well used to housing tourists.

Öz Gaziantep Baklavacısı (☎ 827 7077; Cumhuriyet Caddesi; pastries €0.50-1; 🕑 8am-8pm) Adjoining the Şelale, this is the perfect place to finish your meal off with a triangle of flaky baklava.

Hotel Üstün (☎ 827 9014; Hal Caddesi; s/d €7/14) The family-run Üstün shows signs of wear and tear (read: poo-brown carpets, drab-looking façade, mattresses as comfortable as Thanksgiving's mashed potatoes), but it's tidy and secure, the sheets are immaculate, and there's a functional shower in each room (but the toilets are shared). It's down the side street running by the PTT.

Hotel Dilek (☎ 827 1516; Yeni Çarşı; s/d €14/23) The Dilek stands its ground with spruce, colourful (if a tad compact) rooms with tiled bathrooms and a smart rooftop breakfast room. Pity about the meagre breakfast, though. It's in a street running parallel to the main drag.

Tatvan Kardelen (☎ 825 9500; Belediye Yanı; s/d €25/45) This is usually where tour groups bunk down when in town, which is enough to recommend this sharp-edged concrete lump next to the *belediye*. It features spacious and fastidiously clean rooms. If only the migraine-inducing corridors were smartened up!

Şelale Izgara Salonu (☎ 827 9767; Cumhuriyet Caddesi; mains €2-3; 🕑 11am-10pm) This very well-regarded restaurant evinces a vague sense of style, with yellowish walls adorned with a couple of knick-knacks. It serves kebaps and ready-made meals that will have you walking out belly-first.

Kaşı Beyaz Ocakbaşı (☎ 827 6996; PTT Yanı; mains €3-5; 🕑 10am-10pm) Bona-fide carnivores should head straight to this buzzing eatery, not far from the Hotel Dilek. Meat is grilled to perfection on a big *ocak* (grill) on the ground floor. If you've had your fill of meat dishes, pide is also available.

Şimşek Lokantası (☎ 827 1513; Cumhuriyet Caddesi; mains €3-5; 🕑 10am-10pm) The wood-panelled interior is inviting and the food doesn't disappoint. Don't expect newfangled concoctions – just the standard kebaps.

Getting There & Away

If you're heading to Van, you can take the ferry that crosses the lake twice a day (€3 per person, about four hours). It doesn't have a fixed schedule, though. Buses to Van run round the southern shore of the lake (€6, 2½ hours, 156km).

Minibuses to Ahlat (€2, 30 minutes) and Adilcevaz (€3.50, one hour) leave every hour or so from PTT Caddesi, beside Türk Telekom and the PTT. The minibus stand for Bitlis (€2, 30 minutes) is a bit further up the street.

LAKE VAN (VAN GÖLÜ)

☎ 0432

Lake Van (Van Gölü) is eastern Anatolia's *pièce de résistance*. After the rigours of central Anatolia, this vast expanse of water surrounded by snowcapped mountains sounds deceptively like a holy grail for those in search of beaches and watersport activities, but it's not. Lake Van has great potential for activities, but nothing has been really developed yet and infrastructure is lacking. Water sports? Lakeside resorts? Dream on! But at least this means it's scenic and virtually untouched. A circumnavigation around its shores reveals plenty of surprises.

By far the most conspicuous feature on the map of southeastern Turkey, this 3750-sq-km lake was formed when a volcano (Nemrut Dağı – not to be confused with the one with the statues) north of Tatvan blocked its natural outflow.

North Shore

If anything the journey around the north shore of Lake Van from Tatvan to Van, with first Nemrut Dağı (Mt Nemrut) and then Süphan Dağı (Mt Süphan) looming beside the road, is more beautiful than going around the south shore.

The big bus companies take the shortest route around the south of the lake from Tatvan to Van. If you want to travel around the north shore you'll probably have to break your journey. Regular minibuses run from beside Türk Telekom and the PTT in Tatvan to Ahlat (€2, 30 minutes) and Adilcevaz (€3). From Adilcevaz, there are five direct buses to Van (€6, 2½ hours), but the last one departs at 2.30pm – make sure you start out early in the day.

NEMRUT DAĞI (MT NEMRUT)

This Nemrut Dağı (2935m) rising to the north of Tatvan is an inactive volcano with five crater lakes on its summit – not to be confused with the more famous Nemrut Dağı (Mt Nemrut, topped with the giant heads) near Kahta.

A trip up this Nemrut Dağı is also an unforgettable experience, not least for the fine views back over Lake Van. On the summit the scenery is almost completely unspoilt. In spring and early summer the lower slopes of the mountain are a sea of sweet-smelling wild flowers. Midweek, the only company you're likely to have is the shepherds with their flocks (and dogs) and the hoopoes, nuthatches, skylarks and other birds. A tip: follow the dirt road that leads down to the lake and find your own picnic area. Memorable!

You can visit Nemrut only from around mid-May to the end of October. At other times the summit is under metres of snow.

Several ski lifts were being set up on the outside slopes when we visited. Nemrut Dağı could well become another ski resort in eastern Anatolia in the near future. Stay tuned.

It's not easy to get to Nemrut, as there are no regular services from Tatvan. In high season, you could try to hitch a ride. Your best bet is to ask the staff at your hotel in Tatvan for advice or hire a taxi. Expect to pay about €40 return.

With your own transport, leave Tatvan by the road around the lake and then turn left towards Bitlis; about 300m further, turn right following a sign saying 'Nemrut 13km'. The road is rough but passable in an ordinary car except in wet weather. From the summit you can follow the dirt road that winds down into the crater to the lake shore – another 6km.

AHLAT

A further 42km along the lake shore is the small town of Ahlat, famous for its splendid Seljuk Turkish tombs and graveyard. Don't overlook this largely underrated site, and allow at least one hour to visit the sights.

Founded during the reign of Caliph Omar (AD 581–644), Ahlat became a Seljuk stronghold in the 1060s. When the Seljuk sultan Alp Arslan rode out to meet the Byzantine emperor Romanus Diogenes in battle on the field of Manzikert, Ahlat was his base.

Later, Ahlat had an extraordinarily eventful history even for Anatolia, with emir (tribal leader) defeating prince and king driving out emir; hence, perhaps, the fame of its cemeteries.

Just west of Ahlat you'll see the overgrown polygonal 13th-century tomb, **Usta Şağirt Kümbeti** (Ulu Kümbeti), 300m off the highway and set in the midst of a field near some houses and a new mosque. It's the largest Seljuk tomb in the area.

A bit further along the highway on the left is a little museum, and behind it a vast unique **Seljuk cemetery** (Selçuk Mezarlığı), with stele-like headstones of lichen-covered grey or red volcanic tuff with intricate web patterns and bands of Kufic lettering. It's thought that Ahlat stonemasons were employed on other great stoneworking projects, such as the decoration of the great mosque at Divriği, near Sivas.

Over the centuries earthquakes, wind and water have set the stones at all angles, so they stand out like broken teeth – a striking sight with spectacular Nemrut Dağı as a backdrop. Most stones have a crow as sentinel, and tortoises cruise the ruins.

On the northeastern side of the graveyard is the beautiful and unusual **Bayındır Kümbeti ve Camii** (Bayındır Tomb & Mosque, 1477), with a colonnaded porch and its own *mihrab* (niche indicating the direction of Mecca).

The small **museum** (admission €1.25; ⏰ 8am-noon & 1-5pm) has a reasonable collection including Urartian bronze belts and needles as well as some Byzantine glass-bead necklaces.

Other sites in Ahlat, worth exploring if you have the time, include the **Çifte Kümbet** (Twin Tombs), about 2km from the museum towards the town centre, and the **Ahlat Sahil Kalesi** (Ahlat Lakeside Fortress), south of the Çifte Kümbet, built during the reign of Süleyman the Magnificent. The poplars here are knotted with crows' nests.

It's easy enough to make a half-day trip to Ahlat from Tatvan. Dolmuşes leave for Ahlat (€2, 30 minutes) from beside Türk Telekom and the PTT. Make sure you ask to be let off at the museum on the western outskirts of Ahlat, or you'll have to leg it back from the town centre.

ADİLCEVAZ

About 25km east of Ahlat is the town of Adilcevaz, once a Urartian town but now dominated by a great Seljuk Turkish fortress, the **Kef Kalesi**, and the even greater bulk of **Süphan Dağı** (Mt Süphan, 4434m). It's worth pausing here if you're travelling by car.

Snowmelt from the year-round snowfields on Mt Süphan flows down to Adilcevaz, making its surroundings lush and fertile. As you enter the town along the shore, the highway passes the nice little **Ulu Camii**, built in the 13th century and still used for daily prayer. Now that life in the southeast is slowly returning to normal, it is once again possible to climb Mt Süphan in summer.

If you get stuck, there are a couple of places to stay in Adilcevaz, including **Otel Park** (☎ 311 4150; s/d €23/39) on the waterfront, not far from the otogar. It's a grim building, but the rooms are more colourful and well kept.

South Shore

Travelling south around the lake between Tatvan and Van, the scenery is beautiful, but there's little reason to stop except at a point 5km west of Gevaş, where the 10th-century Church of the Holy Cross at Akdamar is a glorious must.

EDREMİT

About 15km west of Van you'll pass through Edremit, a small lakeside settlement with the feel of a seaside resort: all lilos, beach balls and ice cream.

GEVAŞ

Like Ahlat on the north shore, Gevaş has a cemetery full of tombstones dating from the 14th to 17th centuries. Notable is the polygonal **Halime Hatun Türbesi**, built in 1358 for a female member of the Karakoyunlu dynasty.

AKDAMAR

One of the marvels of Armenian architecture is **Akdamar Kilisesi** (Church of the Holy Cross). It's perched on an island 3km out in the lake, and motorboats ferry sightseers back and forth. Sadly, restoration works were under way when we visited, and the scenery was a bit marred by scaffolding.

In AD 921 Gagik Artzruni, King of Vaspurkan, built a palace, church and monastery on the island. Little remains of the palace and monastery, but the church walls are in superb condition and the wonderful relief carvings are among the masterworks of Armenian art. If you're familiar with biblical stories, you'll immediately recognise Adam and Eve, Jonah and the Whale (with the head of a dog), David and Goliath, Abraham about to sacrifice Isaac, Daniel in the Lions' Den, Samson etc. There are some frescoes inside the church.

Akdamar island is also an ideal spot for a picnic.

North of Akdamar another even more isolated and forgotten 11th-century Armenian church stands on the island of **Çarpanak**, popular with bird-watchers.

ALTINSAÇ KILISESI

Not surprisingly, the well-publicised, easily accessible Akdamar Kilisesi has overshadowed the southern shore's other highlights, and Altınsaç Kilisesi is no exception. Another relatively well-preserved Armenian church, it's perched on a mound overlooking the lake. This is a pearl of a site; if you have your own wheels, be sure to squeeze it into your itinerary. The word is not out, and you'll have the whole place to yourself.

From Akdamar, drive about 11km towards Tatvan until you reach a junction. Turn right onto the road marked for Altınsaç. After 3km the asphalt road ends and becomes a gravel road. The road skirts the shore of the lake for another 14km, until you reach the village of Altınsaç. On a clear day this a wonderfully scenic drive, with breathtaking views over the shimmering waters of the lake and the undulating hills of the steppe. From the village it's another 2km to the church, which is visible from some distance – an awesome vision.

SLEEPING & EATING

Although there are several basic camping grounds at Edremit, the best bet is the **Akdamar Camping ve Restaurant** (☎ 216 1505; camp sites per person €1; mains €2-5; ☼ Apr-Sep) immediately opposite the ferry departure point for Akdamar island. The camping ground here is elevated, with fine views of the lake. The restaurant has a terrace with lake views and an indoor area in case of bad weather; the fish is fresh. Another speciality is the *kürt tavası* (meat, tomato and pepper cooked in a clay pot).

Just east of Edremit, along the main road, you'll find a couple of midrange hotels by the water, including the charmless but well-equipped **Merit Şahmaran** (☎ 214 3479; fax 612 2420; s/d €43/60; ☒), 12km from Van.

GETTING THERE & AWAY

Minibuses run the 44km from near Beş Yol in Van to Akdamar harbour for €1 during high season. At other times, there's an hourly minibus to Gevaş (€1). If you want to be dropped at the boat dock 5km further on, negotiate the price with the driver (about €6). Alternatively, catch a minibus heading to Tatvan and ask to be let off at Akdamar harbour. Make sure you're out on the highway flagging a bus back to Van by 4pm, as soon afterwards the traffic dries up and buses may be full.

Boats to the island run as and when traffic warrants it (minimum 10 people). Provided others are there to share the cost, a return ticket for the 20-minute voyage and admission to the island costs €3. Getting to Çarpanak is harder. The boatmen are likely to want €160 before they'll consider the 2½-hour voyage.

VAN

☎ 0432 / pop 391,000 / elevation 1727m

In the mood for some sophistication? Well, you have come to the right place. It usually comes as a surprise to many travellers to discover that Van is by far the most engaging and liberal urban centre in eastern Anatolia. It feels different from other metropolises in the east, not least because of its sizeable student population. Don't expect too much, though: it's certainly not hedonistic (you're not in Marmaris, baby), but there's a fluid, lively energy to the city and a true *joie de vivre*, as testified by the daily *passegiatta* (promenade). As happens in Italy, the whole town promenades up and down Cumhuriyet Caddesi to window-shop, catch up with friends, see what's new, and generally take things easy. If you want to see young couples walking hand in hand on the main drag or flirting in the pastry shops, this is your chance. The place offers a refreshing change, particularly if you have travelled from rigorous Şanlıurfa or Hakkari.

Beautifully positioned near the eponymous lake, Van doesn't make the most of its enticing location, with few activities on offer. Forget the lake, and focus on the striking monuments, including Van Kalesi (Van Castle or the Rock of Van), which is a true pleasure.

Van is also an ideal base to journey around the lake or explore the ancient Urartian city at Çavuştepe, the craggy mountain fortress of Hoşap and the remote village of Bahçesaray.

History

The kingdom of Urartu, the biblical Ararat, flourished from the 13th to the 7th centuries BC. Its capital was on the outskirts of present-day Van. The Urartians borrowed much of their culture, including cuneiform writing, from the neighbouring Assyrians with whom they were more or less permanently at war. The powerful Assyrians never subdued the Urartians, but when several waves of Cimmerians, Scythians and Medes swept into Urartu and joined in the battle, the kingdom met its downfall.

Later the region was resettled by a people whom the Persians called Armenians. By the 6th century BC it was governed by Persian and Median satraps.

In the 8th century AD, Arab armies flooded through from the south, forcing the Armenian prince to take refuge on Akdamar island. Unable to fend off the Arabs, he agreed to pay tribute to the caliph. When the Arabs retreated, the Byzantines and Persians took their place, and overlordship of Armenia seesawed

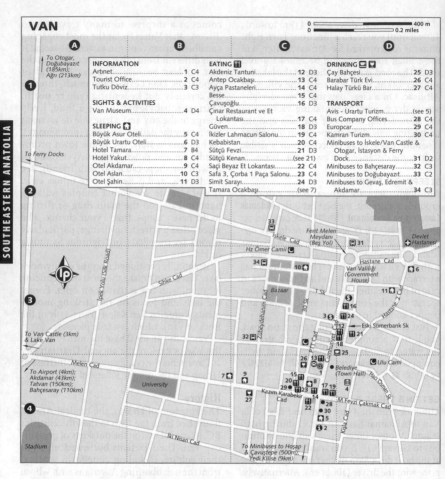

VAN

0 — 400 m
0 — 0.2 miles

INFORMATION
Artınet......................................1 C4
Tourist Office..........................2 C4
Tutku Döviz.............................3 C3

SIGHTS & ACTIVITIES
Van Museum............................4 D4

SLEEPING
Büyük Asur Oteli.....................5 C4
Büyük Urartu Oteli..................6 D3
Hotel Tamara...........................7 B4
Hotel Yakut.............................8 C4
Otel Akdamar..........................9 C4
Otel Aslan..............................10 C4
Otel Şahin..............................11 D3

EATING
Akdeniz Tantuni.....................12 D3
Antep Ocakbaşı......................13 C4
Ayça Pastaneleri....................14 C4
Besse.....................................15 C4
Çavuşoğlu..............................16 D3
Çinar Restaurant ve Et
    Lokantası............................17 C4
Güven....................................18 D3
İkizler Lahmacun Salonu........19 C4
Kebabistan............................20 C4
Sütçü Fevzi............................21 D3
Sütçü Kenan....................(see 21)
Saçı Beyaz Et Lokantası.........22 C4
Safa 3, Çorba 1 Paça Salonu....23 C4
Simit Sarayı...........................24 D3
Tamara Ocakbaşı.............(see 7)

DRINKING
Çay Bahçesi...........................25 D3
Barabar Türk Evi....................26 C4
Halay Türkü Bar.....................27 C4

TRANSPORT
Avis - Urartu Turizm.........(see 5)
Bus Company Offices............28 C4
Europcar................................29 C4
Kamran Turizm......................30 C4
Minibuses to İskele/Van Castle &
    Otogar, İstasyon & Ferry
    Dock..................................31 D2
Minibuses to Bahçesaray........32 C3
Minibuses to Doğubayazıt......33 C2
Minibuses to Gevaş, Edremit &
    Akdamar............................34 C3

between them as one or the other gained military advantage.

After defeating the Byzantines in 1071 at Manzikert, north of Lake Van, the Seljuk Turks marched on, with a flood of Turkoman nomads in tow, to found the sultanate of Rum, based in Konya. The domination of eastern Anatolia by Turkish emirs followed and continued until the coming of the Ottomans in 1468.

During WWI, Armenian guerrilla bands intent on founding an independent Armenian state collaborated with the Russians to defeat the Ottoman armies in Turkey's east. From then on the Armenians, formerly loyal subjects of the sultan, were viewed by the Turks as traitors. Bitter fighting between Turkish and Kurdish forces

on the one side and Armenian and Russian forces on the other brought devastation to the entire region and to Van. For more about this contentious period, see the boxed text, p40.

The Ottomans destroyed the old city of Van (near Van Kalesi) before the Russians occupied it in 1915. Ottoman forces counterattacked but were unable to drive the invaders out, and Van remained under Russian occupation until the armistice of 1917. After the founding of the Turkish Republic, a new planned city of Van was built 4km east of the old site.

Orientation

Everything you'll need (hotels, restaurants, banks, internet cafés, the PTT and the bus company offices) lie on or around Cumhuriyet Caddesi, the main commercial street.

The city's otogar is on the northwestern outskirts, and most bus companies operate *servises* there from the town centre. The main train station is northwest of the centre near the otogar, with another station, İskele İstasyonu, several kilometres to the northwest on the lake shore.

Tours to nearby areas can be organised by Büyük Asur Oteli (see p640).

Information

Banks with ATMs are easily found on Cumhuriyet Caddesi, as are internet cafés.

Artınet (Cumhuriyet Caddesi; per hr €0.60; ☾ 8am-11pm) A modern outlet with flat screens. It's across the street from the *belediye*.

Tourist office (☎ 216 2530; Cumhuriyet Caddesi; ☾ 8.30am-noon & 1-5.30pm Mon-Fri) Hands out some brochures on the Van area.

Tutku Döviz (☎ 214 1847; Cumhuriyet Caddesi; ☾ 8am-6.30pm Mon-Sat) Exchange office.

Sights

VAN CASTLE (VAN KALESİ)

Nothing is quite so impressive in Van as the **Van Castle** (Van Kalesi, Rock of Van; admission €1.25, car parking €1; ☾ 9am-dusk), which dominates the view of the city. About 3km west of the city centre, it's a wonderful place to come for a picnic.

Just past the spot where the minibus drops you, on the northern side of the rock, is a modern mosque and the **tomb** of Abdurrahman Gazi, a Muslim holy man. It's frequently visited by pilgrims including infertile women who are thought to be helped by coming here. Further on, at the northwestern corner, you'll reach the ticket office, then the car park, where there are toilets and a tea garden.

A stairway from the car park leads up the rock. Once you've reached the summit, the old city reveals itself like Pandora's box. Over towards the southern face of the rock you'll see an iron gateway blocking off a lengthy **cuneiform inscription**. This recounts the high points of King Argishti I's reign (786–764 BC). There are also several rock-cut **funeral chambers**, including King Argishti's.

Continue up to the top of the rock, where you can see the fortifications, including the **Sardur Burcu** (Sardur Tower, 840–830 BC) with several cuneiform inscriptions in Assyrian praising the Urartian King Sardur I.

If you look down to the south of the rock, you'll see a flat space broken up by the grass-covered foundations of numerous buildings. This was the site of Tushpa, an Urartian city that flourished almost 3000 years ago, although the foundations you see are those of the **old city** of Van, destroyed during the upheavals of WWI. Time is well spent walking around the base of the rock afterwards and inspecting these ruins, preferably taking someone to guide you for safety and avoid potential hassles from kids. Of the Seljuk **Ulu Cami** only a broken brick minaret remains, but the **Hüsrev Paşa Külliyesi**, dating back to 1567, has been restored and you may be able to get inside to see the fine brick dome and fragmentary murals. If not, you can still inspect the delicate *kümbet* (tomb) attached. The nearby **Kaya Çelebi Camii** (1662) has a similarly striped minaret but is still in use and likely to be locked except at prayer times.

To get to Van Kalesi take a 'Kale' minibus from Beş Yol (Ferit Melen Meydani; €0.40), which will drop you at the eastern edge of the rock. Go right around the base of Van Kalesi to the entrance at the northwestern end. Women should avoid visiting on their own – they may find themselves hassled as they walk to the entrance.

VAN MUSEUM

The small **Van Museum** (Van Müzesi; Kışla Caddesi; admission €1.30; ☾ 8am-noon & 1-5pm Tue-Sun) boasts an outstanding collection of Urartian exhibits. The Urartian gold jewellery is the highlight, but the bronze belts, helmets, horse armour and terracotta figures are also well worth seeing.

The ethnographic exhibits upstairs include local Kurdish and Turkoman kilims and a carpeted sitting area, such as is found in village houses. The Genocide Section is a piece of one-sided propaganda displaying the contents of graves left from the massacres of Turks and Kurds by Armenians at Çavuşoğlu and Zeve.

The museum has a good bookshop with plenty of foreign-language titles about the region.

Sleeping

Van has a decent range of accommodation, though inspiration can be hard to find (please someone – open a boutique hotel!) and it's a wee bit more expensive than elsewhere in eastern Turkey. Most hotels are on or around the main drag, making comparisons relatively easy.

BUDGET

Otel Aslan (☎ 216 2469; Özel İdare İş Merkezi Karşısı; s/d €6-9/9-12) A key player on the Van budget accommodation scene, this hotel-cum-hostel features shoebox-sized colourful rooms with double-glazed windows. And the floor of the rooms is tiled – no brownish, whiffy carpet! Cheaper rooms share toilets and showers, which can be a drag but, in this location for this price, you won't hear anyone complaining. No breakfast is served.

Büyük Asur Oteli (☎ 216 8792; fax 216 9461; Cumhuriyet Caddesi, Turizm Sokak; s/d €20/34; P) This hotel may not be the cheapest option in town, but it's without doubt the most reliable for travellers. Ignore the Soviet-style façade – rooms are freshly painted and come complete with fresh linen, back-friendly beds, TV and prim bathroom. It's also noteworthy for its prime location and its cosy lobby with floor cushions you can sink into with a post-sightseeing beer at hand. The manager, Remzi Bozbay, speaks very good English and is a mine of local information. The hotel can also organise tours to Doğubayazıt, Akdamar Island, Hoşap Castle and other local attractions.

If you have no luck scoring a room at the Aslan or at the Büyük, check out the aging but central **Hotel Yakut** (☎ 214 2832; fax 216 6351; PTT Caddesi; s/d €17/23; P) or the unexciting but acceptable **Otel Şahin** (☎ 216 3062; fax 216 3064; İrfan Baştuğ Caddesi; s/d €14/25; P).

MIDRANGE

Otel Akdamar (☎ 214 9923; fax 212 0868; Kazım Karabekir Caddesi; s/d €29/38; P 🖵) Midrange hotels are thin on the ground, so the Akdamar is destined to do well. Although it has a certain 'could be anywhere' sensibility in its décor and standards, it's well organised and its very central location is a gem, with all the restaurants and pastry shops within easy reach. Amenities are solid, and the bathrooms are clean-smelling. It caters mainly to business travellers. Wi-fi is available.

Büyük Urartu Oteli (☎ 212 0660; www.buyukurartu otel.com; Hastane 2 Caddesi; s/d €37/50; P 🛋) A reassuring choice with no surprises (good or bad) up its sleeves. The monolithic Urartu's primary clientele are business travellers and tour groups, and while all rooms meet modern standards, the hulking great façade is not

too pretty. Still, you don't have to look at that from the inside, and the full array of amenities, including a sauna, rooftop restaurant and a pool, offers ample compensation.

Hotel Tamara (☎ 214 3295; Yüzbaşıoğlu Sokak; s/d €37/62; P 🖵) The newest kid on the block, the ambitious Tamara features smart rooms with all mod cons, and there's not a speck of dirt to be found. It has two restaurants, a bar, a *hamam* and wi-fi access. It caters mainly to businesspeople. Cumhuriyet Caddesi is a wiggle away.

Eating

Simit Sarayı (Cumhuriyet Caddesi; simits €0.60; 😊 8am-8pm) *Simit, simit, simit*, get us our *simit* fix! If you can't find this bustling *simit* shop on the main drag you've either lost your eyesight or your sense of smell.

Safa 3, Çorba 1 Paça Salonu (☎ 215 8121; Kazım Karabekir Caddesi; soups €1; 😊 24hr) If Saçi Beyaz is too trendy for your taste, walk down Kazım Karabekir Caddesi to this quirky little restaurant, which serves soups and other goodies round the clock. If you want to impress your peers (and locals), check out the supposedly palate-pleasing *kelle* (mutton's head) – good luck! The lentil soup, though a bit spicy for the uninitiated, takes you into more traditional culinary territory.

Ayça Pastaneleri (☎ 216 0081; Kazım Karabekir Caddesi; snacks €1-2; 😊 8am-11pm) With its see-and-be-seen glass front on the 1st floor, mellow atmosphere, virginal white walls and sleek furnishings, this place screams trendy. Fortunately, there's substance behind the trappings, with toothsome baklavas and well-prepared snacks. The 1st floor is popular with flirting students. So cute.

İkizler Lahmacun Salonu (☎ 214 9568; M Fevzi Çakmak Caddesi; mains €1-3; 😊 11am-11pm) Make a beeline for this little den off the main drag. It has been serving up pide and *lahmacun* to ravenous locals since 1962, so it really knows what it's doing when it comes to the national dish.

Akdeniz Tantuni (☎ 216 9010; Cumhuriyet Caddesi; mains €2; 😊 11am-10pm) A good spot for a quick bite, this bustling eatery on the main drag features surprisingly pleasant surrounds. Enjoy your chicken sandwich while sitting around low wooden tables.

Kebabistan (☎ 214 2273; Sinemalar Sokak; mains €2-4; 😊 10am-10pm) Another bastion of well-executed Turkish fare, Kebabistan is well regarded for its expertly cooked kebaps. Portions are generous and service swift. Its second branch, across the street, specialises in pide.

Tamara Ocakbaşı (☎ 214 3295; Yüzbaşıoğlu Sokak; mains €2-6; ☺ 10am-11pm) Impressive! In the Hotel Tamara, this eatery wows you with its 40 *ocak* – each table has its own grill. The décor is more over-the-top than recherché, but it makes for a welcome change from the usually mundane dining rooms that characterise many eateries in Anatolia. High-quality meat and fish dishes feature prominently, so prepare to ease out your belt a notch.

Antep Ocakbaşı (☎ 215 9101; Cumhuriyet Caddesi; mains €3-5; ☺ 8am-10pm) This eatery is up some stairs in an unremarkable block. The stomach-groaning menu features all the usual suspects, including mezes, pide, grills and kebaps. The crowd ranges from chattering families to giggling students and crusty old men, giving the place a nice buzz.

Saçi Beyaz Et Lokantası (☎ 214 4016; Kazım Karabekir Caddesi; mains €3-6; ☺ 11am-10pm) Besse's main competitor, this shiny place adds a touch of glitz to Van's restaurant scene (which isn't, of course, saying too much). The food is well presented and of high quality, with service to match, although you can't help but feel you're paying more for the sleek setting than for the food. There's a separate entry for the eponymous pastry shop (on the ground floor), blessed with an agreeable terrace where you can unwind over a cup of tea or a delectable *dondurma*.

Çınar Restaurant ve Et Lokantası (☎ 214 6606; Cumhuriyet Caddesi; mains €3-6; ☺ 11am-10pm) It's more or less the same story as for Kebabistan in this long-standing favourite. The eclectic menu focuses on pide, kebaps, grills and stews. The chef recommends the *kaburga dolması*.

Besse (☎ 215 0050; Sanat Sokak; mains €4-7; ☺ 11am-9.30pm) If you're in search of a bit of sophistication, Besse fits the bill perfectly.

It is done out in soothing yellow tones and features parquet flooring and dim lights. The kitchen turns out superior cooking, with an emphasis on grills, salads and stews – try the excellent *ali nazik*, Besse's signature dish. It's deep in the heart of a vibrant area on the 1st floor of a bland building. If only alcohol was available!

Other temptations in the centre include:
Çavuşoğlu (☎ 214 2669; Cumhuriyet Caddesi; ☺ 8am-10pm) Keep up your strength with a Turkish coffee and a delectable pastry.
Güven (☎ 214 0300; Cumhuriyet Caddesi; ☺ 8am-11pm) Another treasure trove for the sweet tooth, on the main thoroughfare.

Drinking & Entertainment

Van might be a fairly liberal city with an important student population, but if it's Ibiza-style you're after, you're barking up the wrong tree. However, there's a couple of lively hangouts that can be recommended.

Barabar Türk Evi (☎ 214 9866; Sanat Sokak) The closest thing Van has to a pub, the Barabar is a definite rare breed in eastern Turkey. It may be lodged on the 1st floor of an unprepossessing building, but there is a fever-pitch energy with its mainly student crowd of both sexes gulping pints of frothy draught beer (about €3). Yes, BEER! It gets frantic here at weekends, with a live band knocking out Kurdish tunes – tear it up on the dance floor if you dare.

Çay Bahçesi (Cumhuriyet Caddesi; ☺ 8am-8pm) Van's undoubted social hub, this tea garden boasts lots of shade and greenery and is an attractive place to imbibe the atmosphere of central Van. It's deservedly packed with an eclectic crowd any time of the day. Nab a seat under the trees and linger over a cup of tea.

Halay Türkü Bar (☎ 214 8233; Kazım Karabekir Caddesi) Almost a carbon copy of the Barabar. Although it's trying hard and is a great place,

---

THE YUMMIEST BREAKFASTS IN EASTERN TURKEY

Van is famed for its tasty *kahvaltı* (breakfast). Skip the usually bland breakfast that is served in your hotel and head straight to Eski Sümerbank Sokak, also called 'Kahvaltı Sokak' (Breakfast St), a pedestrianised side street running parallel to Cumhuriyet Caddesi. Here you'll find a row of eateries specialising in complete Turkish breakfasts. Drool over *otlu peynir* (cheese mixed with a tangy herb, Van's speciality), *beyaz peynir* (a mild yellow cheese), honey from the highlands (mmm!), olives, *kayma* (clotted cream), butter, tomatoes, cucumbers and *yumurta* (eggs). The **Sütçü Fevzi** (☎ 216 6618; Eski Sümerbank Sokak; ☺ 7am-noon) and the **Sütçü Kenan** (☎ 216 8499; Eski Sümerbank Sokak; ☺ 7am-noon) have a few tables set up outside. A typical Van experience.

the Halay hasn't yet acquired the cool reputation of the Barabar.

Both are resoundingly popular among students of both sexes and make for a great experience. Enjoy!

Getting There & Away

AIR

A bus service leaves from outside the office of Kamran Turizm for the airport, 1½ hours before the departure (€2).

Atlasjet (www.atlasjet.com) Operates a daily flight to/from İstanbul (from €44, two hours).

Kamran Turizm (☎ 216 7031; Cumhuriyet Caddesi; 8am-8pm) An agent for Atlasjet, Pegasus, Sun Express and Turkish Airlines.

Pegasus Airlines (www.flypgs.com) Has a daily flight to/from Ankara (from €44, 1¾ hours) and İstanbul (from €60).

Sun Express (www.sunexpress.com.tr) Has a twice weekly flight to/from İzmir (€55, two hours).

Turkish Airlines (www.thy.com) Has a daily flight to/from İstanbul (from €44) and Ankara (from €44).

BOAT

A ferry crosses Lake Van between Tatvan and Van on a twice-daily basis. There's no fixed schedule. The trip costs €3 per passenger (€6 per car) and takes about four hours. 'İskele' dolmuşes ply İskele Caddesi to the harbour (€0.40).

BUS

Many bus companies have ticket offices at the intersection of Cumhuriyet and Kazım Karabekir Caddesis. They customarily provide *servises* to shuttle passengers to and from the otogar.

Minibuses to Doğubayazıt leave from a small bus stand on İskele Caddesi, a few blocks west of Beş Yol. Minibuses to Bahçesaray (€6, three hours) leave from near a tea house called Bahçesaray Çay Evi, southeast of the bazaar. Minibuses to Hoşap and Çavuştepe (€3, 30 to 45 minutes) leave from Cumhuriyet Caddesi. Minibuses to Gevaş and Akdamar (€1, about 45 minutes) depart from a small bus stand in a side street off Zübeydehanım Caddesi, near the Otel Aslan.

To get to Iran, take a direct bus to Orumiyeh (in Iran) or a bus to Yüksekova (€6, three hours), then get on a shared taxi to Orumiyeh (€6).

Details of some services are listed in the table, right.

SERVICES FROM VAN'S OTOGAR

Destination	Fare	Duration	Distance	Frequency (per day)
Ağrı	€8	3hr	213km	frequent buses
Ankara	€30	22hr	1250km	frequent buses
Diyarbakır	€13	7hr	410km	frequent buses
Doğubayazıt (via Çaldıran)	€6	2½hr	185km	several morning minibuses
Erciş	€3	1¼hr	95km	several buses
Erzurum	€13	6hr	410km	several buses
Hakkari	€6	4hr	205km	a few buses
Malatya	€15	9-10hr	500km	frequent buses
Orumiyeh (Iran)	€12	6hr	311km	at least one bus
Şanlıurfa	€18	9hr	585km	a few buses
Tatvan	€6	2½hr	156km	frequent buses
Trabzon	€14	12hr	733km	a few direct buses, most via Erzurum

CAR

Consider renting a car to journey around Lake Van. Try **Europcar** (☎ 215 8990; Kazım Karabekir Caddesi) or **Avis – Urartu Turizm** (☎ 214 2020; Cumhuriyet Caddesi) next door to the Büyük Urartu Oteli.

TRAIN

The twice-weekly *Vangölü Ekspresi* from İstanbul and Ankara terminates at Tatvan; from Tatvan, the ferry will bring you to the dock at Van. The weekly *Trans Asya Ekspresi* connects İstanbul to Tehran and stops at Van. It leaves for Tehran (€17) at 6.49pm on Friday; for İstanbul (€30), it leaves at 4.53pm.

You can get to the station İstasyon by dolmuş from near Beş Yol (€0.40).

Getting Around

For minibuses to Van Kalesi and the ferry dock *(iskele)*, go to the minibus terminal near Beş Yol at the northern end of Cumhuriyet Caddesi.

AROUND VAN

Yedi Kilise

The poignant, crumbling Yedi Kilise (Seven Churches) is about 9km southeast of Van, in a typical Kurdish village. It used to be a large monastery. The arched portal sports elaborate stone-carvings, and you can also see various Armenian inscriptions above it. Inside, there are some well-preserved frescoes. There's no admission fee but a small donation is expected. If you want to buy souvenirs, women selling knitted gloves and socks usually wait near the building and will be happy to show their handicrafts. After visiting the church, you can mosey around the muddy streets of the village.

There's no reliable public transport to Yedi Kilise. The most practical way to get there is by taxi (about €13 including waiting time), or you could walk back to Van and enjoy the scenery.

Bahçesaray

Wow! Be prepared to run out of superlatives. From Van, the 110km ride to reach this town in the middle of nowhere, set high in the mountains, is exhilarating and makes for a perfect complement to a journey around Lake Van. Bahçesaray's main claim to fame is its isolation: because of the snow it's cut off from the outside world at least six months of the year. 'Half the year we belong to God,' say the locals. From Van, the highly scenic road crosses the steppe before gradually ascending until the Karabel Geçiti, at 2985m – dizzying. On your way look for *zoma* (encampments), with Kurdish shepherds, their flocks and their damn dogs (beware!). The scenery is captivating on a clear day – the air is pure and the surrounding mountains make a perfect backdrop. In late spring, the view of the wild expanses of the highlands ablaze with vivid hues is unforgettable.

Bahçesaray has plenty to keep you busy for a day or two. Why not visit the nearby monuments, including a couple of Armenian churches and an ancient bridge? Or play chess with the locals, who are reputedly the best players in eastern Anatolia? But if all you need is to re-energise, be sure to enjoy the delicious local *bal* (honey). Count on €13 per kilogram.

One of the highlights of this trip is that you'll have to spend the night in a private home, as there's no official accommodation. It shouldn't be a problem, as locals are excessively hospitable and you'll doubtless be warmly received as a *misafir* (guest).

In summer, you could reach Bahçesaray with a normal vehicle, but you should know

that the road is tarred only until Yukarı Narlıca and deteriorates markedly near the pass – a 4WD or a high-clearance vehicle would be more appropriate. If it's wet, this part of the road is impassable with a normal vehicle. There's a *jandarma* (police) checkpoint at Yukarı Narlıca.

One or two minibuses leave daily except Sunday from a small minibus stand in Van (ask for Bahçesaray Çay Evi, off Zubeydehanım Caddesi). The bumpy ride takes about three hours and costs €6.

Hoşap & Çavuştepe

A day excursion southeast of Van along the road to Başkale and Hakkari takes you to the Urartian site at Çavuştepe (25km from Van) and the spectacular Kurdish castle at Hoşap (Güzelsu; 33km further along). Both sites amply reward the effort of visiting them.

Hoşap Castle (admission €1.25) perches photogenically on top of a rocky outcrop alongside Güzelsu, a hicksville truck-stop village. Cross the bridge and follow the signs around the far side of the hill to reach the castle entrance.

Built in 1643 by a local Kurdish chieftain, Mahmudi Süleyman, the castle has a very impressive entrance gateway in a round tower. The guardian will quickly spot you and rush to sell you a ticket. You then enter the fortress via a passage cut through the rock. Many of its hundreds of rooms are still clearly visible, and the view is stunning.

The narrow hill on the left side of the highway at Çavuştepe was once crowned by the fortress-palace **Sarduri-Hinili** (admission €1.25), home of the kings of Urartu and built between 764 and 735 BC by King Sardur II, son of Argishti. These are the best-preserved foundations of any Urartian palace.

From the car park, the **upper fortress** is up to the left, and the vast **lower fortress** to the right. At the upper fortress there is little to see except a platform, possibly used for religious rites, and the ruins of a temple to Haldi, but from here you can see the layout of the lower fortress.

Climb the rocky hill to the lower fortress temple ruins, marked by a gate of black basalt blocks polished to a high gloss; a few blocks on the left side are inscribed in cuneiform. As you walk around, notice other illustrations of Urartian engineering ingenuity: the cisterns under the pathways, the storage vessels and, at the far end where the palace once stood,

---

VISITING TURKEY'S DEEP SOUTHEAST

The southeastern corner of Turkey carries a fearsome reputation among travellers and among Turks from Western Anatolia (who usually know nothing about the area). All right, it was at the epicentre of the Kurdish rebellion during the 1980s and '90s and for a long time was off-limits to travellers. Although the Kurdistan Workers Party (PKK/Kongra-Gel) called off its cease-fire in June 2004, the situation has greatly improved and the whole area is under heavy military control. There are checkpoints, but no hassle to speak of – just have your passport ready at hand and don't deviate from the main road.

It might be a bit intimidating for first-timers, especially women travellers, but you shouldn't believe all the scare stories. Keep in mind that it's the nature of news that you hear more about killing than about living. While a few pockets of the region remain problematic, the vast majority is as warm and welcoming to visitors as anywhere in Turkey. Wild and largely ignored yes, but never dull. At the time of research, we were able to travel without problem (and using public transport) from Mardin to Şirnak (221km), and from Şirnak to Hakkari (181km), and then from Hakkari to Van (203km). From Mardin to Şirnak, there was only one checkpoint, and from Şirnak to Hakkari only three.

Everybody we spoke to in the deep southeast assured us that travelling to the area was perfectly safe. The only thing you need is to be a bit more vigilant and seek local advice before setting off. Anyway, the military will simply not allow you to get too close to trouble – if any. Whatever the situation, you'll probably be the only travellers for miles around.

Check the situation out. If it looks OK, jump right in. You won't regret it, we swear.

---

the royal Urartian loo, said to be the oldest such squat toilet ever excavated. Down on the plains to the south you'll see canals also created by the Urartians.

To get to the Hoşap and Çavuştepe sites, catch a minibus (on Cumhuriyet Caddesi in Van) heading to Başkale and say you want to get out at Hoşap (€3). After seeing the castle, flag down a bus back to Çavuştepe, 500m off the highway, and then catch a third bus back to Van. It's pretty easy to do this trip on your own as frequent minibuses and buses ply the route.

HAKKARI

☎ 0438 / pop 236,000 / elevation 1720m

Tell friends in İstanbul that you intend to go to Hakkari, and the reaction is quite likely to be one of condescending incredulity, at best ('You're going *where*?'), or of warning ('There are some problems out there!'). True, Hakkari is ragged around the edges, as befits a city that was at the epicentre of the Kurdish rebellion during the 1980s and '90s and that is tucked away in Turkey's far southeastern corner, at 1700m, far from any other major urban centre.

But oh, how things have changed. Hakkari is rising from the ashes, and travellers are trickling in, lured by the sensational setting – the city is ringed by the jagged Cilo Dağı moun-

tains – and the great potential for exploration. The Cilo is again accessible, and it won't take long before trekking trips are organised here. You could also take a minibus and explore at your leisure the picturesque nearby town of **Çukurca** and rejuvenate your mind and body in the high pastures of **Kırıkdağ**. Be a pioneer!

Dangers & Annoyances

Women travellers should expect to be the main focus of attention. The area is overwhelmingly male-oriented, and female travellers can be made to feel unwelcome. It's wise to dress modestly. The best place for women travellers is Hotel Şenler.

Sleeping & Eating

Hotel Ümit (☎ 0438-211 2469; Altay Caddesi; s/d €14/17) We prefer Hotel Şenler, but this is a bearable plan B – if you can get past the sombre reception area, that is. It's in the centre.

Hotel Şenler (☎ 0438-211 5512; Bulvar Caddesi; s/d €25/45) Hakkari's best-value and most reassuring hotel, by far. Staff are professional and eager to help (ask for Turan Şimşek), bathrooms are kept in top nick and you won't be tripping over your backpack in the generous-sized rooms. It's also very central. Does it get any better?

Hacibaba Kebap Salonu (☎ 211 3003; Cumhuriyet Caddesi; mains €2-4; ⏰ 8am-10pm) The Hacibaba is heralded as one of the best restaurants in town. After having vacuumed up a satisfying *tavuk şiş* (roast chicken kebap) served with salad and fresh bread, we won't argue. The big grill at the back is impressive. It's just off the main square.

Getting There & Away

From Van to Hakkari, there are regular bus services (€6, four hours). There are also several daily minibuses to Yüksekova (€3, 78km), from where you can cross the border at Esendere–Seró and journey on to Iran. Daily minibuses also ply the route to Çukurca (€3) and Kırıkdağ (€1.50). Westwards you can

take the long but highly scenic haul to Şirnak in the one daily minibus (€9, five to six hours depending on waits at checkpoints).

NORTH OF VAN

If you're bound for Doğubayazıt from Van, you have a choice of routes. Some buses still take the long way round via Erciş, Patnos and Ağrı, but the minibuses all travel via Muradiye, Çaldıran and Ortadirek, a considerably shorter 185km run and one worth taking for the magnificent pastoral scenery along the way, especially if you can pause at the spectacular **Muradiye Waterfalls**. Keep your passport handy for any army checkpoints.

Directory

CONTENTS

ACCOMMODATION

Turkey has accommodation options to suit all budgets with concentrations of good, value-for-money pensions and hotels in all the places – such as İstanbul, Çanakkale, Selçuk, Fethiye and Göreme – most visited by independent travellers. The rates quoted in this book are for peak season (May to September) and include value-added tax (KDV); room prices can be discounted by up to 20% during the low season (October to April, but not during the Christmas period and major Islamic holidays; see p659).

Places within easy reach of İstanbul and Ankara (eg Safranbolu) may hike their prices at summer weekends.

In general, you can expect to spend less than €25 per person (sometimes much less) in places we list as budget options; €25 to €55 in those we list as midrange; and more than €55 in places we list as top end. Prices in İstanbul are considerably higher than those elsewhere in the country – expect to pay at least €10 per person more in a double room in İstanbul. Out east prices are lower. Breakfast is usually included in the price of all accommodation.

If you are planning a stay of a week or more in a coastal resort, check the prices in package-holiday brochures before leaving home. British, French and German tour companies in particular often offer flight-and-accommodation packages to places such as Kuşadası, Bodrum, Marmaris, Dalyan, Fethiye, Antalya, Side and Alanya for much less than you would pay if you make your own bookings.

These days most accommodation has websites for making advance reservations. Once on the travellers' circuit you will find that many pensions operate in informal chains, referring you from one to another. If you've enjoyed staying in one place you will probably enjoy its owner's recommendations, but of course you should hold hard to your right not to sign up to anything sight unseen.

Note that along the Aegean, Mediterranean, the Black Sea coasts and in some parts of Cappadocia, the vast majority of hotels, pensions and camping grounds close from mid-October to late April. These dates are variable, though; see p20 for more information.

Apartments

Apartments for holiday rentals are usually thin on the ground. Wherever possible we have listed them in this book; otherwise your best bet is to try www.ownersdirect.co.uk or www.holidaylettings.co.uk. If you're interested in hiring an apartment along the coast (eg Kaş, Antalya, Bodrum) your best bet is to contact local real estate agents (emlakci) who hold lists of available holiday rentals and are used to dealing with foreigners.

Camping

Most camping facilities are along the coasts and are usually privately run. Inland, camping facilities are fairly rare and are most likely to be on *Orman Dinlenme Yeri* (Forestry Department land). You usually need your own transport to reach these. Other facilities inland tend to be barren, overcrowded options on the outskirts of towns and cities.

If there are no designated camping grounds, ask about at hotels and pensions. Often they will let you camp in their grounds and use their facilities for a small fee (€3 to €6 per person). Otherwise, camping outside official camping grounds is often more hassle than it's worth. Not only may the police drop by to check you out and possibly move you on but also, out east, wolves and Kangal sheep dogs can be a real threat. We recommend female travellers always stick to official camp sites and camp where there are plenty of people around – especially out east.

Hostels

Given that pensions are so cheap, Turkey has no official hostel network, even though a few places claim to be affiliated to the International Youth Hostelling Association (IYHA). However, there are plenty of hostels offering dormitories in touristy destinations. Dorm beds usually cost from €7 to €11 per night.

Hotels

Hotels range from the dirt cheap to the boutique. The cheapest hotels (around €10 per double room) are mostly used by working-class Turkish men on business and are not suitable for lone women. While we don't want to restrict women's freedom of choice, if you're greeted by silence and stony stares in a hotel reception, it may be better to move on.

Moving up a price bracket, one- and two-star hotels may cost around €15 to €35 for a double room with shower but are less oppressively masculine in atmosphere, even when the clientele is mainly male. Three-star hotels are usually used to catering for women travellers.

Hotels in more traditional Turkish towns, however clean and comfortable, normally offer only Turkish TV, Turkish breakfast and none of the 'extras' that are commonplace in pensions.

Prices are usually set by the local authorities and should be displayed at the reception desk. You should never pay more than these official prices; often you will be able to haggle for a lower (sometimes much lower) price.

Unmarried foreign couples don't usually have any problems sharing rooms, although out east you'll usually be given a twin room even if you asked for a double. However, some establishments still refuse to accept an unmarried couple when one of the parties is Turkish. The cheaper the hotel, and the more remote the location, the more conservative its management tends to be.

Not surprisingly, the most difficult places to find really good cheap rooms are İstanbul, Ankara, İzmir and package-holiday resort towns such as Alanya. In most other cities and resorts, good, inexpensive beds are readily available.

BOUTIQUE HOTELS

Increasingly, old Ottoman mansions, caravanserais and other historic buildings are being refurbished or completely rebuilt as hotels equipped with all mod cons and bags of character. Most of these options are in the mid to upper price range. Some are described in this guide; many more are in the excellent *Little Hotel Book*, by Sevan and Müjde Nişanyan, available in bookshops in İstanbul or through www.nisanyan.net.

Pensions & Guesthouses

In all of the destinations popular with travellers you'll be able to find simple family-run pensions and guesthouses (they are one of a kind) where you can get a good, clean single/double for around €20/30. Many also have dorm rooms and sometimes family rooms. These places usually offer a choice of simple meals, book exchanges, laundry services, international TV services etc, and it's these facilities that really distinguish them from traditional small, cheap hotels. Most pensions also have staff who speak at least one foreign language.

In a few places a handful of old-style *ev pansiyonu* (home pensions) survive. These are simply rooms in a family house that are let to visitors at busy times of year and won't normally have these extra facilities let alone anyone who speaks English. Nor do they usually advertise their existence in a formal way: ask locals where to find them and look out for *kıralık oda* (room for rent) in the windows.

In smaller tourist towns such as Fethiye, Pamukkale and Selçuk, touts for the pensions may approach you as you step from your bus and offer you accommodation. Some may string you a line about the pension you're looking for (it's burnt down; was destroyed by earthquake; the owner died) in the hope of getting you to their lair, where they may extract a commission from the owner. Taxi drivers sometimes like to play this game as well. Most people like to politely decline these offers and go to the pension of their choice; however, sometimes it's worth taking them up – especially if you're on a budget – as these touts are often working for newly opened pensions offering cheap rates. Before you let them take you to the pension make it known you're only looking and are under no obligation to stay.

Tree Houses

Olympos (p379), on the Western Mediterranean coast near Antalya, is famous for its 'tree houses' – rough-and-ready permanent shelters of minimal comfort in forested settings near the beach. A few of these places are real tree houses, but many are just tented platforms. They're fun, backpacker hang-outs, with bars, communal dining and internet connections. On the negative side, there's little security and there have been instances of guests falling ill as a result of what they've eaten or drunk. And sewage treatment seems to be an ongoing challenge, so consider swimming well away from the camps and check for odours before you check in. We have also heard of isolated cases of drugged beverages – see p381.

The success of Olympos has started to spawn tree houses elsewhere in Turkey (eg at Saklıkent, near Fethiye). More will probably have appeared by the time you read this.

ACTIVITIES

Outdoor-activity aficionados have started to take notice of Turkey. Water sports abound, be it thrashing the white-water in Yusufeli, paddling over submerged ruins near Kaş or blissfully doing nothing on the sundeck of a *gület* (wooden yacht). Up high you can reconnoitre the best place for your towel while paragliding over Ölüdeniz, catch the breeze over Cappadocia in a hot-air balloon or tackle the wind at famous Alaçatı. In the mountains, Turkey has two way-marked long-distance trails, which are popular with trekkers (see p78), and abseiling, skiing and mountaineering are options as well.

All of these activities you can organise yourself, through your hotel, or check out the tour operators offering activity-based tours on p684. Other tour operators are listed in the various destination chapters; those specialising in trekking are listed on p87.

Bird-Watching

Turkey is on an important migration route for birds travelling from north to south and vice versa, and spring and autumn are particularly good times to visit the country to watch migrating birds. There are several bird sanctuaries (*kuş cennetler,* bird paradises) dotted about the country, although unfortunately they are often popular with noisy, picnicking Turks who frighten the birds away. See p64 for more on birds and conservation issues in Turkey.

East of Gaziantep it's possible to visit one of the last nesting sites of the eastern bald ibis at Birecik (p599).

Boat Trips

Many people want to take a boat trip along the Aegean or Mediterranean coast, preferably in a graceful *gület* (wooden yacht). There are endless possibilities, ranging from day trips out of Kuşadası, Bodrum, Marmaris, Fethiye, Antalya and all the smaller places in between to chartering a *gület* for a week-long tour of the coastline. Marmaris is another yachting centre, while Göcek and Alanya also have marinas. Yachts generally sail from May to October.

The most popular option is probably the four-day, three-night boat trip from Kale (near Olympos) to Fethiye or vice versa; for more details see p356. See p337 for more information on how to charter your own *gület* and p357 for tips on what to look out for.

Canyoning & Abseiling

The glorious 18km-long Saklıkent Gorge, near Fethiye, is a thrilling spot for canyoning, and the icy-cold waters will add punch to your squeals. You can organise trips for six hours or even overnight (see p364). Abseilers head straight for the greatest rockscape in the country, Cappadocia. Ask at **Middle Earth Travel** (☎ 271 2528; www.middleearthtravel.com) in Göreme (p501) for details.

Cycling

The most popular cycling routes are those along the coasts, particularly along the western Mediterranean coast between Marmaris and Antalya, with detours to nearby sites. The coastal road between Amasra and Sinop on the Black Sea passes by some beautiful scenery (see p539). Mountain biking around Cappadocia is popular, too, and plenty of places hire decent mountain bikes. Serious overlanders head out east: some cross to Iran and cycle all the way to India or beyond.

For practical tips on cycling in Turkey, see p679.

Diving

Marmaris, Bodrum and Kaş are Turkey's main diving centres. Bodrum is a great place to take a PADI course with good marine life and coral for experienced divers. It also has plenty of wrecks and the possibility that a handful might open for exploration by the time you read this (see p276). Marmaris (p337) has a larger, more established scene, a legacy of its sponge-diving traditions (see p338). You can also dive off Kaş' shores, too (p373), and it's a much nicer place to base yourself.

A growing number of people enjoy diving off the Gallipoli (Gelibolu) Peninsula to look at old WWI wrecks; see p190 for more details. You can also dive in Ayvalık (p213), which is famous for its red coral.

Scubaturk.net (www.scubaturk.net) is an İstanbul-based group with details about diving schools throughout the country; check out their photo gallery for inspiration!

Horse-Riding

Whether or not Cappadocia means 'Land of Beautiful Horses', as some locals would have you believe, the area is certainly wonderful for exploring on horseback, and a couple of agencies in Avanos (p513) can organise rides of different durations. You can also ride through the mountainous Dilek National Park on the south Aegean coast (see p264).

Hot-Air Ballooning

If you've never tried going up in a hot-air balloon then don't miss the chance at Cappadocia, where several companies compete for your trade. It's not cheap, but looking down on one of the world's most fascinating landscapes is bound to be one of the highlights of your trip. See the boxed text, p512, for more details.

Mountaineering

Turkey's highest mountain is also its most famous: Mt Ararat. Mountaineers can tackle Ararat (Ağrı Dağı; 5137m), near Doğubayazıt, but you need to be cashed-up, organised and extremely patient with all the bureaucracy. See p589 for more information. It may be easier (and cheaper) to opt for climbing Süphan Dağı (Mt Süphan; 4434m), on the north side of Lake Van instead (see p636).

Two relatively easy mountains to climb are Hasan Dağı (Mt Hasan; 3268m) and Erciyes Dağı (Mt Erciyes; 3916m), both in Cappadocia. It's perfectly possible to arrange these climbs yourself; alternatively you could talk to Middle Earth Travel in Göreme (p501).

Paragliding

Ölüdeniz (p359) is home to paragliding in Turkey, and pros come each year to challenge each other at the International Air Games every October. If you're new to dangling yourself in the air, you can tandem paraglide with one of the many operators offering flights.

Swimming & Water Sports

Turkey's beautiful coasts and beaches are perfect for water sports from mid-May to September. The Aegean and Mediterranean coasts offer plentiful opportunities for water-skiing, snorkelling, sea-kayaking, scuba diving and swimming – unlike the chilly Black Sea coast.

There are excellent swimming beaches on Bozcaada (p206); in the Dilek National Park (p263); from Behramkale to Edremit (p212); on the Bodrum peninsula (p281); at İztuzu Beach, near Dalyan (p351); and at Altınkum (p239), near Çeşme. One of the finest is Patara Beach (p366). Note that Black Sea waters, especially close to İstanbul, can be treacherous for swimmers.

Sea-kayaking is a must over the sunken city of Üçağız (Kekova) near Kaş (see p373). Canoeing is possible on the Patara River, also near Kaş (p373).

Trekking

Whatever your level of ability, Turkey is a great place for trekking. Turkey has two way-marked long-distance paths: the Lycian Way (see p78) and St Paul's Trail (p81).

The Kaçkar Mountains offer some of the best mountain hiking, whether you approach from the eastern Black Sea coast near Ayder (p85) or from Yusufeli (p572) on the southern side of the range, though the snow-free season is very short.

For more information on treks available in Turkey, see p87.

Well-Being

Turks need no introduction to pampering themselves. Spend an afternoon in a *hamam* (Turkish bathhouse) and you'll soon see why (see opposite). The well-being industry has therefore found a natural home in Turkey, and opportunities for yoga, health retreats and the like are blossoming over the country. If you're a yoga devotee bring your mat. There are innumerable perfect spots to *asana* in the countryside, and many towns have classes you can join for a few hours, such as in Antalya (p387), which also has meditation instruction.

Kabak (p363) is a remote beach community firmly devoted to well-being, with relaxed accommodation offerings, yoga courses and even a spring-water swimming pool.

The Sultaniye Hot Springs and Mud Baths (p351), close to Dalyan, along the western Mediterranean, is an excellent stopover for a mud bath rich in mineral salts said to aid skin complaints and rheumatism. A similar spa complex with even an open-air pool is Kurşunlu Banyo in Termal (p287). Asthma sufferers might want to head to the two caves near Alanya (p404) – apparently if you inhale the air inside the caves you'll be cured!

For a slightly odd treat visit Balıklı Kaplıca (p480), where teeny 'doctor' fish nibble on your toes, supposedly curing your skin of psoriasis.

White-Water Rafting

The foaming white challenges of the Çoruh Gorge near Yusufeli (p572) are relatively undiscovered by all but those-in-the-know. Rapids junkies swear these are some of the best in the world. Other options include some gentler rapids near Çamlıhemşin (p560), the Köprülü Kanyon near Antalya (p396) and along the Kızılırmak and Zamantı rivers near Avanos (p513). Check out Saklıkent Gorge, near Fethiye, as well (see p364).

Windsurfing

Serious windsurfers need no introduction to Alaçatı (p240), near Çeşme. For the rest of us, it's the windsurfing hotspot of Europe – well, it's almost Europe. Beginners can take comprehensive courses; pros can try their hand with kites. It's definitely worth checking out.

Winter Sports

Ski facilities in Turkey are fairly basic by European or US standards but infinitely cheaper and less cliquey and they provide a great opportunity to after-party with the locals. Snow is generally good and may last well into spring, especially at the country's best ski fields, Palandöken ski resort (p569), near Erzurum. There is also decent skiing at Uludağ (p301), near Bursa, and on Davraz Dağı (p317), near Eğirdir. We also saw ski lifts being constructed on the slopes of Nemrut Dağı (the one near Van; p635) when we visited, so another ski resort in eastern Anatolia could be operating by the time you read this.

An alternative to skiing is snowshoeing, whereby you walk over snow on special shoes. Kirkit Voyage in Avanos (p513) can arrange for you to explore beautiful Cappadocia on snowshoes – but only in years when there is plenty of snow, of course.

THE PLEASURES OF THE TURKISH BATH

After all that vigorous activity few things could be better than relaxing in the nearest *hamam* (Turkish bathhouse).

The steam bath was an institution that passed from the Romans to the Byzantines, and thence to the Turks. It was once a much-anticipated weekly outing for women especially, an opportunity to gossip with friends, groom and pamper, and for mothers to size up potential matches for their sons. Although modern bathrooms have reduced the need for public bathing, the tradition of the leisurely soak is still alive, albeit on a much reduced scale. And unfortunately some of the finest old baths have raised prices for tourists, putting them out of reach for most locals. At the same time they have reduced the quality of their service on the assumption that tourists don't know what to expect and won't be coming back again anyway – boo hiss.

Many people feel anxious the first time they go to a *hamam*. So what should you expect when you cross the threshold? First up, you usually need to choose and pay for the service you'd like at the door. Then you enter the *camekan*, where you'll be shown to a cubicle where you can undress, store your clothes, lock up your valuables and wrap the *peştemal* (cloth) that's provided around you. You'll be given a pair of *nalın* (wooden clogs), which you'll need to attempt to wear to prevent slipping on the marble floors. Then an attendant will lead you through the *soğukluk* (cold room, though it's usually warm) to the *hararet* (steam room) where you sit and sweat for a while.

It's cheapest to wash yourself with the soap, shampoo and towel you brought with you. The steam room will be ringed with individual basins *(kurna)*, that you fill from the taps above. When sluicing the water over yourself with a plastic scoop you should try not to get soap into the water in the basin. Also try to avoid splashing your neighbours, especially on a Friday when someone who has completed their ritual wash would have to start all over again if soaked by a non-Muslim.

But to wash yourself is to miss most of the fun. It's far more enjoyable to let an attendant do it for you, dousing you with warm water and then scrubbing you with a *kese* (a coarse cloth mitten), loosening dirt you never suspected you had. Afterwards you'll be lathered with a sudsy swab, rinsed off and shampooed.

When all this is complete you can have a massage, an experience worth having at least once during your trip. Some massages are carried out on the floor or a table, but usually you'll be spread out on the great marble slab called the *göbektaşı* (belly stone) beneath the great central dome. In touristy areas the massage is likely to be pretty cursory and, unless you're prepared to pay the extra for an 'oil massage', you may be disappointed. Elsewhere, however, a Turkish massage can be an unforgettable and invigorating experience.

Bath etiquette dictates that men should keep the *peştemal* on at all times. In the women's section, the amount of modesty expected varies considerably: in some baths total nudity is fine, in others it would be a blunder to remove your knickers; play safe by keeping your underwear on under your *peştemal* until inside the hot room where you can decide what is appropriate. If you want to shave your legs or armpits, you should do this in the *camekan* rather than in the bath.

Traditional *hamams* have separate sections for men and women or admit men and women at separate times. Opening hours for women are almost invariably more restricted than for men. In tourist areas some *hamams* are more than happy for foreign men and women to bathe together and charge a premium price for the privilege. In traditional *hamams*, women are washed and massaged by other women – no Turkish woman would let a male masseur anywhere near her. Women who accept a massage from a male masseur should have their massage within view of companions and protest loudly at the first sign of impropriety.

BUSINESS HOURS

Government departments, offices and banks usually open from 8.30am to noon and 1.30pm to 5pm Monday to Friday. Shops are open from 9am to 7pm Monday to Saturday. During the summer the working day in some cities, including the Aegean and Mediterranean regions, begins at 7am or 8am and finishes at 2pm. During the month of Ramazan the working day is generally shortened to 2pm or 3pm.

In tourist areas food and souvenir/carpet shops are usually open from around 8am to 11pm or later if it's very busy. Elsewhere, grocery shops are usually open from 7am to 7pm or 8pm daily; other shops are usually closed on Sunday. Friday, the Muslim Sabbath, is a normal working day in Turkey.

Many museums close on Monday, especially in İstanbul. From April to October museums usually open half an hour earlier and close 1½ to two hours later.

Internet cafés usually open from around 9am until late at night, or until the last customer has left.

CHILDREN

Practicalities

Çocuklar (children) may not be well catered for in Turkey, but they are the beloved centrepiece of family life and your children will be welcomed wherever they go. Your baby or young child's journey through the streets will be peppered with *Maşallah* (glory be to God) and your child clutched into the adoring arms of strangers, sometimes even against his/her will. You might want to learn your child's age and sex in Turkish – *ay* (month), *yil* (year), *erkek* (boy) and *kız* (girl). You might also want to make polite inquiries about the other person's children, present or absent: *kaç tane çocuklariniz varmı?* (how many children do you have?)

Pasteurised UHT milk is sold in cartons everywhere, but fresh milk is harder to find. Also hard to find is baby food, and what you do find your baby will understandably find inedible or it will be mashed banana, which you could easily prepare yourself. Consider bringing a supply with you. Migros supermarkets have the best range of baby food in the country. Alternatively you could rely on hotel and restaurant staff to prepare special dishes for your children. Most Turkish women breast-feed their babies (discreetly) in public and no-one is likely to mind you doing the same. You can buy formula and vitamin-fortified rice cereal in all supermarkets. High chairs in restaurants are the exception, not the rule.

Disposable *bebek bezi* (nappies or diapers) are readily available. The best brands are Prima or Huggies, sold in pharmacies and supermarkets – don't bother with the cheaper local brands. Oh, and if you find a public baby-changing facility in the country please let us know!

Most hotels can arrange some sort of baby-sitting service if you ask, but kids' clubs are few and far between and agencies are nonexistent. Many of the seaside towns have children's play equipment, but elsewhere, including İstanbul, the situation is grim. Check the equipment for safety before letting your child use it.

It's important to remember that bus journeys can be very long and that buses do not have toilets on board; trains, planes or automobiles might be the best option. Most car-rental companies provide child-safety seats for a small extra charge. In Turkey, traffic and treacherous road surfaces make travelling by stroller an extreme sport.

Always double check the suitability of prescriptions you may be given in Turkey for children – see p690 for more information.

Check out Lonely Planet's *Travel with Children,* by Cathy Lanigan, which has lots of practical information and advice on how to make travel with children as stress-free as possible.

Sights & Activities

Beaches aside, in terms of things to see and do Turkey doesn't have a lot of attractions that have been designed with children in mind. With the exception of the Rahmi M Koç museum (p123) in İstanbul, most Turkish museums would leave them bored to tears, and there are no zoos or activity centres easily accessible and worthy of mention. For other ideas on how to keep your kids entertained in İstanbul, see p134.

Activity options are a better bet, with boating, ballooning and, depending on their age, horse-riding, snorkelling and white-water rafting all great options.

Apart from the coasts, the area of the country most likely to appeal to older children is Cappadocia, with its underground cities, cave dwellings and kooky landscapes.

Safety Precautions

Parents need to remember that in Turkey ideas of safety consciousness rarely meet the norms of countries such as the UK or the USA. The traffic must be at the forefront of parents' minds constantly, and we've already mentioned the broken-down and poorly de-signed play equipment (grrr). Watch out for open power points in hotels, crudely covered electric mains and open stairwells on the streets. Serious potholes, open drainage and carelessly secured building sites are also a fact of life in Turkey.

If you looking for childcare while in Turkey, you may want to get some tips from **Child Wise** (www.childwise.net/choose-with-care-php).

CLIMATE CHARTS

For meteorologists, Turkey has seven distinct climatic regions, but from the point of view of most casual visitors, the most important distinctions are between the coast with its moderate winter temperatures and hot, humid summers, and the inland areas with their extremely cold winters and excessively hot summers. The further east you travel, the more pronounced these climatic extremes become, so that much of eastern Turkey is unpassable with snow from December through to April, with temperatures sometimes falling to around -12°C. In July and August temperatures rise rapidly and

can exceed 45°C, making travel in the east very uncomfortable.

The Black Sea coast gets two to three times the national average rainfall, along with more moderate temperatures, making it rather like Central Europe but pleasantly warmer. See When to Go in the Getting Started chapter (p19) for more information.

COURSES
Cookery

Cercis Murat Konağı (☎ 0482-213 6841; www.cercis murat.com in Turkish at time of research), run by Ebru Baydemir, runs cookery courses in her restaurant in gorgeous Mardin, southeastern Anatolia. Come here for lessons by female chefs – a rarity anywhere in the country, let alone out east! See p629 for more information.

Gökpinar Retreat (☎ 0252-313 3888; www.caravan turkey.com), run by Caravan Travel, offers an all-inclusive week-long cooking retreat in a

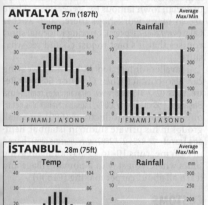

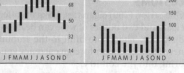

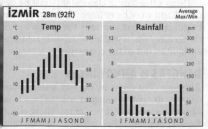

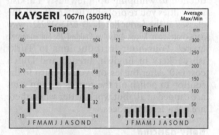

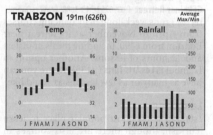

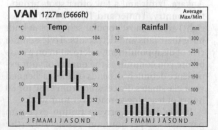

small village out of Bodrum for €500. There are sometimes other low-key courses running at the retreat simultaneously, such as carpet weaving or belly dancing. Jiggling the waistline may be the perfect antidote to a day's taste-testing.

Heritage Travel (☎ 0384-271 2687; www.goreme .com), based in Göreme, Cappadocia, runs one-week cuisine tours (€1050).

İstanbul Food Workshop (☎ 0212-534 4788; www .istanbulfoodworkshop.com; Yıldırım Caddesi 111, Fener, İstanbul) runs small-group workshops in a cosy semiprofessional kitchen. These two- to 20-hour sessions (€20 to €170) are for serious foodies. Add one of their lectures on 15th- and 16th-century Ottoman palace culinary culture, no less, and you're guaranteed top-class kudos at your next dinner soiree. The Australian–Turkish team have recently started gourmet tours of İstanbul too.

If you're more interested in a no-fuss introduction to whipping up a few tasty Turkish specialities you're probably better off with the classes at the **Sarnıç Hotel** (☎ 0212-518 2323; www .sarnichotel.com; Küçük Ayasofya Caddesi 26, Sultanahmet, İstanbul). Four-hour introductions to Turkish cookery in English, French and Dutch cost €40. After the lesson, you adjourn to the rooftop to polish off the results. Group sizes are capped at 10, but work better when there are a few less attendees.

Belly-dancing

Gökpınar Retreat (☎ 0252-313 3888; www.caravantur key.com) runs week-long belly dancing courses from April to November at its retreat near Bodrum from €490, including meals, transfers and 12 hours of lessons. Another option in İstanbul is **Les Arts Turcs** (p135), where you can have as many or as few lessons as you'd like.

Language

İstanbul is the most popular place to learn Turkish, though there are also courses in Ankara, İzmir and a few other spots around the country. Tömer and Taksim Dilmer (see right) are the most popular schools, but both have their fans and detractors. To lessen the risk of disappointment, ask to sit in on a class before you commit, as the quality of your experience definitely depends on the teacher and your classmates. Prices start from €280 for 80 hours of teaching spread over four weeks.

If you'd prefer private tuition expect to pay from €25 per hour; tutors often advertise

in the *Turkish Daily News* and on the expat website www.mymerhaba.com. *Teach Yourself Turkish*, by David and Asuman Çelen Pollard, is by far the best of the many books on teaching yourself Turkish.

Schools to learn Turkish include:

EF Language School (☎ 0212-282 9064; www.turkish lesson.com; Aydin Sokak S Blok 12, 1 Levent, İstanbul)

Spoken Turkish (☎ 0212-244 9000; www.spokeneng lishtr.com; İstiklal Caddesi 212/7, Beyoğlu, İstanbul) A newcomer on the scene offering less intensive courses than its competitors, but relatively untested.

Taksim Dilmer (☎ 0212-292 9696; www.dilmer.com; İnönü Caddesi, Prof Dr Tarık Zafer Tunaya Sokak 18, Taksim, İstanbul)

Tömer (☎ 0212-230 7083; www.tomer.com.tr; Abide-i Hürriyet Sokak 43, Şişli, İstanbul) Affiliated with Ankara University and with many branches throughout the country.

Handicrafts

If you're interested in making pottery, you might like to head to Avanos, the small Cappadocian town famous for its ceramics. There are so many workshops there, such as **Chez Galip** (www.chez-galip.com), offering informal short courses that it's best to just go and see what suits.

Travellers interested in learning weaving can also contact Chez Galip or **Gökpınar Retreat** (☎ 0252-313 3888; www.caravanturkey.com). **Musa Başaran** (☎ 0212-517 0099; musabasaran@ihlas.net.tr) offers 10-hour introductions (€80) for small groups in his private studio in İstanbul. **Heritage Travel** (☎ 0384-271 2687; www.goreme.com), based in Göreme, runs 10- to 15-day kilim-weaving tours where you stay in a nomad village and learn all about carpet making (€1600).

CUSTOMS

One carton (200) cigarettes, 1.5kg of coffee, 10 cigars and two bottles of wine can be imported duty-free. There's no limit to the amount of new Turkish liras or foreign currency you can bring into the country.

Items valued over US$15,000 must be declared and may be entered in your passport to guarantee that you take the goods out of the country when you leave. It's illegal to take antiquities out of the country.

DANGERS & ANNOYANCES

Although Turkey is by no way a dangerous country to visit, it's always wise to be a little cautious, especially if you're travelling alone. Be wary of pickpockets in buses, markets and

TRAVEL ADVISORIES

For the latest travel information log on to
the following websites:
www.smartraveller.gov.au Australian
Government's Travel Advisory & Consular Assistance
Service.
www.fco.gov.uk/travel UK Foreign &
Commonwealth Office.
www.travel.state.gov US Department of State/
Bureau of Consular Affairs.

other crowded places. Keep an eye out for
anyone lurking near ATMs.

In Turkey safety seems a low priority. Holes
in pavements go unmended and unlit at night;
precipitous drops go unguarded; safety belts
are worn only as long as it takes to drive past a
police officer before being released; lifeguards
on beaches are conspicuous by their absence.
Don't even ask yourself how safe it is for a
dolmuş driver to be negotiating a bend while
simultaneously counting out change! Things
are changing slowly, but parents of young
children in particular will need to be on their
guard at all times.

At the time of writing, travelling in the
southeast is safe as the unrest there appears to
have largely subsided. However, the Kurdish
issue is far from resolved, so be sure to check
the situation before setting out.

Flies & Mosquitoes

In high summer, mosquitoes can make a stay
along the coast a nightmare. Some hotel rooms
come equipped with nets and/or plug-in bug-
busters, but it's a good idea to bring your own
mosquito coils to burn as well. As dusk falls,
remember to cover your arms and legs or at
least to slather yourself with insect repellent.

In some towns the authorities try to combat
the more general problem of insects by sending out vans that belch repellent into the sky,
usually at about the time in the evening when
everyone has just sat down on a terrace for
dinner. Some people might consider these
dubious clouds of noxious fumes to be as
alarming as the insects they're supposed to
be eradicating.

Lese-Majesty

The laws against insulting, defaming or making light of Atatürk, the Turkish flag, the
Turkish people, the Turkish Republic etc are
taken very seriously. Be warned that even if
such remarks were never made, Turks have
been known to claim they were in the heat of
a quarrel, which is enough to get the foreigner
carted off to jail.

Traffic

Unfortunately Turkey has a terrible record
when it comes to road safety, which means
that you must drive defensively at all times.
It's particularly unwise to drive in the dark on
country roads where tractors may be ambling
along with unlit trailers. See p681 for more
information. When travelling long distances,
it's worth paying slightly more to use a bus
company with relief drivers, rather than risk
being driven by someone who may be at the
wheel for a straight 18 hours.

As a pedestrian note that there is no such
thing as right of way, despite the little green
man. Give way to cars and trucks in all situations, even if you have to jump out of the way.

Scams & Druggings

Turkey is one of the friendliest and most welcoming countries on the planet, but there will
always be a few sharks in the mix. Although
it wouldn't do to be paranoid about potential
scams, it does pay to be careful, especially in
İstanbul.

One of the most popular scams targeted at
single men is the nightclub-bar shake-down –
it mostly happens in İstanbul. You probably
know the scene: you're strolling through
Sultanahmet, when you're approached by a
dapper young man who starts up a conversation. After your initial hesitation, and once
you realise he's not affiliated with a carpet
shop, you start chatting away. He's says he's
off to meet friends for a drink in Beyoğlu,
as there's nowhere to party in Sultanahmet.
Would you like to go along? Woohoo! You
go into a bar and are approached by some
girls by which time it's way too late to back
out. When the bill arrives, lo and behold the
girls' outrageously expensive drinks appear
on it. It's no good claiming you have no cash
on you – you'll be frogmarched to the nearest ATM and 'persuaded' to cough up. If this
happens to you make sure you report it to the
tourist police; some travellers have taken the
policeman back to the bar and received some
or all of their money back.

Drugging isn't a common problem, but
it's worth mentioning nonetheless. In this

situation a single guy is approached by two or three so-called friends, often claiming to be from Egypt or Lebanon or Romania and often accompanied by the fig leaf of a woman. Fall for this one, and you risk finding your drink spiked and waking up in some unexpected location with all your belongings, right down to your shoes, missing – or worse. When the missing person billboards in 2005 went up for a Korean tourist, most locals knew the fate of this unlucky young man – a month later his body was found on the outskirts of İstanbul. Most likely he was a victim of a drugging gone wrong.

Moral of these stories? Single men should not accept invitations from unknown folk in large cities without sizing the situation up very carefully beforehand. You could also invite your new-found friends to a bar of *your* choice; if they're not keen to go, chances are they are shady characters.

We've also heard reports about two female travellers claiming to have their drinks drugged at a camp in Olympos. See p381 for more information.

Smoking

Turks smoke here, there and everywhere. Our favourite example was a driver holding a newborn with his left hand and a cigarette, the gear stick and the steering wheel with his right! Anti-smoking laws are on the drawing board, but until they come into effect you'll have to endure smoking in restaurants, cafés, bars and hotel lobbies. Public transport is usually smoke-free. Taxi drivers will usually butt out if you ask them to.

DISABLED TRAVELLERS

On the whole, Turkey is a challenging destination for disabled (*engelli* or *özürlü*) travellers. Ramps, wide doorways and properly equipped toilets are extremely rare, and Braille and audio information at sights nonexistent. Crossing most streets is particularly challenging; everyone does so at their peril.

Airlines and the top hotels and resorts have some provision for wheelchair access, and ramps are beginning to appear in a few other places, but very slowly. Hotel Rolli (p417) in Anamur is that rare thing – a hotel truly adapted for wheelchair-users. **Mephisto Voyage** (see p511) offers special tours in Cappadocia for mobility-impaired people, utilising the Joelette system.

Increasingly, dropped kerb edges are being introduced to cities, especially in western Turkey – in cities such as Edirne, Bursa and İzmir they seem to have been sensibly designed. Selçuk, Bodrum and Fethiye have been identified as relatively user-friendly towns for people with mobility problems because their pavements and roads are fairly level. Some towns – and even a few service stations – now have toilets adapted for disabled access, but these are the exception not the rule.

Check out www.everybody.co.uk for information on the facilities for disabled travellers offered by various airlines. Turkish Airlines offers 40% discounts to disabled travellers who are also eligible for discounts on trains and at some museums. In İstanbul, disabled people are eligible for free bus travel. However, to qualify for these discounts you may have to show a doctor's letter as 'proof' of your

---

HAVE WHEELS, WILL TRAVEL *Curtis Palmer (New Zealand)*

I am a C6, C7 quadriplegic who loves to travel. I travel with my partner who assists me where places are not accessible. Travelling around Turkey for six weeks was a total joy. I had some difficulties, but no more than when I travel around Europe.

What makes Turkey such a joy is the people. Turkish people are very laid-back and extremely helpful. Whenever we faced a dilemma there was never a shortage of willing helpers.

Admittedly access was testing at times, and independent travel would be very strenuous. We chose to stay in hostels and pensions, and this often meant my partner had to bump me up and down lots of steps. This proved to be more rewarding than expensive hotels, though, as the people were both friendly and helpful. The bathrooms mostly had one step into them and were small with handheld showers. Accessible toilets were rare, and most were squat toilets.

We used dolmuşes and tourist coaches to get around, which meant 'bumming' my way up the steps, to the astonishment of onlookers.

A lot of tourist sites were big obstacles, but getting in free made up for not being able to see everything.

disability, however obvious it may seem to you. Trams are wheelchair-accessible too.

Organisations

Some information resources dedicated to disabled travellers include:

Access-Able (www.access-able.com) Includes a small list of tour and transport operators in Turkey.

Accessibility.com.au (☎ 02-9692 9322; www.accessibility.com.au; Suite 6, The Cooperage, 56 Bowman St, Pyrmont NSW 2001, Australia)

Radar (☎ 020-7250 3222; www.radar.org.uk; 12 City Forum, 250 City Rd, London EC1V 8AF, UK)

Society for the Advancement of Travel for the Handicapped (SATH; ☎ 212-447 7284; www.sath.org; 347 Fifth Ave, No 610, New York, NY 10016, USA)

The **Physically Disabled Support Association** (Bedensel Engellilerle Dayanışma Derneği; www.bedd.org.tr in Turkish only) has helpful information for visitors to Turkey, but is unfortunately only in Turkish. You could email and someone with English might be able to help.

DISCOUNT CARDS

Currently the only really useful card to lay your hands on is the International Student Identity Card (ISIC); you'll need a letter from your college or university to prove that you are a student before you will be able to get one legally. With an ISIC card you should be able to get discounts of at least 50% on most (but by no means all) museum entry fees. You can also get 20% off domestic and international train tickets.

EMBASSIES & CONSULATES
Turkish Embassies Abroad

The following are Turkish embassies in selected cities around the world. For other countries see the list on www.mfa.gov.tr.

Australia (☎ 02-6295 0227; www.turkishembassy.org .au; 60 Mugga Way, Red Hill, ACT 2603)

Canada (☎ 613-789 4044; www.turkishembassy.com; 197 Wurtemburg St, Ottawa, Ontario KIN 8L9)

France (☎ 01 56 33 33 33; www.tcparbsk.com; 184 blvd Malesherbes, 75017 Paris)

Germany (☎ 030-275 850; www.tcberlinbe.de; Runge Str 9, 10179 Berlin)

Greece (☎ 01-724 5915; 8 Vassileos Gheorgiou B St, 10674 Athens)

Ireland (☎ 01-668 5240; turkembassy@eircom.net; 11 Clyde Rd, Ballsbridge, Dublin 4)

Italy (☎ 06-445 941; www.ambasciataditurchia.it; Via Palestro 28, 00185 Rome)

Spain (☎ 91 319 8064; www.tcmadridbe.org; Calle de Rafael Calvo 18 2A-B, Madrid)

Switzerland (☎ 031 359 7070; www.tr-botschaft.ch; Lombachweg 33, 3006 Berne)

UK (☎ 020-7591 6900; www.turkishconsulate.org.uk; Rutland Lodge, Rutland Gardens, Knightsbridge, London SW7 1BW)

USA (☎ 202-612 6700; www.turkishembassy.org; 2525 Massachusetts Ave, NW Washington, DC 2008)

Embassies & Consulates in Turkey

Most embassies and consulates in Turkey are open from 8am to noon Monday to Friday although some embassies of Muslim countries may be open Sunday to Thursday. Often they also open in the afternoon for people to pick up visas. Exceptions to these opening hours are included below. If you need to ask the way to an embassy say: '[Country] *başkonsolosluğu nerede?*'

For details on getting visas to neighbouring countries, see p674.

Armenia Contact Russian embassy.

Australia (☼ 8.30am-4.30pm Mon-Fri) embassy in Ankara (Map p442; ☎ 0312-459 9521; www.embaustralia.org .tr; Uğur Mumcu Caddesi 88\7, Gaziosmanpaşa); İstanbul (☎ 0212-243 1333; fax 243 1332; 2nd fl, Suzer Plaza, Asker Ocağı Caddesi 15, Elmadağ, Şişli)

Azerbaijan (☼ 8.30am-4.30pm Mon-Fri) embassy in Ankara (☎ 0312-491 1681; Baku Sokak 1, Or-An); İstanbul (☎ 0212-284 9579; Sumbul Sokak 17, Levent 1); Kars (☼ 9.30am-12.30pm Mon-Fri; ☎ 0474-223 6475, 223 1361; fax 223 8741; Eski Erzurum Caddesi)

Bulgaria (☼ 9-11am Mon-Fri) embassy in Ankara (Map p442; ☎ 0312-427 5142; Atatürk Bulvarı 124, Kavaklıdere); Edirne (☎ /fax 0284-214 0617; Talat Paşa Caddesi 31); İstanbul (☼ 9am-noon Mon-Fri) (☎ 0212-281 0114; Mehmet Ahmet Adnan Zeygün Caddesi 44, Ulus, Levent 2)

Canada (☼ 9.30am-5.30pm Mon-Thu, 9.30am-12.30pm Fri) embassy in Ankara (Map p442; ☎ 0312-409 2700; Cinnah Caddesi 58, Çankaya); İstanbul (Map pp100-1; ☎ 0212-251 9838; fax 272 3437; İstiklal Caddesi 373/5, Beyoğlu)

France (☼ 9am-12.30pm Mon-Fri) embassy in Ankara (Map p442; ☎ 0312-455 4545; Paris Caddesi 70, Kavaklıdere); İstanbul (Map pp100-1; ☎ 0212-334 8730; fax 334 8727; İstiklal Caddesi 8, Taksim)

Georgia (☼ 10am-5pm Mon-Fri) embassy in Ankara (☎ 0312-442 6508; Hilal Mahallesi Caddesi 31, Yıldız); Trabzon (Map p550; ☎ 0462-326 2226; fax 326 2296; Pertev Paşa Sokak 10; ☼ 9am-6pm Mon-Fri); İstanbul (Map pp94-5; ☎ 0212-343 9258; Cumhuriyet Caddesi 169)

Germany (☼ 9am-noon Mon-Fri) embassy in Ankara (Map p442; ☎ 0312-455 5100; fax 427 8926; Atatürk Bulvarı 114, Kavaklıdere); İstanbul (Map pp100-1; ☎ 0212-334 6100; fax 249 9920; İnönü Caddesi 16, Taksim)

Iran (🕑 8.30am-12.30pm & 2.30-4.30pm Mon-Thu & Sat, 8.30am-12.30pm Fri & Sun) embassy in Ankara (Map p442; ☎ 0312-468 2820; fax 468 2823; Tahran Caddesi 10, Kavaklıdere); Erzurum (☎ 0442-316 2285; fax 316 1182; off Atatürk Bulvarı); İstanbul (Map pp100-1; 🕑 8.30-11.30am Mon-Thu & Sat; ☎ 0212-513 8230; fax 511 5219; Ankara Caddesi 1/2, Cağaloğlu)

Iraq embassy in Ankara (☎ 0312-468 7421; fax 468 4832; Turan Emeksiz Sokak 11, Gaziosmanpaşa)

Netherlands (🕑 8.30am-5pm Mon-Fri) embassy in Ankara (Map p442; ☎ 0312-409 1800; fax 409 1898; Hollanda Caddesi 3, Yıldız); İstanbul (Map pp100-1; ☎ 0212-393 2121; fax 292 5031; İstiklal Caddesi 393, Beyoğlu)

New Zealand embassy in Ankara (Map p442; ☎ 0312-467 9056; fax 0312-467 9013; level 4, Iran Caddesi 13/4, Kavaklıdere); İstanbul (☎ 0212-251 3895; nzhonconist@hatem-law.com.tr; İnönü Caddesi 92/3, Gümüşuyu)

Russia (🕑 10-11am Mon-Fri) embassy in Ankara (Map p442; ☎ 0312-439 2122; fax 438 3952; Karyağdi Sokak 5, Çankaya); İstanbul (Map pp100-1; ☎ 0212-292 5101; visavi@turk.net; İstiklal Caddesi 443, Beyoğlu); Trabzon (Map p549; ☎ 0462-326 2600; fax 326 2101; Şh Refik Cesur 6, Ortahisar)

Syria embassy in Ankara (☎ 0312-440 9657; fax 438 5609; Sedat Simavi Sokak 40, 06680 Çankaya); İstanbul (☎ 0212-232 6721; fax 230 2215; Maçka Caddesi 59/5, Teşvikiye) There is a newly opened consulate in Gaziantep, but at the time of research it was processing visa applications only for Turkish nationals.

UK embassy in Ankara (☎ 0312-455 3344; fax 455 3351; Şehit Ersan Caddesi 46/A, Çankaya; 🕑 9am-12.30pm & 2-4pm Mon-Fri); İstanbul (Map pp100-1; ☎ 0212-334 6400; fax 334 6407; Meşrutiyet Caddesi 34, Tepebaşı, Beyoğlu; 🕑 9am-12.30pm & 2-3.30pm Mon-Fri); Marmaris (☎ 0412 6486; fax 412 5077; Yeşil Marmaris Travel Agency & Yacht Management Bldg, Barbaros Caddesi 249; 🕑 9.30am-noon Mon-Fri & 2.30-5pm Mon-Thu in summer)

USA (🕑 8.30am-5.30pm Mon-Fri) embassy in Ankara (Map p442; ☎ 0312-455 5555; fax 467 0019; Atatürk Bulvarı 118, Kavaklıdere); Adana (☎ 0322-346 6262; fax 346 7916; Girne Bulvarı No 212 Guzelevler Mahallesi); İstanbul (Map pp100-1; ☎ 0212-335 9000; fax 335 9102; Kaplıcalar Mevkii 2, İstinye)

FESTIVALS & EVENTS

Turkey has loads of festivals – İstanbul seems to have something on almost every week! (See p135 for details of some of these.) The following are some of the national standouts:

January

New Year's Day A surrogate Christmas on 1 January, with the usual decorations, exchange of gifts and greeting cards.

Camel Wrestling On the last Sunday in January be in Selçuk for the camel wrestle of a lifetime. Be a savvy spectator with our wrestling low-down on p250.

March

Nevruz Kurds and Alevis celebrate the ancient Middle Eastern spring festival on 21 March with much jumping over bonfires and general jollity. Banned until a few years ago, Nevruz is now an official holiday with huge parties, particularly in Diyarbakır, that last well into the morning.

April

Children's Day Every 23 April is celebrated with an international children's festival, with kids invited to countrywide events.

Anzac Day The disastrous WWI battles for the Dardanelles are commemorated with dawn services at Gallipoli on 25 April.

June & July

Aspendos Opera & Ballet Festival From mid-June to early July this festival is an excellent excuse to enjoy a performance in one of the finest Roman theatres in the world (p395).

International İzmir Festival Mid-June to mid-July, İzmir, Çeşme and Ephesus host opera, classical and dance (p230).

Kafkasör Kültür ve Sanat Festivalı In the last week-end of June join the crush at the bull-wrestling matches at Artvin (p575).

Kırkpınar Oil Wrestling Competition Every June, Turkey's greatest oil wrestlers slug it out for supremacy in Edirne (p171).

Kültür Sanat ve Turizm Festival During the last week-end of July Doğubayazıt hosts a culture and arts festival celebrating Kurdish music, dance and theatre (p587).

August

Hacı Bektaş Veli Festival From 16 to 18 August, sleepy little Hacıbektaş comes alive for the annual pilgrimage for followers of the Bektaşi order of dervishes (p517).

International Ballet Festival Can you think of a more atmospheric location than the Castle of St Peter in Bodrum for this annual festival? See p276 for more.

December

Mevlâna Festival This Konya festival, honouring Celaleddin Rumi, the great poet and mystic who founded the Mevlevi order of whirling dervishes, usually lasts from around 10 to 17 December (see p486).

FOOD

For information about what you'll find on Turkish menus, see p68.

In the Eating sections of this guide, we usually subdivide eating establishments into restaurants, places for quick, cheap feeds and cafés. Restaurants are the smarter places where you can expect to find tablecloths and alcoholic drinks. Expect to pay between €15 and €30 without drinks to eat in a restaurant in most parts of Turkey (more in İstanbul, less way out east).

Quick eats include all the many *lokantas* that dish up soups, stews and grills – they rarely serve alcohol. A meal is likely to cost you only between €4 and €10, even in the big cities.

Cafés fall somewhere between the two categories. They are usually much smarter than *lokantas* but not as formal as restaurants. Most offer a selection of pastas, sandwiches and salads – you'll pay between €7 and €15. There will probably be alcohol available and may well be music in the evening.

GAY & LESBIAN TRAVELLERS
Homosexuality is legal in Turkey and attitudes are changing thanks to the hard work of groups such as **Kaos GL** (www.kaosgl.com), but prejudice remains strong and there are sporadic reports of violence towards gays – the message is discretion. İstanbul has a flourishing gay scene (see p147), as does Ankara. Elsewhere there may only be a bar or two.

For more information, contact Turkey's gay and lesbian support group, **Lambda İstanbul** (www.lambdaistanbul.org) and Kaos GL, based in Ankara, which publishes the country's only gay and lesbian magazine (in Turkish only).

Gay-friendly travel agents include **Sunset Gay & Lesbian Travel** (www.turkey-gay-travel.com) and **Absolute Sultans** (www.absolutesultans.com).

HOLIDAYS
When you're planning your trip, it's worth noting the dates of Turkish holidays. You should book accommodation and transport ahead of time wherever possible if you're planning to travel during a holiday or a few days either side of one. The biggest Islamic holiday, Kurban Bayramı, sees locals travel all over the

country: for those working in the big cities it may be the only time of the year they get to see their families.

All banks, businesses and most shops are closed on public holidays; however, most restaurants, grocery shops, supermarkets and businesses catering for foreign tourists will remain open. Note that just prior to and after the holidays banks will be extremely busy and ATMs may run out of cash during the holiday period. It's well worth planning ahead so you don't end up having to change money at inflated rates.

Islamic Holidays
The official Turkish calendar is the Gregorian one used in Europe, but religious festivals are celebrated according to the Islamic lunar calendar. Dates in the Major Islamic Holidays table, below, are estimates; exact dates are not confirmed until the moon is sighted.

Turkey celebrates all the main Islamic holidays of which the most important are the month-long Ramazan and, two months later, Kurban Bayramı. Since these holidays are celebrated according to the Muslim lunar calendar, they take place around 11 days earlier each year.

An unofficial half-day holiday for 'preparation' precedes the start of major public and religious holidays; shops and offices close about noon, and the actual festival begins at sunset. Of the religious festivals, only Şeker Bayramı and Kurban Bayramı are also public holidays.

RAMAZAN
The Holy Month (Ramadan in other Muslim countries) is similar in some ways to Lent. Fasting during Ramazan is one of the five pillars of Islam, and for 30 days devout Muslims let *nothing* pass their lips during daylight hours: no eating, drinking, smoking or even downing an Aspirin. Pregnant or nursing women, young children, the infirm and aged, and travellers are not obliged to fast.

MAJOR ISLAMIC HOLIDAYS					
Islamic year	New Year	Prophet's Birthday	Ramazan begins	Şeker Bayramı	Kurban Bayramı
1428	20 Jan 07	31 Mar 07	13 Sep 07	12 Oct 07	20 Dec 07
1429	10 Jan 08	20 Mar 08	2 Sep 08	1 Oct 08	8 Dec 08
1430	29 Dec 09	9 Mar 09	22 Aug 09	21 Sep 09	28 Nov 09

Before dawn, drummers wake the faithful so they can eat before sunrise. Traditionally, a cannon shot signals the end of the fast at sunset whereupon everyone sits down to an *iftar* (the break of fast meal).

During Ramazan, some restaurants may be closed from dawn to nightfall, but most eateries catering to tourists remain open. As non-Muslims, you're allowed to eat and drink when you like – and in the big cities you'll find lots of nonfasting Muslims beside you – but it's still best to be discreet, especially in conservative towns.

Ramazan is not an official public holiday, although many businesses operate in a half-hearted manner, opening late and closing early. Not surprisingly tempers can fray faster than usual at this time, and driving can be a bit more erratic.

ŞEKER BAYRAMI

A three-day festival that celebrates the end of Ramazan, Şeker Bayramı (Sweets Holiday; Ramazan Bayramı) is so named because during this festival children go from door to door asking for sweet treats. Their elders go visiting, and everybody drinks lots of tea in broad daylight after the long fast. Banks and offices close; hotels, buses, trains and planes are booked solid.

KURBAN BAYRAMI

The most important religious and secular holiday of the year, Kurban Bayramı (Festival of the Sacrifice) is just as important to Muslims as Christmas is to Christians. The festival commemorates İbrahim's near-sacrifice of İsmael on Mt Moriah (Quran, Sura 37; Genesis 22), the same story as the biblical one about Abraham and Isaac.

Every year around four million cows and sheep are sacrificed for Kurban Bayramı. Every head of household who can afford to buys a beast to sacrifice. Immediately after early morning prayers on the first day of the holiday the animal's throat is slit. It's then flayed and butchered, and family and friends prepare a feast. Part of the meat is given to the needy; the skin is donated to a charity, which then sells it to a leather products company. These days you won't see the sacrifices in the cities, but out in the countryside it's a different story.

Kurban Bayramı is a four- or five-day holiday, and banks usually close for a full

week. Transport is packed, and hotel rooms, particularly along the coasts, are scarce and expensive.

For more about the part played by food in these festivals, see p70.

Public Holidays

New Year's Day (Yılbaşı; 1 January)
National Sovereignty & Children's Day (Ulusal Egemenlik ve Çocuk Günü; 23 April) Commemorates the first meeting of the Turkish Grand National Assembly in 1920.
Youth & Sports Day (Gençlik ve Spor Günü; 19 May) Dedicated to Atatürk and the youth of the Republic.
Victory Day (Zafer Bayramı; 30 August) Commemorates the republican army's victory over the invading Greek army at Dumlupınar during the War of Independence.
Republic Day (Cumhuriyet Bayramı; 29 October) Commemorates the proclamation of the republic by Atatürk in 1923.

School Holidays

You need to take Turkish school holidays into account when planning your trip. Along with increasing affluence has come a swelling domestic tourism market that gets into its stride in mid-June and continues right through until mid-September. During those months many coastal towns, especially along the north Aegean coast between İstanbul and İzmir, get very busy and transport can become very crowded.

INSURANCE

A travel insurance policy to cover theft, loss and medical expenses is a very good idea. A huge variety of policies is available, so check the small print.

Some policies specifically exclude 'dangerous activities', which can include scuba diving, motorcycling and even trekking. Some policies don't recognise locally obtained motorcycle licences.

Some policies will pay your medical expenses directly, while others will reimburse you later. For more on health insurance, see p687.

Note that some insurance policies may not cover you if you travel to regions of the country where your government warns against travel. Similarly if you decide to cancel your trip on the advice of an official warning against travel your insurer may not cover you.

See p682 for details on motor and health insurance, respectively.

INTERNET ACCESS
Laptop Computers

If you plan to carry your notebook or palmtop with you, remember that the power supply voltage in Turkey may differ from that at home, which entails the risk of damage to your equipment. The best investment is a universal AC adaptor that will enable you to plug your appliance in anywhere without frying the innards. See www.kropla.com for more information.

In four- and five-star hotels, most phone connections are made using the American-style clear plastic RJ11 plug, so it's easy to plug in a laptop. Many of these hotels also have WLANs. In cheaper and older hotels, the phones often use a larger white or beige three-prong Turkish plug. In such cases you'll need to find an electrical shop and buy a cable with one of these plugs on one end and an RJ11 plug on the other.

You'll can find wi-fi in many airports, cafés and top-end hotels throughout the country. See www.winet.turktelekom.com.tr for the hot spots.

Internet Cafés

Turks took to the internet like ducks to water. Wherever you go, you'll be two steps from an internet café, and most have ADSL connections. Most hotels, pensions, travel agencies and carpet shops are also hooked up. Fees are usually around €2 for an hour. Internet cafés are usually open from 9am til late at night, or until the last customer leaves.

The best internet cafés have English keyboards. Others will have Turkish keyboards, in which case you need to be aware that Turkish has two 'i's: the familiar dotted 'i', and the less familiar dotless 'ı'. Unfortunately the one in the usual place on a Turkish keyboard is the dotless 'ı'; ensure you are using the correct dotted 'i' when typing in email addresses.

Likewise, on a Turkish keyboard you will have to create the '@' symbol by holding down the 'q' and ALT keys at the same time.

LEGAL MATTERS

It's important to remember that when you are in Turkey you are subject to Turkish law, *not* the law of your home country. Beyond urging the Turkish authorities to treat you fairly, your embassy won't be able to help you if you break the law.

For most travellers driving is the only thing likely to land them in trouble with the law. You may be stopped by blue-uniformed *trafik polis*. You can be fined on the spot for speeding. However, if you know you have done nothing wrong and the police appear to be asking for money, play dumb. Inevitably, though, you'll have to pay up if they persist.

If you have an accident, don't move the car before finding a police officer and asking for a *kaza raporu* (accident report). The officer may ask you to submit to an alcohol breath-test. Contact your car-rental company within 48 hours.

You could also fall foul of the laws on lese-majesty (see p655), antiquities smuggling or illegal drugs. It goes without saying that Turkish jails are not places where you want to spend any time.

MAPS
Street Maps

Turkish tourist offices stock OK-quality street maps of Adana, Ankara, Antalya, İstanbul and İzmir. Of the local privately produced street maps, Map Medya's are best. It produces proper street maps of many western Turkey cities (€3). You can pick these up in İstanbul at **Azim Dağıtım** (Map pp96-7; ☎ 0212-638 1313; Klodfarer Caddesi 6, Sultanahmet; ☉ 9am-7pm Mon-Sat) or in the good bookshops along İstiklal Caddesi.

Touring Maps

Turkish tourist offices stock a free sheet *Tourist Map* (1:850,000) – it's OK at a pinch, but it's usually out of date. The best sheet map of the whole country you can buy is the *Türkiye Karayolları Haritası* (1:1,000,000; €3), by Map Medya, updated twice a year.

For detailed touring, the *Köy Köy Türkiye* (*Turkey Village by Village*; 1:400,000; €17) atlas is the best. The *Oto Atlas Türkiye* (*Road Atlas Turkey*) at 1:600,000 is another good option. Map Medya also produces excellent regional maps. You can buy these in İstanbul.

MONEY

Turkey's currency is the Yeni Türk Lirası (New Turkish Lira; YTL). Lira comes in coins of 1, 5, 10, 25 and 50 *kuruş* and a 1 lira coin, and notes of 5, 10, 20, 50 and 100 lira.

Prices in this book are quoted in more stable euros. For details on costs in Turkey, see p19. For exchange rates, see the Quick Reference in the inside front cover of this book.

After decades of rampant inflation – as high as 70% – the Turkish lira started to stabilise in 2003; by 2004 inflation was down to around 12%. The Yeni Türk Lirası was introduced in January 2005. However, it still makes sense to wait until you arrive in Turkey to change your money into lira since you will probably get a better exchange rate inside the country than outside. Turkish lira are virtually worthless outside Turkey, so make sure you spend them all before leaving.

Restaurateurs and shop owners don't often carry large-denomination notes on them, so try to keep a supply of small money on you for small payments.

ATMs

ATMs dispense new Turkish lira to Visa, MasterCard, Cirrus and Maestro card holders. Look for these logos on the machines; they are found in most towns. Virtually all the machines offer instructions in English, French and German. It's possible to get around Turkey using only ATMs, provided you remember to draw out money in the towns to tide you through the villages that don't have them, and keep some cash in reserve for the inevitable day when the machine throws a wobbly, or it's a holiday. You can usually draw out about €350 per day.

Note that if your card is swallowed by a stand-alone ATM booth, it may be tricky getting it back in a hurry – these booths are often run by franchisees rather than by the banks themselves.

Cash

US dollars and euros are the easiest currencies to change, although many banks and exchange offices will change other major currencies such as UK pounds and Japanese yen. You may find it difficult to exchange Australian or Canadian currency except at banks and offices in major cities.

Credit Cards

Visa and MasterCard/Access are widely accepted by hotels, shops, bars and restaurants, although not by pensions and local restaurants outside main tourist areas. You can also get cash advances on these cards. Amex cards are rarely accepted.

Moneychangers

It's easy to change major currencies in exchange offices, some post offices (PTTs), shops and hotels, although banks tend to make heavy weather of it. Places that don't charge a commission usually offer a worse exchange rate instead.

Although Turkey has no black market, foreign currencies are readily accepted in shops, hotels and restaurants in many tourist areas.

Exchange rates for several major currencies are listed on the inside front cover of this book.

Tipping

In the cheapest restaurants locals leave a few coins in the change tray. Elsewhere you should tip about 10% to 15% of the bill. Some more expensive restaurants automatically add a 10% or 15% *servis ücreti* (service charge) to your bill, but there's no guarantee this goes to the staff, so you may want to tip the staff directly.

Tips are not expected in cheaper hotels. In more expensive places a porter will carry your luggage and show you to your room. For doing this (and showing you how to turn on the lights and the television) he'll expect about 3% of the room price.

It's usual to round up metered taxi fares to the nearest 50 *kuruş*, so round up YTL4.70 to YTL5. Dolmuş drivers never expect a tip.

In Turkish baths you should tip around 10% to 20% to the masseuse/masseur. In the tourist-oriented *hamams* the fixed price may already be so high that you may assume that service is included, but it usually isn't and a tip is appreciated.

If you are shown around a site that is not normally open to the public or are given a guided tour by the custodian, you should certainly tip them for their trouble. A few YTL for 10 or so minutes is usually fine.

Travellers Cheques

Our advice: don't bring them! Banks, shops and hotels usually see it as a burden to change travellers cheques and will either try to get you to go elsewhere or charge you a premium for changing them.

POST

Postcards to Europe cost €0.55, and to all other destinations €0.65. Letters to Europe cost €0.65, and to all other destinations €0.80. Post your letters in the post office: the *yurtdışı* slot is for mail to foreign countries, the *yurtiçi* for mail to other Turkish cities; the *şehiriçi* for local mail. See www.ptt.gov.tr for information on post offices and rates.

Turkish *postanes* (post offices) are indicated by black-on-yellow 'PTT' signs. Main post offices in large cities are open from 8am to 8pm daily. Smaller post offices keep more limited hours (8.30am to 12.30pm and 1.30pm to 5.30pm) and may be closed on Saturday afternoon and all day Sunday.

Most post offices in tourist areas offer poste-restante services, generally from 8.30am to noon and 1.30pm to 4pm. To collect your mail, go to the *merkez postane* (main post office) with your passport. Letters should be addressed as follows: Name, Poste Restante, Merkez Postahane, District, Postcode, City, Province, Turkey. There are no guarantees you will receive mail, so never have anything valuable or important sent to you.

Letters sometimes take several weeks to arrive (packets even longer), so plan ahead accordingly.

Parcels

If you decide to ship something home from Turkey, don't close your parcel before it has been inspected by a customs official. Take packing and wrapping materials with you to the post office. Parcels sent by surface mail to Europe cost around €14 for the first 1kg, then €2 per kg thereon; to USA, €14 for the first 1kg, then €4 thereon; and to Australia €15 for the first 1kg, then €5 thereon.

If you'd prefer the security of an international courier, DHL, for example, charges €85 for a 2kg parcel to Europe, €105 for the USA and €140 to Australia.

We receive occasional complaints from readers who have bought a beautiful kilim and agreed to have the shopkeeper ship it out, only to find a much cheaper item arriving. This is only likely to happen if the shop is a fly-by-night one. Shops that have been in business a long time have no vested interest in ripping off their customers and are usually well used to shipping parcels worldwide.

SHOPPING

Travellers are usually surprised and delighted by the range and quality of things to buy in Turkey. Sure, there are plenty of chintzy souvenirs, but most of what you buy here won't end up in the cupboard within a week of returning. Goodies here are increasingly being exported to designer boutiques round the world.

If you're wondering about the meaning behind the ubiquitous blue-glass eyes, see (p232).

Note that most shops close on Sunday except in prime tourist locations.

Carpets & Kilims

Turkey is famous for its beautiful carpets and kilims (flat-weave rugs). Most carpet shops have a range of pieces made by a variety of techniques. Besides the traditional pile carpets, they usually offer double-sided flat-woven mats such as kilims. Most are beautiful traditional designs and techniques, but many are patchwork or other contemporary designs.

As well as Turkish carpets, most carpet shops sell pieces from other countries, in particular from Iran, Pakistan, Afghanistan and the ex-Soviet republics of Azerbaijan, Turkmenistan and Uzbekistan. If it matters that your carpet is actually from Turkey, bear in mind that Iran favours the single knot and Turkey the double knot. Turkish carpets also tend to have a higher pile, more dramatic designs and more varied colours than their Iranian cousins.

The carpet market is lucrative and the hard-sell antics of some dealers have tended to bring the trade into disrepute, putting off some potential purchasers. To ensure you get a good buy, spend time visiting shops and comparing prices and quality. It's also worth taking a look in the shops at home before you leave so that you'll know what's available and for what prices at home. When deciding whether to buy a particular carpet it might help to follow some of the guidelines listed here:

- A good-quality, long-lasting carpet or kilim should be 100% wool (*yüz de yüz yün*). Is the wool fine and shiny, with signs of the natural oil? Recycled or cheap wool feels scratchy and has no sheen, and the cheapest carpets may be made from mercerised cotton or 'flosh'. Another way to identify the material is to turn the carpet over and look for the fine, frizzy fibres common to wool. But bear in mind that just being made of wool doesn't guarantee a kilim or carpet's quality. If the dyes and design are ugly, even a 100% woollen piece can be a bad buy.
- Check the closeness of the weave by turning the carpet or kilim over and inspecting the back. In general, the tighter the weave

and the smaller the knots, the higher the quality and durability of the piece.

▪ Beware the salesman who asserts that all his range are coloured with natural dyes. Chemical dyes have been the main method of colouring in the country for the last 50 years. There is nothing wrong with chemical dyes, but natural dyes and colours tend to be preferred and therefore fetch higher prices. Spread the nap with your fingers and look at the bottom of the pile. Both natural and chemical dyes fade (despite what the salesman might tell you). If you see the colours are lighter on the surface than deep in the pile, it's often an indication that the surface has faded in the sun, but not necessarily that it is an antique.

▪ Unless you know something about antique carpets and kilims, which are always more expensive, it's probably best to stick with new productions. New carpets can be made to look old, and damaged or worn carpets can be rewoven (good work, but expensive), patched or even painted.

There's nothing wrong with a dealer offering you a patched or repainted carpet provided they point out these defects and price the piece accordingly.

Ceramics

After carpets and kilims, Turkey's beautiful ceramics would have to be the most successful souvenir industry. Many of the tiles you see in shops have been painted using a silkscreen printing method and this is why they're cheap. One step up are the ubiquitous hand-painted bowls, plates and other pieces; these are made by rubbing a patterned carbon paper on the raw ceramic, tracing the black outline, and filling in the holes with colour. The most expensive pieces are hand-painted by master craftspeople, without the use of patterns.

Note that many ceramics have been covered in lead-based glaze so it's probably safest to use them as ornaments.

Copper

Gleaming copper vessels will greet you in every souvenir shop. Some are old, most

---

THE ART OF BARGAINING

Traditionally, when customers enter a Turkish shop to make a significant purchase, they're offered a comfortable seat and a drink (çay – tea, coffee or a soft drink). There is some general chitchat, then discussion of the shop's goods in general, then of the customer's tastes, preferences and requirements. Finally, a number of items in the shop are displayed for the customer's inspection.

The customer asks the price; the shop owner gives it; the customer looks doubtful and makes a counteroffer 25% to 50% lower. This procedure goes back and forth several times before a price acceptable to both parties is arrived at. It's considered very bad form to haggle over a price, come to an agreement, and then change your mind.

If you can't agree on a price it's perfectly OK to say goodbye and walk out of the shop. In fact, walking out is one of the best ways to test the authenticity of the 'last' offer. If shopkeepers know you can find the item elsewhere for less, they'll probably call out, 'OK, it's yours for what you offered.' Even if they don't stop you, there's nothing to prevent you from returning later and buying the item for what they quoted.

To bargain effectively you must be prepared to take your time, and you must know something about the items in question, not to mention their market price. The best way to do this is to look at similar goods in several shops, asking prices but not making counteroffers. Always stay good humoured and polite when you are bargaining – if you do this the shopkeeper will too. When bargaining you can often get a discount by offering to buy several items at once, by paying in a strong major currency, or by paying cash.

If you don't have sufficient time to shop around, follow the age-old rule: find something you like at a price you're willing to pay, buy it, enjoy it, and don't worry about whether or not you received the world's lowest price.

In general, you shouldn't bargain in food shops or over transport costs. Outside tourist areas, hotels may expect to 'negotiate' the room price with you. In tourist areas pension owners are usually fairly clear about their prices, although if you're travelling in winter or staying a long time it's worth asking about *indirim* (discounts).

are handsome and some are still eminently useful. New copperware tends to be of lighter gauge, but will still have been made by hand.

Copper vessels should not be used for cooking or eating unless they have been tinned inside: that is, washed with molten tin that covers the toxic copper. If you intend to use a copper vessel, make sure the interior layer of tin is intact or negotiate to have it *kalaylı* (tinned). Be sure to ask about the price of the tinning in advance as *teneke* (tin) is expensive.

Inlaid Wood

You'll find cigarette boxes, chess and *tavla* (backgammon) boards and all sorts of items inlaid with different coloured woods, silver or mother-of-pearl on sale all over Turkey. Make sure what you're buying actually is inlay – these days, alarmingly accurate imitations exist. Also, check whether the 'silver' is not actually aluminium or pewter.

Jewellery

Turkey is a wonderful place to buy jewellery, whether new or old. Jewellers' Row in any market is a dazzling strip of glittering shop windows filled with gold for brides-to-be. Serious gold-buyers should check the daily price for unworked gold of so-many carat in the daily papers. Watch carefully as the jeweller weighs the piece in question, and then calculate what part of the price is for gold and what part for labour.

Silver is another matter. You can certainly find sterling silver jewellery (look for the hallmark) but beware nickel silver and pewter-like imitations. Silver, too, is sold by weight as well as labour.

Leather

On any given Kurban Bayramı (Festival of the Sacrifice), more than 2.5 million sheep get the axe in Turkey. Add to that the normal day-to-day needs of a cuisine based on mutton and lamb, and you have a huge amount of raw material to be made into leather; hence the country's thriving leather industry.

Jackets are one of the most popular purchases. To be sure of a good buy, examine the piece thoroughly. Try it on just as carefully and see whether the sleeves are full enough, the buttonholes are positioned well and the collar rubs.

Meerschaum

If you smoke a pipe, you know about meerschaum (*lületaşı*). The world's largest and finest beds of this hydrous magnesium silicate, this soft, white stone, are found near the city of Eskişehir (p303). This porous but heat-resistant material is used most famously to make pipes. Artful carving of the stone produces pipes portraying anything from turbaned paşas to mythological beasts.

SOLO TRAVELLERS

Turkey is a great country for solo travellers since most hotels and pensions have a per-head charge or offer discounts for lone travellers; only rarely will you have to pay the full price of a double (except at the Hilton, Sheraton and their ilk). However, single travellers do need to develop a thick skin as most Turks couldn't conceive of going anywhere alone (except, perhaps, on business). Wherever you go you'll have people double-checking with you that you're really alone and expecting you to justify your solitary status.

If you, too, are having doubts about solitude then Turkey's many small pensions are great places to meet potential travelling companions, as are the hostels in İstanbul.

Lone women inevitably have a harder time of it, although the problems rarely go much further than the occasional unsolicited knock on the hotel door at midnight; see p668 for more information.

TELEPHONE

Türk Telekom (www.telekom.gov.tr) has a monopoly on phone services, and service is efficient if costly. You can direct-dial within Turkey and overseas with little difficulty. When calling Turkey from overseas the country code is ☎ 90, and you drop the 0 on the area codes. The international access code to call abroad from Turkey is ☎ 00.

Kontörlü Telefon

If you're only going to make one call, it's best to look for a booth with a sign saying *kontörlü telefon* (metered telephone); you make your call and the owner reads the meter and charges you accordingly. The cost of a local call depends on what the phone's owner charges for each *kontör* (unit). In touristy areas you can get rates as low as €0.25 per minute to Europe, the UK, USA and Australia. These rates are, however, almost twice as much International

DIRECTORY

Phonecards (see below), but may be the best option if you're only making a quick call.

Mobile Phones

Turks adore mobile (*cep*, pocket) phones, and reception is excellent throughout nearly all of the country. Mobile phone numbers start with a four-figure code beginning with ☎ 05.

If you want use your home phone in Turkey, note that Turkey uses the standard GSM (Global System for Mobile Communications) network operating on 900MHz or 1800MHz. Most phones are GSM so they should be fine but some US-, Canadian- and Scandinavian-bought mobiles phones are not compatible. You should set up an international roaming facility with your home phone provider before you leave home. Mobiles can connect with Turkey's **Turkcell** (www.turkcell.com.tr), **Telsim** (www.telsim.com.tr) or **Avea** (www.avea.com.tr) networks.

If you want to buy a SIM card while you're in Turkey, it's a good idea to stick to the big networks – Turkcell, Avea or MyCep (Telsim) – as you'll get good coverage over the country as well as competitive rates. A SIM card with Turkcell costs around €17 and usually includes some free *kontör* (unit); you'll need to show your passport and ensure the seller sends your details through to Turkcell to activate your account. You can buy prepaid phone cards at any of the little streetside booths around the country. Expect to pay around €7/14 for 120/300 *kontör* with Turkcell, a little more with MyCep or Avea, but it depends on what specials are on.

Pay Phones & Phonecards

Türk Telkom payphones can be found in most major public buildings and facilities, public squares and transportation termini. International calls can be made from all payphones. All payphones require cards that can be bought at telephone centres or, for a small mark-up, at some shops. There are two sets of cards in use: magnetic strip floppy cards and ones with chips on them called Smart cards.

In general, both cards cost about the same. A 30-unit card (€1.50) is sufficient for local calls; 50 units (€2.75) for short domestic intercity calls; and 100 units (€4.75) for longer domestic intercity calls or short international chats. The newer phones also accept major credit cards.

INTERNATIONAL PHONECARDS

The cheapest option for international calls is with phonecards that you use with a land-line (ie the phone in your hotel room) or a public phone. You call the national toll-free number, put in the PIN umber on the card and dial away. Companies such as IPC and Bigalo offer the best rates (note, these are *not* the cards with the Türk Telecom logo). For a 300-*kontör* IPC card (which costs €3) you can speak for 20/6 minutes to a landline/mobile in Australia, and around 26/6 minutes to a landline/mobile to the UK, Europe and the USA. IPC cards are available in 300, 1000 (€8.50) and 1500 (€17) *kontör* lots. It's worthwhile sticking to a reputable phonecard company (such as IPC or Bigalo) as with other companies' cards credit has been known to disappear or calls won't go through. These cards are widely available in the street-side booths in tourist areas of İstanbul and Ankara but can be difficult to find elsewhere. You cannot use these cards through mobile phones.

TIME

Turkish time is two hours ahead of GMT/UTC. Daylight saving (summer time) runs from 3am on the last Sunday in March until 4am on the last Sunday in October. During daylight saving, when it's noon in İstanbul it's 2am in Los Angeles and Vancouver, 5am in New York, 10am in London, 6pm in Tokyo, 7pm in Sydney and 9pm in Auckland. See www.timeanddate.com to calculate other time differences.

Turks use the 24-hour clock.

TOILETS

Although most hotels and public facilities have sit-down toilets, you'll also see hole-in-the-ground models in Turkey. The custom is to wash yourself using the left hand with water from a jug or to use the little copper tube in the toilet, which spurts water where needed. You then dry yourself with tissues, which you usually provide yourself. In most slick, modern bathrooms you can flush paper directly down the toilet, but in many places if you do this you may flood the premises. If you're not sure, play it safe and put it in the bin provided.

Fairly clean public toilets can usually be found at major attractions and transport hubs. In an emergency it's worth remembering that every mosque has a basic toilet.

Most public toilets – even in restaurants or cinemas – require payment of around €0.30.

TOURIST INFORMATION

Every Turkish town of any size has an official tourist office run by the Ministry of Tourism. They're usually open from 8.30am to noon or 12.30pm, and from 1.30pm to 5.30pm Monday to Friday, with longer hours and at weekends in summer in popular tourist locations. Unfortunately only a handful have staff who know anything about the area or who speak any language other than Turkish. If the information you need is not already in this book, you are unlikely to find it by visiting a tourist office. Your best bet is usually to seek out a sympathetic tour operator or pension owner.

Following is a select list of tourist offices outside Turkey:

France (☎ 01 45 62 78 68; www.infoturquie.com; 102 Avenue des Champs-Élysées, 75008 Paris)

Germany Berlin (☎ 030-214 3752; www.tuerkei-kultur -info.de; Tauentzien Str 9-12, 10789) Frankfurt (☎ 069-23 3081; www.reiseland-tuerkei-info.de; Baseler Str 35-37, 60329 Frankfurt)

UK (☎ 0207-839 7778; www.gototurkey.co.uk; 4th fl, 29-30 St James's St, London SW1A 1HB)

USA New York (☎ 212-687 2194; www.tourismturkey .org; 821 UN Plaza, New York, NY 10017) Los Angeles (☎ 323-937 8066; 5055 Wilshire Blvd, Suite 850, Los Angeles, CA 90036) Washington DC (☎ 202-612 6800; 2525 Massachusetts Ave, Washington, DC 20008)

VISAS

Nationals of the following countries (among others) don't need a visa to visit Turkey for up to three months: Belgium, Denmark, Finland, France, Germany, Japan, New Zealand, Norway, Sweden and Switzerland. Nationals of Australia, Austria, Canada, Greece, Ireland, Israel, Italy, Netherlands, Portugal, Spain, the UK and USA do need a visa, but this is just a sticker bought on arrival at the airport or border post rather than at an embassy in advance (make sure to join the queue to buy your visa before the queue for immigration). How much you pay for your visa (essentially a tourist tax) varies; at the time of writing British, Australians and US citizens paid €15, Canadians €45, Spanish, Italians and Irish €10. No photos are required and the procedure is straight forward.

The standard visa is valid for three months and, depending on your nationality, usually allows for multiple entries. See the **Ministry of Foreign Affairs** (www.mfa.gov.tr) for the latest information.

Residency Permits

If you plan to stay in Turkey for more than three months, you can apply for an *ikamet tezkeresi* (residence permit), which is usually valid for one to two years. You'll need to contact the local *emniyet müdürlüğü* (security police) and show that you have some means of supporting yourself (savings, a steady income from outside the country) or legal work within the country. As the permit costs a whopping €320 for a year, many expats find it more convenient and cheaper to cross the border every three months.

Visa Extensions

In theory a Turkish visa can be renewed once after three months at the nearest branch of the *emniyet müdürlüğü*, but the bureaucracy and costs involved mean that it's much easier to leave the country (usually to a Greek island) and then come back in again on a fresh visa. Unless you speak Turkish, dealing with the *emniyet müdürlüğü* is complicated.

Working Visas

It's best to obtain a *çalışma vizesi* (working visa) from the Turkish embassy or consulate before you leave your home country. At least two months before your departure date submit in person the completed visa form, your passport, a photo of yourself, your proof of employment (a contract or letter from your employer) and the required fee (between €140 and €200, depending on your nationality). After about three weeks (*İnşallah*, God willing), your passport will be returned with the visa stamped inside.

Once you arrive in Turkey with a work permit, you must obtain a 'pink book' (a combined work permit and residence permit) from the *emniyet müdürlüğü* (security police). If your employer doesn't do this for you, apply with your passport, five passport photos and the processing fee (€320 for a year, but check as it rises regularly). Your pink book should be ready in three or four working days and replaces the visa in your passport. It's renewable every year as long as you can prove you're still working.

Most people who are working in Turkey illegally (as private English tutors, for example) cross the border into Greece, Northern Cyprus or Bulgaria every three months rather than bother with the cost and hassle of trying to extend their visa or get residency. In theory an immigration officer could query a passport full of recent Turkish stamps. However, in our experience most of them happily turn a blind eye to this bending of the rules.

Note that rules seem to change regularly, so see www.e-konsolosluk.net and the Turkish embassy or consulate in your home country for the latest information about visa requirements.

WOMEN TRAVELLERS

Travelling Turkey as a female traveller is easy and enjoyable, provided you follow some simple guidelines. Tailor your behaviour and your clothing to your surrounds. Look at what local women are wearing. On the streets of Beyoğlu in İstanbul you'll see skimpy tops and tight jeans, but cleavage and short skirts without leggings are always a bit of a no-no. Having a banter with men in restaurants and shops in western Turkey can be great fun, especially since most won't necessarily think anything of it. Out east it's a different story. Passing through some towns you can count the number of women you see on one hand, and those you do see will be headscarved and wearing long jackets. Life here for women is largely restricted to the home. This is not the place to practice your Turkish (or Kurdish) for hours on end with the local *kebapci* and expect him not to get the wrong idea. Keep your dealings with men formal and polite, not friendly. You certainly don't need to don a headscarf, but long sleeves and baggy long pants should attract the least attention.

Men and unrelated women are not expected to sit beside each other in long-distance buses, and lone women are often assigned seats at the front of the bus near the driver. If you're not told where to sit, avoid sitting at the back since that seems to have 'back-of-the-cinema' connotations in some men's minds. We have also received reports of some *yardımcıs* (conductors) on night buses harassing their female customers. If that happens to you, complain loudly, making sure that others on the bus hear, and repeat your complaint on arrival at your destination – you have a right to be treated with respect. When travelling by taxi avoid getting into the seat beside the driver.

When looking for a hotel, you may have to accept that the cheapest fleapits are not suitable for lone women and stick with family-oriented midrange hotels. In 2001 a Taiwanese tourist was murdered in an Urfa hotel and,

while that was undoubtedly a dreadful one-off, if conversation in the lobby invariably grinds to a halt as you cross the threshold it might suggest that this is not really a great place for a woman. If there is a knock on your hotel door late at night, don't open it; in the morning, complain to the manager.

We recommend female travellers always stick to official camp sites and camp where there are plenty of people around – especially out east. A female traveller was raped in mid-2006 while camping beside a waterfall near Van with her male companion and, while this is a very rare occurrence, it's a risk you need to weigh up nonetheless. We should also mention that we've heard reports about two female travellers claiming to have been drugged with drinks at a camp in Olympos. See p381 for more information.

Restaurants that aim to attract women usually set aside a special room (or part of one) for family groups. Look for the term *aile salonu* (family dining room).

WORK

Some travellers come to Turkey for a week and end up staying for months, or even a lifetime. However, jobs aren't all that easy to find (Turkey has a high unemployment level) and most people end up teaching English, though there are other opportunities of course. Job hunters may have luck with the *Turkish Daily News* and the expat websites www.mymerhaba.com, www.expatinturkey .com and http://istanbul.craigslist.org.

Nannying

One of the most lucrative nonspecialist jobs available to foreigners (from €550 to €850 per week) involves nannying for the wealthy city elite; work mainly restricted to English-speaking women who must be prepared for long hours and demanding employers. Contact **Anglo Nannies** (☎ 0212-287 6898; www.anglonannies.com; Bebek Yolu Sokak, Ebru Apt No 25/2 Etiler, İstanbul, 80630), the main agency dealing with placements.

Teaching English

It is also possible to earn a decent living as an English teacher, either privately, for a university, a private *dershane* (school), or for one of the many private language schools around the country.

If you don't have any teaching qualifications, you can usually still find a job, though it'll be private tuition (which pays from €17 to €30 per hour) or at a private language school (where you can expect around €11 an hour). If you have teaching qualifications (at least a Bachelor of Education, majoring in English) you should arm yourself with a TEFL certificate as well to place yourself within reach of the best jobs. Universities will not hire without teaching qualifications, nor will most *dershanes*, and the best private language schools expect at least a TEFL. Pay can be from €750 to €1400 per month, often with accommodation, flights home and a work permit thrown in. The best time of the year to job hunt is near the end of the summer school break, around mid- to late August, when schools are desperate for teachers to replace those who found a spot on a beautiful beach and decided to stay.

As well as those job-hunting resources listed in the introduction to this section, you may also want to log onto www.eslcafe.com and www.tefl.com.

Tourism

Many travellers also find work illegally for room and board in pensions, bars and carpet shops, leaving the country every three months to renew their visas. This sort of work has the advantage that you can take it or leave it at will. But be warned that the authorities take a dim view of foreigners 'stealing' local jobs and that there are occasional shake-outs when they rush around threatening people with prosecution (it rarely actually happens).

Volunteer Work

There are a slowly growing number of volunteering opportunities in Turkey, offering everything from working on organic farms to helping out on an archaeological dig. **Volunteer Abroad** (www.volunteerabroad.com) is a UK-based company listing volunteering opportunities through international organisations in Turkey. Local operators include:

Alternative Camp (www.alternativecamp.org) A fully volunteer-based organisation running camps for disabled people around the country.

Genctur (www.genctur.com) A portal for various volunteering schemes throughout the country, and a good first point of call to see what's on offer in Turkey.

Ta Tu Ta (www.bugday.org/tatuta) Organises work on some 60-odd organic farms around the country, where you can stay for free or for a small donation to cover costs.

Transport

CONTENTS

GETTING THERE & AWAY

ENTERING THE COUNTRY

Generally speaking, entering Turkey by air is pretty painless. The only snag to be aware of is that most people need a 'visa' which is really just a stamp in their passport issued at the point of entry. If you fly into the country you must *first* join the queue to pay for the stamp in your passport before joining the queue for immigration. See p667 for more details. Rarely do customs officers stop you to check your bags at airports.

Entering the country by land can be more trying. Getting a visa is the same deal, but sometimes you can pay for the visa only in euros or US dollars. And at many of the land border crossings there are no facilities for changing money nor ATMs, so make sure you bring enough to pay for your visa. You may also want to consider having some Yeni Türk Lirası (YTL) on you before you get to the border.

Security on borders with countries to the east (Georgia, Iran, Iraq or Syria) is generally tight, so customs officers may want to see what you are bringing in. If you're travelling by train or bus expect to be held up at the border for two to three hours – or even longer if your fellow passengers don't have their paperwork in order.

THINGS CHANGE...

The information in this chapter is particularly vulnerable to change. Check directly with the airline or a travel agent to make sure you understand how a fare (and ticket you may buy) works and be aware of the security requirements for international travel. Shop carefully. The details given in this chapter should be regarded as pointers and are not a substitute for your own careful, up-to-date research.

Passport

Make sure your passport will still have at least three months' life in it after you enter Turkey.

AIR
Airports & Airlines

Turkey's busiest international airport is İstanbul's **Atatürk International Airport** (code IST; ☎ 0212-465 3000; www.dhmiata.gov.tr), 23km west of Sultanahmet (the heart of Old İstanbul). The international *(dış hatlar)* and domestic terminals *(iç hatlar)* are side by side. İstanbul also has a smaller airport, **Sabiha Gökçen International Airport** (code SAW; ☎ 0216-585 5000; www.sgairport.com), some 50km east of Sultanahmet and Taksim Sq on the Asian side of the city. Sabiha Gökçen mainly services cheap flights from Europe, particularly Germany, and some domestic routes.

Throughout the year, but especially during the busy summer months, you can also catch international flights to/from **Antalya** (AYT; ☎ 0242-330 3221; www.aytport.com), **Bodrum** (BJV; ☎ 0252-523 0101), **Dalaman** (DLM; ☎ 0252-692 5899) and the rapidly expanding **İzmir** (ADB; ☎ 0232-274 2424). From Turkey's other airports, including Ankara, you usually have to transit İstanbul.

Turkey's national carrier is Turkish Airlines, which has direct flights from İstanbul to most capital cities around the world. It has a reasonable safety record, and service is usually pretty good too.

AIRLINES FLYING TO & FROM TURKEY

For contact details for most of these airlines in İstanbul, see p155.

Aeroflot (airline code AFL; www.aeroflot.com)
Air France (AF; www.airfrance.com)
Alitalia (AZ; www.alitalia.com)
American Airlines (AA; www.aa.com)
Azerbaijan Airlines (AHY; www.azal.az)
British Airways (BA; www.britishairways.com)
Condor (DE; www.condor.de)
Corendon Airlines (CAI; www.corendon.com)
Cyprus Turkish Airlines (KTHY; www.kthy.net)
EasyJet (EZY; www.easyjet.com)
Emirates Airlines (EK; www.emirates.com)
Fly Air (FLM; www.flyair.com.tr)
German Wings (GWI; www25.germanwings.com)
Hapag Lloyd (HFwww.hlx.com)
Iberia (IB; www.iberia.com)
Iran Air (IR; www.iranair.com)
Japan Airlines (JL; www.jal.co.jp/en)
KLM-Royal Dutch Airlines (KL; www.klm.com)
Lufthansa (LH; www.lufthansa.com)
Olympic Airways (OA; www.olympicairlines.com)
Onur Air (OHY; www.onurair.com.tr/eng/)
Pegasus Airlines (PGT; www.flypgs.com)

Singapore Airlines (SIA; www.singaporeair.com)
Turkish Airlines (Türk Hava Yolları, THY; www.thy.com)

Tickets

If you're after cheap flights, the cheapest routes between Europe and İstanbul are flying through Germany to Turkey, and with EasyJet, which flies between London (Luton) and İstanbul, and Switzerland (Basel) and İstanbul. Sometimes you can also find them by booking on less-usual airlines eg Cyprus Turkish Airlines and Azerbaijan Airlines. Some airlines offer student fares too. Otherwise Turkey is not the best destination for special deals.

It's a good idea to book at least two months in advance for flights to/from Turkey if you plan to arrive in the country any time from early April until late August.

Flights quoted in this chapter are for peak season and include airport taxes.

Australia

You can fly directly to İstanbul with Emirates, Japan, Malaysia and Singapore Airlines for around A$1200/1890 (one-way/return) from Sydney or Melbourne. You can often get cheaper flights with European airlines such as

TRANSPORT

CLIMATE CHANGE & TRAVEL

Climate change is a serious threat to the ecosystems that humans and wildlife rely upon, and air travel is the fastest-growing contributor to the problem. Lonely Planet regards travel, overall, as a global benefit, but believes we all have a responsibility to limit our personal impact on global warming.

Flying & Climate Change

Pretty much every form of motorised travel generates CO_2 (the main cause of human-induced climate change), but planes are far and away the worst offenders, not just because of the sheer distances they allow us to travel, but because they release greenhouse gases high into the atmosphere. The statistics are frightening: two people taking a return flight between Europe and the USA will contribute as much to climate change as an average household's gas and electricity consumption over a whole year.

Carbon Offset Schemes

Climatecare.org and other websites use 'carbon calculators' that allow travellers to offset the level of greenhouse gases they are responsible for with financial contributions to sustainable travel schemes that reduce global warming – including projects in India, Honduras, Kazakhstan and Uganda.

Lonely Planet, together with Rough Guides and other concerned partners in the travel industry, support the carbon offset scheme run by climatecare.org. Lonely Planet offsets all of its staff and author travel.

For more information check out our website: www.lonelyplanet.com.

Lufthansa, but you'll have to transit in a European city first (ie Frankfurt for Lufthansa), before catching a flight back to İstanbul – very frustrating!

Three well-known agencies for cheap fares are **STA Travel** (☎ 1300 733 035; www.statravel.com.au), **Flight Centre** (☎ 133 133; www.flightcentre.com.au) and **Best Flights** (☎ 1300 767 757; www.bestflights.com.au).

Canada
Most flights from Toronto, Ottawa and Vancouver connect with İstanbul-bound flights in the UK and continental Europe. One-way/return fares from İstanbul start at around C$950/1550 with Lufthansa and Air Canada. Try **Travelcuts** (☎ 1866-246 9762; www.travelcuts.com), Canada's national student travel agency, or **Airlineticketsdirect.com** (☎ 1877-679 8500; www .airlineticketsdirect.com).

Continental Europe
Generally, there's not much variation in fares to Turkey from one European city or another. Most European national carriers fly direct to İstanbul for around €200 return. Cheaper return flights can be found for around €160 but usually involve changing planes en route, so if you fly İstanbul–Paris with Lufthansa, you'd fly via Frankfurt each way. **STA Travel** (www .statravel.com/worldwide.htm) has offices throughout Europe. If you plan to visit a resort, check with your local travel agents for flight and accommodation deals.

Germany has the biggest Turkish community outside Turkey, which has enabled some great deals between the two countries. Lufthansa has direct flights to İstanbul, Ankara and İzmir from €160. There are also a number of charter airlines offering flights between several German cities and İstanbul, Antalya, Bodrum, Dalaman and İzmir. Try Condor, Hapag Lloyd, German Wings or Corendon Airlines (see p671 for contact details).

In France, **OTU Voyages** (☎ 01 55 82 32 32; www .otu.fr) is aimed at student travel, but can supply discount tickets to travellers of all ages. **Voyageurs du Monde** (☎ 08 92 68 83 63; www.vdm .com) and **Nouvelles Frontières** (☎ 08 25 00 07 47; www .nouvelles-frontieres.fr) are also recommended.

In Italy, **CTS Viaggi** (☎ 199 501150; www.cts.it) is one of the major travel agencies. In Spain, we recommended **Barcelo Viajes** (☎ 902 11 62 26; www.barceloviajes.com).

Turkish Airlines and Cyprus Turkish Airlines have daily direct services from İstanbul, İzmir and Ankara to Ercan airport at Lefkoşa (Northern Nicosia).

Middle East & Asia
If you want to fly to/from Turkey from any of the central Asian countries, you can usually pick up a flight with Turkish Airlines or the country's national carrier. Turkish Airlines flies İstanbul–Tbilisi (Georgia) and İstanbul–Baku (Azerbaijan) for around €300 each way. Azerbaijan Airlines also offers direct flights between Baku and İstanbul or Ankara, and these are generally cheaper. Because the border between Turkey and Armenia is closed, you can't travel overland between the two countries, but you can fly. Both Armavia Airlines and Fly Air have two flights a week each way between İstanbul and Yerevan. Turkish Airlines has daily flights to Tehran and Tabriz (Iran), for as little as €120.

One of the cheapest ways to get between northeast or southeast Asia and Turkey is to fly via Dubai. Emirates Airlines flies to İstanbul and over nine destinations in India, to Pakistan and further afield to Hong Kong and Bangkok. Fly Air flies to Khartoum for €250. Singapore Airlines often has very good deals on its website between Asia and İstanbul, with return flights between Denpasar and İstanbul as low as €480, Singapore and İstanbul for just €450.

New Zealand
Fares to İstanbul from Auckland start at NZ$1500/2400 one way/return on Air New Zealand, but Singapore Airlines and Qantas fares are also worth checking.

Flight Centre (☎ 0800 243 544; www.flightcentre .co.nz) and **STA Travel** (☎ 0508-782 872; www.statravel .co.nz) are recommended travel agencies.

UK & Ireland
British Airways, Turkish Airlines and EasyJet offer direct flights between London and Turkey. British Airlines flies into İstanbul (from UK£200 return), Dalaman, Ankara and İzmir. Turkish Airlines usually has direct flights only between İstanbul (from UK£200 return) and London. EasyJet flies direct between London (Luton) and İstanbul from UK£80 return.

For most cheap flights you can generally expect to fly to Turkey with a transit in a European city (though EasyJet flies direct). Or you could look into charter flights, which are usually cheaper at the beginning and end of the season. Typical return charter fares, bought in advance, are UK£149/199 for one/two weeks. Charter flights to Turkey go from Birmingham, Bristol, Gatwick, London, Manchester, Nottingham and Newcastle. Try online charter flight agents **Just the Flight** (☎ 0870-758 9589; www.justtheflight.co.uk) and **Thomsonfly.com** (☎ 0870-190 0737; www.thomsonfly.com).

Other recommended travel agencies in the UK and Ireland:

STA Travel (☎ 0870-163 0026; www.statravel.co.uk)
Trailfinders (☎ 0845-058 5858; www.trailfinders.co.uk)
Usit Unlimited (☎ 01 602 1904; www.usitworld.com)

USA

Turkish Airlines offers flights to İstanbul from New York from about US$1400 return. From Los Angeles fares start at US$1650 return. Try Delta and American Airlines, too. You'll probably get a marginally cheaper flight with Lufthansa or KLM-Royal Dutch Airlines, but you'll have to change planes in Europe.

Some leading US travel agencies:

Expedia (☎ 800-397 3342; www.expedia.com)
STA Travel (☎ 800-781 4040; www.statravel.com)
Travelocity (☎ 888-872 8356; www.travelocity.com)

LAND

If you are planning to travel overland, you'll be spoilt for choice since Turkey has land borders with eight countries. Bear in mind, however, that Turkey's relationships with most of its neighbours tend to be tense, which can affect the availability of visas and when and where you can cross. Always check with the relevant embassy for the most up-to-date information before leaving home (see p657).

Border Crossings

Crossing land borders by bus and train is fairly straightforward, but expect delays of between one and three hours. You'll usually have to get off the bus or train and endure a paperwork and baggage check of all travellers on both sides of the border. This is a relatively quick process if you're on a bus, but naturally takes a longer time when there's a trainload of passengers. Before you ditch the idea of trains, however, be aware that delays can be caused by the long line of trucks and cars banked up at some borders – especially at the Reyhanlı–Bab al-Hawa border between Turkey and Syria – not the number of fellow passengers.

Crossing the border with your own vehicle should be fairly straightforward. No special documents are required to import a car for up to six months, but be sure to take it out again before the six months is up. If you overstay your permit, you may have to pay customs duty equal to the full retail value of the car! If you want to leave your car in Turkey and return to collect it later, the car must be put under a customs seal, which is a tedious process.

For more on each country's border crossings, see the relevant country headings following.

Armenia

At the time of writing, the Turkish–Armenian border was closed to travellers. The situation could always change so it's worth checking (the Russian embassy handles Armenian diplomatic interests in Turkey).

If you want to travel from Turkey to Armenia (or vice versa) you can fly (see opposite) or travel by bus via Georgia. At least three buses weekly depart from Trabzon's otogar heading for Yerevan – see p554.

Azerbaijan (Nakhichevan)

At least two daily buses depart from Trabzon's otogar heading for Tbilisi, where you can change for a bus to Baku – see p554.

You can also cross from Turkey to the Azerbaijani enclave of Nakhichevan via the remote Borualan–Sadarak border post, east of Iğdır (see p586). From there you'll need to fly across Armenian-occupied Nagorno-Karabakh to reach the rest of Azerbaijan and Baku.

Bulgaria & Eastern Europe

It's fairly easy to get to İstanbul by direct train or bus from many points in Europe via Bulgaria. There are three border crossings between Bulgaria and Turkey. The main border crossing is the busy Kapitan–Andreevo/Kapıkule, 18km west of Edirne on the E5. The closest town on the Bulgarian side is Svilengrad, some 10km from the border. You have to hitch a lift or hire a taxi rather than walk between the Greek–Turkish border posts. Petrol, foreign-exchange facilities, restaurants and accommodation are available at this crossing, which is open 24 hours daily. For more details, see p172. There is a second, newly opened, crossing at Lesovo–Hamzabeyli, some 25km

VISAS FOR NEIGHBOURING COUNTRIES

Armenia

Most nationalities can get visas upon arrival at the borders (and the airport) for US$30 (valid for 21 days) or three-day transit visas for US$18. You can usually get your visa extended to 35 days on the border; if you want to stay longer you'll need a letter of invitation.

Azerbaijan

Like Syria, the visa conditions for Azerbaijan can be a little tricky to pin down. Officially most nationalities must get a visa prior to arrival costing €63 for two months and coupled with a letter of invitation. If you arrive by air you can get a visa at the airport for €31 (valid for three months) – go figure! We have also heard of European travellers applying at the consulate in Kars, paying only €31 (valid 15 days), with two photos, and having their visa issued in three days. Please let us know your wacky adventures in getting an Azerbaijani visa.

Bulgaria

Currently citizens of Australia, Canada, Ireland, Israel, Japan, New Zealand, the UK and the USA can obtain a free 30-day tourist visa at any Bulgarian border. Citizens of other EU countries are able to get a 90-day visa.

Georgia

Most nationalities (including Australia, Canada, Israel, Japan, Switzerland, EU countries and the USA) can obtain a 90-day tourist visa upon arrival at any Georgian border. Single-entry visas valid for one month cost €8. See www.mfa.gov.ge for the latest information.

Greece

Nationals of Australia, Canada, all EU countries, New Zealand and the USA can enter Greece for up to three months without a visa.

Iran

All would-be visitors to Iran need to get a visa in advance. There is an embassy in Ankara and consulates are located in İstanbul and Erzurum. You will need two photos and a copy of the most important pages of your passport. You must pay a non-refundable application fee of €40 and

north of Edirne; it's a quieter option during the busy summer months than Kapitan-Andreevo/Kapıkule, but takes a little longer to get to and there's no public transport. The third crossing is at Malko Târnovo–Kırıkkale, some 70km northeast of Edirne and 92km south of Burgas.

BUS

There are several departures daily to Sofia, and the coastal cities of Varna and Burgas in Bulgaria from İstanbul's otogar – at least six companies offer services. There are also daily departures to Skopje, Tetovo and Gostivar in Macedonia, and to Constanta and Bucharest in Romania. The following companies run serves from İstanbul's otogar.

Drina Trans (☎ 0212-658 1851; ticket office 88) Daily departures for Skopje, Macedonia (€30, 14 hours)

Metro Turizm (☎ 0212-658 3232; www.metroturizm .com.tr; ticket office 107) Daily departures to Sofia (€20, nine hours), Varna and Burgas in Bulgaria.

Öz Batu (☎ 0212-658 0255; ticket office 149) Daily departures for Sofia, Bulgaria (€17, nine hours) and Skopje, Macedonia (€32, 14 hours).

Özlem (☎ 0212-658 1344; ticket office 97) Daily departures for Constanta (€35; eight hours) and Bucharest (€35; eight hours), Romania.

TRAIN

The *Bosphorus Express* leaves İstanbul daily and runs to Bucsharest, from where you can travel onwards by train to Chişinău (Moldova) and Budapest (Hungary). You can also catch the *Bosphorus Express* as far as Dimitrovgrad (Bulgaria) from where you can travel onwards to Sofia (Bulgaria) and on to Belgrade (Serbia).

then wait at least 10 days to hear whether your application has been granted. Some people wait a day or so, others weeks. Visas are not usually granted to Americans, and the British aren't too popular either, but the Dutch can often get them virtually straight away. If you haven't arranged a visa before arriving in Doğubayazıt you can organise one through the consulate in Erzurum. Although you will need to travel back to Erzurum, in most cases the visa can be arranged in one hour, allowing you to return to Doğubayazıt the same day. You may be asked to show a visa for the country you are travelling to after Iran. Women must be wearing *hijab* (full body cover), the rules for which are more relaxed nowadays so that you can show your fringe, wear make-up and jewellery, and brave colours other than black (although never red).

Northern Cyprus

Visas for the Turkish Republic of Northern Cyprus (TRNC) are available on arrival. If you're planning to visit Greece or the Greek islands, remember that relations between the Greek Cypriot-administered Republic of Cyprus (in the south) and the TRNC remain chilly. Also, if you enter the TRNC and have your passport stamped you may later be denied entry to Greece. The Greeks will only reject a stamp from the TRNC, *not* a stamp from Turkey proper, so have the Turkish Cypriot official stamp a piece of paper instead of your passport, a procedure with which they are familiar.

Russia

The Russian consulate in Trabzon will refer you to Burcu Turizm virtually next door. You will need one photograph and €95 for a visa to be issued the same day.

Syria

Getting a visa to Syria can be taxing as the rules seem changeable. At the time of writing all foreigners wanting to enter Syria need a visa, and most must get it in advance. Some travellers have got visas at the border, but many have been knocked back. It's best to play it safe and apply in your home country, although you can get visas in Ankara or İstanbul. Visa costs vary depending on the nationality, ranging from A$41 for Australians to £32 for UK citizens. Most foreigners also need a letter of recommendation from their embassy. You will not be granted a visa if you have Israeli stamps in your passport.

Essentially the *Bosphorus Express* leaves İstanbul with a line of carriages. There are separate carriages for passengers heading to Budapest, to Sofia and Belgrade, and to Chişinău. The carriages are switched to local trains at either Bucharest or Dimitrovgrad, depending on where you're heading. Confused? Don't worry; bookings are simply from A to B, though there will be some delay as carriages are transferred.

You'll need to take your own food and drinks as there are no restaurant cars on these trains. Note also that the Turkey–Bulgaria border crossing is in the early hours of the morning and you need to leave the train to get your passport stamped – the holdup takes about two hours. We've heard stories of harassment, especially of women, at the border, so lone women may be best taking an alternative route. Travelling in the sleeper cars is always the safest and most comfortable option.

Georgia

The main border crossing is at Sarp on the Black Sea coast, between Hopa (Turkey) and Batum (Georgia). You can also cross inland at the Türkgözü border crossing near Posof, north of Kars (Turkey) and southwest of Akhaltsikhe (Georgia). The Sarp border crossing is open 24 hours a day; Türkgözü is open from 8am to 8pm, though in winter you might want to double-check it's open at all.

Göktaş Ardahan (☎ in İstanbul 0212-658 3476; ticket office 10) runs direct buses between Tiflis and the otogar in İstanbul for €43. The journey takes around 26 hours. At least two daily buses depart from Trabzon's otogar heading for Tbilisi – see p554.

If you're heading to the Türkgözü border from the Turkish side, a convenient starting point is Kars (p585). You need to get to Posof first, then hire a taxi or minibus to take you to the border post (16km, €20). From the border, hire another taxi to take you to the Georgian town of Akhaltsikhe (€15; two hours), from where regular buses head to Tbilisi (which can take up to seven hours).

Greece & Western Europe

An alternative to getting to Turkey from Europe is to make your way to Alexandroupolis in Greece and cross at Kipi–İpsala, 43km northeast of Alexandroupolis, or Kastanies–Pazarkule, 139km northeast, near the Turkish city of Edirne. Both borders are open 24 hours.

To cross at Kipi–İpsala take a bus service from Alexandroupolis to the Greek border point of Kipi, then hitch to the border. From there you can get a taxi (€8.50) to the bus station in İpsala and an onward bus to İstanbul.

If you're crossing from Turkey into Greece, do so as soon after 9am as possible in order to catch one of the few trains or buses from Kastanies south to Alexandroupolis, where there are better connections. Alternatively, take a bus from Edirne to Keşan, then to İpsala and cross to Kipi.

BUS

Bus services to İstanbul run only from Germany, Italy, Austria and Greece, so if you're travelling from other European cities, you'd need to catch a connecting bus. Two of the best Turkish companies – **Ulusoy** (☎ 0212-444 1888 in Turkey; www.ulusoy.com.tr) and **Varan Turizm** (☎ 0212-658 0270 in Turkey; www.varan.com.tr) – operate big Mercedes buses on these routes. Sample one-way fares to İstanbul are: Frankfurt €130 (45 hours), Munich €110 (42 hours), Vienna €105 (36 hours), and Athens €68 (20 hours).

CAR & MOTORCYCLE

The E80 highway makes its way through the Balkans to Edirne and İstanbul, then on to Ankara. Using the car ferries from Italy and Greece can shorten driving time from Western Europe considerably, but at a price (see opposite).

From Alexandroupolis in Greece, the main road goes to the most convenient crossing (Kipi–İpsala) then to Keşan and east to İstanbul or south to Gallipoli, Çanakkale and the Aegean.

TRAIN

From Western European cities (apart from those in Greece) you will come via Eastern Europe; see p673.

The best option travelling between Greece and Turkey is the overnight train between Thessaloniki and İstanbul called the *Filia-Dostluk Express*. The journey takes 12 to 14 hours, including an hour or two's delay at the border, and accommodation is in comfy, air-conditioned sleeper cars. Good-value one-way rates are €48 for 2nd-class between İstanbul and Thessaloniki; or €68 for 2nd-class if you take a connecting Greek Intercity train to/from Athens.

You can buy tickets at the train stations but not online. For more information see the websites of **Turkish State Railways** (TCDD; www.tcdd.gov.tr) or the **Hellenic Railways Organisation** (www.ose.gr).

Iran

There are two border crossings between Iran and Turkey, the busier Gürbulak–Bazargan, near Doğubayazıt (Turkey) and Şahabat (Iran); and the Esendere–Sero border crossing, southeast of Van (Turkey). Gürbulak–Bazargan is open 24 hours. Esendere–Sero is open from 8am until midnight, but double-check in winter as the border might be closed. Travellers are increasingly using this second crossing into Iran, which has the added bonus of taking you through the breathtaking scenery of far Southeastern Anatolia. And to make things easy, there is a direct bus running between Van (Turkey) and Orumiyeh (Iran). See p642 for departure information.

BUS

There are regular buses from İstanbul and Ankara to Tabriz and Tehran. From İstanbul otogar, try **Best Van Tur** (☎ 0212-444 0065; otogar ticket office 147) with daily departures (€55, 35 hours). From Ankara, they leave from the AŞTİ bus terminal.

You may also want to consider taking a dolmuş from Doğubayazıt 35km east to the border at Gürbulak, for about €2, and then walking across the border. The crossing might take up to an hour. From Bazargan there are onward buses to Tabriz; from Sero there are buses to Orumiyeh. You can catch buses to Iran from Van.

TRAIN
The *Trans-Asya Ekspresi* runs between Tehran and İstanbul, travelling via Tabriz, Van and Tatvan. Expect a comfortable journey on connecting Turkish and Iranian trains, a ferry ride across Lake Van, and no showers. See the Iranian Railways site, **RAJA Passenger Train Co** (www.rajatrains.com), for more information.

There's a weekly train service between Tehran (Iran) and Damascus, running through the Turkish cities of Van and Malatya. See www.tcdd.gov.tr for more information.

Iraq
Although we obviously don't suggest that travelling to wider Iraq is at all advisable, a handful of hardy travellers have been travelling into northern Iraq via the Habur–Ibrahim al-Khalil border post. It's near Cizre and Silopi, on the Turkish side; Zakho is the closest town to the border on Iraqi side. There's no town or village at the border crossing and you can't walk across it. A taxi from Silopi to Zakho costs around €20, from Cizre to Zakho US$30.

Travellers report having to give a photocopy of their passport at the Turkish side, and being given a week-long entry stamp (not a visa) on the Iraqi side, as well as having to get a health certificate for a nominal fee. Travelling across the border into Turkey your bags will probably be searched – don't carry patriotic Kurdish items. See p631 for a peep into Tony Wheeler's Iraqi adventures. Check the local situation before crossing into Iraq.

Syria
There are eight border posts between Syria and Turkey, but the border at Reyhanlı–Bab al-Hawa is by far the most convenient, and therefore the busiest. Daily buses link Antakya in Turkey with the Syrian cities of Aleppo (Halab; €3, four hours, 105km) and Damascus (Şam; €5.50, eight hours, 465km). Also close to Antakya is the border post at Yayladağı. For both these crossings see p437. Other popular crossings to Syria include via Kilis, 65km south of Gaziantep (p598), the Akçakale border, 54km south of Şanlıurfa (p606) and the Nusaybin–Qamishle border 5km east of Mardin (p630).

It's possible to buy bus tickets direct from İstanbul to Aleppo or Damascus. **Hatay Pan Turizm** (☎ 0212-658 3911; otogar ticket office 23) has a daily service leaving İstanbul otogar at 6am and arriving in Damascus (€27) at 3am the next morning. **Urfa Seyahat** (☎ 0212-444 6363; otogar ticket office 10) has departures for Aleppo at 1.30pm daily.

The very comfortable *Toros Express* train runs between İstanbul and Aleppo (and *not* all the way to Damascus as it says in the official timetables) – see the table, p157, for details. Bring your own food and drinks as there is no restaurant car. Several comfortable trains link Aleppo and Damascus daily.

There's a weekly train service between Tehran (Iran) and Damascus, running through the Turkish cities of Van and Malatya. See www.tcdd.gov.tr for more information.

SEA
Car ferry services operate between Italian and Greek ports and several Turkish ports, but not to İstanbul. There are also a handful of routes over the Black Sea. **Ferrylines** (www.ferrylines.com) is a good starting point for information about ferry travel in the region.

Greece
Private ferries link Turkey's Aegean coast and the Greek islands, which are in turn linked by air or boat to Athens. Services are usually daily in summer, several times a week in spring and autumn, and perhaps just once a week in winter. The table, p678, summarises the services between the Greek islands and Turkey.

Italy
Marmara Lines (www.marmaralines.com) ferries connect Brindisi and Ancona in Italy with Çeşme. **Turkish Maritime Lines** (www.tdi.com.tr in Turkish) also operates twice-weekly ferries between Brindisi and Çeşme. For more details on these services, see p239.

Northern Cyprus
The main crossing point between northern Cyprus and Turkey is between Taşucu (near Silifke) and Girne on the northern coast of northern Cyprus. **Akgünler Denizcilik** (www.akgunler.com.tr) makes this journey – see p418. You can also travel between Alanya and Girne with **Fergün Denizcilik** (www.fergun.net) – see p414). Finally, you can travel between Mersin and

TRANSPORT

FERRIES BETWEEN TURKEY & GREECE

Route	Frequency	Fare (one way/return)	More details
Ayvalık-Lesvos	daily Jun-Sep; twice a week Oct-May	€40/50	(p217)
Bodrum-Kos	daily May-Oct; three times a week Nov-Apr	(hydrofoil) €60 open return, €30/35 same-day (ferry) €25/25 same-day, €50 open return	(p280)
Bodrum-Rhodes	daily Jun-Sep	€50/60 same-day, €100 open return	(p280)
Çeşme-Chios	five times a week Jun-Sep; twice a week in winter	€25/40 same day, €50 open return	(p239)
Datça-Rhodes & Simi	Sat May-Sep and gület upon demand	(hydrofoil) €35/70 (gület) €50	(p344)
Kaş-Kastellorizo (Meis)	daily	€35 return	(p375)

Gazimağusa (Famagusta) on the east coast of Northern Cyprus, with **Turkish Maritime Lines** (☎ 231 2688, 237 0726 in Mersin) – see p425).

Russia

Ferries travel between Trabzon and Sochi in Russia three times a week; see p553 for more details.

Ukraine

UKR Ferry (www.ukrferry.com) has a comfortable 36-odd hour (each way) weekly service crossing the Black Sea between Odessa and İstanbul from €105 per person (one way).

Another weekly service runs between Sevastopol and İstanbul, departing Sevastopol at 6pm Sunday (arriving at İstanbul 8am Tuesday) for €120 per person in a shared three-bed room, or €400 per person in a private luxury double. Departures from İstanbul are on Thursday nights at 10pm (arriving 8am Saturday). Ferries travel between İstanbul and Yalta too. Ring ☎ in Ukraine 0654-323 064 for more information or email the folk at www.aroundcrimea.com.

TOURS

The following are international tour companies whose trips to Turkey generally receive good reports.

Backroads (☎ 1800 462 2848; www.backroads.com) US-based company offering combined bike and sailing tours of western Turkey.

Cultural Folk Tours of Turkey (☎ 1800 935 8875; www.boraozkok.com) US-based company offering group and private cultural and history tours.

Exodus (☎ 870-240 5550; www.exodus.co.uk) UK-based adventure company offering a wide range of tours including Lycian cruises and kayaking tours.

Imaginative Traveller (☎ 0800 316 2717; www.imaginative-traveller.com) UK-based company offering Anzac Day tours and a variety of overland adventures through Turkey.

Intrepid Travel (☎ 03-9473 2626; www.intrepidtravel.com.au) Australia-based company with a variety of small-group, good-value tours for travellers who like the philosophy of independent travel, but prefer to travel with others.

Pasha Tours (☎ 800 722 4288; www.pachatours.com) US-based company offering general tours as well as special-interest tours such as culinary, Jewish heritage, 'Seven churches of Asia Minor' etc.

See p684 for details of some Turkey-based tour operators.

GETTING AROUND

Many countries could learn a thing or two from Turkey about how to run an effective and affordable transport system. Turkey's inter-city bus system is as good as any you'll find, with modern coaches crossing the country at all hours and with very reasonable prices. The railway network is useful on a few major routes, and becoming an increasingly popular choice as improvements are made. And finally, flying is an excellent option for such a large country, and fierce competition between the many domestic airlines keeps tickets affordable.

AIR
Airlines in Turkey

Domestic airlines fly to some 30 cities throughout the country. Many flights, for instance from Dalaman to Van, go via the hubs of İstanbul or Ankara. Atlasjet is one of the few airlines offering direct flights between west coast and central and eastern destinations.

You can book flights on most airlines' websites. You'll get cheaper seats and more convenient departure times if you book a couple of months ahead.

Domestic flights are available with the following airlines.

Atlasjet (☎ 0216-444 3387; www.atlastjet.com) A growing network, with flights from İzmir, Bodrum, Dalaman and Antalya to many cities throughout the country.

Fly Air (☎ 0212-444 4359; www.flyair.com.tr) A smaller network, mainly with flights to/from İstanbul only, but can offer the cheapest rates.

Onur Air (Map p94-5; ☎ 0212-662 9797; www.onurair.com.tr) Good network and fares from €40 to €80.

Pegasus Airlines (www.pegasusairlines.com) Flies between İstanbul and Nevşehir.

Sun Express Airlines (www.sunexpress.com.tr) A Turkish Airlines subsidiary.

Turkish Airlines (Map p94-5; Türk Hava Yolları, THY; ☎ 0212-444 0849; www.thy.com) State-owned Turkish Airlines provides the main domestic network, and you can book and pay for tickets online. One-way fares from €38.

BICYCLE

Like bike touring anywhere, riding in Turkey is a wonderful adventure, full of surprises, challenges and a whole lotta grunt. Highlights are the spectacular scenery, the easy access to archaeological sites, which you might have all to yourself, and the curiosity and hospitality of locals, especially out east. Take the road-hog drivers, rotten road edges and, out east, stone-throwing children, wolves and ferocious Kangal sheep dogs in your stride. To give yourself the best chance of an enjoyable and safe trip, plan to avoid main roads wherever possible.

You'll be able to find excellent-quality spare parts in İstanbul and Ankara, but bring whatever you think you might need elsewhere. The best bike brand in Turkey is Bisan, with decent models starting at around €150, but you can find leading international brands in bike shops in İstanbul such as **Pedal Sportif** (☎ 0212-511 0654; www.pedalbisiklet.com in Turkish; Mimar Kemalettin Caddesi 29, Sirkeci), or in Ankara at **Delta Bisiklet** (☎ 0212-259 2279; www.deltabisiklet.com; Bosna

Hersek Caddesi 21, Emek). Both these shops have English-speaking staff and come highly recommended by tourers. They service bikes and can send parts throughout the country.

The best map for touring by bike is the *Köy Köy Türkiye Yol Atlası* (€19) available in bookshops in İstanbul; for other map recommendations see p661. You can usually transport your bike by air, bus, train or ferry free of charge, although mini- and midibuses will charge for the space it takes up. You can hire bikes for short rides in tourist towns along the coast and Cappadocia.

BOAT
Sea of Marmara Ferries

İstanbul Fast Ferries (İstanbul Deniz Otobüsleri, İDO; ☎ 0212-444 4436; www.ido.com.tr) operates high-speed car ferry services crossing the Sea of Marmara. There are services from İstanbul (Yenikapı terminal) to Yalova (for Bursa) p287, Bandırma (for İzmir) p202, and a third, to Mudanya (for Bursa).

BUS

Buses form Turkey's most widespread and popular means of transport. Virtually every first-time traveller to the country comments on the excellence of the bus system compared with that in their home country. The buses are well kept and comfortable too, and you'll be treated to snacks and tea along the journey, plus liberal sprinklings of the Turks' beloved *kolonya* (lemon cologne).

Most Turkish cities and towns have a central bus station generally called the otogar, *garaj* or *terminal*. Besides intercity buses, the otogar often handles dolmuşes (minibuses that follow prescribed routes) to outlying districts or villages. Most bus stations have an *emanetçi* (left luggage) room, which you can use for a nominal fee.

These are some of the best companies, with extensive route networks.

Boss Turizm (☎ 444 0880; www.bossturizm.com in Turkish) specialises in super-deluxe İstanbul-Ankara services.

Kamil Koç (☎ 444 0562; www.kamilkoc.com.tr in Turkish)

Ulusoy (☎ 444 1888; www.ulusoy.com.tr)

Varan (☎ 444 8999, 0212-551 5000; www.varan.com.tr)

Costs

Bus fares are subject to fierce competition between companies, and sometimes you can bargain them down by claiming poverty, student status etc. However, this doesn't always work. Prices also reflect what the market will bear, so that the fare from Rich City X to Poor Village Y may not always be the same as from Poor Village Y to Rich City X.

We give sample fares from all Turkey's main bus stations under Getting There & Away in the individual place entries. Typically, a bus ticket from İstanbul to Çanakkale costs €9, from İstanbul to Ankara around €22, and from İstanbul to Göreme (Cappadocia) €17 to €22.

Reservations

Although you can usually walk into an otogar and buy a ticket for the next bus, it's wise to plan ahead for public holidays, at weekends and during the school-holiday period from mid-June to early September. You can reserve seats over the web on most of the bus companies listed (p679).

When you enter an otogar prepare for an onslaught of touts, all offering buses to the destination of your choice. How do you choose which company to go with? It's usually a good idea to stick to the reputable big-name companies we've listed (p679). You may pay a bit more, but at least you can be more confident the bus has been well maintained, will run on time, and that there will be a back-up driver on really long hauls. For shorter trips, you'll find other bus companies have big localised city networks; for example Truva serves the area around Çanakkale, and Uludağ covers destinations around Bursa.

After buying a ticket, getting a refund can be difficult; exchanging it for another ticket with the same company is easier.

All seats are reservable, and your ticket will bear a specific seat number. The ticket agent will have a chart of the seats with those already sold crossed off. Look at the chart and indicate your seating preference, avoiding those right at the back of the bus (which can get stuffy) or immediately over the wheels (which can get bumpy!). On night buses you may also want to avoid the front row of seats behind the driver, which have little legroom (you may have to inhale the driver's cigarette smoke and listen to him chatting to his conductor into the early hours). The seats immediately in front of and behind the middle door are also a bad choice; those in front don't recline, and those behind have no legroom.

Servis

While it obviously makes sense from a town-planning point of view to move the otogars out of the town centres, what this tends to mean is that real journey times are becoming a bit how-long-is-a-piece-of-stringish. The timings we give are from otogar to otogar, but you may need to add up to an hour in either direction for getting to and from the otogars. This is especially true if you're using a *servis* (shuttle minibus) to get there. As otogars move further out of town, so most bus companies provide a *servis* bus to take passengers to and from the city centre. When buying a ticket ask whether there's a *servis* and when it leaves for the otogar. On arrival, say '*Servis var mı?*' to find out whether there's a *servis* into town. Rare cities where there are no *servises* include Bursa, Konya and Safranbolu.

FEZ BUS

A hop-on, hop-off bus service, **Fez Bus** (Map pp96-7; ☎ 0212-516 9024; www.feztravel.com; Akbıyık Caddesi 15, Sultanahmet, İstanbul), links the main tourist resorts of the Aegean and the Mediterranean with İstanbul and Cappadocia. From Cappadocia a loop travels out east to include Şanlıurfa and Nemrut Dağı (Mt Nemrut). A 'Turkish Delight' bus pass, costing €230 (student €205), allows you to travel from İstanbul to Çanakkale, Selçuk, Köyceğiz, Fethiye, Olympos, Cappadocia and then back to İstanbul, with the option of add-on *gület* cruises, the 'Eastern Explorer' and/or a trip to Safranbolu. You can take as long as you like to do the circuit.

The big bonus of using Fez Bus is convenience – although you're not obliged to stay in the places Fez favours, if you do you'll be dropped right at the door. It's also a great way to hook up with fellow travellers, since you'll be following a similar route and maybe even a similar travelling timeframe. The downside to this is that you spend most of your time in Turkey with other travellers rather than with Turks, and it would probably be cheaper to do it yourself with point-to-point buses.

Servis drivers like to allow plenty of time for getting to the otogar, which means that in Göreme, for example, you must usually be at the pick-up point for transfer to Nevşehir a good 45 minutes before the bus is scheduled to leave even though it's just a 15-minute drive.

While these services are free, they do have some snags. You may find yourself waiting around interminably for another busload of passengers to arrive or for your driver to be dragged away from the TV to run his *servis*. Even when he shows up, the journey can still be protracted as he drops each and every passenger off at their doorstep (well, perhaps not literally). If time is more important than money, then forget it and jump into a taxi.

Also, beware pension owners who lead you to believe that the private minibus to their pension is the bus company *servis*. This certainly happens at Nevşehir otogar and probably at other places too.

CAR & MOTORCYCLE

Driving around Turkey gives you unparalleled freedom to enjoy the marvellous countryside and coastline. You can stop at the teeny roadside stalls selling local specialities, explore back roads leading to hidden villages, and picnic at every opportunity, just like locals. Road surfaces and signage is generally good along main roads at least – the most popular route with travellers, along the Aegean and Mediterranean coast, offers excellent driving conditions. Hiring a scooter to explore the rugged Hisarönü Peninsula (p342) of the Western Mediterranean is a day out you'll cherish long after you've recovered from the knuckle-whitening corners.

The bad news is that Turkey has one of the world's highest motor-vehicle accident rates. Turkish drivers are not particularly discourteous, but they are impatient and incautious. They like to drive at high speed and have an irrepressible urge to overtake. To survive on Turkey's highways, drive cautiously and very defensively, and *never* let emotions affect what you do. Avoid driving at night, when you won't be able to see potholes, animals on the road, or even vehicles driving with their lights off!

When you're planning your trip, be mindful that Turkey is a huge country and spending time in the car travelling huge distances will eat up your travel time. Consider planes, trains or buses to cover long distances and hiring a car for localised travel.

Automobile Associations

Turkey's main motoring organisation is the **Türkiye Turing ve Otomobil Kurumu** (Turkish Touring & Automobile Association; ☎ 0212-282 8140; www.turing.org .tr; Oto Sanayi Sitesi Yanı, Seyrantepe 4 Levent, İstanbul).

Motorcyclists may want to check out **One More Mile Riders İstanbul**, (www.ommriders.com), a community resource for riding in Turkey, and the Turkey-related information on **Horizons Unlimited** (www.horizonsunlimited.com/country/turkey/).

Bring Your Own Vehicle

You can bring your vehicle into Turkey for six months without charge. However, the fact that you brought one in with you will be marked in your passport to ensure you take it back out again. Don't plan on selling it here, and be prepared to be charged a hefty fine for any time over the six months. Ensure you have your car registration and insurance policy on you. If you don't have insurance, you'll need to buy it at the border.

Driving Licence

Drivers must have a valid driving licence. Your own national licence will be sufficient; an international driving permit is useful but not required.

Fuel & Spare Parts

In Turkey there is little difference in price between *süper benzin* (normal petrol) and *kurşunsuz* (lead-free); both cost around €1.6 per litre. You can usually pay with credit cards at petrol stations.

There are petrol stations everywhere, at least in western Turkey, and many are mega enterprises. All the same, it's a good idea to have a full tank when you start out in the morning across the vast empty spaces of central and eastern Anatolia.

Yedek parçaları (spare parts) are readily available in the big cities, especially for European models such as Renaults, Fiats and Mercedes-Benz. However, ingenious Turkish mechanics contrive to keep all manner of US models in daily service. Repairs are usually quick and cheap. Roadside repair shops can often provide excellent, virtually immediate service, although they (or you) may have to go somewhere else to get the parts. For tyre repairs find an *oto lastikçi* (tyre repairer). The

TRANSPORT

sanayi bölgesi (industrial zone) on the outskirts of every town will have repair shops.

It's always wise to get an estimate of the repair cost in advance. Repair shops are usually closed on Sunday.

If you bring your motorcycle to Turkey you're bound to have a fine time. Spare parts may be hard to come by everywhere except the big cities, so bring what you might need, or rely on the boundless ingenuity of Turkish mechanics to find, adapt or make you a part. If you do get stuck for a part you could also ring an İstanbul or Ankara repair centre and get the part delivered by bus. **Horizons Unlimited** (www.horizonsunlimited.com/country/turkey/) has a list of repair centres in İstanbul.

Hire

You need to be at least 21 years old, with a year's driving experience, to be able to hire a car. If you don't pay with a major credit card you will have to leave around €500 cash deposit. Most hire cars have standard (manual) transmission; you'll pay more for automatic transmission. Note that most of the big-name companies charge a €100 to €140 drop-off fee (eg pick up in Antalya, and drop-off in Dalaman).

You can hire a car from the big international companies (Avis, Budget, Europcar, Hertz and National) in all main cities, towns and most airport. **Avis** (www.avis.com.tr/english) has the most extensive network of agencies, but **Europcar** (www.europcar.com) is often the best value for money and doesn't charge a drop-off fee. Recommended local companies include **Decar** (www.decar.com.tr), with no drop-off fee, **Car Rental İstanbul** (☎ 0533-467 0724; www.carrentalturkey.info) and **Green Car** (www.greenautorent.com), the largest operator in the Aegean region. **Turkey Car Hire Express** (http://turkey.carhireexpress.co.uk) is also a good place to start your search for a hire car.

If your car incurs any accident damage, or if you cause any, do not move the car before finding a police officer and asking for a *kaza raporu* (accident report). The officer may ask you to take a breath-alcohol test. Contact your car-hire company within 48 hours. Your insurance may be void if it can be shown that you were operating under the influence of alcohol or other drugs, were speeding, or if you did not submit the required accident report within 48 hours.

The total cost of a standard hire vehicle arranged during the summer months (for a week with unlimited kilometres, including tax and insurance) ranges from €400 to €500. Daily hire is from €40 to €70, depending on the size and type of car and the hire location. Hiring on the spot tends to be cheaper than booking ahead, but you run the risk of there not being any cars available. Baby-seat hire is usually available for around €5.50 per day.

Insurance

You *must* have third-party insurance, valid for the entire country (not just for Thrace or European Turkey), or a Turkish policy purchased at the border.

If you hire a car there will be two types of mandatory insurance included in the fee, the Collision Damage Waiver (CDW), which covers damage to the hire car or another, and the Theft Protection (TP) insurance. Personal accident insurance is usually optional; you may not need it if your travel insurance from home covers the costs of an accident.

Parking

Parking around the country is fairly easy to find. You can find parking even in the largest cities – İstanbul, Ankara, İzmir, Antalya and so on – though in some cases it may be a short walk from your accommodation.

Top-end and a handful of midrange hotels offer undercover parking for guests, and most midrange and budget options have a roadside parking place or two that is nominally theirs to use. If they don't, car parking will be close by in an empty block overseen by a caretaker, or on the road, in which case it'll be free or you'll be required to pay an hourly rate to a fee collector. Your best bet is to ring your accommodation and, upon arrival, ask them to point out the nearest and/or cheapest option.

Note that car clamping is a fact of life in Turkey. Park in the wrong place and you risk having your car towed away, with the ensuing costs and hassle.

Road Conditions

There are good *otoyols* (motorways) from the Bulgarian border near Edirne to İstanbul and Ankara, and from İzmir all the way around the coast to Antalya. Elsewhere, roads are being steadily upgraded, although they still tend to be worse in the east. Severe winters play havoc with the surfaces and it's hard for the highways department to keep up with the repairs.

If driving in winter be careful of icy roads. In bad winters you will need chains on your wheels almost everywhere except along the Aegean and Mediterranean coast and the police may stop you in more remote areas to check that you're properly prepared for emergencies.

If driving from İstanbul to Ankara you should be aware of a nasty fog belt around Bolu that can seriously reduce visibility even in summer.

Road Rules

In theory, Turks drive on the right and yield to traffic approaching from the right. In practice, they often drive in the middle and yield to no-one. Be prepared for drivers overtaking on blind curves. If a car approaches from the opposite direction, all three drivers slam on the brakes and pray.

The international driving signs are there but rarely observed. Maximum speed limits, unless otherwise posted, are 50km/h in towns, 90km/h on highways and 130km/h maximum (40km/h minimum) on *otoyols*.

As there are only a few divided highways and many two-lane roads are serpentine, you must reconcile yourself to spending hours crawling along behind slow, seriously overladen trucks. Try to avoid driving at night, but if you do, expect to encounter cars without lights or with lights missing, vehicles stopped in the middle of the road and oncoming drivers flashing their lights just to announce their approach.

DOLMUŞES & MIDIBUSES

Dolmuşes started life as shared taxis that operated on set routes for flat fares, but these days they are very often intercity minibuses. (They also provide local transport within a city – see right.) Some wait until every seat is taken before starting out, others operate at set times. You'll usually use them to get between small towns and villages.

To let the driver know that you want to hop out, say *'inecek var'* (someone wants to get out).

Midibuses generally operate on routes that are too long for dolmuşes, yet not quite popular enough for full-size buses. They usually have narrow seats with rigid upright backs, not at all comfortable on long stretches. Try to avoid the midibuses that ply the long and winding road from Bodrum and Marmaris to Antalya via Fethiye.

HITCHING

Hitching is never entirely safe in any country, and we don't recommend it. Travellers who decide to hitch should understand that they are taking a potentially serious risk.

If you must *otostop* (hitch), you should probably offer to pay something towards the petrol, although most drivers pick up foreign hitchers for their curiosity value. Private cars are not as plentiful as in Europe, so you could be in for a long wait on some routes.

As the country is large and vehicles relatively scarce, short hitches are quite normal. If you need to get from the highway to an archaeological site, you hitch a ride with whatever comes along, be it a tractor, lorry or private car.

Instead of sticking out your thumb for a lift you should face the traffic, hold your arm out towards the road, and wave it up and down as if bouncing a basketball.

LOCAL TRANSPORT
Bus

For most city buses you must buy your *bilet* (ticket) in advance at a special ticket kiosk, either at a major bus terminal or at a transfer point. Some shops near bus stops also sell local bus tickets, which normally cost around €0.65.

In some cities, notably İstanbul, private buses operate on the same routes as municipal buses. The private buses are usually older, accept either cash or tickets, and follow the same routes as municipal buses.

Local Dolmuş

Dolmuşes are minibuses that operate on set routes within a city. They're usually faster, more comfortable and only slightly more expensive than the bus. These days only a few cities still have old-fashioned, shared-taxi dolmuşes (Bursa, Trabzon and İzmir are examples).

Once you've got to grips with a few local routes, you'll feel confident about picking up a dolmuş at the kerb. In the larger cities, stopping places are marked by signs with a black 'D' on a blue-and-white background reading *'Dolmuş İndirme Bindirme Yeri'* (Dolmuş Boarding and Alighting Place). They're usually conveniently located near major squares, terminals or intersections, but you may need to ask the driver: '[your destination] *dolmuş var mı?'*

Metro

Several cities now have underground or partially underground metros, including İstanbul, İzmir, Bursa and Ankara. These are usually quick and simple to use, although you may have to go right through the ticket barriers before you find a route map. Most metros require you to buy a *jeton* (transport token) for around €0.65 and insert it into the ticket barrier.

Taxi

All over Turkey taxis are fitted with digital meters, and most drivers routinely use them. If your driver doesn't, mention it right away by saying '*Saatiniz*' (your meter). The starting rate is about the same as the local bus fare (around €0.65). Check to see the driver is running the right rate: *gündüz* in the daytime, and *gece* at night (which costs 50% more).

Some taxi drivers – particularly in İstanbul – try to demand flat payment from foreigners. Sometimes they offer a decent fare and pocket the money instead of giving the cab owners their share. But most of the time they'll ask an exorbitant amount, give you grief, and refuse to run the meter. If this happens find another cab and, if convenient, complain to the police. Only when you are using a taxi for a private tour involving waiting time (eg to an archaeological site) should you agree a set fare – and then it should always be confirmed in advance to avoid argument later.

Tram

Several cities also have overground *tramvays* (trams), which are a quick and efficient way of getting around; normally you pay around €0.65 to use a tram.

TOURS

Every year we receive complaints from travellers who feel that they have been fleeced by local travel agents, especially some of those operating in the Sultanahmet area of İstanbul. However, there are plenty of very good agents operating alongside the sharks, so try not to get too paranoid. Figure out a ball-park figure for doing the same trip yourself using the prices in this guidebook and shop around before committing.

The list of agents we recommend in İstanbul are on p135. Others are named in the relevant destination chapters. The following are some Turkish tour operators we believe offer a reliable service.

Amber Travel (☎ 0242-836 1630; www.ambertravel .com) Adventure travel specialist based in Kaş; see p371.

Bougainville Travel (☎ 0242-836 3737; www .bougainville-turkey.com) Adventure travel specialist based in Kaş; see p371.

Fez Travel (Map pp96-7; ☎ 0212-516 9024; www.fez travel.com; Akbıyık Caddesi 15, Sultanahmet, İstanbul) Backpacker tours around Turkey, including Gallipoli tours. Also operates the Fez Bus; see the boxed text, p680.

Kirkit Voyage (Map pp96-7; ☎ 0212-518 2282; www .kirkit.com) Customised tours around Turkey (Cappadocia specialists), including İstanbul city and Gallipoli tours; see p135. French spoken too.

Olympica (☎ 0242-836 2049; www.olympicatravel.com) Olympica specialise in 'build your own activity packages'. Based in Kaş; see p371.

TRAIN

Turkish State Railways (Türkiye Cumhuriyeti Devlet Demiryolları, TCDD; ☎ 0216-337 8724; www.tcdd.gov.tr) runs services across the country. Lines laid out during the late Ottoman era rarely follow the shortest route, though a few newer, more direct lines have since been laid, shortening travel times on the best express trains. However, with three nasty train crashes in the space of a few weeks in 2004, including one on the newly inaugurated high-speed İstanbul–Ankara run, some contest that the network needs a complete overhaul. Certainly the government is throwing money at the system, hoping to build a fast-rail network throughout the country. Fast-rail links between İstanbul and Ankara (a new line), Ankara and Konya, Sivas and Kars, and Edirne and Kars have started or are on the drawing board.

The train network covers central and eastern Turkey fairly well, but doesn't go along the coastlines at all, apart from a short stretch between İzmir and Selçuk. For the Aegean and Mediterranean coasts you could go by train to either İzmir or Konya, and take the bus from there.

In terms of what to expect, train travel through Turkey has a growing number of fans embracing the no-rush travel experience: stunning scenery rolling by picture windows, the rhythmic clickity-clacks through a comfy slumber and the immersion with friendly locals. The occasional unannounced hold-up and public toilets gone feral by the end of the long journey are all part of the adventure. And if you're on a budget, an overnight train journey is a great way to save accommodation costs.

TRANSPORT

MAN IN SEAT 61

According to an old Turkish joke, the Germans were paid by the kilometre to build most of Turkey's railways, and they never used a straight line where a dozen curves would do! You'll certainly come to believe this as your train snakes its way across Turkey, round deep valleys and arid mountains, with occasional glimpses of forts on distant hilltops. Turkish train travel is incredibly cheap, but the best trains are air-conditioned and as good as many in Western Europe. The scenery is often better! Chilling out over a meal and a beer in the restaurant car of an İstanbul–Ankara express is a great way to recover from trekking round the sights of İstanbul, and the night trains from İstanbul to Denizli (for Pamukkale) or Konya are a most romantic and time-effective way to go. Other trains are slower and older, but just put your feet up, open a bottle of wine, and let the scenery come to you!

With thanks to Mark Smith, aka the Man in Seat 61, a global rail travel authority and founder of the mighty fine website, www.seat61.com. If you're even remotely interested in travelling by train you'll want to check it out.

The key to enjoying train travel in Turkey is to plan stops en route for long-haul trips and to know what to expect in terms of how long a journey will take. For example, the *Vangölü Ekspresi* from İstanbul to Lake Van (Tatvan), a 1900km trip, takes over 40 hours – and that's an express! The bus takes less than 24 hours, the plane less than two hours. Popular train trips include İstanbul to Ankara, and the overnight trains between İstanbul and Konya, İstanbul and Tehran (Iran), and İstanbul and Aleppo (Syria). Make sure you double-check all train departure times. See the table, p157, for timetable and costs of trains to/from İstanbul.

Note that train schedules usually indicate stations rather than cities. So most schedules refer to Haydarpaşa and Sirkeci rather than İstanbul. For İzmir, you will probably see Basmane and Alsancak, the names of the two main stations.

Classes & Costs

Turkish trains have several seating and sleeping options. Most of the trains have comfortable reclining Pullman seat carriages. Some also have European-style compartments with six seats, usually divided into 1st- and 2nd-class coaches. Sometimes seats can be booked in these compartments, sometimes they're 'first come, best seated'.

There are three types of sleeper. A *küşetli* (couchette) wagon has shared four- or some-

times six-person compartments with seats that fold down into shelf-like beds. Bedding is not provided for these wagons unless it's an *örtülü küşetli* or 'covered' couchette. A *yataklı* wagon has private European-style sleeping compartments, with wash basin and all bedding provided, capable of sleeping one to three people – these are the best option for women travelling on their own on overnight trips.

There is usually a mix of these options on the same service. The *Doğu Express* from İstanbul to Kars, for example, has two pullman carriages, two covered couchettes, two unreserved seating compartments and a sleeper.

Train tickets are usually about half the price of bus tickets. Children, students, seniors, the disabled and return tickets get a 20% discount.

Inter-Rail, Balkan Flexipass and Eurodomino passes are valid on the Turkish railway network; Eurail passes are not.

Reservations

Most seats and all sleepers on the best trains must be reserved. As the *yataklı* (sleeping-car) wagons are very popular, you should make your reservation as far in advance as possible, especially if a religious or public holiday is looming (see p659). Weekend trains tend to be busiest.

You can book and pay for tickets online at www.tcdd.gov.tr.

Health Dr Caroline Evans

CONTENTS

Prevention is the key to staying healthy while travelling in Turkey. Infectious diseases can and do occur in Turkey, but they are usually associated with poor living conditions and poverty, and can be avoided with a few precautions. The most common reason for travellers needing medical help is as a result of accidents – cars are not always well maintained, and poorly lit roads are littered with potholes. Medical facilities can be excellent in large cities, but in remoter areas they may be more basic.

BEFORE YOU GO

A little planning before departure, particularly for pre-existing illnesses, will save you a lot of trouble later. See your dentist before a long trip; carry a spare pair of contact lenses and glasses (and take your optical prescription with you); and carry a first-aid kit with you.

It's tempting to leave it all to the last minute – don't! Many vaccines don't ensure immunity until two weeks after they are given, so visit a doctor four to eight weeks before departure. Ask your doctor for an International Certificate of Vaccination (otherwise known as the yellow booklet), which will list all the vaccinations you've received. This is mandatory for countries that require proof of yellow fever vaccination upon entry, but it's a good idea to carry it wherever you travel.

Travellers can register with the **International Association for Medical Advice to Travellers** (IMAT; www.iamat.org). Its website can help travellers to find a doctor with recognised training.

Bring medications in their original, clearly labelled, containers. A signed and dated letter from your physician describing your medical conditions and medications, including generic names, is also a good idea. If carrying syringes or needles, be sure to have a physician's letter documenting their medical necessity.

MEDICAL CHECKLIST

Here is a list of items you should consider packing in your medical kit.

- Antibiotics (if travelling off the beaten track)
- Antidiarrhoeal drugs (eg loperamide)
- Acetaminophen/paracetamol (Tylenol) or aspirin
- Anti-inflammatory drugs (eg ibuprofen)
- Antihistamines (for hay fever and allergic reactions)
- Antibacterial ointment (eg Bactroban) for cuts and abrasions
- Steroid cream or cortisone (allergic rashes)
- Bandages, gauze, gauze rolls
- Adhesive or paper tape
- Scissors, safety pins, tweezers
- Thermometer
- Pocket knife
- DEET–containing insect repellent for the skin
- Permethrin–containing insect spray for clothing, tents and bed nets
- Sun block (it's very expensive in Turkey)
- Oral rehydration salts
- Iodine tablets (for water purification)
- Syringes and sterile needles (if travelling to remote areas)

INSURANCE

Find out in advance if your insurance plan will make payments directly to providers or reimburse you later for overseas health expenditures (in Turkey doctors generally expect payment in cash). If you are required to pay upfront, make sure you keep all documentation. Some policies ask you to call a centre in your home country (reverse charges) for an immediate assessment of your problem. It's also worth ensuring your travel insurance will cover ambulances or transport either home or to better medical facilities elsewhere. Not all insurance covers emergency medical evacuation home by plane or to a hospital in a major city, which may be the only way to get medical attention in a serious emergency.

Your travel insurance will not usually cover you for anything other than emergency dental treatment.

RECOMMENDED VACCINATIONS

The World Health Organization recommends that all travellers, regardless of the region they are travelling in, should be covered for diphtheria, tetanus, measles, mumps, rubella and polio, as well as hepatitis B. While making preparations to travel, take the opportunity to ensure that all of your routine vaccination cover is complete. The consequences of these diseases can be severe and outbreaks do occur in the Middle East. Rabies is also endemic in Turkey, so if you will be travelling off the beaten track you might want to consider an anti-rabies jab.

INTERNET RESOURCES

There is a wealth of travel health advice on the internet. For further information, the Lonely Planet website (www.lonelyplanet.com) is a good place to start. The **World Health Organization** (www.who.int/ith/en) publishes a superb book, *International Travel and Health*, which is revised annually and is available online at no cost. Another website of general interest is MD Travel Health (www.mdtravelhealth.com), which provides complete travel health recommendations for every country, updated daily, also at no cost. The website for the **Centers for Disease Control & Prevention** (www.cdc.gov) is a very useful source of traveller's health information.

FURTHER READING

Lonely Planet's *Travel With Children* is packed with useful information on topics such as pretrip planning, emergency first aid, immunisation and disease information and what to do if you get sick on the road. Other recommended references include *Traveller's Health* by Dr Richard Dawood, *International Travel Health Guide* by Stuart R Rose MD and *The Travellers' Good Health Guide* by Ted Lankester, an especially useful health guide for volunteers and long-term expatriates working in the Middle East.

IN TURKEY

AVAILABILITY & COST OF HEALTH CARE

The standard of the health care system in Turkey is very variable. Although the best private hospitals in İstanbul and Ankara offer world-class standards of care, they are expensive to use. Elsewhere, even private hospitals don't always offer particularly high standards and their state-run equivalents even less so. Some patients may have contracted hepatitis during their stay in hospital.

For basic care for things such as cuts, bruises and jabs you could ask for the local *sağulık ocağıu* (health centre), but don't expect anyone to speak anything but Turkish. The travel assistance provided by your insurance may be able to locate the nearest source of medical help, otherwise ask at your hotel. In an emergency, contact your embassy or consulate.

Medicine, and even sterile dressings or intravenous fluids, may need to be bought from a local pharmacy. Nursing care is often limited or rudimentary, the assumption being that family and friends will look after the patient.

Standards of dental care are variable and there is a risk of hepatitis B and HIV transmission via poorly sterilised equipment, so watch the tools in use carefully. Your travel insurance will not usually cover you for anything other than emergency dental treatment.

TRAVEL HEALTH WEBSITES

It's a good idea to consult your government's travel health website before departure, if one is available.

Australia (www.smartraveller.gov.au)
Canada (www.travelhealth.gc.ca)
United Kingdom (www.dh.gov.uk/PolicyAnd Guidance/HealthAdviceForTravellers/fs/en)
United States (www.cdc.gov/travel/)

HEALTH

AVIAN INFLUENZA

The H5N1 avian influenza virus was confirmed in Turkey in late 2005 and there were four fatalities, the last in early 2006. All fatalities were linked with ongoing close contact with birds. The risk to humans is considered very low unless the virus develops the ability to spread sustainably and efficiently between humans. For the latest outbreak news and general information log on to the **World Health Organization** (www.who.int).

For minor illnesses, such as diarrhoea, pharmacists can often provide advice and sell over-the-counter medication, including drugs that would require a prescription in your home country. They can also advise when more specialised help is needed.

INFECTIOUS DISEASES
Diphtheria
Diphtheria is spread through close respiratory contact. It causes a high temperature and severe sore throat. Sometimes a membrane forms across the throat requiring a tracheostomy to prevent suffocation. Vaccination is recommended for those likely to be in close contact with the local population in infected areas. The vaccine is given as an injection alone, or with tetanus, and lasts 10 years.

Hepatitis A
Hepatitis A is spread through contaminated food (particularly shellfish) and water. It causes jaundice, and although it is rarely fatal it can cause prolonged lethargy and delayed recovery. Symptoms include dark urine, a yellow colour to the whites of the eyes, fever and abdominal pain. Hepatitis A vaccine (Avaxim, VAQTA, Havrix) is given as an injection: a single dose will give protection for up to a year while a booster 12 months later will provide a subsequent 10 years of protection. Hepatitis A and typhoid vaccines can also be given as a single-dose vaccine (hepatyrix or viatim).

Hepatitis B
Infected blood, contaminated needles and sexual intercourse can all transmit hepatitis B. It can cause jaundice and affects the liver, occasionally causing liver failure. All travellers should make this a routine vaccination,

especially as the disease is endemic in Turkey. (Many countries now give hepatitis B vaccination as part of routine childhood vaccination.) The vaccine is given singly, or at the same time as the hepatitis A vaccine (hepatyrix). A course will give protection for at least five years. It can be given over four weeks or six months.

HIV
HIV is spread via infected blood and blood products, sexual intercourse with an infected partner and from an infected mother to her newborn child. It can be spread through 'blood to blood' contacts such as contaminated instruments during medical, dental, acupuncture and other body-piercing procedures and sharing used intravenous needles.

Leishmaniasis
Spread through the bite of an infected sandfly, leishmaniasis can cause a slowly growing skin lump or ulcer. It may develop into a serious, life-threatening fever usually accompanied by anaemia and weight loss. Infected dogs are also carriers of the infection. Sandfly bites should be avoided whenever possible.

Leptospirosis
Leptospirosis is spread through the excreta of infected rodents, especially rats. It can cause hepatitis and renal failure that may be fatal. It is unusual for travellers to be affected unless living in poor sanitary conditions. It causes a fever and jaundice.

Malaria
You stand the greatest chance of contracting malaria if you travel in southeastern Turkey. The risk of malaria is minimal in most cities, but you should check with your doctor if you are considering travelling to any rural areas. It is important to take antimalarial tablets if the risk is significant. For up-to-date information about the risk of contracting malaria in a specific country, contact your local travel health clinic.

If you're travelling in southeastern Turkey it's as well to be aware of the symptoms of malaria. It is possible to contract malaria from a single bite from an infected mosquito. Malaria almost always starts with marked shivering, fever and sweating. Muscle pain, headache and vomiting are common. Symptoms may occur anywhere from a few days to three weeks after a bite by an infected mosquito. The illness can start while you are taking preventative tablets if they are not fully effective, and may also occur after you have finished taking your tablets.

Poliomyelitis

Generally, poliomyelitis is spread through contaminated food and water. It is one of the vaccines given in childhood and should be boosted every 10 years, either orally (a drop on the tongue) or as an injection. Polio may be carried asymptomatically, although it can cause a transient fever and, in rare cases, potentially permanent muscle weakness or paralysis.

Rabies

Spread through bites or licks on broken skin from an infected animal, rabies is fatal. Animal handlers should be vaccinated, as should those travelling to remote areas where a reliable source of post-bite vaccine is not available within 24 hours. Three injections are needed over a month. If you have not been vaccinated and you suffer a bite, you will need a course of five injections starting within 24 hours or as soon as possible after the injury. Vaccination does not provide you with immunity, it merely buys you more time to seek appropriate medical help.

Tuberculosis

Tuberculosis (TB) is spread through close respiratory contact and occasionally through infected milk or milk products. BCG vaccine is recommended for those likely to be mixing closely with the local population. It is more important for those visiting family or planning on a long stay, and those employed as teachers and health-care workers. TB can be asymptomatic, although symptoms can include a cough, weight loss or fever months or even years after exposure. An X-ray is the best way to confirm if you have TB. BCG gives a moderate degree of protection against TB. It causes a small permanent scar at the site of injection, and is usually only given in specialised chest clinics. As it's a live vaccine it should not be given to pregnant women or immunocompromised individuals. The BCG vaccine is not available in all countries.

Typhoid

This is spread through food or water that has been contaminated by infected human faeces.

The first symptom is usually fever or a pink rash on the abdomen. Septicaemia (blood poisoning) may also occur. Typhoid vaccine (typhim Vi, typherix) will give protection for three years. In some countries, the oral vaccine Vivotif is also available.

Yellow Fever

Yellow fever vaccination is not required for any areas of the Middle East; however, any travellers coming from a yellow-fever-endemic area will need to show proof of vaccination against yellow fever before entry to the Middle East – this normally means if a traveller is arriving directly from an infected country or has been in an infected country during the previous 10 days.

The yellow-fever vaccination must be given at a designated clinic, and is valid for 10 years. It is a live vaccine and must not be given to immunocompromised or pregnant travellers.

TRAVELLER'S DIARRHOEA

To prevent diarrhoea, avoid tap water unless it has been boiled, filtered or chemically disinfected (with iodine tablets). Eat only fresh fruits or vegetables if they're cooked or if you have peeled them yourself, and avoid dairy products that might contain unpasteurised milk. Buffet meals are risky since food may not be kept hot enough; meals freshly cooked in front of you in a busy restaurant are more likely to be safe.

If you develop diarrhoea, be sure to drink plenty of fluids, preferably an oral rehydration solution containing lots of salt and sugar. A few loose stools don't require treatment, but if you start having more than four or five motions a day, you should start taking an antibiotic (usually a quinolone drug) and an antidiarrhoeal agent (such as loperamide). If diarrhoea is bloody, persists for more than 72 hours or is accompanied by fever, shaking chills or severe abdominal pain, you should seek medical attention.

ENVIRONMENTAL HAZARDS
Heat Illness

Heat exhaustion occurs following heavy sweating and excessive fluid loss with inadequate replacement of fluids and salt. This is particularly common in hot climates when taking unaccustomed exercise before full acclimatisation. Symptoms include headache, dizziness and tiredness. Dehydration is already happening by the time you feel thirsty – aim to drink sufficient water such that you produce pale, diluted urine. The treatment of heat exhaustion consists of fluid replacement with water, fruit juice, or both, and cooling by cold water and fans. The treatment of the salt-loss component consists of consuming salty fluids such as soup or broth, and adding a little more table salt to foods than usual.

Heat stroke is much more serious. This occurs when the body's heat-regulating mechanism breaks down. An excessive rise in body temperature leads to sweating ceasing, irrational and hyperactive behaviour, and eventually loss of consciousness and death. Rapid cooling by spraying the body with water and fanning is an ideal treatment. Emergency fluid and electrolyte replacement by intravenous drip is usually also required.

Insect Bites & Stings

Even if mosquitoes do not carry malaria, they can cause irritation and infected bites. Using DEET-based insect repellents will prevent bites. Mosquitoes also spread dengue fever.

There is a risk of bee stings along the Aegean and Mediterranean coastal areas. Bees and wasps only cause real problems for those with a severe allergy (anaphylaxis). If you have a severe allergy to bee or wasp stings you should carry an adrenaline injection or something similar. There is a particularly higher risk of bee stings in the area around Marmaris in southwest Turkey.

Sandflies are located around the Mediterranean beaches. They usually only cause a nasty, itchy bite, but can carry a rare skin disorder called cutaneous leishmaniasis (p688); use a DEET-based repellents to avoid bites.

Scorpions are frequently found in arid or dry climates. Turkey's small white scorpions can give a painful bite which will bother you for up to 24 hours, but they won't kill you.

Snake Bites

Do not walk barefoot or stick your hand into holes or cracks. If bitten by a snake, do not panic. Half of those bitten by venomous snakes are not actually injected with poison (envenomed). Immobilise the bitten limb with a splint (eg a stick) and apply a bandage over the site, with firm pressure, similar to applying a bandage over a sprain. Do not apply a tourniquet, or cut or suck the bite. Get the victim to medical help as soon as possible so that antivenin can be given if necessary.

Water

It's probably not wise to drink Turkey's tap water if you're only here on a short visit. Stick to bottled water, boil water for 10 minutes or use water-purification tablets or a filter. Do not drink water from rivers or lakes since it may contain bacteria or viruses that can cause diarrhoea or vomiting.

TRAVELLING WITH CHILDREN

All travellers with children should know how to treat minor ailments and when to seek medical treatment. Make sure children are up to date with routine vaccinations, and discuss possible travel vaccines well before departure as some vaccines are not suitable for children aged under one year. You may want to consider giving children the BCG vaccine for tuberculosis (TB) if they haven't already had it – see p689 for more information.

In hot, moist climates any wound or break in the skin may lead to infection. The area should be cleaned and then kept dry and clean. Remember to avoid contaminated food and water. If your child is vomiting or experiencing diarrhoea, lost fluid and salts must be replaced. It may be helpful to take rehydration powders for reconstituting with boiled water. Ask your doctor about this.

Children should be encouraged to avoid dogs or other mammals because of the risk of rabies and other diseases. Any bite, scratch or lick from a warm-blooded, furry animal should immediately be thoroughly cleaned. If there is any possibility that the animal is infected with rabies, seek immediate medical assistance.

It always pays to double-check the drug and dosage your child has been prescribed by doctors or pharmacists in Turkey as they may be unsuitable for children. Some information on the suitability of drugs and recommended dosage can be found on the websites listed on p687.

WOMEN'S HEALTH

Emotional stress, exhaustion and travelling through different time zones can all contribute to an upset in the menstrual pattern. If you're using oral contraceptives, remember that some antibiotics, diarrhoea and vomiting can stop the pill from working and lead to the risk of pregnancy. Remember to take condoms with you just in case. Condoms should be kept in a cool, dry place or they may crack and perish.

Emergency contraception is most effective if taken within 24 hours after unprotected sex; ask at a pharmacy for the *ertesi gün hapı* (the morning-after pill). The **International Planned Parent Federation** (www.ippf.org) can advise you about the availability of contraception in Turkey and other countries. Sanitary pads are fairly readily available in the country, but tampons are not always available outside major cities and are expensive – bring your own from home.

Travelling during pregnancy is usually possible, but there are important things to consider. Have a medical check-up before embarking on your trip. The most risky times for travel are during the first 12 weeks of pregnancy, when miscarriage is most likely, and after 30 weeks, when complications such as high blood pressure and premature delivery can occur. Most airlines will not accept a traveller after 28 to 32 weeks of pregnancy,

and in the later stages long-haul flights can be very uncomfortable. Antenatal facilities vary greatly in Turkey and you should think carefully before travelling in out-of-the-way places, bearing in mind the cultural and linguistic difficulties, not to mention poor medical standards you might face if anything goes wrong. Take written records of the pregnancy, including details of your blood group, which is likely to be helpful if you need medical attention while away (in Turkey you have to pay for blood infusions unless a friend supplies the blood for you). Ensure your insurance policy covers birth and postnatal care, but remember that insurance policies are only as good as the facilities available.

If you are pregnant or breastfeeding it always pays to double-check the drug and dosage you have been prescribed by doctors or pharmacists in Turkey. The appropriateness of some drugs and correct dosage for pregnant or lactating women is sometimes overlooked. You can use the earlier websites (p687) to check the generic drug and its recommended dosage.

HEALTH

Language

CONTENTS

Turkish is the dominant language in the Turkic language group, which also includes lesser-known tongues such as Azeri, Kirghiz and Kazakh. Although distantly related to Finnish and Hungarian, the Turkic languages are now seen as comprising their own unique language group. You can find people who speak Turkish, in one form or another, from Belgrade all the way to Xinjiang in China.

In 1928, Atatürk did away with Arabic script and adopted a Latin-based alphabet that was better suited to easy learning and correct pronunciation. He also instituted a language reform process to purge Turkish of Arabic and Persian borrowings, returning it to its 'authentic' roots. The result is a logical, systematic and expressive language with only one irregular noun, *su* (water), one irregular verb, *olmek* (to be) and no genders. It's so logical, in fact, that Turkish grammar formed the basis for the development of Esperanto, an ill-fated artificial international language.

Word order and verb formation in Turkish are very different from what you'll find in Indo-European languages like English. Words are formed by agglutination, meaning affixes are joined to a root word – one scary example is *Avustralyalılaştıramadıklarımızdanmısınız?*, which means 'Are you one of those whom we could not Australianise?' This makes it somewhat difficult to learn at first, despite its elegant logic.

In larger cities and tourist areas you'll usually have little trouble finding someone who speaks English, but a few hints will help you comprehend signs, schedules and menus. For more information on language courses, see p654, and for a comprehensive language guide get Lonely Planet's *Turkish Phrasebook*. You may also want to check out the excellent websites www.turkishclass.com and www.practicalturkish.com.

PRONUNCIATION

Pronouncing Turkish is pretty simple for English speakers as it uses sounds that are very similar to ones you already use. You'll hear some variation in pronunciation in different parts of Turkey, but this language chapter is based on standard pronunciation so you'll be understood wherever you go.

Vowels

Most Turkish vowel sounds can be found in English, although in Turkish they're generally shorter and slightly harsher. When you see a double vowel, such as *saat* (hour) you need to pronounce both syllables separately. Be careful of the symbols ı and i – the ı is undotted in both lower and upper case (like Iğrıdır), while the i has dots in both cases (like İzmir). It's easy to read both of these as an English 'i', but you can be misunderstood if you don't pronounce the two sounds distinctly – *sık* means 'dense', 'tight' or 'frequent' but *sik* is the Turkish equivalent of a certain 'f' word meaning 'to copulate'. The same care should be taken with o/ö and u/ü.

TURKISH PRONUNCIATION GUIDE

TURKISH	PRONUNCIATION GUIDE	
a	a	as in 'father'
ay	ai	as in 'aisle'
e	e	as in 'red'
ey	ay	as in 'say'
ı	uh	as the 'a' in 'ago'
i	ee	as in 'bee'
o	o	as in 'go'
ö	er	as in 'her' with no 'r' sound

| u | oo | as in 'moon' |
| ü | ew | like 'ee' with rounded lips |

Consonants

Most Turkish consonants sound the same as their English counterparts, but there are a couple of exceptions. The Turkish **c** is pronounced like English 'j', **ç** is like English 'c' and **ş** is like English 'sh'. The letter **h** is never silent, so always pronounce it as in 'house'. The **ğ** is a silent letter that extends the vowel before it – it acts like the 'gh' combination in 'weigh', and is never pronounced. The letter **r** is always rolled and **v** is a little softer than the English sound.

TURKISH	PRONUNCIATION GUIDE	
b	b	as in 'big'
c	j	as in 'jam'
ç	ch	as in 'church'
d	d	in as 'day'
f	f	as in 'fun'
g	g	as in 'go'
h	h	as in 'house'
j	zh	as the 's' in 'pleasure'
k	k	as in 'kilo'
l	l	as in 'loud'
m	m	as in 'man'
n	n	as in 'no'
p	p	as in 'pig'
r	r	a strong, rolled 'r'
s	s	as in 'sea'
ş	sh	as in 'ship'
t	t	as in 'tin'
v	v	as in 'van' but softer
y	y	as in 'you'
z	z	as in 'zoo'

Word Stress

Word stress is quite light in Turkish, and generally falls on the last syllable of the word. Most two-syllable place names (eg Kıbrıs) are stressed on the first syllable, and in three-syllable names the stress is usually on the second syllable (eg İstanbul).

ACCOMMODATION

Where can I find a ...?

Nerede ... bulabilirim?	ne·re·de ... boo·la·bee·lee·reem
camping ground	
kamp yeri	kamp ye·ree
guesthouse	
misafirhane	mee·sa·feer·ha·ne

MAKING A RESERVATION
(for written and phone inquiries)

To ...	Alıcı ...	a·luh·juh ...
From ...	Gönderen ...	gern·de·ren ...
Date	Tarih	ta·reeh
in the name of ...	... adına	... a·duh·na
credit card	kredi kartı	kre·dee kar·tuh
number	numara	noo·ma·ra
expiry date	son kullanma tarihi	son kool·lan·ma ta·ree·hee

I'd like to book ...
... ayırtmak istiyorum lütfen.
... a·yurt·mak ees·tee·yo·room lewt·fen
From (2 July) to (6 July).
(2 Temmuz'dan) (6 Temmuz'a) kadar.
(ee·kee tem·mooz·dan) (al·tuh tem·moo·za) ka·dar
Please confirm availability and price.
Lütfen fiyatı ve mal mevcudiyetini teyit eder misiniz?
lewt·fen fee·ya·tuh ve mal mev·joo·dee·ye·tee·nee te·yeet e·der mee·see·neez

---

hotel
| otel | o·tel |
youth hostel
| gençlik hosteli | gench·leek hos·te·lee |
pension
| pansiyon | pan·see·yon |
pension (in a private home)
| ev pansiyonu | ev pan·see·yo·noo |

Can you recommend somewhere cheap?

Ucuz bir yer tavsiye edebilir misiniz?
oo·jooz beer yer tav·see·ye e·de·bee·leer mee·see·neez
What's the address?

Adresi nedir?
ad·re·see ne·deer
Could you write it down, please?

Lütfen yazar mısınız?
lewt·fen ya·zar muh·suh·nuhz

Do you have a ...?

... odanız var mı?	
... o·da·nuz var muh	
single room	
Tek kişilik	tek kee·shee·leek
double room	
İki kişilik	ee·kee kee·shee·leek
twin room	
Çift yataklı	cheeft ya·tak·luh
dormitory room	
Yatakhane	ya·tak·ha·ne

How much is it per night/person?
Geceliği/Kişi başına   ge·je·lee·ee/kee·shee ba·shuh·na
ne kadar?   ne ka·dar
May I see it?
Görebilir miyim?   ger·re·bee·leer mee·yeem
Where's the bathroom/toilet?
Banyo/Tuvalet nerede?   ban·yo/too·va·let ne·re·de
I'm leaving now.
Şimdi ayrılıyorum.   sheem·dee ai·ruh·luh·yo·room

CONVERSATION & ESSENTIALS

Hello.
Merhaba.   mer·ha·ba
Goodbye.
Hoşçakal.   hosh·cha·kal (person leaving)
Güle güle.   gew·le gew·le (person staying)
Yes.
Evet.   e·vet
No.
Hayır.   ha·yuhr
Please.
Lütfen.   lewt·fen
Thank you.
Teşekkür ederim.   te·shek·kewr e·de·reem
You're welcome.
Birşey değil.   beer·shay de·eel
Excuse me.
Bakar mısınız.   ba·kar muh·suh·nuhz
Sorry.
Özür dilerim.   er·zewr dee·le·reem
What's your name?
Adınız nedir?   a·duh·nuhz ne·deer
My name is ...
Benim adım ...   be·neem a·duhm ...
Where are you from?
Nerelisiniz?   ne·re·lee·see·neez
I'm from ...
Ben ...   ben ...
I like ...
... seviyorum.   ... se·vee·yo·room
I don't like ...
... sevmiyorum.   ... sev·mee·yo·room

DIRECTIONS

Can you show me (on the map)?
Bana (haritada)   ba·na (ha·ree·ta·da) gers·te·re·
gösterebilir misin?   bee·leer mee·seen
Where is ...?
... nerede?   ... ne·re·de
It's straight ahead.
Tam karşıda.   tam kar·shuh·da
Turn left.
Sola dön.   so·la dern
Turn right.
Sağa dön.   sa·a dern

SIGNS	
Ada	Island
Belediye	Town Hall
Cami	Mosque
Deniz	Sea
Göl	Lake
Harabeler	Ruins
Havaalanı	Airport
Kale	Castle/Fortress
Kilise	Church
Köprü	Bridge
Liman	Harbour/Port
Meydan	Town Square
Müze	Museum
Otogar	Bus Station
Plaj	Beach
Şehir Merkez	Town Centre
Giriş	Entrance
Çıkışı	Exit
Açık	Open
Kapalı	Closed
Yasak	Prohibited
Sigara İçilmez	No Smoking
Boş Oda	Rooms Available
Boş Yer Yok	Full (No Vacancies)
Tuvaletler	Toilets/WC
Bay	Male
Bayan	Female

at the corner
köşeden   ker·she·den
at the traffic lights
trafik ışıklarından   tra·feek uh·shuhk·la·ruhn·dan

behind   *arkasında*   ar·ka·suhn·da
in front of   *önünde*   er·newn·de
far (from)   *uzak*   oo·zak
near (to)   *yakınında*   ya·kuh·nuhn·da
opposite   *karşısında*   kar·shuh·suhn·da

HEALTH

I'm ill.
Hastayım.   has·ta·yuhm
It hurts here.
Burası ağrıyor.   boo·ra·suh a·ruh·yor
antiseptic
antiseptik   an·tee·sep·teek
condoms
kondom   kon·dom
contraceptives
doğum kontrol ilaçları   do·oom kon·trol ee·lach·la·ruh
diarrhoea
ishali   ees·ha·lee

EMERGENCIES

Help!
İmdat!   *eem·dat*
There's been an accident!
Bir kaza oldu.   beer ka·za ol·doo
I'm lost.
Kayboldum.   kai·bol·doom
Leave me alone!
Git başımdan!   geet ba·shuhm·dan

Call ...!
... çağırın!   ... cha·uh·ruhn
  a doctor
  Doktor   dok·tor
  the police
  Polis   po·lees
  an ambulance
  Ambulans   am·boo·lans

medicine
ilaç   ee·lach
nausea
mide bulantım   mee·de boo·lan·tuhm
sunblock cream
güneş kremi   gew·nesh kre·mee
tampons
tampon   tam·pon

I'm ...
... var.   ... var
  asthmatic
  Astımım   as·tuh·muhm
  diabetic
  Şeker hastalığı   she·ker has·ta·luh·uhm

I'm allergic to ...
... alerjim var.   ... a·ler·zheem var
  antibiotics
  Antibiyotiklere   an·tee·bee·yo·teek·le·re
  aspirin
  Aspirine   as·pee·ree·ne
  penicillin
  Penisiline   pe·nee·see·lee·ne
  bees
  Arılara   a·ruh·la·ra
  nuts
  Çerezlere   che·rez·le·re
  peanuts
  Fıstığa   fuhs·tuh·a

LANGUAGE DIFFICULTIES

Do you speak English?
İngilizce konuşuyor musunuz?
een·gee·leez·je ko·noo·shoo·yor moo·soo·nooz

Does anyone here speak English?
İngilizce bilen var mı?
een·gee·leez·je bee·len var muh
How do you say ...?
... nasıl söylüyorsuhn?
... na·seel say·lew·yor·soohn
Could you write it down, please?
Lütfen yazar mısınız?
lewt·fen ya·zar muh·suh·nuhz
I understand.
Anlıyorum.
an·luh·yo·room
I don't understand.
Anlamıyorum.
an·la·muh·yo·room

NUMBERS

0	*sıfır*	suh·fuhr
1	*bir*	beer
2	*iki*	ee·kee
3	*üç*	ewch
4	*dört*	dert
5	*beş*	besh
6	*altı*	al·tuh
7	*yedi*	ye·dee
8	*sekiz*	se·keez
9	*dokuz*	do·kooz
10	*on*	on
11	*on bir*	on beer
12	*on iki*	on ee·kee
13	*on üç*	on ewch
14	*on dört*	on derrt
15	*on beş*	on besh
16	*on altı*	on al·tuh
17	*on yedi*	on ye·dee
18	*on sekiz*	on se·keez
19	*on dokuz*	on do·kooz
20	*yirmi*	yeer·mee
21	*yirmi bir*	yeer·mee beer
22	*yirmi iki*	yeer·mee ee·kee
30	*otuz*	o·tooz
40	*kırk*	kuhrk
50	*elli*	el·lee
60	*altmış*	alt·muhsh
70	*yetmiş*	yet·meesh
80	*seksen*	sek·sen
90	*doksan*	dok·san
100	*yüz*	yewz
200	*ikiyüz*	ee·kee·yewz
1000	*bin*	been
1,000,000	*bin milyon*	been meel·yon

PAPERWORK

name	*ad*	ad
nationality	*uyrukluk*	ooy·rook·look
date of birth	*doğum günü*	do·oom gew·new

LANGUAGE

place of birth	*doğum yeri*	do-*oom* ye-ree
sex/gender	*cinsiyet*	jeen-see-*yet*
passport	*pasaport*	pa-sa-*port*
surname	*soyad*	*soy*-ad
visa	*vize*	*vee*-ze

QUESTION WORDS

Who?	*Kim?*	keem
What?	*Ne?*	ne
When?	*Ne zaman?*	ne za-*man*
Where?	*Nerede?*	ne-re-de
Which?	*Hangi?*	han-*gee*
How?	*Nasıl?*	na-*seel*

SHOPPING & SERVICES

I'd like to buy ...
... almak istiyorum. al-*mak* ees-*tee*-yo-room
How much is it?
Ne kadar? ne ka-*dar*
May I look at it?
Bakabilir miyim? ba-*ka*-bee-leer mee-yeem
I'm just looking.
Sadece bakıyorum. sa-de-*je* ba-*kuh*-yo-room
The quality isn't good.
Kalitesi iyi değil. ka-lee-te-*see* ee-*yee* de-*eel*
It's too expensive.
Bu çok pahalı. boo chok pa-ha-*luh*
I'll take it.
Tutuyorum. too-*too*-yo-room

Do you accept ...?
... kabul ediyor musunuz?
... ka-*bool* e-*dee*-yor moo-soo-*nooz*
  credit cards
  Kredi kartı kre-dee kar-*tuh*
  travellers cheques
  Seyahat çeki se-ya-*hat* che-kee

more	*daha fazla*	da-*ha* faz-*la*
less	*daha az*	da-*ha* az
smaller	*küçük*	kew-*chewk*
bigger	*büyük*	bew-*yewk*

Where's *... nerede?* *...* ne-re-de
a/the ...?
bank	*Banka*	*ban*-ka
... embassy	*... elçilik*	*...* el-chee-*leek*
hospital	*Hastane*	has-ta-*ne*
market	*Pazar yeri*	pa-*zar* ye-ree
police	*Polis*	po-*lees*
post office	*Postane*	pos-ta-*ne*
public phone	*Telefon*	te-le-*fon*
	kulübesi	koo-lew-be-*see*
public toilet	*Umumi*	oo-moo-*mee*
	tuvalet	too-va-*let*

TIME & DATES

When?	*Ne zaman?*	ne za-*man*
What time is it?	*Saat kaç?*	sa-*at* kach
It's (10) o'clock.	*Saat (on).*	sa-*at* (on)
in the morning	*öğleden evvel*	er-le-den ev-*vel*
in the afternoon	*öğleden sonra*	er-le-den son-ra
week	*hafta*	haf-*ta*
year	*yıl*	yuhl
today	*bugün*	boo-*gewn*
tomorrow	*yarın*	ya-*ruhn*
yesterday	*dün*	dewn

Monday	*Pazartesi*	pa-*zar*-te-see
Tuesday	*Salı*	sa-*luh*
Wednesday	*Çarşamba*	char-sham-*ba*
Thursday	*Perşembe*	per-shem-*be*
Friday	*Cuma*	joo-*ma*
Saturday	*Cumartesi*	joo-*mar*-te-see
Sunday	*Pazar*	pa-*zar*

January	*Ocak*	o-*jak*
February	*Şubat*	shoo-*bat*
March	*Mart*	mart
April	*Nisan*	nee-*san*
May	*Mayıs*	ma-*yuhs*
June	*Haziran*	ha-*zee*-ran
July	*Temmuz*	tem-*mooz*
August	*Ağustos*	a-oos-*tos*
September	*Eylül*	ay-*lewl*
October	*Ekim*	e-*keem*
November	*Kasım*	ka-*suhm*
December	*Aralık*	a-ra-*luhk*

TRANSPORT
Public Transport

What time does the ... leave/arrive?
... ne zaman kalkacak/varır?
... ne za-*man* kal-ka-*jak*/va-*ruhr*
boat	*Vapur*	va-*poor*
bus	*Otobüs*	o-to-*bews*
plane	*Uçak*	oo-*chak*
train	*Tren*	tren

I'd like a ... ticket.
... bir bilet lütfen.
... beer bee-*let* lewt-fen
  one-way
  Gidiş gee-*deesh*
  return
  Gidiş-dönüş gee-deesh-der-*newsh*
  1st-class
  Birinci mevki bee-reen-*jee* mev-*kee*
  2nd-class
  İkinci mevki ee-keen-*jee* mev-*kee*

ROAD SIGNS

Dur	Stop
Girilmez	No Entry
Park Etmek Yasaktir	No Parking
Yol Ver	Give Way
Ücret Ödenir	Toll
Tehlikeli	Danger
Yavaş	Slow Down
Çıkışı	Exit
Giriş	Entry
Otoyol	Freeway
Park Yeri	Parking Garage
Tek Yön	One Way

delayed	*ertelendi*	er·te·len·*dee*
cancelled	*iptal edildi*	eep·*tal* e·deel·*dee*
the first/the last	*ilk/son*	eelk/son
platform	*peron*	pe·*ron*
ticket office	*bilet gişesi*	bee·*let* gee·she·*see*
timetable	*tarife*	ta·ree·*fe*
train station	*istasyon*	ees·tas·*yon*

Private Transport

I'd like to hire a ...
Bir ... kiralamak istiyorum.
beer ... kee·ra·la·*mak* ees·tee·yo·room

car	*araba*	a·ra·*ba*
4WD	*dört çeker*	dert che·*ker*
motorbike	*motosiklet*	mo·to·seek·*let*
bicycle	*bisiklet*	bee·seek·*let*

Is this the road to ...?
... giden yol bu mu? ... gee·*den* yol boo moo

Where's a service station?
Benzin istasyonu ben·*zeen* ees·tas·yo·*noo* ne·re·de
nerede?

Please fill it up.
Lütfen depoyu doldurun. lewt·fen de·po·yoo dol·*doo*·roon

I'd like ... litres.
... litre istiyorum. ... leet·re ees·*tee*·yo·room

diesel	*dizel*	dee·zel
leaded petrol	*kurşunlu*	koor·shoon·*loo*
unleaded petrol	*kurşunsuz*	koor·shoon·*sooz*

(How long) Can I park here?
Buraya (ne kadar süre) park edebilirim?
boo·ra·ya (ne ka·dar sew·re) park e·de·bee·lee·reem

Do I have to pay?
Park ücreti ödemem gerekli mi?
park ewj·re·tee er·de·mem ge·rek·lee mee

I need a mechanic.
Tamirciye ihtiyacım var.
ta·meer·jee·ye eeh·tee·ya·jum var

The car/motorbike has broken down at ...
Arabam/motosikletim ...de bozuldu.
a·ra·*bam*/mo·to·seek·le·*teem* ...·de bo·zool·*doo*

I have a flat tyre.
Lastiğim patladı.
las·tee·*eem* pat·la·*duh*

I've run out of petrol.
Benzinim bitti.
ben·zee·*neem* beet·*tee*

I've had an accident.
Kaza yaptım.
ka·za yap·*tuhm*

TRAVEL WITH CHILDREN

Do you have a/an ...?
... var mı? ... var muh

baby change room
Alt değiştirme odası alt de·eesh·teer·me o·da·suh

baby seat
Bebek koltuğuna be·bek kol·too·oo·na

child-minding service
Çocuk bakım hizmeti cho·jook ba·kuhm heez·me·tee

children's menu
Çocuk menüsü cho·jook me·new·sew

disposable nappies/diapers
Bebek bezi be·bek be·zee

highchair
Mama sandalyesine ma·ma san·dal·ye·see·ne

potty
Oturağa o·too·ra·a

pusher (stroller)
Pusete/Bebek arabası poo·se·te/be·bek a·ra·ba·suh

Where's the nearest toy shop?
En yakın oyuncakçı nerede?
en ya·kuhn o·yoon·jak·chuh ne·re·de

Do you mind if I breast-feed here?
Burada çocuk emzirmemin bir sakıncası var mı?
boo·ra·da cho·jook em·zeer·me·meen beer sa·kuhn·ja·suh
var muh

Are children allowed?
Çocuklar girebilir mi?
cho·jook·lar gee·re·bee·leer mee

Also available from Lonely Planet:
Turkish Phrasebook

Glossary

See p74 in the Food & Drink chapter for useful words and phrases dealing with food and dining. See the Language chapter (p692) for other useful words and phrases.

acropolis – hilltop citadel and temples of a classical Hellenic city
ada(sı) – island
agora – open space for commerce and politics in a Graeco-Roman city
aile salonu – family dining room, for couples, families and single women in a Turkish restaurant
Anatolia – the Asian part of Turkey; also called Asia Minor
arabesk – Arabic-style Turkish music
arasta – row of shops near a mosque, the rent from which supports the mosque
Asia Minor – see Anatolia

bahçe(si) – garden
banliyö treni – suburban train lines
baraj – dam
bedesten – vaulted, fireproof market enclosure where valuable goods are kept
belediye (sarayı) – municipal council, town hall
bey – polite form of address for a man; follows the name
birahane – beer hall
bouleuterion – place of assembly, council meeting place in a classical Hellenic city
büfe – snack bar
bulvar(ı) – often abbreviated to 'bul'; boulevard or avenue

cadde(si) – often abbreviated to 'cad'; street
cami(i) – mosque
caravanserai – large fortified way-station for (trade) caravans
çarşı(sı) – market, bazaar; sometimes town centre
çay bahçesi – tea garden
çayhane – teahouse
çayı – stream
çeşme – spring, fountain
cicim – embroidered rug
Cilician Gates – a pass in the Taurus Mountains in southern Turkey

dağ(ı) – mountain
damsız girilmez – sign meaning that men unaccompanied by a woman will not be admitted
deniz – sea
deniz otobüsü – literally 'seabus'; hydrofoil or catamaran

dere(si) – stream
dervish – member of Mevlevi Muslim brotherhood
dolmuş – shared taxi; can be a minibus or sedan
döviz (burosu) – currency exchange (office)

emanet(çi) – left-luggage (baggage check) office
emir – Turkish tribal chieftain
eski – old (thing, not person)
ev pansiyonu – private home that rents rooms to travellers
eyvan – vaulted hall opening into a central court in a *medrese* or mosque
ezan – the Muslim call to prayer

fasıl – Ottoman classical music, usually played by gypsies
feribot – ferry

GAP – South-East Anatolia Project, a mammoth hydroelectric and irrigation project
gazino – Turkish nightclub, not a gambling den
geçit, -di – (mountain) pass
gişe – ticket booth
göl(ü) – lake
gület – traditional Turkish wooden yacht

hamam(ı) – Turkish bathhouse
han(ı) – caravanserai
hanım – polite form of address for a woman
haremlik – family/women's quarters of a residence; see also *selamlık*
heykel – statue
hisar(ı) – fortress or citadel
Hittites – nation of people inhabiting Anatolia during 2nd millennium BC
hükümet konağı – government house, provincial government headquarters

ilkokul – primary school
imam – prayer leader, Muslim cleric
imaret(i) – soup kitchen for the poor, usually attached to a *medrese*
işhanı – office building
iskele(si) – jetty, quay

jandarma – gendarme, paramilitary police force/officer
jeton – transport token

kale(si) – fortress, citadel
kapı(sı) – door, gate
kaplıca – thermal spring or baths

kahvaltı salonu – breakfast room
Karagöz – shadow-puppet theatre
kaya – cave
kazı – archaeological excavations
KDV – katma değer vergisi, Turkey's value-added tax
kebapçı – place selling kebaps
kervansaray(ı) – Turkish for caravanserai
keyif – relaxation, refined to a fine art in Turkey
kilim – flat-weave rug
kilise(si) – church
köfteci – *köfte*-maker or -seller
konak, konağı – mansion, government headquarters
köprü(sü) – bridge
köşk(ü) – pavilion, villa
köy(ü) – village
kule(si) – tower
külliye(si) – mosque complex including seminary, hospital and soup kitchen
kümbet – vault, cupola, dome; tomb topped by this
küşet(li) – couchette(s), or shelf-like beds, in a six-person train compartment

liman(ı) – harbour
lise – high school
lokanta – restaurant

mağara(sı) – cave
mahalle(si) – neighbourhood, district of a city
medrese(si) – Islamic theological seminary or school, attached to a mosque
mescit, -di – prayer room, small mosque
Mevlâna – also known as Celaleddin Rumi, a great mystic and poet (1207–73), founder of the Mevlevi whirling *dervish* order
meydan(ı) – public square, open place
meyhane – tavern, wine shop
mihrab – niche in a mosque indicating the direction of Mecca
milli parkı – national park
mimber – pulpit in a mosque
minare(si) – minaret, tower from which Muslims are called to prayer
müezzin – cantor who sings the *ezan*, or call to prayer
müze(si) – museum

nargileh – traditional water pipe (for smoking); hookah
necropolis – city of the dead, cemetery

oda(sı) – room
odeon – odeum, small classical theatre for musical performances
örenyeri – ruins
ortaokul – secondary school
otobus – bus
otogar – bus station

otoyol – motorway, limited-access divided highway
Ottoman – of or pertaining to the Ottoman Empire which lasted from the end of the 13th century to the end of WWI

pansiyon – pension, B&B, guesthouse
pastane – pastry shop (patisserie); also *pastahane*
pazar(ı) – weekly market, bazaar
peribacalar – fairy chimneys
peron – gate (at the otogar); platform (train station)
peştimal – *hamam* cloth
petrol ofisi – petrol station
pideci – pide-maker or -seller
PTT – Posta, Telefon, Telegraf; post, telephone and telegraph office

Ramazan – Islamic holy month of fasting

saat kulesi – clock tower
şadırvan – fountain where Muslims perform ritual ablutions
samovar – tea urn
saray(ı) – palace
sarcophagus – a stone or marble coffin or tomb, especially one with inscription
sebil – public fountain or water kiosk
sedir – bench seating that doubled as a bed in Ottoman houses
şehir – city; municipality
şehir merkezi – city centre
selamlık – public/male quarters of a residence (see also *haremlik*)
Seljuk – of or pertaining to the Seljuk Turks, the first Turkish state to rule Anatolia from the 11th to 13th centuries
sema – *dervish* ceremony
serander – granary
servis – shuttle minibus service to and from the otogar
sinema – cinema
sokak, sokağı – often abbreviated to 'sk'; street or lane
Sufi – Muslim mystic, member of a mystic *(dervish)* brotherhood

tabiat parkı – nature park
tavla – backgammon
TC – Türkiye Cumhuriyeti (Turkish Republic); designates an official office or organisation
TCDD – Turkish State Railways
Tekel – government alcoholic beverage and tobacco company
tekke(si) – *dervish* lodge
TEM – Trans-European Motorway
tersane – shipyard
THY – Türk Hava Yolları, Turkish Airlines

TML – Turkish Maritime Lines
tramvay – tram
TRT – Türkiye Radyo ve Televizyon, Turkish broadcasting corporation
tuff, tufa – soft stone laid down as volcanic ash
tuğra – sultan's monogram, imperial signature
türbe(si) – tomb, grave, mausoleum

valide sultan – mother of the reigning sultan
vezir – vizier (minister) in the Ottoman government

vilayet, valilik, valiliği – provincial government headquarters

yalı – grand waterside residence
yarım pansiyon – half-pension, ie breakfast and dinner included
yayla – highland pastures
yeni – new
yol(u) – road, way
yüzyıl – century

Behind the Scenes

THIS BOOK

This 10th edition of *Turkey* was written by Verity Campbell (coordinating author), Jean-Bernard Carillet, Dan Eldridge, Frances Linzee Gordon, Virginia Maxwell and Tom Parkinson. Will Gourlay wrote the History chapter and Kate Clow wrote the Trekking chapter. The Health chapter is based on original research by Dr Caroline Evans. Tom Brosnahan researched and wrote the first five editions of Turkey. Pat Yale joined him in writing the 6th edition, and Richard Plunkett joined Pat and Tom for the 7th edition. Pat Yale, Richard Plunkett and Verity Campbell wrote the 8th edition, and the 9th edition of Turkey was written by Pat Yale, Jean-Bernard Carillet, Virginia Maxwell and Miriam Raphael.

This guidebook was commissioned in Lonely Planet's London office and produced in the Melbourne office by the following:

Commissioning Editor Stefanie Di Trocchio
Coordinating Editor Evan Jones
Coordinating Cartographer Daniel Fennesey
Coordinating Layout Designer Margaret Jung
Managing Cartographer Shahara Ahmed
Assisting Editors Janice Bird, Peter Cruttenden, Michael Day, Trent Holden, Cathryn Game, Simone Egger, Margedd Heliosz
Assisting Cartographers Erin McManus, Katie Cason, Joanne Luke, Anneka Imkamp, Sally Gerdan, Tony Fankhauser, Karina Vitirittl, Darwun Chau
Assisting Layout Designers Wibowo Rusli
Cover Designer Rebecca Dandens
Colour Designer Katie Thuy Bui
Project Manager Sarah Sloane
Language Project Coordinator Quentin Freyne

Thanks to David Burnett, Avril Robertson, Andrew Tudor, Sin Choo, Sally Darmody, Celia Wood, Jacqui Saunders, Brigitte Ellemor, Barbara Delissen, Geoff Howard, Jennifer Garrett, Katie Lynch, Kerryn Burgess, Piers Pickard, David Connolly, Piotr Czajkowski, Emma McNicol, Simon Tillema, Hunor Csutoros and Amanda Sierp

THANKS
Verity Campbell

In İstanbul, greatest thanks must go to the Coşkun brothers, Murat, Mehmet and Metin, for their enduring friendship and constant support. A special thanks also to Erdoğan, whose love for Sultanahmet helps shape the suburb, and to Mark Smith for donating his time and energy. A huge thanks also to Sharon Croxford, who cast her expert eye over the Food & Drink chapter. Cheers to Kate for her travel with children tips, and to Leyla, Kylie, Lou, Esma, Solmaz and Mehmet for helping to keep me sane. Thanks also to Janet, and especially Kay, for their generosity when we were setting up in the city. Thanks to the many family and friends who provided tips and research assistance for the bars, eateries and drinking holes. Thanks especially to Jan, for her help and moral support while Michael was in Bali.

I would like to thank fellow authors Frances, Virginia, Jean-Bernard, Tom, Dan, Will and Kate for their support, enthusiasm, information and the sessions on our İstanbul balcony. It was also fun working with commissioning editor Stefanie Di Trocchio and managing cartographer Shahara Ahmed.

THE LONELY PLANET STORY

The story begins with a classic travel adventure: Tony and Maureen Wheeler's 1972 journey across Europe and Asia to Australia. There was no useful information about the overland trail then, so Tony and Maureen published the first Lonely Planet guidebook to meet a growing need.

From a kitchen table, Lonely Planet has grown to become the largest independent travel publisher in the world, with offices in Melbourne (Australia), Oakland (USA) and London (UK). Today Lonely Planet guidebooks cover the globe. There is an ever-growing list of books and information in a variety of media. Some things haven't changed. The main aim is still to make it possible for adventurous travellers to get out there – to explore and better understand the world.

At Lonely Planet we believe travellers can make a positive contribution to the countries they visit – if they respect their host communities and spend their money wisely. Every year 5% of company profit is donated to charities around the world.

Last but certainly not least, Michael and Jacob, we made it. You've helped me see my beloved city with new eyes.

Jean-Bernard Carillet

A huge thanks to everyone who helped out and made this trip an enlightenment, including Remzi, Celil, Özcan, Tim, Ebru, Zafer, Sadettin and Ayşe, as well as the Diler family, including my guardian angels Ahmet, Tovi and Osman; thanks also to Musa, İhlan and Mehmet for the good vibes in İstanbul, and Pat for the good cheer and discussion over the meaning of an author's life; and the wonderfully hospitable and generous Turks and Kurds who helped along the way.

Verity, coordinating author extraordinaire, deserves huge thanks for her hard work, as does Shahara Ahmed and all the people behind the scenes at LP. I'm also grateful to Stefanie for her constant trust and encouragement.

At home, a phenomenal *gros bisou* to my daughter Eva, who gives a meaning and a direction to my otherwise gypsy life. And I won't forget my mum for her generous care.

Dan Eldridge

First and foremost, an especially sincere thanks to commissioning editor Stefanie Di Trocchio for giving me this unforgettable opportunity, and for so graciously working around my busy schedule. A huge thanks and a big hug to fellow LP author Alex Leviton; without her kindness I likely would not be writing these words today. Thanks and my deepest love go to Carrie Ann, whose selfless assistance with this project went far above and beyond the call of duty, and will never be forgotten. In İstanbul, thanks to Roni Askey-Doran for giving me my first Turkish journalism experience.

In Turkey, thanks to Sedat, Ali and Teresa for their graciousness and friendship. Thanks to Tayfun Eser for his contagious energy and his help. In Adana, thanks to Ethem 'Jack' Kaya for the city tour and the *şalgam:* I hope you put your impressive intelligence to good use. In Kozan, a big thanks to Ayhan Yavuz and his charming family, and also to İbrahim Tenik. Sorry I couldn't stay for dinner!

Finally, *çok teşekkür ederim* to all the incredibly kind Turkish and Kurdish people who gave their time to help me find hotels and highway on-ramps when I was hopelessly lost.

Frances Linzee Gordon

It is impossible to thank the countless individuals who crossed my path and daily demonstrated the legendary hospitality of the Turkish people.

Teşekkürler nevertheless to the following: H Yasemin Güngör, Information Officer in Ayvalık; Songül Parmaksızoğlu of Jale Tour, Ayvalık; Yasemin Demircan and Halil Bölge, Tourism Office, Selçuk; Oğuzhan Kocakulak, Selçuk; Mustafa Askın; Gamze Gümüs, Bozcaada; Alper Taşkıranlar, Anker Travel Agency; Şehnaz Duran, Tourism Office, Bergama; Salın Galişaner & İsmail Bigol, Bergama; Talat Cengiz and Zeliha Kolaş; Murat Azmi Maytere and Samir Büyükkaya, Tourism Office, Foça; Kaan Erge, İzmir Tourism Office; Toygan Üstüntaş, Ercan Zümbüz, Rasim Şener and Osman Bölük, İzmir otogar; Gökhan Alp, Meander Travel, Kuşadasi; Harika Selçuk, Turkish Airlines, Bodrum; Metin Önder, Bodrum Ferryboat Association; Ayjan Golak and Giydem Devrim, Güllük Tourism Office; Sinan Korkmaz, Hotel Dalyan; Ayten Aydın, Dalyan Tourist Office; Nizam Yıldırım, Ocean Turizm & Travel Agency; Mutlu Ulutaş at Saklikent; Bünyamin Şanli, Deniz Bal, Sandra Kayton, Oruç Özkan & Halit Adar in Marmaris; Hasan Cıplak, Knidos Yachting; Serkan Yılmaz, Fisherman House; Tolunay Bükülmez, Yeşilmarmaris Turizm; Cemal Gül; Zekiye Anioğlu; and Mustafa Güglü.

Special thanks to: Mustafa Demircan, Antik Radvan Otel, for putting me up late at night; Clinton Vickers at Behramkale for checking some of the history and archaeology sections in the North Aegean chapter; Diana Elmacioğlu for help with research and insights into Behramkale; Mustafa Kemal Gobi, Bergama, who gave me a great tour of Bergama's best; Hasan Degirmenci (aka Mr Happy) for his tour of Kuşadası's best bars and night spots; Osman Bölük for his help obtaining bus information at İzmir's otogar, and his and his family's hospitality Selçuk; Yaşar Yildiz, Director of Bodrum Underwater Archaeological Museum for granting a long interview and organising special access to exhibits; Bahadir Berkaya at the Bodrum Archaeological Museum for much information on the museum as well as for a fascinating interview; Erol Uysal, Bodrum, for rushing back to Bodrum for an equally fascinating interview about sponge divers; Ferit Paycı, Erman Günay & Chriss Aigner in Kaş for sorting out my complicated travel arrangements; and Metin from the Chez Evy Restaurant for a tour of Kaş' best bars; Elizabeth Maxwell for generously sending me all her best-in-Kaş recommendations; Lisa Lay for her precious time giving invaluable insights into Bozcaada as well as great recommendations (and a delicious cup of tea), and to Nuri Genol, Hikmet Palak, Adem Goban and Sedet Ergün at Kaş *Jandarmarla* for sorting out a minor incident.

Thanks finally to Shaharah Ahmed and her trusty team of cartographers, Stefanie di Trocchio, commissioning editor who made the assignment so much fun, and to Verity Cambell who did a commendable job as coordinating author.

My modest contribution to this book is dedicated to Philip Linzee Gordon, a wonderful brother and a traveller equally enamoured with Turkey.

Virginia Maxwell

In Cappadocia, I would like to thank Mustafa Turgut, Ali Yavuz and all of the staff at the Kelebek, Dawn Köse, Süha Ersöz and Ismail Keremoglu. Greatest thanks of all go to Pat Yale, who once again generously shared her enormous knowledge and love of Turkey.

In Kaş, thanks to Elizabeth Maxwell and Matthew Clarke for outstanding hospitality. Thanks also to Jill and Robert Hollingworth, great friends and travelling companions who have come to love Turkey as much as Peter, Max and I do.

In İstanbul, thanks to Haydar Sarigul and Ann Uysal.

It was great to work with long-time friends and fellow authors Verity Campbell and Frances Linzee Gordon, commissioning editor Stefanie Di Trocchio, mananaging cartographer Shahara Ahmed, coordinating editor Evan Jones and cartographer Daniel Fennesy on this book.

As always, my greatest thanks go to Max and Peter, the best travelling companions imaginable.

Tom Parkinson

Teşekkür ederim abe first and foremost to Süleyman, for driving me around 4000km of Anatolian tarmac (and dirt) in 12 days without even two words of English to smooth the way... As ever, *teşekkürler* and *şerefinize* to everyone who helped me out, kept me company on the road, discussed football and generally kept up Turkey's reputation for hospitality: 'Tom' in Gelibolu; Christian and İbo in Çanakkale; the old goatherds in Binbirkilise; Gulay in Sütçüler; teacher and pupils at Ayazini; İbrahim and Karen in Pamukkale; Fatih in Sivas; Mustafa and the staff at Honça in Tokat; İbby, Yusuf and Cağri, my loyal subjects of Abazhistan, in Amasya; Çif, Mehmet and other friendly folk in Trabzon; M Gürcan in Ordu (thanks for the translation work!); Mehmet and family, mama Demirci and the Altays in Ayder; Carlo, Andrea and Aleko in Tbilisi; my conductor on the night train to Batumi; and the various guys who gave me lifts around the Bulgarian border.

Cheers also to Verity, Michael and Virginia for drinks in İstanbul, Stef for running things smoothly in-house, and Mark 'Danielle' Elliott for the Georgia tips.

OUR READERS

Many thanks to the hundreds of travellers who used the last edition and wrote to us with helpful hints, useful advice and interesting anecdotes: **A** Jane Achermann, Kirsty Agnew, Abid Ahmad, Hass & Leanne Aksu, Sercan Akyildiz, Mick Alexander, Robyn Alexander, Levent Alver, Phil & Hilary André, Talin Ankaraliyan, K Aslan, Armagan Aydedeger, Ibrahim Aydemir, Ibrahim Aydemir **B** Suleyman Babaoglu, Bruce Bachman, Peter Baker, Beverly Ball, Emma Bamford, Elizabeth Bardsley, William Bardsley, Matt Barker, Bron Barnacle, Tracey Barrett, Steve Bassion, Evelyn Bate, Jane Battye, Cloovis Beagle, Laura Beales, Graeme Beardsmore, Nathalie Beauval, Mary Beebe, David Benz, Marjolein Berghuis, Dimitar Berov, L'Vannah Bielsker, Defne Bilge, Susan Blick, Anthony Blount, Diana Bodger, Michael Bodlaender, Marco Bona, David Borella, Matthew Boris, Cliff Bott, Willemijn Bouman, Sara Boys, Derik Bracke, Catherine Bradley, Heather Braiden, Bronwen Brauteseth, Lennart Bredahl, Marianne Britton, Rianne Brouwers, Doris Brown, Ian Brownlie, Jessie Burke, Mary & Andrew Burns, Robert Burns **C** Roderick Campbell, Danielle Carbonneau, John Carroll, David Carter, Owen Carter, Stanislas Casiez, Eli Cesaletti, Filip Ceulemans, Padmaja Chandrasekhar, Robia Charles, Pascale Chausse, John Chiles, Antoine Christiaens, Patricia Cires, Anne Clavreul, Ofir Cochavi, Francien Coenen, Lisa Cohen, Martinez Collazos, Kara & Sky Colley, Alice Conibear, Daniel Cook, Theresa Costigan, Ben Cotsford, Sarah Cox, Michelle Crabb, Matthias Csajka, Armand Cucciniello **D** Carol Dean, Lieve Decaluwé, Allan Dee, Carol Delaney, Teji Dhaliwal, Silvio di Giuseppe, Ainslie

SEND US YOUR FEEDBACK

We love to hear from travellers – your comments keep us on our toes and help make our books better. Our well-travelled team reads every word on what you loved or loathed about this book. Although we cannot reply individually to postal submissions, we always guarantee that your feedback goes straight to the appropriate authors, in time for the next edition. Each person who sends us information is thanked in the next edition – and the most useful submissions are rewarded with a free book.

To send us your updates – and find out about Lonely Planet events, newsletters and travel news – visit our award-winning website: **www.lonelyplanet.com/contact**.

Note: we may edit, reproduce and incorporate your comments in Lonely Planet products such as guidebooks, websites and digital products, so let us know if you don't want your comments reproduced or your name acknowledged. For a copy of our privacy policy visit www.lonelyplanet.com/privacy.

Divers, Colin Doyle, Gary Druce, Jan Dörner, Gill Dugmore **E** Dan Edholm, Elena Eilmes, Steven Eitner, Larry Ellis, Chris Emerson, Senol Erdogan, Birol Erdogmus, Ayhan Eren, Ted & Joyce Eve **F** Andrea Fabbri, Steven Fabian, Nickei Falconer, Suzanne Falconi, Steve Faragher, Simone Fatai, Simone Fausti, Giuliano Federici, Rose Firth, Petra Fleck, Enid Flint, Alexandra Foe, Mark Foley, Polly Foster, Susan Freed, Rich Fromer, Patrick Fry, Mechthild Fuchs **G** Elisenda Galobardes, Richard Gault, Joan Gifford, Val Gijsbers, Bill Glanvill, Ofir Glezer, Janine Gliener, Pili Gonzales, Ayla Gottschlich, Phillip Gray, Stacy Greco, Philip Gregg, Nergiz Gün **H** Chris Hall, Mike Hall, Ole Hansen, Katherine Hargrave, Teresa Harmer, Monica Harrower, Rowan Harvey, Crystal Haynes, K Heath, Rick Held, Ashish Hemrajani, Jolene Henry, Carlos Hernando, Murat Hertzberg, Robin Hethey, Nicola Hirschhorn, Brendan Hoffman, Petra Holc, Rod Holesgrove, Lisa Holliday, Eelko Hooijmaaijers, Jennifer Hosek, Winona Hubbard **I** Trygve & Karen Inda, Nisya Isman **J** Jussi Jaaskelainen, Jordan Jacquard, Bob Jones, Randall Jones, Wilfried Joris, Mirjana Jovanovska **K** Dieter Kamm, Viktor Kaposi, Fulya Kardaslar, Lisa Katavich, Joyce Kawahata, Jeff Kazarian, Anthony Keane, Ann Kelley, Ann Kennefick, Ihsan Khan, Moira Kiggins, Martha Kirmaz, Matthew Klinger, Gerard Kohl, Daniel Koning, Kopal Kopal, TüRkcan Korkmaz, Lilian Kranenburg, Steve Kreiter **L** Tim Lane, Randy Langford, Aaron Langolf, David Latchford, Kimarina Leach, Debbie Lee, Geoff & Robyn Lewis, Ingrid Liboriussen, Chwen Lin, Erik Lindemann, Erwan Lissillour, Paul Lithander, Annemarie Löppenthin, Melissa Lowe, Niki Lunter, James & Kris Luxon, Dyanne Lynne, Annemarie LöPpenthin, Mary Lynch **M** Naoise MacSweeney, Erwin Mah, Michael Manser, Hollie Marett, Erin Marine, Panagiotis Markolefas, Don Marquardt, Fab Marsani, Nicole Mathews, Janez Matos, John Mazuroski, Andy & Sue McCabe, Andrew McCarthy, Melinda McCarthy, Judith McCormick, Kathryn McGregor, Stephen McPhail, Dave McKillop, Jules McNally, Barbara McWilliam, Anthony Melov, Sadie Melov, Kimberly Merris, Gail Michener, Cynthia Miller, Graeme Miller, Tim Mills, Haim Mizrahi, Daniel Montes de Oca, Anita Montvajszki, Lucy

Morel, Kirsten Morgan, Marianne Morin, Shannon Murray **N** Serhat Narsap, Steve Neely, Abhijit Neogy, Kris Nesbitt, Judith Nester, Bao Nguyen, Joris Nicolai, Wolfgang Niebel, Naresh Nirav, Casey Nolan **O** Joe O'Dwyer, Sehsuvar Ongun, Charles Osborne, Raymond Ostelo, Aysin Ozturk **P** Giovanna Pandini, Carla Park, Chris Patrick, Ingeborg Pay, Sehsuvar Peace, Laura Peatling, Line Pedersen, Kendall Peet, Ide Peter, Ron Peterson, Purobi Phillips, Huseyin Piroglu, Tara Pitt, Anne Poepjes, Julie Polzerova, Bradley Posselt, Maja Potocnik, Trish Price, Campbell Price, Anna Ptaszynska **Q** GE Quinan **R** Rebecca Rashbrook, Christ Reiched, Karen & John Reilly, Matthew Richards, Patricia Richter, Isabel Rigolet, Freekand Rijkels, Steve Rock, Kylie Rudge, Jenna Ryan, Greg Ryan, Tim Ryan **S** Fia Salesa, Ken & Marian Scarlett, Paul Schmiede, Jeff Schwartz, KáRoly Schöll, Adrian Scott, Chin Kwang Seah, Tracey Seslen, Yuval Setsemsky, Phil Shacklady, Brody Shappell, Janet Shepherd, Keith & Teresa Simpson, Shirley Smith, Dawn Snider, Jake Soifer, Angelique Solis, Frances Spangler, Tim Spencer, Matthew Spragg, Graham Stagg, Yiannis Staikopoulos, Catherine Stanley, Jennifer Steers, Angus Stewart, Carol Stewart, Elizabeth Stokes, David Stone, Alex Stone, Richard Strange, Pablo Strubell, Nitin Sud, Jrc Sykes **T** Florence Man-Ting Tai, Alison Tanik, Marta Tanrikulu, Andy & Caroline Taylor, Ineke Teijmant, Gonzalez Tejedo, Lisa Teoh, Hugh Thomas, Richard Thompson, Helen Thorne, Penny Tilby, David Tranter, Nerissa Treloar, Emily Troemel, Mitchell Tsai, Denise Turcinov, John Turner **U** Zeynep Uraz **V** Salvador Valencia, Patrick & Sophie van Bree, Jan van Butselaar, Joeri van Holsteijn, Allan Vasconcellos, Alessandro Vernet, Viviana Vestrucci, Ana Vidmar, SašA Vidmar, Kaposi Viktor, Jennifer Vincent, Kate Vogt, Rebecca Vollmer, Michael von Kuelmer **W** Rolf Wahlstrom, Tilmann Waldthaler, Harald Waldvogel, EM Walker, Anne-Maree Walker, Jeffrey Walter, Sarah Ward, Gregor Watson, Beverley Watson, Jeff Wells, Anya Whiteside, Rashy Wilburg, Tim Williams, Donna Williams, Martin Williams, Phoebe Wilson, Glebe Wolfgang, Jason Wright, Eric Wright **X** Debbie Xenophou **Y** Mustafa Yildirim **Z** Marcela Zamora, Sanne Zewald, Lisette Ziere, Volker Zink, John Zubrzycki

Index

INDEX

INDEX

000 Map pages
000 Photograph pages

INDEX

000 Map pages
000 Photograph pages

INDEX

INDEX

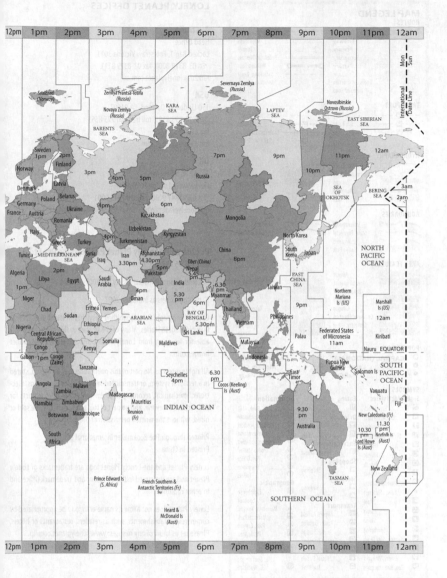

12pm | 1pm | 2pm | 3pm | 4pm | 5pm | 6pm | 7pm | 8pm | 9pm | 10pm | 11pm | 12am

Mon / Sun
International Date Line

Svalbard (Norway)

Zemlya Frantsa-Iosifa (Russia)

Severnaya Zemlya (Russia)

Novaya Zemlya (Russia)

KARA SEA

LAPTEV SEA

Novosibirskie Ostrovo (Russia)

EAST SIBERIAN SEA

BARENTS SEA

Sweden 1pm
Norway
Finland 2pm
Latvia 3pm
4pm 5pm
Russia 7pm
9pm
11pm
12am

SEA OF OKHOTSK

BERING SEA 2am 3am

Denmark
Germany Poland Belarus
France Austria Ukraine 4pm
Italy Romania 4pm
Greece Turkey Kazakhstan 6pm
Tunisia MEDITERRANEAN SEA Syria Iraq Uzbekistan
Algeria 2pm Iran Turkmenistan Kyrgyzstan
Libya Egypt 3.30pm Afghanistan 4.30pm
1pm Saudi Arabia Pakistan
Niger Chad 4pm Oman Nepal 5.45 pm
Sudan India 5.30 pm Myanmar 6.30 pm
Eritrea Yemen 5.30pm
Nigeria Ethiopia 3pm ARABIAN SEA BAY OF BENGAL
Central African Republic Somalia Sri Lanka
Congo Kenya Maldives

Mongolia

North Korea
South Korea Japan 9pm
China 8pm
Tibet (China)
Thailand Vietnam Taiwan
EAST CHINA SEA
Philippines 9pm

NORTH PACIFIC OCEAN

Northern Mariana Is (US)

Marshall Is (US) 12am

Kiribati

Gabon 1pm Congo (Zaire) Tanzania
Angola
Zambia Malawi
Namibia Zimbabwe Mozambique
Botswana
Madagascar Mauritius Réunion (Fr)
South Africa

Seychelles 4pm

6.30 pm Cocos (Keeling) Is (Aust)

INDIAN OCEAN

EQUATOR

Indonesia East Timor

Malaysia

Palau
Federated States of Micronesia 11am

Papua New Guinea Solomon Is

SOUTH PACIFIC OCEAN

Nauru

Vanuatu

New Caledonia (Fr) Fiji

Australia 9.30 pm

10.30 pm Lord Howe Is (Aust)

11.30 pm Norfolk Is (Aust)

New Zealand

Prince Edward Is (S. Africa)

French Southern & Antarctic Territories (Fr)

Heard & McDonald Is (Aust)

SOUTHERN OCEAN

TASMAN SEA

12pm | 1pm | 2pm | 3pm | 4pm | 5pm | 6pm | 7pm | 8pm | 9pm | 10pm | 11pm | 12am

MAP LEGEND

ROUTES

Tollway	One-Way Street
Freeway	Mall/Steps
Primary	Tunnel
Secondary	Pedestrian Overpass
Tertiary	Walking Tour
Lane	Walking Trail
Under Construction	Walking Path
Unsealed Road	Track

TRANSPORT

Ferry	Rail (Underground)
Bus Route	Tram
Rail	Cable Car, Funicular
	Rail (Fast Track)

HYDROGRAPHY

River, Creek	Canal
Intermittent River	Water
Swamp	Lake (Dry)
Mangrove	Lake (Salt)
Reef	Mudflats

BOUNDARIES

International	Regional, Suburb
State, Provincial	Ancient Wall
Disputed	Cliff
Marine Park	

AREA FEATURES

Airport	Land
Area of Interest	Mall
Beach, Desert	Market
Building	Park
Campus	Reservation
Cemetery, Christian	Rocks
Cemetery, Other	Sports
Forest	Urban

POPULATION

CAPITAL (NATIONAL)	CAPITAL (STATE)
Large City	Medium City
Small City	Town, Village

SYMBOLS

Sights/Activities
- Beach
- Castle, Fortress
- Christian
- Diving, Snorkeling
- Hindu
- Islamic
- Jewish
- Monument
- Museum, Gallery
- Point of Interest
- Pool
- Ruin
- Skiing
- Snorkeling
- Surfing, Surf Beach
- Trail Head
- Winery, Vineyard
- Zoo, Bird Sanctuary

Eating
- Eating

Drinking
- Drinking
- Café

Entertainment
- Entertainment

Shopping
- Shopping

Sleeping
- Sleeping
- Camping

Transport
- Airport, Airfield
- Border Crossing
- Bus Station
- General Transport
- Parking Area
- Petrol Station
- Taxi Rank

Information
- Bank, ATM
- Embassy/Consulate
- Hospital, Medical
- Information
- Internet Facilities
- Police Station
- Post Office
- Telephone
- Toilets

Geographic
- Lighthouse
- Lookout
- Mountain, Volcano
- National Park
- Pass, Canyon
- Picnic Area
- River Flow
- Shelter, Hut
- Spot Height
- Waterfall

LONELY PLANET OFFICES

Australia
Head Office
Locked Bag 1, Footscray, Victoria 3011
☎ 03-8379 8000, fax 03-8379 8111
talk2us@lonelyplanet.com.au

USA
150 Linden St, Oakland, CA 94607
☎ 510-893 8555, toll free 800 275 8555
fax 510-893 8572
info@lonelyplanet.com

UK
72–82 Rosebery Ave,
Clerkenwell, London EC1R 4RW
☎ 020-7841 9000, fax 020 7841 9001
go@lonelyplanet.co.uk

Published by Lonely Planet Publications Pty Ltd
ABN 36 005 607 983

© Lonely Planet Publications Pty Ltd 2007

© photographers as indicated 2007

Cover photograph: Female whirling dervishes in İstanbul, © Murat Duzyol/Images&Stories. Many of the images in this guide are available for licensing from Lonely Planet Images: www.lonelyplanet images.com.

Printed through The Bookmaker International Ltd
Printed in China